D1299477

The Torts Process

The Torts Process

Fourth Edition

James A. Henderson, Jr.

Frank B. Ingersoll Professor of Law
Cornell University Law School

Richard N. Pearson

Professor of Law
University of Florida College of Law

John A. Siliciano

Professor of Law
Cornell University Law School

ASPEN LAW & BUSINESS
Aspen Publishers, Inc.

Library of Congress Catalog Card No. 93-80288

ISBN 0-316-35666-2

Fourth Edition

Fourth Printing

MV-NY

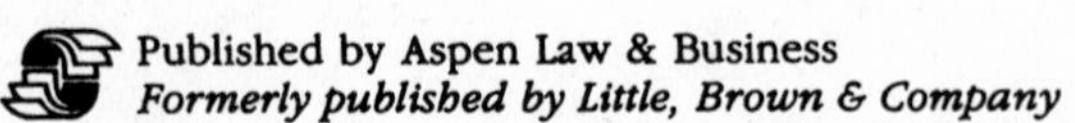

Printed in the United States of America

To Marcie, Danella, and Rosanne

Summary of Contents

Contents

Table of Continuing Notes

Table of Problems

Preface to the Fourth Edition

With this fourth edition, the original co-authors welcome a new co-author, Professor John Siliciano of Cornell Law School. His joining the project imbued it with sufficient freshness and energy to support a fairly substantial updating and revision. The sequencing of the chapters in the middle of the book has been changed to reflect both comments from users and our own judgment that the new arrangement of topics marks an improvement. Users of prior editions may, of course, stick with the old sequencing. But we urge them to consider carefully what we have done. Many new materials, including new problems, have been added, reflecting recent and current developments. At the same time, the fourth edition is somewhat shorter than the third. Wherever we deleted a problem to make room for a new one, we placed the old problem in the supplemental guide made available to teachers, in a format ready for easy duplication. Notwithstanding these changes, the book retains much of its original character. Those who have used earlier editions should find this fourth edition not only freshly invigorated but also comfortably familiar.

James A. Henderson, Jr.
Richard N. Pearson
John A. Siliciano

February 1994

Acknowledgments

This book is now in its fourth edition, and to thank all those who over the years have made significant contributions would make these pages unduly long. But some major contributors to this fourth edition deserve mention. Jylanda Diles and Kathy Wimsatt, at Cornell, took on the task of assembling and typing the manuscript; we could not have completed the task without them. We also would like to thank the student research assistants for this edition: at Cornell Law School, Alex Grant, Lauren Kares and Thomas Lynn; and at the University of Florida College of Law, Megan Kelly, Kristi Kangas, and Jeanine Sadkowski. Both law schools have provided all the assistance and encouragement we could wish for. We thank Deans Russell K. Osgood at Cornell and Jeffrey E. Lewis at Florida for that help.

We also thank the authors and publishers of the following for permitting us to include excerpts from these works:

American Bar Association, Commission on Medical Professional Liability, Designated Compensable Event System: A Feasibility Study (1979). Reprinted by permission.

American Bar Association, excerpts from the Model Code of Professional Responsibility as amended in 1980, copyright © by the American Bar Association. Reprinted by permission.

American Bar Association, excerpts from the Model Rules of Professional Conduct (1992 ed.), copyright © by the American Bar Association. Reprinted by permission.

American Bar Association, 1977 Report on the American Bar Association Commission on Medical Professional Liability. Reprinted by permission.

American Bar Association, Report of the Action Commission to Improve the Tort Liability System (1987), copyright © by the American Bar Association. Reprinted by permission.

American Jurisprudence, Legal Forms 2d. Copyright © by the Lawyers Cooperative Publishing Co. Reprinted by permission.

American Law Institute, II Reporters' Study, Enterprise Responsibility for Personal Injury (1991). Copyright 1991 by the American Law Institute. Reprinted with the permission of the American Law Institute.

American Law Institute, Restatement (First) of Torts, Volume 3. Copyright © 1938 by the American Law Institute. Reprinted with the permission of the American Law Institute.

American Law Institute, Restatement (Second) Agency, Volume 1. Copyright © 1958 by the American Law Institute. Reprinted with the permission of the American Law Institute.

American Law Institute, Restatement (Second) of Torts, Volumes 1 and 2. Copyright © 1965 by the American Law Institute. Reprinted with the permission of the American Law Institute.

American Law Institute, Restatement (Second) of Torts, Volume 3. Copyright © 1977 by the American Law Institute. Reprinted with the permission of the American Law Institute.

American Law Institute, Restatement (Second) of Torts, Volume 4. Copyright © 1979 by the American Law Institute. Reprinted with the permission of the American Law Institute.

American Law Institute, Restatement of Torts, Third: Products Liability (Council Draft, No. 2, 1993). Copyright © 1993 by the American Law Institute. Reprinted with the permission of the American Law Institute.

American Law Institute & National Conference of Commissioners on Uniform State Laws, The Uniform Commercial Code. Copyright © 1978 by The American Law Institute and the National Conference of Commissioners on Uniform State Laws. Reprinted with permission of The American Law Institute and the National Conference of Commissioners on Uniform State Laws.

National Conference of Commissioners on Uniform State Laws, Discussion Draft of the Uniform Defamation Act, December 6, 1991. This Act has been reprinted through the permission of the National Conference of Commissioners on Uniform State Laws, and copies of the Act may be ordered from them at a nominal cost at 676 North St. Clair Street, Suite 1700, Chicago, Illinois, 60611, (312) 915-0195.

National Conference of Commissioners on Uniform State Laws, Model Employment Termination Act. This Act has been reprinted through the permission of the National Conference of Commissioners on Uniform State Laws, and copies of the Act may be ordered from them at a nominal cost at 676 North St. Clair Street, Suite 1700, Chicago, Illinois, 60611, (312) 915-0195.

National Conference of Commissioners on Uniform State Laws, Uniform Comparative Fault Act. This Act has been reprinted through the permission of the National Conference of Commissioners on Uniform State Laws, and copies of the Act may be ordered from them at a nominal cost at 676 North St. Clair Street, Suite 1700, Chicago, Illinois, 60611, (312) 915-0195.

National Conference of Commissioners on Uniform State Laws, Uniform Contribution Among Tortfeasors Act. Copyright © 1955 by West Publishing Co. Sections 1 and 2 reprinted through the permission of the National Conference of Commissioners on Uniform State Laws, and copies of the Act may be ordered from them at a nominal cost at 676 North St. Clair Street, Suite 1700, Chicago, Illinois, 60611, (312) 915-0195.

National Conference of Commisioners on Uniform State Laws, Uniform Correction or Clarification of Defamation Act. This Act has been reprinted through the permission of the National Conference of Commissioners on Uniform State Laws, and copies of the Act may be ordered from them at a nominal cost at 676 North St. Clair Street, Suite 1700, Chicago, Illinois, 60611, (312) 915-0195.

Bailey, Back Injuries, Basic Personal Injury Anatomy 159 (Collins and

Woods, eds.). Copyright © 1966 by California Continuing Education of the Bar. Reprinted by permission.

Bailey, Congress Makes a Law. Copyright © 1950 by Columbia University Press. Reprinted by permission.

Calabresi, The Costs of Accidents. Copyright © 1970 by Yale University Press. Reprinted by permission of Yale University Press.

Dawson, Rewards for the Rescue of Human Life? in The Good Samaritan and the Law 63 (Ratcliffe ed. 1966).

Fuller, The Morality of Law (rev. ed. 1969). Copyright © 1969 by Yale University Press.

Manne, ed., Medical Malpractice Policy Guidebook. Copyright © 1985 by the Florida Medical Association.

Morris and Morris, Morris on Torts 2d ed. Copyright © 1980 by the Foundation Press.

Peck, Negligence and Liability Without Fault in Tort Law. Reprinted by permission.

Polinsky, An Introduction to Law and Economics. Copyright © 1983 by A. Mitchell Polinsky. Reprinted by permission.

Posner, Economic Analysis of Law (4th ed. 1992). Copyright © 1992 by Richard Posner. Reprinted by permission of the author and Little, Brown & Company.

Prosser and Keeton, Handbook of the Law of Torts, 5th ed. Copyright © 1984 by West Publishing Co. Reprinted by permission.

Wahlke, Behavioral Analysis of Representative Bodies, in Essays on the Behavioral Studies of Politics (Ramney ed. 1962).

Bender, A Lawyer's Primer of Feminist Theory and Tort, 38 J. Legal Education 3 (1988). Copyright © 1988 by the Association of American Law Schools. Reprinted with permission.

Bezanson, The Libel Tort Today, 45 Wash. and Lee L. Rev. 535 (1988).

Blumstein, Bovbjerg & Sloan, Beyond Tort Reform: Developing Better Tools for Assessing Personal Injury, 8 Yale J. on Reg. 171 (1990). Copyright © 1990 by the Yale Journal on Regulation, Box 401A Yale Station, New Haven, CT 06520. Reprinted from Volume 8:1 by permission. All rights reserved.

Broeder, The University of Chicago Jury Project, 38 Neb. L. Rev. 744 (1959). Copyright © 1959 by the Nebraska Law Review. Reprinted by permission.

Calabresi and Hirschoff, Toward a Test for Strict Liability in Torts, 81 Yale L.J. 1055 (1972). Copyright © 1972 by The Yale Law Journal Company. Reprinted by permission of The Yale Law Journal Company and Fred B. Rothman & Co. from the Yale Law Journal, Vol. 81, pp. 1055, 1060, 1067-1069.

Ellis, Fairness and Efficiency in the Law of Punitive Damages, 56 So. Cal. L. Rev. 1 (1982). Reprinted with the permission of the Southern California Law Review.

Friedman, Expert Testimony, Its Abuse and Reformation, 19 Yale L.J. 247 (1919). Copyright © by The Yale Law Journal Company. Reprinted by permission of The Yale Law Journal Company and Fred B. Rothman & Co. from The Yale Law Journal, vol. 19, pp. 242, 254-255.

Gifford, A Context-Based Theory of Strategy Selection in Legal Negotiations, 46 Ohio St. L.J. 41 (1985). Copyright © 1985 by The Ohio State University.

J. Henderson, Coping with the Time Dimension in Products Liability, 69 Calif. L. Rev. 919 (1981). Copyright © 1981 by California Law Review, Inc.

J. Henderson, Process Constraints in Torts, 67 Cornell L. Rev. 901 (1982). Copyright © 1982 by Cornell University. All rights Reserved.

J. Henderson, The New Zealand Accident Commission Reform, 48 U. Chi. L. Rev. 781 (1981).

R. Henderson, Should Workmen's Compensation Be Extended to Nonoccupational Injuries?, 48 Tex. L. Rev. 117 (1969). Copyright © 1969 by the Texas Law Review. Reprinted by permission.

James, Functions of Judge and Jury in Negligence Cases, 58 Yale L.J. 667 (1949). Copyright © 1949 by The Yale Law Journal Company. Reprinted by permission of The Yale Law Journal Company and Fred B. Rothman & Company, Vol. 58, pp. 667-690.

Kelley, Proximate Cause in Negligence Law: History, Theory, and the Present Darkness, 69 Wash. U. L.Q. 49 (1991).

Kelman, Cost-Benefit Analysis—An Ethical Critique, Regulation, Jan./Feb. 1981. Reprinted by permission.

Magruder, Mental and Emotional Disturbances in the Law of Torts, 49 Harv. L. Rev. 1033 (1936). Copyright © 1936 by the Harvard Law Review Association. Reprinted by permission.

An Overview of the First Five Program Years (April 1980-March 1985). Institute for Civil Justice, The RAND Corporation, 1700 Main St., P.O. Box 2138, Santa Monica, CA 90406-2138. Reprinted by permission.

Pepper, The Lawyer's Amoral Ethical Role: A Defense, A Problem and Some Possibilities, 1986 Am. Bar Found. Res. J. 613.

Prosser, Insult and Outrage, 44 Calif. L. Rev. 40. Copyright © 1956 by the California Law Review, Inc. Reprinted by permission of the California Law Review, Inc. and Fred B. Rothman & Co.

Prosser, Privacy, 48 Calif. L. Rev. 383. Copyright © 1960 by the California Law Review, Inc. Reprinted by permission of the California Law Review, Inc. and Fred B. Rothman & Co.

Rodgers, Negligence Reconsidered: The Role of Rationality in Tort Theory, 54 S. Calif. L. Rev. 1 (1980). Reprinted with permission of the Southern California Law Review.

Siliciano, Wealth, Equity, and the Unitary Medical Malpractice Standard, 77 Va. L. Rev. 439 (1991).

Sunderland, Verdicts, General and Special, 29 Yale L.J. 253 (1920).

Reprinted by permission of The Yale Law Journal Company and Fred B. Rothman & Company, Vol. 29, pp. 253-267.

Warren and Brandeis, The Right to Privacy, 4 Harv. L. Rev. 193 (1890). Copyright © 1890 by the Harvard Law Review Association.

Weinrib, The Case for a Duty to Rescue, 90 Yale L.J. 247 (1980). Reprinted by permission of The Yale Law Journal Company and Fred B. Rothman & Company, Vol. 90, pp. 247-293.

White, Note, Innovative No-Fault Reform for an Endangered Specialty, 74 Va. L. Rev. 1487 (1988).

Comment, Legislative Process in Alabama: A Microcosm, Alabama L. Rev. 181 (1970).

The Torts Process

Chapter 1

The Intentional Infliction of Harmful and Offensive Bodily Contact—Battery

This chapter serves two functions. First, it provides an overview of the process of resolving torts disputes in our legal system. And second, it introduces one branch of the substantive law of torts—liability for harmful and offensive battery.

A. A Preliminary Look at the Process

Although the substance of this course involves the law of torts, that substance is created, defined, amended, and applied through the process of adjudication. This section is designed to give you a preliminary look at that process in broad outline, so that later, when you study a particular problem or decision, you will know where the case has been and where it might be going.

The Investigation

Of all the potential tort claims that arise when one person harms another, only a few will be brought to a lawyer. For someone to call upon a lawyer for help, he or she must be aware of possibly having a valid claim; must decide to pursue it; must be unwilling, or unable, to handle it alone; must know that a lawyer's help is available; and must be willing to incur the cost, both pecuniary and psychological, of invoking the torts process.

Once a lawyer is consulted, the first step in the process is for the lawyer to listen to the client's story to find out what happened from the client's viewpoint. Deciding to go to a lawyer is a major move, and a client typically will have already decided that he or she is right and that the other person is wrong. For this reason, it takes skill on the part of the lawyer to get a reasonably objective view of what happened without antagonizing the client. It may become readily apparent at this first interview that what the client thinks is a valid claim is clearly without legal merit and for that reason should be dropped. Letting the client down easily when the claim is without merit is a skill that is important both to the lawyer and to the legal profession.

Aside from assessing the potential merit of the claim, the lawyer will want to know when the claim arose. In every jurisdiction, *statutes of limitation* allow injured plaintiffs only a limited length of time to commence legal actions. These periods, which generally range from one to four years, typically begin to run when the plaintiff discovers or should have discovered the injury. Tort actions are usually subject to shorter limitation periods than contract actions, and battery actions are frequently subject to shorter periods than negligence actions. Plaintiffs who do not bring their actions within the time allowed are barred from recovery, although the statutes of limitation for persons under legal disabilities, such as minors, are suspended, or *tolled,* during the periods of disability.

Even if it appears that the claim has legal merit and is not time-barred, it may not be worth pursuing further if the harm suffered by the client is insubstantial. The clearest case of liability may be dropped if the amount of money damages likely to be recovered is insignificant. Of course, this effect of the size of the potential recovery upon the decision to go forward works both ways. If the client is severely harmed, a case in which liability is questionable may still be worth pursuing.

Three categories of money damages may be available to the plaintiff in a torts case: nominal, compensatory, and punitive. Nominal damages, as the name implies, are small in amount, often a dollar. They are available only in intentional tort cases, and they are awarded to establish as a matter of public record that the defendant has wronged the plaintiff even if no actual harm occurred. The hope is that the plaintiff will seek satisfaction in the courtroom rather than resort to violent retaliation. Compensatory damages reflect the harm actually suffered. They include out-of-pocket expenses, such as hospital and doctors' bills, which ordinarily are specific and easy to compute, as well as more generalized elements of harm such as pain and suffering and impairment of earning capacity. Punitive damages are designed to punish the defendant for wrongdoing, and may be substantial in amount. They are ordinarily available only if the defendant is found to have acted with malice, or with reckless indifference to the rights of the plaintiff.

From the point of view of the plaintiff's lawyer, the amount of the potential recovery is of personal relevance. Ordinarily, the plaintiff's lawyer in torts cases works on a contingent fee basis—that is, the lawyer's compensation is a certain percentage of the plaintiff's recovery. (The defendant's lawyer is usually paid on an hourly basis regardless of the outcome in the case.) The lower the recovery, the less the compensation to the plaintiff's lawyer. The normal contingent fee for the plaintiff's lawyer if the case goes to trial is between 30 and 40 percent of the recovery and may be even higher if the case is appealed.

Even if the lawyer determines that the claim has legal merit and that the potential damages will be substantial, as a practical matter the defendant may be unable to pay. In torts cases, liability insurance is the source from which many claims are satisfied. However, the defendant may have no insurance, or it may not cover intentional torts such as battery. In the absence of insurance, a claim must be satisfied, if at all, out of whatever personal assets the defendant may have. The difficulty of satisfying a claim under such circumstances often discourages litigation against uninsured defendants.

If the claim appears to be worth pursuing, the real work for the lawyer begins. The story told by the client is apt to be incomplete and one-sided, so that further investigation will be necessary. Witnesses to the events giving rise to the claim will have to be located and interviewed. Other sources of information include police reports and newspaper stories. The lawyer may also have to consult technical experts such as physicians, automobile mechanics, and engineers to develop a full understanding of the facts. In simpler cases, the law governing the claim may be clear, but with more complex cases, the lawyer is also likely to have to spend considerable time in the law library.

Once the lawyer feels that the facts and the law have been sufficiently mastered, an attempt will usually be made to settle the case. Most torts disputes are resolved by out-of-court settlement. Settlement may occur any time during litigation, but negotiations are almost always initiated well in advance of trying the case. The plaintiff's lawyer will make a tentative evaluation of the damages and of the probability of recovering any amount, and will determine a range within which the case should be settled. The evaluation will be discussed with the client, and the lawyer will then contact the defendant, or more likely the defendant's lawyer, to begin the bargaining process, although sometimes the initiative for settlement will come from the defendant's side. The fact that both sides can save the costs of going to trial pressures them to settle. If the assessments of likely recovery by both sides are in the same range, then the case is likely to be settled, especially if the plaintiff's harm is not serious.

The Pleadings

Formal court proceedings are instituted by the plaintiff with the filing of a *complaint.* The complaint is a document containing the plaintiff's claim for relief and a short statement of the facts upon which the claim is based. For example, in Vosburg v. Putney, the first case we shall examine, the plaintiff's complaint alleged that on February 20, 1889, the defendant "violently assaulted [the plaintiff] . . . kicked him and otherwise ill-treated him and that [he] was thereby made ill and lame and confined to his bed for a long time and suffered great physical pain and mental anguish and was permanently crippled." A complaint typically ends with a demand for damages; in *Vosburg,* for example, the plaintiff demanded what was then the considerable sum of $5,000.

The complaint functions both to initiate the lawsuit and to inform the defendant of the basis of the plaintiff's suit. In the early days of common law pleading, the writ (as the forerunner of the complaint was known) had to comply with many technical rules; a plaintiff who deviated from these rules might lose the cause of action entirely. Modern procedural rules, however, are more forgiving, typically requiring only "a short and plain statement of the claim showing that the pleader is entitled to relief."

After being served with the complaint, the defendant has a short period of time, typically 20 days, in which to file an answer in court. The *answer* must either admit or deny the allegations of fact contained in the complaint, or state that the defendant lacks sufficient knowledge of the facts to admit or deny them. In addition to challenging the plaintiff's version of the facts, the defendant may attack the legal theory upon which the complaint rests. This attack can either be included in the answer or be stated separately by a *motion to dismiss the complaint* asserting that complaint fails to state a claim upon which relief can be granted. The test for whether such a motion should be granted is whether the plaintiff would be entitled to any recovery even if all the factual allegations in the complaint were proven true. A negative answer to this question requires the judge to grant the motion in favor of the defendant.

Even if the complaint states a cause of action, if the parties do not dispute the material facts of a case, the case may not need to go to trial. The method of testing in advance of trial whether a dispute as to material facts exists is the *motion for summary judgment.* This motion is available to both the plaintiff and the defendant, and the party making the motion has the burden of convincing the judge that no real and genuine dispute exists as to any material fact. When all the pleadings and any supporting affidavits have been filed, the judge determines whether any genuine factual disputes remain pertaining to the party's claims and defenses, and grants or denies the motion accordingly. If a dispute remains as to some but not all the relevant facts, the scope of trial may be limited to the disputed facts. Summary judgment is infrequently used for avoiding trial in torts cases, since the resolution of torts claims so often depends upon an evaluation of the conduct of one or more of the parties.

The filing of the initial pleadings and motions does not end the lawyer's pretrial activities. Further investigation into both the law and the facts may be necessary, and in almost all cases negotiations for settlement will continue. If a significant delay is likely before the case is reached for trial, the plaintiff may feel considerable pressure to settle, particularly if the injuries are serious and the plaintiff needs money to pay medical expenses and to replace income lost because of the injuries.

The time period between the filing of the initial pleadings and the trial will depend on a number of factors, and in particular on the degree of congestion in the trial docket. Generally, a case to be tried with a jury will take longer to reach than one without a jury, which is one important reason why many cases that go to trial are tried without a jury. But a plaintiff with serious injuries is more likely to want a jury trial, so it is the serious injury cases that are most affected by crowded dockets. Attorneys for either side may also seek to postpone trial for a variety of tactical reasons.

The Trial

If the case is not settled, the next phase in the process is the trial. If the case is to be tried to a jury, the first important step in the trial process is the selection of jurors. In most states, jurors are selected from a larger panel chosen from citizens of the county in which the court is located. Attorneys for both parties, as well as the presiding judge, participate actively in the jury selection process. What each lawyer hopes for in a jury is not an unbiased cross section of the community, but a jury as many of whom as possible have biases which favor his or her client. Many lawyers believe that characteristics such as race, national origin, occupation, and education will influence the way a juror looks at the evidence and the people involved in the case, although the empirical validity of these intuitions is often open to doubt.

After the jury is selected, the trial itself begins with the plaintiff's lawyer's *opening statement.* The opening statement is an outline of the plaintiff's case and the evidence the lawyer expects to present. It is designed to predispose the jury to accept the plaintiff's view of the case and to enable the jury to relate the evidence as it comes in to the total case. Following this statement, the plaintiff's lawyer presents the evidence. Typically this will consist of oral testimony of the witnesses, documentary evidence, such as medical reports, and occasionally physical evidence. When the plaintiff's lawyer is finished with the direct examination of a witness, the defendant's lawyer has the opportunity to cross-examine. In the course of allowing evidence into the record, the judge rules on objections raised by both sides.

After all the plaintiff's evidence has been presented, the defendant may make a motion that the judge direct the jury to return a verdict in favor of the defendant. This *motion for a directed verdict* will be granted if the judge concludes that the plaintiff has failed to prove one or more of the elements of the case—that is, that a reasonable jury could not find other than for the defendant even if they were to believe all of the testimony favorable to the plaintiff, disbelieve all unfavorable testimony, and draw every reasonable inference favorable to the plaintiff from the testimony. If the judge grants the motion, the judge tells the jury that it must find for the defendant. In effect, granting the defendant's motion for directed verdict on the liability issue ends the trial for that defendant. Directed verdicts are granted in favor of defendants in a significant minority of torts trials, but similar motions by plaintiffs seldom prevail.

Assuming that the judge denies the defendant's motion for directed verdict, the defendant's lawyer then presents the defendant's case. If the defendant's lawyer feels that the plaintiff has not presented evidence that would justify recovery, no further evidence may be presented. But more typically, the defendant's lawyer will begin with an opening statement to the jury and follow up with witnesses and evidence for the defense.

When both sides have finished with the presentation of the evidence, motions for directed verdicts by either party may be made again. Assuming such motions are denied by the judge, lawyers for both sides make their *closing arguments to the jury,* in which they review the evidence in the light most favorable to their case, and indicate why, under the law as the judge will state it in the instructions, the jury ought to return a verdict one way or the other. Following the closing arguments, the trial judge delivers *instructions to the jury* as to the applicable law and what the jury will have to find as facts to support a verdict for the plaintiff.

On most issues of fact in a torts case, the plaintiff has the *burden of proof,* or *burden of persuasion.* What this means is that it is up to the plaintiff's lawyer to persuade the jury that his or her version of the events giving rise to the claim is true; it is not up to the defendant's lawyer to persuade the jury that the plaintiff's version is not true. In civil cases, disputes about the facts are resolved by the jury by assessing probabilities that either side's version is true. For example, in a battery case, the parties may dispute who struck the plaintiff. Putting the burden of proof on the plaintiff means that the plaintiff must persuade the jury that it was the defendant who caused the harm; it is not up to the defendant to persuade the jury that it was someone else. If, after analyzing the evidence, the jury believes that it was someone else, or concludes that there is no more reason to believe that it was the defendant than someone else, the plaintiff has not carried the burden of proof (persuasion), and the jury should return its verdict for the defendant.

After the jury has been instructed on the law by the trial judge, it retires to determine its *verdict.* In a slight majority of jurisdictions, the verdict of a jury in a civil case must be unanimous, and if the jury cannot agree, the parties are entitled to a new trial by a different jury. The remaining jurisdictions allow verdicts by the concurrence of fewer than all the jurors, but typically require more than a bare majority of votes.

After the jury has determined its verdict, it reports that verdict to the trial judge. The verdict may be either "general" or "special." The former is a decision by the jury in favor of either the plaintiff or defendant. The latter contains the jury's specific findings of fact made in response to specific questions put to it by the trial judge, and furnishes the factual basis for the trial judge's decision in favor of either the plaintiff or the defendant. If the verdict is for the plaintiff, it will normally include the jury's determination of the damages the defendant is to pay to the plaintiff. The trial judge then enters *judgment* in accordance with the verdict. (If the case is tried without a jury, the judgment is based on the facts as determined by the judge.) The court's judgment in favor of a torts plaintiff is a written order, signed by the judge, directing the defendant to pay to the plaintiff the amount stated in the verdict. In contrast, a judgment for the defendant is not an order to anyone, but is simply a statement for the record that the defendant has won the trial.

Even after the jury verdict is returned, the losing party has an opportunity to make motions to the trial judge that may "save the day." If the losing party made a motion for a directed verdict earlier, that party may renew the motion by asking the judge to enter judgment for that party, notwithstanding the jury verdict for the other side. This is a motion for *judgment non obstante veridicto* (JNOV). In addition, either side may make a *motion for a new trial.* The latter motion will be granted if the trial judge concludes that the verdict is against the clear weight of the evidence, that the damages awarded are excessive, that procedural errors damaging to the moving party were committed, or that entering judgment on the verdict would cause manifest injustice. The judge will order a new trial on the ground that the verdict is against the clear weight of the evidence only if the judge is convinced that the jury has reached a seriously erroneous result; the order will not issue merely because the judge, if cast in the role of a juror, would have reached a different result.

The Appeal

Few cases proceed past conclusion of the trial process. However, the losing party has one last chance at victory: *appeal.* In all states, there is one highest court to which a final appeal may be taken. In many states, and in the federal judicial system, a system of intermediate appellate courts considers appeals in the first instance, with the highest court hearing most tort cases only when it chooses to hear them.

One reason for the infrequency of appeals is that not all issues that come up at trial can be appealed. The only issues that can be appealed are decisions about the law by the trial judge.[1] Thus, jury verdicts and judicial fact findings may be set aside because of errors of law committed by the trial judge, such as admitting (or refusing to admit) evidence, or erroneously instructing the jury. But absent such an error of law by the judge, the jury's verdict and the trial judge's findings of fact are binding on appeal.

Even if one or more appealable issues of law exist, the further delay and expense discourage the bringing of an appeal. Both sides must file briefs with the appellate court arguing why the result at the trial should or should

1. Appellate review of trial court decisions about the sufficiency of proof to support a given result, or whether a jury verdict is against the weight of the evidence, places the appellate court in a position that comes close to reviewing issues of fact. But strictly speaking the higher court, even in those instances, is reviewing the decisions of law reached by the court below concerning the sufficiency of the proof.

not be overturned, and they must pay to have the relevant portions of the trial record printed. The trial record includes the pleadings, motions, the transcript of the testimony, if one is made, trial briefs, if any, and the orders of the trial judge. The appellate briefs are usually supplemented by oral arguments to the appellate court by the lawyers involved. Thus, the appellate process takes considerable time and money. And even if the party bringing the appeal is successful in having the results at the trial overturned, the victory may only be the right to a second trial.

In most cases, the appellate court announces the result of an appeal in a *written opinion.* This opinion serves a number of functions. It explains to the parties and their lawyers why the court decided the case the way it did, thereby providing some assurance to the parties that their claims and arguments were carefully considered. The opinion is of additional importance to the parties in cases where the result on appeal is the ordering of a new trial. The opinion functions as a lesson in the law to the judge who will preside at the new trial, spelling out the mistakes at the earlier trial that led to the necessity of a new trial.

However, an appellate opinion isn't only a source of psychic satisfaction to the parties and guidance to the trial judge. Appellate opinions are published and are made available to the general public. These appellate opinions are sources of the law. As such, they are a part of the legal and moral environment, and consequently influence the way we conduct ourselves in society. And more particularly, and of greater immediate relevance to the lawyer, they are used in the resolution of subsequent legal disputes. Thus, the function of most opinions transcends the needs of the immediate parties in particular cases. Appellate opinions are part of our jurisprudence and have vitality even many years after they are written.

Mechanisms for Resolving Disputes: Adjudication

The foregoing only sketches the general process by which torts cases are brought and decided. Yet even this brief description suggests a number of reasons why the torts process is currently undergoing critical analysis. It is thought by many to be too cumbersome, too time-consuming, and too expensive for both the immediate parties and society generally. It is also criticized on the ground that its outcomes are often unfair. Much of this criticism focuses on the use of adjudication as the primary means of resolving disputes and many reform efforts involve proposals to modify the adjudication process or to replace it with alternative means of dispute resolution.

Although adjudication is undoubtedly central to the torts process, it is important not to overstate its function. To be sure, adjudication is the most formal method of resolving disputes in our legal system. But it is also the most ponderous and inefficient method, playing practically a far less important role in the day-to-day functioning of the torts process than most laypersons imagine. The truth is that very few torts disputes are resolved by the satisfaction of a judgment obtained in a court action.

Reflect for a moment upon the life cycle of a typical small tort claim. The parties probably would have to wait two years for their case to reach trial. Lawyers for both sides will in all likelihood have been connected with the case for more than three years before it is finally decided. There are expenses in connection with investigating and preparing the case, filing and serving the pleadings and other documents, assembling the witnesses, and providing a court stenographer to record and preserve the testimony, not to mention the judge's time and the use of the courthouse for which the parties are not directly charged but for which they and the rest of us pay out of general tax revenues. And the lawyers expect to be, and are, paid more if the case goes to trial. Moreover, their burdens are substantially increased if the case is tried before a jury. Justice may be blind, but when asked to adjudicate torts disputes it can also be frustratingly slow and expensive.

And yet for all of that, adjudication remains the epitome of the torts lawyer's craft. It is the cutting edge of the system of righting civil wrongs, the basic device against which all else is measured and to which all else is related. Throughout this course we will be encountering mechanisms other than adjudication whereby torts disputes are resolved in our system. Taken together, these other methods dispose of the overwhelming majority of torts claims. Yet all of these other mechanisms for resolving disputes rely for their continued existence on the availability of the adjudicative process, for it is largely in adjudication that the rules of liability undergo the process of adjustment and development so necessary to their continued vitality. And the threat of a trial is a powerful incentive to resolve the dispute in some other way.

It is appropriate, therefore, that the adjudicative process occupy center stage in this course. It is probably appropriate also that a great percentage of attention and effort during law school be directed toward gaining an understanding of the adjudicative process as it functions generally in our legal system. However, it is a premise upon which these materials are based that adjudication is only one of a number of dispute-resolving processes that constitute what is collectively referred to here as the torts process. It is no less appropriate, therefore, that the adjudicative process be put into its proper perspective. As far as the day-to-day process of resolving torts disputes is concerned, adjudication has its greatest impact as a ponderous potentiality rather than as an efficient, useful tool.

B. *The Substantive Law Governing Liability for Battery*

Several reasons support choosing battery as the place to begin the detailed study of the torts process. For one thing, battery is one of the easiest torts to understand. The facts of a battery case are likely to be simple. The law is also relatively uncomplicated, and yet there are enough wrinkles to make it interesting. Moreover, battery is one of the oldest concepts in our law. To study the origins of the common law concept of battery is to study the origins of the common law itself.

A simple and workable definition of the modern concept of battery is the intentional, unprivileged, and either harmful or offensive contact with the person of another. The basic parameters of the battery concept are best described by a hypothetical example. Assume that *A* is walking along the sidewalk and sees *B,* whom *A* dislikes intensely, approaching from the opposite direction. *A* punches *B* on the jaw, knocking out three of *B*'s teeth and rendering *B* unconscious. On these facts *A* has committed a harmful battery upon *B* for which *A* may be held liable in tort. All of the elements of harmful battery are present: *A* intentionally contacted *B*'s person in a harmful manner under circumstances that did not give rise to a privilege on *A*'s part. It should be noted that the fact that *A* dislikes *B* explains *A*'s conduct, but is not a necessary element of the tort. Even if *B* were a stranger to *A, A*'s conduct would be tortious if the above-described elements are present. On the other hand, if we eliminate any of the elements—intent, contact, or absence of privilege—we no longer have a battery. For example, if *A* had missed *B* or if *A* had acted out of sufficient necessity (e.g., in defense of a knife attack by *B*) to justify striking *B, A* would not have committed a battery upon *B* even if *A* in fact dislikes *B* intensely. But where, as in our hypothetical example, *A* intentionally and without justification strikes *B, A*'s liability in tort is clear from our preliminary definition of battery.

Although the informal definition of battery given above is satisfactory for most cases, the formal definitions contained in the Restatement (Second) of Torts are more suitable for detailed analysis:

> §13. BATTERY: HARMFUL CONTACT
>
> An actor is subject to liability to another for battery if
>
> (a) he acts intending to cause a harmful or offensive contact with the person of the other or a third person, or an imminent apprehension of such a contact, and
>
> (b) a harmful contact with the person of the other directly or indirectly results.
>
> §18. BATTERY: OFFENSIVE CONTACT
>
> (1) An actor is subject to liability to another for battery if
>
> (a) he acts intending to cause a harmful or offensive contact with the person of the other or a third person, or an imminent apprehension of such a contact, and
>
> (b) an offensive contact with the person of the other directly or indirectly results. . . .

The source of these rules, the Restatement (Second) of Torts, represents a revision of the original Restatement of Torts, which was first published by the American Law Institute from 1934 to 1939. The American Law Institute was created in 1923 by a distinguished group of judges, lawyers, and scholars. It is a nonprofit organization, whose avowed purpose is improvement of the law. The Restatement of the Law on a variety of topics, including Torts, have been the Institute's chief reason for being. Since its creation, its members have convened annually to review developments in the law and to consider changes in their formal summaries of what the law is in a majority of jurisdictions in this country. Professor Francis H. Bohlen of the University of Pennsylvania was put in charge of the original Restatement of Torts and given the title of Reporter for the project. Professor William L. Prosser of the University of California Law School at Berkeley was appointed Reporter of the Restatement (Second) of Torts. From 1970 to 1981 Dean John Wade of Vanderbilt University Law School acted as Reporter. In 1992, the Institute decided to undertake a Restatement (Third) of Torts, beginning with products liability. Professor James A. Henderson, Jr. of Cornell Law School and Professor Aaron D. Twerski of Brooklyn Law School are Co-Reporters on that portion of the project.

It is important for the law student to appreciate what the Restatement is and what it is not. The original purpose of the Institute was to restate the rules of tort law as recognized by most courts in this country. To some extent, the second Restatement has departed from this model, with the Reporters and Institute adopting what was felt to be the "better" rule, even if not so recognized by a majority of states. Courts cite and rely upon the Restatement, but it is decidedly secondary authority and gives way to statutes and cases where the latter establish a different rule.

Returning to the definitions of battery set forth in §§13 and 18 of the Restatement (Second), the elements of intent and harmful or offensive contact constitute what is known as the plaintiff's prima facie case. To win, the plaintiff must prove these elements, together with the necessary causal connection between the harm incurred and the defendant's conduct. If the defendant had a privilege to inflict harm upon the plaintiff it is up to the defendant to assert this privilege as a defense—it is not up to the plaintiff to assert the absence of privilege as a part of the prima facie case.

1. The Prima Facie Case

a. Intent

Beginning law students are often amazed at the extent to which lawyers can take common, everyday words and concepts and complicate their meanings. The concept of intent in the law of battery provides a good opportunity to test your own reactions in this regard. You have no doubt used the word *intent* for most of your life and never experienced any great difficulties with it. And in what may be called the clear cases, it presents few difficulties even in the legal context of determining whether a battery has been committed. In the earlier hypothetical cases involving *A* and *B*, for example, it is clear that *A* intended to strike and harm *B*. *A* subjectively desired to achieve both of these consequences. And yet, there are other cases that are not so clear. What if *A* had punched *B* on the chin, intending merely to stun *B*, and *B* had fallen to the sidewalk, hit his head, and died from the resulting concussion, a result *A* never intended? Or what if A had mistaken *B*, *A*'s friend, for *C*, *A*'s enemy, and had struck *B* intending to harm *C*? The issue these questions raise in the present context is whether *A* can be said to have acted with sufficient intent to constitute a battery. The important thing at this point is not so much to work out satisfactory responses to these questions (you will be in a better position to do that after working through the following material) as it is to begin to appreciate the potential complexities inherent in the concept of intent. These complexities are well illustrated by Vosburg v. Putney, a famous case that has been used to educate and confound several generations of law students.

Vosburg v. Putney

80 Wis. 523, 50 N.W. 403 (1891)

The action was brought to recover damages for [a] battery, alleged to have been committed by the defendant upon the plaintiff on February 20, 1889. The answer is a general denial. At the date of the alleged [battery] the plaintiff was a little more than fourteen years of age, and the defendant a little less than twelve years of age.

The injury complained of was caused by a kick inflicted by defendant upon the leg of the plaintiff, a little below the knee. The transaction occurred in a schoolroom in Waukesha, during school hours, both parties being pupils in the school. A former trial of the cause resulted in a verdict and judgment for the plaintiff for $2,800. The defendant appealed from such judgment to this court, and the same was reversed for error, and a new trial awarded. 78 Wis. 84.

The case has been again tried in the circuit court, and [the second trial from which the defendant brings the present appeal] resulted in a verdict for plaintiff for $2,500. The facts of the case, as they appeared on both trials, are sufficiently stated in the opinion by Mr. Justice Orton on the former appeal. . . .

[The facts as stated in the first supreme court opinion referred to are: "The plaintiff was about fourteen years of age, and the defendant about eleven years of age. On the 20th day of February, 1889, they were sitting opposite to each other across an aisle in the high school of the village of Waukesha. The defendant reached across the aisle with his foot, and hit with his toe the shin of the right leg of the plaintiff. The touch was slight. The plaintiff did not feel it, either on account of its being so slight or of loss of sensation produced by the shock. In a few moments he felt a violent pain in that place, which caused him to cry out loudly. The next day he was sick, and had to be helped to school. On the fourth day he was vomiting, and Dr. Bacon was sent for, but could not come, and he sent medicine to stop the vomiting, and came to see him the next day, on the 25th. There was a slight discoloration of the skin entirely over the inner surface of the tibia an inch below the bend of the knee. The doctor applied fomentations, and gave him anodynes to quiet the pain. This treatment was continued, and the swelling so increased by the 5th day of March that counsel was called, and on the 8th of March an operation was performed on the limb by making an incision, and a moderate amount of pus escaped. A drainage tube was inserted, and an iodoform dressing put on. On the sixth day after this, another incision was made to the bone, and it was found that destruction was going on in the bone, and so it has continued exfoliating pieces of bone. He will never recover the use of his limb. There were black and blue spots on the shin bone, indicating that there had been a blow. On the 1st day of January before, the plaintiff received an injury just above the knee of the same leg by coasting, which appeared to be healing up and drying down at the time of the last injury. The theory of at least one of the medical witnesses was that the limb was in a diseased condition when this touch or kick was given, caused by microbes entering in through the wound above the knee, and which were revivified by the touch, and that the touch was the exciting or remote cause of the destruction of the bone, or of the plaintiff's injury. It does not appear that there was any visible mark made or left by this touch or kick of the defendant's foot, or any appearance of injury until the black and blue spots were discovered by the physician several days afterwards, and then there were more spots than one. There was no proof of any other hurt, and the medical testimony seems to have been agreed that this touch or kick was the exciting cause of the injury to the plaintiff. . . .

"The learned circuit judge [at the first trial], said to the jury: 'It is a peculiar case, an unfortunate case, a case, I think I am at liberty to say, that ought not to have come into court. The parents of these children ought, in some way, if possible, to have adjusted it between themselves.' "]

On the [second trial from the results of which the present appeal is taken,] the jury found a special verdict, as follows: "(1) Had the plaintiff during the month of January, 1889, received an injury just above the knee, which became inflamed, and produced pus? *Answer.* Yes. (2) Had such injury on the 20th day of February, 1889, nearly healed at the point of the injury? A. Yes. (3) Was the plaintiff, before said 20th of February, lame, as the result of such injury? A. No. (4) Had the *tibia* in the plaintiff's right leg become inflamed or diseased to some extent before he received the blow or kick from the defendant? A. No. (5) What was the exciting cause of the injury to the plaintiff's leg? A. Kick. (6) Did the defendant, in touching the plaintiff with his foot, intend to do him any harm? A. No. (7) At what sum do you assess the damages of the plaintiff? A. $2,500."

The defendant moved for judgment in his favor on the verdict, and also for a new trial. The plaintiff moved for judgment on the verdict in his favor. The motions of defendant were overruled, and that of the plaintiff granted. Thereupon judgment for plaintiff for $2,500 damages and costs of suit was duly entered. The defendant appeals from the judgment.

LYON, J. Several errors are assigned, only three of which will be considered.

1. The jury having found that the defendant, in touching the plaintiff with his foot, did not intend to do him any harm, counsel for defendant maintain that the plaintiff has no cause of action, and that defendant's motion for judgment on the special verdict should have been granted. In support of this proposition counsel quote from 2 Greenl. Ev. §83, the rule that "the intention to do harm is of the essence of an assault." Such is the rule, no doubt, in actions or prosecutions for mere assaults. But this is an action to recover damages for an alleged assault and battery. In such case the rule is correctly stated, in many of the authorities cited by counsel, that plaintiff must show either that the intention was unlawful, or that the defendant is in fault. If the intended act is unlawful, the intention to commit it must necessarily be unlawful. Hence, as applied to this case, if the kicking of the plaintiff by the defendant was an unlawful act, the intention of defendant to kick him was also unlawful.

Had the parties been upon the play-grounds of the school, engaged in the usual boyish sports, the defendant being free from malice, wantonness, or negligence, and intending no harm to plaintiff in what he did, we should hesitate to hold the act of the defendant unlawful, or that he could be held liable in this action. Some consideration is due to the implied license of the play-grounds. But it appears that the injury was inflicted in the school, after it had been called to order by the teacher, and after the regular exercises of the school had commenced. Under these circumstances, no implied license to do the act complained of existed, and such act was a violation of the order and decorum of the school, and necessarily unlawful. Hence we are of the opinion that, under the evidence and verdict, the action may be sustained.

2. [At trial the plaintiff's medical expert was allowed to testify, over the defendant's objection, that in his opinion the exciting cause of the inflammation in the plaintiff's leg was the kick by the defendant. The Supreme Court of Wisconsin concluded that the defendant's objection to such testimony should have been sustained because the form of the question put to the expert witness was improper.]

3. Certain questions were proposed on behalf of defendant to be submitted to the jury, founded upon the theory that only such damages could be recovered as the defendant might reasonably be supposed to have contem-

plated as likely to result from his kicking the plaintiff. The court refused to submit such questions to the jury. The ruling was correct. The rule of damages in actions for torts was held in Brown v. C., M. & St. P.R. Co., 54 Wis. 342, to be that the wrong-doer is liable for all injuries resulting directly from the wrongful act, whether they could or could not have been foreseen by him. . . .

[The judgment for the plaintiff was reversed and the case remanded for yet another new trial on the basis of the evidentiary error described in part 2 of the opinion.]

The possibility of a third trial was precluded when, upon the motion of Putney, the action was dismissed based on Vosburg's failure to pay court costs associated with the prior appeals and to reinstigate the action at the trial level in a timely fashion. This default is perhaps explained by the fact that the Vosburgs were pursuing legal remedies on multiple fronts, including a criminal complaint against Putney and an action by Vosburg's father against Putney to recover his own out-of-pocket expenses and for the loss of his son's services. While the guilty verdict in the criminal action was overturned on appeal, the civil action brought by Vosburg's father was ultimately successful, with a trial judgment in favor of Mr. Vosburg for $1,200 that was affirmed on appeal in Vosburg v. Putney, 86 Wis. 278, 56 N.W. 483 (1893).

Whether the four-year spate of litigation was actually a success for anyone involved is another matter. The Putneys originally offered to settle the suit for $250, while the Vosburgs insisted on $700. Neither party was willing to accept the other's offer or further compromise, and in all likelihood both suffered as a result. When court costs and attorney's fees are considered, it is almost certain that the Vosburgs actually realized less than the Putneys' $250 settlement offer, if indeed they recovered anything at all. It is equally certain that the Putneys, in defending the actions, expended considerably more than the $700 the Vosburgs had originally requested. Thus, the first trial judge's observation that "[t]he parents of these children ought, in some way, if possible, to have adjusted it between themselves" rings true. For a detailed history of the litigation and its aftermath, see Zile, *Vosburg v. Putney:* A Centennial Story, 1992 Wis. L. Rev. 877.

The Law-Fact Distinction: In General

A number of facts appear in and accompany the opinion in *Vosburg*. Which ones are essential to the decision? In attempting to analyze *Vosburg*, it is important to begin to understand one of the most basic concepts of the torts process—the distinction between law and fact.

Whenever the plaintiff brings a torts case before a court, as in Vosburg v. Putney, a legal remedy is being sought based on particular conduct of the defendant that harmed the plaintiff in some way. In deciding whether to grant the remedy asked for, the court performs three functions: (1) it finds the relevant facts, (2) it states the applicable rule of law, and (3) it applies the rule of law to the facts to reach the proper result. When the court finds the facts of a case, it determines what happened—in a torts case, the conduct of the parties, the circumstances surrounding the conduct, and the consequences of that conduct. If the court determines, after hearing the evidence, that the defendant kicked the plaintiff, it concludes that that event took place in time and space, much in the same sense that a scientist might conclude that a given object weighs three grams.

When the court states the law governing the case, it recognizes a generalized rule calling for certain legal consequences to follow from a particular set of facts. For example, the tribunal might declare the rule to be: "If any person shall intentionally kick another in school after the class is called to order, and if the kick causes harm, then that person shall pay damages to the one kicked." Observe that the description of facts appearing in the rule is general, in that it refers to generic kinds of behavior, and is not dependent on the specific identity of the parties. This characteristic of generality would be missing if the facts stated in the rule were: "If the defendant kicks the plaintiff on the right shin on February 20, 1889, in a school room in Waukesha, Wisconsin. . . ."

Observe also that the facts are connected to the consequences in the form of an *if-then* proposition. The portion of the rule following the *if* identifies the relevant facts, and the portion following the *then* describes the legal consequences. Thus, the substantive law of torts consists primarily of rules of conduct that match up generalized descriptions of fact patterns with appropriate legal consequences. In applying the rule of law to the facts of a particular case, the tribunal compares the facts, as it determines them to be, with the general description of the facts in the rule. If the particular facts of the case fit within this general description, the legal consequences described by the rule then follow.

So far we have spoken of the court as if it were composed of a single person who finds the facts, states the law, and applies the law to the facts. In *Vosburg,* however, the lower court consisted of two separate decision-makers—the trial judge and the jury. When a jury is involved in a trial, the three functions of fact finding, law declaring, and law application are split between the judge and the jury, with the judge declaring the law and the jury finding the facts and, in most cases, applying the law to them.[2]

2. The law application function to which this discussion refers is the ultimate application that occurs after the trier of fact has resolved conflicts in the evidence relating to relevant factual issues. The judge performs a preliminary application of law to facts in reacting to motions to dismiss the complaint or to enter summary judgment because there is no substantial disagreement as to material facts. The facts to which the judge applies the law in these

The allocation of the function of fact finding to the jury is generally a matter of constitutional command. The Seventh Amendment to the Constitution of the United States provides for the right to trial by jury in federal courts in all "suits at common law. . . ." The Supreme Court of the United States has never held that the Seventh Amendment applies to state proceedings, but the constitutions of all states provide, with variations, for jury trial in civil cases. The determination of the applicable rules of law is, of course, the exclusive function of the judge. The judge has the legal training necessary for the intelligent resolution of issues of law and the jury does not. To make sure that juries do not have any legal expertise of their own which might impair the exercise of their fact-finding function, in many states lawyers are prohibited from serving on juries.

The means by which the allocation of functions between judge and jury is accomplished are the judge's instructions to the jury and the jury's verdict. The instructions to the jury contain a statement of the law governing the case—that is, a description of the facts that under the law must be found by the jury in order to support recovery for the plaintiff. If the facts found by the jury fit within the fact pattern described in the rules of law contained in the instructions, the jury should return its general verdict for the plaintiff. If the facts do not fit within the rules, the jury should return its general verdict for the defendant.

Occasionally, the trial judge may perform the ultimate law applying function. The procedural device that permits this is the special verdict, which was used in *Vosburg*. In that case, the jury stated its findings of fact in the form of answers to questions, framed by the judge, about the facts. To determine the outcome, the judge then applied the law governing the case to the facts so stated.

The closest that a judge comes to invading the fact-finding province of the jury is when the judge decides whether or not to grant a motion for a new trial on the ground that the verdict is against the clear weight of the evidence. When reacting to a motion for a directed verdict or for a JNOV, the judge may be said to be passing on the sufficiency of the proof itself, rather than on the reaction of the jury to that proof. In contrast, the "against the weight of the evidence" motion invites the trial judge to review the jury's reaction to the evidence, albeit on a standard weighted toward accepting that reaction. It is difficult to avoid the conclusion that in those cases, at least, the trial judge is to some extent acting as a "super-juror." Two constraints lessen the significance of this "non-judge-like" role: first, judges are admonished to grant such motions only in the rare cases when jurors appear grossly in error (some courts hold that the verdict must be against the "great weight

instances are not the facts ultimately found by the fact finder, however, but rather the facts as they are contained in the complaint or in supporting affidavits. In reacting to a motion for directed verdict, or JNOV, the trial judge performs a similar function in reviewing the evidence introduced at the trial, viewing that evidence in the light most favorable to the nonmoving party.

of the evidence"); and second, the judge is limited to ordering a new trial—unlike the situation when reacting to motions for directed verdicts or JNOVs, the judge may not enter judgment for a party that was "robbed" by the jury. If the second jury reacts in the same fashion as the first, presumably the trial judge will conclude that jurors know best, and will deny the defendant's motion for new trial. The special quality of these motions for new trial is reflected in the fact that an appellate court will not overturn the trial judge's denial of such a motion unless the appellate court concludes that the trial judge has committed a clear abuse of discretion.

The division of functions between the judge and jury also has an impact on what issues may be appealed. Just as it is improper for the trial judge to invade the province of the jury and decide issues of fact (except on the rare occasions when an "against the weight of the evidence" motion is granted), it is also improper for an appellate court to review and set aside decisions made by the jury (except on the even rarer occasions when an appellate court decides that the denial of an "against the weight of the evidence" motion was reversible error). The right to a jury trial would be a hollow one if an appellate court were free to substitute its own conclusions of fact for those of the jury. The only issues an appellate court may decide for itself are issues of law—that is, the expressed or implied declarations of law made by the trial judge at the trial.

Mental State Considerations: Offensiveness and Offensive Batteries

A central enigma of *Vosburg* involves the court's conclusion that the defendant could be held liable for a battery despite an express finding by the jury that he did not intend to harm the plaintiff. While an intent to do harm would clearly suffice to establish a battery, the court's opinion suggests that other, less malicious states of mind may establish a battery. The *Vosburg* court specifically refers to an intention to commit an unlawful act, yet this formulation creates as many problems as it resolves. A more modern approach, reflected in §13 of the Restatement (Second) of Torts, quoted on p. 10, defines battery to include the conduct of a defendant who acts "intending to cause . . . offensive contact" with the plaintiff. Following this approach, §18 of the Restatement, also quoted on p. 10, makes clear that plaintiffs can recover for batteries arising from offensive contacts as well as harmful contacts.[3]

3. According to the Restatement (Second) of Torts §7 (1965), *harm* denotes "the existence of loss or detriment in fact of any kind to a person resulting from any cause." Comment b to §7 states:

> "Harm" implies a loss or detriment to a person, and not a mere change or alteration in some physical person, object or thing. Physical changes or alterations may be either beneficial, detrimental, or of no consequence to a person. Insofar as physical changes

The inclusion of "offensive contact" and the intent to cause such contact within the modern definitions of battery helps clarify some of the vagueness of common law decisions like *Vosburg*. Yet, analytical challenges persist. For example, what constitutes "offensive contact?" Does the answer depend on whether or not the defendant actually desired that the contact be offensive? This formulation might work, but what of the defendant who, while not subjectively intending any offense, is unusually insensitive to the obnoxious nature of his behavior? Should, for example, a woman be denied a tort remedy for an unwelcomed pinch on the basis that the man who did it sincerely believed "it was just a harmless joke"? An alternative solution might be to tie liability to whether or not the plaintiff perceived the contact as offensive, regardless of the defendant's actual beliefs or motives. But here again, the subjective perspective causes trouble. Should we allow recovery for the hyper-sensitive plaintiff who is offended by all sorts of everyday human contacts? Imagine, for example, the number of tort complaints a single person of such heightened sensitivities might file after a rush-hour ride on the New York City subway.

The Restatement (Second) of Torts rejects both options in favor of the following approach:

> §19. WHAT CONSTITUTES OFFENSIVE CONTACT
>
> A bodily contact is offensive if it offends a reasonable sense of personal dignity.
>
> COMMENT:
>
> a. In order that a contact be offensive to a reasonable sense of personal dignity, it must be one which would offend the ordinary person and as such one not unduly sensitive as to his personal dignity. It must, therefore, be a contact which is unwarranted by the social usages prevalent at the time and place at which it is inflicted.

---

have a detrimental effect on a person, that person suffers harm.

Another section of the Restatement defines "bodily harm":

> §15. What Constitutes Bodily Harm
>
> Bodily harm is any physical impairment of the condition of another's body, or physical pain or illness.
>
> Comment:
>
> a. There is an impairment of the physical condition of another's body if the structure or function of any part of the other's body is altered to any extent even though the alteration causes no other harm. A contact which causes no bodily harm may be actionable as a violation of the right to freedom from the intentional infliction of offensive bodily contacts. (See §§18-20.)
>
> Illustration:
>
> 1. *A* has a wart on his neck. His physician, *B*, advises him to submit to an operation for its removal. *A* refuses to do so. Later *A* consents to another operation, and for that purpose is anesthetized. *B* removes the wart. The removal in no way affects *A*'s health, and is in fact beneficial. *A* has suffered bodily harm.

Thus, the Restatement uses the hypothetical reaction of "the ordinary person" rather than the actual perception of either the defendant or the plaintiff. What are the justifications and consequences of this choice? How can a court determine what an "ordinary person" would find offensive? These questions, which recur in various forms throughout tort law, are taken up in subsequent notes on Mental State Considerations and in Chapter 11, dealing with dignitary wrongs.

Note: Tort Liability of Minors and Their Parents

In *Vosburg* the defendant was a minor. At common law, minors are not immune from liability for their batteries, although very young children may not be capable of having the intent that liability requires. See, e.g., DeLuca v. Bowden, 42 Ohio St. 2d 392, 329 N.E.2d 109 (1975), in which a child under seven years of age was held to be incapable of committing an intentional tort. Imposing liability on minors for their batteries would not be remarkable if it were not for the fact that, in other areas of the law, minors receive special protection because of their age. One such area we will be dealing with later is negligence—children sometimes are not held to the same standard of care as adults, and young children are often held to be incapable of acting negligently even when they are deemed old enough to commit a battery. There are even more stringent rules for the protection of children in both contract and criminal law. As you develop your knowledge of these other areas of the law, you should ask yourself whether these different rules represent inconsistencies, or whether different considerations of policy permit, if they do not require, different treatment.

Because children typically do not have the financial resources to satisfy tort claims, persons injured by young tortfeasors may try to collect from the youngster's parents. Parents may be liable for their own negligence in failing to supervise their minor children, but under the common law they were not held vicariously liable for their children's torts solely by virtue of the parent-child relationship. This has led all 50 states to enact statutes imposing some degree of liability on parents for the torts of their children. These statutes, which vary significantly in detail, often impose limitations on the amount of damages a parent can be required to pay for the tortious conduct of a child. Such statutes also typically require that the minor's conduct be willful or malicious before the parent can be held liable. Thus, for example, in Travelers Indemnity Company v. Brooks, 60 Ohio App. 2d 37, 395 N.E.2d 494 (1977), the court of appeals of Ohio held that parents were not liable to the owner of an automobile their minor child stole and wrecked. The stealing of the automobile was willful, the court concluded, but the accident was not.

One question that will be important in many battery cases, and which was not raised or discussed in the *Vosburg* opinion, is how the plaintiff can prove what the intent of the defendant was. Suppose that at the trial in *Vosburg* the defendant had testified: "But I didn't intend to kick him. It was just an accident." Would the trial judge have been bound to take his word for it? If not, would the judge or jury be required to explore the innermost recesses of the defendant's mind in order to find out what the defendant really intended? Does the law define intent the same way psychology does? Should it? Some light is shed on the answers to these questions by another landmark case of the law of battery:

Garratt v. Dailey

46 Wash. 2d 197, 279 P.2d 1091 (1955)

HILL, J. The liability of an infant for an alleged battery is presented to this court for the first time. Brian Dailey (age five years, nine months) was visiting with Naomi Garratt, an adult and a sister of the plaintiff, Ruth Garratt, likewise an adult, in the backyard of the plaintiff's home, on July 16, 1951. It is plaintiff's contention that she came out into the backyard to talk with Naomi and that, as she started to sit down in a wood and canvas lawn chair, Brian deliberately pulled it out from under her. The only one of the three persons present so testifying was Naomi Garratt. (Ruth Garratt, the plaintiff, did not testify as to how or why she fell.) The trial court, unwilling to accept this testimony, adopted instead Brian Dailey's version of what happened, and made the following findings:

"III. . . . that while Naomi Garratt and Brian Dailey were in the back yard the plaintiff, Ruth Garratt, came out of her house into the back yard. Some time subsequent thereto defendant, Brian Dailey, picked up a lightly built wood and canvas lawn chair which was then and there located in the back yard of the above described premises, moved it sideways a few feet and seated himself therein, at which time he discovered the plaintiff, Ruth Garratt, about to sit down at the place where the lawn chair had formerly been, at which time he hurriedly got up from the chair and attempted to move it toward Ruth Garratt to aid her in sitting down in the chair; that due to the defendant's small size and lack of dexterity he was unable to get the lawn chair under the plaintiff in time to prevent her from falling to the ground. That plaintiff fell to the ground and sustained a fracture of her hip, and other injuries and damages as hereinafter set forth.

"IV. That the preponderance of the evidence in this case establishes that when the defendant, Brian Dailey, moved the chair in question *he did not have any wilful or unlawful purpose in doing so;* that *he did not have any intent to injure the plaintiff, or any intent to bring about any unauthorized or offensive contact with her person* or any objects appurtenant thereto; that the circumstances which immediately preceded the fall of the plaintiff established that the defendant, *Brian Dailey, did not have purpose, intent or design to perform a prank or to effect an assault and battery upon the person of the plaintiff.*" (Italics ours, for a purpose hereinafter indicated.)

It is conceded that Ruth Garratt's fall resulted in a fractured hip and other painful and serious injuries. To obviate the necessity of a retrial in the event this court determines that she was entitled to a judgment against Brian Dailey, the amount of her damage was found to be eleven thousand dollars. Plaintiff appeals from a judgment dismissing the action and asks for the entry of a judgment in that amount or a new trial.

The authorities generally, but with certain notable exceptions (see Bohlen, "Liability in Tort of Infants and Insane Persons," 23 Mich. L. Rev. 9), state that, when a minor has committed a tort with force, he is liable to be proceeded against as any other person would be.

In our analysis of the applicable law, we start with the basic premise that Brian, whether five or fifty-five, must have committed some wrongful act before he could be liable for appellant's injuries.

The trial court's finding that Brian was a visitor in the Garratt backyard is supported by the evidence and negatives appellant's assertion that Brian was a trespasser and had no right to touch, move, or sit in any chair in that yard, and that contention will not receive further consideration.

It is urged that Brian's action in moving the chair constituted a battery. A definition (not all-inclusive but sufficient for our purpose) of a battery is the intentional infliction of a harmful bodily contact upon another. The rule that determines liability for battery is given in 1 Restatement, Torts, 29, §13, as:

> An act which, directly or indirectly, is the legal cause of a harmful contact with another's person makes the actor liable to the other, if
>
> (a) the act is done with the intention of bringing about a harmful or offensive contact or an apprehension thereof to the other or a third person, and
>
> (b) the contact is not consented to by the other or the other's consent thereto is procured by fraud or duress, and
>
> (c) the contact is not otherwise privileged.

We have in this case no question of consent or privilege. We therefore proceed to an immediate consideration of intent and its place in the law of battery. In the comment on clause (a), the Restatement says:

> Character of actor's intention. In order that an act may be done with the intention of bringing about a harmful or offensive contact or an apprehension

> thereof to a particular person, either the other or a third person, the act must be done for the purpose of causing the contact or apprehension or with knowledge on the part of the actor that such contact or apprehension is substantially certain to be produced.

See also, Prosser on Torts 41, §8.

We have here the conceded volitional act of Brian, i.e., the moving of a chair. Had the plaintiff proved to the satisfaction of the trial court that Brian moved the chair while she was in the act of sitting down, Brian's action would patently have been for the purpose or with the intent of causing the plaintiff's bodily contact with the ground, and she would be entitled to a judgment against him for the resulting damages. Vosburg v. Putney (1891), 80 Wis. 523, 50 N.W. 403.

The plaintiff based her case on that theory, and the trial court held that she failed in her proof and accepted Brian's version of the facts rather than that given by the eyewitness who testified for the plaintiff. After the trial court determined that the plaintiff had not established her theory of a battery (i.e., that Brian had pulled the chair out from under the plaintiff while she was in the act of sitting down), it then became concerned with whether a battery was established under the facts as it found them to be.

In this connection, we quote another portion of the comment on the "Character of actor's intention," relating to clause (a) of the rule from the Restatement heretofore set forth:

> It is not enough that the act itself is intentionally done and this, even though the actor realizes or should realize that it contains a very grave risk of bringing about the contact or apprehension. Such realization may make the actor's conduct negligent or even reckless but unless he realizes that to a substantial certainty, the contact or apprehension will result, the actor has not that intention which is necessary to make him liable under the rule stated in this Section.

A battery would be established if, in addition to plaintiff's fall, it was proved that, when Brian moved the chair, he knew with substantial certainty that the plaintiff would attempt to sit down where the chair had been. If Brian had any of the intents which the trial court found, in the italicized portions of the findings of fact quoted above, that he did not have, he would of course have had the knowledge to which we have referred. The mere absence of any intent to injure the plaintiff or to play a prank on her or to embarrass her, or to commit an assault and battery on her would not absolve him from liability if in fact he had such knowledge. Without such knowledge, there would be nothing wrongful about Brian's act in moving the chair, and, there being no wrongful act, there would be no liability.

While a finding that Brian had no such knowledge can be inferred from the findings made, we believe that before the plaintiff's action in such a case should be dismissed there should be no question but that the trial court had passed upon that issue; hence, the case should be remanded for clarification of the findings to specifically cover the question of Brian's knowledge, because intent could be inferred therefrom. If the court finds that he had such knowledge, the necessary intent will be established and the plaintiff will be entitled to recover, even though there was no purpose to injure or embarrass the plaintiff. Vosburg v. Putney, supra. If Brian did not have such knowledge, there was no wrongful act by him, and the basic premise of liability on the theory of a battery was not established.

It will be noted that the law of battery as we have discussed it is the law applicable to adults, and no significance has been attached to the fact that Brian was a child less than six years of age when the alleged battery occurred. The only circumstance where Brian's age is of any consequence is in determining what he knew, and there his experience, capacity, and understanding are of course material.

From what has been said, it is clear that we find no merit in plaintiff's contention that we can direct the entry of a judgment for eleven thousand dollars in her favor on the record now before us.

Nor do we find any error in the record that warrants a new trial. . . .

The case is remanded for clarification, with instructions to make definite findings on the issue of whether Brian Dailey knew with substantial certainty that the plaintiff would attempt to sit down where the chair which he moved had been, and to change the judgment if the findings warrant it. . . .

Remanded for clarification.

SCHWELLENBACH, DONWORTH, and WEAVER, JJ., concur.

On remand, the trial court found for the plaintiff. On appeal, the Supreme Court of Washington affirmed, 49 Wash. 2d 499, 304 P.2d 681 (1956), disposing of the defendant's argument that the evidence did not support a finding of knowledge on the part of the defendant in the following manner:

> The record was carefully reviewed by this court in Garratt v. Dailey. Had there been no evidence to support a finding of knowledge on the part of the defendant, the remanding of the case for clarification on that issue would have been a futile gesture on the part of the court. As we stated in that opinion, the testimony of the two witnesses to the occurrence was in direct conflict. We assumed, since the trial court made a specific finding that the defendant did not intend to harm the plaintiff, that the court had accepted the testimony of the defendant and rejected that of the plaintiff's witness. However, on remand, the judge who heard the case stated that his findings had been made in the light of his understanding of the law, i.e., that the doctrine of constructive intent does not apply to infants, who are not chargeable with knowledge of the normal consequences of their acts. In order to determine whether the defendant knew that the plaintiff would sit in the place where the chair had been, it was necessary for him to consider carefully the time

> sequence, as he had not done before; and this resulted in his finding that the arthritic woman had begun the slow process of being seated when the defendant quickly removed the chair and seated himself upon it, and that he knew, with substantial certainty, at that time that she would attempt to sit in the place where the chair had been. Such a conclusion, he stated, was the only reasonable one possible. It finds ample support in the record. Such knowledge, we said in Garratt v. Dailey, is sufficient to charge the defendant with intent to commit a battery.

The defendant also argued on the second appeal that the findings on remand were technically inconsistent with the original findings. The Supreme Court refused to address this issue because the defendant had failed to preserve the issue on appeal.

Problem 1

A partner in the law firm in which you are an associate seeks your help in a case she is handling on behalf of Anne Johnson. Johnson's husband, Trenton, was recently killed when the pickup truck he was driving was broad-sided on the driver's side by a car that ran a red light at high speed. Trenton's truck burst into flames; both he and the driver of the other vehicle died in the crash. Because of the intensity of the fire, a post-crash coroner's autopsy was unable to determine whether Trenton died from the impact of the other car or from the fire itself.

In addition to a suit against the other driver's estate, your firm is pursuing a claim against the manufacturer of the truck based on the fire that occurred when the truck was struck. The truck was built in 1985, but used a chassis design that has been in production since 1973. The trucks have twin gas tanks, mounted on the outside of the steel "ladder" structure that forms the truck's frame. Competing truck manufacturers use a single tank nestled inside the ladder structure. The dual tank structure gives the pickup greater fuel capacity, but the placement of the tanks on the outboard side of the truck frame increases their exposure to damage if the truck is hit broadside.

Indeed, other suits against the same manufacturer for similar accidents involving the same truck have produced reliable evidence that the manufacturer was aware of the safety problems of its design as early as 1978. In that year, the manufacturer began reviewing data from actual crashes which indicated that its truck was more than twice as likely to explode or catch fire in side-impact crashes than those of other manufacturers. These data specifically suggested that drivers of the trucks would experience at least a third more fire-related fatalities per year than drivers of competing models, given equal levels of use.

As a result of this empirical information, several of the manufacturer's engineers in 1980 urged the manufacturer to abandon the twin-tank outboard design. The manufacturer explicitly considered and rejected the recommendation, citing the popularity of the high fuel capacity feature, the significant costs of re-engineering the chassis, and the fact that the overall safety record of the truck, considering all types of crashes, was comparable to that of other manufacturers. Thus, the manufacturer continued to produce the truck with its original chassis design, including the 1985 truck that Trenton Johnson was driving when he was killed.

Your firm is considering whether to file a tort suit against the manufacturer. The central claim, based in products liability, is being researched by another lawyer. However, because the state legislature has recently restricted the availability of punitive damages in products liability cases, you have been asked to assess the likelihood of recovery under an intentional tort theory, which, if viable, would allow recovery of punitive damages. You are confident that you can get reliable testimony that will establish the circumstances described above. In analyzing the prospects for recovery for an intentional tort, you should assume that *Garratt* and the Restatement provisions concerning battery are governing law in your jurisdiction.

Mental State Considerations: Long Odds, Bad Shots, and Dirty Tricks

Together, *Vosburg* and *Garratt* sketch the general types of mental states that can be shown as part of establishing a battery: Plaintiff must prove either that the defendant desired to cause harmful or offensive contact or that defendant knew with substantial certainty such contact would occur as a result of defendant's actions. Several other aspects of intent in the context of battery remain to be considered briefly.

First, the "knew with substantial certainty" rule in *Garratt* describes a sufficient, but not an invariably necessary, basis for concluding that an actor intends a result. The *Garratt* rule governs situations where the actor does not subjectively desire the harmful or offensive contact. But when a defendant subjectively desires to harm the plaintiff, there is no requirement that success be highly probable. Instead, as long as the defendant desires to cause the harmful or offensive contact and the contact actually occurs as a result of the defendant's actions, a battery is established. Thus, if the defendant shoots at the plaintiff with a gun from a great distance, with minimal chances of success, a battery is committed as long as the desired result—the wounding of the plaintiff—actually occurs.

What happens, however, when such a defendant misses the intended victim and instead strikes someone else. For example, in the leading case of Carnes v. Thompson, 48 S.W.2d 903 (Mo. 1932), the defendant had been quarrelling with the plaintiff's husband when the defendant struck at his adversary with a pair of pliers. The plaintiff's husband ducked and the pliers struck the plaintiff. Plaintiff brought a battery claim, but faced the seemingly impossible task of establishing the necessary intent, since the defendant neither desired to contact, nor believed he was substantially certain to contact, the plaintiff. Nonetheless, the court concluded that plaintiff could recover:

> If one person intentionally strikes at, throws at, or shoots at another, and unintentionally strikes a third person, he is not excused, on the ground that it was a mere accident, but it is [a] battery of the third person. Defendant's intention, in such a case, is to strike an unlawful blow, to injure some person by his act, and it is not essential that the injury be to the one intended.

Id. at 904.

The court's resolution illustrates what is commonly referred to as *transferred intent;* the ill intent that the defendant bore toward plaintiff's uninjured husband is applied to the conduct that harmed the plaintiff. Some regard the doctrine of transferred intent as a legal fiction, since rather than representing the true reality of defendant's state of mind, it imposes a legally constructed reality in order to achieve a just result. The doctrine raises other interesting questions. For example, what are its limits? Suppose the defendant shoots at a deer out of season, but the bullet strays and wounds a hidden hunter. Is the defendant liable for a battery based on the unlawful intent to harm the deer? Intuition suggests a negative answer, and courts generally follow the Restatement approach and transfer intent only when the target of the defendant's conduct was another person. See Restatement (Second) of Torts, §20(2). Moreover, is the doctrine necessary? In *Carnes,* for example, the plaintiff would presumably be able to recover in negligence and the plaintiff's husband would likely have a claim based on assault. What, then, is the value of the transferred intent doctrine?

Finally, is the intent for a battery established when the defendant merely fakes a desire to cause harmful or offensive contact, but harm actually results? Suppose the defendant swings a stick at the plaintiff, intending only to scare the plaintiff. If the plaintiff, in reaction, stumbles and is injured, a battery is established despite the lack of an intent to cause contact. Thus, in addition to the core mental states identified in *Vosburg* and *Garratt,* an intention to create the imminent apprehension of harmful or offensive contact generally satisfies the mental state requirement for battery. See Restatement (Second) of Torts, §13.

The Law-Fact Distinction: Trials Without Juries

In the law-fact distinction note following *Vosburg,* we spoke of how the functions of fact finding, law declaring, and law applying are divided between the judge and jury. Frequently, however, torts cases are tried without a jury, as was done in Garratt v. Dailey. No constitutional provision requires that torts cases be tried to juries. The only requirement is that the parties be offered the opportunity to have a jury. In many torts cases the parties do not opt for a jury. The most important reason is that in many places, particularly urban areas, it takes much longer for a case which is to be tried by a jury to be reached for trial. Thus, although most lawyers believe, perhaps incorrectly, that juries are more sympathetic to plaintiffs than are trial judges, it may be in the plaintiff's best interests to get on with the trial. In most personal injury cases, defendants pay interest only after judgment is entered against them, so long delays in reaching trial tend to hurt plaintiffs more than defendants.

That a case is tried by a judge without a jury does not mean that the law-fact distinction loses its relevancy. It only means that at the trial the functions of fact finding and law applying, as well as the function of law declaring, are performed by the trial judge. The distinction between law and fact is still important, because the findings of fact by the trial judge, like the findings of fact by a jury, are insulated from appellate review. Thus, the Supreme Court of Washington in Garratt v. Dailey could not properly have directed the trial judge to accept the testimony of the plaintiff's sister rather than that of the defendant.

The nonreviewability of the trial judge's factual findings rests on pragmatic considerations. Because the trial judge is present at the trial and can directly observe the testimony as it comes in, the trial judge is presumed to have a feel for the case that the appellate judges do not have. Thus, if the testimony of witnesses conflicts, the trial judge is better able to tell which witnesses are telling the truth. Further, appellate review of the facts is less needed than review of the law. Because a rule of law is applicable to more than one case, it is important that the law be uniform throughout a given jurisdiction. Review of questions of law by an appellate court that has the final word on what the law is does much to ensure that uniformity. In contrast to the law, the facts of a case are relevant only to that case. Were appellate review of a trial judge's findings of fact allowed, the appellate court would be duplicating the efforts of the trial judge, with no reason to believe that the appellate court would do a better job, and with some reason to believe it would not do as well.

Law and Policy: Preliminary Considerations

The appropriateness of the outcomes in *Vosburg* and *Garratt* is not self-evident. One can easily imagine opinions construing the intent requirement for battery more narrowly, thereby precluding the possibility of recovery in both cases. Why, then, did these courts choose, or at least lend their approval to, those particular rules of tort law? What are the objectives sought to be served by those rules? Indeed, why do we maintain a system of tort liability at all? Our purpose here is not to try to answer these questions, but rather to stimulate thinking about possible answers.

One obvious explanation for the rules adopted by the courts in *Vosburg* and *Garratt* is that they increase the possibility that plaintiffs will succeed and thereby receive compensation for their injuries. This impulse to make victims financially whole undoubtedly influences tort law, but *compensation* as a policy goal fails to explain the precise configuration of rules that courts construct in the tort area. If the overriding objective of tort law is to compensate victims and their families, why do we require that the plaintiff must have been injured by someone's wrongful act? A broken jaw is not less painful, disabling, or expensive when suffered in an accidental fall in the backyard. If the objective of tort liability is to help people who need financial help, why not compensate all needy victims of accidents, irrespective of anyone's wrongdoing? Or why even limit our concern to victims of accidents—why not help the person who becomes ill, or who is the helpless victim of poverty? And couldn't the objective of helping people who need financial help be achieved more directly, equitably, and efficiently under the welfare laws?

These questions reveal that the statement, "tort law aims at compensating victims" begs the underlying question of why we choose to compensate *these particular victims,* rather than victims generally. The search for answers requires us to shift focus from victims to those who have caused the harm, and to ask whether it makes good sense to require them, through the vehicle of tort law, to pay compensation to injured victims.

Two general perspectives are available for analyzing whether particular harm-causing actors should be required to pay their victims under tort law. The first approach asks whether society as a whole will derive future benefits from a particular rule governing recovery. This "instrumental" perspective does not view the imposition of liability as an end in itself, but rather conceives of tort law as an instrument for achieving broader social goals. For most "instrumentalists," the central social goal to be furthered by tort law is to maximize total wealth in society by deterring wasteful injuries and accidents. A prominent proponent of this view, scholar and Judge Richard Posner, argues that the law of battery, like all tort law, deters persons from engaging in activities that a reasonable person would view ahead of time to be socially wasteful.[4] If the harm suffered by the victim exceeds the benefit enjoyed by the actor (in *Vosburg,* if Vosburg's pain and upset over being kicked in the shin exceeds in value Putney's enjoyment derived from doing the kicking), then society will be better off if such activities are deterred by threats of liability. Even if the actor benefits more than the victim suffers, activity such as unprovoked shin-kicking is nonetheless wasteful because it generates higher transaction costs (in the form of the

4. See generally Posner, Economic Analysis of Law 206-211 (4th ed. 1992).

costs of bringing an expensive tort action to make the relevant cost-benefit determination) than would have been generated if the actor had simply gotten the victim's consent ahead of time, perhaps by means of a bribe. As Posner explains it:

> [T]orts [like] simple battery . . . involve a . . . coerced transfer of wealth to the defendant occurring in a setting of low transaction costs. Such conduct is inefficient because it violates the principle . . . that where market transaction costs are low, people should be required to use the market if they can and to desist from the conduct if they can't.[5]

In contrast to the foregoing view, a second, noninstrumental perspective argues that batteries deserve to be punished simply because they are wrongs. Under this view, punishment should accrue regardless of its capacity to deter wasteful conduct and increase societal wealth. Arguments along these lines are often framed in terms of "fairness" or "corrective justice." They are easy to understand in cases in which one person deliberately and without justification inflicts physical harm on another. In these cases, tort liability may be imposed out of some shared sense that punishment, as an end in itself, is an appropriate societal response to these kinds of obvious wrongdoing. Although in its starker forms revenge may be decried by some as uncivilized and barbaric, the psychological need for revenge runs deep. It is hard to deny that in some circumstances punishment for its own sake seems appropriate. In this view, society as well as the plaintiff has been injured, and punishment helps to address the shared sense of loss generated by antisocial conduct. But if revenge were the only purpose served by the law of battery, what explains the results in *Vosburg* and *Garratt*? Levels of wrongfulness sufficient to justify revenge hardly seem to have been reached in those cases. To answer these sorts of questions, noninstrumentalist thinkers have been forced to develop more sophisticated visions of what concepts like "justice" and "fairness" require.[6] One such view, advanced by Richard Epstein, is that the simple fact that *A* causes harm to *B* is enough to start the liability engine running.[7] *A* may be able to avoid liability by justifying or excusing his conduct in some way; but the fact that *A* caused *B*'s harm is the underlying source of *A*'s obligation to pay.

A somewhat different version of noninstrumentalist thinking is offered by George Fletcher. Reacting to the efforts of some instrumental writers "to convert the [tort system] into a makeshift medium of accident insurance

5. Id. 207-208.

6. A significant amount of scholarship is currently being generated in this area. In addition to the ideas of Richard Epstein and George Fletcher, which are discussed in text, major efforts to explain tort law from a corrective justice perspective have been undertaken by Jules Coleman, Ernest Weinrib, Richard Wright, and other scholars. For a useful collection of such efforts, see Symposium, Corrective Justice and Formalism; The Care One Owes One's Neighbors, 77 Iowa L. Rev. *i* (1992).

7. See Epstein, A Theory of Strict Liability, 2 J. Legal Stud. 151 (1973).

or into a mechanism for maximizing social utility," Professor Fletcher insists that achieving fairness between individuals is the important reason for shifting accident losses via rules of liability.[8] Fletcher's vision of fairness is fundamentally grounded in his paradigm of reciprocity, which holds that "a victim has a right to recover for injuries caused by a risk greater in degree and different in order from those created by the victim and imposed on the defendant—in short, for injuries resulting from nonreciprocal risks."[9] Professor Fletcher concludes that the intentional tort of harmful battery embodies the fairness principles reflected in the paradigm of reciprocity:

> To complete our account of the paradigm of reciprocity, we should turn to one of its primary expressions: intentional torts, particularly . . . battery. . . . An intentional . . . battery represents a rapid acceleration of risk, directed at a specific victim. These features readily distinguish the intentional blow from the background of risk. Perceiving intentional blows as a form of nonreciprocal risk helps us understand why the defendant's malice or animosity toward the victim eventually became unnecessary to ground intentional torts. The nonreciprocity of risk, and the deprivation of security it represents, render irrelevant the attitudes of the risk-creator.[10]

The author cites *Vosburg* and *Garratt* as support for his conclusions that the irrelevance of malevolence or actual desire to injure on the part of the defendant in a battery case can only be understood in terms of the fundamental fairness of allowing the injured plaintiff to recover as an innocent victim of unexcused nonreciprocal risks created by the defendant. In Fletcher's view, liability is properly imposed in such cases irrespective of whether young children are likely to be deterred by the threat of liability.

To these brief descriptions of instrumental and noninstrumental perspectives on tort law should be added mention of those writers who reject all attempts to relate tort law to a set of basic normative principles. Richard Abel, for example, argues that while tort law purports to be made up of a set of preference-neutral rules that treat everyone alike, in reality it is designed to help maintain the dominance of the powerful and the wealthy over the weak and the poor. In his Marxist critique of Anglo-American tort law,[11] Professor Abel observes that both efficiency and fairness rationales avoid making any judgment regarding the traditional distributions of wealth and power in our society. Instead, the rightness of those distributions is assumed implicitly, without discussion, and attention focuses on the changes in the status quo ante brought about by harm-causing conduct. These rationales are not to be faulted for having failed to relate their normative principles to questions of wealth distribution—such efforts are doomed to fail in any

8. See Fletcher, Fairness and Utility in Tort Theory, 85 Harv. L. Rev. 537 (1972).
9. Id. at 542.
10. Id. at 550.
11. See Abel, Torts, in The Politics of Law: A Progressive Critique 185-200 (D. Kairys ed. 1982).

event. But given the relevance of distributions of wealth and power to an adequate assessment of any system of government and law and the irrelevance of normative principles to such distributions, attempts to justify tort law on normative grounds are unavoidably incoherent. What bothers Professor Abel is not that the efficiency and fairness rationales fail to justify traditional distributions of wealth and power, but that they skate over the issue as though it does not exist.

Clearly, observers hold widely differing views on the underlying purposes served by tort law. However, debate centers not only on what tort law might be saying, but also on who, if anyone, is listening. In other words, even if one were to conclude that the purpose of tort law is, for example, to encourage socially efficient behavior, one might still question whether tort law was a proper tool to achieve this goal. Consideration of this question, which turns on an examination of the practical impact of tort rules on human behavior, is deferred until later in these materials. Even at this early junction, however, it should be clear that learning the law entails much more than memorizing a received set of rules. It involves, among many other things, both an effort to explore the purposes underlying the rules and an attempt to evaluate what impact, if any, the chosen rules are likely to have on actual human behavior.

b. Contact

The second element of the plaintiff's prima facie case in battery is that there has been a harmful or offensive contact with the plaintiff's person. Although the issue does not appear frequently, cases occasionally test whether a particular contact suffices to establish a battery.

As *Garratt* makes clear, the contact requirement does not mean that a part of the defendant's body must come into direct contact with a part of the plaintiff's body. Indirect contact will suffice. Thus, in *Garratt* the defendant was exposed to liability because his act of moving the chair caused the plaintiff to come into harmful contact with the ground. What should the result be if the plaintiff were to eat a piece of fruit that had been poisoned two hours earlier by the defendant? See Commonwealth v. Stratton, 114 Mass. 303 (1873). Or if the plaintiff were enveloped by the exhaust fumes from the defendant's bus? Cf. Madden v. D.C. Transit System, Inc., 307 A.2d 756 (D.C. App. 1973). In McCracken v. Sloan, 40 N.C. App. 214, 252 S.E.2d 250 (1979), reprinted at p. 823, below, a postal employee brought a battery action against the postmaster, alleging that the postmaster deliberately smoked a cigar in close proximity to the plaintiff, knowing that the smoke was obnoxious to the plaintiff. The court refused to allow recovery in the absence of a showing that the plaintiff had suffered a physical illness from inhaling the smoke.

Similarly, the requirement that there be a contact with the plaintiff's person is not imposed literally. It is sufficient if the defendant strikes something very closely associated with the plaintiff's person, such as the clothing the plaintiff was wearing, the cane he was holding, the horse he was riding, or the car he was driving.

Finally, brief note should be made here of situations in which the defendant intends harmful or offensive contact with the plaintiff, but fails to achieve such contact. The availability of a tort remedy in such situations typically turns on whether the plaintiff was contemporaneously aware of the defendant's unsuccessful effort to cause harmful or offensive contact. If not, recovery is generally barred, perhaps on the theory that forcing the defendant to pay the plaintiff would constitute an unjustified windfall when the plaintiff suffered no actual damages. Note, however, that this outcome is potentially disturbing to both the instrumentalist concerned with deterring dangerous conduct and the noninstrumentalist interested in punishing wrongful behavior. Why should the defendant be absolved of responsibility simply because the potentially tortious efforts went unnoticed? Can you perceive other ways in which the law responds to such concerns? In any event, the outcome is different if the plaintiff actually "sees it coming" but escapes unscathed. Tort law generally provides a remedy through an action for assault, a claim explored in greater detail in Chapter 11.

Problem 2

Cassandra and Warren Miller have come to you to determine whether they have a viable tort claim against Kingston County Hospital. The Millers own a funeral home and work together as morticians. In addition to providing private embalming and funeral services, the Millers are under contract with Kingston County Hospital to embalm and bury unidentified persons, usually homeless alcoholics, who die at the hospital.

Several months ago, the Millers received a call from the hospital to pick up the body of a "John Doe" who had died after being brought into the emergency room unconscious. When Warren Miller picked up the body at the hospital morgue, hospital personnel told him to wear protective clothing when handling the body. Although he found this admonition a bit unusual, the notation of "heart failure" on the death certificate and toe tag tempered his concern that the deceased had died of a contagious disease.

Because the hospital had performed an autopsy to determine the cause of death, the body was quite bloody. Prior to beginning the embalming process, the Millers donned protective gloves, masks, aprons, hats, and booties. During the embalming process, both the Millers were necessarily exposed to the blood, bodily fluids, and tissues of the corpse. Some thirty minutes into the procedure, Cassandra Miller discovered needle marks on the arm that indicated probable intravenous drug use. At this point, Warren relayed the hospital's unusual emphasis on protective clothing, and both

Millers became concerned that the corpse might have been infected with the AIDS virus. The Millers finished the procedure in an abbreviated fashion, removed and discarded their protective garments, and washed with a strong disinfectant.

One day later, the hospital called to inform the Millers that John Doe had been infected with the HIV virus. Since that day, the Millers have suffered greatly. Although both continue to test negatively for the HIV virus, the fear that they might have been infected with the virus has colored their lives and their relationship. Both have suffered from depression, extreme anxiety, and panic attacks. Their sexual relationship has been significantly impaired, and both have sought psychiatric help. The Millers point out that, had they known the full story, they would have insisted on cremating rather than embalming John Doe.

Unfortunately, your jurisdiction generally does not allow recovery for the kinds of emotional harm the Millers have suffered absent some concurrent physical injury. The primary exception to this limitation is when the emotional harm occurs as a result of an intentional tort such as a battery. Hearing this, the Millers seek your opinion on whether they might successfully pursue a battery claim against Kingston County Hospital. How do you respond?

2. Privileges

Even if the plaintiff has succeeded in proving the elements of the prima facie case, the defendant may escape liability by pleading and proving the existence of a privilege to inflict the harm. Privileges are generally divided into two types: consensual privileges, which depend on the plaintiff agreeing to the contact; and nonconsensual privileges, which shield the defendant from liability for harmful or offensive contact even if the plaintiff objects to the contact. We first turn to the privilege of consent, and then to a number of nonconsensual privileges.

a. Consent

What constitutes consent for purposes of barring a plaintiff's recovery in tort? The basic rule is consistent with the meaning of "consent" in everyday speech: "Consent is willingness in fact for conduct to occur. It . . . need not be communicated to the [defendant.]" Restatement (Second) of Torts §892(1). In addition to this general rule, which involves what we might call "actual" or "subjective" consent, there are other meanings of consent within the law of battery. Some, including the type at issue in the following decision of the Supreme Judicial Court of Massachusetts, relate more to the appearance of willingness than to its existence in fact.

O'Brien v. Cunard Steamship Co.

154 Mass. 272, 28 N.E. 266 (1891)

[At trial, the plaintiff advanced counts in negligence and harmful battery. At the close of the evidence, the trial court directed verdicts for defendant on both counts, and plaintiff appealed. Only those portions of the opinion dealing with the battery count are reproduced below.]

KNOWLTON, J. This case presents [the question of] whether there was any evidence to warrant the jury in finding that the defendant, by any of its servants or agents, committed [a battery] on the plaintiff. . . . To sustain [this] count, which was for an alleged [battery,] the plaintiff relied on the fact that the surgeon who was employed by the defendant vaccinated her on shipboard, while she was on her passage from Queenstown to Boston. On this branch of the case the question is whether there was any evidence that the surgeon used force upon the plaintiff against her will. In determining whether the act was lawful or unlawful, the surgeon's conduct must be considered in connection with the circumstances. If the plaintiff's behavior was such as to indicate consent on her part, he was justified in his act, whatever her unexpressed feelings may have been. In determining whether she consented, he could be guided only by her overt acts and the manifestations of her feelings. It is undisputed that at Boston there are strict quarantine regulations in regard to the examination of immigrants, to see that they are protected from small-pox by vaccination, and that only those persons who hold a certificate from the medical officer of the steamship, stating that they are so protected, are permitted to land without detention in quarantine or vaccination by the port physician. It appears that the defendant is accustomed to have its surgeons vaccinate all immigrants who desire it, and who are not protected by previous vaccination, and give them a certificate which is accepted at quarantine as evidence of their protection. Notices of the regulations at quarantine, and of the willingness of the ship's medical officer to vaccinate such as needed vaccination, were posted about the ship, in various languages, and on the day when the operation was performed the surgeon had a right to presume that she and the other women who were vaccinated understood the importance and purpose of vaccination for those who bore no marks to show that they were protected. By the plaintiff's testimony, which in this particular is undisputed, it appears that about two hundred women passengers were assembled below, and she understood from conversation with them that they were to be vaccinated; that she stood about fifteen feet from the surgeon, and saw them form in a line and pass in turn before him; that he "examined their arms, and, passing some of them by, proceeded to vaccinate those that had no mark"; that she did not hear him say anything to any of them; that upon being passed by they each received a card and went on deck; that when her turn came she showed him her arm, and he looked at it and said there was no mark, and that she should be vaccinated; that she told him she had been vaccinated before and it left no mark; "that he then said nothing, that he should vaccinate her again"; that she held up her arm to be vaccinated; that no one touched her; that she did not tell him that she did not want to be vaccinated; and that she took the ticket which he gave her certifying that he had vaccinated her, and used it at quarantine. She was one of a large number of women who were vaccinated on that occasion, without, so far as appears, a word of objection from any of them. They all indicated by their conduct that they desired to avail themselves of the provisions made for their benefit. There was nothing in the conduct of the plaintiff to indicate to the surgeon that she did not wish to obtain a card which would save her from detention at quarantine, and to be vaccinated, if necessary, for that purpose. Viewing his conduct in the light of the circumstances, it was lawful; and there was no evidence tending to show that it was not. The ruling of the court on this part of the case was correct. . . .

[The court did not reach the substance of plaintiff's alternative allegation that the surgeon was negligent in performing the vaccination, concluding that such negligence, if it occurred, could not be legally attributed to the defendant steamship company. Judgment for the defendant affirmed.]

The Law-Fact Distinction: Sufficiency of the Evidence, Directed Verdicts, and Judgments Non Obstante Veredicto

Merely because a party to a lawsuit asserts that there is an issue of fact to be resolved by the jury does not mean that there is such an issue. It is up to the party with the burden of proving the existence of a fact to come forward with sufficient evidence to justify a reasonable person in believing that the fact occurred. Unless the trial judge determines that reasonable persons can disagree about the existence of a fact, the judge will not send the question of whether the fact existed to the jury.[12] Thus, in *O'Brien,* having concluded that no reasonable person could find otherwise than that the plaintiff had manifested consent to the vaccination, the trial judge directed the jury to return their verdict for the defendant. If the judge had reached the same conclusion after the return of a plaintiff's verdict, a JNOV

12. This is not meant to imply that the trial judge will act on his or her own initiative. As the preliminary look at the process in Section A of this chapter makes clear, courts almost always act in response to requests and demands for action from the parties before them. This discussion of the sufficiency of the evidence proceeds on the assumption that the trial judge will take an issue of fact from the jury only when asked to do so by an appropriate motion for directed verdict.

would have been in order. In either event, because the absence of consent was vital to the plaintiff's right to recover in that case, the judge's determination of the consent issue in favor of the defendant also determined the ultimate issue of liability. If the particular assertion of fact that lacks sufficient supporting evidence does not dispose of the ultimate issue of liability, the court will give the question of liability to the jury along with a binding instruction that as a matter of law the jury must decide the particular factual issue for the defendant. Logically, a binding instruction is equivalent to a directed verdict, but it is limited to an issue of fact other than the ultimate issue of the defendant's liability.

In reacting to a request for a binding instruction, a motion for a directed verdict, or a motion for a JNOV, courts in most jurisdictions look at the evidence in the light most favorable to the nonmoving party. For example, in deciding whether to grant the defendant's motion for a directed verdict in *O'Brien,* the trial judge resolved every conflict in the testimony in favor of the plaintiff. This does not mean that the court must accept the plaintiff's view of the law. In *O'Brien* it was appearances, not the reality of the plaintiff's state of mind, that controlled. But in deciding whether to send the question of appearances to the jury, presumably the trial judge drew every reasonable inference from the record favorable to the plaintiff. The judge was authorized to direct a verdict for the defendant only after concluding that no reasonable juror, believing all of the plaintiff's witnesses and drawing every reasonable inference in favor of the plaintiff, could have found otherwise than for the defendant.

The plaintiff as well as the defendant may benefit from binding instructions, directed verdicts, and JNOVs. The trial judge may decide that the proof supporting a factual assertion by the plaintiff is so overwhelming that reasonable persons could only agree that the fact did occur. (Once again, in making this determination the trial judge draws all reasonable inferences and resolves all questions of credibility in favor of the nonmoving party, the defendant.) In that event, the court will either give the jury a binding instruction in favor of the plaintiff or direct the jury to return a verdict in favor of the plaintiff, depending upon whether other facts remain to be decided relating to the question of the defendant's liability. In a battery case, if the trial judge were to decide that as a matter of law the plaintiff did not consent, the liability issue might still be sent to the jury for a determination of the elements in the plaintiff's prima facie case, i.e., intent, contact, and cause-in-fact. Even when the plaintiff wins a directed verdict on the issue of liability, the judge will almost always send the further question of damages to the jury.

But whether the directed verdict or other similar order favors the plaintiff or the defendant, the important point is that in rendering a decision about the sufficiency of the evidence the trial judge is not finding facts. Instead, the judge is making a ruling of law to the effect that a finding of fact by the jury is unnecessary. To be sure, it is a ruling of law which relates directly to the jury's responsibility as fact finder; but it is, nonetheless, a ruling of law. Thus, the trial judge's decision in *O'Brien* to direct a verdict on the consent issue was reviewable by the Supreme Judicial Court on appeal. In a case where the evidence of consent is such that reasonable persons may differ and the judge properly submits the consent issue to the jury, the decision of the jury on that issue is not reviewable on appeal.

Problem 3

Alice Trudlow is seeking your advice regarding a suit she wants to bring against William Jennings. Ms. Trudlow is 32 years old, unmarried, employed by the Postal Service, and the mother of one daughter, Samantha, who will be 15 years old in two months. William Jennings is 18 years old and lives nearby.

Your first interview with Alice Trudlow took place two weeks ago. She was upset over events which had occurred several months earlier. She explained that on the Saturday night on which the events had occurred, she had gone out to a movie and dinner with friends from work. She had, for about a year, been able to leave Samantha home without a baby-sitter; on that night Samantha had assured her mother that she would be busy working on a school paper. Early during the movie, Alice Trudlow developed a migraine headache and decided to return home early. When she opened the front door and walked through the hall to the living room she saw Samantha and William Jennings on the sofa, both partially undressed, and obviously engaged in sexual intercourse. Jennings quickly left the house and Samantha locked herself in her room.

At the first interview, Alice Trudlow reported that, prior to the incident, she had become increasingly concerned with her daughter's interest in William Jennings. The two seemed to spend a lot of time together, even though prior to the incident Samantha claimed the two were "just friends." Alice Trudlow regarded Jennings as "the wrong type"; he reminded her of the teenage boyfriend who had abandoned her after finding out that she was pregnant with Samantha. Alice now deeply fears that Samantha may be heading down the same road. In her first interview, Alice told you "I love Samantha, but having her so early was very hard and changed my life in ways that I couldn't possibly understand at the time. A girl that age just doesn't understand what sex is about. I can't let Sam make the same stupid mistakes I did, but she shuts me out when I try to talk to her about it. For all I know, Jennings tricked her or forced himself on her. I've forbidden her to see him, but I'm really afraid what happened will happen again, and I have to do something."

Specifically, Alice Trudlow wanted you to talk to the District Attorney and have Jennings criminally prosecuted, or bring a civil action against him if the District Attorney won't do anything. Asked whether Samantha had encountered any physical complications as a result of the sexual encounter, Alice Trudlow explained that her daughter had suffered a tubal pregnancy that had to be surgically terminated. Although Alice Trudlow had incurred significant expenses in connection with her daughter's medical care, her main interest in pursuing legal action against Jennings seemed to be to teach him a lesson and scare him from further involvements with Samantha. "Sometimes," Alice Trudlow confessed in her initial interview, "I feel like getting a shotgun and teaching him the old fashioned way."

At the end of the interview, Alice Trudlow agreed, somewhat reluctantly, to permit you to interview Samantha out of Alice's presence. When Samantha came to your office last week, she at first refused to talk about the matter at all. After your assurance that you were trying to help her, she admitted that she had intercourse with Jennings on the night in question, and that she had done so willingly. When asked whether this was the first time, she answered that it was her business. But after a long conversation in which you gained her confidence and in which you explained that it was important for you to have the whole story, she said that it was. She said she had been "sort of going out" with Jennings for about six months, and that on several previous occasions he had suggested that they "go all the way." She had resisted, not knowing what was the right thing to do. When she later asked Bonnie Anderson, a 16-year-old girlfriend, what to do, Bonnie told her that "true love knows no limits." So, when her mother left for the movies, she invited Jennings over and did not resist his obvious moves toward having sexual intercourse.

At the interview, Samantha seemed unsure about her feelings about what had happened. She still wanted to be with Jennings, but reported that he had been decidedly cool toward her since the incident. She was, however, horrified at the thought of anything her mother might do that will make the incident public. She seemed to discount the significance of the physical complications she experienced, and seemed willing and eager to "drop the whole thing." As she left your office, she pleaded, "Can't you talk my mom out of making a big deal out of this?"

You have an appointment with Alice Trudlow to discuss the matter further with her. What advice will you give her? What, if anything, will you tell her if she asks what her daughter told you? Assume that Barton v. Bee Line, Inc., below, and the statutes referred to therein, are governing law in your jurisdiction.

Barton v. Bee Line, Inc.

238 App. Div. 501, 265 N.Y.S. 284 (1933)

LAZANSKY, J. Plaintiff appeals from an order setting aside the verdict of a jury in her favor and ordering a new trial. Plaintiff, who was fifteen years of age at the time, claimed that while a passenger of the defendant, a common carrier, she was forcibly raped by defendant's chauffeur. The chauffeur testified that she consented to their relations. It was conceded that if the chauffeur assaulted plaintiff while a passenger, defendant became liable in damages for failure to perform its duty as a common carrier to its passenger. The jury was charged that plaintiff was entitled to recover even if she consented, although consent might be considered in mitigation of damages. She had a verdict of $3,000. The court set the verdict aside on the ground that if plaintiff consented the verdict was excessive, while if she was outraged the verdict was inadequate. The court is not disposed to interfere with this exercise of discretion. The determination of the trial court was warranted for another reason which may be considered, since the verdict was set aside upon the other grounds set forth in section 549 of the Civil Practice Act as well as upon the ground that it was excessive.

It was error for the trial court to have instructed the jury that plaintiff was entitled to a verdict even if she consented to consort with the chauffeur. By the last paragraph of subdivision 5 of section 2010 of the Penal Law it is provided: "A person who perpetrates an act of sexual intercourse with a female, not his wife, under the age of eighteen years, under circumstances not amounting to rape in the first degree, is guilty of rape in the second degree, and punishable with imprisonment for not more than ten years." Under this subdivision a crime is committed even if the female consents. The effect of the charge of the court was that the provisions of the act are made the basis of a civil liability. The age limitation has been changed from time to time. At first it was ten years, then sixteen, now eighteen. There can be no doubt that the purpose of the legislative enactments was and is to protect the virtue of females and to save society from the ills of promiscuous intercourse. A female over eighteen who is ravished has a cause of action against her assailant. Should a consenting female under the age of eighteen have a cause of action if she has full understanding of the nature of her act? It is one thing to say that society will protect itself by punishing those who consort with females under the age of consent; it is another to hold that, knowing the nature of her act, such female shall be rewarded for her indiscretion. Surely public policy—to serve which the statute was adopted—will not be vindicated by recompensing her for willing participation in that against which the law sought to protect her. The very object of the statute will be frustrated if by a material return for her fall "we should unwarily put it in the power of the female sex to become seducers in their turn." (Smith v. Richards, 29 Conn. 232) Instead of incapacity to consent being a shield to save, it might be a sword to desecrate. The court is of the opinion that a female under the age of eighteen has no cause of action against a male with whom she willingly consorts, if she knows the nature and quality of her act. . . .

Order setting aside verdict in favor of plaintiff unanimously affirmed, with costs.

Clients seldom come into a lawyer's office with problems involving one or perhaps two neatly identifiable legal issues. In addition to a range of legal issues of varying complexity, a case may involve even more difficult problems of professional responsibility and human relations. In this problem, the nonlegal aspects may actually be more difficult to resolve than the purely legal. Moreover, the skills called upon here are much more those of counselor and interviewer than of legal analyst. Indeed, a significant part of a lawyer's time is apt to be spent in one form or another of counseling.

Turning to the legal issues in the problem, Samantha appears to have manifested consent. Indeed, it appears that she subjectively consented as well. But under the *Barton* case, will proof of these facts, if the case does get to trial, be enough to defeat recovery? If not, what are the facts relevant to consent?

Although the facts as Samantha explains them appear to indicate that William Jennings did not trick her or coerce her into consenting, you should understand that conduct of either sort on his part would vitiate any consent given by Samantha regardless of her relative maturity or understanding.

Apart from the merits of the case on the law, there is the decision of whether to take the case at all. This case will not be a pleasant one to handle. The reaction of many lawyers to cases of this sort is, "I should have gone to business school." Is it proper for you to decline to take the case if this is your reaction? Even if you think the case has some legal merit, can you tell Alice Trudlow otherwise, or at least play down the chance of winning, in order to back out gracefully?

Other matters you may wish to think about and resolve before Alice Trudlow comes in are:

1. To what extent are Alice Trudlow's motives important? May you, or should you, decline to take what otherwise might be a meritorious case because your client is partly motivated by revenge?
2. In any event, should your own thoughts about the wisdom of taking legal action be relevant? Should your role as a lawyer be confined to advising Alice Trudlow of her legal rights? May you, or should you, decline to take her case just because you think that her legal rights ought not to be pursued?
3. To what extent should you be influenced by what Samantha wants? And should you reveal to Alice Trudlow what Samantha told you? Who is your client—Alice Trudlow? Samantha? Both?

The Lawyer's Professional Responsibility: Some General Considerations

Lawyers are the trustees of the legal system. They dominate it at almost every level of lawmaking and law applying. The legal system touches people every day of their lives and can follow them to the grave. The public rightfully expects that a group with so much power will exercise it consistent with the public interest. But there is no easy way to compel lawyers to do that. To the layperson, the law is a mysterious thing, so that the understanding necessary for control outside the profession is largely missing. More importantly, the formal agencies that might exercise control, such as legislatures and courts, are themselves controlled substantially or wholly by lawyers. Thus, the public has had to look to the legal profession to control itself. The response by lawyers has been the development of a sense of professional responsibility—responsibility which extends not only to the client but to other lawyers, the courts, and society at large. Put most generally, this responsibility requires a lawyer in the practice of the law to be ethical. To tell a lawyer to be ethical, however, is to tell him or her very little. To give content to this command, bar associations and courts have formulated general rules which define the nature of the lawyer's professional responsibility.

The best known set of rules is the Model Code of Professional Responsibility adopted by the American Bar Association in 1969. The Code itself has no binding effect, but it has been adopted by most states as the basic set of rules of professional conduct. In 1983, reflecting the continuing evolution of ethical thought regarding professional responsibility, the American Bar Association adopted the Model Rules of Professional Conduct. Because most states have adopted or are expected to adopt versions of the Model Rules, the Model Rules will provide the primary basis for discussion of ethical issues presented by these materials. Important distinctions between the Model Rules and the Model Code will be discussed throughout the text.

As the introductory scope section of the Model Rules explains, some of the rules are imperatives, cast in the terms "shall" and "shall not." Other rules are permissive, cast in the term "may," and define areas in which the lawyer has professional discretion. One of the matters left to the discretion of the individual lawyer is the decision of whether or not to take on a particular client. In this age of legal specialization, it is no doubt sound practice for a lawyer to refuse a case in a field with which he or she is substantially unfamiliar. A torts lawyer may well not want to take on a complicated tax case. But the freedom of lawyers to refuse cases permits them to turn down prospective clients for reasons other than professional competency. Thus it is that many people—the alleged child rapist whom everyone knows is guilty, the revolutionary with his deviant political and social ideology—have often been unable to get legal representation quickly and effectively, if they can get it at all. This is in part due to the identification that the general public makes of the lawyer with the client. "He wouldn't take the case if he didn't like the client," is a common lay reaction, and lawyers are as sensitive as most people to public opinion. The choice that a lawyer makes not to represent an unpopular client for fear of losing some popular ones is at least understandable, if not entirely laudable.

Inability to pay the fee is another reason some people have been unable to get legal representation. Recent developments in legal aid, both public and private, and the constitutional right of indigent defendants in criminal cases to publicly paid counsel, have reduced the magnitude of this problem. But there is still more than a little truth to the proposition that the person with the most money can get the best lawyer, although the contingent fee system makes this less true for plaintiffs with torts claims.

Although a lawyer has the right to refuse to take a case for any reason, or for no reason at all, some in the legal profession feel that this is a right that should be exercised with restraint. They feel that if lawyers are to work truly in the public service, they must do more than just meet the minimum requirements of the rules of ethics, and that this "more" includes taking on any meritorious client unless there is a very strong and sound reason for not doing so. The comment to Rule 6.2 recognizes this by providing:

> A lawyer ordinarily is not obliged to accept a client whose character or cause the lawyer regards as repugnant. The lawyer's freedom to select clients is, however, qualified. All lawyers have a responsibility to assist in providing pro bono publico service. An individual lawyer fulfills this responsibility by accepting a fair share of unpopular matters or indigent or unpopular clients. A lawyer may also be subject to appointment by a court to serve unpopular clients or persons unable to afford legal services.

Once a lawyer decides to accept a client, the lawyer's conduct is circumscribed in a number of ways. One of the most important rules of ethics, and one of particular relevance to Problem 3, is that a lawyer must preserve the confidences of the client. The reasons for this, as stated in the Model Code of Professional Responsibility, EC 4-1 (1982) are:

> Both the fiduciary relationship existing between lawyer and client and the proper functioning of the legal system require the preservation by the lawyer of confidences and secrets of one who has employed or sought to employ him. A client must feel free to discuss whatever he wishes with his lawyer and a lawyer must be equally free to obtain information beyond that volunteered by his client. A lawyer should be fully informed of all the facts of the matter he is handling in order for his client to obtain the full advantage of our legal system. It is for the lawyer in the exercise of his independent professional judgment to separate the relevant and important from the irrelevant and unimportant. The observance of the ethical obligation of a lawyer to hold inviolate the confidences and secrets of his client not only facilitates the full development of facts essential to proper representation of the client but also encourages laymen to seek early legal assistance.

One of the most controversial differences between the Model Rules and the Model Code is the extent to which they require a lawyer to preserve the confidences of his or her client. Canon 4 of the Code of Professional Responsibility states the basic duty of client confidentiality: "A lawyer should preserve the confidences and secrets of a client." *Confidence* refers to information protected by the attorney-client privilege however that privilege might be defined by a particular jurisdiction's substantive law. *Secret* has a vaguer definition: "other information gained in the professional relationship that the client has requested be held inviolate or the disclosure of which would be embarrassing or would be likely to be detrimental to the client." (DR 4-101(A)). Limiting *secret* to information "gained in the professional relationship" may produce difficult problems of determining when the relationship begins or ends because information obtained before or after the relationship is not protected.

Rule 1.6(a) of the Model Rules broadens the scope of the information that must be kept confidential: A lawyer shall not reveal "information relating to representation of a client." Under the Model Rules, consequently, when the representation begins or ends is not an issue since the Rule imposes confidentiality on information relating to the representation even if it is acquired before or after the relationship existed.

Do the Model Rules change the scope of protected information as a practical matter? Are Samantha's statements in Problem 3 concerning her sexual relations protected under one regime but not the other? As we will see, there are some practical differences between the Model Rules and the Model Code, especially in the area of exceptions to the confidentiality rule—for example, whether an attorney must divulge a client's revealed intent to commit a crime.

A lawyer today is pulled in many different directions. He or she has duties both to the client and to the courts and may wish to take into account his or her perceptions of the public interest. Moreover, the lawyer cannot, and should not, ignore his or her own self-interest. How individual lawyers resolve the potential conflicts among these duties is important not just to the lawyer, but to the legal profession and society as well. In Problem 3, and in other problems in this book, you will have the opportunity to test your own reactions to difficult questions of professional responsibility.

Note: Minors as Parties to Litigation

In the note on the tort liability of minors and their parents, p. 20, above, we indicated that in a number of ways the law has created special rules that take into account the immaturity of minors. One of these special rules of procedure is that minors usually may not be direct parties to litigation. Instead, two procedural devices allow minors to be represented in court: the guardian ad litem (guardian for the suit) and the next friend. There is little practical difference between the two. Both the guardian ad litem and the next friend are representatives who act on behalf of the minor party. The legal rights at stake in the litigation are not those of the representative but those of the minor. A risk exists, however, that because the representative has no direct interest in the outcome, the litigation will not be conducted in a way that best serves the minor's interest. One method by which the law protects minors from this risk is by giving older minors influence or control over who shall serve as the representative. For example, under §373 of the California Code of Civil Procedure, a minor 14 or over may nominate the guardian ad litem. A court may also dismiss an action brought by a next friend over the objections of a mature minor and his or her parents. But ordinarily, the consent of a minor, even a mature one, is not a prerequisite to the appointment of a representative, although the minor is, of course, entitled to be heard on the matter.

The most important basis for judicial control over the guardian ad litem or next friend is the theory that the minor is a ward of the court. Thus, although the representative has the primary responsibility for managing the litigation, the ultimate responsibility for protecting the rights of the minor is in the court. The court on its own motion can remove the representative if it determines that there is a conflict of interest, that the representative is mishandling the case, or that removal is otherwise necessary to protect the interests of the minor.

Note: The Effect of Criminal Statutes on Consent

One question not discussed in the *Barton* opinion is why the criminal statute proscribing sexual intercourse with a girl under 18 was at all relevant to whether the consenting plaintiff can receive compensation in a private tort action for battery. The rule that makes criminal statutes relevant to civil battery cases may be traceable, in part, to the early relation between tort law and criminal law in England. During the early period of the development of the King's Courts following the Norman Conquest, petitioners seeking redress were required to show themselves to be entitled to one of a limited number of writs by which defendants were ordered to appear in court.[13] The writ of trespass, out of which the substantive law of battery eventually developed, began to be available in the King's Courts in the thirteenth

13. The main concern of the English monarchy during this early period appears to have been consolidating the power of the Crown at the head of the feudal hierarchy that had been introduced by the Norman invaders. The main function of the King's Courts was to reinforce the feudal land system and to maintain the King's peace. This royal court system, which would one day replace in importance the older Anglo-Saxon system of county and village courts, began modestly by hearing cases especially affecting the King's interests. The jurisdiction of these early King's Courts was limited, and they demonstrated no great willingness to expand upon it. The writs, with which actions in these courts were commenced, outlined with rigid particularity the bases upon which relief might be granted. Most of the earlier writs concerned disputes over land. Gradually, a limited number were developed which concerned other matters of particular interest to the Crown. It was through the gradual revision and expansion of the writ system, in effect, that the common law grew and developed during the six or seven centuries following the Conquest. For further reading on the early development of the King's Courts and the origins of the common law action of trespass, see Prosser and Keeton, Law of Torts 28-31 (5th ed. 1984); Plucknett, A Concise History of the Common Law 139-175, 353-378 (5th ed. 1956).

century. It was originally issued at the commencement of a criminal action brought to punish volitional conduct, harmful to persons or property, that might otherwise provoke violent retaliation and thus threaten further breaches of the King's peace. In time, damages came to be awarded to the injured victims of such conduct as an adjunct to the criminal proceeding. By the sixteenth century, the civil trespass action had become fully separated procedurally from the criminal action, the term "misdemeanor" being employed to distinguish the latter from the former. Thus, in light of the early overlap between criminal law and tort law, it is not surprising that American courts today (which inherited the common law of England) would, in a civil case involving battery, look for guidance to a criminal statute establishing the minimum age of consent.

In addition to the historical reasons for the rule, there may be support for it in notions of public policy. One explanation typically given is that it is appropriate for the torts process to reinforce the criminal process. In effect, plaintiffs become private prosecutors in the fight against crime. How likely is it in Problem 3, for example, that Jennings will ever be prosecuted for statutory rape, even though his violation of the criminal law seems clear? Is it the kind of case that ought to be criminally prosecuted? Perhaps in response to policy arguments of this sort, the rule in most states is more rigorous than that adopted in the *Barton* case. The weight of authority is that consent to a criminal act is totally irrelevant in civil cases—in such cases, consent does not constitute a privilege. In addition to statutory rape, these cases involve illegal abortions, illegal fights, illegal purveying of intoxicants, and the like. Thus, the majority rule may help expose and deter clandestine criminal activities by allowing the "willing" victims of such activities to sue for damages.

Critics of the majority rule argue that a consent-based privilege should be available even in cases where the underlying conduct is criminal in nature. The legal recognition of consent as a privilege that will defeat recovery stems, it will be recalled, from an ancient maxim that one who consents to being injured cannot later be heard to complain. To many persons, maxims of this sort do not lose their force simply because the act to which the plaintiff has consented happens to be criminal. Indeed, proponents of the minority rule argue that their position best deters this sort of illegal activity by denying a tort reward to those who are injured as a result of their voluntary participation in illegal activities.

Whichever argument you find more persuasive as a general proposition, special reasons may persuade you to honor the statutory scheme—and thereby refuse to recognize consent as a defense to a battery claim—when the statute in issue was intended to protect minors or others whose capacity for consent is legitimately open to question. Thus, for example, in Hudson v. Craft, 33 Cal. 2d 654, 204 P.2d 1 (1949), the court allowed an 18-year-old boy, who was injured while voluntarily participating in an illegal prize fight, to recover in battery on the ground that the statute prohibiting such fights was specifically intended to protect youth "against their own ill-advised participation in an unregulated match." Consistent with this view, most courts have applied statutory rape statutes in civil cases regardless of proof that the individual plaintiff was able to understand the nature and consequences of her act. And yet, courts occasionally modify the legislative judgments with their own views of public policy. *Barton* took a middle-of-the-road approach and demanded an inquiry into whether the plaintiff really needed the law's protection. *Barton,* however, represents the distinct minority view regarding the effect of statutory rape statutes in battery cases.

Mechanisms for Resolving Disputes: The Decision to Forgo the Claim

The barriers to recovering on a torts claim are substantial. Most laypersons have some familiarity with the judicial process and many are reluctant, for many reasons, to get involved in the process. Thus, a large number of arguably valid claims may never be pursued at all. This is an especially sore point for those who view tort law as part of the political apparatus for maintaining the status quo. Consider this excerpt from Professor Abel's radical critique, described in the Law and Policy Note at p. 31, above (from The Politics of Law: A Progressive Critique 189 (D. Kairys ed. 1982)):

> [C]lass, race, and gender will affect the extent to which and the way in which the experience of injury is transformed into a claim for legal redress: the sense of entitlement to physical, mental, and emotional well-being (women only recently began to resist abuse by their husbands; textile workers are just now coming to view chronic shortness of breath as unnatural); the feeling of competence to assert a claim and to withstand retaliation; the capacity to mobilize the legal process, which includes choosing and controlling a lawyer and preparing evidence; and financial and emotional resources, which will affect the quality of legal representation obtained and the ability of the claimant to overcome opposition and delay in order to pursue negotiation or litigation to a satisfactory conclusion.

Does Abel's critique ring true on this particular issue? Are there many persons in our society who do not realize that, at least if they have suffered serious injury that can be traced to a solvent defendant, a member of the plaintiffs' bar will consider taking the case on a contingent fee basis?

In any event, even if the claim survives the initial decision to pursue it, it may still have a short and unfruitful life. The claimant may handle the case herself. Sometimes this works, but often it does not. If the claimant does not get satisfaction through her own efforts, she will either drop the whole thing or see a lawyer. (Theoretically, a person can pursue her own claim in court without a lawyer, but it is a rarely exercised right.)

But even seeking a lawyer's help hardly assures that the matter will not die a quiet death in the lawyer's office. The claim that looked good to the claimant when she brought it to the lawyer may, on closer inspection of the law or facts, be without merit. Even if there is a solid case on the question of liability, the legally recognized harm may not be sufficient to justify pursuing the matter. In the mid-1980s, in the large urban centers in the eastern part of the United States, skilled plaintiffs' lawyers typically would not take a products liability or medical malpractice claim (both relatively expensive to prepare for, and take to, trial) unless the expected value (the amount likely to be recovered times the probability of recovering it) was in the neighborhood of $100,000. Assuming this figure (adjusted for inflation) holds through time, if a claim has a 50-50 chance of success at trial, the plaintiff must be fairly badly injured to get a big plaintiffs' firm to handle the case.

Or it may be that, regardless of anything else, the plaintiff's claim may be one that ought not to be taken into court. There are cases like this—cases in which the claimant might be better off if she forgot about her legal rights. It is arguable that a lawyer should not be concerned with the general welfare of clients—that the lawyer should only advise the client of her legal rights and leave the decision of what to do with those rights to the client. With experience, however, most lawyers develop a sense about cases that should be dropped, and it is hard to resist the temptation to bring this experience to bear in advising the client. They know that passions cool over time; that bringing in the legal process can exacerbate personal relationships; that in the end, nonlegal solutions to some legal problems are the best. Explaining these things to clients will often give them a different perspective, and will lead them to choose to let the case drop.

Bang v. Charles T. Miller Hospital

251 Minn. 427, 88 N.W.2d 186 (1958)

GALLAGHER, J. Appeal from an order of the district court denying plaintiffs' alternative motion to vacate the dismissal of their action against Frederic E. B. Foley, herein referred to as defendant, or for a new trial.

This was an action for damages for alleged . . . unauthorized operation by the defendant on his patient, Helmer Bang, referred to herein as plaintiff. The latter contends that the question as to whether he expressly or impliedly consented to the operating procedures involved was one of fact for the jury. At the close of plaintiffs' case, the defendant moved for a directed verdict upon the grounds that plaintiffs had failed to prove any actionable negligence or any cause of action against him. This motion . . . was granted. A similar motion was granted with respect to the other defendant, Charles T. Miller Hospital, but that action is not questioned on appeal.

The sole issue raised by the plaintiff on appeal is: Should the question of whether or not there was an . . . unauthorized operation have been submitted to the jury as a fact issue? . . .

. . . [P]laintiff consulted with the defendant on April 6, 1953, at the latter's office in St. Paul. The defendant testified that at that time the patient complained of diminished size and force of the urinary stream and increased frequency of urination. He said that the plaintiff described various urinary symptoms and that a rectal examination of the prostate was performed. Not being certain at that time of the exact nature of the plaintiff's ailment, the defendant informed plaintiff that he wished to make a cystoscopic examination the following day and suggested that plaintiff be admitted to the Miller Hospital in St. Paul for further investigation, which was done. He said that he informed his patient "that the purpose of his going into the hospital was for further investigation with a view to making a prostate operation if the further examination showed that that was indicated."

The important question for determination of the matter presently before us is whether the evidence presented a fact question for the jury as to whether plaintiff consented to the severance of his spermatic cords when he submitted to the operation. Defendant testified on cross-examination under the rules that he did not tell plaintiff at the time of the office visit, April 6, that any examination defendant had made or was going to make had anything to do with the spermatic cords, nor did he recall explaining to his patient what a prostate-gland operation involved. He also said that plaintiff's life was in no immediate danger because of his condition on that day.

He was further questioned:

Q: Did you tell him in your office that if the later examination in the hospital the following day indicated prostate trouble it would be necessary for you as part of your operation to cut his spermatic cords?

A: I am not certain that particular detail of the operation was explained to him.

Q: Dr. Foley, is it not true that the only thing mentioned to Mr. Bang in your office was that a further examination was needed in order to confirm your diagnosis so that you would know what you were going to do next?

A: That is correct.

On the following day the operation was performed. When defendant was asked as to the procedure used, he replied:

A: . . . the cysto-urethroscopic examination was made; following that I went over to the head of the table and talked to Mr. Bang, told him what the findings were, and that in my opinion the transurethral prostatic resection should be done and I had his consent that we proceed with that operation.

Q: Did you at that time as I understand it now ask him for his consent?
A: Yes. . . .
Q: . . . did you at the time you talked to Mr. Bang on the table tell him anything about what you were going to do about his spermatic cords?
A: I do not recall definitely whether that particular detail of the operation was discussed with Mr. Bang or not.

The patient recalled the start of the operation and, when questioned on direct examination, stated:

Q: Did he at any time before the operation began tell you that he cut your spermatic cords?
A: No.
Q: Did he at any time before the operation began tell you that it was necessary to cut your cords?
A: No.

When being questioned on cross-examination with reference to consent, the plaintiff was asked:

Q: And you certainly did consent, didn't you, Mr. Bang, to Dr. Foley doing anything to correct your trouble which in his medical knowledge he felt should be corrected?
A: Not anything he wanted to, no.
Q: Did you put any limitation on his job as a surgeon?
A: No.
Q: When he said, if I find anything that needs correction I will do it at the same time and you said that was all right, that was all of the conversation there was, wasn't it?
A: That was all of the conversation there was.

It is plaintiff's claim that he thought he was discussing his bladder because he understood from his Austin physicians something about burning out the ulcers if there were any ulcers in there. He admitted, however, that defendant said nothing to him about ulcers. Plaintiff also admitted that he did not expect to tell the doctor what to do; that he had faith in him; and that he did not expect to tell him how to perform the operation. He said that he expected the doctor would operate to do what was necessary to right and cure his condition. He testified that he did not ask the doctor what he intended to do and left it up to him to do the right thing.

. . . It is our opinion that under the record here the question as to whether plaintiff consented to the severance of his spermatic cords was a fact question for the jury and that it was error for the trial court to dismiss the action. . . .

While we have no desire to hamper the medical profession in the outstanding progress it has made and continues to make in connection with the study and solution of health and disease problems, it is our opinion that a reasonable rule is that, where a physician or surgeon can ascertain in advance of an operation alternative situations and no immediate emergency exists, a patient should be informed of the alternative possibilities and given a chance to decide before the doctor proceeds with the operation. By that we mean that, in a situation such as the case before us where no immediate emergency exists, a patient should be informed before the operation that if his spermatic cords were severed it would result in his sterilization, but on the other hand if this were not done there would be a possibility of an infection which could result in serious consequences. Under such conditions the patient would at least have the opportunity of deciding whether he wanted to take the chance of a possible infection if the operation was performed in one manner or to become sterile if performed in another.

Reversed and a new trial granted.

The Relationship Between Tort and Contract: Medical Malpractice

Given the difficulties encountered by courts in trying to work out the limits of physicians' responsibilities in medical malpractice cases, it is not surprising that some commentators have urged that the problems be resolved, ahead of time, in contracts entered into by physicians and their patients. Indeed, many health care providers have already turned to contract law as a means of self-help. Consider the following consent form:[14]

Date: ______________

1. I, ______________________________, hereby give my authorization and consent to an operation to be performed on me on or about, ____________________ by Dr. ____________________. The purpose of the operation is to attempt to correct the following condition: ____

____

2. I also consent that Dr. ____________________, during, preceding, and following the operation, perform any other procedure which he deems necessary or desirable in order to achieve the correction of the above-named condition, or any other unhealthy condition he may encounter during the operation.

3. Realizing that an operation by modern methods requires the cooperation of numerous technicians, assistants, nurses, and other personnel, I give my further consent to ministrations, and medical

14. Taken from 15 Am. Jur. Legal Forms 2d §202:146 (1973).

procedures on my body by all such qualified medical personnel working under the supervision of Dr. ________________ before, during, and after the operation to be performed.

4. I consent also to the administration of ________________ anesthesia, to be applied by Dr. ________________.

5. I understand that this operation may not be successful in ________________ the condition named above, and also that there is a danger that certain unfavorable results may follow, namely, ________________.

____

Signature of Patient

I have read the above consent form, signed by my ________________ and join with ________________ in such consent. Paragraph 5 above has been specially pointed out to me and I am aware of the possible unfavorable consequences of the operation, namely, ________________.

____

Signature of Spouse

The most interesting and important question presented by formal agreements of this sort is whether and to what extent courts will look behind them and review the facts of particular cases to see if the consent given by the patient was truly informed and uncoerced. At the extremes, courts could either give such contracts conclusive weight, inquiring only into whether, for example, the plaintiff actually signed the consent form; or give the agreement no weight, making the same full-blown inquiry into the surrounding facts as would be made if the contract never had been entered into. Few courts, if any, take either of these extreme approaches. All courts will allow the plaintiff to escape the contract if it can be shown to be the product of fraud or coercion on the part of the health care provider; all courts purport, at least, to give some weight to contracts to which patients freely agree. The problem most courts have with giving conclusive effect to such agreements is that they appear to be somewhat bootstrapping. Informed consent doctrines rest on the premise that patients lack knowledge of relevant risks and must be informed by the provider before their consent can be meaningful. How then, courts ask, can conclusive effect be given to a written agreement without inquiring into whether the patient did, in fact, understand the relevant risks of injury?

If the contract in question spells out the risks in elaborate, gory detail; if the patient admits signing it after reading it carefully; and if there are no elements suggesting lack of free consent; then we can assume most courts would end their inquiry. But contracts of consent are almost never written that way. Gory detail, spelled out ad nauseum (in the literal as well as the figurative sense) is thought to be counterproductive from the standpoint of the patient's welfare. What many physicians and patients would prefer, at least before the fact, is a contract indicating that the risks (identified in a more general way) were discussed and that consent was freely given. Such contracts, if given effect, would arguably benefit both physicians and patients in many cases. (Can you articulate how and why?) The problem, as courts see it, is that if such contracts are enforced they will also unavoidably insulate some physicians from the unpleasant consequences of their own overbearing conduct. (Again, do you see why?)

Viewed more generally, the possibility of contractually handling informed consent disputes before tort claims arise raises fundamental issues to which we shall return throughout these materials. In the present context, it will be recalled from an earlier law and policy note that the efficiency-based argument in favor of allowing recovery for harmful batteries is that the tortfeasors in these cases have improperly substituted forceful unilateral takings (that require later review under tort law) for peaceful bilateral agreements (that do not). (See pp. 29-30, above.) The appropriate judicial response in battery cases, according to efficiency analysis, is to allow recovery in tort in order to admonish the actors for having "bypassed the market." Interestingly, in the present context of informed consent contracts, the physicians seemingly have done just what they should have done—they have tried to substitute before-the-fact contractual agreements for after-the-fact review under tort law. When courts later set those agreements aside and impose liability on physicians notwithstanding the patients' earlier agreements, the courts are, in effect, admonishing those actors for having tried to rely on the market, rather than trying to bypass it.

Is this an instance of "damned if you do, and damned if you don't?" Can you begin to work out a means of accommodating the sometimes conflicting objectives of contract and tort? Are some of the expectations regarding the nature and quality of medical care best policed by tort, while others are better handled through bargaining between the patient and the health care provider?

Kennedy v. Parrott

243 N.C. 355, 90 S.E.2d 754 (1956)

Civil action to recover damages for personal injuries resulting from an alleged unauthorized operation performed by the defendant, a surgeon.

The plaintiff consulted the defendant as a surgeon. He diagnosed her ailment as appendicitis and recommended an operation to which she agreed. During the operation the doctor discovered some enlarged cysts on her left ovary, and he punctured them. After the operation the plaintiff developed phlebitis in her leg. She testified that Doctor Parrott told her "that while he was puncturing this cyst in my left ovary that he had cut a blood vessel and caused me to have phlebitis and that those blood clots were what was causing the trouble." She also testified that defendant told Dr. Tyndall, who was called in to examine her for her leg condition, "that while he was operating he punctured some cysts on my ovaries, and while puncturing the cyst on my left ovary he cut a blood vessel which caused me to bleed," to which Dr. Tyndall said, "Fountain [the defendant], you have played hell."

The defendant recommended that the plaintiff go to Duke Hospital, and there is evidence he promised he would pay the bill. She also saw Dr. I. Ridgeway Trimble at Johns Hopkins, Baltimore. Dr. Trimble operated on her left leg and side "to try to correct the damage that was done."

Plaintiff had to undergo considerable pain and suffering on account of the phlebitis. . . .

At the conclusion of the testimony, the court, on motion of the defendant, entered judgment of involuntary nonsuit. Plaintiff excepted and appealed.

BARNHILL, C.J. [The court first ruled that the plaintiff's evidence was not sufficient to support recovery in negligence. Although the defendant's conversation with Dr. Tyndall and his willingness to pay for her treatment at Duke Hospital suggest he may have been at fault, defendant's uncontradicted medical testimony (the plaintiff offered none) indicated that defendant had exercised due care.]

On the other hand, if her cause of action is for damages for personal injuries proximately resulting from [a] trespass on her person, as she now asserts, and such operation was neither expressly nor impliedly authorized, she is entitled at least to nominal damages. . . .

Prior to the advent of the modern hospital and before anesthesia had appeared on the horizon of the medical world, the courts formulated and applied a rule in respect to operations which may now be justly considered unreasonable and unrealistic. During the period when our common law was being formulated and applied, even a major operation was performed in the home of the patient, and the patient ordinarily was conscious, so that the physician could consult him in respect to conditions which required or made advisable an extension of the operation. And even if the shock of the operation rendered the patient unconscious, immediate members of his family were usually available. Hence the courts formulated the rule that any extension of the operation by the physician without the consent of the patient or someone authorized to speak for him constituted a battery or trespass upon the person of the patient for which the physician was liable in damages.

However, now that hospitals are available to most people in need of major surgery; anesthesia is in common use; operations are performed in the operating rooms of such hospitals while the patient is under the influence of an anesthetic; the surgeon is bedecked with operating gown, mask, and gloves; and the attending relatives, if any, are in some other part of the hospital, sometimes many floors away, the law is in a state of flux. More and more courts are beginning to realize that ordinarily a surgeon is employed to remedy conditions without any express limitation on his authority in respect thereto, and that in view of these conditions which make consent impractical, it is unreasonable to hold the physician to the exact operation—particularly when it is internal—that his preliminary examination indicated was necessary. We know that now complete diagnosis of an internal ailment is not effectuated until after the patient is under the influence of the anesthetic and the incision has been made.

These courts act upon the concept that the philosophy of the law is embodied in the ancient Latin maxim: Ratio est legis anima; mutata legis ratione mutatur et lex. Reason is the soul of the law; the reason of the law being changed, the law is also changed.

Some of the courts which realize that in view of modern conditions there should be some modification of the strict common law rule still limit the rights of surgeons to extend an operation without the express consent of the patient to cases where an emergency arises calling for immediate action for the preservation of the life or health of the patient, and it is impracticable to obtain his consent or the consent of someone authorized to speak for him.

Other courts, though adhering to the fetish of consent, express or implied, realize "that the law should encourage self-reliant surgeons to whom patients may safely entrust their bodies, and not men who may be tempted to shirk from duty for fear of a law suit." They recognize that "the law does not insist that a surgeon shall perform every operation according to plans and specifications approved in advance by the patient and carefully tucked away in his office-safe for courtroom purposes.". . .

In major internal operations, both the patient and the surgeon know that the exact condition of the patient cannot be finally and definitely diagnosed until after the patient is completely anesthetized and the incision has been made. In such case the consent—in the absence of proof to the contrary—will be construed as general in nature and the surgeon may extend the operation to remedy any abnormal or diseased condition in the area of the original incision whenever he, in the exercise of his sound professional judgment, determines that correct surgical procedure dictates and requires such an extension of the operation originally contemplated. This rule applies when the patient is at the time incapable of giving consent, and no one with authority to consent for him is immediately available.

In short, where an internal operation is indicated, a surgeon may lawfully perform, and it is his duty to perform, such operation as good surgery demands, even when it means an extension of the operation further than was originally contemplated, and for so doing he is not to be held in damages as for an unauthorized operation.

"Where one has voluntarily submitted himself to a physician or surgeon for diagnosis and treatment of an ailment it, in the absence of evidence to the contrary, will be presumed that what the doctor did was either expressly or by implication authorized to be done."

Unexpected things which arise in the course of an operation and incidental thereto must generally at least be met according to the best judgment and skill of the surgeon. And ordinarily a surgeon is justified in believing that his patient has assented to such operation as approved surgery demands to relieve the affliction with which he is suffering.

Here plaintiff submitted her body to the care of the defendant for an appendectomy. When the defendant made the necessary incision he discovered some enlarged follicle cysts on her ovaries. He, as a skilled surgeon, knew that when a cyst on an ovary grows beyond the normal size, it may continue to grow until it is large enough to hold six to eight quarts of liquid and become dangerous by reason of its size. The plaintiff does not say that the defendant exercised bad judgment or that the extended operation was not dictated by sound surgical procedure. She now asserts only that it was unauthorized, and she makes no real showing of resulting injury or damage.

In this connection it is not amiss to note that the expert witnesses testified that the puncture of the cysts was in accord with sound surgical procedure, and that if they had performed the appendectomy they would have also punctured any enlarged cysts found on the ovaries. "That is the accepted practice in the course of general surgery."

What was the surgeon to do when he found abnormal cysts on the ovaries of plaintiff that were potentially dangerous? Was it his duty to leave her unconscious on the operating table, doff his operating habiliments, and go forth to find someone with authority to consent to the extended operation, and then return, go through the process of disinfecting, don again his operating habiliments, and then puncture the cysts; or was he compelled, against his best judgment, to close the incision and then, after plaintiff had fully recovered from the effects of the anesthesia, inform her as to what he had found and advise her that these cysts might cause her serious trouble in the future? The operation was simple, the incision had been made, the potential danger was evident to a skilled surgeon. Reason and sound common sense dictated that he should do just what he did do. So all the expert witnesses testified.

Therefore, we are constrained to hold that the plaintiff's testimony fails to make out a prima facie case for a jury on the theory she brings her appeal to this Court. The judgment entered in the court below is

Affirmed.

As these cases suggest, the issue of consent in medical malpractice cases is complex and arises in diverse contexts. On rare occasions a patient will succeed in proving that consent to treatment was obtained through a physician's fraudulent misrepresentations. Thus, in Mink v. University of Chicago, 460 F. Supp. 713 (N.D. Ill. 1978), the court ruled that a complaint stated a cause of action in battery when it alleged that the plaintiffs had been given diethylstilbestrol (DES) without their knowledge or consent as part of an experiment conducted by a university hospital. Generally, fraud will vitiate consent if the victim is substantially misled concerning the nature and quality of the touching intended by the actor. See generally Restatement (Second) of Torts §892B.

Problems with consent arise even in the absence of fraud. Thus, plaintiffs in medical malpractice cases based on lack of informed consent typically have given some sort of consent to being treated, and the issue for decision is whether that consent is legally adequate to protect the defendant health care provider. The question of legal adequacy takes two basic forms. The first of these, illustrated by the *Kennedy* case, above, is presented when the physician is given consent to perform a certain medical operation or treatment and thereafter extends the operation or treatment beyond the boundaries of the consent as given. On this point, Kennedy v. Parrott is not universally followed. In some states, the consent is implied only if there is an emergency which requires treatment not expressly authorized. The Restatement (Second) of Torts contains the following provision relevant to the question of a physician's (or any actor's, for that matter) privilege to act in an emergency, absent actual consent:

> §892D. EMERGENCY ACTION WITHOUT CONSENT
>
> Conduct that injures another does not make the actor liable to the other, even though the other has not consented to it if
>
> (a) an emergency makes it necessary or apparently necessary, in order to prevent harm to the other, to act before there is opportunity to obtain consent from the other or one empowered to consent for him, and
>
> (b) the actor has no reason to believe that the other, if he had the opportunity to consent, would decline.

The second type of informed consent problem involves cases like *Bang* in which the doctor fails to explain to the patient the risk of side effects of a treatment to which the patient has agreed. In such cases, most courts determine the defendant doctor's liability not by the law of battery, but by the law of negligence. See, e.g., Canterbury v. Spence, 464 F.2d 772 (D.C. Cir.), *cert. denied,* 409 U.S. 1064 (1972) (negligent failure to disclose a 1 percent risk of paralysis inherent in back surgery). The distinction between battery and negligence as the basis of liability is not academic. The applicable statute of limitations, which limits the time after the wrong during which suit can be brought, may be different for the two torts. More importantly, under a battery theory, the only issue of fact is whether the defendant adequately explained the nature of the operation; but under negligence, the doctor may be able to avoid liability by proving that the failure to explain was reasonable. Finally, under negligence, the defendant can avoid liability by proving that even if the collateral risks of the treatment had been fully explained, the plaintiff would have consented—that is, that the failure to inform did not cause the harm. Under battery, whether or not the plaintiff would have consented is irrelevant. What reasons in policy support the distinction between failure to inform as to the nature and extent of the treatment and the failure to inform of collateral risks?

Whatever the legal theory on which these claims are based, plaintiffs are required to prove more than that the physician failed to mention some minor aspect of a pending treatment. Thus, in Henderson v. Milobsky, 595 F.2d 654 (D.C. Cir. 1978), the court of appeals held that a dentist did not owe his patient the duty to warn him of a 1-in-20,000 chance that the patient would suffer some slight loss of sensation to a small section of his face as a result of a tooth extraction. But see Sard v. Hardy, 281 Md. 432, 379 A.2d 1014 (1977), in which the court reversed a directed verdict for the defendant physician when the plaintiff showed that the defendant had failed to tell her that there was a 2 percent chance that an operation would fail in its intended objective of rendering her sterile. Is it likely that the differing outcomes here are solely the result of the differing probabilities of harm?

Problem 4

You have been called in to consult with Lydia Fisher, the director of a public water system that supplies drinking water to a large, primarily rural sector of the state. Like a number of systems serving areas of comparable size, her system filters and chlorinates the water supply but does not add fluoride. The director wants to begin fluoridating the water supply, but is concerned about liability.

When asked about the risks and benefits of fluoridation, Fisher tells you the following story. Fluoridation of public water supplies began about 50 years ago. Public health experts consider it a safe, effective, and inexpensive way of preventing tooth decay in children and osteoporosis among the elderly. Recent studies show that a reduction in tooth decay as high as 65 percent can be achieved for an annual cost of 15 cents per person. More than half of the nation's public water supplies are now fluoridated.

Fisher notes that the benefits of fluoridation can be obtained by taking prescription fluoride tablets orally. However, given the relative poverty and poor education of a significant portion of the population of her district, she does not view this method as an adequate public health response. "What will happen," she says, "is that the well-off and well-educated will take good care of themselves. But the dental health of the poor children of the district is already an enormous problem, and there is no reason to believe that an admonition to take fluoride orally will be the least bit effective."

Indeed, she views this as a classic public health issue, where taking collective action is far more efficacious than relying on individual choice.

As to the risks of fluoridation, the director notes that a small but vocal minority has always resisted fluoridation programs. Some of this resistance stems from a general and unthinking mistrust of all government health efforts. She also explains that fluoridation has been blamed, without any scientific support, for a host of medical problems. She admits that excessive levels of fluoridation can cause discoloration of teeth and unhealthy hardening of long bone structures, and that rare instances of allergic reactions—primarily skin rashes—to fluoridated water do occur. The director further notes that one recent study involving rats and mice raised some possibility that fluoride, in very large doses, might have some carcinogenic properties. She discounts the study on several grounds, however. It is contradicted by 45 years of similar studies that have failed to show such health risks. Also, the results of the study are themselves ambiguous and of marginal statistical significance. And the relevance of rodent studies to humans is open to debate. "At best," she states, "the study indicates that there is a slight risk of a slight risk."

In sum, the director regards the possible known risks of fluoridation as minimal compared to its established health benefits. "It's like not vaccinating kids because one in a million will have an adverse reaction. Life has risks; the only thing we can do is choose among them wisely. Fluoridation benefits people, whether they realize it or not." In this regard, she notes that a state health commission, which oversees public water systems, has just issued a report that again strongly recommends fluoridation.

In short, the director wishes to push ahead with fluoridation and does not intend to announce the change ahead of time. "The only thing I owe the public is a safe and healthy water supply," she explains, "and the state commission report and a half-century of experience make clear that fluoridation distinctly fosters public health. There will be an uproar—there always is—but I'm prepared to weather that. But this is a question for experts. I won't let it be decided by public referendum. The public hears 'cancer' and they lose their common sense. A person would have to drink a swimming pool a week to approximate the levels in the fluoride study, but people don't consider the remoteness of the risk in their thinking. They're just not rational about some things. And those who get hurt are the kids who could really benefit from fluoridation."

The director's only concern involves her potential liability if someone claims to have suffered harm, or perhaps merely offense, from consuming fluoridated water. Assuming that no flat rule of municipal immunity protects the director from liability for intentional torts, what advice would you give her regarding potential liability exposure if she goes ahead with fluoridation? Do you recommend that she announce her plan ahead of time? If so, what should she say about the risks of fluoridation?

In Re Estate of Brooks

32 Ill. 2d 361, 205 N.E.2d 435 (1965)

MR. JUSTICE UNDERWOOD delivered the opinion of the court:

This is an appeal from the probate division of the circuit court of Cook County which entered an order appointing a conservator of the person of Mrs. Bernice Brooks, and allowed the conservator's request to be authorized to consent, on behalf of Mrs. Brooks, to transfusions of whole blood to her. The transfusions were made, and appellants, Mrs. Brooks and her husband, now seek to have all orders in the conservatorship proceedings expunged, and the petition therein filed dismissed. . . .

On and sometime before May 7, 1964, Bernice Brooks was in the McNeal General Hospital, Chicago, suffering from a peptic ulcer. She was being attended by Dr. Gilbert Demange, and had informed him repeatedly during a two-year period prior thereto that her religious and medical convictions precluded her from receiving blood transfusions. Mrs. Brooks, her husband and two adult children are all members of the religious sect commonly known as Jehovah's Witnesses. Among the religious beliefs adhered to by members of this group is the principle that blood transfusions are a violation of the law of God, and that transgressors will be punished by God. . . .

Mrs. Brooks and her husband had signed a document releasing Dr. Demange and the hospital from all civil liability that might result from the failure to administer blood transfusions to Mrs. Brooks. The patient was assured that there would thereafter be no further effort to persuade her to accept blood.

Notwithstanding these assurances, however, Dr. Demange, together with several assistant State's attorneys, and the attorney for the public guardian of Cook County, Illinois, appeared before the probate division of the circuit court with a petition by the public guardian requesting appointment of that officer as conservator of the person Bernice Brooks and further requesting an order authorizing such conservator to consent to the administration of whole blood to the patient. No notice of this proceeding was given any member of the Brooks family. Thereafter, the conservator of the person was appointed, consented to the administration of a blood transfusion, it was accomplished and apparently successfully so, although appellants now argue that much distress resulted from transfusions due to a "circulatory overload.". . .

It is argued by appellants that the absence of notice in any form to Mrs. Brooks or her husband, who were readily available at the hospital, constituted a denial of due process vitiating the entire proceeding; that insufficient proof was presented to establish the patient's incompetency (the doctor testified Mrs. Brooks was "semi-disoriented" and not "fully capable" but also stated "I think she would consent to surgery. It is the fact this is a transfusion of blood she objects to"); and that acceptance of medical treatment previously refused because of religious and medical reasons (blood transfusions are not entirely free from hazard) cannot be judicially compelled under the circumstances here present.

While, under the particular circumstances here, some merit is to be found in all of these contentions, we believe we should predicate our decision upon the fundamental issue posed by these facts, i.e.: When approaching death has so weakened the mental and physical faculties of a theretofore competent adult without minor children that she may properly be said to be incompetent, may she be judicially compelled to accept treatment of a nature which will probably preserve her life, but which is forbidden by her religious convictions, and which she has previously steadfastly refused to accept, knowing death would result from such refusal? So far as we have been advised or are aware, there is no reported decision in which this question has been squarely presented and decided.

. . . It seems to be clearly established that the First Amendment of the United States Constitution as extended to the individual States by the Fourteenth Amendment to that constitution, protects the absolute right of every individual to freedom in his religious belief and the exercise thereof, subject only to the qualification that the exercise thereof may properly be limited by governmental action where such exercise endangers, clearly and presently, the public health, welfare or morals. Those cases which have sustained governmental actions as against the challenge that it violated the religious guarantees of the First Amendment have found the proscribed practice to be immediately deleterious to some phase of public welfare, health or morality. The decisions which have held the conduct complained of immune from proscription involve no such public injury and no danger thereof.

Applying the constitutional guarantees and the interpretations thereof heretofore enunciated to the facts before us we find a competent adult who has steadfastly maintained her belief that acceptance of a blood transfusion is a violation of the law of God. Knowing full well the hazards involved she has firmly opposed acceptance of such transfusions, notifying the doctor and hospital of her convictions and desires, and executing documents releasing both the doctor and the hospital from any civil liability which might be thought to result from a failure on the part of either to administer such transfusions. No minor children are involved. No overt or affirmative act of appellants offers any clear and present danger to society—we have only a governmental agency compelling conduct offensive to appellant's religious principles. Even though we may consider appellant's beliefs unwise, foolish or ridiculous, in the absence of an overriding danger to society we may not permit interference therewith in the form of a conservatorship established in the waning hours of her life for the sole purpose of compelling her to accept medical treatment forbidden by her religious principles, and previously refused by her with full knowledge of the probable consequences. In the final analysis, what has happened here involves a judicial attempt to decide what course of action is best for a particular individual, notwithstanding that individual's contrary views based upon religious convictions. Such action cannot be constitutionally countenanced. . . .

While the action of the circuit court herein was unquestionably well-meaning, and justified in the absence of decisions to the contrary, we have no recourse but to hold that it has interfered with basic constitutional rights.

Accordingly, the orders of the probate division of the circuit court of Cook County are reversed.

Orders reversed.

The ultimate clash of wills between doctor and patient arises when the patient expressly refuses to consent to lifesaving treatment. Given the nature of the physician's mission it is not surprising that the medical profession is reluctant to stand idly by and watch a medically needless death, even if the death is self-chosen. Challenges to the right of doctors to perform, over the objections of the patients, lifesaving operations are not litigated in battery cases. This may be because doctors typically seek judicial approval ahead of time, as in *Estate of Brooks,* and because conceptual difficulty would be involved in calculating damages. Instead, the litigation in which the patient's "right to die" is pitted against the doctor's "duty to save" is initiated by doctors or hospitals seeking judicial authorization to perform the lifesaving treatment.

The litigation is not frequent and the results are diverse, so that any particular judicial response cannot be called typical. In *Estate of Brooks,* the court emphasized the religious basis of the patient's refusal to consent. But should it matter that the reasons given were religious? What if the operation promised survival, but a life of pain? Or immobility? Or what if the patient has just had enough of life? The court in *Estate of Brooks* also seemed to regard as important the fact that the patient had no minor children. What should the relevance of that fact be? For a case in which the court did not authorize the overriding of the patient's refusal for religious reasons to consent to a life-saving blood transfusion even though he was the father of two young children, see In re Osborne, 294 A.2d 372 (D.C. App. 1972). But see Application of the President and Directors of Georgetown College, Inc., 331 F.2d 1000 (D.C. Cir. 1964), *cert. denied sub nom.* Jones v. President and Directors of Georgetown College, Inc., 377 U.S. 978 (1964) (court should prevent the "ultimate abandonment"—death of a parent—of a seven-month-old child by ordering blood transfusion for the mother).

The issue of consent becomes even more problematic when the patient is comatose or otherwise incompetent to make medical decisions. Consider, for example, the situation confronted by the New Jersey high court in In re Conroy, 98 N.J. 321, 486 A.2d 1209 (1985). The patient's condition is described in the majority opinion as follows (98 N.J. at 337, 486 A.2d at 1217):

> At the time of trial, Ms. Conroy was no longer ambulatory and was confined to bed, unable to move from a semi-fetal position. She suffered from arteriosclerotic heart disease, hypertension, and diabetes mellitus; her left leg was gangrenous to her knee; she had several necrotic decubitus ulcers (bed sores) on her left foot, leg, and hip; an eye problem required irrigation; she had a urinary catheter in place and could not control her bowels; she could not speak; and her ability to swallow was very limited. On the other hand, she interacted with her environment in some limited ways: she could move her head, neck, hands, and arms to a minor extent; she was able to scratch herself, and had pulled at her bandages, tube, and catheter; she moaned occasionally when moved or fed through the tube, or when her bandages were changed; her eyes sometimes followed individuals in the room; her facial expressions were different when she was awake from when she was asleep; and she smiled on occasion when her hair was combed, or when she received a comforting rub.

The patient's nephew and guardian sought permission to remove the nasogastric tube through which his aunt was being fed. Without the tube, she would die of dehydration in a short time. The trial court denied the requested relief, and plaintiff appealed. The patient died pending the appeal, but the New Jersey Supreme Court decided to hear arguments and render a decision in order to provide guidance for future cases.

The court concluded that life-sustaining treatment may be withheld or withdrawn from an incompetent patient if one of three separate tests is satisfied: (1) if it is clear that the patient would have refused the treatment under the circumstances involved; (2) if there is some trustworthy evidence that the patient would have refused the treatment, and the decisionmaker is satisfied that it is clear that the burdens of the patient's continued life with the treatment outweigh the benefits of that life; or (3) in the absence of proof of probable intent, if the net burdens of the patient's life with the treatment clearly and markedly outweigh the benefits that the patient derives from life, and the effect of administering painful life-sustaining treatment would be inhumane. Moreover, if tests (2) or (3) are employed, the patient's family or next of kin must concur.

Note: Consent to Harmful Contacts in Sports

Up to this point, the analysis of consent and conduct that exceeds consent has focused primarily on the medical malpractice area. Another significant source of cases involving similar issues is individuals' willing participation in contact sports. What is the actor's exposure to battery-based liability, for example, when the defendant tackles the plaintiff in a football game and breaks the plaintiff's leg? Just as with medical malpractice cases, battery and negligence overlap considerably in the "torts and sports" area. The focus here will be on the participant's exposure to liability in battery.

When someone tackles an opponent in a game of football, clearly the elements of a prima facie case in battery are present. The actor intends a contact that, in the absence of consent, would be both offensive and harmful and, in the broken leg hypothetical, a harmful contact results. Whether the actor will be liable in battery, therefore, depends on whether the other person consented to be tackled. In most instances, a consent-based privilege will be available.[15] In some professional sports, such as boxing, the consent will be formalized in a lengthy contract; in the rest of the cases, the consent will be either implied in fact from the plaintiff's participation or sufficiently apparent (as in *O'Brien*) for the defendant actor to rely on the assumption that the plaintiff is willing to be contacted violently.

But the mere fact that a football player is said to have consented to being tackled while running with the ball does not necessarily mean that he will be said to have consented to any and all intentional contacts with his person. Clearly, a range of football-related contacts fall outside the limits of the privilege extended to the defendant actor. Thus, if the plaintiff is intentionally tackled while standing on the sidelines during a time out, or if the defendant shoots him with a rifle to prevent him from scoring a touchdown, the plaintiff's consent to participating in the game will not bar recovery for his resulting injuries.

The question of how these last examples of excessive violence are worked out is interesting from a conceptual standpoint. Two major analytical approaches are presented by §892A of the Restatement (Second) of Torts: (1) the plaintiff may be said to consent in the first instance only to those contacts that fall within the limits of acceptable conduct in the sport (see §892A(2)(b)); or (2) the defendant actor who engages in excessive violence may be said to have exceeded the otherwise effective consent given by the plaintiff (see §892A(4)). The significance of the choice between these two analytical approaches inheres in the allocation of the burden of proof. Generally speaking, defendants bear the burden of establishing the existence of consent, whereas plaintiffs bear the burden of showing that consent has been exceeded.

If the sport in which the parties were engaged is subject to formal rules or recognized custom and usage, courts will first look to those sources to determine the contours of the consent-based privilege. Contacts prohibited by rules designed to protect participants from injury will not support a privilege; but violations of rules designed merely to secure the better playing of a game as a test of skill will not jeopardize a privilege otherwise available to the defendant. (See Restatement (Second) of Torts §50, Comment *a.*) Thus, in the football hypotheticals presented above, the defendants would be liable in battery for intentionally tackling the plaintiff on the sidelines

15. Of course, one could argue that if the contact was consented to, it is not offensive. But the bone-jarring contact would nonetheless be intentionally harmful, in the sense that it was intended to be physically detrimental, even if the full extent of the resulting harm was neither intended nor even foreseeable.

or for shooting him. But the defendant's conduct would not automatically become tortious simply because the tackle occurred during a play that was called back because of an offsides infraction. In cases in the first category, must the defendant know he is violating a rule? What if a player blocks another and is called for an illegal block, but the play was not flagrant and the player believed what he did was permissible?

These sorts of issues were presented in Hackbart v. Cincinnati Bengals, Inc., 601 F.2d 516 (10th Cir.), *cert. denied,* 444 U.S. 931 (1979), in which a professional football player sued a member of an opposing team and that player's employer for injuries resulting from being struck on the back of the head by the individual defendant after a play had ended. After a trial, judgment was entered for the defendants. From the record in that case it appears that the individual defendant did not intend to injure the plaintiff, but had acted impulsively, out of frustration. The court of appeals concluded, in reversing and remanding for a new trial (601 F.2d at 521):

> The general customs of football do not approve the intentional punching or striking of others. That this is prohibited was supported by the testimony of all of the witnesses. They testified that the intentional striking of a player in the face or from the rear is prohibited by the playing rules as well as the general customs of the game. Punching or hitting with the arms is prohibited. Undoubtedly these restraints are intended to establish reasonable boundaries so that one football player cannot intentionally inflict a serious injury on another. Therefore, the notion is not correct that all reason has been abandoned, whereby the only possible remedy for the person who has been the victim of an unlawful blow is retaliation.

The examples discussed thus far, including the *Hackbart* case, appear to reflect the first analytical approach described earlier—the plaintiffs succeed in these cases because the defendants are unable to demonstrate that their conduct was, on the face of the record, within the rules of the particular game or sport. The sort of cases that are likely to involve the second analytical approach described earlier, in which the plaintiffs succeed in demonstrating that the defendants exceeded the limits of the consent as given, typically involve conduct that is unprivileged because it is accompanied by actual intent to harm the plaintiff. Thus, according to the Restatement, even if the defendant tackles the plaintiff while the plaintiff is carrying the ball during play, the plaintiff will succeed if he can prove that the defendant deliberately injured him. Note, however, the difficulties in proof that confront the plaintiff. If the defendant's behavior—for example, tackling the ball carrier during play—is within the rules of the game, and if such behavior, because it involves forceful physical contact, carries with it an inevitable and significant risk of harm, how is an injured plaintiff to prove that a particular defendant actually desired to cause injury? What kinds of evidence might be useful to a plaintiff in distinguishing such a defendant from one who inadvertently, though in identical fashion, causes harm? And how does this rule operate in the case of the professional boxer, whose central aim, often declared quite boisterously prior to the fight, is to hurt his opponent? See generally Yasser, Torts and Sports 1-30 (1985). Finally note that even if the plaintiff is unable to prevail on an intentional tort claim, many jurisdictions now recognize a right to recover if the plaintiff's harm was the result of recklessness on the part of the defendant. See, e.g., Gauvin v. Clark, 404 Mass. 450, 537 N.E.2d 94 (1989).

b. Self-Defense

Of the nonconsensual privileges, the most important is self-defense. The general rules governing self-defense are set forth in the Restatement (Second) of Torts:

§63. SELF-DEFENSE BY FORCE NOT THREATENING DEATH OR SERIOUS BODILY HARM

(1) An actor is privileged to use reasonable force, not intended or likely to cause death or serious bodily harm, to defend himself against unprivileged harmful or offensive contact or other bodily harm which he reasonably believes that another is about to inflict intentionally upon him.

(2) Self-defense is privileged under the conditions stated in Subsection (1), although the actor correctly or reasonably believes that he can avoid the necessity of so defending himself,

(a) by retreating or otherwise giving up a right or privilege, or

(b) by complying with a command with which the actor is under no duty to comply or which the other is not privileged to enforce by the means threatened.

§65. SELF-DEFENSE BY FORCE THREATENING DEATH OR SERIOUS BODILY HARM

(1) Subject to the statement in Subsection (3), an actor is privileged to defend himself against another by force intended or likely to cause death or serious bodily harm, when he reasonably believes that

(a) the other is about to inflict upon him an intentional contact or other bodily harm, and that

(b) he is thereby put in peril of death or serious bodily harm or ravishment, which can safely be prevented only by the immediate use of such force.

(2) The privilege stated in Subsection (1) exists although the actor correctly or reasonably believes that he can safely avoid the necessity of so defending himself by

(a) retreating if he is attacked within his dwelling place, which is not also the dwelling place of the other, or

(b) permitting the other to intrude upon or dispossess him of his dwelling place, or

(c) abandoning an attempt to effect a lawful arrest.

(3) The privilege stated in Subsection (1) does not exist if the actor correctly

> or reasonably believes that he can with complete safety avoid the necessity of so defending himself by
>
> (a) retreating if attacked in any place other than his dwelling place, or in a place which is also the dwelling of the other, or
>
> (b) relinquishing the exercise of any right or privilege other than his privilege to prevent intrusion upon or dispossession of his dwelling place or to effect a lawful arrest.
>
> §70. CHARACTER AND EXTENT OF FORCE PERMISSIBLE
>
> (1) The actor is not privileged to use any means of self-defense which is intended or likely to cause a bodily harm . . . in excess of that which the actor correctly or reasonably believes to be necessary for his protection. . . .

The Restatement (Second) goes on to provide, in §71, that an actor who uses excessive force in self-defense is liable "for only so much of the force . . . as is excessive."

Note: Rules v. Standards as Means of Guiding and Judging Behavior

The Restatement provisions are noteworthy in their textual detail. They distinguish, for example, between deadly and nondeadly threats and between attacks against the actor which occur in the actor's dwelling and those that occur elsewhere. As such, the provisions might be characterized as *rules* in that they attempt to specify precisely how an actor should behave under carefully defined circumstances. As a means of formulating legal commands, a rule-based approach has several advantages. Before the fact, rules tend to offer relatively unambiguous guidance to those seeking to comply with the law's commands. And after the fact, clear rules make it easier for the judicial process to determine whether an actor has in fact satisfied legal requirements. This, in turn, tends to promote consistency in adjudication. Under a perfectly detailed set of rules, application of the law should be error-proof, for the rules would specify the precise outcome for every conceivable set of facts the fact-finder might determine.

Yet, using highly detailed rules to guide and judge human behavior also has its disadvantages. First, a rule-based approach invites ever more detailed rules. What for example, is a "dwelling place"? Does it include the hallway of an apartment building? What of a homeless person attacked under a highway overpass where he frequently sleeps? It is tempting to answer such questions by formulating more rules, either through judicial decision or legislation. But doing so risks encrusting the law with excessive detail. Moreover, as rules are further refined, their ability to guide human behavior prospectively may, paradoxically, diminish rather than increase; rather than being a beacon informing human conduct, the law may become a thicket through which only the professionally initiated—i.e., the lawyers—can safely pass. Finally, the limits of human foresight, the imprecision of language, and the corrosive effects of time make it highly improbable that any a set of rules can anticipate and account for all possible cases. Thus, we are always left with the problem of the hard case, the one that falls between the rules.

In response to such problems, the law might rely less heavily on detailed rules in favor of *general standards*. Rather than attempting to specify all possible sets of circumstances, such standards simply set a single, general rule of behavior and leave courts the task of determining, on a case by case basis, whether the standard was met. Thus, the law of negligence, which we take up in Chapter 4, essentially takes a standard-based approach; its basic command boils down to something like "be reasonable, or pay the consequences." Can the Restatement provisions regarding self-defense be replaced by such a unified standard? How about: "A defendant is privileged to fight back only as necessary"?

Generally speaking, standards tend to have benefits and drawbacks that are the mirror image of those of detailed rules. Thus, a standard is simple and accessible, and it applies to all cases. Yet, compared to a detailed set of rules, a general standard is of limited value in guiding behavior prospectively or insuring consistent assessments of that behavior retrospectively. For instance, in the two examples of general standards given above, how will individuals, or the courts that will later assess their conduct, know when their behavior is "reasonable" or their actions in self-defense are "necessary"?

At this point, two things may become clear. First, rules and standards are not really distinct approaches, but rather represent ends of a spectrum along which we can formulate legal commands. Thus, a set of rules is simply a highly differentiated standard, or, put conversely, a standard is a highly aggregated and generalized rule. Many legal commands lie somewhere in the middle of the spectrum, offering some detail and some generality. Thus, the Restatement's self-defense provisions, although quite detailed, don't define the circumstances that might lead an actor to "reasonably believe" that harm is imminent. Second, legal regimes are seldom static in their choice of approaches: Over time, very general standards tend toward differentiation, while overly-detailed rules risk recapitulation into a general standard.

The rules-standards spectrum, as well as the dynamic process of movement along that spectrum, can be observed in many areas of law. In the context of this course, it will often prove useful for you to consider where a particular legal command is situated on the spectrum, and why it might make sense for it to be framed in that manner.

Problem 5

The presentation of the evidence in Saunders v. Petrangelo, a case tried before a jury in Hardwick County Superior Court, has been completed.

Defendant has filed a motion for a directed verdict. There is little dispute as to the facts, and a fair summary of the evidence is:

During the summer months prior to August 8, two years ago, there had been a wave of robberies in Central City. The problem was particularly acute in the commercial section of the West End, a predominantly working-class, ethnically and racially diverse section of the city. There had been shootings in the course of several of the robberies, and two of the victims, both liquor store employees, were killed. The defendant, Salvatore Petrangelo, owns and operates a liquor store in the West End. The incident out of which the case arose occurred a few minutes after 10:00 P.M. on August 8. John Saunders, a 35-year-old black man, was shot by the defendant after he entered the store. On direct examination, the plaintiff described what happened in this way:

Q: Now, Mr. Saunders, will you tell us what time you entered Petrangelo's store?
A: Several minutes after ten o'clock, probably two or three minutes after.
Q: That's ten P.M., at night?
A: Yes, I knew that it closes at ten, and I had run to get there before it closed.
Q: You went there to buy some liquor?
A: That's right—a bottle of bourbon.
Q: What was the weather that night?
A: It had been raining off and on; it was raining as I went in.
Q: Tell us about how you went into the store. Did you walk right in frontwards?
A: No. As I walked up to the front of the store, I had my umbrella up. I looked in the window to see if the store was open, and saw someone behind the counter. I tried the door and it was unlocked. Then I closed my umbrella and sort of pushed the door the rest of the way open with my shoulder and went in sort of backwards, with the umbrella behind me. When I got through the door, I stood there for a couple of seconds to shake the water off the umbrella. I didn't want to get water all over the floor of the store.
Q: What happened then?
A: Well, I turned around and saw someone behind the counter with a gun pointed at me. I shouted, "What the hell," or something like that, and next thing I know he shoots me. Hit me in the shoulder and I went down.
Q: How many times did he shoot? Was that in the left shoulder?
A: Yes, in the left shoulder. I don't know how many times he shot. Man, was I scared. It . . . It happened so fast I couldn't count.
Q: How were you dressed that night?
A: Well, I had on a hat, raincoat, rubbers, and . . .
Q: Were you wearing them in a peculiar manner, an unusual manner?
A: What do you mean?

Q: Did you have your hat pulled down over your eyes or your coat collar up around your neck?
A: Well, I might have. I really don't remember. It was windy that night and I might have.
Q: Were you carrying a gun—a rifle, shotgun, or anything like that?
A: No, I wasn't. I really don't like guns. I sure don't now.
Q: How were you holding your umbrella as you entered the store? After you shook the water off?
A: In my hand, or maybe under my arm. I don't know.
Q: Did you point it toward the counter?
A: I might have. I might have sort of held both hands and the umbrella up toward the counter to try and shield myself, you know? I don't remember exactly.

On cross-examination, the plaintiff admitted that he knew that the store usually closed at ten and that it was after ten when he arrived at the store that night. The plaintiff also testified that he had opened the door part way and left it ajar while he turned to close his umbrella. He characterized the length of time from when he first looked in the window until he was shot entering the store as "several seconds, maybe five or six."

On direct examination by his own attorney, the defendant testified in part as follows:

Q: So you were aware of the holdups that had been going on in the West End and the shootings?
A: You bet I was. I bought the gun when I read about the shooting at Foster Brothers Liquors on Fourth Street.
Q: What type of gun did you buy?
A: A 38–caliber revolver.
Q: Did you register the gun?
A: Yes.
Q: Why did you stay open until ten, with all that happening?
A: I do a lot of business after supper. People want some beer to watch a ball game with, or have some friends over. There aren't so many places they can get it. So I stay open. It's good business.
Q: Tell us what happened on the night of August 8.
A: The shooting, you mean. I was about to close—to lock up, to count the cash, and put it in the safe. I usually have quite a bit of cash on hand at closing time. The store was empty. Then I see this guy looking in the window, and when I look up and see him, he ducks back behind the door.
Q: Did you get a good look at the person through the window?
A: No. The light isn't good outside, and the window was wet from the rain. Then the door opens, maybe a foot or so, and no one comes

through the door. I'm getting pretty nervous at this point so I reach for my gun just in case.

Q: Where was your gun?

A: I kept it under the counter.

Q: So then what happened?

A: So then this guy pushes the door open and backs into the store. He just stands there for a minute, and I can see that he's got something in his hands. Then he spins around. He's this big black guy, and points this thing at me and starts yelling. It looks like a shotgun or a rifle; so I shoot. I'm not taking any chances. I remember what happened to Cal Billings, and it's not going to happen to me.

Q: Mr. Petrangelo, who is Cal Billings?

A: A friend of mine. Got shot and killed over on Parker Boulevard in a liquor store holdup a couple of years ago. Before what happened in my store.

Q: Prior to the incident in your store, did you know anything about those other robberies?

A: Not much. Just that they shot first and didn't ask questions.

Q: Did you know at that time whether any black persons had been involved?

A: I don't know, exactly. I guess I heard at least one of them was black. Maybe more. It's hard to remember.

Q: All right, Mr. Petrangelo, returning to the night of August 8, two years ago, when Mr. Saunders turned around in front of you, how many times did you shoot?

A: Once. One time.

Q: Did you pull your revolver out before he turned around?

A: Yes. It was right there, and I had it by the time he stuck that thing in my face.

Q: How did he look when he turned around?

A: Like a thug. He had his hat pulled down over his eyes so you couldn't see much of his face. His coat collar was turned up. He's got this thing in his hands that looks like a rifle, and he's pointing it right at me.

Q: How long would you say it took from the time you first saw someone through the window until the plaintiff spun around and you shot him? How many seconds?

A: I would say 15 or 20 seconds, maybe more. Twenty at least.

Q: Did you have to shoot? Could you have ducked behind the counter, or made it back to the storage room?

A: Frankly, I didn't think about that. It was my store, and I thought there was a gun pointing at me. I just reacted to save myself.

Q: What happened after the shooting?

A: I ran around the counter and out the front door. I was yelling for help. I saw some people running toward me and then I went back inside. When I realized that the guy on the floor didn't have a gun, I did everything I could to help him. I'm sorry this ever happened, but I really thought my number was up.

Q: Getting back to your description of the store. How far is it from your counter to the front door?

A: Twenty feet.

Q: How was the lighting in your store?

A: Overhead fluorescents.

Q: How is your eyesight, Mr. Petrangelo?

A: I wear glasses. I was wearing them then and I could see all right.

Should the defendant's motion for a directed verdict be granted? If the judge sends the case to the jury, what would be the substance of your closing argument to the jury on behalf of the plaintiff? On behalf of the defendant? Assume that the Restatement provisions and the following opinion are governing law in the jurisdiction.

Courvoisier v. Raymond

23 Colo. 113, 47 P. 284 (1896)

Edwin S. Raymond, appellee, as plaintiff below, complains of Auguste Courvoisier, appellant, and alleges that on the 12th day of June, A.D. 1892, plaintiff was a regularly appointed and duly qualified acting special policeman in and for the city of Denver; that while engaged in the discharge of his duties as such special policeman, the defendant shot him in the abdomen, thereby causing a serious and painful wound; that in so doing the defendant acted wilfully, knowingly and maliciously, and without any reasonable cause. . . .

The defendant, answering the complaint, denies each allegation thereof, and, in addition to such denials, pleads five separate defenses. These defenses are all in effect a justification by reason of unavoidable necessity. A trial resulted in a verdict and judgment for plaintiff for the sum of three thousand, one hundred and forty-three (3,143) dollars. To reverse this judgment, the cause is brought here by appeal.

CHIEF JUSTICE HAYT delivered the opinion of the court.

It is admitted or proven beyond controversy that appellee received a gunshot wound at the hands of the appellant at the time and place designated in the complaint, and that as the result of such wound the appellee was seriously injured. It is further shown that the shooting occurred under the following circumstances:

That Mr. Courvoisier, on the night in question, was asleep in his bed in the second story of a brick building, situate at the corner of South Broadway and Dakota streets in South Denver; that he occupied a portion of the lower floor of this building as a jewelry store. He was aroused from his bed shortly after midnight by parties shaking or trying to open the door of the jewelry store. These parties, when asked by him as to what they wanted, insisted upon being admitted, and upon his refusal to comply with this request, they used profane and abusive epithets toward him. Being unable to gain admission, they broke some signs upon the front of the building, and then entered the building by another entrance, and passing upstairs commenced knocking upon the door of a room where defendant's sister was sleeping. Courvoisier partly dressed himself, and, taking his revolver, went upstairs and expelled the intruders from the building. In doing this he passed downstairs and out on the sidewalk as far as the entrance to his store, which was at the corner of the building. The parties expelled from the building, upon reaching the rear of the store, were joined by two or three others. In order to frighten these parties away, the defendant fired a shot in the air, but instead of retreating they passed around to the street in front, throwing stones and brickbats at the defendant, whereupon he fired a second and perhaps a third shot. The first shot fired attracted the attention of plaintiff Raymond and two deputy sheriffs, who were at the Tramway depot, across the street. These officers started toward Mr. Courvoisier, who still continued to shoot, but two of them stopped when they reached the men in the street, for the purpose of arresting them, Mr. Raymond alone proceeding towards the defendant, calling out to him that he was an officer and to stop shooting. Although the night was dark, the street was well lighted by electricity, and when the officer approached him defendant shaded his eyes, and, taking deliberate aim, fired, causing the injury complained of.

The plaintiff's theory of the case is that he was a duly authorized police officer, and in the discharge of his duties at the time; that the defendant was committing a breach of the peace, and that the defendant, knowing him to be a police officer, recklessly fired the shot in question.

The defendant claims that the plaintiff was approaching him at the time in a threatening attitude, and that the surrounding circumstances were such as to cause a reasonable man to believe that his life was in danger, and that it was necessary to shoot in self-defense, and that defendant did so believe at the time of firing the shot. . . .

The next error assigned relates to the instructions given by the court to the jury and to those requested by the defendant and refused by the court. The second instruction given by the court was clearly erroneous. The instruction is as follows: "The court instructs you that if you believe from the evidence, that, at the time the defendant shot the plaintiff, the plaintiff was not assaulting the defendant, then your verdict should be for the plaintiff."

The vice of this instruction is that it excluded from the jury a full consideration of the justification claimed by the defendant. The evidence for the plaintiff tends to show that the shooting, if not malicious, was wanton and reckless, but the evidence for the defendant tends to show that the circumstances surrounding him at the time of the shooting were such as to lead a reasonable man to believe that his life was in danger, or that he was in danger of receiving great bodily harm at the hands of the plaintiff, and the defendant testified that he did so believe.

He swears that his house was invaded shortly after midnight by two men, whom he supposed to be burglars; that when ejected, they were joined on the outside by three or four others; that the crowd so formed assaulted him with stones and other missiles, when, to frighten them away, he shot into the air; that instead of going away someone approached him from the direction of the crowd; that he supposed this person to be one of the rioters, and did not ascertain that it was the plaintiff until after the shooting. He says that he had had no previous acquaintance with plaintiff; that he did not know that he was a police officer, or that there were any police officers in the town of South Denver; that he heard nothing said at the time by the plaintiff or anyone else that caused him to think the plaintiff was an officer; that his eyesight was greatly impaired, so that he was obliged to use glasses, and that he was without glasses at the time of the shooting, and for this reason could not see distinctly. He then adds: "I saw a man come away from the bunch of men and come up towards me, and as I looked around I saw this man put his hand to his hip pocket. I didn't think I had time to jump aside, and therefore turned around and fired at him. I had no doubts but it was somebody that had come to rob me, because some weeks before Mr. Wilson's store was robbed. It is next door to mine."

By this evidence two phases of the transaction are presented for consideration: *First,* was the plaintiff assaulting the defendant at the time plaintiff was shot? *Second,* if not, was there sufficient evidence of justification for the consideration of the jury? The first question was properly submitted, but the second was excluded by the instruction under review. The defendant's justification did not rest entirely upon the proof of assault by the plaintiff. A riot was in progress, and the defendant swears that he was attacked with missiles, hit with stones, brickbats, etc.; that he shot plaintiff, supposing him to be one of the rioters. We must assume these facts as established in reviewing the instruction, as we cannot say what the jury might have found had this evidence been submitted to them under a proper charge.

By the second instruction the conduct of those who started the fracas was eliminated from the consideration of the jury. If the jury believed from the evidence that the defendant would have been justified in shooting one of the rioters had such person advanced towards him as did the plaintiff, then it became important to determine whether the defendant mistook plaintiff for one of the rioters, and if such a mistake was in fact made, was it excusable in the light of all the circumstances leading up to and surrounding the commission of the act? If these issues had been resolved by the jury in favor of the defendant, he would have been entitled to a judgment. . . .

Where a defendant in a civil action like the one before us attempts to justify on a plea of necessary self-defense, he must satisfy the jury not only that he acted honestly in using force, but that his fears were reasonable under the circumstances; and also as to the reasonableness of the means made use of. In this case perhaps the verdict would not have been different had the jury been properly instructed, but it might have been, and therefore the judgment must be reversed.

Reversed.

Focusing on the rules expressed by the Restatement (Second) and by *Courvoisier,* how many separate issues of fact do you see in this problem? What evidence is there in the case that would lead the jury to resolve these issues one way or the other? As to any of these issues, is the evidence so compelling that a reasonable jury could resolve them only one way—that is, in favor of the plaintiff or the defendant?

The Lawyer's Professional Responsibility: Playing to the Prejudices of the Jury

If the defendant's motion for directed verdict were to be denied in Problem 5, and the issue of self-defense were to go to the jury, the lawyers would face a problem that, in a variety of forms, arises fairly frequently in trial practice: To what extent may, or should, a lawyer try to play to the prejudices of the jury? The question arises here in perhaps its starkest form: the plaintiff is black; the possibility exists that some of the jurors will indulge in inappropriate assumptions based on underlying prejudices. Depending on the attitudes of the jurors, the biases could cut either way. Some jurors may feel sympathy for the plaintiff because he is black, and view the defendant's conduct as inherently racist; others may be sympathetic with the defendant because he is white. At the outset of this chapter, in the introductory text in Section A, we observed in general terms that trial lawyers *want* jurors who are biased in their favor, and presumably couch their arguments to play to those biases. Do, or should, the biases to which lawyers play include socially harmful prejudices of the sort we are now considering?

The problem has two dimensions: a substantive law dimension and a professional responsibility dimension. Regarding the first, the trial judge is given fairly broad discretion to grant a motion for new trial on the ground that counsel has appealed to the jury's prejudices against the other side, based on race, nationality, or ethnic background. Note, however, that a lawyer's effort to invoke jury sympathy for a client based on such characteristics is as objectionable as an appeal to be unsympathetic to the other side for the same reason. Thus, in Jackson v. Chicago Transit Authority, 273 N.E.2d 748, 751-752 (Ill. App. 1971), the court of appeals concluded:

> Thereafter, during the closing statement made by plaintiff's counsel to the jury, he alluded to the fact that his client was Negro, as contrasted to the jurors, the attorneys and the court itself, who were all Caucasians. The trial court properly intervened and told the jury to disregard the argument. The trial court acted with complete propriety. An argument of this type should not be made before any tribunal. It is an unmitigated appeal to prejudice and its effect could only be destructive of the proper administration of justice. However, counsel for plaintiff persisted in this argument and again alluded to the racial background of his client. The court properly admonished counsel and again directed the jury to disregard this argument.
>
> Nevertheless, the damage had been done; and, although the jury was thus instructed, it may well be said that the admonition of the court operated only to rivet their attention more firmly to the prejudicial argument. The total and combined impact upon the jury of [this] type of misconduct requires the granting of a new trial.

Regarding the second dimension of the problem being considered, the ethical limitations on a lawyer's appeal to juror prejudice, several provisions in the professional responsibility regulations are relevant. The American Bar Association's Model Code of Professional Responsibility provides as an aspirational standard: "[A] lawyer should not by subterfuge put before a jury matters it cannot properly consider." EC 7-25. A related disciplinary rule prohibits the introduction of irrelevant matters and "engag[ing] in undignified or discourteous conduct which is degrading to a tribunal." DR 7-106(C)(1)&(6). The Model Rules of Professional Conduct contain a similar ban on irrelevant matters and also prohibit a lawyer's seeking to influence jurors by improper means. Rules 3.4(e) & 3.5(a). The American Bar Association Standards Relating to the Administration of Criminal Justice contain similarly worded provisions forbidding prosecutors and defense counsel to use "arguments calculated to inflame the passions or prejudices of the jury." Standards 3-5.8(c) & 4-7.8(c). As a practical matter, however, violation of these provisions is unlikely to lead to formal disciplinary proceedings against the offending lawyer. See generally Wolfram, Modern Legal Ethics 620 (1986).

The Law-Fact Distinction: Evaluation of Conduct

In the law-fact distinction note, p. 15, above, conclusions of fact were described as "what happened," reached by the fact finder "much in the same sense that a scientist might conclude that a given object weighs three grams," and rules of law were defined as "generalized rules calling for certain legal consequences to follow from a particular set of facts." In many cases of harmful battery, these definitions suffice for whatever purpose is to be served by labelling a particular issue as one of fact or law. However, since that first note we have encountered issues that are not so easily classified according to these definitions. For example, one of the issues in a battery case may be whether the contact with the plaintiff is "offensive." (See §§13 and 19 of the Restatement (Second) of Torts discussed in connection with *Vosburg,* above.) Scientists do not typically make scientific assertions as to the offensiveness of contacts. Or consider the question of the reasonableness of the defendant's belief in the preceding problem that he was being robbed—a scientist's function does not typically include answering questions of that sort. Obviously, the assertion that an actor's conduct is offensive, or unreasonable, conveys more than merely "what happened." And yet, if these issues of offensiveness and unreasonableness do not fit the classic definition of an issue of fact, it is equally clear that they do not fit the definition of an issue of law. The assertion that Petrangelo's conduct in the preceding problem was reasonable, or unreasonable, is not a declaration of a prospective, generalized rule to govern behavior. It is a retrospective evaluation of his conduct.

Because issues of this sort do not fit neatly into either of the standard definitions, some commentators have referred to them as "mixed questions of law and fact." See, e.g., Bohlen, Mixed Questions of Law and Fact, 72 U. Pa. L. Rev. 111 (1924); Green, Mixed Questions of Law and Fact, 15 Harv. L. Rev. 271 (1901). Others prefer to talk instead in terms of the process of applying law to fact. See, e.g., Weiner, The Civil Jury Trial and the Law-Fact Distinction, 54 Calif. L. Rev. 1867, 1871-1876 (1966). Regardless of the terminology employed, these issues are almost universally treated, in this country, as issues for the jury to resolve; if there is no jury, they will be the subject of findings of fact by the judge. On balance, this seems to be a commonsense solution. Recall that an offensive contact is one "that offends a reasonable sense of personal dignity." The experience of the ordinary citizen rather than the expertise of the lawyer would seem to be the better authority for gauging offensiveness. Furthermore, offensiveness and unreasonableness usually can be determined only on the facts and circumstances of each individual case. It is not the sort of determination that can have much value as precedent in later cases.

Problem 6

A partner in your firm has asked you for help with a difficult case. Your firm represents the parents of Jason Talco, a small and quiet 12-year-old boy who seriously injured another child with a baseball bat. From interviews with Jason, his parents, and school officials, the following story emerges.

At the time of the incident, Jason was in the sixth grade at Dearborn Middle School. Small for his age, shy, and bookish, Jason was an easy target for the school's bullies. Among them was an eighth-grade student named Louie Chevette, now the plaintiff in a battery action against Jason. Big and mean-spirited, Louie had picked on Jason and several other students from the beginning of the school year. Mostly, this consisted of shoving Jason into lockers, knocking his books loose, and the like. By mid-year, however, the harassment had escalated. Louie had begun using threats of violence to extort lunch money from other students, including Jason. He had also badly beaten up several students after school. Suspensions by the school had failed to temper Louie's behavior.

The incident in question occurred shortly after Jason told his father of the problem. Rather than contact school officials, Jason's father insisted that Jason resolve the conflict himself. He ordered Jason to stop paying Louie and encouraged his son to "get Louie before he can get you." Jason's father freely admits all this. Always disappointed by his son's timidity and small size, he believed this to be a situation where his son could "grow up and learn to handle his problems like a man."

Several days after his conversation with his father, Jason was again accosted by Louie. When Jason refused Louie's demand for money, Louie pinned Jason against a wall and told him: "You will pay. I will get you. I will get you today. I will cut you bad." Jason spent the remainder of the school day in terror. He did not go to school officials, both because of his father's prohibition and because he believed, based on the Louie's past attacks on other students, that such officials would be powerless to protect him.

As Jason was returning from gym before the final period of school, he saw Louie bending over to retrieve something from his locker. Jason's rage and fear exploded, and he attacked the unsuspecting Louie with a baseball bat. Jason's attack took place with stunning speed and ferocity, and Louie was severely injured before several teachers intervened to restrain Jason.

Jason is now facing juvenile disciplinary proceedings and a civil suit by Louie. Under state law, parents are vicariously liable for the intentional wrongdoing of their children. Here, the evidence unequivocally establishes that Jason attacked Louie, and that Louie did not see the attack coming. Before approaching Louie's lawyer concerning settlement, however, the supervising partner wants to know whether any defenses to liability exist. In particular, the partner wonders to what extent the events surrounding the attack might bear on the question of liability.

In this regard, two other aspects of the case may be pertinent. First, Jason has consistently maintained that he remembers little of the attack. He remembers returning from gym class, and seeing Louie's back. He remembers feeling sweaty and "his head boiling." And he recalls several teachers holding him against the wall and shouting at him to calm down. But he claims no direct recollection of the actual attack.

Second, the psychologist for the school system has supplied a written evaluation of Jason that suggests that the nature of the attack may have been partly due to the way Jason was raised. The psychologist believes that in families like the Talcos, where the parents are strict, authoritarian, and reluctant to display emotion, children often have difficulty handling strong feelings. The report notes:

> Such a family system emphasizes controlling rather than processing emotions. The over-constrained range of acceptable behavior within the family unit forces children to suppress feelings that are incompatible with the parental insistence on order. The child eventually internalizes this demand for control and develops internal resources for suppressing emotions. However, when very strong emotions are stimulated by external events, the child's control system often breaks down catastrophically and without warning, resulting in a behavioral manifestation that is inappropriate to context. The events in this case are consistent with this hypothesis.

What is your assessment of Jason's chances of raising a successful defense to Louie's battery claim? What evidence is relevant to such a defense?

Mental State Considerations: Determining Reasonableness

As the preceding law-fact distinction note suggests, the trier of fact is often called upon in a torts case to pass upon the reasonableness of an actor's behavior. Indeed, even in this chapter, which focuses on intentional wrongdoing, issues of reasonableness abound. Would a reasonable person find a kick during class hours to be offensive? Would a reasonable doctor perceive the patient in *O'Brien* to have consented? Would a reasonable person have perceived a need to act in self-defense under the circumstances presented in *Courvoisier?* Such questions continue to percolate throughout the remainder of the materials on intentional torts; and when we reach negligence, they dominate the inquiry, requiring judges and juries constantly to decide whether the conduct in question was reasonable.

At that point, we will explore in greater detail the various tools courts use to resolve the reasonableness inquiry. At this juncture, however, it is useful to raise some preliminary concerns. First, why insist on reasonableness at all? In the self-defense context, for example, shouldn't it be sufficient that the defendant honestly believed that he was in imminent danger of bodily harm? What is gained by requiring, as a condition for escaping liability, that such belief and the attendant response by the defendant also be judged as reasonable by the trier of fact?

An initial response might be that the requirement of objective reasonableness inspires caution and reflection in an actor contemplating potentially harmful activity. One can imagine, for example, the doctor in *O'Brien* thinking: "She appears to consent, but I'm not sure everyone would agree.

Perhaps I should make sure." As a deterrent against imprudence, then, the reasonableness requirement obviously has some value.

Yet it also has limitations. First, situations arise in which prudent deliberation is unlikely to occur. Self-defense is perhaps the best example. As Justice Holmes once noted: "Detached reflection cannot be demanded in the presence of an uplifted knife." Brown v. United States, 256 U.S. 335, 343 (1921). Modern psychological research tends to support this view by suggesting that under situations of extreme stress, the primitive limbic system of the brain, which is programmed to respond vigorously to perceived threats to an individual's survival, is capable of overwhelming the cerebral cortex wherein the capacities for reflection, judgment, and restraint are thought to reside. See R. Restak, The Fiction of the "Reasonable Man," The Washington Post, May 17, 1987 p. C3. Under such circumstances, the law's announced preference for prudence is likely to go unheard.

Moreover, just as situations arise that preclude prudent deliberation, some individuals, by their very nature, have difficulty discerning and meeting the standard of reasonable behavior. For example, young children, such as those involved in *Vosburg* and *Garratt,* are unlikely to have any firm sense of ordinary adult standards of care. Similarly, some adults, because of physical or mental disabilities, will be unable to react to situations in the same manner as would the theoretical "reasonable person."

How, then, can we explain tort law's retention of a reasonableness requirement, particularly in cases like *Courvoisier* where the circumstances conspire against careful deliberation? One answer is that in such situations, the reasonableness requirement helps resolve a "choice of innocents" dilemma. Consider, for example, a case like *Courvoisier* involving a mistaken use of self-defense. From a moral perspective, most would conclude that such a mistake is innocent as long as the defendant was honestly trying to make the best decision under the circumstances. But nonetheless, an equally innocent plaintiff was injured by the defendant's intentional conduct.

In deciding which of two innocent parties should bear the resulting loss, the law might sensibly focus on whether the defendant's honest mistake was reasonable. If it was, then the law can justify a privilege because the defendant only did what any "ordinary" person might have done under the circumstances. In short, the law rejects the claim of wrongdoing by noting that the same outcome might well have occurred had the plaintiff been in the defendant's shoes. But if the defendant's mistake was honest but unreasonable, the innocent plaintiff's claim for compensation arguably becomes more compelling because the plaintiff was exposed to the nonreciprocal risk of unreasonable behavior. Justice Holmes again voices the traditional sentiment:

> [W]hen men live in society, a certain average of conduct, a sacrifice of individual peculiarities going beyond a certain point, is necessary to the general welfare. If, for example, a man is born hasty and awkward, is always

> having accidents and hurting himself or his neighbors, no doubt his congenital defects will be allowed for in the courts of Heaven, but his slips are no less troublesome to his neighbors than if they sprang from guilty neglect. His neighbors accordingly require him, at his proper peril, to come up to their standard, and the courts which they establish decline to take his personal equation into account.

O. W. Holmes, The Common Law 108 (1881). As will be developed further in Chapter 4 on negligence, the law offers other justifications for its frequent decision to assess individual conduct against the behavior of the hypothetical reasonable person.

Moreover, tort law has several means by which it ameliorates the potential harshness, noted by Holmes, that stems from the application of the reasonable person standard to assess the conduct of individuals who, because of circumstance or nature, are not necessarily able to react as an ordinary person might. For example, the law recognizes certain inherent characteristics as affecting individual capacity, and modifies the reasonable person standard accordingly. Holmes continues:

> There are exceptions to the principle that every man is presumed to possess ordinary capacity to avoid harm to his neighbors, which illustrate the rule, and also the moral basis of liability in general. When a man has a distinct defect of such a nature that all can recognize it as making certain precautions impossible, he will not be held answerable for not taking them. A blind man is not required to see at his peril; and although he is, no doubt, bound to consider his infirmity in regulating his actions, yet if he properly finds himself in a certain situation, the neglect of precautions requiring eyesight would not prevent his recovering for an injury to himself, and, it may be presumed, would not make him liable for injuring another.

Id. at 109. Thus, we have the reasonable blind person standard, the reasonable handicapped person, and so on. This ameliorative process is also furthered by the requirement, made clear by *Courvoisier,* that the defendant's conduct must be assessed against the hypothetical reaction of a reasonable person *under similar circumstances.*

Both modifications help give texture and context to the reasonable person standard, and thereby increase the chances that the trier of fact may come to understand why what the unusual defendant did under unusual circumstances was nonetheless reasonable. The difficulty arises in determining how far to carry this process of contextualizing the reasonable person standard. Should personality traits such as aggressiveness or timidity be considered inherent characteristics, so that the actor's self-defense is assessed against the behavior of "reasonable" persons of a like disposition? And against what set of circumstances should we assess the actor's reactions? Is the fact that the actor was drunk at the time, or that the actor chronically overreacts to perceived threats because of abuse suffered as a child, relevant in determining whether acts allegedly done in self-defense were reasonable?

Note here the tension between judging an individual's behavior without understanding him and understanding him so well that we are no longer able to pass judgment on his behavior. The law must draw the line somewhere and refuse to further contextualize the reasonable person standard (can you see why?), but the line so drawn is often waivering and imprecise. Consider, for example, the case of the battered spouse who uses deadly force against her abusive husband. In assessing her self-defense claim, we would certainly want to modify the reasonable person standard to account for the lesser size and strength of the defendant relative to her abuser, perhaps by using a reasonable woman standard. But suppose the defendant acted while her husband was sleeping? Wouldn't the jury balk at a self-defense claim under such circumstances, concluding that no reasonable person would perceive imminent danger from a sleeping spouse and that, in any event, the possibility of leaving or going to the police made the use of deadly force unnecessary?

If the law is willing, the defendant conceivably might be able to answer such questions by introducing evidence, usually through expert testimony, about the psychological condition known as battered woman's syndrome. Roughly summarized, such evidence suggests that, under conditions of serious chronic abuse, an ordinary person may become so psychologically debilitated that she is effectively unable to escape her abuser, even when remaining with him places her life in jeopardy. Under such circumstances, she may reasonably, though perhaps mistakenly, conclude that killing her sleeping spouse represents her only hope of survival. In short, her conduct, while quite at odds with an unmodified reasonable person standard, may become comprehensible if judged against the standard of a reasonable battered spouse.

Yet, refining the reasonable person standard to this extent is not without costs. First, contextualizing the standard eventually defeats one of its chief process values—the jury's ability to use its own collective experience as a proxy for reasonable conduct. Instead, expert testimony, with all its accompanying costs and risks, must often be used to educate the jury about the defendant's particular character and outlook. Moreover, excessive refinement of the reasonable person test defeats the expectation, voiced by Holmes, that people are entitled to expect "a certain average of conduct" from all members of society despite their individual circumstances, histories, and peculiarities. Thus, in the battered spouse context, a key question underlying the ongoing struggle in the courts over the admissibility of such evidence is whether that "average of conduct" includes an expectation that it is never reasonable to attack a sleeping person. See generally Maguigan, Battered Women and Self Defense: Myths and Misconceptions in Current Reform Proposals, 140 U. Pa. L. Rev. 379 (1991).

In short, the reasonableness standard frequently invoked by tort law represents a powerful but somewhat problematic device for judging human behavior. The value as well as the limitations of this standard will become apparent throughout these materials.

c. Defense of Others

Although at early common law the privilege to defend third persons against harmful contacts encompassed only one's family and household, it is now generally agreed that the privilege extends to total strangers as well. The force that may be used by an intervenor to repel an attack on another is measured by the force that the other could lawfully use. Thus, if the attack imperils the life of the third person, the intervenor can use deadly force on behalf of that person.

The one exception to this general rule arises in the case of mistake. The intervenor may be mistaken as to which of two other persons is the aggressor, or mistaken as to the nature of the threat posed by the aggressor. In such cases, there is a split of authority as to whether the intervenor's privilege is derivative from, or independent of, the privilege of the person on whose behalf the actor intervenes. The weight of authority seems to be that the intervenor's privilege is derivative—that is, that the intervenor may use only the force that the person to be protected could legally use. If the intervenor is mistaken, even reasonably mistaken, as to the identity of the aggressor or the severity of the threat, the privilege is unavailable.

In contrast, the Restatement (Second) of Torts, in §76, adopts the view that the intervenor's privilege is independent of that held by the person to be protected. Thus, an intervenor is entitled to use reasonable force to protect a third party as long as the intervenor reasonably believes that intervention is necessary and that the third party would be privileged to use self-defense if able to do so. Comment *c* to this section states: "The actor does not take the risk that the person for whose protection he interferes is actually privileged to defend himself. He may be guided by appearances which would lead a reasonable man in the actor's position to believe that the third person is privileged."

d. Defense of Property

In preceding sections we considered the privilege that sometimes arises to inflict bodily injury intentionally upon another in order to defend oneself or others from imminent threat of physical harm. We now consider the privilege to inflict bodily injury intentionally upon another in order to defend property from imminent threat of theft or destruction. The following sections of the Restatement (Second) of Torts reflect the lower priority afforded the privilege to act in defense of one's property:

§77. DEFENSE OF POSSESSION BY FORCE NOT THREATENING DEATH OR SERIOUS BODILY HARM

An actor is privileged to use reasonable force, not intended or likely to cause death or serious bodily harm, to prevent or terminate another's intrusion upon the actor's land or chattels, if

(a) the intrusion is not privileged . . . and

(b) the actor reasonably believes that the intrusion can be prevented or terminated only by the force used, and

(c) the actor has first requested the other to desist and the other has disregarded the request, or the actor reasonably believes that a request will be useless or that substantial harm will be done before it can be made.

§79. DEFENSE OF POSSESSION BY FORCE THREATENING DEATH OR SERIOUS BODILY HARM

The intentional infliction upon another of a harmful or offensive contact or other bodily harm by a means which is intended or likely to cause death or serious bodily harm, for the purpose of preventing or terminating the other's intrusion upon the actor's possession of land or chattels, is privileged if, but only if, the actor reasonably believes that the intruder, unless expelled or excluded, is likely to cause death or serious bodily harm to the actor or to a third person whom the actor is privileged to protect.

Subsection (c) of §77 is especially interesting in light of the policies underlying the law of battery which support legal recovery as a more civilized alternative to self-help in the form of physical retaliation. Notice that the actor must actually go through a more or less formal procedure of "asking first," in most cases, before the privilege to use reasonable force arises.

The following decision by the Supreme Court of Iowa affords an excellent opportunity to observe these rules in action. Rarely does a decision reflect so starkly the balancing of interests which underlies much of the law of torts. And rarely has a torts decision provoked the sort of public controversy that this one provoked following its publication.

Katko v. Briney

183 N.W.2d 657 (Iowa 1971)

MOORE, C.J. . . . Plaintiff's action is for damages resulting from serious injury caused by a shot from a 20-gauge spring shotgun set by defendants in a bedroom of an old farm house which had been uninhabited for several years. Plaintiff and his companion, Marvin McDonough, had broken and entered the house to find and steal old bottles and dated fruit jars which they considered antiques.

At defendants' request plaintiff's action was tried to a jury consisting of residents of the community where defendants' property was located. The jury returned a verdict for plaintiff and against defendants for $20,000 actual and $10,000 punitive damages.

After careful consideration of defendants' motions for judgment notwithstanding the verdict and for new trial, the experienced and capable trial judge overruled them and entered judgment on the verdict. Thus we have this appeal by defendants. . . .

II. Most of the facts are not disputed. In 1957 defendant Bertha L. Briney inherited her parents' farmland in Mahaska and Monroe Counties. Included was an 80-acre tract in southwest Mahaska County where her grandparents and parents had lived. No one occupied the house thereafter. Her husband, Edward, attempted to care for the land. He kept no farm machinery thereon. The outbuildings became dilapidated.

For about 10 years, 1957 to 1967, there occurred a series of trespassing and housebreaking events with loss of some household items, the breaking of windows and "messing up of the property in general." The latest occurred June 8, 1967, prior to the event on July 16, 1967 herein involved.

Defendants through the years boarded up the windows and doors in an attempt to stop the intrusions. They had posted "no trespass" signs on the land several years before 1967. The nearest one was 35 feet from the house. On June 11, 1967 defendants set "a shotgun trap" in the north bedroom. After Mr. Briney cleaned and oiled his 20-gauge shotgun, the power of which he was well aware, defendants took it to the old house where they secured it to an iron bed with the barrel pointed at the bedroom door. It was rigged with wire from the doorknob to the gun's trigger so it would fire when the door was opened. Briney first pointed the gun so an intruder would be hit in the stomach but at Mrs. Briney's suggestion it was lowered to hit the legs. He admitted he did so "because I was mad and tired of being tormented" but "he did not intend to injure anyone." He gave no explanation of why he used a loaded shell and set it to hit a person already in the house. Tin was nailed over the bedroom window. The spring gun could not be seen from the outside. No warning of its presence was posted.

Plaintiff lived with his wife and worked regularly as a gasoline station attendant in Eddyville, seven miles from the old house. He had observed it for several years while hunting in the area and considered it as being abandoned. He knew it had been uninhabited. In 1967 the area around the house was covered with high weeds. Prior to July 16, 1967 plaintiff and McDonough had been to the premises and found several old bottles and fruit jars which they took and added to their collection of antiques. On the latter date about 9:30 P.M. they made a second trip to the Briney property. They entered the house by removing a board from a porch window which was without glass. While McDonough was looking around the kitchen area plaintiff went to another part of the house. As he started to open the north bedroom door the shotgun went off striking him in the right leg above the ankle bone. Much of his leg, including part of the tibia, was blown away. Only by McDonough's assistance was plaintiff able to get out of the house and after crawling some distance was put in his vehicle and rushed to a doctor and then to a hospital. He remained in the hospital 40 days. . . .

There was undenied medical testimony plaintiff had a permanent deformity, a loss of tissue, and a shortening of the leg.

The record discloses plaintiff to trial time had incurred $710 medical expense, $2056.85 for hospital service, $61.80 for orthopedic service and $750 as loss of earnings. In addition thereto the trial court submitted to the jury the question of damages for pain and suffering and for future disability.

III. Plaintiff testified he knew he had no right to break and enter the house with intent to steal bottles and fruit jars therefrom. He further testified he had entered a plea of guilty to larceny in the nighttime of property of less than $20 value from a private building. He stated he had been fined $50 and costs and paroled during good behavior from a 60-day jail sentence. Other than minor traffic charges this was plaintiff's first brush with the law. On this civil case appeal it is not our prerogative to review the disposition made of the criminal charge against him.

IV. The main thrust of defendants' defense in the trial court and on this appeal is that "the law permits use of a spring gun in a dwelling or warehouse for the purpose of preventing the unlawful entry of a burglar or thief." They repeated this contention in their exceptions to the trial court's instructions 2, 5, and 6. They took no exception to the trial court's statement of the issues or to other instructions.

In the statement of issues the trial court stated plaintiff and his companion committed a felony when they broke and entered defendants' house. In instruction 2 the court referred to the early case history of the use of spring guns and stated under the law their use was prohibited except to prevent the commission of felonies of violence and where human life is in danger. The instruction included a statement breaking and entering is not a felony of violence.

Instruction 5 stated: "You are hereby instructed that one may use reasonable force in the protection of his property, but such right is subject to the qualification that one may not use such means of force as will take human life or inflict great bodily injury. Such is the rule even though the injured party is a trespasser and is in violation of the law himself."

Instruction 6 stated: "An owner of premises is prohibited from willfully or intentionally injuring a trespasser by means of force that either takes life or inflicts great bodily injury; and therefore a person owning a premise is prohibited from setting out 'spring guns' and like dangerous devices which will likely take life or inflict great bodily injury, for the purpose of harming trespassers. The fact that the trespasser may be acting in violation of the law does not change the rule. The only time when such conduct of setting a 'spring gun' or a like dangerous device is justified would be when the trespasser was committing a felony of violence or a felony punishable by death, or where the trespasser was endangering human life by his act."

Instruction 7, to which defendants made no objection or exception, stated:

"To entitle the plaintiff to recover for compensatory damages, the burden of proof is upon him to establish by a preponderance of the evidence each and all of the following propositions:

"1. That defendants erected a shotgun trap in a vacant house on land owned by defendant, Bertha L. Briney, on or about June 11, 1967, which fact was known only by them, to protect household goods from trespassers and thieves.

"2. That the force used by defendants was in excess of that force reasonably necessary and which persons are entitled to use in the protection of their property.

"3. That plaintiff was injured and damaged and the amount thereof.

"4. That plaintiff's injuries and damages resulted directly from the discharge of the shotgun trap which was set and used by defendants."

The overwhelming weight of authority, both textbook and case law, supports the trial court's statement of the applicable principles of law.

Prosser on Torts, Third Edition, pages 116-118, states:

". . . the law has always placed a higher value upon human safety than upon mere rights in property, it is the accepted rule that there is no privilege to use any force calculated to cause death or serious bodily injury to repel the threat to land or chattels, unless there is also such a threat to the defendant's personal safety as to justify a self-defense. . . . Spring guns and other man-killing devices are not justifiable against a mere trespasser, or even a petty thief. They are privileged only against those upon whom the landowner, if he were present in person would be free to inflict injury of the same kind.". . .

In Hooker v. Miller, 37 Iowa 613, we held defendant vineyard owner liable for damages resulting from a spring gun shot although plaintiff was a trespasser and there to steal grapes. At pages 614, 615, this statement is made: "This court has held that a mere trespass against property other than a dwelling is not a sufficient justification to authorize the use of a deadly weapon by the owner in its defense; and that if death results in such a case it will be murder, though the killing be actually necessary to prevent the trespass. The State v. Vance, 17 Iowa 138." At page 617 this court said: "[T]respassers and other inconsiderable violators of the law are not to be visited by barbarous punishments or prevented by inhuman inflictions of bodily injuries."

The facts in Allison v. Fiscus, 156 Ohio 120, 100 N.E.2d 237, 44 A.L.R.2d 369, decided in 1951, are very similar to the case at bar. There plaintiff's right to damages was recognized for injuries received when he feloniously broke a door latch and started to enter defendant's warehouse with intent to steal. As he entered a trap of two sticks of dynamite buried under the doorway by defendant owner was set off and plaintiff seriously injured. The court held the question whether a particular trap was justified as a use of reasonable and necessary force against a trespasser engaged in the commission of a felony should have been submitted to the jury. The Ohio

Supreme Court recognized plaintiff's right to recover punitive or exemplary damages in addition to compensatory damages. . . .

In Wisconsin, Oregon and England the use of spring guns and similar devices is specifically made unlawful by statute. 44 A.L.R., section 3, pages 386, 388.

The legal principles stated by the trial court in instructions 2, 5, and 6 are well established and supported by the authorities cited and quoted supra. There is no merit in defendants' objections and exceptions thereto. Defendants' various motions based on the same reasons stated in exceptions to instructions were properly overruled. . . .

Study and careful consideration of defendants' contentions on appeal reveal no reversible error.

Affirmed.

All Justices concur except LARSON, J., who dissents.

LARSON, J.

I respectfully dissent, first, because the majority wrongfully assumes that by installing a spring gun in the bedroom of their unoccupied house the defendants intended to shoot any intruder who attempted to enter the room. Under the record presented here, that was a fact question. Unless it is held that these property owners are liable for any injury to an intruder from such a device regardless of the intent with which it is installed, liability under these pleadings must rest upon two definite issues of fact, i.e., did the defendants intend to shoot the invader, and if so, did they employ unnecessary and unreasonable force against him?

It is my feeling that the majority oversimplifies the impact of this case on the law, not only in this but other jurisdictions, and that it has not thought through all the ramifications of this holding.

There being no statutory provisions governing the right of an owner to defend his property by the use of a spring gun or other like device, or of a criminal invader to recover punitive damages when injured by such an instrumentality while breaking into the building of another, our interest and attention are directed to what should be the court determination of public policy in these matters. On both issues we are faced with a case of first impression. We should accept the task and clearly establish the law in this jurisdiction hereafter. I would hold there is no absolute liability for injury to a criminal intruder by setting up such a device on his property, and unless done with an intent to kill or seriously injure the intruder, I would absolve the owner from liability other than for negligence. I would also hold the court had no jurisdiction to allow punitive damages when the intruder was engaged in a serious criminal offense such as breaking and entering with intent to steal.

It appears to me that the learned trial court was and the majority is now confused as to the basis of liability under the circumstances revealed. Certainly, the trial court's instructions did nothing to clarify the law in this jurisdiction for the jury. Timely objections to Instructions Nos. 2, 5, and 6 were made by the defendants, and thereafter the court should have been aware of the questions of liability left unresolved, i.e., whether in this jurisdiction we by judicial declaration bar the use in an unoccupied building of spring guns or other devices capable of inflicting serious injury or death on an intruder regardless of the intent with which they are installed, or whether such an intent is a vital element which must be proven in order to establish liability for an injury inflicted upon a criminal invader.

Although the court told the jury the plaintiff had the burden to prove "That the force used by defendants was in excess of that force reasonably necessary and which persons are entitled to use in the protection of their property," it utterly failed to tell the jury it could find the installation was not made with the intent or purpose of striking or injuring the plaintiff. There was considerable evidence to that effect. As I shall point out, both defendants stated the installation was made for the purpose of scaring or frightening away any intruder, not to seriously injure him. It may be that the evidence would support a finding of an intent to injure the intruder, but obviously that important issue was never adequately or clearly submitted to the jury.

Unless, then, we hold for the first time that liability for death or injury in such cases is absolute, the matter should be remanded for a jury determination of defendants' intent in installing the device under instructions usually given to a jury on the issue of intent. . . .

If, after proper instructions, the finder of fact determines that the gun was set with an intent and purpose to kill or inflict great bodily injury on an intruder, then and only then may it be said liability is established unless the property so protected is shown to be an occupied dwelling house. Of course, under this concept, if the finder of fact determines the gun set in an unoccupied house was intended to do no more than to frighten the intruder or sting him a bit, no liability would be incurred under such pleadings as are now presented. If such a concept of the law were adopted in Iowa, we would have here a question for the fact-finder or jury as to whether the gun was willfully and intentionally set so as to seriously injure the thief or merely scare him away.

I feel the better rule is that an owner of buildings housing valuable property may employ the use of spring guns or other devices intended to repel but not seriously injure an intruder who enters his secured premises with or without a criminal intent, but I do not advocate its general use, for there may also be liability for negligent installation of such a device. What I mean to say is that under such circumstances as we have here the issue as to whether the set was with an intent to seriously injure or kill an intruder is a question of fact that should be left to the jury under proper instructions, and that the mere setting of such a device with a resultant serious injury should not as a matter of law establish liability.

In the case of a mere trespass able authorities have reasoned that absolute liability may rightfully be fixed on the landowner for injuries to the trespasser because very little damage could be inflicted upon the property owner and the danger is great that a child or other innocent trespasser might be seriously injured by the device. In such matters they say no privilege to set up the device should be recognized by the courts regardless of the owner's intent. I agree.

On the other hand, where the intruder may pose a danger to the inhabitants of a dwelling, the privilege of using such a device to repel has been recognized by most authorities, and the mere setting thereof in the dwelling has not been held to create liability for an injury as a matter of law. In such cases intent and the reasonableness of the force would seem relevant to liability.

Although I am aware of the often-repeated statement that personal rights are more important than property rights, where the owner has stored his valuables representing his life's accumulations, his livelihood business, his tools and implements, and his treasured antiques as appears in the case at bar, and where the evidence is sufficient to sustain a finding that the installation was intended only as a warning to ward off thieves and criminals, I can see no compelling reason why the use of such a device alone would create liability as a matter of law. . . .

In the case at bar, as I have pointed out, there is a sharp conflict in the evidence. The physical facts and certain admissions as to how the gun was aimed would tend to support a finding of intent to injure, while the direct testimony of both defendants was that the gun was placed so it would "hit the floor eventually" and that it was set "low so it couldn't kill anybody." Mr. Briney testified, "My purpose in setting up the gun was not to injure somebody. I thought more or less that the gun would be at a distance of where anyone would grab the door, it would scare them," and in setting the angle of the gun to hit the lower part of the door, he said, "I didn't think it would go through quite that hard."

If the law in this jurisdiction permits, which I think it does, an explanation of the setting of a spring gun to repel invaders of certain private property, then the intent with which the set is made is a vital element in the liability issue.

In view of the failure to distinguish and clearly give the jury the basis upon which it should determine that liability issue, I would reverse and remand the entire case for a new trial. . . .

Being convinced that there was reversible error in the court's instructions, that the issue of intent in placing the spring gun was not clearly presented to the jury . . . I would reverse and remand the matter for a new trial. . . .

The problem of liability for harm caused by spring guns has been before courts and legislatures for many years. One of the earliest reported cases is Bird v. Holbrook, 4 Bing. 628, 130 Eng. Rep. 911 (C.P. 1828), which imposed liability on a defendant who used a spring gun to protect prize tulips grown in a walled garden. The plaintiff, a teenager seeking to impress the female servant of defendant's neighbor by retrieving a pea-hen that had escaped into the tulip garden, was injured by defendant's trap.

Only rarely have defendants escaped liability in the case of spring guns, in part because the use of such devices is so suggestive of an indiscriminate and malicious intent. A similar, but more problematic, set of cases involves the use of unmarked cables or chains to block off properties from access by motorcycles or similar vehicles. As a means of protecting property from trespassers, such devices can prove as lethal as spring guns, but the success of plaintiffs has been considerably more limited. See Doehring v. Wagner, 80 Md. App. 237, 562 A.2d 762 (1989). Can you see some of the reasons why this might be so? On the subject of spring guns generally (and Katko v. Briney in particular) see Palmer, The Iowa Spring Gun Case: A Study in American Gothic, 56 Iowa L. Rev. 1219 (1971); Posner, Killing or Wounding to Protect a Property Interest, 14 J.L. & Econ. 201 (1971), discussed below; Comment, Tort Law—Use of Mechanical Devices in the Defense of Property, 24 S.C.L. Rev. 133 (1972).

Law and Policy: Why Should We Care About Sneak Thieves?

Katko v. Briney provides an opportunity to develop and apply the ideas presented in the earlier law and policy note, p. 28, above. When the majority opinion quotes Prosser's statement that ". . . the law has always placed a higher value upon human safety than upon mere rights in property," it appears that the noninstrumentalists have carried the day. Professor Fletcher would, presumably, conclude that when the Brineys retaliated against sneak thieves with life-threatening force, they were creating a nonreciprocal risk of injury, and thus in fairness should be liable to their victim. That would clearly be the case if the Brineys, angry at the world, had aimed their shotgun to shoot a passerby in the road. But what about a sneak thief who breaks and enters the Brineys' farmhouse? In a manner of speaking, the sneak thief is the one creating a nonreciprocal risk, inasmuch as he is the one who knowingly commits a wrong to the Brineys in the first instance, without any possible justification. Can you explain the rule in Katko v. Briney in noninstrumental/fairness terms, with or without using the concept of nonreciprocity?

In any event, instrumental/efficiency analysts would seem to have an especially hard time explaining why tort law should invariably favor human safety over property, without inquiring from case to case into the comparative costs of sacrificing one interest or the other. Professor (now Judge) Posner criticized the traditional rule in Katko v. Briney on exactly this basis:

> [N]either blanket permission nor blanket prohibition of spring guns and other methods of using deadly force to protect property interests is likely to be the rule of liability that minimizes the relevant costs. What is needed is a standard of reasonableness that permits the courts to weigh such considerations as the value of the property at stake, its location (which bears not only on the difficulty of protecting it by other means but also on the likelihood of innocent trespass), what kind of warning was given, the deadliness of the device (there is no reason to recognize a privilege to kill when adequate protection can be assured by a device that only wounds), the character of the conflicting activities, the trespasser's care or negligence, and the cost of avoiding interference by other means (including storing the property elsewhere). . . .
>
> All things considered, the approach to tort questions sketched here seems decidedly superior to the "method of maxims"—the pseudo-logical deduction of rules from essentially empty formulas such as "no man should be permitted to do indirectly what he would be forbidden to do directly" or "the interest in property can never outweigh the value of a human life"—that plays so large a role in certain kinds of legal scholarship. . . .[16]

Are you comfortable with this instrumental/efficiency approach? Observe that by implication it would allow a life to be taken under circumstances where that was the least costly alternative from an overall social welfare perspective. Is it appropriate to place values on—and in a real sense "spend"—human lives in this manner? Consider the following excerpt from Professor Guido Calabresi, another prominent spokesperson for what we here describe as the *efficiency rationale* (The Cost of Accidents 17-18 (1970)):

> Our society is not committed to preserving life at any cost. In its broadest sense, the rather unpleasant notion that we are willing to destroy lives should be obvious. Wars are fought. The University of Mississippi is integrated at the risk of losing lives. But what is more pertinent to the study of accident law, though perhaps equally obvious, is that lives are spent not only when the *quid pro quo* is some great moral principle, but also when it is a matter of convenience. Ventures are undertaken that, statistically at least, are certain to cost lives. Thus we build a tunnel under Mont Blanc because it is essential to the Common Market and cuts down the traveling time from Rome to Paris, though we know that about one man per kilometer of tunnel will die. We take planes and cars rather than safer, slower means of travel. And perhaps most telling, we use relatively safe equipment rather than the safest imaginable because—and it is not a bad reason—the safest costs too much. It should be apparent that while some of these accident-causing activities also result in diminution of accidents—the Mont Blanc tunnel may well save more lives by diminishing traffic fatalities than it took to build it—this explanation does not come close to justifying most accident-causing activities. Railroad grade

16. See Posner, Killing or Wounding to Protect a Property Interest, 14 J. Law & Econ. 201, 214, 225 (1971).

crossings are used because they are cheap, not because they save more lives than they take.

One interesting example of the lack of commitment "to preserving life at any cost" is the conclusion some years ago of the National Highway Traffic Safety Administration, a part of the U.S. Department of Transportation, not to require trucks to be equipped with "underride protection." If a truck were to stop short, a car immediately behind it might not be able to stop in time to avoid a collision. The front of the car might then go under the rear of a large truck, so that the first impact of the car with the truck would be by the car's windshield, which results in a high risk of death to the front seat occupants of the car. Underride protection in the form of a metal bar attached to the rear of the truck would prevent direct windshield-truck contacts. The NHTSA declined to require underride protection when it determined that underride protection on trucks would cost $5 million for each life saved, and that any cost over $200,000 a life saved would be societally unacceptable. Another federal agency, the National Traffic Safety Board, argued that underride protection should be required, would cost only $175 a truck to install, and would have an annual per truck maintenance cost of $540. But the NHTSA stuck to its original position. See Business Week, October 14, 1972, at 41.

Do the preceding examples of situations in which society refuses to "preserve life at all costs" convince you that there is no underlying validity to the maxim, recited in *Katko,* that tort law should not tolerate conduct that risks life to preserve property? Are situations like *Katko,* where a defendant deliberately seeks to injure another, fundamentally different than the kinds of general safety compromises that society makes concerning railroad crossings and truck bumpers? See Finnis, Allocating Risks and Suffering: Some Hidden Traps, 38 Cleve. State L. Rev. 193 (1990). Even if it is not so clear, as between the noninstrumental/fairness and the instrumental/efficiency camps, who has the better of the debate over Prosser's "human life wins over property" assertion, is it not clear that the assertion is inconsistent with Professor Abel's "tort law as a capitalist tool" thesis (see p. 31, above)? Prosser's statement and the rule in *Katko* cut against, rather than support, the idea that tort law is designed to further the interests of the propertied classes, do they not?

Ploof v. Putnam

81 Vt. 471, 71 A. 188 (1908)

MUNSON, J. It is alleged as the ground of recovery that on the 13th day of November, 1904, the defendant was the owner of a certain island in Lake Champlain, and of a certain dock attached thereto, which island and dock were then in charge of the defendant's servant; that the plaintiff was then possessed of and sailing upon said lake a certain loaded sloop, on which were the plaintiff and his wife and two minor children; that there then arose a sudden and violent tempest, whereby the sloop and the property and persons therein were placed in great danger of destruction; that to save these from destruction or injury the plaintiff was compelled to, and did, moor the sloop to defendant's dock; that the defendant by his servant unmoored the sloop, whereupon it was driven upon the shore by the tempest, without the plaintiff's fault; and that the sloop and its contents were thereby destroyed, and the plaintiff and his wife and children cast into the lake and upon the shore, receiving injuries.

This claim is set forth in two counts; one in trespass, charging that the defendant by his servant with force and arms wilfully and designedly unmoored the sloop; the other in case, alleging that it was the duty of the defendant by his servant to permit the plaintiff to moor his sloop to the dock, and to permit it to remain so moored during the continuance of the tempest, but that the defendant by his servant, in disregard of this duty, negligently, carelessly and wrongfully unmoored the sloop. Both counts are demurred to generally. [The demurrer was overruled and defendant appeals.]

There are many cases in the books which hold that necessity, and an inability to control movements inaugurated in the proper exercise of a strict right, will justify entries upon land and interferences with personal property that would otherwise have been trespasses. . . .

A traveller on a highway, who finds it obstructed from a sudden and temporary cause, may pass upon the adjoining land without becoming a trespasser, because of the necessity.

An entry upon land to save goods which are in danger of being lost or destroyed by water or fire is not a trespass. In Proctor v. Adams, 113 Mass. 376, 18 Am. Rep. 500, the defendant went upon the plaintiff's beach for the purpose of saving and restoring to the lawful owner a boat which had been driven ashore and was in danger of being carried off by the sea; and it was held no trespass.

This doctrine of necessity applies with special force to the preservation of human life. One assaulted and in peril of his life may run through the close of another to escape from his assailant. One may sacrifice the personal property of another to save his life or the lives of his fellows. In Mouse's Case, 12 Co. 63, the defendant was sued for taking and carrying away the plaintiff's casket and its contents. It appeared that the ferryman of Gravesend took forty-seven passengers into his barge to pass to London, among whom were the plaintiff and defendant; and the barge being upon the water a great tempest happened, and a strong wind, so that the barge and all the passengers were in danger of being lost if certain ponderous things were not cast out, and the defendant thereupon cast out the plaintiff's casket. It was resolved that in case of necessity, to save the lives of the passengers, it was lawful for the defendant, being a passenger, to cast the plaintiff's casket out of the barge; that if the ferryman surcharge the barge the owner shall have his remedy upon the surcharge against the ferryman, but that if there be no surcharge, and the danger accrue only by the act of God, as by tempest, without fault of the ferryman, every one ought to bear his loss, to safeguard the life of a man.

It is clear that an entry upon the land of another may be justified by necessity, and that the declaration before us discloses a necessity for mooring the sloop. But the defendant questions the sufficiency of the counts because they do not negative the existence of natural objects to which the plaintiff could have moored with equal safety. The allegations are, in substance, that the stress of a sudden and violent tempest compelled the plaintiff to moor to defendant's dock to save his sloop and the people in it. The averment of necessity is complete, for it covers not only the necessity of mooring, but the necessity of mooring to the dock; and the details of the situation which created this necessity, whatever the legal requirements regarding them, are matters of proof and need not be alleged. It is certain that the rule suggested cannot be held applicable irrespective of circumstance, and the question must be left for adjudication upon proceedings had with reference to the evidence or the charge. . . .

Judgment affirmed and cause remanded.

Vincent v. Lake Erie Transportation Co.

109 Minn. 456, 124 N.W. 221 (1910)

Action in the district court for St. Louis county to recover $1,200 for damage to plaintiffs' wharf, caused by defendant negligently keeping its vessel tied to it. The defendant in its answer alleged that a portion of the cargo was consigned to plaintiffs' dock and on November 27, 1905, its vessel was placed alongside at the place and in the manner designated by plaintiffs and the discharge of cargo continued until ten o'clock that night, that by the time the discharge of cargo was completed the wind had attained so great a velocity the master and crew were powerless to move the vessel. The case was tried before Ensign, J., who denied the defendant's motion to direct a verdict in its favor, and a jury which rendered a verdict in favor of plaintiffs for $500. From an order denying defendant's motion for judgment notwithstanding the verdict or for a new trial, it appealed. Affirmed.

O'Brien, J. The steamship Reynolds, owned by the defendant, was for the purpose of discharging her cargo on November 27, 1905, moored to plaintiff's dock in Duluth. While the unloading of the boat was taking place a storm from the northeast developed, which at about ten o'clock P.M., when the unloading was completed, had so grown in violence that the wind was then moving at fifty miles per hour and continued to increase during the night. There is some evidence that one, and perhaps two, boats were able to enter the harbor that night, but it is plain that navigation was practically suspended from the hour mentioned until the morning of the twenty-ninth, when the storm abated, and during that time no master would have been justified in attempting to navigate his vessel, if he could avoid doing so. After the discharge of the cargo the Reynolds signaled for a tug to tow her from the dock, but none could be obtained because of the severity of the storm. If the lines holding the ship to the dock had been cast off, she would doubtless have drifted away; but, instead, the lines were kept fast, and as soon as one parted or chafed it was replaced, sometimes with a larger one. The vessel lay upon the outside of the dock, her bow to the east, the wind and waves striking her starboard quarter with such force that she was constantly being lifted and thrown against the dock, resulting in its damage, as found by the jury, to the amount of $500.

We are satisfied that the character of the storm was such that it would have been highly imprudent for the master of the Reynolds to have attempted to leave the dock or to have permitted his vessel to drift away from it. One witness testified upon the trial that the vessel could have been warped into a slip, and that, if the attempt to bring the ship into the slip had failed, the worst that could have happened would be that the vessel would have been blown ashore upon a soft and muddy bank. The witness was not present in Duluth at the time of the storm, and, while he may have been right in his conclusions, those in charge of the dock and the vessel at the time of the storm were not required to use the highest human intelligence, nor were they required to resort to every possible experiment which could be suggested for the preservation of their property. Nothing more was demanded of them than ordinary prudence and care, and the record in this case fully sustains the contention of the appellant that, in holding the vessel fast to the dock, those in charge of her exercised good judgment and prudent seamanship.

It is claimed by the respondent that it was negligence to moor the boat at an exposed part of the wharf, and to continue in that position after it became apparent that the storm was to be more than usually severe. We do not agree with this position. The part of the wharf where the vessel was moored appears to have been commonly used for that purpose. It was situated within the harbor at Duluth, and must, we think, be considered a proper and safe place, and would undoubtedly have been such during what would be considered a very severe storm. The storm which made it unsafe was one which surpassed in violence any which might have reasonably been anticipated.

The appellant contends by ample assignments of error that, because its conduct during the storm was rendered necessary by prudence and good seamanship under conditions over which it had no control, it cannot be held liable for any injury resulting to the property of others, and claims that the jury should have been so instructed. An analysis of the charge given by the trial court is not necessary, as in our opinion the only question for the jury was the amount of damages which the plaintiffs were entitled to recover, and no complaint is made upon that score.

The situation was one in which the ordinary rules regulating property rights were suspended by forces beyond human control, and if, without the direct intervention of some act by the one sought to be held liable, the property of another was injured, such injury must be attributed to the act of God, and not to the wrongful act of the person sought to be charged. If during the storm the Reynolds had entered the harbor, and while there had become disabled and been thrown against the plaintiffs' dock, the plaintiffs could not have recovered. Again, if while attempting to hold fast to the dock the lines had parted, without any negligence, and the vessel carried against some other boat or dock in the harbor, there would be no liability upon her owner. But here those in charge of the vessel deliberately and by their direct efforts held her in such a position that the damage to the dock resulted, and having thus preserved the ship at the expense of the dock, it seems to us that her owners are responsible to the dock owners to the extent of the injury inflicted.

[Discussion of earlier cases, including Ploof v. Putnam, above, is omitted.] Theologians hold that a starving man may, without moral guilt, take what is necessary to sustain life; but it could hardly be said that the obligation would not be upon such person to pay the value of the property so taken when he became able to do so. And so public necessity, in times of war or peace, may require the taking of private property for public purposes; but under our system of jurisprudence compensation must be made.

Let us imagine in this case that for the better mooring of the vessel those in charge of her had appropriated a valuable cable lying upon the dock. No matter how justifiable such appropriation might have been, it would not be claimed that, because of the overwhelming necessity of the situation, the owner of the cable could not recover its value.

This is not a case where life or property was menaced by any object or thing belonging to the plaintiffs, the destruction of which became necessary to prevent the threatened disaster. Nor is it a case where, because of the act of God, or unavoidable accident, the infliction of the injury was beyond the control of the defendant, but is one where the defendant prudently and advisedly availed itself of the plaintiffs' property for the purpose of preserving its own more valuable property, and the plaintiffs are entitled to compensation for the injury done.

Order affirmed.

LEWIS, J. (dissenting). I dissent. . . .

In my judgment, if the boat was lawfully in position at the time the storm broke, and the master could not, in the exercise of due care, have left that position without subjecting his vessel to the hazards of the storm, then the damage to the dock, caused by the pounding of the boat, was the result of an inevitable accident. If the master was in the exercise of due care, he was not at fault. The reasoning of the opinion admits that if the ropes, or cables, first attached to the dock had not parted, or if, in the first instance, the master had used the stronger cables, there would be no liability. If the master could not, in the exercise of reasonable care, have anticipated the severity of the storm and sought a place of safety before it became impossible, why should he be required to anticipate the severity of the storm, and, in the first instance, use the stronger cables?

I am of the opinion that one who constructs a dock to the navigable line of waters, and enters into contractual relations with the owner of a vessel to moor the same, takes the risk of damage to his dock by a boat caught there by a storm, which event could not have been avoided in the exercise of due care, and further, that the legal status of the parties in such a case is not changed by renewal of cables to keep the boat from being cast adrift at the mercy of the tempest.

JAGGARD, J. I concur with LEWIS, J.

The Restatement (Second) of Torts combines the principles of *Ploof* and *Vincent* in §197, and creates a necessity-based privilege (often described as *qualified* or *incomplete*), in favor of an actor to enter the land of another in order to avoid serious harm, coupled with an obligation on the part of the actor to pay for whatever he breaks. In the end, what turns on the characterization of the entry as privileged in cases of this sort, assuming that the entrant must pay for the harm he causes regardless of whether his entry is privileged?

A recent decision in the Ninth Circuit suggests the fact patterns involved in *Ploof* and *Vincent* are apt to recur today. In Protectus Alpha Navigation Co. v. North Pacific Grain Growers, Inc., 767 F.2d 1379 (9th Cir. 1985), the plaintiff's vessel was refueling at the defendant's dock when the vessel caught fire. Local fire fighters and the Coast Guard placed fire fighting equipment on the dock. The fire fighting efforts brought the flames under control, and the fire would have been extinguished within minutes. The defendant's dock manager, however, ordered the vessel cast off and, with the help of another of defendant's employees, did so contrary to the instructions of the fire fighters. The vessel drifted downstream with several fire fighters left on board, and the now unopposed fire destroyed it. Plaintiff sued defendant for negligence. The trial court found for the plaintiff and awarded $7,045,000 in general damages, $2,032,760 in prejudgment interest, and $500,000 in punitive damages for a grand total of $9,577,760. On appeal the Ninth Circuit affirmed, holding that the dock manager's conduct in disobeying the fire fighters had violated state law and was therefore negligence per se. What result if the dock manager had acted before the fire fighters arrived?

Problem 7

Mark Brown and two high school friends were deer hunting in a state forest when caught by a late November blizzard. Poorly dressed for the rapidly deteriorating conditions, Brown and his companions sought to return quickly to their car, but disagreed over the best route. Brown's friends wanted to retrace the arduous and winding trail they had already taken, while Brown argued that taking a straight line over two successive ridges should bring them directly to the trailhead.

Unable to agree, the group split up, and Brown headed toward the first ridge. In the driving snow and dwindling light, however, he became lost. After several hours, Brown emerged onto a plowed field, shivering and slightly disoriented from the onset of hypothermia. He stumbled toward a lighted farmhouse in the distance. When he arrived, he held his hunting rifle behind his back to avoid alarming whoever answered his knock. Sarah Ellman, a single mother of two young children, opened the door a crack without undoing the security chain. His speech slurred and disjointed because of his condition, Brown began explaining that he was lost and freezing and needed to come in. Ellman, however, felt immediately fearful. Brown seemed strange and appeared to be hiding something behind his back. Moreover, since recently divorcing her abusive husband, Ellman had been distrustful of men in general. Without fully understanding Brown's situation, she blurted out, "I'm sorry, I can't help," and quickly closed and locked the door.

Brown pounded on the door for several minutes, but to no avail. He then proceeded to a barn on the property, pried open the door, and huddled among some tarps stored in the barn. A search party, launched after his friends reported him missing, found him five hours later. He had suffered additional severe hypothermia and developed frostbite on several toes.

Brown subsequently sued Ellman for his injuries and medical care. Ellman counterclaimed for damage to the barn door and for the value of a pony that had to be destroyed after it wandered from the open door during the storm and was injured in a drainage ditch. What theories of recovery are the parties likely to advance? What defenses are available to Brown and Ellman? What is the likely outcome if the case goes to trial?

e. Parents and Teachers

In some cases, the privilege to inflict a harmful contact arises primarily out of the status of the parties. The most notable examples are the privileges that, at least to some extent, protect parents and teachers from battery claims brought on behalf of children they have physically disciplined. The common law justifications for the disciplinary privilege are diverse, with the most dominant themes being the ones suggested by courts such as the Supreme

Judicial Court of Maine in Patterson v. Nutter, 78 Me. 509, 7 A. 273, 274 (1886):

> Free political institutions are possible only where the great body of the people are moral, intelligent, and habituated to self-control, and to obedience to lawful authority. The permanency of such institutions depends largely upon the efficient instruction and training of children in these virtues. It is to secure this permanency that the state provides schools and teachers. Schoolteachers, therefore, have important duties and functions. Much depends upon their ability, skill, and faithfulness. They must *train* as well as instruct their pupils. The acquiring of learning is not the only object of our public schools. To become good citizens, children must be taught self-restraint, obedience, and other civic virtues. To accomplish these desirable ends, the master of a school is necessarily invested with much discretionary power. He is placed in charge sometimes of large numbers of children, perhaps of both sexes, of various ages, temperaments, dispositions, and of various degrees of docility and intelligence. He must govern these pupils, quicken the slothful, spur the indolent, restrain the impetuous, and control the stubborn. He must make rules, give commands, and punish disobedience. What rules, what commands, and what punishments shall be imposed are necessarily largely within the discretion of the master, where none are defined by the school board.

While the underlying justifications of instilling discipline and enforcing order are easy enough to state, it is often difficult, in the context of a particular case, to determine whether the harm inflicted by a parent or a teacher was appropriately related to the social goals underlying the privilege. We would all presumably agree that there is no privilege to inflict serious injury on a student for mere inattentiveness. But the rules become more difficult to agree upon as the harm inflicted becomes less serious or the disciplinary problem more serious. Parents, for example, disagree widely over the use and validity of spanking and other measures, with some viewing it as necessary and proper and others equating it with child abuse. As the Vermont Supreme Court observed nearly a century and a half ago in Lander v. Seaver, 32 Vt. 114, 117 (1859):

> [I]t is a point of some difficulty to determine with exact precision when a parent has exceeded the bounds of moderation. That correction which will be considered by some triers as unreasonable will be viewed by others as perfectly reasonable. What may be considered by some a venial folly to which none or very little correction ought to be applied, by others will be considered an offence that requires very severe treatment.

Given the lack of social consensus regarding appropriate discipline, how do tort courts manage to assess the privilege's applicability? Consider the following decision by the Supreme Court of Iowa.

Tinkham v. Kole

252 Iowa 1303, 110 N.W.2d 258 (Iowa 1961)

GARFIELD, CHIEF JUSTICE.

This is a law action in two counts by Michael Tinkham, a minor, through his father-next friend, to recover for personal injury resulting from corporal punishment by defendant Marius L. Kole, a school teacher. For convenience we refer to the boy as plaintiff. Plaintiff's first count alleges negligence, the second assault and battery. At the close of plaintiff's evidence, the trial court directed a verdict for defendant on each count. Plaintiff's appeal from the judgment thereon assigns error in the ruling as to each count.

The vital question presented is whether reasonable minds might conclude from the evidence that the punishment administered by defendant was unreasonable or immoderate under the circumstances. We must answer in the affirmative.

I. Of course it is our duty to view the evidence in the light most favorable to plaintiff.

On October 2, 1958, plaintiff was a student in the eighth grade of the Nevada, Iowa, public school. He was 13, weighed about 110 and was about 5 feet, 2 inches tall. Defendant taught the last period of the day, from 2:30 to 3:30. Jerry Geisler, in the seat in front of plaintiff, was a member of the junior high band to whom white gloves had been issued. When Jerry took his seat he laid his books at the side of his desk and placed his gloves on the books. Plaintiff put the gloves on his hands. There is testimony this was before the bell rang to signal start of the class.

Jerry testifies: "I don't know whether Mr. Kole was in the room or not at that time, but he came in as soon as the bell rang. There wasn't too much order at that time. He (defendant) told us to take our books and most of us did who heard him with the noise. He said, 'Michael, get those gloves off.' Michael started taking them off, one at a time, finger by finger. He said, 'Michael, hurry and get those gloves off.' Mike just kept going like that and he said, 'Mike, you better hurry and get those gloves off.' About that time, Mike took them off real fast, because Mr. Kole was back by his (plaintiff's) desk. Then Mr. Kole started hitting him about the head. He hit him quite a few times. Michael did not say anything to Mr. Kole until he stopped hitting him. He said, 'Are you going to do that again?' Michael said, 'No.' Several times he said it and Mr. Kole started hitting him again for not too long a time. Then he went up in front of the class and gave us a speech. He told us our class was the mangiest, or ornery and wild. . . . He (plaintiff) was not standing up at any time during this and was almost on the floor with us. . . . He was also scared."

[Plaintiff's evidence also indicated that the gloves were tight and difficult to remove, that "the class was not completely 'under way' at the time of the occurrence," and that plaintiff sustained potentially permanent hearing impairment as a result of defendant's actions.]

II. At the close of plaintiff's evidence defendant moved for a directed verdict. . . . The trial court then announced, "This court has about concluded this is not a case which should be submitted to a jury. That we should stop this foolishness right here and now. This teacher had the right to discipline the student and to use such force as was necessary to do so."

In explaining its ruling to the jury the court expressed the opinion "Plaintiff must show the punishment was so cruel and unusual as to be beyond reason. I don't propose to let this case go any further. I think it is time . . . these kids must be taught some means of discipline. . . . For a period of time we sort of said don't spank the little dears, you might spoil their ego. Even parents weren't supposed to do anything to their kids because you would spoil their personality. . . .

"We first must determine whether the punishment was reasonable regardless of the consequences. . . . I don't believe it was unreasonable, any more than it would be for a parent to do something of this kind if his child disobeyed him or didn't do as he was told. If we had a situation where parents chain their kids to a bed and leave them there for days because they run off; that is unusual, unreasonable punishment. Where a father burned his kid's fingers with a cigarette because he was getting things off the table; that would be unreasonable and cruel punishment. But it was the natural thing for this teacher to do where this boy had been causing trouble, and his attitude toward the teacher, disturbing the room, to slap him back and forth on the face."

III. There is no substantial dispute in the law that controls this appeal. It is sufficiently stated in the annotation to Suits v. Glover, 260 Ala. 499, 71 So. 2d 49, from which we quote: ". . . a teacher is immune from liability for physical punishment, reasonable in degree, administered to a pupil. . . .

"But a teacher's right to use physical punishment is a limited one. His immunity from liability in damages requires that the evidence show that the punishment administered was reasonable, and such a showing requires consideration of the nature of the punishment itself, the nature of the pupil's misconduct which gave rise to the punishment, the age and physical condition of the pupil, and the teacher's motive in inflicting the punishment. If consideration of all of these factors indicates that the teacher violated none of the standards implicit in each of them, then he will be held free of liability; but it seems liability will result from proof that the teacher, in administering the punishment, violated any one of such standards.". . .

We are not called upon to decide whether the question of reasonableness of particular punishment would be for the jury in every conceivable case. Our problem is whether under the facts and circumstances here a jury question on such reasonableness is presented. And, as we indicated at the outset, this depends upon whether reasonable minds might fairly so conclude. It is significant that able, industrious counsel for defendant cite no decision of any court which holds a jury question on reasonableness of punishment in a case of this kind was not presented. Nor have we found such a precedent.

In all to which our attention has been called the question of reasonableness was treated as one of fact for the jury, not—as was done here—as one of law for the court. . . .

IV. The jury could find the principal misconduct which gave rise to the punishment of plaintiff was his lack of speed in removing the gloves. The command defendant gave plaintiff was "to get those gloves off" and to hurry in doing so. That the gloves fit "kind of tight" and "you had to pull them off finger by finger" might be found to furnish some justification for the delay in removing them. A circumstance to be considered is that the misconduct occurred at a time when "almost everyone was talking," some of the other pupils were "fooling around" and at least one was "engaged in horseplay." Under all the circumstances reasonable minds might fairly conclude plaintiff's misconduct was not extreme.

There is substantial evidence which stands undisputed that defendant struck plaintiff several times on both sides of his head and this was done in anger. The finding is warranted the boy's eardrum was ruptured and the injury is permanent. Reasonable minds might find injury was liable to result from the manner in which the punishment was inflicted. At least four witnesses testify defendant continued to strike plaintiff after he was scared and had given assurance "he would not do that again." It could fairly be found this added punishment was unnecessary and uncalled for. . . .

Certainly there is room for disagreement among fair-minded persons with the trial court's characterization of the case as foolishness. No authority has come to our attention which supports the court's view "Plaintiff must show the punishment was so cruel and unusual as to be beyond reason." This puts a burden upon plaintiff he was not required to meet. It was his burden to prove the punishment was unreasonable under the circumstances.

Fair-minded persons might also conclude that punishment is unreasonable even though much less cruel than chaining a child to a bed and leaving him there for days or deliberately burning his fingers—the two examples of unreasonable punishment given by the court. It would seem there is no fair room for disagreement that such punishment is unreasonable.

We can readily agree that proper discipline of children is of vital importance and disciplinary lapses seem to be widespread, with regrettable consequences. But, we repeat, the reasonableness of the punishment here was a question of fact for the jury, not one of law for the court.

Reversed and remanded.

All Justices concur.

Leaving constitutional concerns aside, why should the appellate court prefer the jury over the judge as arbiter of reasonable discipline? Presumably, the judge comes from the same community as the jury, and, indeed, may reflect views widely held in the community. Would the appellate court have reached the same result if the trial judge had been of an opposite disposition, prone to coddling "the little dears," and had granted a motion by plaintiff for a directed verdict at the close of evidence?

Note also the trial court's disparaging reference to changing theories about the psychological impact of physical discipline. Both the trial judge and the appellate court in *Tinkham* accept the psychological construct that physical punishment is *useful* in effectively disciplining children; the two courts merely disagree about the permissible bounds of such punishment. But is this psychological assumption valid? Many experts in child psychology now argue that almost all forms of corporal punishment, including spankings, are counterproductive: They are psychologically damaging to the child, they are relatively ineffective in controlling problematic behavior, and they create the propensity in children who receive such punishment to treat *their* children similarly when they become parents. See generally Herman, A Statutory Proposal to Prohibit the Infliction of Violence on Children, 19 Fam. L.Q. 1, 18-39 (Spring 1985). Should such arguments be considered by the court? Can the plaintiff, for example, call a child psychologist as an expert witness to testify about the harm done to children by physical punishment? If so, and if the defendant offers no opposing expert testimony, is the jury bound by such evidence?

In any event, cases like *Tinkham* point out that the privilege to impose reasonable discipline possessed by teachers is largely derivative of that held by parents. Teachers, in essense, stand *in loco parentis* during school hours. Yet it should be noted that parents traditionally have enjoyed additional immunity from liability based simply on the general reluctance of courts to adjudicate disputes between family members. Under this doctrine of intrafamily tort immunity, which also barred tort claims by one spouse against the other, courts declined to hear suits against parents even if the harm inflicted was unrelated to any disciplinary effort and, indeed, even if the conduct violated the criminal law. Thus, for example, in Roller v. Roller, 37 Wash. 242, 79 P. 788 (1905), the Supreme Court of Washington barred a civil damage action by a 15-year-old minor against her father, who had been convicted of raping her, reasoning:

> The rule of law prohibiting suits between parent and child is based upon the interest that society has in preserving harmony in the domestic relations, an interest which has been manifested since the earliest organization of civilized government, an interest inspired by the universally recognized fact that the maintenance of harmonious and proper family relations is conducive to good citizenship, and therefore works to the welfare of the state. This view, in effect, is not disputed by the [plaintiff] who admits the general proposition that the domestic relations of the home and family fireside cannot be disturbed by the members thereof by litigation prosecuted against each other for injuries, real or imaginary, arising out of these relations; but [she] asserts that the law has well-defined limitations, and that every rule of law

> is founded upon some good reason, and the object and purpose intended to be attained must be looked to as a fair test of its scope and limitations; that in the case at bar the family relations have already been disturbed, and that by action of the father the minor child has in reality been emancipated; that the harmonious relations existing have been disturbed in so rude a manner that they never can be again adjusted, and that therefore the reason for the rule does not apply. There seems to be some reason in this argument, but it overlooks the fact that courts, in determining their jurisdiction or want of jurisdiction, rely upon certain uniform principles of law, and, if it be once established that a child has a right to sue a parent for a tort, there is no practical line of demarkation which can be drawn, for the same principle which would allow the action in the case of a heinous crime, like the one involved in this case, would allow an action to be brought for any other tort. The principle permitting the action would be the same. The torts would be different only in degree. Hence all the disturbing confusion would be introduced which can be imagined under a system which would allow parents and children to be involved in litigation of this kind.

Despite such concerns, most courts in recent years have partially or wholly abrogated the near absolute tort immunity of parents at common law. While different courts have drawn the line in different places, a frequent reform has been to allow minors to sue their parents for intentional torts (not arising from an effort to impose reasonable discipline) but to continue to bar such claims if the injuries complained of are due to the negligence of the parent. See Barnes v. Barnes, 603 N.E.2d 1337 (Ind. 1992); Foldi v. Jeffries, 93 N.J. 533, 461 A.2d 1145 (Sup. Ct. N.J. 1983). Can you see why such a line might be reconcilable with the judicial fear, voiced in *Roller*, that allowing tort suits between family members may permanently poison family relations? Intrafamily tort immunities are treated more extensively at pp. 489-495, below.

f. Miscellaneous Privileges

In addition to the defenses mentioned above, tort law has traditionally recognized a number of other nonconsensual privileges that shield an actor from liability for intentionally inflicting harm. Such privileges include those relating to the arrest of lawbreakers and the prevention of crime, the enforcement of military orders, and the recapture of land and possessions. The details of the rules vary, but they all tend to manifest a theme common to the privileges discussed above: The reasonableness of the actor's perception of the need to use force, as well as the reasonableness of the harm actually inflicted, are typically the touchstones upon which the availability of the privilege turns.

Law and Behavior: Does the One Affect the Other?

As noted earlier, one common hope, especially for instrumentalists, is that the decision regarding liability in the context of a particular case can, aside from resolving that conflict, help establish rules of conduct that will deter unnecessary injuries in the future. This assumption regarding the prospective behavioral consequences of tort decisions merits further analysis.

At the outset, a distinction should be drawn between the direct and the indirect effects of legal rules upon primary behavior. Rules that proscribe specific patterns of conduct, as do the rules governing harmful battery, may be said to affect behavior directly when they induce individuals to refrain from engaging in the proscribed conduct. Rules may be said to affect behavior indirectly insofar as they help to reinforce the general moral climate in society which encourages primary actors, unconsciously perhaps, to avoid socially destructive conduct. The difference between direct and indirect effects of rules upon conduct is one of degree. However, as subsequent discussions in these materials will indicate, the distinction between direct and indirect effects is useful, and has been recognized by behavioral scientists investigating the effects of law upon behavior. Clearly, the assumptions in this book up to this point have concerned the direct effects of tort rules upon primary behavior, and it is upon these effects that the remainder of this note will focus.

For legal rules directly and prospectively to affect behavior, three conditions must be present: (1) the rules must be understood by the persons to whom they are addressed; (2) the addressees must desire, perhaps because of fear of sanctions which may be imposed, to follow the rules; and (3) the addressees must be capable of following, and be in a position to follow, the rules. All three conditions are especially open to question in connection with the first two decisions considered in this chapter. In the *Vosburg* case, for example, one might argue that the 11-year-old defendant neither understood the law of battery applicable to his acts nor was he, in his capacity as a naturally rambunctious schoolboy, willing or able to conform his conduct to the law. The question might be asked: Do we really think that imposing liability on young Putney will make schoolchildren in Wisconsin behave any better, or any differently?

Before committing yourself to an answer, consider whether it is even relevant that schoolchildren's behavior will or will not be directly affected by this sort of decision. Are the schoolchildren of Wisconsin, after all, the only, or even the primary, addressees of the rules imposing tort liability upon them for their unlawful conduct? Even if schoolchildren are not likely to behave differently simply because liability is imposed in this manner, can the same thing be said of their parents? Might not the court be tacitly assuming that the behavior of schoolchildren will indirectly be affected to the extent that their parents will learn of the decision and be affected by it?

Implicit in this last question is the assumption that adults are more likely than children to be deterred from committing batteries by the threat of tort liability. Clearly, such an assumption seems sensible by contrasting *Vosburg* and *Tinkham.* The remote prohibitions of tort law probably offer little leverage over the pugnacious Putneys of the world. Indeed, the relative ineffectiveness of tort law as a deterrent in this context may explain, at least in part, why tort law privileges other actors, such as parents and teachers, to use decidedly more tangible and immediate deterrents. These actors, of course, may conceivably abuse the privilege, but they are also more likely, as a general matter, to be deterred from doing so by the legal consequences of their conduct. Thus, it seems likely that teachers in the district in which *Tinkham* arose will, following that decision, think twice before resorting to corporal punishment to bring a class to order.

However, even granting the existence of a differential in the sensitivity of minors and adults to tort law's commands, questions remain concerning the extent to which the conduct of adults may be directly affected. Clearly, the deterrence potential of tort law will vary according to the circumstances in which the defendant finds himself. An actor responding emotionally and spontaneously to outside stimuli—the defendant in *Courvoisier,* for example—is probably unlikely to weigh potential tort liability in the balance before acting. On the other hand, individuals acting with conscious deliberation—the defendants in *Katko,* for example—may be more likely to consider potential liability; and later would-be trap gun setters might be expected to weigh liability even more heavily, on the reasonable assumption (given the publicity that case received) that Iowans know about the trap gun liability rule. Moreover, within the broad category of deliberate actors, doctors, such as the defendants in *Bang* and *Kennedy,* are probably more likely to be aware of and be affected by the law of battery than are landowners such as the defendants in *Katko.* And perhaps even more than doctors, corporations, such as the defendants in *O'Brien, Barton,* and *Vincent,* are likely to know the law and to attempt to guide their employees' conduct accordingly.

Thus, it may be possible to generalize concerning the deterrence potential of the law of battery in relation to the various categories of actors to whom the rules are addressed. As we move up the scale from the schoolchild in *Vosburg* to the doctors in *Bang* and *Kennedy* to the corporations in *O'Brien, Barton,* and *Vincent,* we move from individuals acting on impulse to professionals and institutions acting with a certain amount of planning and deliberation. It seems safe to assume as a general proposition that the more institutional the actor to whom the rules are addressed, the more likely the actor is to be affected in his, or its, behavior by those rules. Managers of corporations are more likely than are schoolchildren to know the legal rules governing liability, and are in a position to conform more effectively their employees' conduct to those rules. (As institutions, they face the same situations over and over again, and can train their employees regarding what to expect and how to behave.) Returning momentarily to the *Vosburg* case and applying these insights to the problem of trying to affect the behavior of schoolchildren in Wisconsin, consider these questions: If the court in that case were to resolve to hold responsible the person who is in the best position to act effectively to prevent schoolchildren from harming each other, who besides the children or their parents might be prime candidates for liability? How might we describe the basis of that liability?

Bear in mind that we have been speaking in terms of *assumptions* regarding the conditions that determine behavior effects of tort law. Later in these materials we will consider the extent to which these assumptions have been the subject of empirical study by behavioral scientists. Many of the studies have focused upon the criminal law, where the extent of the effect of threatened criminal sanctions on behavior has long been a source of hot debate. More recently, the assumptions regarding the effects of tort law on behavior have begun to attract attention. From time to time in this book, we will refer to the published work of behavioral scientists for the purpose of testing and exploring basic assumptions regarding the relationship between law and behavior. In the years to come, lawyers will increasingly be required to be familiar with the methods of inquiry and analysis employed by behavioral scientists.

Law and Policy: Taking Stock

At the close of this treatment of battery, it is useful to take stock of the cases and problems we have considered and how they may reflect various sets of underlying, unifying themes. Earlier, we identified several possible explanations of the objectives that lie behind tort law. Tort law may be seen to reflect noninstrumental values relating to fairness among individuals. It may be explained instrumentally as part of a broader effort to increase social welfare by eliminating unnecessary waste and achieving more efficient allocations of scarce (natural and human) resources. Or it may be viewed more skeptically as lacking any basis in underlying normative values, and thus be viewed as part of the existing American political system designed to promote capitalism and traditional liberalist ideology. For that matter, tort law may reflect some other set of values altogether, or be simply the product of random development. While it is a bit early to try to tie all of tort law into a neat package, what follow are brief observations aimed at stimulating your own thinking along these paths.

As observed earlier, the fairness perspective seems most strongly reflected in the "property never outweighs human life" dictum in connection with the use of deadly force to protect property. Neither the efficiency nor the radical-critique perspectives appears able to do more than observe that this is an exception to their organizing principles. But what about the Vincent

v. Lake Erie decision, in which someone who committed no wrong was forced to pay damages for harm caused to property? Here the efficiency perspective offers an explanation: Liability is imposed on the intruder (in *Vincent,* the boat owner) not because of any "wrong," but because the intruder is the one in the relatively better position to make the appropriate cost-benefit analysis to determine whether it is "worth it" to intrude and cause damage to the owner's property. Thus, the threat of liability will give that party the necessary incentives to avoid wasting scarce resources—the intruder will act in a manner that would be appropriate if the intruder owned all the property interests—boat and dock—threatened with injury. If the parties have contracted ahead of time, as they well might when they enter the contract concerning dockage of the boat, courts presumably will give effect to the contractual assignments of liability. But if they have not, or if before the event contracting is impossible, or too costly, then arguably tort law should impose liability on the one who appears to be the better minimizer of overall costs (total damage to dock and boat, in *Vincent*).

From the noninstrumental/fairness perspective, perhaps *Vincent* represents the view that whenever one person deliberately takes the property or welfare of another for the taker's own benefit, liability should be imposed in order to avoid unjustly enriching the taker. But this explanation may assume the result when it uses the phrase "takes the property or welfare of another." The words "property" and "welfare" imply legally protected entitlements in the victim, and the word "takes" implies violation of the entitlement. And yet the question of entitlement is the one we set out to answer in the first place. Thus, even the noninstrumental/fairness perspective, which *seems* to rely more on the inherent justness of imposing liability, must struggle to explain its underlying assumptions.

On its facts, *O'Brien* appears to support the view that tort law is biased against the lower classes. The rule of law established in that case—that manifestations of consent should count more than uncommunicated, subjective states of mind—seems neutral enough. But its application in that case seems to rest on a tacit assumption that steerage passengers deserve little in the way of a personalized explanation of the relevant risks and had better speak up quickly if they should be so brazen as to object to being treated like cattle at roundup time. Of course, that decision is almost 100 years old. Would the case be decided the same way today, on the same facts?

In any event, the foregoing are meant only as suggestions. Can you explain these decisions, and the others considered in this chapter, more satisfactorily?

Chapter 2

Actual Causation

In all of the battery cases considered in Chapter 1, the plaintiffs sought to recover for physical injuries suffered as a consequence of the tortious conduct of others. Implicit in all of those cases was the requirement that the plaintiffs establish that the defendants' conduct actually caused the harm for which they sought recovery. Indeed, in some of the cases the fact question of actual causation was contested at trial and presented issues of law for decision on appeal. In *Vosburg* (p. 12, above), for example, the causation issue on appeal related to the admissibility of medical expert testimony that the kick by the defendant caused the plaintiff's injuries.

In this chapter, we examine the causation issue more closely, primarily relying on cases involving negligence rather than battery. Negligence cases share with the harmful battery cases in Chapter 1 the requirement that the plaintiff prove that the defendant's conduct caused the harm of which the plaintiff complains. In this chapter we will not focus on the question of what constitutes negligence; that will be deferred until Chapter 4. The focus here is on the issue of actual causation: Did the defendant's wrongful conduct cause the plaintiff's harm?

Actual causation involves two closely related issues. The first issue, reflected in a majority of the cases in this chapter, focuses on the causal relation between defendant's conduct and plaintiff's harm. The relevant question is: "But for defendant having acted at all, would the plaintiff nevertheless have suffered the same harm?" An affirmative answer to this question—"yes, the plaintiff would have suffered the same harm if the defendant had never acted at all"—establishes that defendant's conduct was not an actual cause of plaintiff's injury.

The second issue focuses on the causal effect of the *wrongful* nature of the defendant's conduct. The relevant question is: "But for the wrongful quality of the defendant's conduct would the plaintiff nevertheless have suffered the same harm?" An affirmative answer suggests that the wrongful quality of the defendant's conduct was not an actual cause of plaintiff's harm since the harm would have occurred even if the defendant's conduct had been proper. Both the first and the second but-for questions must be answered negatively for the defendant's wrongful conduct to be the actual cause of the plaintiff's harm.

It will be observed that the first of these but-for issues is entirely factual, whereas the second introduces a legal component in its reference to the "wrongful quality" of the defendant's conduct. This difference has caused some commentators to refer to the first issue as "cause in fact" and the second as part of "proximate cause" or "legal cause." On balance, however, the but-for aspect that both issues share is more significant than the difference between them, justifying treating them together as components of actual causation.

Before examining the actual causation issue in the courts, you should consider why the torts process should impose a causation requirement in the first place. What policy objectives might the causation requirement be viewed as serving? This question cannot be answered once and for all here, at the outset of our inquiry. But it is a question you should consider as you work through this chapter. In developing your answer, the following observations may prove useful. First, although the causation requirement is apt to be viewed as an impediment to plaintiff's recovery, bear in mind that for plaintiffs who succeed in satisfying it, together with the other prerequisites to recovery, the causation concept strongly suggests that they will recover for the full amount of their actual harm, however great that amount might prove to be. From this perspective, the concept of actual cause not only helps to sort out the worthy cases from the unworthy, but also helps to fix the size of the recoveries in worthy cases.

The second point to bear in mind is that the causation requirement may reflect the judgment in some cases that the strength of the signal to be sent to the defendant, from a deterrence perspective, should be proportional to the harm caused. In battery cases, "deterrence for its own sake," or even "quasi-criminal punishment" may seem appropriate in light of the intentionally wrongful nature of defendants' conduct. If the basis of liability is negligence, the attitude seems to be that so long as no harm is caused, the actor will not be exposed to liability.

Finally, the requirement of causation may reflect a shared concern that practical limits be placed on an actor's exposure to liability. Without the actual causation requirement a negligent factory operator might be held liable for all the harm, accidental or otherwise, suffered by anyone in his town, or in his state, for the period during which he acted negligently. Such potential exposure to liability might go a long way toward eliminating the negligent operation of factories, to be sure; but given the unavoidable vagueness of the negligence concept, it might eliminate properly managed factories as well.

Two books explaining the broader meanings of actual causation are Becht and Miller, The Test of Factual Causation in Negligence and Strict Liability Cases (1961), and Hart and Honore, Causation in the Law (2d ed. 1985). A number of the issues covered in this chapter are analyzed in Wright, Causation in Tort Law, 73 Calif. L. Rev. 1735 (1985).

A. *But For the Defendant's Conduct Would the Plaintiff Have Suffered Harm?*

The first but-for inquiry appears quite simple, requiring only that the jury determine whether the defendant's conduct was causally linked to the plaintiff's injury. However, as the subsections that follow illustrate, even simple but-for causation can be surprisingly complicated.

1. Did the Defendant Do It?: Cause-in-Fact

Hoyt v. Jeffers

30 Mich. 181 (1874)

[Defendant owned and operated a steam saw mill located 233 feet from a hotel owned by plaintiff. On August 17, 1870, the hotel was damaged by fire. Plaintiff sued defendant claiming that the fire was caused by sparks emitted from the chimney of defendant's mill, and that defendant was negligent in permitting sparks to escape from the chimney. Judgment was entered upon a jury verdict for plaintiff, and defendant appeals.]

CHRISTIANCY, J. . . . The chimney was a square brick chimney, originally about seventy feet high, but in the spring of 1870 about twelve or twelve and one-half feet were added to the height; but neither before nor after the addition did it have any spark-catcher on it, nor what is called a butterfly valve, with wire netting, nor a hole behind the boiler for the sparks to fall into, so far as the evidence shows. The Sherman House was situated about two hundred and thirty-three feet to the northeast of the mill, and on the other side of the street from it.

There was evidence on the part of the plaintiff relating to the particular time of the fire, which tended to show that the plaintiff's buildings were set on fire and burned by a spark from the mill chimney, though the spark was not seen to fall, or the fire to start from there. But this evidence was greatly strengthened by, and to some extent consisted of, a large amount of testimony showing the action and operation of the chimney in throwing such sparks, endangering and setting fire to property, for a long time previous, and up to the time of the fire, and how the mill had been run, and what measures had been taken or omitted by those running the mill, to avoid such danger to surrounding property, a change made in the height of the chimney, and whether, and how far, that change affected the action of the chimney by increasing or diminishing the escape of, and danger from sparks or cinders.

The evidence on the part of the plaintiff (some of which was received under objection, which will be noticed hereafter) tended to show, *first,* as to the habit of the chimney to throw sparks and the danger to surrounding property:—that from 1862 down to and after the time of this fire, sparks of fire and burning cinders or fragments of fire were frequently and quite generally emitted from the chimney when the mill was running, and carried to considerable distance (as far, and often farther than the Sherman House), falling to the ground and on buildings and sidewalks while still on fire, and sometimes setting fire to buildings and other wooden material they fell upon; that when the wind was from the southwest (especially if strong), and the mill was running, live sparks were frequently seen to fly from the chimney and fall around the Sherman House and near to and upon other buildings, on sidewalks and the yards in and near the same direction; that in 1862 sparks from the chimney were seen to fall and set fire to sawdust near this house; that in 1863 or 1864, and again in 1869, this same Sherman House took fire on the outer south side, when the wind was in the southwest, and mill running, and sparks coming from that direction; that sparks were seen to fall on the sidewalk and set it on fire at one time; that sparks had been picked up on the platform of the Sherman House; that on one occasion clothes were set on fire when out drying on the line near the premises, and that clothes on the line drying in this neighborhood had holes burned in them, and were covered with black, dead sparks, and blackened, and that furniture set out at a cabinet shop about the same distance was rendered smutty in the same way; and that several houses near the Sherman House, and some further off, had to keep their windows shut to avoid injury of this kind to clothes, etc., inside, when the mill was running and the wind coming from the mill; that in 1873, after this fire, the Garvey House, somewhat near the mill, was set on fire under circumstances indicating that it came from such sparks; that fire had caught in several buildings similarly situated, and that all caught on the side towards the mill, and as far as known, when the mill was running, and the wind in the southwest, etc.

The first set of errors assigned [is] based upon exceptions to the admission of evidence tending to show how this chimney had been in the habit of throwing sparks, and setting fire to buildings, etc., for several years previous to the burning of this hotel. The court upon the objection of the defendant, refused to receive evidence extending back over so long a period, except upon the understanding and with the undertaking, on the part of the plaintiff, to follow it up with evidence to show that it was then in the same condition as at the time of the fire; and the plaintiff did produce a large amount of evidence tending to show this, and that the mode of using the mill, the throwing of sparks from the chimney, and the danger to other property in the vicinity, continued substantially the same, from the earliest period to which this evidence referred, down to the time of this fire, and that the raising of the chimney about twelve feet, in the spring prior to the fire, did not appreciably diminish the emission of sparks, or the danger therefrom.

Now, as the evidence of the burning of the plaintiff's property complained of, need not and did not consist of direct evidence, that in that particular instance a particular spark was seen to come from the mill, traced by the same eye through the air and seen to light upon the side of the house and set it on fire, but the plaintiff must be at liberty to show, as he did, circumstances tending to prove that the property was set on fire in this way on the occasion alluded to, I can see no sound reason why he should not be at liberty to show any circumstances fairly tending to prove, or calculated to produce a reasonable belief, that this fire originated in this way on the occasion in question. On principle, I think all such testimony is admissible, and its force or weight to be estimated by the jury. It does not, as is here objected, raise a multitude of distinct issues, any more than in all other cases of circumstantial evidence, where the circumstances are equally numerous. And to show, as was done here, that while the mill and chimney, and the mode of using them, remained the same in all essential respects, the wind in the same direction, and the other surrounding circumstances the same, sparks had been seen to issue from this chimney in large quantities, watched, and seen to fall upon buildings or sidewalks, or other wood material, and to set them on fire, and all the other facts which the evidence given tended to show, as already stated, would strongly tend to produce a reasonable belief of the particular fact of the burning being from this cause on the occasion in question. I therefore see no error in the admission of this evidence.

Upon the same principle, I think the evidence of the Garvey House taking fire, in May, 1873 (though after the burning of plaintiff's building) was admissible, together with all the circumstances tending to show that it was set on fire by sparks from this chimney. . . .

[Judgment affirmed.]

Smith v. Rapid Transit Inc.

317 Mass. 469, 58 N.E.2d 754 (1945)

SPALDING, J. The decisive question in this case is whether there was evidence for the jury that the plaintiff was injured by a bus of the defendant that was operated by one of its employees in the course of his employment. If there was, the defendant concedes that the evidence warranted the submission to the jury of the question of the operator's negligence in the management of the bus. The case is here on the plaintiff's exception to the direction of a verdict for the defendant.

These facts could have been found: While the plaintiff at about 1:00 A.M. on February 6, 1941, was driving an automobile on Main Street, Winthrop, in an easterly direction toward Winthrop Highlands, she observed a bus coming toward her which she described as a "great big, long, wide affair." The bus, which was proceeding at about forty miles an hour, "forced her to turn to the right," and her automobile collided with a "parked car." The plaintiff was coming from Dorchester. The department of public utilities had issued a certificate of public convenience or necessity to the defendant for three routes in Winthrop, one of which included Main Street, and this was in effect in February, 1941. "There was another bus line in operation in Winthrop at that time but not on Main Street." According to the defendant's time-table, buses were scheduled to leave Winthrop Highlands for Maverick Square via Main Street at 12:10 A.M., 12:45 A.M., 1:15 A.M., and 2:15 A.M. The running time for this trip at that time of night was thirty minutes.

The direction of a verdict for the defendant was right. The ownership of the bus was a matter of conjecture. While the defendant had the sole franchise for operating a bus line on Main Street, Winthrop, this did not preclude private or chartered buses from using this street; the bus in question could very well have been one operated by someone other than the defendant. It was said in Sargent v. Massachusetts Accident Co., 307 Mass. 246, at page 250, that it is "not enough that mathematically the chances somewhat favor a proposition to be proved; for example, the fact that colored automobiles made in the current year outnumber black ones would not warrant a finding that an undescribed automobile of the current year is colored and not black, nor would the fact that only a minority of men die of cancer warrant a finding that a particular man did not die of cancer." The most that can be said of the evidence in the instant case is that perhaps the mathematical chances somewhat favor the proposition that a bus of the defendant caused the accident. This was not enough. A "proposition is proved by a preponderance of the evidence if it is made to appear more likely or probable in the sense that actual belief in its truth, derived from the evidence, exists in the mind or minds of the tribunal notwithstanding any doubts that may still linger there." Sargent v. Massachusetts Accident Co., 307 Mass. 246, at page 250. . . .

Exceptions overruled.

One of the more interesting cases involving the use of statistics is People v. Collins, 68 Cal. 2d 319, 438 P.2d 33, 66 Cal. Rptr. 497 (1968). In that case, the court overturned a robbery conviction because it had been obtained improperly through the use of testimony regarding mathematical probabilities. As in *Smith,* the issue was whether the evidence was sufficient to present a jury question as to the defendant identification issue, and it is a case study in the use and misuse of probability analysis. The defendants were convicted on the evidence that the robbery of the victim was committed by two people, a young white woman with blond hair and a ponytail, and a black man with a mustache and beard, who fled the scene in a yellow car. Four days later, the police arrested the defendants, who fit the general description and who owned a yellow car. At the trial, a mathematics instructor from a state college testified as to the *product rule,* which is that the probability of the joint occurrence of a number of mutually independent events is equal to the product of the individual probabilities that each of the events will occur. He was allowed to assume the following probability factors for each of the characteristics:

Yellow automobile	1/10
Man with mustache	1/4
Woman with ponytail	1/10
Woman with blond hair	1/3
Black man with beard	1/10
Interracial couple in car	1/1000

Under the product rule, the prosecutor argued to the jury that there was but one chance in 12 million that any given couple would possess all these distinctive characteristics; therefore, there was only one chance in 12 million that the defendants were innocent. In reversing the convictions, the court ruled that there was no evidence as to the accuracy of the probabilities, and that there was no basis for assuming that the factors were independent. As to the latter point, blacks with beards and men with mustaches obviously represent overlapping categories. The court also observed that the evidence on its face did not exclude the possibility of at least one other couple in the Los Angeles area that would satisfy the characteristics, so there was no basis for concluding that it was the defendants who had committed the robbery.

Understandably, the *Collins* case generated a considerable amount of commentary in the law reviews, all of which seems to have been favorable to the decision reached in that case by the supreme court. See, e.g., Cullison, Identification by Probabilities and Trial by Arithmetic (A Lesson for Beginners in How to Be Wrong with Greater Precision), 6 Hous. L. Rev. 471 (1969); Tribe, Trial by Mathematics: Precision and Ritual in the Legal Process, 84 Harv. L. Rev. 1329 (1971). However, although all of the commentators agree that the particular application of probability analysis in *Collins* was inappropriate, a number of writers insist that as a general proposition probability theory may serve as a useful tool in the fact-finding process. The relationship of probability analysis to the burden of proof is discussed in Cohen, Confidence in Probability: Burdens of Persuasion in a World of Imperfect Knowledge, 60 N.Y.U. L. Rev. 385 (1985).

The Law-Fact Distinction: Sufficiency of the Evidence and Circumstantial Proof of Causation

The preceding cases and the text on mathematical probabilities raise the issue of the sufficiency of the plaintiff's proof of causation in the absence of direct eyewitness testimony linking the defendant's conduct to the plaintiff's harm. In most cases, there will be direct evidence relating to causation. Direct evidence of a particular fact goes directly to the fact in question. It is evidence based on the senses of the witness—what the witness saw, or touched, or heard. In *Hoyt,* for example, if a witness had testified that he saw sparks from the defendant's chimney drift over to and start a fire on the plaintiff's property, the witness would have supplied direct evidence of the cause-in-fact connection between the defendant's conduct and the plaintiff's harm. But, as the preceding cases indicate, reliance on direct evidence is not the only way in which causation may be proved. Causation may also be proved indirectly, on the basis of circumstantial evidence. Where no direct evidence of cause-in-fact is available, as in *Hoyt* where no eyewitness actually saw sparks from the defendant's chimney set fire to the plaintiff's hotel, the plaintiff may be able to prove facts from which an inference of causation may be drawn. Thus, the plaintiff in *Hoyt* was able to prove that sparks had on previous occasions flown from the defendant's mill and started fires. This fact, coupled with others, was considered to be sufficient to establish cause-in-fact circumstantially. Proving a fact circumstantially rather than directly should not be viewed necessarily as a handicap, at least in cases that reach the jury. Direct evidence is, after all, only as strong and convincing as the credibility of the witness who tenders it. In *Hoyt,* for example, the plaintiff was probably better off going to the jury with his circumstantial evidence of causation than he would have been if the only evidence of cause-in-fact had been direct, eyewitness testimony by the plaintiff's brother, a well-known liar.

To the extent that being forced to rely on circumstantial proof of causation is likely to be a handicap, it will be in the plaintiff's ability to get to the jury in the first place. Direct evidence of causation will almost always be sufficient to create a jury question, because it raises issues of credibility of the witnesses. Traditionally, it has been agreed that whenever the resolution of a question of fact depends upon the credibility of witnesses, it is up to the jury to decide whom they will believe. In other words, it is the jury's job to observe the expression on the witness's face, the wringing of his hands and the like, and finally to decide whether he is telling the truth. Only rarely will a trial judge rule that a witness's direct evidence is not believable as a matter of law. Thus, even where the only eyewitness is the plaintiff's untrustworthy brother, the defendant ordinarily will not win a directed verdict on the cause-in-fact issue. However, where direct evidence of causation, or of any other relevant fact, is not available, the plaintiff may encounter difficulties in overcoming the defendant's assertion that the circumstantial evidence is insufficient to warrant sending the case to the jury. Therefore, the cases involving circumstantial proof of causation afford an excellent opportunity to develop and refine your understanding of the law-fact distinction and the allocation of functions between judge and jury.

As was indicated in the law-fact distinction note following O'Brien v. Cunard Steamship Co., p. 36, above, the determination of whether there is evidence sufficient to create a jury issue is one of law, initially to be decided by the trial judge and subject to review on appeal. Whether there is sufficient evidence is a matter about which it is difficult to generalize. Each case tends to be unique and rules of general applicability for measuring sufficiency are difficult to formulate. (*Smith* involves one such rule of general applicability—a jury question is not created if the only evidence of cause is evidence of mathematical probabilities.) The judge's own experience and how he or she views reality are likely to be as important as any other factor in the resolution of close cases. The judge may also be influenced by more or less unarticulated notions of policy.

The appealability of trial judges' rulings as to the sufficiency of the evidence ensures to some extent that these rulings are not entirely whimsical. Appellate review is also important as a way of ensuring that a proper balance is struck across a range of cases in the decisions relating to the sufficiency of evidence. If the power to give binding instructions or to direct verdicts were exercised to an extreme, judges would end up deciding the outcomes in most cases. There might remain a theoretical category of "issues of fact," but in effect most of them would be decided by judges as a matter of law, and this would effectively undermine the jury system. On the other hand, a system under which all cases were sent to the jury with no screening afforded by decisions as to the sufficiency of the evidence would not be a system of law. As Justice Frankfurter once explained: "The easy but timid way out for a trial judge is to leave all cases tried to a jury for jury determination, but in so doing he fails in his duty. . . . A timid judge, like a biased judge, is intrinsically a lawless judge." Wilkerson v. McCarthy, 336 U.S. 53, 65, 69 S. Ct. 413, 419, 93 L. Ed. 497, 506 (1949). Thus, rulings about the sufficiency of the evidence are among the most important decisions that judges make.

2. Does Defendant's Activity Cause This Sort of Injury as a General Matter?

The cause-in-fact material just considered may be said to raise the issue of "specific causation"—whether the defendant's wrongful conduct specifically caused the plaintiff's injuries. In contrast, the issue presented in this section is one of general, or generic, causation—whether the defendant's conduct is of the general sort that is capable of causing injury of the type suffered by the plaintiff. In *Hoyt,* above, the general causation issue was easy; of course a mill emitting showers of burning embers is capable of starting a hotel fire a few blocks downwind. But what if the plaintiff's injury had consisted of a herd of cattle getting sick? In that case the mill operator could well argue that burning embers do not, as a general matter, cause illness in cattle. Even if the plaintiff could somehow establish the necessary general connection between embers and cattle illness, the defendant could nevertheless argue, as in *Hoyt*, "It wasn't *my* embers that caused the illness." But the plaintiff's first task in the embers-cattle context would be to establish the nonobvious general causation link between defendant's conduct and plaintiff's loss.

No area of tort litigation in recent years captures the essence of general causation analysis better than cases involving the widely used prescription drug Bendectin. Approved in 1956 by the Food and Drug Administration as a safe treatment for morning sickness during pregnancy, Bendectin had been used by more than 30 million women between 1957 and 1983, when Richardson-Merrell, Inc., the manufacturer, withdrew it from the market. Merrell withdrew the drug because of fears that it caused severe birth defects in children of mothers who ingested the drug while pregnant. A large number of tort claims had been filed based on scientific studies, including epidemiological studies, allegedly revealing the drug to be a teratogen, or birth-defect-causing agent. By the mid-1980s, Bendectin litigation appeared to be a growing area for plaintiffs' lawyers. See, e.g., Oxendine v. Merrell Dow Pharmaceuticals, 506 A.2d 1100 (D.C. 1986) (Bendectin manufacturer held liable based on epidemiological proof of causation), *cert. denied,* 110 S. Ct. 1121 (1990).

Notwithstanding the optimism that reigned in the early to mid 1980s among plaintiffs regarding the future of Bendectin litigation, the tide began turning against them as the established scientific community concluded in a number of research projects that the link between the drug and the birth defects had not been established at an adequate level of statistical significance—that is, observed correlations between ingestion and injury could have been the product of random chance. Courts hearing these cases began to issue summary judgments for the defendant, Merrell, with increasing frequency. A good example is Richardson v. Richardson-Merrell, Inc., 857 F.2d 823 (D.C. Cir. 1988), *cert. denied,* 110 S. Ct. 218 (1989), in which the court of appeals affirmed a JNOV on behalf of defendant, holding that, given the great weight of scientific opinion to the contrary, plaintiff's expert's testimony on causation was insufficient. The court concluded (857 F.2d at 832):

> The circumstances of the case are tragic and Carita Richardson's plight evokes the utmost sympathy. It would be foolhardy to expect members of the jury to be without compassion for the catastrophe that befell this family. That is a natural response of the human spirit, and is without legal consequence so long as it is properly controlled. But in a case such as this it not only is appropriate but indeed imperative that the court remain vigilant to ensure that neither emotion nor confusion has supplanted reason. . . .

Many of the courts that have rejected plaintiffs' expert testimony in Bendectin cases have relied on Frye v. United States, 293 F.2d 1013, 1014

(D.C. 1923) for the proposition that expert opinion based on a scientific technique is inadmissable unless the technique is "generally accepted" as reliable in the relevant scientific community. In DeLuca v. Merrell Dow Pharmaceuticals, Inc., 911 F.2d 941 (3d Cir. 1990), a Bendectin case, the trial court excluded plaintiff's expert testimony of general causation on the ground that (911 F.2d at 945-947):

> [t]he great weight of scientific opinion, as is evidenced by . . . FDA committee results, sides with the view that Bendectin use does not increase the risk of having a child with birth defects. Sailing against the prevailing scientific breeze is the DeLucas' expert Dr. Alan Done, formerly a Professor of Pharmacology and Pediatrics at Wayne State University School of Medicine, who continues to hold fast to his position that Bendectin is a teratogen. In spite of his impressive curriculum vitae, Dr. Done's opinion on this subject has been rejected as inadmissible by several courts.
>
> Epidemiological studies, of necessity, look to the experience of sample groups as indicative of the experience of a far larger population. Epidemiologists recognize, however, that the experience of the sample groups may vary from that of the larger population by chance. Thus, a showing of increased risk for birth defects among women using Bendectin in a particular study does not automatically prove that Bendectin use creates a higher risk of having a child with birth defects because the discrepancy between the exposed and unexposed groups could be the product of chance resulting from the use of only a small sample of the relevant populations. As a result of the acknowledged risk of this so-called "sampling error," researchers typically have rejected the associations suggested by epidemiological data unless those associations survive the rigors of "significance testing." This practice has also found favor in the legal context. A number of judicial opinions . . . have found Bendectin plaintiffs' causation evidence inadmissible because every published epidemiological study of the relationship of Bendectin exposure to the incidence of birth defects has concluded that there is not a "statistically significant" relationship between these two events.
>
> Significance testing has a "P value" focus; the P value "indicates the probability, assuming [that there is no association between two studied variables], that the observed data will depart from the absence of association to the extent that they actually do, or to a greater extent, by actual chance." [See K. Rothman, Modern Epidemiology 116 (1986).] If P is less than .05 (or 5%) a study's finding of a relationship supportive of the alternative hypothesis is considered statistically significant, if P is greater than 5% the relationship is rejected as insignificant. Accordingly, the results of a particular study are reported as simply "significant" or "not significant" or as P < .05 or P > .05. . . .
>
> Rothman contends that there is nothing magical or inherently important about .05 significance; rather this is just a common value on the tables scholars use to calculate significance. Rothman, supra, at 117. He stresses that the data in a certain study may indicate a strong relationship between two variables but still not be "statistically significant" and that the level of significance which should be required depends on the type of decision being made. . . .

The court of appeals concluded that a remand was appropriate to determine, on a more developed record, what level of confidence the tort system should require for purposes of general causation (911 F.2d at 955):

> By directing such an overall evaluation . . . we do not mean to reject at this point Merrell Dow's contention that a showing of a .05 level of statistical significance should be a threshold requirement for any statistical analysis concluding that Bendectin is a teratogen regardless of the presence of other indicia of reliability. That contention will need to be addressed on remand. The root issue it poses is what risk of what type of error the judicial system is willing to tolerate. This is not an easy issue to resolve and one possible resolution is a conclusion that the system should not tolerate any expert opinion rooted in statistical analysis where the results of the underlying studies are not significant at a .05 level. We believe strongly, however, that this issue should not be resolved in a case where the record contains virtually no relevant help from the parties or from qualified experts. The literature evidences that there are legal scholars and epidemiologists who have given considerable thought to this and related issues and we would hope that this expertise could be made available to the court, on remand, in some acceptable manner. . . .
>
> After considering the reliability of Dr. Done's testimony and the dangers it poses, the district court will have to reach the ultimate determination of whether it is "helpful" and thus admissible. That determination will require an exercise of discretion informed by the . . . record developed on remand. Once made, it will be entitled to deference. . . .

Having determined to remand on the issue of general causation, the court of appeals observed that the issue of specific causation—whether in this specific instance Bendectin caused Amy DeLuca's injuries—might well defeat recovery even if general causation was established.

> If New Jersey law requires the DeLucas to show that it is more likely than not that Bendectin caused Amy DeLuca's birth defects, and they are forced to rely solely on Dr. Done's epidemiological analysis in order to avoid summary judgment, the relative risk of limb reduction defects arising from the epidemiological data Done relies upon will, at a minimum, have to exceed "2":
>
> > A relative risk of "2" means that the disease occurs among the population subject to the event under investigation twice as frequently as the disease occurs among the population not subject to the event under investigation. Phrased another way, a relative risk of "2" means that, on the average, there is a fifty percent likelihood that a particular case of the disease was caused by the event under investigation and a fifty percent likelihood that the disease was caused by chance alone. A relative risk greater than "2" means that the disease more likely than not was caused by the event.
>
> Manko v. United States, 636 F. Supp. 1419, 1434 (W.D. Mo. 1986), *aff'd in relevant part,* 830 F.2d 831 (8th Cir. 1987).
>
> We express no opinion on whether Dr. Done's epidemiological analysis

> fails to meet this threshold requirement. While it is not clear to our untrained eyes that it does, without the benefit of an expert affidavit critiquing that analysis we are not sufficiently confident of our own critical capacities to resolve that issue. Nor do we suggest that the DeLucas will be required to rely solely on Dr. Done's epidemiological analysis at trial or in any subsequent summary judgment proceedings. . . . We note only that even if Dr. Done's epidemiological analysis is found to be admissible, the DeLucas are entitled to get to trial only if the district court is satisfied that this analysis together with any other evidence relevant to the causation issue would permit a jury finding that Amy's birth defects were, when measured against the appropriate burden of proof, caused by her mother's exposure to Bendectin.

In Daubert v. Merrell Dow Pharmaceuticals, Inc., 113 S. Ct. 2786 (1993) the Supreme Court vacated the judgment of the court of appeals in favor of the defendant in a Bendectin case. The Court held that "general acceptance" is not a necessary precondition to the admissibility of scientific evidence under the Federal Rules of Evidence:

> Faced with a proffer of expert scientific testimony . . . the trial judge must make a preliminary assessment of whether the testimony's underlying reasoning or methodology is scientifically valid and properly can be applied to the facts at issue. Many considerations will bear on the inquiry, including whether the theory or technique in question can be (and has been) tested, whether it has been subjected to peer review and publication, its known or potential error rate, the existence and maintenance of standards controlling its operation, and whether it has attracted widespread acceptance within a relevant scientific community. The inquiry is a flexible one, and its focus must be solely on principles and methodology, not on the conclusions that they generate. Throughout, the judge should also be mindful of other applicable Rules. . . . [C]ross examination, presentation of contrary evidence, and careful instruction on the burden of proof, rather than wholesale exclusion under an uncompromising "general acceptance" standard, is the appropriate means by which evidence based on valid principles may be challenged.

Excerpted from official Syllabus, 113 S. Ct. at 2790.

A case involving problems similar to *DeLuca,* quoted in the *DeLuca* opinion, is Manko v. United States, 636 F. Supp. 1419 (W.D. Mo. 1986). At stake was the liability of the United States for a serious disease alleged to have been caused by the plaintiff's innoculation with swine flu vaccine. The government conceded that it would be liable, if cause were established, under a federal statute relieving manufacturers of the vaccine from liability and imposing it on the United States. The court discussed and relied upon detailed statistical analysis showing that the relative incidence of the disease among those who had taken the vaccine was over three times that among those who had not.

Plaintiffs alleging that their lung cancer was caused by cigarette smoking have also been able to get to the jury on the cause issue based on evidence of mathematical probabilities. See Pritchard v. Liggett & Myers Tobacco Co., 295 F.2d 292 (3d Cir. 1961). Although the general causal link between cigarette smoking and lung cancer rests on both statistical and experimental evidence (see The Health Consequences of Smoking: A Report of the Surgeon General, United States Dept. of Health, Education and Welfare, 59-67 (1972)), the conclusion that lung cancer in a particular person was caused by cigarette smoking can only rest upon evidence of mathematical probabilities. For example, recent studies show that the incidence of lung cancer is 460 out of 100,000 for heavy smoking males for the age group of 40 to 64, but only 10 out of 100,000 for nonsmokers. The mortality ratio from lung cancer for the pack-a-day smoking male is nine times that of nonsmokers. Id. at 61.

For an analysis of the problems encountered in attempting to prove that overexposure to radiation causes leukemia, see Estep, Radiation Injuries and Statistics: The Need for a New Approach to Injury Litigation, 59 Mich. L. Rev. 259 (1960). The author states that the natural incidence of leukemia is 107 cases out of 100,000 persons. Exposure to a "doubling dose" of radiation will result in an additional 107 cases of leukemia for every 100,000 persons so exposed. From this, the author concludes that, "Every person [exposed to a doubling dose of radiation], including those whose leukemia results from natural causes rather than the defendant's radiation source, can 'prove' that 'more probably than not' defendant's source 'caused' his particular case. . . . If 100,000 persons receive slightly more than a doubling dose, 214 will get leukemia . . . and can hold the defendants legally liable under existing rules, although defendants 'caused' only 107 of the cases." Id. at 279.

If Estep is correct in his analysis, would any victim of cancer in the area of Three Mile Island, Pennsylvania, be able to recover from the utility owning the nuclear power plant that malfunctioned in the spring of 1979? The Secretary of HEW testified before a congressional committee investigating the incident that radiation from the plant could be expected to cause one to ten cancer deaths among the two million people living within a 50-mile radius of the plant, in which the normal number of cancer deaths would be 325,000. See New York Times, May 4, 1979, §A, at 1, col. 4.

For a consideration of a wide variety of problems involving probabilities and causation, see Symposium, Probability and Inference in the Law of Evidence, 66 B.U. L. Rev. 377-952 (1986).

To some extent, the causation problems considered so far in this chapter exist because of the traditional "all-or-nothing" quality of tort law. If the plaintiff carries his burden of proof that the defendant caused his harm, he recovers in full; if he does not carry that burden, he recovers nothing.

3. When All That Plaintiffs Can Ever Rely On Is Statistical Probability: Loss of a Chance

In Smith v. Rapid Transit Inc., p. 115, the plaintiff attempted to replace eyewitness evidence, which may often be available in such cases, with probabilistic evidence. One effect of the *Smith* decision might be to push plaintiffs to work harder at digging up eyewitness evidence. And in the *DeLuca* case, above, while the plaintiff had no choice but to rely on probabilistic evidence, over time one could expect scientific testing to narrow the gaps of uncertainty in many areas. In the cases in this section, by the very nature of the claim, all plaintiffs will *ever* have available to them is probabilities.

Falcon v. Memorial Hospital

436 Mich. 443, 462 N.W.2d 44 (1990)

LEVIN, Justice . . .

IV

Nena Falcon, a nineteen-year-old woman, gave birth to a healthy baby. . . . Moments after delivery, Nena Falcon coughed, gagged, convulsed, became cyanotic, and suffered a complete respiratory and cardiac collapse. Attempts to revive her were unsuccessful. She was pronounced dead soon thereafter.

The autopsy report indicated that amniotic fluid embolism, an unpreventable complication that occurs in approximately one out of ten or twenty thousand births, was the cause of death. The survival rate of amniotic fluid embolism is, according to Falcon's expert witness, 37.5 percent if an intravenous line is connected to the patient before the onset of embolism. In this case, an intravenous line had not been established.

Falcon's theory is that had a physician or nurse anesthetist inserted an intravenous line before administering the spinal anesthetic to assist the physician in dealing with any of several complications, the intravenous line could have been used to infuse live-saving fluids into Nena Falcon's circulatory system, providing her a 37.5 percent opportunity of surviving. By not inserting the intravenous line, the physician deprived her of a 37.5 percent opportunity of surviving the embolism.

V

The question whether a defendant caused an event is not readily answered, and is especially perplexing in circumstances such as those present in the instant case where the defendant's failure to act is largely responsible for the uncertainty regarding causation.

Had the defendants in the instant case inserted an intravenous line, one of two things would have happened, Nena Falcon would have lived, or she would have died. There would be no uncertainty whether the omissions of the defendants caused her death. Falcon's destiny would have been decided by fate and not possibly by her health care providers. . . .

VI

In an ordinary tort action seeking recovery for physical harm, the defendant is a stranger to the plaintiff and the duty imposed by operation of law is imposed independently of any undertaking by the defendant. In an action claiming medical malpractice, however, the patient generally is not a stranger to the defendant. Generally, the patient engaged the services of the defendant physician. The physician undertook to perform services for the patient, and the patient undertook to pay or provide payment for the services.

The scope of the undertakings by a physician or hospital to the patient and by the patient to the physician or hospital is not generally a matter of express agreement. There is, however, an understanding that the law enforces in the absence of express agreement. The patient expects a physician to do that which is expected of physicians of like training in the community, and the physician expects the patient to pay or provide payment for the services, whether the likelihood of there in fact being any benefit to the patient is only one through fifty percent or is greater than fifty percent.

The defendants assert, in effect, that the scope of their undertaking did not include acts or omissions likely to benefit the patient only to the extent of one through fifty percent—or at least they should not be subject to liability for acts or omissions likely to have caused harm to the extent only of one through fifty percent. They contend that they should be subject to liability only for acts or omissions likely, to the extent of more than fifty percent, to have caused physical harm to the patient. . . .

Patients engage the services of doctors, not only to prevent disease or death, but also to delay death and to defer or ameliorate the suffering associated with disease or death. If the trier of fact were to decide, on the basis of expert testimony, that the undertaking of the defendant physician included the implementation of tasks and procedures that, in the case of Nena Falcon, would have enabled the physician and other medically trained persons, who were present at the time of delivery, to provide her, in the event of the medical accident that occurred, an opportunity to survive the accident, a failure to do so was a breach of the understanding or undertaking.

Nena Falcon, if the testimony of Falcon's expert witness is credited, would have had a 37.5 percent opportunity of surviving had the defendants implemented the procedures Falcon's expert asserts should have been implemented. In reducing Nena Falcon's opportunity of living by failing to insert an intravenous line, her physician caused her harm, although it cannot be said, more probably than not, that he caused her death. A 37.5 percent opportunity of living is hardly the kind of opportunity that any of us would willingly allow our health care providers to ignore. If, as Falcon's expert asserts, the implementation of such procedures was part of the understanding or undertaking, the failure to have implemented the procedures was a breach of the understanding or undertaking. The physician is, and should be, subject to liability for such breach, although Nena Falcon was likely, measured as more than fifty percent, to die as soon as the medical accident occurred and the negligence of the physician eliminated a less than fifty percent opportunity of surviving.

We thus see the injury resulting from medical malpractice as not only, or necessarily, physical harm, but also as including the loss of opportunity of avoiding physical harm. A patient goes to a physician precisely to improve his opportunities of avoiding, ameliorating, or reducing physical harm and pain and suffering.

Women gave birth to children long before there were physicians or hospitals or even midwives. A woman who engages the services of a physician and enters a hospital to have a child does so to reduce pain and suffering and to increase the likelihood of her surviving and the child surviving childbirth in a good state of health even though the likelihood of the woman and child not surviving in good health without such services is far less than fifty percent. That is why women go to physicians. That is what physicians undertake to do. That is what they are paid for. They are, and should be, subject to liability if they fail to measure up to the standard of care.

VII

A number of courts have recognized, as we would, loss of an opportunity for a more favorable result, as distinguished from the unfavorable result, as compensable in medical malpractice actions. Under this approach, damages are recoverable for the loss of opportunity although the opportunity lost was less than even, and thus it is not more probable than not that the unfavorable result would or could have been avoided. . . .

VIII . . .

We are persuaded that loss of a 37.5 percent opportunity of living constitutes a loss of a substantial opportunity of avoiding physical harm. We need not now decide what lesser percentage would constitute a substantial loss of opportunity.

IX

In the instant case, while Nena Falcon's cause of action accrued before her death, she did not suffer conscious pain and suffering from the failure to implement the omitted procedures between the moment that the medical accident occurred and the time of her death a few minutes later—she was sedated throughout the entire time period. In this case, 37.5 percent times the damages recoverable for wrongful death would be an appropriate measure of damages.

We would affirm the Court of Appeals reversal of the entry of summary judgment for the defendants, and remand the case for trial.

[The concurring opinion of BOYLE, J., and the dissenting opinion of RILEY, C.J., are omitted.]

For an article advocating a proportional approach to actual causation in cases of this sort see King, Causation, Valuation, and Chance in Personal Injury Torts Involving Preexisting Conditions and Future Consequences, 90 Yale L.J. 1353 (1981). See also Robinson, Probabilistic Causation and Compensation for Tortious Risk, 14 J. Legal Stud. 779 (1985).

An example of a court taking an "all or nothing" approach to loss of a chance is Hamil v. Bashline, 481 Pa. 256, 392 A.2d 1280 (1978). This was a wrongful death action in which the plaintiff claimed that the defendant hospital negligently failed to take an electrocardiogram (EKG) of the decedent. There was testimony that had an EKG been taken and the decedent's condition properly diagnosed, he would have had a 75 percent chance of surviving. The jury returned a verdict for the defendant. In answer to special interrogatories, the jury stated that while the defendant was negligent, the plaintiff had not proven that the defendant had caused the decedent's death. The intermediate appellate court affirmed, ruling that there was no jury issue as to cause. 243 Pa. Super. 227, 364 A.2d 1366 (1976). In the course of the opinion, the court stated (243 Pa. Super. at 233-234, 236, 364 A.2d at 1369):

> If an expert testified that conduct increased the risk of harm and *may have,* in fact, caused the harm, from what facts can the jury conclude that the conduct in fact *did* cause the harm? If the only evidence of causation is expert testimony, and if the expert, with all his training and experience, can only conclude that the conduct may have caused the harm, any conclusion as to causation on the part of the jury would necessarily be based on speculation. It must therefore be admitted that a jury cannot be permitted to find causation solely from expert testimony of increased risk. . . .
>
> It may be that no expert can ever testify that a person would have survived a heart attack. If it is wrong to forbid recovery under such circumstances, then the fault lies not within the requirement that expert testimony be certain,

but within the requirement that there be a causal link between defendant's conduct and plaintiff's harm. If causation is to be regarded as an element of a cause of action for negligence, then expert testimony must meet a standard of certainty. The expert testimony in this case did not meet that standard. . . .

One judge dissented (243 Pa. Super. at 256, 263, 364 A.2d at 1380, 1384):

Causation in the jurisprudential sense of that term does not involve the kind of mechanistic standard which is necessary to the inductive methodology of a scientist. In the law, causation standards involve considerations of policy which relegate theories of "but-for causation" useless as anything more than starting points in the inquiry whether a defendant should be liable for the injuries sustained by a plaintiff. It would be difficult, if not impossible, to find a legal scholar who believes that causation in the law can be, or should be, limited to scientific precision. . . .

In turning to the evidence presented in the instant case, Dr. Wecht, [plaintiff's expert], testified that had Mr. Hamil [the decedent] been subjected to an EKG and provided with the medication and facilities available at [defendant's hospital], he would have had a seventy-five percent chance for survival. Dr. Wecht also opined that "the substantial chances that Mr. Hamil would have had for survival were terminated, were taken away from him" because of the hospital's negligence. What more positive proof of "causation" can reasonably be required by the law? Even if Dr. Wecht had only testified that Mr. Hamil's chances for survival were reduced from three-in-four to one-in-four, the jury could have concluded that it was *twice as likely* that Mr. Hamil died because of the negligent diagnosis rather than because his condition was necessarily fatal.

The Supreme Court of Pennsylvania reversed, and ordered a new trial. In so doing, the court stated (481 Pa. at 268-271, 392 A.2d at 1286-1288):

We believe that resolution of this conflict lies in the proper interpretation of Section 323(a) of the Restatement, which has been part of our Pennsylvania law of negligence for a dozen years.

Section 323 provides:

§323. NEGLIGENT PERFORMANCE OF UNDERTAKING TO RENDER SERVICES

One who undertakes, gratuitously or for consideration, to render services to another which he should recognize as necessary for the protection of the other's person or things, is subject to liability to the other for physical harm resulting from his failure to exercise reasonable care to perform his undertaking, if

(a) his failure to exercise such care increases the risk of such harm, or

(b) the harm is suffered because of the other's reliance upon the undertaking.

We agree . . . that the effect of §323(a) is to relax the degree of certitude normally required of plaintiff's evidence in order to make a case for the jury

> as to whether a defendant may be held liable for the plaintiff's injuries: Once a plaintiff has introduced evidence that a defendant's negligent act or omission increased the risk of harm to a person in plaintiff's position, and that the harm was in fact sustained, it becomes a question for the jury as to whether or not that increased risk was a substantial factor in producing the harm. Such a conclusion follows from an analysis of the function of Section 323(a).
>
> Section 323(a) recognizes that a particular class of tort actions, of which the case at bar is an example, differs from those cases normally sounding in tort. Whereas typically a plaintiff alleges that a defendant's act or omission set in motion a force which resulted in harm, the theory of the present case is that the defendant's act or omission failed in a duty to protect against harm from another source. To resolve such a claim a fact-finder must consider not only what *did* occur, but also what *might* have occurred, i.e., whether the harm would have resulted from the independent source even if defendant had performed his service in a non-negligent manner. Such a determination as to what *might* have happened necessarily requires a weighing of probabilities. . . .
>
> Such cases by their very nature elude the degree of certainty one would prefer and upon which the law normally insists before a person may be held liable. Nevertheless, in order that an actor is not completely insulated because of uncertainties as to the consequences of his negligent conduct, Section 323(a) tacitly acknowledges this difficulty and permits the issue to go to the jury upon a less than normal threshold of proof.

According to the testimony in *Hamil,* the probability that the defendant caused the decedent's death exceeded 50 percent. What if the uncontradicted testimony had been that the probability was less than 50 percent? Most courts will not permit the plaintiff to get to the jury. See, e.g., McBride v. United States, 462 F.2d 72 (1972); Gooding v. University Hospital Building, Inc., 445 So. 2d 1015 (Fla. 1984); Curry v. Summer, 136 Ill. App. 3d 468, 483 N.E.2d 711 (1985).

Some courts, however, do not insist upon a showing of probabilities in excess of 50 percent. See, e.g., Herskovits v. Group Health Cooperative, 99 Wash. 2d 609, 664 P.2d 474 (1983) (testimony that failure of defendant to diagnose plaintiff's cancer reduced his five-year chance of survival from 39 percent to 25 percent enough to get plaintiff to jury); Kallenberg v. Beth Israel Hospital, 45 A.D.2d 177, 357 N.Y.S.2d 508 (1974), *aff'd* 37 N.Y. 719, 337 N.E.2d 128, 374 N.Y.S.2d 615 (1975) (evidence that had defendant administered a particular drug to decedent she would have had "a 20, say 30, maybe 40 percent chance of survival"). One of the earliest cases upholding the ability of the plaintiff to get to the jury in the face of probabilities of less than 50 percent is Hicks v. United States, 368 F.2d 626 (4th Cir. 1966), which held that it is enough if the plaintiff's evidence establishes a "substantial possibility" of survival that the defendant has destroyed. In Kyriss v. State, 218 Mont. 162, 707 P.2d 5 (1985), the court ruled that the plaintiff could recover if he proved that the defendant's failure to diagnose and treat his condition was a "substantial factor" in producing the harm he ultimately suffered—in this case, the amputation of a leg—but the court did not state what showing of probability is required to justify that conclusion. In Pillsbury-Flood v. Portsmouth Hospital, 128 N.H. 299, 512 A.2d 1126 (1986), the plaintiff argued, unsuccessfully, for a middle ground approach that would shift the burden of proof as to the cause issue to the defendant once the plaintiff has established that the defendant caused the loss of some chance of recovery.

Note, Recovery for Increased Chance of Future Injury: "Chance of a Loss" Litigation

With increasing frequency, persons who have been exposed to toxic substances but who suffer no present harm have attempted to recover for the increased chance that harm will result in the future. Most of these suits have been unsuccessful. See, e.g., Hagerty v. L & L Marine Services, Inc., 788 F.2d 315 (5th Cir. 1986); Johnson v. Armstrong Cork Co., 645 F. Supp. 764 (W.D. La. 1986); Devlin v. Johns-Manville Corp., 495 A.2d 495 (N.J. Super. 1985).

A more generous approach was urged by a concurring judge in Jordan v. Bero, 210 S.E.2d 618, 641 (1974):

> In keeping with the traditional rule, the probability, in the mathematical sense, of future injury must be proved to a reasonable degree of medical certainty. Accordingly a doctor should be permitted to testify that on the basis of his experience and his evaluation of statistical information from recorded cases of similar injuries he believes that there is to a reasonable degree of medical certainty a twenty percent probability of suffering a particular disability. Once it is determined that there is a probability of loss, evidence should then be admitted concerning the maximum expected loss should the victim completely lose in the game of chance he is playing with the fates.
>
> Accordingly the jury would be instructed that from all the evidence they should determine what the overall probability is that the plaintiff will suffer future damages, and that from all of the evidence they should determine the amount of monetary damages to which the plaintiff would be entitled if the disabilities which doctors reasonably believe are possible actually come to pass. The jury would then be instructed to multiply the amount of future damages reasonably to be expected times the probability of those damages actually occurring and arrive at a figure which will compensate the plaintiff for the possibility of future injuries. It would appear that in a major damage suit the jury could be aided by expert testimony with regard to probability analysis to make the problem comprehensible to the average layman.
>
> While this analysis may appear to be overly complicated on first reading, it merely recognizes that mathematical probabilities exist which are less than fifty percent and that when the experts testify that such a probability of under fifty percent exists, it is still possible to award appropriate damages without becoming speculative.

The English cases apportion damages based upon probabilities, along the lines advanced by the foregoing opinion. These cases, as well as the American and somewhat ambivalent Canadian cases are analyzed in Cooper, Assessing Possibilities in Damage Awards—The Loss of a Chance or the Chance of a Loss, 37 Sask. L. Rev. 193 (1973).

4. When One of Several Defendants Did It But We Can't Tell Which One: Alternative Liability

Summers v. Tice

33 Cal. 2d 80, 199 P.2d 1 (1948)

CARTER, J. Each of the two defendants appeals from a judgment against them in an action for personal injuries. Pursuant to stipulation the appeals have been consolidated.

Plaintiff's action was against both defendants for an injury to his right eye and face as the result of being struck by birdshot discharged from a shotgun. The case was tried by the court without a jury and the court found that on November 20, 1945, plaintiff and the two defendants were hunting quail on the open range. Each of the defendants was armed with a 12-gauge shotgun loaded with shells containing 7½ size shot. Prior to going hunting plaintiff discussed the hunting procedure with defendants, indicating that they were to exercise care when shooting and to "keep in line." In the course of hunting plaintiff proceeded up a hill, thus placing the hunters at the points of a triangle. The view of defendants with reference to plaintiff was unobstructed and they knew his location. Defendant Tice flushed a quail which rose in flight to a 10-foot elevation and flew between plaintiff and defendants. Both defendants shot at the quail, shooting in the plaintiff's direction. At that time defendants were 75 yards from plaintiff. One shot struck plaintiff in his eye and another in his upper lip. Finally it was found by the court that as the direct result of the shooting by defendants the shots struck plaintiff as above mentioned and the defendants were negligent in so shooting and plaintiff was not contributorily negligent. . . .

The problem presented in this case is whether the judgment against both defendants may stand. It is argued by defendants that they are not joint tort feasors, and thus jointly and severally liable, as they were not acting in concert, and that there is not sufficient evidence to show which defendant was guilty of the negligence which caused the injuries—the shooting by Tice or that by Simonson. . . .

Considering [this argument], we believe it is clear that the court sufficiently found on the issue that defendants were jointly liable and that thus the negligence of both was the cause of the injury or to that legal effect. It found that both defendants were negligent and "That as a direct and proximate result of the shots fired by *defendants, and each of them,* a birdshot pellet was caused to and did lodge in plaintiff's right eye and that another birdshot pellet was caused to and did lodge in plaintiff's upper lip.". . . Implicit in such finding is the assumption that the court was unable to ascertain whether the shots were from the gun of one defendant or the other or one shot from each of them. The one shot that entered plaintiff's eye was the major factor in assessing damages and that shot could not have come from the gun of both defendants. It was from one or the other only. . . .

. . . Dean Wigmore has this to say: "When two or more persons by their acts are possibly the sole cause of a harm, or when two or more acts of the same person are possibly the sole cause, and the plaintiff has introduced evidence that the one of the two persons, or the one of the same person's two acts, is culpable, then the defendant has the burden of proving that the other person, or his other act, was the sole cause of the harm. . . . The real reason for the rule that each joint tortfeasor is responsible for the whole damage is the practical unfairness of denying the injured person redress simply because he cannot prove how much damage each did, when it is certain that between them they did all; let them be the ones to apportion it among themselves. Since, then, the difficulty of proof is the reason, the rule should apply whenever the harm has plural causes, and not merely when they acted in conscious concert. . . ." (Wigmore, Select Cases on the Law of Torts, §153.) . . .

When we consider the relative position of the parties and the results that would flow if plaintiff was required to pin the injury on one of the defendants only, a requirement that the burden of proof on that subject be shifted to defendants becomes manifest. They are both wrong doers—both negligent toward plaintiff. They brought about a situation where the negligence of one of them injured the plaintiff, hence it should rest with them each to absolve himself if he can. The injured party has been placed by defendants in the unfair position of pointing to which defendant caused the harm. If one can escape the other may also and plaintiff is remediless. Ordinarily defendants are in a far better position to offer evidence to determine which one caused the injury. . . .

Cases are cited for the proposition that where two or more tort feasors acting independently of each other cause an injury to plaintiff, they are not joint tort feasors and plaintiff must establish the portion of the damage caused by each, even though it is impossible to prove the portion of the injury caused by each. In view of the foregoing discussion it is apparent that defendants in cases like the present one may be treated as liable on the same basis as joint tortfeasors, and hence the last-cited cases are distinguishable inasmuch as they involve independent tort feasors.

In addition to that, however, it should be pointed out that the same reasons of policy and justice shift the burden to each of defendants to absolve himself if he can—relieving the wronged person of the duty of apportioning the injury to a particular defendant, apply here where we are concerned with whether plaintiff is required to supply evidence for the apportionment of damages. If defendants are independent tort feasors and thus each liable for the damage caused by him alone, and, at least, where the matter of apportionment is incapable of proof, the innocent wronged party should not be deprived of his right to redress. The wrong doers should be left to work out between themselves any apportionment. Some of the cited cases refer to the difficulty of apportioning the burden of damages between the independent tort feasors, and say that where factually a correct division cannot be made, the trier of fact may make it the best it can, which would be more or less a guess, stressing the factor that the wrongdoers are not in a position to complain of uncertainty. . . .

The judgment is affirmed.

Ybarra v. Spangard

25 Cal. 2d 486, 154 P.2d 687 (1944)

GIBSON, C.J. This is an action for damages for personal injuries alleged to have been inflicted on plaintiff by defendants during the course of a surgical operation. The trial court entered judgments of nonsuit as to all defendants and plaintiff appealed.

On October 28, 1939, plaintiff consulted defendant Dr. Tilley, who diagnosed his ailment as appendicitis, and made arrangements for an appendectomy to be performed by defendant Dr. Spangard at a hospital owned and managed by defendant Dr. Swift. Plaintiff entered the hospital, was given a hypodermic injection, slept, and later was awakened by Doctors Tilley and Spangard and wheeled into the operating room by a nurse whom he believed to be defendant Gisler, an employee of Dr. Swift. Defendant Dr. Reser, the anesthetist, also an employee of Dr. Swift, adjusted plaintiff for the operation, pulling his body to the head of the operating table and, according to plaintiff's testimony, laying him back against two hard objects at the top of his shoulders, about an inch below his neck. Dr. Reser then administered the anesthetic and plaintiff lost consciousness. When he awoke early the following morning he was in his hospital room attended by defendant Thompson, the special nurse, and another nurse, who was not made a defendant.

Plaintiff testified that prior to the operation he had never had any pain in, or injury to, his right arm or shoulder, but that when he awakened he felt a sharp pain about half way between the neck and the point of the right shoulder. He complained to the nurse, and then to Dr. Tilley, who gave him diathermy treatments while he remained in the hospital. The pain did not cease, but spread down to the lower part of his arm, and after his release from the hospital the condition grew worse. He was unable to rotate or lift his arm, and developed paralysis and atrophy of the muscles around the shoulder. He received further treatments from Dr. Tilley until March, 1940, and then returned to work, wearing his arm in a splint on the advice of Dr. Spangard.

Plaintiff also consulted Dr. Wilfred Sterling Clark, who had X-ray pictures taken which showed an area of diminished sensation below the shoulder and atrophy and wasting away of the muscles around the shoulder. In the opinion of Dr. Clark, plaintiff's condition was due to trauma or injury by pressure or strain, applied between his right shoulder and neck.

Plaintiff was also examined by Dr. Fernando Garduno, who expressed the opinion that plaintiff's injury was a paralysis of traumatic origin, not arising from pathological causes, and not systemic, and that the injury resulted in atrophy, loss of use and restriction of motion of the right arm and shoulder.

[Omitted here are several paragraphs in which the court recognizes that the plaintiff has not introduced any direct evidence of negligence on the part of any defendant, but concludes that on the record here established the jury might draw the inference that one or more of the defendants was negligent towards the plaintiff. That is, although the plaintiff is unable to point specifically to the person who harmed him, that person must have been negligent. The court invokes the notion that the plaintiff's injury "speaks for itself," employing a Latin phrase to that effect about which we shall have more to say in a later chapter. Referring to the rule of law that permits an inference of negligence as "the doctrine," the court continues:]

The present case is of a type which comes within the reason and spirit of the doctrine more fully than any other. The passenger sitting awake in a railroad car at the time of a collision, the pedestrian walking along the street and struck by a falling object or the debris of an explosion, are surely not more entitled to an explanation than the unconscious patient on the operating table. Viewed from this aspect, it is difficult to see how the doctrine can, with any justification, be so restricted in its statement as to become inapplicable to a patient who submits himself to the care and custody of doctors and nurses, is rendered unconscious, and receives some injury from instrumentalities used in his treatment. Without the aid of the doctrine a patient who received permanent injuries of a serious character, obviously the result of someone's negligence, would be entirely unable to recover unless the doctors and nurses in attendance voluntarily chose to disclose the identity of the negligent person and the facts establishing liability. If this were the state of the law of negligence, the courts, to avoid gross injustice, would be forced to invoke the principles of absolute liability, irrespective of negligence, in actions by persons suffering injuries during the course of treatment under anesthesia. But we think this juncture has not yet been reached, and that the doctrine . . . is properly applicable to the case before us. . . .

The argument of defendants is simply that plaintiff has not shown an injury caused by an instrumentality under a defendant's control, because he has not shown which of the several instrumentalities that he came in contact with while in the hospital caused the injury; and he has not shown that any one defendant or his servants had exclusive control over any particular instrumentality. Defendants assert that some of them were not the employees of other defendants, that some did not stand in any permanent relationship from which liability in tort would follow, and that in view of the nature of the injury, the number of defendants and the different functions performed by each, they could not all be liable for the wrong, if any.

We have no doubt that in a modern hospital a patient is quite likely to come under the care of a number of persons in different types of contractual and other relationships with each other. For example, in the present case it appears that Doctors Swift, Spangard and Tilley were physicians or surgeons commonly placed in the legal category of independent contractors; and Dr. Reser, the anesthetist, and defendant Thompson, the special nurse, were employees of Dr. Swift and not of the other doctors. But we do not believe that either the number or relationship of the defendants alone determines whether the [jury may draw an inference of negligence]. Every defendant in whose custody the plaintiff was placed for any period was bound to exercise ordinary care to see that no unnecessary harm came to him and each would be liable for failure in this regard. Any defendant who negligently injured him, and any defendant charged with his care who so neglected him as to allow injury to occur, would be liable. The defendant employers would be liable for the neglect of their employees; and the doctor in charge of the operation would be liable for the negligence of those who became his temporary servants for the purpose of assisting in the operation. . . .

It may appear at the trial that, consistent with the principles outlined above, one or more defendants will be found liable and others absolved, but this should not preclude the application of the [doctrine]. The control, at one time or another, of one or more of the various agencies or instrumentalities which might have harmed the plaintiff was in the hands of every defendant or of his employees or temporary servants. This, we think, places upon them the burden of initial explanation. Plaintiff was rendered unconscious for the purpose of undergoing surgical treatment by the defendants; it is manifestly unreasonable for them to insist that he identify any one of them as the person who did the alleged negligent act. . . .

The judgment is reversed.

On remand, a trial was held without a jury, and the trial judge ruled in favor of the plaintiff against all defendants. All defendants, except the hospital's owner, testified that he or she did nothing and saw nothing which would cause the plaintiff's paralysis. The judgment for the plaintiff was affirmed in Ybarra v. Spangard, 93 Cal. App. 2d 43, 208 P.2d 445 (1949). There was a conflict in the medical testimony as to whether the paralysis was traumatic in origin or was caused by an infection. The court on appeal ruled that the conflict was up to the trial judge to resolve as an issue of fact.

Problem 8

You have received the following memorandum from a partner in the firm in which you are an associate:

> We represent Bennett and Rachael Carrington, whose two-year-old son, Robert, was attacked and badly mauled by a dog in the side yard of their house while his mother was inside answering the telephone. The owner of the dog should be liable in damages, which in this case could be quite high. The potential defendants appear to be financially able to pay a large judgment, and there is a good possibility that one or more of them have insurance covering this sort of liability.
>
> On the issue of liability, the difficulty is one of identifying the dog or dogs that attacked the Carrington boy. No one actually saw the attack take place. Mrs. Carrington came upon the scene immediately afterward and saw a German shepherd dog running from the yard. German shepherds appear to be popular in the Carrington neighborhood. Five have been located, and any one of them might have done it. Mrs. Carrington cannot identify any one of them as the attacker. None of the owners of the German shepherds leash or otherwise confine their dogs, and in light of an ordinance making failure to do so a misdemeanor I am sure that we will get to the jury with the negligence issue if we can adequately identify the proper defendant in the case.
>
> I have been called out of town for a week, and this case won't wait until I get back. Therefore, I am handing the file over to you. Take whatever steps you think are reasonably necessary to complete the investigation, bearing in mind that we already have a considerable sum invested in the case to this point. Your main job will be to sift through the file, organize it, and decide whether we have enough as things stand to get to the jury re the identification issue. When I get back, I will want to sit down with you to decide where to go with this thing. Have your conclusions ready for me when I return.

In preparing your response to the partner's memorandum, assume that *Hoyt, Summers,* and *Ybarra* are opinions of the supreme court of your state.

FILE NO. 427-6-708 CARRINGTON

[The actual file in this case consists of correspondence, medical reports, signed statements, memoranda of investigations, and the like. What follows is a summary of the results of the investigation to date. Only material relating to the identification of the dogs has been included.]

GENERAL BACKGROUND

The Carrington family lives in a rural farming area on Forest Road in Webster Township, approximately a quarter-mile north of the intersection of Forest

Road and Long Pond Road, and approximately two miles south of the southern boundary of a state forest. Mr. Carrington is an architect, with an office in Central City. The area within approximately a four-mile radius of the Carrington house has been thoroughly checked, and five German shepherds have been discovered to have been living within that area. All are approximately the same size and color, and all wear collars. None is known to have bitten humans before. The names of the owners of these dogs, together with the dogs' names, age, sex, and the approximate distance of each from the Carrington house, are included in Table 2-1. A map showing the locations of the dog owners relative to the Carrington house is set out in Figure 2-1.

Summary of Interviews

Mrs. Carrington—At approximately 10 minutes after 12 o'clock noon last September 2, Mrs. Carrington was answering the telephone in their home in Webster Township. Robert was in his playpen in the side yard. The Carringtons have no other children and no pets. Mrs. Carrington could not see Robert from inside the house. She heard Robert cry out and heard what sounded like a dog growling. She ran through the kitchen and down the back steps shouting "Bobby! Bobby!" She missed a step and fell to the ground. When she got up she ran around the side of the house in time to see a German shepherd dog disappear into a corn field across Forest Road in front of the Carrington house. The playpen was tipped over and Robert was on the ground, unconscious and severely mauled. She picked Robert up, put him in her car, and drove him to the Central City Hospital.

As far as the identity of the attacking dog is concerned, Mrs. Carrington is certain it was a German shepherd that she saw enter the corn field. The dog was running quite fast and seemed to have just crossed the street in a line directly away from the Carrington house. She says the dog may have been limping but she cannot be sure, nor can she tell whether it had a collar on or not. She has viewed the five suspect dogs, and cannot positively identify any one of them as the dog she saw on September 2, nor can she exclude any of the five. She is certain that the dogs owned by Wilson and Jarvis have visited the Carrington house at one time or other during the year prior to the incident, but she had not seen any dog near the house on the day in question. She does not know whether the Carson's dog had ever come by the Carrington house, as she would not have recognized it on sight. She thinks there may

TABLE 2-1

Owner's Name	*Dog*	*Age*	*Sex*	*Distance from Carrington home*
Ralph Wilson	Chief	5	M	½
	King Henry	4	M	½
	Dolly	7	F	½
Henry Jarvis	Butch	3	M	2
Larry Carson	Queenie	2	F	3

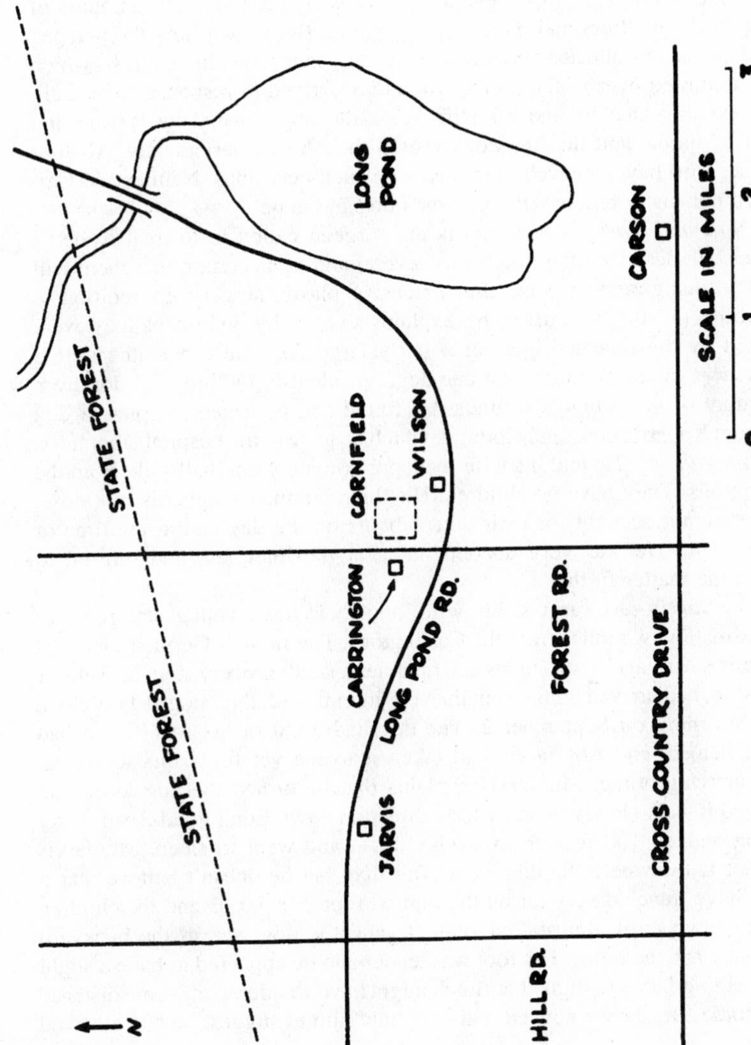
N
STATE FOREST
STATE FOREST
LONG POND
CORNFIELD
WILSON
CARRINGTON
JARVIS
LONG POND RD.
HILL RD.
FOREST RD.
CROSS COUNTRY DRIVE
CARSON
0
1
2
3
SCALE IN MILES

FIGURE 2-1

have been one or two times in the past few months when strange German shepherds came by the house, but she cannot be sure.

Mr. Carrington—A doctor called him from the Central City Hospital shortly after one o'clock in the afternoon of September 2, and he rushed to the hospital from his office. He took his wife home at 3:30 and went out into the yard to examine the playpen area. He found the playpen on its side, with the plastic-covered mattress several feet away. He found small amounts of blood on the mattress and more on the ground. Before washing the playpen and mattress, he collected about two dozen dog hairs from the mattress, which hairs he turned over to the police when they arrived in response to his call.

He explains that he and his wife knew the dogs owned by Wilson and Jarvis by name, and that the dogs visited their house periodically. All four dogs seem to have behaved themselves on such occasions. Neither Mr. Carrington nor his wife knew the Carson's dog by name.

Dr. Edmund Costa—Dr. Costa is the surgeon called in to treat Robert's injuries. He describes the injuries as severe, and he is certain that there will be some disfigurement even after extensive plastic surgery. In addition to describing the boy's injuries, he explains that in his judgment they were inflicted by the repeated bites of a fairly large dog. He can neither tell if Robert was bitten by more than one dog, nor identify the breed of dog from the nature of his patient's wounds. He found and collected samples of dog hair from Robert's body and clothing, which he gave to the hospital laboratory.

Ralph Wilson—He and his wife live approximately one-half mile from the Carringtons. They have no children. His three German shepherds run loose, and he cannot account for their whereabouts on the day and at the time of the accident. He was very uncooperative at the interview and refused to discuss the matter further.

Henry Jarvis—Mr. Jarvis, his wife, and their three young children live approximately two miles from the Carringtons. The Jarvis's German shepherd runs loose. Mr. Jarvis, who owns and operates a small grocery store in Webster Township, had arrived home from the veterinarian with their dog at 11 o'clock in the morning on September 2. The dog had a cut on its foot which had almost healed, and Mr. Jarvis had taken it to the vet for a final checkup. Upon arriving home, Mr. Jarvis explains that he turned the dog loose and observed it walk slowly in an easterly direction down Long Pond Road. After the dog walked 100 feet or so, he lay down and went to sleep. Mr. Jarvis does not know where the dog went after that, but he doesn't believe that it would have traveled very far on the injured foot. Mr. Jarvis and the children were in town until almost four o'clock, and the dog was in the backyard when they arrived home. His foot was tender and he appeared to have a slight limp, leading Jarvis to think that Butch might have wandered off some distance from home. But Jarvis noticed nothing about him to suggest he had attacked Bobby.

Larry Carson—Mr. Carson, his wife, and their two children live on and operate a fairly prosperous dairy farm approximately three miles from the Carringtons. Their dog is not confined, and the Carsons are unable to account for its whereabouts at the time of the attack on September 2.

Walter Palchek—Mr. Palchek is employed as a farmhand by a neighbor of the Carringtons, and was working in a field just south of the cornfield across from the Carrington house on September 2. Shortly after noon, he glanced up to see a large dog leave the southern end of the cornfield. He is sure that it was a German shepherd, but he cannot positively identify it. The dog was moving at a slow trot, southeasterly in the general direction of Wilson's house. Mr. Palchek thought he recognized the dog as King Henry. He called the dog by that name and it stopped for a moment and looked toward him, but then resumed its journey. The dog was never closer than 200 feet or so from Mr. Palchek, and he paid no further attention to it. He does not remember the dog to have been limping, but he cannot be certain due to the distance between him and the dog. He does not know if the dog was wearing a collar.

Other neighbors generally—Questioning of everyone known to live or work within the area surrounding the Carrington home tended generally to confirm the fact that the Wilson, Jarvis, and Carson dogs roam the area frequently. No one remembers having seen any German shepherds other than the five in question for several weeks surrounding the date of the attack on the Carrington boy.

Dr. James Thomas—Dr. Thomas is the veterinarian who treated the Jarvis's dog on September 2. He describes the dog as normally even tempered, but likely to have been a bit more nervous and irritable on that date due to the foot injury. The dog had displayed no noticeable limp during the visit on September 2, but the paw was still tender enough so that a limp might have developed upon extended use of the injured foot. Dr. Thomas says that Jarvis's dog was physically capable of going to the Carrington house on September 2, although less likely to do so because of the residual soreness in the foot. If the dog were to have gone that far, he would have been more likely, once there, to attack a pestering child because of that soreness.

Jack Fagen, Chief of Police, Webster Township—Chief Fagen received a call from Mr. Carrington on the afternoon of September 2, and went right over with a deputy. Inspection of the side yard area where the attack occurred produced no blood or skin samples usable in attempting to identify the attacker. Dog hairs were found at the scene, added to those received from Mr. Carrington, and later sent to the police lab in Central City.

A search of the area in cooperation with the County Health Officer revealed the five German shepherd dogs owned by Wilson, Jarvis, and Carson. Whenever there is an instance of a dog biting a person, an attempt is made to locate the dog to determine if it has rabies. In a case like this, where there is no positive identification, all dogs within the area of the attack generally fitting the description are apprehended for observation. How wide an area is searched depends on a number of factors. Because Webster Township is fairly rural, a somewhat more extensive search was made in this case than would have been made in a more congested area. Because rabies is a very serious disease, the police and public health officials try to be quite certain that the attacking dog is captured.

All five dogs were apprehended on September 3 and confined at the kennel of a local veterinarian in order to check them out for rabies. None showed any outward signs of having been involved in the attack. All five were released ten days later. Chief Fagen thinks that the guilty animal is King Henry. He bases his opinion on observations of the dog during its confinement at the veterinarian's kennel when the dog behaved more aggressively than the others. In addition, King Henry had been the subject of several minor complaints over the past three years. Once he chased a salesman, an incident which led to Mr. Wilson paying a $20 fine for violation of the dog leash ordinance. When asked why the ordinance is not more uniformly or rigorously enforced, Chief Fagen explained that the police department is small and overworked, and that it was customary to overlook violations of the leash law except when a formal complaint is made to the police.

Joseph Brown, technician in police lab, Central City—Mr. Brown examined microscopically the hair samples from the playpen area, and concluded that they are German shepherd hairs. He cannot determine the age or sex of the dog, and he feels that the hairs might even have come from two different dogs. He has compared the hair with samples from all five suspect dogs, and he cannot make any definite inclusionary or exclusionary determination.

Linda Balfours, technician in Central City Hospital lab—Ms. Balfours examined microscopically the hair samples from Robert's body and is reasonably certain that they came from the same German shepherd dog. She cannot determine the sex of the dog, and will only say that it must have been under ten years of age. She has compared these hairs with the samples from the five suspect dogs and can make no definite inclusionary or exclusionary determination.

Dr. Martha Gilley, a lecturer on law-medicine at the state medical school—Dr. Gilley explains that the hair from an attacking dog presents problems in identification. Most authorities agree that the type of dog could probably be determined from a hair sample. However, even this determination could be confused according to where on the dog's body the hair comes from. Back hair is not the same as facial hair or the hair from the inside of the leg. Dr. Gilley concludes that very little can be determined from microscopic examination of the hair. There are other, newer techniques which sometimes allow much more precise identifications, but in her judgment they are not practical or possible in this case.

William Berger—Mr. Berger is the owner and operator of a large kennel in Central City. He has had 27 years of experience working with all breeds of dogs, including German shepherds. He explains that in terms of which breed or sex of dog is more likely to be vicious or to attack other dogs or humans, only the broadest of generalizations are possible. Generally, German shepherds have the reputation of being a slightly more, rather than less, aggressive breed of dog; but they are exceeded by many breeds, both small and large, with respect to their propensity to snap, bite, and attack humans. Generally, males are more aggressive than females, but even this is subject to exceptions—bitches who have just whelped, for example, are likely to be nervous and overprotective, resulting in a belligerent attitude.

The difficulty in Problem 8 from the plaintiff's point of view is that a gap in the evidence as to the issue of causation may prevent the plaintiff from getting to the jury. The investigation so far does not reveal an eyewitness to the attack. Do you think that further investigation to locate such a witness would be worthwhile? Assuming that an eyewitness is not discovered, and that a sense of professional responsibility precludes the manufacturing of one, you are left to do the best you can with circumstantial evidence tending only inferentially to point to one or more defendants.

Circumstantially, there are at least two approaches to the problem of identifying the proper defendant in this case. Either the focus can be narrowed to a single dog, or rather dog owner, as the responsible party; or a limited group of persons whose dogs might have done it can be set up, with the attempt to hold them jointly and severally liable. The first of these approaches, if successful in bringing the case before the jury, ends up exposing a single defendant to liability for harm that he may have caused. Which of the factual elements in this problem tend to narrow the field of potential defendants to a single individual? Do all of these elements point to the same person? If not, is this approach doomed to defeat, or will the court leave it to the jury?

The second approach suggested above—that of asserting the liability jointly and severally of a group of persons because any one of them might have been the person whose dog attacked the boy—is unique not only in the route taken but also in the conclusion reached. Unlike the first approach, which at most exposes a single dog owner to liability, the second could expose two innocent owners to liability for harm they did not cause. What are the legal theories that would support such an approach? Does this case fall into any of the traditional categories, outlined in the following Note, in which joint and several liability is imposed? Do the rules announced in *Summers* and *Ybarra* justify the multidefendant approach to this problem? If so, what factual showing must the plaintiff make to justify getting to the jury against each of the defendants on a joint and several liability theory? And what arguments are available to the defendants to avoid liability under this approach?

Note: Joint and Several Liability

In Summers v. Tice, the court ruled that the defendants in that case should "be treated as liable on the same basis as joint tort feasors." In order to appreciate the implications of this ruling, it is necessary to have a basic understanding of what joint and several liability is, the circumstances under which such liability has traditionally been imposed, and the consequences that flow from such liability. What joint and several liability means can be quickly explained. Defendants who are jointly liable can be joined in a single suit, although they need not be. Defendants who are severally liable are each liable in full for the plaintiff's damages, although the plaintiff is entitled to only one total recovery.

At common law, two situations in which two or more defendants acted tortiously toward the plaintiff gave rise to what is now referred to as joint and several liability: where the defendants acted in concert to cause the harm, and where the defendants acted independently but caused indivisible harm. Liability in the case of concerted action is a form of vicarious liability, in which all the defendants will be responsible for the harm actually caused by only one of them. An example of this is where *A* and *B* engage in an automobile race on a public street and *A* runs over the plaintiff. *B* will be liable to the plaintiff just as much as *A*, although *B* did not actually hit the plaintiff. Joint and several liability will also be imposed if the defendants act independently, each actually causing harm to the plaintiff but under circumstances in which it is impossible to allocate the harm to either defendant's conduct. Thus, if the plaintiff were a passenger in *A*'s automobile which collided with *B*'s automobile due to the fault of both drivers, *A* and *B* will be jointly and severally liable for the harm to the plaintiff.

Because of the procedural limitations relating to the circumstances under which two or more defendants could be joined in a single action, a distinction was made at common law between these two types of cases. Where the defendants acted in concert, they were joint tortfeasors and could be joined in one action. But where they acted independently to cause indivisible harm, they could not be joined. Thus, technically, only defendants acting in concert were called joint tortfeasors. However, modern rules of procedure permit joinder in indivisible harm cases (see James and Hazard, Civil Procedure 473 (3d ed. 1985)), and defendants causing such harm are today commonly referred to as joint tortfeasors.

At common law, if the plaintiff sued just one of the joint tortfeasors and recovered, that defendant was without legal recourse against other tortfeasors to compel them to share the burden of liability. The harshness of this earlier rule has been ameliorated to some extent, and today most states provide for contribution among joint tortfeasors, either by statute or judicial decision. About 20 states have adopted some form of the Uniform Contribution Among Tortfeasors Act. The basic principles of contribution contained in the 1955 Act are:

> §1. [*Right to Contribution*]. (a) Except as otherwise provided in this Act, where two or more persons become jointly or severally liable in tort for the same injury to person or property or for the same wrongful death, there is a right of contribution among them even though judgment has not been recovered against all or any of them.
>
> (b) The right of contribution exists only in favor of a tortfeasor who has paid more than his pro rata share of the common liability, and his total recovery is limited to the amount paid by him in excess of his pro rata share. No tortfeasor is compelled to make contribution beyond his own pro rata share of the entire liability.
>
> (c) There is no right of contribution in favor of any tortfeasor who has intentionally [willfully or wantonly] caused or contributed to the injury or wrongful death.

(d) A tortfeasor who enters into a settlement with a claimant is not entitled to recover contribution from another tortfeasor whose liability for the injury or wrongful death is not extinguished by the settlement nor in respect to any amount paid in a settlement which is in excess of what was reasonable. . . .

§2. [*Pro Rata Shares*]. In determining the pro rata shares of tortfeasors in the entire liability (a) their relative degrees of fault shall not be considered,[1] . . .

§4. [*Release or Covenant Not to Sue*]. When a release or a covenant not to sue or not to enforce judgment is given in good faith to one of two or more persons liable in tort for the same injury or the same wrongful death:

(a) It does not discharge any of the other tortfeasors from liability for the injury or wrongful death unless its terms so provide; but it reduces the claim against the others to the extent of any amount stipulated by the release or the covenant . . . ; and,

(b) It discharges the tortfeasor to whom it is given from all liability for contribution to any other tortfeasor.

The Uniform Act recognizes the distinction between a general release and a covenant not to sue. Both are agreements between the plaintiff and the tortfeasor that formalize an out-of-court settlement. The early law was that any release of liability given by the plaintiff to one joint tortfeasor would also release the others from liability. More recently, some states now give effect to the release only with respect to the persons actually named in it. Even in states in which a general release of one joint tortfeasor releases all, most give legal effect to a covenant not to sue. Such an agreement affects only the legal rights between the particular tortfeasor and the plaintiff, and enables the plaintiff to proceed against the other joint tortfeasors. More on joint and several liability appears at pp. 479-481, below, as it is affected by comparative fault laws.

The Lawyer's Professional Responsibility: Interviewing Witnesses

In the preceding problem, if Mrs. Carrington could have given a positive identification of the dog that was running into the cornfield, the chances of getting to the jury on the cause issue would be substantially increased. A lawyer investigating the case should certainly appreciate this, but what could ethically be done in questioning Mrs. Carrington about the identity of the dog? Certainly, the lawyer ought not to ask her to lie. Not surprisingly, the Model Rules of Professional Conduct prohibit a lawyer from offering evidence to a tribunal that he or she knows to be false. See Rule 3.3 (a)(4). But a layperson is often unaware of the facts necessary to support a cause

1. Contribution among joint tortfeasors proportioned to fault is a common feature of comparative fault schemes. [Eds.]

of action or defense. Is there a risk of subtle subornation of perjury if the lawyer explains in advance, or makes clear through skillful questioning, what facts must be established if the claim or defense is to be successful? Which of the following lines of inquiry, if any, would be improper in interviewing Mrs. Carrington?

1. Did you recognize the dog? Describe it to me to the best of your recollection.
2. Think for a minute. Was the dog limping? Were there any peculiar color markings? Was it wearing a collar? What size was it?
3. I'm sure you realize that it is important for you to remember as much as you can. Are you sure that the dog was not limping?
4. Unless we get a positive identification of the dog, we may very well not be able to collect against anyone. Think about it, and I will see you tomorrow.

These lines of inquiry are a progression from, "Tell me what you know," to "Tell me what I want to hear." Is there a point on this progression beyond which the inquiry would violate the Rules of Professional Conduct? Your own sense of professional responsibility?

Sindell v. Abbott Laboratories

26 Cal. 3d 588, 607 P.2d 924, 163 Cal. Rptr. 132, cert. denied, *449 U.S. 912 (1980)*

[The plaintiff sued several manufacturers of diethylstilbesterol (DES), alleging that her mother took the drug to prevent miscarriage. The plaintiff alleged that as a result, she, the plaintiff, had developed a bladder tumor, which had been surgically removed, and that she might in the future develop a further malignancy. She alleged that DES was ineffective to prevent miscarriage, and that the defendants were negligent in marketing the drug without adequate testing as to its efficacy and as to its cancer-causing properties, and in failing to give adequate warnings. The plaintiff conceded that she would be unable to present proof as to which of the defendants produced the DES used by her mother, or even that the manufacturer that produced her mother's DES was a defendant in this action. The trial judge dismissed the complaint, and the plaintiff appealed.]

MOSK, J.: . . . We begin with the proposition that, as a general rule, the imposition of liability depends upon a showing by the plaintiff that his or her injuries were caused by the act of the defendant or by an instrumentality under the defendant's control. The rule applies whether the injury resulted from an accidental event or from the use of a defective product.

There are, however, exceptions to this rule. . . .

I

Plaintiff places primary reliance upon cases which hold that if a party cannot identify which of two or more defendants caused an injury, the burden of proof may shift to the defendants to show that they were not responsible for the harm. This principle is sometimes referred to as the "alternative liability" theory.

The celebrated case of Summers v. Tice, supra, 33 Cal. 2d 80, 199 P.2d 1, a unanimous opinion of this court, best exemplifies the rule. . . .

. . . There is an important difference between the situation involved in *Summers* and the present case. There, all the parties who were or could have been responsible for the harm to the plaintiff were joined as defendants. Here, by contrast, there are approximately 200 drug companies which made DES, any of which might have manufactured the injury-producing drug.

Defendants maintain that, while in *Summers* there was a 50 percent chance that one of the two defendants was responsible for the plaintiff's injuries, here since any one of 200 companies which manufactured DES might have made the product which harmed plaintiff, there is no rational basis upon which to infer that any defendant in this action caused plaintiff's injuries, nor even a reasonable possibility that they were responsible.

These arguments are persuasive if we measure the chance that any one of the defendants supplied the injury-causing drug by the number of possible tortfeasors. In such a context, the possibility that any of the five defendants supplied the DES to plaintiff's mother is so remote that it would be unfair to require each defendant to exonerate itself. There may be a substantial likelihood that none of the five defendants joined in the action made the DES which caused the injury, and that the offending producer not named would escape liability altogether. While we propose, infra, an adaptation of the rule in *Summers* which will substantially overcome these difficulties, defendants appear to be correct that the rule, as previously applied, cannot relieve plaintiff of the burden of proving the identity of the manufacturer which made the drug causing her injuries.

II

The second principle upon which plaintiff relies is the so-called "concert of action" theory. . . . The gravamen of the charge of concert is that defendants failed to adequately test the drug or to give sufficient warning of its dangers and that they relied upon the tests performed by one another and took advantage of each others' promotional and marketing techniques. These allegations do not amount to a charge that there was a tacit understanding or a common plan among defendants to fail to conduct adequate tests or give sufficient warnings, and that they substantially aided and encouraged one another in these omissions.

The complaint charges also that defendants produced DES from a "common and mutually agreed upon formula," allowing pharmacists to treat the drug as a "fungible commodity" and to fill prescriptions from whatever brand of DES they had on hand at the time. It is difficult to understand how these allegations can form the basis of a cause of action for wrongful conduct by defendants, acting in concert. The formula for DES is a scientific constant. It is set forth in the United States Pharmacopoeia, and any manufacturer producing that drug must, with exceptions not relevant here, utilize the formula set forth in that compendium. (21 U.S.C.A. §351, subd. (b).)

What the complaint appears to charge is defendants' parallel or imitative conduct in that they relied upon each others' testing and promotion methods. But such conduct describes a common practice in industry: a producer avails himself of the experience and methods of others making the same or similar products. Application of the concept of concert of action to this situation would expand the doctrine far beyond its intended scope and would render virtually any manufacturer liable for the defective products of an entire industry, even if it could be demonstrated that the product which caused the injury was not made by the defendant. . . .

. . . There is no allegation here that each defendant knew the other defendants' conduct was tortious toward plaintiff, and that they assisted and encouraged one another to inadequately test DES and to provide inadequate warnings. Indeed, it seems dubious whether liability on the concert of action theory can be predicated upon substantial assistance and encouragement given by one alleged tortfeasor to another pursuant to a tacit understanding to fail to perform an act. Thus, there was no concert of action among defendants within the meaning of that doctrine.

III

A third theory upon which plaintiff relies is the concept of industry-wide liability, or according to the terminology of the parties, "enterprise liability." This theory was suggested in Hall v. E. I. Du Pont de Nemours & Co., Inc. (E.D.N.Y. 1972) 345 F. Supp. 353. In that case, plaintiffs were 13 children injured by the explosion of blasting caps in 12 separate incidents which occurred in 10 different states between 1955 and 1959. The defendants were six blasting cap manufacturers, comprising virtually the entire blasting cap industry in the United States, and their trade association. There were, however, a number of Canadian blasting cap manufacturers which could have supplied the caps. The gravamen of the complaint was that the practice of the industry of omitting a warning on individual blasting caps and of failing to take other safety measures created an unreasonable risk of harm, resulting in the plaintiffs' injuries. The complaint did not identify a particular manufacturer of a cap which caused a particular injury.

The court reasoned as follows: There was evidence that defendants, acting independently, had adhered to an industry-wide standard with regard to the safety features of blasting caps, that they had in effect delegated some functions of safety investigation and design, such as labelling, to their trade association, and that there was industry-wide cooperation in the manufacture and design of blasting caps. In these circumstances, the evidence supported a conclusion that all the defendants jointly controlled the risk. Thus, if plaintiffs could establish by a preponderance of the evidence that the caps were manufactured by one of the defendants, the burden of proof as to causation would shift to all the defendants. The court noted that this theory of liability applied to industries composed of a small number of units, and that what would be fair and reasonable with regard to an industry of five or ten producers might be manifestly unreasonable if applied to a decentralized industry composed of countless small producers.

Plaintiff attempts to state a cause of action under the rationale of *Hall.* She alleges joint enterprise and collaboration among defendants in the production, marketing, promotion and testing of DES, and "concerted promulgation and adherence to industry-wide testing, safety, warning and efficacy standards" for the drug. We have concluded above that allegations that defendants relied upon one another's testing and promotion methods do not state a cause of action for concerted conduct to commit a tortious act. Under the theory of industry-wide liability, however, each manufacturer could be liable for all injuries caused by DES by virtue of adherence to an industry-wide standard of safety. . . . We decline to apply this theory in the present case. At least 200 manufacturers produced DES; *Hall,* which involved 6 manufacturers representing the entire blasting cap industry in the United States, cautioned against application of the doctrine espoused therein to a large number of producers. (345 F. Supp. at p. 378.) Moreover, in *Hall,* the conclusion that the defendants jointly controlled the risk was based upon allegations that they had delegated some functions relating to safety to a trade association. There are no such allegations here, and we have concluded above the plaintiff has failed to allege liability on a concert of action theory.

Equally important, the drug industry is closely regulated by the Food and Drug Administration, which actively controls the testing and manufacture of drugs and the method by which they are marketed, including the contents of warning labels. To a considerable degree, therefore, the standards followed by drug manufacturers are suggested or compelled by the government. Adherence to those standards cannot, of course, absolve a manufacturer of liability to which it would otherwise be subject. But since the government plays such a pervasive role in formulating the criteria for the testing and marketing of drugs, it would be unfair to impose upon a manufacturer liability for injuries resulting from the use of a drug which it did not supply simply because it followed the standards of the industry.

IV

If we were confined to the theories of *Summers* and *Hall,* we would be constrained to hold that the judgment must be sustained. Should we require that plaintiff identify the manufacturer which supplied the DES used by her mother or that all DES manufacturers be joined in the action, she would effectively be precluded from any recovery. As defendants candidly admit, there is little likelihood that all the manufacturers who made DES at the time in question are still in business or that they are subject to the jurisdiction of the California courts. There are, however, forceful arguments in favor of holding that plaintiff has a cause of action.

In our contemporary complex industrialized society, advances in science and technology create fungible goods which may harm consumers and which cannot be traced to any specific producer. The response of the courts can be either to adhere rigidly to prior doctrine, denying recovery to those injured by such products, or to fashion remedies to meet these changing needs. . . .

The most persuasive reason for finding plaintiff states a cause of action is that advanced in *Summers:* as between an innocent plaintiff and negligent defendants, the latter should bear the cost of the injury. Here, as in *Summers,* plaintiff is not at fault in failing to provide evidence of causation, and although the absence of such evidence is not attributable to the defendants either, their conduct in marketing a drug the effects of which are delayed for many years played a significant role in creating the unavailability of proof.

From a broader policy standpoint, defendants are better able to bear the cost of injury resulting from the manufacture of a defective product. . . . The manufacturer is in the best position to discover and guard against defects in its products and to warn of harmful effects; thus, holding it liable for defects and failure to warn of harmful effects will provide an incentive to product safety. These considerations are particularly significant where medication is involved, for the consumer is virtually helpless to protect himself from serious, sometimes permanent, sometimes fatal, injuries caused by deleterious drugs.

Where, as here, all defendants produced a drug from an identical formula and the manufacturer of the DES which caused plaintiff's injuries cannot be identified through no fault of plaintiff, a modification of the rule of *Summers* is warranted. As we have seen, an undiluted *Summers* rationale is inappropriate to shift the burden of proof of causation to defendants because if we measure the chance that any particular manufacturer supplied the injury-causing product by the number of producers of DES, there is a possibility that none of the five defendants in this case produced the offending substance and that the responsible manufacturer, not named in the action, will escape liability.

But we approach the issue of causation from a different perspective: We hold it to be reasonable in the present context to measure the likelihood that any of the defendants supplied the product which allegedly injured plaintiff by the percentage which the DES sold by each of them for the purpose of preventing miscarriage bears to the entire production of the drug sold by all for that purpose. Plaintiff asserts in her briefs that Eli Lilly and Company and 5 or 6 other companies produced 90 percent of the DES marketed. If at trial this is established to be the fact, then there is a corresponding likelihood that this comparative handful of producers manufactured the DES which caused plaintiff's injuries, and only a 10 percent likelihood that the offending producer would escape liability.

If plaintiff joins in the action the manufacturers of a substantial share of the DES which her mother might have taken, the injustice of shifting the burden of proof to defendants to demonstrate that they could not have made the substance which injured plaintiff is significantly diminished. . . .

The presence in the action of a substantial share of the appropriate market also provides a ready means to apportion damages among the defendants. Each defendant will be held liable for the proportion of the judgment represented by its share of that market unless it demonstrates that it could not have made the product which caused plaintiff's injuries. In the present case, . . . one DES manufacturer was dismissed from the action upon filing a declaration that it had not manufactured DES until after plaintiff was born. Once plaintiff has met her burden of joining the required defendants, they in turn may cross-complain against other DES manufacturers, not joined in the action, which they can allege might have supplied the injury-causing product.

Under this approach, each manufacturer's liability would approximate its responsibility for the injuries caused by its own products. Some minor discrepancy in the correlation between market share and liability is inevitable; therefore, a defendant may be held liable for a somewhat different percentage of the damage than its share of the appropriate market would justify. It is probably impossible, with the passage of time, to determine market share with mathematical exactitude. But . . . the difficulty of apportioning damages among the defendant producers in exact relation to their market share does not seriously militate against the rule we adopt. As we said in *Summers* with regard to the liability of independent tortfeasors, where a correct division of liability cannot be made "the trier of fact may make it the best it can." (33 Cal. 2d at p. 88, 199 P.2d at p. 5.)

We are not unmindful of the practical problems involved in defining the market and determining market share,[29] but these are largely matters of proof which properly cannot be determined at the pleading stage of these proceedings. Defendants urge that it would be both unfair and contrary to public policy to hold them liable for plaintiff's injuries in the absence of proof that one of them supplied the drug responsible for the damage. Most of their arguments, however, are based upon the assumption that one manufacturer would be held responsible for the products of another or for those of all other manufacturers if plaintiff ultimately prevails. But under the rule we adopt, each manufacturer's liability for an injury would be approximately equivalent to the damages caused by the DES it manufactured.

The judgments are reversed.

BIRD, C.J., and NEWMAN and WHITE, JJ., concur.

RICHARDSON, J., dissenting.

I respectfully dissent. In these consolidated cases the majority adopts a wholly new theory which contains these ingredients: The plaintiffs were not alive at the time of the commission of the tortious acts. They sue a generation later. They are permitted to receive substantial damages from multiple defendants without any proof that any defendant caused or even probably caused plaintiffs' injuries.

Although the majority purports to change only the required burden of proof by shifting it from plaintiffs to defendants, the effect of its holding is to guarantee that plaintiffs will prevail on the causation issue because defendants are no more capable of disproving factual causation than plaintiffs are of proving it. "Market share" liability thus represents a new high water mark in tort law. The ramifications seem almost limitless. . . . In my view, the majority's departure from traditional tort doctrine is unwise. . . .

The fact that plaintiffs cannot tie defendants to the injury-producing drug does not trouble the majority for it declares that the *Summers* requirement of proof of actual causation by a named defendant is satisfied by a joinder of those defendants who have *together* manufactured *"a substantial percentage"* of the DES which has been marketed. Notably lacking from the majority's expression of its new rule, unfortunately, is any definition or guidance as to what should constitute a "substantial" share of the relevant market. The issue is entirely open-ended and the answer, presumably, is anyone's guess.

Much more significant, however, is the consequence of this unprecedented extension of liability. Recovery is permitted from a handful of defendants *each* of whom *individually* may account for a comparatively small share of the relevant market, so long as the *aggregate* business of those who have been sued is deemed "substantial." In other words, a particular defendant

29. Defendants assert that there are no figures available to determine market share, that DES was provided for a number of uses other than to prevent miscarriage and it would be difficult to ascertain what proportion of the drug was used as a miscarriage preventative, and that the establishment of a time frame and area for market share would pose problems.

may be held proportionately liable *even though mathematically it is much more likely than not that it played no role whatever in causing plaintiffs' injuries.* . . . Furthermore, in bestowing on plaintiffs this new largess the majority sprinkles the rain of liability upon all the joined defendants alike—those who may be tortfeasors and those who may have had nothing at all to do with plaintiffs' injury—and an added bonus is conferred. Plaintiffs are free to pick and choose their targets.

[I]t . . . is readily apparent that "market share" liability will fall unevenly and disproportionately upon those manufacturers who are amenable to suit in California. On the assumption that no other state will adopt so radical a departure from traditional tort principles, it may be concluded that under the majority's reasoning those defendants who are brought to trial in this state will bear effective joint responsibility for 100 percent of plaintiffs' injuries despite the fact that their "substantial" aggregate market share may be considerably less. This undeniable fact forces the majority to concede that, "a defendant may be held liable for a somewhat different percentage of the damage than its share of the appropriate market would justify." (Ante, p. 145 of 163 Cal. Rptr., p. 937 of 607 P.2d.) With due deference, I suggest that the complete unfairness of such a result in a case involving only five of two hundred manufacturers is readily manifest.

Furthermore, several other important policy considerations persuade me that the majority holding is both inequitable and improper. The injustice inherent in the majority's new theory of liability is compounded by the fact that plaintiffs who use it are treated far more favorably than are the plaintiffs in routine tort actions. In most tort cases plaintiff knows the identity of the person who has caused his injuries. In such a case, plaintiff, of course, has no option to seek recovery from an entire industry or a "substantial" segment thereof, but in the usual instance can recover, if at all, only from the particular defendant causing injury. Such a defendant may or may not be either solvent or amenable to process. Plaintiff in the ordinary tort case must take a chance that defendant can be reached and can respond financially. On what principle should those plaintiffs who wholly fail to prove any causation, an essential element of the traditional tort cause of action, be rewarded by being offered both a wider selection of potential defendants and a greater opportunity for recovery?

The majority attempts to justify its new liability on the ground that defendants herein are "better able to bear the cost of injury resulting from the manufacture of a defective product." (Ante, p. 144 of 163 Cal. Rptr., p. 936 of 607 P.2d.) This "deep pocket" theory of liability, fastening liability on defendants presumably because they are rich, has understandable popular appeal and might be tolerable in a case disclosing substantially stronger evidence of causation than herein appears. But as a general proposition, a defendant's wealth is an unreliable indicator of fault, and should play no part, at least consciously, in the legal analysis of the problem. In the absence of proof that a particular defendant caused or at least probably caused plaintiff's injuries, a defendant's ability to bear the cost thereof is no more pertinent to the underlying issue of liability than its "substantial" share of the relevant market. A system priding itself on "*equal* justice under law" does not flower when the *liability* as well as the *damage* aspect of a tort action is determined by a defendant's wealth. The inevitable consequence of such a result is to create and perpetuate two rules of law—one applicable to wealthy defendants, and another standard pertaining to defendants who are poor or who have modest means. Moreover, considerable doubts have been expressed regarding the ability of the drug industry, and especially its smaller members, to bear the substantial economic costs (from both damage awards and high insurance premiums) inherent in imposing an industry-wide liability. . . .

Given the grave and sweeping economic, social, and medical effects of "market share" liability, the policy decision to introduce and define it should rest not with us, but with the Legislature which is currently considering not only major statutory reform of California product liability law in general, but the DES problem in particular. (See Sen. Bill No. 1392 (1979-1980 Reg. Sess.), which would establish and appropriate funds for the education, identification, and screening of persons exposed to DES, and would prohibit health care and hospital service plans from excluding or limiting coverage to persons exposed to DES.) . . .

I would affirm the judgments of dismissal.

CLARK and MANUEL, JJ., concur.

In Murphy v. E. R. Squibb & Sons, Inc., 40 Cal. 3d 672, 710 P.2d 247, 221 Cal. Rptr. 447 (1985), the Supreme Court of California adhered to the "substantial share of the market" requirement set out in *Sindell.* Without shedding any light on what might constitute a substantial share for market share liability purposes, the court ruled that 10 percent does not. Kaus, J., dissented, observing: "[F]rankly, I never could see how [the substantial market share] qualification can logically be squared with [*Sindell's*] general market share decision." 40 Cal. 3d at 701, 710 P.2d at 267, 221 Cal. Rptr. at 467. In rejecting the substantial share requirement, Justice Kaus specifically assumed that the liability of each manufacturing defendant would be limited to its market share.

In Brown v. Superior Court, 44 Cal. 3d 1049, 751 P.2d 470, 245 Cal. Rptr. 412 (1988), the California high court rejected joint liability and ruled that each defendant's liability should be limited to the proportion of the judgment represented by its market share. The Court acknowledged that, unless all manufacturers were joined in the action, the plaintiff would not recover the entire amount of judgment. The court also refused to impose liability for all the plaintiff's damages on those manufacturers before the court, even if they constitute a substantial share of the market.

5. When the Conduct of Two or More Actors Would, Independent of Each Other, Have Caused Plaintiff's Harm: Concurrent and Successive Causation

Dillon v. Twin State Gas & Electric Co.

85 N.H. 449, 163 A. 111 (1932)

The defendant maintained wires to carry electric current over a public bridge in Berlin.

The decedent [age 14] and other boys had been accustomed for a number of years to play on the bridge in the daytime, habitually climbing the sloping girders to the horizontal ones, on which they walked and sat and from which they sometimes dived into the river. No current passed through the wires in the daytime except by chance.

The decedent while sitting on a horizontal girder at a point where the wires from the post to the lamp were in front of him or at his side and while facing outwards from the side of the bridge, leaned over, lost his balance, instinctively threw out his arm and took hold of one of the wires with his right hand to save himself from falling. The wires happened to be charged with a high voltage current at the time and he was electrocuted.

Further facts appear in the opinion.

Transferred . . . on the defendant's exception to the denial of its motion for a directed verdict.

ALLEN, J. . . . The circumstances of the decedent's death give rise to an unusual issue of its cause. In leaning over from the girder and losing his balance he was entitled to no protection from the defendant to keep from falling. Its only liability was in exposing him to the danger of charged wires. If but for the current in the wires he would have fallen down on the floor of the bridge or into the river, he would without doubt have been either killed or seriously injured. Although he died from electrocution, yet if by reason of his preceding loss of balance he was bound to fall except for the intervention of the current, he either did not have long to live or was to be maimed. In such an outcome of his loss of balance the defendant deprived him, not of a life of normal expectancy, but of one too short to be given pecuniary allowance, in one alternative, and not of normal, but of limited, earning capacity, in the other.

If it were found that he would have thus fallen with death probably resulting, the defendant would not be liable unless for conscious suffering found to have been sustained from the shock. In that situation his life or earning capacity had no value. To constitute actionable negligence there must be damage, and damage is limited to those elements the [wrongful death] statute prescribes.

If it should be found that but for the current he would have fallen with serious injury, then the loss of life or earning capacity resulting from the electrocution would be measured by its value in such injured condition. Evidence that he would be crippled would be taken into account in the same manner as though he had already been crippled.

His probable future but for the current thus bears on liability as well as damages. Whether the shock from the current threw him back on the girder or whether he would have recovered his balance, with or without the aid of the wire he took hold of if it had not been charged, are issues of fact, as to which the evidence as it stands may lead to different conclusions.

Exception overruled.

Problem 9

Earlier this past summer, Madolyn Hinkle retained your law firm to represent her in a claim against Vance & Weston Co., the manufacturer of Trophacin, a drug designed to relieve high blood pressure. Three years ago, Madolyn began taking the drug upon her doctor's prescription. Late last year, she was advised by her doctor that Trophacin can cause blindness. She stopped taking the drug, but later tests established that she had begun the irreversible process of losing her sight. Your investigation of the case has revealed that officials at Vance & Weston had been aware for some time that Trophacin causes blindness, but they failed to disclose that information to the medical profession. Madolyn's doctor is certain that had she ceased using the drug when the information first became known to Vance & Weston, her eyesight would not have been affected.

A month ago Madolyn was killed in an automobile accident. She was a passenger in a car driven by her husband, Arthur. They were driving in a sparsely populated part of the state when a severe windstorm arose. As Arthur was driving at a fairly high speed—he doesn't recall the exact rate—to get to a place of shelter, he ran into a large tree that had just fallen into the road. Arthur was unable to stop before hitting the tree, and a large branch crashed through the windshield on the passenger's side. Madolyn was killed in the accident. At the time of her death, Madolyn had over 90 percent of her normal vision. Had she lived, her vision would have started to deteriorate fairly rapidly, so that at the end of a year, she would have been almost totally blind.

The partner in your firm who is handling the case has asked you to help him with several aspects of it. In particular, he wants your thoughts as to what claims, if any, might be made against Vance & Weston Co. with respect to Madolyn's loss of vision. He suggests that you focus primarily on the issues of causation that may be presented.[2]

Assume that Dillon v. Twin State Gas & Electric Co. is an opinion of your supreme court.

Kingston v. Chicago & N.W. Ry.

191 Wis. 610, 211 N.W. 913 (1927)

OWEN, J. . . . We . . . have this situation: [A] fire [to the northeast of the plaintiff's property] was set by sparks emitted from defendant's locomotive. This fire, according to the finding of the jury, constituted a proximate cause of the destruction of plaintiff's property. This finding we find to be well supported by the evidence. We have the northwest fire, of unknown origin. This fire, according to the finding of the jury, also constituted a proximate cause of the destruction of the plaintiff's property. This finding we also find to be well supported by the evidence. We have a union of these two fires 940 feet north of plaintiff's property, from which point the united fire bore down upon and destroyed the property. We therefore have two separate, independent, and distinct agencies, each of which constituted the proximate cause of plaintiff's damage, and either of which, in the absence of the other, would have accomplished such result.

It is settled in the law of negligence that any one of two or more joint tortfeasors, or one of two or more wrongdoers whose concurring acts of negligence result in injury, are each individually responsible for the entire damage resulting from their joint or concurrent acts of negligence. This rule also obtains "where two causes, each attributable to the negligence of a responsible person, concur in producing an injury to another, either of which causes would produce it regardless of the other, . . . because, whether the concurrence be intentional, actual, or constructive, each wrongdoer, in effect, adopts the conduct of his co-actor, and for the further reason that it is impossible to apportion the damage or to say that either perpetrated any distinct injury that can be separated from the whole. The whole loss must necessarily be considered and treated as an entirety." Cook v. M., St. P. & S.S.M.R. Co. 98 Wis. 624 (74 N.W. 561), at p. 642. . . .

From our present consideration of the subject we are not disposed to criticise the doctrine which exempts from liability a wrongdoer who sets a fire which unites with a fire originating from natural causes, such as lightning, not attributable to any human agency, resulting in damage. It is also conceivable that a fire so set might unite with a fire of so much greater proportions,

2. The fact of Madolyn's death does not terminate the cause of action against Vance & Weston in this case. All states have survival statutes which empower the representative of the decedent's estate to recover for causes of action the decedent had at the time of death, and for which the decedent himself could have recovered had he lived.

such as a raging forest fire, as to be enveloped or swallowed up by the greater holocaust, and its identity destroyed, so that the greater fire could be said to be an intervening or superseding cause. But we have no such situation here. These fires were of comparatively equal rank. If there was any difference in their magnitude or threatening aspect, the record indicates that the northeast fire was the larger fire and was really regarded as the menacing agency. At any rate there is no intimation or suggestion that the northeast fire was enveloped and swallowed up by the northwest fire. We will err on the side of the defendant if we regard the two fires as of equal rank.

According to well settled principles of negligence, it is undoubted that if the proof disclosed the origin of the northwest fire, even though its origin be attributed to a third person, the railroad company, as the originator of the northeast fire, would be liable for the entire damage. There is no reason to believe that the northwest fire originated from any other than human agency. It was a small fire. It had traveled over a limited area. It had been in existence but for a day. For a time it was thought to have been extinguished. It was not in the nature of a raging forest fire. The record discloses nothing of natural phenomena which could have given rise to the fire. It is morally certain that it was set by some human agency.

Now the question is whether the railroad company, which is found to have been responsible for the origin of the northeast fire, escapes liability because the origin of the northwest fire is not identified, although there is no reason to believe that it had any other than human origin. An affirmative answer to that question would certainly make a wrongdoer a favorite of the law at the expense of an innocent sufferer. The injustice of such a doctrine sufficiently impeaches the logic upon which it is founded. Where one who has suffered damage by fire proves the origin of a fire and the course of that fire up to the point of the destruction of his property, one has certainly established liability on the part of the originator of the fire. Granting that the union of that fire with another of natural origin, or with another of much greater proportions, is available as a defense, the burden is on the defendant to show that by reason of such union with a fire of such character the fire set by him was not the proximate cause of the damage. No principle of justice requires that the plaintiff be placed under the burden of specifically identifying the origin of both fires in order to recover the damages for which either or both fires are responsible. . . .

. . . There being no attempt on the part of the defendant to prove that the northwest fire was due to an irresponsible origin, that is, an origin not attributable to a human being, and the evidence in the case affording no reason to believe that it had an origin not attributable to a human being, and it appearing that the northeast fire, for the origin of which the defendant is responsible, was a proximate cause of plaintiff's loss, the defendant is responsible for the entire amount of that loss. While under some circumstances a wrongdoer is not responsible for damage which would have occurred in the absence of his wrongful act, even though such wrongful act was a proximate cause of the accident, that doctrine does not obtain "where two causes, each attributable to the negligence of a responsible person, concur in producing an injury to another, either of which causes would produce it regardless of the other." This is because "it is impossible to apportion the damage or to say that either perpetrated any distinct injury that can be separated from the whole," and to permit each of two wrongdoers to plead the wrong of the other as a defense to his own wrongdoing would permit both wrongdoers to escape and penalize the innocent party who has been damaged by their wrongful acts.

The fact that the northeast fire was set by the railroad company, which fire was a proximate cause of plaintiff's damage, is sufficient to affirm the judgment. This conclusion renders it unnecessary to consider other grounds of liability stressed in respondent's brief.

By the Court. Judgment affirmed.

In Capone v. Donovan, 332 Pa. Super. 185, 480 A.2d 1249 (1984), the plaintiff successively saw three doctors in connection with a leg injury, each of whom misdiagnosed the severity of the injury and for that reason provided inadequate treatment. The court ruled that the three doctors would be jointly and severally liable for the resulting harm, stating (480 A.2d at 1251):

> If the tortious conduct of two or more persons causes a single harm which cannot be apportioned, the actors are joint tortfeasors even though they may have acted independently. . . . If two or more causes combine to produce a single harm which is incapable of being divided on a logical, reasonable or practical basis, and each cause is a substantial factor in bringing about the harm, an arbitrary assignment should not be made.

An interesting discussion of the issues presented by the *Dillon* and *Kingston* cases is contained in Peaslee, Multiple Causation and Damage, 47 Harv. L. Rev. 1127 (1934). A variation of these issues was involved in Baker v. Willoughby, [1970] 2 W.L.R. 50; [1969] 3 All E.R. 1528 (H.L.). In this case, the defendant negligently struck the plaintiff with his automobile, causing severe injury to the plaintiff's left leg and ankle. Some time later, but before trial, the plaintiff was shot in the left leg during a robbery at his place of employment. As a result of the gunshot wound, the left leg had to be amputated. At trial, the defendant argued that he should be liable for the plaintiff's damages due to his disability only up to the time of the shooting. The trial judge rejected this argument but the court of appeal accepted it. The judgment of the court of appeal was reversed by the House of Lords, which ruled that the plaintiff's recovery for his disability was not affected by the second injury and amputation. The case is discussed in

McGregor, Successive Causes of Personal Injury, 33 Mod. L. Rev. 378 (1970), and Strachan, The Scope and Application of the "But For" Causal Test, 33 Mod. L. Rev. 386 (1970). In Buchalski v. Universal Marine Corp., 393 F. Supp. 246 (W.D. Wash. 1975), the plaintiff suffered a disabling back injury, and then suffered an unrelated heart attack that would have disabled the plaintiff to the same extent as the back injury. In calculating damages for lost wages, the court ignored the heart attack and awarded the plaintiff recovery in full. In F. Victorson v. Milwaukee & Suburban Transport Co., 70 Wis. 2d 336, 234 N.W.2d 332 (1975), the court ruled that the defendant should be relieved of liability for future damages because a totally disabling stroke, unrelated to the original injury, occurred after that injury. And in Jurney v. Lubeznik, 72 Ill. App. 2d 117, 218 N.E.2d 799 (1966), the court ruled that the plaintiff could not recover for pain and suffering in connection with a leg injury for the period after the leg was amputated for reasons unrelated to the original injury.

Problem 10

If you have already considered Problem 8, p. 137, above, then its facts are incorporated by reference here. If you have not considered Problem 8, use the following summary to consider this problem. On September 2 of this year, an unidentified dog attacked and badly mauled a two-year-old boy, Robert Carrington, in his backyard in Webster Township. The Carringtons have asked your firm to represent them and their son in bringing an action against the owner of the dog that injured the boy. Investigation reveals that the dog was almost certainly a German shepherd, but no eyewitness or other direct evidence is available to identify which, if any, of several German shepherds in Webster Township is the guilty dog. Your firm is considering the possibility of joining all the owners of German shepherds in a single action aimed at holding them jointly and severally liable. All such owners were arguably negligent in failing to restrain their animals in violation of a Township leash law, but joint and several tort liability would result in at least one owner being held liable for harm that his dog did not cause. You have just received the following memorandum from the partner handling the case:

> As you know, the Carrington case presents some very difficult cause-in-fact issues, difficult enough to possibly cause our tort case against the German shepherd owners to fail as a matter of law. The parents are understandably upset over what happened and are frustrated over our inability to identify which dog attacked their son. Mr. Carrington has asked me some questions that I now pass on to you. Assuming for the sake of argument that our tort action does not succeed, he and his wife would feel better about the whole situation if *some* good, at least, could come of their ordeal. After researching

the question of unidentified dog attacks statewide over the last five years, he found evidence of at least seven confirmed episodes. To his knowledge, none of the victims, who were all young children, received tort compensation. He assumes that the medical bills in such cases tend to be substantial—he describes theirs as "already astronomical and going higher"—and he wants to know if some sort of fund could be set up to aid such victims in the future. He thinks maybe a statute at the state level, or an ordinance at the local level, might call for the creation of such a fund.

Mr. Carrington's idea is to have the fund pay all victims of dog attacks "up front," with the fund being reimbursed out of tort proceeds, if any, recovered later on. He is unsure of how such a fund would be set up—that is, who would pay into it ahead of time to get it established. He is also unsure of how the fund would pay out to victims. Which victims? How much? He wants us to consider the problem and come up with recommendations regarding how he might proceed to support such a proposal. He will wait until our tort case is resolved to proceed further but however our case comes out, he intends to pursue his idea so his son's tragedy will not have been totally in vain.

I want you to consider his idea and sketch the way(s) you think best to go with it. What are the major decision points and what are the pros and cons of different resolutions at each point?

B. *But for the Wrongful Quality of Defendant's Conduct, Would the Plaintiff Have Suffered Harm?*

Ford v. Trident Fisheries Co.

232 Mass. 400, 122 N.E. 389 (1919)

Tort by the administratrix of the estate of Jerome Ford . . . against the Trident Fisheries Company . . . for negligently causing the death by drowning of the plaintiff's intestate on December 21, 1916, when he was employed as the mate of the defendant's steam trawler. . . .

. . . At the close of the plaintiff's evidence, which is described in the opinion, the judge, upon motion of the defendant, ordered a verdict for the defendant; and the plaintiff alleged exceptions.

CARROLL, J. The plaintiff's intestate was drowned while employed as mate of the defendant's steam trawler, the Long Island. This action is to recover damages for his death.

On December 21, 1916, about five o'clock in the afternoon, the vessel left T Wharf, Boston, bound for the "Georges," which are fishing banks in Massachusetts waters. About six o'clock, shortly after passing Boston Light, the plaintiff's intestate, Jerome Ford, came on deck to take charge of his watch as mate of the vessel. He came from the galley in the forecastle and walked aft on the starboard side. As he was ascending a flight of four steps leading from the deck to the pilot house, the vessel rolled and he was thrown overboard. At the time of the accident there was a fresh northwest breeze and the vessel was going before the wind; no cry was heard, no clothing was seen floating in the water, and Ford was not seen by any one from the time he fell overboard. . . .

The plaintiff . . . contends that the boat which was lowered to pick up the intestate was lashed to the deck instead of being suspended from davits and in order to launch it the lashings had to be cut; that McCue, who manned it, had only one oar and was obliged to scull, instead of rowing as he might have done if he had had two oars. Even if it be assumed that upon these facts it could have been found the defendant was negligent, there is nothing to show they in any way contributed to Ford's death. He disappeared when he fell from the trawler and it does not appear that if the boat had been suspended from davits and a different method of propelling it had been used he could have been rescued. . . .

Exceptions overruled.

The argument accepted by the court in *Ford* is often made in cases in which the alleged negligence is the failure of the defendant to take adequate security measures to protect the plaintiff against the criminal conduct of others. Many courts considering the issue have held that those who manage commercial premises owe duties of reasonable care to protect those who occupy the premises. See, e.g., Butler v. Acme Markets, Inc., 177 N.J. Super. 279, 426 A.2d 521 (1981), *aff'd,* 89 N.J. 270, 445 A.2d 1141 (1982); Holley v. Mount Zion Terrace Apts., Inc., 382 So. 2d 98 (Fla. App. 1980). One court upheld the argument as an alternative basis for its decision. See Pennington v. Church's Fried Chicken, Inc., 393 So. 2d 360 (La. App. 1980). See also the dissenting opinion of Boyd, J., in Orlando Executive Park, Inc. v. Robbins, 433 So. 2d 491 (Fla. 1983). Some courts have insulated landowners from liability, however, on the grounds that the landowner owes no duty to the plaintiff with respect to the criminal activity, or that the criminal conduct is unforeseeable. See, e.g., Crochet v. Hospital District Number One, 476 So. 2d 516 (La. App.), *cert. denied* 478 So. 2d 1235 (La. 1985); Henley v. Pizitz Realty Co., 456 So. 2d 272 (Ala. 1984); Gillot v. Washington Metropolitan Area Transit Authority, 507 F. Supp. 454 (D.D.C. 1981).

C. *Relationship Between Actual Causation and Proximate Causation*

The materials in this chapter tell only part of the causation story. Even when both but-for causation prerequisites are satisfied, tort law imposes a third requirement: that the resulting harm to the plaintiff have been within the range of foreseeable outcomes one had in mind in labeling the defendant's conduct wrongful in the first instance. Thus, in the *Hoyt* case, p. 113, even if the jury found that the hotel fire was started by a spark from defendant's mill and that proper equipment on the chimney would have prevented the spark from escaping, consider the court's reaction if, as a consequence of the hotel fire, a horse became frightened, ran down the main thoroughfare, jumped through a barber shop window and kicked a customer in the head. Would the barber shop customer have a right to recover against the mill?

The issue thus raised is said to be one of "proximate causation." Observe that it did not arise in any of the cases considered in this chapter, and in most instances when it does arise the questions presented are easily answered. But you should be aware that this third issue is relevant in some cases. Because most proximate causation issues arise in negligence actions and require familiarity with negligence principles, proximate causation is deferred to Chapter 4, which covers negligence. But you can get a sense of how proximate causation might play out in connection with the rules governing battery by considering the following problem.

Problem 11

Kathi Wong, recently widowed at the age of 34, has come to you to determine if she has a claim for recovery in connection with her husband's death. She explains that her husband, Matthew, worked for a news agency for nearly six years prior to his death last year in an airliner bombing incident. He frequently had been called upon in connection with his job to travel to countries in the Middle East. It was on one such assignment that a terrorist group blew up the airliner on which he was traveling, killing Matthew and everyone else on board. Coverage of the incident in the media made it fairly clear to Mrs. Wong that a tort action against the airline company would be unlikely to succeed. The airline company was foreign-based; and the circumstances of the accident (the terrorists fired a surface-to-air missile in commonly used airspace) would make negligence very difficult to establish against the airline.

Recently, however, Mrs. Wong received a letter from her husband's supervisor at the news agency that has her wondering if she may have a tort claim against her husband's employers. The handwritten letter came from Jack Griffith, who had been Matthew Wong's supervisor until Matthew's untimely death. Mr. Griffith explains in the letter that he wants to clear his conscience of something he feels he did to contribute to Matthew Wong's demise. He explains that he has just been diagnosed as suffering from terminal bone cancer and wants to ask Kathi Wong's forgiveness before he dies. He goes on to confess that approximately four years ago he recognized that Matthew Wong had a rare gift for his work and that Matthew would advance rapidly in the ranks of the company if given the right opportunities.

Mr. Griffith also believed that Matthew Wong represented a threat to him personally, as a possible replacement for Mr. Griffith. So Jack Griffith resolved to do everything he could to hinder Matthew Wong's progress in the company.

Part of Griffith's plan involved sending Mr. Wong on an excessive (from the company's viewpoint) number of trips to the Middle East, involving risks to Mr. Wong that could not be justified on the basis of benefits to the company. "I hoped and prayed that your husband would be killed in an incident every time I sent him off on a fool's errand," Mr. Griffith confesses in the letter. "I quietly rejoiced, while outwardly grieving, when we heard he was the victim of a terrorist attack."

Mrs. Wong was understandably upset when she received Mr. Griffith's letter and is in no mood to forgive him. Discrete inquiry has convinced her of several things: first, that Mr. Griffith has sufficient wealth to make him a desirable defendant if a cause of action could be established; second, that if anyone else had been supervising her husband at the relevant time, Matthew would not have been aboard the doomed aircraft; third, that Mr. Griffith's decisions to send Matthew Wong on the trips to the Middle East violated no protocol within the company and in retrospect, ironically, have proved to be very valuable to the company; finally, that Mr. Griffith had nothing whatsoever to do with causing the terrorists to attack the airliner in which her husband was a passenger.

Based on Mr. Griffith's confessions in his letter, together with the just-described assumptions which you may suppose to be true subject to later verification, do you think that Mrs. Wong may have causes of action against either Mr. Griffith or the company, based on counts of harmful battery?

Chapter 3

Vicarious Liability

This chapter is concerned with the extent to which one person may be held liable for harm caused by the tortious conduct of another. The primary focus to this point has been upon the extent of the actor's liability for the actor's own conduct. Here, we assume that the wrongful nature of the actor's conduct has been established, and ask whether liability may be extended beyond the actor to include persons who have not committed a wrong or directly caused any harm, but on whose behalf the wrongdoer acted. When such third persons are held liable for the conduct of others, they are said to be "vicariously" liable.

This concept of vicarious liability is one of considerable practical importance to the plaintiff because it is a most effective means of providing a financially responsible defendant, should the actual harm-causing actor be insolvent or otherwise incapable of satisfying a judgment. By far the largest class of persons to whom the rules in this chapter are applied are employers held liable for the torts of their employees. From the plaintiff's viewpoint, employers make much more desirable defendants than do employees. Not only is the jury likely to be more sympathetic to holding an employer—especially a large, corporate employer—liable in the first place, but they are more likely to be generous in their award of damages. And on top of everything else, employers are more likely than employees to be insured, and are more likely to be financially able to satisfy a judgment when insurance does not cover the liability. It is not surprising that of the opinions reproduced in this book, a significant percentage involve large corporate defendants.

A. *Masters, Servants, and Independent Contractors*

The central principle establishing vicarious liability for the tortious conduct of another is this: A master is vicariously liable for the torts of his servants committed while the latter are acting within the scope of their employment. See generally Restatement (Second) of Agency §219. Often referred to as the principle of respondeat superior—literally, "let the master answer"—its origins may be traced to ancient Greek and Roman law. Although early

English law moved away from the imposition of vicarious liability, by the eighteenth century this trend had reversed itself and respondeat superior was well on its way to assuming its present position of importance.

The use of respondeat superior as a basis of imposing vicarious liability requires, as a threshold matter, the existence of a master-servant relationship. Whatever may be the connotations of the terms "master" and "servant" in a Charles Dickens novel, they do not legally connote menial or manual service slavishly performed. Simply stated, the master-servant relationship is a consensual relationship in which one person, the servant, performs services on behalf of another person, the master, and in which the master controls or has the right to control the conduct of the servant. Thus, the officers of our largest corporations are servants in the legal sense of the word. Moreover, although the concepts of "servant" and "employee" overlap considerably, strictly speaking a servant need not receive a wage in order to bind the master vicariously; someone can be the servant of another even if he is performing services out of a sense of friendship. As a practical matter, however, most servants are employees hired to perform services for their employers.

Not all persons hired to perform work for others are servants who thus expose their employers to vicarious tort liability. In contrast to servants, independent contractors are persons hired to do jobs under circumstances which as a general rule do not call for the application of the principle of respondeat superior. Basically, an independent contractor is one who contracts with another person to do something but who is not controlled by the other person nor subject to the other person's right to control. Where the tortfeasor is an independent contractor, the general rule is that the employer is not vicariously liable for the harm caused by the contractor's wrongful conduct. See Restatement (Second) of Torts, §409. Thus, one of the major questions in cases involving respondeat superior concerns the status of the person acting on the defendant-employer's behalf. If the actor is a servant the employer is, within limits, legally responsible for the actor's conduct; if the actor is an independent contractor, generally speaking the employer is not legally responsible.

To the basic concept of control, the Restatement (Second) of Agency adds a number of considerations in determining whether an actor falls into one category or the other:

> §220. DEFINITION OF SERVANT
>
> (2) In determining whether one acting for another is a servant or an independent contractor, the following matters of fact, among others, are considered:
>
> (a) the extent of control which, by the agreement, the master may exercise over the details of the work;
>
> (b) whether or not the one employed is engaged in a distinct occupation or business;
>
> (c) the kind of occupation, with reference to whether, in the locality, the

work is usually done under the direction of the employer or by a specialist without supervision:

(d) the skill required in the particular occupation;

(e) whether the employer or the workman supplies the instrumentalities, tools, and the place of work for the person doing the work;

(f) the length of time for which the person is employed;

(g) the method of payment, whether by the time or by the job;

(h) whether or not the work is a part of the regular business of the employer;

(i) whether or not the parties believe they are creating the relation of master and servant; and

(j) whether the principal is or is not in business.

The Restatement definition of servant is quite open-ended, and one might question whether it provides sufficient guidance to enable courts to reach consistent results. In this connection, it should be observed that the considerations suggested in §220 do not purport to be exhaustive on the question of whether the actor in a given case is a servant or an independent contractor. What other factors might weigh in the balance on this issue?

Even if the plaintiff establishes that the tortfeasor was a servant at the time the harmful conduct occurred, vicarious liability will not be imposed unless the plaintiff also demonstrates that the servant was acting within the scope of employment. At first blush, this requirement would appear to offer employers a near universal defense, for they would typically be able to claim, quite justifiably, that they did not employ their servants to commit torts. Yet, with limited exceptions, the affirmative desire of employers that their servants act in a nontortious manner does not shield them from vicarious liability. Instead, the factors a court typically considers in determining whether the scope of employment requirement is met are summarized in the Restatement (Second) of Agency, which provides:

§229. KIND OF CONDUCT WITHIN SCOPE OF EMPLOYMENT

(1) To be within the scope of the employment, conduct must be of the same general nature as that authorized, or incidental to the conduct authorized.

(2) In determining whether or not the conduct, although not authorized, is nevertheless so similar to or incidental to the conduct authorized as to be within the scope of employment, the following matters of fact are to be considered:

(a) whether or not the act is one commonly done by such servants;

(b) the time, place and purpose of the act;

(c) the previous relations between the master and the servant;

(d) the extent to which the business of the master is apportioned between different servants;

(e) whether or not the act is outside the enterprise of the master or, if within the enterprise, has not been entrusted to any servant;

(f) whether or not the master has reason to expect that such an act will be done;

(g) the similarity in quality of the act done to the act authorized;

(h) whether or not the instrumentality by which the harm is done has been furnished by the master to the servant;

(i) the extent of departure from the normal method of accomplishing an authorized result; and

(j) whether or not the act is seriously criminal.

These criteria make clear that the servant need not be performing precisely the activity for which he was hired in order to expose the master to liability. Thus, in Riviello v. Waldron, 47 N.Y.2d 297, 391 N.E.2d 1278, 418 N.Y.S.2d 300 (1979), the tavern-owner-employer of a cook-waiter-bartender was exposed to vicarious liability when the latter negligently handled a pocket-knife while exhibiting it to some patrons, causing the loss of the plaintiff's eye. And the tortious conduct for which the master will be held accountable need not involve physical injuries. In Orser v. State, 178 Mont. 126, 582 P.2d 1227 (1978), the Supreme Court of Montana held that liability could be imposed on the state for the malicious prosecution by game wardens of alleged violations of game laws by the plaintiff.

The limits of the scope of employment requirement are most severely pressed when the servant engages in intentional wrongdoing. While it may make sense to hold employers liable for the on-the-job negligence of their employees on the grounds that negligently-caused accidents are a foreseeable part of many human activities, it is harder to explain why an employer should pay for an unauthorized, intentional tort committed by an employee. The early common law categorically barred vicarious liability for the intentional torts of servants unless the master in some way affirmatively solicited or encouraged such conduct.

This view continues to explain the refusal of some courts to impose vicarious liability in cases of intentional wrongdoing. For example, in Boyle v. Anderson Fire Fighters Assn., 497 N.E.2d 1073 (Ind. App. 1986), property owners and their insurers brought actions against striking fire fighters, their unions, and their municipal employer, to recover for property damage caused by the refusal of the fire fighters to extinguish a serious fire and by the fire fighters' prevention of efforts by others to stop the blaze. The trial court entered summary judgment in favor of all defendants. The court of appeals affirmed with respect to the city but reversed with respect to the unions. Regarding the nonliability of the city, the court concluded (497 N.E.2d at 1078):

> Here, the strikers were acting strictly on their own behalf. Their actions were motivated by self-interest—an interest patently inconsistent with the City's interest in providing uninterrupted fire protection. Given that both their refusal to fight the fire and their acts of interference with the efforts of others attempting to extinguish the blaze were intentional as well as unlawful, it is not difficult to conclude that their acts were so outrageous as to be incompatible

> with the duties owed the public and the City and beyond the scope of their employment.

Regarding the potential liability of the unions, the court concluded that the unions would be liable "if the evidence at trial demonstrates that agents of the [unions] participated in or encouraged the wrongful acts of the strikers." (497 N.E.2d at 1083).

Decisions in many jurisdictions, however, reflect an increased willingness to hold employers vicariously liable for the intentional torts of their employees. Although it is difficult to discern a common rationale for these decisions, in general courts focus on a cluster of factors, including whether the misconduct occurred within the time and space of employment, whether the employee was motivated, at least in part, by a concern for the employer's interests, and whether the potential for wrongdoing was foreseeable to the employer. Thus, in LeBrane v. Lewis, 292 So. 2d 216 (La. 1974), the Supreme Court of Louisiana imposed liability on the employer of a supervisor who stabbed a discharged employee while the latter was still on the employer's business premises. Although the argument was substantially a personal affair, it was sufficiently related to the discharge of the employee to render the individual defendant's intentionally wrongful conduct within the scope of his employment.

In sum, the general rule for imposing vicarious liability requires the plaintiff to show both that the employee was a servant rather than an independent contractor and that the employee's tortious behavior fell within the scope of employment. However, even if the plaintiff fails to make these showings, recovery against the employer may still be possible. In particular, the general rule of nonliability for employers of independent contractors, which is summarized in §409 of the Restatement (Second) of Torts, is subject to major exceptions. These exceptions, which are cataloged in §§410-429 of the Restatement, are too numerous to list here, but their general effect is described in the following comments to §409:

> They are so numerous, and they have so far eroded the "general rule," that it can now be said to be "general" only in the sense that it is applied where no good reason is found for departing from it. As was said in Pacific Fire Ins. Co. v. Kenny Boiler & Mfg. Co., 210 Minn. 500, 277 N.W. 226 (1937), "Indeed it would be proper to say that the rule is now primarily important as a preamble to the catalog of its exceptions."
>
> The exceptions have developed, and have tended to be stated, very largely as particular detailed rules for particular situations, which are difficult to list completely, and few courts have attempted to state any broad principles governing them, or any very satisfactory summaries. In general, the exceptions may be said to fall into three very broad categories:
>
> 1. Negligence of the employer in selecting, instructing, or supervising the contractor.

2. Non-delegable duties of the employer, arising out of some relation toward the public or the particular plaintiff.

3. Work which is specially, peculiarly, or "inherently" dangerous.

In the first of these broad categories of exceptions, wherein the employer is negligent in selecting, instructing, or supervising the independent contractor, the employer is not held liable vicariously, but in his own right for his own acts of negligence. Thus, strictly speaking, these cases are not exceptions to the general rule that defendants are not vicariously liable for the torts of their independent contractors, but instead illustrate the potential availability of an alternate, direct remedy against the employer. In some cases where this theory is invoked, the employer's own fault is quite limited. For example, in Becker v. Interstate Properties, 569 F.2d 1203 (3d Cir. 1977), *cert. denied,* 436 U.S. 906 (1978), the court concluded that a developer's failure to employ a "properly solvent or adequately insured subcontractor" violated its own duty to the injured plaintiff.

It is also important to note that this first exception—holding employers directly responsible for their own negligence—applies equally well in the master-servant context. Thus, even though in a particular case a servant may be found to have acted beyond the scope of employment, the master may be held directly liable for negligence in selecting, instructing, supervising, or retaining the employee. For example, in John R. v. Oakland Unified School Dist., 48 Cal. 3d 438, 769 P.2d 948 (1989), the California Supreme Court approved a trial court dismissal of a vicarious liability claim against a school district for the sexual assault of a student by one of its teachers, noting that "the connection between the authority conferred on teachers to carry out their instructional duties and the abuse of that authority to indulge in personal, sexual misconduct is simply too attenuated to deem a sexual assault as falling within the range of risks allocable to a teacher's employer." 48 Cal. 3d at 452, 769 P.2d at 956. The court went on to note, however, that the plaintiff could still seek to impose liability directly on the school district on the ground that it was negligent in hiring and supervising the teacher in question.

The second and third exceptions to the general rule encompass nondelegable duties and work that is especially dangerous. These exceptions are invoked by courts when confronted with defendants engaged in activities which expose the public to significant risks under circumstances where it seems appropriate to make those activities bear the accident costs they generate. See, e.g., Stropes v. Heritage House Childrens Ctr., 547 N.E.2d 244 (Ind. 1990) (center for mentally retarded children assumed nondelegable duty to provide protection and care; vicariously liable for sexual assault by center employee). But see Maguire v. State, 835 P.2d 755 (Mont. 1992) (rejecting liability under similar facts). Defendants to whom these exceptions have been applied typically include common carriers and municipalities, but other extensions have reached hospitals, mental institutions, and security services. Again, it is difficult to discern any hard and fast principles operating here. Indeed, the decision by a particular court to impose liability under one of these exceptions is often based, implicitly or explicitly, on its belief that such a decision would further public policy goals.

Implicit in this summary of the rules governing the vicarious liability of a master for the torts of his servants is the principle that, regardless of whether the master is liable, the servant will be personally liable to the plaintiff for his (the servant's) tortious conduct. From the plaintiff's perspective, the master and servant will be jointly and severally liable when both are joined as defendants. But what about the rights between master and servant—how is the liability to be divided between them? At common law, the general rule was that the master enjoyed a right of full indemnification over against the servant when the master (absent fault on personal part) was held vicariously liable for the wrongs of the servant. This rule remains intact, although some courts and commentators have questioned whether allowing the employer to seek indemnification from the harm-causing employee defeats the social policies that underlie the general doctrine of vicarious liability. See Comment, The Employer's Indemnity Action, 34 La. L. Rev. 79 (1973). These policies are now considered.

Law and Policy: Why Should Masters Be Liable for the Employment-Related Torts of Their Servants?

The somewhat complex and open-ended nature of the vicarious liability rules discussed above should not obscure the stark policy issue that they raise. Specifically, what is the justification for imposing liability on an actor based not on any wrongdoing on that actor's part but *solely* because of that actor's relationship with the actual tortfeasor?[1] Over time, courts and commentators have sought to justify vicarious liability by advancing some of the instrumental and noninstrumental rationales that underlie tort law. The nature and merits of these rationales deserve closer attention.

Some have insisted that masters are held liable on a *deep pocket theory;* that is, masters are held liable because they tend to be wealthier than servants and are thus more easily able to bear the costs of accidents. See Baty, Vicarious Liability 154 (1916). This argument clearly invokes a compensation rationale, but like all unadorned compensation arguments, it is quickly met with the question, "Why me?" In other words, the deepness of a party's pockets, standing alone, can hardly explain the selection of that party as an appropriate defendant. Something else, in the form of a noninstrumental

1. In this sense, vicarious liability represents a form of strict liability in that its imposition does not depend on a finding that the actor intentionally or negligently caused the harm. Thus, many of the policy issues pertaining to strict liability, which are discussed in Chapter 6, are relevant here.

argument based on fairness or an instrumental argument tied to social welfare, is typically needed to justify forcing an otherwise faultless defendant to compensate the plaintiff.

Some have sought to supply this rationale by promoting vicarious liability as a means of allocating to business enterprises the costs of accidents caused by those enterprises, thus spreading those costs in the prices charged for the goods and services marketed by the enterprises. See Prosser and Keeton, Law of Torts 500 (5th ed. 1984); Douglas, Vicarious Liability and the Administration of Risk, 38 Yale L.J. 584, 586 (1929). This argument has both instrumental and noninstrumental strands. From the noninstrumental fairness perspective, one might argue, in Epstein's terms (see p. 30), that the employer "caused" the accident by engaging the servant in the first place. In this regard, the "scope of employment" requirement can be viewed as a means of testing whether the employer's activities "caused" the plaintiff's injuries. However, while employment of the harm-causing worker satisfies the first kind of but-for causation identified in Chapter 2 (see p. 113), in many cases of vicarious liability, the second form of but-for causation, focusing on the *wrongful* nature of the employer's actions, is absent. Alternately, one might attempt a noninstrumental rationale by asking whether, in Fletcher's terminology, liability is justified because the employer's activities have imposed a nonreciprocal risk on others.

In addition to these fairness arguments, the cost-spreading argument suggests an instrumental justification: that accident losses are more detrimental to society when allowed to rest on individual injured plaintiffs than when born generally by the consumers of the employer's products or services. However, even if one subscribes to the premise of this argument—that a spread loss is better than a concentrated loss—it is still necessary to justify the selection of the employer as the loss-spreading mechanism. Why not, for example, spread losses through the plaintiff's own personal insurance company or, alternatively, through government aid for accident victims? Again, we are back to the employer's "Why me?" question.

While a fuller exploration of these questions must wait until we confront similar problems in the strict and products liability areas, a partial answer to why tort law might, for instrumental reasons, choose to impose liability on a faultless employer can be gleaned by examining a third justification for vicarious liability. That argument centers on the longstanding claim that masters are held vicariously liable in order to create the strongest possible incentive for them to be appropriately careful in the selection and supervision of their servants. See Smith, Frolic and Detour, 23 Colum. L. Rev. 444 (1923). Indeed, at first blush, this deterrence-based justification for vicarious liability seems powerful: Employers, faced with the knowledge that they will pay for the torts their servants commit within the scope of their employment, will exercise due care in hiring, training, supervising, and retaining employees. Indeed, the argument goes, without vicarious liability, employers may unfairly profit from the relatively judgment-proof nature of their employees. They will do so by bribing such employees to engage in high risk, high return behavior, knowing that as employers they will be shielded from any liability that such activities generate.

But on closer examination, this explanation proves too much because, as noted earlier, employers can be held *directly* liable to injured plaintiffs if they default on their own obligation to properly select, train, and supervise their employees. In other words, vicarious liability is not theoretically necessary to cause employers to adopt an appropriate level of care for their employees' conduct, since their failure to do so will provide an independent basis for liability.

In light of this apparent redundancy of remedies, does vicarious liability have any independent function in furthering the instrumental goal of deterrence? There are at least several arguments that it does. First, if plaintiffs systematically confront practical difficulties in establishing the employer's negligence at trial—perhaps because of their limited knowledge of the employer's methods of hiring, training, and supervising employees—employers may not experience a level of liability sufficient to force them to exercise appropriate care. Vicarious liability serves to redress this diminished incentive by eliminating altogether the plaintiff's need to show employer negligence. Of course, the plaintiff must still establish the employee's negligence, but that task is generally easier than proving a default by the employer.

Moreover, holding an employer strictly liable as a master not only helps insure that the employer experiences sufficient incentives to monitor and control the manner in which the servant works, but it also creates incentives for the employer to make more socially responsible decisions regarding whether the work ought to be undertaken in the first place. Knowing that it will be liable for *all* the torts its servants cause within the scope of their employment, rather than simply those torts that can be attributed to the employer's own negligence in controlling its employees, the employer may decide against expanding its operations to areas where profitability (and therefore social usefulness) is questionable. Vicarious liability therefore pressures the master to optimize (from the broader social perspective) not only *how* servants act, but also *whether* and *to what extent* they act.

This is an idea we have encountered before. The rules governing battery and trespass, for example, can be said to be aimed more at *whether* one acts than *how.* A physician who fails to obtain a patient's informed consent is strictly liable regardless of the skill exercised in the operation. (See pp. 57-58, above.) The message the physician receives is not that the operation should have been done differently, but that (absent informed consent) it should not have been done at all. And in the context of the dog-bite problems in Chapter 2 (see pp. 160-161 above), if a scheme combining a dog tax and a compensation fund were implemented in which the tax rate varied according to the relative riskiness of the breed of dog, such a scheme of strict liability based on dog ownership would presumably discourage some would-be owners from owning German shepherds rather than beagles, or goldfish.

Obviously, the policy questions raised by vicarious liability are quite complicated. In several subsequent areas of the course, including those dealing with res ipsa loquitor, strict liability, and products liability, you will have a chance to examine in more detail arguments similar to those discussed above. For a further exploration of these questions within the context of vicarious liability, see generally Sykes, The Boundaries of Vicarious Liability: An Economic Analysis of the Scope of Employment Rule and Related Legal Doctrines, 101 Harv. L. Rev. 563 (1988); Kornhauser, An Economic Analysis of the Choice Between Enterprise and Personal Liability for Accidents, 70 Calif. L. Rev. 1345 (1982).

What follow are short problems designed not only to round out your knowledge of this particular subject, but also to test your developing skills in applying generalized rules to particularized fact patterns. In order to achieve the second objective, you should first study the fact pattern of each problem case, along with its preliminary comments, and try to answer the questions it raises before reading the section entitled How the Court Is Likely to React.

The Traveling Salesman

Facts—*P* sues *D* alleging that *D*'s servant, *S*, negligently injured *P* while *S* was acting within the scope of his employment. There is no dispute that *S* caused *P*'s injuries, and there is more than enough evidence that *S* was negligent; thus, the central issue is whether *S* was *D*'s servant at the time of the injury. The uncontradicted evidence shows that *D* is a small company engaged in the manufacture and distribution of medical testing kits, most of which are sold directly to wholesalers throughout the country. *S* was the only salesman employed by *D* to handle sales to wholesalers. *S* would go by the company office four or five times a year, pull cards on wholesale houses, and pick out the ones he desired to visit. *S* took care of his own hotel and traveling expenses out of his commissions. *S* owned the automobile in which he traveled, and *D* paid him 1¼ cents a mile travel expenses. *D* fixed the prices, but *S* often gave greater discounts than were on the discount cards furnished wholesalers, and *D* accepted them. *S* was semi-retired, and sold the goods of at least one other company on his trips. He arranged his trips to coincide with visits to relatives throughout the country. *S* never received more than $1,200 in commissions from *D* in any year, so as not to jeopardize his social security benefits. The company made deductions from payments to *S* for federal withholding tax and paid federal employment compensation. The written contract between *D* and *S* (a letter written by *D*'s president but never signed by *S*) described the manner in which *S* was to call on his accounts; required him to file written reports; and described how he was to make collections, pick up stock from customers, and perform other duties. In fact, *S* rarely filed written reports and in other respects deviated from the express wording of the contract. The accident in which *P* was injured was an auto collision. While he was on a road trip for the purpose of selling *D*'s products, *S* drove his car into a car driven by *P*.

At the conclusion of the evidence *D* requests the court to direct a verdict of no liability, arguing that as a matter of law *D* is not vicariously liable for *S*'s having driven his car in a negligent manner while on a sales trip. Will *D*'s motion be granted?

Preliminary Comments—It seems clear that the issue raised by *D*'s motion comes down to whether there is sufficient evidence upon which a jury could find that *S* was a servant of *D* for purposes of holding *D* liable for *S*'s negligence. It would seem that if there is sufficient evidence to support a finding of master-servant relation, the question of scope of the employment would have to be answered in *P*'s favor by the court. Under the provisions of §220 of the Restatement (Second) of Agency above, could the jury find that *S* was a servant of *D*?

How the Court Is Likely to React—This is a case which is extremely close to the line drawn by the law between servant and independent contractor. In a case decided by the Supreme Court of Arizona on substantially similar facts, Throop v. F. E. Young & Co., 94 Ariz. 146, 382 P.2d 560 (1963), the trial court granted the defendant's motion for a directed verdict. Affirming the judgment below in favor of the defendant, the Arizona Supreme Court explained (94 Ariz. at 153, 382 P.2d at 565):

> Rather than unnecessarily extend this opinion by a discussion of all the "signposts" set forth in plaintiff's assignments of error it suffices to state that the ultimate issue in the servant-independent contractor disputes is "control or right to control." The "matters of fact" or "signposts" listed in the Restatement are but matters to be considered.
>
> An examination of the facts in the instant case makes readily apparent the correctness of the trial court's ruling in directing a verdict in favor of defendant . . . for there is no evidence from which to reasonably infer that the defendant had a right to control [S] in the operation of his automobile. The whole of the United States and anywhere he chose to go in it was [S's] territory. He visited prospects at whatever time he chose and he selected the prospects, visiting the office only four or five times a year. Clearly, no inference of control could stand the scrutiny of a motion for judgment notwithstanding the verdict had the case been submitted to the jury.

Observe that the court concludes that, as a matter of law, *S* was an independent contractor, not a servant. Is this outcome supported by §§220 and 229 of the Restatement (Second) of Agency? Is it in keeping with the general approach of those sections? Might the court in the *Throop* case have come out differently if *S* had dropped one of the medical testing kits on a customer's toe, injuring him? If it might have come out differently, would this be introducing a "scope of employment" limitation into the servant concept itself?

In connection with this last question it might be interesting to note a case in Connecticut in which the plaintiff was injured due to the allegedly negligent disposal by one of the defendant's newsboys of some wires used to bundle the defendant's newspapers prior to distribution. The evidence made it clear that as a general proposition, the newsboy was an independent contractor as a matter of law insofar as the delivery and sale of the papers was concerned. However, the court affirmed a judgment for the plaintiff, explaining that the jury could find that the newsboy was a servant in connection with the disposal of the wires. "A person may be a contractor as to part of his service and a servant as to another part." Scorpion v. American-Republican, Inc., 131 Conn. 42, 45, 37 A.2d 802, 803 (1944).

The Service Station Operator

Facts—*P* sues *D,* a major oil company, alleging that *S,* the operator of one of *D*'s many service stations, negligently injured *P.* The undisputed facts are that *S* leased the premises from *D,* agreeing to pay $70 a month plus a percentage of the receipts from gasoline sold at the station. *S* paid all expenses of operation; paid cash for all oil products purchased from *D;* sold those products at any price he determined; could hire and fire all employees; could sell his products on credit; and stood to gain or lose according to the profits or losses from the business. *D* had responsibility for making certain the building was properly maintained, and its representatives conducted inspections of the premises. *S* was encouraged to wear *D*'s uniforms and to identify with *D*'s products. The only pumps at the station bore *D*'s trademark, and the sale of any other products under *D*'s trademark was forbidden. The manner and nature of delivery of products to *S* was under *D*'s control, and it was customary for *S* to buy all items for sale from *D. D* had established criteria for obtaining operators for its stations; and the operators, including *S,* attended a school where they received instructions on marketing, operations, and safety. The accident in which *P* was injured occurred at the service station operated by *S. P* was helping *S* by pouring gasoline into the carburetor of a car *S* was trying to start. The car backfired, a flash fire broke out, and *P* was badly burned.

D moves for summary judgment, asserting the foregoing to be the undisputed facts and arguing that as a matter of law *S* was an independent contractor for whose conduct *D* is not responsible. Assuming enough evidence to go to the jury on the question of *S*'s negligence, what ruling will the court make on *D*'s motion for summary judgment?

Preliminary Comments—Once again, the scope of employment issue presents no problem in this case; rather, the question is whether *S* is *D*'s servant or an independent contractor. If the average person were to enter the service station and see *D*'s trade name everywhere, including on *S*'s uniforms, might he not reasonably assume that *S* was part of *D*'s organization—i.e., *D*'s employee? If so, is it still open for the court to direct a verdict for *D* on the more technical grounds of "control or right to control"? And in the final analysis, is not *S* obviously controlled by *D* in the economic sense that anything *D* urges *S* to do is likely to be done?

How the Court Is Likely to React—*D*'s motion may very well be granted. In a case on substantially similar facts, Foster v. Steed, 19 Utah 2d 435, 432 P.2d 60 (1967), the plaintiff argued that the written contract between *D* and *S* (on standard forms supplied by *D*) was a subterfuge to conceal the real master-servant relationship between the parties. There, the plaintiff had sued both *S* (Steed) and *D* (Texaco). The court below denied *D*'s motion for summary judgment, and *D* appealed. Reversing the ruling of the trial court and directing that summary judgment be granted in favor of *D,* the Supreme Court of Utah explained (19 Utah 2d at 440, 432 P.2d at 63): "Plaintiff has not pointed to any conduct that would tend to show the contracts were a sham or subterfuge to conceal the true relationship between the parties. The areas of mutual contact demonstrate a mutual interest in the sale of Texaco products and the success of the business. None of the evidence cited by plaintiff indicates that Texaco retained control of the day-to-day operation but, rather, merely influenced the result to be achieved, revealing an independent contractor status." If the accident had occurred due to the breakdown of a piece of equipment which *D* had inspected pursuant to its arrangement with *S,* would *D*'s motion have been granted?

The accident in the *Foster* case, above, occurred during the repair of a vehicle by the filling station operator. Would the same result have been reached if the explosion had occurred while *S* was pumping gasoline? In B.P. Corporation v. Mabe, 279 Md. 653, 370 A.2d 554 (1977), the filling station attendant absent-mindedly filled the plaintiff-customer's radiator (instead of his gas tank) with gasoline, resulting in an explosion. The court refused to hold the gasoline company vicariously liable.

The Traveling Plant Manager

Facts—*P* sues *D,* alleging that *D*'s servant, *S,* drove his automobile negligently and injured *P.* The uncontroverted facts establish that *S* was the manager of one of *D*'s manufacturing plants and frequently used his own automobile to run errands on behalf of *D.* On the day of his accident with *P, S* had driven to a nearby city to obtain parts for some machinery. *S*'s wife, who had a dentist's appointment in the city, accompanied him. After they arrived in the city, *S* waited for his wife to have several teeth extracted and afterwards drove her to the nearby home of a friend. Returning to the downtown area, *S* picked up some pain-killing drugs for his wife and the parts for the machinery. Heading back out of town on the return route to the manufacturing plant and his home, *S* turned off to pick up his wife at their friend's house. Moments after he made the turn, *S*'s car was struck by a car driven by *P*, who was severely injured in the resulting collision. There is more than enough evidence that *S* was negligent in the manner in which he drove his car.

At the close of the evidence, *D* moves for a directed verdict in its favor, arguing that as a matter of law *S* was not acting within the scope of his employment at the time of the collision with *P*. How is the trial court likely to react to *D*'s motion?

Preliminary Comments—*P* must overcome several arguments in order to get to the jury with the scope of employment question. First, *D* may argue that the whole trip to the city was outside the scope of *S*'s employment due to the fact that *S* had as one of his main purposes the taking of his wife to the dentist. Second, *D* may argue that the trip back into the city after dropping his wife off at the friend's house was motivated largely by *S*'s desire to get the drugs for his wife. And third, *D* may argue that *S*'s turn off the route back to the plant was entirely motivated by *S*'s desire to pick up his wife and served no purpose of *D* whatever. The overall picture of this episode, *D* will argue, is that *S* made a trip to the city to take his wife to the dentist and only incidentally did he run an errand for *D*. Moreover, the errand on behalf of *D* bore no relation at all to the detour he made to pick his wife up for the ride home. No jury could find that, while driving toward the friend's house, *S* was acting within the scope of his employment with *D*.

Thus, *D*'s arguments seek to characterize *P* as engaged in what the cases aptly refer to as "frolic and detour." Do you find *D*'s arguments persuasive? How would you counter them on behalf of *P*?

How the Court Is Likely to React—*D*'s motion for a directed verdict will likely be denied. Courts generally treat the significance of the deviation as a question of fact for the jury. Thus, in Van Vranken v. Fence-Craft, 91 Idaho 742, 430 P.2d 488 (1967), on substantially similar facts the Supreme Court of Idaho reversed the granting by the trial court of defendant's motion, offering the following explanation (91 Idaho at 749, 430 P.2d at 495):

> In the instant case, the agent . . . testified to a joint purpose for his trip to Lewiston and, similarly, to a joint immediate purpose for his return to downtown Lewiston after leaving his wife at the Roberts' home. In view of apparent mutual advantage, whether he was acting principally in furtherance of his employer's business at the time and place of his collision with [plaintiff's] car was, on this point, for the determination of the trier of fact, the jury.
>
> Lastly, [defendant] contends that the trial court could nevertheless properly determine as a matter of law that, in turning left . . . for the sole immediate purpose of dropping off the prescription for his wife at the Roberts' home, [S] thereby deviated from the direct return route to [D's plant] and, hence,

> from any purpose to benefit his employer. However, the better reasoned authorities dealing with deviations by an employee from the geodesic route have generally recognized that a proportionately slight or expectable deviation will not relieve an employer of vicarious liability, and except where the deviation is gross, the jury should determine the scope of employment question as one of fact.

How does this compare generally with the approach of the court to the traveling salesman case above? If the cases are different in their approach, is one of them right and the other wrong? In light of the Idaho court's approach to the case of the traveling plant manager, is there anything that the defendant company could have done before *S* made the trip which would have led to a granting of the defendant's motion?

Whether or not a servant-tortfeasor was on a "frolic and detour" can be relevant to issues other than whether the master will be vicariously liable. Thus, in Karangelen v. Snyder, 40 Md. App. 393, 391 A.2d 474 (1978), an on-duty policeman, whose duties involved ticketing illegally parked vehicles, ran over the plaintiff with his motor scooter. At the time of the accident, the policeman was approaching the plaintiff, whom he knew personally, in order to show his vehicle to the plaintiff. The policeman defended on the ground that he was acting within the scope of his employment at the time of the accident, and thus the suit was barred by governmental immunity. The court held that the policeman's deviation from his duties was minor, and denied recovery.

B. Other Forms of Vicarious Liability

In addition to the master-servant rules, other, more limited forms of vicarious liability exist. Two such forms are considered in this section: joint enterprise and the family purpose doctrine.

1. Joint Enterprise

Quite often, two or more persons will join together in an enterprise in which each has an equal right to control the other's conduct. Under such circumstances, one might apply master-servant concepts and speak of each participant being both the master and the servant of all the other participants. However, instead of applying master-servant principles in such cases, the courts have developed a separate legal concept for the purpose, to which they apply the terms "joint enterprise" and "joint venture" interchangeably. Briefly stated, the negligent conduct of each participant in a joint enterprise is imputed to every other participant, assuming the negligent acts to have been committed in the course of the enterprise. The basic elements of a joint enterprise have been generally described as (1) a contract, express or implied, in which the parties enter into an undertaking with (2) a common purpose, (3) a community of interest, and (4) an equal right of control over the agencies employed. See Carboneau v. Peterson, 1 Wash. 2d 347, 95 P.2d 1043 (1939). The doctrine has its clearest application where a formal contract establishes a business enterprise calling for a sharing of profits and losses and mutual control over physical operations.

A decision in the United States Court of Appeals for the Ninth Circuit reveals the manner in which this concept is likely to be applied in a business context. In Shell Oil Co. v. Prestidge, 249 F.2d 413 (9th Cir. 1957), the plaintiff was injured at an oil drilling site maintained and operated by the Rocky Mountain Oil Corporation, a company which had contracted with the Shell Oil Company to conduct oil explorations on land controlled by Shell. The plaintiff joined both Rocky Mountain and Shell in a negligence action and obtained a judgment against both companies. Shell argued on appeal that Rocky Mountain was an independent contractor, with whom Shell had bargained at arm's length, and therefore that Shell should not be responsible for the negligent acts of Rocky Mountain's employees. The court of appeals rejected this argument, concluding that a joint venture between the two companies was established as a matter of law (249 F.2d at 416-417):

> Both companies made substantial contributions to the enterprise. . . . In the event the enterprise did not achieve success, the two companies would share in the losses resulting to the extent of their contributions, and the profits, if any, would be shared. . . .
>
> As to the joint control of the enterprise . . . we think this element too is shown. . . .
>
> Aside from the fact that joint control of the enterprise was provided for in the agreement, and was in fact exercised by Shell through its geologist, there is also the principle . . . that while equal voice and joint control of the enterprise is essential to a joint venture, one of the joint adventurers may entrust actual control of the operation to another, and it still remains a joint venture. This case provides an apt illustration of that principle. As pointed out, the enterprise in which the two companies were engaged was the development of the Give Out Structure. The drilling phase of that enterprise was entrusted by Shell to Rocky Mountain, although as pointed out Shell did exercise some control even over the drilling. However, in the absence of that evidence, the enterprise, with all of the other elements of a joint venture, would not be any the less a joint venture by virtue of Shell entrusting the drilling operation to Rocky Mountain.

The doctrine of joint enterprise has also been applied in informal, nonbusiness contexts. Often, such cases arise out of automobile collisions, with the doctrine either being invoked by the injured plaintiff in an effort to hold the other car's passengers jointly responsible for its driver's negligence, or by the defendant in an effort to establish a contributory negligence defense against the other car's passengers by placing them in a joint enterprise with that car's negligent driver.

As might be expected, jurisdictions vary regarding their willingness to apply the joint enterprise doctrine. Earlier decisions based findings of joint enterprise upon the most casual traveling together of persons for purely social purposes. See, e.g., Delaware and Hudson Co. v. Boyden, 269 F. 881 (3d Cir. 1921). But more recently courts appear to require a business or financial purpose for the trip as a prerequisite to imposition of the joint enterprise doctrine. See Prosser and Keeton, Law of Torts 516-518 (5th ed. 1984); Weintraub. The Joint Enterprise Doctrine in Automobile Law, 16 Cornell L.Q. 320 (1931).

A decision in Illinois suggests the way in which the joint enterprise doctrine is likely to be applied in the context of automobile accidents. In Babington v. Bogdanovic, 7 Ill. App. 3d 593, 288 N.E.2d 40 (1972), the plaintiff and his fiancee, together with the latter's parents and her brother and sister, were injured in an automobile accident while returning from a four-day vacation. The plaintiff had contributed his automobile; his fiancee's family agreed to pay for the gas and oil. The accident occurred at night while the plaintiff's future father-in-law was driving. All the passengers, including the plaintiff, were asleep at the time. The plaintiff brought an action for his resulting injuries against the owner of a tractor trailer which had been parked on the side of the road and into which his future father-in-law had driven. On the plaintiff's appeal from judgment entered upon an adverse jury verdict, the issue was whether the trial court erred in instructing the jury that the automobile driver's negligence, if any, should be imputed to the plaintiff if the jury found a joint venture to have existed. Reversing and remanding for a new trial, the appellate court explained (7 Ill. App. 3d at 600, 288 N.E.2d at 44-45):

> Plaintiff argues that the "business" element is the paramount requirement for a foundation of joint enterprise, and since that element is missing in the case here on appeal, joint enterprise instructions were erroneous. Defendant urges that "the important element is the right of control" and "the sharing of expenses appears to satisfy any requirement as to a business element." We agree that "control" is an important element but we consider the better view to be that the "common business purpose" factor is dominant and must first exist before the joint enterprise doctrine can be viewed as germane. Nor can we agree that the mere sharing of picayune and paltry minimal expenses will satisfy the fundamental "business" factor required. We are faced here with a purely recreational and pleasure outing—a vacation trip. The plaintiff and his future in-laws agreed that his car would be used and that they would furnish the gas and oil. As a matter of fact, the [plaintiff's future in-laws] only paid an undisclosed portion of such expenses. [The plaintiff] and [his future father-in-law] both took turns driving, a fact that is not at all unusual

> under these circumstances. Where was the business element? Does the mere contribution of an unknown portion of the gas and oil money on a vacation trip transform a strictly pleasure excursion into a "common business enterprise"? We think not.
>
> And where is the control element? At the time of the tragic accident, [the plaintiff] (like all others in the car but the driver) was asleep. Does a sleeping owner of an automobile still possess a viable right of control over the driver? Whether that right of control has been abandoned, or whether he has "loaned" the car to [the driver], or whether [the driver] is now a bailee of the auto, to hold that [the plaintiff], while asleep, still possessed control of the automobile appears to us to tax credulity to the breaking point. There was no business enterprise, for it never existed; there was no control, for it had passed from [the plaintiff's] exercisable possession. To our view, the doctrine of joint enterprise has been, in many instances, too loosely applied. We refuse to extend it here.

Observe that the effect of the court's ruling was to prevent the plaintiff passenger from being saddled with the contributory negligence of the car's driver. Would the court have likely reached the same result if the plaintiff had been someone injured by the car and had been using a joint enterprise theory to enhance his prospects of recovery?

2. The Family Purpose Doctrine

In many states, a special rule has been developed judicially which, under certain circumstances, imposes vicarious liability upon automobile owners for harm caused by persons to whom the automobiles have been loaned or made available. Briefly stated, the family purpose doctrine imposes liability upon the owner of a family automobile for harm negligently caused to others by a family member while operating the automobile on a family purpose. Thus, in a strong sense, the family purpose doctrine represents a domestic equivalent of the master-servant rule. See, e.g., Stephens v. Jones, 710 S.W.2d 38, 42 (Tenn. App. 1984) ("[The family purpose] doctrine rests on the presumption that if a family member operates an automobile that is owned and used for family purposes, the family member is the servant of the owner of the automobile and is engaged upon his business at the time the negligence occurred.")

The elements of the doctrine are: (1) ownership of the automobile by the defendant sought to be held liable vicariously; (2) designation of the automobile as a family automobile; (3) status of the driver as a family member; (4) use of the automobile for a family purpose; and (5) use of the automobile with the owner's permission. As might be expected, each of these elements has been the subject of extensive judicial review and refinement. For example, courts have held that the defendant need not actually own the automobile, so long as he controls its use or supplies it to his family. See Gray v. Golden, 301 Ky. 477, 192 S.W.2d 371 (1946). Moreover, for the vehicle in question to be a family automobile, it must be made generally available to the defendant's family and not simply supplied on a single, isolated occasion. See Costanzo v. Sturgill, 145 Conn. 92, 139 A.2d 51 (1958).

Naturally, the definition of "family" provides one of the most challenging questions of interpretation under the doctrine. The spouse and unemancipated children of the defendant owner obviously meet the requirement, but once one ventures beyond the traditional family and considers the wide variety of modern living arrangements, the lines become less clear. In Levy v. Rubin, 181 Ga. 187, 182 S.E. 176 (1935), the court concluded that an unmarried man who lived with, and presumably contributed to the support of, a widowed mother and two sisters was liable under the family purpose doctrine for the negligent operation of his automobile by one of the sisters. Courts have reached contradictory results regarding parental liability for automobile accidents caused by their visiting, emancipated children. See, e.g., Dunn v. Caylor, 218 Ga. 256, 127 S.E.2d 367 (1963); Adkins v. Nanney, 169 Tenn. 67, 82 S.W.2d 867 (1935). Other relationships test the scope of the doctrine. For example, in Liddy v. Hames, 177 Ga. App. 517, 339 S.E.2d 778 (1986), the court summarized the facts as follows (177 Ga. App. at 517, 339 S.E.2d at 778):

> Appellant brought suit against Hames and Britt after being injured when a car in which she was a passenger collided with Britt's car, which was being driven by Hames. The grounds of liability asserted by appellant against Britt were negligent entrustment, respondeat superior, and the family purpose doctrine. In her deposition, Britt denied that Hames had ever had permission to use her car, that Hames was living with her at the time of the collision, and that Hames was driving as her agent when the collision occurred. Hames testified on deposition that although he had once lived with Britt, he lived elsewhere at the time of the collision; that he had borrowed the car on the occasion of the collision without checking with Britt, who was asleep when Hames took the car, but that they had an understanding that he could use her car when he wanted to; and that he was using the car on that occasion for his own purposes. In opposition to Britt's motion for summary judgment, appellant submitted an affidavit in which Hames swore that he was "staying" with Britt at the time and had standing permission to use her car.

On appeal, appellant argued that the conflict in testimony regarding whether Britt and Hames were living together rendered summary judgment erroneous. The court of appeals concluded that the conflict was immaterial. Even if living together, the court explained, both Britt and Hames swore they were just "friends." This would not, as a matter of law, establish a family relationship.

Of course, even the "just friends" defense may fail under some circumstances. Consider Driver v. Smith, 47 Tenn. App. 505, 339 S.W.2d 135,

(1959), in which the defendant's 18-year-old daughter took the family automobile for a pleasure ride with her friends, during which she asked her boyfriend to drive. While her boyfriend was driving, the girl reached over and kissed him, causing him to lose control of the car. Although the court declined to hold the defendant's father liable for the driver's negligence, it imposed liability upon him under the family purpose doctrine for his daughter's negligence in distracting her boyfriend's attention from the road. The court's discussion of the daughter's own negligence again suggests the value to the plaintiff of pursuing direct theories of recovery when derivative claims are stymied.

As the preceding case also suggests, courts have been quite lenient with plaintiffs regarding the requirement that the automobile have been employed on a "family purpose" at the time of the accident. All normal family activities are included, including pleasure driving. In Ferguson v. Gurley, 218 Ga. 276, 127 S.E.2d 462 (1962), the owner of an automobile was held vicariously liable when his wife had an accident while driving herself and a friend to work. The doctrine was held not to apply in Vaughn v. Booker, 217 N.C. 479, 8 S.E.2d 603 (1940), in which a father had expressly directed his son never to take the family automobile to the place where the accident occurred.

Not all states recognize the family purpose doctrine. A New Hampshire decision, Grimes v. Labreck, 108 N.H. 26, 226 A.2d 787 (1967), is fairly typical of those rejecting this form of vicarious liability. In that case, the defendant's daughter had taken his automobile for the purpose of buying fresh corn at a roadside stand. Attempting to pull onto the highway to return to her father's home, she collided with another vehicle. Although the New Hampshire court refused to recognize the family purpose doctrine, it ruled that the question of whether the daughter was acting as her father's agent was one for the trier of fact. Thus, even in jurisdictions which do not recognize the doctrine as a separate rule of law, it may be possible in some cases to establish vicarious liability on the broader basis of master-servant principles. And the plaintiff may be able to reach the vehicle owner's liability insurance carrier even if the owner is not exposed to personal liability. Many policies, in "omnibus clauses," agree to cover nonowner operators driving with the owner's permission.

Chapter 4

Negligence

Negligence is today, and has been for many years, the most important basis of tort liability in the United States. The Industrial Revolution and the mechanization of society have supplied the tools, particularly the automobile, for the mass infliction of unintentionally caused harms; and the general use of liability insurance has vastly increased the number of financially responsible defendants. To be sure, inroads have been made into the dominance of the negligence concept in the torts process. The liability of manufacturers and suppliers for injuries caused by defective products has been expanded beyond negligence. Negligence-based employers' liability arising out of industrial accidents has been replaced substantially by workers' compensation statutes, and systems of nonfault compensation for personal injuries resulting from automobile accidents have been adopted in many states. However, at least for the present, negligence law continues to dominate the torts process.

The basis of liability in negligence is the creation of an unreasonable risk of harm to another. There are few activities that do not involve some risk of harm. Driving an automobile, flying a plane, building a bridge—even mowing a lawn or riding a bicycle—involve risks that someone will be injured. We know with certainty that some accidents will happen, but we nonetheless accept them as a price of the kind of society we have. It is not that we are indifferent to the accident rate. In fact, we have become increasingly concerned in recent years with making things safer. But an accident-free society is impossible to attain, and even reducing accidents as much as humanly possible would cost more than we would be willing to spend on safety. Therefore, an actor who causes harm is not held liable in negligence simply because the activity involves a risk of harm to others. For negligence to be found, the conduct must involve a risk of harm greater than society is willing to accept in light of the benefits to be derived from that activity—that is, the risk of harm must be unreasonable.

A. *The Origins and Development of the Negligence Concept*

Because the negligence concept dominates the torts process today, students understandably tend to assume that it has been an important part of our legal system from the beginning. Actually, it is a relative newcomer. As Professor Peck indicates in the following note, in order to understand fully the law of negligence as it operates today, it will be necessary to know what preceded it, and to appreciate the social pressures in response to which it came into being in the mid-nineteenth century. As shown in the excerpts that follow, the law of negligence shares with the law of battery common origins in the writ system that developed in England in the centuries following the Norman Conquest.

Peck, Negligence and Liability Without Fault in Tort Law

Department of Transportation Study of Automobile Insurance and Compensation 51-56 (1970)

It is frequently assumed that with a few exceptions the principles of negligence constitute the field of tort law and that fault is the most common basis for determining liability for harmful conduct. The space devoted in most torts casebooks used for law school instruction suggests to students and future lawyers that negligence is the dominant principle of tort law, and the emphasis given the subject by teachers, stimulated by the intellectual challenges of defining proximate cause or establishing standards of care, further impresses the importance of negligence principles upon each class of law students. Moreover, most of the tort cases litigated are in fact decided pursuant to principles of negligence, largely because of the litigation-spawning capacity of automobile accidents. And, though these are changing times, the concept persists that what now exists has always been. A survey of tort law produces a somewhat different view and discloses a surprising number of instances in which liability is imposed without fault.

The conclusion reached by most scholars is that until the 19th century a person whose actions caused harm to another was with few exceptions held responsible for that harm simply because he had acted. Holdsworth tells us that this was the case both with respect to early Anglo-Saxon law and the Mediaeval Common Law. Wigmore earlier summarized the primitive German law by writing, "The doer of a deed was responsible whether he acted innocently or inadvertently, because he was the doer. . . ."[5] This absolute responsibility, without regard to blame, persisted, he tells us, until the early 1500s, when sloughing off of the primitive notion took place, permitting a defendant to exempt himself from liability by showing that he was without blame even though he had acted voluntarily. Street agreed, writing that for many hundred years the conception of negligence was unknown to the law of trespass, the consequence being that a defendant

5. Wigmore, Responsibility for Tortious Acts: Its History, 7 Harv. L. Rev. 315, at 317 (1894).

was liable if it was shown that damage had been done by the direct or immediate application of force, without regard to whether he was negligent or not. Justice Holmes, while persuaded that policy and consistency required rejection of the rule of strict liability, recognized that the theory enjoyed the support of some lawyers of his time, and that the common law probably followed such a rule during what he called a period of dry precedent. Scholars today agree that a rule of strict liability prevailed at the early stages of development of the common law, usually rendering an actor liable if he in fact caused injury to another.

Escape from the rule of strict liability evolved and developed slowly in typical common law fashion. There are a number of detailed accounts of the development. Leading among the cases is the early report of The Case of Thorns,[11] in which an action for trespass to real property was brought against a defendant who had cut a hedge of thorns, some of which fell upon plaintiff's land. While holding for the plaintiff, one of the judges noted that the defendant had not alleged that he could not act in any other way, or that he had done all that was in his power to keep the thorns from falling on plaintiff's land, thereby suggesting that establishing these facts would have constituted a valid defense. One hundred and fifty years later a similar suggestion was made in a case holding liable a soldier whose gun accidentally discharged, injuring the plaintiff.[12] The examples given—"as if a man by force take my hand and strike you, or if here the defendant had said that the plaintiff ran across his piece when it was discharging, or had set forth the case with the circumstances so as it had appeared to the court that it had been inevitable, and that the defendant had committed no negligence to give occasion to the hurt"—indicate that liability would have been imposed upon an actor guilty of much less than what is today required to establish negligence.

And so things continued until the 19th century with liability in trespass being imposed upon actors who had caused harm in a series of cases suggesting that inevitability of the accident and lack of any fault upon the part of the defendant would have constituted justification and a defense against liability. Then, three American courts, relying in large part upon dicta from earlier cases, announced the proposition that liability could not be imposed unless the actor were guilty of some fault or neglect. Of the three, the decision of the Supreme Court of Massachusetts in Brown v. Kendall, became the most famous and is now considered the leading case establishing the necessity of proving negligence for the purpose of imposing liability for accidental injury. Perhaps the decision has gained that position because of the esteem enjoyed by its author, Chief Justice Lemuel Shaw; more likely it has gained that position because it so clearly imposed the

11. Y.B. 6 Edw. 4, fo. 7a, pl. 18 (1466).
12. Weaver v. Ward, Hob. 134, 80 Eng. Rep. 284 (K.B. 1617).

burden of proving negligence upon the plaintiff rather than leaving the absence of negligence something to be proved by the defendant. . . .

It is true that after the 14th century liability for causing harm could be established in an action of trespass on the case by showing that the conduct of the defendant was negligent. The action was originated to provide a remedy for harm caused by misfeasance in the performance of an obligation which had been undertaken. In time trespass on the case came to lie for the doing of an unlawful act, if the damage sustained was not "immediate" but instead "consequential." At one time it was fatal error to proceed by case if the harm had been immediately caused by the defendant, but shortly before the development by the American courts of the modern negligence principle, an English court decided that where an injury had been "immediately" caused by a negligent act, the plaintiff might nevertheless make the negligence the ground of his action and declare in case rather than trespass.[22] In effect, one could waive the trespass and sue for negligence. The effect of the mid-19th century American decisions was to bring about a merger of the substantive law of trespass and case and to impose upon a plaintiff who relied upon a trespass theory the same burden which he would formerly have had to carry in an action on the case.

Why the change took place must, of course, remain a matter of speculation. It has been suggested that Chief Justice Shaw may have been motivated by a desire to make the risk-creating enterprises of a developing industrial economy less subject to liability than they had been under the earlier common law. The suggestion has been countered with the observation that Brown v. Kendall, the vehicle by which Chief Justice Shaw announced the change of the law, did not involve industry, but was instead a case growing out of the actions of private persons engaged in separating two fighting dogs. It seems unlikely that Chief Justice Shaw calculatingly selected the case as one which would disguise the ends to be served by making the change in the law, but it seems equally unlikely that he could have written the decision without consideration of what the conditions of society at the time suggested as appropriate standards for allocating responsibility for harms which were unintentionally caused.

Indeed, the common law trespass rule was probably well suited to the conditions which prevailed as it evolved. Most energy sources, if not human, were familiar domestic animals; the implements used in labor or recreation were relatively uncomplicated devices whose functioning was controlled by elementary mechanical principles. One who directly or immediately harmed another by his active conduct probably had departed from community standards of behavior much in the same way that one who is negligent today departs from the standard of the reasonable, prudent man. Proof of "immediate" causation was then a satisfactory standard for allocating

22. Williams v. Holland, 10 Bing. 112, 131 Eng. Rep. 848 (C.P. 1833).

responsibility for harm. It did not have a disruptive effect upon society nor did it deter or misdirect otherwise desirable economic activity.

The development of industry and transportation using steam and other later sources of power changed this, as did the development of new products and devices. One need but read a description of the operation of steam locomotives prior to adoption of the air brake to realize what costs would have been imposed upon railroads if liability for harm caused were to be determined by the common law trespass rule. . . . About the only safety measure at crossings available to railroads was the giving of warning signals by whistle and bell. . . . [T]he reaction of the law predictably was not strict condemnation of an activity which offered escape from the slow, uncomfortable, and jolting transport by stage over roads filled with mud, particularly in a country with rich resources stretching out over thousands of miles of undeveloped territory. The negligence standard provided a legal environment in which rail transportation could grow and prosper. It served other branches of industry and commerce as well. . . .

. . . Society as a whole stood to benefit from the workings of an industrial economy, and as a general proposition it could not afford to burden itself with compensating those individuals who were so unfortunate as to be injured accidentally by an instrument of progress.

Brown v. Kendall

60 Mass. 292 (1850)

This was an action of trespass for assault and battery. . . .

It appeared in evidence, on the trial, . . . that two dogs, belonging to the plaintiff and the defendant, respectively, were fighting in the presence of their masters; that the defendant took a stick about four feet long, and commenced beating the dogs in order to separate them; that the plaintiff was looking on, at the distance of about a rod, and that he advanced a step or two towards the dogs. In their struggle, the dogs approached the place where the plaintiff was standing. The defendant retreated backwards from before the dogs, striking them as he retreated; and as he approached the plaintiff, with his back towards him, in raising his stick over his shoulder, in order to strike the dogs, he accidentally hit the plaintiff in the eye, inflicting upon him a severe injury.

Whether it was necessary or proper for the defendant to interfere in the fight between the dogs; whether the interference, if called for, was in a proper manner, and what degree of care was exercised by each party on the occasion; were the subject of controversy between the parties, upon all the evidence in the case, of which the foregoing is an outline.

The defendant requested the judge to instruct the jury, that "if both the plaintiff and defendant at the time of the blow were using ordinary care, or if at that time the defendant was using ordinary care and the plaintiff was not, or if at that time both plaintiff and defendant were not using ordinary care, then the plaintiff could not recover."

The defendant further requested the judge to instruct the jury, that, "under the circumstances, if the plaintiff was using ordinary care and the defendant was not, the plaintiff [could] recover, and that the burden of proof on all these propositions was on the plaintiff."

The judge declined to give the instructions, as above requested, but left the case to the jury under the following instructions: "If the defendant, in beating the dogs, was doing a necessary act, or one which it was his duty under the circumstances of the case to do, and was doing it in a proper way; then he was not responsible in this action, provided he was using ordinary care at the time of the blow. If it was not a necessary act; if he was not in duty bound to attempt to part the dogs, but might with propriety interfere or not as he chose; the defendant was responsible for the consequences of the blow, unless it appeared that he was in the exercise of extraordinary care, so that the accident was inevitable, using the word inevitable not in a strict but a popular sense."

"If, however, the plaintiff, when he met with the injury, was not in the exercise of ordinary care, he cannot recover, and this rule applies, whether the interference of the defendant in the fight of the dogs was necessary or not. If the jury believe, that it was the duty of the defendant to interfere, then the burden of proving negligence on the part of the defendant, and ordinary care on the part of the plaintiff, is on the plaintiff. If the jury believe, that the act of interference in the fight was unnecessary, then the burden of proving extraordinary care on the part of the defendant, or want of ordinary care on the part of the plaintiff, is on defendant."

The jury under these instructions returned a verdict for the plaintiff; whereupon the defendant alleged exceptions. . . .

SHAW, C.J. . . . The facts set forth in the bill of exceptions preclude the supposition, that the blow, inflicted by the hand of the defendant upon the person of the plaintiff, was intentional. The whole case proceeds on the assumption, that the damage sustained by the plaintiff, from the stick held by the defendant, was inadvertent and unintentional; and the case involves the question how far, and under what qualifications, the party by whose unconscious act the damage was done is responsible for it. We use the term "unintentional" rather than involuntary, because in some of the cases, it is stated, that the act of holding and using a weapon or instrument, the movement of which is the immediate cause of hurt to another, is a voluntary act, although its particular effect in hitting and hurting another is not within the purpose or intention of the party doing the act.

It appears to us, that some of the confusion in the cases on this subject has grown out of the long-vexed question, under the rule of the common law, whether a party's remedy, where he has one, should be sought in an action of the case, or of trespass. This is very distinguishable from the question, whether in a given case, any action will lie. The result of these cases is, that if the damage complained of is the immediate effect of the act of the defendant, trespass vi et armis lies; if consequential only, and not immediate, case is the proper remedy.

In these discussions, it is frequently stated by judges, that when one receives injury from the direct act of another, trespass will lie. But we think this is said in reference to the question, whether trespass and not case will lie, assuming that the facts are such, that some action will lie. These dicta are no authority, we think, for holding, that damage received by a direct act of force from another will be sufficient to maintain an action of trespass, whether the act was lawful or unlawful, and neither wilful, intentional, or careless. . . .

We think, as the result of all the authorities, the rule is correctly stated by Mr. Greenleaf, that the plaintiff must come prepared with evidence to show either that the *intention* was unlawful, or that the defendant was *in fault;* for if the injury was unavoidable, and the conduct of the defendant was free from blame, he will not be liable. If, in the prosecution of a lawful act, a casualty purely accidental arises, no action can be supported for an injury arising therefrom. In applying these rules to the present case, we can perceive no reason why the instructions asked for by the defendant ought not to have been given; to this effect, that if both plaintiff and defendant at the time of the blow were using ordinary care, or if at that time the defendant was using ordinary care, and the plaintiff was not, or if at that time, both the plaintiff and defendant were not using ordinary care, then the plaintiff could not recover.

In using this term, ordinary care, it may be proper to state, that what constitutes ordinary care will vary with the circumstances of cases. In general, it means that kind and degree of care, which prudent and cautious men would use, such as is required by the exigency of the case, and such as is necessary to guard against probable danger. A man, who should have occasion to discharge a gun, on an open and extensive marsh, or in a forest, would be required to use less circumspection and care, than if he were to do the same thing in an inhabited town, village, or city. To make an accident, or casualty, or as the law sometimes states it, inevitable accident, it must be such an accident as the defendant could not have avoided by the use of the kind and degree of care necessary to the exigency, and in the circumstances in which he was placed. . . .

The court instructed the jury, that if it was not a necessary act, and the defendant was not in duty bound to part the dogs, but might with propriety interfere or not as he chose, the defendant was responsible for the consequences of the blow, unless it appeared that he was in the exercise of extraordinary care, so that the accident was inevitable, using the word not in a strict but a popular sense. This is to be taken in connection with the charge afterwards given, that if the jury believed, that the act of interference in the fight was unnecessary (that is, as before explained, not a duty incumbent on the defendant), then the burden of proving extraordinary care on the part of the defendant, or want of ordinary care on the part of plaintiff, was on the defendant.

The court are of opinion that these directions were not conformable to law. If the act of hitting the plaintiff was unintentional, on the part of the defendant, and done in the doing of a lawful act, then the defendant was not liable, unless it was done in the want of exercise of due care adapted to the exigency of the case, and therefore such want of due care became part of the plaintiff's case, and the burden of proof was on the plaintiff to establish it.

Perhaps the learned judge, by the use of the term extraordinary care, in the above charge, explained as it is by the context, may have intended nothing more than that increased degree of care and diligence, which the exigency of particular circumstances might require, and which men of ordinary care and prudence would use under like circumstances, to guard against danger. If such was the meaning of this part of the charge, then it does not differ from our views, as above explained. But we are of opinion, that the other part of the charge, that the burden of proof was on the defendant, was incorrect. Those facts which are essential to enable the plaintiff to recover, he takes the burden of proving. The evidence may be offered by the plaintiff or by the defendant; the question of due care, or want of care, may be essentially connected with the main facts, and arise from the same proof; but the effect of the rule, as to the burden of proof, is this, that when the proof is all in, and before the jury, from whatever side it comes, and whether directly proved, or inferred from circumstances, if it appears that the defendant was doing a lawful act, and unintentionally hit and hurt the plaintiff, then unless it also appears to the satisfaction of the jury, that the defendant is chargeable with some fault, negligence, carelessness, or want of prudence, the plaintiff fails to sustain the burden of proof, and is not entitled to recover.

New trial ordered.

One characteristic of the negligence concept directly traceable to the distinction described by Professor Peck between the writs of trespass and trespass on the case, though not mentioned in his article, is the necessity in negligence cases for the plaintiff to show that the defendant's conduct has caused actual harm. It will be recalled from Chapter 1 that the successful plaintiff in battery may recover nominal damages even if it is clear that no actual harm has been caused by the defendant. This absence of the requirement of harm in battery cases may be traced directly to the common origins, in writs of trespass, of tort law and criminal law, in which the wrongfulness of the defendant's conduct was the dominant element. When the writ of trespass on the case began to be available in the King's courts in England in the thirteenth and fourteenth centuries, one of the elements that plaintiffs had to show from the very beginning, in addition to the indirect and consequential nature of the invasion, was that actual, tangible harm had resulted from the defendant's conduct. This early distinction between trespass and trespass on the case survives today in the very different rules establishing liability for battery and negligence. Thus, in addition to showing that the defendant breached the duty of reasonable care, to recover in a negligence case, the plaintiff must show, as the plaintiff in a battery case need not, that the defendant's breach has caused harm.

Law and Behavior: Influences upon Judicial Decisions

In his treatment of the historical beginnings of the negligence concept, Professor Peck (p. 188, above) suggests that although Chief Justice Shaw may not consciously have been intent on protecting growing industries by his decision in Brown v. Kendall (that case, after all, involved fighting dogs), he could not have avoided being influenced in his decision by the social and political environment surrounding him. Suggestions of this sort raise interesting questions concerning the source and nature of influences upon judicial decisions—questions concerning why judges react the way they do in certain cases. The purpose of this note is to raise these questions and to introduce you in a general way to some of the available literature on the subject of influences upon judicial behavior. We will not directly be concerned in the following discussion with grossly improper and illegal corruptions of the judicial process,[1] such as bribery or extortion of judges.[2] Our interest here is in exploring the influences upon judges in the overwhelming majority of instances in which they are conscientiously trying to decide, within proper bounds, the cases before them.

Until the beginning of this century, it was almost universally asserted and widely believed that the law was the *only* normative factor influencing judicial decisions. The notion was that by carefully searching their law books, judges could find answers to all of the questions brought to them, and that in deciding cases they performed the essentially ministerial functions of applying found law to facts. Such a mechanical view of the judicial process left little room for the possibility that judges might be influenced in their decisions by factors other than found facts and formally realized rules of law.[3]

1. For one well-known writer's lament that the fraternity of judges seems indifferent to the need for developing standards of judicial propriety, see Llewellyn, The Common Law Tradition: Deciding Appeals 47 (1960). For a study of the procedures in this country for the removal and retirement of judges, see Braithwaite, Who Judges the Judges? (1971).

2. During 1970-1977 federal indictments were issued against 44 state judges based on judicial misbehavior. See Noonan, Bribes (1984). For one account of and investigation into judicial impropriety, see Hansen, Operation Court Broom: Police Raid Judges' Homes in Miami-Area Bribery Probe, 77 A.B.A. J. 27 (Sept. 1991).

3. For an analysis of the shortcomings of this earlier mechanical view, see Wasserstrom, The Judicial Decision 12-38 (1961).

The movement away from this formalistic view began toward the end of the nineteenth century[4] and may be said, at least in retrospect, to have culminated with the publication in 1921 of an important book in American jurisprudence—The Nature of the Judicial Process, by Benjamin Cardozo, then a judge on the New York Court of Appeals. In his book, Judge Cardozo argued persuasively that in at least some cases judges do, and ought to, act as law-givers and legislators. Although in the majority of instances, existing rules of law admit of but a single result, cases arise in which the rules are sufficiently ambiguous, or vague, or questionable, requiring the judge to perform a creative, and not strictly a mechanical, function. In performing this legislative function, Cardozo insisted, the judge should endeavor to suppress personal biases and prejudices and strive instead to be guided by "the accepted standards of the community, the *mores* of the times."[5]

Cardozo's view, of course, is the view reflected in Professor Peck's description of the origins of the negligence concept, and it is the view reflected in earlier Law and Policy Notes in this book. In the terms employed earlier in Law and Policy Notes, this view may be described as a mixture of the "noninstrumentalist" and "instrumentalist" perspectives. And yet, it leaves important questions unanswered. Where are judges to look for community standards? How, as a practical matter, are they to separate their own personal biases from what they perceive to be the collective biases of society? Is such a separation possible? Should judges always accede to the desires of the majority? Aren't there circumstances in which a judge may determine the majority to be wrong? In fairness it should be noted that Judge Cardozo raised many of these questions himself;[6] but it also should be noted that he admitted to having answered none of them.[7]

As might have been expected, once the older, mechanical view of the

4. Professor Summers refers to the movement as "American Pragmatic Instrumentalism." See Summers, On Identifying and Reconstructing a General Legal Theory, 69 Cornell L. Rev. 1014, 1016 (1984).

5. Cardozo, The Nature of the Judicial Process 108 (1921). To the extent that public opinion can be said to reflect today's "mores," studies may suggest that Cardozo's ideal does exist in certain instances. One found that with respect to environmental law issues, constituent preferences were a predictor of judicial decisions. Wenner and Dutter, Contextual Influences on Court Outcomes, 41 W. Pol. Q. 115 (Mar. 1988). Other research has demonstrated the tendency of the U.S. Supreme Court to mirror public opinion, and has suggested that deference to public opinion during times of crisis and constancy of decisions mirroring public opinion, contribute to that tendency. See Marshall, Public Opinion and the Supreme Court (1989). Apart from the role that public opinion actually may play, one study revealed that Wisconsin judges believed that while public opinion should be considered, it should not exert great influence over what judges do. Dreschel, Uncertain Dangers: Judges and the News Media, 70 Judicature 264 (Feb.-Mar. 1987).

6. "What is it that I do when I decide a case? To what sources of information do I appeal for guidance? In what proportions do I permit them to contribute to the result? In what proportions ought they to contribute? If a precedent is applicable, when do I refuse to follow it? If no precedent is applicable, how do I reach the rule that will make a precedent for the future? If I am seeking logical consistency, the symmetry of the legal structure, how far shall I seek it? At what point shall the quest be halted by some discrepant custom, by some consideration of the social welfare, by my own or the common standards of justice and morals?" Id. at 10.

7. Id. at 167; Cardozo, The Growth of Law 143-145 (1924).

judicial process began to give way, many legal writers and scholars were attracted to questions relating to influences upon judicial behavior. Paramount in this intellectual movement were a number of lawyers, mostly law teachers, who came to be known as "legal realists."[8] These writers sought to expose the myths of traditional jurisprudence (chief among them the myth that judges never make law) to the "cynical acid of observed reality." One of the most famous of the legal realists was Jerome Frank, who published perhaps the best-known example of the realist approach, Law and the Modern Mind, in 1930. In his book, Frank asserted that the most important influence upon a judge's decision in a close case was not the judge's perception of community standards, but the judge's own personality.[9] Other legal realists ascribed judicial decisions in close cases to the judge's intuition,[10] or to the judge's emotional preferences.[11]

Reacting to the impact of what might be described as the extreme positions taken by some of the realists on the question of external influences upon judicial behavior, Karl Llewellyn (an early and influential legal realist himself) was moved in 1960 to publish The Common Law Tradition: Deciding Appeals,[12] in which he developed what he called "major steadying factors in our appellate courts." Contrary to what he described as the popular and unhappy tendency to assume that judges are free to decide (and do decide) cases before them on personal whim,[13] Llewellyn argued that a number of factors combine to minimize the arbitrary, personal element in appellate decisionmaking. Among these factors he included:[14]

(1) Law-conditioned Officials
(2) Legal Doctrine

8. See generally Patterson, Jurisprudence: Men and Ideas of the Law 537-556 (1953); Schlegel, American Legal Realism and Empirical School Science: From the Yale Experience, 28 Buffalo L. Rev. 459 (1979). For a concise summary of the realist movement, see Segal and Spaeth, The Supreme Court and the Attitudinal Model 65 (1993).

9. Frank, Law and the Modern Mind, Ch. 12 (1930).

10. E.g., Hutcheson, The Judgment Intuitive: The Function of the "Hunch" in Judicial Decision, 14 Cornell L.Q. 274 (1929).

11. E.g., Stoljar, The Logical Status of a Legal Principle, 20 U. Chi. L. Rev. 181 (1953).

12. It should be noted that Llewellyn, The Common Law Tradition: Deciding Appeals 4 (1960), describes a crisis in confidence in the courts as his reason for writing the book:

> You cannot listen to the dirges of lawyers about the death of stare decisis (of the nature of which lovely institution the dirge-chanters have little inkling) without realizing that one great group at the bar are close to losing their faith. You cannot listen to the cynicism about the appellate courts that is stock conversation of the semi- or moderately successful lawyer in his middle years without realizing that his success transmutes into gall even as it comes to him. You cannot watch generations of law students assume, two thirds of them, as of course and despite all your effort, that if the outcome of an appeal is not foredoomed in logic it therefore is the product of uncontrolled will which is as good as wayward, without realizing that our machinery for communicating the facts of life about the work of our central and vital symbol of The Law: the appellate courts has become frighteningly deficient. (Italics omitted.)

13. For a recent discussion of legal realism, see Brigham and Harrington, Realism in the Authority of Law, 5 Social Epistemology 20 (1991).

14. Llewellyn, The Common Law Tradition: Deciding Appeals 4 (1960).

(3) Known Doctrinal Techniques
(4) Responsibility for Justice
(5) The Tradition of One Single Right Answer
(6) An Opinion of the Court
(7) A Frozen Record from Below
(8) Issues Limited, Sharpened, Phrased
(9) Adversary Argument by Counsel
(10) Group Decision
(11) Judicial Security and Honesty
(12) A Known Bench
(13) The General Period-Style and Its Promise
(14) Professional Judicial Office

Professor Llewellyn developed each of these factors individually and in combination in his book. Looking over the list, which of the factors seem relatively more important? To what extent do each of the factors apply to trial courts as well as to appellate courts?

More recently, as we have already observed,[15] two fundamentally opposed views regarding the factors that influence judges' decisionmaking have gathered supporters among lawyers and legal academics. The first, to whom we have referred as "instrumentalist/efficiency" theorists, insist that judges are guided, perhaps subconsciously, by considerations of allocative efficiency.[16] The second, to whom we have referred as "critical legal studies" theorists, assert that judges are guided, even if they consciously deny the fact, by their political preferences.[17] (To a considerable degree, critical scholars may be described as a current-day version of the realists of the 1930s.)

In forming your own reactions to the preceding material, it is important to appreciate the essentially unscientific aspects of the work to which reference has been made. For one thing, the authors described above often adopt a somewhat prescriptive, rather than strictly descriptive, approach to the subject of judicial behavior. That is, they are often arguing for what *ought* to be the pattern of behavior rather than simply describing what the pattern *is*.[18] This is most clearly obvious in Cardozo's writings. Understandably, he is more interested in how judges ought to behave than in how judges

15. See p. 28, below.

16. For assessment of this theory see Hadfield, Bias in the Evolution of Legal Rules, 80 Geo. L.J. 583 (1992); Stake, Status and Incentive Aspects of Judicial Decisions, 79 Geo. L.J. 1447 (1991); Englard, Law and Economics in American Torts Cases: A Critical Assessment of the Theory's Impact on Courts, 41 U. Toronto L.J. 359 (1991); For a symposium on this subject, see Economists on the Bench, 50 L. & Contemp. Probs. 1-286 (1987).

17. For an historical account and analysis of the Critical Legal Studies Movement, see Fischl, Some Realism About Critical Legal Studies, 41 U. Miami L. Rev. 505 (1987).

18. This same tendency to intermingle the *ought* and the *is* will be observed in the questions raised earlier in connection with Cardozo's view of the judicial process. Lawyers are notorious interminglers—see the law-fact distinction note in Chapter 1 at p. 76, above.

do behave. Moreover, even when these authors attempt to describe reality dispassionately, their descriptions tend to be anecdotal and impressionistic. Yet Frank's writings on the subject represent a conscious effort to be descriptive,[19] and the modern descriptions indeed have been based upon systematic, scientific observations.[20]

Another school of thought has developed with a perspective quite different from the preceding philosophies. Feminist jurisprudence suggests that judicial review, judicial restraint, and judicial dependence on precedent are dominated by male points of view, and thus subordinate women in society.[21] However, this philosophy has not been without its critics.[22] Although feminist jurisprudence and the preceding philosophies diverge, it has been proposed that common ground does sometimes exist among the law and economics, critical legal studies, and feminist jurisprudence schools of thought, and that informational exchange between them would be beneficial.[23]

Another important jurisprudential school of thought, one suggesting racial bias in the law and its application, is that of critical race theory.[24] Critical race theory developed as a result of efforts to dismantle societal forces that have perpetuated racism.[25] In view of society's use of law as a vehicle to expound moral judgments, critical race theorists have stated that the absence of laws prohibiting racist speech is revealing.[26] Thus, in response to this void, they have called for a new tort encompassing racial slurs, maintaining that existing causes of action are insufficient to eliminate the harms of racism.[27]

19. In characterizing the work described in the preceding paragraphs as prescriptive and impressionistic, no adverse criticism is intended. Indeed, from the traditional lawyer's perspective that is all that is required of legal philosophy. While the *ought* with which the law primarily concerns itself must never become too aloof from, or inconsistent with, the *is* in which it functions, neither must the *ought* give in to, become overly obsessed with, the *is* lest it lose its efficacy as a guide to the better life. The authors referred to above have performed a great service in awakening lawyers in a general way to the realities of judicial lawmaking, and they have helped to supply philosophies to cope with the more unsettling aspects of their vision. And yet, it would be error to believe that we may look to them with complete confidence for answers to our specific questions concerning how judges behave and why they behave that way.

20. See, e.g., Segal and Spaeth, The Supreme Court and the Attitudinal Model (1993); Henderson, Jr., Judicial Reliance on Public Policy: An Empirical Analysis of Products Liability Decisions, 59 Geo. W. L. Rev. 1570 (1991) (courts relied on public policy, as evidenced by written opinions, in 15 percent of case sample).

21. See MacKinnon, Toward a Feminist Theory of the State (1989).

22. See Letwin, Law and the Unreasonable Woman, 43 National Review 34 (Nov. 18 1991).

23. See Audain, Critical Legal Studies, Feminism, Law and Economics, and the Veil of Intellectual Tolerance: A Tentative Case for Cross-Jurisprudential Dialogue, 20 Hofstra L. Rev. 1017 (1992).

24. See Matsuda, Lawrence III, Delgado, and Crenshaw, Words that Wound: Critical Race Theory, Assaultive Speech, and the First Amendment 11, 47-48 (1993).

25. Id. at 3.

26. Id. at 49.

27. Elements of a claim for racial insult would include the following: language [that] was addressed to him or her by the defendant that was intended to demean through reference to

Prefaced by speculative inquiries in the 1920s into the possibility of systematically investigating influences upon judicial decisions,[28] scientific research began in this field in the late 1930s and 1940s, centering for the most part on the United States Supreme Court.[29] An important book in this early period was C. H. Pritchett's The Roosevelt Court: A Study in Judicial Politics and Values, published in 1948, in which the author quantitatively analyzed the data supplied by the Court's non-unanimous opinions in order to explain the voting behavior of individual justices in terms of their attitudes toward the public policy issues presented in the cases brought to the Court for decision. Pritchett's basic approach—systematically examining sequences of judicial decisions to reveal voting patterns from which the influence of judicial attitudes may be deduced—has been developed and refined,[30] and today constitutes a mainstay in the methodology of judicial behavioralism.[31] Another behaviorial approach increasingly being employed is the analysis of the social background of judges in order to support inferences regarding the values represented on the bench.[32] Efforts also have been made to correlate judges' characteristics with actual decision patterns.[33]

---

race; that the plaintiff understood as intended to demean through reference to race; and that a reasonable person would recognize as a racial insult. Id. at 109.

28. E.g., Haines, General Observations on the Effects of Personal, Political, and Economic Influences on the Decisions of Judges, 17 Ill. L. Rev. 96-116 (1922); Hall, Determination of Methods for Ascertaining the Factors that Influence Judicial Decisions in Cases Involving Due Process of Law, 20 Am. Pol. Sci. Rev. 127-134 (1926).

29. See Grossman and Tanenhaus, Frontiers of Judicial Research 9, n.11 (1969). Modern researchers have also examined the United States Supreme Court decisionmaking. See Segal and Spaeth, The Supreme Court and the Attitudinal Model (1993); Menez, Decision Making in the Supreme Court of the United States: A Political and Behavioral View (1984).

30. A leader in this development has been Glendon A. Schubert. See Quantitative Analysis of Judicial Behavior (1959), Judicial Decision-Making (1963), Judicial Behavior (1964), The Judicial Mind (1965), Comparative Judicial Behavior (1969), Dispassionate Justice (1969), The Constitutional Polity (1970); Human Jurisprudence: Public Law as a Political Science (1975); Political Culture and Judicial Behavior, Volumes One and Two (1985).

31. Goldman and Lamb, Judicial Conflict and Consensus: Behavioral Studies of American Appellate Courts (1986). One study combined analytical approaches to judicial voting behavior, including those studying political attitudes and the nature of the parties, and found the integrated model to strongly suggest that appellate court decisions reflect a complex set of factors. See Songer and Haire, Integrating Alternative Approaches to the Study of Judicial Voting, 36 Am. J. of Pol. Sci. 963 (1992). A number of writers have sought to explore the effect of judges' expectations regarding the judicial role. See, e.g., Hockett, Justices Frankfurter and Black: Social Theory and Constitutional Interpretation, 107 Pol. Sci. Q. 479 (1992); Scheb II, Bowen and Anderson, Ideology, Role Orientations, and Behavior in the State Courts of Last Resort, 19 Am. Pol. Q. 324 (July, 1991); Van Koppen and Ten Kate, Individual Differences in Judicial Behavior: Personal Characteristics and Private Law Decision-Making, 18 L. & Soc. Rev. 225 (1984).

32. See, e.g., Gibson, Judges' Role Orientations, Attitudes, and Decisions: An Interactive Model, 72 Am. Pol. Sci. Rev. 911 (Sept. 1978); Stecher, Democratic and Republican Justice: Judicial Decision-Making on Five State Supreme Courts, 13 Colum. J.L. & Soc. Prob. 137 (1977); Grossman, Social Backgrounds and Judicial Decision-making, 79 Harv. L. Rev. 1551 (1966). One study suggests that social background models are time-bound. See Ulmer, Are Social Background Models Time-Bound?, 80 Am. Pol. Sci. Rev. 957 (Sept. 1986). See also, Idleman, The Role of Religious Values in Judicial Decision Making, 68 Ind. L.J. 433 (1993).

33. See e.g., Hall and Brace, Toward an Integrated Model of Judicial Voting Behavior, 20 Am. Pol. Q. 147 (1992); Spohn, Decision Making in Sexual Assault Cases: Do Black and Female Judges Make a Difference?, 2 Women & Crim. Jus. 83 (1990) (finding no racial

These studies tend to support the assertions of the legal realists that even conscientious judges are influenced in their decisions by extralegal factors having little to do directly with the rules of law which they purport to apply.[34] For example, Stuart Nagel has demonstrated in a national study of appellate court judges that Democratic judges are more likely than their Republican colleagues to favor defendants in criminal cases, administrative agencies in business regulation cases, and employees in employee injury cases.[35] It should be observed that conclusions of this sort are purely statistical in nature.[36] Nagel is not telling us how or why, or even whether, a judge's political affiliation affects his or her decisions.[37] Rather, he is telling us that there is a statistical correlation between party affiliation and judicial reaction to various types of legal issues—that out of a large number of judges selected at random, a larger percentage of Democratic judges than Republican judges will react favorably[38] to criminal defendants, administrative agencies, and employees.[39]

---

differences in sentencing patterns; finding that female judges imposed lengthier sentences than their male counterparts, and suggesting that socialization plays an influential role in judicial decisionmaking); Nagel, The Legal Process From a Behavioral Perspective (1969); Nagel, Judicial Backgrounds and Criminal Cases, 53 Crim. L., Criminology & Police Sci. 333 (1962).

34. One study has found legal factors to substantially affect pretrial release decisions, with extra-legal factors, such as judicial bias, also having some influence. See Ilene H. Nagel, The Legal/Extra-Legal Controversy: Judicial Decisions in Pretrial Release, 17 Law & Soc. Rev. 481 (1983). For an analysis of the influence of precedent from other jurisdictions on judicial decisions see Caldeira, The Transmission of Legal Precedent: A Study of State Supreme Courts, 79 Am. Pol. Sci. Rev. 178 (1985).

35. See Nagel, Political Party Affiliation and Judges' Decisions, 55 Am. Pol. Sci. Rev. 843 (1961). Cf. the observations regarding behavior patterns of jurors, p. 247, below. Another study indicated that while legal norms are the main determinant of judicial actions, political factors often influence the exercise of judicial discretion. See Kritzer, Political Correlates of the Behavior of Federal District Judges: A "Best Case" Analysis, 40 J. Pol. 25 (Feb. 1978).

36. Research has also shown that presidential influence stemming from the appointment process evidences itself by increased tendencies of judges appointed by Democratic presidents to be more liberal than those appointed by Republicans. See Stidham, Carp and Rowland, Patterns of Presidential Influence on the Federal District Courts: An Analysis of the Appointment Process, 14 Presidential Stud. Q. 548 (Fall 1984). With respect to labor and economic relations, another study found that Reagan appointees evidenced decisionmaking similar to previous Republican presidents' appointees, and that Carter appointees evidenced decisionmaking similar to previous Democratic presidents' appointees. See Stidham and Carp, Support for Labor and Economic Regulation Among Reagan and Carter Appointees to the Federal Courts, 26 Soc. Sci. J. 433 (Oct. 1989). As to the response to this pattern, see Schwartz, Unpacking the Supreme Court: What Clinton Could Do, Nation, Oct. 19, 1992, at 434; Moore, Righting the Courts, 24 National Journal 200 (1992); Davis, President Carter's Selection Reforms and Judicial Policymaking: A Voting Analysis of the United States Courts of Appeals, 14 Am. Pol. Q. 328 (1986). For an analysis of the constitutional issues arising from partisan appointments, see Solimine, Constitutional Restrictions on the Partisan Appointment of Federal and State Judges, 61 U. Cin. L. Rev. 955 (1993).

37. For an analysis of political factors that may influence the judiciary, see Yarnold, Politics and the Courts: Toward a General Theory of Public Law 7 (1992).

38. Much of the methodological difficulty in these studies is encountered in trying to establish criteria for determining when a judge may be said to have "reacted favorably" on a particular issue. See Becker, Comparative Judicial Politics 27-34 (1970).

39. In contrast, another study focussing on federal district court judges and civil liberties litigation found no significant relationship between a judge's partisanship and decisional outcomes. See Walker, A Note Concerning Partisan Influence on Trial-Judge Decision Making,

A friendly critic of judicial behavior studies concluded:

> Although such studies reveal some of the correlates of judicial decision, they do not provide us with satisfactory guidance for the next major steps in judicial research. For one thing, while they explain some of the variance in judicial decision, they are unlikely to predict such decisions completely. Anecdotally, we know of enough major changes in orientation by judges once on the bench to be doubtful that background analyses will carry us very far. The influences that operate toward uniformity, so suggestively described by Karl Llewellyn in The Common Law Tradition, probably constitute a powerful counterweight to variations based on background.
>
> More serious, judicial behavior studies have not—for the most part—asked questions concerning judicial behavior that would be most relevant for understanding the functioning of law in society. The kinds of questions I have in mind were those posed by Cardozo more than forty years ago in his Nature of the Judicial Process. It is striking to me that the studies [to date] have told us little about the likelihood that judges in given circumstances will decide a case by the method of precedent, logical construction, custom, or functional considerations.[40]

Aside from the influence of a particular judge's characteristics,[41] such as social background or political partisanship, other factors may be at play. For example, some studies have focused upon factors inherent in the legal system's structure or process that may influence judicial decisionmaking. Studies of this type have included assessments of contemporary commitment practices,[42] the courtroom work group,[43] and presentence recommendations.[44] These studies have indicated that these factors do influence judicial decisionmaking.[45] In addition to process or structural factors, a defendant's traits and characteristics may also exert an influence on decisionmaking.

---

6 Law & Soc. Rev. 645 (1972).

40. Schwartz, A Proposed Focus for Research on Judicial Behavior, appearing in Grossman and Tanenhaus, Frontiers of Judicial Research 490 (1969).

41. Social scientists have also employed psychoanalytical theories in attempting to generalize about how personality affects the decisionmaking process. See Segal and Spaeth, The Supreme Court and the Attitudinal Model 67 (1993); Gibson, Personality and Elite Political Behavior: The Influence of Self-Esteem on Judicial Decision Making, 43 J. Pol. 104 (Feb. 1981); Schubert, The Judicial Mind Revisited (1974).

42. See Holstein, Mental Illness Assumptions in Civil Commitment Proceedings, 16 J. Contemp. Ethnography 147 (July 1987).

43. See Croyle, Measuring and Explaining Disparities in Felony Sentences: Courtroom Work Group Factors and Race, Sex and Socioeconomic Influences on Sentence Severity, 5 Pol. Behav. 135 (1983). See also Hasenfeld and Cheung, The Juvenile Court as a People-Processing Organization: A Political Economy Perspective, 90 Am. J. Sociology 801 (1985).

44. See Bankston, Legal and Extralegal Offender Traits and Decision Making in the Criminal Justice System, 3 Soc. Spectrum 1 (1983).

45. As to the judiciary's structure itself, one study suggests that within the three-judge district court structure, the judge with the highest status was most influential. See Walker, Behavioral Tendencies in the Three-Judge District Court, 17 Am. J. of Pol. Sci. 407 (1973).

Studies have shown that race,[46] gender,[47] and class position[48] may influence judicial decisions.

Given the continued interest among behavioral and social scientists in the judicial process, and the development of additional methodological frameworks from which to analyze judicial behavior,[49] further studies are likely. The importance of a clearer understanding of judicial behavior is readily appreciated. Besides knowledge for its own sake, such an understanding would enable lawyers to be more effective in their arguments before courts,[50] and would provide a rational basis upon which to review and possibly revise our traditional positions on such important matters as the selection of judges, the composition of courts, and the division of functions between judge and jury.

B. *The General Standard*

The general standard applicable in most negligence cases is one of reasonable care under the circumstances. Echoing Chief Justice Shaw's opinion in Brown v. Kendall, above, §283 of the Restatement (Second) of Torts states that "the standard of conduct to which [one] must conform to avoid being negligent is that of a reasonable man under like circumstances." Personifying the standard by the use of a hypothetical reasonable person serves at least

46. See Unnever, Direct and Organizational Discrimination in the Sentencing of Drug Offenders, 30 Soc. Prob. 212 (Dec. 1982); Gibson, Race as a Determinant of Criminal Sentences: A Methodological Critique and a Case Study, 12 Law & Soc. Rev. 455 (Spring 1978) (finding an individual, as opposed to institutional, correlation between judicial background and attitude, and racial discrimination). But see Klein, Petersilia and Turner, Race and Imprisonment Decisions in California, 247 Sci. 812 (Feb. 16, 1990) (finding California courts' sentencing decisions racially equitable).

47. See Bickle and Peterson, The Impact of Gender-Based Family Roles on Criminal Sentencing, 38 Soc. Prob. 372 (August 1991) (including a literature review of past studies finding a correlation between marital status and gender and decisionmaking, and finding that familial criteria influence the sentencing of federal forgers).

48. See Unnever, Direct and Organizational Discrimination in the Sentencing of Drug Offenders, 30 Soc. Prob. 212 (Dec. 1982). In contrast, another study found class position correlated to job loss, but not to incarceration. See Benson, The Influence of Class Position on the Formal and Informal Sanctioning of White-Collar Offenders. 30 Soc. Q. 465 (Fall, 1989).

49. See, e.g., Segal and Spaeth, The Supreme Court and the Attitudinal Model (1993). For Segal and Spaeth's response to attitudinal model critics, see id. at 356. See also Hall and Brace, Order in the Courts: A Neo-Industrial Approach to Judicial Consensus, 42 W. Pol. Q. 391 (Sept. 1989).

50. Llewellyn, The Common Law Tradition: Deciding Appeals 236-255. Moreover, oral argument is sometimes a significant influencing factor in a judge's decision. See Bright, Getting There: Do Philosophy and Oral Argument Influence Decisions? 77 A.B.A. J. 66 (Mar. 1991). See also Menez, Decision Making in the Supreme Court of the United States 99 (1984). However, Segal and Spaeth have maintained that systematic analysis of the influence of oral argument has only begun. See Segal and Spaeth, The Supreme Court and the Attitudinal Model 208-209, n.3 (1993).

two important purposes. For one thing, it makes the standard more comprehensible to the nonexperts who make up the juries to whom the task of determining the defendant's negligence is often given. A description of the standard of care in terms of a flesh and blood image is more apt to be understood by persons of average experience and nonlegal background than some more precise but more abstract and legalistic description. It also serves to impress upon the jury that the standard can be met by something less than superhuman efforts. And second, putting the standard in the form of the reasonable person suggests the objective nature of the standard. In evaluating the defendant's conduct, the jury does not look to what might have been expected of this particular defendant—it is not enough that the defendant "did the best I could." Instead, the defendant is to be judged by what is to be expected of the reasonable person.

The basic objectivity of the standard appears to have been established very early in the development of the negligence concept in England. In Vaughn v. Menlove, 3 Bing. (N.C.) 468, 132 Eng. Rep. 490 (1837), the plaintiff obtained a verdict against the defendant who stacked hay so as to cause it to burn spontaneously and destroy the plaintiff's nearby property. On appeal to the Court of Common Pleas, the defendant argued that the trial judge had erred in instructing the jury to apply the reasonably prudent person standard and in denying the defendant's request that the jury should determine "whether he had acted bona fide to the best of his judgment." Affirming the verdict for plaintiff, Chief Justice Tindal explained (3 Bing. (N.C.) at 475, 132 Eng. Rep. at 493):

> [The subjective standard urged by the defendant] would leave so vague a line as to afford no rule at all, the degree of judgment belonging to each individual being infinitely various. . . . Instead, therefore, of saying that the liability for negligence should be co-extensive with the judgment of each individual, which would be as variable as the length of the foot of each individual, we ought rather to adhere to the rule which requires in all cases a regard to caution such as a man of ordinary prudence would observe.

The court in *Vaughn* was obviously concerned with the variability inherent in a subjective standard. But why? The court suggests that the standard offered by the defendant was too vague. But was the court right on that score? At least with respect to individual actors, the standard proposed by the defendant and rejected by the court may be less vague than the objective standard. The proposed standard tells defendants, in essence, to "do your best," a fairly straightforward command. The objective standard adopted by the court, in contrast, offers only the general instruction to "be reasonable." If vagueness is not really the central concern of the court in *Vaughn,* what is?

In any event, as discussed in an earlier note on mental state considerations, p. 79, the adoption of an objective standard against which an actor's conduct is assessed raises the possibility that some individuals, by virtue of their unique characteristics, will not be able to meet the standard. The challenge for tort law, in this regard, is to determine when, if ever, the objective reasonable person standard should be modified to account for such characteristics. The general approach of courts is reflected in §283B of the Restatement (Second) of Torts, which follows *Vaughn* and refuses to consider mental deficiencies of actors in assessing conduct. The only exception in the Restatement to this general rule appears in §283A, in which children are to be judged according to what might be expected of children of similar age and experience. Thus, in a case involving a ten-year-old defendant, the allegedly negligent conduct is not to be measured against the standard of what a reasonably prudent adult would have done, but rather is to be measured against the standard of a reasonably prudent child of similar age and maturity.

In contrast to the objectivity of their approach to the question of the mental capacity of defendants in negligence cases, the courts have adopted a more subjective, individualized approach to the question of defendants' physical disabilities. Section 283C of the Restatement requires that the individual defendant's physical disabilities be taken into consideration in judging whether the conduct has been negligent. Thus, if the defendant was blind at the time of the allegedly negligent conduct, the jury is to measure his conduct against that of a reasonably prudent blind person under similar circumstances. (Are you able to articulate a rationale with which to explain the willingness of courts to take physical, but not mental, incapacities into account in negligence cases?)

Thus far we have been considering essentially empirical characteristics such as mental competence and physical disability. In the final analysis, the judgment that someone has been negligent is a value judgment—the pivotal concept of reasonableness is normative as well as empirical. Thus, even if we determine with precision which of the various empirical characteristics of mind and body to attribute to the hypothetical reasonable person, the negligence standard will remain vague and indeterminate as long as it relies upon the general reasonableness concept. One judge's attempt to render the value judgment under the negligence standard more precise and manageable follows:

United States v. Carroll Towing Co.

159 F.2d 169 (2d Cir. 1947)

[The incident out of which this admiralty case arose was the sinking of a barge, along with its cargo, allegedly because of the defendant's negligence. A crucial issue in the case involved whether the person in charge of the barge, the bargee, was negligent in being ashore, away from the barge, during the period when the barge got into difficulties and sank. If the bargee's absence was negligence, and if it contributed substantially to the loss of the barge, then the bargee's employer, the owner of the barge, would not receive full recovery from the other parties whose negligence put the barge into difficulties in the first place.]

L. HAND, J. . . .

It appears . . . that there is no general rule to determine when the absence of a bargee or other attendant will make the owner of the barge liable for injuries to other vessels if she breaks away from her moorings. However, in any cases where he would be so liable for injuries to others, obviously he must reduce his damages proportionately, if the injury is to his own barge. It becomes apparent why there can be no such general rule, when we consider the grounds for such a liability. Since there are occasions when every vessel will break from her moorings, and since, if she does, she becomes a menace to those about her; the owner's duty, as in other similar situations, to provide against resulting injuries is a function of three variables: (1) The probability that she will break away; (2) the gravity of the resulting injury, if she does; (3) the burden of adequate precautions. Possibly it serves to bring this notion into relief to state it in algebraic terms: if the probability be called P; the injury L; and the burden, B; liability depends upon whether B is less than L multiplied by P: i.e., whether $B < PL$. Applied to the situation at bar, the likelihood that a barge will break from her fasts and the damage she will do, vary with the place and time; for example, if a storm threatens, the danger is greater; so it is, if she is in a crowded harbor where moored barges are constantly being shifted about. On the other hand, the barge must not be the bargee's prison, even though he lives aboard; he must go ashore at times. We need not say whether, even in such crowded waters as New York Harbor a bargee must be aboard at night at all; it may be that the custom is otherwise . . . and that, if so, the situation is one where custom should control. We leave that question open; but we hold that it is not in all cases a sufficient answer to a bargee's absence without excuse, during working hours, that he has properly made fast his barge to a pier, when he leaves her. In the case at bar the bargee left at five o'clock in the afternoon of January 3rd, and the flotilla broke away at about two o'clock in the afternoon of the following day, twenty-one hours afterwards. The bargee had been away all the time, and we hold that his fabricated story was affirmative evidence that he had no excuse for his absence. At the locus in quo—especially during the short January days and in the full tide of war activity—barges were being constantly "drilled" in and out. Certainly it was not beyond reasonable expectation that, with the inevitable haste and bustle, the work might not be done with adequate care. In such circumstances we hold—and it is all that we do hold—that it was a fair requirement that [the owner of the barge], should have a bargee aboard (unless he had some excuse for his absence), during the working hours of daylight.

The balancing of costs and benefits suggested by Learned Hand in *Carroll Towing* has come to be recognized as the core question in determining whether an actor has been negligent. The Restatement (Second) of Torts states the general rule thus:

> §291. UNREASONABLENESS: HOW DETERMINED: MAGNITUDE OF RISK AND UTILITY OF CONDUCT
>
> Where an act is one which a reasonable man would recognize as involving a risk of harm to another, the risk is unreasonable and the act is negligent if the risk is of such magnitude as to outweigh what the law regards as the utility of the act or of the particular manner in which it is done.

The ultimate question in a negligence case, therefore, is not simply whether a reasonable person would have recognized the risk, but whether recognizing the risk, that person would have acted differently. Even reasonable persons engage in risk-creating conduct in some situations. Every car trip, for example, creates some foreseeable risk of harm. It is only when such risk-taking is unreasonable that the defendant's conduct is negligent. The essence of the bargee's argument in *Carroll Towing* was that even if a reasonable person in the bargee's position might have recognized certain risks in leaving the barge unattended, such a person would nevertheless willingly and reasonably have incurred those risks in the interest of maintaining some freedom of movement.

It is in deciding what the reasonably prudent person would have done that the ultimate value judgment must be made. Thus, when Judge Hand decided that the bargee in the *Carroll Towing* case had taken an unreasonable amount of freedom, he made a value judgment that on these facts the social interest in security of the barge outweighed the social interest in freedom of the bargee. The critical question analytically, therefore, is this: What are the values to be ascribed to the reasonable person in order to judge the reasonableness of the defendant's conduct? The Restatement (Second) of Torts suggests the following formulation:

> §292. FACTORS CONSIDERED IN DETERMINING UTILITY OF ACTOR'S CONDUCT
>
> In determining what the law regards as the utility of the actor's conduct for the purpose of determining whether the actor is negligent, the following factors are important:
>
> (a) The social value which the law attaches to the interest which is to be advanced or protected by the conduct;
>
> (b) The extent of the chance that this interest will be advanced or protected by the particular course of conduct;
>
> (c) The extent of the chance that such interest can be adequately advanced or protected by another and less dangerous course of conduct.

> §293. FACTORS CONSIDERED IN DETERMINING MAGNITUDE OF RISK
>
> In determining the magnitude of the risk for the purpose of determining whether the actor is negligent, the following factors are important:
>
> (a) The social value which the law attaches to the interests which are imperiled;

(b) the extent of the chance that the actor's conduct will cause an invasion of any interest of the other or of one of a class of which the other is a member;

(c) the extent of the harm likely to be caused to the interests imperiled;

(d) the number of persons whose interests are likely to be invaded if the risk takes effect in harm.

Although the balancing process identified by Hand often lurks beneath the language of courts in negligence cases, sometimes the test is used quite explicitly. For example, in Davis v. Consolidated Rail Corp., 788 F.2d 1260 (7th Cir. 1986), the plaintiff railroad car inspector had climbed under a stationary train in order to inspect certain cars leased to the defendant railroad by his employer without setting up the customary blue flags to indicate that the train should not be moved. (He had earlier seen the locomotive decouple and move away.) Unbeknownst to him, a different crew, with orders to move the train, attached another locomotive at the other end. The crew moved the train without blowing the horn or ringing the bell. The plaintiff tried to scramble from under the train when it began to move but was not entirely successful. He lost one leg below the knee and most of his other foot. At trial, the plaintiff urged that the defendant's train crew should have blown the train's horn and rung its bell before moving or that a member of the defendant's crew should have walked the train's entire length and looked under each car. The jury returned a verdict for the plaintiff and defendant appealed.

The court of appeals, in an opinion by Judge Posner, held that requiring the inspection by defendant of the entire train was too burdensome, given the low probability of someone's being under the train and the high cost of the precaution. The court held, however, that the crew should have blown the train's horn and rung its bell, because in that case the B was relatively small and the PL significant, given the range of accidents such a precaution might prevent. "In determining the benefits of a precaution—and PL, the expected accident costs that the precaution would avert, is a measure of the benefits of the precaution—the trier of fact must consider not only the expected cost of this accident, but also the expected costs of any other, similar accidents that the precaution would have prevented." Id. at 1264.

In most cases, however, the court's assessment of the reasonableness of an actor's conduct occurs on a less formal level. Indeed, it is worth noting that in *Carroll Towing* itself, Judge Hand's announcement of his "B/PL" test, was followed by a much more intuitive analysis of the reasonableness of the defendant's conduct. Judge Hand himself later expressed doubt over the wisdom of trying to reduce the negligence concept to precise mathematical formulas. See Moisan v. Loftus, 178 F.2d 148 (2d Cir. 1949). But the basic idea that Hand tried to capture with his "B/PL" formulation has come to be recognized as an appropriate way of expressing the basis for liability for negligence. Although some judges prefer to express the negligence test in the more humanistic terms of "what a reasonable person would have done," even that formulation is consistent with the notion that reasonable persons weigh the costs of activities against their benefits in deciding upon courses of action.

Notwithstanding the foregoing caveats about the possible risks of taking the "B < PL" calculus too seriously, it is important that the student appreciate the underlying concept. Toward that end, consider the following problem:

Problem 12

Assume that a rational actor, *A,* is in a position to reduce the incidence of harm caused by his activity by investing in care. Assume that if *A* makes no effort to be careful, his activity will cause ten accidents per 100 units of activity, at a constant expected cost of $1,000 per accident. Assume further that *A*'s investments in care reduce accidents according to Table 4-1. If the only costs associated with the activity are those included in Table 4-1, how far will *A,* aware of the data in the table, invest in care under a negligence rule perfectly and costlessly applied? See if you can answer this question using the data provided; then fill in columns (6) and (7) either to help reach the answer or to confirm its validity.

The Law-Fact Distinction: The Negligence Issue

Despite Judge Hand's efforts in the *Carroll Towing* case to translate the test into algebraic symbols, the standard against which the conduct of the defendant is to be judged remains a very general standard, and the judgment about that conduct is the judgment of humans, not that of computers. Therefore, as important as the foregoing rules are to an understanding of the negligence concept, it is even more important to appreciate the process by which these rules are applied in concrete cases. Central to such an appreciation is an understanding of the roles played by the judge and the jury in negligence cases that actually are resolved by adjudication. Briefly stated, the determination of the applicable general standard of care is one of law for the judge, and the determination of whether the defendant failed to meet that standard—that is, whether the defendant was negligent—is a question of fact for the jury. If the judge concludes that reasonable minds could not differ regarding the question of the reasonableness of the defendant's conduct, the judge will, upon a proper motion, take the negligence issue from the jury by directing a verdict on that issue for one side or the other. If the evidence warrants submission of the negligence issue to the jury, the judge will communicate the standard to the jury in the instructions at the end of the trial, and the jury will determine, on the basis of the

TABLE 4-1

	(1)	(2)	(3)	(4)	(5)	(6)	(7)
Incremental Reduction in Activity-caused Accidents (per 100 units activity)	*Incremental (marginal) Accident Cost Reduction (per unit of care)*	*Total Accident Cost Reduction (cumulative)*	*Total Remaining (residual) Accident Costs (per 100 units activity)*	*Incremental (marginal) Costs of Care (per unit care)*	*Total Costs of Care (cumulative)*	*Total Social Costs of Care and Accidents (cumulative)*	*Total Actor's Costs of Care and Liability Under Negligence (cumulative)*
10 → 9	1,000	1,000	9,000	100	100		
9 → 8	1,000	2,000	8,000	300	400		
8 → 7	1,000	3,000	7,000	700	1,100		
7 → 6	1,000	4,000	6,000	1,200	2,300		
6 → 5	1,000	5,000	5,000	1,900	4,200		
5 → 4	1,000	6,000	4,000	2,800	7,000		
4 → 3	1,000	7,000	3,000	5,400	12,400		
3 → 2	1,000	8,000	2,000	11,000	23,400		

evidence, whether the defendant's conduct measured up to that standard. Because in most cases the standard to be applied is very general, the judge's task in connection with the negligence issue is relatively simple. The large majority of negligence cases brought to trial are sent to the jury, on instructions that give the jury great latitude in its determination of the negligence issue. Actually, it is only a slight exaggeration to assert that negligence in most cases is whatever the jury says it is.

It warrants repeating here that this division of function between judge and jury is in no way dictated by the meaning inherent in the terms *law* and *fact.* The reasonableness concept on which the law of negligence is predicated is, strictly speaking, neither law nor fact but a conclusion calling for the application of the former to the latter.[51] The negligence issue is labeled *fact* because it is believed to be appropriate for the jury to play an important role in applying law to fact in these cases. If it were generally felt that judges should participate more directly in deciding the negligence issue, such an adjustment could be accomplished by simply changing the label.[52] In fact, Justice Holmes once attempted to move the developing law of negligence in this direction. In his famous lectures on the common law, Holmes argued that over time, judges would increasingly replace jurors in resolving the negligence issue:

> If, now, the ordinary liabilities in tort arise from failure to comply with fixed and uniform standards of external conduct, which every man is presumed and required to know, it is obvious that it ought to be possible, sooner or later, to formulate these standards at least to some extent, and that to do so must at last be the business of the court. It is equally clear that the featureless generality that the defendant was bound to use such care as a prudent man would do under the circumstances, ought to be continually giving place to the specific one, that he was bound to use this or that precaution under these or those circumstances. The standard which the defendant was bound to come up to was a standard of specific acts or omissions, with reference to the specific circumstances in which he found himself. If in the whole department of unintentional wrongs the courts arrived at no further utterance than the question of negligence, and left every case, without rudder or compass, to the jury, they would simply confess their inability to state a very large part of the law which they required the defendant to know, and would assert, by implication, that nothing could be learned by experience. But neither courts nor legislatures have ever stopped at that point.

51. See the law-fact distinction note, p. 76, above.

52. Were courts to label the negligence issue as one of law, and thus to begin to decide that issue themselves, much of the reason-for-being of juries in negligence cases would be eliminated. Were juries retained in such cases, some special verdict procedure would have to be developed as a means of allowing juries to continue to decide preliminary issues of historical fact. See the note on verdicts and instructions, p. 245, below. As a middle ground short of deciding the negligence issue in every case, courts could simply begin to define the standard of care with much greater specificity in these subject matter areas in which greater judicial supervision and control was deemed necessary.

> . . . A judge who has long sat at nisi prius ought gradually to acquire a fund of experience which enables him to represent the common sense of the community in ordinary instances far better than an average jury. He should be able to lead and to instruct them in detail, even where he thinks it desirable, on the whole, to take their opinion. Furthermore, the sphere in which he is able to rule without taking their opinion at all should be continually growing.

Holmes, The Common Law 111-112, 124 (1881). Patience paid off when, 46 years later, Holmes had an opportunity to turn theory into practice. In Baltimore and Ohio R.R. v. Goodman, 275 U.S. 66, 70 S. Ct. 24, 72 L. Ed. 167 (1927), then Justice Holmes led a unanimous Supreme Court to declare as a matter of law the precise conduct required of a driver crossing a railroad track. Holmes wrote (275 U.S. at 69-70):

> . . . When a man goes upon a railroad track he knows that he goes to a place where he will be killed if a train comes upon him before he is clear of the track. He knows that he must stop for the train, not the train stop for him. In such circumstances it seems to us that if a driver cannot be sure otherwise whether a train is dangerously near he must stop and get out of his vehicle, although obviously he will not often be required to do more than to stop and look. It seems to us that if he relies upon not hearing the train or any signal and takes no further precaution he does so at his own risk. If at the last moment [the plaintiff] found himself in an emergency it was his own fault that he did not reduce his speed earlier or come to a stop. It is true . . . that the question of due care very generally is left to the jury. But we are dealing with a standard of conduct, and when the standard is clear it should be laid down once and for all by the Courts.

Seven years later, after Holmes had retired, the Court abandoned the effort to judicially codify the negligence standard. In Pokora v. Wabash Ry., 292 U.S. 98, 54 S. Ct. 580, 78 L. Ed. 1149 (1934), Justice Cardozo buried the "stop, look and listen" rule announced by Holmes (292 U.S. at 104-106):

> Standards of prudent conduct are declared at times by courts, but they are taken over from the facts of life. To get out of a vehicle and reconnoitre is an uncommon precaution, as everyday experience informs us. Besides being uncommon, it is very likely to be futile, and sometimes even dangerous. If the driver leaves his vehicle when he nears a cut or curve, he will learn nothing by getting out about the perils that lurk beyond. By the time he regains his seat and sets his car in motion, the hidden train may be upon him. . . . A train traveling at a speed of thirty miles an hour will cover a quarter of a mile in the space of thirty seconds. It may thus emerge out of obscurity as the driver turns his back to regain the waiting car, and may then descend upon him suddenly when his car is on the track. Instead of helping himself by getting out, he might do better to press forward with all his faculties alert. So a train at a neighboring station, apparently at rest and harmless, may

be transformed in a few seconds into an instrument of destruction. At times the course of safety may be different. One can figure to oneself a roadbed so level and unbroken that getting out will be a gain. Even then the balance of advantage depends on many circumstances and can be easily disturbed. Where was [the plaintiff] to leave his truck after getting out to reconnoitre? If he was to leave it on the switch, there was the possibility that the box cars would be shunted down upon him before he could regain his seat. . . . If he was to leave his vehicle near the curb, there was even stronger reason to believe that the space to be covered in going back and forth would make his observations worthless. One must remember that while the traveler turns his eye in one direction, a train or a loose engine may be approaching from the other.

Illustrations such as these bear witness to the need for caution in framing standards of behavior that amount to rules of law. The need is the more urgent when there is no background of experience out of which the standards have emerged. They are, then, not the natural flowerings of behavior in its customary forms, but rules artificially developed, and imposed from without. Extraordinary situations may not wisely or fairly be subjected to tests or regulations that are fitting for the common-place or normal. In default of the guide of customary conduct, what is suitable for the traveler caught in a mesh where the ordinary safeguards fail him is for the judgment of a jury. The opinion in Goodman's case has been a source of confusion in the federal courts to the extent that it imposes a standard for application by the judge, and has had only wavering support in the courts of the states. We limit it accordingly.

Following Cardozo's logic, courts today seldom decide the negligence issue as a matter of law in cases tried before juries.

Washington v. Louisiana Power and Light Co.

555 So. 2d 1350 (La. 1990)

DENNIS, JUSTICE.

We granted certiorari in this power line accident case to review the Court of Appeal's judgment setting aside a jury award to the adult children of a man who was electrocuted when he accidentally allowed a citizens band radio antenna to come into contact with an uninsulated 8,000 volt electrical wire that spanned the backyard of his residence. We affirm. The jury verdict for the plaintiffs was manifestly erroneous. . . .

[The decedent was electrocuted when the antenna from his CB radio came into contact with the defendant's uninsulated 8,000 volt transmission line, which was about 21½ feet above the ground. Five years before the contact with the line that killed the decedent, the antenna came into contact with the line while the decedent was moving it, causing the decedent and his son, who was helping him move the antenna, to suffer burns on the hand. Several times after the earlier incident, the decedent requested the defendant to insulate the line, or move it underground. The defendant said that it would do so only at the decedent's expense.]

After a trial on the merits, a jury found LP & L at fault in the accident and awarded plaintiffs $500,000 for pain and suffering and the loss of life of the decedent and $75,000 for each plaintiff's loss of love, affection, and support. LP & L appealed suspensively. The Court of Appeal, noting that the decedent had five years earlier received an electrical shock when he touched the antenna to the same line, and had since that time been extremely careful to never move the antenna alone or toward the line until the day of the fatal accident, reversed, concluding that LP & L did not breach any duty owed to the decedent. . . .

When the evidence is clear, as in the present case, that the power company either knew or should have known of the possibility of an accident that materialized in the decedent's electrocution, the remaining negligence issue is whether the possibility of such injury or loss constituted an unreasonable risk of harm. Such a case invites "a sharp focus upon the essential balancing process that lies at the heart of negligence." Malone, Work of Appellate Courts, 29 La. L. Rev. 212, 212 (1969). In this regard, we recently held that the power company's duty to provide against resulting injuries, as in similar situations, is a function of three variables: (1) the possibility that the electricity will escape; (2) the gravity of the resulting injury, if it does; (3) the burden of taking adequate precautions that would avert the accident. When the product of the possibility of escape multiplied times the gravity of the harm, if it happens, exceeds the burden of precautions, the risk is unreasonable and the failure to take those precautions is negligence. [The court referred to other cases, including United States v. Carroll Towing Co., 159 F.2d 169, 173 (2nd Cir. 1947).]

Applying the negligence balancing process, we conclude that although there was a cognizable risk that the antenna stationed in the corner of Mr. Washington's backyard could be lowered and moved to within a dangerous proximity of the power line, that possibility could not be characterized as an unreasonable risk and the power company's failure to take additional precautions against it was not negligence.

Under the circumstances, there was not a significant possibility before the accident that Mr. Washington or anyone acting for him would detach the antenna and attempt to carry it under or dangerously near the power line. Standing alone, Mr. Washington's 1980 accident might have caused an objective observer to increase his estimate of the chances that this particular antenna might be handled carelessly. The other surrounding circumstances, however, overwhelmingly erase any pre-accident enlargement of the risk at that site. Except for the single occasion of the 1980 accident, the antenna was stationed safely in the corner of the backyard for many years, one to three years before the 1980 mishap and five years afterwards. Most of that time it was maintained safely in the pipe receptacle which, by Mr. Washington's design, allowed it to be lowered only in a safe direction.

Between his close call in 1980 and his fatal accident in 1985, Mr. Washington had never been known to handle the antenna carelessly. Indeed, after he and his son narrowly escaped death or serious injury in 1980, his remarks to friends and relatives indicated that the experience had convinced him to keep the antenna far away from the power line. That he continued to be aware of the danger and take exemplary precautions to avoid it until his fatal accident was further illustrated by the care that he and his friend took when they lowered and laid it next to the fence several days before the accident.

The likelihood that the antenna in this case would be brought into contact with the power line was not as great as the chances of an electrical accident in situations creating significant potential for injuries to victims who may contact or come into dangerous proximity with the powerline due to their unawareness of or inadvertence to the charged wire.

Prior to the accident, the anticipated gravity of the loss if the risk were to take effect was, of course, of a very high degree. The deaths and serious injuries in this and other electrical accidents verify that the weight of the loss threatened by a power line accident is not trivial. While some accidents, such as Mr. Washington's 1980 mishap, do not lead to dire consequences, a consideration of all losses resulting from this type of risk indicates that the gravity of the loss if it occurs is usually extreme.

Yet when this high degree of gravity of loss is multiplied by the very small possibility of the accident occurring in this case, we think it is clear that the product does not outweigh the burdens or costs of the precautions of relocating or insulating the power line. This does not mean, of course, that it would not have been worth what it would have cost to place the line underground or to insulate it in order to save the decedent's life if it had been known that the accident would happen or even if the chance of it occurring had been greater. Nor does it mean, on the other hand, that we stop with a consideration of only the burden of an effective precaution in this single case. Common knowledge indicates that within any power company's territory there probably are a great number of situations involving antennas that have been safely installed, but which conceivably could be detached and carelessly moved about dangerously near a power line. In fairness, in this case, in which the coexistence of the power line and the safely installed antenna was no riskier than countless other similar coexistences not considered to involve negligence, the burden to the company of taking precautions against all such slight possibilities of harm should be balanced against the total magnitude of all these risks, including the relatively few losses resulting from the total of all those insignificant risks. Just as single case applications of the Hand formula can understate the benefits of accident prevention by overlooking all other accidents that could be avoided by the same safety expenditures, the burdens of taking precautions in all similar cases may be depreciated by single case consideration here.

The foregoing, of course, is merely a shorthand expression of the mental processes involved in such considerations. We cannot mathematically or mechanically quantify, multiply, or weigh risks, losses, and burdens of precautions. As many scholars have noted, the formula is primarily helpful in keeping in mind the relationship of the factors involved and in centering attention upon which of them may be determinative in any given situation. Nevertheless, the formula would seem to be of greater assistance in cases of the present type, in which the power company's ability to perceive risks is superior and its duty is utmost, than other notions, such as "reasonable man," "duty," or "foreseeability," for example, which must be little more than labels to be applied after some sort of balancing or weighing that the formula attempts to describe. In the present case, the balancing process focuses our attention on the fact that the possibility of an accident appeared to be slight beforehand and on the reality that precautions against such slight risks would be costly and burdensome because they exist in great number and have not usually been considered unreasonable or intolerable.

For the reasons assigned, the judgment of the court of appeals is affirmed.

Weirum v. RKO General, Inc.

15 Cal. 3d 40, 539 P.2d 36, 123 Cal. Rptr. 468 (1975)

MOSK, J. A rock radio station with an extensive teenage audience conducted a contest which rewarded the first contestant to locate a peripatetic disc jockey. Two minors driving in separate automobiles attempted to follow the disc jockey's automobile to its next stop. In the course of their pursuit, one of the minors negligently forced a car off the highway, killing its sole occupant. In a suit filed by the surviving wife and children of the decedent, the jury rendered a verdict against the radio station. We now must determine whether the station owed decedent a duty of due care.

The facts are not disputed. Radio station KHJ is a successful Los Angeles broadcaster with a large teenage following. At the time of the accident, KHJ commanded a 48 percent plurality of the teenage audience in the Los Angeles area. In contrast, its nearest rival during the same period was able to capture only 13 percent of the teenage listeners. In order to attract an even larger portion of the available audience and thus increase advertising revenue, KHJ inaugurated in July of 1970 a promotion entitled "The Super Summer Spectacular." The "spectacular," with a budget of approximately $40,000 for the month, was specifically designed to make the radio station "more exciting." Among the programs included in the "spectacular" was a contest broadcast on July 16, 1970, the date of the accident.

On that day, Donald Steele Revert, known professionally as "The Real Don Steele," a KHJ disc jockey and television personality, traveled in a conspicuous red automobile to a number of locations in the Los Angeles metropolitan area. Periodically, he apprised KHJ of his whereabouts and his intended destination, and the station broadcast the information to its listeners. The first person to physically locate Steele and fulfill a specified condition received a cash prize. In addition, the winning contestant participated in a brief interview on the air with "The Real Don Steele." The following excerpts from the July 16 broadcast illustrate the tenor of the contest announcements:

"9:30 and The Real Don Steele is back on his feet again with some money and he is headed for the Valley. Thought I would give you a warning so that you can get your kids out of the street.". . .

"The Real Don Steele is moving into Canoga Park—so be on the lookout for him. I'll tell you what will happen if you get to The Real Don Steele. He's got twenty-five dollars to give away if you can get it . . . and baby, all signed and sealed and delivered and wrapped up.". . .

In Van Nuys, 17-year-old Robert Sentner was listening to KHJ in his car while searching for "The Real Don Steele." Upon hearing that "The Real Don Steele" was proceeding to Canoga Park, he immediately drove to that vicinity. Meanwhile, in Northridge, 19-year-old Marsha Baime heard and responded to the same information. Both of them arrived at the Holiday Theater in Canoga Park to find that someone had already claimed the prize. Without knowledge of the other, each decided to follow the Steele vehicle to its next stop and thus be the first to arrive when the next contest question or condition was announced.

For the next few miles the Sentner and Baime cars jockeyed for position closest to the Steele vehicle, reaching speeds up to 80 miles an hour. [However, the plaintiff did not contend that Steele exceeded the speed limit at any time.] About a mile and a half from the Westlake offramp the two teenagers heard the following broadcast: "11:13—The Real Don Steele with bread is heading for Thousand Oaks to give it away. Keep listening to KHJ. . . . The Real Don Steele out on the highway—with bread to give away—be on the lookout, he may stop in Thousand Oaks and may stop along the way . . . Looks like it may be a good stop Steele—drop some bread to those folks."

The Steele vehicle left the freeway at the Westlake offramp. Either Baime or Sentner, in attempting to follow, forced decedent's car onto the center divider, where it overturned. Baime stopped to report the accident. Sentner, after pausing momentarily to relate the tragedy to a passing peace officer, continued to pursue Steele, successfully located him and collected a cash prize.

Decedent's wife and children brought an action for wrongful death against Sentner, Baime, RKO General, Inc. as owner of KHJ, and the maker of decedent's car. Sentner settled prior to the commencement of trial for the limits of his insurance policy. The jury returned a verdict against Baime and KHJ in the amount of $300,000 and found in favor of the manufacturer of decedent's car. KHJ appeals from the ensuing judgment and from an order denying its motion for judgment notwithstanding the verdict. Baime did not appeal.

The primary question for our determination is whether defendant owed a duty to decedent arising out of its broadcast of the giveaway contest. The determination of duty is primarily a question of law. It is the court's "expression of the sum total of those considerations of policy which lead the law to say that the particular plaintiff is entitled to protection." (Prosser, Law of Torts (4th ed. 1971) pp. 325-326.) Any number of considerations may justify the imposition of duty in particular circumstances, including the guidance of history, our continually refined concepts of morals and justice, the convenience of the rule, and social judgment as to where the loss should fall. While the question whether one owes a duty to another must be decided on a case-by-case basis, every case is governed by the rule of general application that all persons are required to use ordinary care to prevent others from being injured as the result of their conduct. However, foreseeability of the risk is a primary consideration in establishing the element of duty. Defendant asserts that the record here does not support a conclusion that a risk of harm to decedent was foreseeable.

While duty is a question of law, foreseeability is a question of fact for the jury. The verdict in plaintiffs' favor here necessarily embraced a finding that decedent was exposed to a foreseeable risk of harm. It is elementary that our review of this finding is limited to the determination whether there is any substantial evidence, contradicted or uncontradicted, which will support the conclusion reached by the jury.

We conclude that the record amply supports the finding of foreseeability. These tragic events unfolded in the middle of a Los Angeles summer, a time when young people were free from the constraints of school and responsive to relief from vacation tedium. Seeking to attract new listeners, KHJ devised an "exciting" promotion. Money and a small measure of momentary notoriety awaited the swiftest response. It was foreseeable that defendant's youthful listeners, finding the prize had eluded them at one location, would race to arrive first at the next site and in their haste would disregard the demands of highway safety.

Indeed, "The Real Don Steele" testified that he had in the past noticed vehicles following him from location to location. He was further aware that the same contestants sometimes appeared at consecutive stops. This knowledge is not rendered irrelevant, as defendant suggests, by the absence of any prior injury. Such an argument confuses foreseeability with hindsight, and amounts to a contention that the injuries of the first victim are not compensable. "The mere fact that a particular kind of an accident has not happened before does not . . . show that such accident is one which might not reasonably have been anticipated." (Ridley v. Grifall Trucking Co. (1955), 136 Cal. App. 2d 682, 686 [289 P.2d 31].) Thus, the fortuitous absence of prior injury does not justify relieving defendant from responsibility for the foreseeable consequences of its acts.

It is of no consequence that the harm to decedent was inflicted by third parties acting negligently. Defendant invokes the maxim that an actor is entitled to assume that others will not act negligently. This concept is valid, however, only to the extent the intervening conduct was not to be anticipated. If the likelihood that a third person may react in a particular manner is a hazard which makes the actor negligent, such reaction whether innocent or negligent does not prevent the actor from being liable for the harm caused thereby. Here, reckless conduct by youthful contestants, stimulated by defendant's broadcast, constituted the hazard to which decedent was exposed.

It is true, of course, that virtually every act involves some conceivable danger. Liability is imposed only if the risk of harm resulting from the act is deemed unreasonable—i.e., if the gravity and likelihood of the danger outweigh the utility of the conduct involved.

We need not belabor the grave danger inherent in the contest broadcast by defendant. The risk of a high speed automobile chase is the risk of death or serious injury. Obviously, neither the entertainment afforded by the contest nor its commercial rewards can justify the creation of such a grave risk. Defendant could have accomplished its objectives of entertaining its listeners and increasing advertising revenues by adopting a contest format which would have avoided danger to the motoring public.

Defendant's contention that the giveaway contest must be afforded the deference due society's interest in the First Amendment is clearly without merit. The issue here is civil accountability for the foreseeable results of a broadcast which created an undue risk of harm to decedent. The First Amendment does not sanction the infliction of physical injury merely because achieved by word, rather than act.

We are not persuaded that the imposition of a duty here will lead to unwarranted extensions of liability. Defendant is fearful that entrepreneurs will henceforth be burdened with an avalanche of obligations: an athletic department will owe a duty to an ardent sports fan injured while hastening to purchase one of a limited number of tickets; a department store will be liable for injuries incurred in response to a "while-they-last" sale. This argument, however, suffers from a myopic view of the facts presented here. The giveaway contest was no commonplace invitation to an attraction available on a limited basis. It was a competitive scramble in which the thrill of the chase to be the one and only victor was intensified by the live broadcast which accompanied the pursuit. In the assertedly analogous situations described by defendant, any haste involved in the purchase of the commodity is an incidental and unavoidable result of the scarcity of the commodity itself. In such situations there is no attempt, as here, to generate a competitive pursuit on public streets, accelerated by repeated importuning by radio to be the very first to arrive at a particular destination. Manifestly the "spectacular" bears little resemblance to daily commercial activities. . . .

The judgment and the orders appealed from are affirmed. Plaintiffs shall recover their costs on appeal. The parties shall bear their own costs on the cross-appeal.

Wright, C.J., McComb, J., Tobriner, J., Sullivan, J., Clark, J., and Richardson, J., concurred.

The court in *Weirum* gave no weight to the defendant's First Amendment argument, asserting that the issue rather was one of the defendant's civil accountability "for foreseeable harm caused by the broadcast." In other cases involving personal injuries caused by words, other courts have given greater weight to First Amendment concerns.

Book publishers, for example, have been given extensive First Amendment protection from liability for physical injury caused by the contents of books. See, e.g., Jones v. J.B. Lippincott Co., 694 F. Supp. 1216 (D. Md. 1988) (plaintiff injured after treating herself according to medical text); Smith v. Linn, 563 A.2d 123 (Pa. Super. 1989) (plaintiff injured after following liquid diet in weight loss book); Walter v. Bauer, 109 Misc. 2d 189, 439 N.Y.S.2d 821 (1981) (plaintiff injured in performing a chemical experiment set out in a text book).

In a number of cases, plaintiffs have alleged that the defendant's publication led to violence resulting in injury. By and large, courts have insulated defendants in these cases, ruling that forms of expression which tend to lead to, but do not actually incite, violence are protected by the First Amendment. In Yakubowicz v. Paramount Pictures Corp., 404 Mass. 624, 536 N.E.2d 1067 (1989), for example, a youth was killed by a teenager who was returning home after viewing the motion picture, "The Warriors," which contained many scenes of juvenile gang violence. In a wrongful death action, the plaintiffs alleged that Paramount and the local movie theatre were aware of acts of gang violence perpetrated by youths who had seen the film, and thus had a duty to warn public authorities. The court reasoned, "Although freedom of speech is not absolute and liability may exist for tortious conduct in the form of speech [citing *Weirum*], the recognized exceptions to First Amendment protections are narrowly defined . . ." Id. at 1071. The court held that the film did not fall within the incitement exception since it did "not at any point exhort, urge, entreat, solicit, or overtly advocate or encourage unlawful or violent activity on the part of viewers." Id. See also McCullom v. CBS, Inc., 202 Cal. App. 3d 989, 249 Cal. Rptr. 187 (1988) (decedent alleged to have killed himself after listening to a song, "Suicide Solution," on a record).

The plaintiff had greater success in overcoming First Amendment objections in Braun v. Soldier of Fortune Magazine, Inc., 968 F.2d 1110 (11th Cir. 1992), *cert. denied,* 113 S. Ct. 1028 (1993). The defendant's magazine carried an advertisement which said:

> **GUN FOR HIRE:** 37-year-old professional mercenary desires jobs. Vietnam Veteran. Discrete [sic] and very private. Body guard, courier, and other special skills. All jobs considered.

The plaintiff sued the defendant for the wrongful death of her father, alleging that as a result of the ad, the person who placed it was hired to, and did, kill her father. In affirming a judgment on the jury verdict for the plaintiff, the court stated that even if the advertisement did not explicitly offer illegal services, the magazine would be liable if the advertisement on its face would alert a reasonably prudent publisher to a clearly identifiable risk of harm to the public posed by the advertisement. In Eimann v. Soldier of Fortune Magazine, Inc., 880 F.2d 830 (5th Cir. 1989), the defendant won a case on similar facts, although the advertisement was somewhat more general in nature.

A recent legislative effort to provide a remedy for some persons who suffer personal injury as a result of a publication is the Pornography Victims' Compensation Act of 1989 (S. 1226, 101st Cong., 1st Sess.), which would give rape or sexual assault victims a cause of action for damages against the producers and distributors of pornography, if they could prove that the pornography caused the injury "by influencing or inciting the sexual offender to commit the offense." No action on the bill has been taken.

In general, see Linder, Media Liability for Personal Injuries, 52 U.M.K.C. L. Rev. 421 (1984); Sims, Tort Liability for Physical Injuries Allegedly Resulting from Media Speech: A Comprehensive First Amendment Approach, 34 Ariz. L. Rev. 231 (1992); Note, Modern Day Sirens: Rock Lyrics and the First Amendment, 63 So. Cal. L. Rev. 777 (1990); Note, Tort Liability for Non-libelous Negligent Statements: First Amendment Considerations, 93 Yale L.J. 744 (1984).

The court in *Weirum* stated that the "primary issue" was "whether defendant owed a duty to decedent. . . ." Is that an accurate description of the issue in that case? The answer to this question depends on the sense in which the court used the word "duty." Coburn v. City of Tucson, 143 Ariz. 50, 51-53, 691 P.2d 1078, 1079-1081 (1984), may shed some light on the question:

> Many tort decisions exhibit an unfortunate tendency to confuse the concepts of "duty" and standard of conduct and to argue that the city is, or is not, under a duty to post warning signs, remove obstructions from the road or sidewalks, install traffic control devices, fix potholes, and the like. We believe that an attempt to equate the concept of "duty" with such specific details of conduct is unwise. Attempting to define or evaluate conduct in terms of duty tends to make rigid the concept of negligence—a concept which, by definition, must vary from case to case, depending upon the relationship of the parties and the facts of each case.
>
> The true issue in this case, therefore, is not whether the city had a duty toward [plaintiffs' decedent]. It had a duty to keep the streets reasonably safe for travel by [him] and all others. The issue here is simply whether there is evidence sufficient to create a question of fact on the issue of whether the city's failure to remove the bush was conduct which fell below the standard of care and thus breached the duty.

However the court used, or misused, "duty" in *Weirum,* it does appear that the court's opinion tracks the negligence concept as defined by Judge Hand in *Carroll Towing,* and as set out in §§292 and 293 of the Restatement (Second) of Torts. But does the balancing of costs and benefits provide a useful approach in all negligence cases? Consider the following case.

Young v. Clark

814 P.2d 364 (Colo. 1991)

JUSTICE VOLLACK delivered the Opinion of the Court. . . .

This case arose from a rear-end collision. . . . The plaintiff, John Young (Young), and the defendant, Holly Clark (Clark), were both traveling eastbound in the center lane on Colorado Highway 36. Construction on the highway caused all traffic to slow to an estimated thirty-five to forty-five miles per hour. One unidentified driver, who was four to five cars ahead of Young, pulled out of the center lane into the right-hand lane and then swerved abruptly back into the center-lane traffic, forcing all drivers behind him to apply their brakes. At that time, Clark had looked over her shoulder while attempting to change lanes. Her passenger, Susan Baldwin, yelled to Clark upon seeing that all traffic ahead had stopped. Clark applied her brakes and swerved to the left, but was unable to avoid colliding with the rear of Young's car.

Young filed suit against Clark . . . claiming that he sustained personal injuries as a result of the accident that was caused by Clark's negligent operation of her car. . . . Clark denied that she was negligent. . . .

The trial court submitted the issues of Clark's negligence, John Young's contributory negligence, and the negligence of the designated nonparty to the jury. Included in the court's instructions to the jury was an explanation of the "sudden emergency" doctrine. The trial court submitted this instruction over the objection of the Youngs. . . .

The jury found that the Youngs' injuries were not caused by any negligence on Clark's part. . . . We granted certiorari to determine whether the trial court's submission of a "sudden emergency" instruction was improper . . . under the circumstances of this particular case. . . .

II

The sudden emergency doctrine was developed by the courts to recognize that a person confronted with sudden or unexpected circumstances calling for immediate action is not expected to exercise the judgment of one acting under normal conditions. See W. P. Keeton, D. Dobbs, R. Keeton & D. Owen, Prosser and Keeton on the Law of Torts §33, at 196 (5th ed. 1984) [hereinafter Prosser and Keeton]:

> [T]he basis of the special rule is merely that the actor is left no time for adequate thought, or is reasonably so disturbed or excited that the actor cannot weigh alternative courses of action, and must make a speedy decision, based very largely upon impulse or guess. Under such conditions, the actor cannot reasonably be held to the same accuracy of judgment or conduct as one who has had full opportunity to reflect, even though it later appears that the actor made the wrong decision, one which no reasonable person could possibly have made after due deliberation.

Id. The doctrine does not, however, impose a lesser standard of care on a person caught in an emergency situation; the individual is still expected to respond to the situation as a reasonably prudent person under the circumstances. The emergency is merely a circumstance to be considered in determining whether the actor's conduct was reasonable.

A

In this automobile collision case, the trial court submitted to the jury Colorado's pattern "sudden emergency" instruction, CJI-Civ. 2d 9:10, which states: "A person who, through no fault of his or her own, is placed in a sudden emergency, is not chargeable with negligence if the person exercises that degree of care which a reasonably careful person would have exercised under the same or similar circumstances." The Youngs first contend that the trial court erred by giving this instruction under the circumstances of this case because, they argue, the sudden emergency confronting Clark arose from a common, and thus foreseeable, traffic problem, and because Clark's own negligence caused the emergency situation. . . .

The Youngs contend that it was improper to give the instruction because the rear-end collision was caused by Clark's lack of attention and failure to maintain a safe distance from Young's car. While it is true that the sudden emergency instruction is not available where a defendant, or a plaintiff, is obviously guilty of negligence, the question of whether an emergency arose because of some negligence by Clark was not so clear. No evidence was presented to show that Clark was following too closely to Young's car or that she was driving too fast under the circumstances. In fact, John Young testified that he never saw how close Clark's car was to his or how fast she was driving just prior to the accident. Clark's passenger, Susan Baldwin, testified that Clark was not following Young's car too closely and that she was not speeding or "going faster than the regular flow of the traffic." The factual dispute as to whether Clark was at fault for causing the accident was therefore appropriately submitted to the finder of fact. Indeed, under CJI-Civ. 2d 9:10, the jury's application of the sudden emergency doctrine is explicitly conditioned on a finding that the actor was not placed in a perilous predicament through any fault of his or her own.

Further, it was Clark's theory that the negligence of the unknown driver caused the accident when the driver pulled out of the center lane of traffic and then abruptly reentered the lane several cars ahead of Young, precipitating the sudden stopping of all the cars behind the driver. Young conceded that he had to brake "hard" to avoid hitting the car in front of him and that the unknown driver probably shared some fault in causing the accident between Young and Clark. In our view, the sudden and unexpected reentry of the unknown driver into the flow of traffic provided sufficient evidence to support giving the sudden emergency instruction. . . . We therefore conclude that the trial court did not act improperly in instructing the jury on the sudden emergency doctrine under the circumstances of this case.

Law and Policy: The Values Reflected in the Negligence Concept

In defining negligence in terms of costs and benefits, the courts in *Carroll Towing, Washington,* and *Weirum* clearly fall into the instrumentalist camp.[53] The goal of negligence law is to achieve the optimal level of accident prevention so that the total costs of accidents and accident prevention will be minimized.[54] Not surprisingly, this economic efficiency perspective of negligence law has been attacked as inadequately embodying the right social values.

Consider, for example, the arguments in Kelman, Cost-Benefit Analysis–An Ethical Critique, Regulation, Jan./Feb. 1981, 33, 35-36. Kelman objects to the use of cost/benefit analysis in making decisions about environmental regulation, but his criticisms are relevant to cost/benefit analysis in other contexts as well, including negligence law. He defines cost/benefit analysis (utilitarianism) as involving "a strong presumption that an act should not be undertaken unless its benefits outweigh its costs," and that "it is desirable to attempt to express all benefits and costs in a common scale or denominator, so that they can be compared with each other, even when some benefits and costs are not traded on markets and hence have no established dollar values." Id. at 33. This view of utilitarianism, he argues, is not adequate as a "moral view":

> This does not mean that the question of whether benefits are greater than costs is morally irrelevant. Few would claim such. Indeed, for a broad range

53. See the note, Law and Policy: Preliminary Considerations, p. 28, above.

54. See Calabresi, The Costs of Accidents 26 (1970) ("Apart from the requirements of justice, I take it as axiomatic that the principal function of accident law is to reduce the sum of the costs of accidents and the costs of avoiding accidents."); Posner, A Theory of Negligence, 1 J. Legal Stud. 29, 33 (1972) ("Perhaps, then, the dominant function of the fault system is to generate rules of liability that if followed will bring about, at least approximately, the efficient—the cost-justified—level of accidents and safety.")

of individual and social decisions, whether an act's benefits outweigh its costs is a sufficient question to ask. But not for all such decisions. These may involve situations where certain duties—duties not to lie, break promises, or kill, for example—make an act wrong, even if it would result in an excess of benefits over costs. Or they may involve instances where people's rights are at stake. We would not permit rape even if it could be demonstrated that the rapist derived enormous happiness from his act, while the victim experiences only minor displeasure. We do not do cost-benefit analyses of freedom of speech or trial by jury. . . . The notion of human rights involves the idea that people may make certain claims to be allowed to act in certain ways, even if the sum of benefits does not outweigh the sum of costs. It is this view that underlies the statement that "workers have a right to a safe and healthy work place" and the expectation that OSHA's decisions will reflect that judgment.

In the most convincing versions of non-utilitarian ethics, various duties or rights are not absolute. But each has a *prima facie* moral validity so that, if duties or rights do not conflict, the morally right act is the act that reflects a duty or respects a right. If duties or rights do conflict, a moral judgment, based on conscious deliberation, must be made. Since one of the duties nonutilitarian philosophers enumerate is the duty of beneficence (the duty to maximize happiness), which in effect incorporates all of utilitarianism by reference, a nonutilitarian who is faced with conflicts between the results of cost-benefit analysis and nonutility-based considerations will need to undertake such deliberation. But in that deliberation, additional elements, which cannot be reduced to a question of whether benefits outweigh costs, have been introduced. Indeed, depending on the moral importance we attach to the right or duty involved, cost-benefit questions may, within wide ranges, become irrelevant to the outcome of the moral judgment.

. . . When officials are deciding what level of pollution will harm certain vulnerable people—such as asthmatics or the elderly—one issue involved may be the right of those people not to be sacrificed on the altar of somewhat higher living standards for the rest of us.

Id. at 35-36.

Kelman did not, in the course of his critique of cost/benefit analysis, indicate how regulators should decide how much to spend, for example, on clean air or safe work places. On the assumption that "absolutely clean" air and "absolutely safe" workplaces are not attainable, regulators do have to decide how much to spend. In deciding how safe workplaces, or flying, or driving, should be, should a dollar value be put on a human life? If so, how much? If not, *are* lives to be weighed in considering how much to spend on safety? There is a good bit of debate over these questions. As to the valuing of human lives question, various federal agencies have produced figures that range from $200,000 (see p. 93, above) to several million. See Keller, What Is the Audited Value of Life?, N.Y. Times, Oct. 26, 1984, at A24, col 4.

A noninstrumentalist view, somewhat similar to that of Kelman but aimed directly at tort law, is expressed in Rodgers, Negligence Reconsidered: The Role of Rationality in Tort Theory, 54 So. Calif. L. Rev. 1 (1980). In marked contrast to the efficiency value that underlies the Learned Hand cost/benefit approach, Professor Rodgers asserts:

> The guiding assumption of this Article is that tort liability rules should reflect respect for people. This perception of fairness requires distribution of praise and blame, and the legal consequences of both, in accordance with what people deserve. . . .
>
> The ultimate goal of tort law assumed by the models presented in this Article is not to settle for a stand-off in a search for cost minimization of accidents and accident avoidance. . . . The goal is zero injury, however unattainable that aim may be; that goal follows from the natural duty people have "not to harm or injure others," and the natural right people have not to be harmed or injured.

Id. at 3, 5.

The first of the two models that Professor Rodgers discusses is that of "rational decisionmaking." In this model, actors make conscious choices about risk creation and prevention; actors would be strictly liable for harm caused by those choices, even if the choices are cost effective in the sense that benefits of the choices are greater than their costs. Professor Rodgers relies in part on Vincent v. Lake Erie Transportation Co., (p. 95, above), to support such a strict liability regime.

With respect to "nonrational actors"—those whose conduct is not the product of conscious choices about risk (an example is the defendant in Young v. Clark, p. 220, above, whose "nonrational" conduct was her response to rapidly changing traffic conditions)—the standard should not be that of a reasonable person under the circumstances, but a subjective "best efforts" standard:

> The decision to take wealth from anyone for the benefit of someone else is a moral decision rooted in the idea that the defendant failed to do what could be done and thus should be penalized for that failure. The offender should be judged as he would judge himself, i.e., in light of his capacities and intentions. Ideally, the jury should discover a correct answer to the question of whether the defendant did his best to avoid the accident. The jury therefore would be permitted to take into account the person in all particulars and to make a judgment about whether the actor was able to avoid injury to another.

Id. at 20.

Under Professor Rodger's models, the electric utility in *Washington,* p. 211, above, very likely would have been liable, would it not? How the "nonrational" actor model would affect the outcome in *Young* is perhaps less clear.[55]

A considerably different standard for negligence cases is advanced in Bender, A Lawyer's Primer of Feminist Theory and Tort, 38 J. Legal Educ. 3 (1988). Professor Bender asserts that the traditional objective standard of care was established from a male perspective. Indeed, as she correctly points out, the Restatement of Torts (Second) refers specifically to the "reasonable man." See, e.g., §291, p. 205, above.[56] She also asserts that the more gender-neutral "reasonable person" does not change the underlying male values of the traditional standard. What is needed, she argues, is a fundamental change in the standard to reflect feminine values:

> When the standard of care is equated with economic efficiency or levels of caution, decisions that assign dollar values to harms to human life and health and then balance those dollars against profit dollars and other evidences of benefit become commonplace. Such cost-benefit and risk-utility analyses turn losses, whether to property or to persons, into commodities in fungible dollar amounts. The standard of care is converted into a floor of unprofitability or inefficiency. People are abstracted from their suffering; they are dehumanized. The risk of their pain and loss becomes a potential debit to be weighed against the benefits or profits to others. The result has little to do with care or even with caution, if caution is understood as concern for safety.
>
> There is another possible understanding of "standard of care" . . . rooted in notions of interconnectedness, responsibility, and caring. What would happen if we understood the "reasonableness" of the standard of care to mean "responsibility" and the "standard of care" to mean the "standard of caring" or "consideration of another's safety and interests"? What if, instead of measuring carefulness or caution, we measured concern and responsibility for the well-being of others and their protection from harm? Negligence law could begin with [the] articulation of the feminine voice's ethic of care—a premise that no one should be hurt. We could convert the present standard of "care of a reasonable person under the same or similar circumstances" to a standard of "conscious care and concern of a responsible neighbor or social acquaintance for another under the same or similar circumstances." . . .
>
> The recognition that we are all interdependent and connected and that we are by nature social beings who must interact with one another should lead

55. For an economic analysis of the differences between an objective and a subjective standard, see Schwartz, Objective and Subjective Standards of Negligence: Defining the Reasonable Person to Induce Optimal Care and Optimal Populations of Injurers and Victims, 78 Geo. L.J. 241 (1989).

56. Professor Bender cites the fictional case of Fardell v. Potts, one of the cases penned by A. P. Herbert in his collection of fictional cases called "Misleading Cases in the Uncommon Law." The opinion in *Fardell* held that a woman could not be held liable in negligence since the law did not recognize a "reasonable woman" standard; thus while the jury could have properly found that the defendant woman's conduct did not come up to the standard of the reasonable man, the judge should have told the jury that the defendant's conduct "was only what was expected of a woman, as such." See also Chapter 2, entitled "Reasonable Prudence and the Disadvantaged," in Calabresi, Ideals, Beliefs, Attitudes, and the Law (1985).

> us to judge conduct as tortious when it does not evidence responsible care or concern for another's safety, welfare, or health. Tort law should begin with a premise of responsibility rather than rights, or interconnectedness rather than separation, and a priority of safety rather than profit or efficiency. The masculine voice of rights, autonomy, and abstraction has led to a standard that protects efficiency and profit; the feminine voice can design a tort system that encourages behavior that is caring about others' safety and responsive to others' needs or hurts, and that attends to human context and consequences. . . .
>
> There is a considerable distance between the law's current standard of care and a standard that might exceed our capabilities. A standard that would make us duty-bound to act responsibly and assure that our behavior does not harm someone else is not beyond us. The law should not permit us casually to cast aside another's safety, health, or interests because we do not personally know the random person who might be injured. Just as we would not want "strangers" to discount the human consequences of their actions to someone about whom we care, we must recognize that the person we affect by our "carelessness" is interconnected to other people as well—family, friends, colleagues, neighbors, communities.
>
> Through a feminist focus on caring, context, and interconnectedness, we can move beyond measuring appropriate behavior by algebraic formulas to assessing behavior by its promotion of human safety and welfare. This approach will clearly lead to liability for some behaviors for which there was none before. If we do not act responsibly with care and concern for others, then we will be deemed negligent. Just as we can now evaluate behavior as negligent if its utility fails to outweigh its risks of harm, we could evaluate behavior as negligent if its care or concern for another's safety or health fails to outweigh its risk of harm. From a feminist perspective the duty of care required by negligence law might mean "acting responsibly toward others to avoid harm, with a concern about the human consequences of our acts or failure to act." It is tragic that our law has been insightful enough to use the language of care but has understood it as only carefulness or acting with caution. If the law imposed a duty of care and concern toward others' safety, orienting our behavior toward avoiding and preventing harms to others, and making it impossible for us to dismiss the consequences of our acts to people we do not directly know, our tort law would take on new dimensions.

Id. at 31-32.

To some extent, the feminist perspective that Professor Bender wants to see reflected in the negligence standard of care has been incorporated into other areas of the law. Some courts, for example, recognize the "battered woman" syndrome in criminal cases. See, e.g., Commonwealth v. Craig, 783 S.W.2d 387 (Ky. 1990). And in Ellison v. Brady, 924 F.2d 872 (9th Cir. 1991), the court adopted a "reasonable woman" rather than a "reasonable person" standard as the test of whether the work environment was "hostile" and for that reason violated Title VII of the Civil Rights Act, which prohibits sexual discrimination in employment. See also Cahn, The Looseness of Legal Language: The Reasonable Woman Standard in Theory and Practice,

77 Cornell L. Rev. 1398 (1992). In general, see Bender, An Overview of Feminist Torts Scholarship, 78 Cornell L. Rev. 575 (1993).

C. *Special Rules Governing the Proof of Negligence*

The preceding section explored the nature of the concept of reasonableness that underlies negligence. However, most of the difficulties in a negligence regime arise not in the formulation of the general standard of care, but in the application of that standard to actual situations. To be sure, cases exist where the jury can simply be told to judge the actor's conduct against that of a reasonable person, and the jury's own collective experience, judgment, and wisdom will suffice in applying the standard. Such cases tend to involve conduct that is commonly engaged in and which therefore presents risks and benefits that are easily understood by the fact finder. In a large number of cases, however, an intuitive application of the standard is difficult or impossible. In such cases, tort law has developed a series of devices, or rules, that either supplement or substitute for the fact finder's own resolution of the negligence issue.

1. Violation of Criminal Statutes

Martin v. Herzog

228 N.Y. 164, 126 N.E. 814 (1920)

CARDOZO, J. The action is one to recover damages for injuries resulting in death.

Plaintiff and her husband, while driving toward Tarrytown in a buggy on the night of August 21, 1915, were struck by the defendant's automobile coming in the opposite direction. They were thrown to the ground, and the man was killed. At the point of the collision the highway makes a curve. The car was rounding the curve when suddenly it came upon the buggy, emerging, the defendant tells us, from the gloom. Negligence is charged against the defendant, the driver of the car, in that he did not keep to the right of the center of the highway (Highway Law, sec. 286, subd. 3; sec. 332; Consol. Laws, ch. 25). Negligence is charged against the plaintiff's intestate, the driver of the wagon, in that he was traveling without lights (Highway Law, sec. 329a, as amended by L. 1915, ch. 367). There is no evidence that the defendant was moving at an excessive speed. There is none of any defect in the equipment of his car. The beam of light from his lamps pointed to the right as the wheels of his car turned along the curve toward the left; and looking in the direction of the plaintiff's approach, he was peering into the shadow. The case against him must stand, therefore, if at all, upon the divergence of his course from the center of the highway. The jury found him delinquent and his victim blameless. The Appellate Division reversed, and ordered a new trial.

We agree with the Appellate Division that the charge to the jury was erroneous and misleading. The case was tried on the assumption that the hour had arrived when lights were due. It was argued on the same assumption in this court. In such circumstances, it is not important whether the hour might have been made a question for the jury. A controversy put out of the case by the parties is not to be put into it by us. We say this by way of preface to our review of the contested rulings. In the body of the charge the trial judge said that the jury could consider the absence of light "in determining whether the plaintiff's intestate was guilty of contributory negligence in failing to have a light upon the buggy as provided by law. I do not mean to say that the absence of light necessarily makes him negligent, but it is a fact for your consideration." The defendant requested a ruling that the absence of a light on the plaintiff's vehicle was "*prima facie* evidence on contributory negligence." This request was refused, and the jury were again instructed that they might consider the absence of lights as some evidence of negligence, but that it was not conclusive evidence. The plaintiff then requested a charge that "the fact that the plaintiff's intestate was driving without a light is not negligence in itself," and to this the court acceded. The defendant saved his rights by appropriate exceptions.

We think the unexcused omission of the statutory signals is more than some evidence of negligence. It *is* negligence in itself. Lights are intended for the guidance and protection of other travelers on the highway (Highway Law, sec. 329a). By the very terms of the hypothesis, to omit, willfully or heedlessly, the safeguards prescribed by law for the benefit of another that he may be preserved in life or limb, is to fall short of the standard of diligence to which those who live in organized society are under a duty to conform. That, we think, is now the established rule in this state. . . . In the case at hand, we have an instance of the admitted violation of a statute intended for the protection of travelers on the highway, of whom the defendant at the time was one. Yet the jurors were instructed in effect that they were at liberty in their discretion to treat the omission of lights either as innocent or as culpable. They were allowed to "consider the default as lightly or gravely" as they would (Thomas, J., in the court below). They might as well have been told that they could use a like discretion in holding a master at fault for the omission of a safety appliance prescribed by positive law for the protection of a workman. Jurors have no dispensing power by which they may relax the duty that one traveler on the highway owes under the statute to another. It is error to tell them that they have. The omission of these lights was a wrong, and being wholly unexcused was also a negligent wrong. No license should have been conceded to the triers of the facts to find it anything else. . . .

We must be on our guard, however, against confusing the question of negligence with that of the causal connection between the negligence and the injury. A defendant who travels without lights is not to pay damages for his fault, unless the absence of lights is the cause of the disaster. A plaintiff who travels without them is not to forfeit the right to damages, unless the absence of lights is at least a contributing cause of the disaster. To say that conduct is negligence is not to say that it is always contributory negligence. "Proof of negligence in the air, so to speak, will not do." Pollock, Torts (10th ed.) p. 472. . . .

We are persuaded that the tendency of the charge, and of all the rulings following it, was to minimize unduly, in the minds of the triers of the facts, the gravity of the decedent's fault. Errors may not be ignored as unsubstantial, when they tend to such an outcome. A statute designed for the protection of human life is not to be brushed aside as a form of words, its commands reduced to the level of cautions, and the duty to obey attenuated into an option to conform.

The order of the Appellate Division should be affirmed, and judgment absolute directed on the stipulation in favor of the defendant, with costs in all courts.

[HOGAN, J., dissented.]

Tedla v. Ellman

280 N.Y. 124, 19 N.E.2d 987 (1939)

LEHMAN, J. While walking along a highway, Anna Tedla and her brother, John Bachek, were struck by a passing automobile, operated by the defendant Ellman. She was injured and Bachek was killed. Bachek was a deaf-mute. His occupation was collecting and selling junk. His sister, Mrs. Tedla, was engaged in the same occupation. They often picked up junk at the incinerator of the village of Islip. At the time of the accident they were walking along "Sunrise Highway" and wheeling baby carriages containing junk and wood which they had picked up at the incinerator. It was about six o'clock, or a little earlier, on a Sunday evening in December. Darkness had already set in. Bachek was carrying a lighted lantern, or, at least, there is testimony to that effect. The jury found that the accident was due solely to the negligence of the operator of the automobile. The defendants do not, upon this appeal, challenge the finding of negligence on the part of the operator. They maintain, however, that Mrs. Tedla and her brother were guilty of contributory negligence as matter of law.

Sunrise Highway, at the place of the accident, consists of two roadways, separated by a grass plot. There are no footpaths along the highway and the center grass plot was soft. It is not unlawful for a pedestrian, wheeling a baby carriage, to use the roadway under such circumstances, but a pedestrian using the roadway is bound to exercise such care for his safety as a reasonably prudent person would use. The Vehicle and Traffic Law (Cons. Laws, ch. 71) provides that "Pedestrians walking or remaining on the paved portion, or traveled part of a roadway shall be subject to, and comply with, the rules governing vehicles, with respect to meeting and turning out, except that such pedestrians shall keep to the left of the center line thereof, and turn to their left instead of right side thereof, so as to permit all vehicles passing them in either direction to pass on their right. Such pedestrians shall not be subject to the rules governing vehicles as to giving signals." (§85, subd. 6.) Mrs. Tedla and her brother did not observe the statutory rule and, at the time of the accident, were proceeding in easterly direction on the east-bound or right-hand roadway. The defendants moved to dismiss the complaint on the ground, among others, that violation of the statutory rule constitutes contributory negligence as matter of law. They did not, in the courts below, urge that any negligence in other respect of Mrs. Tedla or her brother bars a recovery. The trial judge left to the jury the question whether failure to observe the statutory rule was a proximate cause of the accident; he left to the jury no question of other fault or negligence on the part of Mrs. Tedla or her brother, and the defendants did not request that any other question be submitted. Upon this appeal, the only question presented is whether, as matter of law, disregard of the statutory rule that pedestrians shall keep to the left of the center line of a highway constitutes contributory negligence which bars any recovery by the plaintiff.

Vehicular traffic can proceed safely and without recurrent traffic tangles only if vehicles observe accepted rules of the road. Such rules, and especially the rule that all vehicles proceeding in one direction must keep to a designated part or side of the road—in this country the right-hand side—have been dictated by necessity and formulated by custom. The general use of automobiles has increased in unprecedented degree the number and speed of vehicles. Control of traffic becomes an increasingly difficult problem. Rules of the road, regulating the rights and duties of those who use highways, have, in consequence, become increasingly important. The Legislature no longer leaves to custom the formulation of such rules. Statutes now codify, define, supplement and, where changing conditions suggest change in rule, even change rules of the road which formerly rested on custom. Custom and common sense have always dictated that vehicles should have the right of way over pedestrians and that pedestrians should walk along the edge of a highway so that they might step aside for passing vehicles with least danger to themselves and least obstruction to vehicular traffic. Otherwise, perhaps, no customary rule of the road was observed by pedestrians with the same uniformity as by vehicles; though, in general, they probably followed, until recently, the same rules as vehicles.

Pedestrians are seldom a source of danger or serious obstruction to vehicles and when horse-drawn vehicles were common they seldom injured pedestrians, using a highway with reasonable care, unless the horse became unmanageable or the driver was grossly negligent or guilty of willful wrong. Swift-moving motor vehicles, it was soon recognized, do endanger the safety of pedestrians crossing highways, and it is imperative that there the relative rights and duties of pedestrians and of vehicles should be understood and observed. The Legislature in the first five subdivisions of section 85 of the Vehicle and Traffic Law has provided regulations to govern the conduct of pedestrians and of drivers of vehicles when a pedestrian is crossing a road. Until, by chapter 114 of the Laws of 1933, it adopted subdivision 6 of section 85, quoted above, there was no special statutory rule for pedestrians walking *along* a highway. Then for the first time it reversed, for pedestrians, the rule established for vehicles by immemorial custom, and provided that pedestrians shall keep to the left of the center line of a highway.

The plaintiffs showed by the testimony of a State policeman that "there were very few cars going east" at the time of the accident, but that going west there was "very heavy Sunday night traffic." Until the recent adoption of the new statutory rule for pedestrians, ordinary prudence would have dictated that pedestrians should not expose themselves to the danger of walking along the roadway upon which the "very heavy Sunday night traffic" was proceeding when they could walk in comparative safety along a roadway used by very few cars. It is said that now, by force of the statutory rule, pedestrians are guilty of contributory negligence as matter of law when they use the safer roadway, unless that roadway is left of the center of the road. Disregard of the statutory rule of the road and observance of a rule based on immemorial custom, it is said, is negligence which as matter of law is a proximate cause of the accident, though observance of the statutory rule might, under the circumstances of the particular case, expose a pedestrian to serious danger from which he would be free if he followed the rule that had been established by custom. If that be true, then the Legislature has decreed that pedestrians must observe the general rule of conduct which it has prescribed for their safety even under circumstances where observance would subject them to unusual risk; that pedestrians are to be charged with negligence as matter of law for acting as prudence dictates. It is unreasonable to ascribe to the Legislature an intention that the statute should have so extraordinary a result, and the courts may not give to a statute an effect not intended by the Legislature.

. . . The appellants lean heavily upon [Martin v. Herzog] and kindred cases and the principle established by them.

The analogy is, however, incomplete. The "established rule" should not be weakened either by subtle distinctions or by extension beyond its letter or spirit into a field where "by the very terms of the hypothesis" it can have no proper application. At times the indefinite and flexible standard of care of the traditional reasonably prudent man may be, in the opinion of the Legislature, an insufficient measure of the care which should be exercised to guard against a recognized danger; at times, the duty, imposed by custom, that no man shall use what is his to the harm of others provides insufficient safeguard for the preservation of the life or limb or property of others. Then the Legislature may by statute prescribe additional safeguards and may define duty and standard of care in rigid terms; and when the Legislature has spoken, the standard of the care required is no longer what the reasonably prudent man would do under the circumstances but what the Legislature has commanded. That is the rule established by the courts and "by the very terms of the hypothesis" the rule applies where the Legislature has prescribed safeguards "for the benefit of another that he may be preserved in life or limb." In that field debate as to whether the safeguards so prescribed are reasonably necessary is ended by the legislative fiat. Obedience to that fiat cannot add to the danger, even assuming that the prescribed safeguards are not reasonably necessary and where the legislative anticipation of dangers is realized and harm results through heedless or willful omission of the prescribed safeguard, injury flows from wrong and the wrongdoer is properly held responsible for the consequent damages.

The statute upon which the defendants rely is of different character. It does not prescribe additional safeguards which pedestrians must provide for the preservation of the life or limb or property of others, or even of themselves, nor does it impose upon pedestrians a higher standard of care. What the statute does provide is rules of the road to be observed by pedestrians and by vehicles, so that all those who use the road may know how they and others should proceed, at least under usual circumstances. A general rule of conduct—and, specifically, a rule of the road—may accomplish its intended purpose under usual conditions, but, when the unusual occurs, strict observance may defeat the purpose of the rule and produce catastrophic results.

Negligence is failure to exercise the care required by law. Where a statute defines the standard of care and the safeguards required to meet a recognized danger, then, as we have said, no other measure may be applied in determining whether a person has carried out the duty of care imposed by law. Failure to observe the standard imposed by statute is negligence, as matter of law. On the other hand, where a statutory general rule of conduct fixes no definite standard of care which would under all circumstances tend to protect life, limb or property but merely codifies or supplements a common-law rule, which has always been subject to limitations and exceptions; or where the statutory rule of conduct regulates conflicting rights and obligations in manner calculated to promote public convenience and safety, then the statute, in the absence of clear language to the contrary, should not be construed as intended to wipe out the limitations and exceptions which judicial decisions have attached to the common-law duty; nor should it be construed as an inflexible command that the general rule of conduct intended to prevent accidents must be followed even under conditions when observance might cause accidents. We may assume reasonably that the Legislature directed pedestrians to keep to the left of the center of the road because that would cause them to face traffic approaching in that lane and would enable them to care for their own safety better than if the traffic approached them from the rear. We cannot assume reasonably that the Legislature intended that a statute enacted for the preservation of the life and limb of pedestrians must be observed when observance would subject them to more imminent danger. . . .

The generally accepted rule and the reasons for it are set forth in the comment to section 286 of the Restatement of the Law of Torts: "Many statutes and ordinances are so worded as apparently to express a universally obligatory rule of conduct. Such enactments, however, may in view of their purpose and spirits be properly construed as intended to apply only to ordinary situations and to be subject to the qualification that the conduct prohibited thereby is not wrongful if, because of an emergency or the like, the circumstances justify an apparent disobedience to the letter of the enactment. . . . The provisions of statutes, intended to codify and supplement the rules of conduct which are established by a course of judicial decision or by custom, are often construed as subject to the same limitations and exceptions as the rules which they supersede. Thus, a statute or ordinance requiring all persons to drive on the right side of the road may be construed as subject to an exception permitting travellers to drive upon the other side, if so doing is likely to prevent rather than cause the accidents which it is the purpose of the statute or ordinance to prevent."

Even under that construction of the statute, a pedestrian is, of course, at fault if he fails without good reason to observe the statutory rule of conduct. The general duty is established by the statute, and deviation from it without good cause is a wrong and the wrongdoer is responsible for the damages resulting from his wrong. . . .

In each action, the judgment should be affirmed, with costs.

CRANE, C.J., HUBBS, LOUGHRAN and RIPPEY, JJ., concur; O'BRIEN and FINCH, JJ., dissent on the authority of Martin v. Herzog (228 N.Y. 164).

A violation of a statute may also be excused if it was impossible for the defendant under the circumstances to comply with the statute (see, e.g., Bush v. Harvey Transfer Co., 146 Ohio St. 657, 67 N.E.2d 851 (1946) (fuse on truck blew out, causing lights to fail)). In general, see Morris, The Role of Criminal Statutes in Negligence Actions, 49 Colum. L. Rev. 21 (1949).

Brown v. Shyne

242 N.Y. 176, 151 N.E. 197 (1926)

LEHMAN, J. The plaintiff employed the defendant to give chiropractic treatment to her for a disease or physical condition. The defendant had no license to practice medicine, yet he held himself out as being able to diagnose and treat disease, and under the provisions of the Public Health Law (Cons. Laws, ch. 45) he was guilty of a misdemeanor. The plaintiff became paralyzed after she had received nine treatments by the defendant. She claims, and upon this appeal we must assume, that the paralysis was caused by the treatment she received. She has recovered judgment in the sum of $10,000 for the damages caused by said injury. . . .

At the close of the plaintiff's case the plaintiff was permitted to amend the complaint to allege "that in so treating the plaintiff the defendant was engaged in the practice of medicine contrary to and in violation of the provisions of the Public Health Law of the State of New York in such case made and provided, he at the time of so treating plaintiff not being a duly licensed physician or surgeon of the State of New York." Thereafter the trial judge charged the jury that they might bring in a verdict in favor of the plaintiff if they found that the evidence established that the treatment given to the plaintiff was not in accordance with the standards of skill and care which prevail among those treating disease. He then continued: "This is a little different from the ordinary malpractice case, and I am going to allow you, if you think proper under the evidence in the case, to predicate negligence upon another theory. The public health laws of this State prescribe that no person shall practice medicine unless he is licensed so to do by the Board of Regents of this State and registered pursuant to statute. . . . This statute to which I have referred is a general police regulation. Its violation, and it has been violated by the defendant, is some evidence, more or less cogent, of negligence which you may consider for what it is worth, along with all the other evidence in the case. If the defendant attempted to treat the plaintiff and to adjust the vertebrae in her spine when he did not possess the requisite knowledge and skill as prescribed by the statute to know what was proper and necessary to do under the circumstances, or how to do it, even if he did know what to do, you can find him negligent." In so charging the jury that from the violation of the statute the jury might infer negligence which produced injury to the plaintiff, the trial justice in my opinion erred.

The provisions of the Public Health Law prohibiting the practice of medicine without a license granted upon proof of preliminary training and after examination intended to show adequate knowledge, are of course intended for the protection of the general public against injury which unskilled and unlearned practitioners might cause. If violation of the statute by the defendant was the proximate cause of the plaintiff's injury, then the plaintiff may recover upon proof of violation; if violation of the statute has no direct bearing on the injury, proof of the violation becomes irrelevant. For injury caused by neglect of duty imposed by the penal law there is civil remedy; but of course the injury must follow from the neglect.

Proper formulation of general standards of preliminary education and proper examination of the particular applicant should serve to raise the standards of skill and care generally possessed by members of the profession in this State; but the license to practice medicine confers no additional skill upon the practitioner; nor does it confer immunity from physical injury upon a patient if the practitioner fails to exercise care. Here, injury may have been caused by lack of skill or care; it would not have been obviated if the defendant had possessed a license yet failed to exercise the skill and care required of one practicing medicine. True, if the defendant had not practiced medicine in this State, he could not have injured the plaintiff, but the protection which the statute was intended to provide was against risk of injury by the unskilled or careless practitioner, and unless the plaintiff's injury was caused by carelessness or lack of skill, the defendant's failure to obtain a license was not connected with the injury. The plaintiff's cause of action is for negligence or malpractice. The defendant undertook to treat the plaintiff for a physical condition which seemed to require remedy. Under our law such treatment may be given only by a duly qualified practitioner who has obtained a license.

The defendant in offering to treat the plaintiff held himself out as qualified to give treatment. He must meet the professional standards of skill and care prevailing among those who do offer treatment lawfully. If injury follows through failure to meet those standards, the plaintiff may recover. The provisions of the Public Health Law may result in the exclusion from practice of some who are unqualified. Even a skilled and learned practitioner who is not licensed commits an offense against the State; but against such practitioners the statute was not intended to protect, for no protection was needed, and neglect to obtain a license results in no injury to the patient and, therefore, no private wrong. The purpose of the statute is to protect the public against unfounded assumption of skill by one who undertakes to prescribe or treat for disease. In order to show that the plaintiff has been injured by defendant's breach of the statutory duty, proof must be given that defendant in such treatment did not exercise the care and skill which would have been exercised by qualified practitioners within the State, and that such lack of skill and care caused the injury. Failure to obtain a license as required by law gives rise to no remedy if it has caused no injury. . . .

It is said that the trial justice did not charge that plaintiff might recover for defendant's failure to obtain a license but only that failure to obtain a license might be considered "some evidence" of defendant's negligence. Argument is made that even if neglect of the statutory duty does not itself create liability, it tends to prove that injury was caused by lack of skill or care. That can be true only if logical inference may be drawn from defendant's failure to obtain or perhaps seek a license that he not only lacks the skill and learning which would enable him to diagnose and treat disease generally, but also that he lacks even the skill and learning necessary for the physical manipulation he gave to this plaintiff. Evidence of defendant's training, learning and skill and the method he used in giving the treatment was produced at the trial and upon such evidence the jury could base finding either of care or negligence, but the absence of a license does not seem to strengthen inference that might be drawn from such evidence, and a fortiori would not alone be a basis for such inference. Breach or neglect of duty imposed by statute or ordinance may be evidence of negligence only if there is logical connection between the proven neglect of statutory duty and the alleged negligence. . . .

For these reasons the judgments should be reversed and a new trial granted, with costs to abide the event.

CRANE, J. (dissenting). . . . The judge fully and completely charged the jury that the defendant was not liable for any of the plaintiff's injuries unless they were the direct and proximate [result] of his acts. The evidence was abundant to prove that the plaintiff's paralysis and injuries resulted from the defendant's manipulation and treatment of her back, neck and head. The jury were justified in finding that whatever he did, whether it were proper or improper, resulted in the plaintiff's painful condition. We start, therefore, the consideration of this point with the fact that the defendant's acts were the direct and proximate cause of the injury. The next question arises as to whether or not the acts were negligent.

As I have stated, the judge charged the jury as if this were the ordinary malpractice case, furnishing for the defendant a standard of the legally authorized physician. It is difficult for me personally to follow this reasoning and the logic of the situation. I think this rule all too liberal to the defendant. What he did was prohibited by law. He could not practice medicine without violating the law. The law did not recognize him as a physician. How can the courts treat him as such? Provided his act, in violation of the law, is the direct and proximate cause of injury, in my judgment he is liable, irrespective of negligence. It seems somewhat strange that the courts, one branch of the law, can hold up for such a man the standards of the licensed physician, while the Legislature, another branch of the law, declares that he cannot practice at all as a physician. The courts thus afford the protection which the Legislature denies.

The judge in this case, however, did not go this far. He charged for the defendant's benefit the ordinary rules of negligence in malpractice cases, and then stated that the violation of the Public Health Law was some evidence of negligence, leaving the whole question to the jury. It is this much milder form of ruling which is challenged. The defendant must be treated, so the appellant claims, as if he were a duly licensed physician, and in this action for damages, resulting from his act, he is only liable if a duly licensed physician would have been liable. Such is the effect of excluding evidence of the defendant's practicing medicine without a license. . . .

The prohibition against practicing medicine without a license was for the very purpose of protecting the public from just what happened in this case. The violation of this statute has been the direct and proximate cause of the injury. The courts will not determine in face of this statute whether a faith healer, a patent medicine man, a chiropractor, or any other class of practitioner acted according to the standards of his own school, or according to the standards of a duly licensed physician. The law, to insure against ignorance and carelessness, has laid down a rule to be followed, namely, examinations to test qualifications, and a license to practice. If a man, in violation of this statute, takes his chances in trying to cure disease, and his acts result directly in injury, he should not complain if the law, in a suit for damages, says that his violation of the statute is some evidence of his incapacity. . . .

The ruling was correct, and the judgments below should be affirmed, with costs.

After *Brown* was decided, the New York legislature enacted the following statute (N.Y. Civ. Prac. L. & R. §4504(d)):

> Proof of negligence: unauthorized practice of medicine. In any action for damages for personal injuries or death against a person not authorized to practice medicine under article 131 of the education law for any act or acts constituting the practice of medicine, when such act or acts were a competent producing proximate or contributing cause of such injuries or death, the fact that such person practiced medicine without being so authorized shall be deemed prima facie evidence of negligence.

Judge Cardozo's approach to the violation of safety statutes in the *Martin* case is clearly the majority position in this country. See generally Restatement (Second) of Torts §288B; Prosser and Keeton, Law of Torts 230, n.1 (5th ed. (1984)). Judge Cardozo's description of the trial in that case suggests that other approaches have been taken. One alternative approach is that adopted in Sheehan v. Nims, 75 F.2d 293 (2d Cir. 1935), in which the court applied Vermont law in a diversity case arising out of a motor vehicle accident. The defendant had run out of gas and parked his truck at dusk on the edge of a highway. The plaintiff's decedent drove his automobile into the defendant's truck. A Vermont statute required a clearance lamp to be displayed by such trucks, and the defendant admittedly did not have one. However, the defendant had hung a lighted kerosene lantern near the left rear corner of the truck. The trial court ruled the defendant negligent as a matter of law, and the defendant appealed. Reversing for a new trial, the court of appeals explained (75 F.2d at 294):

> While it is true that in many states the violation of a standard of care prescribed by statute is held to be negligence per se, the law of Vermont is otherwise. On such a point the federal court will follow the state law. From the foregoing authorities relating to similar safety regulations it appears that a violation of the statute in question gives rise to a rebuttable presumption of negligence which may be overcome by proof of the attendant circumstances

> if they are sufficient to persuade the jury that a reasonable and prudent driver would have acted as did the person whose conduct is in question.
>
> Counsel for the appellee contends that this is so only when the delinquent party is in a position to substitute his own judgment of what is prudent for that of the Legislature. Since the truck was not equipped with clearance lights, it is argued that the appellants were never able to exercise their judgment as to when the lights should be displayed. This argument is specious. Admittedly, while on the highway the appellants had no choice other than to operate without lights; but they had the choice of not being on the highway at all, and their act in operating the truck at the particular time in question might well have involved a decision that to do so was not imprudent. The appellee further urges that not enough was shown to overcome the prima facie case made by proof of absence of a clearance light, and hence the peremptory instruction that negligence existed was justifiable. This contention we are unable to accept. Although it was more than thirty minutes after sunset, it was not yet dark. The truck was standing on a straight stretch of road where it could be expected to be seen from a considerable distance by any motorist approaching from the rear. According to the defendants' testimony, a lighted red lantern was hung near to the left rear corner. The driver intended to leave the truck standing only so long as it should take him to walk three hundred feet to a garage and back again with a borrowed tool with which he would change the gasoline feed pipe from one tank to another so that he could resume his journey. Whether under the same circumstance a reasonable and prudent driver would have done as he did, despite the prohibition of the statute, seems to us a jury question under the Vermont cases.

A somewhat different approach to the question of safety statute violations is the one adopted by the trial judge in the *Martin* case and expressly rejected by Judge Cardozo on appeal—that is, to allow the jury to accept the fact of the violation as some evidence of negligence. In Gill v. Whiteside-Hemby Drug Co., 197 Ark. 425, 122 S.W.2d 597 (1938), the plaintiff was struck by the defendant's motorcycle. Although there was evidence that the defendant had violated several city ordinances by speeding and passing a streetcar at an intersection (the streetcar was moving toward the plaintiff and blocked the plaintiff's view of the defendant's motorcycle), the trial court instructed the jury that such violations would not of themselves conclusively establish negligence. Affirming a verdict and judgment for the defendant, the Supreme Court of Arkansas made it clear that violation of either state law or city ordinances is merely evidence of negligence, and not negligence per se.

The decisions generally do not distinguish between statutes and ordinances in applying the rules described herein.[57] In Peterson v. City of Long Beach,

57. See, e.g., Ferrell v. Baxter, 484 P.2d 250 (Alaska 1971); Prosser and Keeton, Law of Torts 220 (5th ed. 1984); Morris, The Role of Administrative Safety Measures in Negligence Actions, 20 Tex. L. Rev. 143 (1949).

24 Cal. 3d 238, 594 P.2d 477, 155 Cal. Rptr. 360 (1979), the Supreme Court of California held that a policeman's violation of an internal police department regulation gave rise to a rebuttable presumption of negligence. This decision is criticized in Comment, 1979 Wash. U.L.Q. 1154, in part on the ground that it will discourage police departments from establishing rules of conduct for their personnel.

The Law-Fact Distinction: The Effect of Safety Statute Violations upon the Division of Functions Between Judge and Jury

Perhaps the most significant general effect of safety statutes upon negligence cases is that upon the division of functions between judge and jury. Whenever violations of such statutes are held to be relevant to the issue of negligence, the ultimate task of evaluating conduct, usually performed by the jury, is taken over to some extent (perhaps entirely) by the judge. The manner in which this reallocation of functions occurs may be explained very simply. Safety statutes operate to particularize, rather than necessarily to raise, the applicable minimum standard of care. They tend to transform the general standard of reasonableness into a particular standard which can be stated in terms much more closely related to the actual conduct in question. The effect of this particularization is to allow issues to be resolved by the judge as a matter of law which would ordinarily be decided by the jury as issues of fact. This is especially true in cases in which violation of the statute is held to be negligence per se. If there is no dispute over whether the party violated the statute, the judge disposes of the negligence issue as a matter of law. Where the question of violation is disputed, the judge instructs the jury that the negligence issue has become the narrower issue of whether a violation occurred.

Even when statutory violation is only evidence of lack of due care, the judge will play a more influential role in the process of evaluating the defendant's conduct. If the case is close on its facts, the presence of the statute may tip the scales and cause the judge to dispose of the negligence issue as a matter of law. And even where the case goes to the jury, it is accompanied by a special instruction from the judge that the violation does bear upon the central issue of negligence. What has happened in these cases is that the legislature has to some extent performed the task of evaluation in advance; the judge, as interpreter of legislative intent, steps in to play a much more influential role in the evaluative process than would otherwise be the case in the absence of a statutory violation. For further discussion of the impact of safety statute violations upon the division of function between judge and jury, see Weiner, The Civil Jury Trial and the Law-Fact Distinction, 54 Cal. L. Rev. 1867, 1885-1886 (1966).

Problem 13

Sandra Doherty, a partner in your law firm, has asked you for a memorandum discussing the liability issues in a case she is handling. Your client, Mildred Riley, was named as the defendant in a suit by Amanda Salazar. Reliance Insurance Company retained your firm to represent Riley. Specifically, Doherty wants to know if she should file a motion for summary judgment, and if so, what the chances are that it will be granted. The pleadings reveal the following facts, none of which seems to be the subject of any significant dispute:

At 10:00 P.M., on December 16, two years ago, Riley was driving on Route 83 when she witnessed an automobile accident. She stopped immediately and saw that occupants of both cars involved in the accident were seriously injured. She decided that she could better help the injured by reporting the accident, but no house or telephone was available from which to make the report. She then drove to a nearby shopping center. The only parking space near the first telephone she saw was in front of a drug store and was marked as reserved for the handicapped. She quickly looked around and saw no other open space, so she decided to park in that space in order to make the call. Checking her purse, she found that she did not have the correct change for the telephone, so she went into the drug store to get change. At the time that Riley entered the store, the plaintiff drove into the shopping center, intending to pick up a prescription at the drug store. She suffered from severe arthritis in both knees, and had a handicapped parking sticker for her automobile. She wrote down Riley's license plate number, intending to report the violation to the police. A parking space about one hundred yards from the drug store opened up, where she decided to park. She knew that she could walk that distance, although with considerable difficulty and pain. The lighting was not particularly good where she parked, and just as she got out of her car, she was attacked and robbed by a purse snatcher. As a result she suffered serious injuries, for which she brought suit against Riley.

The Uniform Traffic Control Law of your state contains the following statute:

> (1) Any commercial real estate property owner offering parking for the general public shall provide specially designed and marked motor vehicle parking spaces for the exclusive use of physically disabled persons who have been issued parking permits pursuant to subsection (5) of this statute.
>
> (2) Any person who parks a vehicle in any parking space designated with the international symbol of accessibility or the caption "PARKING BY DISABLED PERMIT ONLY," or with both such symbol and caption, is guilty of a traffic infraction, and shall be punished accordingly unless such vehicle displays a parking permit issued pursuant to subsection (5) of this statute, and such vehicle is occupied by a person eligible for such permit.

The parking space occupied by Riley had the sign required by the statute. In preparing your memorandum, assume that Martin v. Herzog and Tedla v. Ellman are controlling precedent.

2. Custom

Trimarco v. Klein

56 N.Y.2d 98, 436 N.E.2d 502 (1982)

FUCHSBERG, JUDGE.

[The plaintiff, a tenant in an apartment owned by the defendant, was severely injured when a glass shower door shattered as he stepped out of the shower. The plaintiff alleged that the defendant was negligent in failing to provide a door made of shatterproof safety glass. In support of this allegation, the plaintiff introduced evidence of a general practice among landlords to use shatterproof materials in showers. At the trial, the judge entered judgment for the plaintiff after a jury verdict for the plaintiff; the Appellate Division reversed and dismissed the complaint, on the ground that the defendant had no duty to replace the glass absent notice of the danger either from the plaintiff or from a similar accident in the building. The Court of Appeals reversed, and ordered a new trial.]

Which brings us to the well-recognized and pragmatic proposition that when "certain dangers have been removed by a customary way of doing things safely, this custom may be proved to show that [the one charged with the dereliction] has fallen below the required standard" (Garthe v. Ruppert, 264 N.Y. 290, 296, 190 N.E. 643). Such proof, of course, is not admitted in the abstract. It must bear on what is reasonable conduct under all the circumstances, the quintessential test of negligence.

It follows that, when proof of an accepted practice is accompanied by evidence that the defendant conformed to it, this may establish due care and, contrariwise, when proof of a customary practice is coupled with a showing that it was ignored and that this departure was a proximate cause of the accident, it may serve to establish liability. Put more conceptually, proof of a common practice aids in "formulat[ing] the general expectation of society as to how individuals will act in the course of their undertakings, and thus to guide the common sense or expert intuition of a jury or commission when called on to judge of particular conduct under particular circumstances" (Pound, Administrative Application of Legal Standards, 44 ABA Rep., 445, 456-457).

The source of the probative power of proof of custom and usage is described differently by various authorities, but all agree on its potency. Chief among the rationales offered is, of course, the fact that it reflects the judgment and experience and conduct of many. Support for its relevancy and reliability comes too from the direct bearing it has on feasibility, for its focusing is on the practicality of a precaution in actual operation and the readiness with which it can be employed. Following in the train of both of these boons is the custom's exemplification of the opportunities it provides to others to learn of the safe way, if that the customary one be.

From all this it is not to be assumed customary practice and usage need be universal. It suffices that it be fairly well defined and in the same calling or business so that "the actor may be charged with knowledge of it or negligent ignorance" (Prosser, Torts [4th ed.], §33, p.168; Restatement, Torts 2d, §295A, p.62, Comment *a*).

However, once its existence is credited, a common practice or usage is still not necessarily a conclusive or even a compelling test of negligence. Before it can be, the jury must be satisfied with its reasonableness, just as the jury must be satisfied with the reasonableness of the behavior which adhered to the custom or the unreasonableness of that which did not. After all, customs and usages run the gamut of merit like everything else. That is why the question in each instance is whether it meets the test of reasonableness. As Holmes' now classic statement on this subject expresses it, "[w]hat usually is done may be evidence of what ought to be done, but what ought to be done is fixed by a standard of reasonable prudence, whether it usually is complied with or not" (Texas & Pacific Ry. Co. v. Behymer, 189 U.S. 468, 470, 23 S.Ct. 622, 622-623, 47 L. Ed. 905).

So measured, the case the plaintiff presented . . . was enough to send it to the jury and to sustain the verdict reached. The expert testimony, the admissions of the defendant's manager, the data on which the professional and governmental bulletins were based, the evidence of how replacements were handled by at least the local building industry for the better part of two decades, these in the aggregate easily filled that bill. Moreover, it was also for the jury to decide whether, at the point in time when the accident occurred, the modest cost and ready availability of safety glass and the dynamics of the growing custom to use it for shower enclosures had transformed what once may have been considered a reasonably safe part of the apartment into one which, in the light of later developments, no longer could be so regarded.

[Nonetheless, the court reversed and ordered a new trial because the trial judge permitted the jury to consider a statute relating to the use of safety materials that the court ruled was not applicable to the defendant.]

The T. J. Hooper

60 F.2d 737 (2d Cir.), cert. denied, *287 U.S. 662 (1932)*

Petition by the Eastern Transportation Company, as owner of the tugs Montrose and T. J. Hooper, for exoneration from, or limitation of, liability; separate libels by the New England Coal & Coke Company and by H. N.

Hartwell & Son, Inc., against the Northern Barge Corporation, as owner of the barge Northern No. 30 and the barge Northern No. 17; and libel by the Northern Barge Corporation against the tugs Montrose and Hooper. The suits were joined and heard together. From the decree rendered [during the limitation proceedings allowing the claims of the cargo owners 53 F.2d 107 (S.D.N.Y. 1931)], the petitioner Eastern Transportation Company and the Northern Barge Corporation, appeal.

[The operator of a tugboat was sued for the value of two barges and their cargoes, which were lost at sea during a coastal storm in March, 1928. The basis of the claim was that the tug was negligently unseaworthy in that it was not equipped with a radio receiver, and thus could not receive reports of an impending storm. There was evidence that the master, had he heard the weather reports, would have turned back.]

L. HAND, J. . . . It is not fair to say that there was a general custom among coastwise carriers so to equip their tugs. One line alone did it; as for the rest, they relied upon their crews, so far as they can be said to have relied at all. An adequate receiving set suitable for a coastwise tug can now be got at small cost and is reasonably reliable if kept up; obviously it is a source of great protection to their tows. Twice every day they can receive these predictions, based upon the widest possible information, available to every vessel within two or three hundred miles and more. Such a set is the ears of the tug to catch the spoken word, just as the master's binoculars are her eyes to see a storm signal ashore. Whatever may be said as to other vessels, tugs towing heavy coal laden barges, strung out for half a mile, have little power to maneuver, and do not, as this case proves, expose themselves to weather which would not turn back stauncher craft. They can have at hand protection against dangers of which they can learn in no other way.

Is it then a final answer that the business had not yet generally adopted receiving sets? There are, no doubt, cases where courts seem to make the general practice of the calling the standard of proper diligence; we have indeed given some currency to the notion ourselves. Indeed in most cases reasonable prudence is in fact common prudence; but strictly it is never its measure; a whole calling may have unduly lagged in the adoption of new and available devices. It never may set its own tests, however persuasive be its usages. Courts must in the end say what is required; there are precautions so imperative that even their universal disregard will not excuse their omission. But here there was no custom at all as to receiving sets; some had them, some did not; the most that can be urged is that they had not yet become general. Certainly in such a case we need not pause; when some have thought a device necessary, at least we may say that they were right, and the others too slack. The statute (section 484, title 46, U.S. Code [46 USCA §484]) does not bear on this situation at all. It prescribes not a receiving, but a transmitting set, and for a very different purpose; to call for help, not to get news. We hold the tugs therefore because had they been properly equipped, they would have got the [weather] reports. The injury was a direct consequence of this unseaworthiness.

Decree affirmed.

For a discussion of custom in general, and of *The T. J. Hooper* in particular, see Epstein, The Path to *The T. J. Hooper:* The Theory and History of Custom in the Law of Tort, XXI (1) J. Legal Stud. 1 (1992).

Problem 14

You are the clerk to the judge presiding at the trial in the case of King v. Marina Costa Co., Inc. The evidence has been completed and the defendant has moved for a directed verdict. Both the plaintiff and the defendant have filed requests for jury instructions in the event that the motion is denied. The judge has asked you to review the record and to give your views as to whether the motion for the directed verdict should be granted and as to which of the requested instructions should be given.

Marina Costa manufactures motorboats for recreational use. The plaintiff bought a boat new from the defendant in 1973. Four years ago, he was operating the boat when it struck a submerged log, throwing him overboard. The motor continued to run and, as the boat circled around the plaintiff, the propeller struck him, causing severe injuries. The plaintiff's complaint alleges that the defendant was negligent in failing to equip the boat with a "kill switch" which would have stopped the motor as soon as the plaintiff was thrown from the seat.

The defendant presented evidence that when the plaintiff bought the boat in 1973, no manufacturer installed kill switches. They had been an optional feature with some manufacturers, including the defendant, beginning in 1969, but they proved to be unpopular. They occasionally malfunctioned, causing motors to be unstartable. In addition, users were apt to trigger the switches inadvertently when they moved away from the motor to perform some task toward the front of the boat. The few customers that bought boats equipped with kill switches from the defendant soon had them disabled, and the defendant stopped installing the switches in 1972.

The plaintiff introduced evidence that kill switches were relatively inexpensive. As public attention to the hazards of boating increased in the 1980s, kill switches began to be installed and used more frequently. Today they are routinely included in all boat and motor designs.

In the event that the motion for directed verdict is denied, the defendant has requested that the jury be instructed that in determining whether the defendant was negligent it should give great weight to the custom in the early 1970s of not having kill switches on motorboats. The plaintiff has requested that the jury be instructed that, under the circumstances, little if any weight should be given to custom, and that the jury should be free to make its own determination of whether the failure to include kill switches was negligent.

Mechanisms for Resolving Disputes: Special Verdicts, General Verdicts, and Instructions to the Jury

In most of the cases set out in this casebook, the judge instructed the jury concerning the law governing liability and damages, often employing instructions the content of which is established by statute or rule of court,[58] and told the jury that they were bound to follow the law as contained in the instructions. The jury's deliberations may result in a general verdict for the defendant or the plaintiff, in the latter event with an assessment of the damages to which the plaintiff is entitled. This general verdict procedure is not followed in all negligence cases. Most states have by rule or statute authorized trial judges to request special verdicts from juries and to require them to answer special interrogatories.[59] Rule 49 of the Federal Rules of Civil Procedure authorizes similar procedures in federal district courts.[60] Essentially, these alternative procedures require the jury in varying degrees to supply findings of fact that are more specific and concrete than are findings relating merely to the ultimate issues of liability and damages. The first case in this book, Vosburg v. Putney, employed the special verdict technique.

Historically, special verdicts may be traced to the earliest developments of juries, called inquests, in England before the Norman Conquest. Members of these ancient forerunners of our modern juries were chosen because they were presumed to have direct, prior knowledge of the facts, and in effect they acted as their own witnesses. If the King's minister responsible for calling such a jury were unhappy with the verdict reached, a second, or attainting, jury could be appointed to decide the case de novo. If the attainting jury reached a verdict different from that reached by the first jury, the second verdict controlled and the members of the first jury were punished. Because the greatest source of possible confusion and error lay in applying the law, these early juries, in order to minimize the risk of punishment, began refusing to return general verdicts and, instead, began merely finding the specific

58. Uniform instructions established by statute or rule of court for either optional or mandatory use by judges are called pattern instructions. For a state-by-state summary of pattern instructions in this country see McBride, The Art of Instructing the Jury (1969).

59. See generally Sunderland, Verdicts, General and Special, 29 Yale L.J. 253 (1920); Wicker, Special Interrogatories to Juries in Civil Cases, 35 Yale L.J. 296 (1926).

60. See Comment, Special Verdicts: Rule 49 of the Federal Rules of Civil Procedure, 74 Yale L.J. 483 (1965).

facts relevant to the case and leaving the application of the law to the judges.[61]

In spite of its historical antecedents in England, implementation of the special verdict in this country has met substantial resistance. Perhaps this resistance is due to a deep-rooted American attitude in favor of increasing the power of the jury system as a distinctly democratic institution. Allowing juries to reach general verdicts gives them wide latitude, especially in negligence cases, to apply their collective common sense, or popular prejudice, in reaching results. In contrast, under the special verdict procedure the judge exerts more control over the application of the law to the facts of the case—either by performing that application in the first instance, or by reviewing the final outcome reached by the jury in light of their more specific, preliminary findings.

As might be expected, the feature of the general jury verdict procedure in negligence cases that is viewed by many to be its major strength—the empowerment of the jury to reach commonsense, ad hoc results—is viewed by others as a serious weakness. For the last 50 years or more, legal commentators have questioned the extent to which the judge's instructions operate as a guide to the jury in reaching general verdicts. Professor James, in Functions of Judge and Jury in Negligence Cases, 58 Yale L.J. 667, 681-682 (1949), typifies the doubts about the effectiveness of jury instructions:

> Now it should be clear . . . that *the instruction is an effective device only to the extent that it is actually followed by the jury.* Moreover there is in many jurisdictions no real way (save through the jurors' own consciences) to make a jury follow instructions.[62]
>
> The question then arises whether juries, having the *power* to decide cases in violation of instructions, actually do so in a significant number of instances. A scientific answer to this question probably cannot be had. There is, however, good reason to believe that instructions are not particularly effective in getting the jury to perform their theoretical function and in keeping them within the bounds charted out for them by the rules of law.[63]

61. See generally Morgan, A Brief History of Special Verdicts and Special Interrogatories, 32 Yale L.J. 575 (1923).

62. If instructions or other rulings are erroneous, or the verdict is unsupported by a sufficiency of the credible evidence, a new trial may be granted. But in many states a new trial may not be granted, in the absence of such a situation, merely because the trial court *believed* that the jury failed to follow a perfectly proper set of instructions (e.g., where the jury might have found for the plaintiff under the evidence and instructions on one ground but where the court believes—on the basis of intuition, or the like—that the jury did find for the plaintiff on grounds which were properly "withdrawn" from their consideration by the charge).

The situation may be different in those states where the trial court has real discretion to set aside a verdict rendered upon conflicting evidence. Franklin v. McGranahan, 119 Kan. 786, 241 P. 113 (1925) (implies that in the judgment of the court the jury has failed to give proper weight to the instructions). [Eds.]

63. Recent studies suggest that things have not improved much, if at all, in the years since Professor James wrote these words. See Steele, Jr. and Thornburg, Jury Instructions: A Persistent Failure to Communicate, 67 N.C. L. Rev. 77 (1988), and *Symposium,* Making Jury Instructions Comprehensible, 8 U. Bridgeport L. Rev. 279 (1987). Both survey studies regarding

Doubts of this sort have led a number of legal writers to the conclusion that universal implementation of the special verdict procedure, especially in negligence cases, is a much needed reform.[64] One of the earliest and most eloquent advocates of the special verdict was Professor Sunderland, who in a classic treatment of the subject, Verdicts, General and Special, 29 Yale L.J. 253, 262 (1920), asserted:

> The real objection to the special verdict is that it is an honest portrayal of the truth, and the truth is too awkward a thing to fit the technical demands of the record. The record must be absolutely flawless, but such a result is possible only by concealing, not by excluding, mistakes. This is the great technical merit of the general verdict. It covers up all the shortcomings which frail human nature is unable to eliminate from the trial of a case. In the abysmal abstraction of the general verdict concrete details are swallowed up, and the eye of the law, searching anxiously for the realization of logical perfection, is satisfied. In short, the general verdict is valued for what it does, not for what it is. It serves as the great procedural opiate, which draws the curtain upon human errors and soothes us with the assurance that we have attained the unattainable.

In recent years, the center of controversy concerning civil juries has shifted from the debate over whether to replace general verdicts with special verdicts to a debate over whether to replace the entire jury-fault system of liability with some type of nonfault system of compensation.[65] Some writers believe that a more sensible resolution of the first controversy would have eliminated the necessity of even considering the second.[66]

Law and Behavior: Influences upon Jury Decisions

In the excerpt from his article on the functions of judge and jury set out in the preceding note, Professor James suggests that a scientific answer "probably cannot be had" to the question of whether and to what extent juries decide cases in violation of instructions. The major reason for his pessimism in this regard may be the traditional judicial antagonism toward

---

the effectiveness, or lack thereof, of jury instructions, and suggest ways in which instructions could be made more effective. [Eds.]

64. For a summary of the commentaries on the reform movement see Comment, Special Verdicts: Rule 49 of the Federal Rules of Civil Procedure, 74 Yale L.J. 483, 488-497 (1965).

65. See Chapter 10, Section B, below.

66. See Green and Smith, Negligence Law, No-Fault, and Jury Trial, (I) 50 Tex. L. Rev. 1093 (1972); (II) 50 Tex. L. Rev. 1297 (1972); (III) 51 Tex. L. Rev. 825 (1973); (IV) 51 Tex. L. Rev. 825 (1973).

efforts to discover what goes on during jury deliberations.[67] Judges are understandably reluctant to cooperate with attempts, even by disinterested scientists, to snoop and pry into the ongoing deliberations of juries. Thus, to some extent at least, Professor James's remarks regarding the unfathomability of the jury decision process have stood, and will probably continue to stand, the test of time.[68] And yet he was writing in the late 1940s, before the upsurge in behavioral scientists' interest in studying the legal process, an upsurge already described in part in the earlier note on judicial behavior. Most of the writing on juror behavior up until that time had been anecdotal, impressionistic, and unavoidably speculative.[69] As might be expected, a considerable amount of empirical work has been done in the intervening years, and as a result it is increasingly possible to generalize with confidence concerning the factors, including the judge's instructions, that influence jury decisions.

Most of the scientific studies in this area have focused, as was true of the studies of judicial behavior described in an earlier law and behavior note, upon extralegal factors which influence the way in which jurors decide the issues presented to them. By studying the records of trials which have been held, and by simulating trials where actual records are unavailable or inadequate for their purposes,[70] behavioral scientists have established correlations between background factors and typical juror responses to particular cases. These correlations include: jurors whose socioeconomic status closely parallels the status of the defendant in a criminal case are more likely to acquit than are jurors whose socioeconomic status is either substantially higher or substantially lower than that of the defendant;[71] jurors with higher education are more likely to place emphasis upon procedure and the instructions in reaching their decisions than are jurors of lower education;[72] persons of higher status are more likely than persons of lower status, to influence the decisions of their fellow jurors;[73] juries composed

67. E.g.: "I[t] is improper and unethical for lawyers, court attaches or judges in a particular case to make public the transactions in the jury room or to interview jurors to discover what was the course of deliberation of a trial jury." Northern Pacific Ry. v. Mely, 219 F.2d 199, 202 (9th Cir. 1954). See also, U.S. v. Kepreos, 759 F.2d 961 (1st Cir. 1985) and U.S. v. Franklin, 546 F. Supp. 1133 (N.D. Ind. 1982).

68. However, study of jury decisionmaking has included participant observation. See Warren and Mauldin, Deliberation in Six Juries: A Participant Observer Study, 3 Symbolic Interaction 157 (1980).

69. See, e.g., Osborn, The Mind of the Juror as Judge of the Facts (1937).

70. For a discussion on mock jury experiments, see MacCoun, Experimental Research on Jury Decision-Making, 244 Science 1046 (June 2, 1989).

71. See Adler, Socioeconomic Factors Influencing Jury Verdicts, 3 N.Y.U. Rev. L. & Social Change 1 (1973). Another study found mock jurors more likely to give harsher penalties to defendants of higher social status when jurors perceived those defendants as having abused capabilities associated with that status. See Bray, Struckman-Johnson, Osborne, McFarlane, and Scott, The Effects of Defendant Status on the Decisions of Student and Community Juries, 41 Soc. Psychol. 256 (Sept. 1978). In general, see Werchick, Jury Selection 77 (2d ed. 1993).

72. See James, Status and Competence of Jurors, 64 A.J. Soc. 563 (1959).

73. See Strodtbeck, James, and Hawkins, Social Status in Jury Deliberations, 22 Am. Soc. Rev. 713 (1957). See also, Werchick, Civil Jury Selection 81-83 (2d ed. 1993) (noting that, except in cases involving gender-related issues, gender may not significantly influence jury

entirely of men are less likely to decide in favor of tort plaintiffs, and more likely to decide in favor of litigants of superior status, than are juries composed of men and women.[74] Past research suggested that jurors of German and British backgrounds are more likely to find criminal defendants guilty than are black jurors and jurors of Slavic and Italian backgrounds,[75] but recent authors have questioned such generalizations;[76] other studies have concluded that jurors with previous jury experience are more likely to reach premature conclusions (apparently based on their past jury experience) than are jurors without such experience;[77] jurors are likely to be prejudiced in favor of parties of their own sex and prejudiced against parties of the opposite sex;[78] and depressed jurors may be more apt to award punitive damages.[79]

This list, by no means exhaustive, tends generally to support the beliefs traditionally held by trial lawyers regarding what may be expected from various types of jurors.[80] The major practical application of these background studies, of course, is in the jury selection process. Trial lawyers working within the system have always wanted to know as much as possible about the jurors and prospective jurors whom they encounter in court.[81] Moreover,

---

decisions). Concerning jury deliberation, see Hastie, Penrod, and Pennington, Inside the Jury 141-142 (1983) (finding that under some conditions males were more likely to dominate jury deliberation). As to jury leadership in general, see Eakin, An Empirical Study of the Effect of Leadership Influence on Decision Outcomes in Different Sized Jury Panels, 11 Kan. J. Soc. 109 (1975).

74. See Snyder, Sex Role Differential and Juror Decisions, 55 Sociology and Social Research 442 (1971). For discussions on the relationship between gender and jury function, see Hastie, Penrod and Pennington, Inside the Jury 140-142 (1983); Roberts, Trial Psychology: Communication and Persuasion in the Courtroom 56-59 (1987).

75. See Broeder, The University of Chicago Jury Project, 38 Neb. L. Rev. 744, 748 (1959).

76. See Sunnafrank and Fontes, General and Crime-Related Racial Stereotypes and Influence on Juridic Decisions, 17 Cornell J. Soc. Rel. 1 (Fall 1983) (reviewing the conflicting research concerning race and jury decisions); Werchick, Civil Jury Selection 81-83 (2d ed. 1993) (extreme caution should be used when making generalizations about race and ethnic background and jury decisionmaking).

77. See Broeder, Previous Jury Trial Service Affecting Juror Behavior, [1965] Ins. L.J. 138. However, a more recent study questioned Broeder's findings, and, in contrast, did not find a significant relationship between prior jury service and jury performance. See, Hastie, Penrod, and Pennington, Inside the Jury 142-143, 150 (1983).

78. See Stephen, Sex Prejudice in Jury Simulation, 88 J. Psych. 305 (1974). For a discussion on the meaning and significance of gender in sociolegal research, see Mendel-Meadow and Diamond, The Content, Method, and Epistemology of Gender in Sociolegal Studies, 25 L. & Soc. Rev. 221 (1991).

79. See Moss, Punitive-Damages Jurors: Study Suggests Selecting Depressed People, 74 A.B.A. J. 18 (Sept. 1, 1988).

80. See Bryan, The Chosen Ones (1971), for an impressionistic exposition by a doctor-lawyer on the psychology of jury selection. For example, the author asserts, without proof, that men tend to accept a woman's testimony in direct proportion to physical beauty, (p. 57). Other research does suggest a potential relationship between a defendant's attractiveness and jury decisions. See MacCoun, The Emergence of Extralegal Bias During Jury Deliberation, 17 Crim. Just. & Behav. 303 (Sept. 1990); Roberts, Trial Psychology: Communication and Persuasion in the Courtroom 74-77 (1987).

81. For trial practice material on jury selection, see, e.g., Blue and Saginaw, Jury Selection: Strategy and Science (Colson and Neely eds. 1993); Vinson, Jury Trials: The Psychology of

knowledge of how background factors influence juror behavior may be valuable to those involved in the ongoing efforts at reforming the system.[82]

The real thrust of Professor James's speculations regarding juror behavior, however, is directed not at the jury selection process but rather at the jury decision process. Given a jury composed by the manner of selection that happens to apply in a given case, how do those jurors set about the task of reaching a verdict? How does what the jury sees and hears in court affect its verdict in a given case? Obviously, statistically supportable correlations between juror backgrounds and juror reactions do not purport to supply answers to these questions. The only means of doing so is to study the decision process itself. Accepting that eavesdropping on actual juries in real cases is improper,[83] two basic methods of investigation are available, both of which have been widely employed by social scientists: Jurors in actual cases may be interviewed after trial, and asked to reconstruct the decision process from memory; or the reactions of mock juries in simulated trials may be observed directly. There are obvious limits to both methodologies. In the former, the reliance upon memory detracts from the accuracy of the data collected, as memories are fallible and selective. The latter technique of simulated trials cures the defect of reliance upon memory, but inevitably some reality is lost because the jurors' reactions are not based on an actual trial but on an obvious fake.[84]

Notwithstanding these shortcomings, valuable work has been done employing both methodologies. One ambitious undertaking was the University of Chicago jury project. In 1966, the first of what was to be at least two volumes was published. This volume covered the project on the jury in criminal trials.[85] No companion volume covering the civil trial jury has been forthcoming. However, an adequate picture of the civil jury studies undertaken may be obtained from the following:

Winning Strategy 149-170 (1986); Werchick, Civil Jury Selection (2d ed. 1993); Roberts, Trial Psychology: Communication and Persuasion in the Courtroom 137-270 (1987).

82. See, e.g., Johnson, Black Innocence and the White Jury, 83 Mich. L. Rev. 1611 (1985); National Jury Project, Jurywork: Systematic Techniques (Krauss and Bonora eds. 1990); Note, The Jury: A Reflection of the Prejudices of the Community, 20 Hast. L.J. 417 (1969). As to the efficacy of social science data for jury selection, see Fulero and Penrod, The Myths and Realities of Attorney Jury Selection Folklore and Scientific Jury Selection: What Works?, 17 Ohio N.U. L. Rev. 229 (1990).

The extent to which lawyers can make use of gender, and racial and ethnic characteristics in the jury selection process through peremptory challenges has become severely limited. See Bray, Reaching the Final Chapter in the Story of Peremptory Challenges, 40 U.C.L.A. L. Rev. 517 (1992); Broderick, Why Peremptory Challenges Should Be Abolished, 65 Temp. L. Rev. 369 (1992); Marko, The Case Against Gender-Based Peremptory Challenges, 4 Hast. Women's L.J. 109 (1993); Swift, Batson's Invidious Legacy: Discriminatory Juror Exclusion and the "Intuitive" Peremptory Challenge, 78 Corn. L. Rev. 336 (1993).

83. See Kalven and Zeisel, The American Jury vi-vii (1961).

84. For an exposition of the main models of jury decisionmaking see Hastie, Inside the Jury: The Psychology of Juror Decision Making (1993).

85. Kalven and Zeisel, The American Jury (1961).

Let us now turn to the most important facet of the project, the development of the experimental jury. Tape recordings of mock trials based on actual trials have been prepared and with the consent of the court and of the jurors themselves—these are persons actually on jury duty at the time—have been played to the jurors. By means of this experimental technique we are able to repeat the same trial before several juries and by comparing the verdicts and the deliberations of groups which have heard different versions of the same trial to test the effects of a given change. In addition, and with the consent of the jurors, the experimental jury has made possible the full recording of the deliberations. Finally the set-up has enabled us to interview the jurors at various stages of the case. Thus they have been asked for their individual decisions at the end of the trial and just before the deliberations and again after the deliberations. Four moot cases have been developed thus far and have been played to over 100 juries.

Only a few illustrations will be attempted from the data and these are drawn from the first experimental case. The case involved an auto-accident in which plaintiff, a forty year old stenographer, was injured when the car in which she was riding as a passenger collided with a car driven by defendant.

The design permitted us to test the effect of several variables at the same time. In three treatments, defendant's liability was very clear; in three it was a little doubtful. These versions were then combined with three different treatments of defendant's liability insurance. In the first, defendant reveals he has no insurance but there is no objection or further attention paid to the disclosure; in the second, the defendant reveals that he has insurance, defense counsel objects and the court directs the jury to disregard; in the third treatment, the defendant again discloses insurance but there is no objection and no further notice is taken. The tapes were then played to sets of juries operating under the unanimity rule and to sets of juries operating under the three-fourths majority rule. In all, the experiment was given to thirty juries.

Here briefly are some of the results. First, twenty-eight verdicts were for plaintiff, one jury hung on the damage issue and one jury found for the defendant. Second, the average award of all verdicts where liability was very clear was $41,000; the average award of all verdicts where liability was somewhat ambiguous was $34,000, $7,000 less. This, of course, supports the suspicion long entertained by the bar that the weaker the proof on liability the lower the verdict is apt to be. However, no significant difference in award level resulted between juries operating under the unanimity rule and juries operating under the three-fourths majority rule.

Then there are the results of the three insurance treatments. Where the defendant disclosed that he had no insurance the average award of all verdicts was $33,000. Where defendant disclosed that he had insurance but there was no objection the average award rose to $37,000. Where, however, the defendant said he had insurance and there was an objection and an instruction to disregard, the average award rose to $46,000, $13,000 more than when the defendant said he was not insured, and $9,000 more than when he said he was insured but where there was no objection or instruction to disregard. The conclusion appears to be two-fold: First, that juries tend to award less when they know that an individual defendant is not insured; and, second, that where they know defendant is insured and a fuss is made over it the verdict will

> be higher than when no such fuss is made. The objection and the instruction to disregard, in other words, sensitize the jurors to the fact that defendant is insured and thereby increase the award. However, the instruction to disregard at least served the purpose of keeping the jurors from talking about insurance during the deliberations.[86]

One of the interesting results of the experiment just described is the way in which the juries apparently attempted consciously to follow the judge's instruction (after all, they did not talk about insurance during deliberations), but were influenced, unconsciously perhaps, by the instruction in exactly the opposite direction from that intended by the judge.

In a jury study conducted at Eastern Michigan University,[87] experimental interview techniques were employed to explore the effects of variations in the judge's instructions on jury decisions. Sixteen different versions of a hypothetical case involving the accidental drowning of a child in a backyard swimming pool were used to test the impact upon 192 individual jurors of four sets of independent, dichotomous variables: (1) the probability that the accident would occur (high density neighborhood with many children versus low density neighborhood with few children); (2) the degree of injury sustained (minor injury vs. death); (3) the extent of the precautions taken by the defendant (pool enclosed by fence six feet high vs. three feet); and (4) the length and content of the instructions to the jury ("decide according to your sense of values" vs. longer, more explicit statement defining the standard of care expected of a reasonable person).[88] The author of the study report reaches the following conclusions regarding the effect upon jurors of differences in the length and complexity of the judge's instructions:

> The functional significance of the charge looms most prominently in the findings which show that within each category of *risk* stratified by *the injury* the difference between the plaintiff and the defendant in the proportion of votes received is generally greater in cases with the short charge than those with the long charge. The vote in cases of *death* with *high risk* under the long form is closely divided between the litigants, 7 for the plaintiff and 5 for the defendant; under the short form the vote is decisive, 10 for the plaintiff and 2 for the defendant. Likewise, in cases of *low risk—minor injury,* the vote is even under the long charge, 6 to 6, but preponderantly for the defendant, 10 to 2, under the short charge. In cases of intermediate liability the length of the charge has less of an influence upon the verdict. The vote for the

86. Broeder, The University of Chicago Jury Project, 38 Neb. L. Rev. 1, 753-754 (1959). For an analysis of the effects of objections to inadmissible testimony, see Reinard and Reynolds, The Effects of Inadmissible Testimony Objections and Rulings on Jury Decisions, 14 J. Am. Forensic Assn. 91 (Fall 1978) (attorney objections may magnify the effect of inadmissible testimony on jury decisions).

87. See Green, The Reasonable Man: Legal Fiction or Psychosocial Reality?, 21 L. & Soc. Rev. 241 (1968).

88. It will be observed that the first three variables are the elements in Judge Hand's famous formulation of the negligence test in United States v. Carroll Towing Co., p. 203, above.

> plaintiff and the defendant under the long and short forms, respectively, in cases of *low risk—death* tallies 3 to 9 and 5 to 7. In cases of *high risk—minor injury* the results under both forms of instruction are 8 to 4 in favor of the plaintiff. In brief, the amount of variance in the vote accruing under the short form . . . significantly exceeds that accruing under the long form. . . . This finding indicates that within each subcategory of cases there is a pronounced consensus among the respondents who received the version with the short form and a rather even division among those who received the version with the long form. Hence, we may infer that the extended charge embodying the calculus of risk formula opposes the purpose for which it was designed by inhibiting rather than facilitating shifts in judgment on the intended dimensions.[89]

Before rushing to accept this conclusion as support for Professor James's suspicions that juries are not particularly helped by formal instructions, we should examine it critically. For example, one might well question the assumption implicit in the preceding quotation that the calculus of risk was designed to facilitate shifts in judgment on the part of jurors. If the jurors' reactions under the shorter charge may be characterized as essentially intuitive or visceral reactions, then the longer charge may help to temper those reactions with reflection and reason. To be sure, in this experiment the longer charge worked to destroy a consensus on the liability issue. However, the jurors reacted individually, and not collectively, in this experiment, and apparently were asked to consider only the liability question to the exclusion of damages. Had the same jurors been confronted with a similar case in real life, with the opportunity to intermingle the issues of liability and damages in group discussions, the effect of the longer charge might have been different. Viewed in this way, the longer charge may be a helpful enhancement of what Leon Green referred to as the ritual aspect of the judge's instructions,[90] saying to the jury, in effect, "Consider this case carefully and weigh the factors thoughtfully."

A somewhat different type of empirical research into jury behavior has come to the fore in the 1980s. The Institute for Civil Justice, established within The Rand Corporation in 1979, has done much of the work. Their studies have focused on trends and patterns of outcomes in thousands of jury trials in actual cases. Not surprisingly, they have found that jury awards in tort cases, even adjusted for inflation, have been rising over the past 20 years, as has the relative frequency of "big" (over $1 million) awards. One study sought to determine the factors that affect outcomes. See Chin & Peterson, Deep Pockets, Empty Pockets: Who Wins in Cook County Jury Trials (1985). Among their findings are the following:

89. 2 L. & Soc. Rev. at 247-248.

90. Green, Judge and Jury 351 (1930). See also Douthwaite, Jury Instructions on Medical Issues (3d ed. 1987 and Supp.). See generally, Steel and Thornburg, Jury Instructions: A Persistent Failure to Communicate, 647 N.C. L. Rev. 77 (1988).

(1) Ninety-eight percent of plaintiffs were individuals. But 25 percent of defendants were corporations and 8 percent were municipalities. One percent of defendants were hospitals or nonprofit organizations.
(2) Among individuals, the least wealthy and educated were more likely to be plaintiffs in jury trials. The proportion of plaintiffs who were unskilled laborers and service workers was nearly twice their proportion in Cook County's population.
(3) Blacks were underrepresented as litigants except in trials involving automobile and common carrier accidents. Surprisingly few blacks brought intentional tort suits (which include claims of discrimination and police abuse), work injury, malpractice, or slip-and-fall or other injury-on-property cases to juries. When blacks were involved in jury trials, in most cases both plaintiff and defendant were black.
(4) Black plaintiffs received, on average, 25 percent less than whites with the same injury. Verdicts against black defendants decreased during the 1970s, where blacks paid 20 percent less than white defendants in similar suits. But black defendants were usually sued by black plaintiffs, who received only 60 percent of what white plaintiffs received from white defendants.
(5) There were no differences in awards between men and women or between workers in different occupations after accounting for the type of lawsuit and plaintiffs' injuries and economic losses. Workers in the prime working age (40-59 years old) received larger awards, but this difference was stronger in the 1960s than in the 1970s.
(6) For most trials, when plaintiffs were not severely injured, government defendants paid the largest awards—50 percent greater than individual defendants paid to plaintiffs with similar injuries in the same type of lawsuit. This pattern was the same in the 1960s and 1970s.
(7) Corporate defendants also paid more than individual defendants, with the premium increasing from 23 percent in the 1960s to 40 percent in the 1970s. Awards against corporations were far greater when plaintiffs were severely injured—over four times greater than those against individual defendants.
(8) Hospitals and other nonprofit organizations paid awards that were smaller than any other defendants, including individuals. These defendants have received even more favorable treatment in recent years.
(9) These differences were most important when plaintiffs were severely injured. Black plaintiffs received \$45,000 less than nonblacks for a very serious work injury. Corporations were paying \$170,000 more than individual defendants when the plaintiff was severely injured.[91]

91. This summary was taken from Institute for Civil Justice (Rand Corporation), An Overview of the First Five Program Years 26-27 (1985).

Other studies sponsored by the Institute for Civil Justice include Peterson, A Summary of Research Results: Trends and Patterns in Civil Jury Verdicts (1986); Peterson, Civil Juries in the 1980s: Trends in Jury Trials and Verdicts in California and Cook County, Illinois (1987); MacCoun, Experimental Research on Jury Decision-Making (1989); MacCoun, Getting Inside the Black Box: Toward a Better Understanding of Civil Juror Behavior (1987); Summary of Research Results on the Tort Liability System: Statement (1986).

Other jury research includes Hastie, Penrod and Pennington, Inside the Jury (1983); National Jury Project, Jurywork: Systematic Techniques (2d ed. 1990); Saks, Jury Verdicts: The Role of Group Size and Social Decision Rule (1977); and Simon, The Jury: Its Role in American Society (1980).

Of course, increased knowledge and understanding of the influences upon jury decisions will present opportunities to affect the outcomes of trials by manipulating the way in which jurors are selected and approached during trial.[92] Given the extent to which the parties to civil litigation are afforded an opportunity to interview prospective jurors and within limits to eliminate those whom they believe on the basis of social science survey data and psychological screening will not react favorably to them,[93] the traditional picture of the jury as a cross section of the community will become outdated. Whether a system in which such sophisticated manipulations are commonplace is preferable to one in which jurors are selected essentially by lot is very much an open question, and one which will have to be answered in the years ahead.

Helling v. Carey

83 Wash. 2d 514, 519 P.2d 981 (1974)

[The plaintiff sued the defendant ophthalmologists in negligence. A trial was held, and the evidence was that the plaintiff suffered from glaucoma, which had seriously impaired her vision. The defendants had given the plaintiff routine eye examinations over a period of several years, but did not administer a test which would have revealed the glaucoma in time to treat it effectively. When her condition was diagnosed, the plaintiff was 32 years old. The uncontradicted expert testimony was that the test for glaucoma is not routinely given to persons under the age of 40, since the incidence of the disease in this age group is only 1 in 25,000. The jury returned its

92. See Blue and Saginaw, Jury Selection: Strategy & Science (Colson and Neely eds. 1993); Starr and McCormick, Jury Selection (2d ed. 1993); Symposium on the Selection and Function of the Modern Jury, 40 Am. U. L. Rev. 541-883 (1991).

93. See authorities cited in notes 77-80, above. For a description of jury selection techniques based on survey analysis and psychological screening employed by the defendants' attorneys in the trial of the "Harrisburg Seven," see Schulman, Shaver, Colman, Emrich and Christie, Recipe for a Jury, 6 Psychol. Today 37 (May 1973).

verdict for the defendants, upon which the trial judge entered judgment. An intermediate appellate court affirmed, and the plaintiff appealed.]

HUNTER, J. . . . In her petition for review, the plaintiff's primary contention is that under the facts of this case the trial judge erred in giving certain instructions to the jury and refusing her proposed instructions defining the standard of care which the law imposes upon an ophthalmologist. As a result, the plaintiff contends, in effect, that she was unable to argue her theory of the case to the jury that the standard of care for the specialty of ophthalmology was inadequate to protect the plaintiff from the incidence of glaucoma, and that the defendants, by reason of their special ability, knowledge and information, were negligent in failing to give the pressure test to the plaintiff at an earlier point in time which, if given, would have detected her condition and enabled the defendants to have averted the resulting substantial loss in her vision.

We find this to be a unique case. The testimony of the medical experts is undisputed concerning the standards of the profession for the specialty of ophthalmology. . . . The issue is whether the defendant's compliance with the standard of the profession of ophthalmology, which does not require the giving of a routine pressure test to persons under 40 years of age, should insulate them from liability under the facts in this case where the plaintiff has lost a substantial amount of her vision due to the failure of the defendants to timely give the pressure test to the plaintiff.

The defendants argue that the standard of the profession, which does not require the giving of a routine pressure test to persons under the age of 40, is adequate to insulate the defendants from liability for negligence because the risk of glaucoma is so rare in this age group. . . .

The incidence of glaucoma in one out of 25,000 persons under the age of 40 may appear quite minimal. However, that one person, the plaintiff in this instance, is entitled to the same protection, as afforded persons over 40, essential for timely detection of the evidence of glaucoma where it can be arrested to avoid the grave and devastating result of this disease. The test is a simple pressure test, relatively inexpensive. There is no judgment factor involved, and there is no doubt that by giving the test the evidence of glaucoma can be detected. The giving of the test is harmless if the physical condition of the eye permits. The testimony indicates that although the condition of the plaintiff's eyes might have at times prevented the defendants from administering the pressure test, there is an absence of evidence in the record that the test could not have been timely given.

Justice Holmes stated in Texas & P. Ry. v. Behymer, 189 U.S. 468, 470, 47 L. Ed. 905, 23 S. Ct. 622 (1903): "What usually is done may be evidence of what ought to be done, but what ought to be done is fixed by a standard of reasonable prudence, whether it usually is complied with or not."

In The T. J. Hooper, 60 F.2d 737 (2d Cir. 1932), Justice Hand stated on page 740: "[I]n most cases reasonable prudence is in fact common prudence; but strictly it is never its measure; a whole calling may have unduly lagged in the adoption of new and available devices. It never may set its own tests, however persuasive be its usages. *Courts must in the end say what is required; there are precautions so imperative that even their universal disregard will not excuse their omission.*" (Italics ours.)

Under the facts of this case reasonable prudence required the timely giving of the pressure test to this plaintiff. The precaution of giving this test to detect the incidence of glaucoma to patients under 40 years of age is so imperative that irrespective of its disregard by the standards of the ophthalmology profession, it is the duty of the courts to say what is required to protect patients under 40 from the damaging results of glaucoma.

We therefore hold, as a matter of law, that the reasonable standard that should have been followed under the undisputed facts of this case was the timely giving of this simple, harmless pressure test to this plaintiff and that, in failing to do so, the defendants were negligent, which proximately resulted in the blindness sustained by the plaintiff for which the defendants are liable.

There are no disputed facts to submit to the jury on the issue of the defendants' liability. Hence, a discussion of the plaintiff's proposed instructions would be inconsequential in view of our disposition of the case.

The judgment of the trial court and the decision of the Court of Appeals is reversed, and the case is remanded for a new trial on the issue of damages only.

HALE, C.J., and ROSELLINI, STAFFORD, WRIGHT, and BRACHTENBACH, JJ., concur.

[The concurring opinion of UTTER, J., in which he urged that the liability of the defendants in this case should be strict, rather than based upon negligence, is omitted.]

As the cases preceding *Helling* in this section indicate, custom may have great weight in determining the particular standard of care, but, as The T. J. Hooper held, it is not ordinarily dispositive. See also Krzywicki v. Tidewater Equipment Co., 600 F. Supp. 629 (D. Md. 1985) and Golden Villa Nursing Home v. Smith, 674 S.W.2d 343 (Tex. App. 1984) (custom itself may tolerate negligence). A different rule has been applied by most courts in medical malpractice cases—professional custom is not just evidence of the standard of care, it *is* the standard of care. See McCoid, The Care Required of Medical Practitioners, 12 Vand. L. Rev. 549 (1959). And, with few exceptions, the plaintiff must establish the professional standard by the use of expert testimony. See Oelling v. Rao, 593 N.E.2d 189 (Ind. 1992). Although some courts have suggested that conclusive effect will not be given to medical custom (see, e.g., Chiero v. Chicago Osteopathic Hospital, 74 Ill. App. 3d 166, 392 N.E.2d 203 (1979)), *Helling* is unique in that it not only permitted plaintiff to recover in the absence of any expert testimony supporting her claim that the defendants were negligent, but it also held that she was entitled to prevail on that issue as a matter of law.

Shortly after *Helling* was decided, the Washington legislature passed a statute requiring that to recover in a malpractice action the plaintiff must prove "that the defendant or defendants failed to exercise that degree of skill, care and learning possessed by other persons in the same profession. . . ." Wash. Rev. Code §4.24.290. In Gates v. Jensen, 92 Wash. 2d 246, 595 P.2d 919 (1979), the court held that this statute did not alter the *Helling* rule. In *Gates,* as in *Helling,* the alleged negligence was the defendants' failure to test the plaintiff for glaucoma. In ruling that the trial judge improperly refused to instruct the jury that it was not bound by medical custom, the court stated that liability can be imposed if the defendant failed to exercise the "skill, care and learning" *possessed* by others in the profession, whether customarily used or not in similar circumstances.

For somewhat differing explanations of the rule that makes medical custom dispositive of the standard of care, see Pearson, The Role of Custom in Medical Malpractice Cases, 51 Ind. L.J. 528 (1976), and the article by McCoid cited above.

At one time, the source to which courts turned to determine medical custom was the locality in which the defendant practiced, or one similar to it. The trend in recent years has been to depart from the "locality rule," and to turn to the country as a whole to determine medical custom, at least with respect to specialists. See, e.g., Brune v. Belinkoff, 354 Mass. 102, 235 N.E.2d 793 (1968). Even applying the broader national standards of practice, however, will not necessarily foreclose the relevance of more limited resources to physicians practicing in less populated areas. See Vergara v. Doan, 593 N.E.2d 185 (Ind. 1992).

The rejection of the locality rule is based on the assumption that the quality of medical care ought not vary with the geographical area in which the defendant practices. Should the quality vary with the ability of patients to pay? The traditional answer of tort law, at least at the level of dictum, is that the standard of care should not vary with a patient's resources. As one court explained, "[w]hether the patient be a pauper or a millionaire, whether he be treated gratuitously or for reward, the physician owes him precisely the same measure of duty, and the same degree of skill and care." Becker v. Janiski, 15 N.Y.S. 675, 677 (1891). This unitary standard of care appeals to the widespread sentiment that, in matters as important as one's health, an individual's wealth should not be a consideration. But as laudable as this sentiment is, is tort law really an effective instrument to achieve this end? In other areas directly related to individual health and welfare, such as the quality of housing or the safety of automobiles, tort law declines to mandate absolute equality. One reason is that doing so may actually disadvantage the poor by pricing such goods and services beyond their means. For a similar argument regarding medical care, see Siliciano, Wealth, Equity, and the Unitary Medical Malpractice Standard, 77 Va. L. Rev. 439 (1991).

The question of the effect of custom has arisen in a variety of medically related contexts. In Osborn v. Irwin Memorial Blood Bank, 5 Cal. App. 4th 234, 271, 7 Cal. Rptr. 2d 101, 120 (1992), the court ruled that "the adequacy of a blood bank's actions to prevent the contamination of blood is a question of professional negligence and fulfillment of a professional standard of care." In another case involving contaminated blood, United Blood Services v. Quintana, 827 P.2d 509 (Colo. 1992), the court held that adherence to the professional standard is not conclusive but rather creates a rebuttable presumption of reasonable care.

The role of custom has arisen in connection with those who are not physicians in the full sense but who do render medical services. For example, the court in Jistarri v. Nappi, 549 A.2d 210 (Pa. Super. 1988), ruled that the standard applicable to a resident orthopedist is higher than the standard applicable to general practitioners, but lower than that for orthopedists that are fully trained. In Kerkman v. Hintz, 142 Wis. 2d 404, 418 N.W.2d 795 (1988), the court ruled that the standard applicable to a chiropractor is that of a reasonable chiropractor under the circumstances, and not that of a "recognized school of the medical profession." This constitutes progress of sorts for chiropractors; in Brown v. Shyne, p. 233, above, the Court of Appeals of New York stated that the defendant chiropractor in that case would be held to the standard of "those who do offer treatment legally."

What should the standard of care be for those who rely on faith healing instead of conventional medicine for the treatment of disease and injury? The issue was presented in Brown v. Laitner, 432 Mich. 861, 435 N.W.2d 1 (1989). The Supreme Court of Michigan vacated an earlier decision to hear an appeal in a case involving the death of a child who had been treated by a Christian Science practitioner. The facts of the case and a discussion of the issues are contained in the dissenting opinion of Justice Levin, who would have heard the appeal. The trial judge determined that the standard applicable to the defendants would be that of a "reasonably prudent Christian Scientist," and that the plaintiff could not prevail on the merits without a constitutionally impermissible inquiry into the sincerity of the defendants' beliefs. The Michigan Court of Appeals agreed, and the plaintiff appealed. After initially granting review, the court vacated its earlier order because "the Court is no longer persuaded that the questions presented should be reviewed by this Court."

Not surprisingly, the standard of care to which veterinarians will be held is the professional standard. King, The Standard of Care for Veterinarians in Medical Malpractice Claims, 58 Tenn. L. Rev. 1 (1990), discusses the issues.

The standard of care applied in attorney malpractice cases is similar to that used in cases involving medical malpractice: The duty of attorneys is "to use such skill, prudence, and diligence as lawyers of ordinary skill and capacity commonly possess and exercise in the performance of tasks which they undertake." Lucas v. Hamm, 56 Cal. 2d 583, 364 P.2d 685, 15 Cal.

Rptr. 821 (1961), *cert. denied,* 368 U.S. 987 (1962). See generally, Wolfram, Modern Legal Ethics 209-217 (1986).

The Relationship Between Tort and Contract: Breach of Promise to Cure as a Basis of Medical Malpractice Liability

As the note on tort and contract following Bang v. Charles T. Miller in Chapter 1, p. 48, above, indicates some commentators have urged greater reliance upon express contract between patient and doctor and lesser reliance upon tort in determining the liability of physicians for medical injuries. In some cases, plaintiffs have relied upon contract as a basis of recovery, although with mixed results.

The major difficulty with express contract as a basis of liability is in separating cases in which the physician has made an express promise to cure from those in which he or she has done no more than to express an opinion that the outcome will be satisfactory, or to make an assurance to a timid and cautious patient. Most courts faced with the issue have required something more than evidence to the effect that the doctor has expressed such opinions or assurances. Thus, some courts have insisted that the plaintiff present "clear proof" that the defendant intended to guarantee a specific result. See, e.g., Clevinger v. Haling, 379 Mass. 154, 394 N.E.2d 1119 (Mass. 1979). Others have required that to be actionable a promise to achieve a particular result must be supported by separate consideration. See, e.g., Dorney v. Harris, 482 F. Supp. 323 (D. Colo. 1980); Wilczynski v. Goodman, 391 N.E.2d 479 (Ill. App. 1979). Some state legislatures have dealt with the problem by statutes declaring that liability cannot be based upon a breach of promise of particular results unless there is a contract to that effect in writing and signed by the physician. See, e.g., Ind. Code §16-9.5-1-4.

A more receptive judicial approach to contract liability was taken in Guilmet v. Campbell, 385 Mich. 57, 188 N.W.2d 601 (1971). The plaintiff had undergone an operation for a bleeding ulcer. He was unsatisfied with his post-operation condition, and sued the surgeons for negligence and breach of express contract to cure. The jury returned a verdict for the defendants on the negligence claim, and for the plaintiff on the contract claim. The Supreme Court of Michigan affirmed the judgment for the plaintiff on the latter claim, pointing to statements made by the defendants as related by the plaintiff (385 Mich. at 68, 88 N.W.2d at 606):

> Once you have an operation it takes care of all your troubles. You can eat as you want to, you can drink as you want to, you can go as you please. Dr. Arena and I are specialists, there is nothing to it at all—it's a very simple operation. You'll be out of work three to four weeks at the most. There is

> no danger at all in this operation. After the operation you can throw away your pill box. In twenty years if you figure out what you spent for Maalox pills and doctor calls, you could buy an awful lot. Weigh it against an operation.

These statements were not all made at the same point in time but were spread out over a lengthy consultation, and the defendants denied making some of them. In ruling that a jury issue was created by the plaintiff's testimony, the court said (385 Mich. at 69, 188 N.W.2d at 606-607):

> What was said, and the circumstances under which it was said always determines whether there was a contract at all and if so what it was. These matters are always for the determination of the factfinder.

If *Guilmet* were a controlling case in your jurisdiction, what advice would you give a doctor who asks how to avoid exposure to contract liability? Would a prospective patient be well advised to consult a lawyer before seeing a doctor? What impact would you expect *Guilmet* to have upon doctor-patient relationships? Perhaps concerns of this sort led the Michigan legislature to substantially undercut *Guilmet* in Mich. Comp. Laws Ann. §566.132(g) (Supp. 1992), requiring that "an agreement, promise, contract, or warranty of cure relating to medical care or treatment" be in writing and signed by the doctor to be enforceable.

Medical malpractice liability based upon contract is discussed in Pearson, The Role of Custom in Medical Malpractice Cases, 51 Ind. L.J. 528, 545-550 (1976); Epstein, Medical Malpractice: The Case for Contract, 76 Am. B. Found. Res. J. 87 (1976); Havighurst, Reforming Medical Malpractice Law Through Consumer Choice, 3 Health Aff. 63 (Winter 1984).

Law and Behavior: Social Science Input into the Judicial Process

In previous notes on the subject of law and behavior we have considered the effects of rules of law upon the conduct of persons to whom those rules are directed. We shall here consider the reverse relationship—that is, the effect of people's conduct upon the rules of law by which they are supposedly governed. At first blush, it might be assumed that the relationship between law and behavior, if such a relationship exists, is essentially a one-way street: the law calls the tune, and people dance to it. However, in many important respects behavior influences the shape of the law to no less significant degree than the law influences behavior. Perhaps the most commonly encountered form of behavior which influences lawmakers, both legislators and judges, is the activity of pressure groups representing special interests.[94] This type of behavior is consciously directed toward influencing the content of the law. Although pressure group activities tend to capture our attention whenever the subject of influencing lawmakers is raised, it is no less true that the behavior patterns of people in general exert a profound effect upon the shape and content of the law. Legislatures, for example, very often investigate existing patterns of behavior as a prelude to the formulation and enactment of statutes, and legislators' perceptions of those behavior patterns undoubtedly exert an important influence in shaping the content of proposed legislation. Much of the work of gathering such information is performed by social scientists specifically retained for that purpose. In fact, legislatively speaking at least, it may fairly be said that we have entered the age of statistics and survey analysis. The main objective of this note will be to consider the extent to which similar social science techniques have been, might be, or should be used by courts in discharging their somewhat more circumscribed but nonetheless vitally important lawmaking responsibility.

Certainly there is nothing in theory that prevents courts from making use of data gathered by means of such techniques. When called upon to extend, modify, or reverse existing rules of law, courts should, and in most instances do, consider the probable effects of their decisions upon the existing patterns of behavior of the persons to whom the rules are directed. In considering those probable effects, courts could make use of the same sorts of social science data as do legislatures. For the most part, however, they have not. Most often judges rely upon their own assumptions regarding general behavior patterns and the likely effects of their decisions upon those patterns. Thus, while it is fair to say that judge-made law is influenced by how people behave, it would be more accurate to say that it is influenced by the judges' "seat-of-the-pants" impressions of how people behave.

Examples of this "seat-of-the-pants" technique abound, varying in the degree to which the judges make explicit their assumptions about behavior. As will be observed later in this chapter, the rule that there is no general duty to rescue appears in part to rest implicitly on the assumption that the law has little to contribute toward increasing altruistic behavior in our society. The only instance thus far in this book where judges have seemed willing to look beyond their assumptions regarding behavior has been in cases involving the admissibility and relevance of evidence of industry

94. A later law and behavior note, p. 360, below, contains a treatment of such influences upon legislative behavior. For a treatment of such influences upon judicial behavior, see Hedman, Friends of the Earth and Friends of the Court: Assessing the Impact of Interest Group Amici Curiae in Environmental Cases Decided by the Supreme Court, 10 Va. Envtl. L.J. 187 (1991). As to social science amicus curiae briefs in general, see Roesch, Golding, Hans, and Reppucci, Social Science and the Courts: The Role of Amicus Curiae Briefs, 15 Law & Human Behav. 1 (1991). On a slightly different note, problems may arise from campaign contributions, including those given by special interest groups. See Champagne, Campaign Contributions in Texas Supreme-Court Races, 17 Crime Law & Soc. Change 91 (Mar. 1992); Johnson and Urbis, Judicial Selection in Texas: A Gathering Storm, 23 Tex. Tech. L. Rev. 525 (1992).

custom. Although courts typically rely on the more informal, personalized testimony of expert witnesses, rather than upon data gathered by social science techniques, they are willing in such cases to admit evidence of customary behavior patterns of industry members. In the discussion that follows we shall explore the possibility of courts opening their doors to the admission of analogous testimony from social scientists regarding the customary behavior patterns of people generally. Are courts reluctant to allow this other kind of testimony and, if so, does their reluctance stem from some deep-seated distrust of the social sciences?[95]

It is certainly difficult to conclude that courts are reluctant to seriously consider social science data merely from the fact that some courts have refused to rely upon such data.[96] Courts may not have relied upon such data largely because they have not been supplied with such data in cases brought before them. Moreover, there is every reason to believe that if social science data were presented to them in the industry custom cases, courts would allow such data into evidence.[97] Therefore, even if one assumes a degree of reluctance on the part of judges to admit testimony by social scientists in cases not involving the question of industry custom, it is difficult to attribute that reluctance to an inherent or insurmountable distrust of the social sciences.[98]

A valuable insight into the question of whether and under what circumstances courts may properly rely upon social science data has been supplied by Professor Kenneth Culp Davis. In articles dealing with the administrative law process and the problem of judicial notice, Professor Davis introduces the distinction between what he calls *adjudicative facts* and *legislative facts*.[99] Adjudicative facts are those facts in a lawsuit that relate specifically to the individual parties and their conduct. They are those facts to which

95. That a certain amount of distrust exists seems to be admitted by even the staunchest supporters of the effort to bring lawyers and social scientists together. See, e.g., Rosenblum, A Place for Social Science Along the Judiciary's Constitutional Law Frontier, 66 Nw. L. Rev. 455 (1971). See also Lindman, Sources of Judicial Distrust of Social Science Evidence: A Comparison of Social Science and Jurisprudence, 64 Ind. L.J. 755 (1989).

96. See Squires v. Squires, 854 S.W.2d 765 (Ky. 1993) (dissenting opinion criticizing the majority's disregard of the significance of social science evidence suggesting potential problems in joint custody arrangements). When such evidence is considered, the courts appear to assess the validity of such data. See U.S. v. Johnson, 970 F.2d 907 (D.C. Cir. 1992) (noting potential difficulties in applying social science findings derived from experimental conditions to the actual trial setting); Penk v. Oregon State Board of Higher Education, 816 F.2d 458 (9th Cir. 1987) (noting problems in the statistical evidence introduced at trial in sex discrimination claim).

97. Sometimes the testimony going to show an industry custom comes very close to the type of survey analysis upon which social scientists frequently rely. See, e.g., Raim v. Ventura, 16 Wis. 2d 67, 113 N.W.2d 827 (1962).

98. For an assessment of various theories offered in explanation of judicial reluctance to rely upon social science data, see Tanford, The Limits of a Scientific Jurisprudence: The Supreme Court and Psychology, 66 Ind. L.J. 137 (1990).

99. See Davis, An Approach to Problems of Evidence in the Administrative Process, 55 Harv. L. Rev. 364, 402 (1942); Davis, Judicial Notice, 55 Colum. L. Rev. 945, 952 (1955); Davis, Facts in Lawmaking, 80 Colum. L. Rev. 931 (1980).

the rules of law are applied, and they usually are given to the jury to decide in a jury case. Legislative facts, on the other hand, are general, background facts that the judge typically considers in framing policies. They do not relate to or concern in a specific way the immediate parties before the court. Applying this distinction to analysis of the judicial admissibility and utility of social science data, one may at least appreciate, if not necessarily accept, how a court might react differently to such data depending on the type of factual issue—adjudicative or legislative—to which it relates. Where social science data is introduced to prove what Davis refers to as an adjudicative fact, one might expect courts to admit it rather freely, as they would admit evidence relating to any fact at issue between the parties. Evidence of custom relates to an adjudicative fact—the individual defendant's negligence—and thus might be expected to encounter little resistance whether or not offered in the form of social science data. And the same judicial reaction might be expected in any other case in which the applicable rules of law raise an issue of adjudicative fact in relation to which social science data is available and would be helpful.[100]

However, it might be expected that courts would react somewhat more hesitantly when confronted with social science data relating to an issue of legislative fact. For one thing, reliance by the judge upon such evidence would tend to expose his lawmaking function more explicitly. Judges undoubtedly have a built-in sensitivity to the charge that they are sitting as one-person legislatures (especially when the charge is true), and traditionally they have preferred to hide their legislative function behind a facade of finding, not making, the law. Moreover, courts typically do not act on their own initiative, as do legislatures, and their budgets do not include funds for independent data-gathering. Consequently, judges would be forced to rely on the parties for such data, and might well suspect the objectivity and hence the validity of much of what they might be given. Even more important, perhaps, is the concern that some judges might have that listening routinely to social science data regarding legislative facts would greatly add to the expense and delays that already pose a serious threat to the efficacy of the judicial process. If it is little else, the "seat-of-the-pants" approach is quick, cheap, and decisive.

The most frequent use of social science data pertaining to legislative facts appears in opinions of the Supreme Court of the United States, where these considerations may be less relevant.[101] As early as 1908, in Muller v.

100. One example is the admissibility of psychiatric and psychological testimony demonstrating the likely effect upon people's minds of allegedly obscene literature. See, e.g., State v. Scope, 46 Del. 519, 86 A.2d 154 (1953); Besig v. United States, 208 F.2d 142 (9th Cir. 1953). For other examples, see Sorensen and Sorensen, The Admissibility and Use of Opinion Research Evidence, 28 N.Y.U. L. Rev. 1212, 1257-1259 (1953); Monahan and Walker, Judicial Use of Social Science Research, 15 Law & Human Behav. 571 (1991).

101. The most important difference between the Supreme Court and other appellate courts in this regard is the extent to which the policy-making function of the Supreme Court is unavoidably visible. See, generally, Rosen, Judicial Interpretation and Extra-Legal Facts: An

Oregon,[102] the Court made reference to economic, sociological, and biological data in sustaining state legislation setting maximum working hours for women.[103]

Professors Larry Walker and John Monahan have recently advanced a third use for social science data. They suggest a new category, the *social framework,* by which they mean "the use of general conclusions from social science research in determining factual issues in a specific case."[104] Walker and Monahan give as examples expert testimony as to the reliability of eyewitnesses' testimony and of the likely recidivism of murderers. In both instances the expert testimony is offered to provide the jury with a frame of reference to decide questions of fact. Would it be contrary to our notions of particularized fact finding for a judge or jury to decide in favor of a litigant based solely upon such social framework considerations? (See the discussion of the *Collins* case, pp. 116-117, above.) In McCleskey v. Kemp[105] a death row inmate challenged his sentence on equal protection grounds, arguing that he had been discriminated against because he was black and his victim was white. The only evidentiary support for the challenge was a statistical analysis of the disproportionate impact of capital punishment upon blacks. The Supreme Court rejected the challenge, in part because the data did not bear sufficient relation to the circumstances of the particular litigant.[106] Even if blacks generally fared worse than whites, that fact did not support the conclusion that this defendant fared worse.

Perhaps the best-known example of the Supreme Court purporting to rely on social science data in framing basic policy is the school desegregation decision, Brown v. Board of Education,[107] in which the Court accepted the finding in the trial court that segregation by race has a detrimental effect.[108]

Analysis of the Supreme Court's Use of Social Science (1972); Davis, Judicial, Legislative, and Administrative Lawmaking: A Proposed Research Service for the Supreme Court, 71 Minn. L. Rev. 1 (1986). See also McCabe, Legislative Facts as Evidence in State Constitutional Analysis, 65 Temp. L. Rev. 1229 (1992).

102. 208 U.S. 412, 28 S. Ct. 324, 52 L. Ed. 551 (1908).

103. The Muller decision introduced the phrase *Brandeis brief* into the vocabulary of the law. Louis D. Brandeis, attorney for petitioners, included extensive citation of social science material to support his policy position.

104. Walker and Monahan, Social Frameworks: A New Use of Social Science in Law, 73 Va. L. Rev. 559, 570 (1987). See also, Mosteller, Legal Doctrines Governing the Admissibility of Expert Testimony Concerning Social Framework Evidence, 52 Law & Contemp. Probs. 85 (Autumn, 1989). As to when a court's reliance on social science data should have precedential value, see Walker and Monahan, Social Facts: Scientific Methodology as Legal Precedent, 76 Cal. L. Rev. 877 (1988).

105. 481 U.S. 279, 107 S. Ct. 1756, 95 L. Ed. 2d 262 (1987).

106. 481 U.S. at 290-294, 107 S. Ct. at 1766-1768, 95 L. Ed. 2d at 278-280.

For an assessment of the United States Supreme Court's use of social science data in 28 capital punishment cases, see Acker, A Different Agenda: The Supreme Court, Empirical Research Evidence, and Capital Punishment Decisions, 1986-1989, 27 L. & Soc. Rev. 65 (1993).

107. 347 U.S. 483, 74 S. Ct. 686, 98 L. Ed. 2d 873 (1954).

108. See generally, Chesler, Sanders, and Kalmuss, Social Science in Court: Mobilizing Experts in the School Desegregation Cases (1988); Levin and Hawley, The Courts, Social Science, and School Desegregation (1977). For an analysis of the use of social science data

Concluding that this finding "is amply supported by modern authority," the court cited the published work of sociologists and social psychologists. As might be expected, this employment of social science data by our highest court has provoked considerable comment and controversy. On the one hand, writers have questioned the methods employed in the studies relied upon in the *Brown* decision,[109] and have advanced the admittedly skeptical view that enterprising lawyers can always put a package of social science data together to support any position whatever.[110] On the other hand, judicial use of such data has been supported,[111] and some commentators posit that it has been widely accepted.[112] Perhaps the greatest contribution of these writers has been their efforts to articulate the essences of the legal and scientific processes and the differences between them.

Two contemporary legal scholars, both very much interested in the interaction between law and the social sciences, have arrived at different conclusions regarding the utility of scientific data input in the judicial formulation of social policy. Having advanced the thesis that the essential difference between the legal and scientific processes is that the former is combative and designed to provide practical resolutions to problems whereas the latter is neutral and is designed to discover truth as an end in itself, Professor Geoffrey Hazard concludes that the scientific process is too remote and expensive to be of much practical utility to the law:

> In the end, as against the exigencies of the law's processes, the uses of behavioral science are relatively remote, its methods relatively expensive, and its results relatively inconsequential. Its findings are, of course, more satisfying to the modern mind than the conclusions advanced from authority.

---

prior to *Brown,* see Hovenkamp, Social Science and Segregation Before Brown, 1985 Duke L.J. 624.

109. See Garfunkel, Social Science Evidence and the School Desegregation Cases, 21 J. Pol. 37 (1959).

110. See Cahn, Jurisprudence, 30 N.Y.U. L. Rev. 150-154 (1955). *Cf.* Elliott, Social Science Data and the APA: The Lockhart Brief as a Case in Point, 15 L. & Human Behav. 59 (1991) (maintaining that the amicus brief of the American Psychological Association was based upon generalizations that went beyond what the data actually supported). For an examination of the criticisms directed toward judicial use of social science data, see Driessen, The Wedding of Social Science and the Courts: Is the Marriage Working?, 64 Soc. Sci. Q. 476 (1983).

111. See, e.g., Auerbach, Issues of Legal Policy in Social Science Perspective, 2 L. & Soc. Rev. 499 (1968); Nagel, Law and the Social Sciences: What Can Social Science Contribute?, 51 A.B.A. J. 356 (1965); Rosenblum, A Place for Social Science Along the Judiciary's Constitutional Law Frontier, 66 Nw. L. Rev. 455 (1971); McCraw, How Do Readers Read? Social Science and the Law of Libel, 41 Cath. U.L. Rev. 81 (1991); Faigman, To Have or Have Not: Assessing the Value of Social Science to the Law as Science and Policy, 38 Emory L.J. 1005 (1989).

112. See, e.g., Levine and Howe, The Penetration of Social Science into Legal Culture, 7 L. & Policy 173 (1985) ("The use of social science data [in judicial opinions] had become so commonplace by 1980 that it was no longer newsworthy in the culture of legal commentators. . . . [I]t is precisely matters which are deeply a part of our culture or world view that we fail even to notice.") See also Tomkins and Oursland, Social and Social Scientific Perspectives in Judicial Interpretations of the Constitution: A Historical Overview and an Overview, 15 L. & Human Behav. 101 (1991).

That, however, is not much consolation for law men, whose concerns are for immediate, cheap, and significant decisionmaking. For them there are continuing attractions in the Delphic Oracle.[113]

In rebuttal, Professor Victor Rosenblum has argued:

Although I don't dispute the estimate of high costs of behavioral research, I would accord it one of the highest priorities regardless of cost since judges frequently make behavioral assumptions in justifying their decisions. Should the judiciary choose to posit decisions on principles of magic, religious authority, or some other talisman that sanctifies the decision-makers, they could do so consistently with society's need for legal processes that resolve questions with speed, economy, and finality. But if the constitutional and political systems make the investiture of authoritarian sources of power unwise or improper, and if attitudinal or behavioral factors are relied upon to support legal stances, there should be empirical validity to the factors cited. They should not partake of facade or ruse whereby the public is duped into believing that science supports contentions when in reality science has been consulted shoddily, if at all.[114]

Lurking beneath the simplicity of these excerpts, of course, is a philosophical difference between the writers that cuts to the core of the question, "What is law?"[115]

3. Expert Testimony

Hines v. Denver & Rio Grande Western Railroad Co.

829 P.2d 419 (Colo. App. 1991), cert. denied, (1992)

METZGER, JUDGE.

In this wrongful death action, defendants, The Denver and Rio Grande Western Railroad Company, engineer Donald Aksamit, and conductor Frank Danicic, appeal the trial court's judgment entered upon a jury verdict awarding compensatory and punitive damages in favor of plaintiff, Thelma Hines, as a result of the death of her husband, Kennedy Hines. . . .

In September 1985, the decedent and a friend were hiking to a fishing spot in a remote area of the Gore Canyon. While walking between the railroad tracks near the east end of the canyon, the decedent was hit by a Rio Grande train and killed. The train, carrying six empty cars and 18

113. Hazard, Limitations on the Uses of Behavioral Sciences in the Law, 19 Case W. Res. L. Rev. 71, 76-77 (1967).

114. Rosenblum, A Place for Social Science Along the Judiciary's Constitutional Law Frontier, 66 Nw. L. Rev. 455, 458-459 (1971).

115. For a comprehensive casebook on the subject of law and social science, see Monahan and Walker, Social Science in Law: Cases and Materials (2d ed. 1990).

cars loaded with liquid petroleum gas, had been traveling at a speed of approximately 40 M.P.H.

Representatives of the Railroad and the Federal Railroad Administration investigated the accident. The results of the pulse events data from the train's "black box" and the crew's statements conflicted in significant respects, most notably the number of warning whistles sounded prior to the time when the brakes were applied. The Railroad did not communicate with decedent's family regarding the investigation, and it did not make its findings available to them until the pretrial discovery process. The jury returned a verdict of $160,000 for the wrongful death claim, which was reduced by 25 percent for the decedent's comparative negligence. . . .

II

Defendants . . . contend that the trial court erred by allowing the plaintiff's expert to express an opinion that their conduct in the operation of the train constituted negligence. We disagree.

Defendants do not contend that the witness was unqualified to give expert testimony. Rather, they argue that the opinion testimony of plaintiff's expert touched impermissibly on the ultimate legal issues involved in the case.

Resolution of this contention rests upon an analysis of CRE 704. Identical in pertinent part to Fed. R. Evid. 704, it provides: "Testimony in the form of an opinion or inference otherwise admissible is not objectionable because it embraces an ultimate issue to be decided by the trier of fact."

As noted in the Advisory Committee's Note to Fed. R. Evid. 704: "The basic approach to opinions, lay and expert, in these rules is to admit them when helpful to the trier of fact." Nevertheless, the rules on expert opinion are not intended to permit experts to "tell the jury what result to reach." See 56 F.R.D. 284 and 285 (Advisory Committee's Note).

Thus, the determination of the admissibility of expert opinions cannot be made by resort to CRE 704 in a vacuum. Instead, the proffered expert opinion should be evaluated by considering the interrelationship of several pertinent evidentiary rules.

For instance, as is the case with all proffered evidence, the expert opinion's relevance should be established. Evidence is relevant when it tends "to make the existence of any fact that is of consequence to the determination of the action more probable or less probable than it would be without the evidence." CRE 401. If the expert opinion is relevant, then it is generally admissible. See CRE 402.

However, CRE 702 imposes a criterion of helpfulness which must be met as well. Thus, the expert witness should be appropriately qualified and the expert opinion should "assist the trier of fact to find a solid path through an unfamiliar and esoteric field." Tabatchnick v. G.D. Searle & Co., 67 F.R.D. 49 (D.N.J. 1975).

To this end, the trial court should determine that the situation is a proper one for expert testimony and, if it is not, should exclude the opinion. Then, the trial court should exercise the considerable discretion afforded it by CRE 403 to exclude statements of expert opinion whose probative value is substantially outweighed by the risks of undue prejudice, confusion, or waste of time. And finally, the court, in its discretion, may require preliminary disclosure of the data underlying the expert opinion pursuant to CRE 705 so that the jury will have adequate material with which to evaluate the opinion.

Plaintiff's expert here testified as follows:

Q: As a bottom line, what are your conclusions on this accident, ma'am?
A: In line with the above facts and circumstances, the death of Mr. Kennedy W. Hines did not have to occur, but did occur because of the negligence of the employees to brake, sound the whistle, or keep a proper lookout.
It's my opinion the D & RGW Railroad was grossly negligent because the company displayed a conscious indifference to Mr. Kennedy W. Hines, Mr. Searle, and other people who walk down the tracks.
Q: Why do you say that, ma'am?
A: Because of all the facts. That they didn't warn this man. He is dead.
Q: Do you feel their conduct was outrageous?
A: I do.
Q: What basis do you have for that?
A: Just from knowing the operation of trains and operating trains myself.

Since one of the crucial issues in this case was when the train's warning whistle sounded, both experts testified extensively concerning that point. Indeed, before opining, the plaintiff's expert recited a litany of examples of specific violations of railroad warning policies and procedures that she asserted had occurred here. Defendants' expert also testified that his "general policy" concerning railroad accidents involving pedestrians is "the more warning the better." Thus, the expert opinions were relevant, helpful, and probative, and were undergirded by sufficient facts to enable the jury to make its own evaluation.

The trial court, in allowing the opinions, ruled:

> In this case it appears that the operation of the train is something outside the knowledge of the ordinary person and that there would be the need for some understanding of that, and that the testimony of an expert could be helpful to the jury.
>
> I am going to deny the Motion in Limine, permit the witness to express an opinion on this, and recognize that it is going to be largely a matter of the weight the jury may wish to give or not give to the opinion of the expert.

We conclude that the trial court correctly evaluated the proffered expert opinions in light of the applicable law. Consequently, we find no abuse of discretion in the ruling.

[The judgment for the plaintiff on the wrongful death claim was affirmed, but the case was remanded for errors not involving the merits of that claim.]

The Lawyer's Professional Responsibility: The Partisan Expert Witness

Two aspects of the use of the expert witness place significant professional strain on lawyers. First, the expert often is not a witness to the events that give rise to the plaintiff's claim, and will testify only if the opinion supports a particular position. Second, the fee payable to an expert may be based on the reasonable value of the services, while the fee payable to the nonexpert is limited to the witness's expenses and income lost because of the testifying.[116] One issue that appears to be undergoing a change in treatment in recent years is the question of whether expert witnesses may be paid on a contingent fee basis. The Code of Professional Responsibility prohibits such a practice.[117] However, the new Model Rules of Professional Conduct would allow contingent fees for expert witnesses where permitted by applicable law.[118]

Unquestionably, these expert-witness-for-hire qualities have led to abuse of expert testimony by some lawyers. See Ford and Holmes, The Professional Medical Advocate, 17 Sw. L.J. 551, 553 (1963):

> Although most doctors, if called upon to testify, adhere to the strict ethical standards of their profession, there are those whose conduct and lack of adherence to the established ethical norms leave an indelible stigma on the entire group. The latter have earned the title of "medical mouthpiece," or, if you will, the "professional medical advocate." The professional medical advocate is retained for his testimonial ability in specifically influencing the outcome of litigation; usually, he presents a plausible diagnosis based on half truth in such a manner that his finality of utterance is more convincing than his medical knowledge or scientific veracity.[119]

116. Code of Professional Responsibility, Canon 7, EC 7-28, DR 7-109(c)(3).

117. Id. See also In re Schapiro, 144 App. Div. 1, 128 N.Y.S. 852 (1911). The New York rule was upheld against constitutional attack in Person v. Assoc. of the Bar of New York, 554 F.2d 534 (2d Cir. 1977). See Comment, 55 N.C.L. Rev. 709 (1977).

118. M.R.P.C. §3.14(b).

119. See also Peck, Impartial Medical Testimony—A Way to Better and Quicker Justice, 22 F.R.D. 21, 23 (1959):

> Under present procedure, where the medical testimony comes from no objective or necessarily qualified source, and only through the hirelings of the parties, partisan experts, medical mouthpieces, the jury is more apt to be confused than enlightened by what it hears. It hears black from one expert, white from the other, a maximizing or minimizing of injuries in accordance with the interest of the source of payment for the testimony.

In those cases in which there is spurious expert testimony, experts and their professions must shoulder part of the blame; but the ultimate responsibility for control in the legal setting lies with the lawyer and the legal profession. See Friedman, Expert Testimony, Its Abuse and Reformation, 19 Yale L.J. 247, 254-255 (1919):

> There can be no question but that the attorneys are no less blameworthy than the experts they use. An attorney who would refuse to present fake testimony to the court in ordinary matter does not hesitate to employ biased or fake expert witnesses. It is the practice and demands of lawyers which have created the "plaintiff's expert" and "defendant's expert." If they did not buy, the doctors would not sell. The average accident lawyer wants the doctors properly labeled. It is a handy short cut and prevents mistakes. It would be embarrassing to call in an expert and find that he was of the opinion that the plaintiff really was suffering the injuries claimed when you are trying a run for luck with the jury in the hope that you may come out better than the offer of settlement. On the other hand, it might be equally fatal to engage an expert to examine your client without knowing in advance that he will be able to help substantiate the claim.
>
> If one expert does not give the lawyer what he demands, he does not hesitate to discard him and search the market until he finds what he wants. If he cannot get the real article, he furbishes up the counterfeit and passes it off on the jury. If he finds that the genuine expert opinion is against him, he may at least deliberately play the game with the counterfeit to disgust the jury with all expert testimony and even up things by leading the jury to disregard it for both sides. There is a doctor in Boston who is notorious about the courts as a plaintiff's expert. He is ingenious and experienced, and when hard pushed an attorney may always go to him and be sure to find what he seeks. Judges and lawyers all know what his appearance in a case signifies, yet he appears in court almost as constantly as any of the regularly retained corporation "defendant's experts." The lawyers who use him and share the spoils of victory with him on a contingent basis retain their standing at the bar.

The abuses have led to occasional expressions of judicial cynicism, such as that of Judge Posner dissenting in Chaulk v. Volkswagen of America, Inc., 808 F.2d 639, 644 (7th Cir. 1986):

> Let us consider the evidence on whether Volkswagen should have foreseen that the design of the door latch was unreasonably dangerous. The design is of a type used on millions of automobiles, including very expensive ones such as Cadillac. The design met or exceeded federal automobile safety standards. There is no evidence that this design has ever caused a door to open in a crash test conducted on the Rabbit, or for that matter on any other car. Indeed, with the disputed exception of the present accident (for Volkswagen presented evidence that the door latch had nothing to do with Chaulk's being flung from the car—that she had been hurled through the window), there is no evidence of any accident—ever—in which a door opened because a broadside crash pushed in the door handle and released the latch.

All Chaulk has is the testimony of Martens, whose involvement in the design of automobile door latches had ended in 1972, thirteen years before the trial. He had gone to work that year for an insurance company, and later he became and he remains a professional expert witness against automobile companies in cases involving issues of door-latch design. On direct examination he testified that other automobile companies had safer latch designs which Volkswagen easily could have adopted and in subsequent model years did adopt. It would have been a jury question whether this evidence outweighed Volkswagen's contrary evidence. But on cross-examination Martens made clear that his position, whether reflecting a genuine and disinterested conviction or pecuniary self-interest, is that almost all door latches, including one for which he holds a patent and Volkswagen's subsequent latch design, are unreasonably dangerous: specifically, all door latches that can be sprung by inward rather than downward pressure; perhaps all automobile door latches, period, except that of Mercedes-Benz; at the very least, the loor latches found in 30 million cars now on American roads. Martens was unwilling to concede that *any* automobile door latch except that of the Mercedes-Benz, including latches he himself had designed, is reasonably safe. Although he believes that some are safer than the one on the 1977 Rabbit, he presented no statistical or other evidence indicating that an accident (with the possible exception of the one in this case) had ever occurred that a safer door latch would have prevented.

Martens' was the testimony either of a crank or, what is more likely, of a man who is making a career out of testifying for plaintiffs in automobile accident cases in which a door may have opened; at the time of trial he was involved in 10 such cases. His testimony illustrates the age-old problem of expert witnesses who are "often the mere paid advocates or partisans of those who employ and pay them, as much so as the attorneys who conduct the suit. There is hardly anything, not palpably absurd on its face, that cannot now be proved by some so-called 'experts.' " Keegan v. Minneapolis & St. Louis R.R., 76 Minn. 90, 95, 78 N.W. 965, 966 (1899).

But the ability of a judge or jury to screen expert testimony in this fashion is necessarily limited. And if the sole penalty attached to misuse is discounting the weight normally given to expert testimony, the lawyer, in deciding whether or not to present testimony which may be suspect, is faced with an everything-to-gain-nothing-to-lose choice. One remedy for the abuse of expert testimony is the use of impartial experts, mentioned in the preceding note. This can be only a limited solution, and may even intensify the pressure on a lawyer to find an expert to rebut the testimony of the impartial expert. In the last analysis, the abuse of expert testimony may be a problem that defies any formal solution, such as the use of impartial experts or increased professional supervision through disciplinary proceedings. A client is entitled to have the best case presented, and the line between spurious and legitimate testimony is not always easy to determine, even for a conscientious lawyer. As with many, if not most, problems of professional responsibility, we have to depend substantially on a lawyer's awareness of the problem and the hope that a sense of professionalism will in most instances result in the line being drawn in the right place.

4. Res Ipsa Loquitur

In most negligence cases, the plaintiff's evidence, if believed, will paint a fairly complete picture of what the defendant did. This will enable the plaintiff to make a detailed argument of how the defendant's conduct missed the mark. But often a serious gap in the evidence remains. We have already encountered such a gap in Problem 8, in Chapter 2, in which the identity of the owner of the dog that attacked the plaintiff was not amenable to direct proof. In this section, we shall consider the reactions of courts to a different type of gap in the evidence—one which prevents the plaintiff from presenting a sufficiently complete picture of the defendant's conduct. In the cases that follow, the plaintiff cannot make an adequately detailed argument as to how the defendant was negligent. One approach to these cases might be for courts to follow the oft-stated injunction that the trier of fact may never be left to speculate, and that every decision in favor of the plaintiff must be based solidly on evidence pointing to the specific manner in which the defendant was negligent. But common sense, and our experience in connection with the earlier dog-bite problem, suggest that such a hard line approach is unlikely to appeal to very many judges. Our sense of justice would be offended if the plaintiff necessarily were to lose because it could not be established exactly what it was that the defendant did that was negligent. We may feel that, even with the evidentiary gap, the facts as we have them clearly indicate that the defendant was negligent. These feelings have been translated into the doctrine of res ipsa loquitur, which allows plaintiffs to win some of the cases in which a gap in the evidence prevents them from proving the specifics of the defendants' negligent conduct.

Res ipsa loquitur is not the happiest of legal phrases. Literally translated, it means "the thing speaks for itself." It was coined by Baron Pollock in Byrne v. Boadle, 2 H. & C. 722, 159 Eng. Rep. 299 (Ex. 1863), a case in which the plaintiff was injured by a barrel of flour which had fallen from a window in the defendant's warehouse. At the trial, the only evidence put in by either party was by the plaintiff, and he made no attempt to show how the barrel fell from the window. On this state of the evidence, the trial judge granted the defendant's motion for a nonsuit. In the course of argument on appeal, the defendant's attorney made this point: "Surmise ought not to be substituted for strict proof. . . . The plaintiff should establish his case by affirmative evidence. . . . The plaintiff was bound to give affirmative proof of negligence." To which Baron Pollock replied: "There are certain cases of which it may be said res ipsa loquitur and this seems one of them. In some cases the Court has held that the mere fact of the accident having occurred is evidence of negligence. . . ." Two years later, in a case involving bags of sugar that fell on the plaintiff, Chief Justice Erle, in Scott v. London & St. Katherine Docks Co., 3 H. & C. 596, 601, 159 Eng. Rep. 665, 667 (Ex. 1865), supplied what is generally recognized as the first formulation of the res ipsa loquitur doctrine:

> There must be reasonable evidence of negligence.
>
> But where the thing is shown to be under the management of the defendant or his servants, and the accident is such as in the ordinary course of things does not happen if those who have the management use proper care, it affords reasonable evidence, in the absence of explanation by the defendants, that the accident arose from want of care.

Although on the surface these judicial expressions seem relatively simple, few concepts in tort law have caused more confusion. Indeed, there is some disagreement over whether res ipsa loquitur is a distinct concept at all. As an American judge asserted in a case brought to his court on appeal (Bond, C.J., dissenting, in Potomac Edison Co. v. Johnson, 160 Md. 33, 40, 152 A. 633, 636 (1930)):

> In this case, as in similar cases, the expression res ipsa loquitur has been the basis of much of the argument, and I venture to urge upon the attention of the profession in the state an objection to the continued use of it. It adds nothing to the law, has no meaning which is not more clearly expressed for us in English, and brings confusion to our legal discussions. It does not represent a doctrine, is not a legal maxim, and is not a rule.
>
> It is merely a common argumentative expression of ancient Latin brought into the language of the law by men who were accustomed to its use in Latin writings. . . . It may just as appropriately be used in argument on any subject, legal or otherwise. Nowhere does it mean more than the colloquial English expression that the facts speak for themselves, that facts proved naturally afford ground for an inference of some fact inquired about, and so amount to some proof of it. The inference may be one of certainty, as when an excessive interest charge appeared on the face of an instrument, or one of more or less probability only, as when negligence in the care of a barrel of flour was found inferable from its fall out of a warehouse.

Judicial deprecations of this sort notwithstanding, in one sense, at least, cases involving res ipsa loquitur are different from other examples of the use of circumstantial evidence. Circumstantial evidence is normally directed at preliminary issues of fact such as "Did sparks from the defendant's mill start the fire at the plaintiff's hotel?" or "Was the defendant traveling in excess of 30 miles an hour?" In res ipsa loquitur cases, however, the circumstantial evidence is directed at the ultimate issue of the defendant's negligence, an issue which calls for a value judgment rather than simply an empirical judgment. (See the Law-Fact Distinction Note, p. 76, above.) Thus, in deciding whether the fact of the plaintiff's injury provides, in and of itself, a sufficient basis upon which to conclude that the defendant has been negligent, the court is necessarily required to assess the relationship between the parties and the nature of the duty owing by the defendant to the plaintiff. Much more than in other cases involving reliance upon circumstantial evidence, here the fact of the accident will "speak for itself" if the court (as the formulator of legal duties) and the jury (as appliers of those legal duties) want it to.

Res ipsa loquitur almost everywhere gives rise to a permissible inference of negligence—that is, it permits, but does not compel, the jury to find that the defendant acted negligently. See Brown v. Scrivner, Inc., 241 Neb. 286, 488 N.W.2d 17 (1992); Wilson v. Honeywell, Inc., 409 Mass. 803, 569 N.E.2d 1011 (1991). See generally, Prosser, The Procedural Effect of Res Ipsa Loquitur, 20 Minn. L. Rev. 241 (1936). In some states, res ipsa gives rise to a rebuttable presumption of negligence. See Stone's Farm Supply, Inc. v. Deacon, 805 P.2d 1109 (Colo. 1991); Ward v. Forrester Day Care, Inc. 547 So. 2d 410 (Ala. 1989). In one state, a plaintiff may be entitled to a permissible inference *or* a rebuttable presumption, depending upon the weight of the evidence. See Bowers v. Schenley Distillers, Inc., 469 S.W.2d 565, 568-569 (Ky. 1971), in which the court states that "the terms 'rebuttable presumption' and 'permissible inference' are merely descriptive of the weight which must be accorded to circumstantial evidence in a particular case, depending upon the degree of probability reflected by the particular facts shown."

Whether the doctrine gives rise to an inference or a presumption, the preliminary factual elements upon which it rests must be proved by a preponderance of the evidence. In most states, if the defendant presents evidence explaining the occurrence, the case will still go to the jury unless the defendant's countervailing proof is so strong that no reasonable person could find the defendant negligent. See Brown v. Racquet Club of Bricktown, 95 N.J. 280, 471 A.2d 25 (1984). On the other hand, in some states, where the elements of res ipsa include the additional requirement of "no evidence to the contrary," courts have held the doctrine inapplicable when the defendant presents evidence of non-negligence. See, e.g., Schmidt v. Gibbs, 305 Ark. 383, 807 S.W.2d 928 (1991).

If the judge determines that res ipsa applies, the jury will be advised as such. Thus, the court may instruct the jury that if they find on a preponderance of the evidence that the defendant had control of the instrumentality in question, and that the accident was one which would not ordinarily have occurred in the absence of defendant's negligence, they may find the defendant to have acted negligently. See Anderton v. Montgomery, 607 P.2d 828 (Utah 1980); Tierney v. St. Michael's Medical Center, 518 A.2d 242 (N.J. Super. 1986).

Boyer v. Iowa High School Athletic Association

260 Iowa 1061, 152 N.W.2d 293 (1967)

Doctrine applied

GARFIELD, C.J. [The plaintiff, a spectator at a basketball game under the management of the defendant, was injured when the bleachers in which she sat collapsed. The bleachers were designed to fold against the gymnasium wall when not in use. As the game ended and the spectators began to leave, the section occupied by the plaintiff and others suddenly folded back toward the wall, throwing the plaintiff to the floor nine feet below. After verdict and judgment for plaintiff, the defendant appealed.]

I. Plaintiff pleaded her case in two counts or divisions, one charging specific acts of negligence, the other in reliance on the doctrine of res ipsa loquitur. We have frequently held this is permissible provided, of course, the doctrine is properly applicable.

The trial court ruled there was no evidence to support the charges of specific negligence and withdrew them from jury consideration. The case was submitted to the jury on the doctrine of res ipsa loquitur.

II. Defendant first assigns error in the court's refusal to withdraw from the jury the division based on res ipsa loquitur.

" 'Under the doctrine referred to, where injury occurs by an instrumentality under the exclusive control and management of defendant and the occurrence is such as in the ordinary course of things would not happen if reasonable care had been used, the happening of the injury permits but does not compel an inference that defendant was negligent.' Shinofield v. Curtis, 245 Iowa 1352, 1360, 66 N.W.2d 465, 470, 50 A.L.R.2d 964, and citations.

" '. . . In considering the applicability of res ipsa loquitur, the question whether the particular occurrence is such as would not happen if reasonable care had been used rests on common experience and not at all on evidence in the particular case that tends in itself to show such occurrence was in fact the result of negligence.' Shinofield v. Curtis, supra." Smith v. Ullerich, 259 Iowa 797, 804, 145 N.W.2d 1, 5.

Thus the two foundation facts for application of the res ipsa doctrine, which permits an inference of defendant's negligence from happening of the injury, are: (1) exclusive control and management by defendant of the instrumentality which causes the injury, and (2) the occurrence is such as in the ordinary course of things would not happen if reasonable care had been used.

We think the jury could properly find these foundation facts existed and infer therefrom plaintiff's injury was caused by defendant's negligence. Bleachers designed for use by spectators at athletic events do not ordinarily collapse, when used as they normally are, without negligence of those having control and management thereof.

Defendant asserts the res ipsa doctrine does not apply, first, because it is said the evidence of the cause of the collapse was accessible to plaintiff and not peculiarly accessible to defendant. As plaintiff admits in argument, under our decisions the underlying reason for the res ipsa rule is that the chief evidence of the true cause of the injury is practically accessible to defendant but inaccessible to the injured person.

In these precedents one or both of the foundation facts above referred to were lacking and the absence of what we have said is the underlying reason for the rule was given as an added reason why it was not applicable to the particular case. We have never held presence of this "underlying reason" is an indispensable requirement for application of the doctrine.

Nor are we persuaded evidence of the true cause of the collapse or partial collapse of the bleachers was not peculiarly accessible to defendant rather than to plaintiff. The athletic director of the Mason City schools was acting manager of the tournament. He and the head custodian at Roosevelt Junior High School must be deemed, under the contract between the school and defendant, to have been acting under the management, supervision and direction of defendant. They had the exclusive control and management of the bleachers at least until game time and had the best opportunity to then discover any defect in them which may have caused the collapse.

We are told plaintiff had as much access to the bleachers immediately after the accident as defendant did and could discover any defect in them. A seriously injured person could hardly be expected to then examine the bleachers for defects rather than to be concerned with proper treatment of her injuries. . . .

The argument the only permissible conclusion to be drawn from the evidence is that the movement of the spectators at the end of the game caused the bleachers to collapse cannot be accepted. Such a conclusion would rest wholly on speculation or conjecture. There is no evidence to support it. Assuming, but not deciding, this would be a defense to the res ipsa doctrine, it was defendant's burden to rebut the inference of negligence.

Such limited control of the bleachers as plaintiff and other spectators may have had during and immediately following the game did not, as a matter of law, render the doctrine of res ipsa loquitur inapplicable. The jury could find defendant and its agents were in control of the bleachers at the time of the negligent act, as failure to inspect, which subsequently resulted in injury to plaintiff and that she and the other spectators did nothing improper or unusual during their occupancy of them. . . .

We find no reversible error in any respect assigned and argued. Affirmed.

[The Concurring opinion of BECKER, J., is omitted.]

Shutt v. Kaufman's, Inc.

165 Colo. 175, 438 P.2d 501 (1968)

En Banc. MR. JUSTICE KELLEY delivered the opinion of the Court. . . .

[Plaintiff, a customer in defendant's shoe store, sat down on a chair which bumped a display table causing a metal shoe stand to topple and strike plaintiff on the head.]

. . . The questions of liability and damages were submitted to a jury which returned a verdict in favor of the defendant. From a denial of her motion for new trial the plaintiff sued out this writ of error.

Plaintiff's grounds for reversal all involve questions arising out of the application of the doctrine of res ipsa loquitur. One phase of alleged error relates to either instructions given or tendered and refused, while the second phase involves the failure of the trial court to direct a favorable verdict for the plaintiff as to liability.

In short, the plaintiff, although having convinced the court that the doctrine of res ipsa loquitur applied, now objects to the manner in which it was applied. On the other hand, the defendant maintains that under the circumstances of this case the doctrine of res ipsa loquitur is not applicable.

The threshold question, therefore, is whether under the circumstances there should have been any instructions given in reference to the doctrine of res ipsa loquitur. An examination of prior pronouncements of this court indicates that a careful analysis of the doctrine or rule and the evidence is necessary to determine that question. . . .

In considering the applicability of res ipsa, some other fundamental rules of law must be integrated into our thinking. We are here concerned with the relationship of a storekeeper and a business visitor. In such relationship the storekeeper owes a duty to one who enters upon the premises at his invitation, express or implied, to protect such visitor not only against known dangers, but also against those which, by the exercise of reasonable care, he might discover.

In short, although the storekeeper must exercise reasonable care for the safety of the business visitor, he is not an insurer of the safety of such visitor; thus, the mere happening of an accident raises no presumption of negligence, except under those circumstances where the doctrine of res ipsa loquitur is applicable.

There is no fundamental disagreement between the parties as to the law. The plaintiff would invoke res ipsa because she "could not possibly have foreseen that by merely sitting down in a proffered chair in a normal manner she would, in effect, spring a concealed trap resulting in a steel and plastic display rack striking her on the head from behind." We are inclined to agree that she probably could not "have foreseen" the accident. But this is not the res ipsa test.

The circumstances here were such that the plaintiff could have shown that the defendant was responsible for her injuries because of its negligence. By way of illustration, it could have been demonstrated, if such were the fact, that the display table was unstable; that it wobbled from a mere touch, and that by placing the shoe display stand on the top shelf the defendant negligently created a dangerous condition. Or it might have been demonstrated that the tripod-based shoe stand was so unstable that the mere use of it on a shelf high above the head of a customer was likely to topple off from the usual and customary bumps which a display table receives. In other words, the plaintiff had the means available to her to establish negligence on the part of the defendant, if any there was. As we pointed out above, the storekeeper is not an insurer.

Under the circumstances of this case, the court erred in submitting any instruction on res ipsa loquitur. Holding as we do, it is not necessary to discuss the correctness of either of the given or the tendered instructions.

No questions have been raised as to the other instructions which the court gave. It appears that, except for the improper res ipsa instruction, the instructions given fairly presented the issues of negligence and contributory negligence. Consequently, the plaintiff, by virtue of the improper instruction, had an unfair advantage, but, even so, failed to prevail. The defendant having won, despite the improper instruction, has therefor not been prejudiced.

The judgment of the trial court is affirmed.

In Marrero v. Goldsmith, 486 So. 2d 530 (Fla. 1986), the plaintiff suffered from numbness, weakness, and pain in her left arm following surgery that did not involve her left arm. She joined the three doctors who performed the surgery and the hospital in a negligence action. Her expert testified that her type of injury does not ordinarily occur in the absence of negligence and that it was probably caused by incorrect arm positioning during surgery. The doctors testified that nothing unusual had happened during the surgery. The trial court denied the plaintiff's request for a res ipsa loquitur jury instruction. The jury found for the defendant doctors. The intermediate appellate court affirmed, on the ruling that res ipsa loquitur was not applicable because the plaintiff had introduced expert testimony regarding specific acts of negligence.

The Supreme Court of Florida reversed and remanded for new trial, concluding (486 So. 2d at 532):

> If a case is a proper res ipsa case in other respects, the presence of some direct evidence of negligence should not deprive the plaintiff of the res ipsa inference. There comes a point, however, when a plaintiff can introduce enough direct evidence of negligence to dispel the need for the inference. According to Prosser:
>
> > Plaintiff is of course bound by his own evidence; but proof of some specific facts does not necessarily exclude inferences of others. When the plaintiff shows that the railway car in which he was a passenger was derailed, there is an inference that the defendant railroad has somehow been negligent. When the plaintiff goes further and shows that the derailment was caused by an open switch, the plaintiff destroys any inference of other causes; but the inference that the defendant has not used proper care in looking after its switches is not destroyed, but considerably strengthened. If the plaintiff goes further still and shows that the switch was left open by a drunken switchman on duty, there is nothing left to infer; and if the plaintiff shows that the switch was thrown by an escaped convict with a grudge against the railroad, the plaintiff has proven himself out of court. It is only in this sense that

> when the facts are known there is no inference, and res ipsa loquitur simply vanishes from the case. On the basis of reasoning such as this, it is quite generally agreed that the introduction of some evidence which tends to show specific acts of negligence on the part of the defendant, but which does not purport to furnish a full and complete explanation of the occurrence, does not destroy the inferences which are consistent with the evidence, and so does not deprive the plaintiff of the benefit of res ipsa loquitur.
>
> Prosser and Keeton §40 (footnotes omitted).

The doctors also argued on appeal that res ipsa was inapplicable because no one of them had exclusive control for the entire period during which the plaintiff may have been injured. The Florida high court concluded (486 So. 2d at 532-533):

> The difficult question presented is whether in the interests of justice, we should slavishly adhere to the exclusive control element normally requisite to res ipsa application or whether we should relax the control element. It is quite clear that under traditional res ipsa loquitur analysis the defendant doctors in this case cannot be said to have each possessed exclusive control at all times when plaintiff's injury may have occurred. Yet the patient is in no position to prove which defendant or combination of defendants caused her injury to an area of her body remote from the site of surgery, because she was unconscious when it occurred. We are persuaded that the fairest course to take under these particular circumstances is to allow the plaintiff to go to the jury with the benefit of a res ipsa loquitur instruction. We agree with the reasoning of the California Supreme Court in the landmark case of Ybarra v. Spangard, 25 Cal. 2d 486, 154 P.2d 687 (1944).

City of Louisville v. Humphrey

461 S.W.2d 352 (Ky. App. 1970)

EDWARD P. HILL, JR., C.J. The appellee obtained judgment on a verdict of $56,534.34 against appellant for injuries, resulting in the death of her husband, which she claimed he received after his arrest or while he was confined in the city's jail. The city appeals. We reverse. Before stating the facts, we should emphasize the appellee's theory of the case that her husband's fatal injuries were inflicted by one or both of the two arresting officers, or by a jail employee, or by a fellow prisoner.

The deceased, Ruel McKinley Humphrey, a hard-working man about 59 years of age with some drinking problems, was highly intoxicated about 2:15 A.M., on the morning of November 21, 1966. He was wandering around in the vicinity of Frankfort and Hite Avenues, near his home, when a report was received by Louisville Police Headquarters that he was shaking doors in that neighborhood. The officers proceeded to arrest him and to deliver him to the booking clerk at the city jail at 2:35 A.M. He was retained in the holdover department in the basement of the city jail until 4:15 A.M., when he was taken by elevator to the third floor of the jail.

The two guards in charge of the third floor of the jail testified that immediately after the deceased stepped off the elevator on the third floor, he began to fall down or collapse. One of the guards caught him and lightened his fall. Shortly thereafter he was dragged by the two guards to the "drunk tank" and left lying on the floor with his feet toward the entrance of the tank. Two of the jail employees testified that no one else was in the "drunk tank" while the deceased was there. However, a third employee testified that he believed there was another prisoner in the "drunk tank" during that time.

At 7:15 A.M. a jail guard attempted to awaken deceased in order that he might appear in court that morning. The guard was unable to arouse him, concluding that Humphrey was in a high state of intoxication. At noon the guard again attempted to arouse him without success. He was then taken to Louisville General Hospital and found to be unconscious with a subdural hematoma from injuries apparently received around the left eye and forehead. He underwent brain surgery and died on December 13, 1966, without ever regaining consciousness.

[The opinion here describes the evidence in the case, which was inconclusive on the question of the cause of the decedent's injuries. Referring to the conduct of the defendant in failing to investigate the incident, the court concludes:]

It would seem that this is a bad way to run a railroad, more especially in a situation where a man imprisoned in the city jail had been injured and dies within a very short period thereafter. Nevertheless, the issue is not the failure of the appellant and its representatives or employees to conduct a proper investigation into the injuries of the deceased, but is whether there was probative evidence that an employee of the city inflicted injuries on the deceased, or that a fellow prisoner did so, and if so, that the city was negligent with respect to the infliction of his injuries by a fellow prisoner.

We may safely say that there is no direct evidence that any of the prison employees inflicted the injuries on the deceased. Neither is there any direct evidence that those injuries were inflicted by a fellow prisoner. The appellee suggests that the proof in the case warrants the application of res ipsa loquitur. With this theory we cannot agree. Although the evidence and circumstances come pretty close to creating an inference that the deceased received his injuries after his arrest and while he was in the custody of the city's employees, yet they fall short of justifying res ipsa. If we assume his injuries were received after his arrest, we are still left to speculate as to whether the injuries were received at the hands of the city employees or whether they were inflicted by a fellow prisoner. We cannot assume either to be the case.

Admitting for the purpose of discussion that the deceased was injured by a fellow prisoner, it is still incumbent upon the appellee to prove negligence on the part of the city in permitting those injuries. The court has written in a similar case that the city will not be liable unless it had knowledge of the violent propensities of the fellow prisoner.

It would appear at first blush that when the officers of the law arrest and confine a highly intoxicated person, the arresting authorities should exercise a degree of care higher than ordinary care, for the simple reason that they are dealing with a helpless human being. Yet, in many prisons, especially large city prisons, large numbers of highly intoxicated persons may be arrested and imprisoned in the short space of a few hours. It would be difficult to provide each and every such prisoner with a padded, injury-proof, individual cell. After all, in a great majority of cases the helpless drunk is safer in prison than outside.

The court is mindful of the hardship placed upon the plaintiff in this class of case by the rule that the plaintiff must prove knowledge of violent propensities of a fellow prisoner before a recovery will be permitted. It is common knowledge that highly intoxicated persons are not given to exercising good judgment or restraint, that they are subject to becoming belligerent on the least provocation.

A majority of this court is of the opinion that to place on the prison keeper the burden of going forward with proof simply upon a showing that a prisoner was injured while in prison would amount to holding that the prison keeper is the absolute insurer of the safety and well-being of the prisoner, which may result in an unfair burden on him.

It is concluded that the appellee did not meet the burden of proof required in our case law above cited. The judgment is, therefore, reversed with directions to enter an order sustaining the appellant's motion for judgment notwithstanding the verdict.

MILLIKEN, NEIKIRK, OSBORNE, REED, and STEINFELD, JJ., concur.

Problem 15

You are an associate in a medium-sized Collegetown law firm. Your supervising attorney wants your evaluation of the applicability of res ipsa loquitur to the following case. The plaintiff, Helen Sims, was severely injured when an empty whiskey bottle struck her in the face. The incident occurred two months ago on the day of Columbia State University's homecoming game against Corning College in Collegetown. Helen was standing on the curb waiting to cross a fairly busy street just off campus when a taxi cab drove past and an empty bottle, apparently thrown from the cab, struck her in the face. Helen's boyfriend, Rob Westin, was standing next to her at the time. He is ready to testify that he saw a passenger in the cab move his hand toward them, releasing the bottle, and then roll up the window. The cab never slowed, proceeding around the corner and out of sight. The passenger who threw the bottle was wearing a red Columbia State scarf. Rob's blue sweatshirt resembled those worn by Corning College students. Rob did not notice the cab's number but is certain it was an Acme Taxicab Company cab. Helen's physician indicates that Helen's injuries were probably enhanced by the bottle's moving thirty to thirty-five miles per hour parallel to her in addition to the impetus imparted by the throw.

The cab company's policy is to require its drivers to report unusual incidents such as this at the end of the day. No report of the incident in question is on file. Your firm questioned several drivers and received no further information. It is quite possible that the driver of the cab could not see or hear what was happening in the back seat due to the thick plastic protective shield between the driver and passengers, included in all Acme cab designs. The cab company says that there is no way to identify the driver who was at that corner at that time.

Your firm has had no luck tracing the scarfed figure through Columbia State's alumni office. It appears that Acme Taxicab Company is the only possible defendant. Your supervising attorney wants to know whether res ipsa loquitur might be applicable. Advise him.

The *Boyer* case, p. 275, above, addressed the issue of whether the comparative unavailability to the plaintiff of direct evidence of negligence should be a prerequisite to application of res ipsa. Contrary to the holding in *Boyer,* some states have actually included the element of the defendant's superior knowledge as a prerequisite. See Bass v. Nooney Co., 646 S.W.2d 765 (Mo. 1983); Goedert v. New Castle Equipment Co., 802 P.2d 157 (Wyo. 1990). See generally, Comment, Res Ipsa Loquitur in Texas: The Element of Superior Knowledge, 1 St. Mary's L.J. 207 (1969).

One source of confusion in the application of res ipsa is the requirement that the "event [be] of a kind which ordinarily does not occur in the absence of negligence." See Restatement (Second) of Torts, §328D. If this phrase is interpreted as meaning "an event which is more likely than not the result of negligence," the res ipsa loquitur doctrine is simply a rule of circumstantial proof based upon probabilities. If the phrase is interpreted more broadly to include events simply because they rarely occur, however, the res ipsa doctrine can reach unusual, and probably improper, results. Assume, for example, that an unfavorable event occurs on the average of once in every 100 times that an activity is engaged in with reasonable care. Assume, further, that a particular actor is, on the average, negligent once in 200 times, resulting in the same unfavorable event. On these assumptions, if the actor engages in the activity 1,000 times, the unfavorable event can be expected to occur approximately 15 times—10 times in spite of due care on the part of the actor and 5 times because of the actor's negligence. If all that is known is that the unfavorable event has occurred, the probabilities are 2 to 1 *against* the event being the result of negligence. And yet, the traditional formulation of the res ipsa loquitur rule might support liability because of the remoteness (1 in 100) of the occurrence of the unfavorable event even when the actor uses due care—that is, the unfavorable event does not "ordinarily" happen when the actor is exercising care, in the sense that it only happens 1 percent of the time. The implications of this sort of misapplication of res ipsa loquitur are explored in Kaye, Probability Theory Meets Res Ipsa Loquitur, 77 Mich. L. Rev. 1456 (1979).

This ambiguity in the res ipsa loquitur doctrine shows up dramatically in medical malpractice cases. In Younger v. Webster, 9 Wash. App. 87, 510 P.2d 1182 (1973), the plaintiff, following an injection of spinal anesthesia, permanently lost all feeling from his navel to his knees. Medical testimony was unanimous to the effect that this consequence was "unusual," but there was no evidence that when it did occur it was usually produced by negligence. The court ruled that on this evidence, res ipsa loquitur was applicable, and reversed the trial judge's dismissal of the action at the end of the plaintiff's evidence. In so doing, the court stated (Id. at 94, 510 P.2d at 1186):

> The present case comes within the reason and spirit of the doctrine. It is difficult to justifiably disregard the application of the doctrine when a patient submits himself to the care and custody of medical personnel, is rendered unconscious, and receives some injury from instrumentalities used in his treatment. Without the aid of the doctrine, a patient who receives permanent injuries of a serious character, apparently the result of someone's negligence, would be unable to recover unless the doctors and nurses voluntarily chose to disclose the facts establishing liability.

Cf. Ybarra v. Spangard, p. 134, above.

More typical of the judicial responses to rare consequences of medical treatment is Riedisser v. Nelsen, 111 Ariz. 542, 534 P.2d 1052 (1975). In this case, the plaintiff developed a ureterovaginal fistula following a vaginal hysterectomy performed by the defendants. In the pretrial affidavits, the plaintiff offered no expert evidence that the consequences were more probably than not the result of negligence. The court ruled that in the absence of such evidence, the defendant's motion for summary judgment was properly granted. In the course of its discussion, the court recognized that in some instances, res ipsa loquitur will be applied to permit a jury to find that the defendant physician was negligent, even though the plaintiff has presented no expert testimony supporting his case. The court cited the commonly given example of a rag left inside a patient after surgery.

Escola v. Coca Cola Bottling Co.

24 Cal. 2d 453, 150 P.2d 436 (1944)

GIBSON, C.J. Plaintiff, a waitress in a restaurant, was injured when a bottle of Coca Cola broke in her hand. She alleged that defendant company, which had bottled and delivered the alleged defective bottle to her employer, was negligent in selling "bottles containing said beverage which on account of excessive pressure of gas or by reason of some defect in the bottle was dangerous . . . and likely to explode." This appeal is from a judgment upon a jury verdict in favor of plaintiff. . . .

[B]eing unable to show any specific acts of negligence, [plaintiff] relied completely on the doctrine of res ipsa loquitur.

Defendant contends that the doctrine of res ipsa loquitur does not apply in this case, and that the evidence is insufficient to support the judgment. . . .

Res ipsa loquitur does not apply unless (1) defendant had exclusive control of the thing causing the injury and (2) the accident is of such a nature that it ordinarily would not occur in the absence of negligence by the defendant.

Many authorities state that the happening of the accident does not speak for itself where it took place some time after defendant had relinquished control of the instrumentality causing the injury. Under the more logical view, however, the doctrine may be applied upon the theory that defendant had control at the time of the alleged negligent act, although not at the time of the accident, *provided* plaintiff first proves that the condition of the instrumentality had not been changed after it left the defendant's possession. As said in Dunn v. Hoffman Beverage Co., 126 N.J. L. 556 [20 A.2d 352, 354], "defendant is not charged with the duty of showing affirmatively that something happened to the bottle after it left its control or management; . . . to get to the jury the plaintiff must show that there was due care during that period." Plaintiff must also prove that she handled the bottle carefully. The reason for this prerequisite is set forth in Prosser on Torts, [1st ed.] at page 300, where the author states: "Allied to the condition of exclusive control in the defendant is that of absence of any action on the part of the plaintiff contributing to the accident. Its purpose, of course, is to eliminate the possibility that it was the plaintiff who was responsible. If the boiler of a locomotive explodes while the plaintiff engineer is operating it, the inference of his own negligence is at least as great as that of the defendant and res ipsa loquitur will not apply until he has accounted for his own conduct." It is not necessary, of course, that plaintiff eliminate every remote possibility of injury to the bottle after defendant lost control, and the requirement is satisfied if there is evidence permitting a reasonable inference that it was not accessible to extraneous harmful forces and that it was carefully handled by plaintiff or any third person who may have moved or touched it. If such evidence is presented, the question becomes one for the trier of fact and, accordingly, the issue should be submitted to the jury under proper instructions.

In the present case no instructions were requested or given on this phase of the case, although general instructions upon res ipsa loquitur were given. Defendant, however, has made no claim of error with reference thereto on this appeal.

Upon an examination of the record, the evidence appears sufficient to support a reasonable inference that the bottle here involved was not damaged by any extraneous force after delivery to the restaurant by defendant. It follows, therefore, that the bottle was in some manner defective at the time defendant relinquished control, because sound and properly prepared bottles of carbonated liquids do not ordinarily explode when carefully handled.

The next question, then, is whether plaintiff may rely upon the doctrine of res ipsa loquitur to supply an inference that defendant's negligence was responsible for the defective condition of the bottle at the time it was delivered to the restaurant. Under the general rules pertaining to the doctrine, as set forth above, it must appear that bottles of carbonated liquid are not ordinarily defective without negligence by the bottling company.

An explosion such as took place here might have been caused by an excessive internal pressure in a sound bottle, by a defect in the glass of a bottle containing a safe pressure, or by a combination of these two possible causes. The question is whether under the evidence there was a probability that defendant was negligent in any of these respects. If so, the doctrine of res ipsa loquitur applies.

The bottle was admittedly charged with gas under pressure, and the charging of the bottle was within the exclusive control of defendant. As it is a matter of common knowledge that an overcharge would not ordinarily result without negligence, it follows under the doctrine of res ipsa loquitur that if the bottle was in fact excessively charged an inference of defendant's negligence would arise. If the explosion resulted from a defective bottle containing a safe pressure, the defendant would be liable if it negligently failed to discover such flaw. If the defect were visible, an inference of negligence would arise from the failure of defendant to discover it. Where defects are discoverable, it may be assumed that they will not ordinarily escape detection if a reasonable inspection is made, and if such a defect is overlooked an inference arises that a proper inspection was not made. A difficult problem is presented where the defect is unknown and consequently might have been one not discoverable by a reasonable, practicable inspection. In [an earlier] case we refused to take judicial notice of the technical practices and information available to the bottling industry for finding defects which cannot be seen. In the present case, however, we are supplied with evidence of the standard methods used for testing bottles.

A chemical engineer for the Owens-Illinois Glass Company and its Pacific Coast subsidiary, maker of Coca Cola bottles, explained how glass is manufactured and the methods used in testing and inspecting bottles. He testified that his company is the largest manufacturer of glass containers in the United States, and that it uses the standard methods for testing bottles recommended by the glass containers association. A pressure test is made by taking a sample from each mold every three hours—approximately one out of every 600 bottles—and subjecting the sample to an internal pressure of 450 pounds per square inch, which is sustained for one minute. (The normal pressure in Coca Cola bottles is less than 50 pounds per square inch.) The sample bottles are also subjected to the standard thermal shock test. The witness stated that these tests are "pretty near" infallible.

It thus appears that there is available to the industry a commonly-used method of testing bottles for defects not apparent to the eye, which is almost infallible. Since Coca Cola bottles are subjected to these tests by the manufacturer, it is not likely that they contain defects when delivered to the bottler which are not discoverable by visual inspection. Both new and used bottles are filled and distributed by defendant. The used bottles are not again subjected to the tests referred to above, and it may be inferred that defects not discoverable by visual inspection do not develop in bottles after they are manufactured. Obviously, if such defects do occur in used bottles there is a duty upon the bottler to make appropriate tests before they are refilled, and if such tests are not commercially practicable the bottles should not be re-used. This would seem to be particularly true where a charged liquid is placed in the bottle. It follows that a defect which would make the bottle unsound could be discovered by reasonable and practicable tests.

Although it is not clear in this case whether the explosion was caused by an excessive charge or a defect in the glass, there is a sufficient showing that neither cause would ordinarily have been present if due care had been used. Further, defendant had exclusive control over both the charging and inspection of the bottles. Accordingly, all the requirements necessary to entitle plaintiff to rely on the doctrine of res ipsa loquitur to supply an inference of negligence are present.

It is true that defendant presented evidence tending to show that it exercised considerable precaution by carefully regulating and checking the pressure in the bottles and by making visual inspections for defects in the glass at several stages during the bottling process. It is well settled, however, that when a defendant produces evidence to rebut the inference of negligence which arises upon application of the doctrine of res ipsa loquitur, it is ordinarily a question of fact for the jury to determine whether the inference has been dispelled.

The judgment is affirmed.

SHENK, J., CURTIS, J., CARTER, J., and SCHAUER, J., concurred.

TRAYNOR, J. I concur in the judgment, but I believe the manufacturer's negligence should no longer be singled out as the basis of a plaintiff's right to recover in cases like the present one. In my opinion it should now be recognized that a manufacturer incurs an absolute liability when an article that he has placed on the market, knowing that it is to be used without inspection, proves to have a defect that causes injury to human beings. McPherson v. Buick Motor Co., 217 N.Y. 382 [111 N.E. 1050, Ann. Cas. 1916C 440, L.R.A. 1916F 696], established the principle, recognized by this court, that irrespective of privity of contract, the manufacturer is responsible for an injury caused by such an article to any person who comes in lawful contact with it.

. . . Even if there is no negligence, however, public policy demands that responsibility be fixed wherever it will most effectively reduce the hazards to life and health inherent in defective products that reach the market. It is evident that the manufacturer can anticipate some hazards and guard against the recurrence of others, as the public cannot. Those who suffer injury from defective products are unprepared to meet its consequences. The cost of an injury and the loss of time or health may be an overwhelming misfortune to the person injured, and a needless one, for the risk of injury can be insured by the manufacturer and distributed among the public as a cost of doing business. It is to the public interest to discourage the marketing of products having defects that are a menace to the public. If such products nevertheless find their way into the market it is to the public interest to place the responsibility for whatever injury they may cause upon the manufacturer, who, even if he is not negligent in the manufacture of the product, is responsible for its reaching the market. However intermittently such injuries may occur and however haphazardly they may strike, the risk of their occurrence is a constant risk and a general one. Against such a risk there should be general and constant protection and the manufacturer is best situated to afford such protection.

As handicrafts have been replaced by mass production with its great markets and transportation facilities, the close relationship between the producer and consumer of a product has been altered. Manufacturing processes, frequently valuable secrets, are ordinarily either inaccessible to or beyond the ken of the general public. The consumer no longer has means or skill enough to investigate for himself the soundness of a product, even when it is not contained in a sealed package, and his erstwhile vigilance has been lulled by the steady efforts of manufacturers to build up confidence by advertising and marketing devices such as trademarks. Consumers no longer approach products warily but accept them on faith, relying on the reputation of the manufacturer or the trade-mark. Manufacturers have sought to justify that faith by increasingly high standards of inspection and a readiness to make good on defective products by way of replacements and refunds. The manufacturer's obligation to the consumer must keep pace with the changing relationship between them. . . .

D. *Modification of the General Standard Arising out of Special Relationships between the Parties*

In a few situations, the general duty of reasonable care may be raised or lowered because of some special relationship existing between the parties. The most common relationships as to which the duty may be modified are those between a possessor of land and entrants on the land, between a common carrier and its passengers, and between a driver of an automobile and guest-passengers.

1. Responsibility of Possessors of Land for the Safety of Trespassers, Licensees, and Invitees

The duty owed by an owner or possessor to those on the land with respect to conditions on the land has traditionally depended upon a rather rigid scheme of classification of the persons on the land as trespassers, licensees, or invitees. These traditional classifications often lower, but never raise, the normal duty of reasonable care, and therefore benefit landowners and possessors generally. Historically, the classifications and their attendant duties owe their existence to the high place that land has occupied in Anglo-American society. At one time, land was the primary source of wealth and social status, and thus the foundation of economic and political power. The importance of private ownership has lessened through the years, and recent cases indicate that we may be in a period of transition toward a single duty of reasonable care to all persons.

a. Invitees and Licensees

Invitees and licensees share the common characteristic of being on the land at least with the permission of the possessor. Beyond that, there are significant differences.

Invitees are defined by the Restatement (Second) of Torts, §332:

> §332. INVITEE DEFINED
>
> (1) An invitee is either a public invitee or a business visitor.
>
> (2) A public invitee is a person who is invited to enter or remain on land as a member of the public for a purpose for which the land is held open to the public.
>
> (3) A business visitor is a person who is invited to enter or remain on land for a purpose directly or indirectly connected with business dealings with the possessor of the land.

The "public invitee" concept is perhaps somewhat narrower than the black letter might indicate. According to Comment *d*:

> It is not enough, to hold land open to the public, that the public at large, or any considerable number of persons, are permitted to enter at will upon the land for their own purposes. As in other instances of invitation, there must be some inducement or encouragement to enter, some conduct indicating that the premises are provided and intended for public entry and use, and that the public will not merely be tolerated, but is expected and desired to come. When a landowner tacitly permits the boys of the town to play ball on his vacant lot they are licensees only; but if he installs playground equipment and posts a sign saying that the lot is open free to all children, there is then a public invitation, and those who enter in response to it are invitees.

The duty owed to an invitee is one of reasonable care under the circumstances. The duty is fleshed out in §343 of the Restatement (Second) of Torts:

> §343. DANGEROUS CONDITIONS KNOWN TO OR DISCOVERABLE BY POSSESSOR
>
> A possessor of land is subject to liability for physical harm caused to his invitees by a condition on the land if, but only if, he
>
> (a) knows or by the exercise of reasonable care would discover the condition, and should realize that it involves an unreasonable risk of harm to such invitees, and
>
> (b) should expect that they will not discover or realize the danger, or will fail to protect themselves against it, and
>
> (c) fails to exercise reasonable care to protect them against the danger.

The definition of licensee is set out in §330 of the Restatement:

> §330. LICENSEE DEFINED
>
> A licensee is a person who is privileged to enter or remain on land only by virtue of the possessor's consent.

The duty to licensees is set out in §342:

> §342. DANGEROUS CONDITIONS KNOWN TO POSSESSOR
>
> A possessor of land is subject to liability for physical harm caused to licensees by a condition on the land if, but only if,
>
> (a) the possessor knows or has reason to know[120] of the condition and should realize that it involves an unreasonable risk of harm to such licensees, and should expect that they will not discover or realize the danger, and
>
> (b) he fails to exercise reasonable care to make the condition safe, or to warn the licensees of the condition and the risk involved, and
>
> (c) the licensees do not know or have reason to know of the condition and the risk involved.

Although the Restatement defines the duties of the possessor to invitees and licensees in different language, in substance are they really the same? Would a warning of the hazardous condition always insulate the possessor from liability, even to invitees? That issue has been presented in cases in which the condition causing harm to the invitee is open and obvious, and the defendant seeks to avoid liability for that reason. Although on occasion a court has ruled that the obviousness of the danger forecloses liability (see, e.g., Baldwin v. Gartman, 604 So. 2d 347 (Ala. 1992)), more often courts

120. According to Comment *a* to §12, Restatement (Second) of Torts, *reason to know* means "that the actor has knowledge of facts from which a reasonable man of ordinary intelligence or one of the superior intelligence of the actor would either infer the existence of the fact in question or would regard its existence as so highly probable that his conduct would be predicated upon the assumption that the fact did exist." [Eds.]

hold that the obviousness is only one factor in determining the negligence of the defendant. See, e.g., Ward v. K mart Corp., 136 Ill. 2d 132, 554 N.E.2d 223 (1990). The court in *Ward* also stated that the obviousness is relevant in assessing the plaintiff's comparative fault.

As might be expected, the distinction between invitees and licensees has generated considerable litigation. The following text discusses a few of the contexts in which the issue has arisen:

Police Officers and Fire Fighters. By and large, courts have characterized police officers visiting the land in their official capacity as licensees. See, e.g., Furstein v. Hill, 218 Conn. 610, 590 A.2d 939 (1991); Scheurer v. Trustee of the Open Bible Church, 175 Ohio St. 163, 192 N.E.2d 38 (1963). The Supreme Court of Ohio distinguished the rule of *Scheurer* in Brady v. Consolidated Rail Corp., 35 Ohio St. 3d 161, 519 N.E.2d 387 (1988), when it held that a police officer is an invitee when on land held open to the public. *Brady* was not mentioned by the Supreme Court of Ohio in Provencher v. Ohio Department of Transportation, 49 Ohio St. 3d 265, 551 N.E.2d 1257 (1990), in which the court rejected the public invitee category. The court in Rosa v. Dunkin' Donuts of Passaic, 122 N.J. 66, 583 A.2d 1129 (1991), extended even less than licensee protection to fire fighters and police officers; it ruled that the owner is liable only for intentional or willful misconduct.

Fire fighters, like police officers, have also been characterized as licensees. See, e.g., Roberts v. Rosenblatt, 146 Conn. 110, 148 A.2d 142 (1959).

The liability of possessors of land to police officers and fire fighters for harm arising out of the risks that called them to the land is discussed at pp. 376-377, below.

Users of Restrooms and Telephones. Restaurants and stores often make restrooms and telephones available to their customers, and customers retain their invitee status while using these facilities. See, e.g., Coston v. Skyland Hotel, 231 N.C. 546, 57 S.E.2d 793 (1950). The law is less clear when the plaintiff's use of such facilities is the sole purpose of the entry to the defendant's premises. In Campbell v. Weathers, 153 Kan. 316, 111 P.2d 72 (1941), the plaintiff was a regular customer of the defendant's lunch counter, but was injured in using the rest room on a visit when he had made no purchase. The court held that he was an invitee, although it did add that a person who has no intent to be a present or future customer would be a licensee only. The latter point is echoed in Argus v. Michler, 349 S.W.2d 389 (Mo. App. 1961), involving a person not a customer using a telephone in a service station. But even regular customers are not invitees in all states. See, e.g., Adams v. Ferraro, 41 A.D.2d 578, 339 N.Y.S.2d 554 (1973), in which the plaintiff, a regular customer of the defendant's bar, was held to be a licensee since his sole purpose for the visit during which he was injured was to use the telephone.

Recreational Users of Land. If a possessor of land holds the land open to others for recreational purposes, such as hunting, fishing, swimming, hiking, and the like, and does not charge a fee, those coming on the land for such purposes would normally be considered licensees. The possessor would have no duty to those persons to make the land reasonably safe, but under §342 of the Restatement would have the duty to use reasonable care to warn of those hazardous conditions of which the possessor knows or has reason to know. Most state legislatures have enacted legislation which codifies the duty of possessors of land to recreational users, although the extent to which these statutes change the common law is not always clear. See, e.g., New York General Obligations Law, §9-103.

b. Trespassers

The lowest duty is owed to a trespasser, who is defined by §329 of the Restatement (Second) as "a person who enters or remains upon land in the possession of another without a privilege to do so created by the possessor's consent or otherwise." In general, the duty of the possessor toward trespassers is to refrain from wanton and willful conduct. See, e.g., Wagner v. Doehring, 315 Md. 97, 553 A.2d 684 (1989). However, if the trespasser is on the land for the purpose of committing a crime, the possessor may be liable only for intentionally injuring the trespasser. See, e.g., Ryals v. United States Steel Corp., 562 So. 2d 192 (Ala. 1990). The circumstances under which the possessor has a privilege to injure trespassers intentionally was the subject of *Katko v. Briney,* the spring gun case set out in Chapter 1, p. 84, above.

Two sections of the Restatement (Second) impose duties to use reasonable care to warn trespassers of hazardous conditions:

§335. ARTIFICIAL CONDITIONS HIGHLY DANGEROUS TO CONSTANT TRESPASSERS ON LIMITED AREA

A possessor of land who knows, or from facts within his knowledge should know, that trespassers constantly intrude upon a limited area of the land, is subject to liability for bodily harm caused to them by an artificial condition on the land, if

(a) the condition

(i) is one which the possessor has created or maintains and

(ii) is, to his knowledge, likely to cause death or serious bodily harm to such trespassers and

(iii) is of such a nature that he has reason to believe that such trespassers will not discover it, and

(b) the possessor has failed to exercise reasonable care to warn such trespassers of the condition and the risk involved.

§337. ARTIFICIAL CONDITIONS HIGHLY DANGEROUS TO KNOWN TRESPASSERS

A possessor of land who maintains on the land an artificial condition which involves a risk of death or serious bodily harm to persons coming in contact with it, is subject to liability for bodily harm caused to trespassers by his failure to exercise reasonable care to warn them of the condition if

(a) the possessor knows or has reason to know of their presence in dangerous proximity to the condition, and

(b) the condition is of such a nature that he has reason to believe that the trespasser will not discover it or realize the risk.

Note that these sections do not apply to natural conditions on the land. If the trespasser stumbles into a quicksand bog on the possessor's land, there is no liability at all for failure to warn. Can you think of any reason why there should be a distinction between artificial and natural conditions in this respect? But also note that the sections do apply even if the possessor has done all that can reasonably be done to keep trespassers from the land. See, e.g., Grant v. City of Duluth, 672 F.2d 677 (8th Cir. 1982).

A higher duty may be owed to young trespassers under the "attractive nuisance doctrine," as set out in §339 of the Restatement (Second):

§339. ARTIFICIAL CONDITIONS HIGHLY DANGEROUS TO TRESPASSING CHILDREN

A possessor of land is subject to liability for physical harm to children trespassing thereon caused by an artificial condition upon the land if

(a) the place where the condition exists is one upon which the possessor knows or has reason to know that children are likely to trespass, and

(b) the condition is one of which the possessor knows or has reason to know and which he realizes or should realize will involve an unreasonable risk of death or serious bodily harm to such children, and

(c) the children because of their youth do not discover the condition or realize the risk involved in intermeddling with it or in coming within the area made dangerous by it, and

(d) the utility to the possessor of maintaining the condition and the burden of eliminating the danger are slight as compared with the risk to children involved, and

(e) the possessor fails to exercise reasonable care to eliminate the danger or otherwise to protect the children.

The attractive nuisance doctrine is sometimes referred to as the "turntable doctrine," after an early case involving a child injured while he was trespassing on a railroad turntable. See Sioux City & Pac. R.R. v. Stout, 84 U.S. (17 Wall) 657, 21 L. Ed. 745 (1873). It is followed by almost all states; among the few still rejecting the doctrine are Macke Laundry Service v. Weber, 267 Md. 426, 298 A.2d 27 (1972), and Elliott v. Nagy, 22 Ohio St. 3d 58, 488 N.E.2d 853 (1986). The court in *Elliott* gave as its reason for refusing to adopt the doctrine (Id. at 60, 488 N.E.2d at 855):

We have not favored attractive nuisance . . . because this doctrine imposes a greater burden to protect children on members of the community (who are often strangers to a child and his family) than is imposed on the parents themselves.

A somewhat similar philosophy was expressed in an early Michigan case:

> There is no more lawless class than children, and none more annoyingly resent an attempt to prevent their trespasses. The average citizen has learned that the surest way to be overrun by children is to give them to understand that their presence is distasteful. The consequence is that they roam at will over private premises, and, as a rule this is tolerated so long as no damage is done. The remedy which the law affords for trifling trespasses of children is inadequate. No one ever thinks of suing them, and to attempt to remove a crowd of boys from private premises by gently laying on of hands, and using no more force than necessary to put them off, would be a roaring farce, with all honors to the juveniles. For a corporation with an empty treasury, and overwhelmed with debt, to be required to be to the expense of preventing children from going across its lots to school, lest it be said that it invited and licensed them to do so, is to our minds an unreasonable proposition.

Ryan v. Towar, 128 Mich. 463, 466, 87 N.W. 644, 645 (1901).

A much different attitude toward trespassing children, and one which would be concurred in by most courts today, is expressed in a later Michigan case, Lyshak v. City of Detroit, 351 Mich. 230, 88 N.W.2d 596 (1958). The plaintiff, together with other boys, went through a hole in a fence surrounding a golf course owned and operated by the defendant. He was injured when he was struck by a flying golf ball. The defendant's employees were aware that children sneaked onto the course, and chased them off whenever they were discovered. In holding that the defendant owed a duty of reasonable care to the plaintiff, even though he was a trespasser, the court said (Id. at 233-234, 88 N.W.2d at 598-599):

> This case, we are told, concerns merely a trespassing child. And, as all know, a trespasser has no rights. A licensee has a few, and an invitee more, but as to a mere trespasser there is no duty of care. There being no duty there can be no negligence, and there being no negligence there can be no recovery by a trespassing child, though grievously hurt.
>
> And yet, if a defendant baits traps with stinking meat and thus lures a trespassing dog to destruction, the defendant has been held liable. There seems to be here a valid (and perplexing) analogy. The theory is that one is liable if he lures something to its destruction. In the case before us, a great city maintained, in a densely populated residential section, a park-like area, a golf course, with ample lawn, trees, and "a little creek." Upon this area, in the summer, children entered daily. They were drawn to it for purposes of play as naturally as the dog to the bait. The city of Detroit knew this, knowing it the only way a "city" can know anything, through the knowledge of its employees, servants, and agents. The professional at [the course] knew it. The supervising greenskeeper, who had charge of all men working on the

golf course, and the repair and control of the fence, knew it. The official in charge of the . . . course knew it. However, knowing of the daily entrance of children onto the course, for purposes of childish play, the city, it is asserted, nevertheless continued to conduct thereon an enterprise of such character as to subject these children to risk of grave bodily injury, resulting in infant plaintiff's loss of one eye.

We will assume that the infant plaintiff, like the dog, was a trespasser. The dog's owner, nevertheless, recovered for his loss. The boy, according to the trial court, is to get nothing. What kind of law is this? . . . It takes great legal skill to distinguish the trespassing boy, having viewed the allurements of the park-like area across the crowded city street, where he had the right to be, from the trespassing dog that followed his instincts to his destruction, denying recovery to the trespassing boy, but granting it to the owner of the trespassing dog. We are not sure we possess the skill required.

Some courts have not extended the protection of the attractive nuisance doctrine to children over 14, although most follow Comment *c* to §339 and reject any arbitrary age limitation in favor of a case-by-case determination of whether "the child is still too young to appreciate the danger. . . ." See Annotation, 16 A.L.R.3d 25 (1967). Regardless of the age of the child, the rule does not apply if the condition is obvious and the child recognizes its danger. See Christon v. Kankakee Valley Boat Club, 504 N.E.2d 263 (Ill. App.), *review denied,* 115 Ill. 2d 539, 511 N.E.2d 426 (1987); Wiles v. Metzger, 238 Neb. 943, 473 N.W.2d 113 (1991).

Problem 16

The presentation of the evidence has been completed in the case of Toth v. Livingston, a case tried to a jury in the Superior Court. The defendant has filed a motion for a directed verdict. There is little dispute as to the facts, and a fair summary of the evidence as it relates to liability is:

The plaintiff, Allen Toth, was injured when he fell through a dock belonging to the defendant, Barry Livingston. The dock extends into Loon Lake from the defendant's property on Snake Island, where the defendant has a summer home. The plaintiff testified that at the time of the accident he was ten years old, and that he went onto the dock, without permission of the defendant, at about 8:30 P.M. on June 16, two and a half years ago, to fish from its end. The plaintiff was large for his age and when he got about 15 feet from the end, a plank gave way under his weight and he fell through and was injured.

The defendant testified that he had built the dock 11 years before the accident. It extended into the lake about 45 feet and was 8 feet wide. The pine planks forming the top of the dock ran the width of the dock, and were 9¾ inches wide and 1¾ inches thick. The broken plank was admitted into evidence. The plaintiff's expert testified that it had rotted from underneath in the area of two knots in the plank. The plank had become sufficiently dry so that the knots would contribute to the weakness caused by the rot. The expert also testified that an inspection of the underside of the dock in the spring before the accident, and probably the previous fall as well, would have revealed the deterioration of the plank. On cross-examination the expert testified that viewed from above the plank would have appeared normal.

The defendant testified that he casually inspected the topside of the dock from time to time and that he had replaced two planks two or three years before the accident. He could not recall if he had made any inspection since then. He knew that he had not looked the dock over during the spring just prior to the accident. He had opened the house around the first of June and had moved his family to the lake the weekend before the accident. He testified that he did not know that this particular plank was in any way defective. He further testified that he was aware that youngsters used his dock for fishing from time to time, that he chased them off whenever this happened, and that he did not see the plaintiff go onto the dock on the evening of June 16. The plaintiff was spending the summer with his family at the lake and did not know that other people had been chased from the dock.

Assuming that your state generally follows the rules set forth in the Restatement (Second) of Torts how would you argue on behalf of the defendant in support of the motion for a directed verdict? On behalf of the plaintiff in opposition to the motion? If the motion is denied, what instructions should the judge give to the jury?

Problem 17

Assume that Rowland v. Christian is an opinion of the supreme court of your state. Should the trial judge on the facts of Problem 16 grant the defendant's motion for a directed verdict? If not, what instructions should be given to the jury?

Rowland v. Christian

69 Cal. 2d 108, 443 P.2d 561, 70 Cal. Rptr. 97 (1968)

[This is an appeal from an order of the trial judge granting the defendant's motion for summary judgment. The facts, as they appeared in the complaint, the answer, and the affidavits supporting and opposing summary judgment, were these: The plaintiff was a social guest in defendant's apartment. The plaintiff asked to use the bathroom, and while he was in the bathroom, a cracked handle of a water faucet broke in his hand, causing severe injuries. The defendant was aware that the handle was cracked, and had so informed her landlord and had asked that the handle be replaced, but she did not warn the plaintiff of the condition of the handle. The pleadings did not indicate whether the condition was obvious, although the defendant alleged in her answer that the plaintiff had failed to use his "eyesight" and that he was aware of the condition.]

PETERS, J. . . . Section 1714 of the Civil Code provides: "Every one is responsible, not only for the result of his willful acts, but also for an injury occasioned to another by his want of ordinary care or skill in the management of his property or person, except so far as the latter has, willfully or by want of ordinary care, brought the injury upon himself. . . ." This code section, which has been unchanged in our law since 1872, states a civil law and not a common law principle.

Nevertheless, some common law judges and commentators have urged that the principle embodied in this code section serves as the foundation of our negligence law. Thus in a concurring opinion, Brett, M. R. in Heaven v. Pender (1883) 11 Q.B.D. 503, 509, states: "whenever one person is by circumstances placed in such a position with regard to another that every one of ordinary sense who did think would at once recognize that if he did not use ordinary care and skill in his own conduct with regard to those circumstances he would cause danger of injury to the person or property of the other, a duty arises to use ordinary care and skill to avoid such danger."

California cases have occasionally stated a similar view: "All persons are required to use ordinary care to prevent others being injured as the result of their conduct." Although it is true that some exceptions have been made to the general principle that a person is liable for injuries caused by his failure to exercise reasonable care in the circumstances, it is clear that in the absence of statutory provision declaring an exception to the fundamental principle enunciated by section 1714 of the Civil Code, no such exception should be made unless clearly supported by public policy.

A departure from this fundamental principle involves the balancing of a number of considerations; the major ones are the foreseeability of harm to the plaintiff, the degree of certainty that the plaintiff suffered injury, the closeness of the connection between the defendant's conduct and the injury suffered, the moral blame attached to the defendant's conduct, the policy of preventing future harm, the extent of the burden to the defendant and consequences to the community of imposing a duty to exercise care with resulting liability for breach, and the availability, cost, and prevalence of insurance for the risk involved.

One of the areas where this court and other courts have departed from the fundamental concept that a man is liable for injuries caused by his carelessness is with regard to the liability of a possessor of land for injuries to persons who have entered upon that land. It has been suggested that the special rules regarding liability of the possessor of land are due to historical considerations stemming from the high place which land has traditionally held in English and American thought, the dominance and prestige of the landowning class in England during the formative period of the rules governing the possessor's liability, and the heritage of feudalism.

The departure from the fundamental rule of liability for negligence has been accomplished by classifying the plaintiff either as a trespasser, licensee, or invitee and then adopting special rules as to the duty owed by the possessor to each of the classifications. Generally speaking a trespasser is a person who enters or remains upon land of another without a privilege to do so; a licensee is a person like a social guest who is not an invitee and who is privileged to enter or remain upon land by virtue of the possessor's consent, and an invitee is a business visitor who is invited or permitted to enter or remain on the land for a purpose directly or indirectly connected with business dealings between them.

Although the invitor owes the invitee a duty to exercise ordinary care to avoid injuring him, the general rule is that a trespasser and licensee or social guest are obliged to take the premises as they find them insofar as any alleged defective condition thereon may exist, and that the possessor of the land owes them only the duty of refraining from wanton or willful injury. The ordinary justification for the general rule severely restricting the occupier's liability to social guests is based on the theory that the guest should not expect special precautions to be made on his account and that if the host does not inspect and maintain his property the guest should not expect this to be done on his account.

An increasing regard for human safety has led to a retreat from this position, and an exception to the general rule limiting liability has been made as to active operations where an obligation to exercise reasonable care for the protection of the licensee has been imposed on the occupier of land. In an apparent attempt to avoid the general rule limiting liability, courts have broadly defined active operations, sometimes giving the term a strained construction in cases involving dangers known to the occupier. . . .

Another exception to the general rule limiting liability has been recognized for cases where the occupier is aware of the dangerous condition, the condition amounts to a concealed trap, and the guest is unaware of the trap. . . .

The cases dealing with the active negligence and the trap exceptions are indicative of the subtleties and confusion which have resulted from application of the common law principles governing the liability of the possessor of land. Similar confusion and complexity exist as to the definitions of trespasser, licensee, and invitee.

In refusing to adopt the rules relating to the liability of a possessor of land for the law of admiralty, the United States Supreme Court stated: "The distinctions which the common law draws between licensee and invitee were inherited from a culture deeply rooted to the land, a culture which traced many of its standards to a heritage of feudalism. In an effort to do justice in an industrialized urban society, with its complex economic and individual relationships, modern common-law courts have found it necessary to formulate increasingly subtle verbal refinements, to create subclassifications among traditional common-law categories, and to delineate fine gradations in the standards of care which the landowner owes to each. Yet even within a single jurisdiction, the classifications and subclassifications bred by the common law have produced confusion and conflict. As new distinctions have been spawned, older ones have become obscured. Through this semantic morass the common law has moved, unevenly and with hesitation, towards imposing on owners and occupiers a single duty of reasonable care in all the circumstances.' " (Footnotes omitted.) (Kermarec v. Compagnie Generale, 358 U.S. 625, 630-631 [79 S. Ct. 406, 3 L. Ed. 2d 550, 554-555].) . . .

There is another fundamental objection to the approach to the question of the possessor's liability on the basis of the common law distinctions based upon the status of the injured party as a trespasser, licensee, or invitee. Complexity can be borne and confusion remedied where the underlying principles governing liability are based upon proper considerations. Whatever may have been the historical justifications for the common law distinctions, it is clear that those distinctions are not justified in the light of our modern society and that the complexity and confusion which has arisen is not due to difficulty in applying the original common law rules—they are all too easy to apply in their original formulation—but is due to the attempts to apply just rules in our modern society within the ancient terminology.

Without attempting to labor all of the rules relating to the possessor's liability, it is apparent that the classifications of trespasser, licensee, and invitee, the immunities from liability predicated upon those classifications, and the exceptions to those immunities, often do not reflect the major factors which should determine whether immunity should be conferred upon the possessor of land. Some of those factors, including the closeness of the connection between the injury and the defendant's conduct, the moral blame attached to the defendant's conduct, the policy of preventing future harm, and the prevalence and availability of insurance, bear little, if any, relationship to the classifications of trespasser, licensee and invitee and the existing rules conferring immunity.

Although in general there may be a relationship between the remaining factors and the classifications of trespasser, licensee, and invitee, there are many cases in which no such relationship may exist. Thus, although the foreseeability of harm to an invitee would ordinarily seem greater than the foreseeability of harm to a trespasser, in a particular case the opposite may be true. The same may be said of the issue of certainty of injury. The burden to the defendant and consequences to the community of imposing a duty to exercise care with resulting liability for breach may often be greater with respect to trespassers than with respect to invitees, but it by no means follows that this is true in every case. In many situations, the burden will be the same, i.e., the conduct necessary upon the defendant's part to meet the burden of exercising due care as to invitees will also meet his burden with respect to licensees and trespassers. The last of the major factors, the cost of insurance, will, of course, vary depending upon the rules of liability adopted, but there is no persuasive evidence that applying ordinary principles of negligence law to the land occupier's liability will materially reduce the prevalence of insurance due to increased cost or even substantially increase the cost. . . .

A man's life or limb does not become less worthy of protection by the law nor a loss less worthy of compensation under the law because he has come upon the land of another without permission or with permission but without a business purpose. Reasonable people do not ordinarily vary their conduct depending upon such matters, and to focus upon the status of the injured party as a trespasser, licensee, or invitee in order to determine the question whether the landowner has a duty of care, is contrary to our modern social mores and humanitarian values. The common law rules obscure rather than illuminate the proper considerations which should govern determination of the question of duty.

It bears repetition that the basic policy of this state set forth by the Legislature in section 1714 of the Civil Code is that everyone is responsible for an injury caused to another by his want of ordinary care or skill in the management of his property. The factors which may in particular cases warrant departure from this fundamental principle do not warrant the wholesale immunities resulting from the common law classifications, and we are satisfied that continued adherence to the common law distinctions can only lead to injustice or, if we are to avoid injustice, further fictions with the resulting complexity and confusion. We decline to follow and perpetuate such rigid classifications. The proper test to be applied to the liability of the possessor of land in accordance with section 1714 of the Civil Code is whether in the management of his property he has acted as a reasonable man in view of the probability of injury to others, and, although the plaintiff's status as a trespasser, licensee, or invitee may in the light of the facts giving rise to such status have some bearing on the question of liability, the status is not determinative.

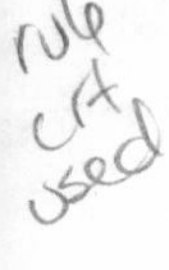

Once the ancient concepts as to the liability of the occupier of land are stripped away, the status of the plaintiff relegated to its proper place in determining such liability, and ordinary principles of negligence applied, the result in the instant case presents no substantial difficulties. As we have seen, when we view the matters presented on the motion for summary judgment as we must, we must assume defendant Miss Christian was aware that the faucet handle was defective and dangerous, that the defect was not obvious, and that plaintiff was about to come in contact with the defective condition, and under the undisputed facts she neither remedied the condition nor warned plaintiff of it. Where the occupier of land is aware of a concealed condition involving in the absence of precautions an unreasonable risk of harm to those coming in contact with it, the trier of fact can reasonably conclude that a failure to warn or to repair the condition constitutes negligence. Whether or not a guest has a right to expect that his host will remedy dangerous conditions on his account, he should reasonably be entitled to rely upon a warning of the dangerous condition so that he, like the host, will be in a position to take special precautions when he comes in contact with it. . . .

The judgment is reversed.

TRAYNOR, C.J., TOBRINER, J., MOSK, J., and SULLIVAN, J., concurred.

BURKE, J. I dissent. In determining the liability of the occupier or owner of land for injuries, the distinctions between trespassers, licensees and invitees have been developed and applied by the courts over a period of many years. They supply a reasonable and workable approach to the problems involved, and one which provides the degree of stability and predictability so highly prized in the law. The unfortunate alternative, it appears to me, is the route taken by the majority in their opinion in this case; that such issues are to be decided on a case by case basis under the application of the basic law of negligence, bereft of the guiding principles and precedent which the law has heretofore attached by virtue of the relationship of the parties to one another.

Liability for negligence turns upon whether a duty of care is owed, and if so, the extent thereof. Who can doubt that the corner grocery, the large department store, or the financial institution owes a greater duty of care to one whom it has invited to enter its premises as a prospective customer of its wares or services than it owes to a trespasser seeking to enter after the close of business hours and for a nonbusiness or even an antagonistic purpose? I do not think it unreasonable or unfair that a social guest (classified by the law as a licensee, as was plaintiff here) should be obliged to take the premises in the same condition as his host finds them or permits them to be. Surely a homeowner should not be obliged to hover over his guests with warnings of possible dangers to be found in the condition of the home (e.g., waxed floors, slipping rugs, toys in unexpected places, etc., etc.). Yet today's decision appears to open the door to potentially unlimited liability despite the purpose and circumstances motivating the plaintiff in entering the premises of another, and despite the caveat of the majority that the status of the parties may "have some bearing on the question of liability . . ." whatever the future may show that language to mean.

In my view, it is not a proper function of this court to overturn the learning, wisdom and experience of the past in this field. Sweeping modifications of tort liability law fall more suitably within the domain of the Legislature, before which all affected interests can be heard and which can enact statutes providing uniform standards and guidelines for the future.

I would affirm the judgment for defendant.

Rowland was the first reported case in which a state court abrogated the rules under which the duty of a landowner depends upon the status of the entrant. The reception given *Rowland* in other jurisdictions has been mixed. Some have rejected it entirely. See, e.g., Payne v. Rain Forest Nurseries, Inc., 540 So. 2d 35 (Miss. 1989); Tate v. Rice, 227 Va. 341, 315 S.E.2d 385 (1984). The Washington Supreme Court rejected *Rowland* in Younce v. Ferguson, 106 Wash. 2d 658, 724 P.2d 991 (1986). The court provides a comprehensive list of cases abolishing and retaining the classifications. It considers the reasons given in *Rowland* for the abolition of the categories, and then some reasons offered for their retention:

> The reasons proffered for continuing the distinctions include that the distinctions have been applied and developed over the years, offering a degree of stability and predictability and that a unitary standard would not lessen the confusion. Furthermore, a slow, piecemeal development rather than a wholesale change has been advocated. Some courts fear a wholesale change will delegate social policy decisions to the jury with minimal guidance from the court. Also, it is feared that the landowner could be subjected to unlimited liability.
>
> We find these reasons to be compelling. . . . We are not ready to abandon [the traditional classifications and exceptions] for a standard with no contours. . . . We do not choose to erase our developed jurisprudence for a blank slate.

106 Wash. 2d at 666, 724 P.2d at 995.

Other courts have abolished the distinction between social guests or licensees and invitees (see, e.g., Burrell v. Meads, 569 N.E.2d 637 (Ind. 1991); Hudson v. Gaitan, 675 S.W.2d 699 (Tenn. 1984)), but have retained the trespasser categories. See, e.g., Mounsey v. Ellard, 363 Mass. 693, 297 N.E.2d 43 (1973), in which the court explained its decision to retain the trespasser category as follows (Id. at 707, 297 N.E.2d at 51-52, fn. 7):

> We feel that there is significant difference in the legal status of one who trespasses on another's land as opposed to one who is on the land under some color of right—such as a licensee or invitee. For this reason, among others, we do not believe they should be placed in the same legal category. For example, one who jumps over a six foot fence to make use of his neighbor's swimming pool in his absence does not logically belong in the same legal classification as a licensee or invitee. Frankly, we are not persuaded as to the logic and reasoning in Rowland v. Christian, 69 Cal. 2d 108, 70 Cal. Rptr. 97, 443 P.2d 561, in placing trespassers in the same legal status as licensees and invitees. The possible difference in classes of trespassers is miniscule compared to the others. These differences can be considered when they arise in future cases.

A few courts have followed *Rowland* entirely and have brought trespassers within landowners' general duty of care. See Mile High Fence Co. v. Radovich, 175 Colo. 537, 489 P.2d 308 (1971); Ouellette v. Blanchard, 116 N.H. 552, 364 A.2d 631 (1976); Scurti v. City of New York, 40 N.Y.2d

433, 354 N.E.2d 794, 387 N.Y.S.2d 55 (1976). The full implications of abolishing the traditional law with respect to trespassers have bothered some judges who advocate such a move, and some limits upon the duty may yet remain. For instance, the court in *Ouellette* stated (116 N.H. at 557, 364 A.2d at 634):

> The character of and circumstances surrounding the intrusion will be relevant and important in determining the standard of care applicable to the landowner. When the intrusion is not foreseeable or is against the will of the landowner many intruders will be denied recovery as a matter of law. In other words, a landowner cannot be expected to maintain his premises in a safe condition for a wandering tramp or a person who enters against the known wishes of the landowner. Essentially the traditional tort test of foreseeability determines the liability or nonliability of the landowner in these cases.

In Soule v. Massachusetts Electric Co., 378 Mass. 177, 390 N.E.2d 716 (1979), the court refused to abandon the position it took in *Mounsey* not to bring trespassers within a general duty of care. A concurring justice would have abolished the special treatment applicable to trespassers, and in the course of his opinion observed (Id. at 188, 390 N.E.2d at 722-723):

> The Chief Justice's concurrence, speaking of the inequity of "abolishing all distinctions among tort plaintiffs who are invitees, licensees, or trespassers," may conjure up in some minds the spectre of an armed robber recovering damages for injuries suffered by him in tripping over a rug while engaged in his criminal adventure. It can be predicted flatly that that would not occur if the court should adopt quite frankly the position I espouse. The robber would be denied recovery, but not for the reason that the common law called him a "trespasser"; rather it would be for good and sufficient functional reasons that appeal to common sense. To make that common law catchword, or any other such as "invitee" or "licensee," in itself determinative, is a gateway to errors, as the history of the problem shows.

2. Responsibility of Common Carriers for the Safety of Their Passengers

In most states, common carriers are held to a duty to their passengers higher than that of reasonable care. The verbalization of the higher standard of care varies somewhat from state to state, with some courts holding carriers to the "highest" degree of care (see Mobile Cab & Baggage Co. v. Busby, 277 Ala. 292, 169 So. 2d 314 (1964), Brinkmoeller v. Wilson, 41 Ohio St. 2d 223, 325 N.E.2d 233 (1975)), and others to a "very high" (see Peoples Checker Cab Co. v. Dunlap, 307 P.2d 833 (Okla. 1957)) or to just a "high" degree of care (see Barrie v. Central R.R., 71 N.J. Super. 587, 177 A.2d 568, *cert. denied,* 37 N.J. 87, 179 A.2d 416 (1962)). Still other courts articulate the standard as "extraordinary care" (see Greyhound Corp. v. Ault, 238 F.2d 198 (5th Cir. 1956)), or "utmost care" (see Pillou v. Connecticut Co., 143 Conn. 481, 123 A.2d 470 (1956)), or "great caution" (see Beaudet v. Boston & Me. R.R., 101 N.H. 4, 131 A.2d 65 (1957)).

A few states have challenged these modifications of the standard of reasonable care. For instance, in McLean v. Triboro Coach Corp., 302 N.Y. 49, 51, 96 N.E.2d 83, 83-84 (1950), the court observed:

> Negligence is defined, broadly and generally speaking, as the failure to employ reasonable care—the care which the law's reasonably prudent man should use under the circumstances of a particular case. That being so, it may well be asked whether it is ever practicable for one to use more care than one reasonably can; whether it is ever reasonable for one to use less; or whether, in sum, there can ever be more than one degree of care. And, indeed, it has been said that to grade care into degrees, to differentiate between various degrees of care, is "unscientific," "most difficult of application," and "perplexing alike to bench and bar."

Even courts that purport to apply the reasonable care standard find the higher standard difficult to avoid. For instance, in Carson v. Boston Elevated Ry., 309 Mass. 32, 35, 33 N.E.2d 701, 703 (1941), the court defined a railway's duty as one of reasonable care under the circumstances, but then added a gloss to that duty: "Among those circumstances are that the carrier has control of the passenger and that the consequences of negligence are likely to be serious. Accordingly it is held that reasonable care under the circumstances is the highest degree of care,—not the highest degree of care imaginable, but the highest degree of care that is consistent with the requirements of the public for speedy and inexpensive as well as safe transportation and with the practical operation of the business."

The definition of a common carrier has also been the subject of some litigation. One early opinion defined a common carrier as "one who engages in the transportation of persons or things from place to place for hire, and who holds himself out to the public as ready and willing to serve the public, indifferently, in the particular line in which he is engaged." Burnett v. Riter, 276 S.W. 347, 349 (Tex. Civ. App. 1925). In more recent times, a ski lift has been characterized as a common carrier (see Squaw Valley Ski Corp. v. Superior Court, 2 Cal. App. 4th 1499, 3 Cal. Rptr. 2d 897 (1992)), as has an elevator in a public building (see Pruneda v. Otis Elevator Co., 828 P.2d 642 (Wash. App. 1992)), and an ambulance (see Nazareth v. Herndon Ambulance Service, Inc., 467 So. 2d 1076 (Fla. App.), *review denied,* 478 So. 2d 53 (Fla. 1985)). In Mount Pleasant Independent School District v. Lindburg, 766 S.W.2d 208 (Tex. 1989), the court ruled that a school bus is not a common carrier; the bus was operated as an incident to the educational enterprise rather than as a carriage for hire.

3. Responsibility of Operators of Motor Vehicles for the Safety of Their Passengers

A few states have laws which lower the standard of care owed by operators of automobiles to their nonpaying guests. Most of these laws are in the form of automobile guest statutes, although the initial development came about through judicial decision. The first state to adopt the lower standard was Massachusetts. In Massaletti v. Fitzroy, 228 Mass. 487, 118 N.E. 168 (1917), the court analogized a nonpaying guest in a horse-drawn wagon to property in the hands of a gratuitous bailee, who is liable only for gross negligence. This rule was later applied to automobiles, and remained the law in Massachusetts until it was overturned in 1971 by legislation, Mass. Gen. L., ch. 231, §85L, imposing a general duty of care on drivers of automobiles toward their passengers. In states in which the lower standard was judicially created, only Georgia continues to adhere to it. See Bickford v. Nolen, 240 Ga. 255, 240 S.E.2d 24 (1977).

By far, the most important source of the lowered duty to nonpaying passengers is automobile guest legislation. But most of that legislation has been repealed, and now only a handful of states retain the modified duty. See, e.g., Code of Ala. §32-1-2, which establishes a "willful or wanton misconduct" standard. The Indiana statute, Ind. Code §34-4-40 (Cum. Supp. 1992), incorporates a similar standard, but is applicable only to hitchhikers and the listed relatives of the operator. The Oregon statute, Or. Rev. Stat. §30.115, applies to operators of aircraft and watercraft, but not to operators of automobiles.

Guest statutes have not been well treated by courts, and some rather strained distinctions have resulted. The California experience is detailed in Brown v. Merlo, 8 Cal. 3d 855, 506 P.2d 212, 106 Cal. Rptr. 388 (1973), in which the California automobile guest statute was held to be unconstitutional on a variety of grounds. But other courts have upheld guest statutes against constitutional attack. See, e.g., Corey v. Jones, 650 F.2d 803 (5th Cir. 1981).

E. *Limitations on Liability*

The preceding sections of this chapter contain the basic analysis of negligence as a basis of liability. In this section, we take up a variety of doctrines that historically have served as limitations on liability for negligence. As you will see, however, the doctrines have been considerably eroded so that with respect to some of them in some states it is fair to say that little in the way of limitation remains.

1. The Absence of a General Duty to Rescue

In the early morning of March 3, 1964, Kitty Genovese was stabbed to death outside an apartment house in New York City. When she was first attacked by her assailant, she screamed: "Oh, my God, he stabbed me! Please help me! Please help me!" Lights in the building went on, and a man called down, "Let that girl alone!" The assailant walked away, but after the lights went out, he returned and stabbed the young woman again. She again screamed, and again the lights went on. Once more, the assailant left, only to return and stab the dying victim a third and final time. The third attack took place 35 minutes after the first and 15 minutes before the police received the first call reporting the incident. The man who finally called the police said that he had given the matter much thought before he called. "I didn't want to get involved," was his explanation. In all, 38 people witnessed the attack. N.Y. Times, March 27, 1964, at 1, col. 4. For a more detailed report of this incident, see Rosenthal, Thirty-Eight Witnesses (1964).

Whatever moral obligation the onlookers may have had, under American common law they had no legal duty to respond in any way to help Kitty Genovese. The absence of a general duty to come to the aid of another is enunciated vividly by Buch v. Amory Mfg. Co., 69 N.H. 257, 261, 44 A. 809, 811 (1897):

> There is a wide difference—a broad gulf—both in reason and in law, between causing and preventing an injury; between doing by negligence or otherwise a wrong to one's neighbor, and preventing him from injuring himself; between protecting him against injury by another and guarding him from injury that may accrue to him from the condition of the premises which he has unlawfully invaded. The duty to do no wrong is a legal duty. The duty to protect against wrong is, generally speaking and excepting certain intimate relations in the nature of a trust, a moral obligation only, not recognized or enforced by law. Is a spectator liable if he sees an intelligent man or an unintelligent infant running into danger and does not warn or forcibly restrain him? . . . I see my neighbor's two-year-old babe in dangerous proximity to the machinery of his windmill in his yard, and easily might, but do not, rescue him. I am not liable in damages to the child for his injuries, nor, if the child is killed, punishable for manslaughter by the common law or under the statute because the child and I are strangers, and I am under no legal duty to protect him.

Although courts do not recognize a general duty to rescue, they have held that some relationships justify the recognition of a limited duty.

Common Carriers. It is universally held that a common carrier owes the duty to use reasonable care to assist its passengers in distress. See Paolone v. American Airlines, Inc., 706 F. Supp. 11 (S.D. N.Y. 1989).

Schools. Schools, whether public or private, have a duty to use care to prevent physical injury to their students. See, e.g., Eisel v. Board of Education of Montgomery County, 324 Md. 376, 597 A.2d 447 (1991) (student committed suicide), and Mullins v. Pine Manor College, 389 Mass. 47, 449 N.E.2d 331 (1983) (student was raped).

Hospital Emergency Rooms. Some courts impose on hospital emergency rooms the obligation to treat persons in need of emergency care, whether those persons can pay for the treatment or not. See, e.g., Thompson v. Sun City Community Hospital, Inc., 141 Ariz. 597, 688 P.2d 605 (1984); Wilmington General Hospital v. Manlove, 54 Del. 15, 174 A.2d 135 (1961). Other courts, however, have refused to impose a duty to render medical care in such circumstances. See, e.g., Harper v. Baptist Medical Center-Princeton, 341 So. 2d 133 (Ala. 1976).

Governmental Employees. The liability of governmental organizations based on the failure of their employees to rescue has risen in a variety of contexts. A major hurdle that plaintiffs face in such cases is the *public duty doctrine*. In general, one cannot recover based on a breach of a duty that a governmental employee owes to the public at large, absent some special relationship that takes the plaintiff out of the general public. See Prosser and Keeton, Law of Torts 1046-1051 (5th ed. 1984).[121] Some courts, however, have rejected the public duty doctrine. See, e.g., Jean v. Commonwealth, 414 Mass. 496, 610 N.E.2d 305 (1993).

Captains of Ships. Ship captains are required by maritime law to attempt to rescue crewmen who have fallen overboard, and can also be held liable for failure to render aid to the crew in cases of illness. See, e.g., Cortes v. Baltimore Insular Line, 287 U.S. 367, 53 S. Ct. 173, 77 L. Ed. 368 (1972); Harris v. Pennsylvania R.R., 50 F.2d 866 (4th Cir. 1931).

Erie R. Co. v. Stewart

40 F.2d 855 (6th Cir. 1930), cert. denied *282 U.S. 843 (1930)*

HICKENLOOPER, C.J. Stewart, plaintiff below, was a passenger in an automobile truck, sitting on the front seat to the right of the driver, a fellow employee of the East Ohio Gas Company. He recovered a judgment in the District Court for injuries received when the truck was struck by one of the defendant's trains at the 123d street crossing in the city of Cleveland. Defendant maintained a watchman at this crossing, which was admittedly heavily traveled, but the watchman was either within the shanty or just outside of it as the train approached, and he gave no warning until too late to avoid the accident. Two alleged errors are relied upon. . . .

The second contention of appellant presents the question whether the court erred in charging the jury that the absence of the watchman, where one had been maintained by the defendant company at a highway crossing

121. A second barrier to recovery in these cases is governmental immunity. See pp. 486-489, below.

over a long period of time to the knowledge of the plaintiff, would constitute negligence as a matter of law. In the present case it is conceded that the employment of the watchman by the defendant was voluntary upon its part, there being no statute or ordinance requiring the same, and that plaintiff had knowledge of this practice and relied upon the absence of the watchman as an assurance of safety and implied invitation to cross. We are not now concerned with the extent of the duty owing to one who had no notice of the prior practice. . . . The question is simply whether there was any positive duty owing to the plaintiff in respect to the maintenance of such watchman, and whether a breach of such duty is so conclusively shown as to justify a peremptory charge of negligence. The question whether such negligence was the proximate cause of the injury was properly submitted to the jury.

Where the employment of a watchman or other precaution is required by statute, existence of an absolute duty to the plaintiff is conclusively shown, and failure to observe the statutory requirement is negligence per se. Conversely, where there is no duty prescribed by statute or ordinance, it is usually a question for the jury whether the circumstances made the employment of a watchman necessary in the exercise of due care. Where the voluntary employment of a watchman was unknown to the traveler upon the highway, the mere absence of such watchman could probably not be considered as negligence toward him as a matter of law, for in such case there is neither an established duty positively owing to such traveler as a member of the general public, nor had he been led into reliance upon the custom. The question would remain simply whether the circumstances demanded such employment. But where the practice is known to the traveler upon the highway, and such traveler has been educated into reliance upon it, some positive duty must rest upon the railway with reference thereto. The elements of invitation and assurance of safety exist in this connection no less than in connection with contributory negligence. The company has established for itself a standard of due care while operating its trains across the highway, and, having led the traveler into reliance upon such standard, it should not be permitted thereafter to say that no duty required, arose from or attached to these precautions.

This duty has been recognized as not only actual and positive, but as absolute, in the sense that the practice may not be discontinued without exercising reasonable care to give warning of such discontinuance, although the company may thereafter do all that would otherwise be reasonably necessary. Conceding for the purposes of this opinion that, in cases where a watchman is voluntarily employed by the railway in an abundance of precaution, the duty is not absolute, in the same sense as where it is imposed by statute, still, if there be some duty, it cannot be less than that the company must use reasonable care to see that reliance by members of the educated public upon its representation of safety is not converted into a trap. Responsibility for injury will arise if the service be negligently performed or abandoned without other notice of that fact. If this issue of negligent performance be disputed, the question would still be for the jury under the present concession. But if the evidence in the case justifies only the conclusion of lack of due care, or if the absence of the watchman or the failure to give other notice of his withdrawal be wholly unexplained, so that but one inference may be drawn therefrom, the court is warranted in instructing the jury that, in that particular case, negligence appears as a matter of law.

So, in the present case, the evidence conclusively establishes the voluntary employment of a watchman, knowledge of this fact and reliance upon it by the plaintiff, a duty, therefore, that the company, through the watchman, will exercise reasonable care in warning such travelers as plaintiff, the presence of the watchman thereabouts, and no explanation of the failure to warn. Therefore, even though the duty be considered as qualified, rather than absolute, a prima facie case was established by plaintiff, requiring the defendant to go forward with evidence to rebut the presumption of negligence thus raised, or else suffer a verdict against it on this point. . . .

The judgment of the District Court is affirmed.

The reliance theory of the preceding case has been used by courts to impose failure to rescue liability in a variety of circumstances. For example, in Mixon v. Dobbs Houses, Inc., 254 S.E.2d 864 (Ga. App. 1979), the court ruled that a cause of action was stated by the plaintiff who alleged that her husband's employer had promised to relay her messages that she had begun labor, but had failed to do so, leaving her to give birth at home alone and unaided. And in Indian Towing Co. v. United States, 350 U.S. 61, 76 S. Ct. 122, 100 L. Ed. 2d 48 (1955), the court ruled that the government was obligated to maintain a lighthouse. But in Brown v. United States, 790 F.2d 199 (1st Cir. 1986), it was held that the government had no duty to maintain a particular weather buoy that had become inoperable. The plaintiffs argued that seamen had come to rely on the presence of the buoy as a part of the government weather forecasting equipment, and that had the buoy been on line, a more accurate weather forecast would have prevented the loss of a ship in a severe storm.

A related, but somewhat different, rescue theory is illustrated by Lacey v. United States, 98 F. Supp. 219 (D. Miss. 1951), in which the plaintiffs alleged that the Coast Guard negligently failed to rescue the occupants of an airplane that had crashed. In the course of the opinion, the court stated (98 F. Supp. at 220):

> It is true that, while the common law imposes no duty to rescue, it does impose on the Good Samaritan the duty to act with due care *once he has undertaken rescue operations*. The rationale is that other would-be rescuers will rest on their oars in the expectation that effective aid is being rendered.

The court, however, ruled that the plaintiff was not entitled to recover because he had not alleged that the Coast Guard had by its conduct deterred potential rescuers from acting. See also Brown v. MacPherson's Inc., 86 Wash. 2d 293, 545 P.2d 13 (1975), in which the court indicated that the state could be liable for the failure of an employee to warn residents of dangerous avalanches that were about to occur. The employee had led an avalanche expert to believe that he would relay warnings, but then did nothing.

Tubbs v. Argus

140 Ind. App. 695, 225 N.E.2d 841 (1967)

PFAFF, J. This appeal arises as a result of demurrer to appellant's Second Amended Complaint which was sustained and judgment entered thereon upon the failure and refusal of the appellant to plead over.

The facts material to a determination of the issues raised on this appeal may be summarized as follows: . . .

. . . [T]he appellant was riding as a guest passenger in the right front seat of an automobile owned and operated by the appellee [when it] was driven over the south curb of West Hampton Drive and into a tree, resulting in injury to the appellant. After the said collision, the appellee abandoned the automobile and did not render reasonable aid and assistance to the injured appellant. Appellant alleges that she suffered additional injuries as a result of appellee's failure to render reasonable aid and assistance and seeks to recover only for these additional injuries.

In her assignment of errors, the appellant avers that the trial court erred in sustaining the demurrer to appellant's Second Amended Complaint. More specifically, the appellant alleges that appellee's failure to render reasonable aid and assistance constituted a breach of a common law duty. . . .

The appellant herein is seeking recovery for additional injuries arising from the appellee's failure to render reasonable aid and assistance, and not for the initial injuries which resulted from the operation of the automobile [since she was precluded from recovering for ordinary negligence under Indiana's automobile guest law].

At common law, there is no general duty to aid a person who is in peril. L. S. Ayres & Company v. Hicks (1941), 220 Ind. 86, 40 N.E.2d 334. However, in L. S. Ayres & Company, supra, page 94, 40 N.E.2d page 337, the Supreme Court of Indiana held that "under some circumstances, moral and humanitarian considerations may require one to render assistance to another who has been injured, even though the injury was not due to negligence on his part and may have been caused by the negligence of the injured person. Failure to render assistance in such a situation may constitute actionable negligence if the injury is aggravated through lack of due care."

Tippecanoe Loan, etc., Co. v. Cleveland, etc., R. Co. (1915), 57 Ind. App. 644, 104 N.E. 866, 106 N.E. 739.

In Tippecanoe Loan, etc., Co. v. Cleveland, etc. R. Co., supra, this court held that a railroad company was liable for failing to provide medical assistance to an employee who was injured through no fault of the railroad company, but who was rendered helpless and by reason of which the employee's injuries were aggravated.

The Supreme Court of Indiana in *L. S. Ayres,* supra, found the appellant liable for aggravation of injuries when it failed to extricate the appellee, a six-year-old boy, whose fingers were caught in the moving parts of an escalator, even though the jury conclusively established that the appellant was not negligent with respect to the choice, construction, or manner of operating the elevator. In so holding, the Supreme Court stated that it may be deduced from Tippecanoe Loan, etc. Co. v. Cleveland, etc. R. Co., supra, "that there may be a legal obligation to take positive or affirmative steps to effect the rescue of a person who is helpless and in a situation of peril, when the one proceeded against is a master or an invitor or when the injury resulted from use of an instrumentality under the control of the defendant."

The doctrine of law as set forth in Restatement (Second) of Torts, §322, p. 133, adds credence to these two Indiana cases. ". . . If the actor knows or has reason to know that by his conduct, whether tortious or innocent, he has caused such bodily harm to another as to make him helpless and in danger of future harm, the actor is under a duty to exercise reasonable care to prevent such further harm.". . .

In the case at bar, the appellant received her injuries from an instrumentality under the control of the appellee. Under the rule stated above and on the authority of the cases cited, this was a sufficient relationship to impose a duty to render reasonable aid and assistance, a duty for the breach of which the appellee is liable for the additional injuries suffered.

We are of the opinion that the court below erred in sustaining the demurrer to appellant's Second Amended Complaint.

This cause is reversed and remanded for proceedings not inconsistent with this opinion.

Judgment reversed.

BIERLY and SMITH, JJ., concur.

The legislatures of at least two states have enacted duty-to-rescue statutes. The Vermont statute, the Duty to Aid the Endangered Act (Vt. Stat. Ann. Tit. 12 §519), which calls for a fine of up to $100 for its violation, provides:

> (a) A person who knows that another is exposed to grave physical harm shall, to the extent that the same can be rendered without danger or peril to himself or without interference with important duties owed to others, give

reasonable assistance to the exposed person unless that assistance or care is being provided by others.

For the Minnesota statute, see Minn. Stat. §604.05. Both statutes insulate would-be rescuers from liability to a rescuee for any negligence in the course of rescue. More common are state statutes that impose duties on those involved in automobile accidents to render or seek medical assistance for others injured in the accident. See, e.g., Ky. Rev. Stat. §189.580(1). Occasionally, civil suits have been brought for injuries resulting from the breaches of such statutes. See Annotation, 80 A.L.R.2d 299 (1961). The legislatures of two states, Massachusetts and Rhode Island, responded to a well-publicized incident by enacting statutes requiring observers of certain specified crimes to report the crimes to the police. The event which prompted the statutes was the alleged "gang rape" of a woman at a bar in the presence of several witnesses, none of whom interfered to prevent the rape or notified the police, and some of whom, it was reported, were on the sidelines cheering. See N.Y. Times, Mar. 17, 1983, at A16, col. 1. The Rhode Island statute (R.I. Gen. Laws §11-37-3.1 (Cum. Supp. 1992)) applies only to rape; the Massachusetts statute (Mass. Ann. Laws ch. 268, §40) applies to some serious crimes other than rape.

Whether or not statutes imposing duties to rescue have affected, or will affect behavior is difficult to tell. Apart from the automobile accident reporting statutes, there does not seem to have been any litigation involving the statutorally created duties. (A note dealing generally with the effect of law upon primary behavior appears at p. 106, below.) The statutes have, however, attracted the attention of a number of commentators. See, e.g., Franklin, Vermont Requires Rescue: A Comment, 25 Stan. L. Rev. 51 (1972); Woozley, A Duty To Rescue: Some Thoughts on Criminal Liability, 69 Va. L. Rev. 1273 (1983); Note, Statutes Establishing a Duty to Report Crimes or Render Assistance to Strangers: Making Apathy Criminal, 72 Ky. L. Rev. 827 (1983-1984).

The preceding efforts at encouraging rescue attempts can be characterized as a "stick" approach—the threat of legal sanctions, either civil or criminal, for the failure to attempt a reasonable rescue effort. The law does not typically resort to "carrot" approaches, by which those attempting to rescue another would be affirmatively rewarded. There are carrots of that sort, but they ordinarily come from private organizations. The law on occasion, however, has used modified carrot approaches by removing what otherwise might be disincentives to rescue. The most common approach in this regard are "Good Samaritan" statutes, which insulate rescuers from liability for their negligence in the course of the rescue effort. Apart from such statutes, courts stand ready to impose negligence liability on the rescuer if the job is botched. See, e.g., Dunson v. Friedlander Realty, 369 So. 2d 792 (Ala. 1979); Farwell v. Keaton, 396 Mich. 281, 240 N.W.2d 217 (1976). A number of states have enacted statutes designed to protect persons from claims arising out of the rendering of gratuitous assistance in an emergency. Some of the statutes protect only medical practitioners; others protect additional persons, such as fire fighters, rescue squad members, and police officers. Still others specify that all persons who render aid are protected against liability for negligence. For a complete listing of the statutes, see 2 Louisell & Williams, Medical Malpractice, §§21.01-21.60 (1986). Whether such statutes are desirable, or even needed, is open to some doubt. See Note, Good Samaritans and Liability for Medical Malpractice, 64 Colum. L. Rev. 1301 (1964); Note, Physicians—Civil Liability for Treatment Rendered at the Scene of an Emergency, 1964 Wis. L. Rev. 494. The conclusions of a federal study group are interesting in this regard. See United States Department of Health, Education, and Welfare, Report of the Secretary's Commission on Medical Malpractice 15-16 (1973):

> While the fears of physicians about their potential liability for rendering emergency aid are undoubtedly real, they appear to be based on little more than rumor or hearsay, generated and perpetuated in large part by the mass media. The States have reacted to the fears of physicians by enacting legislation designed to encourage the provision of on-the-spot emergency care to accident victims by granting some measure of immunity from liability. Many of these statutes apply to nurses as well as physicians. Notwithstanding the passage of such legislation, many health professionals remain convinced that large numbers of their colleagues have been victims of malpractice suits arising out of the rendering of such emergency treatment. . . .
>
> As a Commission, we make no specific findings regarding the real causes behind the reluctance of some physicians to provide emergency aid to accident victims. We do believe, however, that the time has come to set the record straight on at least one issue: the legal risks in rendering emergency medical care to accident victims in non-health-care settings are minimal, if not infinitesimal. Health professionals, as well as the general public, should be so informed. However, we believe that Good Samaritan statutes may be of value even if they induce only a few physicians and other health-care providers to render emergency aid.

Another approach that the law might take to remove disincentives to rescue would be to permit the rescuer to recover his rescue costs from the rescuee. The rescuer's right to recovery, however, is quite limited. He may recover in restitution, if, among other things, he "acted unofficiously and with intent to charge. . . ." Restatement of Restitution, §116. And he may be able to recover in contract if, after the rescue, the rescuee promises to pay him for his rescue efforts. See Restatement (Second) of Contracts §86. In general, see Friedell, Compensation and Reward for Saving Life at Sea, 77 Mich. L. Rev. 1218 (1979). One commentator has opposed more general recovery by rescuers from their rescuees. See Dawson, Rewards for the Rescue of Human Life?, in The Good Samaritan and the Law 63, 68 (Ratcliffe ed. 1966):

> It seems grossly unjust that a drowning woman, herself without fault, should be required (jointly with her husband) to support the widow of the drowned rescuer for the rest of the widow's life, and the children of the rescuer until their majority. . . . The dilemma remains—the claim of the rescuer or his dependents will become more appealing the greater the rescuer's sacrifice; but in the same degree it becomes more unjust to cast the whole loss on the imperilled victim, who was not at fault, who merely responded to the deep human impulse toward survival and called out for help. If any recovery at all is to be given, how can one frame doctrine that will award a little but not too much?

Whether the rescuer can recover for personal injuries suffered in the course of the rescue from the person, including the rescuee, whose negligence caused the need for rescue is taken up in the section on proximate cause. See pp. 372-376, below.

Problem 18

You are the attorney of Thomas Potter, whom you have represented in a variety of matters over the years. Potter is the treasurer of The First National Bank of Canton, is married and the father of three children, and is actively engaged in the community. Potter called you last week after he received a letter from Mark Granger, who identified himself as the lawyer for George Harper. Potter read the letter to you over the telephone, and in substance it stated the following: George Harper is the father of Martha Harper, who was killed in an automobile accident. Martha was a passenger in an automobile driven by Peter Blake. Blake's automobile collided with a tree after being forced off the road by another automobile. Both Blake and Harper were seriously injured, and Harper later died in a local hospital. After the accident, the driver of the other automobile, a man now identified by Blake as Potter, came up to the Blake car. He looked into the window, and told Blake that he would send for help. When help did not arrive after an hour, Blake set out to look for a house from which he could call an ambulance. He was able to locate a telephone and call an ambulance, but too late for Harper who died from the substantial head injuries shortly after her arrival at the hospital. Granger said that he was preparing to sue Potter on behalf of Harper, claiming both that Potter negligently drove his automobile in a way that forced Blake off the road, and for failing to follow through on his promise to call for help.

According to Potter, the actual events leading up to Granger's letter are these: For a period of several months, Potter had an affair with Valerie Whitman, a vice president of the bank. Whitman is also married. About three months ago, Potter drove to a nearby city to confer with a lawyer about a real estate transaction. Whitman had driven to the same city, also on business. When they finished, they had a hurried dinner, and then drove in Potter's automobile to a seldom-used country road. After parking beside the road for about 30 minutes, he pulled back onto the road to return to where Whitman had left her car. But a few minutes later, a car came speeding from the opposite direction, half in Potter's lane. Potter slammed on his brakes and the other car swerved sharply to its right, narrowly avoiding a collision. The other car ran off the road and hit a tree. Potter stopped, got out of his car, and ran back to the other car. When he got there, he found two people in the car, a young man behind the wheel and a young woman next to him. The man was shaken but conscious; the woman was bleeding profusely about her head. Potter panicked, and fearing exposure of his affair, he ran to his car, while the driver was shouting to him to get help. Potter said nothing to Blake at any time. He returned to his car, drove Whitman to her car, and then returned home. Neither Potter nor Whitman reported the accident.

On the day following the accident, a police officer visited Potter at his office. The officer recounted in a general way the occurrence of the accident, and said that Blake stated in his report to the police that he thought that Potter was the driver of the other car and the person, who after the accident, looked into the window of his car and said he would get help. Blake said he was able to identify Potter as he has seen him on several occasions in the bank. In response to the officer's questions, Potter denied that he was there. He told the officer that he had returned home after completing his business by a route that was many miles from the scene of the accident. He explained to the officer that he often took the "back way" home when he wanted to sort out his thoughts about business matters. As the officer was leaving, he expressed outrage that anybody could be so indifferent as not to even call the police. The officer had spoken with the doctor attending Harper at the hospital, and she stated that she couldn't be sure that Harper would have survived even with prompt care. Potter told you that he felt better about the incident after hearing that Harper probably would have died anyway. "What I did can't be so bad, can it? After all, it didn't make any difference." In any event, Potter said that the police and his family have all apparently accepted his story without question.

The police file on the accident contains a statement by Charles Herzog. Just before the accident, Herzog was driving on the same road and a car of the same description as Blake's almost forced him off the road. According to Herzog, the car must have been going 50 to 60 miles an hour. The file also contains a diagram of the scene of the accident made by the investigating police officer showing skid marks leading to the Blake car, starting from a point well into the wrong side of the road. The police report indicated that Blake was arrested for vehicular homicide, reckless driving, speeding, and operating without an operator's license. The case is still pending in Superior Court.

At the time of the accident, Blake was 22 years old, and Harper was 16.

Blake had been convicted on two earlier occasions for speeding and reckless driving. His operator's license had been suspended three weeks before the accident.

Granger is known as a lawyer who processes personal injury cases quickly, and rarely takes cases to court. Potter is coming to your office tomorrow to discuss the matter. In deciding what advice to give him, assume that your state supreme court has adopted the Model Rules of Professional Conduct.

Model Rules of Professional Conduct

American Bar Association (1992)

Rule 1.2 Scope of Representation

(a) A lawyer shall abide by a client's decisions concerning the objectives of representation, subject to paragraphs (c), (d) and (e), and shall consult with the client as to the means by which they are to be pursued. . . .

(d) A lawyer shall not counsel a client to engage, or assist a client, in conduct that the lawyer knows is criminal or fraudulent, but a lawyer may discuss the legal consequences of any proposed course of conduct with a client and may counsel or assist a client to make a good faith effort to determine the validity, scope, meaning or application of the law.

(e) When a lawyer knows that a client expects assistance not permitted by the rules of professional conduct or other law, the lawyer shall consult with the client regarding the relevant limitations on the lawyer's conduct.

Rule 1.6 Confidentiality of Information

(a) A lawyer shall not reveal information relating to representation of a client unless the client consents after consultation, except for disclosures that are impliedly authorized in order to carry out the representation, and except as stated in paragraph (b).

(b) A lawyer may reveal such information to the extent the lawyer reasonably believes necessary:

(1) to prevent the client from committing a criminal act that the lawyer believes is likely to result in imminent death or substantial bodily harm; . . .

Rule 1.16 Declining or Terminating Representation

(a) Except as stated in paragraph (c), a lawyer shall not represent a client or, where representation has commenced, shall withdraw from the representation of a client if:

(1) the representation will result in violation of the rules of professional conduct or other law . . .

(b) Except as stated in paragraph (c), a lawyer may withdraw from representing a client if withdrawal can be accomplished without material adverse effect on the interests of the client, or if:

(1) the client persists in a course of action involving the lawyer's services that the lawyer reasonably believes is criminal or fraudulent;

(2) the client has used the lawyer's services to perpetrate a crime or fraud;

(3) a client insists upon pursuing an objective that the lawyer considers repugnant or imprudent; . . .

Rule 2.1 Advisor

In representing a client, a lawyer shall exercise independent professional judgment and render candid advice. In rendering advice, a lawyer may refer not only to law but to other considerations such as moral, economic, social and political factors, that may be relevant to the client's situation.

Rule 3.1 Meritorious Claims and Contentions

A lawyer shall not bring or defend a proceeding, or assert or controvert an issue therein, unless there is a basis for doing so that is not frivolous, which includes a good faith argument for an extension, modification or reversal of existing law. A lawyer for the defendant in a criminal proceeding, or the respondent in a proceeding that could result in incarceration, may nevertheless so defend the proceeding as to require that every element of the case be established.

Rule 3.3 Candor Toward the Tribunal

(a) A lawyer shall not knowingly:

(1) make a false statement of material fact or law to a tribunal;

(2) fail to disclose a material fact to a tribunal when disclosure is necessary to avoid assisting a criminal or fraudulent act by the client;

(3) fail to disclose to the tribunal legal authority in the controlling jurisdiction known to the lawyer to be directly adverse to the position of the client and not disclosed by opposing counsel; or

(4) offer evidence that the lawyer knows to be false. If a lawyer has offered material evidence and comes to know of its falsity, the lawyer shall take reasonable remedial measures.

(b) The duties stated in paragraph (a) continue to the conclusion of the proceeding, and apply even if compliance requires disclosure of information otherwise protected by Rule 1.6.

(c) A lawyer may refuse to offer evidence that the lawyer reasonably believes is false. . . .

Rule 4.1 Truthfulness in Statements to Others

In the course of representing a client a lawyer shall not knowingly:

(a) make a false statement of material fact or law to a third person; or

(b) fail to disclose a material fact to a third person when disclosure is necessary to avoid assisting a criminal or fraudulent act by a client, unless disclosure is prohibited by Rule 1.6.

The Lawyer's Professional Responsibility: The Relevance of Moral Considerations

It is clear in the preceding problem that the client, Thomas Potter, has committed a crime in lying to the police on the police report. But many might regard lying on a police report to be a venial sin at most—no harm, no foul. And everybody does it, don't they? But his fabricated story, if accepted by George Harper, also will have the effect of foreclosing any claim in tort arising out of the accident he might have had against Potter. Should that have an impact on what advice you will give Potter when you talk to him tomorrow?

Not surprisingly, there is a good deal of controversy over the extent to which a lawyer in representing a client should be influenced by the lawyer's notions of right and wrong—of morality. Most of the debate has been in the context of a client whose goals are legal, but for some reason are repugnant to the lawyer, and perhaps to a large segment of society. One article that argues for a prominent role for the moral views of the lawyer is Wasserstrom, Lawyers as Professionals: Some Moral Issues, 5 Human Rights 1 (1975). He poses a number of hypotheticals in which he suggests that the lawyer should not help a client achieve otherwise lawful aims: the client who wants to disinherit a child because of the child's opposition to the war in Vietnam; the client who wants to take advantage of a loophole in the tax laws available only to the rich; the client who wants to set up a corporation to manufacture a socially harmful product, such as cigarettes. ("Saturday night specials" might also furnish an apt example.)

A different, and the more traditional view, is expressed in Pepper, The Lawyer's Amoral Ethical Role: A Defense, A Problem and Some Possibilities, 1986 Am. Bar Found. Res. J. 613, 617-618:

> Our first premise is that law is intended to be a public good which increases autonomy. The second premise is that increasing individual autonomy is morally good. The third step is that in a highly legalized society such as ours, autonomy is often dependent upon access to the law. Put simply, first-class citizenship is dependent on access to the law. And while access to law—to the creation and use of a corporation, to knowledge of how much overtime one has to pay or is entitled to receive—is formally available to all, in reality it is available only through a lawyer. Our law is usually not simple, usually not self-executing. For most people most of the time, meaningful access to the law requires the assistance of a lawyer. Thus the resulting conclusion: First-class citizenship is frequently dependent upon the assistance of a lawyer. If the conduct which the lawyer facilitates is above the floor of the intolerable—is not unlawful—then this line of thought suggests that what the lawyer does is a social good. The lawyer is the means to first-class citizenship, to meaningful autonomy, for the client.
>
> For the lawyer to have moral responsibility for each act he or she facilitates, for the lawyer to have a moral obligation to refuse to facilitate that which the lawyer believes to be immoral, is to substitute lawyers' beliefs for individual autonomy and diversity. Such a screening submits each to the prior restraint of the judge/facilitator and to rule by an oligarchy of lawyers. (If, in the alternative, the suggestion is that the lawyer's screening should be based not on the lawyer's personal morality, but on the lawyer's assessment of society's moral views or on guidelines spelled out in a professional code of ethics, then one has substituted collective moral decision making for individual moral decision making, contrary to the principle of autonomy. Less room has been left for private decision making through a sub rosa form of lawmaking.) If the conduct is sufficiently "bad," it would seem that it ought to be made explicitly unlawful. If it is not that bad, why subject the citizenry to the happenstance of the moral judgment of the particular lawyer to whom each has access? If making the conduct unlawful is too onerous because the law would be too vague, or it is too difficult to identify the conduct in advance, or there is not sufficient social or political concern, do we intend to delegate to the individual lawyer the authority for case-by-case legislation and policing?

See also Simon, Ethical Discretion in Lawyering, 101 Harv. L. Rev. 1083 (1988) (lawyers should do justice), and Fried, The Lawyer as Friend: The Moral Foundations of the Lawyer-Client Relationship, 85 Yale L.J. 1060 (1976) (lawyers should advance the interests of their clients).

The Model Rules of Professional Conduct, set out above, are tilted somewhat in favor of the traditional view of the lawyer-client relationship. Rule 2.1 does state that a lawyer may refer to considerations other than the law, such as moral factors. The Comments elaborate on this a bit:

> Advice couched in narrowly legal terms may be of little value to a client, especially where practical considerations, such as cost or effects on other people, are predominant. Purely technical legal advice, therefore, can sometimes be inadequate. It is proper for a lawyer to refer to relevant moral and ethical considerations in giving advice. Although a lawyer is not a moral

advisor as such, moral and ethical considerations impinge upon most legal questions and may decisively influence how the law will be applied.

The moral issue you face in the preceding problem is somewhat different from that discussed so far in this Note. This Note has involved clients with lawful, but perhaps morally deficient, goals. In the Problem, what Potter seeks to achieve, the prevention of a claim against him in order to preserve his status in his family and the community, is not so clearly lawful, is it? Or at the least, his methods are questionable. Should that make a difference in how you would advise Potter? Would your advice depend on your assessment of the merits of Harper's case? Might you conclude that even if Potter's involvement in the accident were made public, Harper ought not to be able to recover? That conclusion might be based on your conclusions about the law, or on your view of the facts. From what Potter has told you, Blake is lying in his statement that Potter said that he would get help. Would either of these conclusions be relevant to the ethical problem?

One of the things you might want to discuss with Potter is what the options would be if Harper were to follow through with a suit against Potter; that is something that you would also want to think out before your meeting with him.

Tarasoff v. Regents of University of California

17 Cal. 3d 425, 551 P.2d 334, 131 Cal. Rptr. 14 (1976)

TOBRINER, J. On October 27, 1969, Prosenjit Poddar killed Tatiana Tarasoff. Plaintiffs, Tatiana's parents, allege that two months earlier Poddar confided his intention to kill Tatiana to Dr. Lawrence Moore, a psychologist employed by the Cowell Memorial Hospital at the University of California at Berkeley. They allege that on Moore's request, the campus police briefly detained Poddar, but released him when he appeared rational. They further claim that Dr. Harvey Powelson, Moore's superior, then directed that no further action be taken to detain Poddar. No one warned plaintiffs of Tatiana's peril.

Concluding that these facts set forth causes of action against neither therapists and policemen involved, nor against the Regents of the University of California as their employer, the superior court sustained defendants' demurrers to plaintiffs' second amended complaints without leave to amend. This appeal ensued.

[Plaintiffs' second amended complaints set forth four causes of action: (1) a claim that defendants negligently failed to detain a dangerous patient; (2) a claim that defendants negligently failed to warn Tatiana's parents; (3) a claim for punitive damages on the ground that defendants acted "maliciously and oppressively"; and (4) a claim that defendants breached their duty to their patient and the public. The court concludes that plaintiffs' first and fourth causes of action are barred by governmental immunity, and that plaintiffs' third cause of action is barred by a rule precluding exemplary damages in a wrongful death action. Therefore, the court addresses the question of whether plaintiffs' second cause of action can be amended to state a basis for recovery.]

The second cause of action can be amended to allege that Tatiana's death proximately resulted from defendants' negligent failure to warn Tatiana or others likely to apprise her of her danger. Plaintiffs contend that as amended, such allegations of negligence and proximate causation, with resulting damages, establish a cause of action. Defendants, however, contend that in the circumstances of the present case they owed no duty of care to Tatiana or her parents and that, in the absence of such duty, they were free to act in careless disregard of Tatiana's life and safety.

In analyzing this issue, we bear in mind that legal duties are not discoverable facts of nature, but merely conclusory expressions that, in cases of a particular type, liability should be imposed for damage done. As stated in Dillon v. Legg (1968) 68 Cal. 2d 728, 734, 69 Cal. Rptr. 72, 76, 441 P.2d 912, 916: "The assertion that liability must . . . be denied because defendant bears no 'duty' to plaintiff 'begs the essential question—whether the plaintiff's interests are entitled to legal protection against the defendant's conduct. . . . [Duty] is not sacrosanct in itself, but only an expression of the sum total of those considerations of policy which lead the law to say that the particular plaintiff is entitled to protection.' (Prosser, Law of Torts [3d ed. 1964] at pp. 332-333.)"

In the landmark case of Rowland v. Christian (1968) 69 Cal. 2d 108, 70 Cal. Rptr. 97, 443 P.2d 561, Justice Peters recognized that liability should be imposed "for an injury occasioned to another by his want of ordinary care or skill" as expressed in section 1714 of the Civil Code. Thus, Justice Peters, quoting from Heaven v. Pender (1883) 11 Q.B.D. 503, 509 stated: " 'whenever one person is by circumstances placed in such a position with regard to another . . . that if he did not use ordinary care and skill in his own conduct . . . he would cause danger of injury to the person or property of the other, a duty arises to use ordinary care and skill to avoid such danger.' "

We depart from "this fundamental principle" only upon the "balancing of a number of considerations"; major ones "are the foreseeability of harm to the plaintiff, the degree of certainty that the plaintiff suffered injury, the closeness of the connection between the defendant's conduct and the injury suffered, the moral blame attached to the defendant's conduct, the policy of preventing future harm, the extent of the burden to the defendant and consequences to the community of imposing a duty to exercise care with resulting liability for breach, and the availability, cost and prevalence of insurance for the risk involved."

The most important of these considerations in establishing duty is foreseeability. As a general principle, a "defendant owes a duty of care to all persons who are foreseeably endangered by his conduct, with respect to all risks which make the conduct unreasonably dangerous." As we shall explain, however, when the avoidance of foreseeable harm requires a defendant to control the conduct of another person, or to warn of such conduct, the common law has traditionally imposed liability only if the defendant bears some special relationship to the dangerous person or to the potential victim. Since the relationship between a therapist and his patient satisfies this requirement, we need not here decide whether foreseeability alone is sufficient to create a duty to exercise reasonable care to protect a potential victim of another's conduct.

Although, as we have stated above, under the common law, as a general rule, one person owed no duty to control the conduct of another, nor to warn those endangered by such conduct, the courts have carved out an exception to this rule in cases in which the defendant stands in some special relationship to either the person whose conduct needs to be controlled or in a relationship to the foreseeable victim of that conduct. Applying this exception to the present case, we note that a relationship of defendant therapists to either Tatiana or Poddar will suffice to establish a duty of care; as explained in section 315 of the Restatement Second of Torts, a duty of care may arise from either "(a) a special relation . . . between the actor and the third person which imposes a duty upon the actor to control the third person's conduct, or (b) a special relation . . . between the actor and the other which gives to the other a right of protection."

Although plaintiffs' pleadings assert no special relation between Tatiana and defendant therapists, they establish as between Poddar and defendant therapists the special relation that arises between a patient and his doctor or psychotherapist. Such a relationship may support affirmative duties for the benefit of third persons. Thus, for example, a hospital must exercise reasonable care to control the behavior of a patient which may endanger other persons. A doctor must also warn a patient if the patient's condition or medication renders certain conduct, such as driving a car, dangerous to others.

Although the California decisions that recognize this duty have involved cases in which the defendant stood in a special relationship *both* to the victim and to the person whose conduct created the danger, we do not think that the duty should logically be constricted to such situations. Decisions of other jurisdictions hold that the single relationship of a doctor to his patient is sufficient to support the duty to exercise reasonable care to protect others against dangers emanating from the patient's illness. The courts hold that a doctor is liable to persons infected by his patient if he negligently fails to diagnose a contagious disease or, having diagnosed the illness, fails to warn members of the patient's family. . . .

Defendants contend, however, that imposition of a duty to exercise reasonable care to protect third persons is unworkable because therapists cannot accurately predict whether or not a patient will resort to violence. In support of this argument amicus representing the American Psychiatric Association and other professional societies cites numerous articles which indicate that therapists, in the present state of the art, are unable reliably to predict violent acts; their forecasts, amicus claims, tend consistently to overpredict violence, and indeed are more often wrong than right. Since predictions of violence are often erroneous, amicus concludes, the courts should not render rulings that predicate the liability of therapists upon the validity of such predictions.

The role of the psychiatrist, who is indeed a practitioner of medicine, and that of the psychologist who performs an allied function, are like that of the physician who must conform to the standards of the profession and who must often make diagnoses and predictions based upon such evaluations. Thus the judgment of the therapist in diagnosing emotional disorders and in predicting whether a patient presents a serious danger of violence is comparable to the judgment which doctors and professionals must regularly render under accepted rules of responsibility.

We recognize the difficulty that a therapist encounters in attempting to forecast whether a patient presents a serious danger of violence. Obviously we do not require that the therapist, in making that determination, render a perfect performance; the therapist need only exercise "that reasonable degree of skill, knowledge, and care ordinarily possessed and exercised by members of [that professional specialty] under similar circumstances." Within the broad range of reasonable practice and treatment in which professional opinion and judgment may differ, the therapist is free to exercise his or her own best judgment without liability; proof, aided by hindsight, that he or she judged wrongly is insufficient to establish negligence.

In the instant case, however, the pleadings do not raise any question as to failure of defendant therapists to predict that Poddar presented a serious danger of violence. On the contrary, the present complaints allege that defendant therapists did in fact predict that Poddar would kill, but were negligent in failing to warn.

Amicus contends, however, that even when a therapist does in fact predict that a patient poses a serious danger of violence to others, the therapist should be absolved of any responsibility for failing to act to protect the potential victim. In our view, however, once a therapist does in fact determine, or under applicable professional standards reasonably should have determined, that a patient poses a serious danger of violence to others, he bears a duty to exercise reasonable care to protect the foreseeable victim of that danger. While the discharge of this duty of due care will necessarily vary with the facts of each case, in each instance the adequacy of the therapist's conduct must be measured against the traditional negligence standard of the rendition of reasonable care under the circumstances. . . .

Contrary to the assertion of amicus, this conclusion is not inconsistent with our recent decision in People v. Burnick, supra, 14 Cal. 3d 306, 121 Cal. Rptr. 488, 535 P.2d 352. Taking note of the uncertain character of therapeutic prediction, we held in *Burnick* that a person cannot be committed as a mentally disordered sex offender unless found to be such by proof beyond a reasonable doubt. The issue in the present context, however, is not whether the patient should be incarcerated, but whether the therapist should take any steps at all to protect the threatened victim; some of the alternatives open to the therapist, such as warning the victim, will not result in the drastic consequences of depriving the patient of his liberty. Weighing the uncertain and conjectural character of the alleged damage done the patient by such a warning against the peril to the victim's life, we conclude that professional inaccuracy in predicting violence cannot negate the therapist's duty to protect the threatened victim.

The risk that unnecessary warnings may be given is a reasonable price to pay for the lives of possible victims that may be saved. We would hesitate to hold that the therapist who is aware that his patient expects to attempt to assassinate the President of the United States would not be obligated to warn the authorities because the therapist cannot predict with accuracy that his patient will commit the crime.

Defendants further argue that free and open communication is essential to psychotherapy; that "Unless a patient . . . is assured that . . . information [revealed by him] can and will be held in utmost confidence, he will be reluctant to make the full disclosure upon which diagnosis and treatment . . . depends." (Sen. Com. on Judiciary, comment on Evid. Code, §1014.) The giving of a warning, defendants contend, constitutes a breach of trust which entails the revelation of confidential communications. . . .

We realize that the open and confidential character of psychotherapeutic dialogue encourages patients to express threats of violence, few of which are ever executed. Certainly a therapist should not be encouraged routinely to reveal such threats; such disclosures could seriously disrupt the patient's relationship with his therapist and with the persons threatened. To the contrary, the therapist's obligations to his patient require that he not disclose a confidence unless such disclosure is necessary to avert danger to others, and even then that he do so discreetly, and in a fashion that would preserve the privacy of his patient to the fullest extent compatible with the prevention of the threatened danger.

The revelation of a communication under the above circumstances is not a breach of trust or a violation of professional ethics; as stated in the Principles of Medical Ethics of the American Medical Association (1957), section 9: "A physician may not reveal the confidence entrusted to him in the course of medical attendance . . . *unless he is required to do so by law or unless it becomes necessary in order to protect the welfare of the individual or of the community.*" (Emphasis added.) We conclude that the public policy favoring protection of the confidential character of patient-psychotherapist communications must yield to the extent to which disclosure is essential to avert danger to others. The protective privilege ends where the public peril begins.

Our current crowded and computerized society compels the interdependence of its members. In this risk-infested society we can hardly tolerate the further exposure to danger that would result from a concealed knowledge of the therapist that his patient was lethal. If the exercise of reasonable care to protect the threatened victim requires the therapist to warn the endangered party or those who can reasonably be expected to notify him, we see no sufficient societal interest that would protect and justify concealment. The containment of such risks lies in the public interest. For the foregoing reasons, we find that plaintiffs' complaints can be amended to state a cause of action against defendants Moore, Powelson, Gold, and Yandell and against the Regents as their employer, for breach of a duty to exercise reasonable care to protect Tatiana.

[The majority concludes that the police defendants did not have a special relationship to either Tatiana or Poddar to impose upon them a duty to warn. The court also concludes that the defendant therapists are not protected by governmental immunity in connection with their failure to warn Tatiana's parents because their decisions were not "basic policy decisions" within the meaning of earlier precedent.]

For the reasons stated, we conclude that plaintiffs can amend their complaints to state a cause of action against defendant therapists by asserting that the therapists in fact determined that Poddar presented a serious danger of violence to Tatiana, or pursuant to the standards of their profession should have so determined, but nevertheless failed to exercise reasonable care to protect her from that danger. To the extent, however, that plaintiffs base their claim that defendant therapists breached that duty because they failed to procure Poddar's confinement, the therapists find immunity in Government Code section 856. Further, as to the police defendants we conclude that plaintiffs have failed to show that the trial court erred in sustaining their demurrer without leave to amend.

The judgment of the superior court in favor of defendants Atkinson, Beall, Brownrigg, Hallernan, and Teel is affirmed. The judgment of the superior court in favor of defendants Gold, Moore, Powelson, Yandell, and the Regents of the University of California is reversed, and the cause remanded for further proceedings consistent with the views expressed herein.

WRIGHT, C.J., and SULLIVAN and RICHARDSON, JJ., concur.

MOSK, J. (concurring and dissenting).

I concur in the result in this instance only because the complaints allege that defendant therapists did in fact predict that Poddar would kill and were therefore negligent in failing to warn of that danger. Thus the issue here is very narrow: we are not concerned with whether the therapists, pursuant to the standards of their profession, "should have" predicted potential violence; they allegedly did so in actuality. Under these limited circumstances I agree that a cause of action can be stated.

Whether plaintiffs can ultimately prevail is problematical at best. As the complaints admit, the therapist *did* notify the police that Poddar was planning to kill a girl identifiable as Tatiana. While I doubt that more should be required, this issue may be raised in defense and its determination is a question of fact.

I cannot concur, however, in the majority's rule that a therapist may be held liable for failing to predict his patient's tendency to violence if other practitioners, pursuant to the "standards of the profession," would have done so. The question is, what standards? Defendants and a responsible amicus curiae, supported by an impressive body of literature demonstrate that psychiatric predictions of violence are inherently unreliable. . . .

I would restructure the rule designed by the majority to eliminate all reference to conformity to standards of the profession in predicting violence. If a psychiatrist does in fact predict violence, then a duty to warn arises. The majority's expansion of that rule will take us from the world of reality into the wonderland of clairvoyance.

CLARK, J. (dissenting).

Until today's majority opinion, both legal and medical authorities have agreed that confidentiality is essential to effectively treat the mentally ill, and that imposing a duty on doctors to disclose patient threats to potential victims would greatly impair treatment. . . . Moreover, . . . imposing the majority's new duty is certain to result in a net increase in violence.

Overwhelming policy considerations weigh against imposing a duty on psychotherapists to warn a potential victim against harm. While offering virtually no benefit to society, such a duty will frustrate psychiatric treatment, invade fundamental patient rights and increase violence.

The importance of psychiatric treatment and its need for confidentiality have been recognized by this court. . . .

Assurance of confidentiality is important for three reasons.

Deterrence from Treatment

First, without substantial assurance of confidentiality, those requiring treatment will be deterred from seeking assistance. It remains an unfortunate fact in our society that people seeking psychiatric guidance tend to become stigmatized. Apprehension of such stigma—apparently increased by the propensity of people considering treatment to see themselves in the worst possible light—creates a well-recognized reluctance to seek aid. This reluctance is alleviated by the psychiatrist's assurance of confidentiality.

Full Disclosure

Second, the guarantee of confidentiality is essential in eliciting the full disclosure necessary for effective treatment. The psychiatric patient approaches treatment with conscious and unconscious inhibitions against revealing his innermost thoughts. "Every person, however well-motivated, has to overcome resistances to therapeutic exploration. These resistances seek support from every possible source and the possibility of disclosure would easily be employed in the service of resistance." (Goldstein & Katz, supra, 36 Conn. Bar J. 175, 179; see also, 118 Am. J. Psych. 734, 735.) Until a patient can trust his psychiatrist not to violate their confidential relationship, "the unconscious psychological control mechanism of repression will prevent the recall of past experiences." (Butler, Psychotherapy and Griswold: Is Confidentiality a Privilege or a Right? (1971) 3 Conn. L. Rev. 599, 604.)

Successful Treatment

Third, even if the patient fully discloses his thoughts, assurance that the confidential relationship will not be breached is necessary to maintain his trust in his psychiatrist—the very means by which treatment is effected. "[T]he essence of much psychotherapy is the contribution of trust in the external world and ultimately in the self, modelled upon the trusting relationship established during therapy." (Dawidoff, The Malpractice of Psychiatrists, 1966 Duke L.J. 696, 704). Patients will be helped only if they can form a trusting relationship with the psychiatrist. All authorities appear to agree that if the trust relationship cannot be developed because of collusive communication between the psychiatrist and others, treatment will be frustrated.

Given the importance of confidentiality to the practice of psychiatry, it becomes clear the duty to warn imposed by the majority will cripple the use and effectiveness of psychiatry. Many people, potentially violent—yet susceptible to treatment—will be deterred from seeking it; those seeking it will be inhibited from making revelations necessary to effective treatment; and, forcing the psychiatrist to violate the patient's trust will destroy the interpersonal relationship by which treatment is effected.

Violence and Civil Commitment

By imposing a duty to warn, the majority contributes to the danger to society of violence by the mentally ill and greatly increases the risk of civil commitment—the total deprivation of liberty—and those who should not be confined. The impairment of treatment and risk of improper commitment resulting from the new duty to warn will not be limited to a few patients but will extend to a large number of the mentally ill. Although under existing psychiatric procedures only a relatively few receiving treatment will ever present a risk of violence, the number making threats is huge, and it is the latter group—not just the former—whose treatment will be impaired and whose risk of commitment will be increased. . . .

Neither alternative open to the psychiatrist seeking to protect himself is in the public interest. The warning itself is an impairment of the psychiatrist's ability to treat, depriving many patients of adequate treatment. It is to be expected that after disclosing their threats, a significant number of patients, who would not become violent if treated according to existing practices, will engage in violent conduct as a result of unsuccessful treatment. In short, the majority's duty to warn will not only impair treatment of many who would never become violent but worse, will result in a net increase in violence.

The second alternative open to the psychiatrist is to commit his patient rather than to warn. Even in the absence of threat of civil liability, the doubts of psychiatrists as to the seriousness of patient threats have led psychiatrists to overcommit to mental institutions. This overcommitment has been authoritatively documented in both legal and psychiatric studies. . . .

Given the incentive to commit created by the majority's duty, this already serious situation will be worsened, contrary to Chief Justice Wright's admonition "that liberty is no less precious because forfeited in a civil proceeding than when taken as a consequence of a criminal conviction." (In re W. (1971) 5 Cal. 3d 296, 307, 96 Cal. Rptr. 1, 9, 486 P.2d 1201,1209.) . . .

[T]he majority impedes medical treatment, resulting in increased violence from—and deprivation of liberty to—the mentally ill.

We should accept . . . medical judgment, relying upon effective treatment rather than on indiscriminate warning.

The judgment should be affirmed.

McComb, J., concurs.

Most courts that have addressed the issue have followed *Tarasoff.* Some courts have held that the psychotherapist's duty is triggered only if the patient threatens a particular, identified victim that can be warned. See, e.g., Brady v. Hopper, 751 F.2d 329 (10th Cir. 1984). The plaintiff in this case was shot by the defendant's patient in the course of the latter's attempt to assassinate then President Ronald Reagan. Other courts have rejected the "readily identifiable victim" requirement. See, e.g., Shuster v. Altenberg, 144 Wis. 2d 223, 424 N.W.2d 159 (1988). In Peck v. Counseling Service of Addison County, Inc., 146 Vt. 61, 499 A.2d 422 (1985), *Tarasoff* was applied when the threat was to a building owned by the plaintiff. In Heldund v. Superior Court, 34 Cal. 3rd 695, 669 P.2d 41, 194 Cal. Rptr. 805 (1983), the court extended *Tarasoff* liability for emotional harm to bystanders. The plaintiff was the five-year-old son of the primary victim, who witnessed the shooting of his mother by the defendant's patient. Rejecting *Tarasoff* is Boynton v. Burglass, 590 So. 2d 446 (Fla. App. 1991).

While *Tarasoff* involved the duty warn, in some cases plaintiffs have argued that the defendant may have a duty to go beyond warning and take steps to seek commitment of the patient to prevent harm to the victim. The court in Currie v. United States, 836 F.2d 209 (4th Cir. 1987) refused to accept that argument. But the court in Shuster v. Altenberg, cited above, stated that the duty of the defendant could extend to seeking commitment of the patient.

Tarasoff raises a number of problems not dealt with in the opinion. For example, there is an obvious tension between the duty of the psychotherapist to warn potential victims of the patient's violence and the duty to respect the patient's privacy interests. While the court recognized this tension, it did not recognize the existence of the tort liability dilemma faced by the psychotherapist. On one hand, failure to warn can subject the therapist to tort liability to the victim. On the other hand, overzealous disclosure to the potential victim carries with it the possibility of tort liability to the patient. See, e.g., Alberts v. Devine, 395 Mass. 59, 479 N.E.2d 113, *cert. denied,* 474 U.S. 1083 (1985). Another problem is whether the therapist is under a duty to advise the patient of the duty to disclose what otherwise would be confidential information. In a different context, a lower California court asserted that a duty to advise arises. In People v. Younghanz, 156 Cal. App. 3d 811, 202 Cal. Rptr. 907 (1984), the defendant, whose conviction for child abuse was affirmed by the court, attacked the constitutionality of a statute that required his doctor to report known instances of child abuse. The court concluded that the doctor has an obligation to inform the patient of the duty to report, but that if the patient stays with the doctor in the face of such a warning, he or she waives any constitutional objection to the reporting by the doctor. In any event, according to one survey conducted in 1987, half of the psychologists reported that they say nothing about confidentiality, or tell their patients that everything is confidential. See Simon, Boundaries of Confidence, 22, No. 6, Psychology Today, June 1988, p. 23.

Is the duty to warn imposed by *Tarasoff* having the adverse effects that the dissenting judge predicted? The returns conflict. For support of the dissent on that score, see Stone, The *Tarasoff* Decisions: Suing Psychotherapists to Safeguard Society, 90 Harv. L. Rev. 358 (1976); Note, Where the Public Peril Begins: A Survey of Psychotherapists to Determine the Effects of *Tarasoff,* 31 Stan. L. Rev. 165 (1978). For a different view, see Wexler, Victimology and Mental Health: An Agenda, 66 Va. L. Rev. 681 (1980); Givelber, Bowers, and Blitch, *Tarasoff,* Myth and Reality: An Empirical Study of Private Law in Action, 1984 Wis. L. Rev. 443. For an evaluation of the ability of psychotherapists to predict dangerousness in other contexts, see Slobogin, Dangerousness and Expertise, 133 U. Pa. L. Rev. 97 (1984).

Some state statutes have been passed to provide some protection to therapists in *Tarasoff*-type cases. The California statute (Cal. Civ. Code §43.92 (1992 Supp.)) provides:

> (a) There shall be no monetary liability on the part of, and no cause of action shall arise against, any person who is a psychotherapist as defined in

> Section 1010 of the Evidence Code in failing to warn of and protect from a patient's threatened violent behavior or failing to predict and warn of and protect from a patient's violent behavior except where the patient has communicated to the psychotherapist a serious threat of physical violence against a reasonably identifiable victim or victims.
>
> (b) If there is a duty to warn and protect under the limited circumstances specified above, the duty shall be discharged by the psychotherapist making reasonable efforts to communicate the threat to the victim or victims and to a law enforcement agency.

Would this statute have benefited the defendant in *Tarasoff* had it been in force at that time? A different approach is taken by Pa. Stat. Ann. Tit. 50, ch. 15, §7111 (Cum. Supp. 1992), which limits the persons to whom mental health records and information can be disclosed in a way that would foreclose notifying the victim or the police. The statute applies, however, only to patients who are being treated involuntarily, and to those who are being treated voluntarily as inpatients. See Commonwealth v. Moyer, 595 A.2d 1177 (Pa. Super. 1991).

In the course of its opinion, the majority in *Tarasoff* relied on three contexts in which medical care providers have been liable to third persons:

1. *"[A] hospital must exercise reasonable care to control the behavior of a patient which may endanger other persons."* An example in point, although not involving a hospital, is Dudley v. Offender Aid and Restoration of Richmond, Inc., 241 Va. 270, 401 S.E.2d 878 (1991), in which the defendant failed to keep confined an inmate who had a history of violent crime and who raped and killed his victim.

2. *"A doctor must also warn a patient if the patient's condition or medication renders certain conduct, such as driving a car, dangerous to others."* The court in Myers v. Quesenberry, 144 Cal. App. 3d 888, 193 Cal. Rptr. 733 (1983), relied on this statement to impose liability on a doctor who did not inform a patient that the latter's diabetic condition would impair his ability to drive an automobile. The patient was involved in an automobile accident which injured the plaintiffs. But in Kirk v. Michael Reese Hospital and Medical Center, 117 Ill. 2d 507, 513 N.E.2d 387 (1987), the court refused to impose liability on a physician in similar circumstances. The plaintiff alleged that the defendant failed to warn his patient about the risks of driving while under the influence of a drug the defendant had administered to the patient. The court upheld the decision of the trial judge to dismiss the complaint.

3. *"[A] doctor is liable to persons infected by his patient if he negligently fails to diagnose a contagious disease or, having diagnosed the illness, fails to warn members of the patient's family."* An example is DiMarco v. Lynch Homes-Chester County Inc., 525 Pa. 558, 583 A.2d 422 (1990) (negligence in failing to advise patient about risk of communicating a sexually transmissible disease). But in Britton v. Soltes, 563 N.E.2d 910 (Ill. App. 1990), the

court refused to extend the duty to act with reasonable care to the family of the defendant's patient; the defendant had negligently failed to diagnose the patient's tuberculosis.

Do any of these cases support liability in *Tarasoff*?

Perhaps of more immediate concern to lawyers is whether the rule of *Tarasoff* will be extended to them. While there are no reported opinions involving lawyers, the exposure does exist. The 1980 draft of the ABA Model Rules of Professional Conduct (Rule 1.7(b)) made it mandatory for a lawyer to "disclose information about a client to the extent it appears necessary to prevent a crime that would result in death or serious bodily harm to another person. . . ." The most recent draft is permissive in this regard, rather than mandatory. It states that a lawyer "may reveal" such information. See Rule 1.6(b). Since the rules of professional responsibility are the responsibility of courts, it might be expected that the judicial attitude toward tort liability of lawyers would be reflected in those rules.

Problem 19

Yesterday, you received a telephone call from Elizabeth Green, one of your clients. Green runs Insu-Screen Associates, a company that conducts medical exams on individuals applying for life insurance offered by commercial insurance companies. Upon the request of an insurer, Insu-Screen conducts a full medical exam on applicants for insurance. These exams include a lengthy physical exam, comprehensive blood tests and a detailed medical and family history. Some insurance companies pay Insu-Screen for the testing; others require the applicant to cover the costs of the screening exam.

Green is concerned because Insu-Screen is now finding that a small but growing number of applicants are testing positively for the HIV virus. Under current company policy, Insu-Screen does not inform prospective insurance applicants of the outcome of the tests. Applicants are provided with a written form which indicates that the results of the medical exam are confidential and are the property of the insurance company seeking the test. She notes that most insurers, confronted with a problematic medical report, simply deny the application for life insurance without informing the applicant of the reasons for the denial.

Green is particularly concerned about the legal implications of her company's nondisclosure policy. She notes that such individuals, if uninformed of their HIV-positive status, may delay seeking medical treatments that can prolong the onset of full-blown AIDS. Moreover, such individuals may continue to engage in sexual practices that expose others to HIV infection. Indeed, because of the detailed family histories that constitute part of Insu-Screen's medical exam, Green notes that it is often possible to identify by name the third parties—typically spouses—that are at risk of being infected by the applicant.

Green has asked your advice concerning the outlines of an appropriate disclosure policy. Must she inform insurance applicants when they test positive for HIV? Must she inform known sexual partners of those individuals? Are there other medical findings she must disclose? Assume that the supreme court of your jurisdiction has not yet considered the *Tarasoff* issue.

Law and Policy: A Legal Duty to Rescue?

The Kitty Genovese incident discussed on p. 320, above, provoked a good bit of societal "soul searching." Is there something fundamentally wrong with a society in which 38 people stand by and do nothing, not even call the police, to aid a woman under attack?[122] Not surprisingly, one facet of the debate was whether the legal system should take a more active part in encouraging persons to come to the aid of others in need.[123] A variety of perspectives is contained in The Good Samaritan and the Law (Ratcliffe ed. 1966).

Notwithstanding the widespread concern over the incident, there has been relatively little attempt on the part of legislatures to establish a general duty to rescue. As the preceding material indicates, see pp. 311-312, above, only two states have enacted anything like a general duty to rescue statute. Nor have courts acted to fill the void. Absent a special relationship or a causal connection between the bystander and the harm to the victim, courts have not imposed liability on one who could have, but did not, rescue another from peril. Judicial inaction led one leading treatise to bemoan that "Some of the decisions have been shocking in the extreme. . . . Such decisions are revolting to any moral sense." Prosser and Keeton, The Law of Torts 375-376 (5th ed. 1984).

If the legislatures and the courts have been largely silent, the commentators have not. A number of commentators over the years, reacting to their perceptions that the no-duty-to-rescue law lacks a moral foundation, have argued for a more general duty. One of the early advocates was Professor

122. The explanation of the Kitty Genovese incident may have less to do with collective morality than with the psychology of people in groups. One psychological study following the incident concluded that a bystander is less likely to come to the aid of a person in need of aid if the bystander is one of a group rather than being a lone observer. It is thus not so much a matter of apathy, according to the study, than it is a matter of each person in the group feeling that someone else is doing something. See Darley & Latane, Bystander Intervention in Emergencies: Diffusion of Responsibility, 8 J. of Personality and Soc. Psych. 377 (1968).

123. In other contexts, the legal system does a great deal to encourage, and sometimes compel, citizens to aid others. The Internal Revenue Code permits taxpayers to deduct contributions to a wide range of charitable organizations. The military draft, when it is in effect, compels those drafted to "serve their country." The concern in *Tarasoff* has a narrower focus, dealing with a "one on one" context, in which the law typically has not tried to force bystanders to aid those in distress. It is not a crime, for example, for one to fail to give to a homeless person begging for a handout, and the system does not expose to tort liability the person who does not give to the homeless for any harm caused by the failure to rescue.

Ames in his well-known work, Law and Morals, 22 Harv. L. Rev. 97 (1908). In this article, he urged that tort liability be imposed on those who, with "little or no inconvenience" to themselves, could have rescued another in danger but failed to do so. A similar proposal was advanced in Weinrib, The Case for a Duty to Rescue, 90 Yale L.J. 247 (1980). Here, Professor Weinrib advocated a judicially created tort duty of "easy rescue." While he did not elaborate much on the contours such a duty would have (for instance, he did not state whether the easiness of the rescue would be measured objectively—easy to a reasonable person—or subjectively—easy to this particular defendant), he did state that such a duty ought to be imposed only in "emergency situations where the rescue will not inconvenience the rescuer," and that the rescuer ought not to be compelled to "place himself in physical danger." Id. at 285. See also Levmore, Waiting for Rescue: An Essay on the Evolution and Incentive Structure of the Law of Affirmative Obligations, 72 Va. L. Rev. 879 (1986); Yeager, A Radical Community of Aid: A Rejoinder to Opponents of Affirmative Duties to Help Strangers, 71 Wash. U. L.Q. 1 (1993).

The existing law, however, is not without its defenders. One is Epstein, A Theory of Strict Liability, 2 (1) J. Legal Stud. 151 (1973). Professor Epstein asserted that tort liability should be based on cause, rather than on fault. Since the nonrescuer would not have caused the harm, it would be inappropriate for the law to impose liability. "It may well be," Professor Epstein stated, "that the conduct of individuals who do not aid fellow men is under some circumstances outrageous, but it does not follow that a legal system that does not enforce a duty to aid is outrageous as well." Id. at 201. For an economic analysis of the efficiency implications of the law of rescue, see Landes and Posner, Salvors, Finders, Good Samaritans, and Other Rescuers: An Economic Study of Law and Altruism, 7 (1) J. Legal Stud. 83 (1978). The authors conclude that a law imposing a general duty to rescue would not be more efficient than the existing no-duty law.

Writing from a broader philosophical perspective, though of relevance to the duty to rescue, Professor Fuller in The Morality of Law (rev. ed. 1969) argues that not all goals of society can be accomplished through law. In distinguishing between societal concerns that ought, and those that ought not, to be the subject of legal compulsion, he discusses what he calls the "morality of aspiration" and the "morality of duty." He defines the two concepts as follows (pp. 5-6):

> The morality of aspiration is most plainly exemplified in Greek philosophy. It is the morality of the Good Life, of excellence, of the fullest realization of human powers. . . .
>
> Where the morality of aspiration starts at the top of human achievement, the morality of duty starts at the bottom. It lays down the basic rules without which an ordered society is impossible, or without which an ordered society directed toward certain specific goals must fail of its mark. It is the morality

of the Old Testament and the Ten Commandments. It speaks in terms of "thou shalt not," and, less frequently, of "thou shalt." It does not condemn men for failing to embrace opportunities for the fullest realization of their powers. Instead, it condemns them for failing to respect the basic requirements of social living.

The importance of these concepts lies, according to Fuller, in the inability of the law to "compel a man to live up to the excellences of which he is capable." He makes the argument this way (pp. 9, 27-28):

As we consider the whole range of moral issues, we may conveniently imagine a kind of scale or yardstick which begins at the bottom with most obvious demands of social living and extends upward to the highest reaches of human aspiration. Somewhere along this scale there is an invisible pointer that marks the dividing line where the pressure of duty leaves off and the challenge of excellence begins. The whole field of moral argument is dominated by a great undeclared war over the location of this pointer. There are those who struggle to push it upward; others work to pull it down. Those whom we regard as being unpleasantly—or at least, inconveniently—moralistic are forever trying to inch the pointer upward so as to expand the area of duty. Instead of inviting us to join them in realizing a pattern of life they consider worthy of human nature, they try to bludgeon us into a belief we are duty bound to embrace this pattern. . . .

. . . If the morality of duty reaches upward beyond its proper sphere the iron hand of imposed obligation may stifle experiment, inspiration, and spontaneity. If the morality of aspiration invades the province of duty, men may begin to weigh and qualify their obligations by standards of their own and we may end with the poet tossing his wife into the river in the belief—perhaps quite justified—that he will be able to write better poetry in her absence.

The arguments discussed so far over whether the law should impose a general tort duty to rescue have all involved the merits from a substantive perspective. In Process Constraints in Tort, 67 Cornell L. Rev. 901 (1982), Professor J. Henderson suggests that there are important process considerations which explain the reluctance of courts to adopt a general duty. According to Professor Henderson, to satisfy process requirements, tort law must adequately guide the behavior of two groups of persons: those "whose activities generate the accident costs upon which liability issues focus" (primary behavior); and "the lawyers, judges, and jurors who have responsibility for officially resolving liability disputes" (adjudicative behavior). Id. at 903. With respect to both groups, Professor Henderson asserts that a general duty to rescue would fail to meet the following process criteria (Id. at 905):

First, their clarity must be such as to enable persons to distinguish between modes of conduct that will bring liability and modes that will not. Second,

> they must refer to factual circumstances that can be objectively verified, so that persons can apply the rules with some measure of confidence. Finally, to the extent that the rules describe patterns of behavior to which individuals are expected to conform, they must avoid calling for behavioral patterns that are not achievable by those to whom the rules are directed.

One of the more intriguing uses of rescue theory appears in Regan, Rewriting Roe v. Wade, 77 Mich. L. Rev. 1569 (1979). Professor Regan argues that to compel a woman to carry a fetus to term would be to compel her to be a Good Samaritan, and that for the law to do that without imposing a general duty to rescue on all persons in society would be a violation of the Equal Protection Clause of the Constitution of the United States.

Many European nations do not follow the American view that there should be no general duty to rescue. The European laws are analyzed and compared in Rudzinsky, The Duty to Rescue: A Comparative Analysis, in Ratcliffe, ed., p. 313, above, at 91, and Note, The Failure to Rescue: A Comparative Study, 52 Colum. L. Rev. 631 (1952). Professor Rudzinsky counted 15 countries that have some form of a statutory duty to rescue. Fourteen of the statutes impose criminal sanctions, with penalties varying from fines only (Turkey) to prison terms of up to five years (France). Two countries (Portugal and Czechoslovakia) impose statutory civil penalties. The laws also differ as to who is required to render aid. The Italian and Rumanian statutes impose the duty only on those present at the scene, while the Polish and French statutes reach anyone who is informed of the need for rescue. Under all of the statutes, the would-be rescuer can take into account the risks to himself involved in the rescue. In Rumania, there is no duty if there is danger to the life of the would-be rescuer; in Norway, Denmark and Russia, a serious danger to life or health furnishes a sufficient excuse. Under the statutes of Portugal and France, rescue is required only if no risk is involved. And finally, the statutes vary as to what action is required; most of the laws require personal intervention, but under some, such as those of Italy, Rumania and Russia, the duty can be discharged by summoning the appropriate authorities.

Law and Behavior: The Effect of Legal Rules upon Individual Conduct

One of the questions suggested by the preceding note on law and policy is the extent to which the recognition of a general legal duty to be a Good Samaritan would actually affect behavior in a way that would lead to increased altruism. Earlier notes on law and behavior have considered the influences, including law, upon the behavior of two specialized actors in the torts process—the judge and the jury. In this note, we turn to a consideration of the effect that legal rules have upon the behavior of the person in the street[124]—a question first raised in the note on law and behavior at the end of Chapter 1.

By far the greater number of inquiries by behavioral scientists have been directed toward determining the effectiveness of criminal, rather than civil, liability as a means of discouraging antisocial conduct.[125] The value of these criminal studies to students of the torts process lies primarily in their contribution to the development of general theories explaining how, why, and to what extent people respond to legal rules by seeking to conform their conduct to them. A variety of investigative techniques have been employed. One of these more commonly used involves comparing behavior patterns in two jurisdictions, only one of which imposes a particular criminal sanction. If the patterns of behavior in the two jurisdictions differ significantly, and if other possible explanations for the difference can be eliminated, it may be possible to conclude that the imposition of the sanction does affect behavior.[126] A variation of this basic comparative technique involves observing patterns of behavior in a single jurisdiction both before and after implementation of a change in the criminal law, and comparing them in much the same way as the behavior patterns occurring simultaneously in two or more jurisdictions might be compared.[127]

It should be observed that although these techniques may be useful in demonstrating the presence (or absence) of correlations between particular

124. Perhaps the high-water mark of optimism regarding the potential for influencing human conduct through legal rules is reflected in the following sign observed near a power station in Ireland: "To touch these overhead cables means instant death. Violators will be prosecuted." Quoted in N.Y. Times, Dec. 11, 1969, at 59, col. 2.

125. See generally, Andenaes, Punishment and Deterrence (1974); Geis, White Collar Criminal (1986); Middendorf, The Effectiveness of Punishment (1968); Packer, The Limits of Criminal Sanction; Title, Sanctions and Social Deviance: The Question of Deterrence (1980); Zilboorg, The Psychology of the Criminal Act and Punishment (1954).

126. For a collection of studies employing this comparative technique to determine the effectiveness of capital punishment, see Capital Punishment (Sellin ed. 1967). See also, Amnesty International, United States of America: The Death Penalty 162 (1987) (reviewing death penalty research and concluding that death penalty and nondeath penalty states showed little difference in homicide rates). For concise descriptions and critiques of cross-jurisdictional comparisons see Andenaes, The General Preventative Effects of Punishment, 114 U. Pa. L. Rev. 949, 974-975 (1966); Chambliss, Types of Deviance and the Effectiveness of Legal Sanctions, 1967 Wis. L. Rev. 703, 704-707.

127. For an interesting description and critique of one well-known example of this before-and-after technique, including the development and application by the authors of six common threats to the validity of experiments, see Campbell and Ross, The Connecticut Crackdown on Speeding: Time-Series Data in Quasi-Experimental Analysis, 3 L. & Soc. Rev. 33 (1968). See also, Lempert, Strategies of Research Design in the Legal Impact Study: The Control of Plausible Rival Hypotheses, 1 L. & Soc. Rev. 111 (1966); McDonald, Larson, Wood, Youngs, Rathge, Stead, Examining the Multiple Effects of a Strengthened DUI Law: An Executive Summary of a Three-Year Study, 2 Soc. Prac. Rev. 116 (1991); O'Malley, Wagenaar, Effects of Minimum Drinking Age Laws on Alcohol-Use, Related Behaviors and Traffic Crash Involvement Among American Youth—1976-1987, 52 J. Stud. on Alcohol 478 (1991); Shover, Bankston, and Gurley, Responses of the Criminal Justice System to Legislation Providing More Severe Threatened Sanctions, 14 Criminology 483 (1977); Smith, Hingson, Morelock, Heeren, Mucatel, Mangione, and Scotch, Legislation Raising the Legal Drinking Age in Massachusetts from 18-20: Effect on 16 and 17 Year-Olds, 45 J. Stud. on Alcohol (1984).

criminal sanctions and patterns of behavior, they do not explain how or why people are affected in their behavior by criminal rules of conduct. For explanations of this sort other investigative techniques are required which are designed to explore the psychology of deviance and its control through legal rules. Basically, two techniques are available and have been employed toward that end: persons whose behavior has been observed are, after the fact, asked questions designed to reveal the motivating factors which influenced their conduct;[128] and experiments are conducted in which two or more otherwise identical groups of persons are exposed, before the fact, to different sets of stimuli and their conduct thereafter is observed under controlled conditions to determine the effect, if any, of the differences in stimuli on their subsequent behavior.[129]

Due to the widely varied contexts in which these studies have been undertaken, it is difficult to draw conclusions from what has been accomplished so far. From a review of the literature, the following are offered as tentative formulations:

(1) Behavioral scientists appear generally to agree that legal rules imposing criminal sanctions have a substantial potential for influencing the behavior of persons to whom those rules are addressed.

(2) However, measuring and evaluating the effects of legal rules on behavior is a complicated and difficult task, due largely to the following factors:

(a) "The law," the effects of which are sought to be measured, is often remarkably indeterminate. The realities of the processes by which legal rules are applied and enforced may be very different from what one might have expected from the rules taken at face value, and the effects upon behavior of legal rules will vary greatly depending upon the processes by which they are implemented.[130]

(b) The law itself limits the extent to which scientists may manipulate variables in order to test experimentally the effects of law upon behavior. Rules of due process and equal protection prohibit selective and discriminatory applications of the law, and thus inhibit scientists from making full use of the experimental mode of inquiry.[131]

128. See, e.g., Ball, Social Structure and Rent-Control Violations, 65 Am. J. Soc. 598 (1960); Homel, Policing and Punishing the Drinking Driver: A Study of General and Specific Deterrence (1988).

129. See, e.g., Schwartz and Orleans, On Legal Sanctions, 34 U. Chi L. Rev. 274 (1967).

130. For a recognition of the importance of distinguishing the law "on the books" from the "law in fact," see Lempert, Strategies of Research Design in the Legal Impact Study: The Control of Plausible Rival Hypotheses, 1 L. & Soc. Rev. 111 (1966). For a discussion of the related point that the objectives of legal rules are often indeterminate, see Friedman and Macaulay, Law and the Behavioral Sciences 306-307 (1969). See also, Ansaldi, The German Llewellyn, 58 Brooklyn L. Rev. 705 (1992) (noting that Llewellyn found common law rules lacking in precise wording and that this allowed for their refashioning); Grazin, Essay: Reflections on the Philosophy of Law, 64 Notre Dame L. Rev. 285 (1989).

131. For a thoughtful discussion of the legal and ethical limitations upon legal experimentation, see Zeisel, The New York Expert Testimony Project: Some Reflections on Legal Experi-

(c) It is extremely difficult to sort out the direct effects of law upon behavior from the direct effects of other, nonlegal influences. The complexity of the processes of human thought and action will probably forever frustrate attempts to explain exactly how and why any factors, such as legal rules, affect behavior.

(d) Even if the direct effects of legal rules could be separated from the effects of other factors, these other factors are themselves affected, on a more long-run basis, by the existence of the legal rules. Thus, even if it were possible in a particular instance to conclude that an individual's conduct is more likely to be affected in the short run by his sense of right and wrong than by the existence of a criminal statute threatening a sanction, it nevertheless may be that the individual's moral values are significantly affected in the longer run by the fact that certain actions are publicly branded criminal.[132]

(3) In predicting and evaluating the effects of any legal rule, a number of factors must be considered, among which are:

(a) The broader legal and social environment in which the particular rule is encountered. One important factor determining the effect of legal rules is what might be termed the overall morale of the addressees in the system of which the rules are a part. Apparently, people who have confidence in the basic fairness of the system are more likely than those who do not to conform their conduct to legal rules.[133]

(b) The type of behavior toward which the rule is directed. The more the conduct deemed unlawful is likely to be engaged in as a means of achieving a material objective of the actor, the more the actor is likely to be deterred by the threat of a criminal sanction; the more the conduct tends to be engaged in as a pleasurable end in itself, the less likely the actor is to be deterred by such a threat.[134]

(c) The nature of the rule itself and the accompanying implementation process. The more likely the deviant actor is to be apprehended and punished, and the more severe the punishment, the more likely the rule is to deter the actor's conduct.[135]

---

ments, 8 Stan. L. Rev. 730 (1956). See also, Walker, Perfecting Federal Civil Rules: A Proposal for Restricted Field Experiments, 51 Law & Contemp. Probs. 67 (1988).

132. See generally, Andenaes, Punishment and Deterrence 110 (1974); Berkowitz and Walker, Laws and Moral Judgments, 30 Sociometry 410 (1967): Litwak, Three Ways in Which Law Acts as a Means of Social Control, 34 Social Forces 217 (1956).

133. See generally, Ball, Social Structure and Rent-Control Violations, 65 Am. J. Soc. 598 (1960); Skolnick, Coercion to Virtue: The Enforcement of Morals, 41 S. Cal. L. Rev. 588 (1968); Tyler, Why People Obey the Law (1990).

134. See generally, Chambliss, Types of Deviance and the Effectiveness of Legal Sanctions, 1967 Wis. L. Rev. 703.

135. See generally, Klein and Waller, Causation, Culpability and Deterrence in Highway Crashes 134-135; Kramer, An Economic Analysis of Criminal Attempt: Marginal Deterrence and the Optimal Structure of Sanctions, 81 J. Crim. L. & Criminology 398 (1990); Shavell, Deterrence and the Punishment of Attempts, 19 J. Legal Stud. 435 (1990); Bryjack, The Deterrent Effect of Perceived Severity of Punishment, 59 Soc. Forces 471 (1980). But see Paternoster, Decisions to Participate in and Desist from Four Types of Common Delinquency:

(d) The psychological predispositions of the population of actors to whom the rule is addressed. It is generally agreed that every individual is possessed of certain psychological traits which affect the manner in which behavior is influenced by legal rules, and it is becoming increasingly possible to generalize about these traits.[136]

Of course, even if the foregoing statements are accepted as reasonably accurate, albeit tentative, formulations regarding the effects upon behavior of rules of criminal law, there remains open the question of the effects upon behavior of the imposition of civil tort liability.[137] Compared with what has been accomplished in the criminal law field, relatively little work has been done along similar lines in the field of torts.[138] Certainly, on the face of things, there is a substantial basis upon which to argue that rules of tort law are very much different from rules of criminal law, and that tort rules have for that reason less of an effect upon individual behavior. Tort rules, especially those governing liability in negligence, tend to be more open-ended and vague, and therefore would appear less likely to serve as guides to conduct.[139] There is probably less of a social stigma attached to the imposition of civil, as opposed to criminal, liability. And tort liability is very apt to be insured against, lessening its potential impact upon the individual upon whom liability is imposed.

Deterrence and the Rational Choice Perspective, 23 L. & Soc. Rev. 7 (1989) (deterrence comes from certainty, rather than severity, of punishment).

136. See generally, Schwartz and Orleans, On Legal Sanctions, 34 U. Chi L. Rev. 274 (1967). For a discussion on psychiatric criminology, determinism, and responsibility, see Hall, Law, Social Science and Criminal Theory 104 (1982). In addition, other studies have examined the relationship between demographic factors and the deterrence rationale. See Homel, Policing and Punishing the Drinking Driver: A Study of General and Specific Deterrence 199 (1988); Tittle, Sanctions and Social Deviance: The Question of Deterrence 291 (1980).

137. Criminal law rationales may provide insight into this issue. See Hall, Law, Social Science and Criminal Theory 255-256 (1982) (the deterrence rationale does not support the imposition of criminal sanctions for negligent acts due to their inadvertent nature). However, see Bruce, The Deterrent Effects of Automobile Insurance and Tort Law: A Survey of the Empirical Literature, 6 L. & Pol. 67 (1984) (surveying statistical literature and finding support for the deterrence rationale). Additionally, other writers have expressly or implicitly accepted the proposition that tort law has a deterrent effect. See Evans, School Crime and Violence: Achieving Deterrence Through Tort Law, 3 Notre Dame J.L. Ethics & Public Policy 501 (1988); Judges, Of Rocks and Hard Places: The Value of Risk Choice, 42 Emory L.J. 1 (1993) (arguing that tort law's deterrence rationale interferes with nonparties risk choice); Krent, Preserving Discretion Without Sacrificing Deterrence: Federal Governmental Liability in Tort, 38 U.C.L.A. L. Rev. 871 (1991); Nader, The Assault on Injured Victims' Rights, 64 Den. U.L. Rev. 625 (1988) (noting the deterrent effect that tort liability has on manufacturers and other potential defendants).

138. But see, Bowers, Givelber and Blitch, How Did "Tarasoff" Affect Clinical Practice?, 484 Annals Am. Acad. Pol. & Soc. Sci. 70 (March, 1986); Schwartz and Komesar, Doctors, Damages and Deterrence: An Economic View of Medical Malpractice (1978). For a discussion on the deterrence rationale of tort law, see Williams, Commentary, Second Best: The Soft Underbelly of Deterrence Theory in Tort, 106 Harv. L. Rev. 932 (1993).

139. It should be remembered that we are here concerned with the prospective effect of tort rules upon the behavior patterns of people generally in our society. Obviously, there are a number of more-or-less specific rules directed at institutional actors such as judges, lawyers, and jurors, which presumably do serve as guides for their official conduct, but with which we are not presently concerned.

These considerations, and others, have led many writers to the conclusion that the rules imposing fault-based liability in tort have only a minimal effect directly upon the behavior of individuals to whom they are addressed.[140] Much of the interest in this subject has been stimulated by the enactment into law in many states of no-fault automobile compensation plans.[141] Although some writers have opposed these plans on the grounds that the system of fault-based liability in tort does serve as a deterrence to unreasonably dangerous automobile driving, their arguments appear to be based on the premise that in a general way the fault system reinforces the community's sense of moral and social responsibility, and therefore helps indirectly to curb tendencies on the part of drivers to behave negligently.[142]

2. Proximate Cause

Consider the following hypothetical cases:

(1) The defendant maintains a tar storage tank from which he negligently allows tar to leak onto a public walkway. The plaintiff, a small boy, walks through the tar, and when he gets home, his parents start to remove the tar from his feet with gasoline. A neighborhood boy comes into the yard and fires a cap pistol. A spark from the pistol ignites fumes from the gasoline, causing severe burns to the plaintiff's legs.

(2) The defendant negligently permits oil to escape from his tanker, some of which washes aboard a barge six hours later. The barge was six miles downstream from the tanker. Two days later, the plaintiff, in cleaning the oil from the barge, slips on the oil and is injured.

140. See Keeton and O'Connell, Basic Protection for the Traffic Victim 253 (1965); Klein and Waller, Causation, Culpability, and Deterrence in Highway Crashes 137 (1970); James and Dickinson, Accident Proneness and Accident Law, 63 Harv. L. Rev. 769 (1950); Schwartz and Orleans, On Legal Sanctions, 34 U. Chi. L. Rev. 274, 276 (1967). It should be observed that we are focusing throughout this discussion on the effects of rules of tort law on the behavior of noninstitutional actors—that is, "the person in the street." It must be recognized that the deterrence potential of tort law on the behavior of what might in this context be described as "quasi-institutional actors"—corporations, professionals, etc.—may be higher than the deterrence potential upon private individuals. See the note on law and behavior at the end of Chapter 1, p. 106, above. See also, Cohen, Regulating Regulators: The Legal Environment of the State, 40 U. Toronto L.J. 213 (1990).

141. See Chapter 10, Section B, below.

142. See Lawton, No-Fault: An Invitation to More Accidents, 55 Marq. L. Rev. 73 (1972); Mancuso, The Utility of the Culpability Concept in Promoting Proper Driving Behavior, 55 Marq. L. Rev. 85 (1972). However, other studies have focused on aspects of deterrence. See Kochanowski, Deterrent Aspects of No Fault Automobile Insurance—Some Empirical-Findings; 52 J. Risk & Ins. 269 (1985) (finding no indication that no-fault insurance schemes result in more traffic fatalities); Medoff and Magaddino, An Empirical Analysis of No-Fault Insurance, 6 Evaluation Rev. 373 (1982) (suggesting that adoption of no-fault insurance reduces deterrence); Landes, Insurance, Liability, and Accidents: A Theoretical and Empirical Investigation of the Effect of No-Fault Accidents, 25 J.L. & Econ. 49, 50 (1982) (finding support for the hypothesis that adoption of no-fault insurance increases the number of accidents). For a critique of the Landes study, see O'Connell and Levmore, A Reply to Landes: A Faulty Study of No-Fault's Effect on Fault? 48 Mo. L. Rev. 649 (1983).

(3) The defendant negligently maintains a window—some putty is missing around one of the panes—in a third floor apartment in his apartment building. A boy wanders into the apartment to watch a crowd of people on the street below and pushes against the pane. The pane falls out of the window and into the street below, causing passersby to stampede to avoid the glass. One of the crowd knocks the plaintiff down, severely injuring her.

Is the defendant liable for the plaintiff's injuries in any of these cases? In all of them, the defendants were negligent and their conduct did contribute, in a factual sense, to causing the injuries of which the plaintiffs complain. And yet, in the actual cases upon which the first two hypotheticals are based, the defendants were held not liable as matter of law because the plaintiff in each instance was deemed to have failed to establish that the negligence of the defendant was the proximate cause of the harm.[143] Only in the third case was the plaintiff able to convince the court that the proximate cause requirement was satisfied.[144]

As these cases illustrate, the rules of proximate cause sometimes permit a defendant to escape liability even if all the other elements of the prima facie case—cause-in-fact, negligence, and harm—have been established. But beyond this simple statement of the effect of the rules of proximate cause, there is much disagreement and confusion about what the rules are and how they work.[145] The literature analyzing proximate cause is vast, and greatly exceeds in quantity the importance of the issue in the daily operation of the torts process. But there is much about proximate cause that is intellectually fascinating, and study of the various approaches to this issue serves to illuminate the policies which underlie both the substance and the process

143. Case 1: Hartsock v. Forsgren, 236 Ark. 167, 365 S.W.2d 117 (1963); Case 2: Brown v. Channel Fueling Serv., Inc., 574 F. Supp. 666 (E.D. La. 1983).

144. Case 3: Glasgow Realty Co. v. Metcalfe, 482 S.W.2d 750 (Ky. 1972).

145. "There is perhaps nothing in the entire field of law which has called forth more disagreement, or upon which the opinions are in such a welter of confusion. Nor, despite the manifold attempts which have been made to clarify the subject, is there yet any general agreement as to the proper approach." Prosser and Keeton, The Law of Torts 263 (5th ed. 1984). The authors cite one book and 25 law review articles as attempting to clarify the confusion. The titles of some of the articles indicate what may be unwarranted optimism by their authors—e.g., Carpenter, Workable Rules for Determining Proximate Cause, 20 Calif. L. Rev. 229 (1932); Myers, Causation and Common Sense, 5 Miami L.Q. 238 (1951). A more recent article evincing much more pessimism about proximate cause is Kelley, Proximate Cause in Negligence Law: History, Theory and the Present Darkness, 69 Wash. U. L.Q. 49 (1991). The author concludes his survey and analysis with:

> And so we go round and round, locked in a relentless rivalry between the normative and descriptive poles of a single fallacious theory in which the real proximate cause question cannot be asked.

Id. at 105. Proximate cause, like almost every other aspect of tort law, has been the object of economic analysis. See, e.g., Grady Proximate Cause and the Law of Negligence, 69 Iowa L. Rev. 363 (1984); Landes and Posner, Causation in Tort Law: An Economic Approach, 12 J. Legal Stud. 109 (1983); Rizzo and Arnold, Causal Apportionment in the Law of Torts: An Economic Theory, 80 Colum. L. Rev. 1399 (1980); Shavell, An Analysis of Causation and the Scope of Liability in the Law of Torts, 9 J. Legal Stud. 463 (1980).

of tort law. In this section, we examine a number of the various formulations of the rules of proximate cause.

a. Liability Limited to Foreseeable Consequences

One of the predominating approaches to the proximate cause issue is that of foreseeability, under which the defendant is liable for the foreseeable, but not the unforeseeable, consequences of negligent conduct. This formulation requires an evaluation of the defendant's negligence in terms of the harm that would have been foreseeable to the reasonably prudent person at the time the defendant acted. If the actual consequences of the defendant's conduct fall within the scope of the preliminarily defined risks, the proximate cause requirement is satisfied. If the consequences fall outside the risks, proximate cause is missing, and the defendant is not liable.[146] The foreseeability of the consequences of the defendant's negligent conduct may refer either to the foreseeability of the particular way in which the plaintiff was injured, or to the foreseeability of the plaintiff as a potential victim of the defendant's negligent conduct. We shall deal with each of these—foreseeable results and foreseeable plaintiffs—in the subsections that follow.

Before examining the foreseeability approach in some detail, certain points should be kept in mind: First, if the defendant negligently injures the plaintiff, the defendant is liable even if the *extent* of the plaintiff's injuries was unforeseeable. This *eggshell skull* or *thin skull* rule is illustrated in the context of a battery case in Vosburg v. Putney, p. 12, above. Thus, the defendant is liable if the plaintiff has an unforeseeable eggshell leg, as in *Vosburg,* or an eggshell earning capability, as in Grayson v. Irvmar Realty Corp., p. 695, below, or even an eggshell psyche. See Lockwood v. McCaskill, 262 N.C. 663, 138 S.E.2d 541 (1964), in which the plaintiff—"an insecure person . . . a perfectionist . . . a worrisome individual"—recovered for amnesia traceable to the defendant's negligent operation of an automobile. It has been suggested that this rule is applicable only in personal injury cases and not in property damage cases. Green, Foreseeability in Negligence Law, 61 Colum. L. Rev. 1401, 1405-1409 (1961). As an example of nonliability, Green postulates a case in which the defendant has negligently started a fire which destroys the plaintiff's cottage. The defendant would not be liable for the destruction of the original manuscript of Shakespeare's Hamlet which was stored in the cottage.

Second, the foreseeability approach will result in most proximate cause issues being resolved by the trier of fact, subject to the usual screening as to the sufficiency of the evidence. What the reasonable person would have foreseen as flowing from the defendant's negligent conduct is open-ended

146. The best and clearest explication of this approach is Keeton, Legal Cause in the Law of Torts (1963).

and general and in this regard is very much like the threshold issue of the defendant's negligence. Like that issue, it calls in most cases for resolution by the fact-finding process.

Third, the proximate cause issue is different from the negligence issue, even though both involve notions of foreseeability. The Supreme Court of Florida explained the distinction in McCain v. Florida Power Corp., 593 So. 2d 500, 502 (1992):

> The duty element of negligence focuses on whether the defendant's conduct foreseeably created a broader "zone of risk" that poses a general threat of harm to others. . . . The proximate causation element, on the other hand, is concerned with whether and to what extent the defendant's conduct foreseeably and substantially caused the specific injury that actually occurred.[147]

And finally, in many cases the resolution of the proximate cause issue will depend on the degree of particularity with which the judge or jury defines the reasonably foreseeable consequences. The more general the description, the more likely will be the conclusion that the actual consequences were foreseeable. For example, in Hines v. Morrow, 236 S.W. 183 (Tex. Civ. App. 1921) the defendant negligently permitted a railroad crossing to become full of pot holes. A car became bogged down in the mud at the crossing. The plaintiff, who had one wooden leg, went to the crossing to assist in removing the car. A truck was brought up, and the plaintiff went between the car and the truck to tie a rope to each. When the truck started to back up, the plaintiff attempted to step out from between the two vehicles, but was unable to do so because his wooden leg became stuck in a mud hole. A coil from the tow rope caught the plaintiff's good leg, which was injured so severely that it had to be amputated below the knee. The defendant appealed, unsuccessfully, from a judgment for the plaintiff at the trial, arguing that the condition of the crossing was not the proximate cause of the plaintiff's injury. As Professor Morris has pointed out, had the court focused on the details of the events, the defendant might have prevailed. Morris, Proximate Cause in Minnesota, 34 Minn. L. Rev. 185, 193 (1950). Instead the court adopted the plaintiff's description of the facts: "The case, stated in its briefest form, is simply this: [Plaintiff] was on the highway, using it in a lawful manner, and slipped into this hole, created by [defendant's] negligence, and was injured in undertaking to extricate himself. . . . [To the defendant's argument that it] could not reasonably have been foreseen

147. The similarity between the negligence and proximate cause issues sometimes leads to confusing judicial opinions. See, e.g., Keck v. American Employment Agency, Inc., 279 Ark. 294, 652 S.W.2d 2 (1983), in which the court stated (279 Ark. at 300, 652 S.W.2d at 5), "A decision that the defendant's . . . conduct is not the 'proximate cause' of the result means only that he has not been negligent at all, or that his negligence, if any, does not cover such a risk." And Professor Green once referred to the proximate cause foreseeability issue as a "crude duplication of the negligence issue." See Green, The Causal Relation Issue in Negligence Law, 60 Mich. L. Rev. 543, 562 & n.53 (1962).

that slipping into this hole would have caused the [plaintiff] to have become entangled in a rope, and the moving truck, with such dire results, [the] answer is plain: The exact consequences do not have to be foreseen." 236 S.W. at 187-188.

(1) Foreseeable Outcomes

Marshall v. Nugent

222 F.2d 604 (1st Cir. 1955)

[Plaintiff Marshall was a passenger in an automobile driven by one Harriman in northern New Hampshire during the winter. The road on which they were driving was covered with hard packed snow and ice. As Harriman approached an uphill curve to his right, an oil truck owned by Socony-Vacuum and driven by Prince approached from the opposite direction, and intruded into Harriman's lane as it rounded the curve. To avoid a collision, Harriman cut to his right and went into a skid, coming to a stop completely off of and at right angles to the road. Neither Harriman nor plaintiff was hurt. Prince stopped his truck on the road, blocking his lane of traffic. He offered to help Harriman pull his car back onto the road, and suggested that someone ought to go back up the hill to warn oncoming traffic of the danger in the road. Plaintiff volunteered, and started walking up the hill. After he had walked about seventy-five feet, an automobile driven by Nugent came around the curve and over the hill. Nugent turned to his left to avoid hitting the truck, went into a skid and hit plaintiff.]

MAGRUDER, C.J. . . . Marshall filed his complaint in the court below against both Socony-Vacuum Oil Co., Inc., and Nugent, charging them as joint tortfeasors, each legally responsible for the plaintiff's personal injuries. . . . After a rather lengthy trial, the jury reported a verdict in favor of Marshall as against Socony in the sum of $25,000, and a verdict in favor of the defendant Nugent. The district court entered judgments against Socony and in favor of Nugent in accordance with the verdict.

No. 4867

This is an appeal by Socony from the judgment against it in favor of Marshall. Appellant has presented a great number of points, most of which do not merit extended discussion.

The most seriously pressed contentions are that the district court was in error in refusing Socony's motion for a directed verdict in its favor, made at the close of all the evidence. The motion was based on several grounds, chief of which were . . . (2) that if Socony's servant Prince were found to have been negligent in "cutting the corner" on the wrong side of the road, and thus forcing Harriman's car off the highway, Marshall suffered no hurt from this, and such negligent conduct, as a matter of law, was not the proximate cause of Marshall's subsequent injuries when he was run into by Nugent's car. . . .

Coming then to contention (2) above mentioned, this has to do with the doctrine of proximate causation, a doctrine which appellant's arguments tend to make out to be more complex and esoteric than it really is. To say that the situation created by the defendant's culpable acts constituted "merely a condition," not a cause of plaintiff's harm, is to indulge in mere verbiage, which does not solve the question at issue, but is simply a way of stating the conclusion, arrived at from other considerations, that the causal relation between the defendant's act and the plaintiff's injury is not strong enough to warrant holding the defendant legally responsible for the injury.

The adjective "proximate," as commonly used in this connection, is perhaps misleading, since to establish liability it is not necessarily true that the defendant's culpable act must be shown to have been the next or immediate cause of the plaintiff's injury. In many familiar instances, the defendant's act may be more remote in the chain of events; and the plaintiff's injury may more immediately have been caused by an intervening force of nature, or an intervening act of a third person whether culpable or not, or even an act by the plaintiff bringing himself in contact with the dangerous situation resulting from the defendant's negligence. . . .

Back of the requirement that the defendant's culpable act must have been a proximate cause of the plaintiff's harm is no doubt the widespread conviction that it would be disproportionately burdensome to hold a culpable actor potentially liable for all the injurious consequences that may flow from his act, i.e., that would not have been inflicted "but for" the occurrence of the act. This is especially so where the injurious consequence was the result of negligence merely. And so, speaking in general terms, the effort of the courts has been, in the development of this doctrine of proximate causation, to confine the liability of a negligent actor to those harmful consequences which result from the operation of the risk, or of a risk, the foreseeability of which rendered the defendant's conduct negligent.

Of course, putting the inquiry in these terms does not furnish a formula which automatically decides each of an infinite variety of cases. Flexibility is still preserved by the further need of defining the risk, or risks, either narrowly, or more broadly, as seems appropriate and just in the special type of case.

Regarding motor vehicle accidents in particular, one should contemplate a variety of risks which are created by negligent driving. There may be injuries resulting from a direct collision between the carelessly driven car and another vehicle. But such direct collision may be avoided, yet the plaintiff may fall and injure himself in frantically racing out of the way of the errant car. Or the plaintiff may be knocked down and injured by a human stampede as the car rushes toward a crowded safety zone. Or the plaintiff may faint from intense excitement stimulated by the near collision, and in falling sustain a fractured skull. Or the plaintiff may suffer a miscarriage or other physical illness as a result of intense nervous shock incident to a hair-raising escape. This bundle of risks could be enlarged indefinitely with a little imagination. In a traffic mix-up due to negligence, before the disturbed waters have become placid and normal again, the unfolding of events between the culpable act and the plaintiff's eventual injury may be bizarre indeed; yet the defendant may be liable for the result. In such a situation, it would be impossible for a person in the defendant's position to predict in advance just how his negligent act would work out to another's injury. Yet this in itself is no bar to recovery.

When an issue of proximate cause arises in a borderline case, as not infrequently happens, we leave it to the jury with appropriate instructions. We do this because it is deemed wise to obtain the judgment of the jury, reflecting as it does the earthy viewpoint of the common man—the prevalent sense of the community—as to whether the causal relation between the negligent act and the plaintiff's harm which in fact was a consequence of the tortious act is sufficiently close to make it just and expedient to hold the defendant answerable in damages. That is what the courts have in mind when they say the question of proximate causation is one of fact for the jury. It is similar to the issue of negligence, which is left to the jury as an issue of fact. Even where on the evidence the facts are undisputed, if fairminded men might honestly and reasonably draw contrary inferences as to whether the facts do or do not establish negligence, the court leaves such issue to the determination of the jury, who are required to decide as a matter of common-sense judgment, whether the defendant's course of conduct subjected others to a reasonable or unreasonable risk, i.e., whether under all the circumstances the defendant ought to be recognized as privileged to do the act in question or to pursue his course of conduct with immunity from liability for harm to others which might result.

In dealing with these issues of negligence and proximate causation, the trial judge has to make a preliminary decision whether the issues are such that reasonable men might differ on the inferences to be drawn. This preliminary decision is said to be a question of law, for it is one which the court has to decide, but it is nevertheless necessarily the exercise of a judgment on the facts, just as an appellate court may have to exercise a judgment on the facts, in reviewing whether the trial judge should or should not have left the issue to the jury.

Exercising that judgment on the facts in the case at bar, we have to conclude that the district court committed no error in refusing to direct a verdict for the defendant Socony on the issue of proximate cause. . . .

. . . Plaintiff Marshall was a passenger in the oncoming Chevrolet car, and thus was one of the persons whose bodily safety was primarily endangered by the negligence of Prince, as might have been found by the jury, in "cutting the corner" with the Socony truck in the circumstances above related. In that view, Prince's negligence constituted an irretrievable breach of duty to the plaintiff. Though this particular act of negligence was over and done with when the truck pulled up alongside of the stalled Chevrolet without having actually collided with it, still the consequences of such past negligence were in the bosom of time, as yet unrevealed.

If the Chevrolet had been pulled back onto the highway, and Harriman and Marshall, having got in it again, had resumed their journey and had had a collision with another car five miles down the road, in which Marshall suffered bodily injuries, it could truly be said that such subsequent injury to Marshall was a consequence in fact of the earlier delay caused by the defendant's negligence, in the sense that but for such delay the Chevrolet car would not have been at the fatal intersection at the moment the other car ran into it. But on such assumed state of facts, the courts would no doubt conclude, "as a matter of law," that Prince's earlier negligence in cutting the corner was not the "proximate cause" of this later injury received by the plaintiff. That would be because the extra risks to which such negligence by Prince had subjected the passengers in the Chevrolet car were obviously entirely over; the situation had been stabilized and become normal, and, so far as one could foresee, whatever subsequent risks the Chevrolet might have to encounter in its resumed journey were simply the inseparable risks, no more and no less, that were incident to the Chevrolet's being out on the highway at all. But in the case at bar, the circumstances under which Marshall received the personal injuries complained of presented no such clear-cut situation.

As we have indicated, the extra risks created by Prince's negligence were not all over at the moment the primary risk of collision between the truck and the Chevrolet was successfully surmounted. Many cases have held a defendant, whose negligence caused a traffic tie-up, legally liable for subsequent property damage or personal injuries more immediately caused by an oncoming motorist. This would particularly be so where, as in the present case, the negligent traffic tie-up and delay occurred in a dangerous blind spot, and where the occupants of the stalled Chevrolet, having got out onto the highway to assist in the operation of getting the Chevrolet going again, were necessarily subject to risks of injury from cars in the stream of northbound traffic coming over the crest of the hill. It is true, the Chevrolet car was not owned by the plaintiff Marshall, and no doubt, without violating any legal duty to Harriman, Marshall could have crawled up onto the snowbank at the side of the road out of harm's way and awaited there, passive and inert, until his journey was resumed. But the plaintiff, who as a passenger in the Chevrolet car had already been subjected to a collision risk by the negligent operation of the Socony truck, could reasonably be expected to get out onto the highway and lend a hand to his host in getting the Chevrolet started again, especially as Marshall himself had an interest in facilitating the resumption of the journey in order to keep his business appointment in North Stratford. Marshall was therefore certainly not an "officious intermeddler," and whether or not he was barred by contributory negligence in what he did was a question for the jury, as we have already held. The injury Marshall received by being struck by the Nugent car was not remote, either in time or place, from the negligent conduct of defendant Socony's servant, and it occurred while the traffic mix-up occasioned by defendant's negligence was still persisting, not after the traffic flow had become normal again. In the circumstances presented we conclude that the district court committed no error in leaving the issue of proximate cause to the jury for determination.

Of course, the essential notion of what is meant by "proximate cause" may be expressed to the jury in a variety of ways. We are satisfied in the present case that the charge to the jury accurately enough acquainted them with the nature of the factual judgment they were called upon to exercise in their determination of the issue of proximate cause. . . .

No. 4866

This is an appeal by plaintiff Marshall from the judgment entered in favor of codefendant Nugent pursuant to the jury verdict.

We find no substantial or prejudicial error at the trial which would necessitate our overturning of the verdict in favor of Nugent. . . .

In Socony-Vacuum Oil Co., Inc. v. Marshall, No. 4867, the judgment of the District Court is affirmed.

In Marshall v. Nugent, No. 4866, the judgment of the District Court is affirmed.

In *Marshall,* Judge Magruder posited a hypothetical in which the car in which the plaintiff was riding got back onto the highway, and was involved in an accident, injuring the plaintiff, some miles down the road. Although, according to Magruder, the negligence of the defendant would have caused the later injury to the plaintiff, it would not have been the proximate cause of the injury; the extra risks involved in forcing the automobile off the road would have been over. This type of fact pattern was presented in two Texas cases. In Texas & Pacific Ry. v. McCleery, 418 S.W.2d 494 (Tex. 1967), the plaintiff was injured when the truck in which he was a passenger collided with a train owned and operated by the defendant. The train had exceeded the speed limit, and one of the arguments of the plaintiff was that if the train had not been speeding, the truck would have gotten to the intersection ahead of the train and passed over it without incident. In the other case, Lear Siegler, Inc. v. Perez, 819 S.W.2d 470 (Tex. 1991), the decedent's job was to pull a truck with a flashing arrow sign, manufactured by the defendant, to alert drivers of sweeping operations on the road. The plaintiff alleged that the sign malfunctioned, and when the decedent got out to fix it, he was fatally injured when one Lerma, who had fallen asleep, drove into the sign. In the wrongful death action, the plaintiff argued that if the sign had not malfunctioned, the decedent would not have been in a position to be injured by Lerma's oncoming car. The Supreme Court of Texas rejected the plaintiffs' arguments in both cases, ruling that in neither could it be found that the defendant's negligence caused the harm. Did the court get both cases right? In *Perez,* the court stated (819 S.W.2d at 472):

> It is undisputed that Lerma was asleep, and proper operation of the flashing arrow sign would have had no effect on his conduct. Plaintiffs assert that, had the sign functioned properly, Perez would not have been at the place where the collision occurred at the time it occurred. We conclude that these particular circumstances are too remotely connected with Lear Siegler's conduct to constitute legal cause. If Perez had instead taken the sign back to the highway department office where the roof caved in on him, we likewise would not regard it as a legal cause.

Watson v. Kentucky & Ind. Bridge & Ry.

137 Ky. 619, 126 S.W. 146 (1910)

[Plaintiff alleged that he was injured by the explosion of gasoline that escaped from a railroad tank car which had been derailed as a result of the defendants' negligence. The gasoline flowed into a street, filling gutters and standing in pools. Charles Duerr threw a match into a pool of gasoline, causing the explosion which injured the plaintiff. The evidence as to why Duerr threw the match into the gasoline was conflicting. Duerr's story was that he had lighted a cigar and threw the match away, unaware of the presence of the gasoline. There was other evidence that he had deliberately thrown the match into the gasoline to ignite it. The plaintiff's position was that the several defendants (of which Duerr was not one) were liable for the plaintiff's injuries, notwithstanding the act of Duerr. The trial judge granted the defendant's motion for a directed verdict at the close of the evidence, and this appeal is by the plaintiff from the judgment for defendants.]

SETTLE, J. . . . The lighting of the match by Duerr having resulted in the explosion, the question is, was that act merely a contributing cause, or the efficient and, therefore, proximate cause of appellant's injuries? The question of proximate cause is a question for the jury. In holding that Duerr in lighting or throwing the match acted maliciously or with intent to cause the explosion, the trial court invaded the province of the jury. There was, it is true, evidence tending to prove that the act was wanton or malicious, but also evidence conducing to prove that it was inadvertently or negligently done by Duerr. It was therefore for the jury and not the court to determine from all the evidence whether the lighting of the match was done by Duerr inadvertently or negligently, or whether it was a wanton and malicious act. . . . No better statement of the law of proximate cause can be given than is found in 21 Am. & Eng. Ency. of Law (2d ed.) 490, quoted with approval in Louisville Home Telephone Company v. Gasper, 123 Ky. 128, 93 S.W. 1057, 29 Ky. Law Rep. 578, 9 L.R.A. (N.S.) 548: "It is well settled that the mere fact that there have been intervening causes between the defendant's negligence and the plaintiff's injuries is not sufficient in law to relieve the former from liability; that is to say, the plaintiff's injuries may yet be natural and proximate in law, although between the defendant's negligence and the injuries other causes or conditions, or agencies, may have operated, and, when this is the case, the defendant is liable. So the defendant is clearly responsible where the intervening causes, acts, or conditions were set in motion by his earlier negligence, or naturally induced by such wrongful act or omission, or even, it is generally held, if the intervening acts or conditions were of a nature the happening of which was reasonably to have been anticipated, though they may have been acts of the plaintiff himself. An act or omission may yet be negligent and of a nature to charge a defendant with liability, although no injuries would have been sustained but for some intervening cause, if the occurrence of the latter might have been anticipated. . . . A proximate cause is that cause which naturally led to and which might have been expected to produce the result. . . . The connection of cause and effect must be established. It is also a principle well established that when an injury is caused by two causes concurring to produce the result, for one of which the defendant is responsible, and not for the other, the defendant cannot escape the responsibility. One is liable for an injury caused by the concurring negligence of himself and another to the same extent as for one caused entirely by his own negligence."

If the presence on Madison street in the city of Louisville of the great volume of loose gas that arose from the escaping gasoline was caused by the negligence of the appellee Bridge & Railroad Company, it seems to us that the probable consequences of its coming in contact with fire and causing an explosion was too plain a proposition to admit of doubt. Indeed, it was most probable that someone would strike a match to light a cigar or for other purposes in the midst of the gas. In our opinion, therefore, the act of one lighting and throwing a match under such circumstances cannot be said to be the efficient cause of the explosion. It did not of itself produce the explosion, nor could it have done so without the assistance and contribution resulting from the primary negligence, if there was such negligence, on the part of the appellee Bridge & Railroad Company in furnishing the presence of the gas in the street. This conclusion, however, rests upon the theory that Duerr inadvertently or negligently lighted and threw the match in the gas. . . .

If, however, the act of Duerr in lighting the match and throwing it into the vapor or gas arising from the gasoline was malicious, and done for the purpose of causing the explosion, we do not think appellees would be responsible, for while the appellee Bridge & Railroad Company's negligence may have been the efficient cause of the presence of the gas in the street, and it should have understood enough of the consequences thereof to have foreseen that an explosion was likely to result from the inadvertent or negligent lighting of a match by some person who was ignorant of the presence of the gas or of the effect of lighting or throwing a match in it, it could not have foreseen or deemed it probable that one would maliciously or wantonly do such an act for the evil purpose of producing the explosion. Therefore, if the act of Duerr was malicious, we quite agree with the trial court that it was one which the appellees could not reasonably have anticipated or guarded against, and in such case the act of Duerr, and not the primary negligence of the appellee Bridge & Railroad Company, in any of the particulars charged, was the efficient or proximate cause of appellant's injuries. The mere fact that the concurrent cause or intervening act was unforeseen will not relieve the defendant guilty of the primary negligence from liability, but if the intervening agency is something so unexpected or extraordinary as that he could not or ought not to have anticipated it, he will not be liable and certainly he is not bound to anticipate the criminal acts of others by which damage is inflicted, and hence is not liable therefor. . . .

For the reasons indicated, the judgment is . . . reversed as to the Bridge & Railroad Company, and cause remanded for a new trial consistent with the opinion.

An intervening force that contributes to the plaintiff's injury does not necessarily insulate the defendant from liability, as *Watson* makes clear. Although the court in *Watson* did rule that if Duerr's conduct in igniting the pool of gasoline were done intentionally the defendant would escape liability, intervening intentional, even criminal, conduct will not always have that effect. In Kush v. City of Buffalo, 59 N.Y.2d 26, 449 N.E.2d 725 (1983), the plaintiff was injured by chemicals which she claimed were negligently stored by the defendant, and which were stolen by two 15-year-olds. In affirming a judgment for the plaintiff, the court stated (59 N.Y.2d at 33, 449 N.E.2d at 729):

> Defendant argues that the student employees' stealing of the chemicals was an intentional act and, hence, a superseding cause of plaintiff's injury, relieving it of liability. Defendant is correct that an intervening intentional or criminal act will generally sever the liability of the original tort-feasor, but, on the facts here, it may not rely on this doctrine.
>
> That doctrine has no application when the intentional or criminal intervention of a third party or parties is reasonably foreseeable. Defendant's duty was to take reasonable steps to secure the dangerous chemicals from unsupervised access by children. By its very definition, any breach of this duty that leads

> to injury will involve an intentional, unauthorized taking of chemicals by a child. When the intervening, intentional act of another is itself the foreseeable harm that shapes the duty imposed, the defendant who fails to guard against such conduct will not be relieved of liability when that act occurs.

An issue that arises fairly frequently is whether a negligent defendant who causes injury to another will be held liable for the harm that subsequently results from an accident that occurs in the course of the plaintiff's treatment for his original injuries. Courts in this country have traditionally included a rather broad range of such subsequent accidental injuries within the scope of the risks for which the original tortfeasor will be held liable. See generally Restatement (Second) of Torts §457, Comments *a-c,* Illustrations 1-3 (1965). In Atherton v. Devine, 602 P.2d 634 (Okla. 1979), the defendant was held liable for further injuries suffered by the plaintiff when the ambulance taking the plaintiff to the hospital for treatment after the collision with the defendant was itself involved in a collision. And in Weber v. Charity Hosp. 475 So. 2d 1047 (La. 1985), the plaintiff contracted hepatitis from blood transfusions necessitated by the injuries she received in an automobile accident. The negligent driver who caused the accident was held liable for the hepatitis as well as for the initial injuries.

Should the defendant ever be liable in a wrongful death action if the decedent committed suicide as a consequence of the defendant's negligence? Perhaps the strongest case can be made against health care providers, who might be expected to anticipate and guard against suicide of patients. The cases generally reflect this attitude. See, e.g., Tabor v. Doctors Memorial Hospital, 563 So. 2d 233 (La. 1990). Lawyers sued for malpractice have had greater success in keeping suicide cases from the jury. See, e.g., Snyder v. Baumecker, 708 F. Supp. 1451 (D.N.J. 1989), and McPeake v. Cannon, 553 A.2d 439 (Pa. Super. 1989), both involving alleged negligence in defending criminal cases. In the latter case, the court stated (Id. at 443):

> Because an attorney does not possess the ability either to perceive that a client is likely to commit suicide, or to prevent the suicide, we will not impose liability upon him for failing to prevent a harm that is not a foreseeable result of prior negligent conduct.

One of the more unusual suicide cases, not involving a health care provider or a lawyer, is Zygmaniak v. Kawasaki Motors Corp., 330 A.2d 56 (N.J. Super. 1975), *appeal dismissed,* 68 N.J. 93, 343 A.2d 97 (1975), in which a motorcyclist who had been severely injured in an accident allegedly caused by a defect in his motorcycle manufactured by the defendant was shotgunned to death by his brother at his own request. Given that the macabre request was prompted by the injuries suffered at the hands of the defendant, the court held that the issue of proximate cause was for the jury.

Problem 20

You are clerk to Judge Robert Cohen of the United States Court of Appeals for the circuit in which your state is located, that has before it for decision the appeal of the defendant in Barnett v. Clinton Lumber Co. Clinton Lumber has appealed from decisions of the district judge refusing to grant its motion for a directed verdict and refusing to give certain instructions to the jury. Judge Cohen wants a memorandum concerning the correctness of these decisions.

The following is from the plaintiff's brief. (The jurisdictional statement and references to the record have been omitted.)

STATEMENT OF THE CASE

This is an action for negligence brought by the plaintiff, Gordon Barnett, against the defendant, Clinton Lumber Co., for personal injuries arising out of an accident on Route 102 in Clinton. Trial was held which resulted in a jury verdict for plaintiff in the amount of $53,528.28. Judgment was entered on the verdict.

STATEMENT OF FACTS

There is little dispute as to the facts of this case. The accident giving rise to plaintiff's claim for damages occurred on Route 102 in Clinton at a point 682 feet south of the intersection with Messenger Road. Route 102, at the portions relevant to this case, is a two-lane highway, the traveled portion of which is 45 feet wide. The posted speed limit is 45 miles an hour.

Just prior to the accident plaintiff was proceeding alone in his automobile at about 40 miles an hour in a northerly direction on Route 102. A truck owned by defendant and being operated by its employee, William Mosely, was traveling in a southerly direction at a speed estimated by different witnesses from 40 to 50 miles an hour. The truck was loaded with logs 12 feet in length. The logs were not secured to the truck by means of a rope or chain.

As the defendant's truck approached the automobile driven by plaintiff, several logs fell from the truck and into plaintiff's path. Plaintiff immediately applied the brakes, but was unable to stop in time to avoid colliding with four of the logs. Plaintiff's automobile came to a stop near the easterly edge of the traveled portion of Route 102, and substantially blocking the east lane. There was extensive damage to the front end of plaintiff's automobile, which resulted in both front fenders being crumpled tightly against the front wheels, preventing plaintiff from immediately driving his automobile off the road. It was apparent that it would take some time to remove plaintiff's automobile so that it would not block traffic.

Route 102 curves to the west 280 feet south of the point of the accident. Barry Cook, a passenger in defendant's truck, walked to the curve to warn oncoming traffic of the hazard in the road. Plaintiff and Mosely then worked to pull the fenders back so plaintiff's automobile could be moved. This done, they discovered that the automobile could not be started, so plaintiff and Mosely attempted to push it off the road. While trying to push the automobile off the road, an automobile driven by Harold Craig came around the curve to the south of the accident at a great rate of speed, estimated by Cook to be at least 70 miles an hour. Craig ignored Cook's waves to slow down, and did not apply his brakes until he was 98 feet from where plaintiff and Mosely were trying to push plaintiff's automobile from the road, as indicated by the brake marks left by the Craig automobile. Upon hearing the squealing of Craig's brakes, plaintiff looked back and immediately jumped to the side of the road. Craig's automobile hit plaintiff's, and spun to the right and hit plaintiff, causing the injuries complained of in this suit.

Craig had been drinking heavily at his home for about two hours until he left his home about a half an hour before the accident. A blood test taken less than an hour after the accident showed an alcohol content in Craig's blood of .16 percent. Under General Laws, ch. 86, §27, one who has a blood alcohol content of .10 percent or more is presumed to be under the influence of intoxicating liquor.

STATEMENT OF THE ISSUES

The issues presented on this appeal are whether:

1. The district court properly refused to grant defendant's motion for a directed verdict at the close of the evidence.

2. The district court correctly charged the jury on the issue of proximate cause.

The statements of the facts and issues in the defendant's brief are somewhat different from those in the plaintiff's brief in that they are phrased more favorably to the defendant. But because there is no real dispute as to the primary facts, in essence these statements are the same in both briefs.

The defendant's motion for a directed verdict is as follows:

United States District Court

Gordon Barnett, Plaintiff
v. No. 5,738
Clinton Lumber Co., Defendant

Defendant's Motion for a Directed Verdict

Comes now the defendant in the above entitled action and moves that the Court direct a verdict for defendant on the grounds that as a matter of law any injuries of plaintiff were not the proximate result of the negligence of defendant, if any.

/s/Stanley Winthrop
Attorney for Defendant

The requests for instructions, and the judge's charge to the jury, insofar as relevant to the appeal, are as follows:

PLAINTIFF'S REQUEST FOR INSTRUCTIONS

8. The defendant is responsible for plaintiff's injuries if the negligence of defendant was the proximate cause of those injuries. The negligence of defendant is a proximate cause of the injuries if the negligence was a substantial factor in producing those injuries. The negligence is a substantial factor in producing the injuries if plaintiff would not have been injured if defendant had not been negligent.

9. The fact that the negligence of some third party also helped to cause the plaintiff's injuries does not excuse the responsibility of defendant. If the negligence of defendant created a situation whereby plaintiff was exposed to harm from the wrongful conduct of a third person, defendant's negligence is the proximate cause of the harm that results from the situation.

10. If the defendant's negligence placed plaintiff in a position of increased danger, it is not necessary that defendant foresee the exact way by which the plaintiff was injured. It is enough that the wrongful conduct of a third person is of the same general kind as should have been foreseen by defendant.

DEFENDANT'S REQUEST FOR INSTRUCTIONS

13. Defendant is responsible for plaintiff's injuries only if its negligence is the proximate cause of those injuries.

14. Defendant's negligence may be a condition or circumstance of plaintiff's injuries, but it is not the proximate cause of those injuries if the independent wrongful act of a third person intervenes and causes the injuries. Defendant is responsible only for the consequences of his own acts, and not for the independent, intervening wrongful conduct of another.

15. If you find that the conduct of the third party in this case, Harold Craig, amounted to gross negligence or willful and wanton misconduct, you will return a verdict for defendant.

16. Notwithstanding the negligence of defendant, if you find that defendant exercised reasonable care to alleviate the effects of that negligence, and some intervening and independent negligence nonetheless caused harm to the plaintiff, the original negligence of the defendant is not the proximate cause of those injuries. In this case, should you find that the stationing of Barry Cook as a road guard was reasonably designed to prevent further injury to the plaintiff, you will return your verdict for defendant.

17. Notwithstanding the negligence of the defendant, if you find that by the time the plaintiff was injured, the risk created originally by any negligence of the defendant had terminated and that it was unforeseeable that a person operating under the influence of alcohol would drive at 70 miles an hour and ignore the warning of the road guard posted by the defendant, you will return your verdict for the defendant.

THE DISTRICT COURT'S CHARGE TO THE JURY

If you find that the driver of the defendant's truck was negligent, and that negligence caused plaintiff's car to block the road, then you have to consider the principle of the chain of causation.

You are instructed that in many cases, after an act of negligence has occurred, another force may intervene and become the sole proximate cause of the accident; in such an event, if you find such to be the fact in the present case, there could be no recovery against the defendant.

On the other hand, it is the law that whoever does an unlawful act is answerable for all the consequences that may ensue in the ordinary course of events, even though such consequences are brought about by an intervening cause. If, in fact, such intervening cause was set in motion or made probable by the act of the original wrongdoer, and if the consequences are such as might with reasonable diligence be foreseen, the test is whether or not there was an unbroken connection between the wrongful act and the injury. Did the acts constitute a succession of events so linked together as to make a natural whole, or was there some other new, independent cause intervening between the wrong and the injury?

You are instructed that the driver of the truck which is negligently operated by him in such a manner as to place others in a position where they are struck and injured by an automobile operated by a third person may be held liable therefor, where it is established that such negligence was the proximate cause of the resulting injuries. The fact that the driver of a third car was also negligent is not a defense, provided it is established by the evidence that both drivers were negligent, and that their concurrent negligence was the proximate cause of the resulting injury. It is, of course, essential to a recovery against the first wrongdoer that it be established by the evidence that there was a causal connection between his negligent conduct and the final resulting injury. The ultimate test is whether it appears from all the evidence that the negligence of the first wrongdoer was such that it could have been properly said that it could have been the proximate cause of the later injury; in other words, whether in all the circumstances surrounding the situation he ought reasonably to have foreseen that the later consequences might occur as a result of his negligence.

In negligence cases, the law recognizes that there may be more than one proximate cause of the same injury, and where a chain of events has once been started, due to the negligence of the driver of an automobile, he may be liable for all the mishaps which are, in fact, the proximate results of his unlawful conduct.

The chain of causation is not broken by an intervening act, even if wrongful, which is a normal reaction to the stimulus of a situation created by negligence.

In preparing the memorandum for Judge Cohen, you are to assume that Watson v. Kentucky & Indiana Bridge & Ry. is an opinion of your state's supreme court, and that Marshall v. Nugent is an opinion of the United States Court of Appeals for the circuit in which your state is located. Under the circumstances of this case, the substantive law of negligence to be determined and applied is that of your state. Because of this, the opinion in *Marshall* does not have the binding effect of an opinion of your state's supreme court, but it is an authoritative interpretation of your state's law at the time the opinion was written.

It will be recalled from an earlier section of this chapter that violations of criminal safety statutes may give rise to causes of action in negligence. The next decision illustrates the proximate cause issues that such cases may present.

Gorris v. Scott

[1874] 9. L.R. (Exch.) 125

KELLY, C.B. This is an action to recover damages for the loss of a number of sheep which the defendant, a shipowner, had contracted to carry, and which were washed overboard and lost by reason (as we must take it to be truly alleged) of the neglect to comply with a certain order made by the Privy Council, in pursuance of the Contagious Diseases (Animals) Act, 1869. The Act was passed merely for sanitary purposes, in order to prevent animals in a state of infectious disease from communicating it to other animals with which they might come in contact. Under the authority of that Act, certain orders were made; amongst others, an order by which any ship bringing sheep or cattle from any foreign port to ports in Great Britain is to have the place occupied by such animals divided into pens of certain dimensions, and the floor of such pens furnished with battens or foot-holds. The object of this order is to prevent animals from being overcrowded, and so brought into a condition in which the disease guarded against would be likely to be developed. This regulation has been neglected, and the question is, whether the loss, which we must assume to have been caused by that neglect, entitles the plaintiffs to maintain an action.

. . . And if we could see that it was the object, or among the objects of this Act, that the owners of sheep and cattle coming from a foreign port should be protected by the means described against the danger of their property being washed overboard, or lost by the perils of the sea, the present action would be within the principle.

But, looking at the Act, it is perfectly clear that its provisions were all enacted with a totally different view; there was no purpose, direct or indirect, to protect against such damage; but, as is recited in the preamble, the Act is directed against the possibility of sheep or cattle being exposed to disease on their way to this country. The preamble recites that "it is expedient to confer on Her Majesty's most honourable Privy Council power to take such measures as may appear from time to time necessary to prevent the introduction into Great Britain of contagious or infectious diseases among cattle, sheep, or other animals, by prohibiting or regulating the importation of foreign animals," and also to provide against the "spreading" of such diseases in Great Britain. Then follow numerous sections directed entirely to this object. Then comes s. 75, which enacts that "the Privy Council may from time to time make such orders as they think expedient for all or any of the following purposes." What, then, are these purposes? They are "for securing for animals brought by sea to ports in Great Britain a proper supply of food and water during the passage and on landing," "for protecting such animals from unnecessary suffering during the passage and on landing," and so forth; all the purposes enumerated being calculated and directed to the prevention of disease, and none of them having any relation whatever to the danger of loss by the perils of the sea. That being so, if by reason of the default in question the plaintiffs' sheep had been overcrowded, or had been caused unnecessary suffering, and so had arrived in this country in a state of disease, I do not say that they might not have maintained this action. But the damage complained of here is something totally apart from the object of the Act of Parliament, and it is in accordance with all the authorities to say that the action is not maintainable.

In Morales v. City of New York, 70 N.Y.2d 981, 984, 521 N.E.2d 425, 426 (1988), a gasoline station attendant sold gasoline in plastic milk containers to a person who used the gasoline to burn a building. Actions for personal injury and wrongful death were brought against the station for negligence based on its violation of a statute that made illegal the sale gasoline in unapproved containers; plastic milk containers were not of a type approved by the statute. In upholding the summary judgment for the station, the court stated (70 N.Y. at 984, 521 N.E.2d at 426):

> In the case now before us the requirement that gasoline be sold or delivered only in approved containers bears no relationship to arson. It may be, as the plaintiffs contend, that the harm might not have occurred had the . . . attendant refused to sell the gasoline in an unapproved container because the arsonists may have been unable to obtain one at that hour of the night. However, that fact does not establish the requisite legal connection between the statutory violation and the injuries. The statute was obviously designed to make transport and storage of gas safe by preventing accidental leakage or explosion, not to make it more difficult to buy untanked gasoline at night. Thus, assuming there was a violation by these defendants, it was a mere technical one bearing no practical or reasonable causal connection to the injury sustained.

Statutes requiring automobile operators to remove the keys or otherwise lock unattended automobiles have also generated considerable litigation when the unlocked automobile has been stolen and involved in an accident.

The violation of such a statute is negligence per se in states that give that effect to statutory violations. See, e.g., Johnson v. Manhattan & Bronx Surface Transit Operating Authority, 71 N.Y.2d 198, 519 N.E.2d 326 (1988); Ross v. Hartman, 139 F.2d 14 (D.C. Cir. 1943), *cert. denied,* 321 U.S. 790 (1944). What sort of proximate cause issues might these cases raise? Should the owner of the unlocked automobile be liable for all injuries caused by accidents involving the automobile until it is recovered? In general, see Peck, An Exercise Based upon Empirical Data: Liability for Harm Caused by Stolen Automobiles, 1969 Wis. L. Rev. 909.

Problem 21

A partner in your law firm has asked you for a memorandum of law on an issue raised in a case she is handling. The firm represents Thomas and Phillip Hagen, brothers who have been joined as defendants in a personal injury action. Both Thomas and Phillip live in Wayland. Thomas is married, with three children, and owns and operates a gasoline service station. Phillip is single and is a draftsman with a local engineering firm.

The complaint in the case was filed by Roger Baptiste in Tyler County Superior Court on January 20 of this year. The plaintiff alleges that on June 24 of last year, while walking through woods on the outskirts of Wayland, he was shot and injured with a 22-caliber rifle negligently fired by Phillip Hagen. The complaint further alleges that the rifle was owned by Thomas Hagen, who was with Phillip at the time and who had moments before the accident loaned the rifle to Phillip for the purpose of shooting at some targets the men had erected. The complaint charges the defendants with knowledge that there might be persons in the vicinity, and their conduct in its particulars is described as negligent. In addition, the plaintiff alleges that at the time of the shooting Phillip Hagen was unlicensed to possess a firearm and could not have obtained a license had he applied for one. The complaint alleges that the conduct of the defendants violated Chapter 36, Sections 1, 2, and 6 of the General Laws (the gun registration statute), and was therefore negligent as a matter of law. The complaint prays judgment of $25,000 against the defendants. The relevant portions of the statute follow.

General Laws, Chapter 36, §§1-3, 6, 9

1. *Registration and licensing.* It shall be unlawful for any person to own a firearm unless the same has been registered in accordance herewith and a license issued to the owner thereof. No license shall be issued to any person (a) who is not of good moral character; (b) who has been convicted anywhere of a felony; or (c) who has ever suffered any mental illness or has been

confined to any hospital or institution, public or private, for mental illness. Nor shall any license be issued to any person under the age of 21 years.

2. *Possession.* It shall be unlawful for any person to possess a firearm which has not been registered in accordance herewith. It shall further be unlawful for any person to possess a firearm who for the reasons stated in §1 hereof is ineligible to receive a license for a firearm.

3. *Applications.* Applications for licenses shall be made to the clerk of the town or city in which the applicant resides, and shall be on a form prepared by the Commissioner of Public Safety. The application shall be on oath, and if the clerk is satisfied that the applicant is qualified, he shall register the firearm in a book kept for the purpose, and shall issue to the applicant a license therefor. . . .

6. *Transfer of ownership or possession.* It shall be unlawful for any person to transfer the ownership or possession of a firearm to any person who for the reasons stated in §1 hereof is ineligible to receive a license for a firearm. . . .

9. *Violations.* Any person who violates any provision of this Act shall be punished by a fine of not exceeding five hundred dollars and imprisonment for not more than six months. . . .

The partner wants your advice as to the effect that the gun registration statute is likely to have in this case. There is no question in her mind that both men violated the statute. The gun was properly registered to Thomas, who had a license. However, Phillip did not have a gun license, nor could he have obtained one because of his conviction 12 years ago, at the age of 20, of the felony of unarmed robbery. As a result of his conviction, he was sentenced to 5 years, and served 14 months, in state prison. Phillip explains that he was associating with "the wrong crowd" at the time, and that he has not been in trouble since.

Assuming that Martin v. Herzog, Tedla v. Ellman, and Brown v. Shyne, pp. 227-237, above, are opinions of your state's supreme court, advise the partner on this issue.

Law and Behavior: Influences on Legislative Decisions

In interpreting statutory language, a court typically looks to what it perceives to be the public purpose for which the statute was enacted. In Ross v. Hartman, for example, the court concluded that the purpose of the ordinance requiring unattended parked motor vehicles to be locked was to protect the public from harm caused by children and thieves. It will be recalled that a very similar approach was taken in Martin v. Herzog, p. 227, above, wherein the court stated that the purpose of the statute requiring lights on motor vehicles being driven after dark was to protect highway travelers. In both cases the courts assumed that the legislatures acted openly in the public interest—they never even mentioned the possibility that the statutes might have been enacted to implement some hidden legislative goal, such as the promotion of the purely private interests of the manufacturers of automobile locks and lights. To be sure, the public purpose behind a statute is not always obvious, and courts have often looked to legislative history for evidence of legislative purpose.[148] However, the sources from which courts will accept such history have tended to be limited to formal statements by legislators, made publicly and for the record,[149] and one may ordinarily assume that such statements will conform in content to the judicial presumption that legislators are influenced exclusively by their views of what constitute sound public policies.[150]

Despite occasional arguments to the contrary,[151] it is almost certain that courts will continue to indulge in the traditional presumption that legislatures act in the public interest. The essence of the judicial task is to do the best job possible with what is available, and even a statute known to be the product of underhanded dealings would, if otherwise valid, be treated by the courts as if it had been enacted in the public interest. Thus, even if the realities of the legislative process were shown to diverge greatly from the traditional judicial assumptions, those realities would not likely affect the lawyer's work in court. It does not follow, however, that those realities, if discoverable, would not be valuable to the legal profession. Lawyers are often called upon to deal in one capacity or another with legislators and the legislative process. Knowledge of how that process works and the factors influencing legislative behavior would be of substantial practical value in that context. Moreover, lawyers generally owe a duty to the public to assume a leadership role in law reform.

148. See generally, Folsom, Legislative History: Research for the Interpretation of Laws 1-41 (1972).

149. Courts will look to the reports of legislative committees to whom the proposed legislation was sent prior to final passage (see, e.g., People v. Ameigh, 95 A.D.2d 367, 467 N.Y.S.2d 718 (1983); amendments during the course of its passage (see, e.g., Industrial Comm. v. Milka, 159 Colo. 114, 410 P.2d 181 (1966); Rossiter v. Whitpain, 404 Pa. 201, 170 A.2d 586 (1961)); and statements regarding the purposes and objectives of the statute, made by its sponsors before the legislature in formal session (see, e.g., Mitchell v. Kentucky Finance Co., 359 U.S. 290 (1959)). However, courts will not accept affidavits of individual legislators expressing their opinions, or recollections, regarding the purposes to be achieved by a particular statute. See, e.g., A-NLV-Cab Co. v. State Taxicab Authority, 108 Nev. 92, 825 P.2d 585 (1992).

150. This commonsense assumption is supported by a project recently undertaken by a law student who mailed questionnaires to the 100 United States Senators asking them for their reasons for voting one way or the other on the antiballistics missile proposal in the Senate. Not surprisingly, out of 51 replies received, no one gave what the author considered to be a "political" explanation. See Rees, ABM; A Study of Legislative Decision-Making, 56 A.B.A.J. 475 (1970). The ease with which a public record can be created has led a number of commentators to argue that the traditional legislative history furnishes an unreliable guide to courts in applying statutes. See, e.g., Giles, The Value of Nonlegislators' Contributions to Legislative History, 79 Geo. L.J. 359 (1990); Stringham, Crystal Gazing: Legislative History in Action, 47 A.B.A.J. 466 (1961); Wasby, Legislative Materials as an Aid to Statutory Construction: A Caveat, 12 J. Pub. L. 262 (1963); Wofford, The Blinding Light: The Uses of History in Constitutional Interpretation, 311 U. Chi. L. Rev. 502 (1964).

151. See, e.g., Byrd, Proof of Negligence in North Carolina, Part II, 48 N.C. L. Rev. 731 (1970).

Increased understanding of the realities of the legislative process would provide insights and impetus for reform.

Since 1940, a great deal of research has been undertaken by social scientists in attempting to discover and measure the influences on legislative decisions.[152] Much of this work has taken the form of studies seeking to establish the demographic characteristics of the memberships of legislatures—that is, who the legislators are, where they came from, and how they got to the legislature.[153] Often, attempts are made to correlate elements in legislators' background with patterns of legislative decisionmaking.[154] Other studies have focused upon the behavior of individual legislators in an effort to discover the extent to which factors such as political parties,[155] constituencies,[156] pressure groups,[157] role conceptions,[158] presidential influence,[159]

152. An excellent bibliography may be found in Jewell and Patterson, The Legislative Process in the United States 537-551 (2d ed. 1973). See also Meller, "Legislative Behavior Research" Revised: A Review of Five Years' Publications, 18 W. Pol. Q. 776 (1965); Smith, Advocacy, Interpretation, and Influence in the United States Congress, 78 Am. Pol. Sci. Rev. 44 (1984); Wahlke, Behavioral Analysis of Representative Bodies, in Essays on Behavioral Study of politics 173-190 (Ramney ed. 1962).

153. See, e.g., Barber, The Lawmakers: Recruitment and Adaptation to Legislative Life (1965); Meyer, Legislative Influences—Toward Theory Development Through Causal-Analysis, 5 Legis. Stud. Q. 563 (1980).

154. See, e.g., Duke and Johnson, Religious Affiliation and Congressional Representation, 31 Journal for the Scientific Study of Religion 324 (1992); Reiselbach, The Demography of the Congressional Vote on Foreign Aid, 1939-1958, 58 Am. Pol. Sci. Rev. 577 (1964); Thielemann, Minority Legislators and Institutional Influence, 29 Soc. Sci. J. 411 (1992).

155. See, e.g, Flinn, Party Responsibility in the States: Some Causal Factors, 58 Am. Pol. Sci. Rev. 60 (1964); MacRae, Roll-Call Votes and Leadership, 20 Pub. Opin. Q. 543 (1956); Ward, The Continuing Search for Party Influence in Congress—A View From the Committees, 18 Legis. Stud. Q. 211 (May, 1993).

156. See, e.g., Erikson, Constituency Opinion and Congressional Behavior: A Reexamination of the Miller-Stokes Representation Data, 22 Am. J. Pol. Sci. 511 (1978); McCubbins and Sullivan, Constituency Influences on Legislative Policy Choice, 18 Quality & Quantity 299 (1984); McDonagh, Constituency Influence on House Roll-Call Votes in the Progressive-Era, 1913-1915, 18 Legis. Stud. Q. 185 (May, 1993).

157. See. e.g., Graddy, Interest Groups or the Public Interest—Why Do We Regulate Health Occupations?, 16 J. Health Pol., Pol. & Law 25 (1991); Navarro, An Analysis of the American Medical Association's Recommendations for Change in the Medical Care Sector of the United States, 21 Intl. J. Health Services 685 (1991); Pierce and Lovrich, Trust in the Technical Information Provided by Interest Groups: The Views of Legislators, Activists, Experts and the General Public, 11 Poly. Stud. J. 626 (1983); Smith, Interpretation, Explanation and Political-Action—Interest Group Influence in the United States Congress, 13 Legis. Stud. Q. 141 (1988).

158. See, e.g., Clapp, The Congressman: His Work as He Sees It (1963); Wahlke, The Legislative System (1962); Portnoy, Membership in the Club: Denizens of the Massachusetts House of Representatives, 6 Harv. J. Legis. 199 (1969).

159. James and Pritchard, Presidential Influence on Congress—The Use and Impact of Favors, 12 Legis. Stud. Q. 167 (1987); Kiewiet and McCubbins, Presidential Influence on Congressional Appropriations Decisions, 32 Am. J. Pol. Sci. 713 (1988); Light, Passing Non-Incremental Policy—Presidential Influence in Congress, Kennedy to Carter, 9 Congress & the Presidency—A Journal on Capital Studies 61 (1982); Mouw and MacKuen, The Strategic Configuration, Personal Influence, and Presidential Power in Congress, 45 W. Pol. Q. 579 (1992); Manley, Presidential Power and White House Lobbying, 93 Pol. Sci. Q. 255 (Summer, 1978).

economics,[160] campaign contributions,[161] and individual personalities,[162] influence the way in which legislators react to particular issues.[163] Much of the data that these studies have relied on have come from intensive personal interviews with legislators and examination of various elements of the legislative record such as official journals, speeches, sponsorship of bills, and the like. Perhaps the most important type of legislative decision to be systematically examined and analyzed is roll-call voting.[164]

Substantively, these studies reveal that the image of the legislator earnestly trying to determine the needs and aspirations of his or her constituents and then voting on the merits of proposed legislation consistently with those needs and aspirations—what one writer has termed the rational-man model of legislative behavior[165]—is inaccurate. It is generally recognized that political party affiliation is an important factor influencing legislative voting behavior, and that a complex system of factors interrelate to determine a legislator's reaction to a given issue.[166] To the idealistically inclined, the picture that emerges from some of these studies is disturbing. The author of a study of the congressional lawmaking process leading up to passage of the Employment Act of 1946 concluded:

> Whether the Employment Act of 1946 was a "good thing" or a "bad thing" is, in the context of this book, beside the point. The real question posed by the story of [its passage] is what it suggests about the Congressional formulation of important social and economic policies in the middle of the twentieth century.

160. Shinn and Van Der Slik, The Plurality of Factors Influencing Policymaking: School Reform Legislation in the American States, 1982-1984, 7 Poly. Stud. Rev. 537 (1988).

161. Welch, Campaign Contributions and Legislative Voting: Milk Money and Dairy Price Supports, 35 W. Pol. Q. 478 (Dec. 1982).

162. See, e.g., Froman, The Importance of Individuality in Voting in Congress, 25 J. Pol. 324 (1963); Greenstein, The Impact of Personality on Politics: An Attempt to Clear Away the Underbrush, 61 Am. Pol. Sci. Rev. 629 (1967).

163. For an enlightening treatment of all these subjects, and others, see Jewell and Patterson, The Legislative Process in the United States (2d ed. 1973).

164. See, e.g., Dyson and Soule, Congressional Committee Behavior on Roll Call Votes: The U.S. House of Representatives, 1955-1964, 14 Midwest J. Pol. Sci. 626 (1970); Mouw and MacKuen, The Strategic Agenda in Legislative Politics, 86 Am. Pol. Sci. Rev. 87 (1992); Brooks and Claggett, Black Electoral Power, White Resistance, and Legislative Behavior, 3 Political Behavior 49 (1981); Entman, The Impact of Ideology on Legislative Behavior and Public Policy in the States, 45 J. Pol. 163 (1983); Fowler and Shaiko, The Grass Roots Connection: Environmental Activists and Senate Roll Calls, 31 Am. J. Pol. Sci. 484 (1987).

165. See Wahlke, Behavioral Analysis of Representative Bodies, in Essays on the Behavioral Study of Politics at 178 (Ranney ed. 1962). Professor Wahlke also describes the social-class-interest model (voting to further the interests of a particular social class or pressure group) and the pressure-politics model (voting in direct response to political pressures without regard to the substance of the proposed legislation), and concludes that none of these oversimplified, but traditionally held, views of legislative behavior are adequate.

166. See, e.g., Jewell and Patterson, The Legislative Process in the United States 443 (2d ed. 1973) Goldman, Issue Voting in the Massachusetts House of Representatives, 1969 L. & Soc. Order (1969); Smith and Sullivan, Factors Influencing Senate Voting Patterns on Social Work Related Legislation, 7 J. Sociology & Social Welfare 857 (1980) (finding a significant correlation between party affiliation and voting).

> Certainly one generalization is that the process is almost unbelievably complex. Legislative policy-making appears to be the result of a confluence of factors streaming from an almost endless number of tributaries: national experience, the contributions of social theorists, the class of powerful economic interests, the quality of Presidential leadership, other institutional and personal ambitions and administrative arrangements in the Executive Branch, the initiative, effort, and ambitions of individual legislators and their governmental and non-governmental staffs, the policy commitments of political parties, and the predominant culture symbols in the minds both of leaders and followers in the Congress.
>
> Most of these forces appear to be involved at every important stage in the policy-making process, and they act only within the most general limits of popular concern about a specific issue.
>
> In the absence of a widely recognized crisis, legislative policymaking tends to be fought out at the level of largely irresponsible personal and group strategems and compromises based upon temporary power coalitions of political, administrative, and non-governmental interests.
>
> This type of policy-making is in part responsible for, and is certainly aided and abetted by, the rules, structures, and procedures of the Congress, and by a widely shared folklore of American Constitutional theory which is uncritically accepted by the great majority of our national legislators—the sanctity of Congressional prerogatives and the desirability of competing power systems in the federal government.
>
> Put in its baldest form, the story of [the passage of the Employment Act of 1946] adds up to the fact that majority sentiment expressed in popular elections for a particular economic policy can be, and frequently is, almost hopelessly splintered by the power struggles of competing political, administrative, and private interests, and is finally pieced together, if at all, only by the most laborious, complicated, and frequently covert coalition strategies.[167]

Typical of the studies of legislative behavior is one based upon extensive interviews of members of the Massachusetts House of Representatives that suggests that legislators in that state fall into four separate analytical categories, depending upon how they perceive their roles as legislators.[168] There are *fixers,* who view their role mainly as one of handling petty requests from constituents and dispensing whatever patronage may be at their disposal; *movers,* who view their house membership as a stepping stone to higher office in either the political, professional, or business world; *legisla-*

167. Bailey, Congress Makes Law 236-237 (1950). An examination of the progress of consumer credit bills introduced during the 1969 regular session of the Alabama legislature led to this even more discouraging conclusion: "[F]rom the beginning, debate consisted only of innuendos and insinuations, back-scratching and back-biting, sloganeering and demagoguery, charges and countercharges of payoffs and conflicts of interest." Comment, Legislative Process in Alabama: A Microcosm, 23 Ala. L. Rev. 181 (1970). Other empirical studies of the legislative process include Redman, The Dance of Legislation (1973); Fishman, Evaluation and Congress, 41 New Directions for Program Evaluation 27 (1989); Froman, The Congressional Process, Strategies, Rules and Procedures (1967).

168. See Portnoy, Membership in the Club: Denizens of the Massachusetts House of Representatives, 6 Harv. J. Legis. 199 (1969).

tors, who view themselves as formulators and implementors of policy through the passage of legislation; and *alienated members,* a tiny minority who are disillusioned with the legislative process and who have, therefore, disassociated themselves psychologically from it. Fixers take very little interest or active part in the process of considering and passing upon bills in the legislature and lend their support to various measures essentially on a quid pro quo basis. They tend to make their membership in the legislature a full-time, lifelong job, and are among the most self-satisfied members of the House. In contrast, movers and legislators are part-time lawmakers and tend to be more restless in their positions. More than any other category, legislators tend to study legislation carefully and are more apt than any other to react in a principled fashion to bills on their merits. Alienated legislators are rare individuals about whom generalization is hazardous. They dislike their legislative positions, and their tenure in political office is usually very short.

It is impossible to do more here than supply a general impression of the work that has been undertaken in this field. In the final analysis, the complexity of the interrelationships of factors influencing legislative behavior is probably so immense as to frustrate efforts to understand it fully. In this respect, legislative behavioral research shares with behavioral research generally a tendency to beguile and to frustrate. As one well-known researcher into influences upon legislative behavior reminds us:

> In reality, none of [the] problems [confronting researchers in the field of legislative behavior] will ever be "solved" in the sense that knowledge about representative bodies will be complete and final. Behavioral research aspires to knowledge which, though it may increase in generality and probable truth, will always be fragmentary and hypothetical. To some, this prospect may appear to condemn researchers to a labor of Sisyphus. If so, there is some comfort in the thought that we do not know certainly that our stone must periodically roll back on us forever. But we must still resign ourselves to knowing that the basic tools of future researchers will remain that of their forebears: minds which are finite and human.[169]

(2) *Foreseeable Plaintiffs*

Palsgraf v. Long Island R.R.

248 N.Y. 339, 162 N.E. 99 (1928)

Appeal from a judgment of the Appellate Division of the Supreme Court in the second judicial department . . . affirming a judgment in favor of plaintiff entered upon a verdict.

CARDOZO, C.J. Plaintiff was standing on a platform of defendant's railroad

169. Wahlke, Behavioral Analysis of Representative Bodies, In Essays on the Behavioral Studies of Politics at 190 (Ramney, ed. 1962).

after buying a ticket to go to Rockaway Beach. A train stopped at the station, bound for another place. Two men ran forward to catch it. One of the men reached the platform of the car without mishap, though the train was already moving. The other man, carrying a package, jumped aboard the car, but seemed unsteady as if about to fall. A guard on the car, who had held the door open, reached forward to help him in, and another guard on the platform pushed him from behind. In this act, the package was dislodged, and fell upon the rails. It was a package of small size, about fifteen inches long, and was covered by a newspaper. In fact it contained fireworks, but there was nothing in its appearance to give notice of its contents. The fireworks when they fell exploded. The shock of the explosion threw down some scales at the other end of the platform, many feet away. The scales struck the plaintiff, causing injuries for which she sues.

The conduct of the defendant's guard, if a wrong in its relation to the holder of the package, was not a wrong in its relation to the plaintiff, standing far away. Relative to her it was not negligence at all. Nothing in the situation gave notice that the falling package had in it the potency of peril to persons thus removed. Negligence is not actionable unless it involves the invasion of a legally protected interest, the violation of a right. "Proof of negligence in the air, so to speak, will not do" (Pollock, Torts [11th ed.], p. 455. . . .) The plaintiff as she stood upon the platform of the station might claim to be protected against intentional invasion of her bodily security. Such invasion is not charged. She might claim to be protected against unintentional invasion by conduct involving in the thought of reasonable men an unreasonable hazard that such invasion would ensue. These, from the point of view of law, were the bounds of her immunity, with perhaps some rare exceptions, survivals for the most part of ancient forms of liability, where conduct is held to be at the peril of the actor.

If no hazard was apparent to the eye of ordinary vigilance, an act innocent and harmless, at least to outward seeming, with reference to her, did not take to itself the quality of a tort because it happened to be a wrong, though apparently not one involving the risk of bodily insecurity, with reference to some one else. . . . The plaintiff sues in her own right for a wrong personal to her, and not as the vicarious beneficiary of a breach of duty to another.

A different conclusion will involve us, and swiftly too, in a maze of contradictions. A guard stumbles over a package which has been left upon a platform. It seems to be a bundle of newspapers. It turns out to be a can of dynamite. To the eye of ordinary vigilance, the bundle is abandoned waste, which may be kicked or trod on with impunity. Is a passenger at the other end of the platform protected by the law against the unsuspected hazard concealed beneath the waste? If not, is the result to be any different, so far as the distant passenger is concerned, when the guard stumbles over a valise which a truckman or a porter has left upon the walk? The passenger far away, if the victim of a wrong at all, has a cause of action, not derivative, but original and primary. His claim to be protected against invasion of his bodily security is neither greater nor less because the act resulting in the invasion is a wrong to another far removed. In this case, the rights that are said to have been violated, the interests said to have been invaded, are not even of the same order. The man was not injured in his person nor even put in danger. The purpose of the act, as well as its effect, was to make his person safe. If there was a wrong to him at all, which may very well be doubted, it was a wrong to a property interest only, the safety of his package. Out of this wrong to property, which threatened injury to nothing else, there has passed, we are told, to the plaintiff by derivation or succession a right of action for the invasion of an interest of another order, the right to bodily security. The diversity of interests emphasizes the futility of the effort to build the plaintiff's right upon the basis of a wrong to some one else. The gain is one of emphasis, for a like result would follow if the interests were the same. Even then, the orbit of the danger as disclosed to the eye of reasonable vigilance would be the orbit of the duty. One who jostles one's neighbor in a crowd does not invade the rights of others standing at the outer fringe when the unintended contact casts a bomb upon the ground. The wrongdoer as to them is the man who carries the bomb, not the one who explodes it without suspicion of the danger. Life will have to be made over, and human nature transformed, before prevision so extravagant can be accepted as the norm of conduct, the customary standard to which behavior must conform.

The argument for the plaintiff is built upon the shifting meanings of such words as "wrong" and "wrongful," and shares their instability. What the plaintiff must show is "a wrong" to herself, i.e., a violation of her own right, and not merely a wrong to some one else, nor conduct "wrongful" because unsocial, but not "a wrong" to any one. We are told that one who drives at reckless speed through a crowded city street is guilty of a negligent act and, therefore, of a wrongful one irrespective of the consequences. Negligent the act is, and wrongful in the sense that it is unsocial, but wrongful and unsocial in relation to other travelers, only because the eye of vigilance perceives the risk of damage. If the same act were to be committed on a speedway or a race course, it would lose its wrongful quality. The risk reasonably to be perceived defines the duty to be obeyed, and risk imports relation; it is risk to another or to others within the range of apprehension. . . . The range of reasonable apprehension is at times a question for the court, and at times, if varying inferences are possible, a question for the jury. Here, by concession, there was nothing in the situation to suggest to the most cautious mind that the parcel wrapped in newspaper would spread wreckage through the station. If the guard had thrown it down knowingly and willfully, he would not have threatened the plaintiff's safety, so far as appearances could warn him. His conduct would not have involved, even then, an unreasonable probability of invasion of her bodily security. Liability can be no greater where the act is inadvertent.

Negligence, like risk, is thus a term of relation. Negligence in the abstract, apart from things related, is surely not a tort, if indeed it is understandable at all. . . .

The law of causation, remote or proximate, is thus foreign to the case before us. The question of liability is always anterior to the question of the measure of the consequences that go with liability. If there is no tort to be redressed, there is no occasion to consider what damage might be recovered if there were a finding of a tort. We may assume, without deciding, that negligence, not at large or in the abstract, but in relation to the plaintiff, would entail liability for any and all consequences, however novel or extraordinary. There is room for argument that a distinction is to be drawn according to the diversity of interests invaded by the act, as where conduct negligent in that it threatens an insignificant invasion of an interest in property results in an unforeseeable invasion of an interest of another order, as, e.g., one of bodily security. Perhaps other distinctions may be necessary. We do not go into the question now. The consequences to be followed must first be rooted in a wrong.

The judgment of the Appellate Division and that of the Trial Term should be reversed, and the complaint dismissed, with costs in all courts.

ANDREWS, J. (dissenting). . . .

. . . The result we shall reach [in this case] depends upon our theory as to the nature of negligence. Is it a relative concept—the breach of some duty owing to a particular person or to particular persons? Or where there is an act which unreasonably threatens the safety of others, is the doer liable for all its proximate consequences, even where they result in injury to one who would generally be thought to be outside the radius of danger? This is not a mere dispute as to words. We might not believe that to the average mind the dropping of the bundle would seem to involve the probability of harm to the plaintiff standing many feet away whatever might be the case as to the owner or to one so near as to be likely to be struck by its fall. If, however, we adopt the second hypothesis we have to inquire only as to the relation between cause and effect. We deal in terms of proximate cause, not of negligence. . . .

But we are told that "there is no negligence unless there is in the particular case a legal duty to take care, and this duty must be one which is owed to the plaintiff himself and not merely to others." (Salmond, Torts [6th ed.], 24.) This, I think too narrow a conception. Where there is the unreasonable act, and some right that may be affected there is negligence whether damage does or does not result. That is immaterial. Should we drive down Broadway at a reckless speed, we are negligent whether we strike an approaching car or miss it by an inch. The act itself is wrongful. It is a wrong not only to those who happen to be within the radius of danger but to all who might have been there—a wrong to the public at large. Such is the language of the street. . . . Due care is a duty imposed on each one of us to protect society from unnecessary danger, not to protect A, B or C alone.

It may well be that there is no such thing as negligence in the abstract. "Proof of negligence in the air, so to speak, will not do." In an empty world negligence would not exist. It does involve a relationship between man and his fellows. But not merely a relationship between man and those whom he might reasonably expect his act would injure. Rather, a relationship between him and those whom he does in fact injure. If his act has a tendency to harm some one, it harms him a mile away as surely as it does those on the scene. . . .

In the well-known Polemis Case (1921, 3 K. B. 560), Scrutton, L. J., said that the dropping of a plank was negligent for it might injure "workman or cargo or ship." Because of either possibility the owner of the vessel was to be made good for his loss. The act being wrongful the doer was liable for its proximate results. Criticized and explained as this statement may have been, I think it states the law as it should be and as it is.

The proposition is this. Every one owes to the world at large the duty of refraining from those acts that may unreasonably threaten the safety of others. Such an act occurs. Not only is he wronged to whom harm might reasonably be expected to result, but he also who is in fact injured, even if he be outside what would generally be thought the danger zone. There needs be duty due the one complaining but this is not a duty to a particular individual because as to him harm might be expected. Harm to some one being the natural result of the act, not only that one alone, but all those in fact injured may complain. We have never, I think, held otherwise. . . . Unreasonable risk being taken, its consequences are not confined to those who might probably be hurt.

If this be so, we do not have a plaintiff suing by "derivation or succession." Her action is original and primary. Her claim is for a breach of duty to herself—not that she is subrogated to any right of action of the owner of the parcel or of a passenger standing at the scene of the explosion.

The right to recover damages rests on additional considerations. The plaintiff's rights must be injured, and this injury must be caused by the negligence. We build a dam, but are negligent as to its foundations. Breaking, it injures property down stream. We are not liable if all this happened because of some reason other than the insecure foundation. But when injuries do result from our unlawful act we are liable for the consequences. It does not matter that they are unusual, unexpected, unforeseen and unforeseeable. But there is one limitation. The damages must be so connected with the negligence that the latter may be said to be the proximate cause of the former.

These two words have never been given an inclusive definition. What is a cause in a legal sense, still more what is a proximate cause, depend in each case upon many considerations, as does the existence of negligence itself. Any philosophical doctrine of causation does not help us. A boy throws a stone into a pond. The ripples spread. The water level rises. The history of that pond is altered to all eternity. It will be altered by other causes also. Yet it will be forever the resultant of all causes combined. Each one will have an influence. How great only omniscience can say. You may speak of a chain, or if you please, a net. An analogy is of little aid. Each cause brings about future events. Without each the future would not be the same. Each is proximate in the sense it is essential. But that is not what we mean by the word. Nor on the other hand do we mean sole cause. There is no such thing. . . .

. . . What we do mean by the word "proximate" is, that because of convenience, of public policy, of a rough sense of justice, the law arbitrarily declines to trace a series of events beyond a certain point. This is not logic. It is practical politics. Take our rule as to fires. Sparks from my burning haystack set on fire my house and my neighbor's. I may recover from a negligent railroad. He may not. Yet the wrongful act as directly harmed the one as the other. We may regret that the line was drawn just where it was, but drawn somewhere it had to be. We said the act of the railroad was not the proximate cause of our neighbor's fire. Cause it surely was. The words we used were simply indicative of our notions of public policy. Other courts think differently. But somewhere they reach the point where they cannot say the stream comes from any one source.

Take the illustration given in an unpublished manuscript by a distinguished and helpful writer on the law of torts. A chauffeur negligently collides with another car which is filled with dynamite, although he could not know it. An explosion follows. A, walking on the sidewalk nearby, is killed. B, sitting in a window of a building opposite, is cut by flying glass. C, likewise sitting in a window a block away, is similarly injured. And a further illustration. A nursemaid, ten blocks away, startled by the noise, involuntarily drops a baby from her arms to the walk. We are told that C may not recover while A may. As to B it is a question for court or jury. We will all agree that the baby might not. Because, we are again told, the chauffeur had no reason to believe his conduct involved any risk of injuring either C or the baby. As to them he was not negligent.

But the chauffeur, being negligent in risking the collision, his belief that the scope of the harm he might do would be limited is immaterial. His act unreasonably jeopardized the safety of any one who might be affected by it. C's injury and that of the baby were directly traceable to the collision. Without that, the injury would not have happened. C had the right to sit in his office, secure from such dangers. The baby was entitled to use the sidewalk with reasonable safety.

The true theory is, it seems to me, that the injury to C, if in truth he is to be denied recovery, and the injury to the baby is that their several injuries were not the proximate result of the negligence. And here not what the chauffeur had reason to believe would be the result of his conduct, but what the prudent would foresee, may have a bearing. May have some bearing, for the problem of proximate cause is not to be solved by any one consideration.

It is all a question of expediency. There are no fixed rules to govern our judgment. There are simply matters of which we may take account. . . . There is in truth little to guide us other than common sense.

There are some hints that may help us. The proximate cause, involved as it may be with many other causes, must be, at the least, something without which the event would not happen. The court must ask itself whether there was a natural and continuous sequence between cause and effect. Was the one a substantial factor in producing the other? Was there a direct connection between them, without too many intervening causes? Is the effect of cause on result not too attenuated? Is the cause likely, in the usual judgment of mankind, to produce the result? Or by the exercise of prudent foresight could the result be foreseen? Is the result too remote from the cause, and here we consider remoteness in time and space. . . . Clearly we must so consider, for the greater the distance either in time or space, the more surely do other causes intervene to affect the result. . . .

Here another question must be answered. In the case supposed it is said, and said correctly, that the chauffeur is liable for the direct effect of the explosion although he had no reason to suppose it would follow a collision. "The fact that the injury occurred in a different manner than that which might have been expected does not prevent the chauffeur's negligence from being in law the cause of the injury." But the natural results of a negligent act—the results which a prudent man would or should foresee—do have a bearing upon the decision as to proximate cause. We have said so repeatedly. What should be foreseen? No human foresight would suggest that a collision itself might injure one a block away. On the contrary, given an explosion, such a possibility might be reasonably expected. I think the direct connection, the foresight of which the courts speak, assumes prevision of the explosion, for the immediate results of which, at least, the chauffeur is responsible.

It may be said this is unjust. Why? In fairness he should make good every injury flowing from his negligence. Not because of tenderness toward him we say he need not answer for all that follows his wrong. We look back to the catastrophe, the fire kindled by the spark, or the explosion. We trace the consequences—not indefinitely, but to a certain point. And to aid us in fixing that point we ask what might ordinarily be expected to follow the fire or the explosion.

This last suggestion is the factor which must determine the case before us. The act upon which defendant's liability rests is knocking an apparently harmless package onto the platform. The act was negligent. For its proximate consequences the defendant is liable. If its contents were broken, to the owner; if it fell upon and crushed a passenger's foot, then to him. If it exploded and injured one in the immediate vicinity, to him also as to A in the illustration. Mrs. Palsgraf was standing some distance away. How far cannot be told from the record—apparently twenty-five or thirty feet. Perhaps less. Except for the explosion, she would not have been injured. We are told by the appellant in his brief "it cannot be denied that the explosion was the direct cause of the plaintiff's injuries." So it was a substantial factor in producing the result—there was here a natural and continuous sequence—direct connection. The only intervening cause was that instead of blowing her to the ground the concussion smashed the weighing machine which in turn fell upon her. There was no remoteness in time, little in space. And surely, given such an explosion as here it needed no great foresight to predict that the natural result would be to injure one on the platform at no greater distance from its scene than was the plaintiff. Just how no one might be able to predict. Whether by flying fragments, by broken glass, by wreckage of machines or structures no one could say. But injury in some form was most probable.

Under these circumstances I cannot say as a matter of law that the plaintiff's injuries were not the proximate result of the negligence. That is all we have before us. The court refused to so charge. No request was made to submit the matter to the jury as a question of fact, even would that have been proper upon the record before us.

The judgment appealed from should be affirmed, with costs.

Pound, Lehman and Kellogg, JJ., concur with Cardozo, C.J.; Andrews, J., dissents in opinion in which Crane and O'Brien, JJ., concur.

Judgment reversed, etc.

The range of different circumstances under which courts have been called upon to decide whether injured plaintiffs were within the scope of the risks foreseeably created by defendants' conduct is very wide. Thus, in Ozark Industries v. Stubbs Transports, 351 F. Supp. 351 (W.D. Ark. 1972), the defendant's employee negligently spilled gasoline on a public road. The gasoline flowed into a roadside ditch, from whence it percolated to subterranean waters, eventually reaching the fresh waters of plaintiff's commercial trout farm 2.9 airline miles away. The trial court granted the defendant's motion for summary judgment, concluding that the case was "strikingly similar" to *Palsgraf.* In contrast, in Geyer v. City of Logansport, 346 N.E.2d 634 (Ind. App. 1976), the Indiana Court of Appeals reversed a dismissal by the trial court of a claim for damages arising out of the plaintiff's being shot accidentally by a police officer. A bull had been negligently allowed to escape, and the police officer shot his revolver at the bull to prevent it from injuring others. The plaintiff, who was not within the line of fire, was struck and injured when the bullet ricocheted off one of the bull's horns. The court of appeals held that the issue of the foreseeability of harm to the plaintiff should have been given to the jury.

Solomon v. Shuell

435 Mich. 104, 457 N.W.2d 669 (1990)

[This is a wrongful death action against police officers arising out of the arrest of robbery suspects. The officers were not in uniform, and the decedent, apparently thinking that the suspects needed help, came out of his house with a gun, which was pointed toward the ground. The decedent was shot by one of the officers. The jury found that the defendants and the plaintiff all were negligent, and reduced the plaintiff's recovery according to the Michigan comparative fault regime. The trial judge entered judgment on the jury verdict for the plaintiff, and the plaintiff appealed.]

III

The second question presented is whether the trial court properly instructed the jury on the so-called rescue doctrine. Standard Jury Instruction 13.07 provides:

> "A person who goes to the rescue of another who is in imminent and serious peril caused by the negligence of someone else is not contributorily negligent, so long as the rescue attempt is not recklessly or rashly made."

Over plaintiff's timely objection, the trial court read to the jury a modified version of SJI 13.07:

> "If you find, under the facts, from the evidence, that Alvin Solomon was in imminent and serious peril, a person who goes to the rescue of another who is in imminent and serious peril caused by the negligence of someone else, is not contributorily negligent, so long as the rescue attempt is not recklessly or rashly made."

The basis of plaintiff's objection was that the victim need not be in actual danger in order for the rescue doctrine to apply, and that the instructions misled the jury by stating contributory negligence principles instead of comparative negligence principles.

The Court of Appeals affirmed. Although the Court concluded that the trial court had erroneously instructed the jury, the Court deemed the error harmless. The Court held that the rescue doctrine applies if the rescuer reasonably believes the victim is in actual danger. Consequently, the victim need not ever have been in actual danger in order for the doctrine to apply. The Court found the error harmless, however, because on the whole, the jury instructions adequately presented plaintiff's theory of the case to the jury and properly instructed the jury on comparative negligence principles. Consequently, we must determine whether the Court of Appeals properly held that the trial court erroneously instructed the jury and whether the error was harmless.

A

Under the rescue doctrine, the tortfeasor whose negligence endangers the victim owes the victim's rescuer a duty of reasonable care. Since rescuers, as a class, are foreseeable, the tortfeasor's duty of care owed to the rescuer is independent of that owed to the victim.

Traditionally, the rescue doctrine has served two purposes. First, the doctrine established a causal nexus linking the tortfeasor's negligent conduct to the rescuer's injuries. Consequently, the fact that the rescuer voluntarily exposed himself to an increased risk of harm was not, as a matter of law, deemed to be a superseding cause of the rescuer's injuries that would discharge the tortfeasor's liability. Second, the doctrine also provided that, when the rescue attempt itself was reasonable, the rescuer's recovery was not otherwise absolutely barred by the affirmative defense of contributory negligence merely because the rescuer voluntarily exposed himself to an increased risk of injury in order to save a third person.

An injured rescuer's recovery would still be barred, even if the rescue attempt itself was reasonable, when the rescuer did not exercise reasonable care in the manner in which he carried out the attempt. Thus . . . the application of the rescue doctrine requires a two-step analysis. First, the trier of fact must determine whether a reasonable person under the same or similar circumstances would have acted as did the rescuer. To determine this, the trier of fact must balance the utility of the rescuer's conduct against the magnitude of the increased risk of harm. If the rescue attempt itself is reasonable, then the rescuer is not deemed comparatively negligent merely for voluntarily exposing himself to an increased risk of harm in order to save another. The second step of the analysis is to determine whether the rescuer carried out the rescue attempt in a reasonable manner. If the rescuer did not, then the rescuer's recovery is reduced by his comparative degree of fault.

The Court of Appeals correctly held that the rescue doctrine applies even if the victim never was in actual danger. Although previous Michigan cases held that the victim had to be in actual danger at the time of the rescue attempt, or if not, at least shortly before, it is clear that the dispositive issue determining whether the rescue attempt itself is reasonable is whether the rescuer acted as a reasonable person under the same or similar circumstances. Because the inquiry as to whether the rescue attempt itself was reasonable also rests upon whether the utility of the rescue attempt outweighs the increased risk of harm the rescuer faces, the Court of Appeals correctly determined that the rescue doctrine applies even if the victim never was in actual danger. Because the trial court instructed the jury that Alvin Solomon had to be in actual danger at the time of the rescue attempt, we agree with the Court of Appeals that the instruction was erroneous. Consequently, the instruction was also misleading because it did not clearly charge the jury to undertake its inquiry from the viewpoint of a reasonable person acting under the same or similar circumstances as decedent.

B. . . .

Under the instructions the trial court read to the jury, the jury could not properly analyze plaintiff's theory of the case under the rescue doctrine. Plaintiff's theory of the case was that the rescue attempt itself was reasonable and that decedent carried out the rescue attempt in a reasonable manner. In light of the fact that Alvin never was in actual danger, however, the trial court in effect told the jury that the rescue doctrine did not apply and that the rescue attempt itself was unreasonable. Consequently, the instructions precluded the jury from properly considering whether a reasonable person would have undertaken a rescue attempt under these same circumstances and in the same manner. Thus, it is no comfort to state that the jury was otherwise properly instructed on comparative negligence principles and, notwithstanding the instructional error, undertook an otherwise proper negligence analysis. The simple fact is that the jury, under these instructions, could not determine whether the rescue attempt itself was reasonable. Thus, plaintiff's theory of the case was not adequately presented to the jury. Plaintiff suffered prejudice inconsistent with substantial justice, and, therefore, reversal is required. . . .

The judgment of the Court of Appeals should be reversed, and the case remanded for a new trial consistent with this opinion.

[The concurring opinion of BOYLE, J., and the dissenting opinion of GRIFFIN, J., are omitted.]

Solomon follows what is the well nigh universal rule that a negligent defendant may be liable to one who is injured in an effort to rescue another put at risk by the defendant's negligence. Justice Cardozo, one of the most influential judges shaping American tort law (see, e.g., Martin v. Herzog, p. 227, above, Palsgraf v. Long Island R.R., p. 365, above, and MacPherson v. Buick Motor Co., p. 563, below) wrote an opinion, Wagner v. International Railway, 232 N.Y. 176, 133 N.E. 437 (1921), on the subject that begins with one of his famous epigrams:

> Danger invites rescue. The cry of distress is the summons to relief. The law does not ignore these reactions of the mind in tracing conduct to its consequences. It recognizes them as normal. It places their effects within the range of the natural and probable. The wrong that imperils life is a wrong to the imperilled victim; it is a wrong also to his rescuer. The state that leaves an opening in a bridge is liable to the child that falls into the stream, but liable also to the parent who plunges to its aid. . . . The risk of rescue, if only it be not wanton, is born of the occasion. The emergency begets the man. The wrongdoer may not have foreseen the coming of a deliverer. He is accountable as if he had.
>
> The defendant says that we must stop, in following the chain of causes,

> when action ceases to be "instinctive." By this, is meant, it seems, that rescue is at the peril of the rescuer, unless spontaneous and immediate. If there has been time to deliberate, if impulse has given way to judgment, one cause, it is said, has spent its force, and another has intervened. In this case, the plaintiff walked more than four hundred feet in going to Herbert's aid. He had time to reflect and weigh; impulse had been followed by choice; and choice, in the defendant's view, intercepts and breaks the sequence. We find no warrant for thus shortening the chain of jural causes. We may assume, though we are not required to decide, that peril and rescue must be in substance one transaction; that the sight of the one must have aroused the impulse to the other; in short, that there must be unbroken continuity between the commission of the wrong and the effort to avert its consequences. If all this be assumed, the defendant is not aided. Continuity in such circumstances is not broken by the exercise of volition. . . . The law does not discriminate between the rescuer oblivious of peril and the one who counts the cost. It is enough that the act, whether impulsive or deliberate, is the child of the occasion.

232 N.Y. at 180-181, 133 N.E. at 437-438.

In *Wagner,* the plaintiff and his cousin, Herbert, were passengers on one of the defendant's trains when Herbert was thrown from the train. The plaintiff was injured while attempting to locate Herbert.

One important exception to the rule that permits recovery by rescuers is the "fire fighter's" rule, which bars recovery by professional rescuers for injuries incurred in the course of their duties. The rule reflects the judgment that professional rescuers have been compensated, ahead of time, for the risks inherent in their work. As the name suggests, the rule applies to fire fighters. See, e.g., Krauth v. Geller, 31 N.J. 270, 157 A.2d 129 (1960). And it has been applied to fire fighters in a volunteer fire department, even though they are not monetarily compensated for their services. See Flowers v. Rock Creek Terrace Limited Partnership, 308 Md. 432, 520 A.2d 361 (1987).

The rule has been extended beyond fire fighters to apply to police officers (see, e.g., Winn v. Frasher, 116 Idaho 500, 777 P.2d 722 (1989); Santangelo v. State, 71 N.Y.2d 393, 521 N.E.2d 770 (1988)), and to a member of a voluntary emergency squad (see Siligato v. Hiles, 563 A.2d 1172 (N.J. Super. 1989)), but not to an ambulance attendant (see Krause v. U.S. Truck Co., 787 S.W.2d 708 (Mo. 1990).

Some courts have limited the rule to protect only owners and occupiers of land from liability to professional rescuers. Thus, the rule was held not to be available to a defendant in a products liability case (see Hauboldt v. Union Carbide Corp., 160 Wis. 2d 662, 467 N.W.2d 508 (1991)), to a negligent truck driver (see Lave v. Neumann, 211 Neb. 97, 317 N.W.2d 779 (1982), to a person who wrongfully resisted arrest (see Lang v. Glusica, 393 N.W.2d 181 (Minn. 1986)), and to two defendants, one of whom crashed into a police officer's car while the officer was sitting in it writing out a traffic violation ticket, and the other of whom collided with a fire truck occupied by the plaintiff while the latter was responding to a call (see Benefiel v. Walker, 244 Va. 488, 422 S.E.2d 773 (1992)). The rule also was held not to be available to a defendant whose conduct in causing the injury to the plaintiff was wanton or reckless (see Migdal v. Stamp, 132 N.H. 171, 564 A.2d 826 (1989)), and to a defendant who had misrepresented to the plaintiff the nature of the hazard involved in responding to the call (see Lipson v. Superior Court, 31 Cal. 3d 362, 644 P.2d 822, 182 Cal. Rptr. 629 (1982)).

A few jurisdictions have abolished the fire fighter's rule entirely. See Kaiser v. Northern States Power Co., 353 N.W.2d 899 (Minn. 1984) (by statute); Christensen v. Murphy, 296 Or. 610, 678 P.2d 1210 (1984) (by judicial opinion).

In general, see Comment, The Fireman's Rule: Defining Its Scope Using the Cost-Spreading Rationale, 71 Calif. L. Rev. 218 (1983).

b. Other Approaches to the Proximate Cause Issue

The preceding material suggests that unforeseeability of the consequences is a barrier to recovery. The foreseeability concept might be criticized on two grounds:

1. *It is not workable.* It lacks sufficient substantive content to be capable of rational application across a range of cases.

2. *It is wrong in policy.* The defendant should sometimes be liable for consequences that are not foreseeable.

You should judge the following material in light of both of these criticisms.

RESTATEMENT (SECOND) OF TORTS

§431. WHAT CONSTITUTES LEGAL CAUSE

The actor's negligent conduct is a legal cause of harm to another if

(a) his conduct is a substantial factor in bringing about the harm, and

(b) there is no rule of law relieving the actor from liability because of the manner in which his negligence has resulted in the harm.

COMMENT:

a. *Distinction between substantial cause and cause in the philosophic sense.* In order to be a legal cause of another's harm, it is not enough that the harm would not have occurred had the actor not been negligent. . . . The negligence must also be a substantial factor in bringing about the plaintiff's harm. The word "substantial" is used to denote the fact that the defendant's conduct has such an effect in producing the harm as to lead reasonable men to regard it as a cause, using that word in the popular sense, in which there always lurks the idea of responsibility, rather than in the so-called "philosophic sense," which includes every one of the great number of events without which any happening would not have occurred. Each of these events is a cause in the so-called "philosophic sense," yet the effect of many of them is so insignificant that no ordinary mind would think of them as causes.

§433. CONSIDERATIONS IMPORTANT IN DETERMINING WHETHER NEGLIGENT CONDUCT IS SUBSTANTIAL FACTOR IN PRODUCING HARM

The following considerations are in themselves or in combination with one another important in determining whether the actor's conduct is a substantial factor in bringing about harm to another:

(a) the number of other factors which contribute in producing the harm and the extent of the effect which they have in producing it;

(b) whether the actor's conduct has created a force or series of forces which are in continuous and active operation up to the time of the harm, or has created a situation harmless unless acted upon by other forces for which the actor is not responsible;

(c) lapse of time.

Hill v. Lundin & Associates, Inc.

260 La. 542, 256 So. 2d 620 (1972)

[The defendant was hired to repair damage to a home caused by Hurricane Betsy. The hurricane caused damage to a large number of buildings, and the defendant would deliver materials and equipment to houses to be repaired and pick them up in the way it thought most efficient. This meant that sometimes equipment was not removed from a job until sometime after it was completed. In this case, the defendant left a ladder leaning against a house after the work was finished. Sometime later, someone, not an employee of the defendant, put the ladder on the ground. The plaintiff, an employee of the homeowner, saw a child running toward the ladder, and ran toward him to prevent him from falling over the ladder. But she, the plaintiff, tripped over the ladder and was injured. The trial judge ruled that the plaintiff's negligence barred her recovery. The intermediate appellate court reversed that finding, and ruled that the defendant "was negligent in leaving this ladder on the job site, unattended, for two or three days after the work had been completed, where it was foreseeable that someone could be injured by the ladder." This is an appeal from the decision of the intermediate appellate court.]

BARHAM, J. . . . We are of the opinion that the plaintiff has failed to establish actionable negligence on Lundin's part, and we reverse.

The accident in this case occurred because the plaintiff fell over a ladder lying on the ground. We first inquire whether any causal relationship existed between the harm to the plaintiff and the defendant's allegedly negligent conduct. If the defendant had not left the ladder on the premises, it could not have later been placed on the ground in the yard. To this extent it may be said that the defendant's act had something to do with the harm.

However, if the defendant's conduct of which the plaintiff complains is a cause in fact of the harm, we are then required in a determination of negligence to ascertain whether the defendant breached a legal duty imposed to protect against the particular risk involved.

The Court of Appeal's holding implies that a ladder is a dangerous instrumentality or that simply leaving a ladder unattended is negligence per se. We reject this reasoning as being totally unsound in law. It is only that conduct which creates an appreciable range of risk for causing harm that is prohibited. Leaving a ladder unattended under certain conditions may create an unreasonable risk of harm to others which would impose a reciprocal duty upon the actor. If we assume that the defendant was under a duty not to leave the ladder leaning against the house because of an unreasonable risk of harm, the breach of that duty does not necessarily give rise to liability in this case. Although the defendant would owe a duty to protect certain persons under certain circumstances from this risk, it is not an insurer against every risk of harm which is encountered in connection with the ladder.

Here a third party had moved the ladder to the ground, and the plaintiff was injured as she sought to prevent the child from tripping on the ladder. The basic question, then, is whether the risk of injury from a ladder lying on the ground, produced by a combination of defendant's act and that of a third party, is within the scope of protection of a rule of law which would prohibit leaving a ladder leaning against the house.

Foreseeability is not always a reliable guide, and certainly it is not the only criterion for determining whether there is a duty-risk relationship. Just because a risk may foreseeably arise by reason of conduct, it is not necessarily within the scope of the duty owed because of that conduct. Neither are all risks excluded from the scope of duty simply because they are unforeseeable. The ease of association of the injury with the rule relied upon, however, is always a proper inquiry.

Where the rule of law upon which a plaintiff relies for imposing a duty is based upon a statute, the court attempts to interpret legislative intent as to the risk contemplated by the legal duty, which is often a resort to the court's own judgment of the scope of protection intended by the Legislature. Where the rule of law is jurisprudential and the court is without the aid of legislative intent, the process of determining the risk encompassed within the rule of law is nevertheless similar.

The same policy considerations which would motivate a legislative body to impose duties to protect from certain risks are applied by the court in making its determination. "All rules of conduct, irrespective of whether they are the product of a legislature or are a part of the fabric of the court-made law of negligence, exist for purposes. They are designed to protect *some* persons under *some* circumstances against *some* risks. Seldom does a rule protect every victim against every risk that may befall him, merely because it is shown that the violation of the rule played a part in producing the injury. The task of defining the proper reach or thrust of a rule in its policy aspects is one that must be undertaken by the court in each case as it arises. How appropriate is the rule to the facts of this controversy? This is a question that the court cannot escape." Malone, Ruminations on Cause-In-Fact, 9 Stan. L. Rev. 60, 73 (1956).

This defendant's alleged misconduct, its alleged breach of duty, was in leaving the ladder leaning against the house unattended. The risk encountered by the plaintiff which caused her harm was the ladder lying on the ground where it was placed by another, over which she tripped as she moved to protect the child. The record is devoid of any evidence tending to establish that the defendant could have reasonably anticipated that a third person would move the ladder and put it in the position which created this risk, or that such a "naked possibility" was an unreasonable risk of harm.

A rule of law which would impose a duty upon one not to leave a ladder standing against a house does not encompass the risk here encountered. We are of the opinion that the defendant was under no duty to protect this plaintiff from the risk which gave rise to her injuries. The plaintiff has failed to establish legal and actionable negligence on the part of the defendant.

The judgment of the Court of Appeal is reversed, and plaintiff's suit is dismissed at her costs.

McCaleb, C.J., concurs in the result.

Petition of Kinsman Transit Co.

338 F.2d 708 (2d Cir.), cert. denied, *380 U.S. 944 (1964)*

Friendly, J.: We have here six appeals . . . from an interlocutory decree in admiralty adjudicating liability. The litigation, in the District Court for the Western District of New York, arose out of a series of misadventures on a navigable portion of the Buffalo River during the night of January 21, 1959. The owners of two vessels petitioned for exoneration from or limitation of liability; numerous claimants appeared in these proceedings and also filed libels against the Continental Grain Company and the City of Buffalo, which filed cross-claims. The proceedings were consolidated for trial . . .

The MacGilvray Shiras, owned by The Kinsman Transit Company, was moored at the dock of the Concrete Elevator, operated by Continental Grain Company, on the south side of the river about three miles upstream of the Michigan Avenue Bridge. She was loaded with grain owned by Continental. . . . None of her anchors had been put out. From about 10 P.M. large chunks of ice and debris began to pile up between the Shiras' starboard bow and the bank; the pressure exerted by this mass on her starboard bow was augmented by the force of the current and of floating ice against her port quarter. The mooring lines began to part, and a "deadman," to which the No. 1 mooring cable had been attached, pulled out of the ground—the judge finding that it had not been properly constructed or inspected. About 10:40 P.M. the stern lines parted, and the Shiras drifted into the current. During the previous forty minutes, the shipkeeper took no action to ready the anchors by releasing the devil's claws; when he sought to drop them after the Shiras broke loose, he released the compressors with the claws still hooked in the chain so that the anchors jammed and could no longer be dropped. The trial judge reasonably found that if the anchors had dropped at that time, the Shiras would probably have fetched up at the hairpin bend just below the Concrete Elevator, and that in any case they would considerably have slowed her progress, the significance of which will shortly appear.

Careening stern first down the S-shaped river, the Shiras, at about 11 P.M. struck the bow of the Michael K. Tewksbury, owned by Midland Steamship Line, Inc. . . . The collision caused the Tewksbury's mooring lines to part; she too drifted stern first down the river, followed by the Shiras. The collision caused damage to the Steamer Druckenmiller which was moored opposite the Tewksbury. . . .

The watchman at the elevator where the Tewksbury had been moored phoned the bridge crew to raise the [Michigan Avenue drawbridge, maintained by the city and located downriver from the two ships]. Although not more than two minutes and ten seconds were needed to elevate the bridge to full height after traffic was stopped, assuming that the motor started promptly, the bridge was just being raised when [a half hour after the call], the Tewksbury crashed into its center. . . .

The first crash was followed by a second, when the south tower of the bridge fell. The Tewksbury grounded and stopped in the wreckage with her forward end resting against the stern of the Steamer Farr, which was moored on the south side of the river just above the bridge. The Shiras ended her journey with her stern against the Tewksbury and her bow against the north side of the river. So wedged, the two vessels substantially dammed the flow, causing water and ice to back up and flood installations on the banks with consequent damage as far as the Concrete Elevator, nearly three miles upstream. Two of the bridge crew suffered injuries. Later the north tower of the bridge collapsed, damaging adjacent property.

Judge Burke concluded that Continental and the Shiras had committed various faults . . . and that the City of Buffalo was at fault for failing to raise the Michigan Avenue Bridge. . . .

III. The Allegedly Unexpectable Character of the Events Leading to Much of the Damage

The very statement of the case suggests the need for considering Palsgraf v. Long Island R.R., 248 N.Y. 339, 162 N.E. 99, 59 A.L.R. 1253 (1928), and the closely related problem of liability for unforeseeable consequences. . . . The important question is what was the basis for Chief Judge Cardozo's conclusion that the Long Island Railroad owed no "duty" to Mrs. Palsgraf under the circumstances.

Certainly there is no general principle that a railroad owes no duty to persons on station platforms not in immediate proximity to the tracks, as would have been quickly demonstrated if Mrs. Palsgraf had been injured by the fall of improperly loaded objects from a passing train. . . . Neither is there any principle that railroad guards who jostle a package-carrying passenger owe a duty only to him; if the package had contained bottles, the Long Island would surely have been liable for injury caused to close bystanders by flying glass or spurting liquid. The reason why the Long Island was thought to owe no duty to Mrs. Palsgraf was the lack of any notice that the package contained a substance demanding the exercise of any care toward anyone so far away; Mrs. Palsgraf was not considered to be within the area of apparent hazard created by whatever lack of care the guard had displayed to the anonymous carrier of the unknown fireworks. . . .

We see little similarity between the *Palsgraf* case and the situation before us. The point of *Palsgraf* was that the appearance of the newspaper-wrapped package gave no notice that its dislodgement could do any harm save to itself and those nearby, and this by impact, perhaps with consequent breakage, and not by explosion. In contrast, a ship insecurely moored in a fast flowing river is a known danger not only to herself but to the owners of all other ships and structures down-river, and to persons upon them. No one would dream of saying that a shipowner who "knowingly and willfully" failed to secure his ship at a pier on such a river "would not have threatened" persons and owners of property downstream in some manner. The shipowner and the wharfinger in this case having thus owed a duty of care to all within the reach of the ship's known destructive power, the impossibility of advance identification of the particular person who would be hurt is without legal consequence. Similarly the foreseeable consequences of the City's failure to raise the bridge were not limited to the Shiras and the Tewksbury. Collision plainly created a danger that the bridge towers might fall onto adjoining property, and the crash of two uncontrolled lake vessels, one 425 feet and the other 525 feet long, into a bridge over a swift ice-ridden stream, with a channel only 177 feet wide, could well result in a partial damming that would flood property upstream. As to the City also, it is useful to consider, by way of contrast, Chief Judge Cardozo's statement that the Long Island would not have been liable to Mrs. Palsgraf had the guard willfully thrown the package down. If the City had deliberately kept the bridge closed in the face of the onrushing vessels, taking the risk that they might not come so far, no one would give houseroom to a claim that it "owed no duty" to those who later suffered from the flooding. Unlike Mrs. Palsgraf, they were within the area of hazard. . . .

[A]ll the claimants here met the *Palsgraf* requirement of being persons to whom the actors owed a "duty of care.". . . But this does not dispose of the alternative argument that the manner in which several of the claimants were harmed, particularly by flood damage, was unforeseeable and that recovery for this may not be had—whether the argument is put in the forthright form that unforeseeable damages are not recoverable or is concealed under a formula of lack of "proximate cause."

So far as concerns the City, the argument lacks factual support. Although the obvious risks from not raising the bridge were damage to itself and to the vessels, the danger of a fall of the bridge and of flooding would not have been unforeseeable under the circumstances to anyone who gave them thought. And the same can be said as to the failure of Kinsman's shipkeeper to ready the anchors after the danger had become apparent. The exhibits indicate that the width of the channel between the Concrete Elevator and the bridge is at most points less than two hundred fifty feet. If the Shiras caught up on a dock or vessel moored along the shore, the current might well swing her bow across the channel so as to block the ice floes, as indeed could easily have occurred at the Standard Elevator dock where the stem of the Shiras struck the Tewksbury's bow. At this point the channel scarcely exceeds two hundred feet, and this was further narrowed by the presence of the Druckenmiller moored on the opposite bank. Had the Tewksbury's mooring held, it is thus by no means unlikely that these three ships would have dammed the river. Nor was it unforeseeable that the drawbridge would not be raised since, apart from any other reason, there was no assurance of timely warning. What may have been less foreseeable was that the Shiras would get that far down the twisting river, but this is somewhat negated both by the known speed of the current when freshets developed and by the evidence that, on learning of the Shiras' departure, Continental's employees and those they informed foresaw precisely that.

Continental's position on the facts is stronger. It was indeed foreseeable that the improper construction and lack of inspection of the "deadman" might cause a ship to break loose and damage persons and property on or near the river—that was what made Continental's conduct negligent. With the aid of hindsight one can also say that a prudent man, carefully pondering the problem, would have realized that the danger of this would be greatest under such water conditions as developed during the night of January 21, 1959, and that if a vessel should break loose under those circumstances, events might transpire as they did. But such *post hoc* step by step analysis would render "foreseeable" almost anything that has in fact occurred; if the argument relied upon has legal validity, it ought not be circumvented by characterizing as foreseeable what almost no one would in fact have foreseen at the time.

The effect of unforeseeability of damage upon liability for negligence has recently been considered by the Judicial Committee of the Privy Council, Overseas Tankship (U.K.) Ltd. v. Morts Dock & Engineering Co. (The

Wagon Mound), [1961] 1 All E.R. 404. The Committee there disapproved the proposition, thought to be supported by Re Polemis and Furness, Withy & Co. Ltd., [1921], 3 K.B. 560 (C.A.), "that unforeseeability is irrelevant if damage is 'direct.' " We have no difficulty with the result of *The Wagon Mound,* in view of the finding, 1 All E.R. at 407, that the appellant had no reason to believe that the floating furnace oil would burn, see also the extended discussion in Miller SS. Co. v. Overseas Tankship (U.K) Ltd., The Wagon Mound No. 2, [1963] 1 Lloyd's Law List Rep. 402 (Sup. Ct. N.S.W.). On that view the decision simply applies the principle which excludes liability where the injury sprang from a hazard different from that which was improperly risked. . . . Although some language in the judgment goes beyond this, we would find it difficult to understand why one who had failed to use the care required to protect others in the light of expectable forces should be exonerated when the very risks that rendered his conduct negligent produced other and more serious consequences to such persons than were fairly foreseeable when he fell short of what the law demanded. Foreseeability of danger is necessary to render conduct negligent; where as here the damage was caused by just those forces whose existence required the exercise of greater care than was taken—the current, the ice, and the physical mass of the Shiras, the incurring of consequences other and greater than foreseen does not make the conduct less culpable or provide a reasoned basis for insulation. The oft encountered argument that failure to limit liability to foreseeable consequences may subject the defendant to a loss wholly out of proportion to his fault seems scarcely consistent with the universally accepted rule that the defendant takes the plaintiff as he finds him and will be responsible for the full extent of the injury even though a latent susceptibility of the plaintiff renders this far more serious than could reasonably have been anticipated.

The weight of authority in this country rejects the limitation of damages to consequences foreseeable at the time of the negligent conduct when the consequences are "direct," and the damage, although other and greater than expectable, is of the same general sort that was risked. Other American courts, purporting to apply a test of foreseeability to damages, extend that concept to such unforeseen lengths as to raise serious doubt whether the concept is meaningful; indeed, we wonder whether the British courts are not finding it necessary to limit the language of *The Wagon Mound* as we have indicated.

We see no reason why an actor engaging in conduct which entails a large risk of small damage and a small risk of other and greater damage, of the same general sort, from the same forces, and to the same class of persons, should be relieved of responsibility for the latter simply because the chance of its occurrence, if viewed alone, may not have been large enough to require the exercise of care. By hypothesis, the risk of the lesser harm was sufficient to render his disregard of it actionable; the existence of a less likely additional risk that the very forces against whose action he was required to guard would produce other and greater damage than could have been reasonably anticipated should inculpate him further rather than limit his liability. This does not mean that the careless actor will always be held for all damages for which the forces that he risked were a cause in fact. Somewhere a point will be reached when courts will agree that the link has become too tenuous—that what is claimed to be consequence is only fortuity. Thus, if the destruction of the Michigan Avenue Bridge had delayed the arrival of a doctor, with consequent loss of a patient's life, few judges would impose liability on any of the parties here, although the agreement in result might not be paralleled by similar unanimity in reasoning; perhaps in the long run one returns to Judge Andrew's statement in *Palsgraf,* 248 N.Y. at 354-355, 162 N.E. at 104 (dissenting opinion). "It is all a question of expediency, . . . of fair judgment, always keeping in mind the fact that we endeavor to make a rule in each case that will be practical and in keeping with the general understanding of mankind." It would be pleasant if greater certainty were possible, but the many efforts that have been made at defining the *locus* of the "uncertain and wavering line," 248 N.Y. at 354, 162 N.E. 99, are not very promising; what courts do in such cases makes better sense than what they, or others, say. Where the line will be drawn will vary from age to age: as society has come to rely increasingly on insurance and other methods of loss-sharing, the point may lie further off than a century ago. Here it is surely more equitable that the losses from the operator's negligent failure to raise the Michigan Avenue Bridge should be ratably borne by Buffalo's taxpayers than left with the innocent victims of the flooding; yet the mind is also repelled by a solution that would impose liability solely on the City and exonerate the persons whose negligent acts of commission and omission were the precipitating force of the collision with the bridge and its sequelae. We go only so far as to hold that where, as here, the damages resulted from the same physical forces whose existence required the exercise of greater care than was displayed and were of the same general sort that was expectable, unforeseeability of the exact developments and of the extent of the loss will not limit liability. Other fact situations can be dealt with when they arise. . . .

MOORE, J. (concurring and dissenting): . . .

I cannot agree, . . . merely because "society has come to rely increasingly on insurance and other methods of loss-sharing" that the courts should, or have the power to, create a vast judicial insurance company which will adequately compensate all who have suffered damages. Equally disturbing is the suggestion that "[H]ere it is surely more equitable that the losses from the operators' negligent failure to raise the Michigan Avenue Bridge should be ratably borne by Buffalo's taxpayers than left with the innocent victims of the flooding." Under any such principle, negligence suits would become further simplified by requiring a claimant to establish only his own innocence and then offer, in addition to his financial statement, proof of the financial condition of the respective defendants. Judgment would be entered against the defendant which court or jury decided was best able to pay. Nor am I convinced that it should be the responsibility of the Buffalo taxpayers to reimburse the "innocent victims" in their community for damages sustained. In my opinion, before financial liability is imposed, there should be some showing of legal liability.

Unfortunate though it was for Buffalo to have had its fine vehicular bridge demolished in a most unexpected manner, I accept the finding of liability for normal consequences because the City had plenty of time to raise the bridge after notice was given. Bridges, however, serve two purposes. They permit vehicles to cross the river when they are down; they permit vessels to travel on the river when they are up. But no bridge builder or bridge operator would envision a bridge as a dam or as a dam potential.

By an extraordinary concatenation of even more extraordinary events, not unlike the humorous and almost-beyond-all-imagination sequences depicted by the famous cartoonist, Rube Goldberg, the Shiras with its companions which it picked up en route did combine with the bridge demolition to create a very effective dam across the Buffalo River. Without specification of the nature of the damages, claims in favor of some twenty persons and companies were allowed . . . resulting from the various collisions and from "the damming of the river at the bridge, the backing up of the water and ice upstream, and the overflowing of the banks of the river and flooding of industrial installations along the river banks."

My dissent is limited to that portion of the opinion which approves the awarding of damages suffered as a result of the flooding of various properties upstream. I am not satisfied with reliance on hindsight or on the assumption that since flooding occurred, therefore, it must have been foreseeable. In fact, the majority hold that the danger "of flooding would not have been unforeseeable under the circumstances to anyone who gave them thought." But believing that "anyone" might be too broad, they resort to that most famous of all legal mythological characters, the reasonably "prudent man." Even he, however, "carefully pondering the problem," is not to be relied upon because they permit him to become prudent "[W]ith the aid of hindsight."

The majority, in effect, would remove from the law of negligence the concept of foreseeability because, as they say, "[T]he weight of authority in this country rejects the limitation of damages to consequences foreseeable at the time of the negligent conduct when the consequences are 'direct.' " Yet lingering thoughts of recognized legal principles create for them lingering doubts because they say: "This does not mean that the careless actor will always be held for all damages for which the forces that he risked were a cause in fact. Somewhere a point will be reached when courts will agree that the link has become too tenuous—that what is claimed to be consequence is only fortuity." The very example given, namely, the patient who dies because the doctor is delayed by the destruction of the bridge, certainly presents a direct consequence as a factual matter yet the majority opinion states that "few judges would impose liability on any of the parties here," under these circumstances.

In final analysis the answers to the questions when the link is "too tenuous" and when "consequence is only fortuity" are dependent solely on the particular point of view of the particular judge under the particular circumstances. In differing with my colleagues, I must be giving "unconscious recognition of the harshness of holding a man for what he could not conceivably have guarded against, because human foresight could not go so far." (L. Hand, C.J., in Sinram v. Pennsylvania R. Co., 61 F.2d 767, 770, 2 Cir., 1932.) If "foreseeability" be the test, I can foresee the likelihood that a vessel negligently allowed to break its moorings and to drift uncontrolled in a rapidly flowing river may well strike other ships, piers and bridges. Liability would also result on the "direct consequence" theory. However, to me the fortuitous circumstance of the vessels so arranging themselves as to create a dam is much "too tenuous."

The decisions bearing on the foreseeability question have been so completely collected in three English cases[1] that no repetition of the reasoning pro and con of this principle need be made here. To these cases may be added the many American cases cited in the majority opinion which to me push the doctrine of foreseeability to ridiculous lengths—ridiculous, I suppose, only to the judge whose "human foresight" is restricted to finite limits but not to the judge who can say: It happened; *ergo,* it must have been foreseeable. The line of demarcation will always be "uncertain and wavering," Palsgraf v. Long Island R.R., 248 N.Y. 339, 354, 162 N.E. 99, 59 A.L.R. 1253 (1928), but if, concededly, a line exists, there must be areas on each side. The flood claimants are much too far on the non-liability side of the line. As to them, I would not award any recovery even if the taxpayers of Buffalo are better able to bear the loss.

Dellwo v. Pearson

259 Minn. 452, 107 N.W.2d 859 (1961)

LOEVINGER, J. This case arises out of a personal injury to Jeanette E. Dellwo, one of the plaintiffs. She and her husband, the other plaintiff, were fishing on one of Minnesota's numerous and beautiful lakes by trolling at a low speed with about 40 to 50 feet of line trailing behind the boat. Defendant, a 12-year-old boy, operating a boat with an outboard motor, crossed behind plaintiff's boat. Just at this time Mrs. Dellwo felt a jerk on her line which suddenly was pulled out very rapidly. The line was knotted

1. In re Polemis and Furness, Withy & Co., [1921] 3 K.B. 560 (C.A.); Overseas Tankship (U.K.), Ltd. v. Morts Dock & Engineering Co., Ltd., (The "Wagon Mound"), [1961] 1 All E.R. 404; Miller Steamship Co. Pty., Ltd. v. Overseas Tankship (U.K.) Ltd., [1963] 1 Lloyd's Law List Rep. 402 (Sup. Ct., New South Wales).

to the spool of the reel so that when it had run out the fishing rod was pulled downward, the reel hit the side of the boat, the reel came apart, and part of it flew through the lens of Mrs. Dellwo's glasses and injured her eye. Both parties then proceeded to a dock where inspection of defendant's motor disclosed 2 to 3 feet of fishing line wound about the propeller.

The case was fully tried to the court and jury and submitted to the jury upon instructions which, in so far as relevant here, instructed the jury that: . . . (2) "A person guilty of negligence is liable for all consequences which might reasonably have been foreseen as likely to result from one's negligent act or omissions under the circumstances. . . . A wrongdoer is not responsible for a consequence which is merely possible according to occasional experience, but only for a consequence which is probable according to ordinary and usual experience". . .

The jury returned a general verdict for defendant, and plaintiffs appeal. Plaintiffs contend that the trial court erred in its instruction that a defendant is not responsible for unforeseen consequences of negligence. . . .

There is no subject in the field of law upon which more has been written with less elucidation than that of proximate cause. Cases discussing it are legion. It has challenged many of the most able commentators at one time or another. It is generally agreed that there is no simple formula for defining proximate cause, but this is assumed to be a difficulty peculiar to the law, which distinguishes between "proximate cause" and "cause in fact." However, examination of the literature suggests that neither scientists nor philosophers have been more successful than judges in providing a verbal definition for this concept. We can contrast the concept of cause with that of destiny and of chance, we can use it operationally and pragmatically, but we cannot formulate a precise, rigorous, or very satisfactory verbal definition. Cause seems to be one of those elemental concepts that defies refined analysis but is known intuitively to commonsense.

Although a rigorous definition of proximate cause continues to elude us, nevertheless it is clear, in this state at least, that it is not a matter of foreseeability. We are unable now to make any better statement on this issue than that of Mr. Justice Mitchell many years ago. Speaking for this court, he said: . . .

> What a man may reasonably anticipate is important, and may be decisive, in determining whether an act is negligent, but is not at all decisive in determining whether that act is the proximate cause of an injury which ensues. If a person had no reasonable ground to anticipate that a particular act would or might result in any injury to anybody, then, of course, the act would not be negligent at all; but, if the act itself is negligent, then the person guilty of it is equally liable for all its natural and proximate consequences, whether he could have foreseen them or not. Otherwise expressed, the law is that if the act is one which the party ought, in the exercise of ordinary care, to have

> anticipated was liable to result in injury to others, then he is liable for any injury proximately resulting from it, although he could not have anticipated the particular injury which did happen. Consequences which follow in unbroken sequence, without an intervening efficient cause, from the original negligent act, are natural and proximate; and for such consequences the original wrong-doer is responsible, even though he could not have foreseen the particular results which did follow.[5]

Although language may be found in some opinions dealing with the specific facts of particular cases that seems to be at variance with the statement of Mr. Justice Mitchell, this court has consistently through the years followed the doctrine thus enunciated. We now reaffirm that the doctrine of the *Christianson* case is still the law of Minnesota and, in the words of Mr. Justice Stone, decline the invitation of this case to add further to the already excessive literature of the law dealing, or attempting to deal, with the problem of proximate cause. It is enough to say that negligence is tested by foresight but proximate cause is determined by hindsight.

It follows that the trial court erred in making foreseeability a test of proximate cause. There can be no question that this was misleading to the jury and therefore prejudicial to the plaintiffs, requiring reversal of the judgment. . . .

Reversed and remanded for a new trial.

The conceptual difficulties involved in the proximate cause issue are perhaps best illustrated by three English cases. The first of these is In re Polemis & Furness, Withy & Co., [1921] 3 K.B. 560 (C.A.). The plaintiffs owned a ship which was being unloaded by the defendants. One of the defendants' servants dropped a plank into a hold of the ship which contained cans of benzine. Some of the cans had been broken and when the plank hit the floor of the hold it apparently caused a spark which ignited benzine vapor which had escaped from the broken cans. The resulting fire destroyed the ship. The claim of the plaintiffs for the destruction of the ship was submitted to arbitration, and in addition to the foregoing facts, the arbitrators found that the defendants' servant was negligent in dropping the plank into the hold, in that some damage to the ship could have been foreseen, but that it could not have been reasonably anticipated that the plank would cause a spark. In ruling that the plaintiffs were entitled to judgment, Scrutton L.J. said in part, 3 K.B. at 577:

> To determine whether an act is negligent, it is relevant to determine whether any reasonable person would foresee that the act would cause damage; if he

5. Christianson v. Chicago, St. P. M. & O. Ry., 67 Minn. 94, 96, 69 N.W. 640, 641 (1896).

> would not, the act is not negligent. But if the act would or might probably cause damage, the fact that the damage it in fact causes is not the exact kind of damage one would expect is immaterial, so long as the damage is in fact directly traceable to the negligent act, and not due to the operation of independent causes having no connection with the negligent act, except that they could not avoid its results. Once the act is negligent, the fact that its exact operation was not foreseen is immaterial.

Under the *Polemis* rule, the defendants' liability depended on whether the consequences to the plaintiff could be characterized as direct. The consequences would not be direct if a sufficient new cause intervened between the defendant's negligence and the consequences.

The English law was changed by the first of two cases arising out of a single incident. In Overseas Tankship (U.K.), Ltd. v. Morts Dock and Engineering Co., [1961] 1 All E.R. 404, commonly referred to as *"Wagon Mound (No. 1),"* the charterers of an oil burning vessel, the Wagon Mound, spilled a quantity of oil into the harbor in Sydney, Australia. At the time the oil was spilled, workers were using acetylene torches in effecting repairs upon a wharf adjacent to the harbor. The charterers made no effort to disperse the oil, which drifted in under the wharf on the surface of the water. The wharf owners asked the operators of the nearby wharf at which the Wagon Mound was docked whether the oil would ignite due to the acetylene torch work, and were assured that it would not. Shortly thereafter, the oil did ignite due to embers dropping from the wharf, and the entire wharf area was destroyed by the ensuing fire. The wharf owners sued the charterers of the Wagon Mound, alleging that the spillage of oil was negligent inasmuch as it was foreseeable that it would foul bilge pumps, shipways and other equipment in and around the harbor area. The defendants argued that because the fire in this case was unforeseeable they should not be held liable. The trial court, sitting without a jury in admiralty, specifically found that the fire was unforeseeable, but awarded damages to the plaintiffs for the destruction of the wharf, presumably on the authority of *Polemis.*

On appeal by the defendants to the Privy Council, the English high court reversed the order of the trial court and entered judgment for the defendants based upon the specific finding below that the ignitability of the oil was unforeseeable. The court had this to say about the *Polemis* decision, (1 All E.R. at 413):

> Enough has been said to show that the authority of *Polemis* has been severely shaken, though lip-service has from time to time been paid to it. In their Lordships' opinion, it should no longer be regarded as good law. It is not probable that many cases will for that reason have a different result, though it is hoped that the law will be thereby simplified, and that, in some cases at least, palpable injustice will be avoided. For it does not seem consonant with current ideas of justice or morality that, for an act of negligence, however slight or venial, which results in some trivial foreseeable damage, the actor

should be liable for all consequences, however unforeseeable and however grave, so long as they can be said to be "direct."

The third case arose out of the same occurrence that gave rise to *Wagon Mound (No. 1)*. This was Overseas Tankship (U.K.), Ltd. v. Miller Steamship Co. Pty. Ltd., [1966] 2 All E.R. 709, known as *Wagon Mound (No. 2)*, in which the plaintiff was the owner of two ships damaged by the fire. The court below made the following specific findings with respect to the foreseeability of the oil igniting on water:

(i) Reasonable people in the position of the officers of the Wagon Mound would regard furnace oil as very difficult to ignite on water.
(ii) Their personal experience would probably have been that this had very rarely happened.
(iii) If they had given attention to the risk of fire from the spillage, they would have regarded it as a possibility, but one which could become an actuality only in very exceptional circumstances.
(iv) They would have considered the chances of the required exceptional circumstances happening whilst the oil remained spread on the harbour waters, as being remote.
(v) I find that the occurrence of damage to [the plaintiffs'] property as a result of the spillage, was not reasonably foreseeable by those for whose acts [the defendant] would be responsible.

In ruling that on the basis of these findings the plaintiff was entitled to prevail on the proximate cause issue as a matter of law, the court on appeal distinguished *Wagon Mound (No. 1)* as follows, 2 All E.R. 717-719:

> In *Wagon Mound (No. 1)* the Board were not concerned with degrees of foreseeability because the finding was that the fire was not foreseeable at all. So VISCOUNT SIMONDS had no cause to amplify the statement that the "essential factor in determining liability is whether the damage is of such a kind as the reasonable man should have foreseen". Here the findings show, however, that some risk of fire would have been present to the mind of a reasonable man in the shoes of the ship's chief engineer. So the first question must be what is the precise meaning to be attached in this context to the words "foreseeable" and "reasonably foreseeable.". . .
>
> In the present case there was no justification whatever for discharging the oil into Sydney Harbour. Not only was it an offence to do so, but also it involved considerable loss financially. If the ship's engineer had thought about the matter there could have been no question of balancing the advantages and disadvantages. From every point of view it was both his duty and his interest to stop the discharge immediately.
>
> It follows that in their lordships' view the only question is whether a reasonable man having the knowledge and experience to be expected of the chief engineer of the Wagon Mound would have known that there was a real

risk of the oil on the water catching fire in some way: if it did, serious damage to ships or other property was not only foreseeable but very likely. Their lordships do not dissent from the view of the trial judge that the possibilities of damage "must be significant enough in a practical sense to require a reasonable man to guard against them", but they think that he may have misdirected himself in saying "there does seem to be a real practical difficulty, assuming that some risk of fire damage was foreseeable, but not a high one, in making a factual judgment as to whether this risk was sufficient to attract liability if damage should occur". In this difficult chapter of the law decisions are not infrequently taken to apply to circumstances far removed from the facts which give rise to them, and it would seem that here too much reliance has been placed on some observations in . . . other cases.

In their lordships' view a properly qualified and alert chief engineer would have realized there was a real risk here, and they do not understand [the trial judge] to deny that; but he appears to have held that, if a real risk can properly be described as remote, it must then be held to be not reasonably foreseeable. That is a possible interpretation of some of the authorities; but this is still an open question and on principle their lordships cannot accept this view. If a real risk is one which would occur to the mind of a reasonable man in the position of the defendant's servant and which he would not brush aside as far-fetched, and if the criterion is to be what that reasonable man would have done in the circumstances, then surely he would not neglect such a risk if action to eliminate it presented no difficulty, involved no disadvantage and required no expense.

In the present case the evidence shows that the discharge of so much oil on to the water must have taken a considerable time, and a vigilant ship's engineer would have noticed the discharge at an early stage. The findings show that he ought to have known that it is possible to ignite this kind of oil on water, and that the ship's engineer probably ought to have known that this had in fact happened before. The most that can be said to justify inaction is that he would have known that this could only happen in very exceptional circumstances; but that does not mean that a reasonable man would dismiss such risk from his mind and do nothing when it was so easy to prevent it. If it is clear that the reasonable man would have realised or foreseen and prevented the risk, then it must follow that the appellants are liable in damages. The learned judge found this a difficult case: he said that this matter is "one on which different minds would come to different conclusions". Taking a rather different view of the law from that of the learned judge, their lordships must hold that the respondents are entitled to succeed on this issue.

"The decision would appear to have adopted the American formula of balancing magnitude of risk and gravity of harm against utility of conduct, and to have applied it to foreseeability in relation to 'proximate cause.' The effect would appear to be to let the *Polemis* Case in again by the back door, since cases will obviously be quite infrequent in which there is not some recognizable slight risk of this character." Prosser and Keeton, Law of Torts 296 (5th ed. 1984). Do you agree?

3. Special Instances of Nonliability for Foreseeable Consequences

a. Mental and Emotional Harm

In Mitchell v. Rochester Ry., 151 N.Y. 107, 45 N.E. 354 (1896), the defendant's driver negligently drove a wagon pulled by two horses up to the plaintiff. When the horses stopped, the plaintiff was standing between them, although they did not come into contact with her. The plaintiff was frightened and later suffered a miscarriage, which medical testimony indicated was caused by the fright. In ordering judgment for the defendant notwithstanding a verdict for the plaintiff, the court ruled that there could be no recovery for fright alone without impact. In the court's view, it followed from that ruling that there could be no recovery for any resulting physical manifestations of the fright, such as "nervous disease, blindness, insanity or even a miscarriage." This became known as the impact rule and at one time it was the clear weight of authority.[170] But very few states now adhere to the impact rule. One such case is OB-GYN Associates of Albany v. Littleton, 259 Ga. 663, 386 S.E.2d 146 (1989). The court ruled that not only must there be a physical impact, but that the plaintiff must also suffer physical injury as a result of the impact.

If there has been an impact, the plaintiff can recover damages for pre-impact fright, and if the impact causes immediate harm, damages for the intangible harm that follows from the impact, as set out generally in Chapter 8. In some instances, however, the impact may not cause any immediate harm, but the plaintiff may fear that the harm will be suffered at some indefinite time in the future. In Beeman v. Manville Corp., 496 N.W.2d 247 (Iowa 1993), the court ruled that the plaintiff could recover for "cancerphobia" caused by the inhalation of asbestos fibers, even in the absence of evidence that made it likely that the plaintiff would actually suffer cancer in the future.

Persons alleging emotional harm from fear of future injury have brought suit in a variety of other contexts. In Payton v. Abbott Labs, 386 Mass. 540, 437 N.E.2d 171 (1982), the plaintiffs were daughters of women who had taken DES when they were pregnant. The court ruled that the plaintiffs could recover for fear of developing cancer only if that fear resulted in

170. Two narrow exceptions to the impact rule had developed in some states, permitting recovery for emotional harm resulting from the negligent transmission of telegraph messages and from the negligent handling of corpses. See Prosser and Keeton, The Law of Torts 362 (5th ed. 1984). The latter exception has been extended to a case involving a deceased pet. In Corso v. Crawford Dog & Cat Hosp., 415 N.Y.S.2d 182 (Civ. Ct. N.Y. 1979), the plaintiff retained the defendant to provide a funeral, complete with headstone and epitaph, for the former's 15-year-old poodle. The court ruled that the plaintiff was entitled to recover for the emotional harm she suffered when at the funeral, which was attended by her two sisters and a friend, she opened the casket to discover a dead cat.

physical injury. The court also ruled that the plaintiffs could not recover at all if it were established that they would not have been born at all had the mothers not taken DES.

In Faya v. Almaraz, 329 Md. 435, 620 A.2d 327 (1993), and in Burk v. Sage Products, 747 F. Supp. 285 (E.D. Pa. 1990), the plaintiffs' actions for emotional harm were based on fear of contracting AIDS. In *Faya,* the plaintiffs were patients of a surgeon who died of AIDS shortly after operating on the plaintiffs. Although the plaintiffs' tests were negative, the court ruled that it was error for the trial judge to dismiss the complaints, since the complaints alleged that it would have been possible for the plaintiffs to contract AIDS from the operations. In *Burk,* the plaintiff was pricked with a needle that was available to treat AIDS patients, but he could not prove that the needle had actually come into contact with such a patient. The plaintiff, like the plaintiff in *Faya,* tested negative, and the court refused to permit damages for the fear of contracting AIDS in the future.

Another context that has stimulated considerable litigation involves heart valves. In Brinkman v. Shiley, Inc., 732 F. Supp. 33 (M.D. Pa. 1989), the plaintiff, a wearer of a mechanical heart valve manufactured by the defendant, alleged that he saw a television program detailing the defectiveness of some heart valves of the sort used by the plaintiff and manufactured by the defendant. The valve had not malfunctioned at the time of the suit, but the plaintiff was concerned that it might do so in the future. The court, however, ruled that there could be no recovery. In Khan v. Shiley, Inc., 217 Cal. App. 3d 848, 266 Cal. Rptr. 106 (1990), the court ruled that the plaintiff could not recover for "heart valve anxiety" in a tort-based products liability suit, but could recover on proof of fraud. The manufacturer of the heart valves agreed conditionally to set up a $205 million fund to compensate the 55,000 persons with functioning valves who may fear a future malfunction. The settlement does not affect the suits filed on behalf of the 310 persons who died as a result of valve malfunction. See 20 Prod. Safety & Liab. Rep. (BNA) 117 (1992).

Similar suits may be brought by women who have received silicone breast implants, in light of the stories about the problems many of these women have had. See, e.g., Hilts, Maker Is Depicted as Fighting Tests on Implant Safety, N.Y. Times, Jan. 13, 1992, col. 6, at 1 (N.E.). At least one such suit has already been brought. See 20 Prod. Safety & Liab. Rep. (BNA) 118 (1992).

For an analysis that advocates recovery for psychic harm resulting from exposure to toxic substances, see Bohrer, Fear and Trembling in the Twentieth Century: Technological Risk, Uncertainty and Emotional Distress, 1984 Wis. L. Rev. 83.

Waube v. Warrington

216 Wis. 603, 258 N.W. 497 (1935)

WICKHEM, J. In the statement of facts in both briefs it is said that deceased was looking out the window of her house watching her child cross the highway, and witnessed the negligent killing of the child by defendant. While upon a demurrer the sole question is whether the facts alleged in the complaint state a cause of action, we consider that the statement of facts concurred in by plaintiff and defendant constitutes an informal amendment to the complaint by stipulation, and will determine the questions presented as though the complaint were amended to conform to the statement of facts.

The question presented is whether under the Wisconsin equivalent of Lord Campbell's Act, decedent's husband may recover for her death under such circumstances. Under the provisions of sec. 331.03, Stats., in order that he may recover for her death, the circumstances must have been such as to have entitled Susie Waube, had she lived, to maintain an action for her injuries. Thus the question presented is whether the mother of a child who, although not put in peril or fear of physical impact, sustains the shock of witnessing the negligent killing of her child, may recover for physical injuries caused by such fright or shock.

The problem must be approached at the outset from the view-point of the duty of defendant and the right of plaintiff, and not from the viewpoint of proximate cause. The right of the mother to recover must be based, first, upon the establishment of a duty on the part of defendant so to conduct herself with respect to the child as not to subject the mother to an unreasonable risk of shock or fright, and, second, upon the recognition of a legally protected right or interest on the part of the mother to be free from shock or fright occasioned by the peril of her child. It is not enough to find a breach of duty to the child, follow the consequences of such breach as far as the law of proximate cause will permit them to go, and then sustain a recovery for the mother if a physical injury to her by reason of shock or fright is held not too remote.

Upon this point we adopt and follow the doctrine of Palsgraf v. Long Island R.R. Co., 248 N.Y. 339, 162 N.E. 99. . . .

The right of a plaintiff to recover damages for nervous shock caused by negligence without actual impact has had an interesting history. In Victoria Railways Commissioners v. Coultas (1888), 13 A.C. 222, 226, it was held that plaintiff was not entitled to recover such damages. This became the prevailing doctrine in this country. This doctrine, however, was repudiated in a number of jurisdictions, including Wisconsin, in situations where fright without impact produced physical injuries. . . . The rule followed in Wisconsin appears to represent the modern tendency. . . . In jurisdictions following the liberal rule it has been held consistently . . . that in order to give rise to a right of action grounded on negligent conduct, the emotional distress or shock must be occasioned by fear of personal injury to the person sustaining the shock, and not fear of injury to his property or to the person of another.

Thus it may be said that the doctrine most favorable to plaintiff is not sufficiently broad to entitle him to recover. The question presented is whether there should be an extension of the rule to cases where defendant's conduct involves merely an unreasonable risk of causing harm to the child or spouse of the person sustaining injuries through fright or shock. There are two cases upon this point which deserve consideration in some detail. In Spearman v. McCrary, 4 Ala. App. 473, 58 So. 927, defendant's negligent operation of an automobile caused plaintiff's mule to take fright and run away. The mule was attached to a buggy from which plaintiff and her husband had just alighted but in which plaintiff's two children still remained. The damages alleged were shock and fright resulting in physical injuries. The court there adopted the view that recovery could be had for shock or fright culminating in physical injury although caused without physical impact. The court approaches the problem from the standpoint of proximate cause, and does not discuss the precise point involved here, although in fact recovery appears to have been given for physical injuries sustained through fright occasioned by the peril of the children rather than that of the mother. In the situation presented by that case, however, plaintiff may well have suffered fright and shock as a result of fear for her own safety.

The only case squarely dealing with this problem is Hambrook v. Stokes Bros. (1925), 1 K.B. 141. In this case a servant of defendants was in charge of a motor-truck belonging to defendants, and parked it at the top of a hill on Dover street in Folkestone, leaving it unattended, with the motor running, and without taking proper precautions to prevent it from moving. During his absence the truck started to run down the hill. The street was narrow, being not more than six feet wide in some places, and there was a curve at the lower end of it. The truck eventually came to a standstill by reason of running against the side of a house at a point below the curve. On the day in question Mrs. Hambrook, whose house was at the bottom of Dover street, accompanied her three children, a girl and two boys, part of the distance on their way to school. She walked with them to a point a little below the curve in Dover Street, and then left them. Shortly afterwards she saw the truck coming rapidly around the curve in her direction. She was not in any personal danger, as the truck stopped some distance short of where she was standing, and in any case she would have had ample opportunity to step into a position of safety. She immediately became fearful for the safety of her children. A crowd collected and there were rumors of an accident. She inquired who had been injured, and a friend stated that it was a little girl with glasses. It appeared that her little girl wore glasses. She went to the hospital and found that her daughter had been injured. She sustained a severe shock and consequent physical injuries from which she died. The trial court directed the jury that if the nervous shock was caused by fear of her child's safety, as distinguished from her own, plaintiff could not recover. From a verdict in favor of defendants, plaintiff appealed. The judgment was set aside and a new trial granted for misdirection. . . . Viewing the matter from the standpoint of proximate cause rather than duty, the court held that there should be no distinction between shock sustained by a mother as a result of fear for her own safety, and that sustained by reason of peril to her child. The court considered that defendant ought to have anticipated that if the unattended truck ran down this narrow street it might terrify some woman to such an extent, through fear of some immediate bodily injury to herself, that she would receive a mental shock with resultant physical injuries, and that defendant ought also to have anticipated that such a shock might result from the peril to the child of such a woman. While the majority mistakenly, as it seems to us, approach this problem from the standpoint of proximate cause, the dissenting opinion of SARGANT, L.J., approaches it from the standpoint of duty. The dissenting opinion concedes that since it was defendant's duty to exercise due care in the management of his vehicle so as to avoid physical injury to those on or near the highway, this duty cannot be limited to physical injuries caused by actual physical impact. The dissenting opinion, however, states that the matter is quite different where the shock to plaintiff is due, not to immediate fear of personal impact, but to the sight or apprehension of impact upon a third person. . . .

With due deference to the learned judges who concurred in the decision, we cannot escape the conclusion that the determination in the *Hambrook* case is incorrect, both in its initial approach and in its conclusion, and that the doctrine contended for by plaintiff, and there approved, would constitute an unwarranted enlargement of the duties of users of the highway. Fundamentally, defendant's duty was to use ordinary care to avoid physical injury to those who would be put in physical peril, as that term is commonly understood, by conduct on his part falling short of that standard. It is one thing to say that as to those who are put in peril of physical impact, impact is immaterial if physical injury is caused by shock arising from the peril. It is the foundation of cases holding to this liberal ruling, that the person affrighted or sustaining shock was actually put in peril of physical impact, and under these conditions it was considered immaterial that the physical impact did not materialize. It is quite another thing to say that those who are out of the field of physical danger through impact shall have a legally protected right to be free from emotional distress occasioned by the peril of others, when that distress results in physical impairment. The answer to this question cannot be reached solely by logic, nor is it clear that it can be entirely disposed of by a consideration of what the defendant ought reasonably to have anticipated as a consequence of his wrong. The answer must be reached by balancing the social interests involved in order to ascertain how far defendant's duty and plaintiff's right may justly and expediently be extended. It is our conclusion that they can neither justly nor expediently be extended to any recovery for physical injuries sustained by one out of the range of ordinary physical peril as a result of the shock of witnessing another's danger. Such consequences are so unusual and extraordinary, viewed after the event, that a user of the highway may be said not to subject others to an unreasonable risk of them by the careless management of his vehicle. Furthermore, the liability imposed by such a doctrine is wholly out of proportion to the culpability of the negligent tortfeasor, would put an unreasonable burden upon users of the highway, open the way to fraudulent claims, and enter a field that has no sensible or just stopping point.

It was recognized by the court in the *Hambrook* case that had the mother there merely been told of the injury to her child, instead of having been virtually a witness to the transaction, there would have been no liability. The court thus selected at least one arbitrary boundary for the extension. . . . It was suggested in the dissenting opinion in the *Hambrook* case that if the mother may recover, why not a child whose shock was occasioned by the peril of the mother? It is not necessary to multiply these illustrations. They can be made as numerous as the varying degrees of human relationship, and they shade into each other in such a way as to leave no definite or clear-cut stopping place for the suggested doctrine, short of a recovery for every person who has sustained physical injuries as a result of shock or emotional distress by reason of seeing or hearing of the peril or injury of another. No court has gone this far, and we think no court should go this far. It is our view that fairness and justice, as well as expediency, require the defendant's duty to be defined as heretofore stated, in accordance with the weight of liberal authority and the general statement of the rule by the American Law Institute. Human wrong-doing is seldom limited in its injurious effects to the immediate actors in a particular event. More frequently than not, a chain of results is set up that visits evil consequences far and wide. While from the standpoint of good morals and good citizenship the wrong-doer may be said to violate a duty to those who suffer from the wrong, the law finds it necessary, for reasons heretofore considered, to attach practical and just limits to the legal consequences of the wrongful act. . . .

By the Court. Order reversed, and cause remanded with directions to sustain the demurrer.

Waube adopted what is known as the *zone of danger rule.* That rule came to be the majority rule, and a number of courts have recently reaffirmed commitment to the rule. See, e.g., Williams v. Baker, 572 A.2d 1062 (D.C. App. 1990); Asaro v. Cardinal Glennon Memorial Hospital, 799 S.W.2d 595 (Mo. 1990); Hansen v. Sea Ray Boats, Inc., 830 P.2d 236 (Utah 1992).

What if the plaintiff is not in the zone of danger of physical impact, but reasonably believes that he or she is? According to two courts, the plaintiff must actually be in the zone of danger—reasonable belief on that score is not enough. See Hansen v. Sea Ray Boats, Inc., cited in the previous paragraph, and Outten v. National Railroad Passenger Corp., 928 F.2d 74 (3rd Cir. 1991).

The Supreme Court of Wisconsin expanded somewhat the zone of danger rule in Garrett v. City of New Berlin, 122 Wis. 2d 223, 362 N.W.2d 137 (1985). The court stated, in reversing summary judgment for the defendant, that it was not necessary to rethink *Waube* to permit recovery in a case in which the plaintiff was not in any immediate danger of physical impact. The plaintiff was one of a group of teenagers apparently being sought by a police officer driving a squad car. The plaintiff saw the squad car run over and seriously injure her brother. Although she herself was not at that time in any danger of injury, the court observed that the plaintiff "was not merely an observer who was not directly involved in the tortious activity. She was an object of the police officer's activities since she was a member of the group of children he was pursuing." 122 Wis. 2d at 232, 362 N.W.2d at 142.

In Dillon v. Legg, 68 Cal. 2d 728, 441 P.2d 912, 69 Cal. Rptr. 72 (1968), the Supreme Court of California ruled that the mother of a child killed by an automobile negligently operated by the defendant could recover for the emotional harm she suffered from witnessing the accident. In so doing, the court overruled a decision, Amaya v. Home Ice, Fuel & Supply Co., 59 Cal. 2d 295, 379 P.2d 513, 29 Cal. Rptr. 33 (1963), made only five years earlier which adopted the zone of danger rule. In upholding the plaintiff's complaint in *Dillon,* the court stated (68 Cal. 2d at 739-741, 441 P.2d at 919-921, 69 Cal. Rptr. at 79-81):

> In order to limit the otherwise potentially infinite liability which would follow every negligent act, the law of torts holds defendant amenable only for injuries to others which to defendant at the the time were reasonably foreseeable.
>
> In the absence of "overriding policy considerations . . . foreseeability of risk [is] of . . . primary importance in establishing the element of duty." (Grafton v. Molica (1965) 231 Cal. App. 2d 860, 865 [42 Cal. Rptr. 306]). . . .
>
> This foreseeable risk may be of two types. The first class involves actual physical impact. A second type of risk applies to the instant situation . . .
>
> Since the chief element in determining whether defendant owes a duty or an obligation to plaintiff is the foreseeability of the risk, that factor will be of prime concern in every case. Because it is inherently intertwined with foreseeability such duty or obligation must necessarily be adjudicated only upon a case-by-case basis. We cannot now predetermine defendant's obligation in every situation by a fixed category; no immutable rule can establish the extent of that obligation for every circumstance of the future. We can, however, define guidelines which will aid in the resolution of such an issue as the instant one.
>
> We note, first, that we deal here with a case in which plaintiff suffered a

shock which resulted in physical injury and we confine our ruling to that case. In determining, in such a case, whether defendant should reasonably foresee the injury to plaintiff, or, in other terminology, whether defendant owes plaintiff a duty of due care, the courts will take into account such factors as the following: (1) Whether plaintiff was located near the scene of the accident as contrasted with one who was a distance away from it. (2) Whether the shock resulted from a direct emotional impact upon plaintiff from the sensory and contemporaneous observance of the accident, as contrasted with the learning of the accident from others after its occurrence. (3) Whether plaintiff and the victim were closely related, as contrasted with an absence of any relationship or the presence of only a distant relationship.

The evaluation of these factors will indicate the *degree* of the defendant's foreseeability: obviously defendant is more likely to foresee that a mother who observes an accident affecting her child will suffer harm than to foretell that a stranger witness will do so. Similarly, the degree of foreseeability of the third person's injury is far greater in the case of his contemporaneous observance of the accident than that in which he subsequently learns of it. The defendant is more likely to foresee that shock to the nearby, witnessing mother will cause physical harm than to anticipate that someone distant from the accident will suffer more than a temporary emotional reaction. All these elements, of course, shade into each other; the fixing of obligation, intimately tied into the facts, depends upon each case.

In light of these factors the court will determine whether the accident and harm was *reasonably* foreseeable. Such reasonable foreseeability does not turn on whether the particular [defendant] as an individual would have in actuality foreseen the exact accident and loss; it contemplates that courts, on a case-to-case basis, analyzing all the circumstances, will decide what the ordinary man under such circumstances should reasonably have foreseen. The courts thus mark out the areas of liability, excluding the remote and unexpected.

In the instant case, the presence of all the above factors indicates that plaintiff has alleged a sufficient prima facie case. Surely the negligent driver who causes the death of a young child may reasonably expect that the mother will not be far distant and will upon witnessing the accident suffer emotional trauma. . . .

We are not now called upon to decide whether, in the absence or reduced weight of some of the above factors, we would conclude that the accident and injury were not reasonably foreseeable and that therefore defendant owed no duty of due care to plaintiff. In future cases the courts will draw lines of demarcation upon facts more subtle than the compelling ones alleged in the complaint before us.

Most courts that have considered the matter have rejected the zone of danger rule entirely in favor of a rule patterned after *Dillon.* On rare occasion, a court has advocated a "full recovery rule" under which the test of liability is one of foreseeability of harm. See, e.g., Plaisance v. Texaco, Inc., 937 F.2d 1004 (5th Cir. 1991). Much more common, however, are cases in which some strings are attached to liability based upon foreseeability. See, e.g., Wilder v. City of Keene, 131 N.H. 599, 557 A.2d 636 (1989) (parents who did not see the accident injuring their son but who saw him *in extremis* at the hospital cannot recover); Burris v. Grange Mutual Companies, 46 Ohio St. 3d 84, 545 N.E.2d 83 (1989) (mother not at the scene of injury to her son cannot recover for emotional harm suffered from being informed later of his death). Some courts have not insisted on presence at the scene if the plaintiff arrives shortly after the accident. See, e.g., Champion v. Gray, 478 So. 2d 17 (Fla. 1985). Other courts have permitted recovery in instances where the plaintiff was not at the scene, but saw the primary victim later at the hospital. See, e.g., Masaki v. General Motors Corp., 71 Haw. 1, 780 P.2d 566 (1989); Ferriter v. Daniel O'Connell's Sons, Inc., 381 Mass. 507, 413 N.E.2d 690 (1980). But some geographical relationship to the accident is required even in Hawaii and Massachusetts. In Kelley v. Kokua Sales and Supply, Ltd., 56 Haw. 204, 532 P.2d 673 (1975), recovery was denied in the case of a person who suffered a heart attack and died after being informed of the deaths of his daughter and granddaughter in an automobile accident. The accident occurred in Hawaii; the decedent learned of it a day later while he was in California. In Stockdale v. Bird & Son, Inc., 399 Mass. 249, 503 N.E.2d 951 (1987), the plaintiff, who learned of the accident involving her son several hours after it occurred and first saw him 24 hours later, could not recover.

The nature of the requisite relationship of the plaintiff with the primary victim has also generated considerable litigation. A number of states have limited recovery to persons who bear the traditional family relation to the primary victim. See, e.g., Sollars v. City of Albuquerque, 794 F. Supp. 360 (D.N.M. 1992) (unmarried eight-year cohabitant with primary victim and her children by previous marriage who also lived with primary victim cannot recover); Lindsey v. Visitec, Inc., 804 F. Supp. 1340 (W.D. Wash. 1992) (unmarried cohabitant with primary victim cannot recover). Other courts have permitted recovery beyond those in the traditional family unit. See, e.g., Binns v. Fredendall, 32 Ohio St. 3d 244, 513 N.E.2d 278 (1987) (plaintiff was unmarried cohabitant with primary victim); Leong v. Takasaki, 55 Haw. 398, 520 P.2d 758 (1974) (plaintiff was step-grandson of primary victim). The court in Dunphy v. Gregor, 167 A.2d 1248 (N.J. Super. 1992), opted for an open-ended, case-by-case approach. The plaintiff was engaged to the primary victim, and at the time of the accident they lived together and had plans for marriage. In overruling summary judgment for the defendant, the court stated (Id. at 1255):

> Important considerations in reaching a conclusion on this issue concerning a particular relationship should include whether the plaintiff and the injured person were members of the same household, their emotional reliance on each other, the particulars of their day to day relationship, and the manner in which they related to each other in attending to life's mundane requirements.

What if the plaintiff reasonably believes that the primary victim is her daughter, but in fact she is not? In Barnes v. Geiger, 446 N.E.2d 78 (Mass.

App.), *appeal denied,* 389 Mass. 1011, 448 N.E.2d 767 (1983), the court ruled that the mistaken plaintiff cannot recover.

Courts have also disagreed over whether the plaintiff must suffer some physical injury as a requisite of recovery. Holding that physical injury is a requirement are Champion v. Gray, 478 So. 2d 17 (Fla. 1985), and Reilly v. United States, 547 A.2d 894 (R.I. 1988). But what constitutes a physical injury is a matter of some disagreement. The court in Hayes v. Record, 158 A.D.2d 874, 551 N.Y.S.2d 668 (1990), held that "anxiety attacks" will not suffice. The court in Sullivan v. Boston Gas Co., 414 Mass. 129, 605 N.E.2d 805 (1993), held that "tension headaches . . . tenderness in the back of [the] head . . . concentration and reading problems . . . [and] sleeplessness, gastrointestinal distress, upset stomach, nightmares, depression, feelings of despair, difficulty in driving and working, and an overall 'lousy' feeling" satisfied the physical injury requirement.

Other courts have held that physical injury or manifestation is not required. See, e.g., Folz v. State, 110 N.M. 457, 797 P.2d 246 (1990); Ricottilli v. Summersville Memorial Hospital, 425 S.E.2d 629 (W. Va. 1993). And finally, some courts have held that to recover, the plaintiff must establish that the emotional harm is serious. See, e.g., Rodrigues v. State, 52 Haw. 156, 472 P.2d 509 (1970); Jones v. Howard University, 589 A.2d 419 (D.C. App. 1991).

Some cases have involved primary victims that are not "persons" in the full legal sense. In Johnson v. Ruark Obstetrics and Gynecology Associates, P.A., 327 N.C. 283, 395 S.E.2d 85 (1990), the court held that a fetus was a person for the purposes of emotional harm recovery. What about a pet? Yes, according to the court in Campbell v. Animal Quarantine Station, 63 Haw. 557, 632 P.2d 1066 (1981), which upheld a verdict totalling $1,000 for five plaintiffs for emotional harm caused by the death of their family dog. As to the latter, see Barton and Hill, How Much Will You Receive in Damages from the Negligent or Intentional Killing of Your Pet Dog or Cat?, 34 N.Y.L.S. L. Rev. 411 (1989).

Thing v. La Chusa

48 Cal. 3d 644, 771 P.2d 814, 257 Cal. Rptr. 865 (1989)

EAGLESON, JUSTICE. The narrow issue presented by the parties in this case is whether the Court of Appeal correctly held that a mother who did not witness an accident in which an automobile struck and injured her child may recover damages from the negligent driver for the emotional distress she suffered when she arrived at the accident scene. The more important question this issue poses for the court, however, is whether the "guidelines" enunciated by this court in Dillon v. Legg (1968) 68 Cal. 2d 728, 69 Cal. Rptr. 72, 441 P.2d 912, are adequate, or if they should be refined to create greater certainty in this area of the law.

Although terms of convenience identify the cause of action here as one for negligent infliction of emotional distress (NIED) and the plaintiff as a "bystander" rather than a "direct victim," the common law tort giving rise to plaintiffs' claim is negligence. . . . It is in that context that we consider the appropriate application of the concept of "duty" in an area that has long divided this court—recognition of the right of persons, whose only injury is emotional distress, to recover damages when that distress is caused by knowledge of the injury to a third person caused by the defendant's negligence. Although we again find ourselves divided, we shall resolve some of the uncertainty over the parameters of the NIED action, uncertainty that has troubled lower courts, litigants, and, of course, insurers.

Upon doing so, we shall conclude that the societal benefits of certainty in the law, as well as traditional concepts of tort law, dictate limitation of bystander recovery of damages for emotional distress. In the absence of physical injury or impact to the plaintiff himself, damages for emotional distress should be recoverable only if the plaintiff: (1) is closely related to the injury victim; (2) is present at the scene of the injury-producing event at the time it occurs and is then aware that it is causing injury to the victim and, (3) as a result suffers emotional distress beyond that which would be anticipated in a disinterested witness.

I

[The plaintiff's son was injured in an automobile accident that the plaintiff did not witness. She was near the scene, and, on being informed of the accident, she "rushed to the scene where she saw her bloody and unconscious child, whom she believed was dead, lying in the roadway." She brought suit against the defendants for emotional harm she suffered as a result of witnessing her son in his injured condition. The trial judge granted the defendants' motion for summary judgment, which was reversed by the Court of Appeal.]

III. Limitations in Negligence Actions

[The court surveyed the law preceding Dillon v. Legg, including Amaya v. Home Ice, Fuel & Supply Co.]

The *Amaya* view was short lived, however. Only five years later, the decision was overruled in Dillon v. Legg, supra, 68 Cal. 2d 728, 69 Cal. Rptr. 72, 441 P.2d 912. In the ensuing 20 years, like the pebble cast into the pond, *Dillon*'s progeny have created ever widening circles of liability. Post-*Dillon* decisions have now permitted plaintiffs who suffer emotional distress, but no resultant physical injury, and who were not at the scene of and thus did not witness the event that injured another, to recover damages on grounds that a duty was owed to them solely because it was foreseeable that they would suffer that distress on learning of injury to a close relative. . . .

The difficulty in defining the limits on recovery anticipated by the *Amaya* court was rejected as a basis for denying recovery, but the court did recognize that "to limit the otherwise potentially infinite liability which would follow every negligent act, the law of torts holds defendant amenable only for injuries to others which to defendant at the time were reasonably foreseeable." (*Dillon,* supra, 68 Cal. 2d at p. 739, 69 Cal. Rptr. 72, 441 P.2d 912.) Thus, while the court indicated that foreseeability of the injury was to be the primary consideration in finding duty, it simultaneously recognized that policy considerations mandated that infinite liability be avoided by restrictions that would somehow narrow the class of potential plaintiffs. But the test limiting liability was itself amorphous. . . .

The *Dillon* court anticipated and accepted uncertainty in the short term in application of its holding, but was confident that the boundaries of this NIED action could be drawn in future cases. In sum, as former Justice Potter Stewart once suggested with reference to that undefinable category of materials that are obscene, the *Dillon* court was satisfied that trial and appellate courts would be able to determine the existence of a duty because the court would know it when it saw it. (See Jacobellis v. Ohio (1964) 378 U.S. 184, 197, 84 S. Ct. 1676, 1683, 12 L. Ed. 2d 793 (conc. opn. of Stewart, J.).) Underscoring the questionable validity of that assumption, however, was the obvious and unaddressed problem that the injured party, the negligent tortfeasor, their insurers, and their attorneys had no means short of suit by which to determine if a duty such as to impose liability for damages would be found in cases other than those that were "on all fours" with *Dillon.* Thus, the only thing that was foreseeable from the *Dillon* decision was the uncertainty that continues to this time as to the parameters of the third-party NIED action.

*IV. Post-***Dillon** *Extension*

The expectation of the *Dillon* majority that the parameters of the tort would be further defined in future cases has not been fulfilled. Instead, subsequent decisions of the Courts of Appeal and this court, have created more uncertainty. And, just as the "zone of danger" limitation was abandoned in *Dillon* as an arbitrary restriction on recovery, the *Dillon* guidelines have been relaxed on grounds that they, too, created arbitrary limitations on recovery. Little consideration has been given in post-*Dillon* decisions to the importance of avoiding the limitless exposure to liability that the pure foreseeability test of "duty" would create and towards which these decisions have moved.

[The court's discussion of the post-*Dillon* California cases is omitted.]

V. Clarification of the Right to Recover for NIED

Not surprisingly, this "case-to-case" or ad hoc approach to development of the law that misled the Court of Appeal in this case has not only produced inconsistent rulings in the lower courts, but has provoked considerable critical comment by scholars who attempt to reconcile the cases. . . .

Our own prior decisions identify factors that will appropriately circumscribe the right to damages, but do not deny recovery to plaintiffs whose emotional injury is real even if not accompanied by out-of-pocket expense. Notwithstanding the broad language in some of those decisions, it is clear that foreseeability of the injury alone is not a useful "guideline" or a meaningful restriction on the scope of the NIED action. . . . It is apparent that reliance on foreseeability of injury alone in finding a duty, and thus a right to recover, is not adequate when the damages sought are for an intangible injury. In order to avoid limitless liability out of all proportion to the degree of a defendant's negligence, and against which it is impossible to insure without imposing unacceptable costs on those among whom the risk is spread, the right to recover for negligently caused emotional distress must be limited.

[The court's discussion of the *Dillon* factor involving the relationship of the plaintiff to the primary victim is omitted. The court discussed a variety of contexts in which that issue can arise, including claims for loss of consortium (see Borer v. American Airlines, p. 419) and for wrongful life (see Turpin v. Sortini, p. 439).]

Similar reasoning justifies limiting recovery to persons closely related by blood or marriage since, in common experience, it is more likely that they will suffer a greater degree of emotional distress than a disinterested witness to negligently caused pain and suffering or death. Such limitations are indisputably arbitrary since it is foreseeable that in some cases unrelated persons have a relationship to the victim or are so affected by the traumatic event that they suffer equivalent emotional distress. As we have observed, however, drawing arbitrary lines is unavoidable if we are to limit liability and establish meaningful rules for application by litigants and lower courts.

No policy supports extension of the right to recover for NIED to a larger class of plaintiffs. Emotional distress is an intangible condition experienced by most persons, even absent negligence, at some time during their lives. Close relatives suffer serious, even debilitating, emotional reactions to the injury, death, serious illness, and evident suffering of loved ones. These reactions occur regardless of the cause of the loved one's illness, injury, or death. That relatives will have severe emotional distress is an unavoidable aspect of the "human condition." The emotional distress for which monetary damages may be recovered, however, ought not to be that form of acute emotional distress or the transient emotional reaction to the occasional gruesome or horrible incident to which every person may potentially be exposed in an industrial and sometimes violent society. Regardless of the depth of feeling or the resultant physical or mental illness that results from witnessing violent events, persons unrelated to those injured or killed may not now recover for such emotional upheaval even if negligently caused. Close relatives who witness the accidental injury or death of a loved one and suffer emotional trauma may not recover when the loved one's conduct was the cause of that emotional trauma. The overwhelming majority of "emotional distress" which we endure, therefore, is not compensable.

Unlike an award of damages for intentionally caused emotional distress which is punitive, the award for NIED simply reflects society's belief that a negligent actor bears some responsibility for the effect of his conduct on persons other than those who suffer physical injury. In identifying those persons and the circumstances in which the defendant will be held to redress the injury, it is appropriate to restrict recovery to those persons who will suffer an emotional impact beyond the impact that can be anticipated whenever one learns that a relative is injured, or dies, or the emotion felt by a "disinterested" witness. The class of potential plaintiffs should be limited to those who because of their relationship suffer the greatest emotional distress. When the right to recover is limited in this manner, the liability bears a reasonable relationship to the culpability of the negligent defendant.

The elements which justify and simultaneously limit an award of damages for emotional distress caused by awareness of the negligent infliction of injury to a close relative are those noted in Ochoa [v. Superior Court, 39 Cal. 3d 159, 703 P.2d 1, 216 Cal. Rptr. 661 (1985)]—the traumatic emotional effect on the plaintiff who contemporaneously observes both the event or conduct that causes serious injury to a close relative and the injury itself. Even if it is "foreseeable" that persons other than closely related percipient witnesses may suffer emotional distress, this fact does not justify the imposition of what threatens to become unlimited liability for emotional distress on a defendant whose conduct is simply negligent. Nor does such abstract "foreseeability" warrant continued reliance on the assumption that the limits of liability will become any clearer if lower courts are permitted to continue approaching the issue on a "case-to-case" basis some 20 years after *Dillon*.

We conclude, therefore, that a plaintiff may recover damages for emotional distress caused by observing the negligently inflicted injury of a third person if, but only if, said plaintiff: (1) is closely related to the injury victim; (2) is present at the scene of the injury producing event at the time it occurs and is then aware that it is causing injury to the victim; and (3) as a result suffers serious emotional distress—a reaction beyond that which would be anticipated in a disinterested witness and which is not an abnormal response to the circumstances. These factors were present in *Ochoa* and each of this court's prior decisions upholding recovery for NIED.

The dictum in *Ochoa* suggesting that the factors noted in the *Dillon* guidelines are not essential in determining whether a plaintiff is a foreseeable victim of defendant's negligence should not be relied on. The merely negligent actor does not owe a duty the law will recognize to make monetary amends to all persons who may have suffered emotional distress on viewing or learning about the injurious consequences of his conduct. . . . Experience has shown that, contrary to the expectation of the *Dillon* majority, and with apology to Bernard Witkin, there are clear judicial days on which a court can foresee forever and thus determine liability but none on which that foresight alone provides a socially and judicially acceptable limit on recovery of damages for that injury.

VI. *Disposition*

The undisputed facts establish that plaintiff was not present at the scene of the accident in which her son was injured. She did not observe defendant's conduct and was not aware that her son was being injured. She could not, therefore, establish a right to recover for the emotional distress she suffered when she subsequently learned of the accident and observed its consequences. The order granting summary judgment was proper.

The judgment of the Court of Appeal is reversed.

KAUFMAN, Justice, concurring.

We granted review in this case because of the obvious and continuing difficulties that have plagued trial courts and litigants in the area of negligent infliction of emotional distress. Of course, any meaningful review of the issue necessarily entails reappraising, in the light of 20 years of experience, our landmark holding in Dillon v. Legg (1968) 68 Cal. 2d 728, 69 Cal. Rptr. 72, 441 P.2d 912, that a plaintiff may recover for the emotional distress induced by the apprehension of negligently caused injury to a third person. Two such "reappraisals" have now been suggested.

The majority opinion by Justice Eagleson proposes to convert *Dillon*'s flexible "guidelines" for determining whether the risk of emotional injury was foreseeable or within the defendant's duty of care, into strict "elements" necessary to recovery. While conceding that such a doctrinaire approach will necessarily lead to "arbitrary" results, Justice Eagleson nevertheless concludes that "[g]reater certainty and a more reasonable limit on the exposure to liability for negligent conduct" require strict limitations. (Maj. opn., p. 879 of 257 Cal. Rptr., p. 828 of 771 P.2d.)

Justice Broussard, in dissent, opposes the effort to rigidify the *Dillon* guidelines. He urges, instead, that the court remain faithful to the guidelines as originally conceived—as specific but "flexible" limitations on liability—and adhere to *Dillon*'s original reliance on "foreseeability as a general limit on tort liability." (Dis. opn. of Broussard, J., p. 868 of 257 Cal. Rptr., p. 817 of 771 P.2d.) Justice Broussard denies that *Dillon* has failed to afford adequate guidance to the lower courts or to confine liability within reasonable limits. On the contrary, the *Dillon* approach, in the dissent's view, has provided—and continues to provide—a workable and "*principled* basis for determining liability. . . ." (Id., at p.895 of 257 Cal. Rptr., at p. 844 of 771 P.2d, italics added.)

With all due respect, I do not believe that either the majority opinion or the dissent has articulated a genuinely "principled" rule of law. On the one hand, experience has shown that rigid doctrinal limitations on bystander liability, such as that suggested by Justice Eagleson, result inevitably in disparate treatment of plaintiffs in substantially the same position. To be sure, the majority freely—one might say almost cheerfully—acknowledges that its position is arbitrary; yet nowhere does it consider the cost of such institutionalized caprice, not only to the individuals involved, but to the integrity of the judiciary as a whole.

On the other hand, two decades of adjudication under the inexact guidelines created by *Dillon* and touted by the dissent, has, if anything, created a body of case law marked by even greater confusion and inconsistency of result.

The situation, therefore, calls for a wholesale reappraisal of the wisdom of permitting recovery for emotional distress resulting from injury to others.

[JUSTICE KAUFMAN's discussion of earlier California cases and cases from other states rejecting *Dillon* is omitted.]

B. *Dillon* Rejected as Hopelessly Arbitrary

While the courts rejecting bystander liability have cited a number of reasons, one argument in particular has been considered dispositive: *Dillon*'s confident prediction that future courts would be able to fix just and sensible boundaries on bystander liability has been found to be wholly illusory—both in theory and in practice. . . .

Twenty-five years ago, this court posed a series of rhetorical questions concerning the guidelines later adopted in *Dillon:* "[H]ow soon is 'fairly contemporaneous?' What is the magic in the plaintiff's being 'present'? Is the shock any less immediate if the mother does not know of the accident until the injured child is brought home? And what if the plaintiff is present at the scene but is nevertheless unaware of the danger or injury to the third person until shortly after the accident has occurred. . . ?" (Amaya v. Home Ice, Fuel & Supply Co., supra, 59 Cal. 2d at p. 313, 29 Cal. Rptr. 33, 379 P.2d 513.) As the foregoing sampling of *Dillon*'s progeny vividly demonstrates, we are no closer to answers today than we were then. The questions, however, are no longer hypothetical—they are real: Is there any rational basis to infer that Mrs. Arauz was any less traumatized than Mrs. Dillon because she saw her bloody infant five minutes after it was struck by defendant's car? Was the Hathaways' suffering mitigated by the fact that they witnessed their child literally in death's throes, but failed to witness the precipitating event? Could it be argued that the emotional distress is even more traumatic, more foreseeable, for parents such as the Hathaways who fail to witness the accident and later blame themselves for allowing it to occur?

Clearly, to apply the *Dillon* guidelines strictly and deny recovery for emotional distress because the plaintiff was not a contemporaneous eyewitness of the accident but viewed the immediate consequences, ill serves the policy of compensating foreseeable victims of emotional trauma. Yet once it is admitted that temporal and spatial limitations bear no rational relationship to the likelihood of psychic injury, it becomes impossible to define, as the *Amaya* court well understood, any "sensible or just stopping point." (59 Cal. 2d at p. 311, 29 Cal. Rptr. 33, 379 P.2d 513.) By what humane and principled standard might a court decide, as a matter of law, that witnessing the bloody and chaotic aftermath of an accident involving a loved one is compensable if viewed within 1 minute of impact but noncompensable after 15? or 30? Is the shock of standing by while others undertake frantic efforts to save the life of one's child any less real or foreseeable when it occurs in an ambulance or emergency room rather than at the "scene"?

Obviously, a "flexible" construction of the *Dillon* guidelines cannot, ultimately, avoid drawing arbitrary and irrational distinctions any more than a strict construction. Justice Burke was right when he observed of the *Dillon* guidelines, "Upon analysis, their seeming certainty evaporates into arbitrariness, and inexplicable distinctions appear." (Dillon v. Legg, supra, 68 Cal. 2d at p. 749, 69 Cal. Rptr. 72, 441 P.2d 912, dis. opn. of Burke, J.)

C. *Dillon*'s Arbitrary Approach Should Be Overturned

Of course, it could be argued that recovery—not rationality—is the essential thing; that ultimately justice is better served by arbitrarily denying recovery to some, than by absolutely denying recovery to all. I find this argument to be unpersuasive, however, for two reasons.

First, the cost of the institutionalized caprice which *Dillon* has wrought should not be underestimated. The foremost duty of the courts in a free society is the principled declaration of public norms. The legitimacy, prestige and effectiveness of the judiciary—the "least dangerous branch"—ultimately depend on public confidence in our unwavering commitment to this ideal. Any breakdown in principled decisionmaking, any rule for which no principled basis can be found and clearly articulated, subverts and discredits the institution as a whole.

It is not always easy, of course, to accommodate the desire for individual justice with the need for reasoned, well-grounded, general principles. We sacrifice the latter for the sake of the former, however, only at our peril. For the "power-base" of the courts, as noted above, is rather fragile; it consists of the perception of our role in the structure of American government as the voice of reason, and the faith that the laws we make today, we ourselves will be bound by tomorrow. Any "rule"—such as *Dillon*'s—which permits and even encourages judgments based not on universal standards but individual expediency, erodes the public trust which we serve, and on which we ultimately depend.

There is a second reason, apart from the inherently corrosive effect of arbitrary rules, that points to the conclusion that "bystander" liability should not be retained. The interest in freedom from emotional distress caused by negligent injury to a third party is simply not, in my view, an interest which the law can or should protect. It is not that the interest is less than compelling. The suffering of a parent from the death or injury of a child is terribly poignant, and has always been so. It is the very universality of such injury, however, which renders it inherently unsuitable to legal protection. . . .

A final argument against overruling *Dillon* is, of course, the simple fact that it has been the law for 20 years. Stare decisis should not be lightly dismissed in any thoughtful reconsideration of the law. History and experience, however, are the final judge of whether a decision was right or wrong, whether it should be retained, modified or abandoned. In this case, history and experience have shown, as the *Amaya* court accurately predicted, that the quest for sensible and just limits on bystander liability is "an inherently fruitless one." (59 Cal. 2d at p. 313, 29 Cal. Rptr. 33, 379 P.2d 513.)

Adherence to precedent cannot justify the perpetuation of a policy ill-conceived in theory and unfair in practice. As Justice Harlan aptly observed: "[A] judicious reconsideration of precedent cannot be as threatening to public faith in the judiciary as continued adherence to a rule unjustified in reason, which produces different results for breaches of duty in situations that cannot be differentiated in policy. . . ." (Moragne v. States Marine Lines, Inc. (1970) 398 U.S. 375, 405, 90 S. Ct. 1772, 1790, 26 L. Ed. 2d 339.)

For the foregoing reasons, therefore, I would overrule Dillon v. Legg, supra, 68 Cal. 2d 728, 69 Cal. Rptr. 72, 441 P.2d 912, and reinstate Amaya v. Home Ice, Fuel & Supply Co., supra, 59 Cal. 2d 295, 29 Cal. Rptr. 33, 379 P.2d 513 as the law of this state. Since the plaintiff was indisputably not within the zone of danger and could not assert a claim for emotional distress as the result of fear for her own safety, she could not establish a right to recover. Accordingly, I concur in the majority's conclusion that the order granting summary judgment in this case was proper.

[The dissenting opinion of Mosk, J., is omitted.]

Broussard, Justice, dissenting.

I dissent. . . .

The majority grope for a "bright line" rule for negligent infliction of emotional distress actions, only to grasp an admittedly arbitrary line which will deny recovery to victims whose injuries from the negligent acts of others are very real. In so doing, the majority reveal a myopic reading of Dillon v. Legg, supra, 68 Cal. 2d 728, 69 Cal. Rptr. 72, 441 P.2d 912. They impose a strict requirement that plaintiff be present at the scene of the injury-producing event at the time it occurs and is aware that it is causing injury to the victim. This strict requirement rigidifies what *Dillon* forcefully told us should be a flexible rule, and will lead to arbitrary results. I would follow the mandate of *Dillon* and maintain that foreseeability and duty determine liability, with a view toward a policy favoring reasonable limitations on liability. There is no reason why these general rules of tort law should not apply to negligent infliction of emotional distress actions. . . .

Other courts have also given "bright line" effect to the three factors set out in *Dillon.* See, e.g., Cameron v. Pepin, 610 A.2d 279 (Me. 1992).

Burgess v. Superior Court

2 Cal. 4th 1064, 831 P.2d 1197, 9 Cal. Rptr. 2d 615 (1992)

PANELLI, ASSOCIATE JUSTICE.

Can a mother recover damages for negligently inflicted emotional distress against a physician who entered into a physician-patient relationship with her for care during labor and delivery if her child is injured during the course of the delivery? Because the professional malpractice alleged in this case breached a duty owed to the mother as well as the child, we hold that the mother can be compensated for emotional distress resulting from the breach of the duty. . . .

[The plaintiff underwent a cesarean section, during which she was under a general anesthetic. As she left the recovery room, she was told that something was wrong with her baby, and was given additional sedatives. The baby suffered permanent brain and nervous system damage as a result of oxygen deprivation. The plaintiff felt distress about the condition of the baby for the first time several hours later when she awoke from the sedative. Gupta, the defendant, moved for summary judgment, arguing that the plaintiff did not meet the requirements for recovery of damages for emotional harm established by Thing v. La Chusa. The trial court granted the motion. The intermediate appellate court reversed, ruling that *Thing* was not applicable because the plaintiff was a "direct victim" of the defendant's negligence rather than a "bystander."]

The law of negligent infliction of emotional distress in California is typically analyzed, as it was in this case, by reference to two "theories" of recovery: the "bystander" theory and the "direct victim" theory. In cases involving family relationships and medical treatment, confusion has reigned as to whether and under which "theory" plaintiffs may seek damages for negligently inflicted emotional distress.

Because the use of the "direct victim" designation has tended to obscure, rather than illuminate the relevant inquiry in cases such as the one at hand, we briefly turn our attention to the present state of the law in this area before proceeding to apply this law to the facts that confront us. . . .

Much of the confusion in applying rules for bystander and direct victim recovery to the facts of specific cases can be traced to this court's decision in [Molien v. Kaiser Foundation Hospitals, 27 Cal. 3d 916, 616 P.2d 813, 167 Cal. Rptr. 831 (1980)], which first used the "direct victim" label. In that case, we answered in the affirmative the question of whether, in the context of a negligence action, damages may be recovered for serious emotional distress unaccompanied by physical injury. In so holding, we found that a hospital and a doctor owed a duty directly to the husband of a patient, who had been diagnosed incorrectly by the doctor as having syphilis and had been told to so advise her husband in order that he could receive testing and, if necessary, treatment. We reasoned that the risk of harm to the husband was reasonably foreseeable and that the "alleged tortious conduct of the defendant was directed to him as well as to his wife." (Id. at pp. 922-923, 167 Cal. Rptr. 831, 616 P.2d 813.) Under such circumstances we deemed the husband to be a "direct victim" and found the criteria for bystander recovery not to be controlling. (Id. at p. 923, 167 Cal. Rptr. 831, 616 P.2d 813.)

The broad language of the *Molien* decision coupled with its perceived failure to establish criteria for characterizing a plaintiff as a "direct victim" rather than a "bystander," has subjected *Molien* to criticism from various sources, including this court. (E.g., *Thing,* supra, 48 Cal. 3d at pp. 658-664, 257 Cal. Rptr. 865, 771 P.2d 814.) The great weight of this criticism has centered upon the perception that *Molien* introduced a new method for determining the existence of a duty, limited only by the concept of foreseeability. To the extent that *Molien* stands for this proposition, it should not be relied upon and its discussion of duty is limited to its facts. As recognized in *Thing,* "[I]t is clear that foreseeability of the injury alone is not a useful 'guideline' or a meaningful restriction on the scope of [an action for damages for negligently inflicted emotional distress.]" (48 Cal. 3d at p. 663, 257 Cal. Rptr. 865, 771 P.2d 814.)

Nevertheless, other principles derived from *Molien* are sound: (1) damages for negligently inflicted emotional distress may be recovered in the absence of physical injury or impact, and (2) a cause of action to recover damages for negligently inflicted emotional distress will lie, notwithstanding the criteria imposed upon recovery by bystanders, in cases where a duty arising from a preexisting relationship is negligently breached. In fact, it is this later principle which defines the phrase "direct victim." That label signifies nothing more.

Gupta, however, has succumbed to the confusion in this area by failing to recognize that the distinction between bystander and direct victim cases is found in the source of the duty owed by the defendant to the plaintiff. Gupta argues, relying upon Ochoa v. Superior Court, (1985) 39 Cal. 3d 159, 172-173, 216 Cal. Rptr. 661, 703 P.2d 1 (hereafter *Ochoa*), that, when the emotional distress for which damages are claimed is "purely derivative" of the injury of another, the plaintiff may only recover such damages by satisfying the criteria for bystander recovery. Gupta claims that Burgess's damages are "derivative" because he owed no duty of care to Burgess to avoid injuring her child. Therefore, she may recover for her emotional distress, if at all, only as a bystander. We disagree.

In *Ochoa,* the parents sought damages for the emotional distress that they suffered from witnessing the defendants' failure to provide adequate medical care to their son, who was incarcerated. We held that the parents could state a claim for such damages, but only as bystanders, not as direct victims. In so holding we stated, "the defendants' negligence . . . was directed primarily at the decedent, with Mrs. Ochoa looking on as a helpless bystander as the tragedy of her son's demise unfolded before her." (*Ochoa,* supra, 39 Cal. 3d at pp. 172-173, 216 Cal. Rptr. 661, 703 P.2d 1.) In *Ochoa* the defendants had no preexisting relationship with the parents upon which to premise a duty of care; therefore, Mrs. Ochoa was necessarily in the position of a bystander with respect to her son's health care. The source of the duty, rather than the "derivative nature" of the injuries suffered by Mrs. Ochoa, was determinative.

In contrast to the facts of *Ochoa* and *Molien,* we are presented in this case with a "traditional" plaintiff with a professional negligence cause of action. Gupta cannot and does not dispute that he owed a duty of care to Burgess arising from their physician-patient relationship. Rather, Gupta contends that, while his alleged negligence resulting in injury to Joseph breached a duty of care owed to Joseph, it did not breach a duty of care owed to Burgess. In other words, Gupta claims that the scope of the duty of care owed to Burgess was limited to avoiding physical injury to her during her prenatal care and labor; it did not extend to avoiding injury to her fetus and the emotional distress that would result from such an injury. The origin of these mutually exclusive duties to Burgess and Joseph is apparently Gupta's unsupported assertion that Burgess and Joseph were two separate patients, because his actions could physically injure one and not the other.

To accept Gupta's argument would require us to ignore the realities of pregnancy and childbirth. Burgess established a physician-patient relationship with Gupta for medical care which was directed not only to her, but also to her fetus. The end purpose of this medical care may fairly be said to have been to provide treatment consistent with the applicable standard of care in order to maximize the possibility that Burgess's baby would be delivered in the condition in which he had been created and nurtured without avoidable injury to the baby or to Burgess. Moreover, during pregnancy and delivery it is axiomatic that any treatment for Joseph necessarily implicated Burgess's participation since access to Joseph could only be accomplished with Burgess' consent and with impact to her body.

In addition to the physical connection between a woman and her fetus, there is an emotional relationship as well. The birth of a child is a miraculous occasion which is almost always eagerly anticipated and which is invested with hopes, dreams, anxiety, and fears. In our society a woman often elects to forego general anesthesia or even any anesthesia, which could ease or erase the pain of labor, because she is concerned for the well-being of her child and she anticipates that her conscious participation in and observance of the birth of her child will be a wonderful and joyous occasion. An obstetrician, who must discuss the decision regarding the use of anesthesia with the patient, surely recognizes the emotionally charged nature of pregnancy and childbirth and the concern of the pregnant woman for her future child's well-being. The obstetrician certainly knows that even when a woman chooses to or must undergo general anesthesia during delivery, the receiving of her child into her arms for the first time is eagerly anticipated as one of the most joyous occasions of the patient's lifetime. It is apparent to us, as it must be to an obstetrician, that for these reasons, the mother's emotional well-being and the health of the child are inextricably intertwined.

It is in light of both these physical and emotional realities that the obstetrician and the pregnant woman enter into a physician-patient relationship. It cannot be gainsaid that both parties understand that the physician owes a duty to the pregnant woman with respect to the medical treatment provided to her fetus. Any negligence during delivery which causes injury to the fetus and resultant emotional anguish to the mother, therefore, breaches a duty owed directly anguish to the mother.

Thus, as the Court of Appeal correctly determined in this case, the failure by Burgess to satisfy the criteria for recovery under *Thing* does not end the inquiry. The alleged negligent actions resulting in physical harm to Joseph breached a duty owed to both Joseph and Burgess. Burgess was unavoidably and unquestionably harmed by this negligent conduct. . . .

[The court affirmed the intermediate court of appeals decision reversing summary judgment for the defendant.

[The concurring opinion of Mosk, A.J., is omitted.]

The distinction between "direct victims" and "bystanders" is discussed in Davies, Direct Actions for Emotional Harm: Is Compromise Possible?, 67 Wash. L. Rev. 1 (1992). Are you persuaded by the direct victim/bystander dichotomy of *Burgess*? Did the court in *Burgess* conclude that the plaintiff in *Molien,* discussed in *Burgess,* was, or was not, a direct victim? What do you think the plaintiff in *Molien* was?

In Marlene F. v. Affiliated Psychiatric Medical Clinic, Inc., 48 Cal. 3d 583, 770 P.2d 278, 257 Cal. Rptr. 98 (1989), the plaintiffs were mothers who had taken their children to the defendant clinic for family counseling. The psychologist assigned to the cases treated the mothers as well as the children, believing that the problems of the children stemmed in part from the mother-child relationships. The psychologist sexually molested the children, and the mothers brought suit against the defendant for their own emotional distress. The court held that the plaintiffs were direct victims rather than bystanders (48 Cal. 3d at 591, 770 P.2d at 282-283, 257 Cal. Rptr. at 102-103):

> In these circumstances, the therapist, as a professional psychologist, clearly knew or should have known in each case that his sexual molestation of the child would directly injure and cause severe emotional distress to his other patient, the mother, as well as to the parent-child relationship that was also under his care. His abuse of the therapeutic relationship and molestation of the boys breached his duty of care to the mothers as well as to the children. . . .
>
> It bears repeating that the mothers here were the patients of the therapist along with their sons, and the therapist's tortious conduct was accordingly directed against both. They sought treatment for their children—as they had the right, and perhaps even the obligation, to do—and agreed to be treated themselves to further the purposes of the therapy. They were plainly entitled to recover for the emotional distress they suffered.

In Johnson v. State, 37 N.Y.2d 378, 334 N.E.2d 590 (1975), the defendant notified the sister of a patient, Emma Johnson, that the patient had died, and the sister notified the patient's daughter. At the ensuing wake, the sister and daughter discovered that the body was not that of their Emma Johnson, but of another patient at the hospital also named Emma Johnson. Both the sister and daughter sued the hospital for emotional distress. At the trial, the daughter was awarded damages for that harm, but the sister was not. On appeal to the Appellate Division, the court eliminated the daughter's recovery for emotional harm. The daughter, but not the sister, appealed, and the Court of Appeals held that the daughter was entitled to the emotional harm award (34 N.Y.2d at 383, 334 N.E.2d at 593):

> Tobin v. Grossman is not relevant. In the *Tobin* case, the court held that no cause of action lies for unintended harm sustained by one, solely as a result of injuries inflicted directly upon another, regardless of the relationship and whether the one was an eyewitness to the incident which resulted in the direct injuries. In this case, however, the injury was inflicted by the hospital directly on claimant by its negligent sending of a false message announcing her mother's death. Claimant was not indirectly harmed by injury caused to another; she was not a mere eyewitness of or bystander to injury caused to another. Instead, she was the one to whom a duty was directly owed by the hospital, and the one who was directly injured by the hospital's breach of that duty. Thus, the rationale underlying the *Tobin* case, namely, the real dangers of extending recovery for harm to others than those directly involved, is inapplicable to the instant case.

How would the Supreme Court of California have decided *Johnson*? The commentary, like the cases, is divided over the circumstances under which the plaintiff should be able to recover for emotional harm. An argument for a "full recovery" rule under which recovery would be based on foreseeability is made in Bell, The Bell Tolls: Toward Full Tort Recovery for Psychic Injury, 36 Fla. L. Rev. 333 (1984). A case against full recovery is made in Crump, Evaluating Independent Torts Based upon "Intentional" or "Negligent" Infliction of Emotional Distress: How Can We Keep the Baby from Dissolving in the Bath Water?, 34 Ariz. L. Rev. 439 (1992). An argument for limiting recovery to those in the zone of danger is advanced in Pearson, Liability to Bystanders for Negligently Inflicted Emotional Harm—A Comment on the Nature of Arbitrary Rules, 34 Fla. L. Rev. 477 (1982). One commentator has argued that liability be extended to all foreseeable victims of emotional harm, but that damages be limited to economic loss. See Miller, The Scope of Liability for Negligent Infliction of Emotional Distress: Making "The Punishment Fit the Crime," 1 U. Haw. L. Rev. 1 (1979). See also Ingber, Rethinking Intangible Injuries: A Focus on Remedy, 73 Calif. L. Rev. 772 (1985). For a feminist perspective, see Chamallas and Kerber, Women, Mothers, and the Law of Fright: A History, 88 Mich. L. Rev. 814 (1990). In their introduction (pp. 815-816), the authors state:

> This examination of the history of the law of fright shows that gendered thinking has influenced the law, but has remained unexamined. We make three basic observations. First, we claim that the legal categories of "physical" and "emotional" harm are not unrelated to the gender of the victims. Women who have suffered fright-induced physical injuries have been disadvantaged by the legal classification of their injuries as emotional harm. Second, we demonstrate how the legal system has placed women's fright-based injuries at the margins of the law by describing women's suffering for the injury and death of their unborn and born children as remote, unforeseeable, and unreasonable. Finally, we raise the possibility that the claims of female plaintiffs in these fright cases—plaintiffs such as Margery Dillon—should be viewed as women's rights claims, as attempts to pressure the legal system to recognize and value the interests of women. By constructing a gendered history of this legal claim, we aspire to reclaim *Dillon* for women and to contribute to a feminist reconstruction of tort law.

Problem 22

Your investigation of the *Carrington* case (Problem 8, above) reveals that shortly after Mrs. Carrington left Robert at the emergency ward of the hospital she became extremely distraught. She spent that night at the hospital under sedation, and was released the next day. She still suffers from nervousness, sleeplessness, frequent nausea, and has lost weight. Assuming that it has been decided to bring suit against one or more of the dog owners for Robert's injuries, would you recommend filing a separate complaint seeking to recover damages to compensate Mrs. Carrington for the consequences to her resulting from the attack on Robert? If you would so recommend, prepare a draft of the complaint which maximizes the chances of defeating a motion to dismiss for failure to state a cause of action. Assume that the supreme court of your state generally has followed the law of California with respect to recovery for emotional harm.

b. Injury to Personal Relationships

The earliest cases involving recovery for intangible harm arising out of negligent injury to another occurred in the husband-wife context; recovery was permitted by a husband whose wife was injured. The history of the action is set out in Diaz v. Eli Lilly & Co., 364 Mass. 153, 302 N.E.2d 555 (1973). The first American decision according a wife the right to recover is Hitaffer v. Argonne Co., 183 F.2d 811 (D.C. Cir.), *cert. denied,* 340 U.S. 852 (1950). Since then, a clear majority of states has permitted the wife to recover. See, e.g., Montgomery v. Stephan, 359 Mich. 33, 48-49, 101 N.W.2d 227, 234 (1960):

> The gist of the matter is that in today's society the wife's position is analogous to that of a partner, neither kitchen slattern nor upstairs maid. Her duties and responsibilities in respect of the family unit complement those of the husband, extending only to another sphere. In the good times she lights the hearth with her own inimitable glow. But when tragedy strikes it is a part of her unique glory that, forsaking the shelter, the comfort, the warmth of the home, she puts her arm and shoulder to the plow. We are now at the heart of the issue. In such circumstances, when her husband's love is denied her, his strength sapped, and his protection destroyed, in short, when she has been forced by the defendant to exchange a heart for a husk, we are urged to rule that she has suffered no loss compensable at the law. But let some scoundrel dent a dishpan in the family kitchen and the law, in all its majesty, will convene the court, will march with measured tread to the halls of justice, and will there suffer a jury of her peers to assess the damages. Why are we asked, then, in the case before us, to look the other way? Is this what is meant when it is said that justice is blind?

See also Weaver v. Mitchell, 715 P.2d 1361 (Wyo. 1986). In Hopkins v. Blanco, 457 Pa. 90, 320 A.2d 139 (1974), the court based its decision permitting the wife to recover on a provision of the Pennsylvania constitution prohibiting discrimination based on sex.

A shrinking minority of courts continue to refuse to permit the wife to recover. See, e.g., Karriman v. Orthopedic Clinic, 488 P.2d 1250 (Okla. 1971). Other courts have resolved the issue by refusing to recognize a cause of action by either spouse. See, e.g., Tondre v. Thurmond-Hollis-Thurmond, Inc., 103 N.M. 292, 706 P.2d 156 (1985).

Feliciano v. Rosemar Silver Co.

401 Mass. 141, 514 N.E.2d 1095 (1987)

O'CONNOR, JUSTICE. Marcial Feliciano and the plaintiff Dolores Feliciano commenced an action in the Superior Court against Miguel Costa and Rosemar Silver Company (Rosemar) claiming that Marcial sustained personal injuries and the plaintiff sustained loss of consortium due to Costa's wrongful conduct in the course of his employment by Rosemar. Rosemar moved for summary judgment on the loss of consortium claim. That motion was allowed, and the plaintiff appealed. . . . We now affirm the judgment.

According to the plaintiff's deposition and affidavit submitted in connection with Rosemar's summary judgment motion, Marcial and the plaintiff had lived together as husband and wife for approximately twenty years before Marcial's injuries in 1981 "as a de facto married couple," although they were not legally married until 1983. During those years, the plaintiff used Marcial's surname, and the plaintiff and Marcial held themselves out as husband and wife, had joint savings accounts, filed joint tax returns, jointly owned their home, depended on each other for companionship, comfort, love and guidance, and maintained a sexual relationship to the exclusion of all others. The question on appeal is whether, in those circumstances, the plaintiff may recover for loss of consortium. We answer that question in the negative.

"Marriage is not merely a contract between the parties. It is the foundation of the family. It is a social institution of the highest importance. The Commonwealth has a deep interest that its integrity is not jeopardized." French v. McAnarney, 290 Mass. 544, 546, 195 N.E. 714 (1935). Our recognition of a right of recovery for the loss of a spouse's consortium, see Diaz v. Eli Lilly & Co., 364 Mass. 153, 302 N.E.2d 555 (1973), promotes that value. Conversely, that value would be subverted by our recognition of a right to recover for loss of consortium by a person who has not accepted the correlative responsibilities of marriage. This we are unwilling to do.

Furthermore, as a matter of policy, it must be recognized that tort liability cannot be extended without limit. Distinguishing between the marriage relationship and the myriad relationships that may exist between mere cohabitants serves the purpose of limiting protection to interests and values that are reasonably ascertainable. That cohabitants must have a "stable and significant" relationship to qualify for loss of consortium recovery, a standard relied on in the case of Butcher v. Superior Court of Orange County, 139 Cal. App. 3d 58, 70, 188 Cal. Rptr. 503 (1983), is an unsatisfactorily vague and indefinite standard.

We are not aware that any State court of last resort has recognized a right of recovery for loss of consortium outside of marriage. The two Federal decisions cited by the plaintiff interpreting State law as allowing such recovery, Sutherland v. Auch Inter-Borough Transit Co., 366 F. Supp. 127 (E.D. Pa. 1973), and Bulloch v. United States, 487 F. Supp. 1078 (D.N.J. 1980), were subsequently repudiated in the relevant States. See Leonardis v. Morton Chem. Co., 184 N.J. Super. 10, 445 A.2d 45 (1982); Childers v. Shannon, 183 N.J. Super. 591, 444 A.2d 1141 (1982); Rockwell v. Liston, 71 Pa. D. & C.2d 756 (1975).

Judgment affirmed.

Borer v. American Airlines, Inc.

19 Cal. 3d 441, 563 P.2d 858, 138 Cal. Rptr. 302 (1977)

TOBRINER, ACTING CHIEF JUSTICE. In Rodriguez v. Bethlehem Steel Corp. (1974) 12 Cal. 3d 382, 115 Cal. Rptr. 765, 525 P.2d 669 we held that a married person whose spouse had been injured by the negligence of a third party may maintain a cause of action for loss of "consortium." We defined loss of "consortium" as the "loss of conjugal fellowship and sexual relations" (12 Cal. 3d at p. 385, 115 Cal. Rptr. at p. 766, 525 P.2d at p. 670), but ruled that the term included the loss of love, companionship, society, sexual relations, and household services. Our decision carefully avoided resolution of the question whether anyone other than the spouse of a negligently injured person, such as a child or a parent, could maintain a cause of action analogous to that upheld in *Rodriguez.* We face that issue today: the present case presents a claim by nine children for the loss of the services, companionship, affection and guidance of their mother; the companion case of Baxter v. Superior Court, Cal., 138 Cal. Rptr. 315, 563 P.2d 871 presents the claim of a mother and father for the loss of the companionship and affection of their 16-year-old son.

Judicial recognition of a cause of action for loss of consortium, we believe, must be narrowly circumscribed. Loss of consortium is an intangible injury for which money damages do not afford an accurate measure or suitable recompense; recognition of a right to recover for such losses in the present context, moreover, may substantially increase the number of claims asserted in ordinary accident cases, the expense of settling or resolving such claims, and the ultimate liability of the defendants. Taking these considerations into account, we shall explain why we have concluded that the payment of damages to persons for the lost affection and society of a parent or child neither truly compensates for such loss nor justifies the social cost in attempting to do so. We perceive significant differences between the marital relationship and the parent-child relationship that support the limitation of a cause of action for loss of consortium to the marital situation; we shall therefore further elaborate our reasons for concluding that a child cannot maintain a cause of action for loss of parental consortium. In similar fashion we conclude in the companion case of Baxter v. Superior Court that a parent cannot maintain a cause of action for loss of a child's consortium. . . .

. . . Plaintiffs, the nine children of Patricia Borer, allege that on March 21, 1972, the cover on a lighting fixture at the American Airlines Terminal at Kennedy Airport fell and struck Patricia. Plaintiffs further assert that as a result of the physical injuries sustained by Patricia, each of them has been "deprived of the services, society, companionship, affection, tutelage, direction, guidance, instruction and aid in personality development, all with its accompanying psychological, educational and emotional detriment, by reason of Patricia Borer being unable to carry on her usual duties of a mother". . . Each plaintiff seeks damages of $100,000.

Defendant American Airlines demurred to the complaint for failure to state a cause of action. The trial court sustained the demurrer without leave to amend, and entered judgment dismissing the suit as to defendant American Airlines. Plaintiffs appealed from that judgment.

Our analysis of plaintiffs' appeal begins with our decision in Rodriguez v. Bethlehem Steel Corp., supra, 12 Cal. 3d 382, 115 Cal. Rptr. 765, 525 P.2d 669. In holding that a spouse has a cause of action for loss of consortium, we considered the proffered argument that such a holding would logically require us to uphold an analogous cause of action in the parent-child context or in even more distant relationships; we rejected that contention. . . .

Rodriguez, thus, does not compel the conclusion that foreseeable injury to a legally recognized relationship necessarily postulates a cause of action; instead it clearly warns that social policy must at some point intervene to delimit liability. Patricia Borer, for example, foreseeably has not only a husband (who has a cause of action under *Rodriguez*) and the children who sue here, but also parents whose right of action depends upon our decision in the companion case of Baxter v. Superior Court; foreseeably, likewise, she has brothers, sisters, cousins, inlaws, friends, colleagues, and other acquaintances who will be deprived of her companionship. No one suggests that all such persons possess a right of action for loss of Patricia's consortium; all agree that somewhere a line must be drawn. As stated by Judge Breitel in Tobin v. Grossman (1969) 24 N.Y.2d 609, 619, 301, N.Y.S.2d 554, 561, 249 N.E.2d 419, 424; "Every injury has ramifying consequences, like the ripplings of the waters, without end. The problem for the law is to limit the legal consequences of wrongs to a controllable degree."

The decision whether to limit liability for loss of consortium by denying a cause of action in the parent-child context, or to permit that action but deny any claim based upon more remote relationships, is thus a question of policy. . . .

In the first instance, strong policy reasons argue against extension of liability to loss of consortium of the parent-child relationship. Loss of consortium is an intangible, nonpecuniary loss; monetary compensation will not enable plaintiffs to regain the companionship and guidance of a mother, it will simply establish a fund so that upon reaching adulthood, when plaintiffs will be less in need of maternal guidance, they will be unusually wealthy men and women. To say that plaintiffs have been "compensated" for their loss is superficial; in reality they have suffered a loss for which they can never be compensated; they have obtained, instead, a future benefit essentially unrelated to that loss.

We cannot ignore the social burden of providing damages for loss of parental consortium merely because the money to pay such awards comes initially from the "negligent" defendant or his insurer. Realistically the burden of payment of awards for loss of consortium must be borne by the public generally in increased insurance premiums or, otherwise, in the enhanced danger that accrues from the greater number of people who may choose to go without any insurance. We must also take into account the cost of administration of a system to determine and pay consortium awards; since virtually every serious injury to a parent would engender a claim for loss of consortium on behalf of each of his or her children, the expense of settling or litigating such claims would be sizable.

Plaintiffs point out that courts have permitted recovery of monetary damages for intangible loss in allowing awards for pain and suffering in negligence cases and in sanctioning recovery for loss of marital consortium. The question before us in this case, however, pivots on whether we should recognize a wholly new cause of action, unsupported by statute or precedent; in this context the inadequacy of monetary damages to make whole the loss suffered, considered in light of the social cost of paying such awards, constitutes a strong reason for refusing to recognize the asserted claim. To avoid misunderstanding, we point out that our decision to refuse to recognize a cause of action for parental consortium does not remotely suggest the rejection of recovery for intangible loss; each claim must be judged on its own merits, and in many cases the involved statutes, precedents, or policy will induce acceptance of the asserted cause of action.

A second reason for rejecting a cause of action for loss of parental consortium is that, because of its intangible character, damages for such a loss are very difficult to measure. Plaintiffs here have prayed for $100,000 each; yet by what standard could we determine that an award of $10,000 was inadequate, or one of $500,000 excessive? Difficulty in defining and quantifying damages leads in turn to risk of double recovery: to ask the jury, even under carefully drafted instructions, to distinguish the loss to the mother from her inability to care for her children from the loss to the children from the mother's inability to care for them may be asking too much. . . .

Plaintiffs point out that similar policy arguments could be, and to some extent were, raised in *Rodriguez,* and that our decision to uphold the wife's action for loss of consortium rejected those arguments. We do not, however, read *Rodriguez* as holding that arguments based upon the intangible character of damages and the difficulty of measuring such damages do not merit consideration. Such a holding would imply an indefinite extension of liability for loss of consortium to all foreseeable relationships, a proposition *Rodriguez* plainly repudiates.

Rodriguez, then, holds no more than that in the context of a spousal relationship, the policy arguments against liability do not suffice to justify a holding denying a cause of action. Plaintiffs contend, however, that no adequate ground exists to distinguish a cause of action for loss of spousal consortium from one for loss of parental consortium. We reject the contention for three reasons.

First, as *Rodriguez* pointed out, the spousal action for loss of consortium rests in large part on the "impairment or destruction of the sexual life of the couple." (12 Cal. 3d 382, 405, 115 Cal. Rptr. 765, 780, 525 P.2d 669, 684.) No similar element of damage appears in a child's suit for loss of consortium.

Second, actions by children for loss of parental consortium create problems of multiplication of actions and damages not present in the spousal context. . . .

The instant case illustrates the point. Patricia Borer has nine children, each of whom would possess his own independent right of action for loss of consortium. Even in the context of a consolidated action, the assertion of nine independent causes of action for the children in addition to the father's claim for loss of consortium and the mother's suit for ordinary tort damages, demonstrates the extent to which recognition of plaintiffs' asserted cause of action will multiply the tort liability of the defendant.

Finally, the proposition that a spouse has a cause of action for loss of consortium, but that a child does not, finds overwhelming approval in the decisions of other jurisdictions. Over 30 states, a clear majority of those who have decided the question, now permit a *spousal* suit for loss of consortium. No state permits a child to sue for loss of parental consortium. That claim has been presented, at latest count, to 18 jurisdictions, and rejected by all of them. . . .

In summary, we do not doubt the reality or the magnitude of the injury suffered by plaintiffs. We are keenly aware of the need of children for the love, affection, society and guidance of their parents; any injury which diminishes the ability of a parent to meet these needs is plainly a family tragedy, harming all members of that community. We conclude, however, that taking into account all considerations which bear on this question, including the inadequacy of monetary compensation to alleviate that tragedy, the difficulty of measuring damages, and the danger of imposing extended and disproportionate liability, we should not recognize a nonstatutory cause of action for the loss of parental consortium.

The judgment is affirmed.

CLARK, RICHARDSON, SULLIVAN, WRIGHT, JJ., concur.

MOSK, Justice, dissenting.

I dissent.

Each of the policy arguments which the majority marshal against recognizing the cause of action for loss of consortium in the parent-child relationship was expressly considered and rejected by this court in Rodriguez v. Bethlehem Steel Corp. (1974) 12 Cal. 3d 382, 115 Cal. Rptr. 765, 525 P.2d 669.

First, the majority assert that because deprivation of consortium is an "intangible, nonpecuniary" loss, it is an injury which "can never be compensated." (Ante, p.306 of 138 Cal. Rptr., p. 862 of 563 P.2d.) In *Rodriguez,* however, we held that loss of consortium is principally a form of mental suffering, and like all such subjective disabilities, it is compensable in damages. (Id. 12 Cal. 3d at p.401, 115 Cal. Rptr. 765, 525 P.2d 669.) . . .

The majority reject plaintiffs' claim for a second reason, i.e., that "because of its intangible character, damages for such a loss are very difficult to measure." (Ante, p. 138 of 307 Cal. Rptr., p. 863 of 563 P.2d.) This merely restates the first reason, and was likewise rejected in *Rodriguez.* The loss here is no more and no less "intangible" than that experienced by Mrs. Rodriguez, whose husband became permanently incapacitated, and yet we held the valuation problem to be difficult but manageable. . . .

The majority next reason that the asserted difficulty in measuring damages "leads in turn to risk of double recovery." (Ante, p. 307 of 138 Cal. Rptr., p. 863 of 563 P.2d.) Again we dismissed the identical argument in *Rodriguez,* explaining that the alleged "risk" can be avoided by the use of such well-known procedural devices as joinder of actions and appropriate instructions to the jury. (12 Cal. 3d at pp. 404-407, 115 Cal. Rptr. 765, 525 P.2d 669.)

The majority concede that we rejected the foregoing arguments in *Rodriguez,* but now claim they do not "read"—i.e., interpret—*Rodriguez* as holding that the arguments, "do not merit consideration." (Ante, p. 307 of 138 Cal. Rptr., p. 863 of 563 P.2d.) On this point, however, *Rodriguez* is crystal clear and requires no interpretation: far from implying that the double recovery argument might have some merit in another context, we characterized it in *Rodriguez* as wholly "without substance," and quoted with approval decisions which derided it as "fallacious," "fictional," and a "bogey" that is "merely a convenient cliche" for denying liability. (Id. 12 Cal. 3d at p. 404, 115 Cal. Rptr. 765, 525 P.2d 669.)

The majority next seek to distinguish *Rodriguez* on three grounds, but none is convincing. First, the majority claim *Rodriguez* "pointed out" that the spousal action for loss of consortium rests "in large part" on the impairment of the sexual life of the couple. (Ante, p. 307 of 138 Cal. Rptr., p. 863 of 563 P.2d.) *Rodriguez* "pointed out" no such thing; on the contrary, we there reasoned that the nonsexual loss suffered by a spouse is at least as great as the sexual loss: "Nor is the wife's personal loss limited to her sexual rights. As we recognized in *Deshotel* (v. Atchison, T. & S. F. Ry. Co., 50 Cal. 2d 664, at p. 665, 328 P.2d 449), consortium includes 'conjugal society, comfort, affection and companionship.' An important aspect of consortium is thus the *moral* support each spouse gives the other through the triumph and despair of life. A severely disabled husband may well need all the emotional strength he has just to survive the shock of his injury, make the agonizing adjustment to his new and drastically restricted world, and preserve his mental health through the long years of frustration ahead. He will often turn inwards, demanding more solace for himself than he can give to others. Accordingly, the spouse of such a man cannot expect him to share the same concern for *her* problems that she experienced before his accident. As several of the cases have put it, she is transformed from a happy wife into a lonely nurse. Yet she is entitled to enjoy the companionship and moral support that marriage provides *no less than its sexual side,* and in both cases no less than her husband." (Final italics added; 12 Cal. 3d at pp. 405-406, 115 Cal. Rptr. at p. 780, 525 P.2d at p. 684.)

Precisely the same reasoning can be invoked in the case at bar: a severely disabled mother may well need all her emotional strength to survive the shock of her injury, to adjust to her newly restricted life, and to prepare her mental health through the ensuing years of frustration; and she will therefore often turn inwards, demanding more solace and comfort from her children than she can give to them in return. By its terms, *Rodriguez* applies to such a situation.

Two further points must be made in this connection, however obvious they may seem. *Rodriguez* cannot fairly be limited, as the majority imply, to sexually active couples: surely a husband or wife of advanced years suffers a no less compensable loss of conjugal society when his or her lifetime companion is grievously injured by the negligence of another. And even if *Rodriguez* were to be subjected to such a harsh restriction, surely the majority do not mean to hold that sexual activity is more worthy of the law's concern than the affection, comfort, and guidance which loving parents bestow on their children.

The majority's second purported ground of distinction may conveniently be reduced to syllogistic form: (1) if loss of parental consortium were actionable, a single accident would give rise to as many claims as the victim had minor children; (2) in our society the victim is likely to have several such children but can have only one spouse; therefore (3) to recognize the cause of action for loss of parental consortium would result in a much larger liability for individual defendants and a much larger total cost to the insured community than flow from *Rodriguez.* (Ante, pp. 307-308 of 138 Cal. Rptr., pp. 863-864 of 563 P.2d.)

The minor premise of the majority's argument—that an accident victim is likely to have several children under age 18—is, however, demonstrably inaccurate. In *Rodriguez* we observed that "In our society the likelihood that an injured adult will be a married man or woman is substantial," and supported that statement by a reference to the Statistical Abstract of the United States published annually by the Bureau of the Census. (12 Cal. 3d at p. 400 & fn. 19, 115 Cal. Rptr. at p. 776, 525 P.2d at p. 680.) That document showed, for example, that during the peak working years of ages 25 to 65, the proportion of all men who were married ranged between 77.8

percent and 89.7 percent. (Ibid.) Contrary to the majority's supposition, the same source reveals that the proportion of families with several minor children is very low: as of 1974, 46 percent of the families in the United States had no minor children and an additional 19.2 percent had only 1 such child, making over 65 percent of the total; conversely, only 9.5 percent of families had 3 minor children, and the entire class of "4 or more" such children comprised a mere 7.4 percent.

The last of the quoted figures establishes that, contrary to the majority's implication, the case at bar is completely atypical of American society in the second half of the 20th century. If all the families with 4 or more minor children constitute only 7.4 percent of the total, the proportion of families with, as here, the extremely large number of 9 children—8 of whom were minors at the time the complaint was filed—must be a minute fraction of 1 percent. In these circumstances it is manifestly misleading for the majority to assert that the fact the victim has nine children "illustrates" this ground of distinction. (Ante, p. 307 of 138 Cal. Rptr., p. 863 of 563 P.2d.) . . .

Not only do the statistics show the majority's concern to be unwarranted, they also confirm the verdict of common sense in this matter, i.e., that plaintiffs actually ask us to take a smaller, not a larger, step than we took in *Rodriguez.* Inasmuch as adult, emancipated children who are no longer living in the family home could prove little if any damage from loss of parental consortium, I assume the majority are most troubled by the prospect of claims by minor children. (See ante, p. 307 of 138 Cal. Rptr., p. 863 of 563 P.2d.) Upon reflection, it will be seen that such children inevitably comprise a much more limited class than spouses, for two reasons: not all married persons have children; and of those who do, they are parents of *minor* children for a far shorter period of time than they are spouses. It is therefore not surprising that although more than three-quarters of the adult population is married, almost half of such households—46 percent—have no minor children whatever. It follows that recognition of the cause of action for loss of parental consortium will result in a lesser rather than a greater effect on individual liability and overall insurance costs than our approval of the corresponding action by a spouse in *Rodriguez.*

The majority's third proposed ground of distinction (ante, pp. 307-308 of 138 Cal. Rptr., pp. 863-864 of 563 P.2d) deserves little comment. Emphasis is placed on the fact that no state has recognized the cause of action for loss of parental consortium, while a substantial number had permitted a spousal consortium action by the time we decided *Rodriguez.* (12 Cal. 3d at pp. 389-390, 115 Cal. Rptr. 765, 525 P.2d 669.) But the latter fact was invoked in *Rodriguez* to justify our departure from a directly contrary decision of this court—a hurdle we do not face here. Even while emphasizing the out-of-state authorities, moreover, we expressly warned that although we should be mindful of the trend "our decision is not reached by a process of following the crowd." (Id. at p. 392, 115 Cal. Rptr. at p. 771, 525 P.2d at p. 675.)

When that crowd is marching in the wrong direction, we have not heretofore hesitated to break ranks and strike out on our own. . . .

I conclude that there is no escaping the conflict between the reasoning of the majority herein and the letter and spirit of *Rodriguez.* Yet the majority repeatedly reaffirm the holding of that decision. One can only infer that the majority's true motivation is neither the claimed inadequacy of monetary compensation for this loss, nor the difficulty of measuring damages, nor the danger of disproportionate liability. These are mere window-dressing, designed to lend an appearance of logic and objectivity to what is in fact a purely discretionary exercise of the judicial power to limit the potential liability of common law tortfeasors. The majority suggest their actual incentive earlier in the opinion, when they reason that the victim foreseeably has not only a husband, children, and parents, but also "brothers, sisters, cousins, inlaws, friends, colleagues, and other acquaintances who will be deprived of her companionship. No one suggests that all such persons possess a right of action for loss of [the victim's] consortium; all agree that somewhere a line must be drawn." (Ante, p. 306 of 138 Cal. Rptr., p. 862 of 563 P.2d.) . . .

I agree that it must, but I cannot subscribe to the majority's ad terrorem argument for determining the proper place to draw such a line. The majority raise the spectre of liability not only to the victim's spouse but also to a Gilbert and Sullivan parade of "his sisters and his cousins, whom he reckons up by dozens," then dismiss that possibility with the unimpeachable observation that no one is suggesting the latter be compensated. The implication lingers, however, that such demands will become irresistible if the rights of the victim's children are recognized in the case at bar. . . .

There is, in short, no valid excuse for denying these children their day in court. Justice, compassion, and respect for our humanitarian values require that the "line" in this matter be drawn elsewhere.

I would reverse the judgment.

Most courts that have addressed the issue have, like the Supreme Court of California, denied loss of consortium recovery to both parents and children. See, e.g., Guenther v. Stollberg, 495 N.W.2d 286 (Neb. 1993) (no action by child for injury to parent); Dralle v. Ruder, 124 Ill. 2d 61, 529 N.E. 229 (1988) (no action by parent for injury to child). But some courts have permitted recovery. See, e.g., Shockley v. Prier, 66 Wis. 2d 394, 225 N.W.2d 495 (1975) (parent can recover for injury to child); Reagan v. Vaughn, 804 S.W.2d 463 (Tex. 1990) (child can recover for injury to parent). While Massachusetts permits a child to recover for injury to a parent (see Ferriter v. Daniel O'Connell's Sons, Inc., 381 Mass. 507, 413 N.E.2d 690 (1980)), it does not permit recovery by a parent for injury to a child (see Norman v. Massachusetts Bay Transportation Authority, 403 Mass. 303,

529 N.E.2d 139 (1988)), nor by a step-child for injury to the step-parent (see Mendoza v. B.L.H. Electronics, 403 Mass. 437, 530 N.E.2d 349 (1988)). Arizona permits recovery by both parents and children, but only if the injury is so severe and permanent as to substantially destroy the parent-child relationship. See Pierce v. Casa Adobes Baptist Church, 162 Ariz. 269, 782 P.2d 1162 (1989), and Villareal v. State, 160 Ariz. 474, 774 P.2d 213 (1989).

A Minnesota statute limiting loss of consortium recovery to $400,000 was upheld against a constitutional challenge in Schweich v. Ziegler, Inc., 463 N.W.2d 722 (1990).

c. Prenatal Harm

The issues presented by the cases in this subsection are to a considerable extent conceptually diverse, and thus could have appeared in other places in the book. However, the cases are linked factually; moreover, it is convenient pedagogically to bring them together in one location.

(1) Actions by Parents for Their Own Harm

Werling v. Sandy

17 Ohio St. 3d 45, 476 N.E.2d 1053 (1985)

[This is an action for wrongful death alleging that because of the negligence of the defendants, the plaintiff's child was stillborn. The trial court dismissed the complaint, ruling that there is no action for the wrongful death of a fetus.]

HOLMES, J. Today, this court is confronted with the certified issue of whether an action for wrongful death exists under R.C. 2125.01 where the decedent was a stillborn fetus. More specifically, we are asked to determine whether the statutory beneficiaries of an unborn fetus are entitled to damages for the wrongful death of the fetus where both the alleged negligently inflicted injury and death of the child occurred before birth. To resolve this issue necessarily requires an answer to the question of whether an unborn fetus which dies *en ventre sa mere* may be considered a "person" for the purposes of the statute under consideration. For the reasons which follow, we answer each of the above queries affirmatively as long as it is established that the fetus was viable at the time of its injury. . . .

R.C. 2125.01 provides in pertinent part:

> When the death of a person is caused by wrongful act, neglect, or default which would have entitled the party injured to maintain an action and recover damages if death had not ensued, the person who would have been liable if death had not ensued, or the administrator or executor of the estate of such

> person, as such administrator or executor, shall be liable to an action for damages. . . .

The clear purpose of the wrongful death statute is to provide a remedy whenever there would have been an action in damages had death not ensued. The provision is remedial in nature and was designed to alleviate the inequity perceived in the common law.

In addition, an action for wrongful death is for the exclusive benefit of the statutory beneficiaries. It is rebuttably presumed within the statute that each beneficiary has suffered damages by reason of the wrongful death. R.C. 2125.02. In the present situation, it is the parents who suffer mental anguish and the loss of society *inter alia* due to the death of their child. Our decision is directed to justly compensate those parents for the loss of parenthood.

The rights of an unborn child are no strangers to our law, even though this precise question is one of first impression. The intestate rights of a posthumous child are recognized in R.C. 2105.14. A child in gestation who is subsequently born alive may be considered a life in being throughout the gestation period for purposes of the now statutory rule against perpetuities. R.C. 2131.08(A); Phillips v. Herron (1896), 55 Ohio St. 478, 45 N.E. 720. The definition of "decedent" within the Uniform Anatomical Gift Act includes a stillborn infant or fetus. R.C. 2108.01(B). And, finally, under the Uniform Parentage Act, the personal representative of an unborn child may bring an action on behalf of the infant to establish a father-child relationship. R.C. 3111.04.

While the cause of action herein is statutory, certain common-law decisions of this court assist our resolution of the issue presented. In Williams v. Marion Rapid Transit, Inc. (1949), 152 Ohio St. 114, 87 N.E.2d 334 [39 O.O. 433], the issue before the court was whether a living child injured *en ventre sa mere* was entitled to be heard as a "person" within Section 16, Article I of the Ohio Constitution. In recognizing that the child possessed an action for injuries negligently inflicted during gestation, Judge Matthias, writing for a unanimous court, stated at 128-129, 87 N.E.2d 334:

> To hold that the plaintiff [child] in the instant case did not suffer an injury in her person would require this court to announce that as a matter of law the infant is a part of the mother until birth and has no existence in law until that time. In our view such a ruling would deprive the infant of the right conferred by the Constitution upon all persons, by the application of a time-worn fiction not founded on fact and within common knowledge untrue and unjustified.

This court has also recognized the validity of a wrongful death action on behalf of a child who was born alive but died shortly thereafter as a result of prenatal injuries. . . .

Using these past decisions as a foundation, we are of the opinion that a cause of action may arise under the wrongful death statute when a viable fetus is stillborn since a life capable of independent existence has expired. It is logically indefensible as well as unjust to deny an action where the child is stillborn, and yet permit the action where the child survives birth but only for a short period of time. The requirement of birth in this respect is an artificial demarcation. As hypothetically stated by the court of appeals in *Stidam* [v. Ashmore] (109 Ohio App. 431, 167 N.E.2d 106 [11 O.O.2d 383]), at 434:

> . . . Suppose, for example, viable unborn twins suffered simultaneously the same prenatal injury of which one died before and the other after birth. Shall there be a cause of action for death of one and not for that of the other? Surely logic requires recognition of causes of action for the deaths of both, or for neither.

To allow a cause of action where it is established that the fetus was viable certainly furthers the remedial nature of the wrongful death statute. To hold otherwise would only serve to reward the tortfeasor by allowing him to escape liability upon an increase in the severity of the harm, if such harm results in death to the child. In other words, the greater the harm inflicted, the better the opportunity that a defendant will be exonerated. This result is clearly not acceptable under the statute.

We recognize that our adoption of the viability test will present some practical problems. The term "viability" is an elusive one since not all fetuses arrive at this stage of their development at an identical chronological point in their gestation. The concept may also become increasingly difficult to apply with further developments surrounding the sophisticated medical techniques which allow a child to be conceived outside the mother's womb. Indeed, some commentators have questioned the standard and suggest the adoption of a causation test which permits recovery for an injury sustained by a child at any time prior to his birth if it can be proven that the injury was the proximate result of a wrongful act. However, for the purposes of this appeal, we believe the better reasoned view is to recognize the viable child as a person under the statute rather than to designate the same status to a fetus incapable of independently surviving a premature birth. . . .

We are also cognizant that the United States Supreme Court has held that a fetus is not a person for the purpose of the Fourteenth Amendment, and that states may not enact statutes which prohibit abortions during the first trimester of pregnancy. Roe v. Wade (1973), 410 U.S. 113, 93 S. Ct. 705, 35 L. Ed. 2d 147. However, the court recognized in *Roe* that once a fetus becomes viable, a state may prohibit all abortions except those necessary to preserve the life or health of the mother and that ". . . [s]tate regulation protective of fetal life after viability . . . has both logical and biological justifications." Id. at 163, 93 S. Ct. at 732. The court found the compelling point in the state's legitimate interest of protecting potential life to be at viability, as the fetus, at that time, has the capability of meaningful life outside the mother's womb. It follows, therefore, that our decision is entirely consistent with *Roe* to the effect that a viable fetus is a person entitled to protection and may be a basis for recovery under the wrongful death statute.

Finally, appellees contend that State v. Dickinson (1971), 28 Ohio St. 2d 65, 275 N.E.2d 599 [57 O.O.2d 255], is dispositive of this appeal. We disagree.

In *Dickinson,* it was held in paragraph two of the syllabus that a viable unborn fetus is not a person within the meaning of this state's former vehicular homicide statute, R.C. 4511.181. It is undisputed, however, that criminal statutes are strictly construed against the state and liberally interpreted in favor of the accused. R.C. 2901.-04; Harrison v. State (1925), 112 Ohio St. 429, 442, 147 N.E. 650, *affirmed* (1926), 270 U.S. 632, 46 S. Ct. 350, 70 L. Ed. 771. In fact, *Dickinson* recognizes ". . . that the definition of a word in a civil statute does not necessarily import the same meaning to the same word in interpreting a criminal statute." Id. 28 Ohio St. 2d at 70, 275 N.E.2d 599. Therefore, we find the *Dickinson* case not to be controlling under the facts as presented herein.

Accordingly, we hold that a viable fetus which is negligently injured *en ventre sa mere,* and subsequently stillborn, may be the basis for a wrongful death action pursuant to R.C. 2125.01.

The judgment of the court of appeals is hereby reversed and the cause is remanded to the trial court for further proceedings consistent with this opinion.

Judgment reversed and cause remanded.

CELEBREZZE, C.J., and SWEENEY, FORD, CLIFFORD F. BROWN and WRIGHT, JJ., concur.

DOUGLAS, J., concurs separately.

FORD, J., of the Eleventh Appellate District, sitting for LOCHER, J.

DOUGLAS, J., concurring.

While I agree with the holding of the majority, I am troubled with what appears to be the open-endedness of the decision. In my judgment it would be the better policy of this court to say that for purposes of suit in Ohio, under the wrongful death statute, viability of an unborn child occurs at a time certain during pregnancy. I deem it important that we be precise in our decision and thereby send to the bench and bar under our jurisdiction a clear message. To do otherwise, it seems to me, will be to encourage the filing of multifarious actions to determine, in a descending manner, what this court means as to when viability occurs. Today's case says a full-term pregnancy. Tomorrow's case could be a pregnancy of seven months, then six months and, after that, five months, and so forth.

In addition, I find that the breadth of today's decision will present some very difficult questions, not only for lawyers who advise their clients, but for doctors, organizations and individuals who are concerned with the question in relationship to Roe v. Wade (1973), 410 U.S. 113, 93 S. Ct. 705, 35 L. Ed. 2d 147.

Although wrongful death actions are controlled largely by statutes, as the opinion in *Werling* makes clear, there is considerable room for courts to resolve the statutory interpretation problem on public policy grounds. On this score, consider the following excerpt from the dissenting opinion of Haynsworth, J., in Todd v. Sandidge Construction Co., 341 F.2d 75, 80-81 (4th Cir. 1964), a case arising under South Carolina law:

> Little can be said in favor of allowance of a cause of action for personal injury to a child en ventre sa mère, which thereafter is stillborn for some unrelated reason. When the stillbirth is unrelated to the prenatal injury, the child suffers no economic loss, and it is, at least, highly dubious that it will have endured conscious pain and suffering. The majority here, of course, make no suggestion that a cause of action for personal injury in such circumstances should be recognized or allowed. Yet, and this is where I think they go awry, it is only if an action for personal injury under such circumstances would be allowed that, under their construction of the wrongful death statute, an action for wrongful death would be allowed if the death before birth resulted from the injury rather than from an unrelated cause. Live birth is a prerequisite if we follow the statute's relation of the right to maintain an action for wrongful death to the right to maintain an action for personal injury. There is no right of action for personal injury if the child is stillborn for an unrelated or a related reason, and there is no action for wrongful death if it is stillborn for a related reason. If viability has any usefulness in discovering reasonable answers to the problem—live birth is crucial.
>
> In its social aspects, if a line is to be drawn anywhere, there is much more to be said for placing it at the point of live birth than at any other point after conception.
>
> As noted above, when the child is born alive there are compelling reasons for allowing him to maintain an action for personal injury by him when en ventre sa mère. Those reasons, legal and practical, are unaffected by his viability at the time of injury. Once the cause of action for personal injury matures with the live birth, it, of course, will survive a subsequent death of the child. In the event of a subsequent death after birth, too, if the result of prenatal injury, the wrongful death statute literally and unequivocally applies, and such an action may be maintained.
>
> There are no comparable reasons for allowance of a cause of action for personal injury of a child en ventre sa mère which is later stillborn. If a live birth is a prerequisite to a cause of action for personal injury, it is a prerequisite to a cause of action for wrongful death, for the wrongful death statute is expressly conditioned upon the existence of a cause of action for personal injury. If the need for recognition of a cause of action for wrongful death of a stillborn child were great, then it might be said without too much illogic that the substantive right of action for personal injury of a child later stillborn

exists, but may not be maintained solely because of the absence of recoverable damages. It may be interpolated here that the South Carolina cases contain no shred of a suggestion of recognition of such a need. If such a need exists, however, it exists regardless of the child's maturity at the time of injury or at the time of the stillbirth.

The longer the pregnancy, the greater the parent's expectation and the deeper the sense of loss if there is a miscarriage or the child is stillborn. The potential personal loss the parents may suffer does not spring from nothingness the moment the child becomes viable. It is a progressive thing. The progress is unmarked by the attainment of viability, but it is tremendously enlarged when the child born alive is seen and embraced by its mother and, perhaps, by its father. In some circumstances, the loss of a month-old fetus may be a crushing disappointment to the prospective parents, but the loss of a child born alive and loved, even for a little while, is a cause of much greater grief.

When the child is stillborn, of course, the mother in an action for her injuries can recover the major items of damage, including compensation for her grief. If loss of the child's anticipated companionship is not technically compensable in her action, juries usually take care of the situation. The father is unlikely to have any net recoverable damages. The inevitable consequence of allowance of an action for wrongful death in these circumstances will be multiple recovery for the same items of damage.

This, then is not a particularly deserving plaintiff. Neither reason, analogy nor social considerations dictate allowance of a recovery. Allowance of recovery here, however, by enthroning viability at the time of injury as the touchstone of decision may gravely embarrass recovery by highly deserving plaintiffs, living children crippled by prenatal injuries sustained before they became viable.

Generalizations about whether a fetus is a person for wrongful death purposes should be made cautiously, since wrongful death actions are a matter of statute, and vary considerably from state to state. With that thought in mind, courts have divided on the issue. Agreeing with the majority in *Werling* that viability of the fetus is sufficient for the action are Seef v. Sutkus, 145 Ill. 2d 336, 583 N.E.2d 510 (1991), and DiDonato v. Wortman, 320 N.C. 423, 158 S.E.2d 489, *rehearing den.*, 361 N.C. 799, 320 S.E.2d 73 (1987). Agreeing with Haynsworth's dissent in Todd v. Sandidge that live birth is required are Humes v. Clinton, 246 Kan. 590, 792 P.2d 1032 (1990), and Milton v. Cary Medical Center, 538 A.2d 252 (Me. 1988).

Another context in which courts have reached conflicting results with respect to the legal status of a fetus involves the criminal law. Holding that a fetus is not a person for homicide purposes are Vo v. Superior Court, 836 P.2d 408 (Ariz. App. 1992), and State v. Evans, 745 S.W.2d 880 (Tenn. Ct. App. 1987). Other courts have held that a fetus can be the object of a homicide. See, e.g., People v. Bunyard, 45 Cal. 3d 1189, 756 P.2d 795, 249 Cal. Rptr. 71 (1988); State v. Knapp, 843 S.W.2d 345 (Mo. 1992). State v. Cornelius, 448 N.W.2d 434 (Wis. App. 1989), held that the homicide statute applies to the killing of a fetus if the fetus is born alive.

Fassoulas v. Ramey

450 So. 2d 822 (Fla. 1984)

PER CURIAM . . .

Plaintiffs, Edith and John Fassoulas, were married and had two children, both of whom had been born with severe congenital abnormalities. After much consideration, they decided not to have any more children due to the fear of having another physically deformed child and the attendant high cost of medical care. They then decided that John would undergo a vasectomy. This medical procedure was performed in January 1974 by defendant, Dr. Ramey. However, due to the negligence of the defendant in performing the operation, in giving medical advice concerning residual pockets of sperm, and in examining and judging the viability of sperm samples, Edith twice became pregnant and gave birth to two children. The first of these, Maria, was born in November 1974 and had many congenital deformities. Roussi, the second of the post-vasectomy children and the fourth Fassoulas child, was born in September 1976 with a slight physical deformity which was corrected at birth; he is now a normal, healthy child.

The plaintiffs sued Dr. Ramey and his clinic in tort based on medical malpractice for the two "wrongful births." They sought as damages Edith's past and future lost wages, her anguish and emotional distress at twice becoming pregnant, her loss of the society, companionship and consortium of her husband, John's mental anguish and emotional distress, his loss of the society, companionship and consortium of his wife, medical and hospital expenses and the expenses for the care and upbringing of the two new children until the age of twenty-one.

At trial, the jury found in favor of the plaintiffs, finding the defendants 100% negligent with reference to Maria and 50% negligent with reference to Roussi. The plaintiffs were found to be comparatively negligent as to the birth of Roussi. Damages were assessed in the amount of $250,000 for the birth of Maria and $100,000 for the birth of Roussi, the latter sum being reduced to $50,000 because of the plaintiff's comparative negligence. . . .

The rule in Florida is that "a parent cannot be said to have been damaged by the birth and rearing of a normal, healthy child." Public Health Trust v. Brown, 388 S.2d 1084, 1085 (Fla. 3d DCA 1980), *petition denied,* 399 So. 2d 1140 (Fla. 1981) (footnote omitted). "[I]t has been imbedded in our law for centuries that the father and now both parents or legal guardians of a child have the sole obligation of providing the necessaries in raising the child, whether the child be wanted or unwanted." Ramey v. Fassoulas, 414 So. 2d at 200. "The child is still the child of the parents, not the physician, and it is the parents' legal obligation, not the physician's, to support the child." Id. For public policy reasons, we decline to allow rearing damages for the birth of a healthy child. As stated by the Supreme Court of Wisconsin:

> To permit the parents to keep their child and shift the entire cost of its upbringing to a physician who failed to determine or inform them of the fact of pregnancy would be to create a new category of surrogate parent. Every child's smile, every bond of love and affection, every reason for parental pride in a child's achievements, every contribution by the child to the welfare and well-being of the family and parents, is to remain with the mother and father. For the most part, these are intangible benefits but they are nonetheless real. On the other hand, every financial cost or detriment—what the complaint terms "hard money damages"—including the cost of food, clothing and education, would be shifted to the physician. . . . We hold that such result would be wholly out of proportion to the culpability involved. . . .

Rieck v. Medical Protective Co., 64 Wis. 2d 514, 518, 219 N.W.2d 242, 244-245 (1974) (footnote omitted). We agree with this reasoning and hold that, as a matter of law, the "benefits to the parents outweigh their economic loss in rearing and educating a healthy, normal child." Terrell v. Garcia, 496 S.W.2d 124, 128 (Tex. Civ. App. 1973), *cert. denied,* 415 U.S. 927, 94 S. Ct. 1434, 39 L. Ed. 2d 484 (1974); Public Health Trust v. Brown. The same reasoning forcefully and correctly applies to the ordinary, everyday expenses associated with the care and upbringing of a physically or mentally deformed child. We likewise hold as a matter of law that ordinary rearing expenses for a defective child are not recoverable as damages in Florida.

We agree with the district court below that an exception exists in the case of special upbringing expenses associated with a deformed child. Special medical and educational expenses, beyond normal rearing costs, are often staggering and quite debilitating to a family's financial and social health; "indeed the financial and emotional drain associated with raising such a child is often overwhelming to the affected parents." Ramey v. Fassoulas, 414 So. 2d at 201. There is no valid policy argument against parents being recompensed for these costs of extraordinary care in raising a deformed child to majority. We hold these special upbringing costs associated with a deformed child to be recoverable. . . .

ALDERMAN, C.J., and BOYD, OVERTON and MCDONALD, JJ., concur.

EHRLICH, J., dissents with an opinion with which ADKINS and SHAW, JJ., concur.

EHRLICH, Judge, dissenting. . . . It has often been said that hard cases make bad law. I am afraid that the majority opinion does just that. A look at the instant facts supports this conclusion. John and Edith Fassoulas already had two children and both were born with severe medical problems. They could not afford the medical bills arising out of the treatments required. This was partly a function of the high cost of the medical bills and partly a function of the unemployment of John himself because of ill health. The two decided upon the solution of a vasectomy, both for the stated economic reason and for the reason of their fear that any further children might also be born with defects. They went to Dr. Ramey for the vasectomy but the operation was negligently performed. Thereupon occurred what can only be described as a comedy of errors. The fact that the operation was not successful was not apparent to anyone at the time. Edith soon became pregnant but all concerned thought that the cause was Dr. Ramey's negligent instructions to the couple about how long to wait before resuming intercourse and how long to use birth control because of the presence of residual pockets of sperm. In any event, Maria made her appearance nine months later and was congenitally deformed. She had a short neck, an abnormal shaping of the skull, a skin irregularity that was described as fish-like and scaly in appearance, a heart murmur, hypertension, and malformations of the hands. The very result that John and Edith wished to avoid by having the vasectomy was thus visited upon them, clearly a foreseeable consequence of Dr. Ramey's negligence. Time passed. Dr. Ramey once again erred in his professional conduct, this time by negligently confusing sperm viability with sperm motility in his examination of John's sperm samples. John and Edith were told that John was sterile when in fact he was not. Believing that Maria was born because of the residual sperm pockets extant after the initial operation and that John was now sterile, the couple resumed sexual relations. Again, there resulted a surprise, this time Roussi's birth. Though born with minor infirmities, these were corrected and Roussi can be considered a normal child. But now, instead of having only two children with physical infirmities, John and Edith have a total of four children, three with infirmities and one without. There are now medical bills for three deformed children; John is still out of work; and Edith has to quit work in order to care for the four children. All are now on welfare. While Edith and John testified that they love their two unplanned children greatly (and what parent would not?), they have clearly been wronged by the negligent physician. Can it fairly be said as a matter of law that they have not been damaged by Roussi's birth? Is it fair to say as a matter of law that the nonextraordinary expenses associated with rearing Maria are not recoverable? I think not.

"It is no answer to say that a result which claimant specifically sought to avoid, *might be regarded as a blessing by someone else.*" Rivera v. State, 94 Misc. 2d 157, 162, 404 N.Y.S.2d 950, 954 (Ct. Cl. 1978) (emphasis supplied). "The doctor whose negligence brings about . . . an undesired birth should not be allowed to say, 'I did you a favor,' secure in the knowledge that the courts will give to this claim the effect of an irrebuttable presumption." Terrell v. Garcia at 131 [496 S.W.2d 124 (Tex. C.U. App. 1973, *cert. denied,* 415 U.S. 927 (1974)] (Cadena, J., dissenting).

Dr. Ramey did not do Edith and John a favor. That is what this Court should hold. Since it did not, I must dissent.

ADKINS and SHAW, JJ., concur.

Courts have accepted "wrongful" birth as a theory of recovery with respect to pregnancy-related damages, such as medical expenses, lost wages, and pain and suffering. See, e.g., Johnston v. Elkins, 241 Kan. 407, 736 P.2d 935 (1987); Smith v. Gore, 728 S.W.2d 738 (Tenn. 1987). Claims for emotional harm other than physical pain and suffering have met with mixed reactions. In Berman v. Allan, 80 N.J. 421, 404 A.2d 8 (1979), the court held that the parents could recover for "mental and emotional anguish" they suffered by giving birth to a child with Down's Syndrome. Phillips v. United States, 575 F. Supp. 1309 (D.S.C. 1983), also permitted such recovery, although the trial judge, sitting without a jury, reduced the damages for emotional harm by 50 percent to reflect his assessment of the benefits the parents would get from the child. The court in Viccaro v. Milunsky, 406 Mass. 777, 551 N.E.2d 8 (1990), also ruled that the plaintiffs' recovery for emotional harm caused by the birth of a defective child as a result of the defendant's negligence in genetic counseling should be reduced by any emotional benefit they would get from the child. Furthermore, the court ruled that the emotional harm damages should be reduced by the benefit derived from an earlier born healthy child, apparently on the ground that had the defendant not been negligent, the healthy child, like the defective child, would not have been born. Denying recovery for emotional harm are Smith v. Cote, 128 N.H. 231, 513 A.2d 341 (1986), and Howard v. Lecher 42 N.Y.2d 109, 366 N.E.2d 64 (1977). And in Mears v. Alhadeff, 88 App. Div. 827, 451 N.Y.S.2d 133 (1982), the plaintiff could not recover for humiliation caused by her need to apply for welfare, nor for the "opprobrium and disgrace" she suffered as an unwed mother.

Most courts considering the issue have agreed with the court in *Fassoulas* that the parents cannot recover the cost of raising a healthy child. See, e.g., Smith v. Cote, and Johnston v. Elkins, both cited above, and Johnson v. University Hospitals of Cleveland, 44 Ohio St. 3d 49, 540 N.E.2d 1370 (1989). Courts denying such recovery generally assert that the benefits of having a healthy child more than offset the rearing and education costs. Some courts have suggested that were this not true, the parents either would have had an abortion or put the child up for adoption. See, e.g., Miller v. Johnson, 231 Va. 177, 343 S.E.2d 301 (1986). In McKernan v. Aasheim, 102 Wash. 2d 411, 687 P.2d 850 (1984), the court, quoting from an earlier Florida case, stated that the validity of the total offset approach can be tested by asking the parents the price for which they would sell the child.

A few courts have, however, permitted recovery in full for the costs of raising a healthy child. See, e.g., Lovelace Medical Center v. Mendez, 111

N.M. 336, 805 P.2d 603 (1991); Marciniak v. Lundborg, 153 Wis. 2d 59, 450 N.W.2d 243 (1990). As stated by the court in *Marciniak* (450 N.W.2d at 247):

> We do not consider it reasonable to expect parents to essentially choose between the child and the cause of action. That would truly be a "Hobson's choice." In addition, the decisions concerning abortion or adoption are highly personal matters and involve deeply held moral or religious convictions.

Other courts have suggested a midground approach, and would permit recovery for rearing expenses to the extent that they exceed the benefits of the child to the parents. See, e.g., Jones v. Malinowski, 299 Md. 257, 473 A.2d 429 (1984); Burke v. Rivo, 406 Mass. 764, 551 N.E.2d 1 (1990); University of Arizona Health Sciences Center v. Superior Court, 136 Ariz. 579, 667 P.2d 1294 (1983). These courts, of course, reject what is in effect the "avoidable consequences" rule inherent in the total offset approach. They also provide little guidance as how the benefits of a child to the parents are to be measured on a case-by-case basis.

With respect to children born with birth defects, most courts agree with the Florida Supreme Court in *Fassoulas,* and permit recovery by the parents for at least the out-of-the-ordinary expenses caused by the existence of the birth defect. See, e.g., Ochs v. Borrelli, 187 Conn. 253, 445 A.2d 883 (1982), Smith v. Cote, above; James G. v. Caserta, 332 S.E.2d 872 (W. Va. 1985); Bani-Esraili v. Lerman, 69 N.Y.2d 807, 505 N.E.2d 947 (1987). In *Smith* and *Caserta,* the courts ruled that recovery could be had for projected expenses extending beyond the child's majority, as did the court in Blake v. Cruz, 108 Idaho 253, 698 P.2d 315 (1984). In the latter case, the court pointed to a statute that imposes an obligation on parents to support their children, if they are unable to support themselves, without regard to age. In *Bani-Esraili,* the court held that recovery cannot be had for the period beyond majority because support in that period is the obligation of the state and federal governments and not that of the parents. Even a child with birth defects can provide some intangible benefit to his parents, and the court in *Ochs* stated that recovery is to be reduced by any such benefit. Some courts do not permit recovery for the additional costs of raising an impaired child. See, e.g., Atlanta Obstetrics & Gynecology Group v. Abelson, 260 Ga. 711, 398 S.E.2d 557 (1990).

Should the parents' motive in wanting to take conception prevention steps be relevant? The court in Hartke v. Mckelway, 526 F. Supp. 97 (D.D.C. 1981), said that they are, and denied recovery for the expenses of raising the child since the purpose of the failed sterilization was to prevent the birth of a defective child, and a healthy child was actually born.

If the plaintiff has "avoided the consequences" of the defendant's negligence by having an abortion, it might be expected that the plaintiff would be entitled to recover damages stemming from the abortion. And the court in Lynch v. Bay Ridge Obstetrical and Gynecological Assoc., P.C., 72 N.Y.2d 632, 532 N.E.2d 1239 (1988), so held. The complaint alleged that the defendant was negligent in failing to determine that the plaintiff was pregnant, and prescribed a drug that created a substantial risk that the child would be born with serious defects. The plaintiff opted for an abortion, and sued the defendant, alleging that the negligence "forced her either to risk having a congenitally defective child or to submit to an abortion in violation of her 'personal, moral and religious convictions.'" She sought damages for "her physical, psychological, and emotional injuries resulting from the abortion and from having to decide whether to undergo it." The court reversed the dismissal of the complaint.

Some statutes have limited the right to recover for wrongful birth. In Pennsylvania and Missouri, for example, statutes prohibit wrongful birth actions based on the argument that the child would have been aborted had the defendant not been negligent. See Pa. Cons. Stat. Ann. §8305, and Mo. Ann. Stat. §188.130. In Edmonds v. Western Pennsylvania Hospital Radiology Associates of Western Pennsylvania P.C., 607 A.2d 1083 (Pa. Super. 1992), the court ruled that the statute did not infringe on a woman's right to an abortion, and for that reason did not violate the Fourteenth Amendment to the Constitution of the United States. In Shelton v. St. Anthony's Medical Center, 781 S.W.2d 48 (1989), the Supreme Court of Missouri held that the statute did not preclude an action by the mother for emotional harm based on her physician's failure to advise her that the fetus had congenital defects.

Actions for wrongful birth, at least involving preconception wrongs, have been largely limited to actions against medical care providers. Thus, in Hegyes v. Unjian Enterprises, 234 Cal. 3d 1103, 286 Cal. Rptr. 85 (1991), the court held that a motorist could not be held liable for a preconception tort. In C.A.M. v. R.A.W., 568 A.2d 556 (N.J. Super.), *appeal dismissed,* 127 N.J. 285, 604 A.2d 109 (1990), the court held that a false representation by the father of the plaintiff's child that he had had a vasectomy could not be the basis of a wrongful birth of a healthy, normal child.

(2) Actions on Behalf of Children for Their Own Harm

If a child is born alive, recovery is universally permitted for injuries to the fetus occurring between conception and birth, without regard to viability at the time of the injury. See Prosser and Keeton, The Law of Torts 367-370 (5th ed. 1984).

A number of recent cases have involved harm to the fetus stemming from treatment to the mother before conception. In Renslow v. Mennonite Hospital, 67 Ill. 2d 348, 367 N.E.2d 1250 (1977), the court upheld a complaint alleging that nine years before the plaintiff's birth, the defendant had negligently transfused incompatible blood to the plaintiff's mother, as a result of which she was born prematurely, with permanent brain and nervous system damage. And in Walker v. Rinck, 604 N.E.2d 591 (Ind. 1992), the court ruled that summary judgment in favor of the defendants was improper; the case was based on the failure of the defendants to test the plaintiffs' mother, before their conception, for her blood type, and to administer medicine that would have prevented the plaintiffs' birth defects. The Court of Appeals of New York, however, refused to recognize a cause of action based on preconception injury. See Albala v. City of New York, 54 N.Y.2d 269, 429 N.E.2d 786 (1981), and Enright v. Eli Lilly & Co., 77 N.Y.2d 377, 570 N.E.2d 198 (1991). The complaint in *Albala* alleged that before the plaintiff's conception, the defendant negligently damaged the plaintiff's mother's uterus during the course of an abortion, as a result of which the later-conceived plaintiff was injured. In *Enright,* the plaintiff alleged that she was injured as a result of her grandmother's use of DES. *Enright* was followed in this respect by Grover v. Eli Lilly & Co., 63 Ohio St. 3d 756, 591 N.E.2d 696 (1992), a case involving a DES grandson.

In states that have abrogated the parent-child tort immunity, the question can arise as to the extent to which parents should be held liable for prenatal injuries to their children. This is addressed in the section dealing with the parent-child immunity, at pp. 491-495, below.

Turpin v. Sortini

31 Cal. 3d 220, 643 P.2d 954, 182 Cal. Rptr. 337 (1982)

KAUS, J. This case presents the question of whether a child born with an hereditary affliction may maintain a tort action against a medical care provider who—before the child's conception—negligently failed to advise the child's parents of the possibility of the hereditary condition, depriving them of the opportunity to choose not to conceive the child. Although the overwhelming majority of decisions in other jurisdictions recognize the right of *the parents* to maintain an action under these circumstances, the out-of-state cases have uniformly denied *the child's* right to bring what has been commonly termed a "wrongful life" action. In Curlender v. Bio-Science Laboratories (1980) 106 Cal. App. 3d 811, 165 Cal. Rptr. 477, however, the Court of Appeal, 119 Cal. App. 3d 690, 174 Cal. Rptr. 128, concluded that under California common law tort principles, an afflicted child could maintain such an action and could "recover damages for the pain and suffering to be endured during the limited life span available to such a child and any special pecuniary loss resulting from the impaired condition" (Id., at p. 831, 165 Cal. Rptr. 489), including the costs of medical care to the extent such costs were not recovered by the child's parents. In the case at bar, a different panel of the Court of Appeal disagreed with the conclusion in *Curlender* and affirmed a trial court judgment dismissing the child's cause of action on demurrer. We granted a hearing to resolve the conflict.

[The Turpins, husband and wife, brought suit on behalf of themselves and their two children against their physician and a hospital for negligence for failing to inform them that their offspring would very likely be totally deaf. Subsequent to this alleged negligence, a daughter, Joy, was conceived and was born totally deaf. Four causes of action were alleged. The only one involved in this appeal was brought on behalf of Joy, who sought damages for being "deprived of the fundamental right of a child to be born as a whole, functional human being without total deafness," and for expenses for "specialized teaching, training and hearing equipment."] . . .

[D]efendants' basic position—supported by the numerous out-of-state authorities—is that Joy has suffered no legally cognizable injury or rationally ascertainable damages as a result of their alleged negligence. Although the issues of "legally cognizable injury" and "damages" are intimately related and in some sense inseparable, past cases have generally treated the two as distinct matters and, for purposes of analysis, it seems useful to follow that approach. . . .

Joy's complaint [asserts] that as a result of defendants' negligence she was "deprived of the fundamental right of a child to be born as a whole, functional human being without total deafness. . . ." While the *Curlender* decision did not embrace this approach to "injury" completely—refusing to permit the plaintiff to recover for a reduced lifespan—it too maintained that the proper point of reference for measuring defendant's liability was simply plaintiff's condition after birth, insisting that "[w]e need not be concerned with the fact that had defendants not been negligent, the plaintiff might not have come into existence at all" (106 Cal. App. 3d at p. 829), and rejecting "the notion that a 'wrongful life' cause of action involves any attempted evaluation of a claimed right *not* to be born." (Original italics.) (Id., at pp. 830-831, 165 Cal. Rptr. 477.)

The basic fallacy of the *Curlender* analysis is that it ignores the essential nature of the defendants' alleged wrong and obscures a critical difference between wrongful life actions and the ordinary prenatal injury cases noted above. In an ordinary prenatal injury case, if the defendant had not been negligent, the child would have been born healthy; thus, as in a typical personal injury case, the defendant in such a case has interfered with the child's basic right to be free from physical injury caused by the negligence of others. In this case, by contrast, the obvious tragic fact is that plaintiff never had a chance "to be born as a whole, functional human being without total deafness"; if defendants had performed their jobs properly, she would not have been born with hearing intact, but—according to the complaint—would not have been born at all.

A plaintiff's remedy in tort is compensatory in nature and damages are generally intended not to punish a negligent defendant but to restore an injured person as nearly as possible to the position he or she would have been in had the wrong not been done. . . . Because nothing defendants could have done would have given plaintiff an unimpaired life, it appears inconsistent with basic tort principles to view the injury for which defendants are legally responsible solely by reference to plaintiff's present condition without taking into consideration the fact that if defendants had not been negligent she would not have been born at all. . . .

If the relevant injury in this case is the change in the plaintiff's position attributable to the tortfeasor's actions, then the injury which plaintiff has suffered is that, as a result of defendants' negligence, she has been born with a hereditary ailment rather than not being born at all. Although plaintiff has not phrased her claim for general damages in these terms, most courts and commentators have recognized that the basic claim of "injury" in wrongful life cases is "[i]n essence . . . that [defendants], through their negligence, [have] forced upon [the child] the worse of . . . two alternatives[,] . . . that nonexistence—never being born—would have been preferable to existence in [the] diseased state." (Speck v. Finegold (1979) 268 Pa. Super. 342, 408 A.2d 496, 511-512 (conc. & dis. opn. by Spaeth, J.), *aff'd.* (1981) 439 A.2d 110.)

Given this view of the relevant injury which the plaintiff has sustained at the defendant's hands, some courts have concluded that the plaintiff has suffered no legally cognizable injury on the ground that considerations of public policy dictate a conclusion that life—even with the most severe of impairments—is, as a matter of law, always preferable to nonlife. The decisions frequently suggest that a contrary conclusion would "disavow" the sanctity and value of less-than-perfect human life. . . .

Although it is easy to understand and to endorse these decisions' desire to affirm the worth and sanctity of less-than-perfect life, we question whether these considerations alone provide a sound basis for rejecting the child's tort action. To begin with, it is hard to see how an award of damages to a severely handicapped or suffering child would "disavow" the value of life or in any way suggest that the child is not entitled to the full measure of legal and nonlegal rights and privileges accorded to all members of society.

Moreover, while our society and our legal system unquestionably place the highest value on all human life, we do not think that it is accurate to suggest that this state's public policy establishes—as a matter of law—that under all circumstances "impaired life" is "preferable" to "nonlife." For example, Health and Safety Code section 7186, enacted in 1976, provides in part:

> The Legislature finds that adult persons have the fundamental right to control the decisions relating to the rendering of their own medical care, including the decision to have life-sustaining procedures withheld or withdrawn in instances of a terminal condition.
>
> . . . The Legislature further finds that, in the interest of protecting individual autonomy, such prolongation of life for persons with a terminal condition may cause loss of patient dignity and unnecessary pain and suffering, while providing nothing medically necessary or beneficial to the patient.

This statute recognizes that—at least in some situations—public policy supports the right of each individual to make his or her own determination as to the relative value of life and death. (Cf. Matter of Quinlan (1976) 70 N.J. 10 [355 A.2d 647, 662-664]; Superintendent of Belchertown v. Saikewicz (1977) 373 Mass. 728 [370 N.E.2d 417, 423-427].)

Of course, in the wrongful life context, the unborn child cannot personally make any choice as to the relative value of life or death. At that stage, however, just as in the case of an infant after birth, the law generally accords the parents the right to act to protect the child's interest. As the wrongful birth decisions recognize, when a doctor or other medical care provider negligently fails to diagnose an hereditary problem, parents are deprived of the opportunity to make an informed and meaningful decision whether to conceive and bear a handicapped child. . . . Although in deciding whether or not to bear such a child parents may properly, and undoubtedly do, take into account their own interests, parents also presumptively consider the interests of their future child. Thus, when a defendant negligently fails to diagnose an hereditary ailment, he harms the potential child as well as the parents by depriving the parents of information which may be necessary to determine whether it is in the child's own interest to be born with defects or not to be born at all.

In this case, in which the plaintiff's only affliction is deafness, it seems quite unlikely that a jury would ever conclude that life with such a condition is worse than not being born at all. Other wrongful life cases, however, have involved children with much more serious, debilitating and painful conditions, and the academic literature refers to still other, extremely severe hereditary diseases. Considering the short life span of many of these children and their frequently very limited ability to perceive or enjoy the benefits of life, we cannot assert with confidence that in every situation there would be a societal consensus that life is preferable to never having been born at all.

While it thus seems doubtful that a child's claim for general damages should properly be denied on the rationale that the value of impaired life, as a matter of law, always exceeds the value of nonlife, we believe that out-of-state decisions are on sounder grounds in holding that—with respect to the child's claim for pain and suffering or other general damages—recovery should be denied because (1) it is simply impossible to determine in any rational or reasoned fashion whether the plaintiff has in fact suffered an injury in being born impaired rather than not being born, and (2) even if it were possible to overcome the first hurdle, it would be impossible to assess general damages in any fair, nonspeculative manner. . . .

[T]he practical problems are exacerbated when it comes to the matter of arriving at an appropriate award of damages. [I]n fixing damages in a tort case the jury generally compares the condition plaintiff would have been in but for the tort, with the position the plaintiff is in now, compensating the plaintiff for what has been lost as a result of the wrong. Although the valuation of pain and suffering or emotional distress in terms of dollars and cents is unquestionably difficult in an ordinary personal injury action, jurors at least have some frame of reference in their own general experience to appreciate what the plaintiff has lost—normal life without pain and suffering. In a wrongful life action, that simply is not the case, for what the plaintiff has "lost" is not life without pain and suffering but rather the unknowable status of never having been born. In this context, a rational, nonspeculative determination of a specific monetary award in accordance with normal tort principles appears to be outside the realm of human competence.

The difficulty in ascertaining or measuring an appropriate award of general damages in this type of case is also reflected in the application of what is sometimes referred to as the "benefit" doctrine in tort damages. Section 920 of the Restatement Second of Torts . . . provides that "[w]hen the defendant's tortious conduct has caused harm to the plaintiff . . . and in so doing has conferred a special benefit to the interest of the plaintiff that was harmed, the value of the benefit conferred is considered in mitigation of damages, to the extent that this is equitable."

In requesting general damages in a wrongful life case, the plaintiff seeks monetary compensation for the pain and suffering he or she will endure because of his or her hereditary affliction. Under section 920's benefit doctrine, however, such damages must be offset by the benefits incidentally conferred by the defendant's conduct "to the interest of the plaintiff that was harmed." With respect to general damages, the harmed interest is the child's general physical, emotional and psychological well-being, and in considering the benefit to this interest which defendant's negligence has conferred, it must be recognized that as an incident of defendant's negligence the plaintiff has in fact obtained a physical existence with the capacity both to receive and give love and pleasure as well as to experience pain and suffering. Because of the incalculable nature of both elements of this harm-benefit equation, we believe that a reasoned, nonarbitrary award of general damage is simply not obtainable. . . .

Although we have determined that the trial court properly rejected plaintiff's claim for general damages, we conclude that her claim for the "extraordinary expenses for specialized teaching, training and hearing equipment" that she will incur during her lifetime because of her deafness stands on a different footing.[11]

As we have already noted, in the corresponding "wrongful birth" actions parents have regularly been permitted to recover the medical expenses incurred on behalf of such a child. . . . In authorizing this recovery by the parents, courts have recognized (1) that these are expenses that would not have been incurred "but for" the defendants' negligence and (2) that they

11. As noted, in a separate cause of action Joy's parents seek to recover, inter alia, for the medical expenses which they will incur on Joy's behalf during her minority. Since both Joy and her parents obviously cannot both recover the same expenses, Joy's separate claim applies as a practical matter only to medical expenses to be incurred after the age of majority.

are the kind of pecuniary losses which are readily ascertainable and regularly awarded as damages in professional malpractice actions.

Although the parents and child cannot, of course, both recover for the same medical expenses, we believe it would be illogical and anomalous to permit only parents, and not the child, to recover for the cost of the child's own medical care. If such a distinction were established, the afflicted child's receipt of necessary medical expenses might well depend on the wholly fortuitous circumstance of whether the parents are available to sue and recover such damages or whether the medical expenses are incurred at a time when the parents remain legally responsible for providing such care.

Realistically, a defendant's negligence in failing to diagnose an hereditary ailment places a significant medical and financial burden on the whole family unit. Unlike the child's claim for general damages, the damage here is both certain and readily measurable. Furthermore, in many instances these expenses will be vital not only to the child's well-being but to his or her very survival. . . . If, as alleged, defendant's negligence was in fact a proximate cause of the child's present and continuing need for such special, extraordinary medical care and training, we believe that it is consistent with the basic liability principles of Civil Code section 1714 to hold defendant liable for the cost of such care, whether the expense is to be borne by the parents or by the child. As Justice Jacobs of the New Jersey Supreme Court observed in his dissenting opinion in Gleitman v. Cosgrove, supra, 227 A.2d at page 703: "While the law cannot remove the heartache or undo the harm, it can afford some reasonable measure of compensation toward alleviating the financial burdens."

Moreover, permitting plaintiff to recover the extraordinary, additional medical expenses that are occasioned by the hereditary ailment is also consistent with the established parameters of the general tort "benefit" doctrine discussed above. As we have seen, under that doctrine an offset is appropriate only insofar as the defendant's conduct has conferred a special benefit "to the interest of the plaintiff that was harmed." Here, the harm for which plaintiff seeks recompense is an economic loss, the extraordinary, out-of-pocket expenses that she will have to bear because of her hereditary ailment. Unlike the claim for general damages, defendants' negligence has conferred no incidental, offsetting benefit to this interest of plaintiff. . . . Accordingly, assessment of these special damages should pose no unusual or insoluble problems. . . .

The judgment is reversed and the case is remanded to the trial court for further proceedings consistent with this opinion.

RICHARDSON and BROUSSARD, JJ., concur. [The concurring opinion of NEWMAN, J., and the dissenting opinion of MOSK, J., are omitted.]

Justice Mosk's dissent consists largely of a quotation from the opinion in *Curlender,* discussed by the majority opinion in *Turpin.* In upholding the complaint in *Curlender,* the court in that case stated (165 Cal. Rptr. at 488-489):

> We have no difficulty in ascertaining and finding the existence of a duty owed by medical laboratories engaged in genetic testing to parents and their as yet unborn children to use ordinary care in administration of available tests for the purpose of providing information concerning potential genetic defects in the unborn. The public policy considerations with respect to the individuals involved and to society as a whole dictate recognition of such a duty, and it is of significance that in no decision that has come to our attention which has dealt with the "wrongful-life" concept has it been suggested that public policy considerations negate the existence of such a duty. Nor have other jurisdictions had any difficulty in finding a breach of duty under appropriate circumstances or in finding the existence of the requisite proximate causal link between the breach and the claimed injury; we find no bar to a holding that the defendants owed a duty to the child plaintiff before us and breached that duty.
>
> The real crux of the problem is whether the breach of duty was the proximate cause of an *injury cognizable at law.* The injury, of course, is not the particular defect with which a plaintiff is afflicted—considered in the abstract—but it is the birth of plaintiff with such defect.
>
> The circumstance that the birth and injury have come hand in hand has caused other courts to deal with the problem by barring recovery. The reality of the "wrongful-life" concept is that such a plaintiff both *exists* and *suffers,* due to the negligence of others. It is neither necessary nor just to retreat into meditation on the mysteries of life. We need not be concerned with the fact that had defendants not been negligent, the plaintiff might not have come into existence at all. The certainty of genetic impairment is no longer a mystery. In addition, a reverent appreciation of life compels recognition that plaintiff, however impaired she may be, has come into existence as a living person with certain rights.
>
> One of the fears expressed in the decisional law is that, once it is determined that such infants have rights cognizable at law, nothing would prevent such a plaintiff from bringing suit against its own parents for allowing plaintiff to be born. In our view, the fear is groundless. The "wrongful-life" cause of action with which we are concerned is based upon negligently caused failure by someone under a duty to do so to inform the prospective parents of facts needed by them to make a conscious choice *not* to become parents. If a case arose where, despite due care by the medical profession in transmitting the necessary warnings, parents made a conscious choice to proceed with a pregnancy, with full knowledge that a seriously impaired infant would be born, that conscious choice would provide an intervening act of proximate cause to preclude liability insofar as defendants other than the parents were concerned. Under such circumstances, we see no sound public policy which should protect those parents from being answerable for the pain, suffering and misery which they have wrought upon their offspring. . . .
>
> The extent of recovery, however, is subject to certain limitations due to the nature of the tort involved. While ordinarily a defendant is liable for all

consequences flowing from the injury, it is appropriate in the case before us to tailor the elements of recovery, taking into account particular circumstances involved. . . .

The complaint seeks damages based upon an actuarial life expectancy of plaintiff of more than 70 years—the life expectancy if plaintiff had been born without the Tay-Sachs disease. The complaint sets forth that plaintiff's actual life expectancy, because of the disease, is only four years. We reject as untenable the claim that plaintiff is entitled to damages as if plaintiff had been born without defects and would have had a normal life expectancy. Plaintiff's right to damages must be considered on the basis of plaintiff's mental and physical condition at birth and her expected condition during the short life span (four years according to the complaint) anticipated for one with her impaired condition. In similar fashion, we reject the notion that a "wrongful-life" cause of action involves any attempted evaluation of a claimed right *not* to be born. In essence, we construe the "wrongful-life" cause of action by the defective child as the right of such child to recover damages for the pain and suffering to be endured during the limited life span available to such a child and any special pecuniary loss resulting from the impaired condition.

The early "wrongful life" claims involved children who were born illegitimate and who sought to recover for that allegedly unfortunate circumstance. All such claims were unsuccessful. See Zepeda v. Zepeda, 190 N.E.2d 849 (Ill. App. 1963), *cert. denied,* 379 U.S. 945 (1964); Williams v. State, 18 N.Y.2d 481, 223 N.E.2d 343 (1966); Slawek v. Stroh, 62 Wis. 2d 295, 215 N.W.2d 9 (1974).

Most of the recent cases have involved children born with severe birth defects. A number of courts have denied recovery entirely. See, e.g., Walker v. Mart, 164 Ariz. 37, 790 P.2d 735 (1990); Cowe v. Forum Group, Inc., 575 N.E.2d 630 (Ind. 1991). Others permit, as did the court in *Turpin,* recovery for living expenses attributable to the defect projected to be incurred after the child reaches majority. See, e.g., Kush v. Lloyd, 616 So. 2d 415 (Fla. 1992); Procanik v. Cillo, 97 N.J. 339, 478 A.2d 755 (1984). The New Jersey Supreme Court, however, denied recovery in a case in which the birth of the plaintiff occurred before the decision of Roe v. Wade, 410 U.S. 113, 93 S. Ct. 705, 35 L. Ed. 2d 147 (1973); the allegation was that had the defendant not been negligent in counseling the plaintiff's mother she would have had an abortion. See Hummel v. Reiss, 129 N.J. 118, 608 A.2d 1341 (1992).

The commentators have generally been more receptive to the cause of action for wrongful life than have the courts. See, e.g., Kelly, The Rightful Position in "Wrongful Life" Actions, 42 Hastings L.J. 505 (1991), and Note, Wrongful Life: A Time for a "Day in Court," 51 Ohio St. L.J. 473 (1990). Commentators have not been as receptive, however, when the suit is brought against the parents, as the court in *Curlender* suggested would be appropriate. See Waters, Wrongful Life: The Implications of Suits in

Wrongful Life Brought by Children Against Their Parents, 31 Drake L. Rev. 441 (1981-1982).

d. Purely Consequential Economic Loss

Barber Lines A/S v. M/V Donau Maru

764 F.2d 50 (1st Cir. 1985)

BREYER, C.J. In December 1979 the ship Donau Maru spilled fuel oil into Boston Harbor. The spill prevented a different ship, the Tamara, from docking at a nearby berth. The Tamara had to discharge her cargo at another pier. In doing so, she incurred significant extra labor, fuel, transport and docking costs. The Tamara, her owners, and her charterers sued the Donau Maru and her owners in admiralty. Insofar as is here relevant, they claimed negligence and sought recovery of the extra expenses as damages. The district court denied recovery on the basis of the pleadings. . . . The plaintiffs have appealed. We believe the district court was correct, and we affirm its judgment, for three related sets of reasons.

1. Plaintiffs-appellants seek recovery for a financial injury caused by defendant's negligence. We assume that the injury was foreseeable. Nonetheless controlling case law denies that a plaintiff can recover damages for negligently caused financial harm, even when foreseeable, except in special circumstances. There is present here neither the most common such special circumstance—physical injury to the plaintiffs or to their property—nor any other special feature that would permit recovery. . . .

2. Before affirming the district court on the basis of existing precedent, we have asked ourselves whether that precedent remains good law. After all, courts have sometimes departed from past legal precedent where changing circumstances viewed in light of underlying legal policy deprived that precedent of sound support. Here, however, precedent seems, at least in general, to rest on a firm policy foundation. . . . Much written commentary, which for a time in the 1940's attacked the limitation, has more recently supported it, while offering a variety of refinements. . . .

The cases and commentaries, in making a plausible argument that existing precedent rests on sound considerations of policy, also reveal that these considerations are highly general and abstract. Judges lack the empirical information that would allow measurement of their force or magnitude; and, in particular, judges cannot apply these considerations on a case by case basis.

We have concluded that we could not find for appellants here without ignoring these policy considerations, or at a minimum, applying them case by case, a practice that we believe would be unwise. A brief description of the kinds of policy considerations typically advanced as supporting existing law (perhaps with a few modifications) will show why these considerations have led us to conclude that we must adhere to prior precedent.

First, cases and commentators point to pragmatic or practical administrative considerations which, *when taken together,* offer support for a rule limiting recovery for negligently caused pure financial harm. The number of persons suffering foreseeable financial harm in a typical accident is likely to be far greater than those who suffer traditional (recoverable) physical harm. The typical downtown auto accident, that harms a few persons physically and physically damages the property of several others, may well cause financial harm (e.g., through delay) to a vast number of potential plaintiffs. The less usual, negligently caused, oil spill foreseeably harms not only ships, docks, piers, beaches, wildlife, and the like, that are covered with oil, but also harms blockaded ships, marina merchants, suppliers of those firms, the employees of marina businesses and suppliers, the suppliers' suppliers, and so forth. To use the notion of "foreseeability" that courts use in physical injury cases to separate the financially injured allowed to sue from the financially injured not allowed to sue would draw vast numbers of injured persons within the class of potential plaintiffs in even the most simple accident cases (unless it leads courts, unwarrantedly, to narrow the scope of "foreseeability" as applied to persons suffering physical harm). That possibility—a large number of different plaintiffs each with somewhat different claims—in turn threatens to raise significantly the cost of even relatively simple tort actions. Yet the tort action is already a very expensive administrative device for compensating victims of accidents. Indeed, the legal time, the legal resources, the delay appurtenant to the tort action apparently mean that on average the victim recovers only between 28 and 44 cents of every dollar paid by actual or potential defendants, while victims who insure themselves directly recover at least between 55 and 66 cents of each premium dollar earned by insurance companies and between 85 and 90 cents of every dollar actually paid out to investigate and satisfy claims. The added cost of the increased complexity, while unknowable with precision, seems likely significant.

At the same time many of the "financially injured" will find it easier than the "physically injured" to arrange for cheaper, alternative compensation. The typical "financial" plaintiff is likely to be a business firm that, in any event, buys insurance, and which may well be able to arrange for "first party" loss compensation for foreseeable financial harm. Other such victims will be able to sue under tort principles, for they will suffer at least some physical harm to their property. Still others may have contracts with, or be able to contract with, persons who can themselves recover from the negligent defendant. A shipowner, for example, might contract with a dock owner for "inaccessibility" compensation; and the dock owner (whose pier is physically covered with oil) might recover this compensation as part of its tort damages. Of course, such a tort suit, embodying a "contract-defined" injury, may still raise difficult foreseeability questions, cf. Hadley v. Baxendale, 9 Exch. 341 (1854). But the bringing of one suit, instead of several, still makes the litigation as a whole a less costly compensation device. Finally, some of the "financially injured" will have suffered harm that is, in any event, noncompensable because it is not sufficiently distinguishable from minor harms typical of ordinary living. The law does not compensate, for example, the cost of unused baseball tickets or flowers needed for apology regardless of the cause of delay that foreseeably led to the added expense. Insofar as these considerations, taken as a whole, support recovery limitations, they reflect a fear of creating victim compensation costs that, from an administrative point of view, are unnecessarily high. See Stevenson v. East Ohio Gas Co., 73 N.E.2d 200, 202 (Ohio 1946).

A second set of considerations focuses on the "disproportionality" between liability and fault. Those who argue "disproportionality" are not reiterating the discredited nineteenth century view that tort liability would destroy industry, investment, or capitalism. Rather, they recognize that tort liability provides a powerful set of economic incentives and disincentives to engage in economic activity or to make it safer, see generally G. Calabresi, The Costs of Accidents (1970). And, liability for pure financial harm, insofar as it proved vast, cumulative and inherently unknowable in amount, could create incentives that are perverse.

Might not unbounded liability for foreseeable financial damage, for example, make auto insurance premiums too expensive for the average driver? Is such a result desirable? After all, the high premiums would reflect not *only* the costs of the harm inflicted; they would also reflect administrative costs of law suits, jury verdicts in uncertain amounts, some percentage of unbounded or inflated economic claims, and lessened incentive for financial victims to avoid harm or to mitigate damage. Given the existing liability for physical injury (and for accompanying financial injury), can one say that still higher premiums are needed to make the public realize that driving is socially expensive or to provide greater incentive to drive safely (an incentive that risk spreading through insurance dilutes in any event, see Shavell, On Liability and Insurance, 13 Bell J. of Econ. 120 [1982])?

These considerations, of administrability and disproportionality, offer plausible, though highly abstract, "policy" support for the reluctance of the courts to impose tort liability for purely financial harm. While they seem unlikely to apply with equal strength to every sort of "financial harm" claim, their abstraction and generality, along with the comparative inaccessibility of the empirical information needed to confirm or to invalidate them, mean that courts cannot weigh or apply them case by case. What, for example, in cases like this one, are the added administrative costs involved in allowing all persons suffering pure financial harm to sue the shipowner instead of "channeling" suits (perhaps via contract) through traditionally injured plaintiffs? Is there a problem of "disproportionality"? How far, for example, would additional, unbounded, pure financial loss liability for negligently caused oil spills, when added to the already large potential traditional liability, affect the type of insurance carried, the incentive to mitigate losses, the incentive to transport oil safely, the likelihood that shippers will use pipelines and domestic wells instead of ships and foreign wells, and the consequences of these and other related changes? We do not know the answers to these questions, nor can judges readily answer them in particular cases.

It does not surprise us then that, under these circumstances, courts have neither enforced one clear rule nor considered the matter case by case. Rather they have spoken of a general principle against liability for negligently caused financial harm, while creating many exceptions. (See, e.g., 1) Newlin v. New England Telephone & Telegraph Co., 316 Mass. 234, 54 N.E.2d 929 (1944) (accompanying physical harm); 2) Lumley v. Gye, 2 El. & Bl. 216, 118 Eng. Rep. 749 (1853); Beekman v. Marsters, 195 Mass. 205, 80 N.E. 817 (1907) (intentionally caused harm); 3) Dalton v. Meister, 52 Wis. 2d 173, 188 N.W.2d 494 (defamation), *cert. denied,* 405 U.S. 934, 92 S. Ct. 947, 30 L. Ed. 2d 810 (1971); Systems Operations, Inc. v. Scientific Games Development Corp., 555 F.2d 1131 (3d Cir. 1977) (injurious falsehood); 4) Hitaffer v. Argonne Co., 183 F.2d 811 (D.C. Cir.) (loss of consortium), *cert. denied,* 340 U.S. 852, 71 S. Ct. 80, 95 L. Ed. 624 (1950); 5) Chicago, Duluth & Georgia Bay Transit Co. v. Moore, 259 Fed. 490 (6th Cir.) (medical costs of injured plaintiff paid by a different family member), *cert. denied,* 251 U.S. 553, 40 S. Ct. 118, 64 L. Ed. 411 (1919); 6) Hedley Byrne Co. Ltd. v. Heller & Partners Ltd., A.C. 465 (1964) (negligent misstatements about financial matters); 7) Jones v. Waterman S.S. Corp., 155 F.2d 992 (3d Cir. 1946) (master-servant); 8) Western Union Telegraph Co. v. Mathis, 215 Ala. 282, 110 So. 399 (1926) (telegraph-addressee); 9) Union Oil Co. v. Oppen, 501 F.2d 558 (9th Cir. 1974) (commercial fishermen as special "favorites of admiralty"). These exceptions seem designed to pick out broad categories of cases where the "administrative" and "disproportionality" problems intuitively seem insignificant or where some strong countervailing consideration militates in favor of liability. Thus an award of financial damages to one *also* caused physical harm does not threaten proliferation of law suits, for the plaintiff could sue anyway (for physical damages). Financial harm awards to family members carry with them an obvious self-limiting principle (as perhaps does awarding such damages to fishermen, as "favorites" of admiralty). Awarding damages for financial harm caused by negligent misrepresentation is special in that, without such liability, tort law would not exert significant financial pressure to avoid negligence; a negligent accountant lacks physically harmed victims as potential plaintiffs.

We need not explore the exceptions in detail. Rather, we here simply point to the existence of plausible reasons underlying the judicial hesitance to award damages in a case like this one, and the need to consider exceptions by class rather than case by case. The existence of these factors, together with our comparative inability to evaluate their empirical significance, cautions us against departing from prior law. . . .

We conclude that we should follow existing precedent that requires us, as a matter of law, to deny recovery. That precedent is reasonably consistent. It is supported by plausible considerations of tort policy. Appellants have failed to bring themselves within any recognized class or category in which financial damages are already allowed, and appellants have failed to provide convincing reasons for the creation of any new exception or class that would work to their legal benefit.

For these reasons, the judgment of the district court is affirmed.

The early landmark cases denying recovery for purely consequential economic loss are Robins Dry Dock & Repair Co. v. Flint, 275 U.S. 303, 48 S. Ct. 134, 72 L. Ed. 290 (1927), and Stevenson v. East Ohio Gas Co., 73 N.E.2d 200 (Ohio App. 1946). A number of recent cases, other than *Barber Lines,* have adhered to the traditional rule. See, e.g., FMR Corp. v. Boston Edison Co., 415 Mass. 393, 613 N.E.2d 902 (1993) (power outage caused loss of income and increase in cost of doing business); Floor Craft Floor Covering, Inc. v. Parma Community General Hospital Association, 54 Ohio St. 3d 1, 560 N.E.2d 206 (1990) (negligent design by architect caused problem requiring plaintiff to replace flooring); United Textile Workers of America, AFL-CIO, CLC v. Lear Siegler Seating Corp., 825 S.W.2d 83 (Tenn. App. 1990) (leak in defendant's propane tank forced factory in which plaintiffs worked to close, causing loss of one day's wages).

J'Aire Corp. v. Gregory

24 Cal. 3d 799, 598 P.2d 60, 157 Cal. Rptr. 407 (1979)

BIRD, C.J. Appellant, a lessee, sued respondent, a general contractor, for damages resulting from the delay in completion of a construction project at the premises where appellant operated a restaurant. Respondent demurred successfully and the complaint was dismissed. This court must decide whether a contractor who undertakes construction work pursuant to a contract with the owner of premises may be held liable in tort for business losses suffered by a lessee when the contractor negligently fails to complete the project with due diligence.

I

The facts as pleaded are as follows. Appellant, J'Aire Corporation, operates a restaurant . . . in premises leased from the County of Sonoma. Under the terms of the lease the county was to provide heat and air conditioning. In 1975 the county entered into a contract with respondent for improvements to the restaurant premises, including renovation of the heating and air conditioning systems and installation of insulation.

As the contract did not specify any date for completion of the work, appellant alleged the work was to have been completed within a reasonable time as defined by custom and usage. . . . Despite requests that respondent complete the construction promptly, the work was not completed within a reasonable time. Because the restaurant could not operate during part of the construction and was without heat and air conditioning for a longer period, appellant suffered loss of business and resulting loss of profits.

Appellant alleged two causes of action in its third amended complaint. The first cause of action was based upon the theory that it was a third party beneficiary of the contract between the county and respondent. The second cause of action sounded in tort and was based upon negligence in completing the work within a reasonable time. Damages of $50,000 were claimed.

Respondent demurred on the ground that the complaint did not state facts sufficient to constitute a cause of action. . . . The trial court sustained the demurrer without leave to amend and the complaint was dismissed. On appeal only the sustaining of the demurrer to the second cause of action is challenged.

II

. . . The only question before this court is whether a cause of action for negligent loss of expected economic advantage may be maintained under these facts.

Liability for negligent conduct may only be imposed where there is a duty of care owed by the defendant to the plaintiff or to a class of which the plaintiff is a member. . . . A duty of care may arise through statute or by contract. Alternatively, a duty may be premised upon the general character of the activity in which the defendant engaged, the relationship between the parties or even the interdependent nature of human society. . . . Whether a duty is owed is simply a shorthand way of phrasing what is " 'the essential question—whether the plaintiff's interests are entitled to legal protection against the defendant's conduct.' " (Dillon v. Legg (1968) 68 Cal. 2d 728, 734, 69 Cal. Rptr. 72, 76, 441 P.2d 912, 916, quoting from Prosser, Law of Torts (3d ed. 1964) pp. 332-333. . . .)

This court has held that a plaintiff's interest in prospective economic advantage may be protected against injury occasioned by negligent as well as intentional conduct. For example, economic losses such as lost earnings or profits are recoverable as part of general damages in a suit for personal injury based on negligence. . . . Where negligent conduct causes injury to real or personal property, the plaintiff may recover damages for profits lost during the time necessary to repair or replace the property. . . .

Even when only injury to prospective economic advantage is claimed, recovery is not foreclosed. Where a special relationship exists between the parties, a plaintiff may recover for loss of expected economic advantage through the negligent performance of a contract although the parties were not in contractual privity. . . .

In each of the [other] cases, the court determined that defendants owed plaintiffs a duty of care by applying [certain] criteria . . . Those criteria are (1) the extent to which the transaction was intended to affect the plaintiff, (2) the foreseeability of harm to the plaintiff, (3) the degree of certainty that the plaintiff suffered injury, (4) the closeness of the connection between the defendant's conduct and the injury suffered, (5) the moral blame attached to the defendant's conduct and (6) the policy of preventing future harm. . . .

Applying these criteria to the facts as pleaded, it is evident that a duty was owed by respondent to appellant in the present case. (1) The contract entered into between respondent and the county was for the renovation of the premises in which appellant maintained its business. The contract could not have been performed without impinging on that business. Thus respondent's performance was intended to, and did, directly affect appellant. (2) Accordingly, it was clearly foreseeable that any significant delay in completing the construction would adversely affect appellant's business beyond the normal disruption associated with such construction. Appellant alleges this fact was repeatedly drawn to respondent's attention. (3) Further, appellant's complaint leaves no doubt that appellant suffered harm since it was unable to operate its business for one month and suffered additional loss of business while the premises were without heat and air conditioning. (4) Appellant has also alleged that delays occasioned by the respondent's conduct were closely connected to, indeed directly caused its injury. (5) In addition, respondent's lack of diligence in the present case was particularly blameworthy since it continued after the probability of damage was drawn directly to respondent's attention. (6) Finally, public policy supports finding a duty of care in the present case. The wilful failure or refusal of a contractor to prosecute a construction project with diligence, where another is injured as a result, has been made grounds for disciplining a licensed contractor. . . . Although [the statute] does not provide a basis for imposing liability where the delay in completing construction is due merely to negligence, it does indicate the seriousness with which the Legislature views unnecessary delays in the completion of construction. . . .

To hold under these facts that a cause of action has been stated for negligent interference with prospective economic advantage is consistent with the recent trend in tort cases. This court has repeatedly eschewed overly rigid common law formulations of duty in favor of allowing compensation for foreseeable injuries caused by a defendant's want of ordinary care. (See, e.g., Dillon v. Legg, supra, 68 Cal. 2d at p. 746, 69 Cal. Rptr.

72, 441 P.2d 912 [liability for mother's emotional distress when child killed by defendant's negligence]; Rowland v. Christian (1968) 69 Cal. 2d 108, 119, 70 Cal. Rptr. 97, 443 P.2d 561 [liability of host for injury to social guest on premises]; cf. Brown v. Merlo (1973) 8 Cal. 3d 855, 106 Cal. Rptr. 388, 506 P.2d 212 [liability of automobile driver for injury to nonpaying passenger]; Rodriguez v. Bethlehem Steel Corp. (1974) 12 Cal. 3d 382, 115 Cal. Rptr. 765, 525 P.2d 669 [liability for loss of consortium].) Rather than traditional notions of duty, this court has focused on foreseeability as the key component necessary to establish liability:

> While the question whether one owes a duty to another must be decided on a case-by-case basis, every case is governed by the rule of general application that all persons are required to use ordinary care to prevent others from being injured as a result of their conduct. . . . [F]oreseeability of the risk is a primary consideration in establishing the element of duty.

(Weirum v. RKO General, Inc. (1975) 15 Cal. 3d 40, 46, 123 Cal. Rptr. 468, 471, 539 P.2d 36, 39, fn. omitted.) Similarly, respondent is liable if his lack of ordinary care caused foreseeable injury to the economic interests of appellant. . . .

The chief dangers which have been cited in allowing recovery for negligent interference with prospective economic advantage are the possibility of excessive liability, the creation of an undue burden on freedom of action, the possibility of fraudulent or collusive claims and the often speculative nature of damages. . . . Central to these fears is the possibility that liability will be imposed for remote consequences, out of proportion to the magnitude of the defendant's wrongful conduct.

However, the factors [discussed above] place a limit on recovery by focusing judicial attention on the foreseeability of the injury and the nexus between the defendant's conduct and the plaintiff's injury. These factors and ordinary principles of tort law such as proximate cause are fully adequate to limit recovery without the drastic consequence of an absolute rule which bars recovery in all such cases. (See Dillon v. Legg, supra, 68 Cal. 2d at p. 746, 69 Cal. Rptr. 72, 441 P.2d 912.) Following these principles, recovery for negligent interference with prospective economic advantage will be limited to instances where the risk of harm is foreseeable and is closely connected with the defendant's conduct, where damages are not wholly speculative and the injury is not part of the plaintiff's ordinary business risk.

III

Accordingly, this court holds that a contractor owes a duty of care to the tenant of a building undergoing construction work to prosecute that work in a manner which does not cause undue injury to the tenant's business, where such injury is reasonably foreseeable. The demurrer to appellant's second cause of action should not have been sustained. The judgment of dismissal is reversed.

TOBRINER, MOSK, MANUEL and NEWMAN, JJ., concur.

CLARK and RICHARDSON, JJ., concur in the judgment.

J'Aire Corp. is analyzed in Rabin, Tort Recovery for Negligently Inflicted Economic Loss: A Reassessment, 37 Stan. L. Rev. 1513 (1985), and Schwartz, Economic Loss in American Tort Law: The Examples of *J'Aire* and of Products Liability, 23 San Diego L. Rev. 37 (1986). Professor Rabin's article is generally favorable to *J'Aire Corp.,* while Professor Schwartz's is critical.

People Express Airlines, Inc. v. Consolidated Rail Corp.

100 N.J. 246, 495 A.2d 107 (1985)

HANDLER, J. This appeal presents a question that has not previously been directly considered: whether a defendant's negligent conduct that interferes with a plaintiff's business resulting in purely economic losses, unaccompanied by property damage or personal injury, is compensable in tort. The appeal poses this issue in the context of the defendants' alleged negligence that caused a dangerous chemical to escape from a railway tank car, resulting in the evacuation from the surrounding area of persons whose safety and health were threatened. The plaintiff, a commercial airline, was forced to evacuate its premises and suffered an interruption of its business operations with resultant economic losses.

[The trial court entered summary judgment for the defendant. The appellate division reversed. Defendant appeals.]

II

The single characteristic that distinguishes parties in negligence suits whose claims for economic losses have been regularly denied by American and English courts from those who have recovered economic losses is, with respect to the successful claimants, the fortuitous occurrence of physical harm or property damage, however slight. It is well-accepted that a defendant who negligently injures a plaintiff or his property may be liable for all proximately caused harm, including economic losses. Nevertheless, a virtually *per se* rule barring recovery for economic loss unless the negligent conduct also caused physical harm has evolved throughout this century. . . .

The reasons that have been advanced to explain the divergent results for litigants seeking economic losses are varied. Some courts have viewed the general rule against recovery as necessary to limit damages to reasonably foreseeable consequences of negligent conduct. This concern in a given case is often manifested as an issue of causation and has led to the requirement of physical harm as an element of proximate cause. In this context, the physical harm requirement functions as part of the definition of the causal relationship between the defendant's negligent act and the plaintiff's economic damages; it acts as a convenient clamp on otherwise boundless liability. The physical harm rule also reflects certain deep-seated concerns that underlie courts' denial of recovery for purely economic losses occasioned by a defendant's negligence. These concerns include the fear of fraudulent claims, mass litigation, and limitless liability, or liability out of proportion to the defendant's fault.

The assertion of unbounded liability is not unique to cases involving negligently caused economic loss without physical harm. Even in negligence suits in which plaintiffs have sustained physical harm, the courts have recognized that a tortfeasor is not necessarily liable for *all* consequences of his conduct. While a lone act can cause a finite amount of physical harm, that harm may be great and very remote in its final consequences. A single overturned lantern may burn Chicago. Some limitation is required; that limitation is the rule that a tortfeasor is liable only for that harm that he proximately caused. Proximate or legal cause has traditionally functioned to limit liability for negligent conduct. Duty has also been narrowly defined to limit liability. Compare the majority and dissenting opinions in Palsgraf v. Long Island R.R., supra, 248 N.Y. 339, 162 N.E. 99. Thus, we proceed from the premise that principles of duty and proximate cause are instrumental in limiting the amount of litigation and extent of liability in cases in which no physical harm occurs just as they are in cases involving physical injury.

Countervailing considerations of fairness and public policy have led courts to discard the requirement of physical harm as an element in defining proximate cause to overcome the problem of fraudulent or indefinite claims. . . . In this context, we have subordinated the threat of potential baseless claims to the right of an aggrieved individual to pursue a just and fair claim for redress attributable to the wrongdoing of another. The asserted inability to define damages in cases arising under the cause of action for negligent infliction of emotional distress absent impact or near-impact has not hindered adjudication of those claims. Nor is there any indication that unfair awards have resulted.

The troublesome concern reflected in cases denying recovery for negligently-caused economic loss is the alleged potential for infinite liability, or liability out of all proportion to the defendant's fault. . . .

It is understandable that courts, fearing that if even one deserving plaintiff suffering purely economic loss were allowed to recover, all such plaintiffs could recover, have anchored their rulings to the physical harm requirement. While the rationale is understandable, it supports only a limitation on, not a denial of, liability. The physical harm requirement capriciously showers compensation along the path of physical destruction, regardless of the status or circumstances of individual claimants. Purely economic losses are borne by innocent victims, who may not be able to absorb their losses. In the end, the challenge is to fashion a rule that limits liability but permits adjudication of meritorious claims. The asserted inability to fix chrystalline formulae for recovery on the differing facts of future cases simply does not justify the wholesale rejection of recovery in all cases.

Further, judicial reluctance to allow recovery for purely economic losses is discordant with contemporary tort doctrine. The torts process, like the law itself, is a human institution designed to accomplish certain social objectives. One objective is to ensure that innocent victims have avenues of legal redress, absent a contrary, overriding public policy. This reflects the overarching purpose of tort law: that wronged persons should be compensated for their injuries and that those responsible for the wrong should bear the cost of the tortious conduct.

Other policies underlie this fundamental purpose. Imposing liability on defendants for their negligent conduct discourages others from similar tortious behavior, fosters safer products to aid our daily tasks, vindicates reasonable conduct that has regard for the safety of others, and, ultimately, shifts the risk of loss and associated costs of dangerous activities to those who should be and are best able to bear them. Although these policies may be unevenly reflected or imperfectly articulated in any particular case, we strive to ensure that the application of negligence doctrine advances the fundamental purpose of tort law and does not unnecessarily or arbitrarily foreclose redress based on formalisms or technicalisms. Whatever the original common law justifications for the physical harm rule, contemporary tort and negligence doctrine allow—indeed, impel—a more thorough consideration and searching analysis of underlying policies to determine whether a particular defendant may be liable for a plaintiff's economic losses despite the absence of any attendant physical harm. . . .

III

We may appropriately consider two relevant avenues of analysis in defining a cause of action for negligently-caused economic loss. The first examines the evolution of various exceptions to the rule of nonrecovery for purely economic losses, and suggests that the exceptions have cast considerable doubt on the validity of the current rule and, indeed, have laid the foundation for a rule that would allow recovery. The second explores the elements of a suitable rule and adopts the traditional approach of foreseeability as it relates to duty and proximate cause molded to circumstances involving a claim only for negligently-caused economic injury.

A

Judicial discomfiture with the rule of nonrecovery for purely economic loss throughout the last several decades has led to numerous exceptions in the general rule. Although the rationalizations for these exceptions differ among courts and cases, two common threads run throughout the exceptions. The first is that the element of foreseeability emerges as a more appropriate analytical standard to determine the question of liability than a *per se* prohibitory rule. The second is that the extent to which the defendant knew or should have known the particular consequences of his negligence, including the economic loss of a particularly foreseeable plaintiff, is dispositive of the issues of duty and fault. . . .

We hold therefore that a defendant owes a duty of care to take reasonable measures to avoid the risk of causing economic damages, aside from physical injury, to particular plaintiffs or plaintiffs comprising an identifiable class with respect to whom defendant knows or has reason to know are likely to suffer such damages from its conduct. A defendant failing to adhere to this duty of care may be found liable for such economic damages proximately caused by its breach of duty.

We stress that an identifiable class of plaintiffs is not simply a foreseeable class of plaintiffs. For example, members of the general public, or invitees such as sales and service persons at a particular plaintiff's business premises, or persons travelling on a highway near the scene of a negligently-caused accident, such as the one at bar, who are delayed in the conduct of their affairs and suffer varied economic losses, are certainly a foreseeable class of plaintiffs. Yet their presence within the area would be fortuitous, and the particular type of economic injury that could be suffered by such persons would be hopelessly unpredictable and not realistically foreseeable. Thus, the class itself would not be sufficiently ascertainable. An identifiable class of plaintiffs must be particularly foreseeable in terms of the type of persons or entities comprising the class, the certainty or predictability of their presence, the approximate numbers of those in the class, as well as the type of economic expectations disrupted. . . .

We recognize that some cases will present circumstances that defy the categorization here devised to circumscribe a defendant's orbit of duty, limit otherwise boundless liability and define an identifiable class of plaintiffs that may recover. In these cases, the courts will be required to draw upon notions of fairness, common sense and morality to fix the line limiting liability as a matter of public policy, rather than an uncritical application of the principle of particular foreseeability.

B

Liability depends not only on the breach of a standard of care but also on a proximate causal relationship between the breach of the duty of care and resultant losses. Proximate or legal causation is that combination of "logic, common sense, justice, policy and precedent" that fixes a point in a chain of events, some foreseeable and some unforeseeable, beyond which the law will bar recovery. The standard of particular foreseeability may be successfully employed to determine whether the economic injury was proximately caused, *i.e.,* whether the particular harm that occurred is compensable, just as it informs the question whether a duty exists.

Although not expressly eschewing the general rule against recovery for purely economic losses, our courts have employed a traditional proximate cause analysis in order to decide whether particular claimants may survive motions for summary judgment. These cases embody a distinction between those economic losses that are only generally foreseeable, and thus noncompensable, and those losses the defendant is in a position particularly to foresee. . . .

The particular-general foreseeability axis is also accordant with the policies underlying tort law. For good reason, tortfeasors are liable only for the results falling within the foreseeable risks of their negligent conduct. Assigning liability for harm that fortuitously extends beyond the foreseeable risk of negligent conduct unfairly punishes the tortfeasor for harm that he could not have anticipated and taken precautions to avoid. This comports with an underlying policy of the negligence doctrine: the imposition of liability should deter negligent conduct by creating incentives to minimize the risks and costs of accidents. The imposition of liability for unforeseeable risks cannot serve to deter the conduct that has eventuated in attenuated results, but instead arbitrarily assigns liability unrelated or out of proportion to the defendant's fault. If negligence is the failure to take precautions that cost less than the damage wrought by the ensuing accident, see United States v. Carroll Towing Co., 159 F.2d 169, 173, *reh. den.,* 160 F.2d 482 (2d Cir. 1947), it would be unfair and socially inefficient to assign liability for harm that no reasonably-undertaken precaution could have avoided.

We conclude therefore that a defendant who has breached his duty of care to avoid the risk of economic injury to particularly foreseeable plaintiffs may be held liable for actual economic losses that are proximately caused by its breach of duty. In this context, those economic losses are recoverable as damages when they are the natural and probable consequence of a defendant's negligence in the sense that they are reasonably to be anticipated in view of defendant's capacity to have foreseen that the particular plaintiff or identifiable class of plaintiffs, is demonstrably within the risk created by defendant's negligence.

III

We are satisfied that our holding today is fully applicable to the facts that we have considered on this appeal. Plaintiff has set forth a cause of action under our decision, and it is entitled to have the matter proceed to a plenary trial. Among the facts that persuade us that a cause of action has been established is the close proximity of the North Terminal and People Express Airlines to the Conrail freight yard; the obvious nature of the plaintiff's operations and particular foreseeability of economic losses resulting from an accident and evacuation; the defendants' actual or constructive knowledge of the volatile properties of ethylene oxide; and the existence of an emergency response plan prepared by some of the defendants (alluded to in the course of oral argument), which apparently called for the nearby area to be evacuated to avoid the risk of harm in case of an explosion. We do not mean to suggest by our recitation of these facts that actual knowledge of the eventual economic losses is necessary to the cause of action; rather, particular foreseeability will suffice. The plaintiff still faces a difficult task in proving damages, particularly lost profits, to the degree of certainty required in other negligence cases. The trial court's examination of these proofs must be exacting to ensure that damages recovered are those reasonably to have been anticipated in view of the defendant's capacity to have foreseen that this particular plaintiff was within the risk created by their negligence.

We appreciate that there will arise many similar cases that cannot be resolved by our decision today. The cause of action we recognize, however, is one that most appropriately should be allowed to evolve on a case-by-case basis in the context of actual adjudications. We perceive no reason, however, why our decision today should be applied only prospectively. Our holdings are well grounded in traditional tort principles and flow from well-established exceptional cases that are philosophically compatible with this decision.

Accordingly, the judgment of the Appellate Division is modified, and, as modified, affirmed. The case is remanded for proceedings consistent with this opinion.

Of the courts that have recently considered the issue, it is probably fair to say that a majority have retreated from the no liability rule of *Barber Lines.* It is also fair to say that among the courts that have moved away from the traditional rule, no consensus has emerged as to what the appropriate rule of liability is. The issue was presented to the court in Petitions of Kinsman Transit Co. (Kinsman No. 2), 388 F.2d 821 (2d Cir. 1968), which arose out of the same events as *Kinsman No. 1,* set out at p. 380, above. *Kinsman No. 2* involved claims for extra expenses the petitioners incurred in filling contracts for the delivery of grain and in unloading cargo. The court denied recovery on the facts of the claims presented because the harm for which recovery was sought was "too remote or 'indirect' a consequence of defendants' negligence." 388 F.2d at 824. The court did agree, however, that tested by the usual rules of foreseeability, the consequences could be found to have been foreseeable. In denying recovery, the court relied heavily on Judge Andrews (388 F.2d at 824-825):

> On the previous appeal we stated aptly: "somewhere a point will be reached when courts will agree that the link has become too tenuous—that what is claimed to be consequence is only fortuity." 338 F.2d at 725. We believe that this point has been reached with the Cargill and Cargo Carriers claims. Neither the Gillies nor the Farr suffered any direct or immediate damage for which recovery is sought. The instant claims occurred only because the downed bridge made it impossible to move traffic along the river. Under all the circumstances of this case, we hold that the connection between the defendants' negligence and the claimants' damages is too tenuous and remote to permit recovery. "The law does not spread its protection so far." Holmes, J., in *Robins Dry Dock,* supra, 275 U.S. at 309, 48 S. Ct. at 135.
>
> In the final analysis, the circumlocution whether posed in terms of "foreseeability," "duty," "proximate cause," "remoteness," etc. seems unavoidable. As we have previously noted, 338 F.2d at 725, we return to Judge Andrews' frequently quoted statement in Palsgraf v. Long Island R.R., 248 N.Y. 339, 354-355, 162 N.E. 99, 104, 59 A.L.R. 1253 (1928) (dissenting opinion): "It is all a question of expediency . . . of fair judgment, always keeping in mind the fact that we endeavor to make a rule in each case that will be practical and in keeping with the general understanding of mankind."

In Union Oil Co. v. Oppen, 501 F.2d 558 (9th Cir. 1974), the claims arose out of the escape of oil from one of the defendant's offshore drilling platforms. The plaintiffs were commercial fishermen, and they sought to recover for the resulting reduction of the fishing potential in the waters affected by the spill. In ruling that the trial court properly permitted recovery, the court stated (501 F.2d at 570-571):

> Finally, it must be understood that our holding in this case does not open the door to claims that may be asserted by those, other than commercial fishermen, whose economic or personal affairs were discommoded by the oil spill of January 28, 1969. The general rule urged upon us by defendants has a legitimate sphere within which to operate. Nothing said in this opinion is intended to suggest, for example, that every decline in the general commercial activity of every business in the Santa Barbara area following the occurrences of 1969 constitutes a legally cognizable injury for which the defendants may be responsible. The plaintiffs in the present action lawfully and directly make use of a resource of the sea, viz. its fish, in the ordinary course of their business. This type of use is entitled to protection from negligent conduct by the defendants in their drilling operations. Both the plaintiffs and defendants conduct their business operations away from land and in, on and under the sea. Both must carry on their commercial enterprises in a reasonably prudent manner. Neither should be permitted negligently to inflict commercial injury on the other. We decide no more than this.

In State of Louisiana *ex rel.* Guste v. M/V Testbank, 752 F.2d 1019 (5th Cir. 1985) *cert. denied* 106 S. Ct. 3271 (1986), suit was brought by several plaintiffs arising out of a spill of PCP, a highly toxic substance, in the waters out of which the plaintiffs made their living. After the spill, the area was closed to all navigation. The court upheld summary judgment in favor of the defendants against the "shipping interests, marina and boat rental operators, wholesale and retail seafood enterprises not actually engaged in fishing, seafood restaurants, tackle and bait shops, and recreational fishermen." The trial judge did not grant summary judgment against the plaintiffs who were "commercial oystermen, shrimpers, crabbers and fishermen who had been making a commercial use" of the area, so the legitimacy of their claims was not involved in the appeal. In Pruitt v. Allied Chemical Corp., 523 F. Supp. 975 (E.D. Va. 1981), several groups of plaintiffs sued the defendant for economic harm resulting from the latter's pollution of Chesapeake Bay with Kepone. The court ruled (with no disagreement from the defendant) that commercial fishermen could recover, but those who bought fish from the fishermen could not. However, the groups of plaintiffs made up of the owners of boat shops, bait and tackle shops, and marinas could recover. The court admitted that it found "itself with a perceived need to limit liability, without any articulable reason for excluding any particular set of plaintiffs." 523 F. Supp. at 980. And in Shaughnessy v. PPG Industries, Inc., 795 F. Supp. 193 (W.D. La. 1992), the defendant's motion for summary judgment was denied in a case in which the defendant had polluted several bodies of fresh water near which the plaintiff had a fishing and hunting guide service.

The drift of recent commentary has been in favor of expanding liability for purely economic loss. All writers argue that liability should not extend to the full reach of foreseeability, but beyond that, there is little agreement as to the rules by which liability should be determined. See Probert, Negligence and Economic Damage: The California-Florida Nexus, 33 U. Fla. L. Rev. 485 (1981); Rizzo, A Theory of Economic Loss in the Law of Torts, 11 J. Legal Stud. 281 (1982); Smillie, Negligence and Economic Loss, 32 U. Toronto L.J. 231 (1982); McThenia & Ulrich, A Return to Principles of Corrective Justice in Deciding Economic Loss Cases, 69 Va. L. Rev. 1517 (1983). For a discussion of the English cases, and a criticism of the expansion of liability for economic loss, see Cohen, Bleeding Hearts and Peeling Floors: Compensation for Economic Loss at the House of Lords, 18 U.B.C. L. Rev. 289 (1984).

Problem 23

Your firm represents Reliance Insurance Company, the liability insurer of Willy Reston. Last year, Reston was involved in an accident with a truck owned by Capitol City Refrigeration Company. Reston was driving his car in excess of the speed limit and ran through a stop sign, so there is no issue as to his negligence. At the time of the accident, the Capitol City truck was on its way to the Red Arrow Restaurant. Red Arrow's air conditioning system had broken down, and the manager called Capitol City to make the repairs. The two men in the truck were the only employees of Capitol City who had the know-how to repair the system, but they were both injured, and were unable to get to the restaurant. The manager of Red Arrow was unable to locate another repair company in time to repair the system by noon of the next day. As a result, Red Arrow was forced to cancel an all-afternoon and evening reception for Caroline Saunders, who was running for the United States Senate.

Reliance concedes its liability for the damage to the Capitol City truck and for the injuries to the occupants of the truck. Also making claims against Reston are: Capitol City Refrigeration for the profit it lost on the repair contract with Red Arrow; Red Arrow for the profit it lost because it could not hold the reception at its restaurant; and the Committee to Elect Saunders, for the increase in the cost of holding the reception at another restaurant.

In advising Reliance of its exposure to these claims, assume that no opinion of the supreme court of your state has dealt with the issue of liability for negligently caused, purely consequential economic loss.

4. Contributory Fault

a. Contributory Negligence

Butterfield v. Forrester

11 East. 60, 103 Eng. Rep. 926 (K.B. 1809)

This was an action on the case for obstructing a highway, by means of which obstruction the plaintiff, who was riding along the road, was thrown down with his horse, and injured, &c. At the trial before Bayley J. at Derby, it appeared that the defendant, for the purpose of making some repairs to his house, which was close by the road side at one end of the town, had put up a pole across this part of the road, a free passage being left by another branch or street in the same direction. That the plaintiff left a public house not far distant from the place in question at 8 o'clock in the evening in August, when they were just beginning to light candles, but while there was light enough left to discern the obstruction at 100 yards distance: and the witness, who proved this, said that if the plaintiff had not been riding very hard he might have observed and avoided it: the plaintiff however, who was riding violently, did not observe it, but rode against it, and fell with his horse and was much hurt in consequence of the accident; and there was no evidence of his being intoxicated at the time. On this evidence Bayley J. directed the jury, that if a person riding with reasonable and ordinary care could have seen and avoided the obstruction; and if they were satisfied that the plaintiff was riding along the street extremely hard, and without ordinary care, they should find a verdict for the defendant: which they accordingly did. . . .

LORD ELLENBOROUGH, C.J. A party is not to cast himself upon an obstruction which has been made by the fault of another, and avail himself of it, if he do not himself use common and ordinary caution to be in the right. In cases of persons riding upon what is considered to be the wrong side of the road, that would not authorise another purposely to ride up against them. One person being in fault will not dispense with another's using ordinary care for himself. Two things must concur to support this action, an obstruction in the road by the fault of the defendant, and no want of ordinary care to avoid it on the part of the plaintiff.

Per Curiam. Rule refused.

Butterfield is generally considered to be the first case in which the plaintiff's negligence was held to bar recovery. The doctrine was soon introduced in the United States in Smith v. Smith, 19 Mass. (2 Pick.) (1824), and now appears in §§463-496 of the Restatement (Second) of Torts. Section 463 defines contributory negligence as "conduct on the part of the plaintiff which falls below the standard to which he should conform for his own protection, and which is a legally contributing cause co-operating with the negligence of the defendant in bringing about the plaintiff's harm." Section 464 sets the appropriate standard of conduct as that "of a reasonable man under like circumstances." This parallels the reasonable person standard of care for the protection of others. Some courts, however, have held that the plaintiff's mental as well as his physical disabilities should be taken into account in determining whether he has acted reasonably. See, e.g., Memorial Hospital of South Bend, Inc. v. Scott, 261 Ind. 27, 300 N.E.2d 50 (1973).

In some circumstances, the plaintiff's contributory negligence will not operate to bar his recovery. This result is accomplished by the doctrine of "last clear chance." The Restatement (Second) of Torts provisions relating to the last clear chance doctrine are:

§479. LAST CLEAR CHANCE: HELPLESS PLAINTIFF

A plaintiff who has negligently subjected himself to a risk of harm from the defendant's subsequent negligence may recover for harm caused thereby if, immediately preceding the harm,

(a) the plaintiff is unable to avoid it by the exercise of reasonable vigilance and care, and

(b) the defendant is negligent in failing to utilize with reasonable care and competence his then existing opportunity to avoid the harm, when he

(i) knows of the plaintiff's situation and realizes or has reason to realize the peril involved in it or

(ii) would discover the situation and thus have reason to realize the peril, if he were to exercise the vigilance which it is then his duty to the plaintiff to exercise.

§480. LAST CLEAR CHANCE: INATTENTIVE PLAINTIFF

A plaintiff who, by the exercise of reasonable vigilance, could discover the danger created by the defendant's negligence in time to avoid the harm to him, can recover if, but only if, the defendant

(a) knows of the plaintiff's situation, and

(b) realizes or has reason to realize that the plaintiff is inattentive and therefore unlikely to discover his peril in time to avoid the harm, and

(c) thereafter is negligent in failing to utilize with reasonable care and competence his then existing opportunity to avoid the harm.

The doctrine originated in Davies v. Mann, 10 M. & W. 546, 152 Eng. Rep. 588 (1842). In this case, the plaintiff had left his donkey in the middle of a road, and the defendant ran into it. The plaintiff was permitted, notwithstanding his negligence, to recover for harm to the donkey, because the defendant had the opportunity, last in time, to avoid the accident.

The last clear chance doctrine is generally recognized in this country in the circumstances set out in the Restatement (Second) of Torts, although there are a number of variations. See Annotations, 92 A.L.R. 47 (1934), 119 A.L.R. 1041 (1939), and 171 A.L.R. 365 (1947). One of the most unusual variations is that applied in British Columbia Electric Ry. v. Loach, 1 A.C. 719 (P.C. 1916). In this case, the defendant's train had defective brakes, and for that reason the engineer was unable to stop the train in time to avoid hitting the plaintiff. The Privy Council ruled that the plaintiff could recover, even though his negligence put him in a position to be hit by the train. Adopting what is called the "antecedent last clear chance" rule, the Council observed (1 A.C. at 727) that were the defendant not liable, it "would be in a better position, when they supplied a bad brake but a good motorman, than when the motorman was careless but the brake efficient." This variation of the last clear chance doctrine was rejected in Andersen v. Bingham & Garfield Ry., 117 Utah 197, 214 P.2d 607 (1950).

b. Assumption of the Risk

Meistrich v. Casino Arena Attractions, Inc.

31 N.J. 44, 155 A.2d 90 (1959)

WEINTRAUB, C.J. Plaintiff was injured by a fall while ice-skating on a rink operated by defendant. The jury found for defendant. The Appellate

Division reversed, 54 N.J. Super. 25 (1959), and we granted defendant's petition for certification. 29 N.J. 582 (1959). . . .

The Appellate Division found error in the charge of assumption of the risk. It also concluded there was no evidence of contributory negligence and hence that issue should not have been submitted to the jury.

Defendant urges there was no negligence and therefore the alleged errors were harmless. We think there was sufficient proof to take the case to the jury. There was evidence that defendant departed from the usual procedure in preparing the ice, with the result that it became too hard and hence too slippery for the patron of average ability using skates sharpened for the usual surface. . . .

We however agree with defendant that the issue of contributory negligence was properly left to the trier of the facts. Plaintiff had noted that his skates slipped on turns. A jury could permissibly find he carelessly contributed to his injury when, with that knowledge, he remained on the ice and skated cross-hand with another.

The remaining question is whether the trial court's charge with respect to assumption of risk was erroneous. . . .

The Appellate Division . . . found the trial court failed to differentiate between assumption of risk and contributory negligence. The Appellate Division added:

> We note that contributory negligence involves some breach of duty on the part of the plaintiff. His actions are such as to constitute a failure to use such care for his safety as the ordinarily prudent man in similar circumstances would use. On the other hand, assumption of risk may involve no fault or negligence, but rather entails the undertaking of a risk or a known danger. Hendrikson v. Koppers Co., Inc., 11 N.J. 600, 607 (1953).

As we read the charge, the trial court expressed essentially the same thought, i.e., that assumption of risk may be found if plaintiff knew or reasonably should have known of the risk, notwithstanding that a reasonably prudent man would have continued in the face of the risk. We think an instruction to that effect is erroneous in the respect hereinafter delineated. The error is traceable to confusion in the opinions in our State.

Assumption of risk is a term of several meanings. For present purposes, we may place to one side certain situations which sometimes are brought within the sweeping term but which are readily differentiated from the troublesome area. Specifically we place beyond present discussion the problem raised by an express contract not to sue for injury or loss which may thereafter be occasioned by the covenantee's negligence, and also situations in which actual consent exists, as, for example, participation in a contact sport.

We here speak solely of the area in which injury or damage was neither intended nor expressly contracted to be non-actionable. In this area, assumption of risk has two distinct meanings. In one sense (sometimes called its "primary" sense), it is an alternate expression for the proposition that defendant was not negligent, i.e., either owed no duty or did not breach the duty owed. In its other sense (sometimes called "secondary"), assumption of risk is an affirmative defense to an established breach of duty. In its primary sense, it is accurate to say plaintiff assumed the risk whether or not he was "at fault," for the truth thereby expressed in alternate terminology is that defendant was not negligent. But in its secondary sense, i.e., as an affirmative defense to an established breach of defendant's duty, it is incorrect to say plaintiff assumed the risk whether or not he was at fault. . . .

Hence we think it clear that assumption of risk in its secondary sense is a mere phase of contributory negligence, the total issue being whether a reasonably prudent man in the exercise of due care (a) would have incurred the known risk and (b) if he would, whether such a person in the light of all of the circumstances including the appreciated risk would have conducted himself in the manner in which plaintiff acted.

Thus in the area under discussion there are but two basic issues: (1) defendant's negligence, and (2) plaintiff's contributory negligence. In view of the considerations discussed above, it has been urged that assumption of risk in both its primary and secondary senses serves merely to confuse and should be eliminated. . . .

In short, each case must be analyzed to determine whether the pivotal question goes to defendant's negligence or to plaintiff's contributory negligence. If the former, then what has been called assumption of risk is only a denial of breach of duty and the burden of proof is plaintiff's. If on the other hand assumption of risk is advanced to defeat a recovery despite a demonstrated breach of defendant's duty, then it constitutes the affirmative defense of contributory negligence and the burden of proof is upon defendant.

With the modification expressed above, the judgment of the Appellate Division is affirmed.

For modification—CHIEF JUSTICE WEINTRAUB, and JUSTICES BURLING, JACOBS, FRANCIS and PROCTOR—5.

Opposed—None.

As indicated in *Meistrich,* the principal issue involving assumption of the risk today is the extent to which it should constitute a separate defense in negligence actions. *Meistrich* represents the view that, except in instances of express agreement by the plaintiff to assume the risk involved in the defendant's conduct, the doctrine has no independent legal vitality, and that the plaintiff's conduct is to be gauged by the rules of contributory negligence.

The Restatement (Second) of Torts, in contrast, adopts the view that assumption of the risk constitutes an independent defense. Like *Meistrich,* the Restatement, §496B, bars recovery by a person who expressly agrees to accept the risk of the defendant's negligence. Section 496C provides:

> (1) Except as stated in Subsection (2), a plaintiff who fully understands a risk of harm to himself or his things caused by the defendant's conduct or by the condition of the defendant's land or chattels, and who nevertheless voluntarily chooses to enter or remain, or to permit his things to enter or remain within the area of that risk, under circumstances that manifest his willingness to accept it, is not entitled to recover for harm within that risk.
> (2) The rule stated in Subsection (1) does not apply in any situation in which an express agreement to accept the risk would be invalid as contrary to public policy.

Under §496D, to assume a risk the plaintiff must know that the risk exists and appreciate its unreasonableness. Under §496E, the plaintiff does not assume a risk if as a result of the defendant's tortious conduct the plaintiff has no reasonable alternative to avoid the harm.

Section 496C embodies what is known as "secondary" or "implied" assumption of the risk, and is that aspect of the doctrine that was rejected in *Meistrich.* The magnitude of the disagreement concerning this type of assumption of the risk is revealed by the debate over §496C during the meeting of the American Law Institute that considered the Restatement sections in draft form. The earlier meeting of the Advisors to the Restatement (Second) of Torts was characterized as the "Battle of the Wilderness," and those who supported the limitation of assumption of the risk to instances of express agreement were called the "Confederate Army." The heated debate continued during the meeting of the Institute, and while the forces supporting assumption of the risk as a separate doctrine prevailed on that particular day, the war is not yet over. The most recent editions of the two most widely accepted treatises on torts take opposing views. Not surprisingly, Prosser and Keeton, Law of Torts 493-495 (5th ed. 1984), adheres largely to the Restatement view that express assumption of the risk and no duty cases do not occupy all of the assumption of risk landscape. Dean Prosser was the Reporter for the Restatement (Second) of Torts at the time the law of assumption of the risk was taken up by the American Law Institute. On the other hand, Harper, James and Gray, The Law of Torts 187-199 (2d ed. 1986), argues that assumption of the risk should be limited to express assumption and no duty cases.

Professor Simons in his article, Assumption of Risk and Consent in the Law of Torts: A Theory of Full Preference, 67 B.U. L. Rev. 213 (1987) takes a middle-ground approach. He concludes that while assumption of the risk has room for operation in more types of cases than Harper, James and Gray would recognize, it should be a narrower concept than that set out in the Restatement.

Problem 24

Your client is Security Casualty Insurance Company. The claims manager has sought your advice with respect to an automobile liability claim made against the company. The insured is Robert Dooley. Late one winter's night he was driving home after a party on a country road. He admits that he had had a bit too much to drink at the party and that he had a hard time controlling his car. He saw the claimant, Shirley DeVrees, standing at the roadside waving to him to stop. Dooley did stop, and DeVrees told him that her car had run out of gasoline and that she wanted a ride into town. Dooley told her that given his condition, she might be better off waiting for someone else to come along. DeVrees said that there would be no problem if she were to drive the car, but Dooley insisted that he drive. It was a cold night, and DeVrees had only a lightweight coat, so she told Dooley that she would rather take her chances with him than wait for another car on the lightly traveled country road. DeVrees then got into the car, and a mile or so down the road, Dooley fell asleep. The car ran off the road and into a tree. DeVrees was seriously injured.

The claims manager would like your opinion as to whether DeVrees is barred from recovery. Assume that *Meistrich* is an opinion of your state supreme court.

The Relationship Between Tort and Contract: Exculpatory Clauses and Disclaimers in Contracts

The court in *Meistrich,* in analyzing the circumstances under which the plaintiff may be barred from recovery by his assumption of the risks involved in the defendant's conduct, put to one side the problems raised by express provisions in contracts which by their terms purport to relieve one of the contracting parties from liability in negligence. One might assume that express provisions in contracts allocating losses would be routinely enforced; after all, the parties are in a better position than courts to make loss allocation decisions. To some courts, such exculpatory clauses and disclaimers of liability are unenforceable if they cover personal injuries. See Hiett v. Lake Barcroft Community Association, 244 Va. 191, 418 S.E.2d 894 (1992). Most courts, however, will enforce them, at least under some circumstances. The general rule is that such provisions will be given effect to relieve one party from liability for negligence unless there is a strong public policy against enforcement in a particular case. Furthermore, courts require that the language be clear; any ambiguity or vagueness will be resolved against the existence of a disclaimer. See Williston on Contracts §1750A (Jaeger, 3d ed. 1972). Cf. Restatement of Contracts §§574-575.

Although the hostility of the law toward disclaimers is not new, it has intensified in recent years. The opinion in O'Callaghan v. Waller & Beckwith Realty Co., 15 Ill. 2d 436, 155 N.E.2d 545 (1958), reflects what today would be characterized as an overly tolerant attitude. The plaintiff was a tenant of the defendant, and was injured when she fell on a paved courtyard located between her apartment and the garage. A provision in the lease relieved the defendant from liability for injuries resulting from the defendant's negligence with respect to the premises. In upholding the lease, the court affirmed the traditional principles of freedom of contract. The court relied upon an absence of evidence that the plaintiff was concerned about the clause when she signed the lease, that she had tried to negotiate a lease without the clause, or that she had tried to rent an apartment elsewhere. To the plaintiff's argument that a housing shortage limited her ability to bargain over the terms of the lease, the court answered, "Judicial determinations of public policy cannot readily take account of sporadic and transitory circumstances. They should rather, we think, rest upon a durable moral basis." 15 Ill. 2d at 440-441, 155 N.E.2d at 547. Twenty years later, the Supreme Court of California in Henrioulle v. Marin Ventures, Inc., 20 Cal. 3d 512, 573 P.2d 465, 143 Cal. Rptr. 247 (1978), ruled that exculpatory clauses in leases of residential property are not enforceable. In so doing, the court emphasized that residential shelter is a necessity, and that there is an inequality of bargaining power between landlord and tenant. For an analysis of the law's responses to exculpatory clauses in leases of land, see Love, Landlord's Liability for Defective Premises: Caveat Lessee, Negligence, or Strict Liability?, 1975 Wis. L. Rev. 19, 81-86.

Henrioulle represents a broadening of the grounds upon which disclaimers will be set aside; the court listed as one basis for so doing the fact that the defendant performs an important service, which is of "practical necessity" to the public. In Kopischke v. First Continental Corp., 187 Mont. 471, 610 P.2d 668, 670 (1980), the court refused to give effect to a clause in a contract for the sale of a used car that provided: "All used cars are sold on an as is basis with no guarantee either express or implied except as noted above." The court ruled that this clause cannot be used by the seller to bar recovery for personal injuries resulting from the seller's negligent failure to inspect an automobile before sale. The court stated that liability cannot be disclaimed by one "performing an act in the public interest," and that inspecting used cars before sale to ensure safety is such an act. 610 P.2d at 679. And see Wagenblast v. Odessa School District, 110 Wash. 2d 845, 758 P.2d 968 (1988), holding that school athletic programs are sufficiently infused with the public interest to call for refusing to enforce a release of liability required by the school district as a condition of participation.

These cases suggest that courts might be more receptive toward exculpatory clauses when the "public interest" is not so clearly involved. The court in Young v. City of Gadsden, 482 So. 2d 1158 (Ala. 1985), appeared to draw such a public interest line in upholding the clause in a contract between a go-cart racer and the sponsors of a race. In affirming summary judgment for the defendants, the court stated that the plaintiff could not rely on cases involving landlords and tenants, as those cases "deal with situations having more of an impact on the general public. . . ." 482 So. 2d at 1160. And in BodySlimmer, Inc. v. Sanford, 398 S.E.2d 840 (Ga. App. 1990), the court held that a weight loss facility was not of sufficient public importance to justify invalidating a disclaimer of liability for personal injuries. But in Gross v. Sweet, 49 N.Y.2d 102, 400 N.E.2d 306 (1979), the court refused to enforce an exculpatory clause. In this case, the plaintiff had enrolled in the defendant's parachute jumping school. As a requirement for admission, the plaintiff signed a "Responsibility Release," that provided he waived as to the defendant all claims "for any personal injuries or property damage that I may sustain or which may arise out of my learning, practicing or actually jumping from an aircraft." The plaintiff was seriously injured on his first jump, and sued the defendant for negligence involved in his training. The defendant argued that the release barred recovery. Although the court noted that there was no particular public interest which would preclude enforcement, it did not enforce the clause; the court ruled that the release at most alerted the plaintiff to the inherently risky nature of parachute jumping. It did not, the court said, clearly convey the message that the defendant would be relieved of liability for negligence with respect to training of students or the furnishing of equipment. Three judges dissented, arguing that the clause would be meaningless if it were not applicable to negligence claims.

Courts are more likely to enforce exculpatory clauses covering damage to property than those covering personal injuries. Even the Court of Appeals of New York, which refused to enforce the parachute jumping clause, gave effect to a disclaimer of liability for property damage in a contract calling for the maintenance of a sprinkler system. See S.S.D.W. Co. v. Brisk Waterproofing Co., 76 N.Y.2d 228, 556 N.E.2d 1097 (1990). The court called attention to the fact that the plaintiff is more likely to know the value of property at stake than is the defendant, and for that reason is in a better position to decide what insurance to buy.

Exculpatory clauses and disclaimers which are otherwise enforceable will not operate to preclude recovery for harm caused by aggravated wrongdoing, such as recklessness and gross negligence. See, e.g., Barnes v. Birmingham International Raceway, Inc., 551 So. 2d 929 (Ala. 1989).

c. Comparative Negligence

Contributory negligence as a complete bar to recovery by the plaintiff has been replaced in almost every jurisdiction by a variety of comparative fault regimes, under which the recovery may be reduced, but not necessarily eliminated, by the plaintiff's own fault.

The early attack on contributory fault as a complete bar was on fairness grounds. See, e.g., James, Contributory Negligence, 62 Yale L.J. 691 (1953). More recently, contributory negligence has been examined under the lens of law and economics, and most of the commentary comes down on the side of comparative fault. See, e.g., Cooter and Ulen, An Economic Case for Comparative Negligence, 61 N.Y.U. L. Rev. 1067 (1986); Orr, The Superiority of Comparative Negligence: Another Vote, 20 J. Legal Stud. 119 (1991). Judge Posner argues that the two doctrines are equal from an efficiency perspective, but that comparative fault generates administrative costs that contributory negligence does not. See Posner, Economic Analysis of Law 169-173 (4th ed. 1992).

The comparative negligence concept is not new. The first state to enact a general comparative negligence statute was Mississippi in 1910. Miss. Code Ann. §1454. The Federal Employers Liability Act, enacted in 1906, incorporates the principle of comparative negligence. 45 U.S.C.A. §53. Comparative negligence has long been a rule of admiralty law (see Mole and Wilson, A Study of Comparative Negligence, 17 Cornell L.Q. 333, (1932)), and its origins have been traced to ancient Roman and medieval sea law (see Turk, Comparative Negligence on the March, 28 Chi.-Kent L. Rev. 189 (1950)).

Even in contributory negligence regimes, it has been commonly assumed that juries apply a rough and ready comparative negligence of their own, in violation of the instructions they receive from the judges. See, e.g., Maloney, From Contributory to Comparative Negligence: A Needed Law Reform, 11 U. Fla. L. Rev. 135 (1958); Weinstein, Routine Bifurcation of Jury Negligence Trials: An Example of the Questionable Use of Rule Making Power, 14 Vand. L. Rev. 831 (1961). But others have concluded that jury lawlessness in this regard is not pervasive. See Rosenberg, Comparative Negligence in Arkansas: A "Before and After" Survey, 13 Ark. L. Rev. 89 (1959). Judicial reaction to jury-created comparative fault has been mixed. It was recognized and approved by the court in Karcesky v. Laria, 382 Pa. 227, 114 A.2d 150 (1955). Other courts have expressed disapproval of the practice. See, e.g., Figliomeni v. Board of Education, 38 N.Y.2d 178, 341 N.E.2d 557 (1975); Nourse v. Austin, 140 Vt. 184, 436 A.2d 738 (1981).

A number of cases have involved the issue of whether a trial judge has powers similar to those of additur and remittur (see fn. 5, p. 698 below) to correct what the judge perceives to be an allocation of the percentages of fault unsupported by the evidence. Most courts addressing the issue have held that the judge has no such power. See, e.g., Rowlands v. Signal Construction Co., 549 So. 2d 1380 (Fla. 1989); Schelbauer v. Butler Manufacturing Co., 35 Cal. 3d 442, 673 P.2d 743 198 Cal. Rptr. 155 (1984). Holding that the trial judge does have that power is Gardiner v. Schobel, 521 A.2d 1011 (R.I. 1987).

The basis of the defendant's liability may have an impact on the applicability of comparative fault. For example, what if the basis of the plaintiff's claim is that the defendant is liable without fault? Can the plaintiff's negligence be compared to the defendant's strict liability? That issue is addressed in Chapter 7, Products Liability, p. 603, below. What if the defendant is guilty of aggravated fault, such as willful, wanton or intentional conduct? The court in Burke v. 12 Rothchild's Liquor Mart, Inc., 148 Ill. 2d 429, 593 N.E.2d 522 (1992), held that a defendant guilty of that sort of conduct is not entitled to a reduction in damages based on the plaintiff's fault. But the court in Blazovic v. Andrich, 124 N.J. 90, 590 A.2d 222 (1991), ruled that the comparative fault statute does apply in cases in which the defendant acted intentionally. In general, see Hollister, Using Comparative Fault to Replace the All-or-Nothing Lottery Imposed in Intentional Tort Suits in Which Both Plaintiff and Defendant Are at Fault, 46 Vand. L. Rev. 121 (1993). The court in *Blazovic* also held that comparative fault applies only to compensatory damages; punitive damages, because the purpose is to punish the defendant, are not subject to reduction.

There is also some uncertainty as to the type of plaintiff fault that is subject to comparison. For instance, is postaccident fault in failing to mitigate damages (see Chapter 8, p. 676) a total barrier to recovery of damages that could have been mitigated, or is that failure a form of fault to which comparative fault applies? The court in Ostrowski v. Azzara, 111 N.J. 429, 545 A.2d 148 (1988), held that the negligence in failure to mitigate damages is fault to which the comparative fault statute would apply. This issue has arisen frequently in cases in which the defendant has argued that the severity of the plaintiff's injuries in an automobile accident was increased because of the failure to wear a seat belt and shoulder harness. Courts have taken a variety of approaches to this problem. Some courts treat the failure as negligence which reduces the plaintiff's recovery under the comparative fault law. See, e.g., Law v. Superior Court, 157 Ariz. 147, 755 P.2d 1135 (1988); Waterson v. General Motors Corp., 111 N.J. 238, 544 A.2d 357 (1988). Other courts treat the plaintiff's conduct as the failure to mitigate damages, and preclude recovery for the full increment of harm that could have been avoided by the wearing of an available seat belt. See, e.g., Foley v. City of West Allis, 113 Wis. 2d 475, 335 N.W.2d 824 (1983). Under either approach, the burden of proving that the failure of the plaintiff to wear a seat belt caused harm is usually placed on the defendant. See, e.g., Shahzade v. C.J. Mabardy, Inc., 411 Mass. 788, 586 N.E.2d 3 (1992). Finally, a number of courts have ruled that the plaintiff's failure to wear a seat belt and shoulder harness should be ignored completely in determining both the defendant's liability and the amount of the plaintiff's recovery. See, e.g., Welsh v. Anderson, 228 Neb. 79, 421 N.W.2d 426 (1988); Wright v. Hanley, 182 W. Va. 334, 387 S.E.2d 801 (1989). A statute prohibiting the offering of evidence that the plaintiff failed to wear a seat belt was unsuccessfully attacked as unconstitutional in C.W. Matthews Contracting Co., Inc. v. Gover, 428 S.E.2d 796 (Ga. 1993). The issues, including the effect of a variety of seat belt statutes, are discussed in Cochran, New Seat Belt Defense

Issues: The Impact of Air Bags and Mandatory Seat Belt Use Statutes on the Seat Belt Defense, and the Basis of Damage Reduction under the Seat Belt Defense, 73 Minn. L. Rev. 1369 (1989).

The same sort of problem can arise when the plaintiff has been injured in a motorcycle accident and has not worn a protective helmet. Halvorson v. Voeller, 336 N.W.2d 118 (N.D. 1983) held that such a failure may reduce the plaintiff's damages; Meyer v. City of Des Moines, 475 N.W.2d 181 (Iowa 1991), held that the failure should be ignored.

Not even a handful of states remain without some comparative fault regime. The court in McIntyre v. Balentine, 833 S.W.2d 52 (Tenn. 1992), listed only five: Alabama, Maryland, North Carolina, Virginia, and Tennessee. In *McIntyre,* the court removed Tennessee from that list, adopting a modified comparative fault under which the plaintiff's recovery is reduced so long as the plaintiff's share of the negligence is less than the defendant's. If the plaintiff's share is equal to or exceeds the plaintiff's, the plaintiff can recover nothing. A few states, other than Tennessee, have judicially created comparative fault regimes, although most of these states have adopted pure, rather than modified, comparative fault. See, e.g., Li v. Yellow Cab Co., 13 Cal. 3d 804, 532 P.2d 1226, 119 Cal. Rptr. 858 (1975). Most comparative fault laws are the result of legislation.

Problem 25

You represent Walter Geyer in connection with claims arising out of an automobile accident occurring on December 15 of last year. Your investigation of the accident has revealed the following:

The accident occurred about noon as Geyer was driving home in a northerly direction on School Street. He had been driving at about 40 M.P.H. as he approached the intersection of School with Wilson Avenue. The weather was clear and the road was dry. He saw an automobile to his right on Wilson Avenue stopped at the intersection. There are stop signs at Wilson directing traffic on Wilson to stop at the intersection. Geyer knew the stop signs were there. Suddenly the other car pulled into the intersection and started to cross it. Geyer slammed on his brakes and sounded his horn. Geyer had intended to turn sharply to his right and pass behind the other car, but when he applied the brakes, the car pulled sharply to the left and hit the other car in its left rear. As a result of the impact, Geyer was thrown forward onto the steering wheel, as he was not wearing the seat belt and shoulder harness. He felt a sharp pain in his chest.

After the accident Everett Moreland, the other driver, told Geyer that he had not seen Geyer before he, Moreland, entered the intersection. Moreland did not appear to be hurt. Geyer then called the Oxford police from a nearby house.

Geyer was driving his six-year-old Ford two-door sedan at the time of the accident. There was considerable front end damage to his car, and he was told by the local Ford dealer that the cost of repairs would exceed the fair retail value of the car, which was $3,000 before the accident. Moreland was driving a two-year-old Dodge station wagon. The damage that Geyer could see was to the left rear fender and door.

Three days prior to the accident, Geyer had noticed that his car was pulling to the left when the brakes were suddenly applied. Two weeks earlier, he had had the braking system reconditioned and the brake linings replaced at South End Ford, the local Ford dealership. He had intended to take the car back to South End to have the brakes checked, but had not gotten around to it before the accident. You have had a mechanic look at the car. He thinks that the South End mechanic who worked on the brakes did an inadequate job, and as a result brake fluid leaked into the right front brake drum. This resulted in uneven braking capability in the front wheel, causing the car to pull to the left when the brakes were applied.

On December 17, Geyer saw Dr. Margaret Inman, his personal physician, about the pain in his chest. He was referred to Dr. Carl Shanklin, an orthopedic surgeon, who told him he had a fractured rib. The pain was quite severe for three or four days after the accident, but had disappeared after about a week. On Dr. Shanklin's advice, he stayed away from work, which required a lot of lifting, for five weeks. He took two weeks of paid sick leave, and was unpaid for the other three weeks except for Christmas and New Year's Day, which were paid holidays. His take-home pay at that time was $600 a week. Mr. Geyer's medical expenses totaled $780, of which $702 was covered by his employer-financed medical insurance.

The accident report prepared by Albert Vose, an Oxford police officer, shows that the Geyer automobile left skid marks 89 feet long. When asked about this later, Officer Vose stated that in his opinion, the length of the skid marks indicates that Geyer was going about 40 M.P.H. when he applied his brakes. The posted speed limit for this portion of School Street is 30 M.P.H.

Everett Moreland has refused to give a statement. His explanation of the accident appearing on his report to the Oxford police was: "I was driving on Wilson Avenue. Stopped at School and looked both ways. Saw no one coming. Proceeded into intersection when #2 car came at high rate of speed around curve on School. I accelerated to get through intersection so #2 could pass behind me, but #2 turned left and ran into #1." He stated on the report that he was not injured, and that the cost of repairing his automobile was $2,650.

Your examination of the scene of the accident reveals that the intersection of School Street and Wilson Avenue is in a moderately populated residential area of Oxford. School Street is a main road, and although it has a posted speed of 30 M.P.H., your investigation shows that cars frequently travel at 45 M.P.H. on School Street in the vicinity of the intersection. A state criminal statute requires drivers to travel "at a reasonable speed," having in mind such things as the traffic conditions, weather, and the condition of the road. A speed in excess of the posted speed is, according to the statute, prima facie unreasonable. School Street, as it approaches Wilson from the south, is a flat asphalt road 33 feet wide. South of the intersection, the road curves to the west. A driver traveling north would get his first view of a car heading west on Wilson at the intersection at a distance of about 200 feet from the intersection.

Mr. Geyer will be in to see you next week to get your assessment of his claims against Moreland and the South End Garage. Assume that the legislature of your state has enacted the Uniform Comparative Fault Act.

Uniform Comparative Fault Act

12 Uniform Laws Ann. 43 (1992 Supp.)

Section 1. [Effect of Contributory Fault]

(a) In an action based on fault seeking to recover damages for injury or death to person or harm to property, any contributory fault chargeable to the claimant diminishes proportionately the amount awarded as compensatory damages for an injury attributable to the claimant's contributory fault, but does not bar recovery. This rule applies whether or not under prior law the claimant's contributory fault constituted a defense or was disregarded under applicable legal doctrines, such as last clear chance.

(b) "Fault" includes acts or omissions that are in any measure negligent or reckless toward the person or property of the actor or others, or that subject a person to strict tort liability. The term also includes breach of warranty, unreasonable assumption of risk not constituting an enforceable express consent, misuse of a product for which the defendant otherwise would be liable, and unreasonable failure to avoid an injury or to mitigate damages. Legal requirements of causal relation apply both to fault as the basis for liability and to contributory fault.

Section 2. [Apportionment of Damages]

(a) In all actions involving fault of more than one party to the action, including third-party defendants and persons who have been released under Section 6, the court, unless otherwise agreed by all parties, shall instruct the jury to answer special interrogatories or, if there is no jury, shall make findings, indicating:

(1) The amount of damages each claimant would be entitled to recover if contributory fault is disregarded: and

(2) the percentage of the total fault of all of the parties to each claim

that is allocated to each claimant, defendant, third-party defendant, and person who has been released from liability under Section 6. For this purpose the court may determine that two or more persons are to be treated as a single party.

(b) In determining the percentages of fault, the trier of fact shall consider both the nature of the conduct of each party at fault and the extent of the causal relation between the conduct and the damages claimed.

(c) The court shall determine the award of damages to each claimant in accordance with the findings, subject to any reduction under Section 6, and enter judgment against each party liable on the basis of rules of joint-and-several liability. For the purposes of contribution under Sections 4 and 5, the court also shall determine and state in the judgment each party's equitable share of the obligation to each claimant in accordance with the respective percentages of fault.

(d) Upon motion made not later than one year after judgment is entered, the court shall determine whether all or part of a party's equitable share of the obligation is uncollectible from that party, and shall reallocate any uncollectible amount among the other parties, including a claimant at fault, according to their respective percentages of fault. The party whose liability is reallocated is nonetheless subject to contribution and to any continuing liability to the claimant on the judgment.

Section 3. [Set-off]

A claim and counterclaim shall not be set off against each other except by agreement of both parties. On motion, however, the court, if it finds that the obligation of either party is likely to be uncollectible, may order that both parties make payment into court for distribution. The court shall distribute the funds received and declare obligations discharged as if the payment into court by either party had been a payment to the other party and any distribution of those funds back to the party making payment had been a payment to him by the other party.

Section 4. [Right of Contribution]

(a) A right of contribution exists between or among two or more persons who are jointly and severally liable upon the same indivisible claim for the same injury, death, or harm, whether or not judgment has been recovered against all or any of them. It may be enforced either in the original action or by a separate action brought for that purpose. The basis for contribution is each person's equitable share of the obligation, including the equitable share of a claimant at fault, as determined in accordance with the provisions of Section 2.

(b) Contribution is available to a person who enters into a settlement with a claimant only (1) if the liability of the person against whom contribution is sought has been extinguished and (2) to the extent that the amount paid in settlement was reasonable.

Section 5. [Enforcement of Contribution]

(a) If the proportionate fault of the parties to a claim for contribution has been established previously by the court, as provided by Section 2, a party paying more than his equitable share of the obligation, upon motion, may recover judgment for contribution.

(b) If the proportionate fault of the parties to the claim for contribution has not been established by the court, contribution may be enforced in a separate action, whether or not a judgment has been rendered against either the person seeking contribution or the person from whom contribution is being sought.

(c) If a judgment has been rendered, the action for contribution must be commenced within [one year] after the judgment becomes final. If no judgment has been rendered, the person bringing the action for contribution either must have (1) discharged by payment the common liability within the period of the statute of limitations applicable to the claimant's right of action against him and commenced the action for contribution within [one year] after payment, or (2) agreed while action was pending to discharge the common liability and, within [one year] after the agreement, have paid the liability and commenced an action for contribution.

Section 6. [Effect of Release]

A release, covenant not to sue, or similar agreement entered into by a claimant and a person liable discharges that person from all liability for contribution, but it does not discharge any other persons liable upon the same claim unless it so provides. However, the claim of the releasing person against other persons is reduced by the amount of the released person's equitable share of the obligation, determined in accordance with the provisions of Section 2.

[Sections 7 through 11 are housekeeping sections, and do not add to the substantive features of the act.]

According to the 1992 Supplement to Volume 12 of the Uniform Laws Annotated, two states, Iowa and Washington, have adopted the Uniform Comparative Fault Act. Among the other states that have adopted comparative fault laws, there are significant variations. The following discusses some of the more important differences:

1. *The basis of apportionment of losses between plaintiff and defendant.* The Uniform Act adopts what is known as "pure" comparative negligence. Under this approach, the plaintiff's recovery is reduced, but never eliminated, solely because of the plaintiff's negligence. (If the plaintiff is responsible for 100 percent of the negligence, the defendant would not be negligent at all.) Thus, a plaintiff whose share of the negligence is 99 percent can recover 1 percent of the damages. This is the form that is favored by the courts—of the courts that have adopted comparative negligence, most have chosen pure comparative negligence.

More popular with legislatures is "modified" comparative negligence, under which the plaintiff who is less than 100 percent at fault may be precluded from recovering. There are two principal forms of modified comparative negligence. Under some systems, the plaintiff whose negligence is equal to that of the defendant cannot recover. Under other systems, the bar exists only if the negligence of the plaintiff exceeds that of the defendant. Under both systems, if the plaintiff's negligence has not reached the cut-off point, the recovery is reduced proportionately.

2. *Calculating the shares of fault.* The statutes are singularly unhelpful in determining just how the trier of fact is to determine what share of the total fault is to be allocated to each party. The Uniform Act simply refers to "the nature of the conduct of each party at fault and the extent of the causal relation between the conduct and the damages claimed." Some juries have allocated the fault with considerable precision. For example, in Kaeo v. Davis, 68 Haw. 447, 719 P.2d 387 (1986), the jury was able to determine that one defendant deserved to be allocated 1 percent of the total fault, the remaining 99 percent being allocated to the other defendant. An even finer division was accomplished in Falgoust v. Richardson Industries, Inc., 552 So. 2d 1348 (La. App. 1989), *writ denied,* 558 So. 2d 1126 (La. 1990); the jury's allocation of the fault among the four parties was 60 percent, 37 percent, 1.5 percent and 1.5 percent.

Methods of calculating the shares of fault are discussed in Little, Eliminating the Fallacies of Comparative Negligence and Proportional Liability, 41 Ala. L. Rev. 13 (1989); Pearson, Apportionment of Losses under Comparative Fault Laws—An Analysis of the Alternatives, 40 La. L. Rev. 343 (1980); Sobelsohn, Comparing Fault, 60 Ind. L.J. 413 (1985).

3. *Joint and several liability.* While the basic purpose of comparative fault laws is to reduce, but not necessarily eliminate, the plaintiff's total recovery because of contributory negligence, comparative fault also has implications for the liability of each defendant to the plaintiff in instances where there is more than one defendant. At issue is whether a defendant should be exposed to liability greater than the proportionate share of the fault. Some comparative fault laws as originally enacted abrogated joint and several liability and geared the liability of the defendants to their shares

of fault. See, e.g., Kan. Stat. Ann. §60-258(a)-(b). Other states have retained joint and several liability fully (see Ill. Ann. Stats. ch. 70, ¶304) or partially (see Mass. Gen. Laws Ann. ch. 231, §85).

Joint and several liability has been the focus of intense attack in recent years by those seeking widespread legislative reform of tort law. The argument is that it is unfair to expose a defendant who accounts for only a small share of the total fault to liability out of proportion to fault. The concern is illustrated by Kaeo v. Davis. The plaintiff was seriously injured in a one-car accident. There was evidence that the operator of the car in which the plaintiff was a passenger had consumed several beers the day of the accident. The plaintiff sued the operator and the city of Honolulu, alleging that the latter was negligent in failing to make safe the road on which the accident occurred. The jury returned a verdict of $725,000 against both defendants and apportioned 99 percent of the total negligence to the operator, and 1 percent to the city. In the not unlikely event that the operator would not be financially responsible for his entire share, the 1 percent negligent city would be exposed to liability substantially out of proportion to its negligence. The judgment for the plaintiff was reversed, in part on the ground that the jury should have been told of the effect of apportioning some negligence to the city and of the rules of joint and several liability.

The legislatures of many states have accepted the argument in favor of proportionate liability[171] and have changed the traditional rules of joint and several liability in a variety of ways. Some states have totally abrogated joint and several liability and limit the defendants' damages to their shares of the total fault. See, e.g., Utah Code, tit. 78-27-38. A more common legislative response has been to modify the law, but not to eliminate joint and several liability totally. See, e.g., Fla. Stat. Ann. §768.81 (abrogated except as to cases in which damages do not exceed $25,000, and except, with respect to economic damages, to a defendant whose fault equals or exceeds that of plaintiff); N.Y. Civ. Prac. L. & R. §1601 (1993 Supp.) (retained with respect to economic loss; abrogated with respect to noneconomic loss as to any defendant to whom 50 percent or less of fault allocated).

The American Bar Association Report of the Action Commission to Improve the Tort Liability System, 23-24 (1987), advocates the following:

> The doctrine of joint and several liability should be modified to recognize that defendants whose responsibility is substantially disproportionate to the liability for the entire loss suffered by the plaintiff are to be held liable for

171. Some statutes use the expression *several liability* to describe what here we call *proportionate liability*. See, e.g., Ore. Rev. Stat. §18.485, which provides that liability for noneconomic damages "shall be several only and shall not be joint." Technically, this use of the terms "several" and "joint" is not correct. "Several liability" of joint and several liability means that each defendant is liable for the full amount of the plaintiff's damages, and not just for some lesser proportionate share. "Joint liability" means that the defendants can be joined in the same suit, and not that each is liable for the plaintiff's full damages. See the note on joint and several liability, p. 143, above.

> only their equitable share of the plaintiff's noneconomic loss, while remaining liable for the plaintiff's full economic loss. A defendant's responsibility should be regarded as "substantially disproportionate" when it is significantly less than any of the other defendants; for example, when one of two defendants is determined to be less than 25% responsible for the plaintiff's injury.

This proposal was approved by the American Bar Association at its meeting on February 16, 1987. See 55 U.S.L.W. 2451 (1987). The forces of joint and several liability reform have even taken the battle to the United States Congress. In 1991, a bill was introduced into the Senate which would abrogate joint and several liability entirely. See S. 195, 102nd Cong., 1st Sess. (1991).[172]

For a discussion of the issues, see Wright, Allocating Liability Among Multiple Responsible Causes: A Principled Defense of Joint and Several Liability for Actual Harm and Risk Exposure, 21 U.C. Davis L. Rev. 1141 (1988). See also Colloquy, 22 U.C. Davis L. Rev. 1125 (1989), in which Professors Wright and Twerski carry on the debate over the merits of joint and several liability law and reform.

4. *Contribution.* If joint and several liability is retained, some defendants may end up paying more damages to the plaintiff than would be justified if liability were determined solely by their shares of the negligence—some may pay damages attributable to others. If that happens, should they be able to recover the excess above their shares—should they be able to get contribution—from those who have paid less than their share? As the note on joint and several liability earlier referred to states, the early rule in this country was that there could be no contribution among joint tortfeasors, although the rule has been abandoned in most states. Whatever the historical reasons for the no contribution rule, the basic principle of comparative fault which mandates apportionment between plaintiff and defendant according to relative fault would seem to suggest apportionment between defendants upon the same basis. The commentators generally favor proportional contribution. See, e.g., Berg, Comparative Contribution and Its Alternatives: The Equitable Distribution of Accident Losses, 43 Ins. Counsel J. 577 (1976); Fleming, Forward: Comparative Negligence at Last—By Judicial Choice, 64 Cal. L. Rev. 239 (1976); Griffith, Hemsley and Burr, Contribution, Indemnity, Settlements and Releases: What the Pennsylvania Comparative Negligence Statute Did Not Say, 24 Vill. L. Rev. 494 (1979). Some courts have opted for comparative contribution (see, e.g., Tolbert v. Gerber Indus., Inc., 255 N.W.2d 362 (Minn. 1977)), while others have adhered to the no

172. The confusion in the new use of "several" liability mentioned in the preceeding footnote is clearly demonstrated in this Senate Bill. Section 2(1) of the Bill provides that the defendants' liability "shall be several only and shall not be joint," the clear implication being that several and joint liability are different and inconsistent with each other. But §2(2) states that when the parties have acted in concert, "the liability of each defendant shall be joint and several." Liability could not be both joint and several, as those terms are used in §2(1).

contribution rule (see, e.g., Gomeau v. Forrest, 176 Conn. 523, 409 A.2d 1006 (1979)).

5. *Last Clear Chance.* Most courts addressing the issue have held that the doctrine of last clear chance (see p. 465, above) does not survive comparative fault as a basis for ignoring the negligence of the plaintiff and imposing the full liability on the negligent defendant. See, e.g., Petrove v. Grand Trunk Western R.R., 437 Mich. 31, 474 N.W.2d 711 (1991); Roggow v. Mineral Processing Corp., 698 F. Supp. 1441 (S.D. Ind. 1988), *aff'd* 894 F.2d 246 (7th Cir. 1990).

6. *Assumption of the Risk.* For courts that have eliminated implied or secondary assumption of the risk, incorporating assumption of the risk into comparative fault involves no conceptual problems. Reasonable assumption of the risk will have no effect on the plaintiff's recovery, while unreasonable assumption will be treated as any other contributory negligence for comparison purposes. For example, in Murray v. Ramada Inns, Inc., 521 So. 2d 1123 (La. 1988), the court ruled that assumption of the risk would not bar wrongful death recovery in a case in which the decedent dove several times into the shallow end of a motel pool, finally hitting his head on the bottom of the pool and suffering fatal injuries. A similar result was reached in Mazzeo v. City of Sebastian, 550 So. 2d 1113 (Fla. 1989). In that case, the plaintiff was injured when she dove from a platform into a shallow lake. She claimed that the defendant was negligent in not posting "no diving" or other warning signs at the platform. The jury found that the defendant was negligent, but that the plaintiff was aware of the risks involved in diving into the shallow water. The trial judge entered judgment for the defendant on the ground that the plaintiff assumed the risk. The Supreme Court of Florida reversed, holding that the plaintiff's assumption of the risk should be regarded as contributory negligence, and subject to comparison with the negligence of the defendant.

Knight v. Jewett

3 Cal. 4th 296, 834 P.2d 696, 11 Cal. Rptr. 2d 2 (1992)

GEORGE, JUSTICE.

[The plaintiff sued the defendant for personal injuries arising out of a touch football game. There was some dispute as to the defendant's conduct which caused the plaintiff's injury. According to the plaintiff, after the plaintiff caught a pass, the defendant ran into her from the rear, knocking her down, and stepping on her hand. The defendant's version was that he collided with the plaintiff in an unsuccessful attempt to intercept the pass. The defendant moved for summary judgment, arguing that the plaintiff assumed the risk of injury by participating in the game. The trial judge granted the motion, and that decision was affirmed by the Court of Appeal.

The Court stated that the issue is the extent to which assumption of the risk has survived as a defense after the decision in Li v. Yellow Cab, 13 Cal. 3d 804, 532 P.2d 1226, 119 Cal. Rptr. 858 (1975), in which the Supreme Court of California adopted comparative fault.]

II

A number of appellate decisions, focusing on the language in *Li* indicating that assumption of risk is in reality a form of contributory negligence "where a plaintiff unreasonably undertakes to encounter a specific known risk imposed by a defendant's negligence" (13 Cal. 3d at p. 824, 119 Cal. Rptr. 858, 532 P.2d 1226), have concluded that *Li* properly should be interpreted as drawing a distinction between those assumption of risk cases in which a plaintiff "unreasonably" encounters a known risk imposed by a defendant's negligence and those assumption of risk cases in which a plaintiff "reasonably" encounters a known risk imposed by a defendant's negligence. These decisions interpret *Li* as subsuming into the comparative fault scheme those cases in which the plaintiff acts unreasonably in encountering a specific known risk, but retaining the assumption of risk doctrine as a complete bar to recovery in those cases in which the plaintiff acts reasonably in encountering such a risk. Although aware of the apparent anomaly of a rule under which a plaintiff who acts reasonably is completely barred from recovery while a plaintiff who acts unreasonably only has his or her recovery reduced, these decisions nonetheless have concluded that this distinction and consequence were intended by the *Li* court.

In our view, these decisions—regardless whether they reached the correct result on the facts at issue—have misinterpreted *Li* by suggesting that our decision contemplated less favorable legal treatment for a plaintiff who reasonably encounters a known risk than for a plaintiff who unreasonably encounters such a risk. Although the relevant passage in *Li* indicates that the assumption of risk doctrine would be merged into the comparative fault scheme in instances in which a plaintiff " 'unreasonably undertakes to encounter a specific known risk imposed by a defendant's negligence' " (13 Cal. 3d at p. 824, 119 Cal. Rptr. 858, 532 P.2d 1226), nothing in this passage suggests that the assumption of risk doctrine should survive as a total bar to the plaintiff's recovery whenever a plaintiff acts reasonably in encountering such a risk. Instead, this portion of our opinion expressly contrasts the category of assumption of risk cases which " 'involve contributory negligence' " (and which therefore should be merged into the comparative fault scheme) with those assumption of risk cases which involve " 'a reduction of defendant's duty of care.' " (Id. at p. 825, 119 Cal. Rptr. 858, 532 P.2d 1226.)

Indeed, particularly when the relevant passage in *Li,* supra, 13 Cal. 3d at pp. 824-825, 119 Cal. Rptr. 858, 532 P.2d 1226, is read as a whole *and in conjunction with the authorities it cites,* we believe it becomes clear that the distinction in assumption of risk cases to which the *Li* court referred in this passage was not a distinction between instances in which a plaintiff unreasonably encounters a known risk imposed by a defendant's negligence and instances in which a plaintiff reasonably encounters such a risk. Rather, the distinction to which the *Li* court referred was between (1) those instances in which the assumption of risk doctrine embodies a legal conclusion that there is "no duty" on the part of the defendant to protect the plaintiff from a particular risk—the category of assumption of risk that the legal commentators generally refer to as "primary assumption of risk"—and (2) those instances in which the defendant does owe a duty of care to the plaintiff but the plaintiff knowingly encounters a risk of injury caused by the defendant's breach of that duty—what most commentators have termed "secondary assumption of risk." Properly interpreted, the relevant passage in *Li* provides that the category of assumption of risk cases that is not merged into the comparative negligence system and in which the plaintiff's recovery continues to be completely barred involves those cases in which the defendant's conduct did not breach a legal duty of care to the plaintiff, i.e., "primary assumption of risk" cases, whereas cases involving "secondary assumption of risk" properly are merged into the comprehensive comparative fault system adopted in *Li*. . . .

An amicus curiae in the companion case has questioned, on a separate ground, the duty approach to the post-*Li* assumption of risk doctrine, suggesting that if a plaintiff's action may go forward whenever a defendant's breach of duty has played some role, however minor, in a plaintiff's injury, a plaintiff who voluntarily engages in a highly dangerous sport—for example, skydiving or mountain climbing—will escape *any* responsibility for the injury so long as a jury finds that the plaintiff was not "unreasonable" in engaging in the sport. This argument rests on the premise that, under comparative fault principles, a jury may assign some portion of the responsibility for an injury to a plaintiff only if the jury finds that the plaintiff acted *unreasonably,* but not if the jury finds that the plaintiff knowingly and voluntarily, but reasonably, chose to engage in a dangerous activity. Amicus curiae contends that such a rule frequently would permit voluntary risk takers to avoid all responsibility for their own actions, and would impose an improper and undue burden on other participants.

Although we agree with the general thesis of amicus curiae's argument that persons generally should bear personal responsibility for their own actions, the suggestion that a duty approach to the doctrine of assumption of risk is inconsistent with this thesis rests on a mistaken premise. Past California cases have made it clear that the "comparative fault" doctrine is a flexible, commonsense concept, under which a jury properly may consider and evaluate the relative responsibility of various parties for an injury (whether their responsibility for the injury rests on negligence, strict liability, or other theories of responsibility), in order to arrive at an "equitable apportionment or allocation of loss."

Accordingly, contrary to amicus curiae's assumption, we believe that under California's comparative fault doctrine, a jury in a "secondary assumption of risk" case would be entitled to take into consideration a plaintiff's voluntary action in choosing to engage in an unusually risky sport, whether or not the plaintiff's decision to encounter the risk should be characterized as unreasonable, in determining whether the plaintiff properly should bear some share of responsibility for the injuries he or she suffered. Thus, in a case in which an injury has been caused by both a defendant's breach of a legal duty to the plaintiff and the plaintiff's voluntary decision to engage in an unusually risky sport, application of comparative fault principles will not operate to relieve either individual of responsibility for his or her actions, but rather will ensure that neither party will escape such responsibility. . . .

Accordingly, in determining the propriety of the trial court's grant of summary judgment in favor of the defendant in this case, our inquiry does not turn on the reasonableness or unreasonableness of plaintiff's conduct in choosing to subject herself to the risks of touch football or in continuing to participate in the game after she became aware of defendant's allegedly rough play. Nor do we focus upon whether there is a factual dispute with regard to whether plaintiff subjectively knew of, and voluntarily chose to encounter, the risk of defendant's conduct, or impliedly consented to relieve or excuse defendant from any duty of care to her. Instead, our resolution of this issue turns on whether, in light of the nature of the sporting activity in which defendant and plaintiff were engaged, defendant's conduct breached a legal duty of care to plaintiff. We now turn to that question.

III. . . .

. . . [W]e conclude that a participant in an active sport breaches a legal duty of care to other participants—i.e., engages in conduct that properly may subject him or her to financial liability—only if the participant intentionally injures another player or engages in conduct that is so reckless as to be totally outside the range of the ordinary activity involved in the sport. . . .

Therefore, we conclude that defendant's conduct in the course of the touch football game did not breach any legal duty of care owed to plaintiff. Accordingly, this case falls within the primary assumption of risk doctrine, and thus the trial court properly granted summary judgment in favor of defendant. Because plaintiff's action is barred under the primary assumption of risk doctrine, comparative fault principles do not come into play. The judgment of the Court of Appeal, upholding the summary judgment entered by the trial court, is affirmed.

In Ford v. Gouin, 3 Cal. 4th 339, 834 P.2d 724, 11 Cal. Rptr. 2d 30 (1992), the court held that a water skier was barred by primary assumption of the risk in a claim against the ski boat operator.

Problem 26

In what way would your analysis of Problem 24, p. 469, above, be different under the Uniform Comparative Fault Act?

5. Immunities

a. Governmental Immunity

The rule that a government may not be sued without its consent stems from the ancient English maxim, "the King can do no wrong." The governmental immunity rule was incorporated into American law at an early date, apparently without much thought as to whether this assumption about royal rectitude was appropriate in a democracy. Ultimately, the statement that came to be more or less accepted in this country is that offered by Justice Holmes in Kawananakoa v. Polyblank, 205 U.S. 349, 353, 27 S. Ct. 526, 527, 51 L. Ed. 834, 836 (1907): "A sovereign is exempt from suit, not because of any formal conception or obsolete theory, but on the logical and practical ground that there can be no legal right as against the authority that makes the law on which the right depends." The historical origins of governmental immunity are traced, and the early cases are analyzed, in a series of articles by Borchard entitled Governmental Liabilty in Tort, appearing at 34 Yale L.J. 1, 129, 229 (1924-1925); and Governmental Responsibility in Tort, 36 Yale L.J. 1, 757, 1039 (1926-1927), and 28 Colum. L. Rev. 577, 734 (1928).

The tort liability of the United States government is now controlled by the Federal Torts Claims Act, enacted in 1946.[173] The F.T.C.A. is not a general consent by the United States to be sued in tort, as there are several types of claims which are specifically excluded. Under one exclusion, certain types of tort actions, such as assault, battery, defamation, and interference with contract, may not be brought. 28 U.S.C.A. §2680(h). The conceptual problem courts occasionally face under this exclusion is illustrated in Moos v. United States, 118 F. Supp. 275 (D. Minn. 1954), *aff'd,* 225 F.2d 705 (8th Cir. 1955), in which the plaintiff alleged that he entered a Veterans' Administration hospital for surgery on an injured leg but that the operation was performed instead on his healthy leg. The court dismissed the complaint, ruling that it sounded in battery, rather than in negligence, because the plaintiff had not consented to an operation on that leg.

A more important exclusion under the F.T.C.A. is that which precludes liability for a claim based on the "exercise or performance or the failure

173. 60 Stat. 812. The provisions of the act appear in various sections of the United States Code. Appendix 1 of 3 Jayson, Handling Federal Torts Claims (1992) sets out the locations in the United States Code of the provisions of the act.

to exercise or perform a discretionary function or duty. . . ." 28 U.S.C.A. §2680(a). The leading case interpreting and applying this section is Dalehite v. United States, 346 U.S. 15, 73 S. Ct. 956, 97 L. Ed. 1427 (1953), in which the Supreme Court ruled that the act precludes recovery based upon conduct of administrators "in establishing plans, specifications or schedules of operations." Later cases have interpreted *Dalehite* as distinguishing between conduct at the planning level and conduct at the operational level with liability imposed only in connection with the latter. See Indian Towing Co. v. United States, 350 U.S. 61, 76 S. Ct. 122, 100 L. Ed. 48 (1955). The Federal Torts Claims Act is analyzed in detail in Jayson, Handling Federal Torts Claims (1964, with current supplements).

Sovereign immunity also applies to state and local governments, although a trend toward cutting back the extent of the immunity exists. The change in the immunity rules has been accomplished both by statute (see, e.g., Wash. Rev. Code Ann. §§4.92.090 and 4.96.010 (1993)[174] and by judicial decision; (see McCall v. Batson, 285 S.C. 243, 329 S.E.2d 741 (1985)). The Supreme Court of Ohio, however, has ruled that enough of sovereign immunity remains to bar an award of punitive damages. See Spires v. City of Lancaster, 28 Ohio St. 3d 76, 502 N.E.2d 614 (1986). Although judicial hostility to sovereign immunity is widespread, not all courts have abrogated it. See Comba v. Town of Ridgefield, 177 Conn. 268, 413 A.2d 859 (1979); Worthington v. State, 598 P.2d 796 (Wyo. 1979). And in states that have abrogated the immunity to some extent, it still remains with respect to discretionary or governmental functions. See, e.g., State ex rel. St. Louis Hous. Auth. v. Gaertner, 695 S.W.2d 460 (Mo. 1985) (operation of public housing project); City of Daytona Beach v. Palmer, 469 So. 2d 121 (Fla. 1985) (fire fighting decisions); Hobrla v. Glass, 372 N.W.2d 630 (Mich. App. 1985) (issuance of automobile operators' licenses). Courts have differed as to whether high speed police chases are within the scope of sovereign immunity. They are, according to Colby v. Boyden, 241 Va. 125, 400 S.E.2d 184 (1991); they are not, according to City of Pinellas Park v. Brown, 604 So. 2d 1222 (Fla. 1992).

Statutory attempts to preserve sovereign immunity, in whole or in part, have been subject to constitutional attack. The court in City of Dover v. Imperial Cas. & Indem. Co., 133 N.H. 109, 575 A.2d 1280 (1990), struck down a broad statutory grant of immunity to municipalities for injuries

174. It is commonly held that sovereign immunity is waived by the purchase of liability insurance. See, e.g., Litterilla v. Hospital Authority, 262 Ga. 34, 413 S.E.2d 718 (1992), and Crowell v. School District, 247 Mont. 38, 805 P.2d 522 (1991). However, the Montana legislature responded to this case by passing a statute that provided that the purchase of liability insurance does not constitute a waiver of sovereign immunity. See Hyde v. Evergreen Volunteer Rural Fire Dept., 252 Mont. 299, 828 P.2d 1377 (1992). The Supreme Court of Georgia held that a similar legislative attempt to reverse the immunity-waiving effect of liability insurance was unconstitutional (see Hiers v. City of Barwick, 262 Ga. 129, 414 S.E.2d 647 (1992)); the Supreme Court of West Virginia held that such a statute is constitutional (see Pritchard v. Arvon, 186 W. Va. 445, 413 S.E.2d 100 (1991)).

caused by the operation and maintenance of highways and sidewalks. The court held that the immunity could extend only to legislative, judicial, and other functions involving a high level of judgment or discretion. Other courts have been kinder to legislation preserving the immunity. See, e.g., Brown v. Wichita State University, 219 Kan. 2, 547 P.2d 1015, *appeal dismissed,* 429 U.S. 806 (1976). More limited preservations of sovereign immunity in the form of caps on the amount of damages that can be awarded have generally been upheld. See, e.g., State v. DeFoor, 824 P.2d 783 (Colo. 1992); Meech v. Hillhaven West, Inc., 238 Mont. 21, 776 P.2d 488 (1989); Smith v. City of Philadelphia, 512 Pa. 129, 516 A.2d 306 (1986), *appeal dismissed,* 479 U.S. 1074 (1987).

Governmental units have not been immune in recent years to what has been described as the crisis in tort law and insurance that has also been thought to plague the medical profession and manufacturers and sellers of products. The magnitude of the problem is discussed in Insuring Our Future—Report of the Governor's Advisory Commission on Liability Insurance, Volume I, 137-152 (1986), and in Volume II at 70-85. The first cited pages list the states that have attempted to deal with the liability of governmental units through legislatively established caps on recoverable damages. The Commission recommended no limit on recovery for economic loss—medical expenses and impaired earning capacity—and a $250,000 limit on recovery for intangible harm.

b. Charitable Immunity

The rule that charitable organizations are not liable in tort stems from an early English case, Feoffees of Heriot's Hospital v. Ross, 12 C. & F. 507, 8 Eng. Rep. 1508 (1846), in which the court reasoned that the payment of tort claims would be inconsistent with the purposes of the donors in contributing to the hospital. Charitable immunity eventually gained almost universal acceptance in the United States. However, the doctrine has now been abolished or significantly limited in all but a small handful of states. See Annotation, 25 A.L.R.4th 517 (1983). Most states have abolished the immunity by judicial decision (see, e.g., Albritton v. Neighborhood Centers Association for Child Development, 12 Ohio St. 3d 210, 466 N.E.2d 867 (1984)), although a few have done so by statute (see, e.g., N.C. Gen. Stat. §1-539.9).

The policies behind charitable immunity still have currency, however, and have led to frequent statutory preservation of the immunity. There are two concerns with regard to permitting tort suits against charities. One is with the deterrent effect the abrogation might have on persons who engage in charitable activities without compensation. Imposing liability on such persons may not have the effect of internalizing the cost of injuries; rather, the costs of the abrogation may be externalized to the very people that the charity is intended to benefit by the abandonment of charitable activities by those subject to liability. In general, see Markoff, A Volunteer's Thankless Task, National L.J., Sept. 1, 1988 at 1, col. 1, The New Jersey legislature responded to the judicial abrogation of charitable immunity by insulating volunteers engaged in a variety of charitable activities from liability in negligence. N.J. Stat. Ann. §2A:53-7.1-7.3 (1992 Supp.) This concern prompted the introduction into both houses of Congress in recent years bills which would encourage states to insulate volunteer workers for nonprofit or governmental agencies from negligence liability. See, e.g., S. 1343, 102nd Cong., 1st Sess. (1991).

A second concern is with those who are the beneficiaries of charitable activities "biting the hand that feeds them." Responding to this, the New Jersey legislature also insulated charitable organizations from negligence liability to their beneficiaries. N.J. Stat. Ann. §2A:53A-7. Some modern courts have also preserved the charitable immunity in this respect. See, e.g., Straley v. Urbanna Chamber of Commerce, 243 Va. 32, 413 S.E.2d 47 (1992).

Charitable immunity is analyzed and its vestiges criticized in Note, The Quality of Mercy: "Charitable Torts" and Their Continuing Immunity, 100 Harv. L. Rev. 1382 (1987). See also Comment, Charity Is No Defense: The Impact of the Insurance Crisis on Nonprofit Organizations and an Examination of Alternative Insurance Mechanisms, 22 U. San. Fran. L. Rev. 599 (1988).

c. Intrafamily Immunities

The immunities arising out of family relationships are those barring tort claims between husband and wife and between parent and child.

The husband-wife immunity comes from the old English concept that the two spouses are in legal contemplation one person. See Clark, Law of Domestic Relations 252 (1968). Out of this concept there developed a number of legal disabilities that attached to married women and the broader tort immunity that attached to both spouses. Beginning in the middle of the last century, state legislatures enacted Married Women's Property Acts to remove some of the disabilities of married women. Id. at 222. While these statutes were interpreted to permit interspousal tort suits with respect to property, most courts did not extend them to allow tort actions based on injuries to the person. See 2 Harper, James and Gray, The Law of Torts 562-571 (1986). In recent years, however, most states have either completely or partially abrogated the immunity. See, e.g., Waite v. Waite, 618 So. 2d 1360 (Fla. 1993) (total abrogation); Boblitz v. Boblitz, 296 Md. 242, 462 A.2d 506 (1983) (abrogated in negligence cases; Fernandez v. Romo, 132 Ariz. 447, 646 P.2d 878 (1982) (abrogated in automobile accident cases); Townsend v. Townsend, 708 S.W.2d 646 (Mo. 1986) (abrogated in intentional tort cases). Kansas also permits interspousal suits based on conduct that took place before the marriage. See O'Grady v. Potts, 193 Kan. 644, 396 P.2d 285 (1964). In Robeson v. International Indemnity Co., 248 Ga. 306, 282 S.E.2d 896 (1981), the Georgia Supreme Court adhered to the immunity, but in Harris v. Harris, 252 Ga. 387, 313 S.E.2d 88 (1984), it carved out an exception for cases in which there is no "marital harmony" to be protected by the immunity. In this case, the parties had been separated for ten years, and the defendant husband was living with another woman at the time of the accident.

Illinois has statutorily abrogated the husband-wife immunity for torts committed during marriage. See Ill. Comp. Stat. Ann. ch. 750, §65/1. An earlier Illinois statute barring such suits was held unconstitutional in Moran v. Beyer, 734 F.2d 1245 (7th Cir. 1984). The court stated that the statute did not bear a rational relationship to marital harmony, and did "little more than grant one spouse almost unconditional license to make his marriage partner a sparring partner." 734 F.2d at 1248.

The abrogation of the immunity does not necessarily mean that for tort purposes spouses will always be treated as strangers. In Weicker v. Weicker, 22 N.Y.2d 8, 237 N.E.2d 876 (1968), the court stated that it would not recognize a cause of action for intentional infliction of emotional harm if the dispute arises out of marital differences. In this case, the defendant husband had gotten what the wife alleged was an invalid Mexican divorce and then purported to remarry. The court ruled that her action based on the resulting embarrassment and emotional upset was properly dismissed. The Restatement (Second) of Torts §895F provides that there is no "liability for an act or omission that, because of the marital relationship, is otherwise privileged or is not tortious." The scope of this rule is not made much clearer by Comment *h,* which states:

> The intimacy of the family relationship may also involve some relaxation in the application of the concept of reasonable care, particularly in the confines of the home. Thus, if one spouse in undressing leaves shoes out where the other stumbles over them in the dark, or if one spouse spills coffee on the other while they are both still sleepy, this may well be treated as not negligence. An analogy to the principle of assumption of risk is sometimes drawn.

With the Restatement's "shoes in the dark" hypothetical, compare Brown v. Brown, 381 Mass. 231, 409 N.E.2d 717 (1980), in which the court ruled that the wife stated a cause of action for injuries she received from falling on the slippery driveway of their home. And in S.A.V. v. K.G.V., 708 S.W.2d 651 (Mo. 1986), the court reversed the dismissal of a complaint brought by a wife who alleged that she contracted genital herpes from her husband. One of the more interesting cases on this score is J.P.M. & B.M. v. Schmid Laboratories, Inc., 428 A.2d 515 (N.J. Super. 1981), in which the plaintiffs, husband and wife, sued the manufacturer and retailer of a contraceptive device, alleging that because the device was defective, the wife became pregnant. The manufacturer sought contribution from the husband, arguing that his negligence in using the device contributed to the harm. New Jersey had earlier abrogated the husband-wife immunity concept (see Merenoff v. Merenoff, 76 N.J. 535, 388 A.2d 951 (1978)), although the supreme court had recognized that in some instances such immunity might be appropriate. Here, the husband argued that the failure to recognize his immunity in this contribution action would constitute an unwarranted intrusion into marital privacy. The court rejected this argument, concluding that the plaintiffs had "lifted the veil of secrecy" by bringing the action.

In general, see Tobias, Interspousal Tort Immunity in America, 23 Ga. L. Rev. 359 (1989).

Unlike the other immunities considered in this section, the parent-child immunity rule is homegrown. It originated in Hewellette v. George, 68 Miss. 703, 9 So. 885 (1891), which involved a claim for false imprisonment brought by a minor child against her mother. A common justification for the immunity is that allowing recovery by children against their parents would promote family discord and interfere with parental control. See, e.g., Frye v. Frye, 305 Md. 542, 551-552, 505 A.2d 826, 831 (1986):

> It is clear that for over half a century this Court has recorded its belief in the importance of keeping the family relationship free and unfettered. Our primary concern with regard to matters involving the parent-child relationship was the protection of family integrity and harmony and the protection of parental discretion in the discipline and care of the child. We have steadfastly recognized the authority of parents and their need to fulfill the functions devolved upon them by that position. The parental status should be held inviolate so that there be no undue interference with the dependence of the minor unemancipated child on the parents for such judgment and care needed during the child's minority or with the dependence of the law on the parent for fulfillment of the necessary legal and social functions associated with the office of parent. This Court has declared it to be the public policy that discipline in the family not be impaired and that tranquility of the home be preserved. Matters which tend to disrupt or destroy the peace and harmony of family or home are not to be condoned.

If the parent is protected against liability by the immunity, most courts have refused to permit indirect parental liability through contribution claims brought by others whose negligence has contributed to the child's injury. See, e.g., Jacobsen v. Schroder, 117 Idaho 442, 788 P.2d 843 (1990); Shoemake v. Fogel, Ltd., 826 S.W.2d 933 (Tex. 1992). Illinois does, however, permit such contribution claims. See Hartigan v. Beery, 470 N.E.2d 571 (Ill. App. 1984).

Some courts have abrogated the immunity in cases in which the injury arose out of a business conducted by the parent (see Dzenutis v. Dzenutis, 200 Conn. 290, 512 A.2d 130 (1986)), unless parental discretion or authority is involved (see Holodook v. Spencer, 36 N.Y.2d 35, 324 N.E.2d 338 (1974)).

If the parent is immune to liability, at least one court has held that liability cannot be imposed on the parent's employer based on *respondeat superior.* The court in Davis v. Grinspoon, 570 N.E.2d 1242 (Ill. App.), *appeal denied,* 141 Ill. 2d 538, 580 N.E.2d 111 (1991), ruled that the employer's liability is derivative, and if the parent is not liable, there is no liability to pass on to the employer.

Other courts have limited the abrogation only to the extent that the parents are covered by liability insurance. See, e.g., Unah v. Martin, 676 P.2d 1366 (Okla. 1984). The South Carolina Supreme Court held unconstitutional a statute that abrogated the immunity only in automobile accident cases, the context in which liability insurance is most likely to be present, and went on to eliminate the immunity entirely. See Elam v. Elam, 275 S.C. 132, 268 S.E.2d 109 (1980). But the court in Dellapenta v. Dellapenta, 838 P.2d 1153 (Wyo. 1992), abrogated the immunity in automobile accident cases, in part because the likely presence of insurance eliminates any concern about disruption of family harmony.

The question of who is protected by the immunity has arisen in a number of cases. In Mitchell v. Davis, 598 So. 2d 801 (Ala. 1992), the court ruled that the immunity extended to foster parents and to state and local child care officials. The court in Mayberry v. Pryor, 422 Mich. 579, 374 N.W.2d 683 (1985), refused to extend the immunity to foster parents with whom the child was placed for temporary care by the state Department of Social Services, although the court recognized that the result might be different if there were a more permanent, family-type, relationship. In Lauber v. Doil, 574 N.E.2d 752 (Ill. App. 1989), *appeal denied,* 131 Ill. 2d 560, 553 N.E.2d 396 (1990), the court applied the immunity to the child's step father.

Results are also conflicting as to whether the immunity should apply in cases of intentionally caused harm. The court in Richards v. Richards, 599 So. 2d 135 (Fla. App.), *review dismissed,* 640 So. 2d 487 (Fla. 1992), held that the immunity does extend to intentional torts, here a sexual assault. On the other hand, the court in Barnes v. Barnes, 603 N.E.2d 1337 (Ind. 1992), held that the immunity did not insulate from liability a father who had sexually assaulted his daughter.

A few courts have abrogated the immunity entirely. See, e.g., Stamboulis v. Stamboulis, 401 Mass. 762, 519 N.E.2d 1299 (1988); Shearer v. Shearer, 18 Ohio St. 3d 94, 480 N.E.2d 388 (1985). In Gibson v. Gibson, 3 Cal. 3d 914, 479 P.2d 648, 92 Cal. Rptr. 288 (1971), the court, in responding to the argument that parents should be given legal leeway in bringing up their children, stated (3 Cal. 3d at 921, 479 P.2d at 653, 92 Cal. Rptr. at 293):

> In short, although a parent has the prerogative and the duty to exercise authority over his minor child, this prerogative must be exercised within reasonable limits. The standard to be applied is the traditional one of reasonableness, but viewed in light of the parental role. Thus, we think that the

> proper test of a parent's conduct is this: what would an ordinarily reasonable and prudent *parent* have done in similar circumstances?

The court did not indicate, however, whether it thought that the parental standard of reasonableness is the same as, higher, or lower than the standard that would be applicable in cases of persons who are legal strangers to the child.

The abrogation of the parent-child immunity presents an interesting problem when coupled with the law that permits recovery on behalf of a child for prenatal injuries. (As to the latter law, see pp. 438-446, above). Can an action be brought on behalf of a child against his mother based on injuries resulting from inadequate prenatal care? In Stallman v. Youngquist, 125 Ill. 2d 267, 531 N.E.2d 355, (1988), the court ruled that no such action could be brought in a case based on the claim that the defendant mother was negligent in the operation of an automobile while pregnant, and that as a result an accident occurred which injured the fetus. In rejecting the cause of action, the court stated (Id. at 275-278, 531 N.E.2d at 359-360):

> It is clear that the recognition of a legal right to begin life with a sound mind and body on the part of a fetus which is assertable after birth against its mother would have serious ramifications for all women and their families, and for the way in which society views women and women's reproductive abilities. The recognition of such a right by a fetus would necessitate the recognition of a legal duty on the part of the woman who is the mother; a legal duty, as opposed to a moral duty, to effectuate the best prenatal environment possible. The recognition of such a legal duty would create a new tort: a cause of action assertable by a fetus, subsequently born alive, against its mother for the unintentional infliction of prenatal injuries.
>
> It is the firmly held belief of some that a woman should subordinate her right to control her life when she decides to become pregnant or does become pregnant: anything which might possibly harm the developing fetus should be prohibited and all things which might positively affect the developing fetus should be mandated under penalty of law, be it criminal or civil. Since anything which a pregnant woman does or does not do may have an impact, either positive or negative, on her developing fetus, any act or omission on her part could render her liable to her subsequently born child. While such a view is consistent with the recognition of a fetus' having rights which are superior to those of its mother, such is not and cannot be the law of this State.
>
> A legal right of a fetus to begin life with a sound mind and body assertable against a mother would make a pregnant woman the guarantor of the mind and body of her child at birth. A legal duty to guarantee the mental and physical health of another has never before been recognized in law. Any action which negatively impacted on fetal development would be a breach of the pregnant woman's duty to her developing fetus. Mother and child would be legal adversaries from the moment of conception until birth. The error that a fetus cannot be harmed in a legally cognizable way when the

woman who is its mother is injured has been corrected; the law will no longer treat the fetus as only a part of its mother. The law will not now make an error of a different sort, one with enormous implications for all women who have been, are, may be, or might become pregnant: the law will not treat a fetus as an entity which is entirely separate from its mother. . . .

If a legally cognizable duty on the part of mothers were recognized, then a judicially defined standard of conduct would have to be met. It must be asked, By what judicially defined standard would a mother have her every act or omission while pregnant subjected to State scrutiny? By what objective standard could a jury be guided in determining whether a pregnant woman did all that was necessary in order not to breach a legal duty to not interfere with her fetus' separate and independent right to be born whole? In what way would prejudicial and stereotypical beliefs about the reproductive abilities of women be kept from interfering with a jury's determination of whether a particular woman was negligent at any point during her pregnancy?

The court in Bonte v. Bonte, 136 N.H. 286, 289-290, 616 A.2d 464, 466 (1992), recognized the cause of action:

> The defendant urges us to immunize the mother from tort liability based upon public policy reasons grounded in the unique relationship of the pregnant woman to her fetus. While we recognize that the relationship between mother and fetus is unique, we are not persuaded that based upon this relationship, a mother's duty to her fetus should not be legally recognized. If a child has a cause of action against his or her mother for negligence that occurred after birth and that caused injury to the child, it is neither logical, nor in accord with our precedent, to disallow that child's claim against the mother for negligent conduct that caused injury to the child months, days, or mere hours before the child's birth.
>
> The defendant further argues that public policy dictates against the plaintiff's cause of action because allowing this matter to proceed "deprives women of the right to control their lives during pregnancy . . . [and] unfairly subjects them to unlimited liability for unintended and often unforeseen consequences of every day living." We disagree that our decision today deprives a mother of her right to control her life during pregnancy; rather, she is required to act with the appropriate duty of care, as we have consistently held other persons are required to act, with respect to the fetus. The mother will be held to the same standard of care as that required of her once the child is born. Whether her actions are negligent is a determination for the finder of fact, considering the facts and circumstances of the particular case. Moreover, if a determination based upon public policy can be made denying a cause of action logically recognized by our case law, that determination should be made by the legislature.

If the cause of action against the mother is recognized, is the possibility opened up for actions based upon harm caused by smoking, drinking, drug use, and perhaps even inadequate dietary care? This issue has been discussed in a number of journals. See, e.g., Beal, "Can I Sue Mommy?" An Analysis of a Woman's Tort Liability for Prenatal Injuries to Her Child Born Alive, 21 San Diego L. Rev. 325 (1984); Note, Parental Liability for Prenatal Injury, 14 Colum. J.L. & Soc. Probs. 47 (1978); Note, A Maternal Duty to Protect Fetal Health?, 58 Ind. L.J. 531 (1983). If tort liability comes, can criminal liability be far behind? See Note, Maternal Rights and Fetal Wrongs: The Case Against Criminalization of "Fetal Abuse," 101 Harv. L. Rev. 994 (1988).

Chapter 5

Trespass to Land and Nuisance

The material in this chapter is divided into two parts. The first part consists of a summary of the substantive law of trespass and nuisance, and provides a historical perspective and a general background of the controlling principles. The second part consists of decisions in which courts have applied these principles in actual cases.

A. *Summary of the Substantive Law*

Trespass and nuisance are separated here because traditionally they have been considered as separate concepts involving quite different interests. One of the questions that you will want to consider before leaving this section is the feasibility, and to some extent the possibility, of the continued analytical separation in light of the effects of modern technology upon interests in the possession, enjoyment, and use of real property.

1. Trespass

Most nonlawyers associate the word "trespass" with a deliberate intrusion upon another's land by someone "up to no good." Trespassers tend to be thought of as fence-breaking, chicken-stealing no-accounts. However, the legal concept of trespass is much broader, more technical, and largely devoid of moralistic overtones. The legal interest of the plaintiff protected by the action is the interest in the exclusive possession of the land in question. At early common law, an action for trespass would lie for any unauthorized entry, either by person or thing, upon another's land directly resulting from a volitional act. If the defendant were bodily picked up and thrown upon the plaintiff's land against the defendant's will, no action for trespass would lie, because the defendant's entry did not result from a volitional act by the defendant. But it was no defense that the defendant had stumbled and fallen upon the land, or had entered the land mistakenly believing that the entry was authorized or that no such entry had occurred. It was a trespass even if the defendant had entered the plaintiff's land in reasonable response to physical threats from a third person. And, having committed a trespass, the defendant was liable for all harm resulting from the entry, however unforeseeable. Moreover, because land was deemed to be unique, threatened acts of continuous trespass were enjoinable in equity irrespective of the reasons given by the defendant to justify the entry.

Thus, trespass at early common law had very little, if anything, necessarily to do with moral culpability. To the contrary, it was one of the earliest and strictest forms of strict liability. The main reason for this strictness lay in the fact that an action in trespass was an important legal means by which lawful possessors of land could maintain the integrity of their possessory interests. Even in the absence of substantial harm, the law allowed the plaintiff to establish legally the right to exclude others from the plaintiff's land. Thus, even the innocently motivated but unauthorized entrant would be liable for at least nominal damages, and for compensatory damages if actual harm resulted from the trespass.

To some extent, the strictness of the early common law of trespass has been ameliorated. In the fourteenth, fifteenth, and sixteenth centuries, English courts developed an important distinction between entries resulting *directly* and those resulting *indirectly* from the defendant's conduct. For entries resulting directly from defendant's conduct, trespass would lie; for entries resulting indirectly from defendant's conduct, the proper form of action was trespass on the case.[1] The major difference between these two forms of action was the requirement in connection with the latter, but not the former, that the plaintiff show that the entry was committed either intentionally or negligently and that it caused actual harm.

These differences based upon the directness or indirectness of the entry have largely disappeared, and the forms of action themselves have been abolished. However, the impact of the earlier distinction between trespass and trespass on the case survives in the important distinction drawn by courts today between intrusions upon land that are intentional and those that are unintentional. With respect to intentional intrusions, much of the earlier strictness remains: one who intentionally enters another's land, or causes a thing or a third person to enter, is liable in trespass irrespective of whether the actor causes actual harm and irrespective of any mistake, however reasonable, not induced by the possessor. However, with respect to unintentional intrusions, the earlier strictness has almost entirely been eliminated: One who unintentionally enters land in the possession of another is liable only for recklessness, negligence, or engaging in an extrahazardous activity. Moreover, an unintentional intruder is liable only for harm actually caused by the entry. Thus, the modern system of liability for unintentional entries, which has been freed from responsibility for protecting the possessor's legal title to land, has developed into a flexible system of liability for actual harm to the plaintiff's property.

The rules governing liability for intentional invasions, which continue to bear major responsibility for maintaining the legal integrity of possessory

1. For two somewhat different analyses of the origins of the action of trespass on the case see Plucknett, Case and the Statute of Westminster II, 31 Colum. L. Rev. 778 (1931) and Dix, The Origins of the Action of Trespass on the Case, 46 Yale L.J. 1142 (1937).

interests in land, retain a substantial measure of the earlier strictness and inflexibility. Yet, even here, trespass law has been rendered more flexible by the development and expansion of nonconsensual privileges which, in a variety of circumstances, excuse intentional entries upon the land of another. We have already encountered one such privilege—that of "private necessity"—in the earlier treatment of the duties owed by possessors of land to refrain from committing batteries upon would-be trespassers. See Ploof v. Putnam, p. 93, above. The Restatement (Second) of Torts recognizes no fewer than 20 separate privileges of this sort.

There is much more to the subject of trespass to land than is contained in these few paragraphs, and students interested in exploring this subject further are urged to make use of the sources readily available. Before proceeding to the subject of nuisance, it will be useful to summarize briefly the unique characteristics of trespass so that it can be more easily contrasted to nuisance in the next subsection:

(1) The interest sought to be protected by trespass actions for intentional entries is the plaintiff's interest in the exclusive possession of land.

(2) To constitute a trespass, the defendant must accomplish an entry on the plaintiff's land by means of some physical, tangible agency. The entry must be unauthorized, and (a) intended by the defendant, or (b) caused by defendant's recklessness or negligence, or (c) the result of defendant's carrying on an ultrahazardous activity.

(3) The circumstances in which a defendant may be privileged to commit an unauthorized, intentional entry are carefully limited by judicial decisions, and there exists no broadly based privilege to enter the land of another simply because, on balance, the social benefit of doing so appears to outweigh the risks of harm to the land.

(4) Once the defendant is found to have committed an intentional trespass, in the absence of circumstances giving rise to a privilege the plaintiff is entitled to at least nominal damages and to injunctive relief if further acts by the defendant threaten similar entries upon his land.

As this summary reveals, trespass remains a relatively inflexible concept. Unless an unauthorized entry upon the plaintiff's land has occurred, trespass will not lie no matter how bothersome the defendant's conduct may have been. And whenever an intentional entry is found to have taken place, there is relatively little opportunity for the defendant to talk of justification. Moreover, once a trespass is found to have occurred, the plaintiff may have threatened repetitions enjoined regardless of arguments that to do so would impose a greater hardship on the defendant than would otherwise be suffered by the plaintiff.

2. Nuisance

Some of the confusion that has traditionally surrounded this subject may be avoided if it is understood that two very different legal concepts—public nuisance and private nuisance—are embraced by the single word "nuisance." Public nuisance is defined in §821B of the Restatement (Second) of Torts as "an unreasonable interference with a right common to the general public." It is a very broad concept, having its origins in criminal interferences with the rights of the Crown. A public nuisance need not necessarily involve interference with interests in land. An illegal lottery, for instance, might well constitute a public nuisance even if it is conducted in a perfectly quiet, unobtrusive manner. As the phrase itself suggests, public nuisances are traditionally enjoined or abated in legal proceedings brought by public officials in the name of the state. Private nuisance, on the other hand, is defined in §821D of the Restatement (Second) as "a nontrespassory invasion of another's interest in the private use and enjoyment of land." The law of private nuisance began and was developed entirely independently of the law of public nuisance. Private nuisance is a narrower concept than public nuisance and, as the Restatement definition indicates, necessarily involves interferences with private interests in land. Traditionally, private nuisances are enjoined in actions brought by individuals whose private interests are affected by them.

Although the main concern in this chapter is private nuisance, it is necessary at this point to pursue the subject of public nuisance further because private actions for damages based upon public nuisances are sometimes available to individual plaintiffs. The Restatement (Second) establishes the parameters of the concept of public nuisance in two sections:

> §821B. PUBLIC NUISANCE
>
> (1) A public nuisance is an unreasonable interference with a right common to the general public.
>
> (2) Circumstances that may sustain a holding that an interference with a public right is unreasonable include the following:
>
> (a) Whether the conduct involves a significant interference with the public health, the public safety, the public peace, the public comfort or the public convenience, or
>
> (b) whether the conduct is proscribed by a statute, ordinance or administrative regulation, or
>
> (c) whether the conduct is of a continuing nature or has produced a permanent or long-lasting effect, and, as the actor knows or has reason to know, has a significant effect upon the public right.
>
> §821C. WHO CAN RECOVER FOR PUBLIC NUISANCE
>
> (1) In order to recover damages in an individual action for a public nuisance, one must have suffered harm of a kind different from that suffered by other members of the public exercising the right common to the general public that was the subject of interference.
>
> (2) In order to maintain a proceeding to enjoin to abate a public nuisance, one must
>
> (a) have the right to recover damages, as indicated in Subsection (1), or

(b) have authority as a public official or public agency to represent the state or a political subdivision in the matter, or

(c) have standing to sue as a representative of the general public, as a citizen in a citizen's action or as a member of a class in a class action.

The provisions of greatest relevance to the subject of present concern are subsections (1) and (2) (a) of §821C, providing for individual actions based upon a public nuisance. It is important to note that these subsections are not necessarily limited to interferences with individual plaintiffs' interests in the possession, enjoyment, and use of land. However, very often the cases in which subsections (1) and (2) (a) apply involve conduct by the defendant which does interfere substantially and uniquely with the interests of individual owners and possessors of land. With an illegal lottery, for example, an individual land owner adjacent to the defendant's operation might be uniquely bothered by the coming and going of boisterous participants, and would, in that event, have a private cause of action under subsections (1) and (2) (a) of §821C based upon the public nuisance.

To maintain a private action for public nuisance, the individual plaintiff must suffer harm that is different in kind from that suffered by the public at large. For example, where the defendant without authority digs a ditch across a public highway, obstructing its use as a thoroughfare, an individual inconvenienced thereby will not have a private cause of action based upon the public nuisance simply because by traveling the highway twice as often in the course of a day as do other members of the highway-using public the individual is arguably twice as inconvenienced by defendant's conduct. However, were the plaintiff to fall into the unlighted ditch at night and be injured, a private action for damages would lie. Observe also that subsection (1) of §821C speaks of an action to recover damages, while subsection (2) speaks of a proceeding to enjoin or abate a public nuisance. Just as courts have been willing to enjoin intentional trespass to land, so they have traditionally been willing to enjoin continuing nuisances, both public and private. The important question of the nature of the remedy available to the plaintiff will be raised throughout the materials which follow.

Private nuisance is by far a more important body of law than public nuisance for the protection of private interests in land. Section 821D of the Restatement (Second) defines a private nuisance as an invasion other than a trespass—although there may be an accompanying trespass—of the owner's interests in the use and enjoyment of the land. Thus, private nuisance is different from, but not necessarily inconsistent with, the concept of trespass described in the preceding subsection. The basic difference may be expressed in terms of the different interests protected. A successful action in trespass serves to protect the plaintiff's interest in the exclusive possession of land; an action in private nuisance protects the plaintiff's interest in the use and enjoyment of land. Trespass requires a physical entry; private nuisance does not.

An early English decision illustrates clearly the function served by the law of private nuisance in our legal system. In William Aldred's Case, 9 Co. Rep. 57, 77 Eng. Rep. 816 (1611), the plaintiff brought an action on the case against the defendant alleging that the stench from defendant's hog sty next door constituted a nuisance substantially interfering with the plaintiff's use and enjoyment of his land. Clearly, if the defendant had driven his hogs onto the plaintiff's land without permission, the plaintiff's action would have been in trespass. However, here the defendant kept his hogs at home and sent, instead, their heady smell on the summer breezes to the plaintiff's land. On appeal from a judgment in favor of the plaintiff, the defendant argued "that the building of the house for hogs was necessary for the sustenance of man: and one ought not to have so delicate a nose, that he cannot bear the smell of hogs. . . ." No doubt moved by the plaintiff's appeal to the court's sense of smell as well as to its sense of justice, the King's Bench affirmed the judgment against the defendant. The plaintiff's nuisance action here was brought on the case and it therefore was necessary for the plaintiff to show that harm actually was suffered as a result of the defendant's operating his hog sty. This requirement of harm, reminiscent of a similar requirement in connection with actions for unintentional trespass which also developed out of the common law action on the case, has been carried over into the modern law of nuisance.

In addition to invading the plaintiff's interest in the private use and enjoyment of land and causing substantial harm in the process, in order to constitute a private nuisance the invasion must be wrongful. The Restatement (Second) of Torts sets forth the general rule governing the establishment of the wrongfulness of the defendant's invasion as follows:

> §822. GENERAL RULE
>
> One is subject to liability for a private nuisance if, but only if, his conduct is a legal cause of an invasion of another's interest in the private use and enjoyment of land, and the invasion is either
>
> (a) intentional and unreasonable, or
>
> (b) unintentional and otherwise actionable under the rules controlling liability for negligent or reckless conduct, or for abnormally dangerous conditions or activities.

It is interesting to note the extent to which this formulation of the general rule governing private nuisance parallels the formulation advanced earlier of the rules governing liability for trespass to land. The same distinction is here drawn between invasions that are intentional and those that are unintentional. As for the latter, they are subjected to the same requirements earlier observed in connection with unintentional trespass; that is, that the plaintiff show the defendant to have been negligent, reckless, or to have either engaged in some abnormally dangerous activity or allowed an abnormally dangerous condition to exist.

As for intentional invasions, §822 imposes the more general requirement that they be "unreasonable." It will be recalled that no such additional requirement is imposed in connection with intentional trespass, and that further questions of whether the defendant's intentional entry upon the plaintiff's land might have been justified are left to be handled by the various specific categories of privilege. In effect, the additional requirement that the plaintiff in a nuisance action show the invasion to have been unreasonable brings the question of possible justification of the defendant's conduct into the prima facie case and makes it part of the plaintiff's burden.

The question presenting unique analytical problems peculiar to the law of private nuisance is the question of when an intentional invasion by the defendant is unreasonable. The general rule governing this question of unreasonableness is contained in §826 of the Restatement (Second):

> §826. UNREASONABLENESS OF INTENTIONAL INVASION
>
> An intentional invasion of another's interest in the use and enjoyment of land is unreasonable if
>
> (a) the gravity of the harm outweighs the utility of the actor's conduct, or
>
> (b) the harm caused by the conduct is serious and the financial burden of compensating for this and similar harm to others would not make the continuation of the conduct not feasible.

The concepts of the gravity of the harm to the plaintiff and the utility of the defendant's conduct are developed in subsequent sections of the Restatement (Second):

> §827. GRAVITY OF HARM—FACTORS INVOLVED
>
> In determining the gravity of the harm from an intentional invasion of another's interest in the use and enjoyment of land, the following factors are important:
>
> (a) the extent of the harm involved;
>
> (b) the character of the harm involved;
>
> (c) the social value which the law attaches to the type of use or enjoyment invaded;
>
> (d) the suitability of the particular use or enjoyment invaded to the character of the locality;
>
> (e) the burden on the person harmed of avoiding the harm.

> §828. UTILITY OF CONDUCT—FACTORS INVOLVED
>
> In determining the utility of conduct that causes an intentional invasion of another's interest in the use and enjoyment of land, the following factors are important:
>
> (a) the social value that the law attaches to the primary purpose of the conduct;
>
> (b) the suitability of the conduct to the character of the locality; and
>
> (c) the impracticability of preventing or avoiding the invasion.

These three sections deserve careful consideration. The lists of factors to be considered do not purport to be exhaustive, nor do they appear to be listed in any particular sequence of relative significance. Taken together these three sections afford great latitude to courts in determining the reasonableness of the defendant's invasion of the plaintiff's interest in use and enjoyment. Drawing upon past judicial decisions applying these principles of gravity vs. utility, the first Restatement supplied three sections dealing with applications of §§826-828 to more or less specific circumstances. The invasion of the plaintiff's interest will be found to be unreasonable where the defendant's conduct is malicious or indecent (§829); where the resulting invasion could have been avoided by the defendant relatively easily ("without undue hardship") (§830); or where the plaintiff's use of his land is, and the defendant's conduct is not, suited to the locality in which the invasion occurred (§841). In the Restatement (Second) a fourth illustrative section was added, setting out yet another specific application of the general principles of reasonableness:

> §829A. GRAVITY VS. UTILITY—SEVERE HARM
> An intentional invasion of another's interest in the use and enjoyment of land is unreasonable if the harm resulting from the invasion is severe and greater than the other should be required to bear without compensation.

If §829A is to serve its function of supplying an illustrative example of the application of the rules contained in §§826-828, the latter portion following the "if" must refer to something more specific than the plaintiff's being entitled to compensation under the general rules comprising the law of private nuisance. As the history of this section makes clear, §829A was intended to assert that, quite apart from the traditional considerations of reasonableness reflected in the earlier sections, courts may base a finding of unreasonableness, and hence impose liability, upon the independent ground that the plaintiff cannot afford financially to go without a remedy. Thus, even if the utility of the defendant's conduct outweighs the gravity of the harm it is causing, it would appear that the invasion of the plaintiff's interest may be found to be unreasonable based solely upon the magnitude of the harm to the plaintiff and the accompanying financial burden. Interpreted in this manner, §829A is not so much an illustrative application of the rules contained in §§826-828 as it is a remarkable exception to them.

Any doubt that the Restatement was intended to make relevant the plaintiff's need to be paid is eliminated by turning to an even more explicit recognition that the concomitant consideration—the defendant's ability to pay—is a sufficient, independent basis upon which to impose liability. In subsection (b) of §826 the defendant's intentional invasion of the plaintiff's interest is unreasonable, notwithstanding the fact that the utility of the defendant's conduct outweighs the gravity of the harm, if "the harm caused by the conduct is serious and the financial burden of compensating for this and similar harm to others would not make continuation of the conduct not feasible." Clearly, subsection (b) authorizes the imposition of liability for damages against an otherwise reasonable defendant based solely upon the judgment that the defendant is able to pay and still remain in operation—that is, that the defendant's conduct can financially afford to pay its way. Admittedly, questions of the relative solvency of the parties to a tort action have been in the background of much of what we have considered in this book. However, they have never before been recognized as legitimate independent bases upon which to impose liability on a case-by-case basis.

Thus, into the sections of the Restatement (Second) dealing with private nuisance have been inserted these unique recognitions that both the plaintiff's need to be paid and the defendant's ability to pay may serve as independent bases upon which to impose liability. The sections which accomplish this revision, §§829A and 826(b), respectively, are unquestionably the most intriguing and provocative provisions in the entire Restatement treatment of the subject of private nuisance.

Up to this point, we have been concerned primarily with defining the nuisance concept and describing the elements which must be proved for the plaintiff to succeed in placing the nuisance label upon the defendant's interference with his interest in the enjoyment and use of land. It is also important to consider the question of the remedies available to the plaintiff once the existence of a private nuisance has been shown. It will be recalled that once a trespass is proved, equity has traditionally purported to be willing, based upon the uniqueness of real property and the inadequacy of the legal remedy of damages, to enjoin threatened repetitions. One might have reasonably expected the same underlying recognition of the uniqueness of land to lead courts to enjoin nuisances whenever a substantial and unreasonable interference with the plaintiff's enjoyment and use of his land has been proved. In fact, courts have been willing to adopt this approach whenever the interference is found to be unreasonable in the sense that the harm to the plaintiff's interest outweighs the utility of the defendant's conduct. However, in cases in which judges have concluded that the utility of the defendant's conduct outweighs the gravity of the resulting harm, and yet have found a nuisance to exist based upon the substantiality of the harm and the feasibility of the defendant's enterprise compensating the plaintiff, they have occasionally refused to enjoin the defendant's conduct but have, instead, ordered the defendant to pay damages. These are, of course, precisely the cases covered by §§829A and 826(b), in which the plaintiff's need to be paid and the defendant's ability to pay are made independent bases for concluding the defendant's intrusion to be unreasonable. In both of these new provisions, the clear implication is that the only remedy available to the plaintiff in such cases will be monetary damages, and that injunctive relief will not be forthcoming.

B. *Judicial Applications of the Substantive Law*

It is one thing to offer, as the Restatement attempts to offer, a set of internally consistent rules purporting to solve the problems presented by our traditional commitment to protecting private interests in the possession, enjoyment, and use of land. It is quite another for the courts to develop socially acceptable and judicially manageable solutions when confronted, piecemeal, by these problems in real cases. One of the advantages enjoyed by the American Law Institute (and at the same time, perhaps, one of its weaknesses) is that it need not actually decide difficult cases. It should come as no surprise, therefore, that the rules of law developed in actual cases often lack the conceptual consistency and internal logic of the Restatement. Consistency and logic are often among the first victims when courts are called upon to struggle with major social problems. What follows is a collection of opinions indicating how a number of courts have attempted to harmonize the competing values in difficult cases, and how they have handled the interplay between trespass and nuisance.

Atkinson v. Bernard, Inc.

223 Or. 624, 355 P.2d 229 (1960)

GOODWIN, J. The defendant operator of a small airport appeals, and the plaintiff landowners cross-appeal, from a decree of the circuit court enjoining part, but not all, of the flights from the airport over the lands of the plaintiffs. The parties will be referred to in this opinion as the Airport and the plaintiffs.

In 1918 the Airport commenced operation about one mile north of the city center of Beaverton. The Airport serves mainly single-engine, noncommercial aircraft of the type commonly flown for business and pleasure by persons having private licenses as distinguished from larger aircraft found in military and airline service. The present runway is about 2500 feet long.

Some time after 1948, a suburban residential area known as Cedar Hills was developed directly north of the airport. Building sites and homes were sold to persons desiring to purchase them. Some 68 property owners joined as plaintiffs in 1955 in the present suit, and 21 of them testified at the trial. The plaintiffs located nearest the airport are approximately 1000 feet north of the runway. Others are located at varying distances greater than 1000 feet from the end of the runway, but all are within an area affected in some degree by the sound of aircraft landing and taking off.

The evidence showed that during fair weather the wind commonly blows from the north, and most of the flights take off toward the north during fair weather. The evidence further showed that a substantial number of flights take place early on Sunday mornings when the air is calm but when the plaintiffs are not necessarily ready to greet the new day.

The complaint alleged that, in taking off over the plaintiffs' homes, the planes fly at altitudes varying from 50 to 300 feet above the rooftops, and in so doing create noises and vibrations which substantially interfere with the use and enjoyment of the lands of the plaintiffs. There was testimony in support of these allegations, but the matter of altitude was sharply disputed. . . .

The plaintiffs demanded an injunction of all flights taking off to the north, as such flights necessarily pass over one or more of their homes before gaining cruising altitude. As the only runway lies north and south, such an injunction would, for all practical purposes, put an end to fair-weather flying from the airport. During the winter, the evidence showed, the prevailing winds are from the south.

The trial judge viewed the premises, and, upon stipulation of the parties, observed a demonstration of several flights over the property of the plaintiffs.

The decree enjoined flights taking off over the property of the plaintiffs by all aircraft which make "appreciably more noise than [a certain 1954 Piper Tri-Pacer 135 HP owned at that time by the State of Oregon]."

The Airport appeals from the decree, contending that it is too vague and indefinite for enforcement. The plaintiffs cross-appeal and demand an end to all take-offs over their lands.

No decibel readings or other objective acoustical data were made available to the trial court. The evidence showed that atmospheric conditions have some influence upon what those on the ground may hear as the result of flights over their property, but the nature and extent of such influence was undisclosed.

There are a number of problems raised in the briefs and argued before this court, but the principal question dealt with below was the extent to which the plaintiffs were entitled to noise abatement.

The trial court found, and the evidence supports the finding, that at least some of the plaintiffs were annoyed and inconvenienced by the noise of unspecified "larger" or "noisier" planes taking off over their rooftops. The noise on take-off bears some relation to the kind of engine, the pitch of the propeller, and the angle of climb between the time the plane leaves the runway and the point where it reaches flying or cruising altitude. The evidence left the exact relationship somewhat obscure, but mere size of aircraft alone appeared to be less significant than the other factors.

Here we are dealing with a privately operated airport and the question of enjoining certain flights, all of which, to some extent, invade the airspace below navigable heights and above the surface. . . .

To the facts in the instant case, the trial court applied the "privileged trespass" theory found in the Restatement, 1 Torts 460, §194 (1934). The Restatement rule is as follows:

TRAVEL THROUGH AIR SPACE

An entry above the surface of the earth, in the air space in the possession of another, by a person who is traveling in an aircraft, is privileged if the flight is conducted:

(a) for the purpose of travel through the air space or for any other legitimate purpose,

(b) in a reasonable manner,

(c) at such a height as not to interfere unreasonably with the possessor's enjoyment of the surface of the earth and the air space above it, and

(d) in conformity with such regulations of the State and federal aeronautical authorities as are in force in the particular State.

This court referred to the above-quoted section of the Restatement when it said in a dictum in 1948:

". . . Air travel over a plaintiff's land is still recognized as trespass prima facie imposing liability but the rights of airplane travel are established or recognized by the doctrine of privilege. . . ." Amphitheaters, Inc. v. Portland Meadows, 184 Ore. 336, 344, 198 P.2d 847.

Under the "privileged trespass" theory, two considerations determine whether the invasion of the landowner's airspace will be privileged: (1) the flight itself must be reasonable, thus eliminating stunting, whimsical changes of propeller pitch and the like, at altitudes which affect those on the ground; and (2) the flight must be at such a height as not to interfere unreasonably with the enjoyment of the surface by the person in possession. As will be seen later, reasonableness becomes the key issue in each case. . . .

At the point where "reasonableness" enters the judicial process we take leave of trespass and steer into the discretionary byways of nuisance. Each case then must be decided on its own peculiar facts, balancing the interests before the court.

Whether Oregon courts should meet the airport problem with the ancient and formal doctrine of trespass or the more flexible concept of nuisance is still an open question. Amphitheaters, Inc. v. Portland Meadows, supra, hinted that the law of trespass might apply in this state, and the trial judge in the instant case understandably proceeded accordingly. The decided cases reveal that the same result might well be reached in a given case by following either trespass law or nuisance law, but the distinction is not as academic as it may at first appear to be. For example, in the instant case, the airport attempted to bring into the case the concept of "coming to the nuisance," and was prevented from so doing when the trial court accepted the able argument of counsel for the landowners that the case was, after all, one of trespass.

This case was well tried by able and learned counsel for both parties, and by a capable and experienced trial judge. This court has, therefore, an opportunity to choose the best rule of law to be followed in airport cases upon a record which comes from the trial court in excellent condition.

In re-examining the host of cases in state and federal courts, we are impressed with the logic of those cases which have met the problem frankly as a matter for the application of the law of nuisance. If the mind of man can invent and operate a flying machine, it ought to be able to devise a rule of law which is adequate to deal with the problems flowing from such inventiveness. This is the challenge of the common law.

Reasonableness is so inherent in the judicial balancing of interests in the airport cases that most of the decisions cited by counsel simply proceed to investigate the facts and then grant or deny relief upon the basis of the reasonableness of one interest yielding to another in a given case. In following such a balancing of interests as a means of reaching a decision, the courts employ nuisance concepts with only a passing gesture in the direction of the law of trespass.

In addition to balancing the private interests of the contesting parties, at least one court has recognized that there is a co-existent element of public interest. There are really two public interests: (1) in protecting the property rights of all landowners, and (2) in protecting the freedom of air travel. The point at which the two interests come into conflict is the point where the unreasonable must give way to the reasonable. . . .

We hold that whenever the aid of equity is sought to enjoin all or part of the operations of a private airport, including flights over the land of the plaintiff, the suit is for the abatement of a nuisance, and the law of nuisance rather than that of trespass applies.

The nuisance theory is in accordance with modern thinking in the field, and with common sense. The flexibility of nuisance law enables the trial judge to take into consideration, openly with proper pleadings and evidence, all relevant factors which will assist him in balancing the interests of the parties before the court in light of relevant public interest.

The Restatement rule which attempts to pour new wine into the old bottle of trespass appears to be losing adherents, and does not commend itself to this court as a rule to be cemented into the case law of Oregon.

We have previously said that reasonableness in such cases is primarily a question for the trial judge to determine from all the facts; " . . . whether a particular annoyance or inconvenience is sufficient to constitute a nuisance depends upon its effect upon an ordinarily reasonable man, that is, a normal person of ordinary habits and sensibilities . . . [citing cases]." Amphitheaters, Inc. v. Portland Meadows, supra, 184 Ore. at 349.

The trial judge found that flights which make sufficient noise to constitute an unreasonable interference with the rights of the landowners consisted mainly of isolated flights of planes heavier than those ordinarily using the airport at the time of trial. We are unable to learn from the record just how such aircraft might accurately be described, but presumably the line can be drawn somewhere.

The trial judge attempted to draw the line by using a specific model of plane which he described in the decree. For the purpose of regulating its future conduct, the Airport is entitled to know with greater certainty what flights will be permitted and what flights will be enjoined. The state-owned Tri-Pacer may not always be available as a template for measuring excessive sound.

The landowners are entitled to be relieved from noise and vibration, if any, which in fact substantially limit their enjoyment of their property. This relief, however, cannot be based solely upon the subjective likes and dislikes of a particular plaintiff. Relief, to be workable, must be based upon an objective standard of reasonableness. One witness testified, for example, that aircraft engine noises interfered with the use of the telephone, while another plaintiff said he failed to notice a particular flight because he was talking on the telephone at the time. Difficult as it may be, the trial court should translate its findings as to reasonableness into an objective test. . . .

Before the court can arrive at an objective standard of reasonableness, it will be necessary to perform acoustical studies under the supervision of the trial court. A decree thereafter should be drawn in terms of decibel readings set forth in relation to relevant atmospheric conditions with sufficient latitude for inconsequential deviations. An objective measurement of noise levels will then be established and such a decree can be properly enforced.

The decree appealed from is vacated and the cause remanded for further evidence in accordance with the views expressed herein. Counsel should be given a reasonable time in the trial in which to prepare and submit additional evidence.

In the event that no further evidence is forthcoming, the decree should be reinstated, but modified so that the only flights from the airport to be enjoined would be flights taking off to the north by aircraft capable of carrying more than four adult persons with their usual luggage or by cargo planes of a capacity of more than 1000 pounds plus the crew. . . .

The cause is remanded for further evidence to be ordered by the trial court within a reasonable time from the date of the mandate.

No costs to any party.

Common law nuisance actions seeking injunctive relief against airport noise appear to have been preempted by the federal Noise Control Act of 1972 (42 U.S.C. §§4901-4918), which establishes an administrative scheme to control noise, including airport noise. In City of Burbank v. Lockheed Air Terminal, Inc., 411 U.S. 624, 93 S. Ct. 1854, 36 L. Ed. 2d 547 (1973), the Supreme Court ruled that a city ordinance directed at airport noise reduction could not be enforced because Congress has preempted the field of airport noise control, thus barring, through the operation of the supremacy clause of the United States Constitution, state and local regulation. The act is discussed in Warren, Airport Noise Regulation: Burbank, Aaron, and Air Transport, 5 Envtl. Aff. 97 (1976); Note, Aircraft Noise Abatement: Is There Room for Local Regulation?, 60 Cornell L. Rev. 269 (1975).

However, damages actions for harm caused by airport noise may survive the Noise Control Act. In Alevizos v. Metropolitan Airport Comm., 298 Minn. 471, 216 N.W.2d 651 (1974), the Supreme Court of Minnesota held that the *City of Burbank* opinion does not preclude an action for damages based on the doctrine of inverse condemnation, an action for damages brought against a governmental agency that has effectively appropriated the plaintiff's land without condemnation proceedings. The Minnesota court also ruled that the class of inverse condemnees would include landowners whose land does not lie directly under the flight paths, so long as the market value of the land is substantially reduced. It should be observed that most of the earlier decisions involved actions by owners of land directly under flight paths.

The California Supreme Court ruled in Baker v. Burbank-Glendale-Pasadena Airport Auth., 39 Cal. 3d 862, 705 P.2d 866, 218 Cal. Rptr. 293 *cert. denied,* 475 U.S. 1017 (1986), that an airport authority's lack of eminent domain power does not preclude an inverse condemnation action against it since such an action is constitutionally based. "A landowner whose property has been invaded by a public entity that lacks eminent domain power suffers no less a taking merely because the defendant was not authorized to take." Id. at 866-867, 705 P.2d at 868, 218 Cal. Rptr. at 295. The court also made clear that other state law damage remedies (i.e., nuisance) remain available against an airport proprietor despite the fact that federal law precludes interference by the states with commercial flight patterns and schedules.

The Restatement (Second) of Torts, §159 takes the view that aircraft within the "immediate reaches" of the air space next to the land commit a trespass when they interfere with the use and enjoyment of the landowner's property. The case law, though sparse, supports this approach. See Brenteson Wholesale v. Arizona Pub. Serv. Co., 166 Ariz. 519, 803 P.2d 930 (1990) (overflights can constitute trespass if at such low altitude as to interfere with existing use of land).

Davis v. Georgia-Pacific Corp.

251 Or. 239, 445 P.2d 481 (1968)

HOLMAN, J. Plaintiff Veva Davis owns a residence in the city of Toledo. Subsequent to her occupation of the premises defendant commenced the operation of a pulp and paper plant in close proximity thereto. The plaintiffs, Mrs. Davis and her husband, testified the premises was rendered uninhabitable by the operation of defendant's plant because of the emanation therefrom of vibrations, offensive odors, fumes, gases, smoke and particulates which damaged the residence and plant life. Plaintiffs secured a judgment against defendant for both compensatory and punitive damages for trespass. Defendant appealed.

Defendant's first four assignments of error relate to the admission of evidence and an instruction to the jury which allowed the jury to consider whether the intrusion of fumes, gases, and odors upon the property in question constituted a trespass. Defendant contends such intrusions constitute a nuisance rather than a trespass because there was no direct physical invasion of the property. The traditional concept that a trespass must be a direct intrusion by a tangible and visible object . . . has been abandoned in this state. In Martin et ux v. Reynolds Metals Co., 221 Or. 86, 342 P.2d 790 (1960), we decided that the deposit of airborne particulates upon another's land constituted a trespass even though the particulates were so small as to be invisible in the atmosphere. . . . Error was not committed by allowing the jury to consider an intrusion of fumes, gases, smoke and odors as a trespass.

The next five assignments of error relate to the refusal of the trial court to admit evidence and give instructions relevant to weighing the utility of defendant's conduct of its business and its efforts to prevent harm, against the seriousness of the harm, if any, suffered by plaintiffs. Traditionally, such a weighing process by the jury is one which is permitted in nuisance cases but not in those of trespass. In a trespass case the social value of defendant's conduct, its efforts to prevent the harm and other circumstances that tend to justify an intrusion cannot be considered by the trier of the facts.

This does not mean, however, that a weighing process does not take place when a court decides whether a particular kind of an intrusion, if found by the jury to exist, is of such a nature that it should be classified as a trespass. [A common example of such a weighing process] is the decision of courts that the normal operation of airplanes high in a property's airspace does not constitute a trespass. A similar kind of weighing process takes place when a court decides whether a trespass is privileged. Such classifications however, are ones that are made by courts and not by juries. If the jury finds that an intrusion occurred which is of a kind that courts hold to be an unprivileged trespass, strict liability results. The jury is not allowed to consider the utility of the use to which defendant is putting his land or his efforts to prevent harm to plaintiff in deciding plaintiff's recovery. Therefore, it was proper in this case for the trial court not to allow the jury to consider the evidence and instructions in question in deciding whether defendant should be responsible for *compensatory* damages.

We wish to make clear that no conclusion should be drawn from the above language that such a weighing process is inappropriate in a court's consideration whether an injunction should issue to restrain a continuing unprivileged trespass or whether a plaintiff should be left to his remedy at law for damages. . . .

We have found [no] prejudicial error relevant to . . . compensatory damages. Therefore, the judgment for compensatory damages is affirmed. [The judgment for punitive damages is reversed.]

[The concurring opinions of O'CONNELL and DENECKE, JJ., are omitted.]

Courts have retreated from the old common law rule that smoke, gases and odors could only constitute a nuisance. *Davis* stands for the proposition that trespass need not involve invasions by persons or tangible objects. See, e.g., Ream v. Keen, 314 Or. 370, 838 P.2d 1073 (1992) (smoke from neighboring burning field constitutes trespass; follows *Davis*); Maddy v. Vulcan Materials Co., 737 F. Supp. 1528 (D. Kan. 1990) (airborne pollution constitutes trespass); Maryland Heights Leasing v. Mallinckradt, Inc. 706 S.W.2d 218 (1986) (radioactive emissions constitute trespass).

Underground contamination of neighboring lands may give rise to liability under either nuisance and trespass. See Shockley v. Hoechst Celanese Corp., 793 F. Supp. 670 (D.S.C. 1992) (barrels leaking hazardous chemicals as basis for action based nuisance, trespass, and strict liability; Gulf Park Water Co. v. First Ocean Springs Dev. Co., 530 So. 2d 1325 (Sup. Ct. Miss. 1988) (discharge of waste from sewage plant into lagoon constitutes trespass). But see, Seal v. Naches-Selah Irrigation District, 51 Wash. App. 1, 751 P.2d 873 (1988) (water seepage from canal into orchard rejected as basis for nuisance or trespass action; need to proceed under negligence theory).

The distinction between intentional and unintentional trespass in Oregon was recently relied on in Hoaglin v. Decker, 77 Or. App. 472, 713 P.2d 674 (1986). Since the plaintiff had not shown actual damages as a result of the defendant's inadvertant placement of sand with some debris on his land, the court ruled that the plaintiff could prevail only if the defendants had intentionally trespassed. In the case of an unintentional negligent trespass, actual damage is, consistent with negligence law generally, a necessary element of the cause of action. See §165 of the Restatement (Second) of Torts. In some circumstances, knowledge or reason to know of physical entry may be sufficient for intentional trespass. See, e.g., McGregor v. Barton Sand & Gravel, Inc., 62 Or. App. 24, 660 P.2d 175 (1983).

See also Ward v. Jarnport, 114 Or. App. 466, 835 P.2d 944 (1992) (for nuisance or trespass, defendant's actions must have been intentional, reckless, negligent, or the result of abnormally dangerous activity).

Waschak v. Moffat

379 Pa. 441, 109 A.2d 310 (1954)

STEARNE, J. The appeal is from a judgment of the Superior Court refusing to enter judgment non obstante veredicto for defendants in an action in trespass and affirming the judgment of the Court of Common Pleas of Lackawanna County in favor of plaintiffs.

Gas or fumes from culm banks, the refuse of a coal breaker, damaged the paint on plaintiffs' dwelling. In this action for damages the applicable legal principles are technical and controversial. Considerable confusion appears in the many cases. The field is that of *liability without fault for escape of substances from land.*

Plaintiffs are owners of a dwelling in the Borough of Taylor which is in the center of Pennsylvania's anthracite coal lands. An action in trespass was instituted against two partners, operators of a coal breaker in that Borough. Without fault on the part of defendants, gas known as *hydrogen sulfide* was emitted from two of defendants' culm banks. This caused discoloration of the white paint (with lead base) which had been used in painting plaintiffs' dwelling. The painted surface became dark or black. The sole proven damage was the cost of restoring the surface with a white paint, having a titanium and zinc base, which will not discolor. There was no other injury either to the building or occupants. The verdict was for $1,250.

While the verdict is in a relatively modest amount, the principles of law involved, and their application, are extremely important and far reaching. Twenty-five other cases are at issue awaiting the decision in this case. The impact of this decision will affect the entire coal interest—anthracite and bituminous—as well as other industries. Application of appropriate legal principles is of vital concern to coal miners and to other labor. . . .

In the court below the case was tried on the theory of *absolute liability* for the maintenance of a nuisance. The jury was instructed that it should determine, as a *matter of fact,* whether or not what the defendants did and the conditions resulting therefrom constituted a "reasonable and natural use" of defendants' land.

[The court concludes that the utility of the defendants' conduct clearly outweighed the gravity of the harm thereby caused.]

Even if the reasonableness of the defendants' use of their property had been the *sole* consideration, there could be no recovery here. . . .

In Versailles Borough v. McKeesport Coal & Coke Co., 83 Pittsb. Leg. J. 379, Mr. Justice Musmanno, when a county judge, accurately encompassed the problem when he said:

"The plaintiffs are subject to an annoyance. This we accept, but it is an annoyance they have freely assumed. Because they desired and needed a residential proximity to their places of employment, they chose to found their abode here. It is not for them to repine; and it is probable that upon reflection they will, in spite of the annoyance which they suffer, still conclude that, after all, one's bread is more important than landscape or clear skies.

"Without smoke, Pittsburgh would have remained a very pretty *village.*". . .

In applying [the law of nuisance] it is evident the invasion of plaintiffs' land was clearly *not intentional.* And even if it were, for the reasons above stated, it was not unreasonable. On the contrary, since the emission of gases was not caused by any act of defendants and arose merely from the normal and customary use of their land without negligence, recklessness or ultrahazardous conduct, it was wholly *unintentional,* and no liability may therefore be imposed upon the defendants.

The judgment is reversed and is here entered in favor of defendants non obstante veredicto.

[The dissenting opinion of JONES, J., is omitted.]

MUSMANNO, J. (dissenting). . . .

In 1948 the plaintiffs painted their house with a white paint. Some time later the paint began to turn to a light colored brown, then it changed to a grayish tint, once it burst into a silvery sheen, and then, as if this were its last dying gasp, the house suddenly assumed a blackish cast, the blackness deepened and intensified until now it is a "scorched black." The plaintiffs attribute this chameleon performance of their house to the hydrogen sulfide emanating from the defendants' culm deposits in the town—all in residential areas. The hydrogen sulfide, according to the plaintiffs, not only assaults the paint of the house but it snipes at the silverware, bath tub fixtures and the bronze handles of the doors, forcing them, respectively, into black, yellowish-brown and "tarnished-looking" tints. . . .

The evidence here does not show any *necessity* on the part of the defendants to locate the culm banks in the very midst of the residential areas of Taylor.

The Majority Opinion explores the law of nuisance ably but does not indicate whether the circumstances here make out a case of nuisance, although it does say that the lower Court erred in ruling that this case was one of absolute nuisance. My opinion is that there can be no doubt that the defendants were operating an actionable nuisance. The record, which consists of 600 printed pages, overwhelmingly establishes this fact. The poisonous gases lifting from the defendants' culm banks were destructive of property, detrimental to health and disruptive of the social life of the town.

There was evidence that the poisonous hydrogen sulfide was of such intensity that the inhabitants compelled to breathe it suffered from headaches, throat irritation, inability to sleep, coughing, lightheadedness, nausea and stomach ailments. These grave effects of the escaping gas reached such proportions that the citizens of Taylor held protest meetings and demanded that the municipal authorities take positive action to curb the gaseous invasion. . . .

It must always be kept in mind that these culm banks were not mole hills. The Main Street dump measured 1,100 feet in length, 650 feet in width and 40 feet in height. If these dimensions were applied to a ship, one can visualize the size of the vessel and what would be the state of its odoriferousness if it was loaded stem to stern with rotten eggs. And that is only one of the dumps. There is another dump at Washington Street and, consequently, another ship of rotten eggs. Its dimensions are 800 feet by

750 feet by 50 feet. A third dump measures 500 feet by 500 feet by 40 feet. Then the defendants constructed a silt dam with the same rotten-egg-smelling materials.

I do not think that there can be any doubt that the constant smell of rotten eggs constitutes a nuisance. If such a condition is not recognized by the law, then the law is the only body that does not so recognize it. . . .

The Majority states that the "emission of offensive odors, noises, fumes, violations, etc., must be weighed against the utility of the operation." In this respect, the Majority Opinion does me the honor of quoting from an Opinion I wrote when I was a member of the distinguished Court of Common Pleas of Allegheny County. Versailles Borough v. McKessport Coal & Coke Co., 83 Pittsb. Leg. J. 379. That was an equity case where the plaintiffs sought an injunction against the defendant coal company for maintaining a burning gob pile which emitted smoke. The coal mine was located in the very heart of an industrialized area which contained factories, mills, garbage dumps, incinerators and railroads, all producing their own individualized smoke and vapors so that it could not be said that the discomforts of the inhabitants were due exclusively to the operation of the coal mine. Furthermore, after hearings lasting one month I found that the operation of the mine in no way jeopardized the health of the inhabitants:

"Of course, if the continued operation of this mine were a serious menace to the health or lives of those who reside in its vicinity, there would be another question before us, but there is no evidence in this case to warrant the assumption that the health of anyone is being imperiled."

In the instant case the exact contrary is true. The health of the town of Taylor *is* being imperiled. And then also, as well stated by the lower Court in the present litigation, "Many factors may lead a chancellor to grant or deny injunctive relief which are not properly involved in an action brought to recompense one for injury to his land. . . . A denial of relief by a court of equity is not always precedent for denying redress by way of damages."

Even so, there is a vast difference between smoke which beclouds the skies and gas which is so strong that it peels the paint from houses. I did say in the *Versailles* case, "One's bread is more important than landscape or clear skies." But in the preservation of human life, even bread is preceded by water, and even water must give way to breathable air. Experimentation and observation reveal that one can live as long as 60 or 70 days without food; one can keep the lamp of life burning 3 or 4 days without water, but the wick is snuffed out in a minute or two in the absence of breathable air. For decades Pittsburgh was known as the "Smoky City" and without that smoke in its early days Pittsburgh indeed would have remained a "pretty village." But with scientific progress in the development of smoke-consuming devices, added to the use of smokeless fuel, Pittsburgh's skies have cleared, its progress has been phenomenal and the bread of its workers is whiter, cleaner, and sweeter.

On September 8, 1939, this Court, speaking through Chief Justice Kephart, handed down the monumental decision in the case of Summit Hotel Co. v. National Broadcasting Co., 336 Pa. 182, 8 A.2d 302, 124 A.L.R. 968. Chief Justice Kephart there said: 336 Pa. at page 189, 8 A.2d at page 305.

"In cases of trespass for nuisance, the person responsible may be unable, no matter how careful, to avoid injury to the lands of another, but, again, he knows that injury may result from the nature of his activities regardless of care. *Under such circumstances he also assumes the risk.* The responsibility for injury lies in creating or maintaining the harmful condition.

"In all of these illustrations, the person responsible has, or should have, *prior knowledge of the probable consequences, where the act done, or the instrumentality employed, possesses potentialities of serious harm.*"

There can be no doubt that the defendants were thoroughly aware of the probable consequences of their discarding operations before the plaintiffs suffered the damage of which they complain in this litigation. . . .

Even if the rights of the plaintiffs were to be considered by Restatement Rules they would still be entitled to recover under the proposition that the defendants were so well informed of the probable harmful effects of their operation that their actions could only be regarded as an intentional invasion of the rights of the plaintiff. . . .

If there were *no* other way of disposing of the coal refuse, a different question might have been presented here, but the defendants produced no evidence that they could not have deposited the debris in places removed from the residential districts in Taylor. Certainly, many of the strip-mining craters which uglify the countryside in the areas close to Taylor could have been utilized by the defendants. They chose, however, to use the residential sections of Taylor because it was cheaper to pile the culm there than to haul it away into less populous territory.

This was certainly an unreasonable and selfish act in no way indispensably associated with the operation of the breaker. It brought greater profits to the defendants but at the expense of the health and the comfort of the other landowners in the town who are also entitled to the pursuit of happiness. . . .

I would affirm the decision of the Superior Court.

Jost v. Dairyland Power Cooperative

45 Wis. 2d 164, 172 N.W.2d 647 (1969)

The action is one for damages for injury to crops and loss of market value of farm lands. The plaintiffs are farmers living within, or near, the city limits of Alma, Wisconsin. Their farms are located on the bluffs overlooking the Mississippi River. In 1947 the Dairyland Power Cooperative erected a coal burning electric generating plant at Alma. It is the contention of the farmers that consumption of high-sulfur-content coal at this plant has increased from 300 tons per day in 1948 to 1,670 tons per day in 1967. There was testimony that the 1967 coal consumption resulted in discharging approximately 90 tons of sulphur-dioxide gas into the atmosphere each day. There was substantial evidence to show that the sulphur-dioxide gas, under certain atmospheric conditions, settled on the fields, causing a whitening of the alfalfa leaves and a dropping off of some of the vegetation. There was also testimony to show that the sulphur compounds resulting from the industrial pollution killed pine trees, caused screens to rust through rapidly, and made flower raising difficult or impossible. There was some testimony to show that some of the sulphur came from locomotives or from river barges, but there was testimony that the power plant was the source of most of the contamination. Defendant's witness, a farmer who was "hit" less frequently by the sulphurous fumes, estimated his crop damage at 5 percent. There was also evidence of damage to apple trees, sumac, and wild grape, in addition to the alfalfa damage.

Each of the plaintiff farmers testified that his land had diminished in value as the result of the continuing crop loss. . . .

The trial judge . . . entered [judgment] upon the verdict [for the plaintiffs]. Defendant has appealed from the whole of the judgment, and plaintiffs have filed for a review of the judgment which sustained the jury's finding in regard to loss of market value.

HEFFERNAN, J. [After stating that the evidence compelled the conclusion, as a matter of law, that the harm to the plaintiffs' land was substantial, the court continues:]

Defendant strenuously argues that it was prejudiced by the court's refusal to permit certain testimony, particularly testimony that tended to show that defendant had used due care in the construction and operation of its plant, and to show that the social and economic utility of the Alma plant outweighed the gravity of damage to the plaintiffs.

Defendant's contention that the evidence should have been admitted rests on two theories; one, that due care, if shown, defeats a claim for nuisance, and, two, that, if the social utility of the offending industry substantially outweighs the gravity of the harm, the plaintiffs cannot recover damages. We can agree with neither proposition. . . .

In any event it is apparent that a continued invasion of a plaintiff's interests by non-negligent conduct, when the actor knows of the nature of the injury inflicted, is an intentional tort, and the fact the hurt is administered non-negligently is not a defense to liability.

It is thus apparent that the facts tending to show freedom from negligence would not have constituted a defense to plaintiffs' nuisance action. It was therefore proper that such evidence was excluded (the nominal character of plaintiffs' proof as to negligence has been commented on above.)

While there are some jurisdictions that permit the balancing of the utility of the offending conduct against the gravity of the injury inflicted, it is clear that the rule, permitting such balancing, is not approved in Wisconsin where the action is for damages. . . .

We therefore conclude that the court properly excluded all evidence that tended to show the utility of the Dairyland Cooperative's enterprise. Whether its economic or social importance dwarfed the claim of a small farmer is of no consequence in this lawsuit. It will not be said that, because a great and socially useful enterprise will be liable in damages, an injury small by comparison should go unredressed. We know of no acceptable rule of jurisprudence that permits those who are engaged in important and desirable enterprises to injure with impunity those who are engaged in enterprises of lesser economic significance. Even the government or other entities, including public utilities, endowed with the power of eminent domain—the power to take private property in order to devote it to a purpose beneficial to the public good—are obliged to pay a fair market value for what is taken or damaged. To contend that a public utility, in the pursuit of its praiseworthy and legitimate enterprise, can, in effect, deprive others of the full use of their property without compensation, poses a theory unknown to the law of Wisconsin, and in our opinion would constitute the taking of property without due process of law. . . .

Judgment affirmed in part and reversed in part consistent with this opinion.

As in *Jost,* some courts grant relief for nuisance even with no cost/benefit analysis. In *Waschak,* however, the court held that where the balance tipped in favor of the defendants, they would not be liable in the absence of intent to injure the plaintiff. Indeed, these cases remind one of the *Turner* case, in Chapter 6, in which the court noted that in Texas intentional polluters are liable.

Numerous authorities and courts side with the *Waschak* court. See, e.g., Prosser and Keeton, Law of Torts 622 (5th ed. 1984); Williams v. Amoco Products Co., 241 Kan. 102, 734 P.2d 1113 (1987). Others side with *Jost,* holding that a knowing infliction of injury is sufficient to satisfy the intent requirement, even in the absence of negligence or an ultra hazardous activity. Cf. §822 of the Restatement (Second) of Torts, above at p. 502. See, e.g., Bradley v. American Smelting & Refining Co., 104 Wash. 2d 677, 709 P.2d 782 (1985); Morgan v. Quailbrook Condominium Co., 704 P.2d 573 (Utah 1985). Still other courts eliminate the intent prong entirely, focusing instead on the reasonableness of the defendant's conduct. See, e.g., Davis v. J. C. Nichols Co., 714 S.W.2d 679, 684 (Mo. App. 1986) ("Nuisance is a condition, not an act or failure to act, and it is therefore immaterial in determining liability to inquire whether defendant was negligent and what his intention, design or motive may have been"). If intent is present, Missouri courts have held that punitive damages are also available. See Maryland Heights Leasing, Inc. v. Mallinckrodt, Inc., 706 S.W.2d 218 (Mo. App. 1985).

A third approach to determining whether a nuisance exists is the "reasonableness" test. The reasonableness approach is the majority rule. See generally Lewin, Boomer and the American Law of Nuisance: Past, Present, and

Future, 54 Alb. L. Rev. 189, 292 (1990) (survey of nuisance law shows 32 jurisdictions have adopted some form of the reasonableness test). Thus, in Coty v. Ramsey Assoc. Inc., 149 Vt. 451, 546 A.2d 196 (1988), defendant built a pig farm on property abutting plaintiff's land. Defendant accumulated excessive manure, junked automobiles, and dozens of sickly and dead animals on the farm. The court stated that a nuisance arises when the interference to the use and enjoyment of another's property is "unreasonable and substantial." The court, without citing any factor as having particular importance, concluded that the construction of the pig farm, which created strong odors and attracted flies, was unreasonable and constituted a substantial interference with the use and enjoyment of plaintiff's land. See also, Blanks v. Rawson, 296 S.C. 110, 370 S.E.2d 890 (1988) (improperly maintained dog pen was a nuisance).

Crushed Stone Co. v. Moore

369 P.2d 811 (Okla. 1962)

BLACKBIRD, VICE C.J. This appeal involves an action to enjoin the operation of a limestone rock quarry, located on land belonging to Harry T. Pratt, about one and a half or two miles from where a section line road, known as "Coyote Trail" intersects with the Sapulpa-Sand Springs road.

In 1950, when the Turner Turnpike was being linked with the Will Rogers Turnpike, a road construction business known as "Layman & Sons" operated this quarry to furnish materials for that road.

After an interval, during which there were no operations at the quarry, Crushed Stone Co., Inc., leased the land from Pratt, and commenced operating the quarry with its own equipment, in June, 1957. In December of the same year, said Company, hereinafter referred to by the letters "C.S.C.," suspended its operations at the quarry, but resumed them in June, 1958.

[Plaintiffs] are the owners and inhabitants of premises near the quarry, covering rural acreages of from 5 to 40 acres. They instituted this action to enjoin operations at the quarry in October, 1958. The gist of their alleged cause of action against Pratt and C.S.C. was that the operation of the quarry not only damaged their property, but that it interfered with their rights to the quiet and peaceful occupation, and enjoyment, of them.

The complaints against C.S.C.'s operation, testified to at the trial before the court by four men, who were plaintiffs in the action, together with their wives, and a widow, Lucille Ruddle, were directed against the dust, which filled the air and settled on nearby property; to the noise, concussion, vibration and rock propulsion caused by C.S.C.'s setting off explosives to blast the rock out of the ground; and to the noise and dust caused by the subsequent crushing of the rock into "agricultural limestone" and its loading into dump trucks to be hauled away. Some of said witnesses testified that the air around their homes was so full of dust, after such blasting, that it was hard to breathe; some testified that the dust not only covered the vegetation on their properties, making it look white, but came into their houses—even with the doors and windows closed—coating the furniture and floors and soiling draperies and damaging painted surfaces. Some also testified that the explosions shook the earth as well as their houses, cracking and dislodging the masonry and sheetrock therein and frightening and/or disturbing the occupants. Some also testified that the explosions propelled flying rocks onto the premises, breaking limbs from trees and creating a condition hazardous to both animal and human life. Some of the witnesses also testified that, because of the dust, they could not have the windows and doors of their homes open, and could not hang clothes out in their yards to dry. One witness testified that the dust aggravated his allergies, and worsened his wife's nervous condition. More than one witness testified that the noise from the work at the quarry disturbed, or interrupted, their sleep. . . .

After the trial had been continued from the first week in August, 1959; and, at a further hearing on September 21, 1959, defendants had introduced testimony that they had inaugurated certain corrective measures in their operations which reduced the original ill effects therefrom, and arrangements had been made for the trial judge to go to the quarry a week later, and there watch a test shot being exploded and personally view the situation, the court took the case under advisement and allowed submission of briefs.

Thereafter, in May, 1960, the court adjudged that the manner in which the quarry was being operated constituted a public and private nuisance. He expressed the further opinion, however, that defendants should have an opportunity to "correct" the situation, and gave them until July 17, 1960, for that purpose. After the case was taken under further advisement, until August 8, 1960, and recessed until the next day, both sides were allowed to introduce testimony pertaining to the results of C.S.C.'s attempts to reduce, or prevent, the harmful effects from its operations. After evidence had been introduced, on behalf of defendants, showing that C.S.C. had expended $13,000, or more, making certain improvements in the plant, and had made certain changes in their operations designed to reduce the dust, noise, and vibration from the quarry's operation, and plaintiffs had countered with evidence contemplated to show that operation of the quarry still constituted a nuisance, the court revisited the area and viewed the situation. When the case came on for judgment August 16, 1960, the court announced that evidence introduced since the preceding May 18, was insufficient to show an abatement of the nuisance. In his judgment, the court affirmatively found, and adjudged, that the operation of the quarry continued to constitute both a public and private nuisance, and ordered it abated by cessation of its operation, within 15 days, and removal of the accumulated stock piles (of agricultural limestone) within 30 days. After the overruling of their separate motions for a new trial, defendants perfected the present appeal.

As their first proposition for reversal, defendants have formulated the following: "It is the duty of the court in considering an application of equitable power by injunction to take into account the question of comparative injury." Having called our attention to evidence showing previous disposition, by trial or settlement, of two actions for damages to two of the same home properties, around which plaintiffs built their case for an injunction here, and to the conflict between plaintiffs' and defendants' evidence as to the volume of noise, and intensity of vibrations, from blasting at the quarry, defendants . . . cite the following quotation from City of Harrisonville v. W. S. Dickey Clay Mfg. Co., 289 U.S. 334, 53 S. Ct. 602, 77 L. Ed. 1208, 1211:

". . . Where substantial redress can be afforded by the payment of money and issuance of an injunction would subject the defendant to grossly disproportionate hardship, equitable relief may be denied although the nuisance is indisputable. This is true even if the conflict is between interests which are primarily private. . . ."

Apparently in support of the argument that the losses to be suffered by defendants by cessation of the quarry's operations will be so great in comparison with the (presumably) lesser injuries plaintiffs will suffer from a continuation of same, that the trial court should not have ordered cessation, defendants refer to the testimony of C.S.C.'s President, and principal stockholder, Harold D. Youngman, that the value of the quarry, and his company's rock crusher, is "well over $300,000.00," and that the plant has employed 23 or 24 persons, with a total annual payroll of $140,000. They also cite testimony to the effect that, when, after the first hearing, the court (as hereinbefore indicated) continued the trial to enable C.S.C. to attempt to reduce the blowing of dust from its operations, said company "greatly reduced . . . the dust and noise problem" by installing "washers," and by watering the road leading in and out of the plant. . . .

While we recognize that in proper cases, especially those involving businesses upon which the public's interest, or necessity, depends, the matter of "comparative injury" should be given prominent consideration, this court is among those holding that where damages in an action at law will not give plaintiffs an adequate remedy against a business operated in such a way that it has become a nuisance, and such operation causes plaintiffs substantial and irremediable injury, they are entitled, as a matter of right, to have same abated, by injunction ". . . notwithstanding the comparative benefits conferred thereby or the comparative injury resulting therefrom." See Kenyon v. Edmundson, 80 Okl. 3, 193 P. 739, and other cases cited in the Annotations at 61 A.L.R. 924, 927ff. In the present case, through the trial judge's patience, thoroughness, and evident desire to be fair, and avoid unnecessary hardship to defendants, he afforded ample opportunity for a determination of whether C.S.C.'s quarry operations could be continued in such a way that they might be reasonably tolerated. His subsequent judgment determining, in effect, that they could not, cannot be said to be clearly against the weight of the evidence, nor contrary to law.

As its second, and last proposition, defendants assert: "Persons who live near a lawful business operation, or who moved into such a neighborhood, must necessarily submit to the noise, annoyances and discomforts incident to a proper and ordinary conduct of such business."

From the decisions defendants cite under the above quoted proposition, they seek application to this case of some one, or more, of the principles that have been applied by some courts to cases where plaintiffs had previously bought, or moved into, a residence near the business, whose operation they sought to enjoin. One of the cases refers to the basis of refusing such party's injunctive relief, as "the doctrine of coming to a nuisance." Inherent in such doctrine—and one of its necessary elements—is the plaintiff's knowledge, or notice, that the objectionable business operation was there, when he moved near it, and thus potentially, at least, subjected himself to the condition, or conditions, complained of. The proof establishes without contradiction that all of the plaintiffs, about which there is any evidence on that subject, acquired their homes either before (as far as the record shows) there was any identified operation of the quarry, or during a period in which it was lying dormant, or apparently abandoned, except Carl and Mrs. (Mildred) Smeltzer. Mr. Smeltzer testified that he knew the location of the C.S.C.'s rock crusher before he and his wife purchased their 5-acre tract, about September, 1958. Mrs. Smeltzer testified that, at that time, she didn't know of the crusher and that, because of the wooded area between the two, it could not be seen from their house. She testified that when she and her husband looked at the property, before purchasing same, it was raining, or had been raining, or had been raining so recently that the dust had washed off of the foliage and things.

We do not think the latter evidence is sufficient to render the trial court's judgment erroneous. To hold otherwise would be tantamount to holding that, because of the operation of the quarry before, and at the time, the Smeltzers acquired their property, defendants could restrict its future uses. . . .

After having carefully examined the record, and applied to the evidence therein, the principles approvingly referred to above, we are not convinced that any of defendants' arguments demonstrate substantial ground for reversing the judgment appealed from herein. Said judgment is therefore affirmed.

Boomer v. Atlantic Cement Co.

26 N.Y.2d 219, 257 N.E.2d 870, 309 N.Y.S.2d 312 (1970)

BERGAN, J. Defendant operates a large cement plant near Albany. These are actions for injunction and damages by neighboring land owners alleging injury to property from dirt, smoke and vibration emanating from the plant.

A nuisance has been found after trial, temporary damages have been allowed; but an injunction has been denied.

The public concern with air pollution arising from many sources in industry and in transportation is currently accorded ever wider recognition accompanied by a growing sense of responsibility in State and Federal Governments to control it. Cement plants are obvious sources of air pollution in the neighborhoods where they operate.

But there is now before the court private litigation in which individual property owners have sought specific relief from a single plant operation. The threshold question raised by the division of view on this appeal is whether the court should resolve the litigation between the parties now before it as equitably as seems possible; or whether, seeking promotion of the general public welfare, it should channel private litigation into broad public objectives.

A court performs its essential function when it decides the rights of parties before it. Its decision of private controversies may sometimes greatly affect public issues. Large questions of law are often resolved by the manner in which private litigation is decided. But this is normally an incident to the court's main function to settle controversy. It is a rare exercise of judicial power to use a decision in private litigation as a purposeful mechanism to achieve direct public objectives greatly beyond the rights and interests before the court.

Effective control of air pollution is a problem presently far from solution even with the full public and financial powers of government. In large measure adequate technical procedures are yet to be developed and some that appear possible may be economically impracticable.

It seems apparent that the amelioration of air pollution will depend on technical research in great depth; on a carefully balanced consideration of the economic impact of close regulation; and of the actual effect on public health. It is likely to require massive public expenditure and to demand more than any local community can accomplish and to depend on regional and interstate controls.

A court should not try to do this on its own as a by-product of private litigation and it seems manifest that the judicial establishment is neither equipped in the limited nature of any judgment it can pronounce nor prepared to lay down and implement an effective policy for the elimination of air pollution. This is an area beyond the circumference of one private lawsuit. It is a direct responsibility for government and should not thus be undertaken as an incident to solving a dispute between property owners and a single cement plant—one of many—in the Hudson River valley.

The cement making operations of defendant have been found by the court at Special Term to have damaged the nearby properties of plaintiffs in these two actions. That court, as it has been noted, accordingly found defendant maintained a nuisance and this has been affirmed at the Appellate Division.

The total damage to plaintiffs' properties is, however, relatively small in comparison with the value of defendant's operation and with the consequences of the injunction which plaintiffs seek.

The ground for the denial of injunction, notwithstanding the finding both that there is a nuisance and that plaintiffs have been damaged substantially, is the large disparity in economic consequences of the nuisance and of the injunction. This theory cannot, however, be sustained without overruling a doctrine which has been consistently reaffirmed in several leading cases in this court and which has never been disavowed here, namely that where a nuisance has been found and where there has been any substantial damage shown by the party complaining an injunction will be granted.

The rule in New York has been that such a nuisance will be enjoined although marked disparity be shown in economic consequence between the effect of the injunction and the effect of the nuisance.

The problem of disparity in economic consequence was sharply in focus in Whalen v. Union Bag & Paper Co. (208 N.Y. 1). A pulp mill entailing an investment of more than a million dollars polluted a stream in which plaintiff, who owned a farm, was "a lower riparian owner." The economic loss to plaintiff from this pollution was small. This court, reversing the Appellate Division, reinstated the injunction granted by the Special Term against the argument of the mill owner that in view of "the slight advantage to plaintiff and the great loss that will be inflicted on defendant" an injunction should not be granted (p. 2). "Such a balancing of injuries cannot be justified by the circumstances of this case," Judge Werner noted (p. 4). He continued: "Although the damage to the plaintiff may be slight as compared with the defendant's expense of abating the condition, that is not a good reason for refusing an injunction" (p. 5).

Thus the unconditional injunction granted at Special Term was reinstated. The rule laid down in that case, then, is that whenever the damage resulting from a nuisance is found not "unsubstantial," viz., $100 a year, injunction would follow. This states a rule that had been followed in this court with marked consistency.

[The court refers to several cases where injunctions have been denied, but explains that the damage shown by plaintiffs in those cases "was not only insubstantial, it was nonexistent."]

Although the court at Special Term and the Appellate Division held that injunction should be denied, it was found the plaintiffs had been damaged in various specific amounts up to the time of the trial and damages to the respective plaintiffs were awarded for those amounts. The effect of this was, injunction having been denied, plaintiffs could maintain successive actions at law for damages thereafter as further damage was incurred.

The court at Special Term also found the amount of permanent damage attributable to each plaintiff, for the guidance of the parties in the event both sides stipulated to the payment and acceptance of such permanent damage as a settlement of all the controversies among the parties. The total of permanent damages to all plaintiffs thus found was $185,000. This basis of adjustment has not resulted in any stipulation by the parties.

This result at Special Term and at the Appellate Division is a departure from a rule that has become settled; but to follow the rule literally in these cases would be to close down the plant at once. This court is fully agreed to avoid that immediately drastic remedy; the difference in view is how best to avoid it.[6]

One alternative is to grant the injunction but postpone its effect to a specified future date to give opportunity for technical advances to permit defendant to eliminate the nuisance; another is to grant the injunction conditioned on the payment of permanent damages to plaintiffs which would compensate them for the total economic loss to their property present and future caused by defendant's operations. For reasons which will be developed the court chooses the latter alternative.

If the injunction were to be granted unless within a short period—e.g., 18 months—the nuisance be abated by improved methods, there would be no assurance that any significant technical improvement would occur.

The parties could settle this private litigation at any time if defendant paid enough money and the imminent threat of closing the plant would build up the pressure on defendant. If there were no improved techniques found, there would inevitably be applications to the court at Special Term for extensions of time to perform on showing of good faith efforts to find such techniques.

Moreover, techniques to eliminate dust and other annoying by-products of cement making are unlikely to be developed by any research the defendant can undertake within any short period, but will depend on the total resources of the cement industry nationwide and throughout the world. The problem is universal wherever cement is made.

For obvious reasons the rate of the research is beyond control of defendant. If at the end of 18 months the whole industry has not found a technical solution a court would be hard put to close down this one cement plant if due regard be given to equitable principles.

On the other hand, to grant the injunction unless defendant pays plaintiffs such permanent damages as may be fixed by the court seems to do justice between the contending parties. All of the attributions of economic loss to the properties on which plaintiffs' complaints are based will have been redressed.

The nuisance complained of by these plaintiffs may have other public or private consequences, but these particular parties are the only ones who have sought remedies and the judgment proposed will fully redress them. The limitation of relief granted is a limitation only within the four corners

6. Respondent's investment in the plant is in excess of $45,000,000. There are over 300 people employed there.

of these actions and does not foreclose public health or other public agencies from seeking proper relief in a proper court.

It seems reasonable to think that the risk of being required to pay permanent damages to injured property owners by cement plant owners would itself be a reasonably effective spur to research for improved techniques to minimize nuisance.

The power of the court to condition on equitable grounds the continuance of an injunction on the payment of permanent damages seems undoubted.

[The discussion of authority for permanent damages is omitted.]

Thus it seems fair to both sides to grant permanent damages to plaintiffs which will terminate this private litigation. The theory of damage is the "servitude on land" of plaintiffs imposed by defendant's nuisance. (See United States v. Causby, 328 U.S. 256, 261, 262, 267, where the term "servitude" addressed to the land was used by Justice Douglas relating to the effect of airplane noise on property near an airport.)

The judgment, by allowance of permanent damages imposing a servitude on land, which is the basis of the actions, would preclude future recovery by plaintiffs or their grantees.

This should be placed beyond debate by a provision of the judgment that the payment by defendant and the acceptance by plaintiffs of permanent damages found by the court shall be in compensation for a servitude on the land.

Although the Trial Term has found permanent damages as a possible basis of settlement of the litigation, on remission the court should be entirely free to re-examine this subject. It may again find the permanent damage already found; or make new findings.

The orders should be reversed, without costs, and the cases remitted to Supreme Court, Albany County to grant an injunction which shall be vacated upon payment by defendant of such amounts of permanent damage to the respective plaintiffs as shall for this purpose be determined by the court.

JASEN, J. (dissenting). I agree with the majority that a reversal is required here, but I do not subscribe to the newly enunciated doctrine of assessment of permanent damages, in lieu of an injunction, where substantial property rights have been impaired by the creation of a nuisance.

It has long been the rule in this State, as the majority acknowledges, that a nuisance which results in substantial continuing damage to neighbors must be enjoined. To now change the rule to permit the cement company to continue polluting the air indefinitely upon the payment of permanent damages is, in my opinion, compounding the magnitude of a very serious problem in our State and Nation today.

In recognition of this problem, the Legislature of this State has enacted the Air Pollution Control Act (Public Health Law, §§1264-1299-m) declaring that it is the State policy to require the use of all available and reasonable methods to prevent and control air pollution (Public Health Law, §1265-m).

The harmful nature and widespread occurrence of air pollution have been extensively documented. Congressional hearings have revealed that air pollution causes substantial property damage, as well as being a contributing factor to a rising incidence of lung cancer, emphysema, bronchitis and asthma.

The specific problem faced here is known as particulate contamination because of the fine dust particles emanating from defendant's cement plant. The particular type of nuisance is not new, having appeared in many cases for at least the past 60 years. It is interesting to note that cement production has recently been identified as a significant source of particulate contamination in the Hudson Valley. This type of pollution, wherein very small particles escape and stay in the atmosphere, has been denominated as the type of air pollution which produces the greatest hazard to human health. We have thus a nuisance which not only is damaging to the plaintiffs, but also is decidedly harmful to the general public.

I see grave dangers in overruling our long-established rule of granting an injunction where a nuisance results in substantial continuing damage. In permitting the injunction to become inoperative upon the payment of permanent damages, the majority is, in effect, licensing a continuing wrong. It is the same as saying to the cement company, you may continue to do harm to your neighbors so long as you pay a fee for it. Furthermore, once such permanent damages are assessed and paid, the incentive to alleviate the wrong would be eliminated, thereby continuing air pollution of an area without abatement.

It is true that some courts have sanctioned the remedy here proposed by the majority in a number of cases, but none of the authorities relied upon by the majority are analogous to the situation before us. In those cases, the courts, in denying an injunction and awarding money damages, grounded their decision on a showing that the use to which the property was intended to be put was primarily for the public benefit. Here, on the other hand, it is clearly established that the cement company is creating a continuing air pollution nuisance primarily for its own private interest with no public benefit.

This kind of inverse condemnation may not be invoked by a private person or corporation for private gain or advantage. Inverse condemnation should only be permitted when the public is primarily served in the taking or impairment of property. The promotion of the interests of the polluting cement company has, in my opinion, no public use or benefit.

Nor is it constitutionally permissible to impose servitude on land, without consent of the owner, by payment of permanent damages where the continuing impairment of the land is for a private use. This is made clear by the State Constitution (art. I, §7, subd. [a]) which provides that "[p]rivate property shall not be taken for *public use* without just compensation" (emphasis added). It is, of course, significant that the section makes no mention of taking for a *private* use.

In sum, then, by constitutional mandate as well as by judicial pronouncement, the permanent impairment of private property for private purposes is not authorized in the absence of clearly demonstrated public benefit and use.

I would enjoin the defendant cement company from continuing the discharge of dust particles upon its neighbors' properties unless, within 18 months, the cement company abated this nuisance.

It is not my intention to cause the removal of the cement plant from the Albany area, but to recognize the urgency of the problem stemming from this stationary source of air pollution, and to allow the company a specified period of time to develop a means to alleviate this nuisance.

I am aware that the trial court found that the most modern dust control devices available have been installed in defendant's plant, but, I submit, this does not mean that *better* and more effective dust control devices could not be developed within the time allowed to abate the pollution.

Moreover, I believe it is incumbent upon the defendant to develop such devices, since the cement company, at the time the plant commenced production (1962), was well aware of the plaintiffs' presence in the area, as well as the probable consequences of its contemplated operation. Yet, it still chose to build and operate the plant at this site.

In a day when there is a growing concern for clean air, highly developed industry should not expect acquiescence by the courts, but should, instead, plan its operations to eliminate contamination of our air and damage to its neighbors.

Accordingly, the orders of the Appellate Division, insofar as they denied the injunction, should be reversed, and the actions remitted to Supreme Court, Albany County to grant an injunction to take effect 18 months hence, unless the nuisance is abated by improved techniques prior to said date.

CHIEF JUDGE FULD and JUDGES BURKE and SCILEPPI concur with JUDGE BERGAN; JUDGE JASEN dissents in part and votes to reverse in a separate opinion; JUDGES BREITEL and GIBSON taking no part.

In each action: Order reversed, without costs, and the case remitted to Supreme Court, Albany County, for further proceedings in accordance with the opinion herein.

The *Boomer* case has been the subject of extensive law review commentary. See, e.g., 43 U. Colo. L. Rev. 225 (1971); 19 Kan. L. Rev. 549 (1971); 49 N.C.L. Rev. 402 (1971); 21 Syracuse L. Rev. 1243 (1970). See also Annotations, 40 A.L.R. 3d 601 (1971); 82 A.L.R. 3d 1004 (1978); Symposium on Nuisance Law: Twenty Years after Boomer v. Atlantic Cement Co., 54 Alb. L. Rev. 171; 54 Alb. L. Rev. 189; 54 Alb. L. Rev. 301; 54 Alb. L. Rev. 359 (1990).

The flexibility of nuisance doctrine, as seen in *Boomer,* allows courts to tailor the remedy once they have determined the respective rights of the parties. If the complaining party is entitled to relief, the defendant's activity may be enjoined or the offending party may be subject to paying damages to the "victim."

A recent case enjoining the activity is Armory Park Neighborhood Assn. v. Episcopal Community Services in Arizona, 148 Ariz. 1, 712 P.2d 914 (1985), in which the residents' association sued to stop the community center from providing free meals to indigent persons, alleging that the indigents frequently trespassed, urinated, defecated, drank and littered on residents' property. Acknowledging the social utility of the center, the court noted that "even admirable ventures may cause unreasonable interferences." Id. at 8, 712 P.2d at 921. In Mayes v. Tabor, 77 N.C. App. 197, 334 S.E.2d 489 (1985), the court stated its view that the degree of unreasonableness of the defendant's conduct determines whether damages or permanent injunctive relief is the appropriate remedy for an intentional private nuisance. Injunctive relief requires proof that the defendant's conduct in trying to prevent the interference, rather than the interference itself, be unreasonable.

Professor Lewin has suggested a "comparative nuisance" theory that sees "nuisance" as a problem for both parties, as opposed to traditional doctrine that singles out one actor as the wrongdoer. Under comparative nuisance, the allocation of costs is based on the "relative responsibility" of each party. See Lewin, Comparative Nuisance, 50 U. Pitt. L. Rev. 1009 (1989).

Spur Industries, Inc. v. Del E. Webb Development Co.

108 Ariz. 178, 494 P.2d 700 (1972)

CAMERON, VICE C.J. From a judgment permanently enjoining the defendant, Spur Industries, Inc., from operating a cattle feedlot near the plaintiff Del. E. Webb Development Company's Sun City, Spur appeals, Webb cross-appeals. Although numerous issues are raised, we feel that it is necessary to answer only two questions. They are:

1. Where the operation of a business, such as a cattle feedlot is lawful in the first instance, but becomes a nuisance by reason of a nearby residential area, may the feedlot operation be enjoined in an action brought by the developer of the residential area?

2. Assuming that the nuisance may be enjoined, may the developer of a completely new town or urban area in a previously agricultural area be required to indemnify the operator of the feedlot who must move or cease operation because of the presence of the residential area created by the developer?

[The area involved in this suit is located 15 miles from Phoenix. It began to be used for farming in 1911. It was particularly well suited for cattle feeding, and in 1959 about 8,000 head of cattle were being fed on 35 acres. The defendant purchased these feedlots in 1960, and began expanding its feeding operations. By 1962, the defendant had acquired a total of 114 acres. In May of 1959, the plaintiff began to plan a housing development known as Sun City, and acquired 20,000 acres of ranch land near the cattle feedlots.]

Del Webb's suit complained that the Spur feeding operation was a public nuisance because of the flies and the odor which were drifting or being blown by the prevailing south to north wind over the southern portion of Sun City. At the time of the suit, Spur was feeding between 20,000 and 30,000 head of cattle, and the facts amply support the finding of the trial court that the feed pens had become a nuisance to the people who resided in the southern part of Del Webb's development. The testimony indicated that cattle in a commercial feedlot will produce 35 to 40 pounds of wet manure per day, per head, or over a million pounds of wet manure per day for 30,000 head of cattle, and that despite the admittedly good feedlot management and good housekeeping practices by Spur, the resulting odor and flies produced an annoying if not unhealthy situation as far as the senior citizens of southern Sun City were concerned. There is no doubt that some of the citizens of Sun City were unable to enjoy the outdoor living which Del Webb had advertised and that Del Webb was faced with sales resistance from prospective purchasers as well as strong and persistent complaints from the people who had purchased homes in that area. . . .

May Spur be Enjoined? . . .

It is clear that as to the citizens of Sun City, the operation of Spur's feedlot was both a public and a private nuisance. They could have successfully maintained an action to abate the nuisance. Del Webb, having shown a special injury in the loss of sales, had standing to bring suit to enjoin the nuisance. The judgment of the trial court permanently enjoining the operation of the feedlot is affirmed.

Must Del Webb Indemnify Spur?

A suit to enjoin a nuisance sounds in equity and the courts have long recognized a special responsibility to the public when acting as a court of equity. . . .

In addition to protecting the public interest, however, courts of equity are concerned with protecting the operator of a lawful, albeit noxious, business from the result of a knowing and willful encroachment by others near his business.

In the so-called "coming to the nuisance" cases, the courts have held that the residential landowner may not have relief if he knowingly came into a neighborhood reserved for industrial or agricultural endeavors and has been damaged thereby. . . . Were Webb the only party injured, we would feel justified in holding that the doctrine of "coming to the nuisance" would have been a bar to the relief asked by Webb, and, on the other hand, had Spur located the feedlot near the outskirts of a city and had the city grown toward the feedlot, Spur would have to suffer the cost of abating the nuisance as to those people locating within the growth pattern of the expanding city:

"The case affords, perhaps, an example where a business established at a place remote from population is gradually surrounded and becomes part of a populous center, so that a business which formerly was not an interference with the rights of others has become so by the encroachment of the population. . . ." City of Ft. Smith v. Western Hide & Fur Co., 153 Ark. 99, 103, 239 S.W. 724, 726 (1922).

We agree, however, with the Massachusetts court that:

"The law of nuisance affords no rigid rule to be applied in all instances. It is elastic. It undertakes to require only that which is fair and reasonable under all the circumstances. In a commonwealth like this, which depends for its material prosperity so largely on the continued growth and enlargement of manufacturing of diverse varieties, 'extreme rights' cannot be enforced. . . ." Stevens v. Rockport Granite Co., 216 Mass. 486, 488, 104 N.E. 371, 373 (1914).

There was no indication in the instant case at the time Spur and its predecessors located in western Maricopa County that a new city would spring up, full-blown, alongside the feeding operation and that the developer of that city would ask the court to order Spur to move because of the new city. Spur is required to move not because of any wrongdoing on the part of Spur, but because of a proper and legitimate regard of the courts for the rights and interests of the public.

Del Webb, on the other hand, is entitled to the relief prayed for (a permanent injunction), not because Webb is blameless, but because of the damage to the people who have been encouraged to purchase homes in Sun City. It does not equitably or legally follow, however, that Webb being entitled to the injunction, is then free of any liability to Spur if Webb has in fact been the cause of the damage Spur has sustained. It does not seem harsh to require a developer, who has taken advantage of the lesser land values in a rural area as well as the availability of large tracts of land on which to build and develop a new town or city in the area, to indemnify those who are forced to leave as a result.

Having brought people to the nuisance to the foreseeable detriment of Spur, Webb must indemnify Spur for a reasonable amount of the cost of moving or shutting down. It should be noted that this relief to Spur is limited to a case wherein a developer has, with foreseeability, brought into a previously agricultural or industrial area the population which makes necessary the granting of an injunction against a lawful business and for which the business has no adequate relief.

It is therefore the decision of this court that the matter be remanded to the trial court for a hearing upon the damages sustained by the defendant Spur as a reasonable and direct result of the granting of the permanent injunction. Since the result of the appeal may appear novel and both sides have obtained a measure of relief, it is ordered that each side will bear its own costs.

Affirmed in part, reversed in part, and remanded for further proceedings consistent with this opinion.

HAYS, C.J., STRUCKMEYER and LOCKWOOD, JJ., and UDALL, RETIRED JUSTICE.

The remedy given in *Spur* is uncommon, and courts have been reluctant to follow this innovative approach. See Reynolds, Of Time and Feedlots, 41 Wash. U. J. Urb. & Contemp. L. 75 (1992) (arguing that unique remedy in *Spur* be given only in very similar cases).

The court's dictum that the plaintiff might have been barred by the doctrine of "coming to the nuisance" had its interests been at stake to the exclusion of those of the residents of Sun City suggests a "first come, first served" approach to nuisance law. While the priority of use may be relevant, it is not dispositive, as the *Crushed Stone* case (p. 520) suggests. See also §840D of the Restatement (Second) of Torts. The doctrine is discussed in Rabin, Nuisance Law: Rethinking Fundamental Assumptions, 63 Va. L. Rev. 1299 (1977). Professor Rabin's principal concern in this article is with the range of remedies available in nuisance actions, and he approves the unique approach taken by the court in *Spur Industries* in this respect. See also Polinsky, Resolving Nuisance Disputes: The Simple Economics of Injunctive and Damage Remedies, 32 Stan. L. Rev. 1075 (1980) and Wittman, First Come, First Served: An Economic Analysis of "Coming to the Nuisance," 9 J. Legal Stud. 557 (1980).

"Right to Farm" statutes, designed to protect farms from nuisance actions, may make a coming to the nuisance defense dispositive in some instances. Often, residential developments grow up around farms in formerly rural areas, making farming incompatible with the changed character of the neighborhood. A "right to farm" statute insulates the farm from nuisance liability in these situations. See N.C. Gen. Stat. §106-701 (1988 & Supp. 1992) (agricultural operation not a nuisance when it was commenced will not become a nuisance due to "changed conditions"). See also Burgess-Jackson, 9 Harv. J.L. & Pub. Poly. 481 (1986) (appendix) (listing of the 47 states that have right to farm statutes).

Chapter 6

Strict Liability

As we saw in Chapter 4, a defendant is liable under negligence for causing another to suffer harm only if the defendant's conduct is determined to be negligent. If, however, the defendant behaved reasonably and harm to another nevertheless resulted, recovery is denied. In such cases, the *residual accident costs* generated by the defendant's activities remain with the plaintiff who, absent insurance, charity, or some other form of relief, must bear those losses personally. In contrast to negligence, strict liability makes no distinction based on the presence or absence of fault on the part of the defendant. Instead, under strict liability an actor whose conduct proximately causes harm to another is liable regardless of whether reasonable, or, indeed, even extraordinary, care was exercised. Thus, as used in this chapter, strict liability equals *liability without fault* for harm proximately caused by certain categories of conduct.[1] Those categories are now examined.

A. *Animals*

The common law developed a complex set of rules dealing with harm caused by animals. These rules distinguished, among other things, between property damage caused by the trespass of livestock and other harms caused by animals. With respect to the former, the common law mirrored traditional trespass rules and held livestock owners strictly liable for harm caused to real property by wandering livestock. Section 504 of the Restatement (Second) of Torts essentially adopts the common law position, providing that "a possessor of livestock which intrude upon the land of another is liable for their intrusion and for any harm done while upon the land . . . although the possessor of the livestock exercised the utmost care to prevent them from intruding." In some states, this rule is modified to the extent that landowners cannot recover for harm caused by wandering livestock unless they have protected their property with appropriate fencing.

1. Courts and commentators sometimes use the phrase *absolute liability,* and distinguish it from *strict liability.* The former phrase has several different meanings, depending on the context. Sometimes it means that the defendant is liable for certain bad outcomes even if the actor did not proximately cause them. When used in this way, *absolute liability* is synonymous with *insurer's liability.* In products liability, which is dealt with in Chapter 7, *absolute liability* is sometimes used to suggest liability caused by defendant's products whether or not defective.

It should be observed that these rules apply only to *livestock,* which includes, according to Comment *a* of §504, "those kinds of domestic animals and fowls which are normally susceptible of confinement within boundaries without seriously impairing their utility and the intrusion of which upon the land of others normally causes harm to the land or to crops thereon." Wild, undomesticated animals are clearly not included in the livestock category. Neither are dogs and cats that, although domesticated, are difficult to restrain and unlikely to do substantial harm to the land or crops of others.

With respect to both wild animals and domesticated animals other than livestock, the common law rules are somewhat more complicated, but they retain strong elements of strict liability. Thus, although wild animals are not "livestock" under §504 of the Restatement, owners and possessors of wild animals are strictly liable for harm, including personal injuries, caused by their animals' escape. The general rule is set forth in §507 of the Restatement. The leading English decision imposing strict liability upon the owners and possessors of wild animals is Filburn v. People's Palace & Aquarium, Ltd., 25 Q.B. Div. 258 (1890). The plaintiff in that case had been attacked by an elephant owned by the defendants and exhibited publicly by them. Although the jury specifically found that the defendants did not know that the elephant was dangerous, the trial court entered judgment for the plaintiff. The Court of Appeal affirmed, Lord Esher explaining in his opinion (25 Q.B. Div. at 260):

> Unless an animal . . . is shown to be either harmless by its very nature, or to belong to a class that has become so by what may be called cultivation—it falls within the class of animals as to which the rule is that a man who keeps one must take the responsibility of keeping it safe. It cannot possibly be said that an elephant comes within the class of animals known to be harmless by nature, or within that shewn by experience to be harmless in this country, and consequently it falls within the class of animals that a man keeps at his peril, and which he must prevent from doing injury under any circumstances, unless the person to whom the injury is done brings it on himself. It was, therefore, immaterial in this case whether the particular animal was a dangerous one, or whether the defendants had any knowledge that it was so.

The strict liability rule in the *Filburn* case is widely followed in the United States today. The major exception is for public zookeepers, who are generally liable only for their negligence in keeping wild animals. Thus, a Colorado court applied negligence principles in a case brought by a plaintiff whose finger had been bitten off by a zebra at the Denver Zoo. See Kennedy v. City and County of Denver, 506 P.2d 764 (Colo. App. 1972). When the zoo is privately owned and operated for profit, however, strict liability may be imposed. See Isaacs v. Powell, 267 So. 2d 864 (Fla. App. 1972), in which the two-year-old plaintiff was injured when a chimpanzee attacked him through the bars of its cage at defendants' monkey farm, a well-known tourist attraction. The court of appeals reversed a verdict and judgment for the defendant on the grounds that the trial court erred in limiting the defendant's liability to negligence (267 So. 2d at 865-866):

> [W]e are of the view that the older and general rule of strict liability, which obviates the issue of the owner's negligence, is more suited to the fast growing populous and activity-oriented society of Florida. Indeed, our society imposes more than enough risks upon its members now, and we are reluctant to encourage the addition of one more, particularly when that one more is increasingly contributed by those who, for profit, would exercise their "right" to harbor wild animals and increase exposure to the dangers thereof by alluring advertising.

What if, instead of a vicious zebra or chimpanzee, the defendant owns a vicious dog that bites off the finger of a visitor? The general rule in this country is that the owner of a domestic animal will be liable to injured persons if, but only if, the owner knows of the vicious tendencies of the animal. This rule is set forth in Restatement (Second) §509:

> §509. HARM DONE BY ABNORMALLY DANGEROUS DOMESTIC ANIMALS
>
> (1) A possessor of a domestic animal which he knows or has reason to know has dangerous propensities abnormal to its class, is subject to liability for harm done by the animal to others, although he has exercised the utmost care to prevent it from doing the harm.
>
> (2) Such liability is limited to harm which results from the abnormal dangerous propensity of which the possessor knows or has reason to know.

In cases to which this section applies, the most important issue is likely to be the one of prior knowledge—that is, did the defendant know or have reason to know that the animal was vicious? The greatest percentage of such cases involve dogs. When the defendant's dog bites the plaintiff, must the plaintiff show that the dog has previously bitten others? The popular adage, "Every dog deserves one bite," suggests that the plaintiff must show prior attacks in order to establish liability. But are there not some situations in which, even absent a first bite, a dog's owner should be aware of the dog's dangerous propensities? For example, should a harmed plaintiff be able to invoke strict liability against the owner of a dog that has been trained to attack others, or that belongs to a notoriously vicious breed? Cf. Colorado Dog Fanciers, Inc. v. City and County of Denver, 820 P.2d 644 (Colo. 1991) (rejecting constitutional challenges to municipal ordinance prohibiting ownership of pit bull terriers).

In many states, the liability of dog owners is expressly covered by statute. Many of these statutes change the common law rule and impose liability irrespective of the owner's prior knowledge of the dog's viciousness. The Michigan statute, Mich. Comp. Laws Ann. §287.351 (Mich. Stat. Ann. §12.544), is fairly typical:

> The owner of any dog which shall without provocation bite any person while such person is on or in a public place, or lawfully on or in a private place, including the property of the owner of such dog, shall be liable for such damages as may be suffered by the person bitten, regardless of the former viciousness of such dog or the owner's knowledge of such viciousness.

These statutes holding dog owners strictly liable are reminiscent of the statutes considered in Chapter 1, p. 20, holding parents strictly liable for the actions of their minor children, except that in this context the owners are not being held "vicariously" liable because their animals are incapable of performing legal acts. In substance, however, both types of statutes impose strict liability in the sense that the defendants are held liable irrespective of fault on their parts. Moreover, even in situations where neither common law nor statute imposes strict liability, owners of domestic animals can still be held liable in negligence for failing to exercise reasonable control over their animals. See, e.g., Ryman v. Alt, 266 N.W.2d 504 (Minn. 1978); Westberry v. Blackwell, 282 Or. 129, 577 P.2d 75 (1978).

B. *Abnormally Dangerous Activities*

Fletcher v. Rylands

L.R. 1 Exch. 265 (1866)

[This action was originally tried at the Liverpool Summer Assizes in 1862, and resulted in a verdict for the plaintiff. An arbitrator, appointed to assess damages, was later empowered by court order to state a special case in the Exchequer for the purpose of obtaining that court's opinion on the novel question of law presented. In the Exchequer, two judges voted for the defendants and one for the plaintiff, and judgment was entered for the defendants. The plaintiff appealed to the next higher court, the Exchequer Chamber, the decision of which follows.]

BLACKBURN, J. This was a special case stated by an arbitrator, under an order of nisi prius, in which the question for the Court is stated to be, whether the plaintiff is entitled to recover any, and, if any, what damages from the defendants, by reason of the matters thereinbefore stated.

In the Court of Exchequer, the Chief Baron and Martin, B., were of opinion that the plaintiff was not entitled to recover at all, Bramwell, B., being of a different opinion. The judgment in the Exchequer was consequently given for the defendants, in conformity with the opinion of the majority of the court. The only question argued before us was, whether this judgment was right, nothing being said about the measure of damages in case the plaintiff should be held entitled to recover. We have come to the conclusion that the opinion of Bramwell, B., was right, and that the answer to the question should be that the plaintiff was entitled to recover damages from the defendants, by reason of the matters stated in the case, and consequently, that the judgment below should be reversed, but we cannot at present say to what damages the plaintiff is entitled.

It appears from the statement in the case, that the plaintiff was damaged by his property being flooded by water, which, without any fault on his part, broke out of a reservoir constructed on the defendants' land by the defendants' orders, and maintained by the defendants.

It appears from the statement in the case that the coal under the defendants' land had, at some remote period, been worked out; but this was unknown at the time when the defendants gave directions to erect the reservoir, and the water in the reservoir would not have escaped from the defendants' land, and no mischief would have been done to the plaintiff, but for this latent defect in the defendants' subsoil. And it further appears, that the defendants selected competent engineers and contractors to make their reservoir, and themselves personally continued in total ignorance of what we have called the latent defect in the subsoil; but that these persons employed by them in the course of the work became aware of the existence of the ancient shafts filled up with soil, though they did not know or suspect that they were shafts communicating with old workings.

It is found that the defendants, personally, were free from all blame, but that in fact proper care and skill was not used by the persons employed by them, to provide for the sufficiency of the reservoir with reference to these shafts. The consequence was, that the reservoir when filled with water burst into the shafts, the water flowed down through them into the old workings, and thence into the plaintiff's mine, and there did the mischief.

The plaintiff, though free from all blame on his part, must bear the loss, unless he can establish that it was the consequence of some default for which the defendants are responsible. The question of law therefore arises, what is the obligation which the law casts on a person who, like the defendants, lawfully brings on his land something which, though harmless whilst it remains there, will naturally do mischief if it escape[s] out of his land. It is agreed on all hands that he must take care to keep in that which he has brought on the land and keeps there, in order that it may not escape and damage his neighbours, but the question arises whether the duty which the law casts upon him, under such circumstances, is an absolute duty to keep it in at his peril, or is, as the majority of the Court of Exchequer have thought, merely a duty to take all reasonable and prudent precautions, in order to keep it in, but no more. If the first be the law, the person who has brought on his land and kept there something dangerous, and failed to keep it in, is responsible for all the natural consequences of its escape. If the second be the limit of his duty, he would not be answerable except on proof of negligence, and consequently would not be answerable for escape arising from any latent defect which ordinary prudence and skill could not detect.

Supposing the second to be the correct view of the law, a further question arises subsidiary to the first, viz., whether the defendants are not so far identified with the contractors whom they employed, as to be responsible for the consequences of their want of care and skill in making the reservoir in fact insufficient with reference to the old shafts, or the existence of which they were aware, though they had not ascertained where the shafts went to.

We think that the true rule of law is, that the person who for his own purposes brings on his lands and collects and keeps there anything likely to do mischief if it escapes, must keep it in at his peril, and, if he does not do so, is prima facie answerable for all the damage which is the natural consequence of its escape. He can excuse himself by shewing that the escape was owing to the plaintiff's default; or perhaps that the escape was the consequence of vis major, or the act of God; but as nothing of this sort exists here, it is unnecessary to inquire what excuse would be sufficient. The general rule, as above stated, seems on principle just. The person whose grass or corn is eaten down by the escaping cattle of his neighbour, or whose mine is flooded by the water from his neighbour's reservoir, or whose cellar is invaded by the filth of his neighbour's privy, or whose habitation is made unhealthy by the fumes and noisome vapours of his neighbour's alkali works, is damnified without any fault of his own; and it seems but reasonable and just that the neighbour, who has brought something on his own property which was not naturally there, harmless to others so long as it is confined to his own property, but which he knows to be mischievous if it gets on his neighbour's, should be obliged to make good the damage which ensues if he does not succeed in confining it to his own property. But for his act in bringing it there no mischief could have accrued, and it seems but just that he should at his peril keep it there so that no mischief may accrue, or answer for the natural and anticipated consequences. And upon authority, this we think is established to be the law whether the things so brought be beasts, or water, or filth, or stenches.

The case that has most commonly occurred, and which is most frequently to be found in the books, is as to the obligation of the owner of cattle which he has brought on his land, to prevent their escaping and doing mischief. The law as to them seems to be perfectly settled from early times; the owner must keep them in at his peril, or he will be answerable for the natural consequences of their escape; that is with regard to tame beasts, for the grass they eat and trample upon, though not for any injury to the person of others, for our ancestors have settled that it is not the general nature of horses to kick, or bulls to gore; but if the owner knows that the beast has a vicious propensity to attack man, he will be answerable for that too. . . .

. . . But it was further said by Martin, B., [a majority judge in the Court of Exchequer] that when damage is done to personal property, or even to the person, by collision, either upon land or at sea, there must be negligence in the party doing the damage to render him legally responsible; and this is no doubt true, and as was pointed out by Mr. Mellish during his argument before us, this is not confined to cases of collision, for there are many cases in which proof of negligence is essential, as for instance, where an unruly horse gets on the footpath of a public street and kills a passenger; or where a person in a dock is struck by the falling of a bale of cotton which the defendant's servants are lowering; and many other similar cases may be found. But we think these cases distinguishable from the present. Traffic on the highways, whether by land or sea, cannot be conducted without exposing those whose persons or property are near it to some inevitable risk; and that being so, those who go on the highway, or have their property adjacent to it, may well be held to do so subject to their taking upon themselves the risk of injury from that inevitable danger; and persons who by the license of the owner pass near to warehouses where goods are being raised or lowered, certainly do so subject to the inevitable risk of accident. In neither case, therefore, can they recover without proof of want of care or skill occasioning the accident; and it is believed that all the cases in which inevitable accident has been held an excuse for what prima facie was a trespass, can be explained on the same principle, viz., that the circumstances were such as to shew that the plaintiff had taken that risk upon himself. But there is no ground for saying that the plaintiff here took upon himself any risk arising from the uses to which the defendants should choose to apply their land. He neither knew what these might be, nor could he in any way control the defendants, or hinder their building what reservoirs they liked, and storing up in them what water they pleased, so long as the defendants succeeded in preventing the water which they there brought from interfering with the plaintiff's property.

The view which we take of the first point renders it unnecessary to consider whether the defendants would or would not be responsible for the want of care and skill in the persons employed by them, under the circumstances stated in the case.

We are of the opinion that the plaintiff is entitled to recover, but as we have not heard any argument as to the amount, we are not able to give judgment for what damages. The parties probably will empower their counsel to agree on the amount of damages; should they differ on the principle, the case may be mentioned again.

Judgment for the plaintiff.

Rylands v. Fletcher

L.R. 3 H.L. 330 (1868)

THE LORD CHANCELLOR (Lord Cairns):. . . . My lords, the principles on which this case must be determined appear to me to be extremely simple. The Defendants, treating them as the owners or occupiers of the close on which the reservoir was constructed, might lawfully have used that close for any purpose for which it might in the ordinary course of the enjoyment of land be used; and if, in what I may term the natural user of that land, there had been any accumulation of water, either on the surface or underground, and if, by the operation of the laws of nature, that accumulation of water had passed off into the close occupied by the Plaintiff, the Plaintiff could not have complained. . . .

On the other hand if the Defendants, not stopping at the natural use of their close, had desired to use it for any purpose which I may term a nonnatural use, for the purpose of introducing into the close that which in its natural condition was not in or upon it, for the purpose of introducing water either above or below ground in quantities and in a manner not the result of any work or operation on or under the land,—and if in the consequence of their doing so, or in consequence of any imperfection in the mode of their doing so, the water came to escape and to pass off into the close of the Plaintiff, then it appears to me that that which the Defendants were doing they were doing at their own peril; and, if in the course of their doing it, the evil arose to which I have referred, the evil, namely, of the escape of the water and its passing away to the close of the Plaintiff and injuring the Plaintiff, then for the consequence of that, in my opinion, the Defendants would be liable. . . .

My Lords, these simple principles, if they are well founded, as it appears to me they are, really dispose of this case. . . .

Judgment of the Court of Exchequer Chamber affirmed.

Turner v. Big Lake Oil Co.

128 Tex. 155, 96 S.W.2d 221 (1936)

MR. CHIEF JUSTICE CURETON delivered the opinion of the court.

The primary question for determination here is whether or not the defendants in error, without negligence on their part, may be held liable in damages for the destruction or injury to property occasioned by the escape of salt water from ponds constructed and used by them in the operation of their oil wells. . . .

The defendants in error in the operation of certain oil wells in Reagan County constructed large artificial earthen ponds or pools into which they ran the polluted waters from the wells. On the occasion complained of, water escaped from one or more of these ponds, and, passing over the grass lands of the plaintiffs in error, injured the turf, and after entering Garrison draw flowed down the same into Centralia draw. In Garrison draw there were natural water holes, which supplied water for the livestock of plaintiffs in error. The pond, or ponds, of water from which the salt water escaped were, we judge from the map, some six miles from the stockwater holes to which we refer. The plaintiffs in error brought suit, basing their action on alleged neglect on the part of the defendants in error in permitting the levees and dams, etc., of their artificial ponds to break and overflow the land of plaintiffs in error, and thereby pollute the waters to which we have above referred and injure the turf in the pasture of plaintiffs in error. The question was submitted to a jury on special issues, and the jury answered that the defendants in error did permit salt water to overflow from their salt ponds and lakes down Garrison draw and on to the land of the plaintiffs in error. *However, the jury acquitted the defendants in error of negligence in the premises.* . . .

. . . [T]he immediate question presented is whether or not defendants in error are to be held liable as insurers, or whether the cause of action against them must be predicated upon negligence. We believe the question is one of first impression in this Court, and so we shall endeavor to discuss it in a manner in keeping with its importance.

Upon both reason and authority we believe that the conclusion of the Court of Civil Appeals that negligence is a prerequisite to recovery in a case of this character is a correct one. There is some difference of opinion on the subject in American jurisprudence brought about by differing views as to the correctness or applicability of the decision of the English courts in Rylands v. Fletcher, L.R. 3 H.L. 330. . . .

In Rylands v. Fletcher the Court predicated the absolute liability of the defendants on the proposition that the use of land for the artificial storage of water was not a natural use, and that, therefore, the land owner was bound at his peril to keep the waters on his own land. This basis of the English rule is to be found in the meteorological conditions which obtain there. England is a pluvial country, where constant streams and abundant rains make the storage of water unnecessary for ordinary or general purposes. When the Court said in Rylands v. Fletcher that the use of land for storage of water was an unnatural use, it meant such use was not a general or an ordinary one; not one within the contemplation of the parties to the original grant of the land involved, nor of the grantor and grantees of adjacent lands, but was a special or extraordinary use, and for that reason applied the rule of absolute liability. This conclusion is supported by the fact that those jurisdictions which adhere to the rule in Rylands v. Fletcher do not apply that rule to dams or reservoirs constructed in rivers and streams, which they say is a natural use, but apply the principle of negligence. In other words, the impounding of water in streamways, being an obvious and natural use, was necessarily within the contemplation of the parties to the original and adjacent grants, and damages must be predicated upon negligent use of a granted right and power; while things not within the contemplation of the parties to the original grants, such as unnatural uses of the land, the land owner may do only at his peril. As to what use of land is or may be a natural use, one within the contemplation of the parties to the original grant of land, necessarily depends upon the attendant circumstances and conditions which obtain in the territory of the original grants, or the initial terms of those grants.

In Texas we have conditions very different from those which obtain in

England. A large portion of Texas is an arid or semi-arid region. West of the 98th meridian of longitude, where the rainfall is approximately 30 inches, the rainfall decreases until finally, in the extreme western part of the State, it is only about 10 inches. This land of decreasing rainfall is the great ranch or livestock region of the State, water for which is stored in thousands of ponds, tanks, and lakes on the surface of the ground. The country is almost without streams; and without the storage of water from rainfall in basins constructed for the purpose, or to hold waters pumped from the earth, the great livestock industry of West Texas must perish. No such condition obtains in England. With us the storage of water is a natural or necessary and common use of the land, necessarily within the contemplation of the State and its grantees when grants were made, and obviously the rule announced in Rylands v. Fletcher, predicated upon different conditions, can have no application here.

Again, in England there are no oil wells, no necessity for using surface storage facilities for impounding and evaporating salt waters therefrom. In Texas the situation is different. Texas has many great oil fields, tens of thousands of wells in almost every part of the State. Producing oil is one of our major industries. One of the by-products of oil production is salt water, which must be disposed of without injury to property or the pollution of streams. The construction of basins or ponds to hold this salt water is a necessary part of the oil business. In Texas much of our land was granted without mineral reservation to the State, and where minerals were reserved, provision has usually been made for leasing and operating. It follows, therefore, that as to these grants and leases the right to mine in the usual and appropriate way, as, for example, by the construction and maintenance of salt water pools such as here involved, incident to the production of oil, were contemplated by the State and all its grantees and mineral lessees, that being a use of the surface incident and necessary to the right to produce oil. . . .

The judgments of the Court of Civil Appeals and of the District Court are affirmed.

In Atlas Chemical Industries, Inc. v. Anderson, 514 S.W.2d 309 (Tex. Civ. App. 1974), the Texas Court of Appeals reviewed a verdict and judgment for the plaintiff in a case involving the deliberate dumping by the defendant of industrial wastes on 60 acres of the plaintiff's land. The defendant conceded that the discharge was intentional, but claimed that it was not done with the intent to harm the plaintiff. The court of appeals affirmed the judgment for the plaintiff, concluding that strict liability will attach under Texas law whenever pollutants are intentionally discharged. The court explained (514 S.W.2d at 315-316):

> We recognize that the rule of law hereinabove set out by this court may be a departure from the rules heretofore established by our courts and may be in conflict with some of those decisions. However, we believe that the common law rules of tort liability in pollution cases arising out of the intentional discharge of pollutants should be in conformity with the public policy of this state as declared by the Legislature in the Texas Water Code, (1971). . . . Basically, the public policy is that the quality of water in this State shall be maintained free of pollution. . . . Texas Water Code, Sec. 21.003(11) states that " 'Pollution' means the alteration of the physical, thermal, chemical, or biological quality of, or the contamination of, any water in the state that renders the water harmful, detrimental, or injurious to humans, animal life, vegetation, or property, or to public health, safety, or welfare, or impairs the usefulness or the public enjoyment of the water for any lawful or reasonable purpose.". . .
>
> We further believe the public policy of this State to be that however laudable an industry may be, its owners or managers are still subject to the rule that its industry or its property cannot be so used as to inflict injury to the property of its neighbors. To allow industry to inflict injury to the property of its neighbors without just compensation amounts to inverse condemnation which is not permitted under our law. We know of no acceptable rule of jurisprudence which permits those engaged in important and desirable enterprises to injure with impunity those who are engaged in enterprises of lesser economic significance. The costs of injuries resulting from pollution must be internalized by industry as a cost of production and borne by consumers or shareholders, or both, and not by the injured individual.

Is the Texas court correct in its claim that "no acceptable rule of jurisprudence" allows actors to impose accident costs on others? What about the rule of negligence? In any event, liability for the discharge or release of hazardous substances is not always covered by strict liability. In Indiana Harbor Belt Co. v. American Cyanamid Co., 916 F.2d 1174 (7th Cir. 1990), the court rejected an effort to apply strict liability to the manufacturer and shipper of acrylonitrile, a flammable, highly toxic, and possibly carcinogenic chemical used in many manufacturing processes. The plaintiff, a company operating a railroad switching yard, brought suit against the defendant to recover almost a million dollars in decontamination costs it incurred when the acrylonitrile leaked from a railroad tank car. In rejecting the plaintiff's strict liability claim, the court noted (916 F.2d at 1178):

> Acrylonitrile is one of a large number of chemicals that are hazardous in the sense of being flammable, toxic, or both; acrylonitrile is both, as are many others. A table in the record . . . contains a list of the 125 hazardous materials that are shipped in highest volume on the nation's railroads. Acrylonitrile is the fifty-third most hazardous on the list. Number 1 is phosphorus (white or yellow), and among the other materials that rank higher than acrylonitrile on the hazard scale are anhydrous ammonia, liquified petroleum gas, vinyl chloride, gasoline, crude petroleum, motor fuel antiknock compound, methyl and

> ethyl chloride, sulphuric acid, sodium metal, and chloroform. The plaintiff's lawyer acknowledged at argument that the logic of [recognizing strict liability for acrylonitrile] dictated strict liability for all 52 materials that rank higher than acrylonitrile on the list, and quite possibly for the 72 that rank lower as well, since all are hazardous if spilled in quantity while being shipped by rail. Every shipper of any of these materials would therefore be strictly liable for the consequences of a spill or other accident that occurred while the material was being shipped. . . . No cases recognize so sweeping a liability. Several reject it, though none has facts much like those of the present case.

Finding precedent unhelpful, the court concluded that the application of strict liability was inappropriate, in part because there was "no reason . . . for believing that a negligence regime is not perfectly adequate to remedy and deter, at reasonable cost, the accidental spillage of acrylonitrile from railroad cars." Id. at 1179.

Siegler v. Kuhlman

81 Wash. 2d 448, 502 P.2d 1181 (1972)

HALE, J. Seventeen-year-old Carol J. House died in the flames of a gasoline explosion when her car encountered a pool of thousands of gallons of spilled gasoline. She was driving home from her after-school job in the early evening of November 22, 1967, along Capitol Lake Drive in Olympia; it was dark but dry; her car's headlamps were burning. There was a slight impact with some object, a muffled explosion, and then searing flames from gasoline pouring out of an overturned trailer tank engulfed her car. The result of the explosion is clear, but the real cause of what happened will remain something of an eternal mystery.

[Testimony revealed that on the night in question defendant Aaron Kuhlman was driving a gasoline truck and trailer unit, owned by co-defendant Pacific Inter-Mountain Express and fully loaded with gasoline, along a freeway in Olympia, Washington. Without warning, the trailer came loose from the truck, catapulted off the freeway and through a chain link fence, and landed upside down on Capitol Lake Drive. Moments later, the plaintiff's decedent drove into the gasoline, somehow ignited it, and perished in the flames. What caused the trailer to come loose, and the gasoline to ignite, is not revealed in the record. Plaintiff joined the driver, the owner and the manufacturer of the truck and trailer, seeking recovery on the bases of negligence and strict liability. The trial court refused the plaintiff's request for an instruction on res ipsa loquitur and strict liability, and the jury returned a verdict for defendants. From a judgment for defendants entered on the verdict, the plaintiff appealed. The intermediate court of appeals affirmed, 3 Wash. App. 231, 473 P.2d 445 (1970).]

In the Court of Appeals, the principal claim of error was directed to the trial court's refusal to give an instruction on res ipsa loquitur, and we think that claim of error well taken. Our reasons for ruling that an instruction on res ipsa loquitur should have been given and that an inference of negligence could have been drawn from the event are found, we believe, in our statements on the subject. . . . We think, therefore, that plaintiff was entitled to an instruction permitting the jury to infer negligence from the occurrence.

But there exists here an even more impelling basis for liability in this case than its derivation by allowable inference of fact under the res ipsa loquitur doctrine, and that is the proposition of strict liability arising as a matter of law from all of the circumstances of the event.

Strict liability is not a novel concept; it is at least as old as Fletcher v. Rylands, L.R. 1 Ex. 265, 278 (1866), *aff'd,* House of Lords, 3 H.L. 330 (1868). . . . The basic principles supporting the Fletcher doctrine, we think, control the transportation of gasoline as freight along the public highways the same as it does the impounding of waters and for largely the same reasons.

In many respects, hauling gasoline as freight is no more unusual, but more dangerous, than collecting water. When gasoline is carried as cargo—as distinguished from fuel for the carrier vehicle—it takes on uniquely hazardous characteristics, as does water impounded in large quantities. Dangerous in itself, gasoline develops even greater potential for harm when carried as freight—extraordinary dangers deriving from sheer quantity, bulk and weight, which enormously multiply its hazardous properties. And the very hazards inhering from the size of the load, its bulk or quantity and its movement along the highways presents another reason for application of the Fletcher v. Rylands, supra, rule not present in the impounding of large quantities of water—the likely destruction of cogent evidence from which negligence or want of it may be proved or disapproved. It is quite probable that the most important ingredients of proof will be lost in a gasoline explosion and fire. Gasoline is always dangerous whether kept in large or small quantities because of its volatility, inflammability and explosiveness. But when several thousand gallons of it are allowed to spill across a public highway—that is, if, while in transit as freight, it is not kept impounded—the hazards to third persons are so great as to be almost beyond calculation. As a consequence of its escape from impoundment and subsequent explosion and ignition, the evidence in a very high percentage of instances will be destroyed, and the reason for and causes contributing to its escape will quite likely be lost in the searing flames and explosions. . . .

Thus, the reasons for applying a rule of strict liability obtain in this case. We have a situation where a highly flammable, volatile and explosive substance is being carried at a comparatively high rate of speed, in great and dangerous quantities as cargo upon the public highways, subject to all of the hazards of high-speed traffic, multiplied by the great dangers inherent in the volatile and explosive nature of the substance, and multiplied again by the quantity and size of the load. Then we have the added dangers of ignition and explosion generated when a load of this size, that is, about 5,000 gallons of gasoline, breaks its container and, cascading from it, spreads over the highway so as to release an invisible but highly volatile and explosive vapor above it. . . .

The rule of strict liability, when applied to an abnormally dangerous activity, as stated in the Restatement (Second) of Torts §519 (Tent. Draft No. 10, 1964), was adopted as the rule of decision in this state in Pacific Northwest Bell Tel. Co. v. Port of Seattle, 80 Wash. 2d 59, 64, 491 P.2d 1037, 1039-1040 (1971), as follows:

> (1) One who carries on an abnormally dangerous activity is subject to liability for harm to the person, land or chattels of another resulting from the activity, although he has exercised the utmost care to prevent such harm.
> (2) Such strict liability is limited to the kind of harm, the risk of which makes the activity abnormally dangerous.

As to what constitutes an abnormal activity, section 520 states:

> In determining whether an activity is abnormally dangerous, the following factors are to be considered:
> (a) Whether the activity involves a high degree of risk of some harm to the person, land or chattels of others;
> (b) Whether the gravity of the harm which may result from it is likely to be great;
> (c) Whether the risk cannot be eliminated by the exercise of reasonable care;
> (d) Whether the activity is not a matter of common usage;
> (e) Whether the activity is inappropriate to the place where it is carried on; and
> (f) The value of the activity to the community.

. . . Transporting gasoline as freight by truck along the public highways and streets is obviously an activity involving a high degree of risk; it is a risk of great harm and injury; it creates dangers that cannot be eliminated by the exercise of reasonable care. That gasoline cannot be practicably transported except upon the public highways does not decrease the abnormally high risk arising from its transportation. Nor will the exercise of due and reasonable care assure protection to the public from the disastrous consequences of concealed or latent mechanical or metallurgical defects in the carrier's equipment, from the negligence of third parties, from latent defects in the highways and streets, and from all of the other hazards not generally disclosed or guarded against by reasonable care, prudence and foresight. Hauling gasoline in great quantities as freight, we think, is an activity that calls for the application of principles of strict liability.

The case is therefore reversed and remanded to the trial court for trial to the jury on the sole issue of damages.

HAMILTON, C.J., FINLEY, ROSELLINI, and HUNTER, JJ., and RYAN, J. PRO TEM., concur.

ROSELLINI, J. (concurring) I agree with the majority that the transporting of highly volatile and flammable substances upon the public highways in commercial quantities and for commercial purposes is an activity which carries with it such a great risk of harm to defenseless users of the highway, if it is not kept contained, that the common-law principles of strict liability should apply. In my opinion, a good reason to apply these principles, which is not mentioned in the majority opinion, is that the commercial transporter can spread the loss among his customers—who benefit from this extrahazardous use of the highways. Also, if the defect which caused the substance to escape was one of manufacture, the owner is in the best position to hold the manufacturer to account.

I think the opinion should make clear, however, that the owner of the vehicle will be held strictly liable only for damages caused when the flammable or explosive substance is allowed to escape without the apparent intervention of any outside force beyond the control of the manufacturer, the owner, or the operator of the vehicle hauling it. I do not think the majority means to suggest that if another vehicle, negligently driven, collided with the truck in question, the truck owner would be held liable for the damage. But where, as here, there was no outside force which caused the trailer to become detached from the truck, the rule of strict liability should apply. . . .

HAMILTON, C.J., FINLEY, J., and RYAN, J. PRO TEM., concur with ROSELLINI, J.

[The dissenting opinion of NEILL, J., is omitted.]

On the subject of strict liability for the transportation of hazardous substances see Note, Common Carriers and Risk Distribution: Absolute Liability for Transportation of Hazardous Materials, 67 Ky. L.J. 441 (1979); Note, Strict Liability for Generators, Transporters and Disposers of Hazardous Wastes, 64 Minn. L. Rev. 949 (1980).

In Oja & Assocs. v. Washington Park Towers, Inc., 89 Wash. 2d 72, 569 P.2d 1141 (1977), the Supreme Court of Washington affirmed a strict liability judgment based on property damage caused by pile-driving activities. But in Jennings Buick, Inc. v. City of Cincinnati, 56 Ohio St. 2d 459, 384 N.E.2d 303 (1978), the Supreme Court of Ohio refused to impose strict liability on the city when a 12-inch water main, controlled and maintained by the city, allowed water to escape causing damage to the plaintiff's property.

Not surprisingly, transporters and storers of explosives are frequently held strictly liable for harm caused by accidental explosions. Thus, in Chevez v. So. Pac. Transp. Co., 413 F. Supp. 1203 (E.D. Calif. 1976), a railroad was held strictly liable for the harm caused when 18 bomb-loaded boxcars exploded in the railroad's yard. The court refused to recognize an exception to the general rule of strict liability for ultrahazardous activities based on the fact that the railroad was authorized by law to transport the explosives. And in Yukon Equip., Inc. v. Fireman's Fund Ins. Co., 585 P.2d 1206 (Alaska 1978), the Supreme Court of Alaska imposed strict liability on the storers of explosives even when it was proven that the harmful explosion was deliberately caused by thieves who were attempting to prevent discovery of the fact that they had stolen some explosives. See also Klein v. Pyrodyne Corp., 117 Wash. 1, 810 P.2d 917 (1991) (fireworks company strictly liable for injuries caused by fireworks display).

In Kelley v. R.G. Industries, Inc., 304 Md. 2d 124, 497 A.2d 1143 (1985), the Maryland Court of Appeals became the first court of last resort to recognize a cause of action in products liability against the manufacturer of a small, inexpensive handgun, commonly known as a Saturday night special, when the victim was shot by a criminal who made use of this particular type of handgun. The court reasoned that those who market Saturday night specials know that they have no legitimate function other than to be used for the commission of a crime. The court was careful to point out that it was not finding that Saturday night specials were "unreasonably dangerous" within the meaning of §402A. Nor was it prepared to expand the category of abnormally dangerous activity under Restatement (Second) of Torts §§519-520 to include marketing dangerous handguns. Rather, the court said it was drawing on basic common law principles to impose liability for the sale of this particular product, which was manufactured and marketed for the sole purpose of facilitating crime. Other courts that have faced the question have refused to impose strict liability. See, e.g., Martin v. Harrington and Richardson, Inc., 743 F.2d 1200 (7th Cir. 1984); Richman v. Charter Arms Corp., 571 F. Supp. 192 (E.D. La. 1983), *rev'd sub nom.* Perkins v. F.I.E. Corp., 762 F.2d 1250 (5th Cir. 1985); Coulson v. DeAngelo, 493 So. 2d 98 (Fla. Dist. Ct. App. 1986); Linton v. Smith & Wesson, 127 Ill. App. 3d 676, 469 N.E.2d 339 (1984).

Law and Policy: Why Strict Liability?

As described in Chapter 4, pp. 186-189, the early common law flirted with both fault-based and strict liability concepts before adopting negligence as the dominant regime for American tort law. This choice was applauded by observers of tort law like Holmes, who viewed the imposition of liability without fault as violating basic notions of fairness and who, therefore, favored negligence's focus on the defendant's efforts to take reasonable care. See Holmes, The Common Law 77-96 (1881).

Given the supposed superiority of a negligence system, why have courts (and to some extent legislatures) embraced strict liability in scattered areas of tort law? More specifically, is strict liability in some sense "fairer," from a noninstrumental perspective, than negligence, at least in certain contexts? And from an instrumental, efficiency-oriented viewpoint, does strict liability offer advantages—in terms of minimizing socially wasteful accidents—over a negligence rule?

Beginning with the noninstrumental perspective, it is useful to reflect on the court's emphasis in *Rylands v. Fletcher* on the fact that the defendants had exposed the plaintiff to risks due to the defendants' "nonnatural use" of their land. Although the scope of the court's conception of "nonnatural uses" is far from clear, if we assume that the court was referring to activities that create unusual or uncommon risks to others, the outlines of a fairness argument for strict liability emerge. Recall that an earlier note (p. 28) offered an analysis by Professor George Fletcher in which tort liability is justified on fairness grounds when the defendant imposes unusual or nonreciprocal risks on the plaintiff. As Fletcher observes, the concept of nonreciprocal risks is especially relevant to the justification of strict liability (85 Harv. L. Rev. at 547-548):

> Expressing the standard of strict liability as unexcused, nonreciprocal risk-taking provides an account not only of the *Rylands* . . . decision, but of strict liability in general. It is apparent, for example, that . . . uncommon, ultrahazardous activities . . . are readily subsumed under the rationale of nonreciprocal risk-taking. If uncommon activities are those with few participants, they are likely to be activities generating nonreciprocal risks. Similarly, dangerous activities like blasting, fumigating, and crop dusting stand out as distinct, nonreciprocal risks in the community. They represent threats of harm that exceed the level of risk to which all members of the community contribute in roughly equal shares.
>
> The rationale of nonreciprocal risk-taking accounts as well for [other] pockets of strict liability. . . . For example, an individual is strictly liable for damage done by a wild animal in his charge, but not for damage committed by his domesticated pet. Most people have pets, children, or friends whose presence creates some risk to neighbors and their property. These are risks that offset each other; they are, as a class, reciprocal risks. Yet bringing an unruly horse into the city goes beyond the accepted and shared level of risks in having pets, children, and friends in one's household. If the defendant creates a risk that exceeds those to which he is reciprocally subject, it seems fair to hold him liable for the results of his aberrant indulgence. Similarly, according to the latest version of the Restatement, airplane owners and pilots are strictly liable for ground damage, but not for mid-air collisions. Risk of ground damage is nonreciprocal; homeowners do not create risks to airplanes flying overhead. The risks of mid-air collisions, on the other hand, are generated reciprocally by all those who fly the air lanes. Accordingly, the threshold of liability for damage resulting from mid-air collisions is higher than mere involvement in the activity of flying. To be liable for collision damage to

> another flyer, the pilot must fly negligently or the owner must maintain the plane negligently; they must generate abnormal risks of collision to the other planes aflight.

While Fletcher's focus on the unusual or imbalanced risk is useful in identifying some situations in which courts have imposed strict liability, its strength as a fairness justification for strict liability is more open to question. Why, for example, should a plaintiff be able to invoke strict liability simply because the plaintiff's injury occurred through the operation of an unusual risk? Fletcher's analysis suggests an answer similar to an inverse Golden Rule: "I didn't expose the defendant to such risks; the defendant shouldn't have exposed me to them." Indeed, Fletcher characterizes the creation of nonreciprocal risks as an "aberrant indulgence" that justifies strict liability on fairness grounds. While this may be true with respect to the keeping of panthers and pit bulls, many activities that are subject to strict liability—such as the gasoline transportation involved in *Siegler*—are economically important. Despite the fact that such activities generate asymmetrical risks in society, they are arguably more socially valuable than other risk-generating activities—such as dog-owning or Sunday driving—that typically are governed by negligence rules. In such cases, it is hard to see why the nonreciprocity of the risk, standing alone, should trigger strict liability.

Perhaps because of these problems, most theorists have sought to justify strict liability on instrumental rather than noninstrumental grounds. Indeed, the instinctive reaction of many beginning law students is that strict liability is better at deterring accident-producing behavior than negligence because, simply put, it is "more strict." But is this common assumption—that a rational actor will invest more in care under a strict liability rule than under a negligence rule—really true? The following hypothetical example will permit you to test the validity, at least in theory, of that assertion. Assume that a rational actor, *A*, is in a position to reduce the incidence of harm caused by its activity by investing in care. Assume that if *A* makes no effort to be careful, its activity will cause ten accidents per 100 units of the activity, at a constant expected cost of $1,000 per accident. Assume further that *A*'s investments in care reduce accidents according to Table 6-1, below. If the only costs associated with the activity are those included in Table 6-1, how far will *A*, aware of the data in the table, invest in care under a negligence rule perfectly and costlessly applied? How far under a rule of strict liability? See if you can answer this question using the data provided in the table; then fill in columns (6), (7), and (8) either to help reach the answer or to confirm its validity.

Perhaps surprisingly, this exercise reveals that, in theory at least, moving from negligence to strict liability will not cause actors to act any more carefully. Under negligence, actors will invest a socially optimal amount in accident avoidance. The costs of accidents that continue to occur even after such optimal investment—the "residual" losses not deemed worth

TABLE 6-1

Incremental Reduction in Activity-caused Accidents (Per 100 Units Activity)	(1) *Incremental (Marginal) Accident Cost Reduction (Per Unit of Care)*	(2) *Total Accident Cost Reduction (Cumulative)*	(3) *Total Remaining (Residual) Accident Costs (Per 100 Units Activity)*	(4) *Incremental (Marginal) Costs of Care (Per Unit Care)*	(5) *Total Costs of Care (Cumulative)*	(6) *Total Social Costs of Care and Accidents (Cumulative)*	(7) *Total Actor's Costs of Care and Liability Under Negligence (Cumulative)*	(8) *Total Actor's Costs of Care and Liability Under Strict Liability (Cumulative)*
10 → 9	1,000	1,000	9,000	100	100			
9 → 8	1,000	2,000	8,000	300	400			
8 → 7	1,000	3,000	7,000	700	1,100			
7 → 6	1,000	4,000	6,000	1,200	2,300			
6 → 5	1,000	5,000	5,000	1,900	4,200			
5 → 4	1,000	6,000	4,000	2,800	7,000			
4 → 3	1,000	7,000	3,000	5,400	12,400			
3 → 2	1,000	8,000	2,000	11,000	23,000			

Observe that this exercise builds on the one included in Section B of Chapter 4, above, (Problem 12, p. 207). If you already considered that problem, then you have already filled in columns (6) and (7), and your task here is to consider the implications of column (8) to your earlier analysis.

avoiding through further precautions—will remain on the victims of such accidents. But even if actors were held strictly liable for all accident losses, including such residual accident costs, they would not increase their investment in care. Instead, because the residual losses are, by hypothesis, cheaper to incur than to prevent, actors under strict liability will simply pay for such losses (through insurance, perhaps) rather than make the additional investments in safety necessary to avoid them.

If strict liability and negligence give actors identical incentives to invest in socially optimal levels of care, is there any reason, from an instrumental perspective, to prefer strict liability over negligence? There are several possible responses. First, despite their ability in theory to encourage the same optimal level of care, strict liability and negligence may vary in practice in the incentives they impose on harm-causing actors. Under negligence, a plaintiff must show not only that the defendant caused the harm, but also that the defendant's behavior was unreasonable. As the materials in Chapter 4 illustrate, this additional showing can be messy. If plaintiffs experience systematic problems in their efforts to establish fault on the part of defendants—perhaps because of the loss or unavailability of evidence—defendants as a class will experience insufficient levels of liability. In *Siegler*, for example, the court noted that the explosive nature of gasoline created a risk of "the likely destruction of cogent evidence from which negligence . . . may be proved or disproved." Strict liability redresses this potential deficiency in the process of proof by removing the issue of fault from the test for liability. In this sense, strict liability functions similarly to *res ipsa* in correcting perceived imbalances in the trial process.[2]

More importantly, from an instrumental perspective, holding an actor strictly liable for the residual losses caused by his activity may affect the actor's threshold decision of *whether*, and to what extent, to engage in the activity in the first place. As noted above, the actor's investment in care and the overall social costs of the activity, when it is engaged in, in theory will not change when the liability regime changes from negligence to strict liability. But the residual costs borne by accident victims under negligence

2. Of course, this analysis assumes that a negligence system is prone to systematic errors that favor defendants over plaintiffs, and therefore exposes defendants to levels of liability that are insufficient to encourage optimal investments in accident prevention. This assumption, however, is quite speculative. Some have argued that the opposite situation, in which the practical operation of the negligence system forces defendants to *over-invest* in accident avoidance, may be more descriptively accurate. For example, if defendants under a negligence regime experience systematic difficulties in determining ahead of time what amount of precaution constitutes reasonable care, they will tend to "err on the side of caution," that is, to over-invest in care. They will do so because a slight shortfall below what a court later determines to be adequate care will make the defendant liable for all the plaintiff's losses, while over-investment in care will insure that the defendant pays no accident losses. Under strict liability, in contrast, the defendant faces no such incentive to spend excessively on precaution because the defendant pays all accident costs regardless of the level of care adopted. A comparison of columns 7 and 8 in Table 6-1 reveals this difference between the two liability regimes. For more extensive analysis of this question, see Coffee & Craswell, Some Effects of Uncertainty on Compliance with Legal Standards, 70 Virg. L. Rev. 965 (1984).

will now be borne under strict liability by the ones making the decisions whether or not to engage in the particular activity. Some of these actors, who may have found the activity marginally profitable when victims bore the residual losses, presumably will conclude that the activity is no longer economically feasible now that they must bear those losses. Those decisions, of course, will depend on the aggregate, "all costs considered" profitability of the activity.

This "activity level" effect of strict liability is described by Judge Posner in Indiana Belt Harbor R.R. Co. v. Am. Cyanamid Co., 916 F.2d 1174, 1177 (7th Cir. 1990):

> The baseline common law regime of tort liability is negligence. When it is a workable regime, because the hazards of an activity can be avoided by being careful (which is to say, nonnegligent), there is no need to switch to strict liability. Sometimes, however, a particular type of accident cannot be prevented by taking care but can be avoided, or its consequences minimized, by shifting the activity in which the accident occurs to another locale, where the risk or harm of an accident will be less. . . , or by reducing the scale of the activity in order to minimize the number of accidents caused by it. . . . Shavell, Strict Liability versus Negligence, 9 J. Legal Stud. 1 (1980). By making the actor strictly liable—by denying him in other words an excuse based on his inability to avoid accidents by being more careful—we give him an incentive, missing in a negligence regime, to experiment with methods of preventing accidents that involve not greater exertions of care, assumed to be futile, but instead relocating, changing, or reducing (perhaps to the vanishing point) the activity giving rise to the accident. . . . The greater the risk of an accident . . . and the costs of an accident if one occurs . . . , the more we want the actor to consider the possibility of making accident-reducing activity changes; the stronger, therefore, is the case for strict liability. Finally, if an activity is extremely common, . . . like driving an automobile, it is unlikely either that its hazards are perceived as great or that there is no technology of care available to minimize them; so the case for strict liability is weakened.

To be sure, the negligence system itself could have accommodated such a result by labeling as "negligent" the threshold decision to engage in an activity whose residual losses exceeded its gains-net-of-all-other-costs. But for reasons we will not go into here, the negligence system has never chosen to grapple with such "macroefficiency" questions. Thus, it falls to strict liability to address the "whether to engage" question.

Of course, if one accepts either of these arguments—that strict liability improves the clarity of the deterrent signal actually produced by the torts process or that strict liability encourages actors to adopt optimal levels of activity—the title of this note may seem to require rewriting. Rather than asking what explains the adoption of strict liability, perhaps the more appropriate question is what justifies the retention of negligence in many areas of the law. It is unlikely that the practical problems inherent in proving negligence are restricted only to those areas where courts already have invoked strict liability. Moreover, controlling excessive levels of harm-causing activity would surely be beneficial in some areas, such as driving, that are often governed by negligence principles.

Not surprisingly, then, the perceived advantages of strict liability over negligence have led to calls for its application to practically every area of tort law. Yet, the widescale adoption of strict liability simply has not occurred. The reasons for limited spread of strict liability are complex and their detailed examination lies beyond the scope of this note. Briefly, however, they include the noninstrumental argument that it is generally unfair to impose liability on those who are acting reasonably; the problems of high administrative costs and excessive liability that arise in some areas if the test for liability is too simple; and the advantages of a negligence system in monitoring plaintiff behavior. For a sampling of the extensive writings on this question, see Landes and Posner, The Economic Structure of Tort Law 54-84 (1987); Jones, Strict Liability for Hazardous Enterprises, 92 Colum. L. Rev. 1705 (1992); Henderson and Twerski, Closing the American Products Liability Frontier: the Rejection of Liability without Defect, 66 N.Y.U. L. Rev. 1263 (1991).

Thus, the border between the two liability systems is not clearly established, and probably never will be. Each system offers an array of appealing justifications, both in instrumental and noninstrumental terms. The challenging and perhaps unending task of the torts system is to determine whether, in any given set of cases, the choice of one rule is preferable to the other.

Foster v. Preston Mill Co.

44 Wash. 2d 440, 268 P.2d 645 (1954)

HAMLEY, J. Blasting operations conducted by Preston Mill Company frightened mother mink owned by B. W. Foster, and caused the mink to kill their kittens. Foster brought this action against the company to recover damages. His second amended complaint, upon which the case was tried, sets forth a cause of action on the theory of absolute liability, and, in the alternative, a cause of action on the theory of nuisance.

After a trial to the court without a jury, judgment was rendered for plaintiff in the sum of $1,953.68. The theory adopted by the court was that, after defendant received notice of the effect which its blasting operations were having upon the mink, it was absolutely liable for all damages of that nature thereafter sustained. The trial court concluded that defendant's blasting did not constitute a public nuisance, but did not expressly rule on the question of private nuisance. Plaintiff concedes, however, that, in effect, the trial court decided in defendant's favor on the question of nuisance. Defendant appeals.

[The court describes the operation of the plaintiff's mink ranch, explaining that during the whelping season, which lasts several weeks, female mink are very excitable. The defendant had been engaged in a logging operation adjacent to the plaintiff's land for more than fifty years. They began the blasting in order to clear a path for a road, approximately two and one-quarter miles away from the ranch. The vibrations at the ranch excited the mother mink, who began killing their young. After the plaintiff told the defendant about the loss of mink kittens, the defendant reduced the strength of the dynamite charges, but continued blasting throughout the remainder of the whelping season. Defendant's experts testified that unless the road had been cleared, the logging operation would have been delayed and the company's log production disrupted, with attendant costs to the defendant company.]

In this action, respondent sought and recovered judgment only for such damages as were claimed to have been sustained as a result of blasting operations conducted after appellant received notice that its activity was causing loss of mink kittens.

The primary question presented by appellant's assignments of error is whether, on these facts, the judgment against appellant is sustainable on the theory of absolute liability.

The modern doctrine of strict liability for dangerous substances and activities stems from Justice Blackburn's decision in Rylands v. Fletcher. As applied to blasting operations, the doctrine has quite uniformly been held to establish liability, irrespective of negligence, for property damage sustained as result of casting rocks or other debris on adjoining or neighboring premises.

There is a division of judicial opinion as to whether the doctrine of absolute liability should apply where the damage from blasting is caused, not by the casting of rocks and debris, but by concussion, vibration, or jarring. This court has adopted the view that the doctrine applies in such cases. . . .

However the authorities may be divided on the point just discussed, they appear to be agreed that strict liability should be confined to consequences which lie within the extraordinary risk whose existence calls for such responsibility. This limitation on the doctrine is indicated in the italicized portion of the rule as set forth in Restatement of Torts, [§519]:

> Except as stated in §§521-4, one who carries on an ultra-hazardous activity is liable to another whose person, land or chattels the actor should recognize as likely to be harmed by the unpreventable miscarriage of the activity for harm resulting thereto *from that which makes the activity ultra-hazardous,* although the utmost care is exercised to prevent the harm. (Italics ours.)

This restriction which has been placed upon the application of the doctrine of absolute liability is based upon considerations of policy. As Professor Prosser has said:

> It is one thing to say that a dangerous enterprise must pay its way within reasonable limits, and quite another to say that it must bear responsibility for every extreme of harm that it may cause. The same practical necessity for the restriction of liability within some reasonable bounds, which arises in connection with problems of 'proximate cause' in negligence cases, demands here that some limit be set. . . . This limitation has been expressed by saying that the defendant's duty to insure safety extends only to certain consequences. More commonly, it is said that the defendant's conduct is not the 'proximate cause' of the damage. But ordinarily in such cases no question of causation is involved, and the limitation is one of the policy underlying liability. Prosser on Torts, 457, §60.

Applying this principle to the case before us, the question comes down to this: Is the risk that any unusual vibration or noise may cause wild animals, which are being raised for commercial purposes, to kill their young, one of the things which make the activity of blasting ultrahazardous?

We have found nothing in the decisional law which would support an affirmative answer to this question. The decided cases, as well as common experience, indicate that the thing which makes blasting ultrahazardous is the risk that property or persons may be damaged or injured by coming into direct contact with flying debris, or by being directly affected by vibrations of the earth or concussions of the air. . . .

The relatively moderate vibration and noise which appellant's blasting produced at a distance of two and a quarter miles was no more than a usual incident of the ordinary life of the community. The trial court specifically found that the blasting did not unreasonably interfere with the enjoyment of their property by nearby landowners, except in the case of the respondent's mink ranch.

It is the exceedingly nervous disposition of mink, rather than the normal risks inherent in blasting operations, which therefore must, as a matter of sound policy, bear the responsibility for the loss here sustained. We subscribe to the view . . . that the policy of the law does not impose the rule of strict liability to protect against harms incident to the plaintiff's extraordinary and unusual use of land. This is perhaps but an application of the principle that the extent to which one man in the lawful conduct of his business is liable for injuries to another involves an adjustment of conflicting interests.

It is our conclusion that the risk of causing harm of the kind here experienced, as a result of the relatively minor vibration, concussion, and noise from distant blasting, is not the kind of risk which makes the activity of blasting ultrahazardous. The doctrine of absolute liability is therefore inapplicable under the facts of this case, and respondent is not entitled to recover damages.

The judgment is reversed.

GRADY, C.J., MALLERY, FINLEY, AND OLSON, JJ., concur.

The specific result in *Foster* is supported by §524A of the Restatement (Second) of Torts, which bars the application of strict liability to harms that "would not have resulted but for the abnormally sensitive character of the plaintiff's activity." Other defenses based on the plaintiff's actions or activity can sometimes defeat the application of strict liability. The Restatement, for example, recognizes an assumption of risk defense in §523. It also precludes liability based on the plaintiff's contributory negligence, but only if the plaintiff "knowingly and unreasonably subject[ed] himself to the risk of harm. . . ." §524(2). Suppose, however, that the plaintiff knowingly but *reasonably* subjected himself to the risk of harm?

Problem 27

Your firm has been retained by Midvalle Grass Seed Company to handle a spate of litigation arising from a runaway grass fire. Midvalle owns a large grass farm in the central region of the state. It grows special grasses that produce grass seed for sale. Late each summer, after the seed is harvested but before the rainy season begins, Midvalle follows the long-standing tradition of grass seed farmers by "firing" its fields. Specifically, Midvalle intentionally sets fire to the dried grasses in its fields so that they burn completely. This process returns nutrients to the soil and sterilizes the top layer of soil, thereby killing all leftover seeds so that any grasses planted the next year will "run true" and not cross-breed with seeds from previous years.

Midvalle controls grass fires using a standard method used by seed farmers in the state. A 20-foot-wide swath is tilled around the perimeter of its farm. This bare soil acts as a firebreak, making it difficult for the burning grass to ignite grass on the other side. Midvalle also waits for a day with light winds. Using handheld torches, employees light the upwind portion of the field, and monitor the fire as it burns across its fields. A water truck is kept on hand as an extra precaution.

Last summer, when Midvalle lit its fields, things went badly. An unusually dry summer had left the grasses with a very low moisture content. When lit, the fields burned with near explosive speed and intensity despite the fact that Midvalle deliberately picked a day with almost no wind. The shear heat of the grass fire soon created its own wind, which generated a small firestorm that raced across the farm. Although the water truck was dispatched, it was unable to contain the quickly spreading fire. When the fire reached the downwind edge of the farm, burning stalks and grasses were blown well over the firebreak and ignited grasses on the other side.

This portion of Midvalle's farm adjoins a 2,000 acre forested hillside owned by Western Timber Co. When the fire escaped the farm, Midvalle quickly alerted both Western and the National Forest Service, which dispatched a fire fighting crew to the fire. Normally, a fire on Western's land would not pose a terrible risk, since most forest fires simply burn the undergrowth without igniting or killing the trees. In fact, the subsequent release of nutrients is believed to be beneficial to the forest ecosystem, and hence the Forest Service often lets such fires burn under careful supervision.

Unfortunately, many of the trees in the central section of Western's land were killed the year before by an infestation of the Western Pine Weevil. The dead trees, while still saleable as lumber, were extremely dry and flammable. The Forest Service had issued an advisory, urging timber companies to harvest any large stands of dead timber to reduce fire risk, but Western had held off harvesting the trees in the hopes that lumber prices would improve.

The firefighting team dispatched to the fire was unaware of the special fire danger presented by the section of dead trees, and hence did not aggressively attack the fire while it was still confined to the underbrush in the nondamaged part of Western's land. When the team realized the risk, it was too late to take effective action. The fire reached the dead trees, and again exploded into a firestorm, destroying most of the trees, both alive and dead, on Western's property. The value of the destroyed timber was over $1 million. In the process of fighting the fire, a fire fighter from the Forest Service was seriously injured when burning debris from the firestorm struck him.

A heavy rainstorm two weeks later washed great amounts of ash from the burned forest into a tributary of the Rogue River. The run-off temporarily fouled the water, killing large numbers of game fish. As a result, High Country Expeditions, a commercial enterprise that runs fishing trips on the river, lost a significant amount of business.

Midvalle has already received a complaint from Western, and is anticipating litigation from the injured fire fighter and from High Country Expeditions. The supervising partner has asked you to assess the likely outcome of a strict liability claim brought by any of the potential plaintiffs. Assume that there is no controlling precedent in your jurisdiction, but that courts follow the general approach suggested by the materials in this chapter.

Chapter 7

Products Liability

Some of the most dramatic developments in tort law in the last three decades have occurred in connection with manufacturers' and suppliers' liability for harm caused by defective products. As might be expected, these changes in the law have produced confusion, much of which may be traced to two sources: first, the development of no fewer than three distinct but overlapping legal theories of liability; second, a tendency for courts and commentators to insist upon applying the same rules of decision in all products liability cases notwithstanding the fact that different categories of cases require significantly different solutions.

This chapter is organized on the basis of the different types of defects for which products liability is imposed: manufacturing defects, failures to instruct or warn, and unsafe designs. *Manufacturing defects* (sometimes referred to as *construction defects* or *production defects*), are features in a few product units that make those few units different from, and inferior to, the vast majority of units in the same product line. Some manufacturing defects are merely cosmetic and do not interfere with the product's intended function. Others interfere with the functioning, but in ways that are not particularly dangerous. The defects with which we shall be concerned are those that dangerously interfere with product function and are likely to cause personal injury or property damage. In contrast to manufacturing defects, *design defects* are shared by each unit in the product line, causing the products to be generically dangerous. *Marketing defects,* which also produce generic defectiveness, include failures to instruct regarding proper product use and failures to warn of hidden dangers.

A. Liability for Manufacturing Defects

Manufacturing defects are inadvertent imperfections that cause products to fail to perform their intended functions. These defects find their source in the fallibility of the manufacturing process, and in the fact that the social costs of zero defect rates would be unacceptably high. Usually, only a small percentage of the total number of products in any product run turn out to be defective in a way posing unreasonable risks of harm, and only relatively few defective products actually cause injuries that become the subject of the sorts of actions considered in this section. Manufacturing defect cases do not present many theoretically difficult problems relating to the determination of defectiveness, but there are a few difficult issues involving the circumstances under which liability for harm caused by a manufacturing defect should be imposed.

1. The Plaintiff's Prima Facie Case: Bases of Liability

In the subsections that follow we shall consider the three basic theories upon which liability is based: negligence, warranty, and strict liability. Although they are distinct theories of liability, each has influenced the development of the others, and they will often be combined in the plaintiff's claim for relief.

a. Negligence

Although the basic concept of negligence as it is applied in products liability cases is the same as that developed in Chapter 4, the early law distinguished products liability cases from other negligence cases, affording substantial insulation from liability to manufacturers and suppliers of defective goods. The most significant early decision was Winterbottom v. Wright, 10 M. & W. 109 (Exch. 1842). The plaintiff was a mail coach driver who was injured when the coach broke down. The defendant had contracted with the Postmaster General to supply a number of coaches, including the coach in question, for the transport of mail. Under the terms of the contract, the defendant had promised the Postmaster General to keep the coaches in good repair. The plaintiff was employed by one Atkinson who, with knowledge of the defendant's contract, had contracted with the Postmaster General to supply horses and coachmen to operate the coaches. The plaintiff's declaration alleged that the defendant negligently failed to carry out his duties of maintenance and repair under the contract, and that as a consequence the coach had become weakened and dangerous, causing the plaintiff's injuries. Lord Abinger, writing for a unanimous court, denied liability as a matter of law, concluding (10 M. & W. at 114):

> There is no privity of contract between these parties; and if the plaintiff can sue, every passenger, or even any person passing along the road, who was injured by the upsetting of the coach, might bring a similar action. Unless we confine the operation of such contracts as this to the parties who entered into them, the most absurd and outrageous consequences, to which I can see no limit, would ensue.

The rule in the *Winterbottom* case came generally to be recognized in this country by the second half of the nineteenth century. See Lebourdais v. Vitrified Wheel Co., 194 Mass. 341, 80 N.E. 482 (1907); Burkett v. Studebaker Bros. Mfg. Co., 126 Tenn. 467, 150 S.W. 421 (1912). A number of exceptions to the privity requirement were judicially developed, the most interesting of which occurred in New York, commencing with the decision of the court of appeals in Thomas v. Winchester, 6 N.Y. 397 (1852). The injured plaintiff in *Thomas* was a woman who had purchased from a retail druggist a bottle of poison falsely labeled as a mild medicine. Taking the poison believing it to be medicine, she was injured. She brought a negligence action against both the retail druggist and the chemist who had erroneously labelled the bottle and sold it to the druggist. The jury returned a verdict in favor of the druggist and against the chemist, and judgments were entered accordingly. The defendant chemist appealed. Citing the *Winterbottom* decision for the general rule, the court of appeals nevertheless affirmed the judgment, concluding that the falsely labeled poison, unlike the defective mail coach, was "imminently dangerous to the lives of others."

In the years following Thomas v. Winchester, the New York Court of Appeals refined and extended the concept of "imminently dangerous products." These extentions culminated in one of the most famous American products liability decisions.

MacPherson v. Buick Motor Co.

217 N.Y. 382, 111 N.E. 1050 (1916)

CARDOZO, J. The defendant is a manufacturer of automobiles. It sold an automobile to a retail dealer. The retail dealer resold to the plaintiff. While the plaintiff was in the car, it suddenly collapsed. He was thrown out and injured. One of the wheels was made of defective wood, and its spokes crumbled into fragments. The wheel was not made by the defendant; it was bought from another manufacturer. There is evidence, however, that its defects could have been discovered by reasonable inspection, and that inspection was omitted. There is no claim that the defendant knew of the defect and willfully concealed it. . . . The charge is one, not of fraud, but of negligence. The question to be determined is whether the defendant owed a duty of care and vigilance to any one but the immediate purchaser.

[At this point, Justice Cardozo reviews the New York decisions, beginning with Thomas v. Winchester, and proceeds to formulate a general rule of liability:]

We hold, then, that the principle of Thomas v. Winchester is not limited to poisons, explosives, and things of like nature, to things which in their normal operation are implements of destruction. If the nature of a thing is such that it is reasonably certain to place life and limb in peril when negligently made, it is then a thing of danger. Its nature gives warning of the consequences to be expected. If to the element of danger there is added knowledge that the thing will be used by persons other than the purchaser, and used without new tests, then, irrespective of contract, the manufacturer of this thing of danger is under a duty to make it carefully. That is as far as we are required to go for the decision of this case. There must be knowledge of a danger, not merely possible, but probable. It is *possible* to use almost anything in a way that will make it dangerous if defective. That is not enough to charge the manufacturer with a duty independent of his contract. Whether a given thing is dangerous may be sometimes a question for the court and sometimes a question for the jury. There must also be knowledge that in the usual course of events the danger will be shared by others than the buyer. Such knowledge may often be inferred from the nature of the transaction. But it is possible that even knowledge of the danger and of the use will not always be enough. The proximity or remoteness of the relation is a factor to be considered. We are dealing now with the liability of the manufacturer of the finished product, who puts it on the market to be used without inspection by his customers. If he is negligent, where danger is to be foreseen, a liability will follow. We are not required at this time to say that it is legitimate to go back of the manufacturer of the finished product and hold the manufacturers of the component parts. To make their negligence a cause of imminent danger, an independent cause must often intervene; the manufacturer of the finished product must also fail in *his* duty of inspection. It may be that in those circumstances the negligence of the earlier members of the series is too remote to constitute, as to the ultimate user, an actionable wrong. We leave that question open. We shall have to deal with it when it arises. The difficulty which it suggests is not present in this case. There is here no break in the chain of cause and effect. In such circumstances, the presence of a known danger, attendant upon a known use, makes vigilance a duty. We have put aside the notion that the duty to safeguard life and limb, when the consequences of negligence may be foreseen, grows out of the contract and nothing else. We have put the source of the obligation where it ought to be. We have put its source in the law.

From this survey of the decisions, there thus emerges a definition of the duty of a manufacturer which enables us to measure this defendant's liability. Beyond all question, the nature of an automobile gives warning of probable danger if its construction is defective. This automobile was designed to go fifty miles an hour. Unless its wheels were sound and strong, injury was almost certain. It was as much a thing of danger as a defective engine for a railroad. The defendant knew the danger. It knew also that the car would be used by persons other than the buyer. This was apparent from its size; there were seats for three persons. It was apparent also from the fact that the buyer was a dealer in cars, who bought to resell. The maker of this car supplied it for the use of purchasers from the dealer just as plainly as the contractor in Devlin v. Smith supplied the scaffold for use by the servants of the owner. The dealer was indeed the one person of whom it might be said with some approach to certainty that by him the car would not be used. Yet the defendant would have us say that he was the one person whom it was under a legal duty to protect. The law does not lead us to so inconsequent a conclusion. Precedents drawn from the days of travel by stage coach do not fit the conditions of travel to-day. The principle that the danger must be imminent does not change, but the things subject to the principle do change. They are whatever the needs of life in a developing civilization require them to be. . . .

We think the defendant was not absolved from a duty of inspection because it bought the wheels from a reputable manufacturer. It was not merely a dealer in automobiles. It was a manufacturer of automobiles. It was responsible for the finished product. It was not at liberty to put the finished product on the market without subjecting the component parts to ordinary and simple tests. Under the charge of the trial judge nothing more was required of it. The obligation to inspect must vary with the nature of the thing to be inspected. The more probable the danger, the greater the need of caution. . . .

[The dissenting opinion of CHIEF JUSTICE BARTLETT is omitted.]

HISCOCK, CHASE, and CUDDEBACK, JJ., concur with CARDOZO, J., and HOGAN, J., concurs in result; WILLARD BARTLETT, C.J., reads dissenting opinion; POUND, J., not voting.

Judgment affirmed.

The holding in *MacPherson*—abrogating the privity requirement in negligence cases—gained rapid and widespread acceptance and is today universally recognized. See Prosser and Keeton, Law of Torts 683 (5th ed. 1984); Restatement (Second) of Torts §395. However, the *MacPherson* decision did not eliminate the necessity of the plaintiff's proving negligence on the part of the manufacturer. Thus, the injured plaintiff was still required to prove not only that the product's breakdown and resulting injuries were proximately caused by a product defect but also that negligence attributable to the manufacturer caused the defect to be present. (You can review how one court coped with the problem of proving negligence in a manufacturing case by rereading Escola v. Coca Cola Bottling Co., p. 284, above.)

b. Breach of Warranty

Centuries ago, a body of law developed in England regulating commercial dealings between and among merchants. The substance of this specialized *law merchant* drew heavily from the customs of the marketplace and reflected a shared desire to give effect to commercial agreements and to uphold the reasonable expectations of participants when the market broke down. Among the features of this complex body of law were *warranties*—obligations imposed by law on sellers of goods requiring them to stand behind the quality of their goods and to make buyers whole when the quality fell short of promised performance levels or reasonable expectations.

Given the practical significance of the law merchant and the accompanying need for uniformity and predictability, the rules tended through time to be codified by statute. In the United States, the first great statute governing sales warranties was the Uniform Sales Act, which controlled commercial practices dealing with the sale of goods until the late 1950s and early 1960s. Beginning in 1954, state legislatures replaced the Sales Act and other commercial law statutes with the Uniform Commercial Code (U.C.C.), Article 2 of which governs sale-of-goods transactions. Today, the law of commercial sales warranties in this country is governed largely by the U.C.C. Courts in recent years, as we shall see, have developed special warranty rules to cover sellers' liabilities for personal injuries caused by defective products. But the place to begin to understand sales warranties is Article 2.

Article 2 of the Uniform Commercial Code establishes three types of sales warranties: (1) express warranties (§2-313), which are promises by the seller that the product will perform in a certain manner; (2) implied warranties of merchantability (§2-314), which are implied-in-law obligations of the seller that his products are free of defects and meet generalized standards of acceptability; and (3) implied warranties of fitness for a particular purpose (§2-315), which are implied-in-law obligations that a product recommended by a knowledgeable seller will meet special needs of the purchaser communicated to the seller at the time of sale.

Implied warranties of merchantability were in the forefront of the movement to achieve strict, fault-free liability for harm caused by defective products. One product area that developed more rapidly than others involved goods for human consumption and intimate bodily use. An interesting subset of these cases involved food served in restaurants. The earliest rule was that restaurants dispensed services rather than goods. Thus, the implied-in-law warranties that imposed liability without fault on commercial sellers of food generally and on retail food sellers (grocers, and the like), did not apply to restaurants, against whom plaintiffs had to prove negligence. Cushing v. Rodman, 82 F.2d 864 (D.C. Cir. 1936), is typical of the decisions that began extending sales warranties to restaurants. In that case, the plaintiff was injured when he bit into a breakfast roll and broke his tooth on a hidden pebble. He sought to recover against the lunch counter at which he had ordered the roll on the basis of breach of implied warranty of wholesomeness. Judgment at trial was for the defendant, but the Court of Appeals reversed, holding that a warranty of wholesomeness ran from defendant to plaintiff under those circumstances. The plaintiff had not proven negligence—the breakfast rolls had been purchased by defendant from a reputable bakery, and the pebble could not have been discovered by reasonable inspection.

But the implied warranty meant the restaurant operator was strictly liable to his customer.

The warranty law applied by the court in Cushing v. Rodman came from the Uniform Sales Act, then in effect in most American jurisdictions. Today, as mentioned earlier, the dominating influence is the Uniform Commercial Code. The implied warranty in the *Cushing* case was the equivalent of the implied warranty of merchantability under §2-314 of the Code:

> §2-314. IMPLIED WARRANTY: MERCHANTABILITY; USAGE OF TRADE
>
> (1) Unless excluded or modified,[1] a warranty that the goods[2] shall be merchantable is implied in a contract for their sale[3] if the seller is a merchant[4] with respect to goods of that kind. Under this section the serving for value of food or drink to be consumed either on the premises or elsewhere is a sale.
>
> (2) Goods to be merchantable must be at least such as
>
> (a) pass without objection in the trade under the contract description; and
>
> (b) in the case of fungible goods, are of fair average quality within the description; and
>
> (c) are fit for the ordinary purposes for which such goods are used; and
>
> (d) run, within the variations permitted by the agreement, of even kind, quality and quantity within each unit and among all units involved; and
>
> (e) are adequately contained, packaged, and labeled as the agreement may require; and
>
> (f) conform to the promises or affirmations of fact made on the container or label if any.

1. Section 2-316 of the Code explicitly allows for the exclusion or modification of implied warranties. When the seller disclaims in writing it must be conspicuous. Section 2-316(3)(a) provides:

> Unless the circumstances indicate otherwise, all implied warranties are excluded by expressions like "as is", "with all faults" or other language which in common understanding calls the buyer's attention to the exclusion of warranties and makes plain that there is no implied warranty. . . .

Section 2-719 of the Code deals with the effect to be given contractual modification or limitation of remedy. It includes the following language: "Consequential damages may be limited or excluded unless the limitation or exclusion is unconscionable. Limitation of consequential damages for injury to the person in the case of consumer goods is prima facie unconscionable but limitation of damages where the loss is commercial is not." The Code also contains a general provision dealing with unconscionable contracts or clauses. [Eds.]

2. The term "goods" is defined in §2-105(1): " 'Goods' means all things (including specially manufactured goods) which are movable at the time of identification to the contract for sale other than the money in which the price is to be paid, investment securities and things in action, 'Goods' also includes the unborn young of animals and growing crops and other identified things attached to realty. . . ." [Eds.]

3. The term "sale" is defined in §2-106(1): "A 'sale' consists of the passing of title from the seller to the buyer for a price." [Eds.]

4. The term "merchant" is defined in §2-104(1): " 'Merchant' means a person who deals in goods of the kind or otherwise by his occupation holds himself out as having knowledge or skill peculiar to the practices or goods involved in the transaction or to whom such knowledge or skill may be attributed by his employment of an agent or broker or other intermediary who by his occupation holds himself out as having such knowledge or skill. . . ." [Eds.]

(3) Unless excluded or modified other implied warranties may arise from course of dealing or usage of trade.

OFFICIAL COMMENT

13. In an action based on breach of warranty, it is of course necessary to show not only the existence of the warranty but the fact that the warranty was broken and that the breach of the warranty was the proximate cause of the loss sustained. In such an action an affirmative showing by the seller that the loss resulted from some action or event following his own delivery of the goods can operate as a defense. Equally, evidence indicating that the seller exercised care in the manufacture, processing or selection of the goods is relevant to the issue of whether the warranty was in fact broken. Action by the buyer following an examination of the goods which ought to have indicated the defect complained of can be shown as matter bearing on whether the breach itself was the cause of the injury.

Observe that §2-314 expressly resolves the primary issue presented for decision in the *Cushing* case.

One issue not presented by the facts in Cushing v. Rodman is whether the implied warranty accompanying the serving of food in a restaurant runs to those not in privity of contract with the defendant. Privity was not a problem in the plaintiff's action against the remote manufacturer in *Escola,* you will remember, because the plaintiff sought to recover in negligence. But in a case such as *Cushing,* in which the plaintiff relies on implied warranty, can plaintiff succeed against a remote seller with whom plaintiff is not in privity? Section 2-314 suggests that such warranties run only between sellers and their purchasers, and it should not surprise you to learn that the privity requirement survived in warranty actions long after MacPherson v. Buick Motor Company had eliminated that requirement in negligence cases. Indeed, the privity requirement in warranty cases involving personal injuries survived until relatively recently, as the following landmark products liability decision indicates.

Henningsen v. Bloomfield Motors, Inc.

32 N.J. 358, 161 A.2d 69 (1960)

FRANCIS, J. Plaintiff Claus H. Henningsen purchased a Plymouth automobile, manufactured by defendant Chrysler Corporation, from defendant Bloomfield Motors, Inc. His wife, plaintiff Helen Henningsen, was injured while driving it and instituted suit against both defendants to recover damages on account of her injuries. Her husband joined in the action seeking compensation for his consequential losses. The complaint was predicated upon breach of express and implied warranties and upon negligence. At the trial the negligence counts were dismissed by the court and the cause was submitted to the jury for determination solely on the issues of implied warranty of merchantability. Verdicts were returned against both defendants and in favor of the plaintiffs. Defendants appealed and plaintiffs cross-appealed from the dismissal of their negligence claim. The matter was certified by this court prior to consideration in the Appellate Division.

The facts are not complicated, but a general outline of them is necessary to an understanding of the case.

On May 7, 1955 Mr. and Mrs. Henningsen visited the place of business of Bloomfield Motors, Inc., an authorized De Soto and Plymouth dealer, to look at a Plymouth. They wanted to buy a car and were considering a Ford or a Chevrolet as well as a Plymouth. They were shown a Plymouth which appealed to them and the purchase followed. The record indicates that Mr. Henningsen intended the car as a Mother's Day gift to his wife. He said the intention was communicated to the dealer. When the purchase order or contract was prepared and presented, the husband executed it alone. His wife did not join as a party.

[The court describes the purchase order form as consisting of a single page, with print of various sizes appearing on the front and back. The two most important paragraphs on the front were in very fine type:

> The front and back of this Order comprise the entire agreement affecting this purchase and no other agreement or understanding of any nature concerning same has been made or entered into, or will be recognized. I hereby certify that no credit has been extended to me for the purchase of this motor vehicle except as appears in writing on the face of this agreement.
>
> I have read the matter printed on the back hereof and agree to it as a part of this order the same as if it were printed above my signature. I certify that I am 21 years of age, or older, and hereby acknowledge receipt of a copy of this order.

On the back of the form, also in fine type, appeared ten "conditions" numbered consecutively. The warranty was contained in paragraph seven:

> 7. It is expressly agreed that there are no warranties, express or implied, made by either the dealer or the manufacturer on the motor vehicle, chassis, or parts furnished hereunder except as follows:
>
> The manufacturer warrants each new motor vehicle (including original equipment placed thereon by the manufacturer except tires), chassis or parts manufactured by it to be free from defects in material or workmanship under normal use and service. Its obligation under this warranty being limited to making good at its factory any part or parts thereof which shall, within ninety (90) days after delivery of such vehicle to the original purchaser or before such vehicle has been driven 4,000 miles, whichever event shall first occur, be returned to it with transportation charges prepaid and which its examination shall disclose to its satisfaction to have been thus defective; this warranty being expressly in lieu of all other warranties expressed or implied, and all other obligations or liabilities on its part, and it neither assumes nor authorizes

any other person to assume for it any other liability in connection with the sale of its vehicle. . . .

Mr. Henningsen testified that he did not read the foregoing provisions of the contract before signing it, nor were they called to his attention.]

The new Plymouth was turned over to the Henningsens on May 9, 1955. No proof was adduced by the dealer to show precisely what was done in the way of mechanical or road testing beyond testimony that the manufacturer's instructions were probably followed. Mr. Henningsen drove it from the dealer's place of business in Bloomfield to their home in Keansburg. On the trip nothing unusual appeared in the way in which it operated. Thereafter, it was used for short trips on paved streets about the town. It had no servicing and no mishaps of any kind before the event of May 19. That day, Mrs. Henningsen drove to Asbury Park. On the way down and in returning the car performed in normal fashion until the accident occurred. She was proceeding north on Route 36 in Highlands, New Jersey, at 20-22 miles per hour. The highway was paved and smooth, and contained two lanes for northbound travel. She was riding in the right-hand lane. Suddenly she heard a loud noise "from the bottom, by the hood." It "felt as if something cracked." The steering wheel spun in her hands; the car veered sharply to the right and crashed into a highway sign and a brick wall. No other vehicle was in any way involved. A bus operator driving in the left-hand lane testified that he observed plaintiff's car approaching in normal fashion in the opposite direction; "all of a sudden [it] veered at 90 degrees . . . and right into this wall." As a result of the impact, the front of the car was so badly damaged that it was impossible to determine if any of the parts of the steering wheel mechanism or workmanship or assembly were defective or improper prior to the accident. The condition was such that the collision insurance carrier, after inspection, declared the vehicle a total loss. It had 468 miles on the speedometer at the time.

The insurance carrier's inspector and appraiser of damaged cars, with 11 years of experience, advanced the opinion, based on the history and his examination, that something definitely went "wrong from the steering wheel down to the front wheels" and that the untoward happening must have been due to mechanical defect or failure: "something down there had to drop off or break loose to cause the car" to act in the manner described.

As has been indicated, the trial court felt that the proof was not sufficient to make out a prima facie case as to the negligence of either the manufacturer or the dealer. The case was given to the jury, therefore, solely on the warranty theory, with results favorable to the plaintiffs against both defendants.

I. The Claim of Implied Warranty Against the Manufacturer

[The court begins its analysis with a review of the nature of common law warranties, both express and implied, and their fairly recent codification and liberalization by the Uniform Sales Act, which was in effect when Mr. Henningsen purchased his new automobile. The court proceeds to criticize the terms of the warranty in this case, calling them "a sad commentary upon the automobile manufacturers' marketing practices."]

Putting aside for the time being the problem of the efficacy of the disclaimer provisions contained in the express warranty, a question of first importance to be decided is whether an implied warranty of merchantability by Chrysler Corporation accompanied the sale of the automobile to Claus Henningsen. . . .

Chrysler points out that an implied warranty of merchantability is an incident of a contract of sale. It concedes, of course, the making of the original sale to Bloomfield Motors, Inc., but maintains that this transaction marked the terminal point of its contractual connection with the car. Then Chrysler urges that since it was not a party to the sale by the dealer to Henningsen, there is no privity of contract between it and the plaintiffs, and the absence of this privity eliminates any such implied warranty.

There is no doubt that under early common-law concepts of contractual liability only those persons who were parties to the bargain could sue for a breach of it. In more recent times a noticeable disposition has appeared in a number of jurisdictions to break through the narrow barrier of privity when dealing with sales of goods in order to give realistic recognition to a universally accepted fact. The fact is that the dealer and the ordinary buyer do not, and are not expected to, buy goods, whether they be foodstuffs or automobiles, exclusively for their own consumption or use. Makers and manufacturers know this and advertise and market their products on that assumption; witness, the "family" car, the baby foods, etc. The limitations of privity in contracts for the sale of goods developed their place in the law when marketing conditions were simple, when maker and buyer frequently met face to face on an equal bargaining plane and when many of the products were relatively uncomplicated and conducive to inspection by a buyer competent to evaluate their quality. With the advent of mass marketing, the manufacturer became remote from the purchaser, sales were accomplished through intermediaries, and the demand for the product was created by advertising media. In such an economy it became obvious that the consumer was the person being cultivated. Manifestly, the connotation of "consumer" was broader than that of "buyer." He signified such a person who, in the reasonable contemplation of the parties to the sale, might be expected to use the product. Thus, where the commodities sold are such that if defectively manufactured they will be dangerous to life and limb, then society's interests can only be protected by eliminating the requirement of privity between the maker and his dealers and the reasonably expected ultimate consumer. In that way the burden of losses consequent upon use of defective articles is borne by those who are in a position to either control the danger or make an equitable distribution of the losses when they do occur. . . .

Although only a minority of jurisdictions have thus far departed from the requirement of privity, the movement in that direction is most certainly gathering momentum. Liability to the ultimate consumer in the absence of direct contractual connection has been predicated upon a variety of theories. Some courts hold that the warranty runs with the article like a covenant running with land; others recognize a third-party beneficiary thesis; still others rest their decision on the ground that public policy requires recognition of a warranty made directly to the consumer. . . .

Most of the cases where lack of privity has not been permitted to interfere with recovery have involved food and drugs. In fact, the rule as to such products has been characterized as an exception to the general doctrine. But more recently courts, sensing the inequity of such limitation, have moved into broader fields. . . .

We see no rational doctrinal basis for differentiating between a fly in a bottle of beverage and a defective automobile. The unwholesome beverage may bring illness to one person, the defective car, with its great potentiality for harm to the driver, occupants, and others, demands even less adherence to the narrow barrier of privity. . . .

Under modern conditions the ordinary layman, on responding to the importuning of colorful advertising, has neither the opportunity nor the capacity to inspect or to determine the fitness of an automobile for use; he must rely on the manufacturer who has control of its construction, and to some degree on the dealer who, to the limited extent called for by the manufacturer's instructions, inspects and services it before delivery. In such a marketing milieu his remedies and those of persons who properly claim through him should not depend "upon the intricacies of the law of sales. The obligation of the manufacturer should not be based alone on privity of contract. It should rest, as was once said, upon 'the demands of social justice.' ". . .

Accordingly, we hold that under modern marketing conditions, when a manufacturer puts a new automobile in the stream of trade and promotes its purchase by the public, an implied warranty that it is reasonably suitable for use as such accompanies it into the hands of the ultimate purchaser. Absence of agency between the manufacturer and the dealer who makes the ultimate sale is immaterial.

II. The Effect of the Disclaimer and Limitation of Liability Clauses on the Implied Warranty of Merchantability

[The court takes judicial notice of the extensive advertising programs undertaken by automobile manufacturers, and the increasing willingness of courts to find express and implied warranties based upon that advertising.]

In the light of these matters, what effect should be given to the express warranty in question which seeks to limit the manufacturer's liability to replacement of defective parts, and which disclaims all other warranties, express or implied? In assessing its significance we must keep in mind the general principle that, in the absence of fraud, one who does not choose to read a contract before signing it, cannot later relieve himself of its burdens. And in applying that principle, the basic tenet of freedom of competent parties to contract is a factor of importance. But in the framework of modern commercial life and business practices, such rules cannot be applied on a strict, doctrinal basis. The conflicting interests of the buyer and seller must be evaluated realistically and justly, giving due weight to the social policy evinced by the Uniform Sales Act, the progressive decisions of the courts engaged in administering it, the mass production methods of manufacture and distribution to the public, and the bargaining position occupied by the ordinary consumer in such an economy. The history of the law shows that legal doctrines, as first expounded, often prove to be inadequate under the impact of later experience. In such case, the need for justice has stimulated the necessary qualifications or adjustments. . . .

The warranty before us is a standardized form designed for mass use. It is imposed upon the automobile consumer. He takes it or leaves it, and he must take it to buy an automobile. No bargaining is engaged in with respect to it. In fact, the dealer through whom it comes to the buyer is without authority to alter it; his function is ministerial—simply to deliver it. The form warranty is not only standard with Chrysler but, as mentioned above, it is the uniform warranty of the Automobile Manufacturers Association. Members of the Association are: General Motors, Inc., Ford, Chrysler, Studebaker-Packard, American Motors (Rambler), Willys Motors, Checker Motors Corp., and International Harvester Company. Of these companies, the "Big Three" (General Motors, Ford, and Chrysler) represented 93.5% of the passenger-car production for 1958 and the independents 6.5%. And for the same year the "Big Three" had 86.72% of the total passenger vehicle registrations.

The gross inequality of bargaining position occupied by the consumer in the automobile industry is thus apparent. There is no competition among the car makers in the area of the express warranty. Where can the buyer go to negotiate for better protection? Such control and limitation of his remedies are inimical to the public welfare and, at the very least, call for great care by the courts to avoid injustice through application of strict common-law principles of freedom of contract. Because there is no competition among the motor vehicle manufacturers with respect to the scope of protection guaranteed to the buyer, there is no incentive on their part to stimulate good will in that field of public relations. Thus, there is lacking a factor existing in more competitive fields, one which tends to guarantee the safe construction of the article sold. Since all competitors operate in the same way, the urge to be careful is not so pressing. . . .

Public policy at a given time finds expression in the Constitution, the statutory law and in judicial decisions. In the area of sale of goods, the legislative will has imposed an implied warranty of merchantability as a general incident of sale of an automobile by description. The warranty does not depend upon the affirmative intention of the parties. It is a child of the law; it annexes itself to the contract because of the very nature of the transaction. . . . True, the Sales Act authorizes agreements between buyer and seller qualifying the warranty obligations. But quite obviously the Legislature contemplated lawful stipulations (which are determined by the circumstances of a particular case) arrived at freely by parties of relatively equal bargaining strength. The lawmakers did not authorize the automobile manufacturer to use its grossly disproportionate bargaining power to relieve itself from liability and to impose on the ordinary buyer, who in effect has no real freedom of choice, the grave danger of injury to himself and others that attends the sale of such a dangerous instrumentality as a defectively made automobile. In the framework of this case, illuminated as it is by the facts and the many decisions noted, we are of the opinion that Chrysler's attempted disclaimer of an implied warranty of merchantability and of the obligations arising therefrom is so inimical to the public good as to compel an adjudication of its invalidity.

III. The Dealer's Implied Warranty

The principles that have been expounded as to the obligation of the manufacturer apply with equal force to the separate express warranty of the dealer. This is so, irrespective of the absence of the relationship of principal and agent between these defendants, because the manufacturer and the Association establish the warranty policy for the industry. The bargaining position of the dealer is inextricably bound by practice to that of the maker and the purchaser must take or leave the automobile, accompanied and encumbered as it is by the uniform warranty. . . .

For the reasons set forth in Part 1 hereof, we conclude that the disclaimer of an implied warranty of merchantability by the dealer, as well as the attempted elimination of all obligations other than replacement of defective parts, are violative of public policy and void. . . .

IV. Proof of Breach of the Implied Warranty of Merchantability

Both defendants argue that the proof adduced by plaintiffs as to the happening of the accident was not sufficient to demonstrate a breach of warranty. Consequently, they claim that their motion for judgment should have been granted by the trial court. We cannot agree. In our view, the total effect of the circumstances shown from purchase to accident is adequate to raise an inference that the car was defective and that such condition was causally related to the mishap. Thus, determination by the jury was required. . . .

V. The Defense of Lack of Privity Against Mrs. Henningsen

Both defendants contend that since there was no privity of contract between them and Mrs. Henningsen, she cannot recover for breach of any warranty made by either of them. On the facts, as they were developed, we agree that she was not a party to the purchase agreement. Her right to maintain the action, therefore, depends upon whether she occupies such legal status thereunder as to permit her to take advantage of a breach of defendant's implied warranties.

[The court concludes that "the cause of justice . . . can be served only by" allowing Mrs. Henningsen to recover.]

It is important to express the right of Mrs. Henningsen to maintain her action in terms of a general principle. To what extent may lack of privity be disregarded in suits on such warranties? In that regard, [precedent] points the way. By a parity of reasoning, it is our opinion that an implied warranty of merchantability chargeable to either an automobile manufacturer or a dealer extends to the purchaser of the car, members of his family, and to other persons occupying or using it with his consent. It would be wholly opposed to reality to say that use by such persons is not within the anticipation of parties to such a warranty of reasonable suitability of an automobile for ordinary highway operation. Those persons must be considered within the distributive chain. . . .

For affirmance—CHIEF JUSTICE WEINTRAUB, and JUSTICES BURLING, JACOBS, FRANCIS, PROCTOR and SCHETTINO—6.

For reversal—None.

c. Strict Liability in Tort

The decision generally recognized to have been the first to avoid reliance on warranty terminology and explicitly to apply the rule of privity-free strict liability in tort to manufacturers of defective products is Greenman v. Yuba Power Products, Inc., 59 Cal. 2d 57, 377 P.2d 897, 27 Cal. Rptr. 697 (1962). Citing Henningsen v. Bloomfield Motors, Inc., above, the California court in *Greenman* concluded that the manufacturer's liability for defective products "is not one governed by the law of contract warranties but by the law of strict liability in tort." (59 Cal. 2d at 63, 377 P.2d at 901, 27 Cal. Rptr. at 701). The court concluded (59 Cal. 2d at 64), 377 P.2d at 901, 27 Cal. Rptr. at 701:

> Implicit in the machine's presence on the market, however, was a representation that it would safely do the jobs for which it was built. Under these circumstances, it should not be controlling whether plaintiff selected the machine because of the statements in the brochure, or because of the machine's own appearance of excellence that belied the defect lurking beneath the

surface, or because he merely assumed that it would safely do the jobs it was built to do. It should not be controlling whether the details of the sales from manufacturer to retailer and from retailer to plaintiff's wife were such that one or more of the implied warranties of the sales act arose. . . . To establish the manufacturer's liability it was sufficient that plaintiff proved that he was injured while using the Shopsmith in a way it was intended to be used as a result of a defect in design and manufacture of which plaintiff was not aware that made the Shopsmith unsafe for its intended use.

Three years after Greenman was decided, the American Law Institute, relying on *Greenman* and inspired by the scholarly work of the Reporter for the Restatement (Second) of Torts, William Prosser, adopted its well-known strict products liability rule:

RESTATEMENT OF TORTS, SECOND

§402A. SPECIAL LIABILITY OF SELLER OF PRODUCT FOR PHYSICAL HARM TO USER OR CONSUMER

(1) One who sells any product in a defective condition unreasonably dangerous to the user or consumer or to his property is subject to liability for physical harm thereby caused to the ultimate user or consumer, or to his property, if

(a) the seller is engaged in the business of selling such a product, and

(b) it is expected to and does reach the user or consumer without substantial change in the condition in which it is sold.

(2) The rule stated in Subsection (1) applies although

(a) the seller has exercised all possible care in the preparation and sale of his product, and

(b) the user or consumer has not bought the product from or entered into any contractual relation with the seller.

COMMENT

g. Defective condition. The rule stated in this Section applies only where the product is, at the time it leaves the seller's hands, in a condition not contemplated by the ultimate consumer, which will be unreasonably dangerous to him. The seller is not liable when he delivers the product in a safe condition, and subsequent mishandling or other causes make it harmful by the time it is consumed. The burden of proof that the product was in a defective condition at the time that it left the hands of the particular seller is upon the injured plaintiff; and unless evidence can be produced which will support the conclusion that it was then defective, the burden is not sustained.

Safe condition at the time of delivery by the seller will, however, include proper packaging, necessary sterilization, and other precautions required to permit the product to remain safe for a normal length of time when handled in a normal manner.

i. Unreasonably dangerous. The rule stated in this Section applies only where the defective condition of the product makes it unreasonably dangerous

> to the user or consumer. Many products cannot possibly be made entirely safe for all consumption, and any food or drug necessarily involves some risk of harm, if only from over-consumption. Ordinary sugar is a deadly poison to diabetics, and castor oil found use under Mussolini as an instrument of torture. That is not what is meant by "unreasonably dangerous" in this Section. The article sold must be dangerous to an extent beyond that which would be contemplated by the ordinary consumer who purchases it, with the ordinary knowledge common to the community as to its characteristics. Good whiskey is not unreasonably dangerous merely because it will make some people drunk, and is especially dangerous to alcoholics; but bad whiskey, containing a dangerous amount of fusel oil, is unreasonably dangerous. Good tobacco is not unreasonably dangerous merely because the effects of smoking may be harmful; but tobacco containing something like marijuana may be unreasonably dangerous. Good butter is not unreasonably dangerous merely because, if such be the case, it deposits cholesterol in the arteries and leads to heart attacks; but bad butter, contaminated with poisonous fish oil, is unreasonably dangerous.
>
> m. "Warranty." The liability stated in this Section does not rest upon negligence. It is strict liability, similar in its nature to that covered by Chapters 20 and 21. The basis of liability is purely one of tort.

Since 1965, courts in virtually every jurisdiction in this country have recognized the rule of privity-free strict products liability in manufacturing defect cases, although a few employ "implied warranty" language instead of "strict liability in tort" language.

The American Law Institute attached a caveat to §402A in which it expressed no opinion as to whether §402A applied (1) to harm to persons other than users or consumers; (2) to the seller of a product expected to be processed or otherwise substantially changed before it reaches the user or consumer; or (3) to the seller of a component part of a product to be assembled later. The issue regarding the availability of §402A to nonusers and nonconsumers, which came to be known as the *bystander issue,* has been resolved in favor of plaintiffs. The leading case is Elmore v. American Motors Corp., 70 Cal. 2d 578, 451 P.2d 84, 75 Cal. Rptr. 652 (1969).

The application of the second caveat accompanying §402A, dealing with products expected to be processed or otherwise substantially changed before they reach users or consumers, is less clear. Certainly the seller of nondefective raw materials, such as bulk sulfuric acid, is not liable when his purchaser turns those materials into a commercially distributed drain cleaner that is defective (see, e.g., Walker v. Stauffer Chemical Corp., 19 Cal. App. 3d 669, 96 Cal. Rptr. 803 (1971)), unless the original seller knows or has reason to know of the dangerous use to which his component will be put and is in a position to act to prevent harm to the plaintiff (see, e.g., Dunson v. S. A. Allen, Inc., 355 So. 2d 77 (Miss. 1978)).

Regarding the third caveat, a consensus has been reached that the strict liability rule applies to component part manufacturers. See, e.g., Suvada v. White Motor Co., 32 Ill. 2d 612, 210 N.E.2d 182 (1965).

In the Spring of 1992, the American Law Institute decided to revise the Restatement of Torts, Second, beginning with the subject of products liability. It appointed Professors James A. Henderson, Jr. (Cornell) and Aaron D. Twerski (Brooklyn) Co-Reporters. The first four sections of the Council Draft, No. 1A, as of January, 1994, appear on pp. 671-673, below.

Vandermark v. Ford Motor Co.

61 Cal. 2d 256, 391 P.2d 168, 37 Cal. Rptr. 896 (1964)

TRAYNOR, J. In October 1958 plaintiff Chester Vandermark bought a new Ford automobile from defendant . . . Maywood Bell Ford. About six weeks later, while driving on the San Bernardino Freeway, he lost control of the car. It went off the highway to the right and collided with a light post. He and his sister, plaintiff Mary Tresham, suffered serious injuries. They brought this action for damages against Maywood Bell Ford and the Ford Motor Company, which manufactured and assembled the car. They pleaded causes of action for breach of warranty and negligence. The trial court granted Ford's motion for a nonsuit on all causes of action and directed a verdict in favor of Maywood Bell on the warranty causes of action. The jury returned a verdict for Maywood Bell on the negligence causes of action, and the trial court entered judgment on the verdict. Plaintiffs appeal.

Vandermark had driven the car approximately 1,500 miles before the accident. He used it primarily in town, but drove it on two occasions from his home in Huntington Park to Joshua Tree in San Bernardino County. He testified that the car operated normally before the accident except once when he was driving home from Joshua Tree. He was in the lefthand westbound lane of the San Bernardino Freeway when traffic ahead slowed. He applied the brakes and the car "started to make a little dive to the right and continued on across the two lanes of traffic till she hit the shoulder. Whatever it was then let go and I was able to then pull her back into the road." He drove home without further difficulty, but before using the car again, he took it to Maywood Bell for the regular 1,000-mile new car servicing. He testified that he described the freeway incident to Maywood Bell's service attendant, but Maywood Bell's records do not indicate any complaint was made.

After the car was serviced, Vandermark drove it in town on short trips totaling approximately 300 miles. He and his sister then set out on another trip to Joshua Tree. He testified that while driving in the right-hand lane of the freeway at about 45 to 50 miles per hour, "the car started to make a little shimmy or weave and started pulling to the right. . . . I tried to pull back, but it didn't seem to come, so I applied my brakes gently to see if I could straighten her up, but I couldn't seem to pull her back to the left. So, I let off on the brakes and she continued to the right, and I tried again to put on the brakes and she wouldn't come back, and all of a sudden this pole was in front of me and we smashed into it." Plaintiff Tresham testified to a substantially similar version of the accident. A witness for plaintiffs, who was driving about 200 feet behind them, testified that plaintiffs' car was in the right-hand lane when he saw its taillights come on. The car started to swerve and finally skidded into the light post. An investigating officer testified that there were skid marks leading from the highway to the car.

Plaintiffs called an expert on the operation of hydraulic automobile brakes. In answer to hypothetical questions based on evidence in the record and his own knowledge of the braking system of the car, the expert testified as to the cause of the accident. It was his opinion that the brakes applied themselves owing to a failure of the piston in the master cylinder to retract far enough when the brake pedal was released to uncover a bypass port through which hydraulic fluid should have been able to escape into a reservoir above the master cylinder. Failure of the piston to uncover the bypass port led to a closed system and a partial application of the brakes, which in turn led to heating that expanded the brake fluid until the brakes applied themselves with such force that Vandermark lost control of the car. The expert also testified that the failure of the piston to retract sufficiently to uncover the bypass port could have been caused by dirt in the master cylinder, a defective or wrong-sized part, distortion of the firewall, or improper assembly or adjustment. The trial court struck the testimony of the possible causes of the failure of the piston to retract, on the ground that there was no direct evidence that any one or more of the causes existed, and it rejected plaintiffs' offer to prove that all of the possible causes were attributable to defendants. These rulings were erroneous, for plaintiffs were entitled to establish the existence of a defect and defendants' responsibility therefor by circumstantial evidence, particularly when, as in this case, the damage to the car in collision precluded determining whether or not the master cylinder assembly had been properly installed and adjusted before the accident.

Accordingly, for the purpose of reviewing the nonsuit in favor of Ford and the directed verdict in favor of Maywood Bell on the warranty causes of action, it must be taken as established that when the car was delivered to Vandermark, the master cylinder assembly had a defect that caused the accident. Moreover, since it could reasonably be inferred from the description of the braking system in evidence and the offer of proof of all possible causes of defects that the defect was owing to negligence in design, manufacture, assembly, or adjustment, it must be taken as established that the defect was caused by some such negligence.

Ford contends, however, that it may not be held liable for negligence in manufacturing the car or strictly liable in tort for placing it on the market without proof that the car was defective when Ford relinquished control over it. Ford points out that in this case the car passed through two other authorized Ford dealers before it was sold to Maywood Bell and that Maywood Bell removed the power steering unit before selling the car to Vandermark.

In Greenman v. Yuba Power Products, Inc., 59 Cal. 2d 57, 62 [337 P.2d 897, 27 Cal. Rptr. 697], we held that "A manufacturer is strictly liable in tort when an article he places on the market, knowing that it is to be used without inspection for defects, proves to have a defect that causes injury to a human being." Since the liability is strict it encompasses defects regardless of their source, and therefore a manufacturer of a completed product cannot escape liability by tracing the defect to a component part supplied by another. (Goldberg v. Kollsman Instrument Corp., 12 N.Y.2d 432, 437 [240 N.Y.S.2d 592, 191 N.E.2d 81].) Moreover, even before such strict liability was recognized, the manufacturer of a completed product was subject to vicarious liability for the negligence of his suppliers or subcontractors that resulted in defects in the completed product. These rules focus responsibility for defects, whether negligently or nonnegligently caused, on the manufacturer of the completed product, and they apply regardless of what part of the manufacturing process the manufacturer chooses to delegate to third parties. It appears in the present case that Ford delegates the final steps in that process to its authorized dealers. It does not deliver cars to its dealers that are ready to be driven away by the ultimate purchasers but relies on its dealers to make the final inspection, corrections, and adjustments necessary to make the cars ready for use. Since Ford, as the manufacturer of the completed product, cannot delegate its duty to have its cars delivered to the ultimate purchaser free from dangerous defects, it cannot escape liability on the ground that the defect in Vandermark's car may have been caused by something one of its authorized dealers did or failed to do.

Since plaintiffs introduced or offered substantial evidence that they were injured as a result of a defect that was present in the car when Ford's authorized dealer delivered it to Vandermark, the trial court erred in granting a nonsuit on the causes of action by which plaintiffs sought to establish that Ford was strictly liable to them. Since plaintiffs also introduced or offered substantial evidence that the defect was caused by some negligent conduct for which Ford was responsible, the trial court also erred in granting a nonsuit on the causes of action by which plaintiffs sought to establish that Ford was liable for negligence.

Plaintiffs contend that Maywood Bell is also strictly liable in tort for the injuries caused by the defect in the car and that therefore the trial court erred in directing a verdict for Maywood Bell on the warranty causes of action. Maywood Bell contends that the rule of strict liability in the *Greenman* case applies only to actions against manufacturers brought by injured parties with whom the manufacturers did not deal. . . .

Retailers like manufacturers are engaged in the business of distributing goods to the public. They are an integral part of the overall producing and marketing enterprise that should bear the cost of injuries resulting from defective products. (See Greenman v. Yuba Power Products, Inc., 59 Cal. 2d 57, 63 [27 Cal. Rptr. 697, 377 P.2d 897].) In some cases the retailer may be the only member of that enterprise reasonably available to the injured plaintiff. In other cases the retailer himself may play a substantial part in insuring that the product is safe or may be in a position to exert pressure on the manufacturer to that end; the retailer's strict liability thus serves as an added incentive to safety. Strict liability on the manufacturer and retailer alike affords maximum protection to the injured plaintiff and works no injustice to the defendants, for they can adjust the costs of such protection between them in the course of their continuing business relationship. Accordingly, as a retailer engaged in the business of distributing goods to the public, Maywood Bell is strictly liable in tort for personal injuries caused by defects in cars sold by it. . . .

Although plaintiffs sought to impose strict liability on Maywood Bell on the theory of sales-act warranties, they pleaded and introduced substantial evidence of all the facts necessary to establish strict liability in tort. Accordingly, the trial court erred in directing a verdict for Maywood Bell on the so-called warranty causes of action. . . .

The judgment of nonsuit in favor of Ford Motor Company is reversed. The judgment in favor of Maywood Bell Ford on the negligence causes of action is affirmed and in all other respects the judgment in favor of Maywood Bell Ford is reversed.

GIBSON, C.J., SCHAUER, J., MCCOMB, J., PETERS, J., TOBRINER, J., and PEEK, J., concurred.

Courts have differed in their attitudes regarding the extent to which plaintiffs will be allowed to prove the existence of defects by means of circumstantial evidence. In Scanlon v. General Motors Corp., 65 N.J. 582, 326 A.2d 673 (1974), the plaintiff was injured when the automobile he was driving suddenly increased in speed, went out of control, and hit a telephone pole. The plaintiff argued that the cause of the sudden acceleration was a defective carburetor. The court ruled that the trier of fact would be permitted to find that the plaintiff's car was defective at the time of the accident upon proof that it malfunctioned while being properly operated by him. But since at the time of the accident the vehicle was nine months old and had been driven 4,000 miles, the plaintiff had to produce more evidence than that to permit the fact finder to determine that the carburetor was defective when the automobile left the defendant's control. Thus, in the absence of additional proof of prior defectiveness, the defendant was entitled to a judgment as a matter of law. The New Jersey court reacted differently a short time later in a case involving a slightly newer automobile, and permitted a finding that it was defective on otherwise similar facts. See Moraca v. Ford Motor Co., 66 N.J. 454, 332 A.2d 599 (1975). Several justices dissented on the

older v. newer car
→ more lenient on circ. evid.

ground that the two decisions could not be reconciled. See also §§1 and 2 of Council Draft No. 1A of the Restatement (Third) of Torts: Products Liability, p. 671, below.

It will be observed that the court in *Vandermark* imposed strict liability not only on the manufacturer, Ford Motor Company, but also on the retailer, Maywood Bell. This is consistent with §402A of the Restatement, which imposes duties on *all* commercial sellers. Thus, in most jurisdictions all commercial entities in the vertical chain of distribution are held jointly and severally liable to injured plaintiffs for harm caused by defects attributable to the manufacturer. Moreover, although generalizations are difficult in this area, as a general rule each seller in the chain has a right of indemnity against those sellers above him in the chain. (For the effectiveness of disclaimers between commercial sellers in the chain of distribution, see the tort and contract note at the end of this section.)

One of the interesting developments in recent years has been the movement (or at least the beginnings of a movement) to let retailers and wholesalers off (or at least partway off) the strict liability hook. Under traditional rules governing contribution and indemnity among the members of the distributive chain, the tendency is for the liability to be passed up the chain from retailers and wholesalers to the manufacturer by means of implied rights of indemnity. Although this tendency reduces the ultimate exposures to liability of retailers and wholesalers, those categories of sellers are routinely joined as defendants and, even if eventually they escape liability to the plaintiff, they incur substantial costs defending against liability and otherwise protecting their interests.

Earlier, in the days when implied warranty and res ipsa loquitur were the vehicles by which product sellers' liabilities were expanded, some jurisdictions recognized exceptions for retailers and wholesalers to whom products came wrapped in packaging that prevented inspection for defects. These *sealed package* or *sealed container* exceptions were not recognized under §402A, and gave way to a more pro-plaintiff regime of strict seller's liability in tort. In recent years, however, retailers and wholesalers have increasingly objected to being held strictly liable.

In recent years some states have enacted statutes immunizing nonmanufacturer sellers from strict liability when the manufacturer is a viable defendant from whom the plaintiff may recover damages. The Kansas statute is typical:

Kansas Statutes Annotated (1982-1990)

60-3306. SELLER NOT SUBJECT TO LIABILITY

A product seller shall not be subject to liability in a product liability claim arising from an alleged defect in a product, if the product seller establishes that:

(a) Such seller had no knowledge of the defect;

(b) such seller in the performance of any duties the seller performed, or was required to perform, could not have discovered the defect while exercising reasonable care;

(c) the seller was not a manufacturer of the defective product or product component;

(d) the manufacturer of the defective product or product component is subject to service of process either under the laws of the state of Kansas or the domicile of the person making the product liability claim; and

(e) any judgment against the manufacturer obtained by the person making the product liability claim would be reasonably certain of being satisfied.

Problem 28

Your firm represents the El Papagayo Verde restaurant, defendant in a suit brought by a restaurant patron. The complaint contains counts in both negligence and strict liability. The senior partner handling the case asked for your assistance. At the time of the accident eight months ago, the plaintiff, Tom Walters, and his wife, Mary Jean, had just ordered dinner at the restaurant. Mr. Walters was tasting the wine they had chosen to celebrate their anniversary when the glass shattered in his hand, causing deep cuts and possible permanent injury. The plaintiff seeks to recover against El Papagayo Verde on the basis of negligence and strict liability. Pedro Nejarte, the waiter who served the wine, and Mrs. Walters insist that Mr. Walters was drinking normally and did not mishandle the glass. El Papagayo Verde opened nine months before the accident. When it began its operation, all glasses used by the restaurant were new. El Papagayo Verde continually replaces glasses that break, so it is unclear exactly how long the particular glass in this case had been in service. The turnover rate among the kitchen staff at El Papagayo Verde is quite high. Consequently, the plaintiff has been unable to gather direct evidence supporting the conclusion that El Papagayo Verde's employees were negligent in their handling of glasses in general or this particular glass.

The partner in charge of this case wants you to prepare a memorandum assessing the strengths of both the negligence and strict liability counts. He also wants you to anticipate, and meet, the plaintiff's likely arguments in support of his claims.

The Relationship Between Tort and Contract: Products Liability Theory and Pure Economic Loss

The materials in this section provide an opportunity to observe the interplay between tort and contract doctrines in the working out of the rules of decision in a significant area of private law. During the period following the *MacPherson* decision in New York, American courts gradually moved the traditional tort concepts of negligence closer to strict liability by increasingly generous applications of the doctrine of res ipsa loquitur. This development of a *fault-free negligence rule* culminated in the *Escola* decision in California, p. 284, above, with Traynor urging his colleagues to take the last step of breaking free from negligence traditions. Over the same period, courts were heading in essentially the same direction by gradually stripping implied warranty concepts of their contract trappings in products liability cases. This development of a *contract-free warranty rule* culminated in the *Henningsen* decision, p. 568, above, in which the court retained what it liked in warranties (negligence-free strict liability) and rejected what it did not like (the privity requirement and disclaimers.) By the time courts had all but eliminated the element of fault from negligence and all but eliminated the element of contract from warranty, it was but a short step for the California high court in the Greenman case in 1962, and the American Law Institute in 1965, to embrace strict liability in tort.

At least from a tort/contract perspective, it would appear that tort has won the day, albeit with a helpful boost along the way from the contract warranties. Simply stated, tort concepts dominate present-day products liability. However, lest the erroneous impression be created that contract warranties have no continuing role to play in products liability, several important caveats are necessary. First, some jurisdictions in recent years have decided to retain implied warranty as the primary conceptual vehicle for imposing strict liability. Thus, the Supreme Judicial Court of Massachusetts in Back v. Wickes Corp., 375 Mass. 633, 378 N.E.2d 964 (1978) retained §2-314(2)(c) of the U.C.C. as the basis for strict manufacturers' liability in that state, although the court readily admitted that "the duty which the plaintiff sues to enforce in a 'warranty' action for personal injuries is one imposed by law as a matter of social policy, and not necessarily one which the defendant has acquired by contract." (Id. at 640, 378 N.E.2d at 969.)

Even in those jurisdictions that recognize §402A as their primary conceptual vehicle, two types of warranties—express warranties and implied warranties of fitness for a particular purpose—continue to serve unique and useful purposes in products liability cases. For example, if a product seller promises that a product will perform in a certain manner, a disappointed or injured plaintiff will have rights based on express warranty that might not otherwise be available under strict tort liability. And when a seller recommends a particular product as appropriate to the plaintiff's particular purpose, knowing that the buyer is relying on the seller's expertise, the seller will be liable if the product fails dangerously to serve the buyer's purpose, resulting in injury.

Perhaps the most significant caveat to the earlier pronouncement that tort law has won out over contract law in the products liability area concerns the limits of what is here referred to as "products liability." By its terms, §402A applies only to actions to recover for personal injuries and property damage caused by defective, unreasonably dangerous products. What of purely consequential economic loss? A majority of courts deny recovery on the basis of strict tort and relegate plaintiffs to the U.C.C. See, e.g., Seely v. White Motor Co., 63 Cal. 2d 9, 403 P.2d 145, 45 Cal. Rptr. 17 (1965); In Pennsylvania Glass Sand Corp. v. Caterpillar Tractor Co. (652 F.2d 1165, 1172-1173 (3d Cir. 1981), the court supported this position by the following reasoning:

> Although strict liability in tort developed out of the law of warranties, the courts of most states have recognized that the principles of warranty law remain the appropriate vehicle to redress a purchaser's disappointed expectations when a defect renders a product inferior or unable adequately to perform its intended function. These courts have classified the damages consequent to qualitative defects, such as reduced value, return of purchase price, repair and replacement, or lost profits, as economic loss, and have relegated those who suffer such commercial loss to the remedies of contract law.
>
> On the other hand, almost all courts have adopted the view that the benefit-of-the-bargain approach of warranty law is ill-suited to correct problems of hazardous products that cause physical injury. Manufacturers are better able to bear the risk or to take action to correct flaws that pose a danger. Accordingly, tort law imposes a duty on manufacturers to produce safe items, regardless of whether the ultimate impact of the hazard is on people, other property, or the product itself.

The leading case allowing recovery in strict liability for pure economic loss is Santor v. A & M Karagheusian, Inc., 44 N.J. 52, 207 A.2d 305 (1965) in which the plaintiff purchased carpeting manufactured by the defendant from a third-party seller. After several months, unsightly lines began to appear on the surface of the carpet. The trial court determined that there was an implied warranty of merchantability and concluded that the defendant breached that warranty. The Supreme Court of New Jersey affirmed and held that the plaintiff could maintain a breach of implied warranty claim directly against the manufacturer despite the lack of privity between them. In dicta, the court stated that the plaintiff also possessed a cause of action in strict tort liability. As with cases involving personal injuries and property damage caused by defective products, said the court, a manufacturer of an unsatisfactory product is better able to insure against and to spread the risk of economic losses than are individual customers. (Id. at 64-65, 207 A.2d at 311-312). The court observed:

> [W]hen the manufacturer presents his goods to the public for sale he accompanies them with a representation that they are suitable and safe for the intended use. . . . The obligation of the manufacturer thus becomes what in justice it ought to be—an enterprise liability, and one which should not depend upon the intricacies of the law of sales. The purpose of such liability is to insure that the cost of injuries or damage, either to the goods sold or to other property,

> resulting from defective products, is borne by the makers of the products who put them in the channels of trade, rather than by the injured or damaged persons who ordinarily are powerless to protect themselves.

In Spring Motors Distributors, Inc. v. Ford Motor Co., 98 N.J. 555, 489 A.2d 660 (1985), the New Jersey Supreme Court refused to apply *Santor* to a case involving a commercial, rather than a consumer, transaction. The plaintiff, a commercial lessor of trucks, purchased trucks from the defendant. The trucks were defective, and the plaintiff sued to recover damages for repair, towing, and replacement part expenses, for lost profits resulting from the termination of lease agreements for the trucks with its customers, and for a decrease in the market value of the trucks. Defendant sought protection under the four-year U.C.C. statute of limitations, §2-725. In rejecting the plaintiff's position, the court concluded (Id. at 575-577, 489 A.2d at 670-671):

> In the present case, which involves an action between commercial parties, we need not reconsider the *Santor* rule that an ultimate consumer may recover in strict liability for direct economic loss. To determine whether a commercial buyer may recover economic loss, however, we must reconsider the policies underlying the doctrine of strict liability and those underlying the U.C.C. Those policy considerations include, among others, the relative bargaining power of the parties and the allocation of the loss to the better risk-bearer in a modern marketing system. As a general rule, the rights and duties of a buyer and seller are determined by the law of sales which throughout this century has been expressed first in the Uniform Sales Act and more recently in the U.C.C. As indicated, however, strict liability evolved as a judicial response to inadequacies in sales law with respect to consumers who sustained physical injuries from defective goods made or distributed by remote parties in the marketing chain. . . .
>
> Insofar as risk allocation and distribution are concerned, Spring Motors is at least as well situated as the defendants to assess the impact of economic loss. Indeed, a commercial buyer, such as Spring Motors, may be better suited than the manufacturer to factor into its price the risk of economic loss caused by the purchase of a defective product.
>
> Presumably the price paid by Spring Motors for the trucks reflected the fact that Ford was liable for repair or replacement of parts only. By seeking to impose the risk of loss on Ford, Spring Motors seeks, in effect, to obtain a better bargain than it made. In such a context, the imposition of the risk of loss on the manufacturer might lead to price increases for all of its customers, including individual consumers. As between commercial parties, then, the allocation of risks in accordance with their agreement better serves the public interest than an allocation achieved as a matter of policy without reference to that agreement.

In East River Steamship Corp. v. Transamerica Delaval Inc., 476 U.S. 858, 106 S. Ct. 2295, 90 L. Ed. 2d 865 (1986), the Supreme Court, in admiralty, confronted the question of whether the plaintiff could recover in tort when the defect injured only the product itself causing purely economic loss. After carefully reviewing the case law, the Court sided with the majority of jurisdictions and denied tort recovery.

On the issue of tort recovery for economic loss see generally Perlman, Interference with Contract and Other Economic Expectations: A Clash of Tort and Contract Doctrine, 49 U. Chi. L. Rev. 61 (1982); Rabin, Tort Recovery for Negligently Inflicted Economic Loss: A Reassessment, 37 Stan. L. Rev. 1513 (1985); Schwartz, Economic Loss in American Tort Law: The Examples of J'Aire and of Products Liability, 23 San Diego L. Rev. 37 (1986).

Law and Policy: Policy Objectives Supporting Strict Liability in Tort for Defective Products

A number of policy objectives have been advanced by courts and commentators in support of imposing strict liability in tort on commercial sellers of defective products. Among these objectives are (1) compensating injured plaintiffs more adequately; (2) spreading losses among those who consume products; (3) forcing sellers to make good on implied representations of safety; (4) redressing the disappointment of consumer expectations; (5) deterring the marketing of defective products; (6) easing the evidentiary burden on plaintiffs to prove the sellers' negligence; and (7) controlling wasteful accident costs. Is there any way to tie these objectives together into an overarching philosophy? Consider the following excerpt.

Henderson, Coping with the Time Dimension in Products Liability

69 Calif. L. Rev. 919, 931-939 (1981)

In general, strict liability is thought to be preferable to negligence because it better enhances social utility by reducing the costs associated with accidents and because it promotes fairness. Strict liability is believed to increase utility by satisfying four major objectives: encouraging investment in product safety, discouraging consumption of hazardous products, reducing transaction costs, and promoting loss spreading. . . .

Strict liability promotes investment in product safety, the so-called "risk control" objective, by imposing liability rules that encourage manufacturers to find ways to reduce or eliminate avoidable product risks. Although in theory this same objective is satisfied by holding manufacturers liable only for their negligence, those who advocate strict liability suggest that manufacturers escape a significant portion of negligence-based liability. An action sounding in negligence presents the plaintiff with difficult issues of proof, such as what a manufacturer with expertise in the field should have known. Manufacturers also may be able to destroy adverse test results and frustrate plaintiffs' attempts to demonstrate that the defendant knew of the hazards. Knowing that the average plaintiff has difficulty in establishing negligence, manufacturers may be willing to bet on escaping liability, or at least large judgments, and thus may limit their efforts to reduce product risks. A regime of strict liability, which does not consider the manufacturer's knowledge, eliminates the practical difficulties involved in litigating a negligence claim. Manufacturers will be less likely to escape liability and will have a greater incentive to invest in efforts to reduce product risks.

Strict liability has also been justified on the ground that it reduces the consumption of risky products by increasing their cost and so placing them at a disadvantage in the market. This second objective, frequently referred to as "market deterrence," rests on the assumption that consumers tend to underassess the risks associated with various products. Unless consumers are reminded of these risks by price increments reflecting manufacturers' liability insurance costs, including the costs of insuring against accidents not worth trying to prevent, they will overconsume relatively risky products. Lower consumption of these products will result in fewer accidents, thereby reducing the costs of product liability insurance. Unlike the risk control objective, market deterrence is not achieved to the same extent, even in theory, by imposing liability only for negligence: a relatively hazardous product will escape liability if its benefits are sufficient to justify its risks and a reasonable person would not have made it safer at the time of its distribution. In that event, the product will reflect the relevant avoidance costs, but will not reflect the costs of insuring against those accidents that are not worth trying to prevent.

The third objective traditionally thought to be promoted by strict liability is the reduction of transaction costs, which include the costs of operating the accident reparation system. Strict liability reduces these costs by simplifying the proof necessary to establish liability. Since the plaintiff need not put forward evidence of the defendant's negligence, often a difficult, costly, and time consuming process, the costs of trials under a strict liability rule should be lower than they would be under a negligence rule.

The final utility objective concerns reducing dislocation costs that occur when a single individual or business must bear the full accident loss. The costs of repairing the damage or replacing what has been lost, whether borne by an unsuccessful plaintiff or by a liable defendant, may financially destroy the loss bearer. The additional social costs represented by the uncompensated victim who becomes a public charge, or by the manufacturer who goes into bankruptcy, must also be counted as costs of accidents. These dislocation costs can be reduced by spreading accident losses among a large number of persons by means of insurance. In general, manufacturers are believed to be better able to obtain insurance than are consumers, and are assumed to be able to pass on most, if not all, of the insurance costs by raising the prices of products. Under a negligence approach, manufacturers who are not negligent escape liability; even very large accident costs caused by dangerous products will not be shifted to defendants who have acted reasonably. Under strict liability, more of such costs are shifted to manufacturers and their insurers, thus decreasing dislocation costs to the extent of the increased liability.

In addition to the first four objectives aiming at the promotion of social utility, strict products liability traditionally has been supported on the ground that it responds to shared notions of fairness. This writer confesses to a certain degree of skepticism regarding the relevance of fairness, as a consideration separate from utility, to the question of whether producers should be held strictly liable. When a producer is negligent in designing, manufacturing, or marketing a product, it is easy to appreciate the relevance of fairness principles to the question of liability. But the allocation of accident losses to producers irrespective of fault seems to be primarily a means of reducing social waste rather than a means of achieving fairness. Yet, the fact that courts and commentators persist in rationalizing strict products liability in terms of fairness strongly suggests that fairness should be examined. Thus, rather than circumventing fairness in this analysis, or attempting once and for all to settle the question of its relevance to strict products liability, an effort will be made to identify those fairness rationales that seem to support strict liability.

Of the many fairness rationales relied upon by courts and commentators, three offer possible justifications for strict products liability. All three rationales rely to some extent on intuition for their support, and all present analytical difficulties. In order to understand these rationales, it will be useful to consider how they support the traditional imposition of strict liability for harm caused by manufacturing defects.

First, strict liability may be justified on fairness grounds because the product that contains a hidden manufacturing defect that causes harm disappoints the consumer's or user's reasonable expectations with regard to safety. The producer may not have been negligent, and the plaintiff may have understood as a general proposition that mistakes can happen. However, when the plaintiff has paid value for the product, he has a right to expect that it will not fail dangerously in its intended use. Moreover, producers typically try to communicate impressions of infallibility that create consumer confidence in the product. Intuitively it seems appropriate to allow the plaintiff in such a case to claim compensation based on the unfair disappointment of his reasonable expectations.

Second, strict liability for manufacturing defects may be justified because in distributing its products, some of which contain hidden manufacturing defects, the producer may be said to be deliberately taking the physical well-being of those who are injured by the product. The producer is like an actor who shoots into a crowd. The producer, like the shooter, does not know who will be injured; but as surely as the shooter knows that someone will be shot, the producer knows that someone will be injured. Both the shooter and the producer can also estimate the number of victims. The shooter loads his gun with a certain number of bullets, and the producer accepts a certain defect rate when setting the level of quality control for its products. Having set a defect rate, the producer can predict the number of accidents, and thus, the number of accident victims. Choosing to limit quality control means accepting a certain number of accidents; so in a sense, the eventual victims of this choice are harmed deliberately. Of course, the shooter is presumably not privileged, and thus commits a battery when he shoots into the crowd. In contrast, the producer is here assumed to have made the economically reasonable decision in choosing to limit quality control. Consequently, the producer can be said to be privileged in the sense that it will not be found liable under a system of negligence even though its conduct caused harm to others. However, there is precedent for holding an actor liable to others for harm deliberately inflicted even when the actor is privileged to act. The best that can be said for the manufacturer is that it has behaved in an economically rational manner; but that does not alter the fact that its deliberate decision has condemned users and consumers to suffer harm. On this view, the manufacturer should in fairness be required to compensate the injured victims.

Finally, strict liability for manufacturing defects may be justified on fairness grounds because it causes the financial burden of accidents to be borne by those who use, and therefore benefit directly from, the product. From this perspective, the producer is a conduit through which accident costs are shifted from injured persons who do not directly benefit from the product to those persons who do. When a defective product distributed by a nonnegligent producer causes an accident in which a nonuser or nonconsumer bystander is injured, the producer who is held strictly liable shifts the costs to those who purchase and use or consume the product. The bystander-plaintiff's claim is supported by the fairness principle that "those who benefit should pay." Of course, the principle applies only crudely. Some nonusers and nonconsumers benefit indirectly from the use and consumption of the products that cause them injury. Also, spreading the costs pro rata on a per-product rather than on a per-use basis causes some users and consumers to bear more, and some less, than their fair share of the burden. Moreover, recovery on the basis of strict liability is not restricted to bystanders; users and consumers also recover for harm caused by manufacturing defects. However, within these narrow limitations strict liability for manufacturing defects seem to be supported by the "benefits/burdens" fairness principle.

All three fairness rationales represent responses to situations in which accident costs are imposed on certain persons without their express or tacit consent. The "benefits/burdens" rationale, with its concern for bystanders who in no way consent to being victims, is most clearly concerned with consent. The other rationales reflect similar perspectives. The "consumer expectations" rationale relies on the assumption that producers, through advertising, entice purchasers into a misplaced sense of security so that the consent seemingly given by purchasers to their exposure to product-related risks is more properly viewed as involuntary. Finally, the "deliberate taking" rationale, although it purports to focus on the deliberateness of the manufacturer's quality control decisions, relies on the idea of nonconsensual "taking."

For an empirical study on the frequency with which courts explicitly invoke public policy in published products liability opinions see Henderson, Judicial Reliance on Public Policy: An Empirical Analysis of Products Liability Decisions, 59 Geo. Wash. L. Rev. 101 (1991). The author concludes that courts rely on policy in fifteen percent of their published opinions. Fairness/rightness reasons are more often invoked than are efficiency/cost reduction reasons.

So far, all of the cases we have examined have involved commercial sellers of new products who are in the business of selling the product causing the injury. To a large extent, although not completely, §402A reaches only such sellers. To what extent should, and has, strict liability in tort been applied in other contexts? In reacting to the following discussion of this question, it is important to appreciate that the issue is not one of liability or no liability. Even if strict liability in tort does not apply, the defendant may still be exposed to liability in negligence or breach of implied warranty. But you should also appreciate that to the extent that it is more difficult for the plaintiff to recover under one of those other bases, the issue as a practical matter may be one of liability or no liability.

Courts disagree on the question of whether to impose liability on commercial sellers of used products. In Crandell v. Larkin and Jones Appliance Co., 334 N.W.2d 31 (S.D. 1983), the seller of a used clothes dryer was held strictly liable for harm caused by a fire that started when a thermostat failed. The defendant had sold the dryer as a "Quality Reconditioned Unit." In a somewhat narrower opinion than *Crandell,* the New Jersey Supreme Court held that strict liability applies to defective repairs or new component parts replaced by a dealer who sells used products. Realmuto v. Straub Motors, 65 N.J. 336, 344-345, 322 A.2d 440, 444 (1974). Accord Sell v. Bertsch and Co., 577 F. Supp. 1393 (D. Kan. 1984); Peterson v. Lou Bachrodt Chevrolet Co., 61 Ill. 2d 17, 329 N.E.2d 785 (1975).

Other courts believe that strict liability is not appropriate in used products cases in which the seller does not introduce the defect into the product. See, e.g., La Rosa v. Superior Court, 122 Cal. App. 3d 741, 176 Cal. Rptr. 224 (1981); Tillman v. Vance Equipment Co., 286 Or. 747, 596 P.2d 1299 (1979). See generally Henderson, Extending the Boundaries of Strict Products Liability: Implications of the Theory of the Second Best, 128 U. Pa. L. Rev. 1036, 1081-1085 (1980).

Another area of controversy concerns defendants who supply products in the course of performing what are essentially services. In Newmark v. Gimbel's Inc., 54 N.J. 585, 258 A.2d 697 (1969), the Supreme Court of New Jersey held that a beauty parlor patron who was injured by defective permanent wave solution could hold the beauty parlor strictly liable in tort. The court distinguished an earlier decision refusing to impose strict liability on a dentist (see the *Magrine* decision, discussed below) on the ground that "the essence of the relationship [of the dentist] with his patient was the furnishing of professional skill and services," whereas the beautician was engaged "in a commercial enterprise." Id. at 596, 258 A.2d at 702. The decision in *Newmark* highlights an interesting aspect of products liability law: the apparent ease with which the strict liability doctrine may be rendered inapplicable by characterizing what the defendant has supplied as "service" rather than "goods." Doctrinally, the distinction has support. Both the Uniform Commercial Code (§2-102), and §402A of the Restatement (Second), purport to apply only to transactions characterizable as sales of goods or products. Many of the early cases raising the "goods vs. services" issue were brought by plaintiffs injured by contaminated food served in restaurants. Cf. Cushing v. Rodman, discussed at p. 566, above.

One of the most interesting contexts in which the distinction between goods and services arises is the tendering of professional medical and dental services. In another New Jersey decision, Magrine v. Krasnica, 94 N.J. Super. 228, 227 A.2d 539 (1967), *aff'd sub nom.,* Magrine v. Spector, 53 N.J. 259, 250 A.2d 129 (1969), the New Jersey intermediate appellate court refused to hold a dentist strictly liable for injuries to a patient suffered when a defective needle broke off in the patient's jaw. The court distinguished the New Jersey Supreme Court decision in Cintrone v. Hertz Truck Leasing & Rental Service, discussed below, on the ground that, unlike the Hertz rental company in that case, the dentist in *Magrine* did not put the needle into the stream of commerce. Moreover, the court reasoned, the dentist has no control over this sort of accident, and dentists' and doctors' bills are already too high. One judge dissented in the appellate division, pointing out that dentists almost always have insurance, and thus have a ready means of spreading the costs of these accidents. The dissenting opinion concluded (100 N.J. Super. at 240-241, 241 A.2d at 646-647):

> The law of torts should seek to compensate the injured, to encourage safety practices and to distribute losses justly. These objectives may be taken to express the needs of justice. In my view these objectives are advanced by granting plaintiff an award in this case. Dentistry as an enterprise should pay its own way. Denying compensation is to require an injured person who bears the loss alone to subsidize the risk-creating activities by which others profit.

Compare with the *Magrine* decision Cheshire v. Southampton Hospital Association, 53 Misc. 2d 355, 278 N.Y.S.2d 531 (1967), in which a hospital was held not liable for having supplied a defective surgical pin during an operation; and Silverhart v. Mount Zion Hospital, 20 Cal. App. 3d 1022, 98 Cal. Rptr. 187 (1971), in which a hospital was held not liable for having supplied a defective hypodermic needle during surgery. See generally Farnsworth, Implied Warranties of Quality in Non-Sales Cases, 57 Colum. L. Rev. 653 (1957); Sales, The Service-Sales Transaction: A Citadel Under Assault, 10 St. Mary's L.J. 13 (1978); Note, A New Principle of Products Liability in Service Transactions, 30 U. Pitt. L. Rev. 508 (1969).

In Murphy v. E. R. Squibb & Sons, Inc., 40 Cal. 3d 672, 710 P.2d 247, 221 Cal. Rptr. 447 (1985), the California high court faced the question of whether a retail pharmacist might escape strict liability on the ground that it dispensed services rather than sold products. A majority held that strict liability would not be imposed, concluding (40 Cal. 3d at 678-679, 710 P.2d at 251, 221 Cal. Rptr. at 451):

> It seems clear to us that the pharmacist is engaged in a hybrid enterprise, combining the performance of services and the sale of prescription drugs. It is pure hyperbole to suggest, as does plaintiff, that the role of the pharmacist is similar to that of a clerk in an ordinary retail store. With a few exceptions, only a licensed pharmacist may dispense prescription drugs, and as indicated above there are stringent educational and professional requirements for obtaining and retaining a license. A pharmacist must not only use skill and care in accurately filling and labelling a prescribed drug, but he must be aware of problems regarding the medication, and on occasion he provides doctors as well as patients with advice regarding such problems. In counseling patients, he imparts the same kind of information as would a medical doctor about the effects of the drugs prescribed. A key factor is that the pharmacist who fills a prescription is in a different position from the ordinary retailer because he cannot offer a prescription for sale except by order of the doctor. In this respect, he is providing a service to the doctor and acting as an extension of the doctor in the same sense as a technician who takes an X-ray or analyzes a blood sample on a doctor's order.

In Cintrone v. Hertz Truck Leasing & Rental Service, 45 N.J. 434, 212 A.2d 769 (1965), the Supreme Court of New Jersey faced the question whether strict liability applied to a commercial lessor of trucks. The plaintiff was injured when the brakes on a truck rented from defendant by the plaintiff's employer failed, causing an accident. The defendant had rented a fleet of trucks to the employer, along with a promise to maintain them in good working order. At the time of the accident the truck was over two years old. Reversing the trial court's dismissal of the plaintiff's strict liability count, the New Jersey high court held that a commercial vehicle lessor impliedly warrants that its vehicles are in safe working order regardless of the actual age of the vehicle. The court concluded (45 N.J. at 450-451, 212 A.2d at 778):

> When the implied warranty or representation of fitness arises, for how long should it be considered viable? Since the exposure of the user and the public to harm is great if the rented vehicle fails during ordinary use on a highway, the answer must be that it continues for the agreed rental period. The public interests involved are justly served only by treating an obligation of that nature as an incident of the business enterprise. The operator of the rental business must be regarded as possessing expertise with respect to the service life and fitness of his vehicles for use. That expertise ought to put him in a better position than the bailee to detect or to anticipate flaws or defects or fatigue in his vehicles. Moreover, as between bailor for hire and bailee the liability for flaws or defects not discoverable by ordinary care in inspecting or testing ought to rest with the bailor just as it rests with a manufacturer who buys components containing latent defects from another maker, and installs them in the completed product, or just as it rests with the retailer at the point of sale to the consumer. And, with respect to failure of a rented vehicle from fatigue, since control of the length of the lease is in the lessor, such risk is one which in the interest of the consuming public as well as of the members of the public traveling the highways, ought to be imposed on the rental business.

In Mason v. General Motors Corp., 397 Mass. 183, 490 N.E.2d 437 (1986), a man and his son were killed when the Chevrolet Corvette that the father was driving between 70 and 80 M.P.H. ran into a roadside guardrail. The plaintiff claimed that the automobile should have been designed to reduce the decedents' injuries and prevent their deaths. The plaintiff included a breach of implied warranty claim, the equivalent in Massachusetts of strict liability. The decedents had gone to their local Chevrolet dealer to discuss repair work on the father's Chevrolet. While there, the father noticed the Corvette parked in the lot, told the manager his son had never ridden in one, and asked if he could take the car for a drive. The manager agreed, and ten minutes later both father and son were fatally injured. Prior to the accident, the dealership had used the Corvette for demonstration purposes, but there was no mention of a possible purchase by the father in this instance. The trial court granted the dealer's motion for summary judgment on the ground that no sale had occurred and hence no action for implied warranty/ strict liability would lie. (The case against General Motors proceeded to trial and ended in a jury verdict for the defendant.) The Massachusetts high court affirmed, explaining:

> . . . [I]n Massachusetts, under G.L. c. 106, §2-314, a warranty of merchantability is implied in present sales of goods and in contracts for the future sale of goods, and, as a result of judicial extension of warranty liability sanctioned by the Legislature, §2-318, a warranty of merchantability is implied in leases of goods. There is no statutory language, however, that reasonably

> may be construed as either creating or sanctioning the judicial creation of a warranty in connection with a bailment of the kind that occurred in this case. It is true, as the plaintiffs have been careful to remind us, that we have said that "[a]mendments to the Massachusetts version of the Uniform Commercial Code make clear that the Legislature has transformed warranty liability into a remedy intended to be fully as comprehensive as the strict liability theory of recovery that has been adopted by a great many other jurisdictions," id., and that we have said that warranty liability in Massachusetts is "as comprehensive as that provided by §402A of the Restatement [(Second) of Torts (1965)]." Swartz v. General Motors Corp. 375 Mass. 628, 630 (1978). . . . Our statements [to that effect] were made in cases in which sales had in fact taken place. Once a transaction has occurred in which a warranty is implied by our statute. . . . the nature of the warranty and the parties benefited by it are the same as, or at least very similar to, the warranties and beneficiaries recognized in §402A of the Restatement, and the remedies are congruent. However, unlike our warranty law, under §402A an injured plaintiff may recover damages resulting from a defective product regardless of whether title to the product passed or there was a contract to pass title to the product or the product was leased. We did not intend our statements to encompass transactions other than contracts of sale and leases. In any event, our statements did not insert in the statute words that the Legislature had not put there. [Id. at 189-190, 490 N.E.2d at 441-442.]

For general treatments of the policy questions implicit in extending the boundaries of strict products liability see Ghiardi, Products Liability—Where Is the Borderline Now?, 13 Forum 206 (1977); Henderson, Extending the Boundaries of Strict Product Liability: The Implications of the Theory of the Second Best, 128 U. Pa. L. Rev. 1036 (1980); Owen, Rethinking the Policies of Strict Products Liability, 33 Vand. L. Rev. 681 (1980); Note, Strict Liability in Hybrid Cases, 32 Stan. L. Rev. 391 (1980).

2. The Plaintiff's Prima Facie Case: Causation

The actual cause and proximate cause requirements developed in Chapters 2 and 4, above, apply in products liability cases regardless of whether the theory relied on is negligence, warranty, or strict liability in tort, and regardless of the type of defect involved. Section 2-715 of the Uniform Commercial Code establishes that "consequential damages resulting from the seller's breach include. . . . injury to person or property *proximately resulting* from any breach of warranty" (emphasis added); and §402A of the Restatement (Second) of Torts establishes seller's liability "for physical harm . . . *caused* to the ultimate user and consumer, or to his property (emphasis added)." These provisions have been interpreted so as to impose actual cause and proximate cause requirements similar to the requirements under negligence principles. Thus, the plaintiff must show that the product that caused the

injury was distributed by the defendant and that, but for the defect, the accident either would not have happened or would not have been so harmful to the plaintiff. The plaintiff must also show that the resulting harm to the plaintiff was within the range of foreseeable risks created by the defect. Moreover, courts will occasionally recognize the conduct of third persons as "efficient intervening causes" sufficient to relieve the defendant seller of liability to the plaintiff.

One of the more interesting causation issues arose in Anderson v. Somberg, 67 N.J. 291, 338 A.2d 1, *cert. denied,* 423 U.S. 929 (1975). Plaintiff was undergoing a back operation performed by Dr. Somberg when the tip of a rongeur, a forceps-like instrument, broke off in plaintiff's spinal canal causing injury. Plaintiff sued Dr. Somberg, alleging medical malpractice; the hospital, alleging negligent storage and handling of the rongeur; the medical distributor who supplied the rongeur to the hospital, alleging breach of warranty; and the rongeur manufacturer, alleging strict liability in tort. The jury returned verdicts in favor of all defendants. On appeal, the New Jersey Supreme Court reversed and remanded, holding that the jury should be instructed it must return a verdict against at least one of the defendants. On remand, the jury returned a verdict in favor of the plaintiff against the manufacturer and the distributor. The judgment on this verdict was affirmed in Anderson v. Somberg, 158 N.J. Super. 348, 386 A.2d 413 (1978).

The most difficult gap-in-the-proof causation cases are those in which the plaintiff is harmed by a defective product that is both unidentified by trademark or insignia and in no way unique to the defendant. In the classic example of such a defendant identification case, the plaintiff is harmed by a defective unit of a type of product manufactured and distributed by many companies, under circumstances where the plaintiff cannot prove which company actually produced and distributed the defective, harm-causing product unit. These difficult causation cases usually involve generically dangerous products rather than manufacturing flaws. One of the most famous examples in recent years involved personal injuries allegedly resulting from plaintiffs' prenatal exposure to diethylstilbestrol (DES). The harmful products in those cases were allegedly defective by reason of their design and marketing; they did not contain manufacturing defects. Some courts have responded in ways that allow injured plaintiffs to overcome otherwise fatal gaps in their proofs of causation by joining as defendants all, or most, of the companies manufacturing and distributing DES during the time periods relevant to their cases. The best known of these decisions, following in the footsteps of Summers v. Tice, p. 132, above, is Sindell v. Abbott Laboratories, 26 Cal. 3d 588, 607 P.2d 924, 163 Cal. Rptr. 132, *cert. denied,* 449 U.S. 912 (1980), p. 146, above. *Sindell* dropped like a bombshell on the American legal scene. It became the focal point of much controversy as to whether private tort litigation was capable of dealing with mass tort. Courts and commentators have lined up on both sides of the issue.

Once the seminal market share opinion was set in type, other courts fashioned their own versions to conform to their own sense of fairness. Thus, in Collins v. Eli Lilly Co., 116 Wis. 2d 166, 342 N.W.2d 37, *cert. denied sub. nom.,* F.R. Squibb & Co. v. Collins, 469 U.S. 826 (1984), Wisconsin rejected market share in favor of "risk share." The court explained (116 Wis. 2d at 193-198, 342 N.W.2d at 50-52):

> Thus, the plaintiff need commence suit against only one defendant and allege the following elements: that the plaintiff's mother took DES; that DES caused the plaintiff's subsequent injuries; that the defendant produced or marketed the type of DES taken by the plaintiff's mother; and that the defendant's conduct in producing or marketing the DES constituted a breach of a legally recognized duty to the plaintiff. In the situation where the plaintiff cannot allege and prove what type of DES the mother took, as to the third element the plaintiff need only allege and prove that the defendant drug company produced or marketed the drug DES for use in preventing miscarriages during pregnancy. . . .
>
> If the plaintiff is able to prove these elements, the plaintiff may recover all damages from the one defendant. If, however, more than one defendant is joined, the plaintiff should recover from each defendant damages proportionate to the jury's assignment of liability under the comparative negligence scheme developed below. . . .
>
> . . . [I]n order to assure that liability in multiple defendant DES cases is equitably distributed among as many defendants as possible, any defendant may. . . . implead as third-party defendants other drug companies which it can allege produced or marketed the type of DES taken by the plaintiff's mother. This will permit any originally named defendant to share liability with other defendants, and will thereby result in damages being more equitably distributed among all those defendants found liable for the plaintiff's injuries. . . .
>
> Once the plaintiff has proven a prima facie case under either cause of action, the burden of proof shifts to the defendant to prove by a preponderance of the evidence that it did not produce or market the subject DES either during the time period the plaintiff was exposed to DES or in the relevant geographical market area in which the plaintiff's mother acquired the DES. In utilizing these defenses, the defendant must establish that the DES it produced or marketed could not have reached the plaintiff's mother. We conclude that it is appropriate to shift the burden of proof on time and geographical distribution to the defendant drug companies because they will have better access to relevant records than the plaintiff. Further, if relevant records do not exist, we believe that the equities of DES cases favor placing the consequences on the defendants.
>
> We believe that this procedure will result in a pool of defendants which it can reasonably be assumed could have caused the plaintiff's injuries. We note in this regard that, in cases where the plaintiff's mother took DES over a period of time and had the prescription refilled, it is possible that DES from several drug companies may have contributed to the plaintiff's injuries. This still could mean that some of the remaining defendants may be innocent, but we accept this as the price the defendants, and perhaps ultimately society, must pay to provide the plaintiff an adequate remedy under the law.

In Martin v. Abbott Laboratories, 102 Wash. 2d 581, 606, 689 P.2d 368, 383 (1984), the Supreme Court of Washington was troubled by the fact that under *Sindell-Collins* a defendant who had proved its market share would be liable to pay for the damages caused by unnamed or insolvent defendants. The court explained how it would administer its rule of probabilistic causation:

> Application of this rule of apportionment is illustrated by the following hypotheticals. Assume that plaintiff's damages are $100,000 and defendants *X* and *Y* remain subject to liability after exculpation by other named defendants. If neither establishes its market share then they are presumed to have equal shares of the market and are liable respectively for 50 percent of the total judgment, *X*, $50,000 and *Y*, $50,000
>
> Assume defendant *X* establishes that it occupies 20 percent of the relevant market, and defendant *Y* fails to prove its market share. Defendant *X* is then liable for 20 percent of the damages, or $20,000, and defendant *Y* is subject to the remaining 80 percent, or $80,000.
>
> Assume that defendant *X* establishes a market share of 20 percent and defendant *Y* a 60 percent market share. Then defendant *X* is subject to 20 percent of the judgment, $20,000, and defendant *Y* to 60 percent of the judgment, $60,000. The plaintiff does not recover her entire judgment because the remaining 20 percent of the market share is the responsibility of unnamed defendants.
>
> The defendants may implead third party defendants in order to reduce their presumptive share of the market or in order to establish an actual reduced market share.
>
> This ability of a defendant to reduce its liability reduces the disproportion between potential liability that a particular defendant caused the injury by imposing liability according to respective market shares. In the case where each party carries its burden of proof, no defendant will be held liable for more harm than it statistically could have caused in the respective market.

In Conley v. Boyle Drug Co., 570 So. 2d 275 (Fla. 1990), the Supreme Court of Florida adopted a modified version of the marketshare alternate theory of liability for DES cases set forth in *Martin.* The Court held that the plaintiff could bring a cause of action against a defendant for negligently manufacturing and marketing DES of the type which caused a plaintiff's injury when the plaintiff, after a reasonable effort, is unable to establish that a particular defendant was responsible for the injury. The Court, in requiring plaintiff's reasonable effort, incorporated due diligence as a prerequisite to recovery. Market-share liability, the Court stated, is generally looked upon as a theory of last resort, developed to provide a remedy where there is an inherent inability to identify the manufacturer of the product that caused the injury.

Further refining *Martin*'s approach, the Court narrowed the definition of relevant market by the specificity of the evidence as to geographic market area, time of ingestion, and type of DES. The narrower the market, the greater the likelihood that liability will be imposed only on those drug companies who could have manufactured the DES which caused plaintiff's injuries. Finally, the Court restricted application of the market-share alternate theory to actions sounding in negligence, disallowing its use in conjunction with allegations of fraud, breach of warranty or strict liability. Like *Martin,* recovery according to joint and several liability was rejected.

At least two other courts have adopted rulings that help resolve the problem of the indeterminate defendant. In Abel v. Eli Lilly & Co., 418 Mich. 311, 343 N.W.2d 164 (1984), *cert. denied,* 105 S. Ct. 123 (1984), the Michigan high court said that it would hold all the defendants as joint tortfeasors (thus jointly and severally liable for all the plaintiff's damages) if the plaintiff joined all the defendants that were responsible for the sale of DES in the Michigan market. The *Abel* decision relied heavily on the Summers v. Tice theory of alternative liability. This theory was extensively discussed in the *Collins* decision, above.

The New York high court entered the DES fray in Hymowitz v. Eli Lilly Co., 73 N.Y.2d 487, 541 N.Y.2d 941, 539 N.E.2d 1069 (1989). The court began by noting that the New York legislature had enacted a special statute instituting a discovery rule for DES cases, and also reviving for one year cases previously barred under the traditional, accrual-at-time-of-exposure rule. The court observed (73 N.Y.2d at 507-508, 541 N.Y.S.2d at 947, 539 N.E.2d at 1075):

> [I]t would be inconsistent with the reasonable expectations of a modern society to say to these plaintiffs that because of the insidious nature of an injury that long remains dormant, and because so many manufacturers, each behind a curtain, contributed to the devastation, the cost of injury should be borne by the innocent and not the wrongdoers. This is particularly so where the legislature consciously created these expectations by reviving hundreds of DES cases. Consequently, the ever-evolving dictates of justice and fairness, which are the heart of our common-law system, require formation of a remedy for injuries caused by DES (see, Woods v. Lancet, 303 N.Y. 349, 355; see also, Kaye, The Human Dimension in Appellate Judging: A Brief Reflection on a Timeless Concern, 73 Cornell L. Rev. 1004).
>
> We stress, however, that the DES situation is a singular case, with manufacturers acting in a parallel manner to produce an identical, generically marketed product, which causes injury many years later, and which has evoked a legislative response reviving previously barred actions. Given this unusual scenario, it is more appropriate that the loss be borne by those that produced the drug for use during pregnancy, rather than by those who were injured by the use, even where the precise manufacturer of the drug cannot be identified in a particular action. We turn then to the question of how to fairly and equitably apportion the loss occasioned by DES, in a case where the exact manufacturer of the drug that caused the injury is unknown.

The court proceeded to review and reject approaches adopted elsewhere. The court concluded (73 N.Y.2d at 511-513, 541 N.Y.S.2d at 949-950, 539 N.E.2d at 1077-1078):

> Turning to the structure to be adopted in New York, we heed both the lessons learned through experience in other jurisdictions and the realities of the mass litigation of DES claims in this State. Balancing these considerations, we are led to the conclusion that a market share theory, based upon a national market, provides the best solution. . . .
>
> . . . We are aware that the adoption of a national market will likely result in a disproportion between the liability of individual manufacturers and the actual injuries each manufacturer caused in this State. Thus our market share theory cannot be founded upon the belief that, over the run of cases, liability will approximate causation in this State (see, Sindell v. Abbott Laboratories). Nor does the use of a national market provide a reasonable link between liability and the risk created by a defendant to a particular plaintiff (see, Collins v. Lilly & Co., Martin v. Abbott Laboratories). Instead, we choose to apportion liability so as to correspond to the overall culpability of each defendant, measured by the amount of risk of injury each defendant created to the public at large. Use of a national market is a fair method, we believe, of apportioning defendants' liabilities according to their total culpability in marketing DES for use during pregnancy. Under the circumstances, this is an equitable way to provide plaintiffs with the relief they deserve, while also rationally distributing the responsibility for plaintiffs' injuries among defendants.
>
> To be sure, a defendant cannot be held liable if it did not participate in the marketing of DES for pregnancy use; if a DES producer satisfies its burden of proof of showing that it was not a member of the market of DES sold for pregnancy use, disallowing exculpation would be unfair and unjust. Nevertheless, because liability here is based on the overall risk produced, and not causation in a single case, there should be no exculpation of a defendant who, although a member of the market producing DES for pregnancy use, appears not to have caused a particular plaintiff's injury. It is merely a windfall for a producer to escape liability solely because it manufactured a more identifiable pill, or sold only to certain drugstores. These fortuities in no way diminish the culpability of a defendant for marketing the product, which is the basis of liability here.
>
> Finally, we hold that the liability of DES producers is several only, and should not be inflated when all participants in the market are not before the court in a particular case. We understand that, as a practical matter, this will prevent some plaintiffs from recovering 100% of their damages. However, we eschewed exculpation to prevent the fortuitous avoidance of liability, and thus, equitably, we decline to unleash the same forces to increase a defendant's liability beyond its fair share of responsibility. . . .

The cancers that developed in women who were exposed to DES in utero frequently led to malformations of their reproductive organs. As a result, their children have allegedly suffered premature births and prenatal injuries, thus creating a class of third-generation plaintiffs. As of this writing, these DES grandchildren have not met with much success. Thus, in Grover v. Eli Lilly, 63 Ohio St. 3d 756, 591 N.E.2d 696 (1992), the court denied the third-generation claim of a child born 11 weeks premature and with cerebral palsy to a mother whose malformed uterus, allegedly caused by her in utero exposure to DES, led to the plaintiff's injuries. In answer to a certified question from the federal district court trying the case, the highest state court held that drug manufacturers owe no duty to such plaintiffs. The court found as a matter of law that "[a] pharmaceutical company's liability for the distribution or manufacture of a defective prescription drug does not extend to persons who were never exposed to the drug, either directly or in utero." Id. at 700-701. The injuries to grandchildren of women who used DES were too remote "in time and causation" to give rise to a legal duty. Id. at 700.

Justice Resnick's dissenting opinion in *Grover* rejects the majority's rationale, relying instead on the substantive issues of the case. The widespread use and inadequate testing of DES before 1971, as well as the defendants' apparent disregard of early studies demonstrating the dangers of DES, should have satisfied the foreseeability test. (Resnick, J., dissenting). Furthermore, the dissent characterizes the case as one sounding in strict products liability, rather than negligence, thus invoking a more relaxed standard for foreseeability. See also Sparapany v. Rexall, 249 Ill. App. 3d 388, 618 N.E.2d 1098 (1993), (upheld summary judgment for the defendant in a third-generation DES case because at the time the drug was prescribed and ingested the defendant owed no legal duty to the unborn plaintiff).

DES is not the only product to present *Sindell*-type problems. In Minnich v. Ashland Oil Co., 15 Ohio St. 3d 396, 473 N.E.2d 1119 (1984), the court followed the burden-shifting approach of Summers v. Tice, above, in a claim against two manufacturers of cleaning solvent. In Hardy v. Johns-Manville Sales Corp, 509 F. Supp. 1353 (E.D. Tex. 1981), *rev'd on other grounds,* 681 F.2d 334 (5th Cir. 1982), the court accepted the market share approach in an asbestos case. In Smith v. Cutter Biological, Inc., 72 Haw. 416, 439, 823 P.2d 717, 729 (1989), the Supreme Court of Hawaii recognized the basic market share theory in a suit against manufacturers of a blood concentrate by a hemophiliac who allegedly contracted AIDS from injections of the protein.

A substantial number of courts have rejected the market share approach even in the DES cases. See, e.g., Ryan v. Eli Lilly & Co., 514 F. Supp. 1004 (D.S.C. 1981); Mizell v. Eli Lilly & Co., 526 F. Supp. 589 (D.S.C. 1981); Mulcahy v. Eli Lilly & Co., 386 N.W.2d 67 (Iowa 1986); Zafft v. Eli Lilly & Co., 676 S.W.2d 241 (Mo. 1984) (en banc). The attempt to apply market share to the asbestos litigation has also met with some hostility. See Celotex Corp. v. Copeland, 471 So. 2d 533 (Fla. 1985), for a full listing of the cases. (The Florida court emphasized that while DES presented uniform levels of risk-per-unit, asbestos products have widely divergent toxicities; thus, a producer with a relatively low market share of a particular product might, if its product were especially toxic, have contributed a larger proportion of the risks of injury.) See also Bateman v. Johns-Manville Sales Corp., 781 F.2d 1132 (5th Cir. 1986). For negative commentary on market share, see Fischer, Products Liability—An Analysis of Market Share Liability, 34 Vand. L. Rev. 1623 (1981); Note, Market Share Liability—The California Roulette of Causation Eliminating the Identification Requirement, 11 Seton Hall L. Rev. 610 (1981).

Problem 29

Frank Tarbuckle seeks your advice regarding possible products liability claims he may have in connection with injuries he suffered in a workplace accident 11 months ago. At the time of the accident, Mr. Tarbuckle was employed at a sheet metal fabricating plant in your city. He worked as part of a "finishing crew," grinding and sanding fabricated metal units in preparation for painting and shipment. Mr. Tarbuckle's job was to grind off rough edges and excess welding material, eliminating unsightly lumps and dangerous sharp edges. On the day in question, he was using a No. 10 abrasive disk on a half-inch portable drill to smooth the welds on metal pickup truck roof units. He explains that he had just put a new abrasive disk on the drill and was routinely grinding a weld on a roof unit when the disk exploded, causing injuries to his arms, face, neck and upper torso. He was wearing safety goggles, which prevented serious injury to his eyes, but his injuries are substantial and disfiguring.

An expert retained by your law firm has examined the fragments from the disk that disintegrated. Based on his examination and the surrounding facts he is prepared to testify that the abrasive disk in question contained a latent manufacturing defect that caused it to explode violently when Mr. Tarbuckle began using it to grind the welds. The client explains that he had worked on the same job for six years and had never known such an accident to happen. "It was like a bomb went off," he explains. "Normally a disk is good for 30 minutes or so until the abrasive coating wears off. This one blew up the minute I started using it."

Mr. Tarbuckle's employer, Freeman Fabricators, Inc., (hereafter Freeman) purchases abrasive disks in a variety of sizes from a variety of suppliers and keeps a large inventory on hand. In most instances, it is not possible from a physical examination to determine who made or distributed any particular disk. Our expert is unable to identify, based on his examination, the original source of the disk that exploded. Freeman tries to rotate its stock of expendable equipment, such as abrasive disks, periodically. It makes no effort to keep track of which equipment comes from which source. The disk in question had been in Freeman's possession for between one and six months. During that five-month period, Freeman purchased No. 10 abrasive disks from four different wholesalers: Acme, Best, Cost-Less and Dorchester. Of the No. 10 disks purchased during that period, approximately 40 percent come from Acme, 30 percent from Best and 15 percent each from Cost-Less and Dorchester. Given the nature of Freeman's stock rotation system, the percentages from each source of disks on hand at the time of the accident could have been different. All four wholesalers deal with a number of different disk manufacturers, and it would be very difficult to determine the relative likelihoods that various producers manufactured the defective disk that injured the plaintiff. Freeman appears to have handled the disks carefully and, in any event, is immune from tort liability to Tarbuckle under the workers' compensation statute.

Assuming that Collins v. Ely Lilly Co., discussed above, was decided by your supreme court, what are your chances of reaching the jury in products liability actions against Acme, Best, Cost-Less and Dorchester? What arguments are available in overcoming the gaps in proof of causation? What further investigation should be undertaken?

3. Affirmative Defenses Based on User's Conduct

To the extent that the plaintiff relies on traditional negligence principles in a products liability case, presumably he will be barred from recovery, or have his recovery reduced, if he is found to have been contributorily negligent. When the plaintiff relies on the theory of strict liability, however, he may find his way to recovery made easier in this regard. The Restatement position is stated in the following comment to §402A:

> n. Contributory negligence. Since the liability with which this Section deals is not based upon negligence of the seller, but is strict liability, the rule applied to strict liability cases applies. Contributory negligence of the plaintiff is not a defense when such negligence consists merely in a failure to discover the defect in the product, or to guard against the possibility of its existence. On the other hand the form of contributory negligence which consists in voluntarily and unreasonably proceeding to encounter a known danger, and commonly passes under the name of assumption of risk, is a defense under this Section as in other cases of strict liability. If the user or consumer discovers the defect and is aware of the danger, and nevertheless proceeds unreasonably to make use of the product and is injured by it, he is barred from recovery.

Murray v. Fairbanks Morse

610 F.2d 149 (3d Cir. 1979)

ROSENN, CIR. J. This appeal raises several issues, including novel and important questions as to whether a comparative negligence statute may be applied and, if so, to what extent, in an action for personal injuries brought under twin theories of strict products liability and common law principles of negligence. The jury returned a verdict in favor of the plaintiff, Norwilton Murray, in the sum of two million dollars against the manufacturer, Beloit Power Systems, Inc. (Beloit). The jury, in response to special interrogatories, found that plaintiff's negligence was a proximate cause of his injuries and that he was at fault to the extent of five percent. The trial judge reduced the verdict accordingly and judgment was thereupon entered for the plaintiff. Beloit's motion for a new trial was denied and it appealed. . . .

I

At the time of the accident, Norwilton Murray, a thirty-four year old experienced instrument fitter, was employed by Litwin Corporation, an installer of equipment. On July 21, 1974, Murray and a co-worker were installing an electrical control panel at the Hess Oil Refinery in the Virgin Islands. The panel was built by Beloit to Litwin's specifications and Litwin's engineer approved it at Beloit's factory before it was shipped. Litwin intended to install the panel on a platform over an open space approximately ten feet above the concrete floor of the refinery. There was evidence, however, that Beloit had not been so informed. At Litwin's request the unit had been purposely left open at the bottom so that conduits from below could be attached to it. The control panel was removed from its shipping crate and a cherry-picker hoisted it by its metal lifting eyes onto the platform. In order to protect the integrity of the delicate instrumentation inside the panel, Beloit had attached two iron cross-members to the open bottom of the unit to stabilize it during shipping. Murray's task was to align the holes in the base of the control panel with pre-drilled holes in the platform and secure the unit with mounting bolts. Because the holes were not perfectly aligned when the cherry-picker deposited the unit on the foundation, Murray chose to use a crow-bar to rock the approximately one and a half ton unit into alignment.

The accident occurred when Murray put his weight on one of the iron cross-members by leaning over the open space at the bottom of the unit to bolt it to the platform. The cross-member gave way and Murray fell approximately ten feet to the concrete floor incurring severe injuries to his spine. It was determined at trial that the cross-member gave way because it had been only temporarily or "tack-welded" to the unit, instead of being secured by a permanent or "butt-weld.". . .

Murray brought a products liability action against Beloit alleging alternative theories of strict liability under Restatement (Second) of Torts §402A and common law negligence. He contended that the control panel was defective because the cross-member had been only tack-welded to the unit. Beloit defended with expert evidence to prove that Murray's method of installation was highly dangerous and Beloit argued that Murray assumed the risk of injury posed by his manner of installation. The district court, holding that the Virgin Islands comparative negligence statute, 5 V.I.C. §1451 (1978) was applicable to a strict products liability action, instructed the jury that if they found Beloit liable and Murray negligent, to reduce Murray's award by the percentage attributable to his fault.

The jury returned a verdict finding Beloit liable under both the strict products liability and the negligence counts. The jury also found Murray's negligence in installing the unit to constitute five percent fault for the injuries. The jury awarded Murray $2,000,000 in damages. This sum, when reduced by the five percent fault attributable to Murray and the reduction to present value of his future earnings, amounted to $1,747,000. Although noting that the verdict was very high, the district court denied defendant's motion for a new trial.

[The court's discussion of preliminary issues is omitted.]

III

Contrib. Neg.

We now turn to the claims of both parties that damages were improperly apportioned. Murray has cross-appealed and we shall first consider whether his award should have been reduced by the five percent fault attributed to his negligence in causing his injuries. We must determine whether the district court was correct in applying the Virgin Islands comparative negligence statute, 5 V.I.C. §1451 in a strict products liability action. . . .

In the present case, Beloit requested a jury instruction that Murray's voluntary assumption of risk would constitute a complete bar to recovery. Murray, on the other hand, requested an instruction that ordinary contributory negligence was not a defense to a section 402A action. The district court declined to issue either instruction and instead, applying the Virgin Islands comparative negligence statute, instructed the jury that they could reduce any award for Murray by whatever fault they ascribed to his negligence in causing the accident. Judge Young later explained his position:

> The Court is of the opinion that neither of the positions advanced by the parties should govern the law of strict products liability in the Virgin Islands, but that both plaintiff's want of ordinary due care in his use of the product and plaintiff's unreasonable exposure to a known and appreciable risk of injury should work to diminish plaintiff's recovery in a §402A type action in proportion to the amount of causative culpable conduct attributable to plaintiff. The mere failure of plaintiff to discover or guard against the existence of a defect where plaintiff had no reason to suspect the same would not constitute a defense in a §402A type action.

Murray v. Beloit Power Systems, Inc., 450 F. Supp. 1145, 1147 (D.V.I. 1978) (footnote omitted). . . .

IV

We are faced with an initial problem not fully considered by the district court. As indicated above, comparative negligence has been adopted by statute in the Virgin Islands, 5 V.I.C. §1451. The statute provides that contributory negligence is replaced by comparative negligence "[i]n any action based upon *negligence* to recover for injury to person or property. . . ." 5 V.I.C. §1451(a) (emphasis supplied). . . .

In applying the Virgin Islands comparative negligence statute to this suit, the district court expressly adopted the "position and policy considerations advanced by the Wisconsin Supreme Court in Powers v. Hunt-Wesson Foods, Inc., 64 Wis. 2d 532, 219 N.W.2d 393 (1974) and Dippel v. Sciano, 37 Wis. 2d 443, 155 N.W.2d 55 (1967)." 450 F. Supp. at 1147. The *Dippel* case was the first decision to apply a comparative negligence statute to a strict products liability action. . . . The Wisconsin approach is to review the strict products liability action as "akin to negligence per se" and therefore within the purview of the comparative negligence statute. 155 N.W.2d at 64. By adopting the Wisconsin approach, the district court justified the application of the Virgin Islands comparative negligence statute, arguably limited to negligence actions, to strict products liability.

We disagree with the district court's adoption of Wisconsin's gloss on section 402A actions as negligence per se. The Restatement makes it quite clear that strict liability is imposed on the defendant even if he has exercised "all possible care in the preparation and sale of his products." Restatement (Second) of Torts §402A(2)(a). The focus of the strict products liability action is on the condition of the product and not on the conduct of the defendant. . . . The advantage of strict products liability theory is that the plaintiff need only prove the existence of a product defect and not that negligence caused it. The problem is that products liability cases are often tried on alternative theories of negligence and strict liability and the temptation to view strict liability as a species of presumptive negligence is inviting. We decline any such invitation because we believe that a satisfactory union of strict liability and comparative negligence principles cannot be conceptually achieved by converting an action predicated upon a product defect into a hybrid action adulterated by proof of personal misconduct. . . .

V

We agree with the district court that the use of comparative principles in section 402A actions can achieve a more equitable allocation of the loss from product related injuries. We are mindful, however, of the current conceptual confusion among the courts, and the difficulties confronting us in comparing plaintiff's personal conduct with the strict liability of the defendant for his product defect. . . .

The elimination of the need to prove defendant's negligence has led some to view strict products liability as a "no-fault" doctrine to which the application of comparative negligence principles is simply not conceptually feasible. According to Dean Wade, however, fault is still present in strict products liability cases despite the focus on the product defect:

> In the case of products liability, the fault inheres primarily in the nature of the product. The product is "bad" because it is not duly safe; it is determined to be defective and (in most jurisdictions) unreasonably dangerous. . . . [S]imply maintaining the bad condition or placing the bad product on the market is enough for liability. . . . One does not have to stigmatize conduct as negligent in order to characterize it as fault.

Wade, [Products Liability and Plaintiff's Fault, 29 Mercer L. Rev. 373, 377 (1978)] (footnotes omitted). Dean Aaron Twerski adds perspective on the relationship between defect and fault: "In this imperfect world it is not an outrageous inference that a bad defect most probably stems from serious fault—even if the fault need not nor cannot be established." Twerski, From Defect to Cause to Comparative Fault—Rethinking Some Product Liability Concepts, 60 Marq. L. Rev. 297, 331 (1977).

The substitution of the term fault for defect, however, would not appear to aid the trier of fact in apportioning damages between the defect and the conduct of the plaintiff. The key conceptual distinction between strict liability theory and negligence is that the plaintiff need not prove faulty *conduct* on the part of the defendant in order to recover. The jury is not asked to determine if the defendant deviated from a standard of care in producing his product. There is no proven faulty conduct of the defendant to compare with the faulty conduct of the plaintiff in order to apportion the responsibility for an accident. Although we may term a defective product "faulty," it is qualitatively different from the plaintiff's conduct that contributes to his injury. A comparison of the two is therefore inappropriate. The characterization of both plaintiff's negligent conduct and the defect as faulty may provide a semantic bridge between negligence and strict liability theories, but it provides neither a conceptual nor pragmatic basis for apportioning the loss for a particular injury.

We believe that if the loss for a particular injury is to be apportioned between the product defect and the plaintiff's misconduct, the only conceptual basis for comparison is the causative contribution of each to the particular loss or injury. In apportioning damages we are really asking how much of the injury was caused by the defect in the product versus how much was caused by the plaintiff's own actions. We agree with the Ninth Circuit when it noted that comparative causation "is a conceptually more precise term than 'comparative fault' since fault alone without causation does not subject one to liability." Pan-Alaska Fisheries, Inc. v. Marine Construction & Design Co., 565 F.2d 1129, 1139 (9th Cir. 1977). The appropriate label for the quality of the act is insignificant. . . . Thus, the underlying task in each case is to analyze and compare the causal conduct of each party regardless of its label. Although fault, in the sense of the defendant's defective product or the plaintiff's failure to meet a standard of care, must exist before a comparison takes place,[12] the comparison itself must focus on the role each played in bringing about the particular injury. . . .

The relevant causation inquiry in a strict products liability suit should be whether the product defect "caused-in-fact" some or all of the injury and whether the plaintiff's faulty conduct "caused-in-fact" all or some of the injury. If the answer to both these questions is affirmative, the issue of proximate cause becomes relevant. Were there any intervening causes or unforeseeable consequences which would absolve the defendant of liability for the defect or the plaintiff for his conduct? It is conceivable that in any given accident, both the product defect and the plaintiff's conduct may be substantial factors in bringing about the injury. Under a comparative causation approach, once the jury has determined that the product defect caused the injury, the defendant is strictly liable for the harm caused by his defective product. The jury, however, would be instructed to reduce the award of damages "in proportion to the plaintiff's contribution to his own loss or injury." *Pan-Alaska Fisheries,* supra, 565 F.2d at 1139.

The use of causation as the conceptual bridge between the plaintiff's conduct and the defendant's product in no way jeopardizes the conceptual integrity of the strict products liability action. The focus is still on the product defect. Semantically, apportioning damages in strict products liability cases may be termed a system of "comparative fault" but the real division occurs along lines of causation.[13] However, "because the term 'comparative fault' appears to be commonly accepted and used," id., we shall use that label to represent a system of apportioning damages in strict products liability cases. . . .

VI

Once a conceptually viable way of apportioning damages in section 402A actions is established, the key inquiry is whether such a system is consistent

12. We believe the initial determination of fault is necessary to avoid situations in which conduct that is reasonable on the part of the plaintiff might contribute causally to an injury and the plaintiff would accordingly bear part of the loss. Only when conduct fails to meet a societal standard of reasonable care should the casual link between conduct and injury be examined.

13. Indeed, this appears to be the thrust of the new Proposed Uniform Comparative Fault Act. Under this proposed model act, strict liability is included definitionally within the scope of the term "fault." Uniform Comparative Fault Act §1(b). This is accomplished by attributing fault to the defectiveness of the product. See Wade, supra 29 Mercer L. Rev. at 377. However, the Uniform Act recognizes that "[l]egal requirements of causal relation apply both to fault as the basis for liability and to contributory fault." Uniform Comparative Fault Act §1(b). In determining the percentages of fault attributed to each

with the policy goals of strict product liability. As we have indicated already, a central goal of the strict liability action is to relieve the plaintiff of proof problems associated with existing negligence and warranty theories. A system of comparative fault which proceeds to apportion damages on the basis of causation in no way disturbs the plaintiff's burden of proof. The plaintiff still need only prove the existence of a defect causally linked to the injury. The defendant's burden is to prove plaintiff's contributory fault. . . .

The recognition of contributory fault as an absolute bar to recovery would improperly shift the total loss to the plaintiff. Under a system of comparative fault, however, there are good reasons for allowing some form of contributory fault to be considered in reducing damages. When plaintiff's conduct is faulty, i.e., he exposes himself to an unreasonable risk of harm which causes part of his injuries, the manufacturer should not be required to pay that portion of the loss attributable to the plaintiff's fault. Under a comparative system, the future cost of the defendant's product will accurately represent the danger it has caused and not the danger caused by plaintiff's own fault.[14]

[The court left unresolved the question of whether to apply comparative fault to assumption of the risk and product misuse.]

VII

The foregoing analysis leads us to conclude that a system of comparative fault may effectively operate in strict products liability cases and will result in a more equitable apportionment of the loss for product related injuries while furthering the valid policy goals behind the strict products liability action. We accordingly hold that a system of pure comparative fault should be applied to Restatement §402A actions in the Virgin Islands. Under this system, fault is ascribed to the defendant once his product is found to be defective. If fault on the part of the plaintiff is also present, the trier of fact shall reduce the damage award in proportion to the plaintiff's causal

part, the Uniform Act states that "the trier of fact shall consider both the nature of the conduct and the damages claimed." Id. §2(b).

14. There is a legitimate concern, however, that if contributory negligence, in the sense of failing to discover the product defect, is recognized as a category of plaintiff's fault, almost every case of products liability will be open to loss apportionment through protracted litigation. Defendants will always argue that the plaintiff negligently failed to find the defect. Such a defense might intrude on another goal of strict products liability, that of discouraging the introduction of obviously defective products into the stream of commerce. If the plaintiff can be held responsible for not discovering the defect, there is an incentive to make defects obvious and not eliminate them from products. But when the plaintiff is contributorily at fault, in the sense of exposing himself to an unreasonable risk of harm in the use of the product, such conduct is to be considered plaintiff's legal fault, thereby triggering the comparative causation analysis. This view is consistent with the position adopted by Judge Young in his memorandum opinion in the instant case. 450 F. Supp. at 1147.

contribution to his own injury. Under our holding, the plaintiff shall not be barred from recovery even if his fault is determined to be greater than that of the defendant.

The task before us now is to determine what effect our holding has on the apportionment of the loss for Murray's injuries. . . .

Our review of the record reveals that Beloit introduced expert testimony to prove that Murray's method of installation was highly dangerous. Beloit's expert testified that Murray could have taken safety measures to avoid or minimize the risk of a fall. . . .

Balanced against this evidence was testimony from Murray's supervisor and co-worker that the method used to install the unit was commonly employed without difficulty. Murray's supervisor testified that over an eighteen-year period he had installed approximately 400 units in this fashion. . . .

We cannot say as a matter of law that the jury's assessment of five percent fault to Murray under the strict liability count was against the weight of the evidence. . . .

Because we perceive no error in the district court's judgment under either the strict products liability or negligence counts, the judgment of the district court is affirmed. . . .

In Conti v. Ford Motor Co., 578 F. Supp. 1429 (E.D. Pa. 1983), *rev'd on other grounds,* 743 F.2d 195 (3d Cir. 1984), *cert denied,* 470 U.S. 1028 (1985), the court addressed the question of whether the Pennsylvania comparative fault statute applied in strict products liability actions. Concluding that it did not, and that a judicially crafted comparative fault doctrine would be inappropriate, the district court (Fullam, J.) made these observations regarding the *Murray* case, above.

> . . . I note that it is far from clear that the *Murray* decision would require the result sought by defendant in this case. In *Murray,* and in most if not all of the cases applying comparative fault or comparative causation in product-liability cases, the courts were dealing with what might be termed independent or additional negligence on the part of the user of the defective product; that is, negligence other than mere failure to learn of, and guard against, the defect alleged. In *Murray,* for example, there was evidence that the plaintiff was pursuing a dangerous method of installing the equipment in question, and was not exercising reasonable care for his own safety, in ways totally unrelated to the inadequate welds which rendered the product defectively dangerous. Notwithstanding the generality of the language in the *Murray* opinion, it is reasonable to suppose that the court might reach a different conclusion in a case, for example, where the operator of a vehicle is traveling at grossly excessive speeds when the wheel falls off, than in a case in which the operator merely was negligent in failing to inspect the wheel and observe that its

> fastenings were inadequate. And the concurrent negligence of a third party, such as an employer who fails to supply guarding omitted by the manufacturer, falls more comfortably within the comparative-fault realm than the negligence of a user of the product, when his negligence consists of failure to discover the defect or to avoid the harm. Invocation of the comparative-fault doctrine in the latter situation would severely undermine the policies served by §402A strict liability. [Id. at 1435.]

A considerable body of literature has grown up around the subject of comparative fault and its applicability to products litigation. Two early articles were influential: Levine, Buyer's Conduct as Affecting the Extent of Manufacturer's Liability in Warranty, 52 Minn. L. Rev. 627 (1968); Noel, Defective Products: Abnormal Use, Contributory Negligence, and Assumption of Risk, 25 Vand. L. Rev. 93 (1972). See also Fischer, Products Liability—Applicability of Comparative Negligence, 43 Mo. L. Rev. 431 (1978); Leff & Pinto, Comparative Negligence in Strict Products Liability: The Courts Render the Final Judgment, 89 Dick. L. Rev. 915 (1985); Thode, Some Thoughts on the Use of Comparisons in Products Liability Cases, 1981 Utah L. Rev. 3; Woods, The Trend Toward Comparative Fault, 7 J. Prod. Liab. 399 (1984).

One form of contributory fault—the seat belt defense—has become a serious topic of debate in recent years. (See p. 473-474, above.) Auto manufacturers contend that even if they have contributed to causing the plaintiff's injury by supplying a defective vehicle, the plaintiff has co-authored the injury by failing to buckle up. Several courts have allowed for some form of reduction of the plaintiff's damages based on the failure to wear a seat belt. See, e.g., Insurance Co. of North America v. Pasakarnis, 451 So. 2d 447 (Fla. 1984); Spier v. Barker, 35 N.Y.2d 444, 323 N.E.2d 164, 363 N.Y.S.2d 916 (1974); Bentzler v. Braun, 34 Wis. 2d 362, 149 N.W.2d 626 (1967). But resistance to the defense persists notwithstanding the overwhelming acceptance of the comparative fault doctrine. See, e.g., Dare v. Sobule, 674 P.2d 960 (Colo. 1984); Melesko v. Riley, 32 Conn. Supp. 89, 339 A.2d 479 (1975); Clarkson v. Wright, 108 Ill. 2d 129, 483 N.E.2d 268 (1985); Taplin v. Clark, 6 Kan. App. 2d 66, 626 P.2d 1198 (1981); Kopischke v. First Continental Corp., 187 Mont. 471, 610 P.2d 668 (1980). For a discussion of the different methods of computing the reduction of damages, see Twerski, The Use and Abuse of Comparative Negligence in Products Liability, 10 Ind. L. Rev. 797, 819-822 (1977).

B. Liability for Failure to Instruct and Warn

Whenever a commercial seller markets a product he must provide needed instructions regarding proper use and he must warn of hidden risks. If adequate instructions and warnings are not provided to purchasers and users, the seller may be liable for supplying a defective product even if the product in question is free from manufacturing defects and even if the product design is not, judged on its own merits, unreasonably dangerous. In many cases the plaintiff will rely on traditional negligence principles, alleging that the defendant's duty of care has been breached. Failure to provide adequate instructions or warning can also support a conclusion that the product, as marketed, is defective. The following comment to §402A of the Restatement explains the relationship between failure to provide instructions or warning and strict liability in tort:

> j. Directions or warning. In order to prevent the product from being unreasonably dangerous, the seller may be required to give directions or warning, on the container, as to its use. The seller may reasonably assume that those with common allergies, as for example to eggs or strawberries, will be aware of them, and he is not required to warn against them. Where, however, the product contains an ingredient to which a substantial number of the population are allergic, and the ingredient is one whose danger is not generally known, or if known is one which the consumer would reasonably not expect to find in the product, the seller is required to give warning against it, if he has knowledge, or by the application of reason, developed human skill and foresight should have knowledge, of the presence of the ingredient and the danger. Likewise in the case of poisonous drugs, or those unduly dangerous for other reasons, warnings as to use may be required.
>
> But a seller is not required to warn with respect to products, or ingredients in them, which are only dangerous, or potentially so, when consumed in excessive quantity, or over a long period of time, when the danger, or potentiality of danger, is generally known and recognized. Again the dangers of alcoholic beverages are an example, as are also those of foods containing such substances as saturated fats, which may over a period of time have a deleterious effect upon the human heart.
>
> Where warning is given, the seller may reasonably assume that it will be read and heeded; and a product bearing such a warning, which is safe for use if it is followed, is not in defective condition, nor is it unreasonably dangerous.

One question raised by the preceding comment, with its requirement that the seller know of the risks or be in the position that he should have known, is whether the approach in §402A is different in substance from traditional negligence principles.

Sheckells v. AGV Corp.

987 F.2d 1532 (11th Cir. 1993)

BIRCH, CIRCUIT JUDGE:

Plaintiff Charles Sheckells ("Sheckells"), the natural father and guardian of John Sheckells, an incapacitated adult, appeals from the grant of summary judgment in favor of AGV, a defendant in the underlying product liability action. The grant of summary judgment in favor of AGV is AFFIRMED IN PART and REVERSED IN PART.

I. Background

John Sheckells was injured when he lost control of his motorcycle after striking debris in the road. At the time of the accident, he was wearing a helmet manufactured by AGV. On behalf of his son, Sheckells filed suit against AGV alleging that the helmet was defectively designed and manufactured and that the defendants failed to warn that the helmet would not afford any significant protection from certain reasonably foreseeable impacts. On appeal, Sheckells has abandoned his theory of defective design and appeals the judgment only upon the failure to warn theory.

When purchased, the helmet contained a warning label affixed to the inside of the helmet, stating in substance that "some reasonably foreseeable impacts may exceed this helmet's capability to protect against severe injury or death." In addition, the helmet was packaged with a consumer notice that informs the purchaser that "[y]our helmet is the single most important piece of safety equipment you own and should be treated as such." The notice further states that "NO HELMET, including your AGV helmet, can protect the wearer against all foreseeable impacts" and that "NO WARRANTY OR REPRESENTATION IS MADE AS TO THIS PRODUCT'S ABILITY TO PROTECT THE USER FROM ANY INJURY OR DEATH. THE USER ASSUMES ALL RISKS."

In opposition to summary judgment, Sheckells offered the deposition testimony of Dr. Joseph L. Burton, the Chief Medical Examiner for the City of Atlanta. With regard to the failure to warn claim, Dr. Burton testified that Department of Transportation and Snell Memorial Foundation impact tests are conducted at speeds of only 15 to 20 miles an hour and that no motorcycle helmet marketed today provides any assurance of protecting the wearer from facial or brain injury at speeds of 30 or 45 miles an hour. Further, he opined that the average purchaser of a helmet would not know these facts.

The district court entered summary judgment in favor of AGV on the failure to warn theory on the ground that it was open and obvious that the AGV helmet would not protect an operator traveling at 30 to 45 miles an hour. Sheckells appeals the grant of summary judgment.

II. Discussion. . . .

In this diversity action, AGV's duty to warn of hazards posed by the use of its products is determined by Georgia law. . . . Under Georgia law, a manufacturer is subject to liability for failure to warn if it "(a) knows or has reason to know that the chattel is or is likely to be dangerous for the use for which it is supplied, and (b) has no reason to believe that those for whose use the chattel is supplied will realize its dangerous condition and (c) fails to exercise reasonable care to inform them of its dangerous condition or of the facts which make it likely to be dangerous." Greenway v. Peabody Intl. Corp., 163 Ga. App. 698, 703, 294 S.E.2d 541, 545-546 (1982) (quoting Restatement (Second) of Torts §388). Georgia law imposes no duty on a manufacturer to warn of a danger associated with the use of its product if that danger is open or obvious.

> [T]here is no duty resting upon the manufacturer or seller to warn of a product-connected danger which is obvious, or of which the person who claims to be entitled to warning knows, should know, or should, in using the product, discover.

294 S.E.2d at 546 (quoting Annotation, Products Liability—Duty to Warn, 76 A.L.R.2d 9, 28-29 (1961)).

At his deposition, Dr. Burton testified that, although no motorcycle helmet on the market today would provide any assurance of protecting an operator from facial or brain injury at a speed of 30 to 45 miles an hour, "the average buyer of a helmet would not know that." Dr. Burton also testified that representations made by vendors of motorcycles and helmets may lull a purchaser into a false sense of security regarding the amount of protection provided by a helmet. Dr. Burton concluded that, in order to dispel this impression, some warning should accompany the helmet to educate the user that the helmet provides no significant protection at speeds exceeding 30 to 45 miles an hour. Thus, Dr. Burton's deposition, viewed in the light most favorable to the plaintiff, suggests that the failure of a motorcycle helmet to protect the wearer at speeds over 30 to 45 miles an hour is not an open or obvious danger.

AGV presented no evidence tending to show that it is open or obvious that its helmet would not protect the wearer at speeds of 30 to 45 miles an hour. That the parties' experts agree that no helmet currently marketed could protect a wearer traveling at speeds of 45 miles an hour does not mean that this fact is patent to a purchaser. Presumably, these experts are "expert" for the reason that they possess knowledge not generally shared with the public. As noted by the Greenway court, the focus of the open or obvious danger rule is upon "those for whose use the chattel is supplied." 294 S.E.2d at 545-546.

The district court relied on several Georgia cases for the proposition that "it is a matter of common knowledge that operating a motorcycle carries with it certain inherent dangers." While recognizing the inherent hazard of operating a motorcycle, these cases do not establish as a matter of Georgia law that safety precautions, such as a helmet, openly and obviously provide insignificant protection at speeds of 30 to 45 miles an hour. Further, those cases where the Georgia courts have concluded that a peril associated with a product is open or obvious suggest that summary judgment was inappropriate based on the factual record before the district court. The Georgia courts have determined that, under certain circumstances, operating a product without the safety features included by the manufacturer is an open or obvious hazard. See, e.g., Weatherby v. Honda Motor Co., 195 Ga. App. 169, 393 S.E.2d 64, 67 (1990) (danger in operating motorcycle with uncapped fuel tank is open and obvious). Additionally, the Georgia cases reveal that the observable absence of a safety feature is likely to be considered an open and obvious danger. In each of these cases, however, the absence of the safety feature in question was apparent to the purchaser by a simple visual inspection. By contrast, it is not obvious from an observation of the AGV helmet that this product provides only minimal protection against collision when the motorcycle is operated at speeds of 30 to 45 miles an hour. Conceivably, a purchaser might expect more from "the single most important piece of safety equipment" that he or she owns. Further, Dr. Burton's testimony suggests that the limited degree of protection afforded by wearing a helmet is not common knowledge. The evidence presented by the plaintiff was sufficient to raise an issue of fact regarding the open or obvious nature of this hazard. Thus, in granting summary judgment for AGV with respect to the failure to warn claim, the district court erred by resolving a material and genuinely disputed issue of fact against the plaintiff.

AGV further contends that summary judgment was appropriate based on either of two issues not reached by the district court. First, AGV argues that John Sheckells did not read the allegedly inadequate warnings, and, thus, the failure to warn was not a proximate cause of his injuries. AGV relies on John Sheckells's deposition testimony that he did not remember reading the warning label affixed to the helmet or the literature that was packaged with the helmet. John Sheckells did not testify that he did not read the warnings, only that he did not remember doing so. Based on the factual record before the district court, it is possible that this failure to remember was due to his memory loss, suffered as a result of the accident. Additionally, Charles Sheckells testified at his deposition that he discussed the consumer warnings with his son at the time the helmet was purchased. Therefore, there is a genuine dispute of material fact as to proximate cause, and summary judgment is inappropriate.

AGV also maintains that summary judgment was proper since the warnings included with the helmet were adequate as a matter of law. The district court did not reach this issue. The consumer information packaged with the helmet explains that no helmet "can protect the wearer against all foreseeable impacts." While this warning informs the purchaser that certain foreseeable impacts exceed the helmet's capacity to protect the wearer, it falls short of informing the purchaser that the helmet will not provide any significant degree of protection at speeds of 30 to 45 miles an hour. Dr.

Burton's testimony, viewed in the light most favorable to Sheckells, establishes a lack of consumer awareness of the degree of protection provided by a helmet at median and high speeds. AGV has not, at this stage of the litigation, proffered sufficient facts to show that this warning was sufficient as a matter of law.

The consumer information sheet also informs the purchaser that no warranty or representation is made as to the helmet's ability to protect the user from any injury or death and that the user assumes all risks. AGV contends that this statement, couched in language typically used in disclaimers of legal responsibility, also serves as a warning to purchasers. Whether this language was sufficient to warn the user that the helmet, which was described in the consumer information as "the single most important piece of safety equipment you own," would provide no significant protection at speeds of over 30 to 45 miles an hour is, at this stage of the proceeding, a disputed issue of fact.

III. Conclusion

The grant of summary judgment in favor of AGV is AFFIRMED with regard to the claim of defective design or manufacture. In granting summary judgment on the failure to warn theory, however, the district court erred by resolving a disputed and material issue of fact regarding the open or obvious nature of the limited protection provided by AGV's helmet. Summary judgment on the failure to warn claim is therefore REVERSED.

In Westry v. Bell Helmets, Inc., 194 Mich. App. 366, 487 N.W.2d 718 (1992), on substantially similar facts, the court of appeals affirmed a summary judgment for defendant manufacturer on the ground that the risks of serious injury were open and obvious.

In Watson v. Uniden Corp. 775 F.2d 1514 (11th Cir. 1985), the Eleventh Circuit ruled on the adequacy of a warning supplied with a cordless telephone. The handset of the phone had a switch that, in the "standby" position, allowed the phone to ring. To talk on the phone, the user had to push the switch to the "talk" position. The use of the phone, including the switch, was explained in the instruction manual, which the plaintiff said she read: "CAUTION—LOUD RING. Move switch to talk position before holding receiver to ear." The first time plaintiff answered the phone after it was installed, she forgot to push the switch to "talk." As she put the receiver to her ear, it rang again and permanently impaired her hearing. The district court granted summary judgment for the defendant-manufacturer. The court of appeals reversed and sent the case back for trial on the sufficiency of the warning.

One group of cases in which the obviousness of the risks has been the subject of continuing controversy involves alcoholic beverages. The general rule is that the risks of excessive drinking are obvious and therefore need not be warned against. See, e.g., Maguire v. Pabst Brewing Co., 387 N.W.2d 565 (Iowa 1986) (no duty to warn of the dangers of drinking too much beer prior to driving automobile).

But there have been exceptions. In Hon v. Stroh Brewery Co., 835 F.2d 510 (3d Cir. 1987), plaintiff's decedent died from pancreatitis at the age of 26. Medical experts supported plaintiff's claim that relatively moderate consumption of beer distributed by defendant—two or three cans per night on an average of four nights a week for a period of six years—caused his fatal disease. The district court granted summary judgment for defendant, relying on the general rule that the risks of drinking alcohol are widely known. The court of appeals reversed, concluding (835 F.2d at 514):

> [The medical] affidavits provide evidence tending to show that beer in the quantity and manner [decedent] consumed it can have fatal consequences. Nothing in the record suggests that [decedent] was aware of this fact, however. Moreover [one medical] affidavit tends to show that the general public is unaware that consumption at this level and in this manner can have any serious adverse effects. There is no evidence in the record that the public appreciates any hazard that may be associated with this kind of consumption.

A startling exception to the general rule that risks of drinking alcohol are obvious was made in McGuire v. Joseph E. Seagram & Sons, Inc., 790 S.W.2d 842 (Tex. Civ. App. 1990). The plaintiffs were chronic alcoholics who sought damages from several distillers for "certain diseases, bodily injury, financial ruin, mental anguish and loss of consortium caused by the addictive drug, alcohol." They alleged that the defendants failed to communicate to consumers twenty-four separate items of information relating to alcoholic beverages. Notwithstanding the defendants' argument that the dangers of long-term overconsumption of alcohol were well known, the intermediate appellate court held that given the "vastly increasing complexities in relationships between and among human beings, (coupled with entire new fields of scientific knowledge and empirical wisdom)" (790 S.W.2d at 852), there was reason to reexamine the law and to "implant correlative duties." Although the Texas Supreme Court reversed and held that knowledge of the dangers of massive overconsumption of alcohol is widespread, (814 S.W.2d 385 (Tex. 1991)), the intermediate court decision is the starkest example yet of a court turning its back on the traditional rule.

Late in 1988 the 100th Congress enacted into law the Alcoholic Beverage Labelling Act of 1988, 102 Stat. 4518 (Nov. 18, 1988), containing the following provisions:

> Section 204. (a) On and after the expiration of the 12-month period following the date of enactment of this title, it shall be unlawful for any person to

manufacture, import, or bottle for sale or distribution in the United States any alcoholic beverages unless the container of such beverage bears the following statement:

> **GOVERNMENT WARNING:** (1) according to the Surgeon General, women should not drink alcoholic beverages during pregnancy because of the risk of birth defects. (2) Consumption of alcoholic beverages impairs your ability to drive a car or operate machinery, and may cause health problems.

Section 205. No statement relating to alcoholic beverages and health, other than the statement required by section 204 of this title, shall be required under State law to be placed on any container of an alcoholic beverage, or on any box, carton, or other package, irrespective of the material from which made, that contains such a container.

What effect will this statute have on claims such as the one in *Hon,* supra, that accrue after the effective date of the statute?

For an argument that the failure-to-warn doctrine defies consistent, coherent application by the courts see Henderson & Twerski, Doctrinal Collapse in Products Liability: The Empty Shell of Failure to Warn, 65 N.Y.U. L. Rev. 265 (1990). The authors' position is summarized in the following excerpt from Henderson & Twerski, Stargazing: The Future of American Products Liability Law, 66 N.Y.U. L. Rev. 1332, 1337 (1991):

> The only area that remains truly troublesome is failure-to-warn. It has been the sleeper of products liability law. Precisely because it is so unpretentious, it has the ability to wreak havoc. After all, a warnings claim is so modest, asking only for a small tidbit of information that would inform the plaintiff of some risk or other. Only an ogre would deny consumers relevant information. Nonetheless, failure-to-warn products litigation only appears unpretentious. In fact, it asks the judiciary to deliver a verdict on little more than empty rhetoric or say-so. Failure-to-warn must be recognized as a legitimate basis of liability. But courts will have to cut back on the more flighty warning cases. We predict that the next decade will bring to warnings cases what the last decade brought to design cases. Courts will deal more rigorously with claims that slight modifications in language would have altered consumer behavior and they will read the rule that one need not warn of obvious dangers much more broadly.

Problem 30

Your firm represents the Bambi Peanut Butter Company (BPB) in an action recently brought against it. Karen and Peter Jones have brought the action to recover as guardians for their two-year-old daughter, Pamela, and on their own behalf. The complaint alleges that nine months ago, when Pamela was 16 months old, Karen Jones fed her a peanut butter sandwich made with Bambi Peanut Butter. The complaint alleges that the child choked on the peanut butter when the sticky, viscous substance lodged in the back of her mouth and in her throat, cutting off her breathing capacity. By the time Karen could clear the baby's throat, Pamela had suffered irreversible brain damage. The complaint does not allege that the peanut butter was different from ordinary peanut butter. Instead, it alleges that BPB failed to supply a warning to Karen Jones that babies under two years of age cannot manage eating peanut butter and should not be fed it given the risk of possible fatal choking. No warning accompanied the Bambi Peanut Butter, and the complaint alleges that Karen Jones did not know of the dangers. Had she been warned, the complaint asserts, she never would have fed the peanut butter sandwich to Pamela.

The Joneses seek to recover as guardians for their daughter and also for Karen's mental upset and emotional distress at witnessing the tragedy and Peter's, at learning of it shortly after it occurred. How will you defend this case on behalf of BPB?

Harmful side effects caused by prescription drugs give rise to an interesting subset of failure-to-warn cases. The general rule is that drug companies owe patients duties to use reasonable care in testing their products and in warning prescribing and treating physicians regarding harmful side effects. If timely and adequate warnings are given to doctors, the companies will not be liable for injuries caused by the drugs. See, e.g., Cochran v. Brooke, 243 Or. 89, 409 P.2d 904 (1966). In most cases, warnings need not be given directly to the patients. But consider the following case.

MacDonald v. Ortho Pharmaceutical Corp.

394 Mass. 131, 475 N.E.2d 65, cert. denied, *794 U.S. 920 (1985)*

ABRAMS, J.: This products liability action raises the question of the extent of a drug manufacturer's duty to warn consumers of dangers inherent in the use of oral contraceptives. The plaintiffs brought suit against the defendant, Ortho Pharmaceutical Corporation (Ortho), for injuries allegedly caused by Ortho's birth control pills, and obtained a jury verdict in their favor. The defendant moved for a judgment notwithstanding the verdict. The judge concluded that the defendant did not owe a duty to warn the plaintiffs, and entered judgment for Ortho. The plaintiffs appealed. We transferred the case to this court on our own motion and reinstate the jury verdict.

We summarize the facts. In September, 1973, the plaintiff Carole D. MacDonald (MacDonald), who was twenty-six years old at the time, obtained from her gynecologist a prescription for Ortho-Novum contraceptive pills, manufactured by Ortho. As required by the then effective regulations promulgated by the United States Food and Drug Administration (FDA), the pill dispenser she received was labeled with a warning that "oral contraceptives are powerful and effective drugs which can cause side effects in some users and should not be used at all by some women," and that "[t]he most serious known side effect is abnormal blood clotting which can be fatal."[3] The warning also referred MacDonald to a booklet which she obtained from her gynecologist, and which was distributed by Ortho pursuant to FDA requirements. The booklet contained detailed information about the contraceptive pill, including the increased risk to pill users that vital organs such as the brain may be damaged by abnormal blood clotting. The word "stroke" did not appear on the dispenser warning or in the booklet.

MacDonald's prescription for Ortho-Novum pills was renewed at subsequent annual visits to her gynecologist. The prescription was filled annually. On July 24, 1976, after approximately three years of using the pills, MacDonald suffered an occlusion of a cerebral artery by a blood clot, an injury commonly referred to as a stroke. The injury caused the death of approximately twenty per cent of MacDonald's brain tissue, and left her permanently disabled. She and her husband initiated an action in the Superior Court against Ortho, seeking recovery for her personal injuries and his consequential damages and loss of consortium.

MacDonald testified that, during the time she used the pill, she was unaware that the risk of abnormal blood clotting encompassed the risk of stroke, and that she would not have used the pills had she been warned that stroke is an associated risk. The case was submitted to a jury on the plaintiffs' theories that Ortho was negligent in failing to warn adequately of the dangers associated with the pills and that Ortho breached its warranty of merchantability. These two theories were treated, in effect, as a single claim of failure to warn. The jury returned a special verdict, finding no negligence or breach of warranty in the manufacture of the pills. The jury also found that Ortho adequately advised the gynecologist of the risks inherent in the

3. FDA regulations in effect during the time period relevant to this litigation required that the following warning be included in or with the pill dispenser:

Do Not Take This Drug Without Your Doctor's Continued Supervision.

The oral contraceptives are powerful and effective drugs which can cause side effects in some users and should not be used at all by some women. The most serious known side effect is abnormal blood clotting which can be fatal.

Safe use of this drug requires a careful discussion with your doctor. To assist him in providing you with the necessary information, (Firm name) has prepared a booklet (or other form) written in a style understandable to you as the drug user. This provides information on the effectiveness and known hazards of the drug including warnings, side effects and who should not use it. Your doctor will give you this booklet (or other form) if you ask for it and he can answer any questions you may have about the use of this drug.

Notify your doctor if you notice any unusual physical disturbance or discomfort.

21 C.F.R. §130.45(d)(1), 35 Fed. Reg. 9002-9003 (1970), recodified at 21 C.F.R. §310.501(a)(4), 39 Fed. Reg. 11680 (1974), 40 Fed. Reg. 5354 (1975).

pills; the jury found, however, that Ortho was negligent and in breach of warranty because it failed to give MacDonald sufficient warning of such dangers. The jury further found that MacDonald's injury was caused by Ortho's pills, that the inadequacy of the warnings to MacDonald was the proximate cause of her injury, and that Ortho was liable to MacDonald and her husband.

After the jury verdict, the judge granted Ortho's motion for judgment notwithstanding the verdict, concluding that, because oral contraceptives are prescription drugs, a manufacturer's duty to warn the consumer is satisfied if the manufacturer gives adequate warnings to the prescribing physician, and that the manufacturer has no duty to warn the customer directly.

The narrow issue, on appeal, is whether, as the plaintiffs contend, a manufacturer of birth control pills owes a direct duty to the consumer to warn her of the dangers inherent in the use of the pill. We conclude that such a duty exists under the law of this Commonwealth.

1. *Extent of duty to warn.* . . .

The rule in jurisdictions that have addressed the question of the extent of a manufacturer's duty to warn in cases involving prescription drugs is that the prescribing physician acts as a "learned intermediary" between the manufacturer and the patient, and "the duty of the ethical drug manufacturer is to warn the doctor, rather than the patient, [although] the manufacturer is directly liable to the patient for a breach of such duty." Oral contraceptives, however, bear peculiar characteristics which warrant the imposition of a common law duty on the manufacturer to warn users directly of associated risks. Whereas a patient's involvement in decision-making concerning use of a prescription drug necessary to treat a malady is typically minimal or nonexistent, the healthy, young consumer of oral contraceptives is usually actively involved in the decision to use "the pill," as opposed to other available birth control products, and the prescribing physician is relegated to a relatively passive role.

Furthermore, the physician prescribing "the pill," as a matter of course, examines the patient once before prescribing an oral contraceptive and only annually thereafter. At her annual checkup, the patient receives a renewal prescription for a full year's supply of the pill. Thus, the patient may only seldom have the opportunity to explore her questions and concerns about the medication with the prescribing physician. Even if the physician, on those occasions, were scrupulously to remind the patient of the risks attendant on continuation of the oral contraceptive, "the patient cannot be expected to remember all of the details for a protracted period of time."

Last, the birth control pill is specifically subject to extensive Federal regulation. The FDA has promulgated regulations designed to ensure that the choice of "the pill" as a contraceptive method is informed by comprehensible warnings of potential side effects. These regulations, and subsequent amendments, have their basis in the FDA commissioner's finding, after hearings, that "[b]ecause oral contraceptives are ordinarily taken electively by healthy women who have available to them alternative methods of treatment, and because of the relatively high incidence of serious illnesses associated with their use, . . . users of these drugs should, without exception, be furnished with written information telling them of the drug's benefits and risks." . . .

The oral contraceptive thus stands apart from other prescription drugs in light of the heightened participation of patients in decisions relating to use of "the pill"; the substantial risks affiliated with the product's use; the feasibility of direct warnings by the manufacturer to the user; the limited participation of the physician (annual prescriptions); and the possibility that oral communications between physicians and consumers may be insufficient or too scanty standing alone fully to apprise consumers of the product's dangers at the time the initial selection of a contraceptive method is made as well as at subsequent points when alternative methods may be considered. We conclude that the manufacturer of oral contraceptives is not justified in relying on warnings to the medical profession to satisfy its common law duty to warn, and that the manufacturer's obligation encompasses a duty to warn the ultimate user. Thus, the manufacturer's duty is to provide to the consumer written warnings conveying reasonable notice of the nature, gravity, and likelihood of known or knowable side effects, and advising the consumer to seek fuller explanation from the prescribing physician or other doctor of any such information of concern to the consumer.

2. *Adequacy of the warning*. Because we reject the judge's conclusion that Ortho had no duty to warn MacDonald, we turn to Ortho's separate argument, not reached by the judge, that the evidence was insufficient to warrant the jury's finding that Ortho's warnings to MacDonald were inadequate. Ortho contends initially that its warnings complied with FDA labeling requirements, and that those requirements preempt or define the bounds of the common law duty to warn. We disagree. The regulatory history of the FDA requirements belies any objective to cloak them with preemptive effect. In response to concerns raised by drug manufacturers that warnings required and drafted by the FDA might be deemed inadequate by juries, the FDA commissioner specifically noted that the boundaries of civil tort liability for failure to warn are controlled by applicable State law. Although the common law duty we today recognize is to a large degree coextensive with the regulatory duties imposed by the FDA, we are persuaded that, in instances where a trier of fact could reasonably conclude that a manufacturer's compliance with FDA labeling requirements or guidelines did not adequately apprise oral contraceptive users of inherent risks, the manufacturer should not be shielded from liability by such compliance. Thus, compliance with FDA requirements, though admissible to demonstrate lack of negligence, is not conclusive on this issue, just as violation of FDA requirements is evidence, but not conclusive evidence, of negligence. We therefore concur with the plaintiffs' argument that even if the conclusion

that Ortho complied with FDA requirements were inescapable, an issue we need not decide, the jury nonetheless could have found that the lack of a reference to "stroke" breached Ortho's common law duty to warn. . . .

Ortho argues that reasonable minds could not differ as to whether MacDonald was adequately informed of the risk of the injury she sustained by Ortho's warning that the oral contraceptives could cause "abnormal blood clotting which can be fatal" and further warning of the incremental likelihood of hospitalization or death due to blood clotting in "vital organs, such as the brain." We disagree. . . . We cannot say that this jury's decision that the warning was inadequate is so unreasonable as to require the opposite conclusion as a matter of law. The jury may well have concluded, in light of their common experience and MacDonald's testimony, that the absence of a reference to "stroke" in the warning unduly minimized the warning's impact or failed to make the nature of the risk reasonably comprehensible to the average consumer. Similarly, the jury may have concluded that there are fates worse than death, such as the permanent disablement suffered by MacDonald, and that the mention of the risk of death did not, therefore, suffice to apprise an average consumer of the material risks of oral contraceptive use. . . .

We reverse the judgment, which the judge ordered notwithstanding the verdict, and remand the case to the Superior Court for the entry of judgment for the plaintiffs.

So ordered.

O'CONNOR, J. (dissenting). . . .

In order to fulfill its duty to warn consumers of risks associated with its product, a manufacturer of a nonprescription ("over-the-counter") drug must place on the drug's package printed warnings. That duty "derives from the basic marketing predicate of the over-the-counter drug industry, namely, that nonprescription drugs are purchased by consumers for the purpose of self-medication *typically without any intended or actual intervention by a physician.*" Torsiello v. Whitehall Laboratories, 165 N.J. Super. 311, 322 (1979) (emphasis added). In contradistinction, a manufacturer of a prescription drug fulfills its duty to warn a consumer by adequately informing the consumer's physician—a "learned intermediary between the purchaser and the manufacturer." . . . of the drug's associated risks. That rule results from the fact that, by definition, before a consumer uses a prescription drug, that consumer must have some interaction with a doctor. In cases involving manufacturers of contraceptive pills, every court but one has adhered to the "prescription drug" rule. The one court that went beyond the prescription drug rule imposed on Ortho the duty to adequately inform physicians of the contraceptive pill's risks and to comply with applicable FDA regulations. To my knowledge, no other court has embraced the rule laid down today by the court. . . .

I believe that the "prescription drug" rule most fairly and efficiently allocates among drug manufacturers, physicians, and drug users, the risks and responsibilities involved with the use of prescription drugs. Furthermore, I believe that those rules best ensure that a prescription drug user will receive in the most effective manner the information that she needs to make an informed decision as to whether to use the drug. The rules place on drug manufacturers the duty to gather, compile, and provide to doctors data regarding the use of their drugs, tasks for which the manufacturers are best suited, and the rules place on doctors the burden of conveying those data to their patients in a useful and understandable manner, a task for which doctors are best suited. Doctors, unlike printed warnings, can tailor to the needs and abilities of an individual patient the information that that patient needs in order to make an informed decision whether to use a particular drug. Manufacturers are not in position to give adequate advice to those consumers whose medical histories and physical conditions, perhaps unknown to the consumers, make them peculiarly susceptible to risk. Prescription drugs—including oral contraceptives—differ from other products because their dangers vary widely depending on characteristics of individual consumers. Exposing a prescription drug manufacturer to liability based on a jury's determination that, despite adequately informing physicians of the drug's risks and complying with FDA regulations, the manufacturer failed reasonably to warn a particular plaintiff-consumer of individualized risks is not essential to reasonable consumer protection and places an unfair burden on prescription drug manufacturers.

It will be observed that in the *MacDonald* case, the oral contraceptive might cause injuries even if an adequate warning is given. There may be cases in which plaintiffs who are adequately warned will nevertheless take the drug and will suffer injury. Why shouldn't the manufacturer be strictly liable in such cases, especially if the plaintiff's decision to consume the drug is, on balance, reasonable?

RESTATEMENT (SECOND) OF TORTS (1965)

§402A. SPECIAL LIABILITY OF SELLER OF PRODUCT FOR PHYSICAL HARM TO USER OR CONSUMER

COMMENT

k. Unavoidably unsafe products. There are some products which, in the present state of human knowledge, are quite incapable of being made safe for their intended and ordinary use. These are especially common in the field of drugs. An outstanding example is the vaccine for the Pasteur treatment of rabies, which not uncommonly leads to very serious and damaging consequences when it is injected. Since the disease itself invariably leads to a dreadful death, both the marketing and the use of the vaccine are fully justified, notwithstanding the unavoidable high degree of risk which they involve. Such a product, properly prepared, and accompanied

> by proper directions and warning, is not defective, nor is it *unreasonably* dangerous. The same is true of many other drugs, vaccines, and the like, many of which for this very reason cannot legally be sold except to physicians, or under the prescription of a physician. It is also true in particular of many new or experimental drugs as to which, because of lack of time and opportunity for sufficient medical experience, there can be no assurance of safety, or perhaps even of purity of ingredients, but such experience as there is justifies the marketing and use of the drug notwithstanding a medically recognizable risk. The seller of such products, again with the qualification that they are properly prepared and marketed, and proper warning is given, where the situation calls for it, is not to be held to strict liability for unfortunate consequences attending their use, merely because he has undertaken to supply the public with an apparently useful and desirable product, attended with a known but apparently reasonable risk.

Comment *k* has been interpreted by most courts to mean that prescription drugs and medical devices are the one category of products for which judicial review of the reasonableness of product designs is inappropriate. Why do you suppose prescription drugs and devices are thought to be unique in this regard? In any event, as the materials in the next section indicate, courts in recent years have begun to question the validity of treating prescription products differently in this regard.

For the treatment of prescription drugs in the Council Draft No. 1A of the Restatement of Torts, Third: Products Liability, see §4, pp. 672-673, below.

The courts in the cases considered thus far have all spoken as if the basis of liability were negligence. Indeed, it is difficult to imagine how strict liability for failure to warn could have been applied in those cases—"failure," after all, implies some sort of shortcoming on the part of the defendant. (See comment j to §420A, p. 612, above.) One court, however, has purported to apply genuine strict liability for failure to warn. In Beshada v. Johns-Manville Products Corp., 90 N.J. 191, 447 A.2d 539 (1982), the plaintiffs were workers and survivors of deceased workers who claimed to have contracted various lung ailments, including lung cancer, from exposure to defendant's asbestos products. The defendants asserted that at the time of the exposure they did not know and could not have known that their products caused such ailments. The trial court refused plaintiffs' motion to strike that defense and the plaintiffs appealed. The Supreme Court of New Jersey reversed and ordered the defense stricken.

The New Jersey Supreme Court recently addressed the question of whether the holding in *Beshada* applied in prescription drug cases, and held that it did not. See Feldman v. Lederle Laboratories, 97 N.J. 429, 479 A.2d 374 (1984). In Gogol v. Johns-Manville Sales Corp., 595 F. Supp. 971 (D.N.J. 1984), the district court concluded that "the import of *Feldman* . . . is that one rule applies to asbestos products, and a different rule applies to non-asbestos products." Id. at 974. The court recognized that the defendant's equal protection arguments were not without merit, but declined to upset the New Jersey rule on that ground.

Anderson v. Owens-Corning Fiberglas Corp.

53 Cal. 3d 987, 810 P.2d 549, 281 Cal. Rptr. 528 (1991)

PANELLI, J. Defendants are or were manufacturers of products containing asbestos. Plaintiff Carl Anderson filed suit in 1984, alleging that he contracted asbestosis and other lung ailments through exposure to asbestos and asbestos products (i.e., preformed blocks, cloth and cloth tape, cement, and floor tiles) while working as an electrician at the Long Beach Naval Shipyard from 1941 to 1976. Plaintiff allegedly encountered asbestos while working in the vicinity of others who were removing and installing insulation products aboard ships. . . .

Plaintiff's amended complaint alleged a cause of action in strict liability for the manufacture and distribution of "asbestos, and other products containing said substance . . . which caused injury to users and consumers, including plaintiff." . . . Plaintiff alleged that defendants marketed their products with specific prior knowledge, from scientific studies and medical data, that there was a high risk of injury and death from exposure to asbestos or asbestos-containing products; that defendants knew consumers and members of the general public had no knowledge of the potentially injurious nature of asbestos; and that defendants failed to warn users of the risk of danger. Defendants' pleadings raised the state-of-the-art defense, i.e., that even those at the vanguard of scientific knowledge at the time the products were sold could not have known that asbestos was dangerous to users in the concentrations associated with defendants' products.

Plaintiff moved before trial to prevent defendants from presenting state-of-the-art evidence. . . . The trial court granted the motion. . . . The defendants then moved to prevent plaintiff from proceeding on the failure-to-warn theory. . . . In response to the court's request for an offer of proof on the alleged failure to warn, plaintiff referred to catalogs and other literature depicting workers without respirators or protective devices and offered to prove that, until the mid-1960's, defendants had given no warnings of the dangers associated with asbestos, that various warnings given by some of the defendants after 1965 were inadequate, and, finally, that defendants removed the products from the market entirely in the early 1970's. Defendants argued in turn that the state of the art, i.e., what was scientifically knowable in the period 1943-1974, was their obvious and only defense to any cause of action for failure to warn, and that, in view of the court's decision to exclude state-of-the-art evidence, fairness dictated that plaintiff be precluded from proceeding on that theory. With no statement of reasons, the trial court granted defendants' motion. . . . After a four-week trial, the jury returned a verdict for defendants. . . .

Plaintiff moved for a new trial, asserting that the court erred in precluding proof of liability on a failure-to-warn theory. . . . The court granted the motion. . . . Plaintiff . . . urged that knowledge or knowability, and thus state-of-the-art evidence, was irrelevant in strict liability for failure to warn. . . . The trial court agreed.

The Court of Appeal, in a two-to-one decision, upheld the order granting a new trial. . . . The appellate court added that, "in strict liability asbestos cases, including those prosecuted on a failure to warn theory, state of the art evidence is not admissible since it focuses on the reasonableness of the defendant's conduct, which is irrelevant in strict liability." The dissenting justice urged that the majority had imposed "absolute liability," contrary to the tenets of the strict liability doctrine, and that the manufacturers' right to a fair trial included the right to litigate all relevant issues, including the state of the art of scientific knowledge at the relevant time. We granted review. . . .

Failure to Warn Theory of Strict Liability . . .

In Cavers v. Cushman Motor Sales, Inc. (1979) 95 Cal. App. 3d 338, 157 Cal. Rptr. 142, the first case in which failure to warn was the sole theory of liability, the appellate court approved the instruction that a golf cart, otherwise properly manufactured, could be defective if no warning was given of the cart's propensity to tip over when turning and if the absence of the warning rendered the product substantially dangerous to the user. *Cavers* was principally concerned with the propriety of the term "substantially dangerous" and concluded that it is necessary to weigh the degree of danger involved when determining whether a warning defect exists.

[Early] cases did not address the specific factual question whether or not the manufacturer or distributor knew or should have known of the risks involved in the products, either because the nature of the product or the risk involved made such a discussion unnecessary or because the plaintiff limited the action to risks about which the manufacturer/distributor obviously knew or should have known. Moreover, the appellate courts in these same cases did not discuss knowledge or knowability as a component of the failure to warn theory of strict liability. However, a knowledge or knowability component clearly was included as an implicit condition of strict liability. In that regard, California was in accord with authorities in a majority of other states.

Only when the danger to be warned against was "unknowable" did the knowledge component of the failure-to-warn theory come into focus. Such cases made it apparent that eliminating the knowledge component had the effect of turning strict liability into absolute liability.

[The court reviews other California Court of Appeals decisions.]

In sum, the foregoing review of the decisions of the Courts of Appeal persuades us that California is well settled into the majority view that knowledge, actual or constructive, is a requisite for strict liability for failure to warn and that [our earlier decision], if not directly, at least by implication, reaffirms that position.

However, even if we are implying too much from the language in [our earlier decision,] the fact remains that we are now squarely faced with the issue of knowledge and knowability in strict liability for failure to warn in other than the drug context. Whatever the ambiguity of [our earlier decision,] we hereby adopt the requirement, as propounded by the Restatement Second of Torts and acknowledged by the lower courts of this state and the majority of jurisdictions, that knowledge or knowability is a component of strict liability for failure to warn.

One of the guiding principles of the strict liability doctrine was to relieve a plaintiff of the evidentiary burdens inherent in a negligence cause of action. . . . Indeed, it was the limitations of negligence theories that prompted the development and expansion of the doctrine. The proponents of the minority rule, including the Court of Appeal in this case, argue that the knowability requirement, and admission of state-of-the-art evidence, improperly infuse negligence concepts into strict liability cases by directing the trier of fact's attention to the conduct of the manufacturer or distributor rather than to the condition of the product. Similar claims have been made as to other aspects of strict liability, sometimes resulting in limitations on the doctrine and sometimes not.

[The court discusses earlier decisions not involving failure to warn.]

As these cases illustrate, the strict liability doctrine has incorporated some well-settled rules from the law of negligence and has survived judicial challenges asserting that such incorporation violates the fundamental principles of the doctrine. It may also be true that the "warning defect" theory is "rooted in negligence" to a greater extent than are the manufacturing- or design-defect theories. The "warning defect" relates to a failure extraneous to the product itself. Thus, while a manufacturing or design defect can be evaluated without reference to the conduct of the manufacturer . . . the giving of a warning cannot. The latter necessarily requires the communicating of something to someone. How can one warn of something that is unknowable? If every product that has no warning were defective per se and for that reason subject to strict liability, the mere fact of injury by an unlabelled product would automatically permit recovery. That is not, and has never been, the purpose and goal of the failure-to-warn theory of strict liability. Further, if a warning automatically precluded liability in every case, a manufacturer or distributor could easily escape liability with overly broad, and thus practically useless, warnings. . . .

We therefore reject the contention that every reference to a feature shared with theories of negligence can serve to defeat limitations on the doctrine of strict liability. Furthermore, despite its roots in negligence, failure to warn in strict liability differs markedly from failure to warn in the negligence context. Negligence law in a failure-to-warn case requires a plaintiff to prove that a manufacturer or distributor did not warn of a particular risk for reasons which fell below the acceptable standard of care, i.e., what a reasonably prudent manufacturer would have known and warned about. Strict liability is not concerned with the standard of due care or the reasonableness of a manufacturer's conduct. The rules of strict liability require a plaintiff to prove only that the defendant did not adequately warn of a particular risk that was known or knowable in light of the generally recognized and prevailing best scientific and medical knowledge available at the time of manufacture and distribution. Thus, in strict liability, as opposed to negligence, the reasonableness of the defendant's failure to warn is immaterial.

Stated another way, a reasonably prudent manufacturer might reasonably decide that the risk of harm was such as not to require a warning as, for example, if the manufacturer's own testing showed a result contrary to that of others in the scientific community. Such a manufacturer might escape liability under negligence principles. In contrast, under strict liability principles the manufacturer has no such leeway; the manufacturer is liable if it failed to give warning of dangers that were known to the scientific community at the time it manufactured or distributed the product. Whatever may be reasonable from the point of view of the manufacturer, the user of the product must be given the option either to refrain from using the product at all or to use it in such a way as to minimize the degree of danger. Davis v. Wyeth Laboratories, Inc. (9th Cir. 1968) 399 F.2d 121, 129-130, described the need to warn in order to provide "true choice": "When, in a particular case, the risk qualitatively (e.g., of death or major disability) as well as quantitatively, on balance with the end sought to be achieved, is such as to call for a true choice judgment, medical or personal, the warning must be given. [Footnote omitted.]" . . . Thus, the fact that a manufacturer acted as a reasonably prudent manufacturer in deciding not to warn, while perhaps absolving the manufacturer of liability under the negligence theory, will not preclude liability under strict liability principles if the trier of fact concludes that, based on the information scientifically available to the manufacturer, the manufacturer's failure to warn rendered the product unsafe to its users.

The foregoing examination of the failure-to-warn theory of strict liability in California compels the conclusion that knowability is relevant to imposition of liability under that theory. Our conclusion not only accords with precedent but also with the considerations of policy that underlie the doctrine of strict liability.

We recognize that an important goal of strict liability is to spread the risks and costs of injury to those most able to bear them. However, it was never the intention of the drafters of the doctrine to make the manufacturer or distributor the insurer of the safety of their products. It was never their intention to impose absolute liability.

Conclusion

Therefore, in answer to the question raised in our order granting review, a defendant in a strict products liability action based upon an alleged failure to warn of a risk of harm may present evidence of the state of the art, i.e., evidence that the particular risk was neither known nor knowable by the application of scientific knowledge available at the time of manufacture and/or distribution. The judgment of the Court of Appeal is affirmed with directions that the matter be remanded to the trial court for proceedings in accord with our decision herein.

LUCAS, C.J., and KENNARD, ARABIAN and BAXTER, JJ., concur. . . .

MOSK, J., concurring and dissenting.

In my view the trial court properly granted a new trial and the Court of Appeal, in a thoughtful analysis of the law, correctly affirmed the order. I thus concur in the result.

I must express my apprehension, however, that we are once again retreating from "[t]he pure concepts of products liability so pridefully fashioned and nurtured by this court." (Daly v. General Motors Corp. (1978) 20 Cal. 3d 725, 757, 144 Cal. Rptr. 380, 575 P.2d 1162 (dis. opn. by Mosk, J.).) . . .

The majority distinguish failure-to-warn strict liability claims from negligence claims on the ground that strict liability is not concerned with a standard of due care or the reasonableness of a manufacturer's conduct. This is generally accurate. However in practice this is often a distinction without a substantial difference. Under either theory, imposition of liability is conditioned on the defendant's actual or constructive knowledge of the risk. Recovery will be allowed only if the defendant has such knowledge yet fails to warn. . . .

We should consider the possibility of holding that failure-to-warn actions lie solely on a negligence theory. "[A]lthough mixing negligence and strict liability concepts is often a game of semantics, the game has more than semantic impact—it breeds confusion and inevitably, bad law." (Henderson & Twerski, Doctrinal Collapse in Products Liability: The Empty Shell of Failure to Warn, 65 N.Y.U. L. Rev. at p. 278.) If, however, the majority are not ready to take that step, I would still use this opportunity to enunciate a bright-line rule to apply in failure-to-warn strict liability actions.

Here plaintiff alleged, among other claims, that defendants marketed their products "with specific prior knowledge" of the high risks of injury and death from their use. If plaintiff can establish at the new trial that defendants had actual knowledge, then state of the art evidence—or what everyone else was doing at the time—would be irrelevant and the trial court could properly exclude it. Actual knowledge may often be difficult to prove, but it is not impossible with adequately probing discovery. Defendants, of course, can produce evidence that they had no such prior actual knowledge.

On the other hand, if plaintiff is only able to show, by medical and scientific data or other means, that defendants should have known of the risks inherent in their products, then contrary medical and scientific data and state-of-the-art evidence would be admissible if offered by defendants.

Thus I would draw a clear distinction in failure-to-warn cases between evidence that the defendants had actual knowledge of the dangers and evidence that the defendants should have known of the dangers.

With the foregoing rule in mind, the parties should proceed to the new trial ordered by the trial court and upheld by the Court of Appeal. Thus I would affirm the judgment of the Court of Appeal.

C. *Liability for Defective Design*

1. The Plaintiff's Prima Facie Case: Duty/Breach

Cases involving allegedly defective product designs began to play a significant role in products liability only in recent years. Until the late 1960s and early 1970s, when something of an explosion in product design litigation occurred, claims based on defective design succeeded only in two limited categories of cases. The first of these might be called *flawed design cases.* If the plaintiff could show that the design caused the product to fail to perform its intended function—if the design was self-defeating in a dangerous way so as to cause injury—courts would treat the design defect the same as if it were a manufacturing defect. Indeed, given the functional similarities between manufacturing defects and these types of inadvertent design errors, it is often difficult to tell from reading the earlier decisions whether the defect was a manufacturing defect or a bad design. Thus, in the California decision in Greenman v. Yuba Power Products, Inc., p. 575, above, the defect that caused the plaintiff's injuries was a loose set screw on a home power lathe which allowed a piece of wood to fly out of the machine and strike the plaintiff. It is not clear from the opinion whether the wrong screw had been mistakenly installed in the particular machine used by the plaintiff, in which case the particular power tool had a manufacturing defect, or whether the screw was the one called for in the tool's specifications, in which case the power tool had a defective design. Either way, the tool was unreasonably dangerous because of the self-defeating characteristic of the inadequate set screw, and the court had no trouble in concluding that it could be found to be defective.

But when the product designs in earlier cases were not self-defeating in the just-described way, plaintiffs had a more difficult time convincing courts to condemn them as defective. Thus, if the power lathe in the *Greenman* case had functioned exactly as the designer had intended, and if the plaintiff had been injured when he caught his fingers in the drive belt connecting the motor to the spindle, it is not clear that a court 20 years ago would have imposed liability on the manufacturer. The plaintiff could have argued that the belt should have been shielded in some manner; but earlier courts would have been disposed to blame the accident on the carelessness of the plaintiff-user in failing to cope with an obvious risk, rather than on any shortcomings in the tool's design. Indeed, in a leading case close on its facts to the power lathe hypothetical, the New York Court of Appeals established the general rule that there would be no liability for injuries caused by an obvious risk created by a product's design. Campo v. Scofield, 301 N.Y. 468, 95 N.E.2d 802 (1950). This rule, which came to be known as the *patent danger rule,* effectively insulated manufacturers from most of the risks presented by their conscious design choices,[5] such as the decision in the hypothetical not to put a guard on the drive belt of the power tool.

The second basic category of cases in which courts have traditionally imposed liability for defective designs was where the seller had expressly warranted that the product would perform safely and not cause injuries of the sort suffered by the plaintiff. Thus, in the hypothetical case involving the power lathe, the injured plaintiff would have had a better chance of recovery if the manufacturer had promised that "your hand cannot get caught in the belt."

One of the best known express warranty decisions from this earlier era is Baxter v. Ford Motor Co., 168 Wash. 456, 12 P.2d 409 (1932), in which the defendant car manufacturer advertised that the windshields in its new cars would not shatter "under the hardest impact." The plaintiff was injured when a rock struck his windshield and shattered the glass, blinding him in one eye. The court permitted recovery on the basis of express warranty, even though the plaintiff was not in privity with the defendant manufacturer. Express warranty is today available to an injured plaintiff whenever the injury-causing feature of the design fails to measure up to promises of safety made by the defendant. The general rule governing express warranties is set out in the Uniform Commercial Code as follows:

§2-313. EXPRESS WARRANTIES BY AFFIRMATION, PROMISE, DESCRIPTION, SAMPLE

(1) Express warranties by the seller are created as follows:

(a) Any affirmation of fact or promise made by the seller to the buyer which relates to the goods and becomes part of the basis of the bargain creates an express warranty that the goods shall conform to the affirmation or promise.

(b) Any description of the goods which is made part of the basis of the bargain creates an express warranty that the goods shall conform to the description.

(c) Any sample or model which is made part of the basis of the bargain

5. This phrase is taken from Henderson, Judicial Review of Manufacturers' Conscious Design Choices: The Limits of Adjudication, 73 Colum. L. Rev. 1531 (1973).

creates an express warranty that the whole of the goods shall conform to the sample or model.

(2) It is not necessary to the creation of an express warranty that the seller use formal words such as "warrant" or "guarantee" or that he have a specific intention to make a warranty, but an affirmation merely of the value of the goods or a statement purporting to be merely the seller's opinion or commendation of the goods does not create a warranty.

It will be observed that §2-313 does not require that the plaintiff rely on the express warranty, but only that the warranty "become part of the basis of the bargain." This has been interpreted to require that the warranties be made in reasonable proximity, in time and space, to the sale. The plaintiff need not even be aware that the warranties have been made. Consistent with the holding in *Baxter,* there is no requirement that the plaintiff be in privity of contract with the defendant.

McCormack v. Hankscraft Co.

278 Minn. 322, 154 N.W.2d 488 (1967)

ROGOSHESKE, J. Plaintiff appeals from the judgment entered upon an order of the district court granting judgment n.o.v. and a conditional new trial in favor of defendant, Hankscraft Company, Inc. . . .

Viewing, as we must, the evidence and all permissible inferences most favorably to the sustaining of the verdict [for the plaintiff for $150,000] the jury reasonably could have found the following facts.

In October 1957, Andrea's father, Donald McCormack, purchased from a retail drugstore an electric Hankscraft steam vaporizer manufactured by defendant. It was purchased pursuant to the advice of a doctor to be used as a humidifier for Andrea, then 8 months old, who had just returned from being hospitalized for croup and pneumonia. After unpacking the vaporizer, Andrea's parents read the instruction booklet accompanying the unit from "cover to cover." Then, following defendant's printed instructions, they put the vaporizer to use in the treatment of Andrea. Thereafter, from time to time as the need arose, it was used for the young children of the family in the prescribed manner, including the use of it unattended throughout the night, without any problem. . . .

In the spring of 1960, the children had colds and Mrs. McCormack desired to use the vaporizer but found it "wasn't working." She went to the same self-service drugstore and purchased another Hankscraft vaporizer similar to the first unit. She personally selected it without the aid or recommendation of any clerk because it was a Hankscraft, knowing defendant to be a manufacturer of a number of products for children and relying upon defendant's prior representations contained in the booklet accompanying the first vaporizer that its vaporizers were "safe" and "practically foolproof," as well as advertisements representing them to be "tip-proof." This second vaporizer, purchased in a sealed carton, was known as Model 202A, and its general appearance as to size and shape and its method of operation were identical with the first unit. It was accompanied by an instruction booklet substantially identical to that furnished with the first vaporizer, which Mrs. McCormack again completely read.

This second vaporizer had been used about a half dozen times without incident when, on November 20, 1960, it was again set up for use in a small bedroom in the northwest corner of the house, occupied by Andrea, then 3 years and 9 months old, and her baby sister, Alison, 1 year and 10 months old. Andrea slept in a regular single bed and Alison in a crib. To the east of the doorway of this bedroom is an adjoining bathroom, which Andrea frequently used during the night. The doors of the bedrooms and bathroom were habitually left open and a light was usually burning in the bathroom. Andrea's bed was located in what might be described as the southwest corner of the room with the headboard against the doorway wall. The crib was in the northeast corner. A chifforobe stood next to the crib against the north wall. Andrea's mother set up the vaporizer at about 8 P.M. on a seat-step-type metal kitchen stool about 2½ feet high. She placed the stool in front of and against the chifforobe. The electric cord was extended behind the chifforobe and plugged into an outlet located there. The stool was about 4 feet from the foot of Andrea's bed. When steam started coming from the hole in the top of the unit, Mrs. McCormack left the room. After visiting a neighbor until about 11 P.M., she did some ironing, and at about 1:30 A.M. she returned to the room to replenish the water supply in the vaporizer. Using some type of "mitt," she lifted the cap and poured water from a milk bottle into the jar. She then went to bed.

At about 2:30 A.M., Mrs. McCormack heard a terrible scream and got out of bed. She found Andrea lying on the floor of her bedroom, screaming. The metal stool was upright, but the vaporizer was on the floor and the water had come out of the jar. The vaporizer had separated into its three component parts—a glass jar, a metal pan, and a plastic top-heating unit. The electric cord was still plugged into the electric outlet. In some manner, Andrea, while intending to go to the bathroom, had tipped over the vaporizer and caused the water in the jar to spill upon her body.

Andrea was rushed to the hospital for treatment. More than 30 percent of her body had severe burns; she was suffering from shock; and her condition was critical for some time. She had third-degree burns on her chest, shoulders, and back. Skin-graft surgery was performed on her twice. She was hospitalized for 74½ days. Ten days later she was admitted to the Kenny Institute for treatment. She remained there 102 days and thereafter was taken to the Mayo Clinic, where she had further surgery in August 1961. At the time of the trial, Andrea had heavy scar tissue on her chest, stomach, legs, arms, and neck; a deformed jaw; restricted movement of her head; an irregular posture; and the prospect of 6 to 12 more surgical procedures during her lifetime. Her condition is largely permanent.

The "automatic-electric" vaporizer in question is of normal design and consists of three component parts—an aluminum pan which serves as a base, a 1-gallon glass jar or water reservoir which is inserted into the pan, and a black plastic cap to which is fastened a black plastic heating-chamber tube.

The glass jar, 6⅝ inches square and 8 inches high, is a so-called "standard gallon pickle jar" not specially manufactured as a component part. The top opening is 4½ inches in diameter and its outer neck has a male-type glass thread. To fill the jar to a designated fill mark requires .73 gallon of water.

The aluminum pan, which is made to fit the bottom of the jar, is 4 inches high. It has two plastic lifting and carrying handles. Four projections, ¾ inch in diameter and ⅛ inch in height, are regularly spaced on the bottom of the pan and serve as feet for the unit.

The plastic cap and heating chamber assembly has a domelike appearance in its upper portion, which is 5 inches in diameter and 2¾ inches high. Enclosed in a plastic tube which attaches to the upper portion are two narrow, 8-inch-long steel electrodes which extend from the underside of the cap and are fastened to terminals which connect to an electric plug-in type cord. This cord, about 6 feet long, is attached to the terminals through a hole in the cap. Opposite the electric cord is a round steam hole 3⁄16 inch in diameter. . . . The cap and heating chamber assembly, by its own weight, rests loosely upon the glass jar with the black tube extending down into the jar. There are no threads inside the plastic cap or any other means provided to fasten the cap to the threaded neck of the jar. This design and construction were intended by defendant to serve as a safety measure to avoid any buildup of steam in the glass jar, but it also has the result of allowing the water in the jar to gush out instantaneously when the vaporizer is tipped over. This unit can be tipped over easily by a child through the exertion of about 2 pounds of force.

To operate the vaporizer in accordance with the instructions contained in defendant's booklet, the "entire plastic cover" is removed, the glass jar is filled to the filling marker with tap water containing minerals, and the cord is plugged into an electric outlet, whereupon "[t]he vaporizer will produce a gentle cloud of steam within a few minutes." The heating unit is designed so that it automatically turns off whenever the water in the jar decreases to a certain point. As the booklet pictorially illustrates, the water from the jar enters the lower section of the heating chamber through the small hole at the bottom. Here it is heated until it boils and is vaporized into steam, which passes out of the unit through the hole in the cap.

Tests made of the unit established that after about 4 minutes of operation the water in the heating chamber reaches 212 degrees Fahrenheit and steam emanates from the steam port. Although the water in the jar outside the heating chamber does not reach the boiling point, the upper portion of this water does reach 211 degrees within 35 minutes of operation and the middle portion reaches 211 degrees within 3 hours. The temperature of the outside of the jar ranges from 172 degrees after about 1 hour to 182 degrees after 5 hours. Thus, during most of the 6- to 8-hour period in which the unit is designed to operate without refilling, the water in the reservoir is scalding hot, since water of 145-degree temperature will burn and 180-degree water will cause third-degree burns on a child 5 years old.

By touch, a user can determine that the water in the jar outside the heating unit, as well as the jar and the plastic cap, becomes hot during the operation of the vaporizer. However, there is no movement of the water in the jar and no means by which a user could discern by sight or touch that this reserve water in the jar became and remained scalding hot. Plaintiff's parents, relying upon their understanding of what defendant represented in its instruction booklet, were reasonably led to believe up to the time of plaintiff's injury that, since steam was generated only in the heating unit, the temperature of the water in the jar during the entire operation of the vaporizer remained the same as when put in. At all of the times when replenishing the water in either the first or second vaporizer, plaintiff's mother followed the routine of removing the entire plastic cover by using some "glove" or "mitt" as a precaution against the steam. She would leave the cord plugged in, add water to the jar, replace the cover, wait until steam appeared, and then leave the unit unattended in the room. As her testimony implied, she at no time discovered by touching or handling the unit when it was in use that the temperature of any part of the water in the jar became hot.

The instruction booklet furnished by defendant did not disclose the scalding temperatures reached by the water in the jar, not was any warning given as to the dangers that could result from an accidental upset of the unit. While plaintiff's mother realized that the unit could be tipped over by a sufficient external force, she justifiably relied upon defendant's representations that it was "safe," "practically foolproof," and "tip-proof." She understood this to mean that the unit "was safe to use around [her] children" and that she "didn't have to worry" about dangers when it was left unattended in a child's room since this was the primary purpose for which it was sold.

In its booklet and advertising, defendant in fact made the representations relied upon by plaintiff's mother. In addition to the simple operating instructions and a pictorial "cut-away" indicating how the steam is generated by the electrodes in the heating chamber, the booklet stated:

"WHY THE HANKSCRAFT VAPORIZER IS SUPERIOR TO OTHERS IN DESIGN

"Your vaporizer will run all night on one filling of water, directing a steady, gentle flow of medicated steam exactly where it is needed. No attention is necessary.

"It's safe, too, and practically foolproof. Since the water itself makes the electric contact, the vaporizer shuts off automatically when the water is gone. The electric unit cannot burn out."

The booklet also had a picture of a vaporizer sending steam over a baby's crib alongside which was printed:

"For most effective use, the vaporizer should be placed at least four feet away from the person receiving treatment, and should not be placed above the patient's level."

Defendant's officers realized that the vaporizers would be primarily used in the treatment of children and usually would be unattended. They had knowledge that the water in the jar got scalding hot; that this water would cause third-degree burns on a small child; that the water in the jar would gush out instantaneously if the unit were tipped over; that the unit was not "tip-proof"; that the combination of the unsecured top and the hot water in the jar was dangerous because of the possibility that a child might tip it over during operation; and that, prior to plaintiff's injury, at least 10 to 12 children had been burned in this manner. Furthermore, defendant's officers realized that the fact the water in the jar got hot was not discernible during operation except by touching or handling the unit and that a user could conclude from their booklet that steam was generated in the plastic core and be led to believe that the reserve water in the jar did not itself become scalding hot.

Plaintiff called two expert witnesses, whose qualifications in the field of product design were unquestioned. Both testified that the design of the vaporizer was defective principally in that it failed to provide a means for securing the plastic cover to the jar in a manner which would prevent the water in the jar from instantaneously discharging when the unit tipped over. In the opinion of both, the unit could be tipped over with little force and this defective design created a risk of bodily harm to a child if the unit were left operating and unattended in the room. This defect could have been eradicated by the adoption of any one of several practical and inexpensive alternative designs which utilized simple and well-known techniques to secure the top to the jar. Any of these alternative designs could have been employed by defendant prior to its production of the second vaporizer by the application of sound product-design principles current at that time. Among these alternative designs was that of making threads on the inside of the plastic top so it could screw onto the jar and the putting of two or three small holes in the top, which would take care of any danger that steam would build up inside the jar. Both witnesses stated that such a change in design was essential to make the unit safe for its intended use because the presence of near-boiling water in the jar was not discernible by sight or touch and no warning of the risk of harm was contained in defendant's instruction booklet. . . .

Plaintiff urges that defendant was negligent both in its failure to give any warning of the dangers inherent in the use of the vaporizer and in its adoption of an unsafe design. Plaintiff claims among other things that defendant, in undertaking to instruct as to the use of its vaporizer, violated its duty to use due care when it failed to inform that the water in the jar got scalding hot with temperatures up to 211 degrees Fahrenheit and to warn of the dangers of serious injury if the unit were upset during operation. Defendant concedes it gave no such warning but vigorously argues that a warning was not necessary since the fact that the water in the jar becomes and remains hot should be obvious to any user.

In support of its position, defendant claims that anyone touching the jar or plastic top after the vaporizer had been working for some time would realize they are hot and conclude the water in the jar is also hot, and that because the instructions indicate that steam is produced in the plastic heating chamber, a reader would necessarily conclude the water in the jar is hot since the heating unit obviously comes into direct contact with such water. Plaintiff, on the other hand, contends that a warning is necessary because the average user would not realize that this water becomes hot, much less that it becomes scalding hot. Plaintiff relies upon the undisputed evidence that there is no boiling activity of the reserve water in the jar and that there is no way short of actual temperature measurements to discern by sight or touch that this water reaches the dangerous temperature of 211 degrees. Further, plaintiff relies upon the evidence that the instructions furnished by defendant served to allay any suspicions a user might otherwise have as to the near-boiling temperature of the water or any apprehension of danger by indicating that the vaporizer was safe to use unattended in a child's room throughout the night. Moreover, both of plaintiff's parents testified that neither had in fact become aware of the temperature of the water nor realized the danger that, if the unit were upset while in use, the water could scald and inflict third-degree burns on a child.

We have little difficulty in reaching the conclusion that the evidence justified the jury in finding that defendant failed to exercise reasonable care to inform users, including plaintiff's parents, of the scalding temperatures of the water and to warn of the dangers reasonably foreseeable in the use of the vaporizer. Surely the evidence does not as a matter of law compel a conclusion that the true nature and gravity of the dangers which could result from the scalding water in the jar were sufficiently obvious to most potential users as to preclude the jury from finding that due care required an appropriate warning. Under the court's instruction, the jury could, and quite likely did, conclude that defendant knew or should have reasonably foreseen that the primary use of its vaporizer involved the danger that a child might be severely burned by the rapid discharge of near-boiling water upon an intentional or accidental upset, and that a substantial number of users would not become aware of the scalding temperature of the water nor realize the potential dangers of using the vaporizer unattended in a child's room unless adequate information and an appropriate warning were given so that parents would take extraordinary precautions. These findings, together with defendant's utter failure to warn, and the finding that the dangers inherent in the vaporizer's use were not obvious and were outside the realm of common knowledge of potential users (especially in view of defendant's representations of safety) are, we hold, supported by the evidence and alone justified the jury's verdict of liability.

We similarly conclude and hold that the evidence is also sufficient to support the jury's verdict of liability on the ground that defendant was negligent in adopting an unsafe design. It is well established that a manufacturer, despite lack of privity of contract, has a duty to use reasonable care in designing its product so that those it should expect will use it are protected from unreasonable risk of harm while the product is being used for its intended use. A breach of such duty renders the manufacturer liable. Clearly, such a duty was owed to plaintiff for defendant admitted that the primary, intended use of the vaporizer was for the treatment of children's colds and croup.

The proof is sufficient to support plaintiff's claim of defective design in that, among other defects, defendant failed to exercise reasonable care in securing the plastic cover to the jar to guard against the reasonably foreseeable danger that a child would tip the unit over when it was in use and be seriously burned by coming in contact with the scalding water that would instantaneously gush out of the jar.

[In a footnote the court concludes that the plaintiff's proof on the tippability issue failed in that there was no showing that the design modifications suggested by the plaintiff's experts would have prevented the vaporizer from tipping in this case.]

To urge that a vaporizer is not a dangerous instrumentality is not persuasive to a reviewing court when the evidence reasonably permits a finding that a simple, practical, inexpensive, alternative design which fastened the top to the jar would have substantially reduced or eliminated the danger which caused plaintiff's injuries. Defendant's experts testified that the design adopted was to guard against an explosion because of a buildup of steam in the heating unit and jar, but the jury could have accepted the testimony of plaintiff's experts which indicated the use of defendant's design was not necessary to accomplish this purpose. Moreover, the fact that at the time the second vaporizer was purchased many other brands of vaporizers on the market were designed in basically this same manner, while certainly relevant, did not necessarily bar the jury from concluding that the exercise of due care required the adoption of a different design.

We also find no merit in defendant's contention that it was not negligent because any defect caused by its failure to secure the heating unit to the jar was obvious. Clearly the jury could have justifiably found that users, particularly children such as plaintiff who was a mere child of 3 years of age, are incapable of meaningfully comprehending the true nature and gravity of the risk to them that results from a product's design and of effectively acting so as to avoid the danger. The jury could have concluded that protection of this class of persons required that defendant in the exercise of due care should have adopted one of the safe alternative designs. While the evidence with respect to this issue required a resolution of the conflicts in the testimony of expert witnesses, the jury was free to adopt the opinions of plaintiff's witnesses and to reach a verdict of liability on this ground of negligence also.

We also conclude that the evidence was sufficient to support a finding of liability upon a breach of an express warranty.

We are persuaded that whether the previously quoted language of the booklet, particularly in combination with the picture of a vaporizer sending steam over a baby's crib, amounted to an express warranty that it was "safe" for a user to let this vaporizer run all night in a child's room without attention was a jury question. No particular words are required to constitute an express warranty, and the representations made must be interpreted as an ordinary person would understand their meaning, with any doubts resolved in favor of the user. Since parents instinctively exercise great care to protect their children from harm, the jury could justifiably conclude that defendant's representations were factual (naturally tending to induce a buyer to purchase) and not mere "puffing" or "sales talk." . . .

We also hold the evidence adequate to support a reasonable inference that defendant's negligence and breach of warranty proximately caused plaintiff's injury. From the fact that plaintiff sustained third-degree burns by coming in contact with near-boiling water, the obvious and reasonable inference is that her injuries were directly caused by the undisclosed presence and rapid discharge of the scalding water in the vaporizer jar. At best, under the court's instructions, defendant was permitted to argue that the negligence of plaintiff's mother was a superseding cause, for it is clear that the failure of plaintiff's parents to discover the defect or any other negligent conduct on the part of plaintiff's mother under any theory of liability cannot be imputed to plaintiff. The jury found against defendant on this issue, and we doubt that a contrary finding could be sustained. We discover no evidentiary basis for a claim that the vaporizer was abnormally used or, indeed, was so placed in plaintiff's room that the propensity of children to tip things over when going to the bathroom at night was deliberately or negligently ignored, amounting to unforeseeable negligent conduct or assumption of risk by plaintiff's mother. Foreseeable intervention by a third party is not a superseding cause. . . .

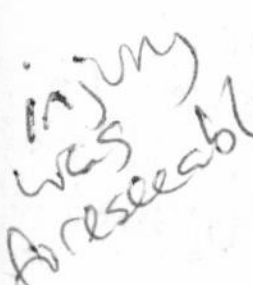

Reversed with directions to enter judgment upon the verdict.

In Uloth v. City Tank Corp., 376 Mass. 874, 384 N.E.2d 1188 (1978), the court carefully considered the capabilities of warning and design to reduce risk. Plaintiff's foot was severed from his leg when he caught it in a pincer between the blade and compaction chamber of a garbage truck on which he was working. Plaintiff claimed that he jumped on the back step of the garbage truck as it was moving from one stop to the next. In the process he lost his balance and his left foot went toward the loading sill of the garbage compaction chamber. When the blade meets the loading sill it creates a shear point, with the blade and sill acting like scissors. The descending panel caught the plaintiff's foot and dragged it into the trash hopper, severing it from his leg.

The defendant argued that the simple and obvious scissor-like quality of the machine was itself a totally adequate warning of the dangers of the garbage truck. Plaintiff argued that a design alternative such as a stop-bar, an interrupted cycle, or a "dead-man control" would have reduced the danger of a shear point accident. Affirming judgment for plaintiff, the Massachusetts high court rejected the defendant's warning argument:

> An adequate warning may reduce the likelihood of injury to the user of a product in some cases. We decline, however, to adopt any rule which permits a manufacturer or designer to discharge its total responsibility to workers by simply warning of the dangers of a product. Whether or not adequate warnings are given is a factor to be considered on the issue of negligence, but warnings cannot absolve the manufacturer or designer of all responsibility for the safety of the product. . . .
>
> [A] warning is not effective in eliminating injuries due to instinctual reactions, momentary inadvertence, or forgetfulness on the part of a worker. One of the primary purposes of safety devices is to guard against such foreseeable situations.
>
> Balanced against the somewhat limited effectiveness of warnings is the designer's ability to anticipate and protect against possible injuries. If a slight change in design would prevent serious, perhaps fatal, injury, the designer may not avoid liability by simply warning of the possible injury. [Id. at 879-880, 384 N.E.2d at 1192.]

The *Uloth* court rejected defendant's argument that the simple and obvious nature of a danger absolved the defendant of liability where the defendant could have made a "slight change in design," preventing "serious, perhaps fatal injury." In Camacho v. Honda Motor Co., Ltd., 741 P.2d 1240 (Colo. 1987), a similar finding was made by the Supreme Court of Colorado. In *Camacho,* the plaintiff collided with an automobile at an intersection while operating a motorcycle purchased new from a Honda dealership. The accident resulted in serious leg injuries. Plaintiffs alleged that the motorcycle was a defectively designed, unreasonably dangerous product under the Restatement (Second) of Torts §402A because it was not equipped with "crash bars"—tubular steel bars attached to the motorcycle frame to protect the rider's legs in the event of a collision. Plaintiffs asserted that if crash bars had been installed, the leg injuries would have been mitigated.

Honda, the defendant, moved for summary judgment arguing that as a matter of law a motorcycle lacking crash bars cannot be deemed unreasonably dangerous. The trial court granted the motion, concluding that because the danger was obvious and foreseeable, Honda had no duty to totally alter the nature of its product by installing crash bars. The Court of Appeals affirmed, stating that whether or not a product is unreasonably dangerous depends on the extent of danger that "would have been fully anticipated by or within the contemplation of the ordinary user or consumer." Camacho v. Honda Motor Co., 701 P.2d 628, 631 (Colo. App. 1985).

The Supreme Court of Colorado rejected the consumer expectation test invoked by the Court of Appeals and held that "the fact that the dangers of a product are open and obvious does not constitute a defense to a claim alleging that the product is unreasonably dangerous." *Camacho,* 741 P.2d at 1245. The Court went on to state that:

> [An] uncritical rejection of design defect claims in all cases wherein the danger may be open and obvious thus contravenes sound public policy by encouraging design strategies which perpetuate the manufacture of dangerous products."

Id. at 1246. The Court found the granting of summary judgment in error, reversed and remanded for a determination of whether plaintiff's expert witnesses were correct in stating that effective injury-reducing leg protection devices were feasible at the time of the accident.

See also McWilliams v. Yamaha Corp., USA, 987 F.2d 200 (3rd Cir. 1993), holding that although the purchase of a motorcycle is covered by the "open and obvious" danger exception to liability under §3(a)(2) of the New Jersey Products Liability Law, §3(a)(2) also provides that the open and obvious danger defense was not intended to apply to dangers posed by products such as machinery or equipment that can be feasibly eliminated without impairing the usefulness of the product. The court remanded to the district court for a determination of whether the danger of injury to the plaintiff could feasibly be eliminated by the installation of crash bars or similar protective devices without impairing the usefulness of the motorcycle. But see Toney v. Kawasaki Heavy Industries Ltd., 975 F.2d 162 (5th Cir. 1992) (because its lack of leg protection and concomitant danger were open and obvious to ordinary consumer, the motorcycle was not "unreasonably dangerous" and plaintiffs' strict liability claim, as a matter of law, is barred).

In Eads v. R.D. Werner Co., 847 P.2d 1370 (Nev. 1993), the plaintiff suffered injury in a fall from an allegedly defective ladder. Plaintiff claimed that the design of the ladder was defective; defendant manufacturer argued that if plaintiff had heeded its warnings the accident would not have happened. The trial court instructed the jury as follows, quoting comment *j* of the Restatement (Second) of Torts §402A (1965):

> Where an instruction or warning is given, the manufacturer may reasonably assume that it will be read and heeded; and the product bearing such a

> warning, that is safe for use if it is followed, is not in defective condition, nor is it unreasonably dangerous.

The jury returned a defendant's verdict and plaintiff appealed. The Nevada high court reversed, holding that the instruction was erroneous. The court observed (847 P.2d at 1372):

> Given the erroneous instruction, the jury could have easily concluded that since the warning was given, the ladder was not defective even if there was a commercially feasible design available when it was manufactured that probably would have prevented the accident.

Troja v. Black & Decker Manufacturing Co.

62 Md. App. 101, 488 A.2d 516 (1985)

GILBERT, C.J. This appeal involves a personal injury action grounded in strict liability.

On January 10, 1979, Michael Troja accidentally amputated his thumb while he was operating a radial arm saw manufactured by Black and Decker Manufacturing Company, Inc. . . .

At the close of Troja's case before Judge Raymond G. Thieme and a jury, the judge granted Black and Decker's motion for a directed verdict on the defective design portion of Troja's strict liability count. Judge Thieme ruled that Troja had failed to produce any legally sufficient evidence of the economic feasibility of a proposed alternative radial arm saw design, or of the existence of the technology necessary to produce such a product in 1976, the year the particular saw was manufactured. . . .

Troja argues that the trial court: 1) abused its discretion in precluding an expert witness from stating an opinion in regard to the economic and technological feasibility of a proposed safeguard for the radical arm saw; 2) erred in directing a verdict on the issue of design defect based on the court's findings that Troja failed to produce legally sufficient evidence to warrant submission of that issue to the jury. . . .

The alleged villain in this litigation is a twelve inch radial arm saw, DeWalt Model No. 780, manufactured by Black and Decker in 1976. Troja had borrowed the saw from Robert Krohn, who had hired Troja to build a bar. Troja and Krohn removed the saw from its metal base and stand in order that it could be carried from Krohn's basement to the work site in the bar. The guide fence and metal base were left behind. Bereft of its base, the saw was placed directly on the floor. Troja rigged a makeshift guide fence by securing an aluminum level to the saw with two "C" clamps. At the time of his injury, Troja was using the saw to make a cross-cut. He had dispensed with his makeshift fence and guided the wood into the saw blade with his bare hand.

A "DeWalt Instruction & Maintenance Manual" accompanied the 1976 DeWalt Model No. 780. The manual contained instructions, illustrated with photographs, on the subjects of assembly, operation, and maintenance of the saw. The manual included instructions for performing various types of cuts. The proper procedure for executing a cross-cut was explained and illustrated.

The Design Defect

Troja contends that because the saw was designed so that the guide fence was easily removable, the absence of a safety feature that would prevent the saw from running when the fence was not in place rendered it unreasonably dangerous.

Maryland, in Phipps v. General Motors Corp., 278 Md. 337, 363 A.2d 955 (1976), embraced the theory of strict liability in tort actions. There the Court expressly adopted the elements contained in the Restatement (Second) of Torts, §402A (1965). . . .

Section 402A requires a court, in a design defect case, to weigh "the utility of risk inherent in the design against the magnitude of the risk." Phipps v. General Motors Corp., 278 Md. at 345, 363 A.2d at 959. The court, *Phipps* tells us, ought to implement a balancing process to decide whether the product in question was unreasonably dangerous.

One helpful guide to the balancing process was recommended in Wade, On the Nature of Strict Tort Liability for Products, 44 Miss. L.J. 825, 837-838 (1973). Wade suggests seven factors that should be weighed in determining whether a given product is "reasonably safe." Those factors are:

(1) The usefulness and desirability of the product—its utility to the user and to the public as a whole.

(2) The safety aspects of the product—the likelihood that it will cause injury, and the probable seriousness of the injury.

(3) The availability of a substitute product which would meet the same need and not be as unsafe.

(4) The manufacturer's ability to eliminate the unsafe character of the product without impairing its usefulness or making it too expensive to maintain its utility.

(5) The user's ability to avoid danger by the exercise of care in the use of the product.

(6) The user's anticipated awareness of the dangers inherent in the product and their avoidability, because of general public knowledge of the obvious condition of the product, or of the existence of suitable warnings or instructions.

(7) The feasibility, on the part of the manufacturer, of spreading the loss by setting the price of the product or carrying liability insurance.

In some instances the risk is "inherently unreasonable," and no balancing test is necessary. An example of an inherently unreasonable risk is where, as in *Phipps,* the gas pedal of a new automobile suddenly and without warning sticks, causing the vehicle to accelerate.

The failure of the manufacturer, in the case sub judice, to incorporate a safety system such as the one proposed by Troja is not an inherently unreasonable risk. Therefore, in order to create a jury issue on the liability of Black and Decker because of a defective design, Troja was required to produce evidence from which the jury could determine the former's unreasonableness in manufacturing a saw, in 1976, without a safety system. In Singleton v. International Harvester Co., 685 F.2d 112 (4th Cir. 1981), the Fourth Circuit held that in order to carry a case to the jury, the evidence should show: the technological feasibility of manufacturing a product with the suggested safety device at the time the suspect product was manufactured; the availability of the materials required; the cost of production of the suggested device; price to the consumer, including that of the suggested device; and the chances of consumer acceptance of a model incorporating such features. The design alternative proposed in *Singleton* was a roll-over protective structure for a tractor which had upended or toppled, trapping the operator beneath it. Because Singleton's experts failed to provide the foundation information required, the court affirmed the trial court's directed verdict on the issue of defective design.

Troja contends that Judge Thieme erred when he refused to allow an expert in the field of "machine guarding safety systems" to testify that a radial saw design, incorporating a safety device described as an "interlock system," could have been developed in 1976. Gerald Rennell, who was offered by Troja as an expert, testified that he had taken courses in machine guarding and industrial safety. He said that he had been employed as a "safety engineer" and a "loss-control inspector." Although Rennell suggested that Black and Decker could have incorporated a "safety interlock feature," which would have prevented the saw from running when the guide fence was not in place, he acknowledged that he had no experience in radial arm saw design. Rennell was unable to furnish a design demonstrating the actual placement of such a system, or to explain how it could be integrated in the saw without interfering with the functions for which the fence would normally not be employed. The expert's bald statement that a safety interlock device could be implemented without great cost to the manufacturer was not supported by any data regarding the cost of the materials necessary to include such a feature. Moreover, Rennell did not conduct any tests to determine the feature's actual utility. Despite the trial court's pointed comments that it would exclude Rennell's testimony as to the feasibility of incorporating the proposed safety device, unless the expert established a foundation, Troja opted not to question his witness with respect to those areas. Inasmuch as there was an absence of a proper foundation for the expert's statement relative to a safety interlock device, the trial court excluded all testimony regarding the economic/technological feasibility in 1976 of producing a saw with the proposed safety system. We agree with Judge Thieme. The record simply does not support Troja's assertion that the trial court incorrectly excluded Rennell's testimony. . . .

When we view the evidence and all the inferences which may reasonably be drawn therefrom in a light most favorable to Troja, we are left with the inescapable conclusion that there simply was no legally sufficient evidence of design defect for the jury to consider. . . . The trial court properly granted the manufacturer's motion for a directed verdict on the issue of design defect. . . .

Judgment affirmed.

Not only have many courts articulated their strict liability tests in risk-utility terms (see, e.g., Wilson v. Piper Aircraft Corp., 282 Or. 61, 577 P.2d 1322 (1978); Turner v. General Motors Corp., 584 S.W.2d 844 (Tex. 1979); Morningstar v. Black & Decker Mfg. Co., 162 W. Va. 857, 253 S.E.2d 666 (1979)), but some have also mandated that the jury be instructed as to the risk-utility factors. The New York Court of Appeals in Voss v. Black & Decker Mfg. Co., 59 N.Y.2d 102, 450 N.E.2d 204, 463 N.Y.S.2d 398 (1983), was explicit on this matter. After reiterating Wade's seven factors, set out in *Troja,* the court concluded: "Pertinent factors in the individual case, when evaluated as to whether or not they are applicable, should form the basis for charging the jury as to how it should evaluate the evidence in order to decide whether a product is not reasonably safe." Id. at 109, 450 N.E.2d at 209, 463 N.Y.S.2d at 403. Other courts have held that risk-utility factors are only for the court in deciding whether plaintiff has established a prima facie case and are not to be given to the jury. See, e.g., Turner v. General Motors Corp., above.

Not only has risk-utility been widely adopted by the courts, but also it has the support of the overwhelming majority of commentators. See, e.g., Birnbaum, Unmasking the Test for Defect: From Negligence [to Warranty] to Strict Liability to Negligence, 33 Vand. L. Rev. 593 (1980); Epstein, Products Liability: The Search for the Middle Ground, 56 N.C.L. Rev. 643 (1978); Henderson, Renewed Judicial Controversy over Defective Product Design: Toward the Preservation of an Emerging Consensus, 63 Minn. L. Rev. 773 (1979); Hoenig, Product Designs and Strict Tort Liability: Is There a Better Approach?, 8 Sw. U.L. Rev. 109 (1976); Powers, The Persistence of Fault in Products Liability, 61 Tex. L. Rev. 777 (1983); Twerski, A

Moderate and Restrained Federal Product Liability Bill: Targeting the Crisis Areas for Resolution, 18 U. Mich. J.L. Ref. 575 (1985).

Problem 31

A partner in your law firm has asked you to prepare a memorandum analyzing the potential merits of a products liability case he is handling. Your client, Robert Condlin, suffered severe injuries when the 1985 Volkswagen Rabbit he was driving was involved in a head-on collision with a 1986 Chevrolet station wagon. The accident occurred on a four lane highway in Grovesburg, Columbia. Mr. Condlin was driving within the 45 M.P.H. speed limit when the Chevrolet wagon, coming toward him from the opposite direction, crossed the median strip and entered Mr. Condlin's traffic lane. Both vehicles braked before the head-on impact, which an expert estimates occurred at a combined speed of between 35 and 45 M.P.H. The impact crushed the front end of the VW Rabbit, pushing the engine rearward. Mr. Condlin's right leg was caught between the engine and the frame of his car, and was substantially severed below the knee. The leg was surgically amputated later at the hospital. Mr. Condlin was wearing his seat belt and shoulder harness at the time of the accident.

The file contains a memorandum prepared by an automotive design expert retained by your firm which describes in general terms the relative crashworthiness of the VW Rabbit compared with other cars. The expert explains that although Volkswagen tried to design the Rabbit so as to minimize the risks to occupants in high speed collisions, the risks to the driver in an accident of the sort involved in this case are "unacceptably high." The memo explains that out of 11 small 1985 vintage foreign cars crash tested by the Department of Transportation during the summer of 1986, ten, including the 1985 Volkswagen Rabbit, failed to meet unofficial standards of safety developed by the Department. The major reason for their failure in this regard appears to be closely connected with the reason for their popularity among the car-owning public in recent years—their small size, which enables them to deliver relatively high gas mileage. The memo prepared by your firm's expert explains that the 1985 VW Rabbit is designed so that the engine will tend to be pushed downward as well as backward in a front end crash, and thus avoid being pushed into the occupants of the front seat. In the expert's opinion, however, the front end of the Rabbit is not substantial enough to afford adequate protection to the driver and passengers in accidents at speeds exceeding 40 M.P.H. The expert offers several suggestions as to how the design of the Rabbit's front end could be changed to afford more protection against injuries of the sort suffered by Mr. Condlin, but he candidly admits that they would all require adding to the weight of the car and hence would require a sacrifice in fuel efficiency. The expert adds that he is prepared to state as his opinion that the gains in safety achieved by his suggested changes would more than outweigh any losses in reduced fuel economy.

The main issue which the partner would like you to address in your memorandum is whether there is any substantial chance of reaching the jury with a claim that the crashworthiness of the 1985 VW Rabbit is inadequate. He recognizes that the file is far from complete, and that further factual inquiry will be necessary if your firm proceeds with the case. What he wants at this stage is for you to identify the legal issues likely to be involved and to assess the client's chances of success with respect to each, making reasonable factual assumptions wherever necessary. He would also like you to identify the major avenues for further investigation. Assuming that Troja v. Black & Decker, above, is the latest decision in your jurisdiction on the subject of defective design, prepare an outline of the memorandum requested.

Heaton v. Ford Motor Co.

248 Or. 467, 435 P.2d 806 (1967)

GOODWIN, J. The plaintiff appeals a judgment entered after an involuntary nonsuit in a products-liability case involving a wheel on a Ford 4-wheel-drive pickup truck. The principal question is whether the plaintiff produced sufficient evidence to support his allegation that the wheel was dangerously defective.

Plaintiff purchased the truck new in July 1963 to use for hunting and other cross-country purposes as well as for driving upon paved highways. He drove the truck some 7,000 miles without noticing anything unusual about its performance. Prior to the day of the accident the truck had rarely been off the pavement, and plaintiff swore that it had never been subjected to unusual stress of any kind.

On the day of the accident, however, the truck, while moving on a "black-top" highway at normal speed, hit a rock which plaintiff described as about five or six inches in diameter. The truck continued uneventfully for about 35 miles, when it left the road and tipped over.

After the accident, the rim of the wheel was found to be separated from the "spider." Witnesses described the "spider" as the interior portion of the wheel which is attached to the vehicle by the lug nuts. The twelve rivets connecting the rim to the spider appeared to have been sheared off. The spider, according to one witness, showed signs of having been dragged along the ground. There was also a large dent in the rim and a five-inch cut in the inner tube at a spot within the tire that was adjacent to the dent in the rim. Only three of the rivets which had held the rim on the spider were found after the accident. . . .

In the type of case in which there is no evidence, direct or circumstantial, available to prove exactly what sort of manufacturing flaw existed, or exactly how the design was deficient, the plaintiff may nonetheless be able to establish his right to recover, by proving that the product did not perform in keeping with the reasonable expectations of the user. When it is shown that a product failed to meet the reasonable expectations of the user the inference is that there was some sort of defect, a precise definition of which is unnecessary. If the product failed under conditions concerning which an average consumer of that product could have fairly definite expectations, then the jury would have a basis for making an informed judgment upon the existence of a defect. The case at bar, however, is not such a case. . . .

The court's function is to decide whether the evidence furnishes a sufficient basis for the jury to make an informed decision. If the record permits, the jury determines whether the product performed as an ordinary consumer would have expected. In the case at bar the record furnishes no basis for a jury to do anything but speculate.

Where the performance failure occurs under conditions with which the average person has experience, the facts of the accident alone may constitute a sufficient basis for the jury to decide whether the expectations of an ordinary consumer of the product were met. High-speed collisions with large rocks are not so common, however, that the average person would know from personal experience what to expect under the circumstances. Nor does anything in the record cast any light upon this issue. The jury would therefore be unequipped, either by general background or by facts supplied in the record, to decide whether this wheel failed to perform as safely as an ordinary consumer would have expected. To allow the jury to decide purely on its own intuition how strong a truck wheel should be would convert the concept of strict liability into the absolute liability of an insurer.

The argument has been made that the question of the ordinary consumer's expectations should be treated for jury purposes in the same way that the question of reasonable conduct in a negligence case is treated. But in deciding in a negligence case what is reasonable conduct, the jury is deciding in a context of "right and wrong" how someone *should* have behaved. In making this decision they are presumed to know the relevant factors. If not, such information is provided, as in a medical malpractice case where there is expert testimony as to the proper standards.

In the defective-product area, courts have already decided how strong products *should* be: They should be strong enough to perform as the ordinary consumer expects. In deciding what the reasonable consumer expects, the jury is not permitted to decide how strong products should be, nor even what consumers should expect, for this would in effect be the same thing. The jury is supposed to determine the basically factual question of what reasonable consumers do expect from the product. Where the jury has no experiential basis for knowing this, the record must supply such a basis. In the absence of either common experience or evidence, any verdict would, in effect, be the jury's opinion of how strong the product *should* be. Such an opinion by the jury would be formed without the benefit of data concerning the cost or feasibility of designing and building stronger products. Without reference to relevant factual data, the jury has no special qualifications for deciding what is reasonable. . . .

While the matter was never presented to the trial court, and thus requires no extended discussion in this appeal, the plaintiff has referred in this court to certain advertising published by the defendant, to reinforce the plaintiff's claim that a consumer would have expected the wheel in question to be engineered and manufactured in such a manner as to withstand the kind of force applied to it in this case. The plaintiff does not contend that the advertising constituted misrepresentation under Restatement (Second) of Torts §402B, but rather that the advertising in general tends to create expectations of strength and durability under Section 402A. A general impression of durability, however, does not help a customer to form an expectation about the breaking point of a wheel. A "rugged" Ford truck could be expected to negotiate rough terrain, including five-or-six-inch rocks, at appropriate off-the-road speeds, but it does not follow that a user could expect the same thing at highway speeds. If such expectations do exist, the record should contain evidence to support the inference that they do.

Affirmed.

O'CONNELL, J. (dissenting).

. . . It is plaintiff's position that the theory of strict liability should be deemed applicable whenever a person is injured as a result of exposing himself to a hazard in reasonable reliance upon the capabilities of a product as represented by the seller. The gist of plaintiff's argument is summed up as follows:

> . . . It is not unreasonable to suggest that the driver of a vehicle promoted as "solid," "rugged" and "built like a truck" will subject that vehicle and its passengers to hazards to which he would not subject a vehicle otherwise promoted. With specific reference to this case, it is not unreasonable to surmise that a driver of a vehicle so promoted who runs over a rock on the highway will not even consciously consider the possibility of stopping to check for damage because he takes it for granted that such an impact will not harm a vehicle which he has been conditioned to think of as "solid," "rugged," and "like a truck."

Plaintiff, then, is asking us to "take judicial notice of facts which form part of the common knowledge of people who possess average intelligence. . . .

Apparently the majority opinion would hold that there was a failure of proof, irrespective of whether the question of strict liability is for the court or jury in a case of this kind. I disagree. If we had been presented with the same facts with the modification that plaintiff had struck a rock one inch in diameter rather than a five-inch rock, I am sure that the majority would have held that at least a jury question was made out. The beginning point of our reasoning would be that a manufacturer of automobiles must construct wheels of sufficient durability to withstand the impact of one-inch rocks, because one-inch rocks are not an uncommon obstacle on highways. A buyer could reasonably expect to have the wheel withstand such an impact and it would not be unreasonable for him to proceed on his journey after the impact. However, the buyer could not reasonably expect a wheel to remain safe after striking a rock two feet in diameter at seventy miles an hour. Somewhere along the continuum between one inch and two feet it will be necessary to draw a line. The line is drawn by deciding whether a manufacturer should be required to construct a wheel of such durability as to withstand the impact of a rock of the size in question. Whether the manufacturer has that duty in a particular case should depend, it seems to me, upon whether the manufacturer could reasonably foresee the likelihood that the hazard would be encountered by those using the product, and this would, of course, depend to some extent upon the representations made by the manufacturer with respect to the durability of the product.

The manufacturer's conduct must be measured against a standard of reasonableness, a standard similar to that employed in determining whether a defendant is negligent. Here, however, we do not measure defendant's conduct in terms of fault but simply upon the basis of its foreseeability. A jury is just as well equipped to judge the reasonableness of defendant's conduct on this score as it is when the inquiry is made as to defendant's negligence. The members of the jury draw upon their experiences and observations and set up some kind of a standard as a measure against which to appraise the defendant's conduct in the particular case. They would be justified in concluding that the wheel in this case was unreasonably dangerous according to the test stated in Restatement (Second) of Torts §402A, p. 352 (1965), requiring a finding that "[t]he article sold must be dangerous to an extent beyond that which would be contemplated by the ordinary consumer who purchases it, with the ordinary knowledge common to the community as to its characteristics."

The majority apparently would require some evidence of what this community standard is. How is this to be done? Certainly this is not the type of question which calls for the testimony of an expert witness. Are we to call lay witnesses to testify what "would be contemplated by the ordinary customer"? If that is required in the present case, it would be equally necessary in an ordinary negligence case to inform the jury of the community standard on such questions as the reasonableness of conduct in driving a car with respect to speed, lookout and control.

But we submit these questions of the reasonableness of defendant's conduct to the jury and, subject to the right of the court to decide as a matter of law that the standard was or was not met, we are willing to trust the jury's judgment as to the community standard and to appraise the defendant's conduct in light of it.

I believe that the question of defendant's liability is kept from the jury in the present case not because there is a lack of evidence upon which to sustain a verdict for plaintiff, but because the majority of the court, finding the imposition of strict liability a severe burden upon the seller, attempts to limit that burden by distorting the concept of the jury's function.

SLOAN, J., joins in this dissent.

One question under the consumer expectations test is whether the court is concerned with the expectations of a reasonable person or with the actual expectations of the plaintiff. The Supreme Court of California has made it clear that "the jury considers the expectations of a hypothetical reasonable consumer, rather than those of the particular plaintiff in the case." Campbell v. General Motors Corp., 32 Cal. 3d 112, 126 n.6, 649 P.2d 224, 233 n.6, 184 Cal. Rptr. 891, 900 n.6 (1982).

A fair number of courts have couched their tests for defect in whole or in part in terms of "consumer expectations." See, e.g., Lester v. Magic Chef, Inc., 230 Kan. 643, 641 P.2d 353 (1982); Voss v. Black & Decker Mfg. Co., 59 N.Y.2d 102, 450 N.E.2d 204, 463 N.Y.S.2d 398 (1983); Leichtamer v. American Motors Corp., 67 Ohio St. 2d 456, 424 N.E.2d 568 (1981).

A well known decision that combined a consumer expectations test for design defect with a risk utility standard is Barker v. Lull Engineering Co., 20 Cal., 20 Cal. 3d 413, 573 P.2d 443, 143 Cal. Rptr. 225 (1978). The plaintiff in that case was a young, relatively inexperienced worker whose supervisor asked him to operate a high lift loader on a sloping work site. The regular operator, learning of the location at which the loader would be operated that day and realizing the dangers presented by the rough, sloping terrain, had called in sick. The loader was a large machine capable of lifting heavy loads on forks similar to a forklift.

On the day of the accident in which he received injuries, the plaintiff first leveled the loader by means of a lever on the floor between his legs. As he was lifting a load of lumber to the second story of a building under construction, the loader appeared to begin to tip. Heeding the warnings from several coworkers, the plaintiff jumped from the loader and started to run. The loader tipped over, causing the load to fall on the plaintiff. The plaintiff's expert testified that the loader's relatively narrow wheel base made it unstable and likely to tip. Outriggers could have been incorporated in the design that would have made it more stable, preventing the accident. Also, the loader should have been equipped with a roll bar and a seat belt. In addition, the expert testified the lever used to level the machine should have been protected from accidental bumping, and the transmission should have had a "park" position.

Defendant's experts contradicted all of plaintiff's arguments. The court instructed the jury "that strict liability for a defect in design of a product is based on a finding that the product was unreasonably dangerous for its intended use." The jury returned its verdict for the defendant manufacturer. On appeal, the Supreme Court of California reversed and remanded (20 Cal. 3d at 435, 573 P.2d at 457-458, 143 Cal. Rptr. at 239-240):

> If a jury in determining liability for a defect in design is instructed only that it should decide whether or not there is "a defective design," it may reach to the extreme conclusion that the plaintiff, having suffered injury, should without further showing, recover; on the other hand, it may go to the opposite extreme and conclude that because the product matches the intended design the plaintiff, under no conceivable circumstance, could recover. The submitted definition eschews both extremes and attempts a balanced approach.
>
> We hold that a trial judge may properly instruct the jury that a product is defective in design (1) if the plaintiff demonstrates that the product failed to perform as safely as an ordinary consumer would expect when used in an intended or reasonably foreseeable manner, or (2) if the plaintiff proves that the product's design proximately caused his injury and the defendant fails to prove, in light of the relevant factors discussed above, that on balance the benefits of the challenged design outweigh the risk of danger inherent in such design.

The consumer expectation test has drawn fire from respected academic commentators. Professor Page Keeton, for example, argues that:

> It is quite clear that to the extent that a maker knows, or in the exercise of ordinary care should know, of a risk or hazard that users may not discover or appreciate, liability results for breach of the duty to disclose what a reasonable person would disclose. This ground of liability protects users and consumers to a considerable extent from harm resulting from unappreciated dangers. It is submitted, however, that an inquiry as to whether the danger in fact of the design outweighed the benefits of the design would better protect users and consumers, without placing an undue burden on manufacturers and suppliers. The court's primary justification for the retention of the contemplation test is the ease with which the plaintiff can establish a design defect under this test by circumstantial evidence. If a claimant proves that a product fails under circumstances the ordinary purchaser or user would not have expected, a case has been made. That is clearly so, but the question is, should it be so? I think not. If the court would permit the defendant to show under a risk-utility analysis by way of rebuttal that it would not be feasible, then the position would be supportable. [Keeton, Products Liability—Design Hazards and the Meaning of Defect, 10 Cumb. L. Rev. 293, 310 (1979).]

A similar note is sounded by Professor Gary Schwartz in Foreword: Understanding Products Liability, 67 Calif. L. Rev. 435 (1979), in which he roundly criticizes the consumer expectation test. Schwartz notes that

> [t]he thesis works well if the "portrayal" is concrete enough to entail a U.C.C. express warranty or a Restatement product representation. Absent this concreteness, the thesis does not easily test out. Consider, for example, the advertisements for Datsun automobiles, advertisements that have always praised the car for both economy and quality, but with varying emphases. For several years, this advertising stressed economy through the slogan, "Datsun Saves." After a well-publicized change of advertising agencies, in 1977-1978 Datsun's message became "We Are Driven," suggesting quality and performance. With inventories swelling in dealer's lots in fall 1978, its advertising shifted to "We Are Dealing," pointing to temporary low prices. To my mind, these changes in advertising themes, conspicuous though they are, do not justify a legal rule that measures Datsun's personal injury liability to its 1976 purchasers by standards less demanding than those applicable to its 1977-1978 purchasers. Nor should Datsun's liability differ in any material respect from Toyota's ("If You Can Find a Better-Built Small Car, Buy It.") [Id. at 476 n.241.]

The second prong of *Barker*'s two-step test for liability, which shifts the burden of proof to the defendant to establish that its product is not defective in light of risk-utility factors, has come under heavy fire. The critics contend that the party who bears the burden of proof rarely is able to obtain a directed verdict. This suggests that even the flimsiest of design claims may go to jury verdict. Risk-utility balancing thus becomes an open-ended test not subject to significant judicial control. See Henderson, Renewed Judicial Controversy over Defense Product Design: Toward the Preservation of an Emerging Consensus, 63 Minn. L. Rev. 773 (1979); Schwartz, Foreword: Understanding Products Liability, 67 Calif. L. Rev. 435, 468 (1979).

Professor Sheila Birnbaum disagrees. In her article, Unmasking the Test for Design Defect: From Negligence [to Warranty] to Strict Liability to Negligence, 33 Vand. L. Rev. 593 (1980), she observes:

> The question remains. . . . as to whether the dual-standard test, as a practical matter, eliminates the "ring of negligence" and significantly alters the evidentiary burdens in a strict products liability action. Conceptually, shifting the burden of proof to the defendant undoubtedly lessens the plaintiff's burden; but pragmatically, this is not as dramatic a benefit as it might seem at first blush. In practice, defendants have typically come forward with sufficient evidence of complicated technological factors under a risk-utility test to convince the jury that trade-offs were in fact made in designing the product, thus tipping the balance in favor of utility and diminished risk. [Id. at 606.]

Several other courts have adopted the *Barker* two-prong test for liability. See, e.g., Lamer v. McKee Industries, Inc., 721 P.2d 611 (Alaska 1986);

Caterpillar Tractor Co. v. Beck, 593 P.2d 871 (Alaska 1979); Knitz v. Minster Mach. Co., 69 Ohio St. 2d 460, 432 N.E.2d 814, *cert. denied,* 459 U.S. 857 (1982). However, it appears that only *Barker* and *Beck* have coupled the two-prong liability test with a shift to defendant of the burden of proof on the risk-utility issue. For decisions specifically rejecting *Barker*'s shifting of the burden, see, e.g., Vineyard v. Empire Mach. Co., 119 Ariz. 502, 581 P.2d 1152 (Ct. App. 1978); Armentrout v. FMC, 842 P.2d 175 (Colo. 1992); Wilson v. Piper Aircraft Corp., 282 Or. 411, 579 P.2d 1287 (1978).

In Campbell v. General Motors Corp., 32 Cal. 3d 112, 649 P.2d 224, 184 Cal. Rptr. 891 (1982), the Supreme Court of California shed light on the meaning of its holding in *Barker.* The plaintiff, a 62-year-old woman, fell and injured herself in a bus manufactured by defendant GM and operated by the city of San Francisco. She had been sitting in the first forward-facing seat on the right side. The bus rounded a corner to the right and she slid leftwards, off the seat and onto the floor. She testified that she reached in front of her to stop herself from sliding, but "there was nothing there to grab." The plaintiff sued GM on the basis of an allegedly defective design, relying on *Barker.* The trial court granted GM's motion for nonsuit at the end of the plaintiff's proof, holding that the plaintiff had failed to introduce any evidence whatever that a hand-hold in a position to help her would have been feasible in a bus already festooned with handholds, railings and the like.

The California Supreme Court reversed, concluding that under *Barker* it was up to the defendant GM to prove that its design was reasonable. The plaintiff had carried her burden of production merely by reciting she had fallen in the bus. No further proof was required. The court concluded (Id. at 124-127, 649 P.2d at 231-233, 184 Cal. Rptr. at 898-900):

> In the case before this court, there was sufficient evidence from which the jury could infer that the lack of a restraining pole or rail within plaintiff's reach was a proximate cause of the injury. Plaintiff's seat, unlike the other forward-facing seats, did not have a metal "grab bar" at shoulder level in front of it. There was also no vertical pole in front of the seat. As she was being propelled from her seat, plaintiff reached for some object to grab on to, but found none. From this evidence, the jury could reasonably conclude that if a bar or pole had been present, plaintiff would not have been thrown to the other side of the bus and injured.
>
> [It is] clear that plaintiff produced sufficient evidence to establish a prima facie case of causation. The evidence justified a conclusion that a design feature of the bus—the absence of a restraining bar or pole—was a substantial factor in causing the injury. Under the second prong of *Barker,* plaintiff discharged her evidentiary burden. At this point, the burden of proof should have shifted to defendant to offer evidence relevant to a risk-benefit evaluation of the design of the bus. Of course, defendant also could have attempted to refute plaintiff's theory of causation by producing evidence (including expert testimony, if desired) that a bar or pole would not have prevented the accident.

However, the trial court's grant of the motion for nonsuit prematurely and erroneously withdrew these issues from the jury.

Alternatively, if a plaintiff proceeds under the first prong of *Barker,* in addition to establishing a prima facie case regarding causation, the plaintiff must also produce evidence that the product failed to satisfy ordinary consumer expectations as to safety.

Here, plaintiff presented sufficient evidence to have the case submitted to the jury on this theory as well. Not only did she testify about the accident (her use of the product), but she also introduced photographic evidence of the design features of the bus. This evidence was sufficient to establish the objective conditions of the product. The other essential aspect of this test involves the jurors' own sense of whether the product meets ordinary expectations as to its safety under the circumstances presented by the evidence. Since public transportation is a matter of common experience, no expert testimony was required to enable the jury to reach a decision on this part of the *Barker* inquiry.

Indeed, it is difficult to conceive what testimony an "expert" could provide. The thrust of the first *Barker* test is that the product must meet the safety expectations of the general public as represented by the ordinary customer, not the industry or a government agency. "[O]ne can hardly imagine what credentials a witness must possess before he can be certified as an expert on the issue of ordinary consumer expectations." (Schwartz, Foreward: Understanding Products Liability (1979) 67 Cal. L. Rev. 435, 480.)

The quantum of proof necessary to establish a prima facie case of design defect under the first prong of *Barker* cannot be reduced to an easy formula. However, if the product is one within the common experience of ordinary consumers, it is generally sufficient if the plaintiff provides evidence concerning (1) his or her use of the product; (2) the circumstances surrounding the injury; and (3) the objective features of the product which are relevant to an evaluation of its safety. That evidence was provided in this case. Therefore, appellant was entitled to a jury determination concerning whether the bus satisfied ordinary consumer expectations.

For the treatment of design defects in the Council Draft No. 1A of the Restatement (Third) of Torts: Products Liability, see §2(b), p. 671, below.

Tobin v. Astra Pharmaceutical Products, Inc.

993 F.2d 528 (6th Cir. 1993)

RALPH B. GUY, JR., CIRCUIT JUDGE.

Defendant Astra Pharmaceutical Products, Inc., appeals the denial of its motion for judgment notwithstanding the verdict, or in the alternative for a new trial, in this diversity products liability action. On appeal, Astra argues that its motion for a j.n.o.v. should have been granted, because the causation hypothesis of plaintiff's expert does not have a generally accepted scientific basis and the risk/benefit theory and failure to warn theory proposed by the plaintiff cannot establish liability under Kentucky law. Astra also argues that its motion for a new trial should have been granted . . . because the verdict was against the clear weight of the evidence. We reject defendant's arguments and affirm.

I

In 1986, Kathy Tobin was 19 years old and pregnant with twins. Her expected date of delivery was in early April 1987. Other than a mitral valve prolapse, or heart murmur, a rather common finding in reproductive-age women, Tobin was a healthy young woman. In mid-October 1986, Tobin was hospitalized for dehydration. She was having difficulty keeping down food and fluids and required hydration. Her condition was diagnosed as viral in origin. She was released after a few days and her pregnancy progressed. In January 1987, Tobin was admitted to the hospital for management of preterm labor. She was given an injection of magnesium sulphate and then was placed on an oral maintenance dose of ritodrine. Dosage levels varied, being increased when contractions returned.

Tobin testified that after each dose of ritodrine her pulse would race and her heart felt as if "it was going to jump out of my skin"; her face would also flush and her hands and legs would swell. She was advised that these symptoms were normal side effects of ritodrine. On March 9, 1987, Tobin's obstetricians reduced the dosage because of her rapid heart rate. On March 16, 1987, Tobin informed her doctors that she could not breathe when lying down, and she was told to further reduce the ritodrine dosage. At 1:30 A.M. on March 17, she was admitted to the hospital with symptoms of tachypnea (rapid breathing), dyspnea (shortness of breath), and a gallop rhythm of the heart. At this time, it also was noted that Tobin had a grade I/IV systolic murmur of the heart. X-rays revealed that she had pulmonary edema (fluid in the lungs) and cardiomegaly (enlargement of the heart) caused by congestive heart failure. An electrocardiogram revealed advanced dilated cardiomyopathy. Ritodrine was discontinued, and that afternoon plaintiff delivered healthy twins having a gestational age of 37 weeks.

On March 20, Tobin was discharged from the hospital with instructions to follow up with a cardiologist. The next day she was readmitted for treatment of congestive heart failure, cardiomyopathy, and pulmonary edema. After five days in the hospital, she was again released. She was readmitted on April 10, and on April 15 a mechanical heart, or ventricular assist device, was inserted until a donated heart for a heart transplant could be found. On April 16, Tobin underwent a heart transplant.

Plaintiff filed suit against Duphar B.V., the corporation in the Netherlands that manufactures ritodrine, and against Astra Pharmaceutical, Duphar's United States distributor. After removal to federal court on diversity grounds, the district court granted Duphar's motion to dismiss for lack of personal jurisdiction. Plaintiff proceeded against Astra. After a two-week trial, the jury returned a verdict in favor of the plaintiff. The jury awarded Tobin approximately $4.5 million, finding Astra liable on the basis of defective design and failure to warn for the conditions that led to her heart transplant. The district court denied Astra's motion for j.n.o.v. or in the alternative for a new trial, and Astra timely appealed.

II

[The court next addresses defendant's argument that plaintiff's expert testimony regarding the causal link between taking ritodrine and plaintiff's subsequent heart failure was inadequate. Rejecting defendant's assertion that plaintiff's expert relied on "junk science," the court affirms the jury's finding that plaintiff's ingestion of ritodrine caused her injury.]

III

Having concluded that plaintiff's evidence of causation was appropriate expert testimony from which the jury could find causation, we turn to the two theories of liability offered by the plaintiff. The jury was instructed that it should find for the plaintiff if:

> (a) ritodrine, as manufactured and marketed by Astra and as used by the plaintiff, was in a defective condition unreasonably dangerous to the user, and
> (b) the defective and unreasonably dangerous condition of the ritodrine was a substantial factor in causing the plaintiff's injuries.
> Or, if Astra failed to comply with the duty to exercise ordinary care to provide such warnings and instructions as would afford reasonable notice of the proper use and consequences of use of ritodrine.
> . . . [A]nd that such failure was a substantial factor in causing the injuries sustained by the plaintiff. . . .

Separate verdict forms were used for each theory of liability, and the jury found Astra liable under both theories.

A. Failure to Warn

Astra argues that under Kentucky law it was error to submit a separate instruction on failure to warn because the nature of the warning is one of several factors to be considered on the issue of product defect. Indeed, the design defect instruction given to the jury included the statement:

> In determining whether the ritodrine was in a defective condition unreasonably dangerous to the user, you may consider the adequacy of the warnings and instructions for use set forth in the package insert and in the Physician's Desk Reference. A warning is adequate if it affords fair and adequate notice of the possible consequences of use of the product.

However, under Kentucky law, when a plaintiff has made a claim of negligence in addition to a product defect claim, a separate "negligence instruction is warranted." Ingersoll-Rand Co. v. Rice, 775 S.W.2d 924, 932 (Ky. Ct. App. 1989). The instruction on Astra's duty to warn was a negligence instruction, using the standard of "ordinary care," and expressly explained that phrase to the jury. Therefore, Astra's challenge to the separate instruction is rejected. . . .

Plaintiff's other argument regarding failure to warn relates to the studies on efficacy of ritodrine. Plaintiff argues that, because the duty to warn includes the duty to provide adequate instructions for safe use, the warnings Astra provided were deficient because they "failed to inform physicians that ritodrine has not been proven effective in extending pregnancy beyond 24 to 48 hours, nor in improving neonatal outcome." Plaintiffs are essentially arguing that the package insert should have included a warning that ritodrine is not effective. We prefer to analyze the evidence regarding efficacy under the second theory of liability presented to the jury—defective product design, unreasonably dangerous to the user.

B. Strict Liability-Defective Design

Under Kentucky law, the test for whether a product is in a defective condition and unreasonably dangerous to the user is whether an ordinarily prudent manufacturer, being fully aware of the risks, would have placed the product on the market. Plaintiff argues that the only way to decide whether an ordinarily prudent manufacturer would place a product on the market is to balance the product's risks, its harmful side effects, against its benefits. Defendant argues that Kentucky has never adopted the risk/benefit analysis proffered by plaintiff. To support its position, defendant cites Ingersoll-Rand, 775 S.W.2d at 932, where the Kentucky Court of Appeals stated it was "disturbed by the risk/benefit analysis provided in" a jury instruction. Defendant fails to note two critical points.

First, the *Ingersoll-Rand* court specifically stated that it was not expressing an opinion on the appropriateness of the "risk/benefit analysis" instruction in future cases, but that in the case before it such an instruction was not appropriate because "[t]here was simply no evidence before the jury in this case which would allow the jury to evaluate the risks and benefits associated with the design and manufacture of [the product] in order for them to use this instruction in any meaningful way." Id. at 933. In the case at bar, evidence of the risks and benefits associated with ritodrine were a main focus of the case. Second, the jury in this case was not given a "risk/benefit analysis" instruction; it was given the standard strict liability instruction, approved in Kentucky. Thus, *Ingersoll-Rand* is inapplicable.

As summarized by the Kentucky Supreme Court, the standard for strict liability is formulated:

> The manufacturer is presumed to know the qualities and characteristics, and the actual condition, of his product at the time he sells it, and the question is whether the product creates "such a risk" of an accident of the general nature of the one in question "that an ordinarily prudent company engaged in the manufacture" of such a product "would not have put it on the market."

In the context of her defective design claim, plaintiff's arguments regarding the weighing of the risks against the benefits of ritodrine were not improper, given the evidence presented in this case. The district judge did not instruct the jury to weigh the risks against the benefits, but only instructed them that "ritodrine was in a defective condition unreasonably dangerous to the user if an ordinarily prudent manufacturer of such a drug, being fully aware of the risks associated with the use of ritodrine, would not have put the drug on the market." The instruction that was given is consistent with Kentucky law.

In a nutshell, plaintiff claims that oral ritodrine is bereft of benefits as far as improving neonatal outcome. Weighing no benefits against the serious risks posed by the drug and suffered by the plaintiff, it is clear, plaintiff asserts, that the risks outweigh the benefits and thus no "ordinarily prudent manufacturer" would put the drug on the market. Astra maintains that oral ritodrine is effective in prolonging pregnancy, and therefore in improving neonatal outcome, and that the risks to maternal and fetal health associated with oral ritodrine are outweighed by the benefits of reducing neonatal morbidity and mortality. Astra also maintains that, because of FDA approval, ritodrine's effectiveness is not open to question.

[The court concludes that FDA approval of ritodrine does not preclude judicial review of the drug's effectiveness.]

We do not sit to review the findings of the FDA; our only role in this appeal is to decide if there was sufficient evidence on which the jury could base its verdict. Plaintiff introduced evidence, through the cross-examination of Astra officials, that a reasonably prudent manufacturer would not market ritodrine if the evidence of its efficacy was inconclusive. Plaintiff also introduced sufficient evidence regarding the various clinical studies concerning the efficacy of ritodrine. The jury found that ritodrine, as manufactured and marketed by Astra, was in a defective condition and unreasonably dangerous to plaintiff. We find that there was sufficient evidence before the jury to conclude that a prudent manufacturer knowing all the risks would not market ritodrine.

Defendant argues that if the warning accompanying ritodrine was adequate then it cannot be held strictly liable. The cases cited by defendant to support its position, that a drug manufacturer should be shielded from liability, so hold based on Comment *k* of the Restatement (Second) of Torts §402A. Comment *k* provides that the seller of "unavoidably unsafe products" . . . "is not to be held to strict liability for unfortunate consequences attending their use. . . ." For Comment *k* to apply, however, the product must be "an apparently useful and desirable product." It is the useful or effective nature of ritodrine which plaintiff has called into question. Kentucky has ruled that Comment *k* shields manufacturers from liability for "highly useful and desirable product[s] attended with a known but reasonable risk." McMichael v. American Red Cross, 532 S.W.2d 7, 9 (Ky. 1975) (citing Comment *k*). A drug that prolongs pregnancy in order to reduce infant morbidity and mortality, if effective, is a highly useful and desirable product. Plaintiff, however, has attacked the linchpin of this theory—effectiveness—with various evidence. The jury was instructed:

> A product such as ritodrine is not in a defective condition unreasonably dangerous if it cannot be made completely safe for all users, but is nevertheless a useful and desirable product which is accompanied by proper directions and warnings.

The jury verdict rejecting this argument is supported by the evidence that was presented.

We affirm the district court's denial of defendant Astra's motion for judgment notwithstanding the verdict or in the alternative for a new trial.

2. Affirmative Defenses: Misuse

Jurado v. Western Gear Works

131 N.J. 375, 619 A.2d 1312 (1993)

POLLOCK, J.

Our focus is on the meaning of "misuse" as that term is used in a strict-liability design-defect products-liability case. In the present case, the problem arises from confusion inherent in Model Civil Charge 5.34I pertaining to product misuse. The trial court relied on that charge, which confuses the purpose for which a product is used with the manner of using it, in submitting special interrogatories to the jury. Those interrogatories apparently misled the jury about the meaning of "misuse."

Before submitting the case to the jury, the court reserved decision on a motion for a directed verdict by plaintiff Alfonso Jurado. After the jury returned a verdict for defendants Western Gear Corporation and Bucyrus-Erie Company, the court granted Jurado's motion for a judgment notwithstanding the verdict. The Appellate Division affirmed the judgment on liability in Jurado's favor and remanded to the Law Division for a trial on damages only.

We granted certification. We now reverse that part of the Appellate Division's judgment that affirmed the judgment on liability and remand the matter to the Law Division for a trial on both liability and damages.

I

Jurado, an employee of N & W Printing, injured his right hand when it became caught in an "in-running nip point" located between a rotating cylinder and a support bar underneath a collating machine. The machine, which was designed to collate and assemble business forms, was manufactured and distributed by defendants.

During the collating process, excess paper salvage would enter a vacuum tube beneath the machine. Frequently, the paper would build up at the mouth of the tube, forcing the operator to clear it by hand. The tube was located near the rotating cylinder underneath the collator.

On the date of the accident, Jurado reduced the speed of the machine and tried to clear salvage that was blocking the vacuum tube. As he crouched and reached under the collator with his left hand, he lost his balance and tried with his right hand to prevent himself from falling. Jurado's right hand was injured when it was drawn into the in-running nip point. He claimed that he had not turned off the collator before attempting to unclog the vacuum tube because his employer had warned that the interruption would confuse the collating sequence. N & W Printing disputes this claim.

Jurado's expert witness, Gerald Weiner, a mechanical engineer, testified that the collator did not conform to proper design standards because of the absence of a guard on the in-running nip point. Weiner stated that at the time the collator was manufactured, defendants easily and inexpensively could have installed a sheet-metal fixed-barrier guard around the nip point. According to Weiner, the guard would not have affected the function of the machine and could have been installed for as little as $40 to $50 per unit.

He testified that since 1948 design engineers have recognized the potential danger posed by nip points. Defendants should have known, according to Weiner, that salvage would obstruct the mouth of the vacuum, and that an operator of the machine ultimately would have to clear the vacuum manually. In addition, he claimed that production engineers know that employees will typically take "shortcuts" to increase their productivity. Thus, according to Weiner, a machine designer should have taken precautionary steps to prevent accidents that may result from such foreseeable shortcuts by employees.

He also noted that the area of the machine containing the in-running nip point was not "guarded by its location." He defined a guarded location as one either located more than eight feet off the floor or that could not be reached without removing a part of the machine. Weiner intimated that defendants had indirectly acknowledged that the location of the nip point did not constitute a guard because defendants had placed fixed-barrier guards over other nip points in the same area of the collator. He concluded that the in-running nip point was a foreseeable hazard and that defendants had avoided the use of well-known inexpensive methods of installing a guard.

Defendants' expert, Edward Schwalje, a mechanical engineer, asserted that the existence of the nip point did not require the installation of a sheet-metal guard. In his opinion, the nip point was already guarded by its location. Schwalje said that the location served as a guard because Jurado would not have placed his hands in the nip point during the normal course of operating the machine. He pointed out that Jurado had to squat and reach under the machine to touch the nip point, which was twenty-eight inches off the ground.

Schwalje acknowledged that the gears near the location of the injury were properly covered with fixed guards. He stated, however, that the collator had numerous moving parts that created nip points that were potentially dangerous if the operator "tamper[ed]" with the collator while it was in operation. According to Schwalje, the collator was not designed to be adjusted or repaired while in operation. Further, in the case of "salvage jams," the machine was designed to be stopped and cleaned while in "static condition." He concluded that the machine was "safe for use as intended" and met the design standards for safety when it was manufactured and distributed by defendants in the early- to mid-1960s.

Finally, Schwalje testified that he did not know whether defendants had reasonably anticipated when they had manufactured and distributed the machine that salvage would build up at the mouth of the vacuum tube. He stated, however, that similarly-designed collators occasionally jam because of excess salvage.

At the close of the entire case, Jurado moved for a directed verdict. He asserted that Schwalje's testimony constituted a "net opinion" and that "reasonable minds could not differ" on the outcome in favor of Jurado. After reserving decision, the court charged the jury, instructing it to reach a verdict on damages even if it found for defendants on liability. Relying on Model Civil Jury Charge 5.34I, the court instructed the jury to answer four special interrogatories. The interrogatories and the jury's answers are: 1. Was the product as designed, manufactured, or sold defective, in that it was not reasonably safe for its intended or reasonably foreseeable uses? No. 2. Did the defect exist when the product left the hands and control of the defendant? No. 3. At the time of the accident was the product being used for an intended or reasonably foreseeable purpose, that is, that it was not being misused or had not been substantially altered in a way that was not reasonably foreseeable? Yes. 4. Was the defect in the product a proximate cause of the accident? No. The jury returned a verdict in favor of defendants on liability and awarded Jurado hypothetical damages of $65,000.

In his motion for a judgment notwithstanding the verdict, Jurado argued that the jury's answers to the special interrogatories were inconsistent with the evidence presented at trial. The court granted that motion, but denied Jurado's subsequent motion for additur or a new trial on damages. It then entered a verdict in favor of Jurado for $92,514.18 (the $65,000 award plus prejudgment interest).

The Appellate Division affirmed the judgment on liability n.o.v., but reversed the denial of a new trial on damages. It found that the affirmative answer to interrogatory three constituted a rejection of the defense expert's testimony and therefore left the opinion of Jurado's expert uncontradicted. The court interpreted the jury's response to the third interrogatory as a finding that "plaintiff's use of the machine was reasonably foreseeable, and it was not being misused at the time of the accident." This, according to the court, constituted a denial of the plausibility of the defense expert's theory that the nip point was guarded by its location. Thus, the court found that the judgment notwithstanding the verdict was warranted. We have a different view.

II

We cannot tell whether the jury simply concluded that Jurado was using the collator for its intended purpose, as the trial court apparently believed, or that Jurado was not misusing the machine, as the Appellate Division believed. In fairness to the lower courts, some confusion inheres in Model Civil Jury Charge 5.34I. That charge states in relevant part: If you find that the plaintiff has shown by the preponderance of the credible evidence that (1) the product as designed, manufactured, or sold was defective, in that it was not reasonably safe for its intended or reasonably foreseeable uses, (2) the defect existed when the product left the hands and control of the defendant, (3) that at the time of the accident the product was being used for an intended or reasonably foreseeable purpose, that is, that it was not being misused or had not been substantially altered in a way that was not reasonably foreseeable, . . . and (5) that the defect in the product was a proximate cause of the accident, then you must find for the plaintiff. If plaintiff has failed to establish any one of the just mentioned elements, then you must find for defendant.

Initially, subparagraph 3 of Model Civil Jury Charge 5.34I leads a jury to believe that the focus of the question is the purpose for which the product was used. The charge, however, proceeds to define "use for an intended or reasonably foreseeable purpose" in terms of whether the product was "misused" or "substantially altered." Thus, the charge could be understood to define misuse solely in terms of the purpose for which the collator was being used without mentioning the manner of use.

As read by the Appellate Division, the answer to the third interrogatory, which was based on subparagraph three, confuses the purpose for which a product is used with the manner in which it is used. If the jury found in answering interrogatory three that Jurado was using the collator for its intended purpose, that finding would constitute only a partial resolution of the issue of misuse. The Appellate Division assumed that the jury's response necessarily found not only that the product was being used for a reasonably foreseeable purpose, but also that Jurado's manner of use was reasonably foreseeable.

A. . . .

The decision whether a product is defective because it is "not reasonably fit, suitable, and safe" for its intended purposes reflects a policy judgment under a risk-utility analysis. That analysis seeks to determine whether a particular product creates a risk of harm that outweighs its usefulness. Risk-utility analysis is especially appropriate when a product may function satisfactorily under one set of circumstances and yet, because of a possible design defect, presents an unreasonable risk of injury to the user in other situations.

Under a risk-utility analysis, a defendant may still be liable when a plaintiff misused the product, if the misuse was objectively foreseeable.

The absence of misuse is part of the plaintiff's case. Misuse is not an affirmative defense. Thus, the plaintiff has the burden of showing that there was no misuse or that the misuse was objectively foreseeable.

Essentially, product misuse contemplates two kinds of conduct. One is the use of a product for an improper purpose. "If, for instance, a plaintiff undertakes to use his power saw as a nail clipper and thereby snips his digits, he will not be heard to complain. . . ." Suter [v. San Angelo Foundry & Mach. Co., 81 N.J. 150, 194, 406 A.2d 140 (1979).] (Clifford, J., concurring). For a plaintiff to recover, the purpose for which the product is used at the time of the accident must be objectively foreseeable. When a plaintiff is injured while using the product for a purpose that is not objectively foreseeable, the injury does not establish that the product is defective.

The other kind of misuse concerns the manner in which the plaintiff used the product. When, for example, the operator of a high-lift forklift is injured while using the forklift on steep, instead of level, terrain, the emphasis should be on the manner, not the purpose, of the misuse. As Comment *h* of Restatement (Second) of Torts §402A states: "A product is not in a defective condition when it is safe for normal handling or consumption." . . .

Product misuse theoretically could relate to the existence of a defect, the issue of causation, or that of comparative fault. See James A. Henderson, Jr. and Aaron D. Twerski, Products Liability Problems and Process 669 (2d ed. 1992). In a workplace setting, when, because of a design defect, an employee is injured while using a machine in a reasonably foreseeable manner, the employee's comparative fault is irrelevant. . . .

If the jury concludes that the product is defective, it must then determine whether the misuse proximately caused the injury. Even if a defect is a contributing or concurring cause, but not the sole cause, of an accident, the manufacturer will be liable. For example, if, in the present case, the accident had happened when a co-employee negligently or playfully bumped plaintiff while he crouched in front of the collator, the manufacturer could be found liable notwithstanding the untoward conduct of the co-employee. In that situation, the jury should consider whether the absence of the guard was the proximate, contributing, or concurring cause of the injury.

In some situations, however, the issue of proximate cause is predetermined by the finding that the product is defective solely because of the manufacturer's failure to protect against a foreseeable misuse. As Professor Aaron D. Twerski explains:

> If a court determines that a design defect exists [solely] because the manufacturer has failed to include safety devices, there is no proximate cause question of any moment left to consider. The very reason for declaring the design defective was to prevent this kind of foreseeable misuse. Proximate cause could not, in such a case, present an obstacle on the grounds of misuse. To do so would negate the very reason for declaring the design defective in the first instance.

[The Many Faces of Misuse: An Inquiry Into the Emerging Doctrine of Comparative Causation, 29 Mercer L. Rev. 403, 421 (1978).]

In sum, when misuse is an issue in a design-defect case, the jury should first determine whether the plaintiff used the product for an objectively foreseeable purpose. If the jury finds that the plaintiff's purpose was not foreseeable, the defendant did not breach any duty owed to the plaintiff. If, however, the jury finds that the plaintiff's purpose was foreseeable, it must then decide whether the product was defective.

Under the risk-utility analysis, the jury must then determine whether the plaintiff used the product in an objectively foreseeable manner. The effect of a finding that the plaintiff did not so use the product, like a determination that the product was not used for a foreseeable purpose, is that the jury will have found that the defendant did not breach any duty owed to the plaintiff. If, however, the jury finds that the plaintiff used the product in an objectively foreseeable manner, it should then evaluate the product's utility. That evaluation entails the determination whether the defendant feasibly could have modified the product's design to prevent the injury or whether that modification would have either unreasonably impaired the utility of the product or excessively increased its cost.

If the jury finds that the product is defective, it must then decide whether the misuse proximately caused the injury. In cases in which the product is defective solely because of a foreseeable misuse, the determination of defect predetermines the issue of proximate cause. In other cases, however, where a product is defective for reasons other than the particular misuse, the jury must separately determine proximate cause.

Here, the jury found that the product was not defective as designed, that it was reasonably safe for its intended or reasonably foreseeable uses, that it was not defective when it left defendants' hands, and that it was not a proximate cause of the accident. It also found that at the time of the accident, the product was being used for an intended or reasonably foreseeable purpose in that "it was not being misused or had not been substantially altered in any way that was not reasonably foreseeable." The Appellate Division concluded that the jury had found that Jurado had used the machine in a foreseeable manner and that the jury's finding was a rejection of the defense expert's theory that "the in-running nip point was guarded by reason of its location. . . ." Special interrogatory number three, the jury's answer to which was the predicate for that conclusion, however, does not mention the word "manner." Instead, the interrogatory focuses on the purpose for which the product was being used at the time of the accident.

Consequently, the Appellate Division should not have assumed that the jury had decided the issue of misuse based on the manner in which Jurado had used the collator. In particular, the Appellate Division states: "The jury found that plaintiff had to put his hand into the nip point area during foreseeable operation." In effect, the Appellate Division defined away the alternative that the jury found only that the machine had been used for its intended purpose. The inconsistency in the jury's findings requires a retrial on liability as well as damages.

The record suggests that if on retrial the jury determines that plaintiff's misuse was objectively foreseeable, that determination will predetermine that the defect was the proximate cause of the accident. If so, the trial court should instruct the jury that its determination of the existence of a defect will have that further effect.

The Appellate Division, after concluding that the jury must have determined that Jurado had not used the collator in an improper manner, implicitly concluded further that the jury must have determined that the defect was the proximate cause of the accident. As previously stated, however, we cannot ascertain whether the jury found that plaintiff had used the collator in an improper manner or for an improper purpose. Contrary to the Appellate Division's implicit conclusion, moreover, the jury explicitly found that the defect was not the proximate cause of the accident. Given our concern about the possible inconsistency of the jury's finding on the existence of a defect and the implications of that finding for the issue of proximate cause, we believe that the interests of justice are better served by a retrial.

The judgment of the Appellate Division on liability is reversed, and the matter is remanded to the Law Division for a trial on both liability and damages.

CLIFFORD, J., dissenting.

When in a querulous mood, our colleagues at the trial bench sometimes grumble that while trial judges devote their energies to the pursuit of justice, appellate judges spend their time hunched over the record, pawing through it in an unrelenting search for error. One might find support for that dyspeptic observation in today's decision to remand this case for a new trial, given the fact that the jurors rendered a verdict after a charge that, although not squeaky clean, nevertheless fairly put the single critical issue to them in simple, comprehensible terms: Was defendants' product as designed, manufactured, or sold defective in that it was not reasonably safe for its intended or reasonably foreseeable uses? Answer: No.

That question and answer should have been the end of the case. In theory, there was no need for the jury to address questions two, three, and four. We have seen many other jury verdict forms in product-liability failure-to-warn cases that state that if the jury finds no defect, it should cease deliberations and return a verdict for defendant. Viewed in that way, the jury's answers to questions two through four become irrelevant, and the sole focus of appellate inquiry becomes whether a reasonable jury could have concluded that the product was not defective. . . .

D. *Statutory Reform of Products Liability*

1. At the State Level

Legislative activity at the state level has, until recently, been sporadic and piecemeal. Only a few states have passed comprehensive products liability legislation. See, e.g., Idaho Code §§6-1401 et seq. (Supp. 1985); Ill. Ann. Stat. ch. 735, para. 2-621 (Smith-Hurd 1983); Ind. Code Ann. §§33-1-1.5-1 et seq. (West Supp. 1985); Ky. Rev. Stat. Ann. §§411.300 et seq. (Baldwin 1979); Wash. Rev. Code Ann. §§7.72.010 et seq. (Supp. 1986). By 1993, many states had passed legislation in direct response to what sponsors of such measures perceived to be a mounting crisis. Most of the legislation seeks to provide some measure of protection to manufacturers who claim to be hard-hit by the far-reaching decisions of courts.

In addition to legislation directed specifically at products liability, in recent years many states have enacted reform statutes dealing generally with tort law. These statutes are, of course, applicable to products liability and have been considered at a number of junctures throughout this book.

2. Uniform Laws Approaches

In 1976, the United States Department of Commerce commenced an 18-month interagency study on the topic of products liability. Its final report, issued in November 1977, recommended that a uniform product liability law be prepared. In early 1979, a "Draft Uniform Product Liability Law" was published in the Federal Register for public comment. 44 Fed. Reg. 2996. A final version of the uniform act was promulgated later in 1979 under the name of "Model Uniform Product Liability Act" and is now generally known by its acronym, MUPLA. See 44 Fed. Reg. 62, 714 (1979).

MUPLA explicitly identifies the problems that brought it into existence. Section 101, entitled "Findings," proclaims:

> (A) Sharply rising product liability insurance premiums have created serious problems in commerce resulting in:
>
> (1) Increased prices of consumer and industrial products;
>
> (2) Disincentives for innovation and for the development of high-risk but potentially beneficial products;
>
> (3) An increase in the number of product sellers attempting to do business without product liability insurance coverage, thus jeopardizing both their continued existence and the availability of compensation to injured persons; and
>
> (4) Legislative initiatives enacted in a crisis atmosphere that may, as a result, unreasonably curtail the rights of product liability claimants.
>
> (B) One cause of these problems is that product liability law is fraught with uncertainty and sometimes reflects an imbalanced consideration of the interests it affects. The rules vary from jurisdiction to jurisdiction and are subject to rapid and substantial change. These facts militate against predictability of litigation outcome.
>
> (C) Insurers have cited this uncertainty and imbalance as justifications for setting rates and premiums that, in fact, may not reflect actual product risk or liability losses.
>
> (D) Product liability insurance rates are set on the basis of country-wide, rather than individual state, experience. Insurers utilize country-wide experience because a product manufactured in one state can readily cause injury in any one of the other states, the District of Columbia, or the Commonwealth of Puerto Rico. One ramification of this practice is that there is little an individual state can do to solve the problems caused by product liability.
>
> (E) Uncertainty in product liability law and litigation outcome has added to litigation costs and may put an additional strain on the judicial system.
>
> (F) Recently enacted state product liability legislation has widened existing disparities in the law. . . .

Although MUPLA emphasizes the need for certainty and uniformity so that insurers may be able to set rates with greater confidence in their predictions as to ultimate exposure, clearly the act seeks substantive changes that favor the business community. It is important to note that MUPLA was not proposed by the Department of Commerce as a federal products liability bill. It was offered as a model for voluntary use by the states. To date, several states have borrowed some of its provisions. However, not a single state has enacted it in whole or even in significant part, and there does not appear to be even a remote chance that widespread adoption will ever take place. Unlike the Uniform Commercial Code, which was built upon a broad consensus of the business and banking community, the important sectors of the body politic disagree over what rules should govern products liability. Consumer groups, labor unions, and the trial bar see the world from very different perspectives than do manufacturers and distributors. Given the diverse political make-ups of the various states, even middle-of-the-road reform will almost certainly not take place at the state level in a way that will promote uniformity. The atmosphere is too charged and the voices too strident for a national consensus to develop and manifest itself.

3. Substantive Reform at the Federal Level

With state legislatures going their own ways and demonstrating no inclination to adopt MUPLA, and with state court systems all possessing their own, individualized doctrinal biases, the quest for a uniform solution to the products liability crisis has turned to Congress. Beginning in 1979, bills have been introduced each year (in either the House or the Senate) to "federalize" and thus (it was hoped by the sponsors) to render uniform, much of present-day products liability law. Some of these proposals have been modest and directed toward a limited number of issues; others have attempted to regulate all aspects of products litigation. Nonetheless, most of the proposals have not sought radical restructuring of the tort system, contenting themselves with offering corrections of present-day products liability law. Some observers believe that nothing short of radical change will bring about the necessary improvements.

Several comprehensive products bills that are corrective in nature have, as of 1994, been unable to gain sufficient political support. The preemption clause of one much-discussed federal bill demonstrates the wide sweep of the "corrective" legislation:

> This Act supersedes any State law regarding recovery for any loss or damage caused by a product to the extent that this Act establishes a rule of law applicable to any civil action brought against a manufacturer or product seller for loss or damage caused by a product, including any action which before the effective date of this Act would have been based on (A) strict or absolute

liability in tort; (B) negligence or gross negligence; (C) breach of express or implied warranty; (D) failure to discharge a duty to warn or instruct; or (E) any other theory that is the basis for an award for damages for loss or damage caused by a product. Any issue arising in such an action that is not governed by any such rule of law shall be governed by applicable State law. This Act shall not be construed to waive or affect any defense of sovereign immunity asserted by any State under any provision of law. [Kasten bill, S. 100, 99th Cong., 1st Sess. §3(b)(1), 131 Cong. Rec. 571 (1985).]

Nothing short of a full recitation of the various federal products liability bills could give the student a full appreciation of the changes they seek to impose, but a short list of subjects covered will provide some flavor as to their ambition. The Kasten bill, for example, covers all phases of the cause of action, including manufacturing defect, design defect, failure to warn, express warranty, contributory fault, assumption of risk, obvious dangers, technological feasibility, liability of wholesalers and retailers, joint and several liability, statutes of repose and statutes of limitation, worker compensation, and punitive damages.

E. *The Restatement of Torts, Third: Products Liability*

As mentioned earlier in this chapter, in the Spring of 1992, the American Law Institute decided to undertake a revision of the Restatement of Torts, Second. Moreover, the Institute determined to begin its work with the subject of products liability. In May, 1992, the Institute appointed Professor James A. Henderson, Jr. (Cornell Law School) and Aaron D. Twerski (Brooklyn Law School) Co-Reporters on the project. The following, as of January, 1994, are the provisions in Council Draft No. 1A dealing with product defect.

TOPIC 1. PRODUCT DEFECTIVENESS

§1. COMMERCIAL SELLER'S LIABILITY FOR HARM CAUSED BY DEFECTIVE PRODUCTS

(a) One engaged in the business of selling products who sells a defective product is subject to liability for harm to persons or property caused by the product defect.

(b) A product is defective only if, at the time of sale, it contains a manufacturing defect, is defective in design or is defective due to inadequate instructions or warnings.

§2. CATEGORIES OF PRODUCT DEFECTS

For purposes of determining liability under Section 1:

(a) a product contains a manufacturing defect when the product departs from its intended design even though all possible care was exercised in the preparation and marketing of the product;

(b) a product is defective in design when the foreseeable risks of harm posed by the product could have been reduced by the adoption of a reasonable alternative design by the seller or a predecessor in the commercial chain of distribution and the omission of the alternative design renders the product not reasonably safe;

(c) a product is defective due to inadequate instructions or warnings when the foreseeable risks of harm posed by the product could have been reduced by the provision of reasonable instructions or warnings by the seller or a predecessor in the commercial chain of distribution and the omission of reasonable instructions or warnings renders the product not reasonably safe.

§3. INFERENCE OF MANUFACTURING DEFECT WITHOUT PROOF OF SPECIFIC DEFECT

When a product fails to function as it should reasonably be expected to function and causes harm under circumstances where it is more probable than not that the malfunction was caused by a manufacturing defect, the trier of fact may infer that such a defect caused the harm and plaintiff need not specify the nature of such defect.

§4. LIABILITY OF SELLERS FOR HARM CAUSED BY PRESCRIPTION DRUGS AND MEDICAL DEVICES

(a) A manufacturer of a prescription drug or medical device who sells a defective product is subject to liability for harm to persons caused by the product defect. A prescription drug or medical device is one that can be sold legally only pursuant to a health care provider's prescription.

(b) For purposes of liability under Subsection (a), product defectiveness is established only if at the time of sale by the manufacturer:

(1) the drug or medical device contained a manufacturing defect as defined in Section 2(a); or

(2) reasonable instructions or warnings regarding foreseeable risks of harm posed by the drug or medical device were not provided to prescribing and other health care providers who were in a position to reduce the risks of harm in accordance with the instructions or warnings; or

(3) reasonable instructions or warnings regarding foreseeable risks of harm posed by the drug or medical device were not provided directly to the patient when:

(i) the manufacturer knew or had reason to know that no medical provider was in the position described in Subsection (b)(2); or

(ii) governmental regulations required that direct warnings be provided; or

(4) the foreseeable risks of harm posed by the drug or medical device were sufficiently great in relation to its therapeutic benefits as to deter a reasonable medical provider, possessing knowledge of such foreseeable risks and therapeutic benefits, from prescribing the drug or medical device for any patient.

(c) A retail seller of a prescription drug or medical device is subject to liability only if, at the time of sale:

(1) the drug or medical device contained a manufacturing defect as defined in Section 2(a); or

(2) the retail seller failed to exercise reasonable care in preparing, packaging, labelling, instructing or warning about the drug or medical device.

Chapter 8

Damages

In Section A of this chapter, we take up the rules by which the injury to the plaintiff is translated into a dollar amount. In working through this section, it is important to keep in mind the practical interrelationship between the damages covered here and the liability issues covered in the preceding chapters. These issues are not resolved in isolation from each other; particularly in the settlement process, the parties' assessments of liability and damages are combined so that the amount, if any, that the plaintiff receives depends as much on the extent of the injury as it does on the clarity of the defendant's liability. Even in cases that go to trial, it is commonly assumed that juries, and perhaps even judges, fuse the issues in reaching compromise verdicts. Thus, while it is necessary for pedagogical reasons to focus here on the rules of damages largely to the exclusion of liability considerations, this is not an accurate reflection of the torts process.

In Section B, we cover punitive damages.

A. *Compensatory Damages*

The basic tort measure of compensatory damages is the amount of money necessary to restore the plaintiff to his preinjury condition. Often, a complete restoration cannot physically be accomplished, and in such cases damages include the monetary value of the difference between the plaintiff's preinjury and postinjury conditions. In this section, we consider the rules of compensatory damages in cases of personal injury, wrongful death, and property damage.[1]

1. Personal Injury

a. Medical Expenses

Because they tend to be made up of the most concrete and objectively demonstrable items advanced by the plaintiff, the subject of medical ex-

1. Compensatory damages in tort cases are not limited to the damages taken up in this section. Other categories of damages are taken up in the chapters dealing with the substantive bases of liability to which they are appropriate. See, e.g., Chapter 12, Defamation, and Chapter 14, Commercial Torts.

penses presents relatively few difficult problems. In order to be compensable, the expense must be reasonably related to the defendant's wrongful conduct. The most common items are doctors' bills, X-rays, hospital bills, and the like. Psychiatric care is also an allowable item of medical expense. See Browning v. United States, 361 F. Supp. 17 (E.D. Pa. 1973). Recovery has also been permitted for an assortment of expenses related to the plaintiff's physical condition or to medical treatment. For example, in Isgett v. Seaboard Coast Line R.R., 332 F. Supp. 1127 (D.S.C. 1971), the plaintiff, whose legs had been amputated, recovered for the cost of a specially equipped automobile. And in Blissett v. Frisby, 249 Ark. 235, 458 S.W.2d 735 (1970), expenses for baby-sitters while the plaintiff was in the hospital, travel expenses for visits to an out-of-state doctor, and telephone expenses in connection with the making of the doctor's appointments were all recoverable.

Not only must the expenses have been reasonably necessitated by the invasion of the plaintiff's person, but also they must be reasonable in amount. The plaintiff who goes for treatment to three medical specialists when a reasonable person would have gone to one will probably not recover for the expense of the extra two. Nor will the plaintiff recover fully for bills from even a single doctor that are later found to be excessively high.

Related to the question of whether the plaintiff has spent too much on medical treatment is the question of whether the plaintiff has spent too little. Under the "avoidable consequences rule," the plaintiff generally cannot recover for the consequences of the defendant's wrong that the plaintiff could have been avoided by taking reasonable harm-reducing measures. See 2 Dobbs, Law of Remedies§8.7(2) (2d ed. 1993). Thus, in personal injury cases, to recover fully the plaintiff ordinarily must take reasonable steps to mitigate the injuries, including, according to one court, the losing of weight if that is necessary to reduce the extent of the plaintiff's injuries. See Aisole v. Dean, 574 So. 2d 1248 (La. 1991). If the plaintiff has unreasonably refused medical care, the damages will be based on what would have happened had the reasonable care been followed, including, according to one court (see Sette v. Dakis, 133 Conn. 55, 48 A.2d 271 (1946)), the cost of reasonable medical expenses not in fact incurred. Of course, the important question here is whether the plaintiff's failure or refusal to submit to a certain treatment is reasonable. Should the plaintiff's tort recovery be reduced because of a refusal to undergo an operation that involves some risk of death? Risk of paralysis? Do not all operations involve some degree of risk?

What if the refusal of the plaintiff to seek what otherwise would be reasonable medical care is based on religious beliefs? Some courts have held that it is up to the jury to determine whether the refusal was reasonable, and in making that judgment the jury can take the plaintiff's beliefs into account. See, e.g., Lange v. Hoyt, 114 Conn. 590, 159 A. 575 (1932), and Christiansen v. Hollings, 44 Cal. App. 2d 332, 112 P.2d 723 (1941), both involving Christian Scientists, who believe in faith healing. Other courts, however, have refused to recognize religious beliefs as providing a valid reason for refusing medical treatment. See, e.g., Munn v. Algee, 924 F.2d 568 (5th Cir.), *cert. denied,* 112 S. Ct. 277 (1991), involving a member of the Jehovah's Witnesses, whose beliefs do not permit blood transfusions. The court was concerned that the "case-by-case" approach of *Lange* and *Christiansen* would require the jury to assess the reasonableness of the religious basis of the plaintiff's refusal to accept medical treatment. The court felt that such an assessment might violate the "establishment clause" of the First Amendment of the United States Constitution; however, because of the procedural posture of the case, the court did not have to resolve that issue. These issues are discussed in Note, Medical Care, Freedom of Religion, and Mitigation of Damages, 87 Yale L.J. 1466 (1978), which argues that the avoidable consequences rule violates the First Amendment rights of those whose religious beliefs prevent them from seeking medical care. See also Calabresi, Ideals, Beliefs, Attitudes, and the Law (1985). Chapter 3 of that book, entitled "The Beliefs of a Reasonable Person," is particularly relevant.

The plaintiff in Munn v. Southern Health Plan, 719 F. Supp. 525 (N.D. Miss. 1989), *aff'd sub nom.* Munn v. Algee, cited above, also argued that the "egg shell skull" rule should apply in such cases. Under this rule, the defendant is liable to the plaintiff for all harm, including unforeseeable harm, caused by the wrongful conduct of the defendant. Recall that in *Vosburg v. Putney,* p. 12, the court ruled that the defendant would be liable for the unforeseeable harm to the plaintiff's leg caused by the battery. The court in *Munn* rejected the argument:

> Every authority which this court can find which states the "egg shell skull rule" speaks only of physical conditions which pre-exist the injury for which compensation is sought and lead to unforeseeably severe results. The religious beliefs of the plaintiff simply are not covered by the rule.

719 F. Supp. at 529.

In support of limiting the rule to physical injuries, the court cited the Restatement (Second) of Torts, §461, which refers only to the "physical condition" of the plaintiff. Are there any arguments in policy that might be made for applying the rule to the plaintiff's "moral" or "religious condition"?

Future medical expenses are also recoverable, but they must be proven with reasonable certainty (see Hendrix v. Raybestos-Manhattan Inc., 776 F.2d 1492 (11th Cir. 1985)). Future expenses will also be reduced to present value. See Thorpe v. Bailey, 386 A.2d 668 (Del. 1978). Even if the plaintiff has not established a present injury, there may be recovery for future medical monitoring expenses if a reasonable person could conclude that an injury caused by the defendant will become manifest in the future. See, e.g., In re Paoli Railroad Yard PCB Litigation, 916 F.2d 829 (3rd Cir. 1990), *cert. denied sub nom.* General Electric Co. v. Knight, 111 S. Ct. 1584 (1991).

Even more basic than the question of whether or not the plaintiff's expenses are "reasonable" is the question of whether or not the plaintiff has undergone an "expense." Where the plaintiff is fully compensated by medical insurance, for example, is there an expense for which recovery from the defendant will be allowed? The general rule in this country regarding the effect of plaintiff's obtaining benefits from sources other than the defendant is stated in Bell v. Primeau, 104 N.H. 227, 228, 183 A.2d 729, 730 (1962), as follows:

> The rule of law . . . known as the "collateral source rule," which provides that the damages may not be mitigated on account of payments received by the plaintiff from sources other than the defendant has been adopted in one or more of its applications by many jurisdictions, including this one. While the rule has been criticized by commentators and text writers as anomalous, and illogical, it continues to find support in litigated cases.

The plaintiffs were servicemen who received their pay and their medical care without charge from the Air Force. Nevertheless, they were allowed to recover both for reduced earning capacity and medical expenses. Would the New Hampshire court have reached the same result in the following case as did the New York Court of Appeals?

Coyne v. Campbell

11 N.Y.2d 372, 183 N.E.2d 891 (1962)

FROESSEL, J. On July 5, 1957, plaintiff sustained a whiplash injury when his automobile was struck in the rear by a motor vehicle driven by defendant. Inasmuch as plaintiff is a practicing physician and surgeon, he received medical treatment, physiotherapy and care from his professional colleagues and his nurse, and incurred no out-of-pocket expenses therefor. Nevertheless, in his bill of particulars, he stated that his special damages for medical and nursing care and treatment amounted to $2,235. The trial court ruled that the value of these services was not a proper item of special damages, and that no recovery could be had therefor since they had been rendered gratuitously. He thus excluded evidence as to their value. The sole question here presented is the correctness of this ruling.

In the leading case of Drinkwater v. Dinsmore (80 N.Y. 390) we unanimously reversed a plaintiff's judgment entered upon a jury verdict, because defendant was precluded from showing that plaintiff had been paid his wages by his employer during the period of his incapacitation. We held such evidence admissible on the theory that plaintiff was entitled to recover only his pecuniary losses, of which wages gratuitously paid were not an item. With respect to medical expenses, we stated (p. 393) that "the plaintiff must show what he paid the doctor, and can recover only so much as he paid or was bound to pay." Although decided more than 80 years ago, the *Drinkwater* case has continuously been and still is recognized as the prevailing law of this State.

As recently as 1957, the Legislature declined to enact a proposed amendment to the Civil Practice Act, the avowed purpose of which (1957 Report of N.Y. Law Rev. Comm., p. 223) was "to abrogate the rule of Drinkwater v. Dinsmore, 80 N.Y. 390 (1880) and to conform New York law to the rule followed in most states that payments from collateral sources do not reduce the amount recoverable in a personal injury action." . . . The Legislature and not the judiciary is the proper body to decide such a policy question involving the accommodation of various interests. We should not now seek to assume their powers and overrule their decision not to change the well-settled law of this State. No matter what may be the rule in other jurisdictions, *Drinkwater* is still the law in this State.

We find no merit in plaintiff's contention that the medical and nursing services for which damages are sought were supported by consideration. Plaintiff testified that he did not have to pay for the physiotherapy, and his counsel confirmed the fact that "these various items were not payable by the doctor nor were they actual obligations of his, and that he will not have to pay them."

Plaintiff's colleagues rendered the necessary medical services gratuitously as a professional courtesy. It may well be that as a result of having accepted their generosity plaintiff is under a moral obligation to act for them in a similar manner, should his services ever be required; such need may never arise, however, and in any event such a moral obligation is not an injury for which tort damages, which "must be compensatory only" may be awarded. A moral obligation, without more, will not support a claim for legal damages. . . .

We are also told that the physiotherapy treatments which plaintiff received from his nurse consumed approximately two hours per week, and that they were given during the usual office hours for which she received her regular salary. Plaintiff does not claim that he was required to or in fact did pay any additional compensation to his nurse for her performance of these duties, and, therefore, this has not resulted in compensable damage to plaintiff.

Finally, we reject as unwarranted plaintiff's suggestion that our decision in Healy v. Rennert (9 N.Y.2d 202, 206) casts doubt on the continued validity of the *Drinkwater* rule in a case such as the instant one. In *Healy,* we held that it was error to permit defendants to establish on cross-examination that plaintiff was a member of a health insurance plan and that he was receiving increased disability pension benefits. In that case, however, the plaintiff had given value for the benefits he received; he paid a premium for the health insurance, and had worked for 18 years, in order to be eligible for the disability retirement benefits. We were not confronted with—and did not attempt to pass upon—a situation where the injured plaintiff received wholly gratuitous services for which he had given no consideration in return and which he was under no legal obligation to repay. In short, insurance, pension, vacation and other benefits which were contracted and paid for are not relevant here. Gratuitous services rendered by relatives, neighbors and friends are not compensable.

. . . It would hardly be fair in a negligence action, where damages are compensatory and not punitive, to change the *Drinkwater* rule of long standing in the face of the Legislature's refusal to do so, and to punish a defendant by requiring him to pay plaintiff for a friend's generosity. If we were to allow a plaintiff the reasonable value of the services of the physician who treated him gratuitously, logic would dictate that the plaintiff would then be entitled to the reasonable value of such services, despite the fact that the physician charged him but a fraction of such value. Such a rule would involve odd consequences, and in the end simply require a defendant to pay a plaintiff the value of a gift.

The judgment appealed from should be affirmed.

CHIEF JUDGE DESMOND (concurring). The reason why this plaintiff cannot include in his damages anything for physicians' bills or nursing expense is that he had paid nothing for those services. . . .

Settled and consistent precedents provide the answer to the question posed by this appeal. Neither justice nor morality require a different answer. Diminution of damages because medical services were furnished gratuitously results in a windfall of sorts to a defendant but allowance of such items although not paid for would unjustly enrich a plaintiff.

I vote to affirm.

FULD, J. (dissenting). It is elementary that damages in personal injury actions are awarded in order to compensate the plaintiff, but, under an established exception, the collateral source doctrine—which we recognized in Healy v. Rennert (9 N.Y.2d 202)—a wrongdoer will not be allowed to deduct benefits which the plaintiff may have received from another source. To put the matter broadly, the defendant should not be given credit for an amount of money, or its equivalent in services, received by the plaintiff from other sources. "The rationale of the collateral source doctrine in tort actions," it has been said, "is that a tort-feasor should not be allowed to escape the pecuniary consequences of his wrongful act merely because his victim has received benefit from a third party" (Note, 26 Fordham L. Rev. 372, 381).

In the *Healy* case, this court held that, if one is negligently injured by another, the damages recoverable from the latter are diminished neither (1) by the fact that the injured party has been indemnified for his loss by insurance effected by him nor (2) by the fact that his medical expenses were paid by HIP or some other health insurance plan (p. 206). In the case before us, the plaintiff suffered injuries and required medical and nursing care. He had no health insurance, but he received the necessary medical care and services from fellow doctors without being required to pay them in cash. In addition, he received physiotherapy treatments from the nurse employed by him in his office and to whom he, of course, paid a salary.

I fail to see any real difference between the situation in Healy v. Rennert and the case now before us. In neither case was the injured person burdened with any charges for the medical services rendered and, accordingly, when the defendant is required to pay as "damages" for those services or their value, such damages are no less "compensatory" in the one case than in the other. Nor do I understand why a distinction should be made depending upon whether the medical services were rendered gratuitously or for a consideration.[1] What difference should it make, either to the plaintiff or to the defendant, whether an injured plaintiff has his medical bills taken care of by an insurer or by a wealthy uncle or by a fellow doctor? Certainly, neither the uncle, who acted out of affection, nor the doctor, impelled by so-called professional courtesy, intended to benefit the tort-feasor.

The crucial question in cases such as this is whether the tort-feasor would, in fairness and justice, be given credit for the amounts, or their equivalent in services, which the plaintiff has received from some collateral source. The collateral source doctrine is not, and should not be, limited to cases where the plaintiff had previously paid consideration (in the form of insurance premiums, for instance) for the benefit of services which he receives or where there has been a payment of cash or out-of-pocket expenses. The rationale underlying the rule is that a wrongdoer, responsible for injuring the plaintiff, should not receive a windfall. Were it not for the fortuitous circumstance that the plaintiff was a doctor, he would have been billed for the medical services and the defendant would have had to pay for them. The medical services were supplied to help the plaintiff, not to relieve the defendant from any part of his liability or to benefit him. It should not matter, in reason, logic or justice, whether the benefit received was in return for a consideration or given gratuitously, or whether it represented money paid out or its equivalent in services.

The rule reflected by the decision in Drinkwater v. Dinsmore (80 N.Y. 390) is court made and, accordingly, since I believe . . . that it is not only "completely opposite to the majority rule", but also "unfair, illogical and unduly complex", I cannot vote for its perpetuation. Indeed, as I have already indicated, an even stronger case for its repudiation is made out by our recent decision in Healy v. Rennert (9 N.Y.2d 202, supra).

I would reverse the judgment appealed from and direct a new trial.

1. I shall assume that in this case the doctors' services were given gratuitously, though a strong argument could be made to the contrary, that is, that they were supported by consideration in that the plaintiff came under a duty to reciprocate and render medical services to his colleagues. Be that as it may, though, I see no basis for labeling the physiotherapy treatments given by the plaintiff's salaried nurse gratuitous. They were given during the nurse's normal working day for which she received wages from the plaintiff. Had she not been required to give such treatments, she would undoubtedly have been free to perform other work for the plaintiff.

JUDGES DYE, VAN VOORHIS, BURKE and FOSTER concur with JUDGE FROESSEL; CHIEF JUDGE DESMOND concurs in a separate opinion; JUDGE FULD dissents in an opinion.

Judgment affirmed.

It may, of course, be difficult to determine whether the service is really gratuitous. For example, one court permitted recovery of expenses already paid for by Medicare (Berg v. United States, 806 F.2d 978 (10th Cir. 1986), *cert. denied,* 482 U.S. 913 (1987)), but not for expenses paid for by a different governmental program, the Civilian Health and Medical Program of the Uniformed Services (Mays v. United States, 806 F.2d 976 (10th Cir. 1986)). The court stated that the important distinction between the two sources is that the former is supported by a special social security tax paid for by its beneficiaries, while the latter is paid for out of general governmental revenue.

Most courts have applied the collateral source rule to gratuitously rendered services, such as free medical care rendered by a veterans' hospital (see Hudson v. Lazarus, 217 F.2d 344 (D.C. Cir. 1954)), and a state operated mental health facility (see Werner v. Lane, 393 A.2d 1329 (Me. 1978)); special services for students with handicaps furnished by a public school (see Williston v. Ard, 611 So. 2d 274 (Ala. 1992)); and the value of nursing and domestic help rendered gratuitously by the plaintiff's mother (see Bandel v. Friedrich, 122 N.J. 235, 584 A.2d 800 (1991)).

Several states have by statute substantially abrogated the collateral source rule in torts cases. Some statutes abrogating the rule have provided an offset to the reduction by some amount, reflecting the fact that the collateral source benefits may have been paid for by the plaintiff, or someone else acting on the plaintiff's behalf. See, e.g., N.Y. CPLR §4545(c), which provides that the collateral source reduction is to be offset by the amount of premiums paid by the plaintiff for the benefits for the two-year period immediately preceding the accrual of the cause of action, and by the projected future cost to the plaintiff of maintaining the benefits.

The constitutionality of a number of statutes abrogating the collateral source rule has been challenged on a variety of grounds. Some courts have upheld the statutes (see, e.g., Imlay v. City of Lake Crystal, 453 N.W.2d 326 (Minn. 1990); Murray v. Nicol, 540 A.2d 239 (N.J. Super. 1988)), and others have found the abrogation unconstitutional (see, e.g., Thompson v. KFB Insurance Co., 252 Kan. 1010, 850 P.2d 773 (1993)).

Another way of avoiding double recovery, which is the main concern of statutes abrogating the collateral source rule, is to permit the collateral source to be subrogated to the rights of the plaintiff against the defendant. Subrogation is a device which puts the collateral source "in the shoes of the plaintiff," so that the collateral source can recover from the defendant to the extent of the payment to the plaintiff. The right of the collateral source to subrogation will ordinarily arise only out of contract. For example, if a medical expense insurer has paid the plaintiff for the latter's bills, the insurer will be able to recover the amount of such payment from the tortfeasor only if the insurance contract authorizes it.

If no subrogation agreement exists, the insurer who has paid medical expenses usually has no right to subrogation. Courts following this view generally perceive medical insurance more as a form of investment by the insured which imposes on the insurer simply a duty to pay, rather than as a form of indemnification protecting the insured from medical expense losses. Courts have been willing, however, to examine the insurance policy to determine if it is one of indemnification rather than investment. If the policy appears to be written more in the language of the former, courts may allow subrogation even in the absence of an express clause. See, e.g., Cunningham v. Metropolitan Life Ins. Co., 121 Wis. 2d 437, 360 N.W.2d 33 (1985). The Florida statute abrogating the collateral source rule, Fla. Stat. Ann. Ch. 768.76, provides that the defendant is not entitled to a reduction to the extent that the collateral source is entitled to subrogation.

Problem 32

You have received the following memorandum from a partner in your firm:

> My client is Sandra Fuller, the daughter of an old friend. Sandra, who was 23 at the time, was injured in an automobile accident about a year ago. The liability issues are fairly routine, but there is a problem with respect to damages that I need your help on. Sandra's back was severely injured. Her doctor has prescribed conservative treatment, but the pain has persisted. The doctor told her that there are medicines that would substantially reduce the pain, but she has refused to take them. As a teenager, Sandra became involved with cocaine. About three years ago, she realized that she was addicted, and at the recommendation of a friend, joined the "Martinists," a religious group that opposes the use of all drugs, including those for purely medicinal purposes. The Martinists were very effective in dealing with Sandra's addiction. She was able to kick the cocaine habit, and is a dedicated believer in the Martinists.
>
> Three months ago, Sandra's father met a Dr. Wolverton at a party. Dr. Wolverton has studied pain for many years, and has been experimenting with ultra-sound and electrical shock treatments for the relief of pain. His methods are very controversial and have not been accepted by the medical profession. Dr. Wolverton told Sandra's father that he would treat Sandra for her back pain at no cost. While Sandra would have been willing to pay for the treatment,

she agreed to volunteer since it offered a drug-free treatment for pain. She has been undergoing treatment by Dr. Wolverton for two months, and reports that the treatments have helped but have not eliminated the pain. Dr. Wolverton has told me that with time the pain will be completely eliminated, but he has refused to say just how long it will take. I have talked with an orthopedic surgeon at the University of Columbia Medical School, and he is very doubtful as to the efficacy of the Wolverton treatments. He is confident that the accepted drug therapy would be more effective, relatively inexpensive, and nonaddictive.

I have a meeting next week with Catherine Riggs, who represents the insurance company of Lawrence Melby, the driver of the other car. I want to work up an initial demand, and I would like your help determining how these facts will affect Sandra's claim for pain and suffering and medical expenses.

b. Lost Earnings and Impairment of Earning Capacity

(1) The Basic Measure of Recovery

From a strictly economic point of view, impairment of ability to earn may be the most justifiable element of general compensatory damages. The loss or impairment of a person's capacity to earn a living, unless compensated, may result in a life of subsistence and dependence on others. In a typical case involving serious bodily injury, the plaintiff is totally incapacitated for a period, during which some or all of the earnings that the plaintiff otherwise would have received are lost; later, the condition improves to the point that the plaintiff is able to return to work, albeit with difficulty, and to achieve something less than the former earnings level. The plaintiff in such a case will be seeking to recover for both the earnings actually lost up to the time of the trial or settlement and the diminution in the capacity to earn in the future. In this type of case, the dividing line between lost earnings and impairment of earning capacity is drawn in time: out-of-pocket losses up to the time of trial or settlement constitute the former; anticipated losses in the future constitute the latter. Thus, for example, if the plaintiff had been earning $1,000 a month prior to the accident (that is, with a demonstrated earning capacity of $1,000 a month) and thereafter experiences a three-month total disability during which no earnings are received, followed by a return to work at a diminished earnings rate of $750 a month (that is, a permanent 25 percent disability), and the trial takes place 18 months after the accident, the plaintiff will be seeking to recover $6,750 in lost earnings ($3,000 for three months total disability and $3,750 for fifteen months partial disability) and a lump sum for impairment of earning capacity equal to the anticipated loss of $250 a month for the rest of plaintiff's life.

Of course, not all cases are so simple, as the following decisions make clear.

Holton v. Gibson

402 Pa. 37, 166 A.2d 4 (1960)

Opinion by MR. JUSTICE EAGEN. . . .

This appeal is from the entry of judgment after refusal of the court below to grant defendant's motions for a new trial and for judgment non obstante veredicto in an action of trespass wherein the jury returned a verdict of $24,416.75 in favor of plaintiffs. Appellees are husband and wife, the former alone having sustained personal injury and the latter joined solely because of her rights of partial ownership in the damaged vehicle involved.

[The plaintiff husband was injured in an automobile collision with the defendant. The portions of the opinion dealing with the issue of liability are omitted.]

Now, as to the motion for new trial, we agree with the lower court that appellee's failure to show a diminution in wages, subsequent to his return to work (approximately three months after the accident) did not make improper the court's submission to the jury of the issue of loss of earning power or capacity. Appellee at the time of trial was out of work and, although his unemployment was not shown to have been due to his injuries, it was shown that he continued to suffer, since the date of the accident, from severe headaches which, when visiting him during work, had necessitated his taking unauthorized rests for "half an hour or so." The injury to his leg caused him pains which persisted even to the date of trial and which then were occurring, as he put it, "when I am on my leg considerable." Moreover, the surgery to his head resulted in the removal of skull structure, the absence of which renders one more prone to suffer from later slight injury. As this Court said in Bochar v. J. B. Martin Motors, Inc., 374 Pa. 240, 244, 97 A.2d 813 (1953): "A tortfeasor is not entitled to a reduction in his financial responsibility because, through fortuitous circumstances or unusual application on the part of the injured person, the wages of the injured person following the accident are as high or even higher than they were prior to the accident. . . . It is not the status of the immediate present which determines capacity for remunerative employment. Where permanent injury is involved, the whole span of life must be considered. Has the economic horizon of the disabled person been shortened because of the injuries sustained as the result of the tortfeasor's negligence? That is the test. And it is no answer to that test to say that there are just as many dollars in the patient's pay envelope now as prior to his accident. The normal status of a healthy person is to progress, and to the extent that his progress has been curtailed, he has suffered a loss which is properly computable in damages." Appellee, in the instant case, was no longer able to inspect the various stations that it was his duty to check as guard. He was relegated to the role of telephone message taker. As of the date of trial he had not yet been able to drive an automobile. Out of work at that time, his "economic horizon" was necessarily less broad than it would have been but for the accident. The fact that immediately after his return to work his pay scale had not been cut and the fact that he later received customary periodic pay increases does not obscure the inescapable conclusion that he is now, as a result of his injuries, less able to perform certain services that, but for the accident, he would readily accept as incident to desirable employment. . . .

The judgment of the lower court is affirmed.

The task of placing a dollar value on diminution of earning capacity can involve a good deal of guesswork. The variables that determine, at least theoretically, the size of the award for diminished earning capacity are: (1) the plaintiff's basic earning capacity; (2) the percentage by which the plaintiff's earning capacity has been diminished—which is often difficult to assess with any certainty, and rough fractions such as 25 or 50 percent, supported by expert medical testimony, are typically employed; (3) the expected duration of the disability; and, if permanent, (4) the life expectancy of the plaintiff—obviously, the longer the plaintiff is likely to live, the greater will be the cumulative loss of earnings potential. On this last point, life expectancy tables are usually employed, such as Table 8-1, which is taken from the Internal Revenue Regulations (Reg. §1.72-9).

In states which do not establish the controlling life expectancy table by statute,[2] this may become the subject of disagreement between the parties. Life expectancy tables vary considerably depending upon when they were constructed and the type of data that was used. There are even "work life expectancy" tables, prepared by the Office of Manpower, Automation and Training in the Manpower Administration of the United States Department of Labor, and others, upon which defense lawyers often base their calculations of diminished earning capacity. See, e.g., Poust, A Breadwinner's Value—Considered From Another Perspective, 60 Ill. B.J. 96 (1971). Courts sometimes accept this idea of the plaintiff's "expected working life," and use it instead of the more ordinarily employed "life expectancy." See, e.g., Williams v. United States, 435 F.2d 804 (1st Cir. 1970), a case arising under the Federal Employers' Liability Act,[3] in which the court assumed the

2. For an example of a statutory life expectancy table, see N.C. Gen. Stat. §8-46 (Supp. 1979). The table set out in this statute is a unisex table, in contrast to Table 8-1.

3. The Federal Employers' Liability Act (45 U.S.C.A. §§51-60) provides for compensation to railroad employees injured as the result of work-related activities. Liability of the employer-railroad is based on negligence. Assumption of the risk and contributory negligence are not defenses, but the contributory negligence of the employee serves to reduce recovery, except in cases in which the railroad's negligence constitutes a violation of a statute enacted for the safety of employees.

TABLE 8-1
Ordinary Life Annuities—One Life—Expected Return Multiples
[i.e., Life Expectancies]

Ages		*Multiples*	*Ages*		*Multiples*	*Ages*		*Multiples*
Male	*Fe-male*	*[Life Ex-pectancies)*	*Male*	*Fe-male*	*[Life Ex-pectancies]*	*Male*	*Fe-male*	*[Life Ex-pectancies)*
6	11	65.0	41	46	33.0	76	81	9.1
7	12	64.1	42	47	32.1	77	82	8.7
8	13	63.2	43	48	31.2	78	83	8.3
9	14	62.3	44	49	30.4	79	84	7.8
10	15	61.4	45	50	29.6	80	85	7.5
11	16	60.4	46	51	28.7	81	86	7.1
12	17	59.5	47	52	27.9	82	87	6.7
13	18	58.6	48	53	27.1	83	88	6.3
14	19	57.7	49	54	26.3	84	89	6.0
15	20	56.7	50	55	25.5	85	90	5.7
16	21	55.8	51	56	24.7	86	91	5.4
17	22	54.9	52	57	24.0	87	92	5.1
18	23	53.9	53	58	23.2	88	93	4.8
19	24	53.0	54	59	22.4	89	94	4.5
20	25	52.1	55	60	21.7	90	95	4.2
21	26	51.1	56	61	21.0	91	96	4.0
22	27	50.2	57	62	20.3	92	97	3.7
23	28	49.3	58	63	19.6	93	98	3.5
24	29	48.3	59	64	18.9	94	99	3.3
25	30	47.4	60	65	18.2	95	100	3.1
26	31	46.5	61	66	17.5	96	101	2.9
27	32	45.6	62	67	16.9	97	102	2.7
28	33	44.6	63	68	16.2	98	103	2.5
29	34	43.7	64	69	15.6	99	104	2.3
30	35	42.8	65	70	15.0	100	105	2.1
31	36	41.9	66	71	14.4	101	106	1.9
32	37	41.0	67	72	13.8	102	107	1.7
33	38	40.0	68	73	13.2	103	108	1.5
34	39	39.1	69	74	12.6	104	109	1.3
35	40	38.2	70	75	12.1	105	110	1.2
						106	111	1.0
36	41	37.3	71	76	11.6	107	112	.8
37	42	36.5	72	77	11.0	108	113	.7
38	43	35.6	73	78	10.5	109	114	.6
39	44	34.7	74	79	10.1	110	115	.5
40	45	33.8	75	80	9.6	111	116	0

plaintiff would have worked until age 60. It should be observed that in every instance it is the individual plaintiff's actual life expectancy immediately preceding the accident which is the measure of recovery. Except where by statute the trier of fact must rely exclusively upon the standard life expectancy tables, the defendant may attempt to prove that the individual plaintiff had a shorter than average life expectancy. See, e.g., Wachovia Bank & Trust Co. v. Atlantic Greyhound Lines, 210 N.C. 293, 186 S.E. 320 (1936).

Where the injuries caused by the defendant's conduct have the effect of shortening the plaintiff's expected life, the plaintiff will recover, at 100 percent disability, for the total impairment in his earning capacity for the number of years by which his life expectancy has been shortened. Plaintiffs on occasion have sought compensation for a shortening of life expectancy separate from other economic and noneconomic elements of damages, but American courts have rejected such claims. See, Burke v. United States, 605 F. Supp. 981 (D. Md. 1985); Rhone v. Fisher, 224 Md. 223, 167 A.2d 773 (1961). The reason usually given for denying recovery is stated by the court in Downie v. U.S. Lines Co., 359 F.2d 344, 347 (3rd Cir. 1966), *cert. denied,* 385 U.S. 897 (1966):

> We believe that the rule [that the shortening of one's life expectancy is a compensable element of damages] is not feasible because of the incalculable variables which may enter into any attempt to place value on life; absent some workable criteria, a damage award would be base speculation.

In general, see Smith, Psychic Interest in Continuation of One's Own Life: Legal Recognition and Protection, 98 U. Pa. L. Rev. 781 (1950). See generally Fleming, The Lost Years: A Problem in the Computation and Distribution of Damages, 50 Calif. L. Rev. 598 (1962).

In attaching a dollar value to the plaintiff's earning capacity, it is necessary in cases involving self-employed persons to separate out from the plaintiff's income any return from business investments. See Wesson v. F.M. Heritage Co., 174 Conn. 236, 386 A.2d 217 (1978).

One of the most difficult elements in the impairment of earning capacity formula is the first one suggested above—the assessment of the plaintiff's basic capacity to earn. One source of difficulty is the fact that the plaintiff's earning capacity probably would not have remained constant. The plaintiff will often be able to establish that, but for the injuries, further training and experience would have led to an increased earning capacity (see, e.g., Folse v. Fakouri, 371 So. 2d 1120 (La. 1970)); but the defendant will almost always be able to argue that the earning capacity would have declined toward the end of plaintiff's life (see, e.g., Aretz v. United States, 456 F. Supp. 397 (S.D. Ga. 1978)).[4] For an interesting case study which traces the

4. There is a lengthy subsequent history to this case, none of which changes the point for which it is cited in the text. The last opinion in the history is Aretz v. United States, 660 F.2d 531 (5th Cir. 1981).

projected earning capacity of a plaintiff year by year, see Horvitz and Krist, Measuring the Loss of Earning Capacity, 36 Tex. B.J. 411 (1973). As the following cases make clear, predictions of future earning capacity may require considerable speculation.

Mauro v. Raymark Industries, Inc.

116 N.J. 126, 561 A.2d 257 (1989)

STEIN, J. . . .

I

Plaintiffs, Roger Mauro (hereinafter plaintiff) and Lois Mauro, his wife, instituted this action against several manufacturers of asbestos products based on injuries allegedly sustained as a result of inhalation of asbestos fibers in the course of Mauro's employment at Ancora State Psychiatric Hospital. . . .

In 1981 plaintiff and his co-workers participated in tests conducted by the New Jersey Department of Health to determine the prevalence of asbestos-related disease among plumbers and steamfitters in state institutions. Plaintiff was informed by Dr. Peter Gann, the department's Chief of Occupational Medicine, that although the results of his physical examination and lung function test were "normal," he had bilateral thickening of both chest walls and calcification of the diaphragm. Dr. Gann's letter informing plaintiff of his condition stated: "[Y]our exposure to asbestos has been significant and there is some evidence that this exposure may increase the risk of development of lung cancer."

Mauro testified that when informed of his condition, he became "very angry, very upset." He feared contracting cancer because his mother and a prior employer had died of the disease. He subsequently consulted a pulmonary specialist, by whom he has been examined every six months since 1982. Mauro has also had annual chest x-rays. He testified that the reason for his medical surveillance is "to find out if I'm going to get cancer and when I'm going to get it."

[Plaintiff's expert] Dr. Guidice . . . acknowledged that he did not testify that it was probable that Mauro would contract cancer: "There's a risk. . . . I certainly can't predict he's going to get cancer. All I can say is there's a high probability he's at risk because he's a young man and therefore he's at increased risk . . . for developing cancer." . . .

In its charge to the jury at the conclusion of the trial, the trial court rejected Mauro's claim for enhanced risk of developing cancer. The court explained:

> There's no testimony that the Plaintiff Roger has cancer or that he likely will get cancer. In New Jersey damages may not be awarded for any future injury which is merely possible but not probable.
>
> The reason for this rule is simple. In this state, if the Plaintiff were to get cancer sometime in the future and claim same to have been due to an alleged asbestos exposure, at that point he could file a new lawsuit seeking damages for that cancer.
>
> Accordingly, even if you conclude that the plaintiff has an enhanced risk of developing cancer, you may not award any damages for that risk.

However, the court permitted the jury to consider Mauro's claim for damages caused by emotional distress relating to his fear of developing cancer, provided the jury found that Mauro sustained an asbestos-related injury. The court also permitted the jury to consider Mauro's claim for damages caused by his present medical condition, as well as the cost of future medical surveillance.

[The jury returned a verdict for the plaintiff Roger Mauro for $7,500. The judgment for the plaintiff on the jury verdict was affirmed by the Appellate Division.]

***II* . . .**

The long-standing rule in New Jersey is that prospective damages are not recoverable unless they are reasonably probable to occur. [The court's discussion of New Jersey cases, law review commentary, and cases from other states is omitted.]

Nor is there any question concerning the right of a plaintiff who has sustained physical injury because of exposure to toxic chemicals to recover damages for emotional distress based on a reasonable concern that he or she has an enhanced risk of further disease. . . . On appeal, defendants urged that the claim was not cognizable because of a lack of physical symptoms evidencing plaintiff's distress. . . . [A]lthough we need not and do not reach the question whether exposure to toxic chemicals without physical injury would sustain a claim for emotional distress damages based on a reasonable fear of future disease, such a damage claim is clearly cognizable where, as here, plaintiff's exposure to asbestos has resulted in physical injury. . . .

Although the weight of authority compellingly argues against recognition of an enhanced-risk-of-cancer claim by a plaintiff with an asbestos-related injury absent proof that satisfies the standard of reasonable medical probability, our analysis would be incomplete without consideration of policy arguments that oppose the general rule. Foremost among these is the concern that deferral of the prospective-injury claim may preclude any recovery when the disease eventually occurs because of the substantial difficulties inherent in attempting to prove causation in toxic-tort cases. If the enhanced-risk claim is deferred, a plaintiff asserting the claim when the second injury occurs will inevitably confront the defense that the injury did not result from exposure to toxic chemicals but was "the product of intervening events or causes."

Recognition of a claim for significantly enhanced risk of disease would also enhance the tort-law's capacity to deter the improper use of toxic chemicals and substances, thereby addressing the contention that tort law cannot deter polluters who view the cost of proper use or disposal as exceeding the risk of tort liability.

The rule of reasonable medical probability is also challenged as an artificial, all-or-nothing standard that rejects future-injury claims supported by substantial evidence that barely falls short of the required quantum of proof. . . .

Other considerations weigh in favor of limiting recognition of enhanced-risk claims to those that prove to a reasonable medical probability the likelihood of future injury. Those claims that fail to meet this standard, if presented to juries, would require damage awards for diseases that are prospective, speculative, and less than likely to occur. The more speculative the proof of future disease, the more difficult would be the juries' burden of calculating fair compensation. Inevitably, damage awards would be rendered for diseases that will never occur, exacting a societal cost in the form of higher insurance premiums and higher product costs.

The vast number of asbestos-related claims now pending in state and federal courts throughout the country is a matter of public record. The formidable burden of litigating such claims would be significantly greater if a substantial percentage of these cases also involved disposition of damage claims for the relatively unquantified enhanced risk of future disease.

Equally persuasive to this Court, however, is the availability of a future opportunity to assert such claims if and when the disease occurs, combined with the present availability of medical surveillance and emotional distress damages in appropriate cases. In our view, removal of the statute-of-limitations and single-controversy doctrines as a bar to the institution of suit when the disease for which plaintiff is at risk ultimately occurs enhances the quality of the remedy that tort law can provide in such cases. If the disease never occurs, presumably there will be no claim and no recovery. If it does occur, the resultant litigation will involve a tangible claim for present injury, rather than a speculative claim for future injury. Hence, juries will be better able to award damages in an amount that fairly reflects the nature and severity of the plaintiff's injury.

We acknowledge that our resolution of this issue is imperfect. In asbestos cases, for example, the available statistical evidence correlating asbestos-related disease with the future onset of cancer appears to fall short—as was evident from the evidence proffered in this case—of establishing the occurrence of cancer as a matter of reasonable medical probability. Undoubtedly, there will be individual cases in which statistical evidence, combined with the particular degree of exposure and injury sustained by the plaintiff, will establish the likelihood of future disease as a matter of probability. With respect to those cases in which the evidence that future disease will occur falls substantially short of the reasonable-medical-probability standard, we are satisfied that the interests of justice are well served by excluding such claims from jury consideration. Of course, there will be close cases, and for their resolution our use of the reasonable-medical-probability standard "to draw judicial lines beyond which liability will not be extended is fundamentally . . . an instrument of fairness and policy." Caputzal v. The Lindsay Co., 48 N.J. 69, 77, 222 A.2d 513 (1966). The standard of reasonable medical probability has been applied in New Jersey since at least 1957. See Budden v. Goldstein, 43 N.J. Super. at 347, 128 A.2d 730 [(1957)]. The rationale then advanced for the rule bears repetition here:

> [A] consequence of an injury which is possible, which may possibly ensue, is a risk which the injured person must bear because the law cannot be administered so as to do reasonably efficient justice if conjecture and speculation are to be used as a measure of damages. On the other hand, a consequence which stands on the plane of reasonable probability, although it is not certain to occur, may be considered in the evaluation of the damage claim against the defendant. In this way, to the extent that men can achieve justice through general rules, a just balance of the warring interests is accomplished. [Id.]

By adapting the statute-of-limitations and the single-controversy doctrines to the realities of toxic-tort cases, we have ameliorated the potential unfairness of applying the reasonable-probability standard to this type of litigation. Moreover, our case law affords toxic-tort plaintiffs the right to receive full compensation for any provable diminution of bodily health, accommodating all damage claims attributable to present injury and deferring compensation only for disease not yet incurred and not reasonably probable to occur. Recognition of present claims for medical surveillance and emotional distress realistically addresses significant aspects of the present injuries sustained by toxic-tort plaintiffs, and serves as an added deterrent to polluters and others responsible for the wrongful use of toxic chemicals. In our view, these developments in New Jersey law affecting toxic-tort plaintiffs argue persuasively against modification of the reasonable-probability standard in such cases. We therefore will not disturb the trial court's refusal to submit to the jury plaintiff's damage claim based on his enhanced risk of cancer. . . .

Judgment affirmed.

HANDLER, J., dissenting. . . .

The Court refuses to allow any recovery by a plaintiff now suffering from pre-cancerous lung disease for the palpable and demonstrable risk that he or she will incur cancer. The Court purports to follow ancient wisdom, namely, our traditional legal rules that over the years have sufficed to define compensable injury. These conventional rules of damages . . . do not permit the recovery of damages for prospective injury unless it is reasonably probable to occur. Such a rule has always been considered adequate and just because it generates a greater assurance that the measurement of such damages would not be suffused by undue conjecture and speculation.

However, the Court's invocation of that rule to the difficult question of damages posed by the current case is ritualistic. The traditional rule, at least considered in the context of this case, can no longer be reconciled with the knowledge and experience that has emerged in recent years. This common knowledge and experience confirms for us that there is a genuine, substantial, and palpable risk that a person with defendant's condition will incur cancer as a result of exposure to asbestos. The Court effectively smothers that understanding when it insists on applying the traditional rule of damages. I stress what seems truly indisputable—the genuineness, actuality, and gravity of the risk of cancer to one exposed to asbestos over a long period of time and currently manifesting asbestos-related disease. . . .

Indeed, the Court's solution, which denies any present recovery, nevertheless would allow recovery where plaintiff's claim for increased risk amounts to reasonable medical probability. This suggests, for example, that if a plaintiff has a 51% chance of developing cancer, his or her damage claim would be decided by a jury. This line drawing, however, seems unfair and arbitrary. For example, why should a plaintiff recover for a 51% risk of developing prostate cancer where the normal person's risk may be 30% (a 21% increase due to defendant's conduct) but not an individual who has a 25% risk of skin cancer where the normal person's risk is 1% (a 24% increase due to defendant's conduct)? It would be more fair and just if the jury could weigh the enhanced risk of cancer with the defendant's conduct in causing plaintiff's current condition and then assess the appropriate damages to compensate plaintiff adequately.

In my view, the majority's solution of allowing the plaintiff to sue defendant later if he develops cancer is unfair and unjust and does not comport with broader notions of sound public policy. In light of current knowledge and experience, there is no valid reason why plaintiff's enhanced risk of cancer should not be considered an element of a present injury caused by the defendant and to be compensated now. Due to this injury, plaintiff may have to alter his lifestyle to avoid cancer-causing agents that may be present in foods or the environment and atmosphere to prevent the likelihood of developing cancer. Plaintiff may also be prevented from obtaining certain jobs—such as in chemical factories—because his enhanced risk of cancer make him more vulnerable to other workplace injuries. In addition, his health and life insurance premiums will be greater because the insurance companies will charge plaintiff for his enhanced risk of developing cancer.

I return to the fairness and feasibility of permitting a current recovery for the present risk of cancer. It seems disingenuous, if not callous, to suggest that plaintiff's risk of cancer is not palpable and serious—why quibble between probable and possible when it is agreed that the risk is significant? When the reality of this risk is confirmed by the fact that plaintiff is now required to submit to bi-annual cancer medical examinations and defendant is more than willing to pay for the cost of this medical surveillance? If the rest of the society treats plaintiff's enhanced risk of cancer as a present injury, why should the courts deny its existence by denying its compensability? Plaintiff does not ask for damages for having cancer, he only wants to recover for the unusual risk to his health and life and the tangible and significant likelihood of developing cancer. He seeks only fair compensation, which a jury should be quite capable of assessing. . . .

In my opinion, Mr. Mauro . . . has a cognizable injury in the form of a palpable and serious risk of incurring cancer that should be compensated for now.

Most courts that have addressed the issue have agreed with the majority in *Mauro* and have permitted recovery for future harm only if the plaintiff has evidence that such harm is probable. See, e.g., Pollock v. Johns-Manville Sales Corp., 686 F. Supp. 489 (D. N.J. 1988). Occasionally, however, a court will permit the plaintiff to get to the jury when the evidence is that the chance of future harm is "substantial," although not necessarily greater than 50 percent. See, e.g., Davis v. Graviss, 672 S.W.2d 928 (Ky. 1984).

While Judge Handler would have permitted the plaintiff in *Mauro* to get to the jury although the chance of future harm was, according to the evidence, less than 51 percent, he did not state how the evidence should affect the jury's decision. Perhaps implicit in his opinion is the thought that the jury would reduce, but not eliminate, the plaintiff's recovery based on the evidence relating to the chance of future harm. That thought was made explicit by a concurring judge in Jordan v. Bero, 158 W. Va. 28, 65, 210 S.E.2d 618, 641 (1974):

> In keeping with the traditional rule, the probability, in the mathematical sense, of future injury must be proved to a reasonable degree of medical certainty. Accordingly a doctor should be permitted to testify that on the basis of his experience and his evaluation of statistical information from recorded cases of similar injuries he believes that there is to a reasonable degree of medical certainty a twenty percent probability of suffering a particular disability. Once it is determined that there is a probability of loss, evidence should then be admitted concerning the maximum expected loss should the victim completely lose in the game of chance he is playing with the fates.
>
> Accordingly the jury would be instructed that from all the evidence they should determine what the overall probability is that the plaintiff will suffer future damages, and that from all of the evidence they should determine the amount of monetary damages to which the plaintiff would be entitled if the

disabilities which doctors reasonably believe are possible actually come to pass. The jury would then be instructed to multiply the amount of future damages reasonably to be expected times the probability of those damages actually occurring and arrive at a figure which will compensate the plaintiff for the possibility of future injuries. It would appear that in a major damage suit the jury could be aided by expert testimony with regard to probability analysis to make the problem comprehensible to the average layman.

While this analysis may appear to be overly complicated on first reading, it merely recognizes that mathematical probabilities exist which are less than fifty percent and that when the experts testify that such a probability of under fifty percent exists, it is still possible to award appropriate damages without becoming speculative.

In Patriello v. Kalman, 215 Conn. 377, 576 A.2d 474 (1990), the Supreme Court of Connecticut overruled an earlier case, Healy v. White, 173 Conn. 438, 378 A.2d 540 (1977) that, like *Mauro,* had held that the plaintiff could recover for future harm only if the probability of the harm exceeded 50 percent. The court ruled that a plaintiff who has suffered a "present injury which has resulted in an increased risk of future harm is entitled to compensation to the extent that the future harm is likely to occur." Id. at 398, 576 A.2d at 484.

Arguments for dividing damages between the plaintiff and defendant based on the chances of future injury are made in King, Causation, Valuation and Chance in Personal Injury Torts Involving Preexisting Conditions and Future Consequences, 90 Yale L.J. 1353 (1981) and Robinson, Probabilistic Causation and Compensation for Tortious Risk, 14 J. Legal Stud. 779 (1985).

Grayson v. Irvmar Realty Corp.

7 A.D.2d 436, 184 N.Y.S.2d 33 (1959)

BREITEL, J. The principal issue raised in this personal injury negligence case is whether the court, in permitting the jury to award substantial damages to plaintiff for impairment or frustration of her inchoate operatic career, committed error. In addition, defendant contends that the damages awarded are, in any event, excessive. Some question is also raised as to liability, but it does not merit discussion.

Plaintiff, a young woman who is engaged seriously in the study of music looking to the development of an operatic career, sustained a fractured leg and an alleged impairment of her hearing as a result of a fall on the sidewalk in front of defendant's premises. The act of negligence charged was the failure to light properly a construction sidewalk bridge. . . . The jury awarded damages in the amount of $50,000.

There is no dispute that one tortiously injured may recover damages based upon the impairment of future earning capacity. There is also no dispute that the assessment of damages may be based upon future probabilities and is not confined to actual earnings prior to the accident. The unusual issue tendered in this case is whether there may be a similar assessment where the probability of future earnings is not based upon any prior actual engagement in the vocational earning of income. In that respect it is not unlike the situation in death actions where the pecuniary benefit to survivors must be determined with respect to children or very young people whose income potentiality has not yet been developed. The situation, on the other hand, is a little different, again, from that of young persons training for occupations, especially professions, where the probability of completion of training is high, and the resultant earning of at least a modal income is equally highly probable. The reason for this last difference is that in the case of persons of rare and special talents many are called but few are chosen. For those who are not chosen, the probabilities of exploiting their talents financially are minimal or totally negative. In this class would fall the musical artist, the professional athlete, and the actor.

It should be clear that one possessed of rare and special talents is entitled to recover damages for tortious injury to the development of those talents. This, too, may have a pecuniary value which is assessable, albeit without the degree of precision one would require in a commercial case. On this view, the court properly submitted to the jury the question of assessing the damages to plaintiff's operatic career, inchoate though it may have been. But, in the light of the proper distinctions, the jury's award of $50,000 was grossly excessive.

At the time of the accident plaintiff was twenty-one and had been graduated from high school. Since some undisclosed age as a child, she had studied music and singing. This included five years of instrumental instruction. In the later years she had a professional teacher of voice and studied under an opera coach. When she left school she participated successively in operatic workshops. As part of her operatic studies it was necessary to learn the various foreign languages closely associated with classic opera. While engaged in her studies she made a large number of appearances, all without income, on the radio, in benefit performances, and in workshop-productions of opera. Her voice teacher and opera coach testified that she had a superior voice and, as a consequence, had a bright future, in their opinion, in the opera. There was testimony that plaintiff was preparing for a European debut.

Plaintiff sustained her injuries when she fell, catching her foot in a hole. Her leg was then fractured. At the same time her head struck the surface, as a result of which she claims she sustained an impairment of hearing. The alleged hearing impairment has largely cleared up, leaving, however, a sequela of an impairment of pitch. Although she has continued to study singing and made a number of appearances of the same character as she had made before the accident, it is claimed that the impairment of pitch has limited her performance and that this is likely to be permanent. This claim was supported by her voice teacher and by medical testimony. However, there was highly credible proof from an eminent physician selected from the court-designated medical panel, offered by defendant, to the effect that any impairment of hearing she had was due to a diseased condition which existed before the accident. The jury might well have, but did not, accept this testimony, despite still other proof that plaintiff had had ear trouble prior to the accident.

As already noted, it is undisputed that a person tortiously injured is entitled to recover for impairment of future earning capacity, without limitation to the actual earnings which preceded the accident. In death actions, and in the cases of injuries, involving very young people whose vocational potentialities have not yet been developed, the courts have allowed assessment of damages based on future, and not presently realized, earning capacity. . . .

In the case of young people engaged in the study for occupations or professions requiring a great deal of preliminary or formal training the courts have also permitted the assessment of damages based on future earning potential after the training period would have been completed. And even in the case of singers, and presumably, therefore, in the case of other musical artists, some courts in other jurisdictions have had occasion to permit juries to assess damages based on future earning potential although at the time of the accident the would-be artist's career is inchoate.

On this analysis the jury in this case was very properly permitted to assess the damages with respect to plaintiff's inchoate operatic career. But the award it made was highly excessive.

It is at this point that the distinction must be made between persons who largely exploit native talents and those who exploit intensive training. It is notable that those who exploit rare and special talents may achieve exceedingly high financial rewards, but that the probability of selection for the great rewards is relatively low. On the other hand, those who, provided they have the intelligence and opportunities, train for the more skilled occupations and professions, not so heavily dependent upon unusual native gifts, will more likely achieve their objectives.

The would-be operatic singer, or the would-be violin virtuoso, or the would-be actor, are not assured of achieving their objectives merely because they have some gifts and complete the customary periods of training. Their future is a highly speculative one, namely, whether they will ever receive recognition or the financial perquisites that result from such recognition. Nevertheless, the opportunities exist and those opportunities have an economic value which can be assessed, although, obviously, without any precision. But a jury may not assume that a young student of the opera who has certain gifts will earn the income of an operatic singer, even in the median group.

In determining, therefore, the amount to be recovered, the jury may consider the gifts attributed to plaintiff; the training she has received; the training she is likely to receive; the opportunities and the recognition she already has had; the opportunities she is likely to have in the future; the fact that even though the opportunities may be many, that the full realization of those opportunities is limited to the very few; the fact that there are many other risks and contingencies, other than accidents, which may divert a would-be vocal artist from her career; and, finally, that it is assessing directly not so much future earning capacity as the opportunities for a practical chance at such future earning capacity.

The foregoing factors to be considered must reflect substantial development in the would-be artist's career. Every gleam in a doting parent's eye and every self-delusion as to one's potentialities must be skeptically eradicated. The jury is not to assess within the limits of wishful thinking but is to assess the genuine potentialities, although not yet realized, as evidenced by objective circumstances. Thus viewed, plaintiff here was undoubtedly serious about her operatic career; but, except from her teachers, she had not achieved any spectacular or extraordinary recognition for her talents. It is not the dilettante interest that has a pecuniary value, but the genuine opportunity to engage in a serious artistic career. In this context no effort has been made to consider the possible issues, sometimes tendered, as to the compensability for artistic pursuits indulged in solely for self-enjoyment, but impaired as a result of tortious injury.

Based on the preceding discussion and the proof in this case, and allowing for the injury sustained by plaintiff to her leg, any verdict in excess of $20,000 is excessive[5]. . . .

Judgment reversed, on the law and on the facts, and a new trial granted, unless plaintiff stipulates to accept a judgment in the reduced amount of $20,000, in which event the judgment is modified in that respect and, as so modified, affirmed, with costs to defendant-appellant. Settle order on notice.

All concur except VALENTE and MCNALLY, JJ., who concur in part and dissent in part. . . .

In *Grayson,* there was little doubt that the plaintiff's injury was permanent, but she had no well-defined existing occupation which could function as the basic measure of the value of impaired capacity to earn. The two groups

5. If the trial judge, or the court on appeal, determines that the damages as set by the jury clearly exceed or are clearly less than is warranted by the evidence, a remittitur or additur can be ordered. In the case of remittitur, if the plaintiff refuses to accept the lower amount of damages determined by the court to be the most the jury on the evidence could award, a new trial will be awarded. In the case of additur, the choice is put to the defendant—agree to the increased award the court has determined as the least amount supported by the evidence or face a new trial. Remittitur and additur cannot be ordered simply because the judge disagrees with the amount of the jury award; the standard is usually stated to be whether the jury award "shocks the conscience" of the court. [Eds.]

of persons most likely to present problems of this sort are homemakers and the young. The problems with respect to homemakers are likely to occur less frequently as more of them join the labor force. If a woman is injured during what is clearly a temporary withdrawal from the labor market during, for example, the early years of child rearing, she may have a career which would furnish the basis of a claim for impaired earning capacity. More troublesome are cases involving women who have never worked, or have worked only sporadically, outside the home. A number of approaches have been used or suggested. Some courts permit a homemaker to recover for impaired earning capacity based upon existing, though unused, capacity. In this approach it is irrelevant that the homemaker was not engaged in any particular commercial employment outside the home at the time of injury. See, e.g., Nelson v. Patrick, 326 S.E.2d 45 (N.C. App. 1985), which held that a homemaker who had not been employed outside the home for 15 years was not deprived of the right to recover damages for loss of earning capacity. One factor which might be taken into account in determining the impaired earning capacity of a homemaker is the likelihood that he or she would have entered the workforce at some time in the future. See, e.g., the following statistics from the 1991 Statistical Abstract of the United States, p. 391:

	Percentage of Women with Children in Civilian Work Force in 1989
Children 14-17 years old	74.4%
Children 6-13 years old	72.6%
Children under 6	58.4

Perhaps the most common approach attempts to put a market value upon the services which a typical homemaker performs for the family, to reach a figure that represents their total replacement cost. See, e.g., DeLong v. Erie County, 89 A.D.2d 376, 455 N.Y.S.2d 887 (1982), *aff'd* 60 N.Y.2d 296, 457 N.E.2d 717 (1983), in which there was expert testimony that the replacement cost of services performed by a 28-year-old housewife with three children was $527,659. Occasionally, courts seem to permit a subjective assessment of the impaired value by the jury, much in the same way it is permitted to attach a value to other intangible elements of damages, such as pain and suffering. See, e.g., Florida Greyhound Lines Inc. v. Jones, 60 So. 2d 396 (Fla. 1952).

The commentators, particularly those with an economics outlook, seem to prefer the method of assessing damages that refers to "opportunity costs"—the income that the homemaker could have earned in the market had she worked there. See Posner, Economic Analysis of Law 192-196 (4th ed. 1992).

Cases involving permanent injury to young persons are even more difficult to deal with. With the very young, there is likely to be a total absence of proof that the plaintiff could or would enter any particular occupation. In such cases, courts permit, within a fairly wide range, pure guesswork as to the amount of damages. See, e.g., Capriotti v. Beck, 264 Minn. 39, 117 N.W.2d 563 (1962), and Lesniak v. County of Bergen, 117 N.J. 12, 563 A.2d 795 (1989).

Some of the factors upon which courts have based their determinations of a child's future earning capacity are the minimum wage (see McNeil v. United States, 519 F. Supp. 283 (D.S.C. 1981)), and intelligence and skill tests administered by a school prior to the child's injury (see Martin v. United States, 471 F. Supp. 6 (D. Ariz. 1979)). In considering the effect of societal factors, one court ruled that a female child would receive lower wages throughout her life as well as leave the workplace for ten years to have children, and ordered a reduction of her award accordingly. See Caron v. United States, 410 F. Supp. 378 (D.R.I.), *aff'd,* 548 F.2d 366 (1st Cir. 1976). The problems involved in assessing damages in cases of injured children are surveyed in Note, Children Take Their Lumps—The Sorry State of Children's Tort Recovery, 12 U. Cal.-Davis L. Rev. 797 (1979), in which the author proposes a system of deferred periodic payments. For a brief analysis of a more scientific approach to measuring the lost earnings of children, see Lees-Haley, Earnings Regression Analysis—Paying a Child's Lost Earnings, Trial, Feb. 1986, p. 37.

Of more immediate concern to law students is the question of the point in a student's educational development at which a claim for impaired ability to become a lawyer might be recognized. In one case, Kenton v. Hyatt Hotels Corp., 693 S.W.2d 83 (Mo. 1985), the plaintiff was a law student when she was injured, and she was permitted to recover impaired earning capacity damages based on what she would have earned as a lawyer. On the other hand, the plaintiff in Waldorf v. Shuta, 896 F.2d 723 (3rd Cir. 1990), was not able to recover such damages. In this case, the plaintiff's aspirations of a legal profession amounted to little more than a "gleam in the eye;" the plaintiff was a high school drop out, although he had gotten a high school equivalency diploma while in the military. He had worked as a paralegal; he had been denied admission to a four-year college, but had completed one year of a two-year program, in which he had taken courses in tennis, acting, and photography. The court stated that while the plaintiff did want to become a lawyer, no evidence supported the conclusion that he had the ability to do so.

(2) *Adjustments in Reaching the Final Recovery Figure*

Thus far, the tacit assumption has been that once the difficult assessments of earning capacity and percentage of disability are made, the plaintiff's recovery for future impairment of earning capacity is calculated by multiplying those two elements together and then multiplying their product by the plaintiff's expected period of disability. Thus, in the earlier example of the plaintiff with a $1,000 a month earning capacity and a 25 percent permanent disability, if we posit a life expectancy of 30 years it might be assumed that his recovery for future impairment would be $90,000 (that is, $1,000 a month × .25 × 360 months). However, in most jurisdictions the plaintiff would, on the forgoing assumptions, receive something less than the full $90,000, in order to take into account the fact that the recovery will be received immediately, in a lump sum, rather than in increments, over the years. Because the money can be put into the bank and earn interest, the amount received is in most states adjusted downward. What the plaintiff will receive is the present value of the right to receive $250 a month for 30 years—that is, the sum of money which, invested at a given rate of interest, will permit the plaintiff to withdraw $250 a month for 30 years, the fund to be exhausted upon the final withdrawal.

Courts in this country refer to the process of calculating this lump sum as reducing the recovery to present value. Actually, this phrase is misleading insofar as it suggests that a gross sum is first reached (e.g., the $90,000 figure in the preceding hypothetical example) and then reduced to a lower figure to reflect the earning power of the lump sum. Instead, the present value of the right to receive a certain income for a certain period is calculated in the first instance, from standard charts prepared for the purpose. These charts, such as Table 8-2, show the present value of the right to receive one dollar for *x* number of years at *y* rate of interest.

The manner in which this chart is used to calculate the plaintiff's recovery for impairment of earning capacity is best illustrated with an example. Assume that a court were to determine that a fair and conservative rate of interest to expect the plaintiff in the earlier example to earn on his recovery is 6 percent. What is the present value at 6 percent of the right to receive $3,000 a year ($250 a month for 12 months) for 30 years? Locating year "30" on the chart, and running it over to the "6%" column, we find the value of the right to receive one dollar a year at 6 percent for 30 years is

TABLE 8-2
Present Value of One Dollar Per Annum
(Payable at the end of each year for the number of years indicated)

Yr.	*3%*	*4%*	*5%*	*6%*
1	.971	.962	.952	.943
2	1.914	1.886	1.859	1.833
3	2.829	2.775	2.723	2.673
4	3.717	3.630	3.546	3.465
5	4.580	4.452	4.330	4.212
6	5.417	5.242	5.076	4.917
7	6.230	6.002	5.786	5.582

TABLE 8-2
(Continued)

Yr.	3%	4%	5%	6%
8	7.020	6.733	6.463	6.210
9	7.786	7.435	7.108	6.802
10	8.530	8.111	7.722	7.360
11	9.253	8.761	8.306	7.887
12	9.954	9.385	8.863	8.384
13	10.635	9.986	9.394	8.853
14	11.296	10.563	9.899	9.295
15	11.938	11.118	10.380	9.712
16	12.561	11.652	10.838	10.106
17	13.166	12.166	11.274	10.477
18	13.754	12.659	11.690	10.828
19	14.324	13.134	12.085	11.158
20	14.878	13.590	12.462	11.470
21	15.415	14.029	12.821	11.764
22	15.937	14.451	13.163	12.042
23	16.444	14.857	13.489	12.303
24	16.936	15.247	13.799	12.550
25	17.413	15.622	14.094	12.783
26	17.877	15.983	14.375	13.003
27	18.327	16.330	14.643	13.211
28	18.764	16.663	14.898	13.406
29	19.189	16.984	15.141	13.591
30	19.600	17.292	15.373	13.765
31	20.000	17.589	15.593	13.929
32	20.389	17.874	15.803	14.084
33	20.766	18.148	16.003	14.230
34	21.132	18.411	16.193	14.368
35	21.487	18.665	16.374	14.498
36	21.832	18.908	16.547	14.621
37	22.167	19.143	16.711	14.737
38	22.493	19.368	16.868	14.846
39	22.808	19.585	17.017	14.949
40	23.115	19.793	17.159	15.046
41	23.412	19.993	17.294	15.138
42	23.701	20.186	17.423	15.225
43	23.982	20.371	17.546	15.306
44	24.254	20.549	17.663	15.383
45	24.519	20.720	17.774	15.456

$13.765. The right to receive $3,000 a year at the same rate is 3,000 times as great, or $41,295, a figure slightly less than one-half of the $90,000 figure calculated earlier. The reason why a $41,295 lump sum recovery will allow the plaintiff to receive $3,000 a year for 30 years is reflected in the fact that, at 6 percent, $2,477.70 will be generated in interest in the first year.[6] Thus, of the first $3,000 presumably withdrawn by the plaintiff at the end of the first year, only $522.30 will actually come from the principal, that is, the lump sum paid by the defendant.

In some states, damages for future impaired capacity are not reduced to present value. In Beaulieu v. Elliott, 434 P.2d 665 (Alaska 1967), the court gave the following as its reason for declining to follow the majority rule (434 P.2d at 671):

> [W]e believe that the rule for reducing awards, including the formula applied by the Washington court, ignores facts which should not be ignored. Annual inflation at a varying rate is and has been with us for many years. There is no reason to expect that it will not be with us in the future. This rate of depreciation offsets the interest that could be earned on government bonds and many other "safe" investments. As a result the plaintiff, who through no fault of his own is given his future earnings reduced to present value must, in order to realize his full earnings and not be penalized by reduction of future earnings to present value, invest his money in enterprises, other than those which are considered "safe" investments, which promise a return in interest or dividends greater than the offsetting rate of annual inflation. But ours is a competitive economy. By their very nature some enterprises backed by investors' money are going to fail with resulting loss to individuals. Thus, instead of being assured of earnings at rates greater than the annual rate of inflation, the injured plaintiff stands a chance of entirely losing his future earnings by unlucky or unwise investments. Since the plaintiff, through the defendant's fault and not his own, has been placed in the position of having no assurance that his award of future earnings, reduced to present value, can be utilized so that he will ultimately realize his full earnings, we believe that justice will best be served by permitting the trier of fact to compute loss of future earnings without reduction to present value. The plaintiff is more likely to be restored to his original condition under the rule we adopt than under the prevailing rule which calls for a discounting of the award for future earnings.[7]

While most courts addressing the matter have rejected the total offset method used by the court in *Beaulieu,* they will consider evidence of strong

6. The plaintiff may withdraw the money more often than once a year, in smaller increments—e.g., at the rate of $250 a month. We are here assuming an annual withdrawal of $3,000 in order to keep the calculations as simple as possible and in order to make relevant the discount chart which is based on interest compounded annually rather than monthly.

7. The general rule in the United States in torts actions is that each party bears its own attorney's fees. Alaska departs from the norm in this respect. The court's discussion of the attorney's fees question appears at 434 P.2d 677-678. [Eds.]

and persistent inflation in estimating the present value of lost future wages. Some courts increase the amount of recovery based upon a predicted inflation rate. See, e.g., In re Eastern and Southern Districts Asbestos Litigation, 772 F. Supp. 1380 (E. & S.D. N.Y. 1991), *aff'd in part and rev'd in part (on other grounds) sub nom.* In re Brooklyn Navy Yard Asbestos Litigation, 971 F.2d 831 (2d Cir. 1992); Stringham v. United Parcel Service, Inc., 536 N.E.2d 1292 (Ill. App. 1989). More courts, however, have adopted an inflation-adjusted rate for discounting to present value and use a rate lower than the then current low risk rate of return on investments. The leading case is Feldman v. Allegheny Airlines, Inc., 524 F.2d 384 (2d Cir. 1975), in which the predicted annual inflation rate of 2.87 percent was subtracted from the current savings bank interest rate of 4.14 percent and rounded off to an adjusted discount rate of 1.5 percent. Many courts continue to reduce the plaintiff's recovery to present value without any adjustment for inflation. See, e.g., Welch v. Keene Corp., 575 N.E.2d 766 (Mass. App. 1992); Baublitz v. Heinz, 535 A.2d 497 (Md. App. 1988).

Yet another possible adjustment in the plaintiff's recovery for impaired earning capacity stems from the fact that such damages are not subject to taxation under §104(a)(2) of the Internal Revenue Code, which excludes as taxable income the "amount of any damages received (whether by suit or agreement and whether as lump sums or as periodic payments) on account of personal injuries or sickness." Notwithstanding the nontaxability of awards for impaired earning capacity, at one time most courts refused to adjust downward the award to reflect a hypothetical after-tax income. The leading case was McWeeney v. New York, N.H. & H.R.R., 282 F.2d 34 (2d Cir.), *cert. denied,* 364 U.S. 870 (1960). However, in a wrongful death action arising under the Federal Employers' Liability Act, the Supreme Court of the United States later ruled that damages for lost earning capacity must be reduced to an after-tax amount. See Norfolk & W. Ry. v. Liepelt, 444 U.S. 490, 100 S. Ct. 755 62 L. Ed. 2d 689 (1980). In Fanetti v. Helenic Lines, Ltd., 678 F.2d 424 (2d Cir. 1982), *cert. denied,* 463 U.S. 1206 (1983), the court ruled that *Liepelt* applies to all actions brought under federal law.

Some states have adopted *Liepelt* (see, e.g., Ruff v. Weintraub, 195 N.J. 233, 519 A.2d 1384 (1987)), but a far greater number have rejected a reduction of damages to an after-tax amount (see, e.g., Stover v. Lakeland Square Owners Association, 434 N.W.2d 866 (Iowa 1989)). It is worth noting that while the Supreme Court in *Liepelt* found a worker's after-tax income to be the appropriate basis upon which to project future lost earnings, the court, in dicta, also indicated that the lump sum damage award should be increased by the amount of income tax that would have to be paid on the earnings of the award. This suggestion was accepted by the court in DeLucca v. United States, 670 F.2d 843 (9th Cir. 1982).

In general, see Burke and Friel, Tax Treatment of Employment-Related Personal Injury Awards: The Need for Limits, 50 Mont. L. Rev. 13 (1989); Dodge, Taxes and Torts, 77 Cornell L. Rev. 143 (1992).

Problem 33

A partner in your firm has asked you to help her in connection with a case she is handling for Henry Milo. Milo, who is now 37 years old, owned and operated a plumbing business until two years ago. About three years ago, he was involved in an automobile accident that resulted in the loss of his left arm. The partner has sued Andrew Trumball, who was driving the automobile in which Milo was a passenger. The legal issues involved in the case are fairly routine, except with respect to Milo's damages for impaired earning capacity.

At the time of the accident, Milo's gross income from his plumbing business was $75,000 a year. Without his left arm, Milo could no longer function as a plumber, and about a year after the accident he sold the business to an employee. He now is in a Baptist seminary where he is studying to become a minister. In current dollars, Milo can expect to make about $20,000 a year when he graduates later this year. If he does well, he can expect to get a church of his own in three or four years after graduating, with a salary in current dollars of about $25,000. His future income will be hard to predict—it will depend on the size and location of his church. Ministers in urban churches earn more than those in small town and rural churches. Milo is at the top of his class, and he could pretty much choose among available churches. His current intention is to find a rural, relatively poor church where he feels he could accomplish more than in a larger, wealthier situation.

For several years before the accident, Milo had been thinking of getting out of the plumbing business and following his father's footsteps into the clergy. In fact, he had applied to several seminaries in the month before the accident. Milo is quite philosophical about the loss of his arm and has come to view it as a message from God directing him to leave his business and join the ministry.

The partner would like a memorandum indicating how you would present the impairment of earning capacity element most favorably to the client.

c. Pain, Suffering, and Other Intangible Elements

Walters v. Hitchcock

237 Kan. 31, 697 P.2d 847 (1985)

McFarland, J. This is a medical malpractice action wherein plaintiff Lillian K. Walters received a $2,000,000 damage award against defendant C. Thomas Hitchcock, M.D. The defendant physician appeals from the jury's verdict and certain pretrial and posttrial rulings of the district court.

The facts may be summarized as follows. In December, 1979, a lump on the neck of Lillian Walters was discovered by her family physician. Mrs. Walters was, at the time, approximately 32 years of age, married, with four minor children. She was not employed outside the home. The family physician conducted a number of tests and advised her to consult with a surgeon. Mrs. Walters was seen by defendant Hitchcock, a surgeon, on January 7, 1980. As a result of the prior testing and his physical examination of her, Dr. Hitchcock recommended surgical removal of diseased areas of the thyroid gland. There were indications of a possibly malignant condition. Surgery was scheduled for January 22, 1980. Mrs. Walters was advised the operation was a relatively low risk procedure with an anticipated three-day hospital stay and a small residual scar.

The operation proceeded in what appeared at the time to be a routine manner. Specimens were sent to the pathology laboratory and no malignancy was detected. The patient was sutured and sent to the recovery room. One day later. Mrs. Walters' condition rapidly deteriorated. Her head ballooned in size, she became blind and suffered extreme respiratory distress. She was taken to the intensive care unit where a breathing tube was inserted. Shortly thereafter, Dr. Hitchcock was advised by the hospital pathology department that a one inch by one and one-half inch piece of esophagus tissue was connected to the thyroid specimen sent to the laboratory during surgery. Mrs. Walter's wound was now badly infected. She was taken to surgery. Dr. Hitchcock reopened the wound and observed a significant hole in the left front portion of her esophagus. He concluded that repair was not possible and sewed the esophagus shut—thereby closing it permanently.

At this point feeding was possible only through a tube inserted directly into Mrs. Walters' stomach. She regained her vision. Numerous hospitalizations and surgical procedures followed. Ultimately, colon interposition surgery was performed which involved making a sort of bypass esophagus from a portion of Mrs. Walters' colon. Additional facts relative to Mrs. Walters' condition and the quality of her life will be set forth in the discussion of the issue relative to the amount of damages awarded herein.

Mrs. Walters brought this action against Dr. Hitchcock based upon negligence in cutting into the esophagus and in failing to make prompt repair thereof. She sought $4,000,000 in damages. Dr. Hitchcock denied negligence and blamed the injury to the esophagus on the abnormal physiology of Mrs. Walters. The jury awarded Mrs. Walters $2,000,000 in damages and Dr. Hitchcock appeals therefrom.

The first issue on appeal concerns alleged misconduct of plaintiff's counsel during closing argument. In his closing argument plaintiff's counsel stated: "Who would sell their esophagus for $4 million? I would not sell mine."

Defendant contends this constitutes a prohibited "golden rule" argument. This term relates to arguments of counsel that jurors should place themselves in the position of the plaintiff. Such arguments are usually improper and may constitute reversible error. See 75 Am. Jur. 2d., Trial §282, pp. 357-358.

Plaintiff argues the remarks were not asking the jurors to place themselves in plaintiff's shoes, and were merely hypothetical in nature.

The remarks actually span two categories. The comment commencing "Who would sell. . . ." is, we believe, a fair argument relative to claimed damages and is not a "golden rule" argument. The comment that counsel would not sell his esophagus for that sum is testimonial in nature as it is a statement of counsel's personal opinion. This is an improper argument. Does this improper comment constitute reversible error? We believe not. To constitute reversible error there must be a likelihood that the improper remarks changed the result of the trial. We have examined the record and conclude that, in the totality of the circumstances, the improper comment constituted only harmless error. . . .

For his final issue, defendant challenges the size of the verdict. In his brief defendant states:

> In advancing this argument, the defendant is definitely aware of the long line of Kansas cases on the subject and the guidelines that have evolved in those cases. The defendant realizes that the trial court will not be reversed in an order denying new trial *unless* the amount of the verdict, in light of the evidence, shocks the conscience of the appellate court.

Defendant, in support of his argument that the verdict was excessive, directs our attention to the following:

> 1. Plaintiff's medical bills by the time of trial were approximately $59,000.
>
> 2. There was no claim nor was the jury instructed with regard to lost wages or diminished future earning capacity as Mrs. Walters was not employed during the course of her 19-year marriage.
>
> 3. The repair surgery and reconstruction by colon interposition were working properly at the time of trial, and no further surgery, with respect to the surgical complication that occurred during the thyroidectomy, was contemplated. . . . No further evidence was presented regarding future medical expenses.

The evidence herein bears out that medical science has done all that it can do to alleviate plaintiff's condition and no further surgery is contemplated, although the same is not ruled out. This does not mean the damage done to Mrs. Walters has been undone and that she has been restored to her previous condition. It simply means her condition cannot be helped by further surgery or treatment. The substitute esophagus fashioned from a part of Mrs. Walters' colon is, apparently, functioning as well as can be expected but that level of function is a source of permanent problems for Mrs. Walters. When she swallows, food does not automatically go to her stomach. It piles up in grotesque bulges in her throat and upper chest. It is necessary for her to manually massage the bulges downward to force the food to her stomach. The process is physically painful. As there is no valve to keep the contents of her stomach from traveling back up the makeshift esophagus, she cannot lie flat and must remain in a position where gravity will keep the contents of her stomach in place. Her condition is embarrassing, distasteful to persons around her, and a major obstacle to leading a normal life. She has serious ongoing digestive problems. At the time of trial her life expectancy was 41.9 years. The years between Mrs. Walters' injury and attainment of her present level of functioning were a nightmare of pain, disability, hospitalizations and surgical procedures. She has severe disfiguring scars on her neck and torso. Many activities, such as eating and sitting, continue to be painful.

After having reviewed the record, we conclude our collective conscience are not shocked by the size of the verdict herein.

The judgment is affirmed.

SCHROEDER, C.J., dissenting:

The magnitude of the verdict in this case is the result of trial error and what purports to be misconduct of the jurors. . . .

By reason of the . . . trial court errors and speculation on the part of the jurors, the magnitude of the verdict in this case demonstrates *prejudice on its face.* In light of the evidence it shocks my conscience.

The plaintiff, Lillian K. Walters, at the time of trial had a life expectancy of 41.9 years. Her medical bills at the time of trial were approximately $59,000. She made no claim for lost-earning capacity, or diminished earning capacity; no evidence of future surgery or medical expenses was presented. The $2 million verdict included $1,940,000 in the general damage categories.

On an annual basis this gives the plaintiff the principal sum of $47,733 per year for the rest of her life. Assuming one-half of the damage award is paid on expenses and attorney fees, the remaining $1 million invested at 10% simple interest (present interest rates compounded quarterly on money invested in C.D.'s will exceed 10%), payable annually, will provide an annual income of $100,000 without invading the principal sum invested.

The law in Kansas regarding an excessive verdict has been well defined. One of our leading cases is Kirk v. Beachner Construction Co., Inc., 214 Kan. 733, 522 P.2d 176 (1974). The rules there stated are confined to a situation which is based solely on the amount of the verdict. The case stands for the proposition that no verdict is right which more than compensates—and none is right which fails to compensate. The legal test is one of reasonable compensation.

In my opinion, courts of last resort must exercise a degree of economic judgment to provide stability in our free enterprise system if justice is to be administered fairly and within reason. Courts should not declare serious errors made by the trial court to be harmless, or permit a verdict permeated with speculation and conjecture to go unchallenged, particularly where the amount of the verdict is clearly excessive on its face and indicates prejudice.

Many articles appearing in journals and periodicals address the crisis in the medical profession. The tremendous growth in malpractice liability has resulted in higher insurance premiums which insured physicians pass along in higher prices to health care consumers. In DeVito, Abuse of Litigation: Plague of the Medical Profession, 56 N.Y. St. B.J. 23, 25 (1984), the author says:

> The jury system is a free society's precious gift to its citizens. The adversary system within which it functions is an effective guardian of our rights, but, as obtains in any free society, these rights carry with them commensurate obligations and responsibilities. This is especially true of lawyers who, in their capacity as officers of the court, have a unique duty to preserve, protect and perpetuate the founding spirit of our judicial process. Abuse of that process, whether in civil or criminal law, whether by the courts or by lawyers, is to guarantee its ultimate demise. . . .

Where state courts of last resort fail to respond with reasonable action to fairly administer justice, public opinion shifts the control to legislative bodies. In the 1985 session of the Kansas Legislature, Senate Bill No. 110 has been introduced by the Judiciary Committee. The Bill is designed to limit liability in malpractice actions of this nature. In the Journal of the Kansas Trial Lawyers Association, Vol. VIII, No. 4, p. 25, this legislation is described as "extremely regressive." Similar instances where state courts of last resort have failed to act with reason have resulted in legislation introduced in the Congress of the United States. Carryover bills in the 99th Congress from the 98th Congress are bills concerning Federal Trade Commission regulation of the Bar, and federal preemption of product liability law of the states.

It is respectfully submitted this court should reverse the trial court and grant a new trial on the ground of misconduct of counsel for the plaintiff in closing argument and, failing this, that the court should remand the case for a hearing on the motion for new trial concerning the charge of misconduct on the part of the jury in fixing the damage award.

From a purely monetary point of view, recovery for noneconomic loss has become the preeminent element of recovery in personal injury cases. It has been estimated that in products liability and medical malpractice cases, recovery for intangible harm accounts for nearly 50 percent of the total recovery. See II The American Law Institute, Reporters Study—Enterprise Responsibility for Personal Injury 201 (1991).

Pain and suffering is the most difficult element of recovery to measure. One device permitted in some states as a guide to juries is the *per diem argument,* under which the plaintiff's attorney suggests to the jury a dollar value for the plaintiff's pain for whatever time segment the attorney chooses.

The common rationale for the per diem approach is stated in Beaulieu v. Elliott, p. 703, above, (434 P.2d 676):

> We agree [that] there is no fixed measure of compensation in awarding damages for pain and suffering, and such an award necessarily rests in the good sense and deliberate judgment of the tribunal assigned by law to ascertain what is just compensation. We can see nothing manifestly unfair or unjust about the method used by the trial court in assessing damages for future pain and suffering. In fact . . . it appears to be a fair argument and a rational approach to treat damages for pain the way it is endured—day by day, month by month, year by year. Ultimately, however, the question for decision is whether the total sum is reasonable or not, regardless of how it was arrived at. We find no error in the method used by the trial court in awarding damages for future pain and suffering.

The Supreme Court of New Hampshire in Duguay v. Gelinas, 104 N.H. 182, 185-187, 182 A.2d 451, 453-454 (1962) expressed the commonly stated reasons for not permitting per diem arguments:

> The chief vice of the formula is that it is an attempt by counsel to distort and exaggerate the measurement of what is immeasurable by such a mathematical method. The second vice of this type of argument in our opinion is that it will more often mislead a jury than aid them, since the jury are given an illusion of certainty by the use of figures which are not and cannot be substantiated by evidence. . . .
>
> The mathematical formula applied to the plaintiff's pain and suffering, or to her anguish and embarrassment resulting from facial defects due to the accident for her life expectancy of 233,600 hours can result in any amount that the imagination of counsel deems advantageous. It is only necessary to change either the period of time involved or the specific amount of money selected for the hourly rate. A small sum multiplied by the number of hours in plaintiff's life expectancy introduces an element of apparent precision that is illusory and compounds the dangers of conjecture. In the present case counsel deducted eight hours a day for sleep but this deduction could be increased or decreased as well as the hourly rate. . . . The tendency of the mathematical formula to mislead a jury is a strong factor in persuading us that it should be rejected in this state.

Courts are divided on whether recovery for pain and suffering should be reduced to present value. Holding that the reduction should be made is Oliveri v. Delta S.S. Lines, Inc., 849 F.2d 742 (2d Cir. 1988). Holding that the reduction should not be made is Friedman v. C & C Car Service, 108 N.J. 72, 527 A.2d 871 (1987).

Pain and suffering is a broad concept that may include a number of more or less separate factors, the most common of which is the physical pain associated with the injury. To recover for this, the injured person must have been conscious. See Estate of Swarthout v. Beard, 190 N.W.2d 373 (Mich. App. 1971), *rev'd on other grounds sub nom.* Smith v. City of Detroit, 388 Mich. 637, 202 N.W.2d 300 (1972); Blunt v. Zinni, 32 A.D. 882, 302 N.Y.S.2d 504 (1969). But the plaintiff need not necessarily be aware of what is happening. See Capelouto v. Kaiser Foundation Hospitals, 7 Cal. 3d 889, 500 P.2d 880, 103 Cal. Rptr. 856 (1972), in which the court ruled that a baby one week old at the time of the injury can recover for pain and suffering. In some cases, a relatively brief period of consciousness before death has been held sufficient to support a verdict for physical pain and suffering. In Wiggins v. Lane & Co., 298 F. Supp. 194 (E.D. La. 1969), the plaintiff's decedent was knocked with great force from a pile-driving rig on which he was working and fell 50 feet to the deck below. Medical experts testified that he probably died when he hit the deck, but offered no opinions as to whether he was conscious during the fall. On this evidence, the jury was permitted to find that the decedent suffered pain from the time he was struck until he died, and the trial judge refused to set aside an award of $10,000 for that period.

Recovery for mental suffering associated with bodily disfigurement is also includible as an element of pain and suffering. In Kravenas v. Algonquin Township, 13 Ill. App. 3d 1000, 301 N.E.2d 490 (1973), for example, the plaintiff suffered permanent scarring from deep cuts on his forehead which required 69 stitches. As a result, he became "self-conscious with a change in personality." The court upheld a total award of $30,000, with special damages of approximately $900.00.

McDougald v. Garber

73 N.Y.2d 246, 536 N.E.2d 372 (1989)

WACHTLER, Chief Judge. This appeal raises fundamental questions about the nature and role of nonpecuniary damages in personal injury litigation. By nonpecuniary damages, we mean those damages awarded to compensate an injured person for the physical and emotional consequences of the injury, such as pain and suffering and the loss of the ability to engage in certain activities. Pecuniary damages, on the other hand, compensate the victim for the economic consequences of the injury, such as medical expenses, lost earnings and the cost of custodial care.

The specific questions raised here deal with assessment of nonpecuniary damages and are (1) whether some degree of cognitive awareness is a prerequisite to recovery for loss of enjoyment of life and (2) whether a jury should be instructed to consider and award damages for loss of enjoyment of life separately from damages for pain and suffering. We answer the first question in the affirmative and the second question in the negative.

I

On September 7, 1978, plaintiff Emma McDougald, then 31 years old, underwent a Caesarean section and tubal ligation at New York Infirmary. Defendant Garber performed the surgery; defendants Armengol and Kulkarni provided anesthesia. During the surgery, Mrs. McDougald suffered oxygen deprivation which resulted in severe brain damage and left her in a permanent comatose condition. This action was brought by Mrs. McDougald and her husband, suing derivatively, alleging that the injuries were caused by the defendants' acts of malpractice.

A jury found all defendants liable and awarded Emma McDougald a total of $9,650,102 in damages, including $1,000,000 for conscious pain and suffering and a separate award of $3,500,000 for loss of the pleasures and pursuits of life. The balance of the damages awarded to her were for pecuniary damages—lost earnings and the cost of custodial and nursing care. Her husband was awarded $1,500,000 on his derivative claim for the loss of his wife's services. On defendants' posttrial motions, the Trial Judge reduced the total award to Emma McDougald to $4,796,728 by striking the entire award for future nursing care ($2,353,374) and by reducing the separate awards for conscious pain and suffering and loss of the pleasures and pursuits of life to a single award of $2,000,000 (McDougald v. Garber, 132 Misc. 2d 457, 504 N.Y.S.2d 383). Her husband's award was left intact. On cross appeals, the Appellate Division affirmed (135 A.D.2d 80, 524 N.Y.S.2d 192) and later granted defendants leave to appeal to this court.

II

. . . At trial, defendants sought to show that Mrs. McDougald's injuries were so severe that she was incapable of either experiencing pain or appreciating her condition. Plaintiffs, on the other hand, introduced proof that Mrs. McDougald responded to certain stimuli to a sufficient extent to indicate that she was aware of her circumstances. Thus, the extent of Mrs. McDougald's cognitive abilities, if any, was sharply disputed.

The parties and the trial court agreed that Mrs. McDougald could not recover for pain and suffering unless she were conscious of the pain. Defendants maintained that such consciousness was also required to support an award for loss of enjoyment of life. The court, however, accepted plaintiffs' view that loss of enjoyment of life was compensable without regard to whether the plaintiff was aware of the loss. Accordingly, because the level of Mrs. McDougald's cognitive abilities was in dispute, the court instructed the jury to consider loss of enjoyment of life as an element of nonpecuniary damages separate from pain and suffering. . . .

We conclude that the court erred, both in instructing the jury that Mrs.

McDougald's awareness was irrelevant to their consideration of damages for loss of enjoyment of life and in directing the jury to consider that aspect of damages separately from pain and suffering.

III

We begin with the familiar proposition that an award of damages to a person injured by the negligence of another is to compensate the victim, not to punish the wrongdoer. The goal is to restore the injured party, to the extent possible, to the position that would have been occupied had the wrong not occurred. To be sure, placing the burden of compensation on the negligent party also serves as a deterrent, but purely punitive damages—that is, those which have no compensatory purpose—are prohibited unless the harmful conduct is intentional, malicious, outrageous, or otherwise aggravated beyond mere negligence.

Damages for nonpecuniary losses are, of course, among those that can be awarded as compensation to the victim. This aspect of damages, however, stands on less certain ground than does an award for pecuniary damages. An economic loss can be compensated in kind by an economic gain; but recovery for noneconomic losses such as pain and suffering and loss of enjoyment of life rests on "the legal fiction that money damages can compensate for a victim's injury" (Howard v. Lecher, 42 N.Y.2d 109, 111, 397 N.Y.S.2d 363, 366 N.E.2d 64). We accept this fiction, knowing that although money will neither ease the pain nor restore the victim's abilities, this device is as close as the law can come in its effort to right the wrong. We have no hope of evaluating what has been lost, but a monetary award may provide a measure of solace for the condition created.

Our willingness to indulge this fiction comes to an end, however, when it ceases to serve the compensatory goals of tort recovery. When that limit is met, further indulgence can only result in assessing damages that are punitive. The question posed by this case, then, is whether an award of damages for loss of enjoyment of life to a person whose injuries preclude any awareness of the loss serves a compensatory purpose. We conclude that it does not.

Simply put, an award of money damages in such circumstances has no meaning or utility to the injured person. An award for the loss of enjoyment of life "cannot provide [such a victim] with any consolation or ease any burden resting on him . . . He cannot spend it upon necessities or pleasures. He cannot experience the pleasure of giving it away" (Flannery v. United States, 4th Cir., 718 F.2d 108, 111, *cert. denied,* 467 U.S. 1226, 104 S. Ct. 2679, 81 L. Ed. 2d 874).

We recognize that, as the trial court noted, requiring some cognitive awareness as a prerequisite to recovery for loss of enjoyment of life will result in some cases "in the paradoxical situation that the greater the degree of brain injury inflicted by a negligent defendant, the smaller the award the plaintiff can recover in general damages" (McDougald v. Garber, 132 Misc. 2d 457, 460, 504 N.Y.S.2d 383, supra). The force of this argument, however—the temptation to achieve a balance between injury and damages—has nothing to do with meaningful compensation for the victim. Instead, the temptation is rooted in a desire to punish the defendant in proportion to the harm inflicted. However relevant such retributive symmetry may be in the criminal law, it has no place in the law of civil damages, at least in the absence of culpability beyond mere negligence.

Accordingly, we conclude that cognitive awareness is a prerequisite to recovery for loss of enjoyment of life. We do not go so far, however, as to require the fact finder to sort out varying degrees of cognition and determine at what level a particular deprivation can be fully appreciated. With respect to pain and suffering, the trial court charged simply that there must be "some level of awareness" in order for plaintiff to recover. We think that this is an appropriate standard for all aspects of nonpecuniary loss. No doubt the standard ignores analytically relevant levels of cognition, but we resist the desire for analytical purity in favor of simplicity. A more complex instruction might give the appearance of greater precision but, given the limits of our understanding of the human mind, it would in reality lead only to greater speculation. We turn next to the question whether loss of enjoyment of life should be considered a category of damages separate from pain and suffering.

IV

There is no dispute here that the fact finder may, in assessing nonpecuniary damages, consider the effect of the injuries on the plaintiff's capacity to lead a normal life. Traditionally, in this State and elsewhere, this aspect of suffering has not been treated as a separate category of damages; instead, the plaintiff's inability to enjoy life to its fullest has been considered one type of suffering to be factored into a general award for nonpecuniary damages, commonly known as pain and suffering.

Recently, however, there has been an attempt to segregate the suffering associated with physical pain from the mental anguish that stems from the inability to engage in certain activities, and to have juries provide a separate award for each.

Some courts have resisted the effort, primarily on the ground that duplicative and therefore excessive awards would result. Other courts have allowed separate awards, noting that the types of suffering involved are analytically distinguishable. Still other courts have questioned the propriety of the practice but held that, in the particular case, separate awards did not constitute reversible error. . . .

We do not dispute that distinctions can be found or created between the concepts of pain and suffering and loss of enjoyment of life. If the term "suffering" is limited to the emotional response to the sensation of pain, then the emotional response caused by the limitation of life's activities may be considered qualitatively different. But suffering need not be so limited—it can easily encompass the frustration and anguish caused by the inability to participate in activities that once brought pleasure. Traditionally, by treating loss of enjoyment of life as a permissible factor in assessing pain and suffering, courts have given the term this broad meaning.

If we are to depart from this traditional approach and approve a separate award for loss of enjoyment of life, it must be on the basis that such an approach will yield a more accurate evaluation of the compensation due to the plaintiff. We have no doubt that, in general, the total award for nonpecuniary damages would increase if we adopted the rule. That separate awards are advocated by plaintiffs and resisted by defendants is sufficient evidence that larger awards are at stake here. But a larger award does not by itself indicate that the goal of compensation has been better served.

The advocates of separate awards contend that because pain and suffering and loss of enjoyment of life can be distinguished, they must be treated separately if the plaintiff is to be compensated fully for each distinct injury suffered. We disagree. Such an analytical approach may have its place when the subject is pecuniary damages, which can be calculated with some precision. But the estimation of nonpecuniary damages is not amenable to such analytical precision and may, in fact, suffer from its application. Translating human suffering into dollars and cents involves no mathematical formula; it rests, as we have said, on a legal fiction. The figure that emerges is unavoidably distorted by the translation. Application of this murky process to the component parts of nonpecuniary injuries (however analytically distinguishable they may be) cannot make it more accurate. If anything, the distortion will be amplified by repetition.

Thus, we are not persuaded that any salutary purpose would be served by having the jury make separate awards for pain and suffering and loss of enjoyment of life. We are confident, furthermore, that the trial advocate's art is a sufficient guarantee that none of the plaintiff's losses will be ignored by the jury.

The errors in the instructions given to the jury require a new trial on the issue of nonpecuniary damages to be awarded to plaintiff Emma McDougald. Defendants' remaining contentions are either without merit, beyond the scope of our review or are rendered academic by our disposition of the case.

Accordingly, the order of the Appellate Division, insofar as appealed from, should be modified, with costs to defendants, by granting a new trial on the issue of nonpecuniary damages of plaintiff Emma McDougald, and as so modified, affirmed.

TITONE, Judge (dissenting).

The majority's holding represents a compromise position that neither comports with the fundamental principles of tort compensation nor furnishes a satisfactory, logically consistent framework for compensating nonpecuniary loss. Because I conclude that loss of enjoyment of life is an objective damage item, conceptually distinct from conscious pain and suffering, I can find no fault with the trial court's instruction authorizing separate awards and permitting an award for "loss of enjoyment of life" even in the absence of any awareness of that loss on the part of the injured plaintiff. Accordingly, I dissent.

It is elementary that the purpose of awarding tort damages is to compensate the wronged party for the actual loss he or she has sustained. Personal injury damages are awarded "to restore the injured person to the state of health he had prior to his injuries because that is the only way the law knows how to recompense one for personal injuries suffered" (Romeo v. New York City Tr. Auth., 73 Misc. 2d 124, 126, 341 N.Y.S.2d 733; [other citations omitted]). Thus, this court has held that "[t]he person responsible for the injury must respond for all damages resulting directly from and as a natural consequence of the wrongful act" (Steitz v. Gifford, 280 N.Y. 15, 20, 19 N.E.2d 661).

The capacity to enjoy life—by watching one's children grow, participating in recreational activities, and drinking in the many other pleasures that life has to offer—is unquestionably an attribute of an ordinary healthy individual. The loss of that capacity as a result of another's negligent act is at least as serious an impairment as the permanent destruction of a physical function, which has always been treated as a compensable item under traditional tort principles. Indeed, I can imagine no physical loss that is more central to the quality of a tort victim's continuing life than the destruction of the capacity to enjoy that life to the fullest.

Unquestionably, recovery of a damage item such as "pain and suffering" requires a showing of some degree of cognitive capacity. Such a requirement exists for the simple reason that pain and suffering are wholly subjective concepts and cannot exist separate and apart from the human consciousness that experiences them. In contrast, the destruction of an individual's capacity to enjoy life as a result of a crippling injury is an objective fact that does not differ in principle from the permanent loss of an eye or limb. As in the case of a lost limb, an essential characteristic of a healthy human life has been wrongfully taken, and, consequently, the injured party is entitled to a monetary award as a substitute, if, as the majority asserts, the goal of tort compensation is "to restore the injured party, to the extent possible, to the position that would have been occupied had the wrong not occurred" (majority opn., at 254, at 939 of 538 N.Y.S.2d, at 374 of 536 N.E.2d).

Significantly, this equation does not suggest a need to establish the injured's awareness of the loss. The victim's ability to comprehend the degree to which his or her life has been impaired is irrelevant, since, unlike "conscious pain and suffering," the impairment exists independent of the victim's ability to apprehend it. Indeed, the majority reaches the conclusion that a degree of awareness must be shown only after injecting a new element into the equation. Under the majority's formulation, the victim must be aware of the loss because, in addition to being compensatory, the award must have "meaning or utility to the injured person." (Majority opn., at 254, at 940 of 538 N.Y.S.2d, at 375 of 536 N.E.2d.) This additional requirement, however, has no real foundation in law or logic. "Meaning" and "utility" are subjective value judgments that have no place in the law of tort recovery, where the primary goal is to find ways of quantifying, to the extent possible, the worth of various forms of human tragedy.

Moreover, the compensatory nature of a monetary award for loss of enjoyment of life is not altered or rendered punitive by the fact that the unaware injured plaintiff cannot experience the pleasure of having it. The fundamental distinction between punitive and compensatory damages is that the former exceed the amount necessary to replace what the plaintiff lost. As the Court of Appeals for the Second Circuit has observed, "[t]he fact that the compensation [for loss of enjoyment of life] may inure as a practical matter to third parties in a given case does not transform the nature of the damages" (Rufino v. United States, 2nd Cir., 829 F.2d 354, 362).

Ironically, the majority's expressed goal of limiting recovery for non-pecuniary loss to compensation that the injured plaintiff has the capacity to appreciate is directly undercut by the majority's ultimate holding, adopted in the interest of "simplicity," that recovery for loss of enjoyment of life may be had as long as the injured plaintiff has " 'some level of awareness' ", however slight (majority opn., at 255, at 940 of 538 N.Y.S.2d, at 375 of 536 N.E.2d). Manifestly, there are many different forms and levels of awareness, particularly in cases involving brain injury. Further, the type and degree of cognitive functioning necessary to experience "pain and suffering" is certainly of a lower order than that needed to apprehend the loss of the ability to enjoy life in all of its subtleties. Accordingly, the existence of "some level of awareness" on the part of the injured plaintiff says nothing about that plaintiff's ability to derive some comfort from the award or even to appreciate its significance. Hence, that standard does not assure that loss of enjoyment of life damages will be awarded only when they serve "a compensatory purpose," as that term is defined by the majority.

In the final analysis, the rule that the majority has chosen is an arbitrary one, in that it denies or allows recovery on the basis of a criterion that is not truly related to its stated goal. In my view, it is fundamentally unsound, as well as grossly unfair, to deny recovery to those who are completely without cognitive capacity while permitting it for those with a mere spark of awareness, regardless of the latter's ability to appreciate either the loss sustained or the benefits of the monetary award offered in compensation. In both instances, the injured plaintiff is in essentially the same position, and an award that is punitive as to one is equally punitive as to the other.

Of course, since I do not subscribe to the majority's conclusion that an award to an unaware plaintiff is punitive, I would have no difficulty permitting recovery to both classes of plaintiffs.

Having concluded that the injured plaintiff's awareness should not be a necessary precondition to recovery for loss of enjoyment of life, I also have no difficulty going on to conclude that loss of enjoyment of life is a distinct damage item which is recoverable separate and apart from the award for conscious pain and suffering. The majority has rejected separate recovery, in part because it apparently perceives some overlap between the two damage categories and in part because it believes that the goal of enhancing the precision of jury awards for nonpecuniary loss would not be advanced. However, the overlap the majority perceives exists only if one assumes, as the majority evidently has (see, majority opn., at 256-257, at 940-942 of 538 N.Y.S.2d, at 375-377 of 536 N.E.2d), that the "loss of enjoyment" category of damages is designed to compensate only for "*the emotional response* caused by the limitation of life's activities" and "*the frustration and anguish caused by* the inability to participate in activities that once brought pleasure" (emphasis added), both of which are highly *subjective* concepts.

In fact, while "pain and suffering compensates the victim for the physical and mental discomfort caused by the injury; . . . loss of enjoyment of life compensates the victim for the limitations on the person's life created by the injury," a distinctly objective loss (Thompson v. National R.R. Passenger Corp., [6th Cir., 621 F.2d 814, 824, *cert. denied,* 449 U.S. 1035, 101 S. Ct. 611, 66 L. Ed. 2d 497]). In other words, while the victim's "emotional response" and "frustration and anguish" are elements of the award for pain and suffering, the "limitation of life's activities" and the "inability to participate in activities" that the majority identifies are recoverable under the "loss of enjoyment of life" rubric. Thus, there is no real overlap, and no real basis for concern about potentially duplicative awards where, as here, there is a properly instructed jury.

Finally, given the clear distinction between the two categories of nonpecuniary damages, I cannot help but assume that permitting separate awards for conscious pain and suffering and loss of enjoyment of life would contribute to accuracy and precision in thought in the jury's deliberations on the issue of damages. . . . In light of the concrete benefit to be gained by compelling the jury to differentiate between the specific objective and subjective elements of the plaintiff's nonpecuniary loss, I find unpersuasive the majority's reliance on vague concerns about potential distortion owing to the inherently difficult task of computing the value of intangible loss. My belief in the jury system, and in the collective wisdom of the deliberating jury, leads me to conclude that we may safely leave that task in the jurors' hands.

For all of these reasons, I approve of the approach that the trial court adopted in its charge to the jury. Accordingly, I would affirm the order below affirming the judgment.

In general, see Comment, Nonpecuniary Damages for Comatose Tort Victims, 61 Geo. L.J. 1547 (1973).

In recent years, legislatures have been critical of recovery for pain and suffering, and as a part of the recent explosion in legislative tort reform, a number of states have enacted statutes limiting recovery for that element of harm. See, e.g., Alaska Stat. §09.17.010 (Supp. 1991) (noneconomic damages, except in cases of "disfigurement and severe physical impairment" limited to $500,000 "for each claim based on a separate incident or injury"); Colo. Rev. Stat. §13-21-102.5 (noneconomic damages limited to $500,000, but may not exceed $250,000 unless "the court finds justification by clear and convincing evidence"); Md. Cts. & Jud. Proc. Code Ann. §11-108 (noneconomic damages limited to $350,000); N.H. Rev. Stat. Ann. (Supp. 1991) (noneconomic damages limited to $875,000). Statutes with damage caps have been the subject of constitutional attack, with varying results explainable in part because of the differences in the state constitutions. Upholding the statutes are Samsel v. Wheeler Transport Services, Inc., 246 Kan. 336, 789 P.2d 541 (1990), and Murphy v. Edmonds, 325 Md. 342, 601 A.2d 102 (1990). Ruling that the damage cap statutes are unconstitutional are Brannigan v. Usitalo, 134 N.H. 50, 587 A.2d 1232 (1991) (state constitutional right to equal protection violated), and Sofie v. Fibreboard Corp., 112 Wash. 2d 636, 771 P.2d 711, *modified,* 780 P.2d 260 (1989) (state constitutional right to jury trial violated). Legislation of this sort expresses a concern that the absolute amount of compensation for intangible harm is too high.

Another concern expressed by critics of the existing process is that it involves "horizontal" unfairness—plaintiffs with substantially similar injuries recover significantly different amounts. This results from the fact that the jury in each case hears only the evidence in that case, and does not have a basis for comparing that case with other similar cases. One way to achieve greater equality between similar cases would be to provide juries with information about the awards for intangible harm in those similar cases. Such a suggestion was made in II Reporters' Study—Enterprise Responsibility for Personal Injury—Approaches to Legal and Institutional Change 223-229 (1991). For a more detailed proposal, see Bovbjerg, Sloan and Blumstein, Valuing Life and Limb in Tort: Scheduling "Pain and Suffering," 83 Nw. U.L. Rev. 908 (1989).

Problem 34

A partner in the firm with which you are an associate has asked for your assistance on the Sidney Rothman case. Rothman is seeking to recover against Tompkins Department Stores, Inc., in whose store in Fairfield, Columbia, Mr. Rothman recently fell and suffered what his doctor has diagnosed as a herniated disc in his lower back. The lawyer for Reliance Insurance Company, which carries the liability insurance covering Tompkins Department Stores, Inc., has an appointment to see the partner next week to discuss settlement of the case. The partner wants you to analyze the file so that you can make a recommendation as to the range within which the case should be settled.

In responding to this assignment, you are to consider the case that follows to be the most recent reported Columbia case dealing with the subject of recovery for low back injuries. In addition, there exist in Columbia rules of thumb which are routinely referred to (though by no means followed unswervingly) in settlement negotiations. Generally, in what are usually referred to as the smaller cases, insurance companies recognize a range of from three to five times out-of-pocket loss, including work time lost (this amount is usually referred to as the "specials"), depending upon such factors as the severity and duration of pain and the like.[8] Where the plaintiff is represented by a lawyer, insurance companies may on occasion go as high as ten times specials in these smaller cases. For cases of a more serious or unusual nature, the rule of thumb multiples just described tend to give way to more individualized consideration of the unique factors of the particular case. One of the senior partners in your firm, who has had a great deal of trial experience in personal injury cases, recently explained his views of what a lawyer might expect a Columbia jury to return in a herniated disc case. Without a myelogram or subsequent laminectomy confirmation, the range of probable recovery is approximately $6,500 to $35,000. With myelographic confirmation but no surgery, the range is $35,000 to $75,000. And where surgery has been performed, the range jumps to $100,000 to $150,000 or more. The partner explained that these are at best only general categories with respect to which he gears his expectations in low back cases. The first category, for example, includes what he calls the "doubtful diagnosis" cases. Even without a myelogram, if the diagnosis is firm, the case may be treated almost as favorably as other cases with myelographic confirmation. Moreover, the categories reflect a range of cases as to the certainty of liability, from rather doubtful liability to clear liability. "Clear liability always adds to the value of a case—even if only a sprained finger is involved" he suggests. The partner referred you to a few Columbia Supreme Court cases somewhat in point; the most recent is the *Delaney* case (reproduced at p. 730, below). A couple of the cases were decided some time ago and thus are of more limited usefulness. One case, decided on appeal in 1973, upheld a judgment of $25,000 for a woman who had a 15 percent permanent disability as a result of a neck injury and a 5 percent permanent

8. It is not proper, however, for the trial judge to use this approach in calculating damages. In Hayhurst v. LaFlamme, 441 A.2d 544 (R.I. 1982), the court reversed the trial judge's method of calculating damages for pain and suffering by multiplying lost wages and medical expenses by five.

disability in her lower back. There was no evidence of future loss of income, but she did testify that she could "no longer ride horses, build corrals, or dance as she had before the accident." Her remaining life expectancy at the time of the trial was 26 years. The other case, decided on appeal in 1975, involved a 46-year-old male with a herniated disc, which was confirmed by a myelogram. His annual earnings before the accident ranged from $2100 to $5800. His disability appears to have been total. The judgment for damages of $36,000 for loss of future earnings, and of $15,000 for pain and suffering was upheld. "In the final analysis," the partner added, "while generalizations are helpful, each case has its own twists, and in working up any case, particularly the bigger ones, it is important to focus on the particular facts of that case."

The documents on pp. 721-728 are from the file on the Sidney Rothman case.

Client's Statement

Name: Sidney L. Rothman *Date:* March 17
Address: 15 Beacon Road
Fairfield, Columbia
Telephone: 361-0020

My name is Sidney L. Rothman. I am 42 years old, married, with three children, ages 11, 13 and 15. I am employed as a civil engineer with Grayson & Sons, Fairfield National Bank Building, 382 Main Street, Fairfield, Columbia.

On November 20 last year, I had driven into downtown Fairfield to do some shopping for my wife's birthday. At about 3:00 in the afternoon, I entered Tompkins Department Store to look for a wrist watch. I went first to the sporting goods department on the sixth floor to look at tennis racquets. I had taken the elevator. I decided not to buy one and took the elevator down to the second floor to the jewelry department. I bought a watch and had it wrapped. Straight ahead from the counter where I bought the watch is a stairway leading to the main floor. I started

/s/ David J. Richards 1. */s/ Sidney L. Rothman*

down the stairs toward the main floor. I would guess that it was around 3:45 or 4:00 by then. I don't know how many steps there are in that staircase or how high the staircase is. It is covered with carpeting. I was about a third of the way down the stairs when a clerk approached me coming up the stairs with a pile of boxes. He turned to say hello to someone to my left, and walked right into me, causing me to lose my balance. I could feel that I was falling and I tried to keep my balance by pushing against the wall. I was too far from the railing on the right side to grab it. I must have spun around, because I landed very heavily in a sitting position on the bottom step. There wasn't anyone ahead of me on the stairs so I had a clear fall to the bottom. I didn't have any packages or anything else in my hands. I was looking straight ahead, as I always do when I go down stairs. I don't remember anything else about the fall because it all happened so fast.

I experienced immediate and terrible pain in my right lower back and I was unable to rise from the position in

/s/ David J. Richards 2. */s/ Sidney L. Rothman*

which I had fallen. Several persons who identified themselves as store personnel, whose names I do not know, helped me walk to a rest area nearby in the store, from which I was taken shortly after in an ambulance to the Great Oaks Hospital in Fairfield. The ambulance was from Shafer's Ambulance Service, in Fairfield.

I spent seven nights in the hospital, undergoing various tests and treatments. My doctor, Dr. William M. Peters, of Fairfield, decided against an operation at this time. I was discharged on November 27, and spent approximately one week in bed at home, during which time my wife cared for me.

I returned to work on December 18, but as yet I have been unable to return to my normal activities, which include field trips of various sorts to construction jobs being performed by our company. At the present time I am

/s/ David J. Richards 3. */s/ Sidney L. Rothman*

on a salary with Grayson & Sons, making $73,000 a year before taxes. Since I came with the firm, I have advanced steadily and am presently in charge of our heavy construction department.

The pain in my back has diminished some since the fall in the department store, but I have been unable to engage in many of the activities which I was accustomed to before the accident, such as tennis and doing jobs around the house. Since my discharge from the hospital I have worn a brace on my back, and I have seen my doctor a number of times. However, the pain and the accompanying incapacity continue. I have had recurrent attacks of pain in my lower back throughout most of my adult life, but it has never lasted more than two or three days and it has never incapacitated me in any appreciable way.

I have read this statement of four pages, and it is true to the best of my knowledge and belief.

/s/ David J. Richards 4. */s/ Sidney L. Rothman*

William M. Peters, M.D.
240 West Plain Street
Fairfield, Columbia

March 23

Richards & Berger, Attorneys
4000 Main Street
Fairfield, Columbia

Dear Sirs:

Mr. Sidney Rothman has been a patient of mine for over 11 years. I was called to see him at the Great Oaks Hospital on the afternoon of November 20, last year. The patient reported having fallen earlier that day, injuring his lower back. He complained of severe pain in the lumbo-sacral area with accompanying pain in the posterior right calf, indicating some sciatic nerve root involvement in the right thigh and leg. Examination of the patient on November 20, including employment of the Nafzigger test and the straight leg raising test indicated the strong possibility of a herniated disc being present at the L5-S1 levels. X-ray examination the following day revealed a narrowing of the lumbar 4-5 sacral interspace, suggesting that the herniation was located at the level of the fifth lumbar disc space. No earlier X-rays of the lumbar area are available for purposes of comparison. Based upon my examination of the patient and the X-rays, it is my opinion that the patient is suffering from a herniated disc at the L5 level. During the patient's stay in the hospital, I called Dr. Hall Gordon, an orthopedic surgeon with a great deal of experience in these matters. His diagnosis was consistent with mine.

In cases of this sort I advise my patients to employ conservative treatment for an indefinite period of time before resorting to surgery. Therefore, I recommended several weeks bed rest and extended diathermy treatments of the area affected. In addition, a Williams-type back brace has been employed in an effort to achieve stabilization of the patient's lower spine in order to promote a resolution of the nerve root involvement. However, in some cases of this type, despite physiotherapy to the patient's spine, low back pain persists. If the pain persists in Mr. Rothman's case, I will recommend that he undergo a CAT scan, and if that shows a problem, it will probably be necessary for him to undergo a myelographic examination. Eventually, surgical stabilization and removal of the herniated disc may be required. Surgery of this sort is expensive and involves some risks of paralysis to the patient, and I therefore prefer to give conservative treatment every chance in cases of this sort.

As for the cause of the herniation in this case, it was probably produced by the patient's fall on November 20. There is no indication of any other possible cause. The patient has a history of some back pain in the past, but it is doubtful it would have been caused by a herniated disc in light of the active nature of his life during this period. The X-rays reveal no arthritis or any other congenital defects or traumatically produced conditions other than the herniation in question which could in any way be contributing to Mr. Rothman's present incapacity.

Sincerely,

William M Peters

William M. Peters, M.D.

Randolph Copich, M.D.
Sanford Medical Building
Fairfield, Columbia

March 27

Richards & Berger, Attorneys at Law
4000 Main Street
Fairfield, Columbia

Dear Sirs:

At the request of the Reliance Insurance Company, I have examined Sidney L. Rothman for the purpose of evaluating the condition of his lower back in connection with a fall he is said to have had on a stairway in Tompkins Department Store. The results of my examination are as follows:

First, it is by no means certain that the patient, Mr. Rothman, has experienced any injury to his back beyond the spraining of certain ligaments in the lumbar region. I have examined the X-rays taken later on November 22, last year, and I have had additional X-rays taken at my clinic, and in both instances it is impossible to detect a fracture of any of the vertebrae or a herniation of any of the intervertebral discs. There is at most a slight narrowing of the lumbar 4-5 sacral interspace, but that is perfectly consistent with the natural condition of the patient's spine. Without a CAT scan and myelographical examination of the area in question, which I am told the attending physician, Dr. Peters, is opposed to, it is impossible to conclude that the patient is suffering from a herniated disc.

Second, it is not at all clear that any traumatically produced injury to the patient's lower back originated with his fall on November 20. My interview of the patient indicates that he has suffered some intermittent lower back pain for more than twenty years. It appears that he played football both in high school and in college, and it is very possible that some injury to his lower back occurred during that period. It is possible (and, in light of the patient's history of low back pain, probable) that he exposed the lumbar region to severe shock and trauma resulting in a chronic instability of the vertebrae at the L5-S1 level. The fall on November 20 may have merely aggravated what could properly be described as a preexisting condition of instability.

In any event, it is my opinion that the patient has a marked tendency to exaggerate the pain he claims to be suffering in this case, and that the physical indications do not support his subjective descriptions of pain.

Sincerely,

Randolph Copich

Randolph Copich, M.D.

Grayson & Sons
Civil Engineers
382 Main Street
Fairfield, Columbia

March 24

Richards & Berger, Attorneys
4000 Main Street
Fairfield, Columbia

Dear Sirs:

Mr. Sidney Rothman has been part of our organization here at G. & S. for 9 years. He is a most competent engineer and, at least until his recent accident, was one of our most valuable supervisors. His salary for this year will, with bonuses, exceed $73,000. He missed approximately 4 weeks of work due to the accident, but we paid him without deduction for the time he lost. We have assured him that he need not worry over his position with our firm, but frankly his present physical condition does cause some concern in our minds over his future usefulness to us. As you probably know, civil engineering of the sort we are engaged in is an active, "get up and go" occupation requiring a lot of physical activity. Jobs must be checked at construction sites, and so on. Sid Rothman was probably headed for a position of major responsibility in our construction operations. It is possible that in another 5 years or so he might have been part of our executive management picture, at a salary in excess of $95,000 a year. If he does not manage eventually to pull himself together physically, however, it is difficult to predict the role he may be playing in the future growth and development of our company.

Sincerely,

Parker G. Grayson

Parker G. Grayson, President

15 Beacon Road
Fairfield, Columbia
October 15

Richards & Berger, Attorneys at Law
4000 Main Street
Fairfield, Columbia

Dear Mr. Richards:

As you requested when I visited your office, I am writing this letter to keep you up to date on my physical condition at the present time. I don't know if this hurts our case or not, but I have followed Dr. Peters' orders and have avoided all strenuous physical exercise and the like, and it seems to be paying off. At my last visit to Dr. Peters' office earlier this week, we discussed my progress and more or less concluded that an operation won't be necessary after all. As he explained, it is my decision. The way things are going, it looks like this thing will resolve itself with just taking it easy. I have had to give up tennis, and I haven't gotten back to a full schedule at work, but I honestly think that in time I will be able to return to these activities.

I have finally collected all the bills for my medical expenses, which I am enclosing. As you can see, they total $6,978.23. Of that amount, $5,582.58 was covered by my medical insurance, and I am enclosing the statements from Blue Cross.

If I can be of any further help in preparing our case, just let me know.

Best regards,

Sidney L. Rothman

William M. Peters, M.D.
240 West Plain Street
Fairfield, Columbia

October 16

Richards & Berger, Attorneys
4000 Main Street
Fairfield, Columbia

Dear Mr. Richards:

Pursuant to your request by letter dated October 11, I am writing to bring you up to date on the progress of Sidney Rothman. Briefly stated, he appears to be responding quite favorably to the conservative treatments that I have prescribed, and it does not appear that, barring some unforeseeable mishap or reinjury to his lower back, an operation will be necessary. He is still somewhat restricted in his physical activities, and may never be able fully to return to his former routine of heavy physical exercise without suffering a recurrence of pain. He is a remarkably fit individual, however, and I personally believe, at his present rate of recovery, that he will have achieved what might be called a "return to normal activity" within six months to a year. Whether he will ever play tennis again is somewhat in doubt, but he should be able to return to full activities in connection with his job.

In your letter, you asked what the medical costs of an operation on Mr. Rothman's back would be, if it were to come to that. It is impossible to be precise, but I can assure you that it would be expensive. My conservative estimate is that it would be between $50,000 and $60,000. It is possible that it could be a bit less, and may even be more, depending on what would be determined to be needed at the time of the surgery, and how much medical costs will have gone up. As I have indicated, I believe that surgery will not be necessary, but of course it can't be ruled out completely.

Sincerely,

William M. Peters

William M. Peters, M.D.

Contingent Fee Agreement

Date March 17, 1987

The Client, Sidney L. Rothman, Fairfield, Cal.

(Name and Address)

Retains the Attorney Richards & Berger, 4000 Main St.

(Name and Address)

To represent him in the following matter:

The Client hereby agrees to pay the Attorney from any recovery in the above matter in accordance with the following schedule:

1. Settlement before suit is instituted 25%
2. Settlement after suit is instituted but before trial 33⅓%
3. Recovery or settlement after commencing trial but before entry of case in appellate court 40%
4. Recovery or settlement after entry of case in appellate court 50%

These percentages shall apply to the full amount of recovery or settlement without deduction for expenses and disbursements. The Client shall be liable to the Attorney regardless of the outcome of the case for such expenses and disbursements.

Sidney L. Rothman

(Signature of Client)

David J. Richards

(Signature of Attorney)

Bailey, Back Injuries

Basic Personal Injury Anatomy 159, 161-163, 165-167, 171 (Collins and Wood, eds. 1965)

I. Anatomy of Back

A. Spinal Column

1. [§5.1] Components

The spinal column is a flexible assemblage of individual segments of bone called vertebrae. There are normally seven cervical (neck) vertebrae, twelve dorsal or thoracic (chest) vertebrae, and five lumbar (low back) vertebrae. Each section moves with the structures above and below. The sacrum is composed of five vertebrae that fused during the early stage of embryonic life to form a solid body mass. . . .

Each vertebra is described by a number: C-2, L-1, D-12, etc. . . .

B. Vertebrae

1. [§5.3] Vertebral Body . . .

The bodies of the vertebrae are connected by the intervertebral disc structures made up of a tough ring of annulus fibrosus and a semigelatinous nucleus pulposus. On its upper (superior) and lower (inferior) surfaces, each vertebral body is covered with a thin plate of hyaline cartilage.

C. Intervertebral Disc

1. [§5.5] Location . . .

The discs or fibrocartilages are interposed between the surfaces of the vertebral bodies from the second cervical vertebra to the sacrum, and they form strong bonds between the adjacent vertebra. . . .

2. Components

a. [§5.6] Annulus Fibrosus

Each intervertebral disc has two constituents, the annulus fibrosus and the nucleus pulposus. The annulus fibrosus is composed of laminae (layers) of fibrous tissue. . . .

b. [§5.7] Nucleus Pulposus

The nucleus pulposus has a pulpy or mucoid character, is yellowish in color, and has a consistency somewhat like gristle. . . . The nucleus is somewhat plastic in nature, and because of this it tends to obey the law of fluids when there is movement of the vertebral column—it is neither compressible nor expansible. . . .

3. [§5.8] Function

The elasticity of the disc under pressure indicates that it functions as a shock absorber for the vertebrae. . . .

It should be evident that the amount of force to which the annulus fibrosus is subjected with various activities of the spine is tremendous. Its anatomy suggests great strength. Not only must it resist the pressures exerted on it by the nucleus pulposus, but it must act also as a retainer, during extreme bending, because it binds the vertebral bodies together. . . .

II. Mechanics of Rupture

A. [§5.15] Location

About 95 percent of all ruptures of the lumbar intervertebral disc occur between the fourth and fifth lumbar, or fifth lumbar and first sacral, vertebrae. The remaining 5 percent occur between the third and fourth or second and third lumbar vertebrae. Rupture of the annulus fibrosus fibers allows displacement or herniation of the nucleus pulposus.

Delaney v. The Empire Insurance Co.

469 So. 2d 1173 (La. App. 1985)

GUIDRY, J. This suit arose out of a vehicular collision on June 11, 1980, in which a vehicle driven by Lloyd Pickens rear-ended an automobile occupied by plaintiffs, Doris and Robert Delaney. Plaintiffs named as defendants Pickens, his employer, Kimbel Trucking Company, and Empire Insurance Company, the latter's insurer. . . .

On January 24, 1984, jury selection began in this case and, on January 27, 1984, the jury returned a verdict in favor of plaintiffs as follows: . . .

Robert Delaney	
Special Damages	$11,550.00
General Damages	43,350.00
Total	54,900.00

Judgment was rendered and signed accordingly. Empire has appealed urging that the jury awards are excessive. . . .

Mr. Delaney was brought to the emergency room at St. Francis Cabrini Hospital minutes after the rear-end collision took place. Mr. Delaney was given medication for his complaints of lower back pain and sent home. The following day, June 12, 1980, Mr. Delaney's pain had not subsided so he sought medical attention from Dr. Defee. After examining Mr. Delaney, Dr. Defee admitted him to the Doctors Hospital of Tioga where he remained until June 28, 1980. During his stay in the hospital, Mr. Delaney was treated with muscle relaxers, anti-inflammatory drugs and physical therapy.

Over the next two years, Mr. Delaney was treated by a number of physicians for his back ailment. Finally, in April of 1982, Mr. Delaney checked into the Diagnostic Center Hospital in Houston, Texas. Dr. Enrigue Raso, a neurosurgeon, recommended surgery to Mr. Delaney after examining the results of a myelogram performed on him.

According to Dr. Raso, the myelogram indicated a narrowing of the lumbar spaces at two levels, L2-3 and L3-4, and also scar tissue from previous back surgeries. On May 4, 1982, Dr. Raso performed a laminectomy on Mr. Delaney. Fragments of an extruded disc and scar tissue were excised at the L4-5 level, additionally, nerves in this region were freed by a procedure known as a foraminotomy. Dr. Raso explained that an extruded disc means that a fragment of the disc has come out of place. Dr. Raso observed that Mr. Delaney also had spinal stenosis, which is a narrowing of the spine. Dr. Raso opined that the vehicular collision of June, 1980, did not cause the pathology he observed in Mr. Delaney but it could very well have made it symptomatic.

Mr. Delaney had two laminectomies performed on him in 1976. The laminectomies were the result of a serious back injury sustained by him while employed by the City of Alexandria. The injury left him permanently disabled.

Empire argues, on appeal, that the surgery conducted by Dr. Raso was for a condition which was caused by his injury in 1976, not the June, 1980 accident.

Undoubtedly, Mr. Delaney's back problems do relate to the injury of 1976. However, as noted by Dr. Raso, Mr. Delaney's complaints of severe pain did not occur until after the 1980 accident, which suggests that the 1980 accident made the condition symptomatic. Although Mr. Delaney did experience some back pain prior to June, 1980, the pain was much more severe after the accident.

According to Mr. Delaney, the 1976 injury severely restricted his activities but he was able to fish, camp, do a little yard work and travel. However, Mr. Delaney added that subsequent to the 1980 accident, he has been unable to engage in any of these activities because of the severe pain he must endure. Members of Mr. Delaney's family corroborated his testimony in this connection. . . .

In light of the jury's wide discretion in quantum awards, we cannot say that the jury's award of $46,350.00 in general damages to Mr. Delaney was an abuse of that discretion. Moreover, there is ample evidence in the record to support the jury's award of $11,550.00 in special damages. . . .

Affirmed. . . .

Mechanisms for Resolving Disputes: Settlement

One of the main purposes of the materials in this section is to introduce the student to the settlement process as an indispensable mechanism for resolving disputes in our system. For every torts dispute that is resolved by means of the formal adjudicative process, many more are resolved by means of settlement. The expense and delay incident to adjudication contribute to the pressures on both parties to settle, especially in smaller cases of up to $1,000 or $2,000. Indeed, one practicing attorney estimated that it would take a verdict of $2,700 to cover the plaintiff's lawyer's overhead and expenses involved in the trial of the case. See Hermann, Fair Dealing in Personal Injury Cases, 10 Clev.-Mar. L. Rev. 449, 450 (1961). No doubt this figure has increased considerably in the intervening years. The inherent unpredictability of adjudication also exerts pressure to settle, even in the minority of cases where the damages may be very large. Contrary to what one might have otherwise assumed, it is the uncertainty, and not the certainty, of a given case that exerts the greater pressure upon the parties to settle prior to final judicial determination. Whenever the plaintiff and defendant in a torts dispute enter into settlement negotiations, they assume the roles of seller and buyer in a contractual setting. If a mutually agreeable settlement figure is reached, the plaintiff sells to the defendant the right to bring legal action and receives from the defendant a liquidated, lump sum payment in money. The promise not to sue that the plaintiff makes it legally binding to the same extent as any other promise given for adequate consideration, and may be raised by the defendant as an absolute bar to any later action by the plaintiff based upon the claim in question. It follows that in order for a settlement to take place, both sides to a dispute must believe that they stand to gain from the contemplated contractual exchange. Both parties must believe, in other words, that they have something to lose by proceeding further with the formal torts process. It is the uncertainty inherent in most cases that helps to provide the setting necessary for both parties to see some substantial benefit in resorting to the settlement process.

One method to encourage the settlement of disputes without trial in cases brought in federal court is embodied in Rule 68 of the Federal Rules of Civil Procedure. Under this rule, if one party makes an offer of settlement that is rejected by the other, the rejecting party must pay the costs incurred after the offer is made if the outcome to that party is not more favorable than the offer. For a discussion of the application and limitations of the rule, see Varon, Promoting Settlements and Limiting Litigation Costs by Means of Offer of Judgment: Some Suggestions for Using and Revising Rule 68, 33 Am. U.L. Rev. 813 (1984).

The preceding paragraphs may carry the implication that settlement occurs, if at all, before trial and judgment. In the vast majority of settled cases, that is the point in the process where settlement does occur. But a case may be settled after judgment is entered at the trial, and even after the case has been appealed. In fact, one recent study of Rand Corporation's Institute for Civil Justice indicates that 20 percent of plaintiffs end up recovering less than their judgments at the trials, and that settlements account for 62 percent of that number. See L.A. Times, July 7, 1987, at 3, col. 1.

The plaintiff's lawyer conducts a great many, perhaps the substantial majority of, settlement negotiations with representatives of insurance companies. Were it not for the insurance money it would not be worth the lawyer's time and the plaintiff's expense to advance the claim in many cases. In any event, it is worthwhile to reflect a moment upon the manner in which insurance companies approach the settlement process. In a word, they approach it with a singular absence of sentimentality. They are not charitable organizations; they are privately owned business institutions designed and operated to maximize profits. Short of fraudulent or otherwise illegal conduct, the company managers are encouraged in our free enterprise system to settle cases brought against their insureds for as little as possible. The representative of the insurance company assigned to handle a claim seeks to determine what is commonly referred to as the company's exposure to liability—that is, the amount (up to applicable policy limits) representing the maximum which the company reasonably might be called upon by a jury to pay upon a finding of liability, adjusted by a factor representing the realistic probability of such a finding. From this base figure a reserve is created on the books of the company which statistical experience dictates should cover the company's exposure to liability. The reserve is an amount out of the general assets of the company that has been set aside for application, when and if needed, to the case until it is finally resolved. It appears as a liability on the company's books. If the plaintiff ultimately obtains a judgment in excess of this reserve, then of course the company must pay it up to (and sometimes exceeding) policy limits. But the reserve represents the company's expert's opinion of what the plaintiff is likely to receive, adjusted by the probability of receiving it. It is never revealed to the plaintiff and represents from the company's point of view a ceiling on what they will be willing to settle for. Actually, the goal of the claims manager will be to settle for a figure substantially below the reserve in a particular case, thereby creating at least the impression that the manager has saved his company money. It should come as no surprise that in order to provide enough room to maneuver comfortably below the reserve figure, the first figure the claims manager advances will often appear depressingly low to the plaintiff.

From the point of view of the plaintiff's attorney, an evaluation process is followed which is very similar to that just described, except that no reserve is created and the figures arrived at are, therefore, not formalized to the same extent. The plaintiff's lawyer is in a more flexible position relative to the bargaining process. The client may and probably will place pressure upon his attorney to obtain a generous settlement. But the client is rarely in a position to judge what is "generous," relatively speaking, and may in the end look largely to the attorney for assurances that the settlement obtained is a fair one. In any event, it is clear that the plaintiff will start off asking for more than the insurer is likely to pay to leave adequate room for the give and take of bargaining. The plaintiff's lawyer ordinarily will not ask what he or she believes to be a preposterous figure. Not only must the lawyer appear to be minimally desirous of settling the case in order for the insurance company to take the offer seriously and begin to make serious counteroffers; but also the lawyer faces the difficult task of explaining to even the timid client why "we asked for 10,000 but settled for 10."

And so the settlement process is formally launched with a demand by the plaintiff who usually (but by no means always) goes first, and a responding counteroffer by the defendant. Usually, these figures are separated by some distance, but not be too far apart, so that the settlement process breaks down. Essentially, it is like the bartering that accompanies the purchase and sale of any item of questionable or arguable value.

The literature on the settlement process is rich and varied. Many articles appear in lawyers' professional journals and are written from the perspective of either the plaintiff's or defendant's lawyer. In recent years, the negotiation process has been the subject of more neutral academic study and many law schools now have courses in negotiation. See Bastress and Harbaugh, Interviewing, Counseling, and Negotiating—Skills for Effective Representation (1990). The article from which the following excerpts are taken surveys the literature. Of relevance to the preceding problem is Professor Gifford's analysis of negotiation strategies.

Gifford, A Context-Based Theory of Strategy Selection in Legal Negotiations

46 Ohio St., L.J. 41, 45-58, 60-64, 66-67, 71, 87 (1985)

II. A Basic Typology of Negotiation Strategies

The type of negotiation strategy likely to yield the most favorable outcome for a client is an important question, because the attorney is professionally obligated to seek an advantageous result for her client in all negotiations. During the last twenty years, negotiation theorists from various disciplines including law, social psychology, economics, and international relations have debated vigorously the attributes of various approaches to negotiation. This section defines the characteristics of three primary negotiation strategies and suggests that the negotiator's view of his relationship with the other party is the primary determinant that identifies each theory and distinguishes it from the others. The competitive negotiator seeks to force the opposing party to a settlement favorable to the negotiator by convincing the opponent that his case is not as strong as previously thought and that he should settle the case. The cooperative strategy mandates that the negotiator make concessions to build trust in the other party and encourage further concessions on his part. The third strategy, integrative bargaining, seeks to find solutions to the conflict which satisfy the interests of both parties. . . .

A negotiation strategy is a separate and distinct concept from the negotiator's personal characteristics; a strategy is the negotiator's planned and systematic attempt to move the negotiation process toward a resolution favorable to his client's interests. Negotiation strategy consists of the decisions made regarding the opening bid and the subsequent modifications of proposals. Admittedly, strategy and personal style are frequently intertwined. A negotiator who has a "forceful, aggressive, and attacking" personal style frequently will succeed in causing an opponent to lose confidence in himself or his case thereby inducing substantial unilateral concessions, a goal of the competitive strategy. In another instance, however, a negotiator who is "courteous, personable, and friendly" may, through competitive strategic moves such as high opening demands and infrequent concessions, be even more successful in destroying the opponent's confidence in his case and inducing unilateral concessions from the opponent. Usually, a negotiator's personal characteristics positively correlate with his preferred negotiating strategy. Separating personal style and negotiation strategies, however, yields new flexibility for the negotiator. It is possible for negotiators with cooperative personal characteristics to adopt a competitive strategy when it would be advantageous, and naturally competitive individuals can adopt a cooperative strategy. Further, a negotiator should often make competitive, cooperative, and integrative moves within a single negotiation. If negotiation strategies are recognized as something distinct from the personal style of negotiators, then the essential elements of each strategy can be disseminated in writing and taught to prospective negotiators. Short of psychoanalysis, however, it might be difficult or impossible to transform a naturally "courteous, personable, and friendly" individual, even temporarily, into someone who is "attacking, forceful, and aggressive."

A. The Competitive Strategy

The competitive negotiator tries to maximize the benefits for his client by convincing his opponent to settle for less than she otherwise would have at the outset of the negotiation process. The basic premise underlying the competitive strategy is that all gains for one's own client are obtained at the expense of the opposing party. The strategy aims to convince the opposing party that her settlement alternative is not as advantageous as she previously thought. Competitive tactics are designed to lessen the opponent's confidence in her case, thereby inducing her to settle for less than she originally asked. The competitive negotiator moves "psychologically against the other person," with behavior designed to unnerve the opponent. Competitive negotiators expect similar behavior from their opponents and therefore mistrust them. In undermining their opponents' confidence, competitive negotiators employ a strategy which often includes the following tactics:

1. a high initial demand;
2. limited disclosure of information regarding facts and one's own preferences;
3. few and small concessions;
4. threats and arguments; and
5. apparent commitment to positions during the negotiating process.

A negotiator who utilizes the competitive strategy begins with a high initial demand. Empirical research repeatedly demonstrates a significant positive relationship between a negotiator's original demand and his payoff. A high initial demand conceals the negotiator's minimum settlement point and allows the negotiator to grant concessions during the negotiating process and still achieve a favorable result. The negotiator's opening position may also include a false issue—a demand that the negotiator does not really care about, but one that can be traded for concessions from the opponent during the negotiation. Generally, the more that the negotiator insists upon a particular demand early in the negotiation, the larger the concession that ultimately will be obtained from the opponent in exchange for dropping that demand. In addition, the opponent may have evaluated the negotiator's case more favorably than the negotiator has; a high demand protects the negotiator from quickly agreeing to a less favorable settlement than one which he might later obtain. If the demand is high but credible, the opponent's response to the demand may also educate the negotiator about how the opponent evaluates her own case.

The competitive negotiator selectively and strategically shares information with his opponent. He does not disclose the least favorable terms to which his client would agree, that is, his minimum reservation point. He prefers to obtain an even more favorable settlement in excess of his reservation point. If the negotiator reveals his reservation point too quickly, the opponent has no incentive to offer anything more than the reservation price. Therefore, the competitive negotiator carefully hides not only his reservation point, but also any information which would allow the opponent to determine his true reservation point. For example, in a criminal case, the prosecutor might conceal from the defense attorney information regarding her caseload, her familiarity with the case, her own vacation plans, and the attitude of the victim toward the case. Conversely, the competitive negotiator selectively discloses information which strengthens his case and which undermines the opponent's case. The competitive negotiator should also pursue tactics that glean information about his opponent's reservation price, his opponent's attitude toward the case, and specific facts about the case.

The competitive strategy of negotiations mandates that the party make as few concessions as possible. If a concession must be made, it should be as small as possible. The competitive negotiator makes concessions reluctantly, because concessions may weaken one's position through both "position loss" and "image loss." Position loss occurs because in most negotiations a norm exists against withdrawing a concession. Further, an early concession results in an opportunity loss for something that might have been extracted in exchange for the concession later in the negotiation process. Image loss occurs because after a concession, the opponent perceives that the negotiator is flexible; in the opponent's mind this may suggest that further concessions can be obtained. Obviously, however, concessions are generally an inevitable part of the negotiating process. Concessions made by a negotiator build an expectation of reciprocity and lead to further concessions by the opponent which bring the parties closer to agreement. Granting concessions prevents premature deadlock and impasse and maintains goodwill with the adversary. This may be necessary to complete the negotiations or to foster a continued cooperative venture in the future. When possible, the competitive negotiator seeks to create the illusion in his opponent's eye that he is making a concession without diminishing his own satisfaction. This is done by either conceding on an issue the negotiator does not care about or appearing to make a concession without really making one.

The competitive negotiator obviously strives to force his opponent into making as many and as large concessions as possible while he makes few concessions, small in degree. To force concessions from his opponent, he employs both arguments and threats. . . .

B. The Cooperative Strategy

A view of human nature different than that upon which the competitive strategy is premised, with its emphasis on undermining the confidence of opposing counsel, underlies most collaborative interaction. In everyday events, even when they are deciding how to divide a limited resource between them, two negotiators often seek to reach an agreement which is fair and equitable to both parties and seek to build an interpersonal relationship based on trust. This approach to negotiation can be designated the cooperative strategy. The cooperative negotiator initiates granting concessions in order to create both a moral obligation to reciprocate and a relationship built on trust that is conducive to achieving a fair agreement.

The cooperative negotiator does not view making concessions as a necessity resulting from a weak bargaining position or a loss of confidence in the value of her case. Rather, she values concessions as an affirmative negotiating technique designed to capitalize on the opponent's desire to reach a fair and just agreement and to maintain an accommodative working relationship. Proponents of the cooperative strategy believe that negotiators are motivated not only by individualistic or competitive desires to maximize their own utilities, but also by collectivistic desires to reach a fair solution. Cooperative negotiators assert that the competitive strategy often leads to resentment between the parties and a breakdown of negotiations.

According to Professor Otomar Bartos, an originator of the cooperative strategy, the negotiator should begin negotiations not with a maximalist position, but rather with a more moderate opening bid that is both favorable to him and barely acceptable to the opponent. Once two such opening bids are on the table, the negotiators should determine the midpoint between the two opening bids and regard it as a fair and equitable outcome. External facts, such as how large a responsive concession the negotiator expects from the opponent, whether she is representing a tough constituency that would view large concessions unfavorably, and whether she is under a tight time deadline and wants to expedite the process by making a large concession, affect the size of the negotiator's first concession. According to Professor Bartos, the negotiator should then expect the opponent to reciprocate with a concession of similar size so that the midpoint between the parties' positions remains the same as it was after the realistic opening bids were made. The concessions by the parties are fair, according to Bartos, as long as the parties do not need to revise their initial expectations about the substance of the agreement.

The term cooperative strategy embraces a larger variety of negotiation tactics than Bartos' detailed model. Cooperative strategies include any strategies that aim to develop trust between the parties and that focus on the expectation that the opponent will match concessions ungrudgingly. Endemic to all cooperative strategies is the question of how the negotiator should respond if the opponent does not match her concessions and does not reciprocate her goodwill. The major weakness of the cooperative approach is its vulnerability to exploitation by the competitive negotiator. The cooperative negotiator is severely disadvantaged if her opponent fails to reciprocate her concessions. Cooperative negotiation theorists suggest a variety of responses when concessions are not matched. Professor Bartos recommends that the negotiator "stop making further concessions until the opponent catches up."

Because of its vulnerability to exploitation, the cooperative theory may not initially appear to be a viable alternative to the competitive strategy. As mentioned previously, in tightly controlled experiments with simulated negotiations, the competitive strategy generally produces better results. However, in actual practice, the competitive approach results in more impasses and greater distrust between the parties. . . .

C. The Integrative Strategy

Both the competitive and cooperative strategies focus on the opposing positions of the negotiators—each negotiator attempts to achieve as many concessions from the other as possible. These concessions move the negotiations closer to an outcome favorable to the negotiator; however, each concession diminishes the opponent's satisfaction with the potential agreement. Integrative bargaining, on the other hand, attempts to reconcile the parties' interests and thus provides high benefits to both. Integrative bargaining is usually associated with a situation in which the parties' interests are not directly opposed and the benefit of one widget for one party does not necessarily result in the loss of one widget for the opponent. Instead, the parties use a problem-solving approach to invent a solution which satisfies the interests of both parties.

Integrative bargaining recently has received widespread attention as the result of the publication of Professors Roger Fisher and William Ury's popular text, *Getting to Yes: Negotiating Agreement Without Giving In.* Professors Fisher and Ury's negotiation strategy is largely based on integrative bargaining theory, although it goes beyond integrative theory in important ways. The authors call their strategy principled negotiation and identify four basic points to this approach:

People: Separate the people from the problem.
Interests: Focus on interests, not positions.
Options: Generate a variety of possibilities before deciding what to do.
Criteria: Insist that the result be based on some objective standard.

The first point distinguishes integrative bargaining from both cooperative bargaining and competitive bargaining, according to Professors Fisher and Ury. The competitive bargainer believes that his relationship with the opponent is important, because he seeks to change the opponent's position through sheer willpower. The cooperative negotiator builds trust in order to reach a fair agreement. In contrast, Professors Fisher and Ury's principled negotiator attempts to separate the interpersonal relationship between the negotiators from the merits of the problem or conflict.

Professors Fisher and Ury's second and third points are the standard components of integrative bargaining theory. The negotiation dance of concession matching or positioning, which is a part of both competitive and cooperative behavior, often obscures the parties' real interests. A major component of integrative bargaining is the free exchange of information between the negotiators so that each party's motives, goals, and values are understood and appreciated. . . .

Traditional integrative bargaining strategy does not have universal applicability. The strategy is utilized most easily when the parties share a problem-solving orientation, and either an identifiable mutual gain option is available or multiple issues which can be traded off against one another exist. It is less useful when the parties disagree on only a single issue and the parties' interests are inherently opposed. Examples of situations that present direct conflicts include personal injury litigation and plea bargaining. . . .

The Lawyer's Professional Responsibility: Problems of the Plaintiff's Lawyer in the Settlement Process

As the preceding note indicates, a substantial body of literature addresses the techniques that are available to lawyers to maximize their clients' positions in the settlement process. In contrast, commentators pay relatively little attention to the professional problems that may arise during the settlement negotiations. And yet, many such problems that put a substantial professional strain on lawyers do arise.

Many of the problems arise because in making the decision to settle or not, the lawyer may find that his or her own personal interests are at odds with those of the client. One example of this potential conflict stems from the fact that most successful, experienced plaintiffs' lawyers make a good portion of their livelihood from settling, not trying, cases. As younger lawyers, they established reputations as fierce and effective trial adversaries. Later, with their reputations accepted, defendants and insurance companies are more willing to settle with them at more acceptable figures. Of course, if what has just been described is accepted at least as a possibility, then it is equally possible that a younger, less well-established attorney may have a personal interest in taking a relatively higher percentage of cases to formal adjudication—how else is he or she to establish the reputation upon which to base the more profitable practice of settling almost all cases?

Another potential source of ethical problems is the contingent fee contract, an example of which is set out above. Under such a contract, the lawyer's compensation does not depend directly on how much effort has been expended to achieve a particular recovery, but rather on the phase the case is at when recovery is achieved. Thus, a lawyer may in a particular case be able to shift from one phase to another by, for example, filing suit or commencing trial, without a substantial increase in work. And with larger cases such a shift may result in a significant increase in compensation even if there is no increase in recovery. Pressures of a different sort operate with smaller cases. In such cases, the higher fee percentage applicable to a later phase will often not provide sufficient additional dollars to make the extra effort of moving to that phase worthwhile to the lawyer. The very human temptation exists, then, to accept many more cases than would otherwise be feasible and then to resolve every doubt in favor of settlement. The lawyer may thus come to have a vested interest in settling all but the most glaring examples of inadequate compensation. The torts practice pursued in this direction takes on the features of a volume wholesaler. Some of the stresses and strains resulting from the contingent fee system are discussed in MacKinnon, Contingent Fees for Legal Services: A Study of Professional Economics and Responsibilities (1964).

Some states have adopted rules relating to contingent fees which set limits on the amount of the fee without regard to the phase at which the case is disposed of. In New Jersey, for instance, contingent fees in tort cases are limited to 50 percent of the first $1,000, 40 percent of the next $2,000, 33⅓ percent of the next $47,000, 25 percent of the next $50,000, 20 percent of the next $150,000, and 10 percent of any amount over $250,000. Rule 1:21-7, Rules Governing the Courts of the State of New Jersey (1980). The constitutionality of this system was upheld in American Trial Lawyers Assn. v. New Jersey Supreme Court, 126 N.J. Super. 577, 316 A.2d 19 (1974). A few moments of reflection will suggest that this system generates its own set of professional stresses. Since the lawyer's percentage share of the recovery may decrease as the recovery increases, the extra effort needed to produce a higher recovery for the client may not be worth it from the lawyer's point of view. This fee system can also exacerbate the problem mentioned below that arises when a lawyer is handling more than one case with the same insurer. Because the lawyer will get a larger portion of the lower settlement, it will be possible for multicase settlements to be so structured as to increase the lawyer's fee while decreasing the overall recovery.

The lawyer's personal financial condition may also influence the decision whether or not to settle. Settling claims rather than trying them, or settling them earlier than they should be, may be the answer to a lawyer's immediate need for funds. This would be particularly true in urban areas, where delay before trial can be measured in years. Another situation in which the temptation is presented to place the client's interests in a secondary position arises when a lawyer who has several different clients with separate claims against the same defendant, or against the same insurance company, meets with the opposing party to settle the several claims together. It is obvious that such a practice puts the plaintiff's lawyer in the position of potentially divided loyalty with respect to the several clients. If the lawyer strikes what he or she believes to be a "hard bargain" with respect to claim number one, this may put the lawyer at a disadvantage when the negotiating parties immediately turn their attention to claim number two. One particularly bad practice is settlement in the aggregate, whereby a single figure for all the claims the lawyer has with the company is agreed upon, with the lawyer dividing this figure among the clients as he or she sees best.

It is difficult to determine how often lawyers engage in these practices. In one study of settlement practices, the author concluded that such conduct did not appear to be a major problem.[9] Part of the difficulty in judging the performance of lawyers in this respect is that it is almost impossible to determine if hidden, but improper, motives lead to unwise settlements. And apart from aggregate settlements, which, in the absence of informed consent by each client, are clear violations of the rules of ethics (Model Rules of Professional Conduct 1.8(g)), no objective standard is available by which

9. See Ross, Settled Out of Court: The Social Process of Insurance Claims Adjustment 83 (1980).

most settlements can be characterized as good or bad. Each case tends to have enough unique aspects so that the range of acceptability is wide enough to make firm, critical judgments difficult. This is not to suggest that lawyers frequently engage in these practices; but the pressures do exist. As with so many problems of professional responsibility, the most effective control is the lawyer's awareness of these personal pressures and a willingness to put the client's interests first. See also Thomason, Are Attorneys Paid What They Are Worth? Contingent Fees and the Settlement Process, 20 J. Legal Stud. 187 (1991), in which the author, using economic analysis, answers in the negative the question posed by the title.

Other problems of professional responsibility occur in the context of settlement negotiations, not because the interests of the lawyer and client conflict, but because of the lawyer's desire to do the best he or she can for the client. One particularly stressful situation, even for the conscientious lawyer, arises in cases involving relatively serious injury. In such cases, clients may have an immediate need for funds to meet their living expenses. A prompt settlement may satisfy this need, but the amount obtained will probably be lower than could have been had if the client were financially able to wait out the negotiation process for a longer time. The lawyer's own interest may be on the side of postponing settlement in order to reach a higher figure, because under the contingent fee contract he or she receives more compensation from higher settlements. Under these circumstances, the temptation is great for the lawyer to advance living expenses to the hard-pressed client to remove the pressure for an early but unwise settlement. The rules of ethics prohibit this (see Model Rules of Professional Conduct 1.7(e)) but nevertheless it does occur. See Carlin, Lawyers on Their Own: A Study of Individual Practitioners in Chicago 74 (1962).

2. Wrongful Death

One of the peculiarities of the common law was the effect of the plaintiff's death upon the right to recover damages in a tort action. No cause of action existed for the death itself, and any cause of action to recover for physical injuries tortiously caused by the defendant's conduct abated—terminated—with the plaintiff's death. See Malone, The Genesis of Wrongful Death, 17 Stan. L. Rev. 1043 (1965); Smedley, Wrongful Death—Bases of the Common Law Rules, 13 Vand. L. Rev. 605 (1960). Thus, if the plaintiff were killed outright by the defendant, no civil action would lie, and if the plaintiff died—even of old age—before obtaining a judgment against the defendant, any cause of action would have died. Similarly, if the defendant were to die before judgment, the cause of action abated.

This state of the law has been changed in England and in every state in the United States. Today, by statute, the death of the plaintiff before judgment has far less devastating effects upon existing or potential rights of recovery against the tortious defendant. Two basic types of statutes accomplish this result. In all jurisdictions, survival statutes prevent abatement of existing causes of action due to the death of either party, and in many jurisdictions, wrongful death statutes create causes of action that allow recovery when tortious conduct of the defendant causes someone's death. Many states have separate statutes of both types. In those jurisdictions which do not have a separate wrongful death statute, the courts have construed the general survival statute to create rights of recovery based upon tortiously caused deaths.

The measures of recovery under these two types of statute differ, reflecting the differences in the underlying statutory objectives. Under survival statutes, the basic measure of recovery is what the plaintiff's decedent would have been able to recover had he or she survived; under wrongful death statutes, the basic measure of recovery is the harm caused to the decedent's family by the defendant's conduct. There are at least three different approaches to measuring the plaintiff's recovery under wrongful death statutes. One approach, found today only in Alabama, is punitive in nature, measuring wrongful death recovery by the degree of fault of the defendant.[10] The two remaining approaches reflect the statutes more commonly encountered throughout the United States. One type of wrongful death statute is patterned after the earliest English statute, Lord Campbell's Act, 1846, 9 & 10 Vict., ch. 93, and measures recovery by the loss (including, in many states, grief and mental anguish) suffered by the surviving family members and next of kin of the decedent. This is by far the most widely adopted measure of recovery for wrongful death in this country. The other type of statute, in effect in a relatively small minority of states, measures recovery by the pecuniary loss suffered by the decedent's estate.

Apart from the preceding broad generalizations, the wrongful death statutes vary considerably from state to state with respect to most of the important provisions. Therefore, the point of departure in any wrongful death case is the controlling statute.

3. Damage to Personal Property

Compared to the rules involved in measuring damages for personal injury and death, the rules in cases of damage to personal property are simple and straightforward. The basic measure is the difference between the market value of the property before the injury and its market value after. If for practical purposes the item has been totally destroyed, the market value after the injury will be the salvage value, if any. Furthermore, in some jurisdictions a plaintiff's total recovery may be limited to an amount not exceeding the preaccident value of the property (see, e.g., Magnolia Petro-

10. See Estes Health Care Center, Inc. v. Bannerman, 411 So. 2d 109 (Ala. 1982).

leum Co. v. Harrell, 66 F. Supp. 559 (W.D. Okla. 1946). See generally Dobbs, Remedies 375-421 (1973).

For an interesting argument that damages should not be available for negligent harm to property, see Abel, Should Tort Law Protect Property Against Accidental Loss?, 23 San Diego L. Rev. 79 (1986).

B. Punitive Damages

Owens-Illinois, Inc. v. Zenobia

325 Md. 420, 601 A.2d 633 (1992)

ELDRIDGE, JUDGE. [The plaintiff sued for damages alleged to have been caused by asbestos manufactured by the defendants. The jury awarded punitive damages against some defendants, including Owens-Illinois. The intermediate appellate court affirmed the punitive damage award against Owens-Illinois, who appealed that issue, among others.]

We issued a writ of certiorari in these cases to consider several important questions [including] some of the principles governing awards of punitive damages in tort cases. . . .

IV

In granting the petitions for a writ of certiorari in these cases, this Court issued an order requesting that the briefs and argument encompass the following issue:

> [W]hat should be the correct standard under Maryland law for the allowance of punitive damages in negligence and products liability cases, i.e., gross negligence, actual malice, or some other standard. . . .

[I]n recent years there has been a proliferation of claims for punitive damages in tort cases, and awards of punitive damages have often been extremely high. . . .

Accompanying this increase in punitive damages claims, awards and amounts of awards, is renewed criticism of the concept of punitive damages in a tort system designed primarily to compensate injured parties for harm. In Maryland the criticism has been partly fueled and justified because juries are provided with imprecise and uncertain characterizations of the type of conduct which will expose a defendant to a potential award of punitive damages. Accordingly, we shall (1) examine these characterizations of a defendant's conduct in light of the historic objectives of punitive damages,

(2) more precisely define the nature of conduct potentially subject to a punitive damages award in nonintentional tort cases, and (3) heighten the standard of proof required of a plaintiff seeking an award of punitive damages.

These cases, along with two others heard by us on the same day, directly raise the problem of what basic standard of wrongful conduct should be used for the allowance of punitive damages in negligence actions generally, and in products liability actions based on either negligence or on strict liability. The jury in these cases received the following instruction on punitive damages:

> Implied malice, which the plaintiffs have to prove in order to recover punitive damages in this case, requires a finding by you of a wanton disposition, grossly irresponsible to the rights of others, extreme recklessness and utter disregard for the rights of others. . . .

[The] court required the plaintiffs to show by a preponderance of evidence that the defendants acted with "implied" rather than "actual" malice. That is, the plaintiffs were not required to show that the defendants' conduct was characterized by evil motive, intent to injure, fraud, or actual knowledge of the defective nature of the products coupled with a deliberate disregard of the consequences. Instead, the plaintiffs were required to show only that the defendants' conduct was grossly negligent.

The standard applied by the trial court . . . results from, and consequently requires reexamination of, some of the decisions of this Court relating to punitive damages. . . .

B . . .

In 1972 this Court, for the first time in a nonintentional tort action, allowed an award of punitive damages based upon implied malice. The Court . . . allow[ed] the plaintiff to recover punitive damages upon a showing that the defendant was guilty of "gross negligence," which was defined as a "wanton or reckless disregard for human life.". . .

The gross negligence standard has led to inconsistent results and frustration of the purposes of punitive damages in nonintentional tort cases. . . .

In the face of "a literal explosion of punitive damage law and practice," many states have acted to define more accurately the type of conduct which can form the basis for a punitive damages award. In Tuttle v. Raymond, 494 A.2d 1353 (Me. 1985), the Supreme Judicial Court of Maine reviewed its law on punitive damages. The implied malice standard applied by the lower courts in *Tuttle* allowed recovery of punitive damages upon a showing that the defendant's conduct was "wanton, malicious, reckless or grossly negligent." 494 A.2d at 1360. The court rejected this standard, stating (494 A.2d at 1361):

> "Gross" negligence simply covers too broad and too vague an area of behavior, resulting in an unfair and inefficient use of the doctrine of punitive damages. . . . A similar problem exists with allowing punitive damages based merely upon "reckless" conduct. "To sanction punitive damages solely upon the basis of conduct characterized as heedless disregard of the consequences would be to allow virtually limitless imposition of punitive damages."

The Maine court went on to point out that the implied malice standard "overextends the availability of punitive damages" and consequently "dulls the potentially keen edge of the doctrine as an effective deterrent of truly reprehensible conduct." Ibid. . . .

As previously indicated, arbitrary and inconsistent application of the standard for awarding punitive damages frustrates the dual purposes of punishment and deterrence. Implied malice as that term has been used, with its various and imprecise formulations, fosters this uncertainty. As pointed out by Professor Ellis, (D. Ellis, Fairness and Efficiency in the Law of Punitive Damages, 56 S. Cal. L. Rev. 1, 52-53 (1982)): "[T]he law of punitive damages is characterized by a high degree of uncertainty that stems from the use of a multiplicity of vague, overlapping terms. . . . Accordingly, there is little reason to believe that only deserving defendants are punished, or that fair notice of punishable conduct is provided.". . .

The implied malice test . . . has been overbroad in its application and has resulted in inconsistent jury verdicts involving similar facts. It provides little guidance for individuals and companies to enable them to predict behavior that will either trigger or avoid punitive damages liability, and it undermines the deterrent effect of these awards. . . . In a nonintentional tort action, the trier of facts may not award punitive damages unless the plaintiff has established that the defendant's conduct was characterized by evil motive, intent to injure, ill will, or fraud, i.e., "actual malice.". . .

E

The defendant Owens-Illinois and some amici have argued that, in order for a jury to consider a punitive damages award, a plaintiff should be required to establish by clear and convincing evidence that the defendant's conduct was characterized by actual malice. . . .

A growing majority of states requires that a plaintiff prove the defendant's malicious conduct by clear and convincing evidence before punitive damages

Many states have adopted the clear and convincing
e. Other states have adopted the standard by judicial

and convincing standard of proof will help to insure ages are properly awarded. We hold that this heightened priate in the assessment of punitive damages because of and potential for debilitating harm. Consequently, in any tiff must establish by clear and convincing evidence the rd of punitive damages. . . .

ng opinion of MCAULIFFE, J. is omitted.]

ELL, JUDGE, concurring and dissenting. . . .

y with the majority on the question of what is the appropriate termining the cases in which punitive damages are appropriate. Whi... have no quarrel with requiring that, in some cases, "actual malice," characterized as "evil motive," "intent to injure," "ill will," "fraud," or, in the case of products liability actions, "actual knowledge of the defective nature of the product, coupled with a deliberate disregard of the consequences," be shown, I am opposed to excising from the standard the concept . . . : "wanton or reckless disregard for human life," sometimes characterized as "gross negligence." That standard, now the old one, is a floor, not a ceiling; it sets a minimum requirement, not a maximum. Therefore, if a defendant acts with "actual malice," however characterized, he or she will be subject to an award of punitive damages under the old standard. On the other hand, by adopting the "actual malice" standard, the majority does much more than excise a useless phrase, it places outside the scope of punitive damages eligibility numerous deserving cases, differing from cases that remain punitive damages eligible only in the subjective element. That change simply goes too far.

The perception is that more claims for punitive damages, involving conduct so diverse that predictability and, therefore, the ability to choose the proper conduct and avoid being culpable, than were justified, were being brought and allowed with the result that the purposes of punitive damages were being undermined. The changes proposed are for the purpose of making the awards more uniform and consistent with the historical bases for punitive damages awards: punishment and deterrence. The purposes of punitive damages are better served, it has been determined, by requiring a more stringent standard for assessing punitive damages and by requiring a greater burden of proof. To be sure, one of the goals of today's decision is to set a higher threshold for punitive damages eligibility. That is accomplished by changing the burden of proof, that clearly will exclude some undeserving cases, no doubt, a large number, even applying the old standard. But, by both changing the burden of proof and the standard, an even greater percentage of deserving cases, heretofore eligible for punitive damages awards, is affected. Indeed, by so doing, not only is the threshold raised, but excluded is an entire category of cases, nonintentional torts, involving, in many instances, injuries of greater severity than in cases that still qualify and, thus, not necessarily those least deserving of an award of punitive damages. And the distinction causing the exclusion is the subjective intent of the defendant. While I can agree, as I have previously indicated, to raising the threshold by raising the level of the proof required, I cannot agree that punitive damages should be awarded only in cases of "actual malice," where there is a subjective intent element. In cases where there is no actual malice, the totality of the circumstances may reveal conduct on the part of a defendant that is just as heinous as the conduct motivated by that actual malice and, so, for all intents and purposes is the same.

Although not intentional, i.e., willful, conduct, nevertheless, may be outrageous and extreme in the context in which it occurs, and may produce injuries commensurate with those caused by intentional conduct. In other words, conduct may be so reckless and outrageous as to be the equivalent of intentional conduct. . . .

Permitting punitive damages when one acts with actual malice, but not when, given the totality of the circumstances, that same person acts in total disregard for the safety of others has no reasoned basis.

Consider the following example. A hot water pipe bursts in a crowded apartment complex quite near an open area upon which young people are playing baseball. A repair team dispatched to make repairs observes young people playing baseball nearby. It also sees that the area of the affected pipe is in easy reach of a baseball hit to the outfield. Nevertheless, they dig a hole, but, being unable to proceed due to the temperature of the water, suspend operations. Although aware of the young people playing in the area, they leave without warning them of the hole or its contents or in any way marking or obstructing the hole. One of the outfielders, having chased and caught a ball hit to the outfield, falls into the hole and is severely injured.

Under the new standard, if it could be proved that a member of the repair team harbored ill will toward the outfielder and, in the back of his mind, entertained a hope that the outfielder, or one of the other players, would fall in the unattended hole, then, in addition to compensable damages, the outfielder could recover punitive damages. On the other hand, if none of the members of the repair team knew any of the ball players and, in fact, harbored no evil motive at all, no punitive damages could be recovered, notwithstanding that they acted, given the circumstances, in total disregard of the safety of the ballplayers. I can see no reasoned difference between these scenarios. The state of mind of the individual simply is not so important a factor as to permit recovery in one case and not in the other.

I am satisfied that allowing punitive damages for "wanton and reckless conduct," . . . serves the purposes of punishment and deterrence. Gross negligence, outrageous conduct, etc. cannot be defined in a vacuum. To have meaning, the terms must be viewed in a factual context. The conduct described in the example is not only outrageous and extraordinary, it is the sine qua non of reckless conduct. Such conduct should be punished. And that scenario presents a striking example of the kind of conduct a defendant must not engage in if he or she is to avoid paying punitive damages. The example I have proffered is not the only one that can be posited. There are hundreds of such cases. The long and short of it is that changing the standard for punitive damages will eliminate numbers of cases, in which, heretofore, punitive damages would have been appropriate and those cases now are eliminated not because their facts are not egregious enough to justify such an award but because other, less serious, and perhaps, undeserving, cases may also qualify for such damages. With all due respect, that is not a sufficiently good reason to change the rules of the game.

Insulating a defendant from an award of punitive damages except when he or she acts with actual malice, meaning with an evil intent, ill will, with intent to injure, or to defraud, provides a disincentive for that defendant to act reasonably. Since, from the standpoint of a defendant's pocketbook, it makes no difference in the award of damages, whether he or she is negligent or grossly negligent, that is, his or her conduct is extreme to a point just short of being intentional, requiring that defendant to pay compensatory damages for the victims's injuries is not likely to have a deterrent effect; it is not likely to cause him or her to consider, not to mention, change, his or her conduct. . . .

Punitive damages have occupied center stage of the torts process in recent years. The critics of punitive damages have argued that a significant and unjustified increase has occurred in the frequency and amount of punitive damage awards. See, e.g., Huber, Liability—The Legal Revolution and Its Consequences 127-132 (1988). A study by the Institute for Civil Justice of the Rand Corporation commissioned by the American Bar Association gives partial support to the assertion that there has been an increase in the frequency and amount of such awards. See Peterson, Sarma, and Shanley, Punitive Damages—Empirical Findings. See also Punitive Damages Explosion: Fact or Fiction? (Am. Tort Reform Assn. 1992). Other studies have concluded that punitive damage awards have remained fairly stable over the years. See Daniels and Martin, Myth and Reality in Punitive Damages, 75 Minn. L. Rev. 1 (1990). However that debate is resolved, if it ever is, no one can doubt that there have been substantial changes in the law of punitive damages in the past two decades or so. What follows is a brief summary of the more significant issues:

1. The constitutionality of punitive damages has been the subject of considerable litigation. In Browning-Ferris Industries of Vermont, Inc. v.

Kelko Disposal, Inc., 492 U.S. 257, 109 S. Ct. 2909, 106 L. Ed. 2d 219 (1989), the Supreme Court ruled that the "excessive fines" clause in the Eighth Amendment to the United States Constitution does not bar punitive damages. In Pacific Mutual Insurance Co. v. Haslip, 499 U.S. 1, 111 S. Ct. 1032, 113 L. Ed. 2d 1 (1991), the Court considered, and rejected, a due process attack on the punitive damages regime of Alabama. In upholding the Alabama law, the Court said (499 U.S. at 18, 21-22, 111 S. Ct. at 1043, 1045, 113 L. Ed. 2d at 20, 22):

> One must concede that unlimited jury discretion—or unlimited judicial discretion for that matter—in the fixing of punitive damages may invite extreme results that jar one's constitutional sensibilities. We need not, and indeed we cannot, draw a mathematical bright line between the constitutionally acceptable and the constitutionally unacceptable that would fit every case. We can say, however, that general concerns of reasonableness and adequate guidance from the court when the case is tried to a jury properly enter into the constitutional calculus. With these concerns in mind, we review the constitutionality of the punitive damages awarded in this case. . . .
>
> [B]efore its ruling in the present case, the Supreme Court of Alabama had elaborated and refined the . . . criteria for determining whether a punitive award is reasonably related to the goals of deterrence and retribution. It was announced that the following could be taken into consideration in determining whether the award was excessive or inadequate: (a) whether there is a reasonable relationship between the punitive damages award and the harm likely to result from the defendant's conduct as well as the harm that actually has occurred; (b) the degree of reprehensibility of the defendant's conduct, the duration of that conduct, the defendant's awareness, any concealment, and the existence and frequency of similar past conduct; (c) the profitability to the defendant of the wrongful conduct and the desirability of removing that profit and of having the defendant also sustain a loss; (d) the "financial position" of the defendant; (e) all the costs of litigation; (f) the imposition of criminal sanctions on the defendant for its conduct, these to be taken in mitigation; and (g) the existence of other civil awards against the defendant for the same conduct, these also to be taken in mitigation.
>
> The application of these standards, we conclude, imposes a sufficiently definite and meaningful constraint on the discretion of Alabama fact finders in awarding punitive damages. The Alabama Supreme Court's post-verdict review ensures that punitive damages awards are not grossly out of proportion to the severity of the offense and have some understandable relationship to compensatory damages. While punitive damages in Alabama may embrace such factors as the heinousness of the civil wrong, its effect upon the victim, the likelihood of its recurrence, and the extent of defendant's wrongful gain, the fact finder must be guided by more than the defendant's net worth. Alabama plaintiffs do not enjoy a windfall because they have the good fortune to have a defendant with a deep pocket.

The lower courts have not viewed *Haslip* as foreclosing inquiry into the constitutionality of punitive damage awards. See, e.g., Mattison v. Dallas

Carrier Corp., 947 F.2d 95 (4th Cir. 1991), in which the court held the South Carolina punitive damage regime unconstitutional because it left no guidance to the jury in determining the amount of the award. The court held that the jury must, as a matter of constitutional law, be told to consider the following (947 F.2d at 110):

> (1) Relationship to harm caused: Any penalty imposed should take into account the reprehensibility of the conduct, the harm caused, the defendant's awareness of the conduct's wrongfulness, the duration of the conduct, and any concealment. Thus any penalty imposed should bear a relationship to the nature and extent of the conduct and the harm caused, including the compensatory damage award made by the jury.
>
> (2) Other penalties for the conduct: Any penalty imposed should take into account as a mitigating factor any other penalty that may have been imposed or which may be imposed for the conduct involved, including any criminal or civil penalty or any other punitive damages award arising out of the same conduct.
>
> (3) Improper profits and plaintiff's costs: The amount of any penalty may focus on depriving the defendant of profits derived from the improper conduct and on awarding the costs to the plaintiff of prosecuting the claim.
>
> (4) Limitation based on ability to pay: Any penalty must be limited to punishment and thus may not effect economic bankruptcy. To this end, the ability of the defendant to pay any punitive award entered should be considered.

See also Johnson v. Hugo's Skateway, 974 F.2d 1408 (4th Cir. 1992) (instruction to jury that it "may add to the award of actual damages such amount as you shall unanimously agree to be proper as punitive or exemplary damages" does not meet the *Haslip* requirements).

In general, see Riggs, Constitutionalizing Punitive Damages: The Limits of Due Process, 52 Ohio St. L.J. 859 (1991).

2. Even though the constitutionality of punitive damages has largely been put to rest, the debate over whether such damages serve a socially useful purpose continues, at least among legal academics. Calling punitive damages into question is Ellis, Fairness and Efficiency in the Law of Punitive Damages, 56 So. Cal. L. Rev. 1, 76, 77 (1982):

> The case for punitive damages is a limited one. Although a number of objectives have been suggested for punitive damages, only two survive scrutiny: retribution and deterrence. Retribution implies desert, which is controlled by the broader principle of fairness. Deterrence seeks to provide a better state of the world through efficient means.
>
> Principles of fairness justify punitive damages only when a wrongful act has been committed with the objective of harming another or when the utility of an act was unequivocally known by the actor to fall far short of the danger created. The vagueness of the criteria for determining punitive damage liability and the attendant discretion accorded to juries extend liability far beyond that

justified by fairness. Notice of activities that will be punished is obscured, and juries are left free to exercise biases and indulge in wealth redistribution. Rather than forgoing the punishment of some guilty persons to avoid punishing the innocent, punishment is imposed on more of the latter group. . . .

Vicarious liability and insurability of punitive damages cause detriments to be imposed on unarguably innocent people, in amounts that far exceed, at least in the aggregate, the amount that the guilty actors could have been assessed.

Without better empirical evidence, it is impossible definitively to establish that the present law of punitive damages does not promote efficiency. The most that can be said is that there is no empirical basis for believing that it does and that the intuitive arguments supporting the proposition are weaker than those against it. Punitive damages can be shown to promote efficient levels of deterrence only in those cases where expected liability for compensatory damages is less than expected harm to society or where harm is deliberately caused and the satisfaction obtained by the actor is "illicit." Present punitive damage law extends far beyond these categories, however, and imposes additional costs on society. The uncertainty of the criteria, the lack of standards for determining the magnitude of damage assessments, the use of the defendant's wealth as a variable, the principle that punitive damages must bear a reasonable relationship to the actual harm caused, vicarious liability, and insurability each result in increased litigation costs. Uncertainty causes litigants and courts to consume additional resources. These resources are expended both in cases where punitive damages are appropriate and in cases where they are not. The other factors mentioned increase the stakes at risk and, therefore, also increase litigation costs. In tandem, their adverse effects on litigation costs are compounded. Litigation resources are attracted to cases involving large actual damages and wealthy, insured, vicarious defendants.

See also Note, An Economic Analysis of the Plaintiff's Windfall from Punitive Damage Litigation, 105 Harv. L. Rev. 1900 (1992) ("[P]unitive damages, in their current form, are economic folly."); Johnston, Punitive Liability: A New Paradigm of Efficiency in Tort Law, 87 Colum. L. Rev. 1385 (1987), and the Symposia in 56 S. Cal. L. Rev 1 (1982) and 40 Ala. L. Rev. 687 (1989).

3. The Supreme Court in *Haslip* found constitutional comfort in the Alabama law because of the relevance of the award to harm actually and likely to be caused by the defendant's conduct. The pre-*Haslip* law as to that relationship was varied. Some courts held that no relationship of the punitive award to compensatory damages was required. See, e.g., Hospital Authority of Gwinnett County v. Jones, 261 Ga. 613, 409 S.E.2d 501 (1991); Kirkbride v. Lisbon Contractors, Inc., 521 Pa. 97, 555 A.2d 800 (1989). Among the courts that do require some relationship between the punitive and compensatory awards, a rather high ratio is sometimes permitted. See, e.g., TXO Production Corp. v. Alliance Resources Corp., 419 S.E.2d 870

(W. Va. 1992), *aff'd* 113 S. Ct. 2711, 125 L. Ed. 2d 366 (1993) (punitive award 500 times compensatory award approved).

Whether the rule that the amount of compensatory damages is irrelevant will survive *Haslip* is questionable. The court in *Mattison* ruled that as a matter of constitutional law, the jury must be told that the punitive award must bear a reasonable relationship to the compensatory award. See also Garnes v. Fleming Landfill, Inc., 186 W. Va. 656, 413 S.E.2d 897 (1991). However, in Caterpillar, Inc. v. Hightower, 605 So. 2d 1193 (Ala. 1992), the Supreme Court of Alabama reaffirmed an early holding that punitive damages may be awarded absent an award for either compensatory or nominal damages, if the plaintiff has suffered least some nominal harm.

4. Debate has also stirred over whether the defendant's wealth should be relevant to the amount of the punitive damage award. Ruling that such evidence is not admissible is Industrial Chemical & Fiberglass Corp. v. Chandler, 547 So. 2d 812 (Ala. 1989), a position supported in Abraham and Jeffries, Jr., Punitive Damages and the Rule of Law: The Role of the Defendant's Wealth, 18(2) J. Legal. Stud. 415 (1989). Most courts, however, have made the defendant's wealth relevant. See, e.g., Adams v. Murakami, 54 Cal. 3d 105, 813 P.2d 1348, 284 Cal. Rptr. 318 (1991). The court in Wollersheim v. Church of Scientology of California, 10 Cal. App. 4th 370, 6 Cal. Rptr. 2d 532, *rev. granted* 10 Cal. Rptr. 2d 182, 832 P.2d 898 (1992), upheld the constitutionality of the California punitive damages awards regime, but ruled that an award of $16 million, which was 150 percent of the defendant's net worth, was clearly excessive and ordered a remittitur to $2 million. An appendix to this opinion lists California punitive damage awards reviewed on appeal from 1981, with a comparison of the amount of the awards to the wealth of the defendants and the amount of compensatory damages.

5. Given the purpose of punitive damages as stated by the Supreme Court in *Haslip*—deterrence and punishment—it might be expected that such damages would not be insurable. To permit the defendant to avoid personally paying the damages would undercut the deterrent and punishment message that the award is intended to convey. And some courts have so ruled. See, e.g., Public Service Mutual Insurance Co. v. Goldfarb, 53 N.Y.2d 392, 425 N.E.2d 810, 442 N.Y.S.2d 422 (1981). Other courts have held that punitive damages are insurable, if the insurance policy provides for such coverage. See, e.g., South Carolina State Budget & Control Board v. Prince, 304 S.C. 241, 403 S.E.2d 643 (1991). And still other courts have ruled that punitive damages are insurable only if they are imposed vicariously on the defendant. See, e.g., U.S. Concrete Pipe Co. v. Bould, 437 So. 2d 1061 (Fla. 1983).

6. Since the punitive damage award, in theory at least, is geared to the wrongdoing of the defendant, it might be expected that where there are multiple defendants, punitive damages would not be subject to joint and several liability. And some courts have so held. See, e.g., Owens-Illinois,

Inc. v. Armstrong, 326 Md. 107, 604 A.2d 47 (1992), and Straudacher v. City of Buffalo, 115 A.D.2d 956, 547 N.Y.S.2d 770 (1989). But other courts have imposed joint and several liability for punitive damages. See, e.g., Radford v. J.J.B. Enterprises, Ltd., 472 N.W.2d 790 (Wis. App. 1991).

7. The Supreme Court in *Haslip* suggested a concern with the problem of multiple punishment for the same conduct, and the Court of Appeals for the 4th Circuit in *Mattison* ruled that juries must be told to consider other punishments that have been or may be imposed on the defendant. In one case, Juzwin v. Amtorg Trading Corp., 705 F. Supp. 1053 (D. N.J. 1989), the court held that multiple punitive awards based on the same conduct are unconstitutional. However, the court vacated the order, in part on the grounds that later awards could not be prohibited by that court. Juzwin v. Amtorg Trading Corp., 718 F. Supp. 1233 (D. N.J. 1989). Taking a different view of the constitutional issues, the court in McBride v. General Motors Corp., 737 F. Supp. 1563 (M.D. Ga. 1990), held that a "one award" punitive damages statute violated the equal protection and due process clauses of the Federal and Georgia constitutions. The statute provided that a punitive damages award could be assessed against a products liability defendant only once, regardless of how many separate causes of action arose out of the defendant's conduct. At least two courts have held that punitive damages can be awarded against a defendant who has been convicted of a crime for conduct upon which the punitive award is based. See Eddy v. McGinnis, 523 N.E.2d 737 (Ind. 1988); Whittman v. Gilson, 70 N.Y.2d 970, 520 N.E.2d 514 (1988). Presumably, the defendant is now entitled to have the jury consider the earlier awards or criminal convictions, but for tactical reasons a defendant may be reluctant to make any earlier award or conviction known to the jury.

A Missouri statute permits the defendant in a post-verdict motion to ask the judge for credit for punitive damages earlier awarded based on the same conduct. See Mo. Stat. Ann. §510.263 (Supp. 1992).

8. Considerable state legislation aims at controlling the amount of punitive damage awards, evidencing a mistrust in the ability or willingness of courts to control jury discretion in this respect. A fairly common method is the establishing of a maximum that can be awarded. See, e.g., Code of Va. §8.01-38.1 (total punitive damages cannot exceed $350,000 in "any action"); Tex. Civ. Prac. & Rems. Code §41.008 (Supp. 1992) (except where harm intentionally caused, punitive damage award cannot exceed $200,000 or four times actual damages, whichever is greater). A more flexible approach to limiting the amount of the award is contained in Fla. Stat. Ann. Ch. 768.73, which provides that an award in excess of three times compensatory damages is presumed to be excessive; the plaintiff can recover the higher amount only by establishing by clear and convincing evidence that the award is supported by the facts.

Some legislatures have addressed the "windfall" aspect of punitive damages (see Note, An Economic Analysis of the Plaintiff's Windfall from

Punitive Damage Litigation, 105 Harv. L. Rev. 1900 (1992)) by channeling part of the award to the state. See, e.g., Fla. Stat. Ann. ch. 768.73(2)(a) (1992 Supp.) (35 percent of the award paid to either of two state funds); N.Y. CPLR §8701 (1992 Supp.) (20 percent of the award paid to the state). The constitutionality of the Florida statute was upheld in Gordon v. State, 608 So. 2d 800 (Fla. 1992), *cert. denied* 113 S. Ct. 1647 (1993), against a charge that it takes private property without compensation. A similar constitutional claim succeeded in Kirk v. Denver Publishing Co., 818 P.2d 262 (Colo. 1991), in which the court held that a statute requiring one-third of punitive awards to be paid to the state's general fund was an unconstitutional taking. The venturesome trial judge in Smith v. States General Life Insurance Co., 592 So. 2d 1021 (Ala. 1992), allocated, with no legislative authority, one-half of the punitive award to the American Heart Association. On appeal, the Supreme Court of Alabama ruled that the trial judge lacked power to so divert any part of the plaintiff's recovery.

Chapter 9

Liability Insurance: Settlement Conflicts

Liability insurance began in England in the 1880s to protect employers against liability to injured employees. Since then, it has become an integral part of the torts process, and is available to protect against tort liability arising from almost every human activity. Although precise statistics are not available, in the larger proportion of torts claims the defendant is to some extent insured against liability. Insurance has even hyphenated its way into the description of the torts process, and the phrases "fault-insurance" and "negligence-insurance" are commonly applied to the system of allocating accident losses in this country.

It is beyond the limited scope of this chapter to deal with the full range of liability insurance problems. Extended coverage must be left to upper class courses in insurance. Rather, we focus here on a recurring problem of immediate concern to lawyers involved in a tort claim in which liability insurance is available: the obligations of insurers and insureds to handle tort settlements in good faith. See Syverud, Toward a Workable Duty to Settle for Liability Insurers: A Reply, 77 Va. L. Rev. 1597 (1991).

Although this chapter is sharply focussed on settlement, a bit of general background will be helpful. The basic mechanics of liability insurance are relatively simple. The insurance company and the insured enter into a contract, embodied in the policy, whereby in exchange for the premium paid by the insured the company agrees to defend any claim against the insured covered by the policy and to pay to the claimant any amount, up to the limits stated in the policy,[1] that the insured becomes legally obligated to pay to the claimant. In addition to having the duty to defend, the insurer also has the right to defend, and thus takes over the effective management of the claim. Thus, when the claim is within policy limits and the company admits coverage, the insured assumes a decidedly secondary role and is more like a witness than a party. Typically, the insured does not even participate in the settlement negotiations, and any unauthorized settlement agreed to by the insured is not binding on the insurer. Indeed, the decision to settle the claim within policy limits or defend the claim is more often than not made by the insurer with little or no consultation with the insured.

1. Liability insurance is available with different limits of liability. With automobile insurance, the limits are usually stated as a certain amount for each person injured, and generally a higher amount for each accident.

See Marginian v. Allstate Insurance Co., 18 Ohio St. 3d 345, 481 N.E.2d 600 (1985), in which the court ruled that the insurer could settle the claims against the insured within policy limits in the face of specific objection to the settlement by the insured. And if the claim does go to trial, in most instances the lawyer for the defense will be selected and paid by the insurer. Thus, from the perspective of everyone involved with the claim, the real defender of the claim in most cases is the insurer.[2]

Everything said above is relevant only when the company admits coverage and the tort claim is within policy limits. When the company disputes coverage, the company has several options. It can notify the insured that it denies coverage and will not participate in the tort defense, leaving the defense and the associated expenses to the insured. A separate action is commenced to determine the issue of coverage. If the company loses on coverage, it owes the insured the coverage on the policy up to applicable limits; reasonable costs of the tort defense; and, in some states, tort damages for mental upset and the like.

The other option open to the company is to agree to defend the tort claim under a reservation of rights or a nonwaiver agreement that preserves the company's right to dispute coverage in a separate proceeding. In that instance, the company advises the insured of the potential conflict of interest and of the possible need for the insured to retain independent counsel in connection with the tort proceedings. Jurisdictions vary over whether the company must pay for plaintiff's independent counsel. Many states call for payment by the company if insurance coverage is subsequently found. In San Diego Navy Federal Credit Union v. Cumis Insurance Society, Inc., 162 Cal. App. 3d 358, 208 Cal. Rptr. 494 (1984), an intermediate appellate

2. What has been said about the relative roles of the insured and the insurer is true in all but a comparatively small handful of those cases in which the tort claim is within policy limits. Lawyers, doctors, and other professionals are much more likely to take an active part in any professional malpractice claim because they see themselves as having an interest in the outcome—their professional reputations may be at stake—notwithstanding the fact that the insurer will be the one to pay. Indeed, insureds who are professionals, such as physicians, frequently pay an extra premium for the right to veto the company's acceptance of settlement offers within policy limits.

However, see Shuster v. South Broward Hospital District Physicians' Professional Liability Insurance Trust, 591 So. 2d 174 (1992) (court held that where insurance contract provision provided that insurer may make such investigation and such settlement of any claim or suit as it deems expedient, a cause of action for breach of good faith duty owing to insured will not lie for failure to defend or investigate a claim when insurer has settled the claim for an amount within the limits of the insurance policy).

A Florida statute, effective after the decision in *Shuster*, requires clauses similar to the one in that case be included in medical malpractice policies. The statute also asserts:

> However, any offer of admission of liability, settlement offer, or offer of judgment made by an insurer or self-insurer shall be made in good faith and in the best interests of the insured.

See Brant, Medical Malpractice Insurance: The Disease and How to Cure It, 6 Val. U.L. Rev. 152, 162-163 (1972); Denenberg, Ehre, and Huling, Lawyers' Professional Liability Insurance: The Peril, the Protection, and the Price, [1970] Ins. L.J. 389, 394.

court required the insurer to pay for an independent lawyer to defend, or help to defend, the tort claim and protect the insured's interests whenever a potential conflict of interest arises, regardless of the outcome in the coverage dispute. Thus, the insured receives a free defense even if it turns out that there is no coverage. In 1987 the California legislature enacted the Obligation to Defend Action statute (California Civil Code §2860) which permits insurance contracts to provide measures to protect companies from excessive behavior by insureds. These measures include minimum qualifications for defense lawyers, limiting the insured to reasonable defense fees, mutual rights to cooperation, and the like.

The other great source of conflicts of interest between liability insurance companies and their insureds is when the tort claim exceeds, or threatens to exceed, the policy limits. What should be the court's reaction when a company refuses to settle the tort claim within policy limits and the resulting tort judgment ends up exceeding those limits? Consider the following decisions.

Crisci v. Security Insurance Co.

66 Cal. 2d 425, 426 P.2d 173, 58 Cal. Rptr. 13 (1967)

PETERS, J. In an action against The Security Insurance Company of New Haven, Connecticut, the trial court awarded Rosina Crisci $91,000 (plus interest) because she suffered a judgment in a personal injury action after Security, her insurer, refused to settle the claim. Mrs. Crisci was also awarded $25,000 for mental suffering. Security has appealed.

June DiMare and her husband were tenants in an apartment building owned by Rosina Crisci. Mrs. DiMare was descending the apartment's outside wooden staircase when a tread gave way. She fell through the resulting opening up to her waist and was left hanging 15 feet above the ground. Mrs. DiMare suffered physical injuries and developed a very severe psychosis. In a suit brought against Mrs. Crisci the DiMares alleged that the step broke because Mrs. Crisci was negligent in inspecting and maintaining the stairs. They contended that Mrs. DiMare's mental condition was caused by the accident, and they asked for $400,000 as compensation for physical and mental injuries and medical expenses.

Mrs. Crisci had $10,000 of insurance coverage under a general liability policy issued by Security. The policy obligated Security to defend the suit against Mrs. Crisci and authorized the company to make any settlement it deemed expedient. Security hired an experienced lawyer, Mr. Healy, to handle the case. Both he and defendant's claims manager believed that unless evidence was discovered showing that Mrs. DiMare had a prior mental illness, a jury would probably find that the accident precipitated Mrs. DiMare's psychosis. And both men believed that if the jury felt that the fall triggered the psychosis, a verdict of not less than $100,000 would be returned.

An extensive search turned up no evidence that Mrs. DiMare had any prior mental abnormality. As a teenager Mrs. DiMare had been in a Washington mental hospital, but only to have an abortion. Both Mrs. DiMare and Mrs. Crisci found psychiatrists who would testify that the accident caused Mrs. DiMare's illness, and the insurance company knew of this testimony. Among those who felt the psychosis was not related to the accident were the doctors at the state mental hospital where Mrs. DiMare had been committed following the accident. All the psychiatrists agreed, however, that a psychosis could be triggered by a sudden fear of falling to one's death.

The exact chronology of settlement offers is not established by the record. However, by the time the DiMares' attorney reduced his settlement demands to $10,000, Security had doctors prepared to support its position and was only willing to pay $3,000 for Mrs. DiMare's physical injuries. Security was unwilling to pay one cent for the possibility of a plaintiff's verdict on the mental illness issue. This conclusion was based on the assumption that the jury would believe all of the defendant's psychiatric evidence and none of the plaintiff's. Security also rejected a $9,000 settlement demand at a time when Mrs. Crisci offered to pay $2,500 of the settlement.

A jury awarded Mrs. DiMare $100,000 and her husband $1,000. After an appeal, the insurance company paid $10,000 of this amount, the amount of its policy. The DiMares then sought to collect the balance from Mrs. Crisci. A settlement was arranged by which the DiMares received $22,000, a 40 percent interest in Mrs. Crisci's claim to a particular piece of property, and an assignment of Mrs. Crisci's cause of action against Security. Mrs. Crisci, an immigrant widow of 70, became indigent. She worked as a babysitter, and her grandchildren paid her rent. The change in her financial condition was accompanied by a decline in physical health, hysteria, and suicide attempts. Mrs. Crisci then brought this action.

The liability of an insurer in excess of its policy limits for failure to accept a settlement offer within those limits was considered by this court in Comunale v. Traders & General Ins. Co., 50 Cal. 2d 654 [328 P.2d 198]. It was there reasoned that in every contract, including policies of insurance, there is an implied covenant of good faith and fair dealing that neither party will do anything which will injure the right of the other to receive the benefits of the agreement; that it is common knowledge that one of the usual methods by which an insured receives protection under a liability insurance policy is by settlement of claims without litigation; that the implied obligation of good faith and fair dealing requires the insurer to settle in an appropriate case although the express terms of the policy do not impose the duty; that in determining whether to settle the insurer must give the interests of the insured at least as much consideration as it gives to its own interests; and that when "there is great risk of a recovery beyond the policy limits so that the most reasonable manner of disposing of the claim is a settlement which can be made within those limits, a consideration in good faith of the insured's interest required the insurer to settle the claim." (50 Cal. 2d at p. 659.)

In determining whether an insurer has given consideration to the interests of the insured, the test is whether a prudent insurer without policy limits would have accepted the settlement offer.

Several cases, in considering the liability of the insurer, contain language to the effect that bad faith is the equivalent of dishonesty, fraud, and concealment. Obviously a showing that the insurer has been guilty of actual dishonesty, fraud, or concealment is relevant to the determination whether it has given consideration to the insured's interest in considering a settlement offer within the policy limits. The language used in the cases, however, should not be understood as meaning that in the absence of evidence establishing actual dishonesty, fraud, or concealment no recovery may be had for a judgment in excess of the policy limits. Comunale v. Traders & General Ins. Co., supra, 50 Cal. 2d 654, 658-659, makes it clear that liability based on an implied covenant exists whenever the insurer refuses to settle in an appropriate case and that liability may exist when the insurer unwarrantedly refuses an offered settlement where the most reasonable manner of disposing of the claim is by accepting the settlement. Liability is imposed not for a bad faith breach of the contract but for failure to meet the duty to accept reasonable settlements, a duty included within the implied covenant of good faith and fair dealing. Moreover . . . recovery may be based on unwarranted rejection of a reasonable settlement offer and . . . the absence of evidence, circumstantial or direct, showing actual dishonesty, fraud, or concealment is not fatal to the cause of action.

Amicus curiae argues that, whenever an insurer receives an offer to settle within the policy limits and rejects it, the insurer should be liable in every case for the amount of any final judgment whether or not within the policy limits. As we have seen, the duty of the insurer to consider the insured's interest in settlement offers within the policy limits arises from an implied covenant in the contract, and ordinarily contract duties are strictly enforced and not subject to a standard of reasonableness. Obviously, it will always be in the insured's interest to settle within the policy limits when there is any danger, however slight, of a judgment in excess of those limits. Accordingly the rejection of a settlement within the limits where there is any danger of a judgment in excess of the limits can be justified, if at all, only on the basis of interests of the insurer, and, in light of the common knowledge that settlement is one of the usual methods by which an insured receives protection under a liability policy, it may not be unreasonable for an insured who purchases a policy with limits to believe that a sum of money equal to the limits is available and will be used so as to avoid liability on his part with regard to any covered accident. In view of such expectation an insurer should not be permitted to further its own interests by rejecting opportunities to settle within the policy limits unless it is also willing to absorb losses which may result from its failure to settle.

The proposed rule is a simple one to apply and avoids the burdens of a determination whether a settlement offer within the policy limits was reasonable. The proposed rule would also eliminate the danger that an insurer, faced with a settlement offer at or near the policy limits, will reject it and gamble with the insured's money to further its own interests. Moreover, it is not entirely clear that the proposed rule would place a burden on insurers substantially greater than that which is present under existing law. The size of the judgment recovered in the personal injury action when it exceeds the policy limits, although not conclusive, furnishes an inference that the value of the claim is the equivalent of the amount of the judgment and that acceptance of an offer within those limits was the most reasonable method of dealing with the claim.

Finally, and most importantly, there is more than a small amount of elementary justice in a rule that would require that, in this situation where the insurer's and insured's interests necessarily conflict, the insurer, which may reap the benefits of its determination not to settle, should also suffer the detriments of its decision. . . .

We need not, however, here determine whether there might be some countervailing considerations precluding adoption of the proposed rule because, under Comunale v. Traders & General Ins. Co., supra, 50 Cal. 2d 654, and the cases following it, the evidence is clearly sufficient to support the determination that Security breached its duty to consider the interests of Mrs. Crisci in proposed settlements. Both Security's attorney and its claims manager agreed that if Mrs. DiMare won an award for her psychosis, that award would be at least $100,000. Security attempts to justify its rejection of a settlement by contending that it believed Mrs. DiMare had no chance of winning on the mental suffering issue. That belief in the circumstances present could be found to be unreasonable. Security was putting blind faith in the power of its psychiatrists to convince the jury when it knew that the accident could have caused the psychosis, that its agents had told it that without evidence of prior mental defects a jury was likely to believe the fall precipitated the psychosis, and that Mrs. DiMare had reputable psychiatrists on her side. Further, the company had been told by a psychiatrist that in a group of 24 psychiatrists, 12 could be found to support each side.

The trial court found that defendant "knew that there was a considerable risk of substantial recovery beyond said policy limits" and that "the defendant did not give as much consideration to the financial interests of its said insured as it gave to its own interests." That is all that was required. The award of $91,000 must therefore be affirmed.

We must next determine the propriety of the award to Mrs. Crisci of $25,000 for her mental suffering. In Comunale v. Traders & General Ins.

Co., supra, 50 Cal. 2d 654, 663, it was held that an action of the type involved here sounds in both contract and tort and that "where a case sounds both in contract and tort the plaintiff will ordinarily have freedom of election between an action of tort and one of contract. An exception to this rule is made in suits for personal injury caused by negligence, where the tort character of the action is considered to prevail [citations], but no such exception is applied in cases, like the present one, which relate to financial damage [citations].". . .

Fundamental in our jurisprudence is the principle that for every wrong there is a remedy and that an injured party should be compensated for all damage proximately caused by the wrongdoer. Although we recognize exceptions from these fundamental principles, no departure should be sanctioned unless there is a strong necessity therefor.

The general rule of damages in tort is that the injured party may recover for all detriment caused whether it could have been anticipated or not. In accordance with the general rule, it is settled in this state that mental suffering constitutes an aggravation of damages when it naturally ensues from the act complained of, and in this connection mental suffering includes nervousness, grief, anxiety, worry, shock, humiliation and indignity as well as physical pain. The commonest example of the award of damages for mental suffering in addition to other damages is probably where the plaintiff suffers personal injuries in addition to mental distress as a result of either negligent or intentional misconduct by the defendant.

Such awards are not confined to cases where the mental suffering award was in addition to an award for personal injuries; damages for mental distress have also been awarded in cases where the tortious conduct was an interference with property rights without any personal injuries apart from the mental distress.

We are satisfied that a plaintiff who as a result of a defendant's tortious conduct loses his property and suffers mental distress may recover not only for the pecuniary loss but also for his mental distress. No substantial reason exists to distinguish the cases which have permitted recovery for mental distress in actions for invasion of property rights. The principal reason for limiting recovery of damages for mental distress is that to permit recovery of such damages would open the door to fictitious claims, to recovery for mere bad manners, and to litigation in the field of trivialities. Obviously, where, as here, the claim is actionable and has resulted in substantial damages apart from those due to mental distress, the danger of fictitious claims is reduced, and we are not here concerned with mere bad manners or trivialities but tortious conduct resulting in substantial invasions of clearly protected interests.

Recovery of damages for mental suffering in the instant case does not mean that in every case of breach of contract the injured party may recover such damages. Here the breach also constitutes a tort. Moreover, plaintiff did not seek by the contract involved here to obtain a commercial advantage but to protect herself against the risks of accidental losses, including the mental distress which might follow from the losses. Among the considerations in purchasing liability insurance, as insurers are well aware, is the peace of mind and security it will provide in the event of an accidental loss, and recovery of damages for mental suffering has been permitted for breach of contracts which directly concern the comfort, happiness or personal esteem of one of the parties.

It is not claimed that plaintiff's mental distress was not caused by defendant's refusal to settle or that the damages awarded were excessive in the light of plaintiff's substantial suffering.

The judgment is affirmed.

TRAYNOR, C.J., MCCOMB, J., TOBRINER, J., MOSK, J., and BURKE, J. concurred.

Although the *Crisci* opinion suggests that it might be appropriate to impose strict liability upon an insurer for an excess judgment after the insurer has refused a settlement offer within policy limits, California continues to apply the traditional negligence test.

The liability of an insurer for an excess judgment is not confined to instances where the insurer has refused a firm settlement offer within the policy limits. See Davis v. Nationwide Mutual Fire Ins. Co., 370 So. 2d 1162 (Fla. App. 1979) (insurer's understatement of policy limits to claimant deterred claimant from making a settlement offer within actual limits); Alt v. American Family Mutual Ins. Co., 71 Wis. 2d 340, 237 N.W.2d 706 (1976) (firm offer by claimant to settle not a prerequisite of excess liability recovery); Young v. American Casualty Co., 416 F.2d 906 (2d Cir. 1969), *cert. dismissed,* 396 U.S. 997 (1970) (insurer failed to respond to offer exceeding policy limits, but jury could find that a settlement within limits could have been achieved).

Most jurisdictions hold that the insurer is liable to the insured for an excess judgment even if the insured has not actually satisfied the judgment. See Camp v. St. Paul Fire & Marine Ins. Co., 616 So. 2d 12, 15 (Fla. 1993), where Supreme Court of Florida held that an action for bad faith may be claimed by a bankruptcy trustee of an insured who was discharged from liability prior to exposure to excess judgment. But in Frankenmuth Mutual Insurance Co. v. Keeley, 436 Mich. 372, 461 N.W.2d 666 (1990), the insurer's liability was limited to the amount that could be collected by the plaintiff from the insured. And in Harris v. Standard Accident and Ins. Co., 297 F.2d 627 (2d Cir. 1961), *cert. denied,* 369 U.S. 843 (1962), the insurer was not liable for the excess judgment when the insured had been discharged in bankruptcy before the judgment was rendered. Under these circumstances the court found that the insured had not been injured by the excess judgment. In Young v. American Casualty Co., above, the insurer was held liable when the discharge in bankruptcy occurred after the excess judgment. See generally Comment, Bad Faith Failure to Settle Within Policy Limits: Recovery by Semi-Solvent Insureds, 61 Geo. L.J. 1525 (1973). In a case involving a related problem—damages caused by the insurer's failure to defend the claim—one court held that the insured's damages in connection with a judgment in excess of the policy limits are limited to the value of his assets exempt from legal process. See Stockdale v. Jamison, 416 Mich. 217, 330 N.W.2d 389 (1982).

In most states, the insured's right against the insurer for the excess judgment may be assigned to the claimant. See Annotation, 12 A.L.R.3d 1158 (1967). However, absent such an assignment, or other explicit statutory or policy authorization, the claimant usually has no action directly against the insurer. See, e.g., Murray v. Allstate Insurance Co., 507 A.2d 247 (N.J. Super. 1986); Bean v. Allstate Insurance Co., 285 Md. 572, 403 A.2d 793 (1979). Florida, however, permits the claimant to bring a direct action against the insurer without an assignment from the insured. See Thompson v. Commercial Union Ins. Co., 250 So. 2d 259 (Fla. 1971). *Thompson* was followed by Jones v. National Emblem Insurance Co., 436 F. Supp. 1119 (E.D. Mich. 1977). A direct action without assignment was also permitted in Bourget v. Government Employees Insurance Co., 287 F. Supp. 108 (D. Conn. 1968), in which the court relied on a Connecticut statute giving a judgment creditor of the insured all the insured's rights against the insurer if the judgment is not satisfied within 30 days.

Some states have imposed upon insurers a duty to third-party claimants to effectuate prompt, fair, and equitable settlements of claims. Cf. Thaler v. American Ins. Co., 614 N.E.2d 1021, 1023-1024 (Mass. App. 1993) (court held that insistence on a release by an insurer as a condition of payment of the policy limits, where liability of its insured is undisputed and damages clearly exceed the policy limits, amounts to an unfair settlement practice in violation of a state statute).

Problem 35

A partner of the firm in which you are an associate has given you the file dealing with the claim of Matilda Jones against Diedre Gertzweiler. Your firm represents Eagle Insurance Company, Gertzweiler's insurer. Jones and Gertzweiler are neighbors, and both are in their mid-50s. A little over a year ago, Jones dropped in at Gertzweiler's home for a morning cup of coffee. After finishing her coffee, Jones started to walk to the kitchen counter. On the way, she tripped on the corner of a rug, fell, and hit her head on the edge of the counter. She suffered serious and permanent head injuries. You have concluded that while liability is doubtful, the injuries, apart from any doubts about liability, would support recovery of somewhere near $150,000. The file indicated that the limits on Gertzweiler's policy were $200,000 per person and $500,000 per accident.

Taking into account both the doubtful liability and the seriousness of the injuries, you concluded that Eagle should make an initial offer of settlement of $25,000, and in no event go higher than $40,000. On the basis of your evaluation, an offer of $25,000 was submitted to Jones's lawyer. At a conference with the partner last week, she told you that Jones's lawyer has responded with a demand of $50,000. This turns out to be the limit of Gertzweiler's liability coverage—someone at Eagle had made a mistake in reporting the higher limits to your firm. The partner has also told you that the highest court of your jurisdiction has just handed down an opinion that follows *Crisci.* The partner asked you whether you would now abandon your resistance point of $40,000 and recommend that the offer of $50,000 be accepted. The partner is concerned that if Eagle rejects the $50,000 offer, and Jones wins at the trial, the company will be exposed to a claim for bad faith refusal to settle and may end up paying an amount well in excess of the $50,000 policy limit. If your assessment of damages is accurate, the company's liability could amount to as much as $150,000, apart from the possibility of recovery by the insured of punitive damages or damages for mental upset. The partner wonders if it would be wise for the company to avoid that exposure at the cost of $10,000, the difference between your initial resistance point and the policy limits.

What advice will you give to the partner with respect to whether Eagle Insurance should settle for the policy limits, or stay with your initial resistance point of $40,000?

The Lawyer's Professional Responsibility: Conflicts of Interest in Liability Insurance Cases

Under the typical liability insurance policy, the insurer has both the right and the duty to defend the claim against its insured. If the insurer is unable to settle the claim through its own claims process, it will usually name an attorney to handle the case. While the lawyer is selected by the insurer, and for that reason must look after its interests, the insurer's interests may conflict with those of the insured. When that occurs, the lawyer must act carefully to avoid representing persons with conflicting interests.

The rules of professional responsibility permit a lawyer to represent clients with differing interests in the same matter so long as the lawyer "reasonably believes the representation will not adversely affect" either client, and both have consented, after consultation, to the dual representation. Model Rules of Professional Conduct, Rule 1.7 (1983).

In liability insurance cases, the lawyer appointed by the insurer to represent the insured owes primary loyalty to the insured. As stated by the court in American Employers Ins. Co. v. Goble Aircraft Specialties, Inc., 205 Misc. 1066, 131 N.Y.S.2d 393 (1954), the lawyer owes the insured "an undeviating and single allegiance." Thus, on one hand, it has been held that the attorney-client privilege does not bar access by the insured to communications between the company and the attorney. See Henke v. Iowa Home Mut. Casualty Co., 249 Iowa 614, 87 N.W.2d 920 (1958). On the other hand, the attorney may not divulge information gotten from the insured indicating a lack of coverage, if the attorney got the information under circumstances indicating an expectation by the insured that it would not be divulged to the company. See American Bar Association, National Conference of Lawyers and Liability Insurers—Guiding Principles.[3]

One of the more frequently recurring conflict of interest situations is that involved in *Crisci,* in which the claim exceeds the policy limits. The common procedure in such cases is for the company, or its attorney, to write the insured an "excess claim" letter inviting the insured to secure her own attorney to protect her interests. Occasionally, the insured will secure her own attorney, but more often she will not. If the insured does not secure independent representation, the excess claim letter does not relieve the attorney retained by the company from his or her duties to the insured. The attorney is under a continuing duty to represent the interests of the insured, and must advise of any offers of settlement from the claimant, and may later have to withdraw from representing the insured if the conflict becomes irreconcilable. See Hamilton v. State Farm Mut. Auto. Ins. Co., 511 P.2d 1020 (Wash. App. 1973).

The possible existence of a policy defense can also be the source of a conflict of interest. In Employers Casualty Co. v. Tilley, 496 S.W.2d 552 (Tex. 1973), the court ruled that it was improper for an attorney, retained by the insurer to represent the insured, to gather evidence, unknown to the insured, on which to base a defense that the insured had failed to give the insurer timely notice of the accident. One of the more troublesome of the policy defense cases involves a claim that the insured intentionally injured the claimant, a claim not normally covered by liability insurance. While the insurer and the insured both would prefer the insured to prevail no matter what theory is relied on at the trial, the insurer may be able to avoid liability by supporting the intentional harm claim. The insured, if he is to lose at all, would naturally prefer a judgment based on negligence or recklessness, which would make the insurer ultimately liable. In Burd v. Sussex Mut. Ins. Co., 56 N.J. 383, 267 A.2d 7 (1970), the court held in such a case that it was proper for the attorney to withdraw from representing the insured, compelling the insured to select his own attorney to defend the claim. The coverage question would then be litigated in a later case, and if it were determined that the claim was covered by the policy, the insurer would be liable

3. These principles, reproduced at 5 Forum 296 (1970), are one of a set of guiding principles developed jointly by the American Bar Association and various professional groups, such as engineers, realtors and social workers. The full set of Principles has been published in a pamphlet entitled Statements of Principles with Respect to the Practice of Law Formulated by Representatives of the American Bar Association and Various Business and Professional Groups (1972).

not only for the judgment against the insured, but also for the latter's attorney's fees and expenses. A different resolution was suggested in Employers' Fire Ins. Co. v. Beals, 103 R.I. 623, 240 A.2d 397 (1968)—the appointment of two attorneys by the insurer, one to represent the insurer and one the insured.

Commercial Union Assurance Companies v. Safeway Stores, Inc.

164 Cal. Rptr. 709, 610 P.2d 1038 (1980)

BY THE COURT:

We granted a hearing herein in order to resolve a conflict between Court of Appeal opinions in this case and the earlier case of Transit Casualty Co. v. Spink Corp., 94 Cal. App. 3d 124, 156 Cal. Rptr. 360 (1979). After an independent study of the issue, we have concluded that the thoughtful opinion of Justice Sabraw (assigned) for the Court of Appeal, First Appellate District, 158 Cal. Rptr. 97, in this case correctly treats the issues, and that we should adopt it as our own opinion. That opinion, with appropriate deletions and additions,* is as follows:

This case presents the question of whether an insured owes a duty to its excess liability insurance carrier which would require it to accept a settlement offer below the threshold figure of the excess carrier's exposure where there is a substantial probability of liability in excess of that figure.

Facts:

At all times relevant herein Safeway Stores, Incorporated (hereafter Safeway) had liability insurance coverage as follows:

(a) Travelers Insurance Company and Travelers Indemnity Company (hereafter Travelers) insured Safeway for the first $50,000 of liability.

(b) Safeway insured itself for liability between the sums of $50,000 and $100,000.

(c) Commercial Union Assurance Companies and Mission Insurance Company (hereafter conjunctively referred to as Commercial) provided insurance coverage for Safeway's liability in excess of $100,000 to $20 million.

One Hazel Callies brought an action against Safeway in San Francisco Superior Court and recovered judgment for the sum of $125,000. Thereafter, Commercial was required to pay $25,000 of said judgment in order to discharge its liability under the excess insurance policy.

Commercial, as excess liability carrier, brought the instant action against

* Brackets together, in this manner ( ), are used to indicate deletions from the opinion of the Court of Appeal; brackets enclosing material (other than the editor's parallel citations) are, unless otherwise indicated, used to denote insertions or additions by this court.

its insured Safeway and Safeway's primary insurance carrier, Travelers, to recover the $25,000 which it had expended. Commercial alleged that Safeway and Travelers had an opportunity to settle the case for $60,000, or possibly even $50,000, and knew or should have known that there was a possible and probable liability in excess of $100,000. It was further alleged that said defendants had a duty to settle the claim for a sum less than $100,000 when they had an opportunity to do so. Commercial's complaint attempts to state two causes of action against Safeway and Travelers, one in negligence and another for breach of the duty of good faith and fair dealing.

Safeway demurred to the complaint on the grounds of failure to state a cause of action. The court sustained the demurrer with 20 days' leave to amend. When Commercial failed to amend its complaint, the complaint was dismissed as to Safeway. Commercial now appeals from the judgment of dismissal.

The present case is unusual in that the policyholder, Safeway, was self-insured for liability in an amount below Commercial's initial exposure. While this status may explain Safeway's reluctance to settle, it remains to be determined if the insured owes an independent duty to his excess carrier to accept a reasonable settlement offer so as to avoid exposing the latter to pecuniary harm. (Both of Commercial's theories of recovery, negligence and breach of good faith, depend upon the existence of such a duty.)

It is now well established that an insurer may be held liable for a judgment against the insured in excess of its policy limits where it has breached its implied covenant of good faith and fair dealing by unreasonably refusing to accept a settlement offer within the policy limits (Crisci v. Security Ins. Co., 66 Cal. 2d 425, 429 (58 Cal. Rptr. 13, 426 P.2d 173)). . . .

It has been held in California and other jurisdictions that the excess carrier may maintain an action against the primary carrier for (wrongful) refusal to settle within the latter's policy limits. . . . This rule, however, is based on the theory of equitable subrogation: Since the insured would have been able to recover from the primary carrier for a judgment in excess of policy limits caused by the carrier's wrongful refusal to settle, the excess carrier, who discharged the insured's liability as a result of this tort, stands in the shoes of the insured and should be permitted to assert all claims against the primary carrier which the insured himself could have asserted. . . . Hence, the rule does not rest upon the finding of any separate duty owed to an excess insurance carrier. [Because the insured in this case agreed with the primary insurer to take the case to judgment, no subrogation rights extend to the excess carrier.]

Commercial argues that the implied covenant of good faith and fair dealing is reciprocal, binding the policyholder as well as the carrier. . . . It is further contended, in effect, that turnabout is fair play: that the implied covenant of good faith and fair dealing applies to the insured as well as the insurer, and thus the policyholder owes a duty to his excess carrier not to unreasonably refuse an offer of settlement below the amount of excess coverage where a judgment of liability above that amount is substantially likely to occur.

This theory, while possessing superficial plausibility and exquisite simplicity, cannot withstand closer analysis. We have no quarrel with the proposition that a duty of good faith and fair dealing in an insurance policy is a two-way street, running from the insured to his insurer as well as vice versa. . . . However, what that duty embraces is dependent upon the nature of the bargain struck between the insurer and the insured and the legitimate expectations of the parties which arise from the contract.

The essence of the implied covenant of good faith in insurance policies is that " 'neither party will do anything which injures the right of the other to receive the benefits of the agreement' " (Murphy v. Allstate Ins. Co., supra, 17 Cal. 3d at p. 940, 132 Cal. Rptr. at p. 426, 553 P.2d at p. 586, quoting from Brown v. Superior Court (1949) 34 Cal. 2d 559, 564 (212 P.2d 878)). One of the most important benefits of a maximum limit insurance policy is the assurance that the company will provide the insured with defense and indemnification for the purpose of protecting him from liability. Accordingly, the insured has the legitimate right to expect that the method of settlement within policy limits will be employed in order to give him such protection.

No such expectations can be said to reasonably flow from an excess insurer to its insured. The object of the excess insurance policy is to provide additional resources should the insured's liability surpass a specified sum. The insured owes no duty to defend or indemnify the excess carrier; hence, the carrier can possess no reasonable expectation that the insured will accept a settlement offer as a means of "protecting" the carrier from exposure. The protection of the insurer's pecuniary interests is simply not the object of the bargain.

. . . Where, as here, the policyholder is self-insured for an amount below the beginning of the excess insurance coverage, he is gambling as much with his own money as with that of the carrier. The crucial point is that the excess carrier has no legitimate expectation that the insured will " 'give at least as much consideration to the financial well-being' " of the insurance company as he does to his " 'own interests' " (Shapero v. Allstate Ins. Co. (1971) 14 Cal. App. 3d 433, 437-438 [92 Cal. Rptr. 244], 247), in considering whether to settle for an amount below the excess policy coverage. In fact, the primary reason excess insurance is purchased is to provide an available pool of money in the event that the decision is made to take the gamble of litigating. . . .

In the instant case, whether Commercial could harbor any legitimate expectation that its insured would settle a claim for less than the threshold amount of the policy coverage must be determined in the light of what the parties bargained for. The complaint makes no reference to any language in the policy which would give rise to such expectation. We must therefore ask the question: Did Safeway, when it purchased excess coverage, impliedly promise that it would take all reasonable steps to settle a claim below the limits of Commercial's coverage so as to protect Commercial from possible exposure? Further, did Commercial extend excess coverage with the understanding and expectation that it would receive such favorable treatment from Safeway under the policy? We think not.

At this point, a recent appellate decision which bears upon this issue, deserves mention.

. . . In the case of Kaiser Foundation Hospitals v. North Star Reinsurance Corp. (1979) 90 Cal. App. 3d 786 (153 Cal. Rptr. 678), the Court of Appeal for the Second District, Division Five, concluded that the relationship between an insured and primary carrier vis-à-vis the excess carrier was governed by an implied covenant of good faith and fair dealing (p. 792, 153 Cal. Rptr. 678). That decision, however, dealt with a situation where the insured and its primary carrier acted in collusion to wrongfully allocate certain dates of loss so as to maximize the liability of the excess carrier. It appears that the aggravated conduct on the part of the insured and the primary carrier in taking advantage of the excess carrier prompted the Court of Appeal to invoke the basic principles of good faith and fair dealing in order to give proper redress to the excess carrier. It is to be noted that the opinion takes careful pains to emphasize that in speaking of a good faith and fair dealing duty owed by the insured to the excess carrier under these circumstances, it was expressly not amplifying on the nature of such duty: "(W)e make no attempt to define precisely what rights and duties that entails in a case such as this. Such questions are best decided in the light of concrete facts . . ." (p. 794, 153 Cal. Rptr. p. 683).

We acknowledge that equity requires fair dealing between the parties to an insurance contract. We view the Kaiser . . . case as pointing up a recognition in the law that the insured status as such is not a license for the insured to engage in unconscionable acts which would subvert the legitimate rights and expectations of the excess insurance carrier.

However, we are unable to derive from this sound principle, the precipitous conclusion that the covenant of good faith and fair dealing should be extended to include a . . . duty which would require an insured contemplating settlement to put the excess carrier's financial interests on at least an equal footing with his own. Such a duty cannot reasonably be found from the mere existence of the contractual relationship between insured and excess carrier in the absence of express language in the contract so providing.

We observe that an apparently contrary conclusion has been reached by the Third District in the recent case of Transit Casualty Co. v. Spink Corp. ( ) (supra) 94 Cal. App. 3d 124, 156 Cal. Rptr. 360. ( ) (We disapprove that case) insofar as it holds that an insured's duty of good faith and fair dealing to his excess carrier compels him to accept a settlement offer or proceed at his peril where there is a substantial likelihood that an adverse judgment will bring excess insurance coverage into play.

In conclusion, we hold that a policy providing for excess insurance coverage imposes no implied duty upon the insured to accept a settlement offer which would avoid exposing the insurer to liability. Moreover such a duty cannot be predicated upon an insured's implied covenant of good faith and fair dealing. If an excess carrier wishes to insulate itself from liability for an insured's failure to accept what it deems to be a reasonable settlement offer, it may do so by appropriate language in the policy. We hesitate, however, to read into the policy obligations which are neither sought after nor contemplated by the parties. . . .

The judgment is affirmed.

American Home Assurance Co. v. Hermann's Warehouse Corp.

521 A.2d 903, 215 N.J. Super. 260 (1987)

MORTON I. GREENBERG, P.J.A.D.

This matter comes before this court on appeal by plaintiff American Home Assurance Company from an order of February 18, 1986 denying plaintiff's motion for summary judgment and granting defendant Hermann's Warehouse Corporation's cross-motion for summary judgment dismissing this action. Plaintiff, which had issued a liability insurance policy with a $2,000,000 limit of coverage to defendant to protect its warehouse business, settled a claim by a third party against defendant and brought this action to recover the deductible provided in the policy. The deductible was for $20,000 on all losses except for inventory shortages or unexplained disappearances in which cases it was for $40,000.

The basic facts are not in dispute. On August 4, 1980, All Freight Trucking Company contacted defendant to make arrangements for the delivery to defendant for storage of a number of cargo trailers containing Christmas ornaments for Kurt S. Adler, Inc. According to defendant, it advised All Freight that because of a full work schedule it could not unload and take possession of the trailers that day. Nevertheless, All Freight dropped off three trailers in defendant's yard and requested it to unload them the next morning. While defendant permitted the trailers to be left in its yard, it did so without charge solely for the convenience of All Freight. Consequently, defendant did not unload the vehicles or formally acknowledge the receipt of their contents or issue a warehouse receipt for them. The following morning two of the three trailers were missing leading Adler to make a claim against defendant for $76,382.80 for lost merchandise.

Inasmuch as Adler's claim was not paid, it instituted an action against defendant for the loss. While we do not have the pleadings from that action, plaintiff asserts that Adler's possible recovery was $100,000, calculated as $76,382.80 damages with the balance as interest. Defendant does not deny that representation. As provided in the insurance policy, defendant turned the case over to plaintiff for defense. Thereafter, pursuant to a provision in the policy that reserved to it "the right to settle any claim, suit or other proceedings as it may deem expedient," plaintiff settled Adler's claim for $67,500 without defendant's consent.

Following the settlement, plaintiff requested defendant to reimburse it for the $20,000 deductible in accordance with a provision in the policy specifying that: "If the Company shall have paid such deductible amount, the Assured shall promptly reimburse the Company therefor." Defendant refused to reimburse plaintiff claiming that it could not have been liable to Adler, had not consented to the settlement, had urged Adler's claim be rejected and had requested a jury trial. Consequently, plaintiff instituted this action to recover the deductible. Evidently, plaintiff is in doubt as to whether the $20,000 or $40,000 figure is applicable as it seeks either amount alternatively.

After an answer was filed, the parties served cross-motions for summary judgment. The motion judge disposed of the case with the following opinion:

> As to American Home Assurance Company versus Hermann's Warehouse Corporation, there are motions for summary judgment. The plaintiff, American Home Assurance Company, settled the case and seeks recovery of the deductible. Defendant opposes the motion for summary judgment and seeks motion for summary judgment in its own behalf arguing that it did not participate in the settlement, did not approve the settlement and should not be required to pay the deductible. I am satisfied from the arguments of counsel that the defendant's position is the sound one. In fact, it did not approve the settlement and should not be required to pay the deductible. I am going to grant summary judgment for the defendant. Accordingly, I will deny summary judgment on behalf of the plaintiff.

The order of February 18, 1986 was then entered and this appeal followed.

On this appeal, plaintiff contends that it was empowered to settle Adler's claim without defendant's consent, it acted reasonably and in good faith in doing so and it is entitled to recover the deductible. Defendant contends plaintiff acted in bad faith, did not adequately represent it and may not recover the deductible as it settled Adler's claim without its consent. Defendant further contends that plaintiff cannot recover because the policy provides that no action shall lie against the company unless, as a condition precedent thereto, defendant's obligation to pay is established by judgment against it or by written agreement among plaintiff, defendant and the claimant.

There is, of course, no doubt but that the policy empowered plaintiff to settle Adler's claim. While some insurance policies provide that a settlement may be made only with the consent of the insured, this policy did not. Further, the provision that plaintiff cannot be liable until defendant's liability is established by judgment or agreement is not intended to bar voluntary settlements. It simply attempts to establish when an action will lie against plaintiff as the insurance carrier. Thus, absent some overriding principle of law, plaintiff should have been granted summary judgment.

Defendant finds that principle in decisions emphasizing an insurance company's duty to act in good faith toward its insured in settlement of claims and urges that plaintiff breached this obligation, thereby barring it from recovery. . . . Though we do not doubt that insurance companies must act in good faith in settling claims, the case law defining this duty has developed when companies have refused to settle following which judgments are obtained against insureds in excess of the policy limits. We are aware of no case in New Jersey, however, which indicates that a company may be held to have acted in bad faith in settling a claim within the policy limits when its power to do so is not conditioned upon obtaining the consent of the insured. The Supreme Court's decision in Lieberman v. Employers Ins. of Wausau, 84 N.J. 325, 419 A.2d 417 (1980), though indicating that a carrier may be liable for settling a claim within the policy limits, is not contrary as the policy there had a provision that any settlement required the consent of the insured which, though originally obtained, had been revoked before the settlement.

We are convinced that an insurance company may not be held liable or be held to lose its rights to recover a deductible on a claim of bad faith to its insured when it settles a case within the policy limits. A contrary ruling would encourage a carrier proposing a settlement to consult with its insured before agreeing to it. While this in itself would not be unreasonable, in practice if a carrier settling without the insured's consent could be held to have acted in bad faith, there would be a loss of potential settlements. Persons subject to claims frequently consider their own actions to have been faultless in situations where juries, judges and professional claims evaluators view them as having been negligent. Thus, some insureds would tend to object to objectively prudent settlements requiring contribution from them, particularly in cases such as this one where the insured runs no risk that a failure to settle could result in a verdict in excess of the policy limits. Such an objection might cause a carrier to decline to settle a case even though it considered a settlement desirable. Inasmuch as the law gives a high priority to settlement of lawsuits, we should not adopt a rule of law which discourages them. . . .

A second reason to avoid incorporation of the requirement that a carrier act in good faith in settling a case within a policy limit is that the good faith requirement is ordinarily imposed to protect an insured from an insurance carrier's refusal to settle within the policy limit thereby putting the insured's personal assets at peril. . . . Here, the insured did get the benefit of a settlement within the policy limits and thus the reason for the imposition of a duty of good faith is absent.

We also point out that liability insurance policies with deductibles are written for commercial risks. Consumers purchasing homeowners', tenants' and automobile liability protection receive policies without deductibles. We think that business persons should recognize that when they accept a liability policy with a deductible they may be called upon to pay it. We also point out that at least in some situations a commercial insured may be able to negotiate for the terms of a policy and thereby obtain a policy according it the right to approve a liability claim settlement. . . .

Another consideration leading to our result is that defendant could have had the jury trial it sought by defending Adler's action itself. We are certain that plaintiff would not have objected if defendant had waived its insurance protection, defended Adler's action at its own expense and, if Adler obtained a judgment, satisfied it. It is obvious, however, that defendant did not want to run the risk of a judgment as it called on plaintiff for a defense. In reality, defendant contends that it should have the most favorable aspects of two inconsistent positions. It wanted to control the litigation by rejecting the settlement but it claimed the advantage of its insurance, thereby receiving a defense at plaintiff's expense and protection from Adler's claim. Inasmuch as defendant sought the protection of its insurance, it had to accept the burdens that went with it. . . .

In reaching our result, we have not overlooked the fact that an insurance company might act unreasonably in settling a case for less than the policy limits. For example, a carrier might settle a doubtful claim for the amount of the deductible or some lesser amount to save attorney's fees. Nevertheless, we think that for the practical considerations we have stated and because of the agreement between the insured and the company, our result should be reached. In the event that a carrier does act unreasonably in settling within the policy limits, the insured's remedy will be to look elsewhere for coverage in the future.

The order of February 18, 1986 is reversed and the matter is remanded to the Superior Court, Law Division, Middlesex County, for entry of an order for partial summary judgment for liability in favor of plaintiff and for further proceedings. Inasmuch as the parties have not briefed the issue of which deductible is applicable, that issue shall be determined on the remand. We do not retain jurisdiction.

Chapter 10

Compensation Systems as Alternatives to the System of Tort Liability Based on Fault

In this chapter, we take up systems that provide compensation to injured persons largely without regard to fault. Section A deals with one of the oldest compensation systems—workers' compensation. Section B considers a relative newcomer—no-fault automobile insurance. Section C explores the possibility of a system that would provide no-fault compensation for injuries caused by medical treatment. Finally, Section D, with its analysis of the New Zealand system, presents the possibility of almost total replacement of the tort system of allocating personal injury losses.

Compensation without regard to fault is not limited to the systems discussed in this chapter. For example, self-insurance against a variety of losses, such as property damage, medical expense and loss of income, is widely available and commonly used. What distinguishes the no-fault compensation systems discussed here from such insurance is that the former have been created as substitutes, in whole or part, for tort liability. This also serves to distinguish broad, governmentally administered social welfare programs such as social security.

The compensation systems examined in this chapter are also different from other areas of tort law considered in this book under which liability may be imposed without regard to fault. Such areas of liability without fault include some forms of battery (Chapter 1), vicarious liability (Chapter 3), nuisance (Chapter 5), strict liability (Chapter 6), products liability (Chapter 7), and, at least until recently, defamation (Chapter 12). The compensation systems about to be examined are products of the legislative process, while the other forms of liability without fault have been developed largely by courts as a part of the common law. The compensation systems in this chapter also make much more explicit use of insurance—insurance is often required, and claims are made directly against insurers rather than against persons who cause harm. Compensation under these systems is usually limited to the more objectively determinable economic losses (such as loss of wages and medical expenses), with little or no compensation for pain and suffering.

There is one other significant difference between the statutory schemes covered in this chapter and the common law systems of liability without fault considered elsewhere: the potential for increased efficiency which the statutory schemes present by simplifying the liability and damages issues, thus reducing the need for resorting to the judicial process in most claims. Under workers' compensation and no-fault automobile insurance, the liability issues are likely to be simpler and the compensation easier to measure than under the common law rules of damages. One of the principal arguments advanced in favor of no-fault automobile insurance is that it reduces the costs of processing claims, resulting in a greater share of the insurance premium dollar being used to compensate the injured victims of automobile accidents and a lesser share being absorbed as a cost of processing claims. From a public policy perspective, the issue raised by this chapter is whether the concept of no-fault compensation, with its potentially greater efficiency and more universal compensation, should be extended beyond workers' compensation and no-fault automobile insurance to other areas now occupied by the fault system.

A. *Workers' Compensation*

One of the significant impacts of the Industrial Revolution in this country in the latter half of the nineteenth century was the rapid increase in industrial accidents and employee injuries. Unsafe working conditions combined with expansion of the industrial work force to produce a steady stream, and then a flood, of disabling accidents. Many injured employees who were no longer able to earn wages became charges on the public. And for every worker injured or killed on the job there were likely to be dependent family members who would also have to look to public assistance for economic survival. The problem was compounded by the difficulties the disabled worker encountered in recovering compensation from the employer in the form of tort damages. In the first place, fault had to be shown on the part of someone as the proximate cause of his injuries. Even if negligence could be proved, if the person at fault happened to be a co-worker, as was very often the case, the employer was immunized from liability by the fellow servant rule, which barred recovery from a common master for the negligence of a fellow servant.[1] And even where the employer was shown to be directly at fault, or where some exception to the fellow servant rule was available, the doctrines of assumption of the risk and contributory negligence often barred recovery. Injured employees might, in appropriate cases, succeed in actions against third persons. However, because the great majority of industrial accidents did not involve strangers to the employment relationship, the availability of tort actions against third persons remained almost totally

1. The landmark case is Priestley v. Fowler [1837] 3 M. & W. 1, 150 Reprint 1030. The leading American case is Farwell v. Boston & Worcester R., 4 Metc. (Mass.) 49 (1842).

theoretical. Studies of the economic impact of industrial accidents prior to workers' compensation reveal a system under which most workers injured on the job received little or no compensation. See 1 Larson, The Law of Workmen's Compensation §4.50 (1993).

Legislative and public concern over the mounting problem of disabled, uncompensated workers led, early in this century, to the enactment of workers' compensation statutes in several states. By 1920, all but eight states had such statutes. The last state to fall in line was Mississippi in 1949.

Workers' compensation replaces the common law tort action with a system of absolute liability for injury or death suffered in work-related activities. Compensation is measured by economic loss, primarily medical expense and incapacity to work, with no compensation for pain and suffering. But there are a number of limits on the amount of compensation payable so that in many instances the compensation is not complete even for economic loss. Typically, workers' compensation is funded by insurance paid for by the employer, and is administered by a specialized agency whose primary function is the processing of claims. Thus, workers' compensation replaces the all-or-nothing common law fault system of employer liability under which most injured workers received little or nothing, with a system of absolute liability under which such workers are guaranteed compensation for a portion of their economic losses from work-related injuries.[2]

A fairly representative workers' compensation statute is that of Massachusetts (Mass. Ann. Laws ch. 152), enacted in 1911 and amended from time to time since then. To provide the compensation required by the Massachusetts act, an employer must either obtain insurance or qualify as a licensed self-insurer. The great majority of covered employers purchase insurance. A fine is imposed for failure to comply with the insurance requirements, substantially eliminating deliberate noncompliance with the act. In addition to the fine, if an employer as to whom coverage is required fails to insure or to qualify as a self-insurer, that employer is exposed to absolute liability in tort without regard to negligence and without recourse to the common law defenses of assumption of the risk, contributory negligence, or the fellow servant rule. Employers who are either insured or self-insured are immune from employee actions in tort for injuries compensable under the act, as are fellow employees. An employee may elect, at the time of hiring, to forgo workers' compensation coverage and retain the common law tort action against the employer, although such elections are rare. An injured employee retains the right to sue in tort any third person who has caused a work-related injury, and the insurer is subrogated to any such claim to the extent that it has paid workers' compensation benefits.

2. Workers' compensation has not completely replaced the traditional fault system with respect to claims against employers for injuries arising out of job-related accidents. See the law and policy note, p. 788, below.

Not all employees and employers are covered by the workers' compensation statute. Section 1 of the statute defines an employee as a "person in the service of another under any contract of hire, express or implied, oral or written. . . ." Some employees are excluded from coverage, such as professional athletes whose contracts call for continued compensation during periods of work-related injury, and real estate brokers who work only on commission. The section defines an employer as a person "employing an employee . . . subject to this chapter," with minor exceptions.

For an employee to be entitled to compensation, there must be "a personal injury arising out of and in the course of his employment." The concept of personal injury is sufficiently broad to include diseases and bodily wear and tear as well as accidental injuries. There is no requirement that the employer or any other person have been at fault, and the contributory fault of the employee is no bar to recovery unless the injury is "by reason of his serious and wilful misconduct."

The phrase "arising out of and in the course of employment" has been the subject of considerable litigation. Although each case involving the issue of work relation is likely to raise its own unique problems of interpretation, a few generalizations are possible. The Supreme Judicial Court of Massachusetts has interpreted the phrase as imposing two requirements. The first requirement, that the injury "arise out of" the employment, is one of causation and is satisfied if the employment brought the employee into contact with the risk that in fact caused the injury. There is no necessity that the risk be one peculiar to the job—a machine operator who stumbles against the machine may recover for an injury just as may the operator whose hand gets caught in the machine. The act expressly includes injuries "arising out of an ordinary risk of the street while the employee is actually engaged . . . in the business affairs or undertakings of [the] employer." The second requirement, that the injury occur "in the course of employment," relates to the circumstances, time, and place of the injury. Most industrial accidents occur while employees are on the job during working hours and at the place of employment. But Massachusetts court decisions have extended coverage beyond this, and it is clear that lunch hour injuries, for example, are compensable unless they occur off the job premises and are unconnected with the particular requirements imposed upon the employee by the contract of employment. If the employee away from the job premises is on an errand for the employer, or furthering the employer's interests in some material way, the injury also will likely be compensable.

The basic elements of recovery under the act are medical expenses and incapacity to work. Included in medical expenses are doctor and hospital bills and expenses of rehabilitation, all of which are compensable without limit. The act classifies incapacity to work as partial, total, and total and permanent. Compensation for incapacity is subject to two limits, one relating to the maximum weekly amount payable, and the other to the overall amount payable for any one injury. The act provides for additional compensation for injuries which result in specific consequences, such as the loss of sight, hearing, or a limb. Benefits also are payable to dependents in cases of employee death. The act adopts the collateral source rule by providing that "savings, . . . insurance [and] benefits derived from any source other than the insurer" shall not reduce the amount of compensation payable. However, if the employee has an insurance policy providing medical expense or income loss benefits which excludes coverage for injuries compensable under the act, and if compensation payments have been made pending resolution of a workers' compensation claim, the insurer is entitled to reimbursement to the extent of the payments from any compensation award. The right of reimbursement is also given to the state department of public welfare with respect to welfare payments made because of an injury determined to be compensable under the act.

The procedure for processing most workers' compensation claims is relatively simple. An injured employee is required to notify the employer in writing immediately after the injury, and the employer in turn notifies the insurer. Following receipt of the notice, the insurer will investigate the claim by taking necessary statements from the employee and others, including attending physicians and hospitals. The insurer will typically have the employee examined by its doctor. When the investigation by the insurer is complete, the insurer will either notify the board, the employer, and the employee of its intent to contest the claim, or commence payments called for by the act. The insurer and the employee may agree to a lump sum payment, instead of weekly payments, which will satisfy the insurer's obligation to make future payments. However, a lump sum payment must be approved by the board, and then only after a thorough review based on a number of factors designed to protect the interests of the employee. If the lump sum payment is approved, it is final and binding as to all issues presented by the original claim. If the claim is not "lump summed," the case may later be reconsidered, based on changes in the employee's condition.

As the act was originally conceived and drafted, it was not anticipated that it would be necessary for an injured employee to be represented by a lawyer when filing a claim. However, there are cases involving disputes which do require a lawyer's services. The Industrial Accident Board is given statutory authority to supervise the setting of fees in exceptional cases, and where the negotiations break down and the claim goes to hearing, there are several provisions which allow all costs, including the employee's attorney's fees, to be assessed against the insurer. Although instances of the parties' failure to agree voluntarily are common enough to suggest that a system of rapid and efficient compensation has not altogether been realized, in most cases the act achieves the desired ends—most claims are settled quickly and informally. The act puts pressure on both employees and insurers to handle claims fairly and quickly by permitting the board to award the costs of hearings and attorneys' fees against an employee who unreasonably prosecutes a claim or against an insurer who unreasonably defends one.

If the insurer elects to contest the claim, the employee, to pursue the claim, must file a request for a hearing before the board. Although the board functions as a court in resolving disputes, in some ways the board has less power than a court. For example, the board has no authority to enforce its orders—if the parties to a controversy do not voluntarily choose to abide by the board's decision, the party aggrieved must petition the superior court for enforcement. In other ways, however, the board's authority and responsibility under the act exceeds that of courts. The board has extensive supervisory power over the setting of attorneys' fees in workers' compensation cases, and the board may investigate on its own initiative cases brought before it and call expert witnesses of its own choosing.

Although the board consists of 16 members, initial hearings are held before a single member. The only appeal from the decision of the single member is to a reviewing board composed of at least three members from the full board. Cases may be argued orally before the reviewing board, and the reviewing board may reach its own conclusions of fact and law. Judicial review of a board decision may be had by either party by appealing the decision to the superior court. Generally speaking, the superior court is limited to deciding whether the board's decision is either supported by evidence or affected by an erroneous interpretation of the law; the board's findings of fact are given the same status as those returned by a jury in a court action. Thus, the superior court is not free to decide questions of fact, and may not choose to substitute the findings of the single member for those of the reviewing board where the findings differ and where the evidence supports both.

While the Massachusetts statute is representative of the workers' compensation principle, there are many variations, both major and minor, among the states. These variations result not only from differences in the statutes, but from differing judicial interpretations of essentially similar statutory language. The basic coverage formula—"arising out of and in the course of employment"—is the phrase used in most statutes. A few states, such as Pennsylvania, omit the "arising out of" requirement entirely. See Penn. Stat. Ann. tit. 77, §431.

Even in those states that have the full coverage formula, there are important differences in interpretation and application. The most significant difference involves whether the formula expresses two requirements, both of which must be independently satisfied, or only one requirement. An example of the two-requirement approach is Collier's Case, 331 Mass. 374, 119 N.E.2d 191 (1954). The claimant had refused, on the order of her employer, to serve a drink to a customer in the bar in which she worked. The customer became angry, and attacked and injured the claimant an hour later while she was on her way home. The court denied compensation, ruling that since the claimant had left her place of employment, the injury did not occur in the course of her employment. In some states the coverage formula is interpreted as expressing a single requirement—that of "work connection."

See, e.g., Thornton v. Chamberlain Mfg. Corp., 62 N.J. 235, 300 A.2d 146 (1973) in which the Supreme Court of New Jersey ordered compensation paid to a claimant attacked and injured by a former coemployee who was motivated by an on-the-job dispute, although the attack took place off the employment premises and nine days after the claimant left the employment.

Significant differences in coverage also exist because certain types of employment are exempted from various statutes. The most common exemption is that for domestic servants; many states also exempt agricultural workers. Another exemption appearing on occasion is geared to the number of employees working for the employer. Some statutes exempt employers having fewer than a stated number of employees. See 1C Larson, The Law of Workmen's Compensation §52.00 (1993).

The early doubts about the constitutionality of workers' compensation laws led many states to make coverage entirely elective. Retention of the elective feature as to some employees is not unusual, but a majority of states make coverage compulsory as to some categories of employees.

There is a wide variation among the states as to the limits on the amount of compensation payable. No statute provides full wage loss replacement; the limits may be on the amount of the weekly payment, the total amount payable, the number of weeks during which compensation is payable, or a combination of these.

In most states, workers' compensation claims are handled by a specialized administrative agency, similar to the Massachusetts Industrial Accident Board. However, doubts about the constitutionality of committing adjudicative responsibilities to administrative agencies caused some states, such as Louisiana (see La. Rev. Ann. tit. 23, §1311), to assign the task of processing claims to the courts.

Problem 36

You have been retained by Sidney Rothman to represent him in pressing a workers' compensation claim against Reliance Insurance Company. The preliminary investigation has been completed, and you must decide whether Mr. Rothman has a valid claim worth pursuing beyond the amount of Reliance's offer, and if so, how to proceed to recover upon that claim. The file on the Rothman claim follows:

Memo for file — March 13
Re: Sidney L. Rothman

I had a conference with Mr. Rothman this morning, and I have agreed to represent him in his comp claim against Reliance Insurance. Rothman is an engineer at Grayson & Sons. He is married, and has three children, aged 11, 13, and 15.

On Nov. 20 last year he fell down a flight of stairs at work on his way out to lunch. He said that as a result of the fall, he suffered a ruptured disc. He spent a week in the hospital and another week at home in bed. He said that he still suffers severe pain. Although he returned to work on Dec. 18, he has been unable to adequately do all that his job requires or engage in his normal off-work activities, such as working around the house and playing tennis.

Grayson has continued to pay Rothman his full salary, but he has been unable to do outside consulting work, from which he estimates he would have earned about $60 a week since the accident. Rothman's medical expenses were $6,978.23, of which $5,582.58 were picked up by medical insurance he has through Grayson's. He made over $73,000 last year, but is concerned that he will not get the promotion he is after unless his back improves considerably. He also indicated that he has run into some unusual family expenses since the accident, and could use the money as soon as he can get it.

Reliance has offered Rothman $1,640 for 4 weeks of total disability, plus his medicals, I told him I thought that he is entitled to more, but that I would have to get all the facts before expressing any final opinion. I also told him that my usual fee in comp cases is 20 percent of whatever recovery there is, plus my expenses. He agreed to this.

Attached is Reliance's letter of last Dec. 20, relating to the claim.

Reliance Insurance Company
205 Main Street
Central City, Columbia

December 20

Mr. Sidney L. Rothman
15 Beacon Road
Fairfield, Columbia

Dear Mr. Rothman:

We received a Notice of Compensable Injury from your employer and our insured, Grayson & Sons, on December 4. We have received copies of your hospital records and we have reports from both the attending physicians and our own examining physician, Dr. Randolph Copich. We have given your claim careful consideration and are ready to pay your medical expenses to date, supplemented by necessary medical expenses which you may incur in the future, and the sum of $1,640 representing the maximum disability compensation to which you are entitled.

Please complete the enclosed Form of Voluntary Agreement, sign it, and give it to your employer who will verify it and forward it to us.

Sincerelv.

James Parker

James Parker
District Manager

The file of Problem 34, beginning at p. 719, above, is incorporated here. Assume that the Columbia Workers' Compensation Act, of which the following sections are a part, is the same as that of Massachusetts, and that the opinion in Shaw's Case is by the Columbia Supreme Court. You should also refer to the excerpts from Bailey, Back Injuries, set out in connection with Problem 34, above.

COLUMBIA WORKERS' COMPENSATION ACT

§34A. TOTAL AND PERMANENT INCAPACITY

While the incapacity for work resulting from the injury is both permanent and total, the insurer shall pay to the injured employee, following payment of compensation provided in sections thirty-four and thirty-five, a weekly compensation equal to two-thirds of his average weekly wage before the injury, but not more than the maximum weekly compensation rate nor less than the minimum weekly compensation rate.

§35. PARTIAL INCAPACITY

While the incapacity for work resulting from the injury is partial, during each week of incapacity the insurer shall pay the injured employee a weekly compensation equal to sixty percent of the difference between his or her average weekly wage before the injury and the weekly wage he or she is capable of earning after the injury, but not more than seventy-five percent of what such employee would receive if he or she were eligible for total incapacity benefits under section thirty-four. An insurer may reduce the amount paid to an employee under this section to the amount at which the employee's combined weekly earnings and benefits are equal to two times the average weekly wage in the commonwealth at the time of such reduction.

The total number of weeks of compensation due the employee under this section shall not exceed two hundred sixty.

§35A. ADDED COMPENSATION FOR DEPENDENTS; PAYMENT; PRESUMED DEPENDENTS; DEPENDENCY DETERMINED BY FACTS

Where the injured employee has persons conclusively presumed to be dependent upon him or in fact so dependent, the sum of six dollars shall be added to the weekly compensation payable under sections thirty-four, . . . and thirty-five, for each person wholly dependent on the employee, but in no case shall the aggregate of such amounts exceed the average weekly wages of the employee. No weekly payment to the employee under this section shall allow the employee to receive an amount in excess of one hundred and fifty dollars per week when combined with the compensation due under sections thirty-four, . . . and thirty-five. For the purposes of this section the following persons shall be conclusively presumed to be wholly dependent for support upon an employee:

(a) A wife upon a husband with whom she lives at the time of his injury.

(b) A husband upon a wife with whom he is living at the time of her injury.

(c) Children under the age of eighteen years, or over said age but physically or mentally incapacitated from earning, if living with the employee at the time of his injury. . . .

An administrative judge or reviewing board may in his or its discretion order the insurer or self-insurer to make payment of the six dollars aforesaid directly to the dependent.

§51. COMPENSATION OF YOUNG EMPLOYEE

Whenever an employee is injured under circumstances entitling him to compensation, if it be established that the injured employee was of such age and experience when injured that, under natural conditions, in the open labor market, his wage would be expected to increase, that fact may be considered in determining his weekly wage. A determination of an employee's benefits under this section shall not be limited to the circumstances of the employee's particular employer or industry at the time of injury.

The *maximum weekly compensation rate* referred to in the foregoing is defined in an earlier section of the act to be the average weekly wage in the state as determined from time to time by the Commissioner of the Department of Employment and Training. The most recent average weekly wage has been determined to be $410. The *minimum weekly compensation rate* is defined to be 20 percent of the average weekly wage.

Shaw's Case

247 Mass. 157, 141 N.E. 858 (1923)

BRALEY, J. The employee on February 14, 1919, fractured his right patella in the course of, and arising out of his employment by the subscriber the Taunton Hotel Company, hereafter referred to as the employer, and "the insurer entered into an agreement to pay him $16 a week for total incapacity for work, based on an average weekly wage of $28, and compensation was paid in accordance with this agreement up to and through January 21, 1922. Since that date the insurer paid the employee $4 for the week ending April 1, and $4 each for the week ending April 29, May 6, 13, 20, 27, June 3, and June 10." The record states that the question for decision was the employee's "incapacity since January 21, 1922."

The board member, who heard the case in the first instance and whose findings and decision were adopted and affirmed by the Industrial Accident Board on review under the insurer's appeal, was warranted in finding on the evidence of the employee and of the impartial physician, that at the date of the hearing, July 5, 1922, he was still incapacitated "for the performance of many of the duties which his employment calls for and which he performed before the injury." While the insurer does not question this finding, it contends, that there was no evidence warranting the further findings which fixed his earning capacity at $16 a week during the period in question. The statute provides, "While the incapacity for work resulting from the injury is partial, the insurer shall pay the injured employee a weekly compensation equal to two-thirds of the difference between his average weekly wages before the injury and the average weekly wages which he is able to earn thereafter, but not more than sixteen dollars a week; and the amount of such compensation shall not be more than four thousand dollars." G.L. c. 152, §35.

It was undisputed that before the injury his earning capacity was at least $24 a week, and the extent of its impairment after January 1, 1922, to the date of the hearing was the question for decision. In substance the employee testified that he received no money from the employer while he was out of work, although "after the insurance company stopped paying," quite often "the hotel gave him money to help him because he had a big family." In reply to questions by the board member he said that "he was back there working some of the time," and notified the insurance company he had "gone to work," but could not tell the date when he resumed work or of the notice, and that the insurer subsequently paid him $4 for two weeks only, when the payments ceased. The evidence of the employer's treasurer, a witness called by the insurer, shows, however, that on January 21, 1922, he was engaged in such work as he was able to perform, receiving $24 a week, except that on April 1 and April 4 the payments were $20, to which the payments for those weeks by the insurer of $4 for each week afforded a weekly revenue of $24. It is true, as contended by the insurer, this witness also said that for the last few weeks the employee "has earned his full wages and he also earned it back in January . . . working along the same lines as previous to the accident but he is not able to do a ceiling; he is doing the greater part of the general repair work." If this were all the evidence, the employee was earning $24 a week, the amount of his average weekly wages prior to the injury. But the witness further testified, that while "he was disabled the hotel paid him the balance between what the insurance company was paying him and his wages so that he got his full wages," and that before "he came back to work the hotel gave him $8 a week . . . all the time he was out; the idea of the company was to make up the difference; if they did not have him insured they would have paid him his full wages." The board member found that during the weeks under review the subscriber paid full wages not because the employee was able to earn them, but because the insurer had stopped payments. "From the time the employee was injured the subscriber has paid him enough money each week to make up the $24 he earned before his injury." This $24 was his regular wage, overtime raising it to $28.

The statute awards compensation for loss of earning capacity caused by the injury as compared with the employee's average weekly wage received by him before the injury, and, the findings having been supported by the board member's view of the evidence, and of the credibility of the witnesses, we cannot say as matter of law that they are erroneous. It follows from these findings and the findings of continuing partial incapacity that the employee is entitled to compensation, the amount of which was to be determined.

The insurer contends that there is reversible error in the further findings fixing the employee's earning capacity at $16, and that "he still is limited to that amount." It could be found on all the evidence that while the employer gave the employee $24 a week for many weeks, $8 of the amount was a gratuity, apparently leaving his earning capacity at $16 for a very substantial portion of the period, and on this basis he was allowed partial compensation at the rate of $8 a week for twenty-three weeks from January 21 to July 1, 1922. But at the date of the hearing by a single member of the Industrial Accident Board, July 5, 1922, he was "getting the same wages as he earned previous to his injury"; and "for the past few weeks" previous to the hearing he "earned his full wages." The insurer therefore cannot be held for the full amount awarded where for any appreciable part of the time the employee was earning the average weekly wages not including overtime he had formerly received.

It is also contended that even if the claimant finally prevails, the insurer should be credited with alleged overpayments from September 12, 1921, to January 1, 1922, as well as the payments for eight weeks allowed by the board member. But on the employee's evidence it could be found there were no overpayments. The inquiry moreover was limited to a period which did not include payments made prior to January 21, 1922.

While error appears for the reasons stated, and the decree must be reversed, the case is recommitted to the Industrial Accident Board for further proceedings not inconsistent with this opinion.

Ordered accordingly.

Law and Policy: Whither the Workers' Compensation Concept?

In the introductory text to this chapter, we stated that "from a public policy perspective, the issue raised by this chapter is whether the concept of no-fault compensation . . . should be extended beyond workers' compensation . . . to . . . other areas now occupied by the fault system." Such an extension is urged in R. Henderson, Should Workmen's Compensation Be Extended to Nonoccupational Injuries?, 48 Tex. L. Rev. 117 (1969). Professor Roger Henderson argues that courts have eroded the distinction between occupational and nonoccupational injuries in cases involving the requirement that to be compensable an injury must arise out of and in the course of the employment. Among the cases he discusses as illustrating the erosion is Gargiulo v. Gargiulo, 13 N.J. 8, 97 A.2d 593 (1953), wherein the Supreme Court of New Jersey ruled that an employee was entitled to compensation for injuries caused by his being accidentally struck by an arrow shot by a child while the employee was working. Henderson also cites O'Leary v. Brown-Pacific-Maxon, Inc., 340 U.S. 504, 71 S. Ct. 470, 95 L. Ed. 483 (1951), in which the United States Supreme Court permitted to stand an award of compensation to the dependent mother of an employee who drowned in an unsuccessful rescue attempt. The employee had spent an afternoon away from work at an employer-owned recreation area near the ocean. Next to the shoreline was a dangerous channel, and a sign erected by the employer prohibited swimming in it. As the employee was leaving the area, he saw two men standing on a reef beyond the channel signaling for help. Along with others, he jumped into the channel to rescue the two men, but drowned before he could reach them. Relying on these and other cases, Henderson asserts that the policies underlying workers' compensation statutes have undergone a metamorphosis (48 Tex. L. Rev. at 126-127):

> The original purpose was to compensate employees when the injury was one caused by a risk growing out of the employment and to pass the cost of that compensation along to the consumer. The policy was that society should pay, through the mechanism devised, for injuries caused to the working man while he was engaged in his employment, and which were caused by that employment. Now that policy is playing less and less of a role in the compensation decision process. The emphasis now seems to be on the right of a working man to recover regardless of the origin of the risk, as long as the employment has some substantial effect on the conduct or life of the employee when the injury occurs. The unarticulated, but apparently emerging policy, as evidenced by the decisions referred to above, seems to be a desire to provide economic security and medical care for society in general. It is a limited but natural application of this policy to want to provide economic security for the productive persons in our society, and their dependents, and when possible, to assist them to return to a productive capacity as quickly as possible with a minimum of permanent disability. This desire to provide medical and vocational rehabilitation, with attendant economic security as a means of achieving that goal, is easily carried out for employees by the courts because of the basic compensation insurance scheme that already exists. The inefficacy of the "work-connected" distinction now blurs to a great extent any clear identification of this policy, but it is submitted that this will be the undergirdings of the future decisions in this area, since there is no longer any clear rationale by which to identify injuries "arising out of and in the course of the employment."

> The courts will not be able to avoid the language of the statutes entirely, but by paying them a certain amount of lip service, they can still extend the scope of the compensation acts to include the great bulk of injuries befalling employees. It is not a matter of erecting a whole new system and exposing it to the political process through proposed legislation, but merely a matter of broadening the scope of existing coverage by judicial decision.

The blurring of the distinction between occupational and nonoccupational injuries under workers' compensation statutes is, according to the author, a reflection of a policy calling for a "healthy, productive society," regardless of the cause of the injury. The choice now is how best to implement that policy. Henderson argues that workers' compensation can be an important vehicle for implementing the new policy, together with other social welfare programs covering those not covered by workers' compensation. He does not favor absorbing the entire nonoccupational injury problem into other governmental programs, such as social security (48 Tex. L. Rev. at 155-156):

> The organization, capital outlay, and expertise now exist in the realm of private enterprise to handle the program. The argument that the Government through social security can do it more efficiently—which is questionable when viewed over the long run—proves too much. Under that theory we should abandon private enterprise entirely for the socialist state. Until a convincing practical case is made for changing our basic economic structure, we should not be any more ambitious to replace the private insurance industry with social security any more than we should replace the present social security program with private enterprise.

According to the author, national legislation will be required to accomplish the proposed expansion of workers' compensation coverage. This is because no state will want to be the first state to increase the costs associated with the expansion out of a fear of putting local industry at a competitive disadvantage compared to industries in states which do not have expanded coverage. However, existing methods of financing would be retained, which in most states is through private insurance companies. The program would be funded by contributions from both employers and employees with the latter paying for the nonoccupational injury coverage. Henderson asserts that the retention of the occupational-nonoccupational distinction for this purpose will not result in the litigation that the distinction now generates when the issue is whether the employee is entitled to compensation.

Henderson does not suggest that expanded workers' compensation be made an injured employee's exclusive remedy (48 Tex. L. Rev. at 144):

> No one is arguing that the fault system is basically unsound, but only that in particular instances it has not worked out to the advantage of those most concerned—the employee and the motorist. Thus, the need to make the

> proposed workmen's compensation plan any more exclusive than it already is has not been demonstrated, at least in so far as changing the existing system other than in the area of motor vehicle accidents. As to the employer, workmen's compensation should be retained as the exclusive remedy, and as to third-party tortfeasors, the common law liability system should be available to the employee, just as it now is in most states.

The author concludes his article with these observations (48 Tex. L. Rev. at 157):

> Whether the basic workmen's compensation system, or some other scheme, will be used to meet the growing demands of society for economic security and medical care will be a historical fact in the not too distant future. The present fractionated approach is destined for some drastic change. The problems of attempting to maintain the occupational-nonoccupational distinction in the existing compensation system and social setting have been explored. Hopefully, this Article has indicated, in rather sweeping strokes, how social insurance can meet these problems and, at the same time, respond in a way compatible with the private enterprise economic system in the United States. Basically, ours is a system built on reciprocity—a trading or exchange economy. This is a system that lends dignity to the members of the society involved. In keeping with that ideal, people should be compensated for disability as a matter of right and not as a matter of grace. The proposal presented would continue that overall scheme of things. At the very least, it provides a meaningful alternative to that of allowing the matter to pass by default into a tax supported government plan such as social security.

Whether or not the extensions of worker compensation envisioned by Professor Henderson are accomplished in this country in the coming years, it is interesting to observe that such extensions have been accomplished in at least one common law country. The New Zealand Accident Compensation Act of 1972, together with subsequent amendments, bars all causes of action for death or personal injury suffered by accident and substitutes therefor rights in accident victims to collect on a no-fault basis from state administered compensation funds. The New Zealand system is analyzed in Section D of this chapter.

A different view of workers' compensation is presented in Note, Exceptions to the Exclusive Remedy Requirements of Workers' Compensation Statutes, 96 Harv. L. Rev. 1641 (1983). The note argues that partial payment for economic loss and lack of payment for pain and suffering provide inadequate compensation for injured workers and insufficient employer incentive to invest in workplace safety. Because of this, the note recommends that the tort system should play an increasing role in compensating for work-related injuries through inroads into the exclusivity feature of workers' compensation statutes.

Generally, workers' compensation statutes provide the exclusive remedy against employers for employees' work-related injuries. The statutes require employers to provide compensation to employees without regard to employer fault; in return, the employees give up the common law right to recover from employers in tort. However, some states recognize certain exceptions to the rule that workers' compensation is the exclusive remedy for work related injuries.

One common exception to the exclusivity rule concerns intentional torts committed by the employer. Some states have statutory exceptions allowing employees to sue for such torts. See, e.g., Ky. Rev. Stat. §342.610(4). In other jurisdictions, the intentional tort exception has been judicially created.

It is not surprising that the scope of the intentional tort exception to the exclusivity of worker's compensation varies considerably from state to state, in part because the statutes themselves vary from state to state. Keeping in mind, then, that generalization is difficult, the following cases indicate some of the contexts in which the issue has arisen:

Intentional Failure of the Employer to Maintain Safe Working Conditions. In most courts, this kind of employer behavior is not sufficient to take the case out of the exclusivity provision. See, e.g., Abbott v. Gould, Inc., 232 Neb. 907, 443 N.W.2d 591 (1988) (allegation that employer intentionally misrepresented the safety of working conditions). But in Bradfield v. Stop-N-Go Foods, Inc., 17 Ohio St. 3d 58, 477 N.E.2d 621, *appeal dismissed* 474 U.S. 805 (1985), the court held that a convenience store employee who alleged that the employer failed to provide adequate security was not necessarily barred from tort recovery.

Intentional Infliction of Emotional Harm. McSwain v. Shei, 304 S.C. 25, 402 S.E.2d 890 (1991) (claim not barred); Livitsanos v. Superior Court, 2 Cal. 4th 744, 828 P.2d 1195, 7 Cal. Rptr. 2d 708 (1992) (test is whether employer's misconduct "exceeds normal risks of employment relationship").

Sexual Harassment. Irvin Investors, Inc. v. Superior Court, 166 Ariz. 113, 800 P.2d 979 (Ariz. App. 1990) (claim barred); Byrd v. Richardson-Greenshields Securities, Inc., 552 So. 2d 1099 (Fla. 1989) (claim not barred).

Defamation. Snead v. Harbaugh, 241 Va. 524, 404 S.E.2d 53 (1991) (law professor's action against dean and other law professors not barred).

Another exception to the exclusivity of worker's compensation as a remedy for work-related injuries followed by some courts is the *dual capacity doctrine.* It is applied most frequently in products liability actions, in which the employee alleges injury in the course of employment by a product manufactured and supplied by the employer. The theory is that the employee is not suing the employer as employer, but as a manufacturer of the injury-causing product. See, e.g., Bell v. Industrial Vangas, Inc., 30 Cal. 3d 268, 637 P.2d 266, 179 Cal. Rptr. 30 (1981). (After this case, the California legislature passed a statute barring the application of the dual capacity doctrine in products liability cases. Cal. Labor Code §3602.) The overwhelming majority of courts have rejected the dual capacity doctrine in products liability actions. See, e.g., Schump v. Firestone Tire and Rubber Co., 44 Ohio 3d 148, 541 N.E.2d 1040 (1989); Stewart v. CMI Corp., 740 P.2d 1340 (Utah 1987).

In a number of contexts, employers have sought refuge in exclusivity clauses from claims by persons other than injured employees. One type of claim involves an action of indemnity or contribution against the employer by a third party who is liable in tort to the injured employee. The court in Dole v. Dow Chemical Co., 38 N.Y.2d 142, 282 N.E.2d 288 (1972) permitted the action. But other courts have overwhelmingly rejected such actions as impermissible "end runs" around the exclusivity of the worker's compensation system. See, e.g., Lake v. Construction Machinery Inc., 787 P.2d 1027 (Alas. 1990); Henning v. GM Assembly Division, 143 Wis. 1, 419 N.W.2d 551 (1988). The court in Kotecki v. Cyclops Welding Corp., 146 Ill. 155, 585 N.E.2d 1023 (1991), permitted the third party to claim contribution to the extent of the employer's workers' compensation liability; the employee had not filed a claim against the employer and, presumably, would be foreclosed from pursuing a workers' compensation claim if recovery is had against the third party. The action is also permitted if the employer has entered into an express contract of indemnity with the third party. See, e.g., Barsness v. General Diesel & Equipment Co., Inc., 422 N.W.2d 819 (N.D. 1988).

Other third person claims have been brought against employers by persons whose claim is in some sense derivative from the injury to the employee. One claim frequently made, and just as frequently denied, is a loss of consortium claim by a spouse of the injured employee. See, e.g., Dobrydnia v. Indiana Group, Inc., 568 N.E.2d 1002 (Ill. App.), *review denied,* 139 Ill. 2d 594, 575 N.E.2d 912 (1991); Sama v. Cardi Corp., 569 A.2d 432 (R.I. 1990). Recovery has also been attempted in prenatal injury cases, with mixed results. See Bell v. Macy's California, 212 Cal. App. 3d 1442, 261 Cal. Rptr. 447 (1989) (action denied); Cushing v. Time Saver Stores, Inc., 552 So. 2d 730 (La. App. 1990) (action permitted).

It is fair to say that most courts today adhere rather rigidly to the exclusivity provisions of their workers' compensation laws, and that they have yet to bring tort law into an integrated system of compensation for work-related injuries.

In general, see King, The Exclusiveness of an Employee's Workers' Compensation Remedy Against His Employer, 55 Tenn. L. Rev. 405 (1988).

B. Compensation for Victims of Automobile Accidents

Much of the criticism directed at the torts system of allocating losses from personal injuries has focused on those stemming from automobile accidents.

In general, the system stands accused of overcompensating the slightly injured, undercompensating the seriously injured, delaying the payment of claims, absorbing high costs in processing claims, encouraging dishonesty in the making and paying of claims, and causing high, to the point of being unaffordable, liability insurance premiums. The most comprehensive empirical study of automobile accidents was conducted by the United States Department of Transportation, which culminated in a multi-volume report released in 1970.

The most influential work kindling an interest in moving automobile accident losses out of the torts system is that of then Professor, now Judge, Robert Keeton and Professor Jeffrey O'Connell. In their book, Basic Protection for the Traffic Victim: A Blueprint for Reforming Automobile Insurance, (1965), they presented a detailed proposal that would replace much of the traditional negligence-insurance system of compensation for personal injuries caused by automobile accidents. The key features of the Basic Protection Plan are:

(1) Compulsory insurance providing for compensation for economic loss of up to $10,000, without regard to fault, for injuries "arising out of the ownership, maintenance, or use of a motor vehicle." Economic loss consists of income actually lost, expenses reasonably incurred by the injured person for services he would have performed for himself but for the injury, and reasonable medical and rehabilitation expenses.

(2) Reduction of the amount of compensation due by any amount received from a collateral source, such as medical insurance and sick leave plans (but not life insurance or "gratuities"), and by an amount representing the income tax that would be paid were the compensation taxable.

(3) Exemption from liability in tort for the first $5,000 of damages for pain and suffering and for the first $10,000 of other tort damages.

(4) Periodic payments of benefits on a monthly basis, with lump sum payment only when a court rules that it "is in the best interests of the claimant."

Massachusetts was the first state to enact a no-fault automobile insurance statute. In 1967, a bill patterned after the Keeton-O'Connell Basic Protection Plan was passed by the House of Representatives, but was defeated in the Senate. This setback for no-fault was only temporary, and the Massachusetts legislature enacted the Personal Injury Protection Act (Mass. Gen. L. ch. 90, §§34A, 34M and 34N, and ch. 231, §6D), which became effective in 1971.

No-fault statutes were subsequently adopted by a number of states and they come in almost endless variations. In some states, no-fault insurance is compulsory, and in others it is only elective—insurance companies must offer the coverage, but it need not be purchased. The statutes also vary in the amount of no-fault benefits that are payable. No-fault compensation is limited to out-of-pocket expenses, usually medical and related expenses and lost wages. Some statutes have an aggregate limit for both; others specify separate limits.

"True" no-fault requires some sort of tort exemption applicable to the operator causing the injury. All such statutes exempt the operator from tort liability for out-of-pocket no-fault benefits that are paid, and, to some extent, from liability for pain and suffering. As to the latter, some tort liability exemptions are geared to the amount of medical expenses, so that no recovery can be had under no-fault unless the medical expenses exceed a specified threshold. Other statutes gear pain and suffering recovery to the nature of the claimant's injury. Under that system, there can be no recovery unless the injury is relatively severe and permanent.

The state-to-state variations in the statutes have led to a number of proposals to bring about a uniform approach. One such proposal is the Uniform Motor Vehicle Reparations Act, approved by the National Conference of Commissioners on Uniform State Laws in 1972. Legislation has been introduced into Congress from time to time which would establish comprehensive minimum requirements for each state to incorporate into a no-fault statute. See, e.g., S. 354, 93rd Cong., 2nd Sess. (1974).

Florida was one of the early states to enact no-fault legislation and the important sections of the Florida statute are set out below. Following the statute are questions which will aid you in understanding how the statute works and how it meets the criticisms of the negligence-insurance system.

Florida Motor Vehicle No-Fault Law

Florida Statutes

627.730 Short Title

Sections 627.730-627.7405 may be cited and known as the "Florida Motor Vehicle No-Fault Law."

627.732 Definitions

As used in §§627.730-627.7405:

(1) "Motor vehicle" means any self-propelled vehicle with four or more wheels which is of a type both designed and required to be licensed for use on the highways of this state and any trailer or semitrailer designed for use with such vehicle and includes:

(a) A "private passenger motor vehicle," which is any motor vehicle which is a sedan, station wagon, or jeep-type vehicle and, if not used primarily for occupational, professional, or business purposes, a motor vehicle of the pickup, panel, van, camper, or motor home type.

(b) A "commercial motor vehicle," which is any motor vehicle which is not a private passenger motor vehicle.

The term "motor vehicle" does not include a mobile home or any motor vehicle which is used in mass transit or public school transportation and designed to transport more than five passengers exclusive of the operator of the motor vehicle and which is owned by a municipality, a transit or public school transportation authority, or a political subdivision of the state.

(2) "Named insured" means a person, usually the owner of a vehicle, identified in a policy by name as the insured under the policy.

(3) "Owner" means a person who holds the legal title to a motor vehicle; or, in the event a motor vehicle is the subject of a security agreement or lease with an option to purchase with the debtor or lessee having the right to possession, then the debtor or lessee shall be deemed the owner for the purposes of §§627.730-627.7405.

(4) "Relative residing in the same household" means a relative of any degree by blood or by marriage who usually makes his home in the same family unit, whether or not temporarily living elsewhere.

627.733 Required Security

(1) Every owner or registrant of a motor vehicle required to be registered and licensed in this state shall maintain security [which in most instances will be an insurance policy providing coverage as set out in this statute] in effect continuously throughout the registration or licensing period. . . .

(4) An owner of a motor vehicle with respect to which security is required by this section who fails to have such security in effect at the time of an accident shall have no immunity from tort liability, but shall be personally liable for the payment of benefits under §627.736. With respect to such benefits, such an owner shall have all of the rights and obligations of an insurer under §§627.730-627.7405. . . .

627.736 Required Personal Injury Protection Benefits; Exclusions; Priority

(1) Required benefits.—Every insurance policy complying with the security requirements of §627.733 shall provide personal injury protection to the named insured, relatives residing in the same household, persons operating the insured motor vehicle, passengers in such motor vehicle, and other persons struck by such motor vehicle and suffering bodily injury while not an occupant of a self-propelled vehicle, subject to the provisions of subsection (2) and paragraph (4)(d), to a limit of $10,000 for loss sustained by any such person as a result of bodily injury, sickness, disease, or death

arising out of the ownership, maintenance, or use of a motor vehicle as follows:

(a) Medical benefits.—Eighty percent of all reasonable expenses for necessary medical, surgical, X-ray, dental, and rehabilitative services, including prosthetic devices, and necessary ambulance, hospital, and nursing services. Such benefits shall also include necessary remedial treatment and services recognized and permitted under the laws of the state for an injured person who relies upon spiritual means through prayer alone for healing, in accordance with his religious beliefs.

(b) Disability benefits.—Sixty percent of any loss of gross income and loss of earning capacity per individual from inability to work proximately caused by the injury sustained by the injured person, plus all expenses reasonably incurred in obtaining from others ordinary and necessary services in lieu of those that, but for the injury, the injured person would have performed without income for the benefit of his household. All disability benefits payable under this provision shall be paid not less than every 2 weeks.

(c) Death benefits.—Death benefits of $5,000 per individual. The insurer may pay such benefits to the executor or administrator of the deceased, to any of the deceased's relatives by blood or legal adoption or connection by marriage, or to any person appearing to the insurer to be equitably entitled thereto. . . .

(2) Authorized exclusions.—Any insurer may exclude benefits:

(a) For injury sustained by the named insured and relatives residing in the same household while occupying another motor vehicle owned by the named insured and not insured under the policy or for injury sustained by any person operating the insured motor vehicle without the express or implied consent of the insured.

(b) To any injured person, if such person's conduct contributed to his injury under any of the following circumstances:

1. Causing injury to himself intentionally; or
2. Being injured while committing a felony.

Whenever an injured is charged with conduct as set forth in subparagraph 2, the 30-day payment provision of paragraph (4)(b) shall be held in abeyance, and the insurer shall withhold payment of any personal injury protection benefits pending the outcome of the case at the trial level. If the charge is nolle prossed or dismissed or the insured is acquitted, the 30-day payment provision shall run from the date the insurer is notified of such action.

(3) Insured's rights to recovery of special damages in tort claims.—No insurer shall have a lien on any recovery in tort by judgment, settlement, or otherwise for personal injury protection benefits, whether suit has been filed or settlement has been reached without suit. An injured party who is entitled to bring suit under the provisions of §§627.730-627.7405, or his legal representative, shall have no right to recover any damages for which personal injury protection benefits are paid or payable. The plaintiff may

prove all of his special damages notwithstanding this limitation, but if special damages are introduced in evidence, the trier of facts, whether judge or jury, shall not award damages for personal injury protection benefits paid or payable. In all cases in which a jury is required to fix damages, the court shall instruct the jury that the plaintiff shall not recover such special damages for personal injury protection benefits paid or payable.

(4) Benefits; when due.—Benefits due from an insurer under §§627.730-627.7405 shall be primary, except that benefits received under any workers' compensation law shall be credited against the benefits provided by subsection (1) and shall be due and payable as loss accrues, upon receipt of reasonable proof of such loss and the amount of expenses and loss incurred which are covered by the policy issued under §§627.730-627.7405. . . .

(d) The insurer of the owner of a motor vehicle shall pay personal injury protection benefits for:

1. Accidental bodily injury sustained in this state by the owner while occupying a motor vehicle, or while not an occupant of a self-propelled vehicle if the injury is caused by physical contact with a motor vehicle.

2. Accidental bodily injury sustained outside this state, but within the United States of America or its territories or possessions or Canada, by the owner while occupying the owner's motor vehicle.

3. Accidental bodily injury sustained by a relative of the owner residing in the same household, under the circumstances described in subparagraph 1 or subparagraph 2, provided the relative at the time of the accident is domiciled in the owner's household and is not himself the owner of a motor vehicle with respect to which security is required under §§627.730-627.7405.

4. Accidental bodily injury sustained in this state by any other person while occupying the owner's motor vehicle or, if a resident of this state, while not an occupant of a self-propelled vehicle, if the injury is caused by physical contact with such motor vehicle, provided the injured person is not himself:

a. The owner of a motor vehicle with respect to which security is required under §§627.730-627.7405; or

b. Entitled to personal injury benefits from the insurer of the owner or owners of such a motor vehicle.

627.737 Tort Exemption; Limitation on Right to Damages; Punitive Damages

(1) Every owner, registrant, operator, or occupant of a motor vehicle with respect to which security has been provided as required by §§627.730-627.7405, and every person or organization legally responsible for his acts or omissions, is hereby exempted from tort liability for damages because of bodily injury, sickness, or disease arising out of the ownership, operation,

maintenance, or use of such motor vehicle in this state to the extent that the benefits described in §627.736(1) are payable for such injury, or would be payable but for any exclusion authorized by §§627.730-627.7405, under any insurance policy or other method of security complying with the requirements of §627.733, or by an owner personally liable under §627.733 for the payment of such benefits, unless a person is entitled to maintain an action for pain, suffering, mental anguish, and inconvenience for such injury under the provisions of subsection (2).

(2) In any action of tort brought against the owner, registrant, operator, or occupant of a motor vehicle with respect to which security has been provided as required by §§627.730-627.7405, or against any person or organization legally responsible for his acts or omissions, a plaintiff may recover damages in tort for pain, suffering, mental anguish, and inconvenience because of bodily injury, sickness, or disease arising out of the ownership, maintenance, operation, or use of such motor vehicle only in the event that the injury or disease consists in whole or in part of:

(a) Significant and permanent loss of an important bodily function.

(b) Permanent injury within a reasonable degree of medical probability, other than scarring or disfigurement.

(c) Significant and permanent scarring or disfigurement.

(d) Death. . . .

(4) In any action brought against an automobile liability insurer for damages in excess of its policy limits, no claim for punitive damages shall be allowed.

627.7372 Collateral Sources of Indemnity

(1) In any action for personal injury or wrongful death arising out of the ownership, operation, use, or maintenance of a motor vehicle, the court shall admit into evidence the total amount of all collateral sources paid to the claimant, and the court shall instruct the jury to deduct from its verdict the value of all benefits received by the claimant from any collateral source.

(2) For purposes of this section, "collateral sources" means any payments made to the claimant, or on his behalf, by or pursuant to:

(a) The United States Social Security Act; any federal, state, or local income disability act; or any other public programs providing medical expenses, disability payments, or other similar benefits.

(b) Any health, sickness, or income disability insurance; automobile accident insurance that provides health benefits or income disability coverage; and any other similar insurance benefits except life insurance benefits available to the claimant, whether purchased by him or provided by others.

(c) Any contract or agreement of any group, organization, partnership, or corporation to provide, pay for, or reimburse the costs of hospital, medical, dental, or other health care services.

(d) Any contractual or voluntary wage continuation plan provided by employers or any other system intended to provide wages during a period of disability.

(3) Notwithstanding any other provision of this section, benefits received under Medicare or any other federal program providing for a federal government lien on the plaintiff's recovery, the Worker's Compensation Law or the Medicaid program of Title XIX of the Social Security Act, or from any medical services program administered by the Department of Health and Rehabilitative Services shall not be considered a collateral source.

627.739 Personal Injury Protection; Optional Limitations; Deductibles

(1) The named insured may elect a deductible to apply to the named insured alone or to the named insured and dependent relatives residing in the same household, but may not elect a deductible to apply to any other person covered under the policy. Any person electing a deductible or modified coverage, or subject to such deductible or modified coverage as a result of the named insured's election, shall have no right to claim or to recover any amount so deducted from any owner, registrant, operator, or occupant of a vehicle or any person or organization legally responsible for any such person's acts or omissions who is made exempt from tort liability by §§627.730-627.7405.

(2) Insurers shall offer to each applicant and to each policyholder, upon the renewal of an existing policy, deductibles, in amounts of $250, $500, $1,000, and $2,000, such amount to be deducted from the benefits otherwise due each person subject to the deduction. However, this subsection shall not be applied to reduce the amount of any benefits received in accordance with §627.736(1)(c).

(3) Insurers shall offer coverage wherein, at the election of the named insured, all benefits payable under 42 U.S.C. §1395, the federal "Medicare" program, or to active or retired military personnel and their dependent relatives shall be deducted from those benefits otherwise payable pursuant to §627.736(1).

(4) Insurers shall offer coverage wherein, at the election of the named insured, the benefits for loss of gross income and loss of earning capacity described in §627.736(1)(b) shall be excluded.

627.7405 Insurers' Right of Reimbursement

Notwithstanding any other provisions of §§627.730-627.7405, any insurer providing personal injury protection benefits on a private passenger motor vehicle shall have, to the extent of any personal injury protection benefits paid to any person as a benefit arising out of such private passenger motor vehicle insurance, a right of reimbursement against the owner or the insurer of the owner of a commercial motor vehicle, if the benefits paid result from such person having been an occupant of the commercial motor vehicle or having been struck by the commercial motor vehicle while not an occupant of any self-propelled vehicle.

Questions About the Florida No-Fault Statute

1. As to what kinds of motor vehicles is no-fault insurance required?

2. What are the elements of personal injury loss for which no-fault benefits are recoverable? How is each element measured? What are the limits on the amount of benefits that may be recovered? To what extent are collateral sources taken into account in calculating benefits?

3. Are all persons who are injured as the result of the operation or use of a motor vehicle, and who suffer loss described in the answer to Question 2, entitled to no-fault benefits? If not, what circumstances leading to the injury are necessary for entitlement to benefits?

4. To what extent are conventional actions in tort for personal injury retained?

5. What conduct on the part of a claimant will serve to reduce or eliminate recovery of no-fault benefits?

6. What are the territorial and residential restrictions on entitlement to no-fault benefits?

7. Does the statute appear to deal effectively with the criticisms of the negligence-insurance system.

8. What would be an acceptable formula for setting individual insurance premium rates? Should the rate be the same for everyone? If not, what factors should be taken into account?

C. Compensation for Victims of Medical Accidents

In the early 1970s, and several times since then, there have been what many observers have characterized as medical malpractice crises—fear of runaway damage awards, the practice of defensive medicine, physicians leaving areas of practice involving high risks of malpractice suits, and rapidly rising liability insurance premiums—that appeared to many to threaten the viability of the health care delivery system. This section will provide a brief look at the nature and sources of the medical malpractice problems, together with representative examples of how the law, primarily through legislation, has reacted to those problems. The section will also focus on the potential for no-fault solutions.

1. The Nature and Sources of the Medical Malpractice Problems

To a considerable extent, the existence of a crisis is in the eye of the beholder. But in recent years sufficient empirical evidence has emerged to justify the conclusion that medical malpractice claims do affect the availability and cost of medical care. For example, obstetrical care in some communities is not available because of the high price of malpractice insurance premiums.[3] A comprehensive study of the malpractice scene in Florida concluded that the primary cause of the dramatic increase in insurance premiums in the nine years preceding the study was the substantial increase in loss payments to claimants. The increase was due primarily to an increase in payment size, rather than to an increase in the frequency of claims; the latter had remained fairly steady when adjusted for the increased number of physicians.[4] The Florida study also concluded that excessive insurance company profits did not contribute to the crisis, since such profits were not out of line with profits in other fields generally. The underwriting cycle[5] did contribute, in the short run, to the timing and suddenness of the increases. But in the long run, the study concluded, the primary factor was the increase in the amount paid to claimants.

A somewhat different, although clearly related, explanation of the crisis was offered in the 1977 Report of the American Bar Association Commission of Medical Professional Liability. While the Report is several years old, its conclusions have validity in the current time:[6]

1977 Report of the American Bar Association Commission on Medical Professional Liability

9-12

General Perspective

When the Commission was established in February, 1975, a crisis in the delivery of medical care seemed imminent because of the unavailability of

3. See Nye, Gifford, Webb and Dewar, The Causes of the Medical Malpractice Crisis: An Analysis of Claims Data and Insurance Company Finances, 76 Geo. L.J. 1495-1496 (1988).

4. Id. at 1540.

5. The underwriting cycle begins with an increase in demand for insurance, which attracts new investment to the industry. After the expansion, price competition sets in, and companies tend to sell insurance at rates that in the long run are not profitable. Then underwriting losses become excessive, and some insurers withdraw from the market, either voluntarily or because of insolvency. This permits the remaining companies to raise rates, and the cycle begins again. Id. at 1525.

6. The following excerpt from the Report is reproduced with the permission of the American Bar Association.

liability insurance at a cost which was acceptable to high-risk providers [of medical services.]

The immediate cause of the . . . crisis was the withdrawal of many commercial insurers from the market as a result of sharp increases in the frequency and severity of claims, the magnitude of which was largely unforeseen; a shrinkage in capacity to write insurance due to casualty line losses and the 1974 market decline; the particular difficulty in this line of predicting future trends due to its "long tail" characteristic [i.e., the fact that some effects of medical malpractice do not manifest themselves for many years]; and very large rate increases by those companies which remained. The underlying causes are many and diverse and may never be fully known. However, the following factors appear to have played a part:

- Particularly in the last decade, the dramatic growth in medical technology and the more frequent use of complicated machines and procedures. Complex technology has resulted in striking gains in medical care, the extension of lives and greater expectations by patients, but it has also increased the risk of serious adverse results.
- The involvement of more professional and non-professional personnel in the treatment sequence, thus increasing the risk of communication and follow-up errors.
- The increased readiness of patients to question the quality of care given them and to ascribe responsibility for poor outcomes to health care providers. To some extent this may be attributable to unreasonable expectations as to the ability of medicine to cure; it may reflect increased medical specialization and impersonalization and the resultant decrease in continuous physician-patient relationships; and it may also reflect a greater litigiousness in the population.
- Inadequate efforts by hospitals to prevent the occurrence of adverse incidents.
- Inadequate medical discipline.
- Liberalization by appellate courts, at least in some states, of substantive and procedural rules of law so that it is easier for a plaintiff to prove entitlement to damages.
- A general growth in the last decade in the number of practicing attorneys, as well as some increase in the number of competent, experienced attorneys available to represent persons who feel they may have been injured through medical negligence.
- The rapid escalation, in cases of severe, permanent injury, in the amounts of damages awarded by juries.

A more recent comprehensive look at the medical malpractice problem, Weiler, Medical Malpractice on Trial (1991), concludes that the existing tort system does not do a very good job of what it is supposed to do: compensate those who have suffered injury as a result of negligent medical treatment. According to Professor Weiler, one substantial study indicated treatment-related injuries to one out of twenty-two hospital patients, another to one out of twenty-seven. Only one in eight of the potentially valid malpractice claims were filed, and of these only half would result in compensation to the plaintiff. Of the more serious medical injuries, only one in three victims ended up with compensation.[7]

2. Legislative Responses to the Crises

Whether or not the medical malpractice liability situation deserves to be called a crisis, insurance carriers and the medical profession have lobbied actively in the state legislatures for changes in tort law which they feel will ameliorate whatever problems do exist. These efforts have generated counter lobbying efforts by consumer groups and the plaintiffs' bar. The clear winners are the forces for change. Almost all states have enacted legislation designed to make it more difficult for torts plaintiffs generally to recover, or to recover as much, and many states have enacted legislation directed specifically to medical malpractice cases. The extent of the response by the mid-1980s is described in Florida Medical Association, Medical Malpractice Guidebook 53-54 (Manne ed. 1985):

> In reaction to an assumed crisis in medical malpractice insurance rates and availability, in the mid 1970s all 50 states passed some form of legislation regulating various aspects of the patient-health care provider (HCP) relationship. . . .
>
> . . . Although the number of different medical malpractice statutes is as great as the number of states, analysis of the most important features of the various statutes shows that the states can be categorized in terms of two statutory patterns. These patterns are defined by the presence or absence of certain of the nine most important provisions found in the medical malpractice statutes across the states. The provisions are:
>
> 1) new statutes of limitations applicable only to medical malpractice claims;
> 2) prohibition of specification of dollar amounts in the ad damnum clause of the complaint;
> 3) a collateral source evidentiary rule;
> 4) limitations on attorneys' fees;
> 5) a medical review panel (MRP) to which institution of malpractice claims must be submitted;
> 6) limitations on plaintiffs' total recovery
> 7) limitations on the dollar liability of the health care provider;

7. Medical Malpractice on Trial, pp. 12-13.

8) institution of a state-run patient's compensation fund;
9) limitations of plaintiff's recovery to annual payments ("structured recovery").

Most of the medical malpractice legislation has been subject to constitutional attack, sometimes successfully, sometimes not. The attack has been principally under state constitutions, and to some extent the state-to-state variations in the outcomes can be explained by the differences in the state constitutions.

3. No-Fault Compensation Alternatives to the Medical Malpractice System

The legislative reforms just discussed, while in the aggregate are significant, do not alter the basic system of liability based upon a determination that the medical care provider was negligent. Thus, many of what are viewed to be the faults of this traditional system remain untouched. For this reason, there have emerged in recent years proposals for more drastic changes—changes that will eliminate fault as the basis of liability entirely. These proposals also call for the reduction in the amount of compensation available, usually limiting compensation to economic loss, and perhaps some limited compensation for intangible harm. Two of the proposals, one which bases compensation on the existence of a designated compensable event, the other on the existence of birth-related neurological injuries, are outlined below.

Designated Compensable Events. The following is taken from the most complete elaboration of this approach:

ABA Commission on Medical Professional Liability, Designated Compensable Event System: A Feasibility Study

1-3, 5, 10 (1979)

In considering fundamental ways to improve the medical professional liability system, the Commission decided that any system for compensating injured persons should ideally:

1. Encourage the prompt availability of remedial medical services to injured persons;
2. Compensate all persons deemed compensable under the mechanism;
3. Pay a victim of a compensable medical incident at least the net economic loss occasioned by the incident;
4. Provide for the prompt resolution of claims;
5. Charge a minimum of administrative costs (including attorneys' fees) and make a maximum amount available for the injured person;

6. Insure maximum predictability of outcome as an aid to planning by health care providers and insurers;

7. Discourage the bringing of baseless or contrived claims and provide for their prompt elimination if brought;

8. Contribute to the prevention of malpractice incidents by introducing incentives for improving health care and improving the supervision and discipline of health care personnel;

9. Distribute losses through insurance or otherwise in a way which does not leave an unfair burden on any segment of the health care systems; and

10. Disrupt to the least possible degree the relationships of trust and confidence between health care providers and patients. . . .

The Commission concluded that the most promising alternative of those considered is a designated compensable event (DCE) system which would predefine compensable outcomes according to established criteria. Such a DCE approach would largely but not solely predicate the payment of compensation on the conclusion of a representative group of clinicians that an injury probably would have been avoidable by adherence to accepted medical practice. Thus if a medical mishap resulting in injury is an occurrence which has been predefined, the patient would receive reparation without the necessity of bringing a tort liability claim and proving negligence. Mishaps not covered by the list of designated compensable events would remain under the tort liability system.

The Commission cited the following reasons in its 1977 Report for selecting the DCE approach for study (at pages 94-95):

1. The DCE approach offers a conceptually sound "middle ground" between retaining negligence as the basis for compensation and compensating all who are medically injured. It offers an opportunity to retain a general relationship between avoidable conduct and compensation while not restricting the system to a "fault" label or to a costly case-by-case determination of negligence.

2. DCE is a flexible tool. It permits a modest start on the enumeration of compensable events and the periodic expansion and updating of any such list. Such an incremental approach permits program costs to be taken into account in deciding whether to expand the number of covered events.

3. DCE offers the possibility of creating links between quality of care efforts, malpractice prevention, and compensation. The health care and tort systems now relate only in jarring, discordant ways. By predefining compensable events and by relating those events to general quality of care efforts (particularly in the hospital setting), a strong impetus can be given to prevention efforts.

4. DCE might improve the predictability of outcomes by setting forth in detail the outcomes which would give rise to compensation. To the extent that predictability of outcomes increases, the practice of defensive medicine should decrease.

5. If the decision to compensate or not follows fairly automatically when there has been an injury, based upon enumerated outcomes, then transaction

costs should be considerably reduced and claims closed out much more quickly than under the present system.

The study methodology consisted of five basic tasks. The first task was a data analysis of treatment-related injuries in order to develop lists of candidate compensable events, each to be identified by as many of the following variables as possible: frequency; degree of disability; amount of indemnity paid; expense; procedure involved; and medical specialty. The second task was to refine the criteria for determining DCEs and to select two medical specialties for intensive efforts to develop and validate DCE lists. The third task envisaged a review of available literature on the relative efficacy of particular treatments and procedures and attendant risks. The fourth task was to discuss, modify and augment the tentative DCE lists through review panels consisting principally of practicing physicians in the selected specialties. The fifth task was an analysis of the implementation of a DCE system in terms of elements of damages, benefit systems, dispute resolution mechanisms, pros and cons of statutory vis-à-vis voluntary systems and constitutional basis. . . .

It is the consensus of the Commission that the feasibility of developing lists of designated compensable events has been established by this study. The Commission recognizes that the study has not proved the feasibility of a DCE compensation system. This will only be established after a DCE-based compensation system has been constructed and tested. Nonetheless, the Commission is encouraged by the work which has been done and strongly recommends that those who are involved with medical professional liability—such as the organized bar, health care providers, consumers and insurers—proceed with the further work which must be done before a DCE system can be designed and tested.

The important point is that this study has shown that DCE lists can be developed from universes of treatment-related injuries. In fact, starting from the real world of treatment-related injuries appears to be the most practical and effective methodology for developing DCE lists. . . .

The attractiveness of this proposal in theory is apparent when it is considered in light of the list of ideal attributes of a compensation system promulgated by the ABA Commission on Medical Professional Liability and reproduced in Part I. By eliminating the necessity for findings of fault on the part of individual health care providers, much of the "sting," and hence the accompanying tendency toward breakdown in provider-patient relationships, will be removed from decisions to compensate the victims of medical accidents; by focusing primary attention upon the quality of outcomes, together with a commitment to experience-rating in the setting of insurance premiums,[8] incentives will be created for improving the quality of health care; and by defining the compensable events specifically, and

8. "Experience rating" in this context means that each insured's premiums reflect the insured's claims experience; the more claims an insured has experienced, and is likely to experience, the higher the liability insurance premium.

thus allowing decisions to compensate to follow fairly automatically when there has been an injury, transaction costs and dislocation costs will be substantially reduced.

The following questions will help you to make a tentative assessment of the DCE plan:

1. If the DCE lists include outcomes that are beyond the control of health care providers, will the hoped-for incentives toward improving health care quality be undermined?
2. Would a DCE system create incentives for health care providers to avoid risky procedures in favor of alternative procedures which, though less beneficial to the patient, are less risky?
3. What would be an appropriate process for preparing and revising the DCE lists?
4. Would that process likely become the subject of intense political fighting among interest groups?
5. Even if a workable DCE system could be devised, is it likely that the overall payout of benefits might be so substantial as to cause unacceptable increases in premium costs to health care providers?

A no-fault proposal somewhat similar to the DCE plan is advanced by Professor Weiler in his book, Medical Malpractice on Trial 132-158 (1991). Like the DCE plan, Professor Weiler's would compensate on the basis of injuries caused by medical treatment to hospital patients. Professor Weiler argues that while compensation decisions may be difficult, they can be made. In one study, review of files by medical reviewers resulted in "close calls" in only five percent of the cases. Professor Weiler would limit compensation to those with serious injuries—those who are disabled six months or more.

Compensation under Professor Weiler's proposal would be much more limited than under the tort system. While compensation for medical expenses would be in full, there could be no recovery to the extent that the claimant has been compensated under social and first-person insurance programs. Compensation for lost income would not be full: two-thirds of lost wages, not to exceed a limit of somewhere between 100 percent and 150 percent of the state average wage. The primary aim would be to compensate for economic loss; compensation for intangible harm would be limited to the very seriously injured, and then would be based on schedules that would take into account the nature of the injury and the claimant's age.

Another variation on the DCE no-fault proposal is that advanced by Professor O'Connell, who was the co-author of the automobile no-fault proposal discussed at p. 794, above. He prefers mandatory no-fault, but until such a plan is enacted into law, he feels that health care providers and patients could agree ahead of time to no-fault compensation for medical injury. See O'Connell, An Alternative to Abandoning Tort Liability: Elective No-Fault Insurance for Many Kinds of Injuries, 60 Minn. L. Rev. 501 (1976). Elective no-fault would apply to all medical injuries, not just to serious, hospital-related injury; compensation would be limited to net out-of-pocket loss, and would not include any compensation for pain and suffering. Elective no-fault, with some variations from the O'Connell model, was advanced, at least as an intermediate step, by II Reporters' Study, Enterprise Responsibility for Personal Injury 514-515 (American Law Institute 1991):

> Elective no-fault would operate this way: legislation would be enacted explicitly to empower hospitals and other health care organizations to offer their patients an administrative compensation scheme for iatrogenic injuries in return for a waiver of common law tort liability. The legislation would require that the benefits meet certain standards of generosity. This might mean full out-of-pocket medical expenses, 80 percent of net lost earnings up to 150 percent of the state average, plus specified payments for the loss of enjoyment of life due to different physical impairments. The health care facility would also have to operate an effective quality assurance program that would include measures for reporting and accountability for all adverse events identified through this claims process. The claims administration procedure would have to meet acceptable standards of neutrality and due process. The program would cover all injuries inflicted on the hospital's patients, even injuries caused by non-employee doctors with admitting privileges to the hospital. Appropriate adjustments would have to be made in the health care reimbursement schedules for all the participants, both the hospitals that were shouldering the new liability and the doctors being relieved of the old tort liability. The data assembled by the Harvard Medical Practice Study could be used by insurance actuaries to make projections of the cost of this new no-fault insurance, which would permit hospital administrators and medical staff to judge whether it was worthwhile to offer the new package to their patients in return for relief from the financial and psychological burdens of tort litigation. The patients, in turn, would have to be fully informed, in easily comprehensible terms approved by the state insurance department, of both the tort rights they were surrendering and the no-fault benefits they would be eligible to receive before deciding whether to accept medical care offered under no-fault auspices or instead to patronize an institution and doctors that were still governed by the existing tort regime.

Birth-Related Neurological Injuries. Broadly applicable no-fault plans for medical injuries of the sort just discussed have yet to be implemented anywhere in this country. A more narrow plan, however, has. In 1987, the Virginia legislature enacted a limited no-fault compensation system entitled the Birth-Related Neurological Injury Compensation Act, Code of Va. §§38.2-5000 to .2-5021. The following description is taken from Note,

Innovative No-Fault Reform for an Endangered Specialty, 74 Va. L. Rev. 1487, 1489-1494 (1988) (footnotes have been omitted):

> The Injured Infant Act was created for the purpose of
>
> > seeking to assure the lifetime care of infants with birth-related neurological injuries, fostering an environment that will increase the availability of medical malpractice insurance at a reasonable cost for physicians and hospitals providing obstetrical services, and promoting the availability of obstetrical care to indigent and low-income patients.
>
> The Act creates a program similar to workers' compensation in that those who recover under its terms give up whatever right they may have had to bring a tort action against the health care providers attending the delivery. The definition of eligible infants is narrow—the drafters of the Act estimate that it will apply to only about forty births in the state per year. The Act applies only to live births in which there is
>
> > injury to the brain or spinal cord of an infant caused by the deprivation of oxygen or mechanical injury occurring in the course of labor, delivery or resuscitation in the immediate post-delivery period in a hospital which renders the infant permanently nonambulatory, aphasic [having a defect or loss in the power of expression], incontinent, and in need of assistance in all phases of daily living.
>
> In addition, the birth must have occurred on or after January 1, 1988 at a hospital participating in the program, and a participating physician must have provided obstetric services. Specifically excluded from coverage under the Act are claims involving "disability or death caused by genetic or congenital abnormalities." Claims filed more than ten years after the birth of the injured child are barred.
>
> The Act creates the Virginia Birth-Related Neurological Injury Compensation Program (Program), which is governed by a Board of Directors (Board), each member of which is appointed by the Governor for a three-year term. The Board administers the Birth-Related Neurological Injury Compensation Fund (Fund). Participation in the Program is not mandatory for either physicians or hospitals. Obstetricians who want to participate in the Program pay $5,000 into the Fund each year, while all other physicians licensed in the state, including those who do not practice obstetrics, are assessed $250 per year. Participating hospitals pay a sum equal to $50 multiplied by the number of deliveries made during the prior year, with a cap of $150,000 per hospital per year. If these assets are inadequate to maintain the Fund on an actuarially sound basis, a premium tax of up to one-quarter of one percent of net direct premiums written in the state will be assessed on all liability insurance carriers in the state. All of these payments will go directly into the Fund, which is designed to be self-sufficient—none of the money for the Program is to come from the state's general revenues.
>
> Claims filed pursuant to the Act are heard and determined by the Industrial Commission of Virginia (Commission), which also handles the state's workers' compensation claims. A panel of three physicians chosen pursuant to a

> plan developed by the deans of the state's medical schools review each claim and make a recommendation to the Commission "as to whether the injury alleged is a birth-related neurological injury" coming within the statutory scheme. This provision establishes an automatic source of independent, expert medical opinion in lieu of that which a malpractice plaintiff would produce for trial. The Commission is required to hold a hearing on any claim within 120 days of its filing, assuring swifter compensation for those newborns covered by the Act than is currently available through the tort system. The only parties to the hearing are the claimant and the Program. Although compensation is awarded under the Act without regard to fault, each claim is automatically referred to the state licensing agencies of the physicians and hospital involved for investigation of any possible substandard care. All factual findings of the Commission are conclusive and binding.
>
> Upon a determination by the Industrial Commission that an infant comes within the terms of the Act, the Commission will award a remedy limited to net economic loss less any amount received from collateral sources. The award is paid out as it accrues, rather than in a lump sum as a civil remedy typically would be. In addition to reasonable medical expenses, the award compensates for reasonable expenses, including attorney's fees, and loss of earnings from the age of eighteen.
>
> In addition to its goal of making liability insurance for obstetricians more available and affordable by removing from the tort system the claims of catastrophically injured newborns, the Act also attempts to facilitate access to medical care for indigents. This problem has become especially acute for the indigent, because physicians are increasingly reluctant to handle these often "high-risk" deliveries. To address this problem, the Injured Infant Act requires obstetricians and hospitals who wish to obtain the advantages of the Act's coverage to agree to work with local health departments in developing "a program to provide obstetrical care to patients eligible for Medical Assistance Services and to patients who are indigent, and upon approval of such program by the Commissioner of Health, to participate in its implementation."

In addition to the note cited above, the statute is analyzed in Epstein, Market and Regulatory Approaches to Medical Malpractice: The Virginia Obstetrical No-Fault Statute, 74 Va. L. Rev. 1451 (1988); O'Connell, Pragmatic Constraints on Market Approaches: A Response to Professor Epstein, 74 Va. L. Rev. 1475 (1988).

Florida has a similar statute. See Fla. Stat. ch. 766.301-766.316, and 1992 Supp.

D. *Replacing the Tort System—Universal Compensation for Accident Losses*

As should be clear from the materials in the casebook so far, the tort system of allocating personal injury losses has come under considerable attack.

Those who have sought to change the system have proceeded along two very different lines. One line has been to work within the system and to seek changes in the substantive rules and procedures by which tort law allocates losses. The most dramatic of the recent changes have come largely through legislation, and involve such items as caps on damages and the abrogation of joint and several liability and of the collateral source rule. These changes, and others, are discussed at various points throughout this casebook.

The second line of attack, documented in the preceding sections of this chapter, seeks to replace the torts system in part with one not based on fault. Workers' compensation is such a system. A more limited inroad into the torts system is no-fault automobile insurance.

As yet, proposals in this country to replace the tort system entirely with a compensation system in which fault plays no part have not reached the legislative halls. There is, however, some sentiment for such a move. See, e.g., American Bar Association, Report of the Action Commission to Improve the Tort Liability System 6 (1987):

> There are . . . members of the Commission who hold the view that meaningful improvement in the system of compensating injury victims can better be achieved by adopting a social insurance or no-fault recovery scheme that assures compensation of basic economic loss to every accident victim and promotes incentives to greater safety either through contributions to the funding of the reparation scheme, utilization of criminal and administrative sanctions, or a combination of these strategies.

See also Sugarman, Doing Away with Personal Injury Law (1989); Abraham and Liebman, Private Insurance, Social Insurance, and Tort Reform: Toward a New Vision of Compensation for Illness and Injury, 93 Colum. L. Rev. 75 (1993).

Sweeping changes in the system of allocating personal injury losses has been in effect in New Zealand since the early 1970s. As a response to a number of perceived problems of the tort system, especially the failure to provide adequate compensation to accident victims, New Zealand enacted the Accident Compensation Act of 1972.[9] The Act created a government administered no-fault compensation system which provided benefits to those suffering "injury by accident." An essential element of the Act was that

9. The following description of the New Zealand system is taken from Miller, An Analysis and Critique of the 1992 Changes to New Zealand's Accident Compensation Scheme, 52 Md. L. Rev. 1070 (1993).

Professor Miller conducted a comprehensive study of the New Zealand system before the 1992 amendments and concluded, among other things, that the system, by removing the incentives of tort law, has had an adverse effect on overall safety. See Miller, The Future of New Zealand's Accident Compensation Scheme, 11 U. Haw. L. Rev. 1 (1989). A brief response by the New Zealand Law Commission disagreed with some of Professor Miller's conclusions in this regard. See Comment on "The Future of New Zealand's Accident Compensation Scheme" by Richard S. Miller, 12 U. Haw. L. Rev. 339 (1990).

no showing of fault was required to recover under the plan. In exchange for the many generous benefits under the Act, accident victims were barred from exercising common law rights to sue in tort for damages for death or personal injury. However, in the rare situation where a particular injury was not covered by the Act (possibly by virtue of a restrictive interpretation of "injury by accident") the victim was not precluded from bringing a tort action for damages.

The original Act was based on an underlying philosophy of collective responsibility, and was designed to establish a program of social welfare or social insurance. Thus, although the plan at first provided benefits only for accident victims, it was hoped that the plan would eventually cover victims of disease and illness as well. However, a recent change in the governing party of New Zealand has resulted in a changed perception of the purpose of the plan as well as reforms of the benefits provided. The new government no longer views the no-fault system as a social insurance scheme, but rather maintains the plan as a system of accident insurance. The change in philosophy is reflected in the new title of the Act, the Accident Rehabilitation and Compensation Insurance Act 1992 (ARCIA).

The prior Act provided benefits for "personal injury by accident," which was defined to include the physical and mental consequences of any injury from an accident; medical, surgical, dental, or first aid misadventure; incapacity resulting from occupational disease or industrial deafness; and actual bodily harm arising from certain sexual crimes. Except for "mental or nervous shock" suffered by victims of sexual crimes, the new Act, ARCIA, excludes benefits for emotional harm unconnected with any physical injury, thereby eliminating coverage for negligently or intentionally inflicted emotional distress. This leaves it to the courts to decide whether common law actions to recover for emotional distress shall be allowed. Moreover, the new Act spells out in great detail what constitutes medical misadventure, a form of injury previously undefined.

ARCIA covers most accident victims, including visitors injured in New Zealand and New Zealand residents injured abroad. However, not every benefit extends to all accident victims. ARCIA benefits in varying degrees wage earners including the self-employed, non-wage earners. The extent and type of benefits received vary according to the category or type of victim injured in the accident. The most important distinction is that, with insignificant exceptions, only wage earners are entitled to earnings-related compensation; loss of earning capacity of injured non-earners, such as those working at home, remains largely uncompensated.

ARCIA significantly reformed the benefits provided under the plan. However, the earnings-related compensation system remains intact. This benefit provides 80 percent of lost earnings after an initial one week period of nonpayment. If the accident is work-related, the employer must ordinarily pay for the first week. After the first week, a government corporation pays for all earners' injuries, whether sustained on or off the job. The plan provides initially for a maximum of (NZ) $1,179 a week for loss of earnings, for as long as the victim is unable to work, or until retirement age. However, if the earner's capacity to work is determined to be at least 85 percent a year after the injury, payment ceases regardless of whether employment is available. This is significantly less generous than the previous Act, which continued payment if there was no appropriate work available (which was often the case because until recently New Zealand was suffering from a serious recession). Furthermore, the new Act, unlike the previous Act, requires a periodic reassessment of the permanency of incapacity.

While the prior Act may have encouraged injured workers to feign permanent incapacity, the new Act may discourage efforts at rehabilitation, because decreased incapacity could lead to reduced benefits.

The new Act attempts to address a complaint raised under the prior Act that non-wage earners were not compensated for the loss of earning capacity or potential. Under ARCIA, certain non-wage earners are allowed to pay premiums to purchase the right to receive compensation for lost earning capacity as a result of an accident. However, there are significant limitations on which non-earners are eligible to participate, and the benefits paid as compensation are not generous.

As with the prior Act, ARCIA is more generous in its coverage of medical treatment and hospital care, and offers wider options of care from the private sector, than that which New Zealand's socialized medical system offers to victims of illness that is not accident-related. The plan also pays for ambulance expenses, nursing care expenses, dental expenses, and expenses for artificial limbs. These benefits accrue to any victim injured in an accident. However, in an attempt to restrict the escalating costs of the program, the government hopes to make the victims responsible for payment of some medical services. Thus, accident victims are required to pay "user part charges" for pharmaceuticals, laboratory diagnostic tests, and some public hospital services on the same basis as the sick. It is also possible that the government will reduce the maximum the plan will pay for use of private hospitals, forcing accident victims to pay a greater share of the expense or seek treatment in less costly public hospitals.

In addition to providing medical expenses, the plan is charged with the responsibility of promoting the rehabilitation of accident victims. To this end, resources are provided to assist victims in assessing their needs and options. Financial assistance for purchase or modification of motor vehicles, modification of a residence, child care, and equipment are also provided when necessary to further the independence of the injured.

The earlier Act provided lump-sum payments of up to (NZ) $27,000 for permanent loss or impairment of bodily functions, loss of capacity for enjoying life, disfigurement, and pain and suffering. These payments for noneconomic losses were provided in lieu of the potentially large awards granted under common law tort actions. Often such payments constituted the principal compensation to disabled non-wage earners. However, ARCIA has eliminated compensation for these noneconomic losses, moving the system away from its origin as a substitute for the tort action, and leaving non-wage earners with little real means of compensation. In place of payments for noneconomic loss, the new Act creates an "independence allowance," which is supposed to enable the injured to meet the additional, miscellaneous costs of disability. As of 1992, the allowance was (NZ) $40 per week for a person with a 100 percent disability. A reduced allowance is given to those with a lesser disability. The payment cannot be lump-summed, and is adjusted annually to reflect changes in the consumer price index. Lastly, the Act pays for several miscellaneous benefits, including compensation for funeral expenses, constant personal attention for a victim when such care is necessary, substitute household services previously provided by the victim, and earnings-related compensation to the surviving dependent family members of an earner who dies as a result of an accident.

In addition to modifying some of the benefits, ARCIA is no longer funded by "levies" but rather by "premiums." This change reflects the new philosophical basis for the plan; moreover the funding for the plan now stems from different sources. Previously, levies on employers funded compensation for work and non-work-related accidents of earners; levies on motor vehicle owners funded compensation for motor vehicle accidents; and general taxes funded the compensation for victims of accidents falling inside neither category. Under ARCIA, employers still fund work-related accidents through the payment of premiums. These premiums are adjusted by industry class, based upon the injury experience of persons working in that industry. However, employees, rather than employers, now fund, through premiums withheld by their employers, the compensation for non-work-related accidents of earners.

The owners of motor vehicles will continue to fund the compensation for motor vehicle accidents through premiums paid during the annual registration and licensing of vehicles. However, a two cent per liter tax has been imposed on motor vehicle fuel in order to "alert individual drivers to the real costs of accidents. . . ." The revenue so generated will be used to supplement the funds collected from the motor vehicle premiums. Compensation for non-motor vehicle accidents to non-wage earners will continue to be funded by general tax revenue.

The new Act significantly changed the coverage for and funding of injuries caused by medical treatment. Compensation is provided for "medical misadventure," which, briefly stated, is personal injury resulting either from medical error (failure of a registered health professional to observe a standard of care and skill reasonably to be expected in the circumstances, i.e., negligence), or "medical mishap" (a "rare" and "severe" adverse consequence of treatment given by a registered health professional). Under the earlier Act, levies on health care professionals were based on the rate of injury to persons working in that industry; because the medical field is relatively safe for those who work in it, the levies were fairly low. However, in order to introduce an element of deterrence, ARCIA now imposes premiums on health care professionals based on the cost of injuries they cause to patients. Because such experience-rating has been introduced for medical professionals, and because those who are found to have committed medical errors are referred to "the appropriate body with a view to the institution of disciplinary proceedings," the affected professionals are given an opportunity to comment or object at hearings and also to seek review or appeals of adverse findings through the courts.[10]

For a critical analysis of the New Zealand plan, see J. Henderson, The New Zealand Accident Compensation Reform, 48 U. Chi. L. Rev. 781 (1981).

10. Professor Miller, in the article on which this summary is based, suggested that the effect of this procedure is to turn a claim to establish medical error into what is likely to become an adversarial medical malpractice action. Because the level of compensation does not approach that available in a common law action, however, and because lawyers in New Zealand cannot accept contingent fees, Miller believes the new act is likely to discourage the pursuit of such claims, or, at the least, seriously delay their payment while the claims wind their way through the courts. For this reason, Professor Miller characterized the new medical misadventure scheme "as an unnatural union of fault and no-fault, grossly unfair to many victims of medical error." 52 Md. L. Rev. at 1086.

Chapter 11

Dignitary Wrongs, Intentional Infliction of Mental Upset, and Violations of Civil Rights

In this chapter, we bring together five categories of intentional torts having at their core the protection of interests in peace of mind and basic human dignity. Three—assault, offensive battery, and false imprisonment—have their roots in the early common law[1] and are well-established legal wrongs. The fourth, intentional infliction of emotional harm, is a more recent development, and functions as a means of reaching conduct that does not fall squarely within the definitions of the other torts. The fifth, based primarily on the federal civil rights act, has grown in importance in recent years.

A. *Assault*

RESTATEMENT (SECOND) OF TORTS

§21. ASSAULT

(1) An actor is subject to liability to another for assault if

(a) he acts intending to cause a harmful or offensive contact with the person of the other or a third person, or an imminent apprehension of such a contact, and

(b) the other is thereby put in such imminent apprehension.

(2) An action which is not done with the intention stated in Subsection (1,a) does not make the actor liable to the other for an apprehension caused thereby although the act involves an unreasonable risk of causing it and, therefore, would be negligent or reckless if the risk threatened bodily harm.

§29. APPREHENSION OF IMMINENT AND FUTURE CONTACT

(1) To make the actor liable for an assault he must put the other in apprehension of an imminent contact.

(2) An act intended by the actor as a step toward the infliction of a future

1. Indeed, one of the earliest recorded opinions in tort law involves assault. I de S v. W de S, [1348] Y.B. Lib. Ass. fo. 99, placitum 60. In this classic torts case, the defendant had banged on the door of a tavern with a hatchet, and swung the hatchet in the direction of the tavern keeper's wife after she informed him that the tavern was closed. For this assault, the defendant was held liable for damages of half a mark.

contact, which is so recognized by the other, does not make the actor liable for an assault under the rule stated in §21.

Read v. Coker

[1853] 13 C.B. 850, 138 Eng. Rep. 1437

The cause was tried before TALFOURD, J., at the first sitting in London in Easter Term last. The facts which appeared in evidence were as follows:—The plaintiff was a paper-stainer, carrying on business in the City Road, upon premises which he rented of one Molineux, at a rent of 8s. per week. In January 1852, the rent being sixteen weeks in arrear, the landlord employed one Holliwell to distrain for it. Holliwell accordingly seized certain presses, lathes, and other trade fixtures, and, at the plaintiff's request, advanced him 16£ upon the security of the goods, for the purpose of paying off the rent. The plaintiff, being unable to redeem his goods, on the 23rd of February applied to the defendant for assistance. The goods were thereupon sold to the defendant by Holliwell, on the part of Read, for 25£. 11s.6d.; and it was agreed between the plaintiff and the defendant, that the business should be carried on for their mutual benefit, the defendant paying the rent of the premises and other outgoings, and allowing the plaintiff a certain sum weekly.

The defendant becoming dissatisfied with the speculation, dismissed the plaintiff on the 22nd of March. On the 24th, the plaintiff came to the premises, and refusing to leave when ordered by the defendant, the latter collected together some of his workmen, who mustered round the plaintiff, tucking up their sleeves and aprons, and threatened to break his neck if he did not go out; and, fearing that the men would strike him if he did not do so, the plaintiff went out. This was the assault complained of in the first count. Upon this evidence, the learned judge left it to the jury to say, whether there was an intention on the part of the defendant to assault the plaintiff, and whether the plaintiff was apprehensive of personal violence if he did not retire. The jury found for the plaintiff on this count, damages one farthing. . . .

Byles, Serjt., on a former day in this term, in pursuance of leave reserved to him at the trial, moved for a rule nisi to enter the verdict for the defendant . . . or for a new trial on the ground of misdirection, and that the verdict was not warranted by the evidence. That which was proved . . . clearly did not amount to an assault. . . . To constitute an assault, there must be something more than a threat of violence. An assault is thus defined in Buller's Nisi Prius, p. 15,—"An assault is an attempt or offer, by force or violence, to do a corporal hurt to another, as, by pointing a pitchfork at him, when standing within reach; presenting a gun at him [within shooting distance]; drawing a sword, and waving it in a menacing manner, &c. But no words can amount to an assault, though perhaps they may in some cases serve to explain a doubtful action, as, if a man were to lay his hand upon his sword, and say, 'If it were not assize time, he would not take such language'; the words would prevent the action from being construed to be an assault, because they shew he had no intent to do him any corporal hurt at that time: Tuberville v. Savage, 1 Mod. 3.". . . [JERVIS, C.J. If a man comes into a room, and lays his cane on the table, and says to another, "If you don't go out, I will knock you on the head," would not that be an assault?] Clearly not: it is a mere threat, unaccompanied by any gesture or action towards carrying it into effect. The direction of the learned judge as to this point was erroneous. He should have told the jury, that, to constitute an assault, there must be an attempt, coupled with a present ability to do personal violence to the party; instead of leaving it to them, as he did, to say what the plaintiff thought, and not what they (the jury) thought was the defendant's intention. There must be some act done denoting a present ability and an intention to assault.

[A rule nisi was granted.]

JERVIS, C.J. I am of opinion that this rule . . . must be discharged. If anything short of actual striking will in law constitute an assault, the facts here clearly shewed that the defendant was guilty of an assault. There was a threat of violence exhibiting an intention to assault, and a present ability to carry the threat into execution. . . .

MAULE, CRESSWELL, and TALFOURD, JJ., concurring. Rule discharged. . . .

Beach v. Hancock

27 N.H. 223 (1853)

Trespass, for an assault.

Upon the general issue it appeared that the plaintiff and defendant, being engaged in an angry altercation, the defendant stepped into his office, which was at hand, and brought out a gun, which he aimed at the plaintiff in an excited and threatening manner, the plaintiff being three or four rods distant. The evidence tended to show that the defendant snapped the gun twice at the plaintiff, and that the plaintiff did not know whether the gun was loaded or not, and that, in fact, the gun was not loaded.

The court ruled that the pointing of a gun, in an angry and threatening manner, at a person three or four rods distant, who was ignorant whether the gun was loaded or not, was an assault, though it should appear that the gun was not loaded, and that it made no difference whether the gun was snapped or not.

The court, among other things, instructed the jury that, in assessing the damages, it was their right and duty to consider the effect which the finding of light or trivial damages in actions for breaches of the peace, would have to encourage a disregard of the laws and disturbances of the public peace.

The defendant excepted to these rulings and instructions.

The jury, having found a verdict for the plaintiff, the defendant moved for a new trial by reason of said exceptions.

GILCREST, C.J. . . . One of the most important objects to be attained by the enactment of laws and the institutions of civilized society is, each of us shall feel secure against unlawful assaults. Without such security society loses most of its value. Peace and order and domestic happiness, inexpressively more precious than mere forms of government, cannot be enjoyed without the sense of perfect security. We have a right to live in society without being put in fear of personal harm. But it must be a reasonable fear of which we complain. And it surely is not unreasonable for a person to entertain a fear of personal injury, when a pistol is pointed at him in a threatening manner, when, for aught he knows, it may be loaded, and may occasion his immediate death. The business of the world could not be carried on with comfort, if such things could be done with impunity.

We think the defendant guilty of an assault, and we perceive no reason for taking any exception to the remarks of the court. Finding trivial damages for breaches of the peace, damages incommensurate with the injury sustained, would certainly lead the ill-disposed to consider an assault as a thing that might be committed with impunity. But, at all events, it was proper for the jury to consider whether such a result would or would not be produced.

Judgment on the verdict.

In Bouton v. Allstate Insurance Co., 491 So. 2d 56 (La. App. 1986), the plaintiff claimed that a thirteen-year-old boy committed an assault upon him by going to the front door of plaintiff's house on Halloween night dressed in military fatigues and carrying a plastic model submachine gun. The plaintiff shot and killed the boy, believing him to be an armed assailant. After plaintiff's acquittal on second degree murder charges, plaintiff brought this action against the boy's insurers, alleging that the boy's assault caused plaintiff to be tried criminally, incur legal expenses, lose his job, and suffer a damaged reputation. The court rejected this claim as a matter of law, stating that a reasonable person under these circumstances would not have been apprehensive of imminent harmful bodily contact.

Damages are often difficult to prove in assault cases where no actual contact occurs. In some cases, plaintiffs seek to enjoin threats of violence and intimidation. In Vietnamese Fisherman's Association v. Knights of the Ku Klux Klan, 518 F. Supp. 993 (S.D. Tex. 1981), the court granted plaintiff's motion for declaratory and injunctive relief. The court found that the defendants' behavior of rallying, burning fishing boats, pointing guns at certain plaintiffs and their families and wearing Klan robes and hoods while bearing arms was intended to and did cause the members of the plaintiff association apprehension of imminent harm.

B. *Offensive Battery*

As indicated in Chapter 1, a physical contact with the plaintiff may be actionable as a battery even if no bodily harm results. At this point, you should reread the sections of the Restatement (Second) of Torts pertaining to battery, p. 10, and the note on Mental State Considerations: Offensiveness and Offensive Batteries, p. 18.

Fisher v. Carrousel Motor Hotel

424 S.W.2d 627 (Tex. 1967)

GREENHILL, J. This is a suit for actual and exemplary damages growing out of an alleged assault and battery. The plaintiff Fisher was a mathematician with the Data Processing Division of the Manned Spacecraft Center, an agency of the National Aeronautics and Space Agency, commonly called NASA, near Houston. The defendants were the Carrousel Motor Hotel, Inc., located in Houston, the Brass Ring Club, which is located in the Carrousel, and Robert W. Flynn, who as an employee of the Carrousel was the manager of the Brass Ring Club. Flynn died before the trial, and the suit proceeded as to the Carrousel and the Brass Ring. Trial was to a jury which found for the plaintiff Fisher. The trial court rendered judgment for the defendants notwithstanding the verdict. The Court of Civil Appeals affirmed. 414 S.W.2d 774. The questions before this Court are whether there was evidence that an actionable battery was committed, and, if so, whether the two corporate defendants must respond in exemplary as well as actual damages for the malicious conduct of Flynn.

The plaintiff Fisher had been invited by Ampex Corporation and Defense Electronics to a one day's meeting regarding telemetry equipment at the Carrousel. The invitation included a luncheon. The guests were asked to reply by telephone whether they could attend the luncheon, and Fisher called in his acceptance. After the morning session, the group of 25 or 30 guests adjourned to the Brass Ring Club for lunch. The luncheon was buffet style, and Fisher stood in line with others and just ahead of a graduate student of Rice University who testified at the trial. As Fisher was about to be served, he was approached by Flynn, who snatched the plate from Fisher's hand and shouted that he, a Negro, could not be served in the club.

Fisher testified that he was not actually touched, and did not testify that he suffered fear or apprehension of physical injury; but he did testify that he was highly embarrassed and hurt by Flynn's conduct in the presence of his associates.

The jury found that Flynn "forceably dispossessed plaintiff of his dinner plate" and "shouted in a loud and offensive manner" that Fisher could not be served there, thus subjecting Fisher to humiliation and indignity. It was stipulated that Flynn was an employee of the Carrousel Hotel and, as such, managed the Brass Ring Club. The jury also found that Flynn acted maliciously and awarded Fisher $400 actual damages for his humiliation and indignity and $500 exemplary damages for Flynn's malicious conduct.

The Court of Civil Appeals held that there was no assault because there was no physical contact and no evidence of fear or apprehension of physical contact. However, it has long been settled that there can be a battery without an assault, and that actual physical contact is not necessary to constitute a battery, so long as there is contact with clothing or an object closely identified with the body. . . .

Under the facts of this case, we have no difficulty in holding that the intentional grabbing of plaintiff's plate constituted a battery. The intentional snatching of an object from one's hand is as clearly an offensive invasion of his person as would be an actual contact with the body. . . .

. . . Damages for mental suffering are recoverable without the necessity for showing actual physical injury in a case of willful battery because the basis of that action is the unpermitted and intentional invasion of the plaintiff's person and not the actual harm done to the plaintiff's body. Personal indignity is the essence of an action for battery; and consequently the defendant is liable not only for contacts which do actual physical harm, but also for those which are offensive and insulting. We hold, therefore, that plaintiff was entitled to actual damages for mental suffering due to the willful battery, even in the absence of any physical injury. . . .

We now turn to the question of the liability of the corporations for exemplary damages. In this regard, the jury found that Flynn was acting within the course and scope of his employment on the occasion in question; that Flynn acted maliciously and with a wanton disregard of the rights and feelings of plaintiff on the occasion in question. There is no attack upon these jury findings. The jury further found that the defendant Carrousel did not authorize or approve the conduct of Flynn. It is argued that there is no evidence to support this finding. The jury verdict concluded with a finding that $500 would "reasonably compensate plaintiff for the malicious act and wanton disregard of plaintiff's feelings and rights. . . ."

The rule in Texas is that a principal or master is liable for exemplary or punitive damages because of the acts of his agent, but only if: (a) the principal authorized the doing and the manner of the act, or (b) the agent was unfit and the principal was reckless in employing him, or (c) the agent was employed in a managerial capacity and was acting in the scope of employment, or (d) the employer or a manager of the employer ratified or approved the act.

. . . At the trial of this case, the following stipulation was made in open court: "It is further stipulated and agreed to by all parties that as an employee of the Carrousel Motor Hotel the said Robert W. Flynn was manager of the Brass Ring Club." We think this stipulation brings the case squarely within part (c) of the rule. . . .

The judgments of the courts below are reversed, and judgment is here rendered for the plaintiff for $900 with interest from the date of the trial court's judgment, and for costs of this suit.

McCracken v. Sloan

252 S.E.2d 250 (N.C. 1979)

WEBB, JUDGE. JUDGES PARKER and ARNOLD concur.

[The plaintiff alleged that the defendant twice committed a battery upon him by smoking cigars in his presence. At a pretrial conference, the parties stipulated what the evidence most favorable to the plaintiff would be, and, based on that evidence, the trial court ordered the case dismissed on the ground that "that plaintiff could not prove a sufficient case to carry his cause to the jury." The stipulated evidence showed that the plaintiff had been a postal employee in the City of Charlotte and the defendant was the postmaster in that city. The plaintiff had a documented medical history of being allergic to tobacco smoke. The plaintiff had made complaints and distributed literature within the post office building in regard to the dangers of smoking. He had requested and been denied sick leave for his allergic condition. On two occasions, the plaintiff attended meetings in the office of the defendant at which the plaintiff's application for sick leave was discussed. At both of these meetings, defendant smoked a cigar. At one of these meetings, the defendant said: "Bill, I know you claim to have an allergy to tobacco smoke and you have presented statements from your doctor stating this, but there is no law against smoking, so I'm going to smoke."]

Although the court below made detailed findings of fact in its order, we are not bound by them. The parties stipulated and made a part of the record what the plaintiff's evidence would tend to show. It is from this stipulation as to what the evidence would be that we must determine whether there is enough evidence to be submitted to the jury to support a claim for assault and battery.

We have found no case with a factual situation which controls this case. North Carolina follows the common law principles in the civil actions of assault and battery. . . . It has been said that assault and battery, which are two separate common law actions, "go together like ham and eggs." The interest in freedom from apprehension of a harmful or offensive contact with the person is protected by the action for assault. The interest in freedom from intentional and unpermitted contacts with the plaintiff's person is protected by the action for battery. It is not necessary that the contact be brought about by a direct application of force. It is enough that the defendant set a force in motion which ultimately produces the result. The gist of the action for battery is not the hostile intent of the defendant, but rather the absence of consent to the contact on the part of the plaintiff. At the same time, in a crowded world, a certain amount of personal contact is inevitable and must be accepted. Consent is assumed to all those ordinary contacts which are customary and reasonably necessary to the common intercourse of life. Smelling smoke from a cigar being smoked by a person in his own office would ordinarily be considered such an innocuous and generally permitted contact. In this case there is the added factor that the defendant was on notice that the smelling of cigar smoke was personally offensive to the plaintiff who considered it injurious to his health. In examining the plaintiff's claim, we observe that it has been said "it may be questioned whether any individual can be permitted, by his own fiat, to erect a glass cage around himself, and to announce that all physical contact with his person is at the expense of liability." See Prosser on Torts, at 37.

From a reading of what the plaintiff's evidence would tend to show, we can find no evidence that the plaintiff suffered any physical illness from inhaling the cigar smoke. Each of the doctor's statements says the plaintiff is allergic to tobacco smoke, but neither says that the smoking of the cigars by defendant on [the two occasions alleged in the complaint] could have caused a physical illness to plaintiff. There is nothing in the record to show what the plaintiff's own testimony would have been. The statements of the other witnesses do not go to the question of any physical illness to the plaintiff resulting from inhaling cigar smoke. There being no competent evidence that the plaintiff suffered a physical illness from smelling the cigar smoke, we are left with evidence that defendant smoked cigars in his own office when he knew it was obnoxious to a person in the room for him to do so. That person did experience some mental distress as a result of inhaling the cigar smoke. We hold this is not enough evidence to support a claim for assault or battery.

We express no opinion as to what the result would be if there were evidence of some physical injury, but on the facts of this case we cannot hold it is an assault or battery for a person to be subjected either to the apprehension of smelling cigar smoke or the actual inhaling of the smoke. This is an apprehension of a touching and a touching which must be endured in a crowded world.

Affirmed.

Note the date and jurisdiction of the court's decision. Would the same result occur if a case presenting similar facts was brought today, in California, for example? The question reveals the elasticity of the tort of offensive battery. Because it is based on contacts that a reasonable person would find offensive, the tort has the ability to change in response to changing social standards.

Yet, in another sense, the tort is remarkably limited. What would have happened in *Fisher,* for example, if the defendant's employee had made the same remarks to the plaintiff, but had not grabbed the plaintiff's plate? Surely, the employee's remarks, rather than the plate snatching, were the primary source of the plaintiff's distress. What, then, is the value, if any, of the contact requirement?

Problem 37

Lloyd Anderson is consulting you about a difficult family problem involving his 14-year-old daughter, Megan. Eight years ago, you handled Lloyd's divorce from his wife, Sylvia Birnbaum. The divorce was unpleasant, but not particularly hostile, and the parties ultimately agreed to a custody arrangement in which Megan would spend the week with Lloyd and the weekends with Sylvia.

A year after the divorce, Sylvia married Ralph Dennison. According to Lloyd, Dennison is a gregarious sort who has generally been a decent and affectionate step-father to Megan. Over the last few years, however, a chronic problem has developed. At about age 12, Megan, a fairly shy and reserved girl, began complaining after her weekends with her mother that Dennison touched her too much. The touching was not overtly sexual in nature and consisted mainly of Dennison putting his arm around Megan, patting her back, or stroking her hair. On occasion, Dennison has had Megan sit in his lap. Dennison had always behaved this way, and indeed it had never previously bothered Megan or alarmed Lloyd.

Lloyd attributes Megan's increased discomfort with the behavior largely to her reaching puberty, although he does harbor a lingering but unsubstantiated fear that Dennison's motivations might not be altogether innocent. He believes quite firmly that Megan's preferences on this subject must control absolutely. "I always taught her," he tells you, "that no one had the right to touch her unless it was okay with her."

Several months after Megan first complained about Dennison's behavior, Lloyd confronted Sylvia and her husband. The conversation apparently was a disaster. Dennison insisted that he was just "being himself" and that his conduct was utterly harmless and normal. "She's like a daughter to me," Dennison had remarked. Sylvia, in turn, claimed that Lloyd was being "paranoid," "uptight," and "controlling" and insisted that Megan was merely going through a phase. Subsequent conversations on the issue have only served to further polarize the parties. Megan, for her part, is increasingly distressed by Dennison's behavior, but has been unable to do anything more than complain to her father about it.

Lloyd is now asking you about the possibility of legal action. He does not want to go to family court to challenge the basic custody division, partly because he realizes that Megan needs time with her mother and partly because he fears that reopening the custody question may result in a disposition that is less favorable to him than the current arrangement. You are also aware that the current family law judge is very reluctant to micro-manage intra-family disputes. Lloyd thinks, however, that if he could make a credible threat of bringing a civil lawsuit on behalf of Megan, the problem might resolve itself quickly and favorably. "They don't want to be in a court any more than I do," he notes, "and if they know I'm serious, they will back down." He is concerned, however, that if he were to end up going to court and losing, the result might be very damaging to Megan. He therefore asks you for an accurate assessment of whether Megan has a cause of action, and if so, whether the chance of success is good. Assume that the Restatement provisions on battery and the foregoing cases are the controlling law of your jurisdiction. Assume also that no intra-family immunity protects stepfathers from tort liability for harms to their stepchildren. What would you advise?

C. *False Imprisonment*

RESTATEMENT (SECOND) OF TORTS

§35. FALSE IMPRISONMENT

(1) An actor is subject to liability to another for false imprisonment if

(a) he acts intending to confine the other or a third person within boundaries fixed by the actor, and

(b) his act directly or indirectly results in such a confinement of the other, and

(c) the other is conscious of the confinement or is harmed by it.

(2) An act which is not done with the intention stated in Subsection (1,a) does not make the actor liable to the other for a merely transitory or otherwise harmless confinement, although the act involves an unreasonable risk of imposing it and therefore would be negligent or reckless if the risk threatened bodily harm.

Whittaker v. Sanford

110 Me. 77, 85 A. 399 (1912)

SAVAGE, J. Action for false imprisonment. The plaintiff recovered a verdict for $1100. The case comes up on defendant's exceptions and motion for a new trial.

[The plaintiff had been a member of a religious sect which had colonies in Maine and in Jaffa, Syria, and of which the defendant was the leader. Some months prior to the alleged imprisonment, the plaintiff, while in Jaffa, announced her intention to leave the sect. The defendant, with the help of the plaintiff's husband, persuaded the plaintiff to return to the United States aboard the sect's palatial yacht, the Kingdom. The defendant promised the plaintiff that she and her children would be free to leave the ship any time they were in port. After their arrival in Maine, the plaintiff asked to be put ashore with her children and baggage, and the defendant refused. (The plaintiff eventually gained her release on a writ of habeas corpus.) There was evidence that the plaintiff had been ashore a number of times, had been on numerous outings and had been treated as a guest during her stay aboard the yacht. According to the uncontradicted evidence, at no time did anyone physically restrain the plaintiff except for the defendant's refusal, once the plaintiff announced her decision to quit the yacht, to let the plaintiff use a small boat to take herself, her children, and her belongings ashore. Throughout the entire episode, the plaintiff's husband was with her and repeatedly tried to persuade her to change her mind and remain with the sect.]

. . . The court instructed the jury that the plaintiff to recover must show that the restraint was physical, and not merely a moral influence, that it must have been actual physical restraint, in the sense that one intentionally locked into a room would be physically restrained, but not necessarily involving physical force upon the person; that it was not necessary that the defendant, or any person by his direction, should lay his hand upon the plaintiff, that if the plaintiff was restrained so that she could not leave the yacht Kingdom by the intentional refusal to furnish transportation as agreed, she not having it in her power to escape otherwise, it would be a physical restraint and unlawful imprisonment. We think the instructions were apt and sufficient. If one should, without right, turn the key in a door, and thereby prevent a person in the room from leaving, it would be the simplest form of unlawful imprisonment. The restraint is physical. The four walls and the locked door are physical impediments to escape. How is it different when one who is in control of a vessel at anchor, within practical rowing distance from the shore, who has agreed that a guest on board shall be free to leave, there being no means to leave except by rowboats, wrongfully refuses the guest the use of a boat? The boat is the key. By refusing the boat he turns the key. The guest is as effectually locked up as if there were walls along the sides of the vessel. The restraint is physical. The impassable sea is the physical barrier. . . .

But the damages awarded seem to us manifestly excessive. The plaintiff, if imprisoned, was by no means in close confinement. She was afforded all the liberties of the yacht. She was taken on shore by her husband to do shopping and transact business at a bank. She visited neighboring islands with her husband and children, on one of which they enjoyed a family picnic.

The case lacks the elements of humiliation and disgrace that frequently attend false imprisonment. She was respectfully treated as a guest in every way, except that she was restrained from quitting the yacht for good and all.

The certificate will be,

Exceptions overruled. If the plaintiff remits all of the verdict in excess of $500, within 30 days after the certificate is received by the clerk, motion overruled; otherwise, motion sustained.

The "moral influence" aspects of the *Whittaker* decision arise today in the context of struggles of parents to free their children from the control and influence of religious sects. If the children are unemancipated minors, presumably their parents may legally establish and restore their rights to custody. But because the children in these cases are more often than not adults, parents must resort to allegations that their children are being held tortiously against their wills. Consistent with the holding in *Whittaker,* an action based on allegations of false imprisonment will not lie when the only restraints on the children are moral—allegations by parents that their adult children have been brainwashed, and must be returned to their parents for "deprogramming," will not suffice even when the parents' right to custody in such circumstances are established by special statutes. Thus, in Katz v. Superior Court, 73 Cal. App. 3d 952, 141 Cal. Rptr. 234, (1977), the court granted the petition of the adult children to prohibit the enforcement of court orders appointing their parents temporary guardians for the purpose of permitting the children to be deprogrammed from the ideas and attitudes allegedly instilled in them by the Rev. Sun Myung Moon's Unification Church.

Although courts are reluctant to support efforts by parents to gain custody of their adult children, they are also reluctant to interfere with those efforts by imposing tort liability upon persons who attempt to persuade members to leave religious sects. Thus, in Weiss v. Patrick, 453 F. Supp. 717 (D.R.I. 1978), *aff'd,* 588 F.2d 818 (1st Cir. 1978), *cert. denied,* 442 U.S. 929 (1979), the plaintiff, a member of the Unification Church, brought an action alleging that the defendants had conspired to violate her civil rights and claiming damages for assault, battery and false imprisonment. The defendants had been hired by the plaintiff's mother to help persuade the plaintiff to leave the church. Although the plaintiff testified that she had been kidnapped and held forceably against her will, the district court found that the plaintiff had merely been exposed to lawful efforts to convince her to change her way of life.

Rougeau v. Firestone Tire & Rubber Co.

274 So. 2d 454 (La. App. 1973)

SAVOY, J. Deryl D. Rougeau instituted this tort suit against his exemployer, Firestone Tire and Rubber Company, seeking damages for . . . false imprisonment . . . alleged to have occurred during the investigations by agents of defendant concerning missing property at defendant's Lake Charles plant. The trial judge denied recovery to plaintiff, and we affirm the judgment of the trial judge.

Plaintiff was employed as a guard-fireman at defendant's plant in Lake Charles. Two lawnmowers belonging to the defendant were allegedly stolen during plaintiff's working shift. Local management enlisted the aid of E. E. Drummond, Corporate Security Manager of Firestone Tire and Rubber Company, to investigate the thefts. . . .

. . . The facts revealed that Drummond and two employees of defendant and plaintiff went to his home to search for the missing property. Plaintiff, on advice of his attorney, refused to allow the search. Drummond, the employees of defendant, and plaintiff returned to the plant. Plaintiff was asked to wait in the guardhouse. Two guards were instructed to keep plaintiff in the guardhouse. However, both guards stated they did not consider plaintiff to be a prisoner. Plaintiff was allowed to leave when he fell ill. The total amount of time which plaintiff spent in the guardhouse did not exceed thirty minutes.

We agree with the trial judge that plaintiff was not falsely imprisoned. At no time was he totally restrained. Additionally, plaintiff never revealed to anyone that he did not want to stay in the guardhouse, thus showing his implied consent to stay.

In Faniel v. Chesapeake and Potomac Telephone Company of Maryland, 404 A.2d 147 (D.C. 1979), an employee who was suspected by her employer of stealing telephone equipment brought an action for false imprisonment based on allegations that she had been forced against her will to accompany her employer's security personnel to her home to locate and recover the equipment. The trial court entered judgment for the defendant employer notwithstanding a jury verdict for the plaintiff. On evidence similar to that in the *Rougeau* case the court of appeals affirmed, holding that there was no evidence that the plaintiff employee, who agreed to accompany the security officers to her home, had yielded to threats, either express or implied, or to physical force. In response to plaintiff's argument that she had not agreed to a detour during the trip to her home, the court of appeals pointed out that the plaintiff had not objected or asked to leave the car, and thus had failed to negate her prior consent to take the trip.

Another issue that might have been addressed by the court in *Rougeau* is whether the plaintiff must be aware of the confinement in order to recover. Section 35 of the Restatement, above, requires that the plaintiff must either be aware of the confinement or be harmed by it. This limitation has been attacked by commentators as overly restrictive. See, e.g., Fleming, The Law of Torts 27 (6th ed. 1983); 1 Harper, James and Gray, The Law of Torts

286-287 (2d ed. 1986); Cohen, False Imprisonment: A Reexamination of the Necessity for Awareness of Confinement, 43 Tenn. L. Rev. 109 (1975).

Sindle v. New York City Transit Authority

33 N.Y.2d 293, 307 N.E.2d 245 (1973)

JASEN, J. At about noon on June 20, 1967, the plaintiff, then 14 years of age, boarded a school bus owned by the defendant, New York City Transit Authority, and driven by its employee, the defendant Mooney. It was the last day of the term . . . and the 65 to 70 students on board the bus were in a boisterous and exuberant mood. Some of this spirit expressed itself in vandalism, a number of students breaking dome lights, windows, ceiling panels and advertising poster frames. There is no evidence that the plaintiff partook in this destruction.

The bus made several stops at appointed stations. On at least one occasion, the driver admonished the students about excessive noise and damage to the bus. When he reached the Annadale station, the driver discharged several more passengers, went to the rear of the bus, inspected the damage and advised the students that he was taking them to the St. George police station.

The driver closed the doors of the bus and proceeded, bypassing several normal stops. As the bus slowed to turn onto Woodrow Road, several students jumped without apparent injury from a side window at the rear of the bus. Several more followed, again without apparent harm, when the bus turned onto Arden Avenue.

At the corner of Arden Avenue and Arthur Kill Road, departing from its normal route, the bus turned right in the general direction of the St. George police station. The plaintiff, intending to jump from the bus, had positioned himself in a window on the right-rear side. Grasping the bottom of the window sill with his hands, the plaintiff extended his legs (to mid-thigh), head and shoulders out of the window. As the bus turned right, the right rear wheels hit the curb and the plaintiff either jumped or fell to the street. The right rear wheels then rolled over the midsection of his body, causing serious personal injuries.

The plaintiff, joined with his father, then commenced an action to recover damages for negligence and false imprisonment. At the outset of the trial, the negligence cause was waived and plaintiffs proceeded on the theory of false imprisonment. At the close of the plaintiffs' case, the court denied defendants' motion to amend their answers to plead the defense of justification. The court also excluded all evidence bearing on the justification issue.

We believe that it was an abuse of discretion for the trial court to deny the motion to amend and to exclude the evidence of justification. It was the defendants' burden to prove justification—a defense that a plaintiff in an action for false imprisonment should be prepared to meet—and the plaintiffs could not have been prejudiced by the granting of the motion to amend. The trial court's rulings precluded the defendants from introducing any evidence in this regard and were manifestly unfair. Accordingly, the order of the Appellate Division must be reversed and a new trial granted.

In view of our determination, it would be well to outline some of the considerations relevant to the issue of justification. In this regard, we note that, generally, restraint or detention, reasonable under the circumstances and in time and manner, imposed for the purpose of preventing another from inflicting personal injuries or interfering with or damaging real or personal property in one's lawful possession or custody is not unlawful. . . . Also, a parent, guardian or teacher entrusted with the care or supervision of a child may use physical force reasonably necessary to maintain discipline or promote the welfare of the child.

Similarly, a school bus driver, entrusted with the care of his student-passengers and the custody of public property, has the duty to take reasonable measures for the safety and protection of both—the passengers and the property. In this regard, the reasonableness of his actions—as bearing on the defense of justification—is to be determined from a consideration of all the circumstances. At a minimum, this would seem to import a consideration of the need to protect the persons and property in his charge, the duty to aid the investigation and apprehension of those inflicting damage, the manner and place of the occurrence, and the feasibility and practicality of other alternative courses of action.

With regard to the proper measure of damages, an ancillary but nevertheless important question of law is presented—namely, whether a plaintiff's negligence in attempting to extricate himself from an unlawful confinement should diminish his damages for bodily injuries sustained as a result of the false imprisonment. In this regard, plaintiff has been awarded damages of $500 for mental anguish and $75,000 for bodily injuries. The plaintiff father has been awarded damages of $750 for loss of services and $5,797 for medical expenses.

Where the damages follow as a consequence of the plaintiff's detention without justification an award may include those for bodily injuries. And although confinement reasonably perceived to be unlawful may invite escape, the person falsely imprisoned is not relieved of the duty of reasonable care for his own safety in extricating himself from the unlawful detention. In this regard, it has been held that alighting from a moving vehicle, absent some compelling reason, is negligence per se. Therefore, upon retrial, if the trier of fact finds that plaintiff was falsely imprisoned but that he acted unreasonably for his own safety by placing himself in a perilous position in the window of the bus preparatory to an attempt to alight, recovery for the bodily injuries subsequently sustained would be barred.

For the reasons stated, the order of the Appellate Division should be reversed and the case remitted for a new trial.

FULD, C.J., and BURKE, BREITEL, GABRIELLI, JONES and WACHTLER, JJ., concur.

Order reversed, without costs, and a new trial granted.

Coblyn v. Kennedy's, Inc.

359 Mass. 319, 268 N.E.2d 860 (1971)

SPIEGEL, J. This is an action of tort for false imprisonment. At the close of the evidence the defendants filed a motion for directed verdicts which was denied. The jury returned verdicts for the plaintiff in the sum of $12,500. The case is here on the defendants' exceptions to the denial of their motion and to the refusal of the trial judge to give certain requested instructions to the jury.

We state the pertinent evidence most favorable to the plaintiff. On March 5, 1965, the plaintiff went to Kennedy's, Inc. (Kennedy's), a store in Boston. He was seventy years of age and about five feet four inches in height. He was wearing a woolen shirt, which was "open at the neck," a topcoat and a hat. "[A]round his neck" he wore an ascot which he had "purchased . . . previously at Filenes." He proceeded to the second floor of Kennedy's to purchase a sport coat. He removed his hat, topcoat and ascot, putting the ascot in his pocket. After purchasing a sport coat and leaving it for alterations, he put on his hat and coat and walked downstairs. Just prior to exiting through the outside door of the store, he stopped, took the ascot out of his pocket, put it around his neck, and knotted it. The knot was visible "above the lapels of his shirt." The only stop that the plaintiff made on the first floor was immediately in front of the exit in order to put on his ascot.

Just as the plaintiff stepped out of the door, the defendant Goss, an employee, "loomed up" in front of him with his hand up and said: "Stop. Where did you get that scarf?" The plaintiff responded, "[W]hy?" Goss firmly grasped the plaintiff's arm and said: "[Y]ou better go back and see the manager." Another employee was standing next to him. Eight or ten other people were standing around and were staring at the plaintiff. The plaintiff then said, "Yes, I'll go back in the store" and proceeded to do so. As he and Goss went upstairs to the second floor, the plaintiff paused twice because of chest and back pains. After reaching the second floor, the salesman from whom he had purchased the coat recognized him and asked what the trouble was. The plaintiff then asked: "[W]hy 'these two gentlemen stop me?' " The salesman confirmed that the plaintiff had purchased a sport coat and that the ascot belonged to him.

The salesman became alarmed by the plaintiff's appearance and the store nurse was called. She brought the plaintiff to the nurse's room and gave him a soda mint tablet. As a direct result of the emotional upset caused by the incident, the plaintiff was hospitalized and treated for a "myocardial infarct."

Initially, the defendants contend that as a matter of law the plaintiff was not falsely imprisoned. They argue that no unlawful restraint was imposed by either force or threat upon the plaintiff's freedom of movement. However, "[t]he law is well settled that '[a]ny genuine restraint is sufficient to constitute an imprisonment . . .' and '[a]ny demonstration of physical power which, to all appearances, can be avoided only by submission, operates as effectually to constitute an imprisonment, if submitted to, as if any amount of force had been exercised. If a man is restrained of his personal liberty by fear of a personal difficulty, that amounts to a false imprisonment' within the legal meaning of such term." Jacques v. Childs Dining Hall Co., 244 Mass. 438, 438-439, 138 N.E. 843.

We think it is clear that there was sufficient evidence of unlawful restraint to submit this question to the jury. Just as the plaintiff had stepped out of the door of the store, the defendant Goss stopped him, firmly grasped his arm and told him that he had "better go back and see the manager." There was another employee at his side. The plaintiff was an elderly man and there were other people standing around staring at him. Considering the plaintiff's age and his heart condition, it is hardly to be expected that with one employee in front of him firmly grasping his arm and another at his side the plaintiff could do other than comply with Goss's "request" that he go back and see the manager. . . .

The defendants next contend that the detention of the plaintiff was sanctioned by G.L. c. 231, §94B, inserted by St. 1958, c. 337. This statute provides as follows: "In an action for false arrest or false imprisonment brought by any person by reason of having been detained for questioning on or in the immediate vicinity of the premises of a merchant, if such person was detained in a reasonable manner and for not more than a reasonable length of time by a person authorized to make arrests or by the merchant or his agent or servant authorized for such purpose and if there were reasonable grounds to believe that the person so detained was committing or attempting to commit larceny of goods for sale on such premises, it shall be a defence to such action. If such goods had not been purchased and were concealed on or amongst the belongings of a person so detained it shall be presumed that there were reasonable grounds for such belief."

The defendants argue in accordance with the conditions imposed in the statute that the plaintiff was detained in a reasonable manner for a reasonable length of time and that Goss had reasonable grounds for believing that the plaintiff was attempting to commit larceny of goods held for sale.

It is conceded that the detention was for a reasonable length of time. We need not decide whether the detention was effected in a reasonable manner for we are of opinion that there were no reasonable grounds for believing that the plaintiff was committing larceny and, therefore, he should not have been detained at all. However, we observe that Goss's failure to identify himself as an employee of Kennedy's and to disclose the reasons for his inquiry and actions, coupled with the physical restraint in a public place imposed upon the plaintiff, an elderly man, who had exhibited no aggressive intention to depart, could be said to constitute an unreasonable method by which to effect detention.

The pivotal question before us as in most cases of this character is whether the evidence shows that there were reasonable grounds for the detention. At common law in an action for false imprisonment, the defense of probable cause, as measured by the prudent and cautious man standard, was available to a merchant. In enacting G.L. c. 231, §94B, the Legislature inserted the words, "reasonable grounds." Historically, the words "reasonable grounds" and "probable cause" have been given the same meaning by the courts. . . .

The defendants assert that the judge improperly instructed the jury in stating that "grounds are reasonable when there is a basis which would appear to the reasonably prudent, cautious, intelligent person." In their brief, they argue that the "prudent and cautious man rule" is an objective standard and requires a more rigorous and restrictive standard of conduct than is contemplated by G.L. c. 231 §94B. The defendants' requests for instructions, in effect, state that the proper test is a subjective one, viz., whether the defendant Goss had an honest and strong suspicion that the plaintiff was committing or attempting to commit larceny. . . .

If we adopt the subjective test as suggested by the defendants, the individual's right to liberty and freedom of movement would become subject to the "honest . . . suspicion" of a shopkeeper based on his own "inarticulate hunches" without regard to any discernible facts. In effect, the result would be to afford the merchant even greater authority than that given to a police officer. In view of the well established meaning of the words "reasonable grounds" we believe that the Legislature intended to give these words their traditional meaning. This seems to us a valid conclusion since the Legislature has permitted an individual to be detained for a "reasonable length of time.". . .

Applying the standard of reasonable grounds as measured by the reasonably prudent man test to the evidence in the instant case, we are of opinion that the evidence warranted the conclusion that Goss was not reasonably justified in believing that the plaintiff was engaged in shoplifting. There was no error in denying the motion for directed verdicts and in the refusal to give the requested instructions.

Exceptions overruled.

The court's opinion implies that the decisions of shopowners to detain potential shoplifters should be subject to the same level of scrutiny as that applied to police officers. But might there be good reason to afford shopowners greater latitude? Note that an erroneous detention imposes costs not only on the falsely-accused patron, but also on the business itself in terms of an immediate and probably permanent loss of the customer's good will. Thus, a merchant will have a natural incentive to avoid overzealous efforts to detect shoplifting. Perhaps, then, there is a greater justification than acknowleged by the *Coblyn* court for deferring to the "honest suspicions" of shopowners. Indeed, some courts do appear more deferential to the decisions of shopowners concerning the need to detain potential shoplifters. See, e.g., Meadows v. F.W. Woolworth Co., 254 F. Supp. 907 (N.D. Fla. 1966) (detention of three teenagers based on general description). Are there limits, however, to this market-based argument for deference to the detention decisions of shopowners? Specifically, might a shopowner affirmatively seek to alienate certain consumer groups—teenagers, for example—by excessive vigilance against shoplifting? Should tort law be more willing to second-guess detention decisions in such cases?

D. *Intentional Infliction of Mental Upset*

Prosser, Insult and Outrage

44 Calif. L. Rev. 40, 40-43 (1956)

By the middle of this century, it appears to be quite generally recognized that the nameless wrong which, for lack of anything better, usually is called the intentional infliction of mental suffering, or mental anguish or mental disturbance, or emotional distress, has such distinct and definite features of its own that it is entitled to be regarded as a separate tort.

. . . [I]t is no longer disputed that in a proper case the action for such a tort will lie, without resort to any assault, defamation, or other traditional basis of liability. . . .

Certain assumptions may be made at the outset. The . . . tort . . . encountered from the beginning the same objections which have been raised against any liability for mental disturbance negligently inflicted: the unsatisfactory character of the injury, "too subtle and speculative to be capable of admeasurement by any standard known to the law," and so evanescent, intangible, peculiar and variable with the individual as to be beyond prediction or anticipation; and the "wide door" which might be opened, not only to fictitious claims, but to litigation in the field of trivialities and mere bad manners. The leading case which broke through the shackles in 1897 was Wilkinson v. Downton in England, in which a practical joker amused himself by telling a woman that her husband had been smashed up in an accident and was lying at The Elms at Leytonstone with both legs broken, and that she was to go at once in a cab with two pillows to fetch him home. The shock to her nervous system produced serious and permanent physical consequences, which at one time threatened her reason, and entailed weeks of suffering and incapacity. The court no doubt regretted that the defendant could not, like that other false informer Titus Oates, be whipped from

Aldgate to Newgate and from Newgate to Tyburn; and as in many another hard case, the enormity of the outrage overthrew the settled rule of law.

As other outrageous cases began to accumulate, the courts continued to struggle to find some familiar and traditional basis of liability; and wherever it was possible without too obvious pretense, the recovery was rested upon a technical assault, battery, false imprisonment, trespass to land, nuisance, or invasion of the right of privacy. The independent cause of action served as a peg upon which to hang the mental damages; and there are many such cases which on their facts fall fairly within the scope of the "new tort." Gradually too many cases appeared in which no such traditional ground could be discovered; and somewhere around 1930 it began to be generally recognized that the intentional infliction of mental disturbance, at least by extreme and outrageous conduct, could be a cause of action in itself. . . .

It may . . . be assumed that "mental anguish" requires no definition. By whatever name it passes, from nervous shock to emotional upset, it is familiar enough as an element of compensable damages in cases of personal injury, where the admitted difficulty of measuring its financial equivalent never has been regarded as an insuperable obstacle. . . . It includes all highly unpleasant mental reactions, such as fright, horror, grief, shame, humiliation, anger, embarrassment, chagrin, disappointment, worry and nausea. It must of course be proved; and since it is easily feigned and difficult to deny, the courts have tended quite naturally to insist upon some guarantee of genuineness, either in the form of physical consequences which can be attested objectively, or in the nature of the defendant's conduct and the circumstances of the case.

Magruder, Mental and Emotional Disturbances in the Law of Torts

49 Harv. L. Rev. 1033, 1035 (1936)

[I]t is true . . . that the common law has been reluctant to recognize the interest in one's peace of mind as deserving of general and independent legal protection, even as against intentional invasions. Conceivably a principle might have been developed that mental distress purposely caused is actionable unless justified, thus casting upon the defendant the burden of establishing some privilege by way of rebutting the prima facie liability. That this was not done is hardly to be ascribed to any inherent difficulty in assessing damages. . . . Rather it was due to policy considerations of a different sort. Adoption of the suggested principle would open up a wide vista of litigation in the field of bad manners, where relatively minor annoyances had better be dealt with by instruments of social control other than the law. Quite apart from the question how far peace of mind is a good thing in itself, it would be quixotic indeed for the law to attempt a general securing of it. Against a large part of the frictions and irritations and clashing of temperaments incident to participation in a community life, a certain toughening of the mental hide is a better protection than the law could ever be. Furthermore, in an ad hoc manner, and perhaps not very scientifically, the courts have in large measure afforded legal redress for mental or emotional distress in the more outrageous cases, without formulating too broad a general principle.

Prosser's attempt to outline this "new tort" and his effort to limit its scope to avoid the problems suggested by Magruder are embodied in §46 and accompanying commentary of the Restatement (Second) of Torts:

§46. OUTRAGEOUS CONDUCT CAUSING SEVERE EMOTIONAL DISTRESS

(1) One who by extreme and outrageous conduct intentionally or recklessly causes severe emotional distress to another is subject to liability for such emotional distress, and if bodily harm to the other results from it, for such bodily harm.

(2) Where such conduct is directed at a third person, the actor is subject to liability if he intentionally or recklessly causes severe emotional distress

(a) to a member of such person's immediate family who is present at the time, whether or not such distress results in bodily harm, or

(b) to any other person who is present at the time, if such distress results in bodily harm. . . .

COMMENT:

d. Extreme and outrageous conduct. The cases thus far decided have found liability only where the defendant's conduct has been extreme and outrageous. It has not been enough that the defendant has acted with an intent which is tortious or even criminal, or that he has intended to inflict emotional distress, or even that his conduct has been characterized by "malice," or a degree of aggravation which would entitle the plaintiff to punitive damages for another tort. Liability has been found only where the conduct has been so outrageous in character, and so extreme in degree, as to go beyond all possible bounds of decency, and to be regarded as atrocious, and utterly intolerable in a civilized community. Generally, the case is one in which the recitation of the facts to an average member of the community would arouse his resentment against the actor, and lead him to exclaim, "Outrageous!"

The liability clearly does not extend to mere insults, indignities, threats, annoyances, petty oppressions, or other trivialities. The rough edges of our society are still in need of a good deal of filing down, and in the meantime plaintiffs must necessarily be expected and required to be hardened to a certain amount of rough language, and to occasional acts that are definitely inconsiderate and unkind. There is no occasion for the law to intervene in every case where some one's feelings are hurt. There must still be freedom to express an unflattering opinion, and some safety valve must be left through which irascible tempers may blow off relatively harmless steam. See Magruder, Mental and Emotional Disturbance in the Law of Torts, 47 Harvard Law Review 1033, 1053 (1936). It is only where there is a special relation between the parties, as stated in §48,[2] that there may be recovery for insults not amounting to extreme outrage.

State Rubbish Collectors Association v. Siliznoff

38 Cal. 2d 330, 240 P.2d 282 (1952)

TRAYNOR, J. On February 1, 1948, Peter Kobzeff signed a contract with the Acme Brewing Company to collect rubbish from the latter's brewery. Kobzeff had been in the rubbish business for several years and was able to secure the contract because Acme was dissatisfied with the service then being provided by another collector, one Abramoff. Although Kobzeff signed the contract, it was understood that the work should be done by John Siliznoff, Kobzeff's son-in-law, whom Kobzeff wished to assist in establishing a rubbish collection business.

Both Kobzeff and Abramoff were members of the plaintiff State Rubbish Collectors Association, but Siliznoff was not. The by-laws of the Association provided that one member should not take an account from another member without paying for it. Usual prices ranged from five to ten times the monthly rate paid by the customer, and disputes were referred to the board of directors for settlement. After Abramoff lost the Acme account he complained to the association, and Kobzeff was called upon to settle the matter. Kobzeff and Siliznoff took the position that the Acme account belonged to Siliznoff, and that he was under no obligation to pay for it. After attending several meetings of plaintiff's board of directors Siliznoff finally agreed, however, to pay Abramoff $1,850 for the Acme account and join the association. The agreement provided that he should pay $500 in 30 days and $75 per month thereafter until the whole sum agreed upon was paid. Payments were to be made through the association, and Siliznoff executed a series of promissory notes totaling $1,850. None of these notes was paid, and in 1949 plaintiff association brought this action to collect the notes then payable. Defendant cross-complained and asked that the notes be cancelled because of duress and want of consideration. In addition he sought general and exemplary damages because of assaults made by plaintiff and its agents to compel him to join the association and pay Abramoff for the Acme account. The jury returned a verdict against plaintiff and for defendant on the complaint and for defendant on his cross-complaint. It awarded him $1,250

2. §48. Special Liability of Public Utility for Insults by Servants.
A common carrier or other public utility is subject to liability to patrons utilizing its facilities for gross insults which reasonably offend them, inflicted by the utility's servants while otherwise acting within the scope of their employment. [Eds.]

general and special damages and $7,500 exemplary damages. The trial court denied a motion for a new trial on the condition that defendant consent to a reduction of the exemplary damages to $4,000. Defendant filed the required consent, and plaintiff has appealed from the judgment.

Plaintiff's primary contention is that the evidence is insufficient to support the judgment. Defendant testified that shortly after he secured the Acme account, the president of the association and its inspector, John Andikian, called on him and Kobzeff. They suggested that either a settlement be made with Abramoff or that the job be dropped, and requested Kobzeff and defendant to attend a meeting of the association. At this meeting defendant was told that the association "ran all the rubbish from that office, all the rubbish hauling," and that if he did not pay for the job they would take it away from him. " 'We would take it away, even if we had to haul for nothing'. . . [O]ne of them mentioned that I had better pay up, or else." Thereafter, on the day when defendant finally agreed to pay for the account, Andikian visited defendant at the Rainier Brewing Company, where he was collecting rubbish. Andikian told defendant that " 'We will give you up till tonight to get down to the board meeting and make some kind of arrangements or agreements about the Acme Brewery, or otherwise we are going to beat you up.' . . . He says he either would hire somebody or do it himself. And I says, 'Well, what would they do to me?' He says, well, they would physically beat me up first, cut up the truck tires or burn the truck, or otherwise put me out of business completely. He said if I didn't appear at that meeting and make some kind of an agreement that they would do that, but he says up to then they would let me alone, but if I walked out of that meeting that night they would beat me up for sure." Defendant attended the meeting and protested that he owed nothing for the Acme account and in any event could not pay the amount demanded. He was again told by the president of the association that "that table right there [the board of directors] ran all the rubbish collecting in Los Angeles and if there was any routes to be gotten that they would get them and distribute them among their members. . . ." After two hours of further discussion defendant agreed to join the association and pay for the Acme account. He promised to return the next day and sign the necessary papers. He testified that the only reason "they let me go home, is that I promised that I would sign the notes the very next morning." The president "made me promise on my honor and everything else, and I was scared, and I knew I had to come back, so I believe he knew I was scared and that I would come back. That's the only reason they let me go home." Defendant also testified that because of the fright he suffered during his dispute with the association he became ill and vomited several times and had to remain away from work for a period of several days.

Plaintiff contends that the evidence does not establish an assault against defendant because the threats made all related to action that might take place in the future; that neither Andikian nor members of the board of directors threatened immediate physical harm to defendant. We have concluded, however, that a cause of action is established when it is shown that one, in the absence of any privilege, intentionally subjects another to the mental suffering incident to serious threats to his physical well-being, whether or not the threats are made under such circumstances as to constitute a technical assault.

In the past it has frequently been stated that the interest in emotional and mental tranquillity is not one that the law will protect from invasion in its own right. As late as 1934 the Restatement of Torts took the position that "The interest in mental and emotional tranquillity and, therefore, in freedom from mental and emotional disturbance is not, as a thing in itself, regarded as of sufficient importance to require others to refrain from conduct intended or recognizably likely to cause such a disturbance." (Restatement, Torts, §46, Comment *c.*) The Restatement explained the rule allowing recovery for the mere apprehension of bodily harm in traditional assault cases as an historical anomaly (§24, Comment *c*), and the rule allowing recovery for insulting conduct by an employee of a common carrier as justified by the necessity of securing for the public comfortable as well as safe service. (§48, Comment *c.*)

The Restatement recognized, however, that in many cases mental distress could be so intense that it could reasonably be foreseen that illness or other bodily harm might result. If the defendant intentionally subjected the plaintiff to such distress and bodily harm resulted, the defendant would be liable for negligently causing the plaintiff bodily harm. (Restatement, Torts, §§306, 312.) Under this theory the cause of action was not founded on a right to be free from intentional interference with mental tranquillity, but on the right to be free from negligent interference with physical well-being. A defendant who intentionally subjected another to mental distress without intending to cause bodily harm would nevertheless be liable for resulting bodily harm if he should have foreseen that the mental distress might cause such harm.

The California cases have been in accord with the Restatement in allowing recovery where physical injury resulted from intentionally subjecting the plaintiff to serious mental distress.

The view has been forcefully advocated that the law should protect emotional and mental tranquillity as such against serious and intentional invasions and there is a growing body of case law supporting this position. In recognition of this development the American Law Institute amended section 46 of the Restatement of Torts in 1947 to provide: [see §46, p. 837, above].

There are persuasive arguments and analogies that support the recognition of a right to be free from serious, intentional, and unprivileged invasions of mental and emotional tranquillity. If a cause of action is otherwise established, it is settled that damages may be given for mental suffering naturally ensuing from the acts complained of, and in the case of many torts, such as assault, battery, false imprisonment, and defamation, mental suffering will frequently constitute the principal element of damages. In cases where mental suffering constitutes a major element of damages it is anomalous to deny recovery because the defendant's intentional misconduct fell short of producing some physical injury.

It may be contended that to allow recovery in the absence of physical injury will open the door to unfounded claims and a flood of litigation, and that the requirement that there be physical injury is necessary to insure that serious mental suffering actually occurred. The jury is ordinarily in a better position, however, to determine whether outrageous conduct results in mental distress than whether that distress in turn results in physical injury. From their own experience jurors are aware of the extent and character of the disagreeable emotions that may result from the defendant's conduct, but a difficult medical question is presented when it must be determined if emotional distress resulted in physical injury. Greater proof that mental suffering occurred is found in the defendant's conduct designed to bring it about than in physical injury that may or may not have resulted therefrom.

That administrative difficulties do not justify the denial of relief for serious invasions of mental and emotional tranquillity is demonstrated by the cases recognizing the right of privacy. Recognition of that right protects mental tranquillity from invasion by unwarranted and undesired publicity. As in the case of the protection of mental tranquillity from other forms of invasion, difficult problems in determining the kind and extent of invasions that are sufficiently serious to be actionable are presented. Also the public interest in the free dissemination of news must be considered. Nevertheless courts have concluded that the problems presented are not so insuperable that they warrant the denial of relief altogether.

In the present case plaintiff caused defendant to suffer extreme fright. By intentionally producing such fright it endeavored to compel him either to give up the Acme account or pay for it, and it had no right or privilege to adopt such coercive methods in competing for business. In these circumstances liability is clear. . . .

Plaintiff contends finally that the damages were excessive. The question of excessiveness is addressed primarily to the discretion of the trial court, and an award that stands approved by that court will not be disturbed on appeal unless it appears that the jury was influenced by passion or prejudice. With respect to the general damages the trial court concluded that the jury was not so influenced, and on the record before us we cannot say that it was. The excessiveness, if any, of the award of exemplary damages was cured by the trail court's reduction of those damages to $4,000.

The judgment is affirmed. GIBSON, C.J., SHENK, EDMONDS, CARTER, SCHAUER, and SPENCE, JJ., concurred.

The judicial fear of a "runaway tort" is not triggered by cases like *Siliznoff.* Serious threats of grievous physical harm are plainly not part of the everyday friction of life, and the likelihood that such threats will produce severe emotional distress in their recipient is open to little doubt. Similarly, several other limited categories of cases have typically provoked untroubled applications of the tort of intentional infliction of emotional distress. One area involves debt collection practices that, while not as physically threatening as those involved in *Siliznoff,* nonetheless pass beyond the realm of acceptable business practice. For example, in Ford Motor Credit Co. v. Sheehan, 373 So. 2d 956 (Fla. App.), *cert. dismissed,* 379 So. 2d 204 (Fla. 1979), judgment for the plaintiff was affirmed based on proof that the defendant, in order to locate the debtor, falsely represented that the debtor's children had been involved in a serious automobile accident. In Boyle v. Wenk, 378 Mass. 592, 392 N.E.2d 1053 (1979), the Supreme Judicial Court of Massachusetts held that it was for the jury to determine whether the defendant creditor's conduct in telephoning the plaintiff, whom defendant knew had just returned from the hospital, resulting in serious emotional and physical harm to the plaintiff, was merely "rude and clumsy" or was "extreme and outrageous." And in Moorhead v. J. C. Penney Co., 555 S.W.2d 713 (Tenn. 1977), the Supreme Court of Tennessee reversed the trial court's dismissal of a complaint that alleged repeated and threatening demands, over an extended period, for the repayment of a nonexistent debt. The fact that the defendant apologized when the accounting error was finally corrected would not bar recovery for its prior conduct.

Another established foothold for intentional infliction of emotional distress claims involves the mishandling of corpses and related funeral and burial services. In Meyer v. Nottger, 241 N.W.2d 911 (Iowa 1976), for example, the high court of Iowa reversed a trial court dismissal and held that the plaintiff's complaint had stated a claim for intentional infliction of severe emotional stress, based on the following allegations:

> 5. That Defendant advised Plaintiff and his family that the deceased's wife had died subsequent to the deceased, said statement being untrue, and was intended and did induce Plaintiff to retain only the Defendant to undertake the services and duties incident to the funeral and burial.
>
> 6. That Defendant advised Plaintiff that a more expensive sealer casket had to be purchased due to the objectionable odor of the deceased, when, in fact, there was no objectionable odor and a sealer casket was not necessary.
>
> 7. That Defendant advised Plaintiff that he and his family could not view the body of the deceased because of the gruesome condition and noxious odor of the body, when, in fact, the body was not in such gruesome condition, nor did it have such noxious odor.
>
> 8. That Plaintiff was delayed in joining the procession to the cemetery and Defendant was advised to delay the procession until Plaintiff was present. The Defendant did not comply, causing the procession to proceed without Plaintiff's presence and resulting in Plaintiff's inability to view the interment on that date.

241 N.W.2d at 917. Similarly, the Missouri Court of Appeals in Golston v. Lincoln Cemetery, Inc., 573 S.W.2d 700 (Mo. App. 1978), held that members

of the family of a decedent were entitled to recover compensatory and punitive damages from a mortuary for mental anguish resulting from the mortuary's failing to bury the decedent in a vault as called for by contract and instead permitting burial in a shallow grave. The defendant's handling of the burial caused the body to be uncovered during subsequent excavations.

Both decisions are at a considerable remove from cases like *Siliznoff.* The defendant mortuaries, for example, were hardly attempting to distress the bereaved plaintiffs; instead, they were undoubtedly hoping that their shady practices would go entirely unnoticed by the mourners. Indeed, in this regard, it is open to debate whether the defendants' actions satisfied even the "reckless" requirement of §46 of the Restatement (Second) of Torts. The willingness of courts nonetheless to recognize intentional infliction claims in this context probably reflects several considerations.

One reason that plaintiffs often succeed in actions against funeral parlors may be the peculiar vulnerability to emotional upset of family members in the context of the death and burial of a loved one. This factor may have influenced the decision in Wood v. United Air Lines, Inc., 404 F.2d 162 (10th Cir. 1968), in which the trial court's granting of defendant's motion for summary judgment was reversed on appeal. Affidavits filed by the plaintiffs revealed that upon inquiring of the fate of one Mrs. Wood, a family member, following the crash of the plane on which she had been a passenger, the plaintiffs were told that Mrs. Wood was not on the passenger list and may have gotten off in Denver to meet a man. The court concluded that the suggestion of an illicit liaison might be found to be outrageous under such "aggravated circumstances."

Another possible argument explaining the judicial leniency toward plaintiffs in such cases follows from deterrence theory. In general, the law's ability to discourage unacceptable behavior is a combined function of the wrongdoer's likelihood of being caught, the ease with which liability is imposed on the apprehended, and the magnitude of the punishment thus imposed. In certain classes of cases, including the shady behavior of funeral homes, the chances of detecting wrongful behavior are seriously impaired. The grief and vulnerability of bereaved family members undermines their ability to police the conduct of funeral home personnel. Most wrongful behavior goes undetected, and even when it is found out, potential plaintiffs are often too distraught to pursue legal remedies. In such cases, the law, in an effort to send a deterrent signal of sufficient strength, may lower the barriers to imposing liability and amplify the damages that are consequently imposed.

Somewhat similar concerns are presented by cases involving mental upset caused by the conduct of hospitals and other health care providers. In Burges v. Perdue, 721 P.2d 239, 239 Kan. 473 (1986), the plaintiff agreed to a partial autopsy of her son's body, but specifically refused to consent to an examination of his brain. The doctor who obtained the consent failed to inform the county coroner of its limited nature, and the decedent's brain was removed and sent to the Kansas Neurological Institute for examination.

Upon discovering the error, another doctor called the plaintiff, told her that the Institute had her son's "brain in a jar," and asked her what she would like to have done with it. The court found that the behavior of the latter doctor was not outrageous, because the doctor who called the plaintiff had done so out of concern and a desire to resolve any impropriety. In Johnson v. Woman's Hospital, 527 S.W.2d 133 (Tenn. App. 1975), the court of appeals affirmed an award of compensatory and punitive damages to the mother of a premature baby on proof that, after the baby died, the defendant hospital attempted to dispose of the body as a surgical specimen and then, on inquiry by the mother some six weeks later, exhibited it to her preserved in formaldehyde. The court concluded that recovery could be justified on either tort or contract theories.

Quite obviously, however, not all cases of upset involve botched burials and mishandled bodies. Most potential cases arise in less unusual circumstances, and therefore force courts to pay more attention to the appropriate boundaries of liability. As we have seen throughout these materials, a central method by which courts define the parameters of liability is through their decisions to enter judgment on the pleadings, direct verdicts, or allow cases to go to the jury. The decisions that follow represent a sampling of the efforts of courts to draw a meaningful line between outrageousness and mere obnoxiousness.

Samms v. Eccles

11 Utah 2d 289, 358 P.2d 344 (1961)

CROCKETT, JUSTICE.

Plaintiff Marcia G. Samms sought to recover damages from David Eccles for injury resulting from severe emotional distress she claims to have suffered because he persistently annoyed her with indecent proposals.

The parties presented their respective contentions to the court at pretrial. The court entered a pretrial order noting that, "plaintiff bases her cause of action on . . . the infliction of severe emotional distress by wilful and wanton conduct of an outrageous and intolerable nature," and dismissed the action upon the ground that plaintiff had shown no basis upon which relief could be granted. She appeals.

Plaintiff alleged that she is a respectable married woman; that she has never encouraged the defendant's attentions in any way but has repulsed them; that all during the time from May to December, 1957, the defendant repeatedly and persistently called her by phone at various hours including late at night, soliciting her to have illicit sexual relations with him; and that on one occasion came to her residence in connection with such a solicitation and made an indecent exposure of his person. She charges that she regarded his proposals as insulting, indecent, and obscene; that her feelings were deeply wounded; and that as a result thereof she suffered great anxiety and fear for her personal safety and severe emotional distress for which she asks $1,500 as actual, and a like amount as punitive, damages. . . .

Due to the highly subjective and volatile nature of emotional distress and the variability of its causations, the courts have historically been wary of dangers in opening the door to recovery therefor. This is partly because such claims may easily be fabricated: or as sometimes stated, are easy to assert and hard to defend against. They have, therefore, been reluctant to allow such a right of action unless the emotional distress was suffered as a result of some other overt tort. Nevertheless, recognizing the reality of such injuries and the injustice of permitting them to go unrequited, in many cases courts have strained to find the other tort as a peg upon which to hang the right of recovery.

Some of these have been unrealistic, or even flimsy. For instance, a technical battery was found where an insurance adjuster derisively tossed a coin on the bed of a woman who was in a hospital with a heart condition, and because of this tort she was allowed to recover for distress caused by his other attempts at intimidation in accusing her of gold-bricking and attempting to defraud his company; courts have also dealt with trespass where hotel employees have invaded rooms occupied by married couples and imputed to them immoral conduct; and other similar torts have been used as a basis for such recovery. But a realistic analysis of many of these cases will show that the recognized tort is but incidental and that the real basis of recovery is the outraged feelings and emotional distress resulting from some aggravated conduct of the defendant. The lengths to which courts have gone to find a basis for allowing such recoveries serves to emphasize their realization that justice demands that grossly wrong conduct which causes such an injury to another should be held accountable.

In recent years courts have shown an increasing awareness of the necessity and justice of forthrightly recognizing the true basis for allowing recovery for such wrongs and of getting rid of the shibboleth that another tort peg is necessary to that purpose. . . .

Our study of the authorities, and of the arguments advanced, convinces us that, conceding such a cause of action may not be based upon mere negligence, the best considered view recognizes an action for severe emotional distress, though not accompanied by bodily impact or physical injury, where the defendant intentionally engaged in some conduct toward the plaintiff, (a) with the purpose of inflicting emotional distress, or, (b) where any reasonable person would have known that such would result; and his actions are of such a nature as to be considered outrageous and intolerable in that they offend against the generally accepted standards of decency and morality. This test seems to be a more realistic safeguard against false claims than to insist upon finding some other attendant tort, which may be of minor character, or fictional.

It is further to be observed that the argument against allowing such an action because groundless charges may be made is not a good reason for denying recovery. If the right to recover for injury resulting from the wrongful conduct could be defeated whenever such dangers exist, many of the grievances the law deals with would be eliminated. That some claims may be spurious should not compel those who administer justice to shut their eyes to serious wrongs and let them go without being brought to account. It is the function of courts and juries to determine whether claims are valid or false. This responsibility should not be shunned merely because the task may be difficult to perform.

We quite agree with the idea that under usual circumstances the solicitation to sexual intercourse would not be actionable even though it may be offensive to the offeree. It seems to be a custom of long standing and one which in all likelihood will continue. The assumption is usually indulged that most solicitations occur under such conditions as to fall within the well-known phrase of Chief Judge Magruder that, 'there is no harm in asking.' The Supreme Court of Kentucky in Reed v. Maley [115 Ky. 816, 74 S.W. 1079 (1903)] pertinently observed that an action will not lie in favor of a woman against a man who, without trespass or assault, makes such a request; and that the reverse is also true: that a man would have no right of action against a woman for such a solicitation.

But the situations just described, where tolerance for the conduct referred to is indulged, are clearly distinguishable from the aggravated circumstances the plaintiff claims existed here. Even though her complaint may not flawlessly state such a cause of action, the facts were sufficiently disclosed that the case she proposes to prove could be found to fall within the requirements hereinabove discussed. Therefore, the trial court erred in dismissing the action.

Reversed.

CALLISTER, JUSTICE (dissenting).

I dissent. The opinion correctly states the law in cases of this nature. However, the complaint in the instant case is deficient and fails to state a cause of action. It fails to show that the defendant deliberately intended to injure the plaintiff by his unwelcome attentions, or that he knew or should have known that his conduct would result in severe emotional distress to the plaintiff. In fact, the plaintiff specifically alleges that "The defendant has wilfully, wantonly, and with intent to commit unlawful acts caused plaintiff severe emotional distress in the following particulars: Defendant has telephoned plaintiff late at night, and at other hours, upon at least 15 and possibly more than 25 separate occasions and has made statements and proposals to plaintiff of a highly insulting, obscene and indecent nature, *with the avowed purpose of inducing plaintiff to have illicit sexual relations with defendant*. . . ."

The complaint only shows that the alleged conduct of the defendant amounted to a moral, rather than a legal or actionable, wrong.

I would affirm the trial court.

Alcorn v. Anbro Engineering, Inc.

2 Cal. 3d 493, 468 P.2d 216, 86 Cal. Rptr. 88 (1970)

EN BANC:

Plaintiff appeals from an order of dismissal entered after defendants' demurrer to the third amended complaint was sustained without leave to amend. The complaint seeks to recover actual and exemplary damages against defendants, based upon their alleged intentional infliction of emotional distress. . . . We have concluded that the complaint states a cause of action for intentional infliction of emotional distress, and that the order of dismissal must be reversed. . . .

[P]laintiff alleged that he is a Negro employed as a truck driver by defendant Anbro Engineering, Inc., a corporation owned and operated by defendants Thomas Anderson, Sr., and Harlon Anderson, doing business as Anderson Bros., a partnership. On the day of the incident at issue, plaintiff informed defendant Palmer, Anbro's Caucasian field superintendent and plaintiff's foreman, that plaintiff, in his capacity as shop steward for the Teamster's Union, had advised another Anbro employee that he should not drive a certain truck to the job site, since that employee was not a teamster. Plaintiff's remarks to Palmer allegedly were neither rude, insubordinate nor otherwise violative of plaintiff's duties as an employee.

Immediately thereafter, Palmer allegedly shouted at plaintiff in a rude, violent and insolent manner as follows: "You goddam 'niggers' are not going to tell me about the rules. I don't want any 'niggers' working for me. I am getting rid of all the 'niggers'; go pick up and deliver that 8-ton roller to the other job site and get your pay check; you're fired." Plaintiff thereupon delivered the roller and reported the incident to defendant Thomas Anderson, Jr., a Caucasian and Anbro's secretary, who allegedly ratified and confirmed Palmer's acts, including plaintiff's discharge, on behalf of Anbro and the other defendants.

As a result of the foregoing incident, plaintiff allegedly suffered humiliation, mental anguish and emotional and physical distress. Plaintiff was sick and ill for several weeks thereafter, was unable to work, and sustained shock, nausea and insomnia.

Plaintiff further alleged that defendant Palmer's conduct was intentional and malicious, and done for the purpose of causing plaintiff to suffer humiliation, mental anguish and emotional and physical distress, and that defendant Anderson, Jr.'s conduct in confirming and ratifying Palmer's conduct and in discharging plaintiff, was done with knowledge that plaintiff's emotional and physical distress would thereby increase, and was done intentionally or with a wanton and reckless disregard of the consequences to plaintiff.

Plaintiff also alleged that Negroes such as plaintiff are particularly susceptible to emotional and physical distress from conduct such as committed by defendants.

Plaintiff was reinstated with Anbro through grievance and arbitration procedures, and has received back pay. This action seeks the recovery of actual and exemplary damages for the emotional and physical distress allegedly suffered by him. . . . [T]he courts of this state have . . . acknowledged the right to recover damages for emotional distress alone, without consequent physical injuries, in cases involving extreme and outrageous intentional invasions of one's mental and emotional tranquility. [citing State Rubbish Collectors Assn. v. Siliznoff, supra] . . .

Plaintiff has alleged facts and circumstances which reasonably could lead the trier of fact to conclude that defendants' conduct was extreme and outrageous, having a severe and traumatic effect upon plaintiff's emotional tranquility. Thus, according to plaintiff, defendants, standing in a position or relation of authority over plaintiff,[2] aware of his particular susceptibility to emotional distress,[3] and for the purpose of causing plaintiff to suffer such distress, intentionally humiliated plaintiff, insulted his race,[4] ignored his union status, and terminated his employment, all without just cause or provocation. Although it may be that mere insulting language, without more, ordinarily would not constitute extreme outrage, the aggravated circumstances alleged by plaintiff seem sufficient to uphold his complaint as against defendants' general demurrer. "Where reasonable men may differ, it is for the jury, subject to the control of the court, to determine whether, in the particular case, the conduct has been sufficiently extreme and outrageous to result in liability." (Rest. 2d Torts, §46, Comment *h*).

The multitude of cases upholding on various theories complaints alleging similar circumstances strongly indicates at least that plaintiff has pleaded a situation in which reasonable men may differ regarding defendants' liability. That being so, the order of dismissal should be reversed as to plaintiff's first cause of action.

2. The cases and commentators have emphasized the significance of the relationship between the parties in determining whether liability should be imposed. Thus, plaintiff's status as an employee should entitle him to a greater degree of protection from insult and outrage than if he were a stranger to defendants. As provided in Labor Code section 1412: "The opportunity to . . . hold employment without discrimination because of race, religious creed, color, national origin, or ancestry is hereby recognized as and declared to be a civil right."

3. Plaintiff's susceptibility to emotional distress has often been mentioned as significant in determining liability. With respect to the susceptibility of Negroes to severe emotional distress from discriminatory conduct, see Colley, Civil Actions for Damages Arising out of Violations of Civil Rights (1965-1966) 17 Hast. L.J. 189, 201.

4. Although the slang epithet "nigger" may once have been in common usage, along with such other racial characterizations as "wop," "chink," "jap," "bohunk," or "shanty Irish," the former expression has become particularly abusive and insulting in light of recent developments in the civil rights' movement as it pertains to the American Negro. Nor can we accept defendants' contention that plaintiff, as a truck driver must have become accustomed to such abusive language. Plaintiff's own susceptibility to racial slurs and other discriminatory conduct is a question for the trier of fact, and cannot be determined on demurrer.

. . . The judgment of dismissal of the first cause of action is reversed, and the trial court is hereby instructed to overrule the demurrer and allow defendants to answer.

Does the use of a racial or ethnic slur always create a claim for intentional infliction of emotional distress? In Irving v. J. L. Marsh, Inc., 360 N.E.2d 983 (Ill. App. 1977), the plaintiff sought a refund for returned merchandise. The defendant's employee wrote on the refund slip he gave the plaintiff: "arrogant nigger refused exchange/says he doesn't like product." The court found that the employee's conduct was insufficient to support a valid cause of action. Similarly, in Lay v. Roux Laboratories, Inc., 379 So. 2d 451 (Fla. App. 1980), the court affirmed the dismissal of a complaint based on the intentional infliction of emotional distress. In that case, an employee of Roux Laboratories who was responsible for administering and policing parking spaces for the company's employees called plaintiff a "nigger" during an argument over a parking space. The court held that the employee's conduct did not reach such level of outrageousness and atrociousness as to serve as a predicate for the independent tort of intentional infliction of emotional distress. Likewise, in Dawson v. Zayre Dept. Stores, 499 A.2d 648 (Pa. Sup. 1985), the Superior Court of Pennsylvania upheld the trial courts dismissal of a complaint alleging that the defendant's employee, a store clerk, had called the plaintiff a "nigger" during a dispute over a layaway ticket. The court observed: "Although we by no means condone the derogatory and offensive language used by Appellee's employee, and while we understand Appellant's rightful resentment, we believe that this conduct merely constitutes insulting namecalling from which no recovery may be had." 499 A.2d at 649.

Do the courts in these cases simply disagree with the *Alcorn* court concerning the offensiveness of such language, or are there other bases to distinguish the result reached in *Alcorn*? For general treatments of tort liability for racial and ethnic slurs, see Delgado, Words That Wound: A Tort Action for Racial Insults, Epithets, and Name-Calling, 17 Harv. C.R.-C.L. L. Rev. 133 (1982); Love, Discriminatory Speech and the Tort of Intentional Infliction of Emotional Distress, 47 Wash & Lee L. Rev. 123 (1990).

The court in *Alcorn* appears to credit plaintiff's claim that he, individually, and all members of his racial group, collectively, were especially sensitive to racial slurs. However, in Wiggs v. Courshon, 355 F. Supp. 206 (S.D. Fla. 1973), the court seemed to take an opposite tack. Although the court refused to grant the defendant's motion for a new trial after a jury returned a verdict in favor of the plaintiffs, who were called "niggers" and "a black son-of-a-bitch" by defendant's waitress in a dispute over a dinner order, the court nonetheless concluded that the damages were excessive and therefore ordered a remittitur. The court observed:

As to the amount of the verdicts, not only were the judicial eyebrows raised at the size of these verdicts, but the judicial conscience was profoundly shocked. As reluctant as the court is to interfere with the amounts arrived at by a jury comprising three blacks and three whites, four women and two men, the court concludes that the amounts of the verdicts were outrageously excessive. This jury plainly embarked on a giveaway program far out of line with common sense and experience.

The court condemns the uncivil outburst and rude remarks made by defendant's waitress, but does such an inexcusable insult justify the award of $25,000 under these circumstances? Plainly not. We all have ethnic and racial backgrounds and the court notes that there is at least one and usually several epithets ascribed to any ethnic group members, the use of which offends some members of the group. Despite that, it is certain a line would quickly form by members of any ethnic group to receive $25,000 as balm for an ethnic or racial epithet. The indefensibility of the size of the verdict is plainer still when we place it in context of an epithet delivered in a dispute over the ingredients of a dinner entree when that remark caused neither out-of-pocket expenses to the members of the ethnic group nor any apparent mental or emotional injury.

In its order of remittitur, the court set appropriate damages for the plaintiffs collectively at $2,500. But does the court's analysis make sense in terms of the test set out in §46 of the Restatement (Second) of Torts. Can the plaintiff be outraged, but just a little?

Finally, note that the *Alcorn* court observes that the expression "nigger" has "become particularly abusive and insulting in light of recent developments in the civil rights movement as it pertains to the American Negro." Id. at footnote 4. What does the court mean by this? Was the epithet less offensive to African-Americans before the civil rights movement? Or is the court really saying that judges, who are overwhelming caucasian, are simply more sensitive to the offensiveness of the term as a result of the changed social consciousness brought about by the civil rights movement? This raises an important question that recurs whenever liability depends on the reactions of the hypothetical reasonable person. Consider the following case.

Logan v. Sears, Roebuck & Co.

466 So. 2d 121 (Ala. 1985)

MADDOX, J.:

Robert Logan operates a beauty salon in Birmingham. On May 11, 1982, an employee of Sears, Roebuck and Company phoned Logan at his place of business to inquire whether he had made his monthly charge account payment. While looking for his checkbook, Logan heard the Sears employee tell someone on her end of the line, "This guy is as queer as a three-dollar bill. He owns a beauty salon, and he just told me that if you'll hold the line I will check my checkbook." No one on Logan's end of the conversation, other than Logan, heard the statement.

Logan brought suit against Sears, seeking damages based on the torts of outrage and invasion of privacy. Sears moved for summary judgment as to both causes of action. The trial court granted Sears's motion, holding that although the statement of the Sears employee was insulting, it was not sufficient to support a claim of outrage or invasion of privacy. Logan appeals here.

It is undisputed that the Sears employee indeed made the statement complained of by Logan. It is further undisputed that Logan is, in fact, a homosexual. Thus, the only issue presented is whether the trial court erred in granting summary judgment. We find that it did not.

The tort of outrage, as proposed in Restatement (Second) of Torts §46 (1948), and adopted by this Court in American Road Service Co. v. Inmon, 394 So. 2d 361 (Ala. 1980), provides that:

> One who by extreme and outrageous conduct intentionally or recklessly causes severe emotional distress to another is subject to liability for such emotional distress, and if bodily harm to the other results from it, for such bodily harm.

While *Inmon* did recognize a cause of action in Alabama based solely upon insulting language, it did not create a cause of action which arises from every insult. As this Court stated therein, the tort of outrage "does not recognize recovery for 'mere insults, indignities, threats, annoyances, petty oppressions, or other trivialities.' The principle applies only to unprivileged, intentional or reckless conduct of an extreme and outrageous nature, and only that which causes severe emotional distress. . . . The emotional distress thereunder must be so severe that no reasonable person could be expected to endure it. Any recovery must be reasonable and justified under the circumstances, liability ensuing only when the conduct is extreme. . . . By extreme we refer to conduct so outrageous in character and so extreme in degree as to go beyond all possible bounds of decency, and to be regarded as atrocious and utterly intolerable in a civilized society." 394 So. 2d at 365. . . .

We are unwilling to say that the use of the word "queer" to describe a homosexual is atrocious and intolerable in civilized society. We recognize that there are other words favored by the homosexual community in describing themselves, but the word "queer" has been used for a long time by those outside that community. It has been in use longer than the term "gay," which has recently become the most frequently used term to describe homosexuals.

Since Logan is admittedly a homosexual, can it be said realistically that being described as "queer" should cause him shame or humiliation? We think not. In order to create a cause of action, the conduct must be such that would cause mental suffering, shame, or humiliation to a person of ordinary sensibilities, not conduct which would be considered unacceptable merely by homosexuals. . . .

We hold that the statement was one of those relatively trivial insults for which the law grants no relief; therefore, the trial court did not err in granting summary judgment.

Affirmed.

TORBERT, C.J., JONES, SHORES, and BEATTY, JJ., concur.

To what extent does the First Amendment protect the defendant from an intentional infliction of emotional distress claim brought by a plaintiff as a result of something the defendant said? The answer is unclear. Most courts have avoided the issue, either by finding that the plaintiff's injury was caused by conduct as well as speech on the part of the defendant, or by concluding that the defendant's speech was not sufficiently outrageous to satisfy the substantive requirements of the tort. But in Hustler Magazine v. Falwell, 485 U.S. 46, 108 S. Ct. 876, 99 L. Ed. 2d 41 (1988), the Supreme Court held that a public figure, televangelist Jerry Falwell, could not recover for intentional infliction of emotional distress arising from the publication of a vicious "ad parody," absent a showing that the ad contained a false statement of fact and that the defendant, in publishing the ad, acted with actual malice. Thus, the decision appeared to subject claims for the intentional infliction of emotional distress to constitutional constraints similar to those applying to the tort of defamation, which are discussed in detail in Chapter 12. The scope of the constitutional privilege remains unclear, however. The *Falwell* decision focused on the status of the plaintiff as a public figure, as well as the value of the ideas expressed in the ad parody. But these considerations may be lacking in other cases, and hence the scope of First Amendment protection for outrageous speech will need to be clarified by future decisions.

Ford v. Revlon, Inc.

153 Ariz. 38, 734 P.2d 580 (1987)

Facts

Leta Fay Ford worked for the purchasing department of Revlon, Inc. (Revlon) in Phoenix, Arizona. She began her employment in 1973 as a secretary. She worked her way up to junior buyer and buyer positions over the ten years of her employment at Revlon. In October 1979, Revlon hired Karl Braun as the new manager for the purchasing department, which made him Ford's supervisor.

On 3 April 1980, Braun invited Ford to a dinner ostensibly to discuss business away from the office. Ford agreed and met Braun at a Phoenix restaurant. The business discussion, however, turned to more personal topics. At the end of the dinner, Ford started to leave. Braun told her that she was not going anywhere and to sit down because he planned to spend the night with her. When Ford rejected his advances, Braun told her, "you will regret this." Ford testified at trial that after this incident her working relationship with Braun was strained and uncomfortable. Ford did not report the dinner incident nor the adverse working atmosphere to Revlon management.

On 3 May 1980, Revlon held its annual service awards picnic. Braun followed Ford for most of the day. At one point, [Braun actually assaulted Ford, submitted her to unwanted touching of a sexual nature, and made repeated vulgar statements regarding what he planned to do to her.]

Later in May of 1980, Ford began a series of meetings with various members of Revlon management to report her complaints. Ford first spoke with the Phoenix Revlon comptroller, Robert Lettieri, who had authority to recommend hiring, firing, discipline, and promotions. Ford told him about the incidents with Braun and that she was afraid of Braun and wanted help. Lettieri said that he would speak to someone in personnel about her complaint and that she also should talk to personnel.

In early June of 1980, Ford spoke to Cecelia Domin, the personnel manager for the clerical and technical group in the Phoenix plant. In the Revlon management hierarchy, Domin reported directly to the director of personnel and worked with the plant manager of executives. When meeting with Domin, Ford was very emotional, her hands were shaking, and she was crying. Ford told Domin about the incidents and said that she was afraid of Braun. On 23 June 1980, Ford spoke to Robert Kosciusko, the personnel manager for executives. Ford also told him about the incidents, that she was afraid of Braun, and that the strain was making her sick.

In August of 1980, Ford met again with Domin and additionally with Martin Burstein, the director of personnel at the Phoenix plant. Again Ford complained about the incidents and told them that she was afraid of Braun. Burstein told Ford that he would talk to a Revlon vice president and that he would get back to her. Also in August, Ford spoke to John Maloney, a manager in receiving and stores. Maloney suggested that Ford contact Marie Kane at Revlon headquarters in New Jersey. Kane, a manager of human resources, was a "trouble shooter" and a veteran of the Phoenix personnel department.

In November of 1980, Ford telephoned Kane in New Jersey to report her concerns about Braun and her frustrations about the work situation. At this time, it had been six months since Ford first complained of Braun's conduct and no action had been taken. Kane then reported the details of her conversation with Ford to her boss, David Coe, the vice president of industrial relations and operations. Kane also informed Coe that Ford was becoming ill because of the problem. Coe's response was that the matter was not their concern at the corporate level and that the matter should be sent back to the local level and handled in Phoenix. Coe instructed Kane to telephone Burstein so that he could solve the problem. Kane did speak to Burstein, who promised to take care of the problem immediately.

When, as of December 1980, no action had been taken on Ford's complaint, Ford telephoned Kane again and informed her that Braun was continuing his harassment by calling her into his office and telling her that he wanted to destroy her, that she made him nervous, and that so long as she worked for him she was never going to go anywhere. He also called her into his office and did not allow her to sit down and would stare at her and not speak to her. According to Ford, Kane responded that it was a lot to absorb and that she would have to talk to someone else about it and that she would get back to Ford. After a few days had elapsed and Kane had not telephoned Ford, Ford again called Kane, who was out, and left a message. It was January 1981 before Kane returned Ford's call. Kane told Ford that the situation was too hot for her to handle and that she did not want to be involved. Kane suggested that Ford put the matter in the back of her mind and try to forget the situation.

Around this time, Ford also contacted Gene Tucker, a corporate Equal Employment Opportunity (EEO) specialist, and asked him for help. Tucker said that he would have to talk to Harry Petrie, the vice president of industrial relations and personnel in New York. Tucker did not get back to Ford.

During the time of the harassment, Ford developed high blood pressure, a nervous tic in her left eye, chest pains, rapid breathing, and other symptoms of emotional stress. Ford felt weak, dizzy, and generally fatigued. Ford consulted a physician about her condition.

On 23 February 1981, Ford submitted a written request for a transfer out of the purchasing department. On 24 February 1981, Braun placed Ford on a 60-day probation because of her allegedly poor work performance. On 25 February 1981, a meeting finally was held in personnel at Ford's demand so she could have something done about her situation with Braun. Ford was able to have Tucker arrange a meeting with them and with Domin and Burstein. Ford again gave the details of her complaint against Braun and her fear of him. Ford also submitted a handwritten complaint which read in part:

> I want to officially register a charge of sexual harassment and discrimination against K. Braun.
>
> I am asking for protection from Karl Braun. I have a right to be protected.
>
> I am collapsing emotionally and physically and I can't go on.

At this meeting on 25 February 1981, Braun was called in and confronted. After the meeting, Burstein and Domin told Ford that Braun would be closely monitored. Burstein also testified that he investigated Ford's allegation, which he said took him about three weeks.

Not until three months later, on 8 May 1981, however, did Burstein submit a report on Ford's complaint to vice president Coe; the report confirmed Ford's charge of sexual assault and recommended that Braun be censured. On 28 May 1981, a full year and one month after Braun's initial act of harassment, Braun was issued a letter of censure from Revlon.

In October of 1981, Ford attempted suicide.

On 5 October 1981, Revlon terminated Braun. Braun testified at trial that the reason given him for his termination was that he did not fit into the Revlon organization, partially because of the way he handled the "Ford situation."

In April of 1982, Ford sued both Braun and Revlon for assault and battery, and for intentional infliction of emotional distress.

The jury found Braun liable for assault and battery but not liable for intentional infliction of emotional distress. The jury found Revlon liable for intentional infliction of emotional distress but not liable for assault and battery. Damages awarded to Ford by the jury were assessed against Braun in the amount of $100 compensatory damages and $1,000 punitive damages, and assessed against Revlon in the amount of $10,000 compensatory damages and $100,000 punitive damages. Only Revlon appealed. Therefore, the only issue on appeal was whether Revlon was liable for intentional infliction of emotional distress. The court of appeals in a memorandum decision reversed the judgment of the trial court, holding that since Braun (as agent) was found not guilty of intentional infliction of emotional distress, then Revlon (as principal) could not be found guilty. We granted review because we disagreed with this limitation on the liability of Revlon.

Independent Tort Liability of the Employer

The court of appeals held that Revlon could not be liable for intentional infliction of emotional distress if Braun was not liable. The court of appeals stated:

> Even though the jury found Braun did assault Ford on May 3, 1980, it found that the assault and his subsequent acts, whatever they were found to be, were insufficient to hold him liable for intentional or reckless infliction of emotional distress. Revlon's liability is inextricably tied to the acts of Braun. Since Braun's acts did not constitute intentional or reckless infliction of emotional distress, then the inaction of Revlon on Ford's complaint certainly could not reach that level.

We disagree. Admittedly, when the master's liability is based solely on the negligence of his servant, a judgment in favor of the servant is a judgment in favor of the master. DeGraff v. Smith, 62 Ariz. 261, 157 P.2d 342 (1945).

When the negligence of the master is independent of the negligence of the servant, the result may be different. As noted by the court of appeals:

> We recognize that where there is independent negligence on the part of the master, the master may be liable, apart from his derivative liability for his servant's wrongful acts. In such a case, a judgment in favor of the servant will not ordinarily bar a recovery against the master. However, the master must have " 'been guilty of acts on which *independently of the acts of the servant,* liability may be predicated.' " (Emphasis supplied.)

We believe that the analysis should be the same in intentional tort cases. In a case factually similar to this one, the U.S. Court of Appeals for the Fourth Circuit recognized that a corporation could be liable for intentional infliction of emotional distress because its supervisor was aware of the sexual harassment of an employee by a manager and failed to stop it even though the *underlying* harassment might not rise to the level of either assault and battery or intentional infliction of emotional distress. Davis v. United States Steel Corp., 779 F.2d 209, 211 (4th Cir. 1985). The Fourth Circuit held that although the acts and behavior of the manager were despicable, they did not rise to the level of providing a basis for recovery by the complainant against the corporation for assault and battery or intentional infliction of emotional distress. The court went on to say, however, that "the situation is otherwise with respect to [the employer] and [its] failure to take any action." Id. at 212. We believe that Revlon's failure to investigate Ford's complaint was independent of Braun's abusive treatment of Ford.

Is Revlon Liable for Intentional Infliction of Emotional Distress?

Elements of the tort of intentional infliction of emotional distress have been set out by this court, relying upon the language of the Restatement of Torts.

The three required elements are: *first,* the conduct by the defendant must be "extreme" and "outrageous"; *second,* the defendant must either intend to cause emotional distress or recklessly disregard the near certainty that such distress will result from his conduct; and *third,* severe emotional distress must indeed occur as a result of defendant's conduct.

We believe that the conduct of Revlon met these requirements. First, Revlon's conduct can be classified as extreme or outrageous. Ford made numerous Revlon managers aware of Braun's activities at company functions. Ford did everything that could be done, both within the announced policies of Revlon and without, to bring this matter to Revlon's attention. Revlon ignored her and the situation she faced, dragging the matter out for months and leaving Ford without redress. Here is sufficient evidence that Revlon acted outrageously.

Second, even if Revlon did not intend to cause emotional distress, Revlon's reckless disregard of Braun's conduct made it nearly certain that such emotional distress would in fact occur. Revlon knew that Braun had subjected Ford to physical assaults, vulgar remarks, that Ford continued to feel threatened by Braun, and that Ford was emotionally distraught, all of which led to a manifestation of physical problems. Despite Ford's complaints, Braun was not confronted for nine months, and then only upon *Ford's* demand for a group meeting. Another three months elapsed before Braun was censured. Revlon not only had actual knowledge of the situation but it also failed to conduct promptly any investigation of Ford's complaint.

Third, it is obvious that emotional distress did occur. Ample evidence, both medical and otherwise, was presented describing Ford's emotional distress. Ford testified about her emotional distress and her development of physical complications caused by her stressful work environment. The evidence convinced the jury, which found that emotional distress had occurred.

We also note that Revlon had set forth a specific policy and several guidelines for the handling of sexual harassment claims and other employee complaints, yet Revlon recklessly disregarded these policies and guidelines. Ford was entitled to rely on the policy statements made by Revlon.

Once an employer proclaims a policy, the employer may not treat the policy as illusory. We hold that Revlon's failure to take appropriate action in response to Ford's complaint of sexual harassment by Braun constituted the tort of intentional infliction of emotional distress.

Arizona Workers' Compensation Law

Revlon contends that this matter is controlled by Arizona Workers' Compensation laws and not by tort law. We disagree. Ford's severe emotional distress injury was found by the jury to be not unexpected and was essentially nonphysical in nature. As the trial court stated:

> Evidence established that this tort was committed through defendant's action and inaction to plaintiff's complaints made over a period in excess of eight months. Such action and inaction and the resulting emotional injury to the plaintiff were therefore not "unexpected," accidental, or physical in nature so as to limit plaintiff's recovery to the workmen's compensation claim under A.R.S. §§23-1021(B) and 1043.01(B).

Ford v. Revlon, Inc., No. C-457854, slip op. at 15 (Super. Ct. Maricopa County, June 15, 1984). A.R.S. §23-1021(B) provides, in relevant part, that

> Every employee covered by insurance in the state compensation fund who is injured *by accident* arising out of and in the course of employment . . . shall be paid such compensation (emphasis added). . . .

A.R.S. §23-1043.01(B) sets forth the limiting standard for compensation under the statute for physiological injury. This section states: "A mental injury . . . shall not be considered a personal injury by accident . . . and is not compensable . . . unless . . . unexpected, unusual or extraordinary stress . . . or some physical injury . . . was a substantial contributing cause."

The acts by Braun and Revlon were not "accidents." Indeed, the jury found both parties liable for the intentional offenses in which they engaged: Braun for assault and battery and Revlon for emotional distress. An injured employee may enforce common-law liability against his or her employer if not encompassed by statute.

The decision of the court of appeals is vacated. The judgment of the trial court is reinstated.

GORDON, C.J., and JACK D. H. HAYS, RETIRED J., concur.

[The concurring opinion of FELDMAN, VICE CHIEF JUSTICE, is omitted.]

Sexual harassment often combines elements of assault, battery, and intentional infliction of emotional distress. In addition to the challenge of getting a court to recognize intentional infliction of emotional harm as independent of assault or battery, a plaintiff must also avoid the pitfalls of workers' compensation and respondeat superior limitations. Workers' compensation statutes were enacted to spread the costs of injuries resulting from natural workplace hazards and are intended to be an employee's exclusive remedy against his or her employer. (See pp. 778-793, above.) Courts have split on whether sexual harassment should be considered compensable under the statutes. As *Ford* demonstrates, some jurisdictions allow recovery outside of workers' compensation for sexual harassment in the workplace. Other courts hold that sexual harassment claims fit within the plain language of the statutes and, absent legislative determination otherwise, workers' compensation remedies preclude tort recovery. In Florida, for example, the courts have used workers' compensation and respondeat superior principles to deny tort recovery in three recent cases. In Studstill v. Borg Warner Leasing, 806 F.2d 1005 (11th Cir. 1986), the court held that the verbal harassment the plaintiff suffered did not "constitute conduct sufficiently heinous to support a claim for intentional infliction of emotional distress," id. at 1008, and the sexual battery claim was barred by the exclusivity limitation of workers' compensation. In *Studstill,* plaintiff's supervisor had physically and verbally harassed her during her second term of employment with defendant. In affirming the lower court's judgment for defendant on the claims for intentional infliction of emotional distress and civil assault and battery, the court found the sexual harassment alleged by the plaintiff was covered under Florida's Workers' Compensation Law. In Brown v. Winn-Dixie Montgomery, Inc., 469 So. 2d 155 (Fla. App. 1985), the court determined that the plaintiff's emotional distress resulting from being "grabbed" by her supervisor was directly caused by the battery and thus was covered under workers' compensation as an accidental injury. The court went on to state that while the plaintiff was precluded from pursuing her tort claims against her employer, she was free to do so against the supervisor individually. On the same day, the court denied tort recovery to two plaintiffs in a consolidated action against their employer. See Schwartz v. Zippy Mart, Inc., 470 So. 2d 720 (Fla. App. 1985). Both plaintiffs had been harassed by a supervisor who had physically attacked them on numerous occasions. In affirming the lower court's granting of summary judgment for the defendant, the court held that workers' compensation was the plaintiffs' sole remedy because the batteries occurred during the course and scope of their employment with the defendant. The court also found no employer liability for the tortious behavior of the supervisor because his acts were not within the scope of his employment.

Paralleling state law rules allowing tort recovery for sexual harassment, Congress enacted the Civil Rights Act of 1964 with a provision that provides a cause of action against an employer who discriminates on the basis of sex. See 42 U.S.C. §2000e et seq. (1982). Successful plaintiffs under Title VII may obtain "such affirmative action as may be appropriate," which often includes reinstatement, back pay, retroactive seniority benefits and sometimes even punitive damages. See Note, Damages for Sexual Harassment under Title VII and State Tort Law, 10 Cap. U.L. Rev. 657, 662-666 (1981). Thus plaintiffs typically join Title VII claims with state law tort actions in attempting to obtain full recovery for injuries suffered from sexual harassment. Unfortunately for plaintiffs, some courts consider the tort claims to be part of the Title VII claims and deny separate recovery on both. See, e.g., Otto v. Heckler, 781 F.2d 754 (9th Cir. 1986).

In addition to struggling with the issue of damages under Title VII, courts have continued to confront the question of what sort of employer conduct will constitute a cause of action for sexual harassment. Courts easily determine that denial of a tangible employment benefit is actionable. Thus in Barnes v. Costle, 561 F.2d 983 (D.C. 1977), the plaintiff could recover when her job was terminated after she refused her supervisor's sexual demands. (Some states provide broad protection to employees discharged for socially unacceptable reasons. See the note on wrongful discharge, Chapter 14, p. 1033, below.) Later decisions have expanded the criteria regarding whether harassment affected the "terms, conditions, or privileges of employment" under Title VII. Recently, the Supreme Court held that harassment creating a "hostile workplace" is actionable under the statute. See Meritor Savings Bank v. Vinson, 477 U.S. 57, 106 S. Ct. 2399, 91 L. Ed. 2d 49 (1986), in which a supervisor's demands for the plaintiff to participate in sexual activity were held to have created an "intimidating, hostile or offensive" environment, regardless of whether such demands were linked to the offering or denial of economic job benefits. In a subsequent decision, Harris v. Forklift Systems, Inc., 114 S. Ct. 367 (1993), the Supreme Court clarified the *Vinson* test by holding that a plaintiff asserting a "hostile workplace" claim need not establish that the conduct in issue caused a tangible psychological injury. Instead, the plaintiff need show only that the conduct created an environment that a reasonable person would find hostile or abusive. The Court observed:

> Whether an environment is "hostile" or "abusive" can be determined only by looking at all the circumstances. These include the frequency of the discriminatory conduct; its severity; whether it is physically threatening or humiliating, or a mere offensive utterance; and whether it unreasonably interferes with an employee's work performance. The effect on the employee's psychological well-being is, of course, relevant to determining whether the plaintiff actually found the environment abusive. But while psychological harm, like any other relevant factor, may be taken into account, no single factor is required.

114 S. Ct. at 371. See generally, Estrich, Sex at Work, 43 Stan. L. Rev. 813 (1991); Ehrenreich, Pluralist Myths and Powerless Men: The Ideology of Reasonableness in Sexual Harassment Law, 99 Yale L.J. 117 (1990); Abrams, Gender Discrimination and the Transformation of Workplace Norms, 42 Vand. L. Rev. 1183 (1989).

E. Violations of Civil Rights

In civil rights litigation, tort and constitutional issues frequently overlap. In recent years the volume of cases in which plaintiffs seek damages in tort for alleged violations of rights guaranteed to them by the constitutions and laws of the federal and state governments has risen significantly. Because the issues raised by these cases are too numerous and diverse to be examined in this limited framework, this section seeks to acquaint the student with only a few of the areas in which the relationship between tort and constitutional law continues to evolve.

Many modern civil rights actions, including those to be examined here, are based on alleged violations of §1 of the Civil Rights Act of 1871, which provides (42 U.S.C. §1983):

> Every person who, under color of any statute, ordinance, regulation, custom, or usage, of any State or Territory or the District of Columbia, subjects, or causes to be subjected, any citizen of the United States or other person within the jurisdiction thereof to the deprivation of any rights, privileges, or immunities secured by the Constitution and laws, shall be liable to the party injured in an action at law, suit in equity, or other proper proceeding for redress. For the purposes of this section, any Act of Congress applicable

exclusively to the District of Columbia shall be considered to be a statute of the District of Columbia.

This legislation was originally enacted during Reconstruction in response to the abuses of civil rights inflicted by the Ku Klux Klan with the tacit, and often active, sanction of local authorities. The Civil Rights Act was an attempt by Congress to force the Southern states to implement federal constitutional guarantees, especially those contained in the then-recently ratified Fourteenth Amendment.

In spite of its seeming breadth and importance, §1983 lay virtually dormant for many years. It was not until after the middle of this century that §1983 became an active part of civil rights litigation. The case many commentators regard as having opened the floodgates is Monroe v. Pape, 365 U.S. 167, 81 S. Ct. 473, 5 L. Ed. 2d 492 (1961). (The case was overruled in part on grounds not relevant to this discussion by Monell v. Department of Social Services, 436 U.S. 658, 98 S. Ct. 2018, 56 L. Ed. 2d 611 (1978)). The defendants in *Monroe* included thirteen Chicago police officers who conducted a search of plaintiffs' home in violation of state and federal law. They argued that their conduct was outside the scope of their legal authority and thus they could not be acting under color of state law. The Supreme Court nevertheless held that they were acting under color of state law for §1983 purposes. The Court also refused to require, as an element of the claim, that the defendants act "willfully"—i.e., that they have a specific intent to deprive the plaintiffs of a federal right. Rather, the Court determined that §1983 "should be read against the background of tort liability" making one liable for the natural consequences of one's acts. 365 U.S. at 187, 81 S. Ct. at 484, 5 L. Ed. 2d at 505.

Section 1983 specifies no state-of-mind requirement. Must the act be intentional, reckless, or merely negligent? Or is the liability strict? The Supreme Court considered these questions in the following case.

Daniels v. Williams

474 U.S. 327, 106 S. Ct. 662, 88 L. Ed. 2d 662 (1986)

JUSTICE REHNQUIST delivered the opinion of the Court.

In Parratt v. Taylor, 451 U.S. 527, 101 S. Ct. 1908, 68 L. Ed. 2d 420 (1981), a state prisoner sued under 42 U.S.C. §1983, claiming that prison officials had negligently deprived him of his property without due process of law. After deciding that §1983 contains no independent state-of-mind requirement, we concluded that although petitioner had been "deprived" of property within the meaning of the Due Process Clause of the Fourteenth Amendment, the State's postdeprivation tort remedy provided the process that was due. Petitioner's claim in this case, which also rests on an alleged Fourteenth Amendment "deprivation" caused by the negligent conduct of a prison official, leads us to reconsider our statement in *Parratt* that "the alleged loss, even though negligently caused, amounted to a deprivation." Id., at 536-537, 101 S. Ct., at 1913, 68 L. Ed. 2d at 429. We conclude that the Due Process Clause is simply not implicated by a *negligent* act of an official causing unintended loss of or injury to life, liberty or property.

In this §1983 action, petitioner seeks to recover damages for back and ankle injuries allegedly sustained when he fell on a prison stairway. He claims that, while an inmate at the city jail in Richmond, Virginia, he slipped on a pillow negligently left on the stairs by respondent, a correctional deputy stationed at the jail. Respondent's negligence, the argument runs, "deprived" petitioner of his "liberty" interest in freedom from bodily injury; because respondent maintains that he is entitled to the defense of sovereign immunity in a state tort suit, petitioner is without an "adequate" state remedy. Accordingly, the deprivation of liberty was without "due process of law."

The District Court granted respondent's motion for summary judgment. A panel of the Court of Appeals for the Fourth Circuit affirmed, concluding that even if respondent could make out an immunity defense in state court, petitioner would not be deprived of a meaningful opportunity to present his case. 720 F.2d 792 (1983). On rehearing, the en banc Court of Appeals affirmed the judgment of the District Court, but under reasoning different from that of the panel. 748 F.2d 229 (1984). [In addition to the reasons relied upon by the Court of Appeals panel, the Court of Appeals held en banc that negligent infliction of bodily injury was not a constitutional deprivation.]

Because of the inconsistent approaches taken by lower courts in determining when tortious conduct by state officials rises to the level of a constitutional tort and the apparent lack of adequate guidance from this Court, we granted certiorari. We now affirm.

In Parratt v. Taylor, we granted certiorari, as we had twice before, "to decide whether mere negligence will support a claim for relief under §1983." 451 U.S., at 532, 101 S. Ct., at 1911, 68 L. Ed. 2d at 427. After examining the language, legislative history and prior interpretations of the statute, we concluded that §1983, unlike its criminal counterpart, 18 U.S.C. §242, contains no state-of-mind requirement independent of that necessary to state a violation of the underlying constitutional right. We adhere to that conclusion. But in any given §1983 suit, the plaintiff must still prove a violation of the underlying constitutional right; and depending on the right, merely negligent conduct may not be enough to state a claim. . . .

Upon reflection, we . . . overrule *Parratt* to the extent that it states that mere lack of due care by a state official may "deprive" an individual of life, liberty or property under the Fourteenth Amendment.

The Due Process Clause of the Fourteenth Amendment provides: "[N]or shall any State deprive any person of life, liberty, or property, without due process of law." Historically, this guarantee of due process has been applied to *deliberate* decisions of government officials to deprive a person of life, liberty or property. No decision of this Court before *Parratt* supported the view that negligent conduct by a state official, even though causing injury, constitutes a deprivation under the Due Process Clause. This history reflects the traditional and common-sense notion that the Due Process Clause, like its forebear in the Magna Carta, was " 'intended to secure the individual from the arbitrary exercise of the powers of government,' " Hurtado v. California, 110 U.S. 516, 527, 4 S. Ct. 111, 116, 28 L. Ed. 232, 236 (1884) (quoting Bank of Columbia v. Okely, 4 Wheat. (17 U.S.) 235, 244, 4 L. Ed. 559, 561 (1819)). By requiring the government to follow appropriate procedures when its agents decide to "deprive any person of life, liberty, or property," the Due Process Clause promotes fairness in such decisions. And by barring certain government actions regardless of the fairness of the procedures used to implement them, it serves to prevent governmental power from being "used for purposes of oppression," Murray's Lessee v. Hoboken Land & Improvement Co., 18 How. (59 U.S.) 272, 277, 15 L. Ed. 372, 374 (1856) (discussing Due Process Clause of Fifth Amendment).

We think that the actions of prison custodians in leaving a pillow on the prison stairs, or mislaying an inmate's property, are quite remote from the concerns just discussed. Far from an abuse of power, lack of due care suggests no more than a failure to measure up to the conduct of a reasonable person. To hold that injury caused by such conduct is a deprivation within the meaning of the Fourteenth Amendment would trivialize the centuries-old principle of due process of law.

The Fourteenth Amendment is a part of a constitution generally designed to allocate governing authority among the branches of the Federal Government and between that Government and the States, and to secure certain individual rights against both State and Federal Government. When dealing with a claim that such a document creates a right in prisoners to sue a government official because he negligently created an unsafe condition in the prison, we bear in mind Chief Justice Marshall's admonition that "we must never forget, that it is *a constitution* we are expounding," McCulloch v. Maryland, 4 Wheat. (17 U.S.) 316, 407, 4 L. Ed. 579, 602 (1819) (emphasis in original). Our Constitution deals with the large concerns of the governors and the governed, but it does not purport to supplant traditional tort law in laying down rules of conduct to regulate liability for injuries that attend living together in society. We have previously rejected reasoning that "would make of the Fourteenth Amendment a font of tort law to be superimposed upon whatever systems may already be administered by the States," Paul v. Davis, 424 U.S. 693, 701, 96 S. Ct. 1155, 1160, 47 L. Ed. 2d 405, 413 (1976), quoted in Parratt v. Taylor, 451 U.S., at 544, 101 S. Ct., at 1917, 68 L. Ed. 2d at 534.

The only tie between the facts of this case and anything governmental in nature is the fact that respondent was a sheriff's deputy at the Richmond city jail and petitioner was an inmate confined in that jail. But while the Due Process Clause of the Fourteenth Amendment obviously speaks to some facets of this relationship, we do not believe its protections are triggered by lack of due care by prison officials. "Medical malpractice does not become a constitutional violation merely because the victim is a prisoner," Estelle v. Gamble, 429 U.S. 97, 106, 97 S. Ct. 285, 292, 50 L. Ed. 2d 251, 261 (1976), and "false imprisonment does not become a violation of the Fourteenth Amendment merely because the defendant is a state official." Baker v. McCollan, 443 U.S. 137, 146, 99 S. Ct. 2689, 2695, 61 L. Ed. 2d 433 (1979). Where a government official's act causing injury to life, liberty or property is merely negligent, "no procedure for compensation is *constitutionally* required." *Parratt,* 451 U.S., at 548, 101 S. Ct., at 1919 (POWELL, J., concurring in result) (emphasis added.)

That injuries inflicted by governmental negligence are not addressed by the United States Constitution is not to say that they may not raise significant legal concerns and lead to the creation of protectible legal interests. The enactment of tort claim statutes, for example, reflects the view that injuries caused by such negligence should generally be redressed. It is no reflection on either the breadth of the United States Constitution or the importance of traditional tort law to say that they do not address the same concerns. . . .

Petitioner also suggests that artful litigants, undeterred by a requirement that they plead more than mere negligence, will often be able to allege sufficient facts to support a claim of intentional deprivation. In the instant case, for example, petitioner notes that he could have alleged that the pillow was left on the stairs with the intention of harming him. This invitation to "artful" pleading, petitioner contends, would engender sticky (and needless) disputes over what is fairly pleaded. What's more, requiring complainants to allege something more than negligence would raise serious questions about what "more" than negligence—intent, recklessness or "gross negligence"—is required, and indeed about what these elusive terms mean. But even if accurate, petitioner's observations do not carry the day. In the first place, many branches of the law abound in nice distinctions that may be troublesome but have been thought nonetheless necessary. . . . More important, the difference between one end of the spectrum—negligence—and the other—intent—is abundantly clear. In any event, we decline to trivialize the Due Process Clause in an effort to simplify constitutional litigation.

Affirmed. JUSTICES MARSHALL, BLACKMUN, and STEVENS concurred in the result.

In Davidson v. Cannon, 474 U.S. 344, 106 S. Ct. 668, 88 L. Ed. 2d 677 (1986), decided on the same day as *Daniels,* an inmate alleged that prison officials were negligent in not preventing another inmate from attacking him. After citing *Daniels* as controlling, the Court added: "The guarantee of due process has never been understood to mean that the State must guarantee due care on the part of its officials." 474 U.S. at 348, 106 S. Ct. at 670, 88 L. Ed. 2d at 683.

Although most §1983 actions are brought against government officials, under some circumstances civil rights claims may be brought against private actors if their harm-causing activity occurred "under color of law." Thus, for example, in Lugar v. Edmonson Oil Co., 457 U.S. 922, 102 S. Ct. 2744, 73 L. Ed. 2d 482 (1982), the Supreme Court upheld the use of a §1983 action by a debtor against a creditor who had used the state's attachment statute to obtain prejudgment attachment of some of the debtor's property. The Court, while reluctant to conclude that any reliance by a private party on state law would satisfy the "under color of law" requirement of §1983, found that the requirement was satisfied if the private party's harm causing actions could be fairly attributed to the state. The court adopted a two-part approach to the question of "fair attribution":

> First, the deprivation must be caused by the exercise of some right or privilege created by the State or by a rule of conduct imposed by the state or by a person for whom the State is responsible. . . . Second, the party charged with the deprivation must be a person who may fairly be said to be a state actor. This may be because he is a state official, because he has acted together with or has obtained significant aid from state officials, or because his conduct is otherwise chargeable to the State.

One of the most important issues under §1983 is whether a government actor or entity is immune from liability. In Monell v. Dept. of Social Servs., 436 U.S. 658, 98 S. Ct. 2018, 56 L. Ed. 2d 611 (1978), the Supreme Court held that local governing bodies are "persons" within the meaning of the statute and could be sued directly. However, states are immune from §1983 liability under the Eleventh Amendment, and Supreme Court decisional law has extended immunity from damage actions to state legislators, judges, and prosecutors.

The damages issue also plays an important role in §1983 actions. The language of the statute does not define any uniform system of compensation or specify any form or amount of relief for plaintiffs who have successfully proven that their rights under the statute have been violated. Therefore, as a general rule damages in §1983 actions have been determined by application of traditional tort principles. As developed in Chapter 8, compensatory damages principles have as their purpose the restoration of the plaintiff to his preinjury condition.

Although lower courts have awarded punitive damages in §1983 actions for some time, it was not until 1983 that the Supreme Court explicitly approved this remedy. In Smith v. Wade, 461 U.S. 30, 103 S. Ct. 1625. 75 L. Ed. 2d 632 (1983), the Court ruled that "a jury may be permitted to assess punitive damages in an action under §1983 when the defendant's conduct is shown to be motivated by evil motive or intent, or when it involves reckless or callous indifference to the federally protected rights of others." 461 U.S. at 50, 103 S. Ct. at 1640, 75 L. Ed. 2d at 651. However, cities are immune from liability for punitive damages. City of Newport v. Fact Concerts, Inc., 453 U.S. 247, 101 S. Ct. 2748, 69 L. Ed. 2d 616 (1981).

Special difficulties concerning the awarding of damages in §1983 cases arise when the plaintiffs prove that their rights have been violated, but are unable to show substantial resulting harm. The following decision illustrates how the Supreme Court has addressed this problem.

Memphis Community School District v. Stachura

477 U.S. 299, 106 S. Ct. 2537, 91 L. Ed. 2d 249 (1986)

JUSTICE POWELL delivered the opinion of the Court.

This case requires us to decide whether 42 U.S.C. §1983 authorizes an award of compensatory damages based on the fact finder's assessment of the value or importance of a substantive constitutional right.

I

Respondent Edward Stachura is a tenured teacher in the Memphis, Michigan, public schools. When the events that led to this case occurred, respondent taught seventh-grade life science, using a textbook that had been approved by the school board. The textbook included a chapter on human reproduction. During the 1978-1979 school year, respondent spent six weeks on this chapter. As part of their instruction, students were shown pictures of respondent's wife during her pregnancy. Respondent also showed the students two films concerning human growth and sexuality. These films were provided by the county health department, and the principal of respondent's school had approved their use. Both films had been shown in past school years without incident.

After the showing of the pictures and the films, a number of parents complained to school officials about respondent's teaching methods. These complaints, which appear to have been based largely on inaccurate rumors about the allegedly sexually explicit nature of the pictures and films, were discussed at an open school board meeting held on April 23, 1979. Following the advice of the school superintendent, respondent did not attend the meeting, during which a number of parents expressed the view that respondent should not be allowed to teach in the Memphis school system. The day after the meeting, respondent was suspended with pay. The school board later confirmed the suspension, and notified respondent that an "administration evaluation" of his teaching methods was underway. No such evaluation was ever made. Respondent was reinstated the next fall, after filing this lawsuit.

Respondent sued the school district, the board of education, various board members and school administrators, and two parents who had participated in the April 23 school board meeting. The complaint alleged that respondent's suspension deprived him of both liberty and property without due process of law and violated his First Amendment right to academic freedom. Respondent sought compensatory and punitive damages under 42 U.S.C. §1983 for these constitutional violations.

At the close of the trial on these claims, the District Court instructed the jury as to the law governing the asserted bases for liability. Turning to damages, the court instructed the jury that on finding liability it should award a sufficient amount to compensate respondent for the injury caused by petitioners' unlawful actions:

> You should consider in this regard any lost earnings; loss of earning capacity; out-of-pocket expenses; and any mental anguish or emotional distress that you find the Plaintiff to have suffered as a result of conduct by the Defendants depriving him of his civil rights.

In addition to this instruction on the standard elements of compensatory damages, the court explained that punitive damages could be awarded, and described the standards governing punitive awards. Finally, at respondent's request and over petitioners' objection, the court charged that damages also could be awarded based on the value or importance of the constitutional rights that were violated.

> If you find that the Plaintiff has been deprived of a Constitutional right, you may award damages to compensate him for the deprivation. Damages for this type of injury are more difficult to measure than damages for a physical injury or injury to one's property. There are no medical bills or other expenses by which you can judge how much compensation is appropriate. In one sense, no monetary value we place upon Constitutional rights can measure their importance in our society or compensate a citizen adequately for their deprivation. However, just because these rights are not capable of precise evaluation does not mean that an appropriate monetary amount should not be awarded.
>
> The precise value you place upon any Constitutional right which you find was denied to Plaintiff is within your discretion. You may wish to consider the importance of the right of our system of government, the role which this right has played in the history of our republic, [and] the significance of the right in the context of the activities which the Plaintiff was engaged in at the time of the violation of the right.

The jury found petitioners liable, and awarded a total of $275,000 in compensatory damages and $46,000 in punitive damages. The District Court entered judgment notwithstanding the verdict as to one of the defendants, reducing the total award to $266,750 in compensatory damages and $36,000 in punitive damages.

In an opinion devoted primarily to liability issues, the Court of Appeals for the Sixth Circuit affirmed, holding that respondent's suspension had violated both procedural due process and the First Amendment. Stachura v. Truszkowski, 763 F.2d 211 (1985). Responding to petitioners' contention that the District Court improperly authorized damages based solely on the value of constitutional rights, the court noted only that "there was ample proof of actual injury to plaintiff Stachura both in his effective discharge . . . and by the damage to his reputation and to his professional career as a teacher. Contrary to the situation in Carey v. Piphus, 435 U.S. 247, 98 S. Ct. 1042, 55 L. Ed. 2d 252 (1978) . . . there was proof from which the jury could have found, as it did, actual and important damages." Id., at 214.

We granted certiorari limited to the question whether the Court of Appeals erred in affirming the damages award in the light of the District Court's instructions that authorized not only compensatory and punitive damages, but also damages for the deprivation of "any constitutional right." We reverse, and remand for a new trial limited to the issue of compensatory damages.

II

Petitioners challenge the jury instructions authorizing damages for violation of constitutional rights on the ground that those instructions permitted the jury to award damages based on its own unguided estimation of the value of such rights. Respondent disagrees with this characterization of the jury instructions, contending that the compensatory damages instructions taken as a whole focused solely on respondent's injury and not on the abstract value of the rights he asserted.

We believe petitioners more accurately characterize the instructions. The damages instructions were divided into three distinct segments: (i) compensatory damages for harm to respondent, (ii) punitive damages, and (iii) additional "compensat[ory]" damages for violations of constitutional rights. No sensible juror could read the third of these segments to modify the first. On the contrary, the damages instructions plainly authorized—in addition to punitive damages—two distinct types of "compensatory" damages: one based on respondent's actual injury according to ordinary tort law standards, and another based on the "value" of certain rights. We therefore consider whether the latter category of damages was properly before the jury.

III

A

We have repeatedly noted that 42 U.S.C. §1983 creates " 'a species of tort liability' in favor of persons who are deprived of 'rights, privileges, or immunities secured' to them by the Constitution." Carey v. Piphus, 435 U.S. 247, 253, 98 S. Ct. 1042, 1047, 55 L. Ed. 2d 252, 258 (1978), quoting Imbler v. Pachtman, 424 U.S. 409, 417, 96 S. Ct. 984, 988, 47 L. Ed. 2d 128, 136 (1976). Accordingly, when §1983 plaintiffs seek damages for violations of constitutional rights, the level of damages is ordinarily determined according to principles derived from the common law of torts.

Punitive damages aside, damages in tort cases are designed to provide "*compensation* for the injury caused to plaintiff by defendant's breach of duty." 2 F. Harper & F. James, Law of Torts §25.1, p. 1299 (1956) (emphasis in original), quoted in Carey v. Piphus, supra, 435 U.S., at 255, 98 S. Ct., at 1047, 55 L. Ed. 2d at 259. To that end, compensatory damages may include not only out-of-pocket loss and other monetary harms, but also such injuries as "impairment of reputation . . . , personal humiliation, and mental anguish and suffering." Gertz v. Robert Welch, Inc., 418 U.S. 323, 350, 94 S. Ct. 2997, 3012, 41 L. Ed. 2d 789, 811 (1974). Deterrence is also an important purpose of this system, but it operates through the mechanism of damages that are *compensatory*—damages grounded in determinations of plaintiff's actual losses. Congress adopted this common-law system of recovery when it established liability for "constitutional torts." Consequently, "the basic purpose" of §1983 damages is "to *compensate persons for injuries* that are caused by the deprivation of constitutional rights." Carey v. Piphus, 435 U.S., at 254, 98 S. Ct., at 1047, 55 L. Ed. 2d at 259 (emphasis added).

Carey v. Piphus represents a straightforward application of these principles. *Carey* involved a suit by a high school student suspended for smoking marijuana; the student claimed that he was denied procedural due process because he was suspended without an opportunity to respond to the charges against him. The Court of Appeals for the Seventh Circuit held that even if the suspension was justified, the student could recover substantial compensatory damages simply because of the insufficient procedures used to suspend him from school. We reversed, and held that the student could recover compensatory damages only if he proved actual injury caused by the denial of his constitutional rights. We noted that "[r]ights, constitutional and otherwise, do not exist in a vacuum. Their purpose is to protect persons from injuries to particular interests. . . ." Id., at 254, 98 S. Ct., at 1047, 55 L. Ed. 2d at 259. Where no injury was present, no "compensatory" damages could be awarded.

The instructions at issue here cannot be squared with *Carey,* or with the principles of tort damages on which *Carey* and §1983 are grounded. The jurors in this case were told that, in determining how much was necessary to "compensate [respondent] for the deprivation" of his constitutional rights, they should place a money value on the "rights" themselves by considering such factors as the particular right's "importance . . . in our system of government," its role in American history, and its "significance . . . in the context of the activities" in which respondent was engaged. These factors focus, not on compensation for provable injury, but on the jury's subjective perception of the importance of constitutional rights as an abstract matter. *Carey* establishes that such an approach is impermissible. The constitutional right transgressed in *Carey*—the right to due process of law—is central to our system of ordered liberty. We nevertheless held that *no* compensatory damages could be awarded for violation of that right absent proof of actual injury. *Carey* thus makes clear that the abstract value of a constitutional right may not form the basis for §1983 damages.

Respondent nevertheless argues that *Carey* does not control here, because in this case a *substantive* constitutional right—respondent's First Amendment right to academic freedom—was infringed. The argument misperceives our analysis in *Carey.* That case does not establish a two-tiered system of constitutional rights, with substantive rights afforded greater protection than "mere" procedural safeguards. We did acknowledge in *Carey* that "the elements and prerequisites for recovery of damages" might vary depending on the interests protected by the constitutional right at issue. Id., at 264-265, 98 S. Ct., at 1053. But we emphasized that, whatever the constitutional basis for §1983 liability, such damages must always be designed "to *compensate injuries* caused by the [constitutional] deprivation." Id., at 265, 98 S. Ct., at 1053, 55 L. Ed. 2d at 266 (emphasis added). That conclusion simply leaves no room for non-compensatory damages measured by the jury's perception of the abstract "importance" of a constitutional right.

Nor do we find such damages necessary to vindicate the constitutional rights that §1983 protects. Section 1983 presupposes that damages that compensate for actual harm ordinarily suffice to deter constitutional violations. Moreover, damages based on the "value" of constitutional rights are an unwieldly tool for ensuring compliance with the Constitution. History and tradition do not afford any sound guidance concerning the precise value that juries should place on constitutional protections. Accordingly, were such damages available, juries would be free to award arbitrary amounts without any evidentiary basis, or to use their unbounded discretion to punish unpopular defendants. Such damages would be too uncertain to be of any great value to plaintiffs, and would inject caprice into determinations of damages in §1983 cases. We therefore hold that damages based on the abstract "value" or "importance" of constitutional rights are not a permissible element of compensatory damages in such cases.

B

Respondent further argues that the challenged instructions authorized a form of "presumed" damages—a remedy that is both compensatory in nature and traditionally part of the range of tort law remedies. Alternatively, respondent argues that the erroneous instructions were at worst harmless error.

Neither argument has merit. Presumed damages are a *substitute* for ordinary compensatory damages, not a *supplement* for an award that fully compensates the alleged injury. When a plaintiff seeks compensation for an injury that is likely to have occurred but difficult to establish, some form of presumed damages may possibly be appropriate. In those circumstances, presumed damages may roughly approximate the harm that the plaintiff suffered and thereby compensate for harms that may be impossible to measure. As we earlier explained, the instructions at issue in this case did not serve this purpose, but instead called on the jury to measure damages based on a subjective evaluation of the importance of particular constitutional values. Since such damages are wholly divorced from any compensatory purpose, they cannot be justified as presumed damages. Moreover, no rough substitute for compensatory damages was required in this case, since the jury was fully authorized to compensate respondent for both monetary and non-monetary harms caused by petitioner's conduct.

Nor can we find that the erroneous instructions were harmless. . . . the jury awarded respondent a very substantial amount of damages, none of which could have derived from any monetary loss. It is likely, although not certain, that a major part of these damages was intended to "compensate" respondent for the abstract "value" of his due process and First Amendment rights. For these reasons, the case must be remanded for a new trial on compensatory damages.

IV

The judgment of the Court of Appeals is reversed, and the case is remanded for further proceedings consistent with this opinion.

It is so ordered.

JUSTICE BRENNAN and JUSTICE STEVENS join the opinion of the Court and also join JUSTICE MARSHALL'S opinion concurring in the judgment.

JUSTICE MARSHALL, with whom JUSTICE BRENNAN, JUSTICE BLACKMUN, and JUSTICE STEVENS join, concurring in the judgment.

I agree with the Court that this case must be remanded for a new trial on damages. Certain portions of the Court's opinion, however, can be read to suggest that damages in §1983 cases are necessarily limited to "out-of-pocket loss," "other monetary harms," and "such injuries as 'impairment of reputation . . . , personal humiliation, and mental anguish and suffering.' " I do not understand the Court so to hold, and I write separately to emphasize that the violation of a constitutional right, in proper cases, may itself constitute a compensable injury.

The instructions given the jury in this case were improper because they did not require the jury to focus on the loss actually sustained by respondent. Rather, they invited the jury to base its award on speculation about "the importance of the right in our system of government" and "the role which this right has played in the history of our republic," guided only by the admonition that "[i]n one sense, no monetary value we place on Constitutional rights can measure their importance in our society or compensate a citizen adequately for their deprivation." These instructions invited the jury to speculate on matters wholly detached from the real injury occasioned respondent by the deprivation of the right. Further, the instructions might have led the jury to grant respondent damages based on the "abstract value" of the right to procedural due process—a course directly barred by our decision in *Carey.*

The Court therefore properly remands for a new trial on damages. I do not understand the Court, however, to hold that deprivations of constitutional rights can never themselves constitute compensable injuries. Such a rule would be inconsistent with the logic of *Carey,* and would defeat the purpose of §1983 by denying compensation for genuine injuries caused by the deprivation of constitutional rights.

Bringing an action under §1983 can be expensive. In order to encourage meritorious suits to vindicate civil rights, Congress provided in 42 U.S.C. §1988 for the award of attorney's fees to the prevailing party. The award of fees is at the discretion of the trial court. No attorney's fees, however, are available for the pursuit of state administrative remedies. Webb v. Board of Education, 471 U.S. 234, 105 S. Ct. 1923, 85 L. Ed. 2d 233 (1985). The Supreme Court has declined to require that the award of attorney's fees be proportionate to the damages actually recovered. City of Riverside v. Rivera, 477 U.S. 561, 106 S. Ct. 2686, 91 L. Ed. 2d 466 (1986) (plurality). Attorney's fees are available even if the lawyer did not actually charge the client. Blum v. Stenson, 465 U.S. 886, 104 S. Ct. 1541, 79 L. Ed. 2d 891 (1984). An agreement to waive attorney's fees, given as a bargaining chip, is enforceable. Evens v. Jeff D., 475 U.S. 717, 106 S. Ct. 1531, 89 L. Ed. 2d 747 (1986). For more on attorney's fees, see Note, Surveying the Law of Fee Awards Under the Attorney's Fees Award Act of 1976, 59 Notre Dame L. Rev. 1293 (1984).

Law review treatments include Blackmun, Section 1983 and Federal Protection of Individual Rights—Will the Statute Remain Alive or Fade

Away?, 60 N.Y.U. L. Rev. 1 (1985); Mead, Evolution of the "Species of Tort Liability" Created by 42 U.S.C. §1983: Can Constitutional Tort Be Saved From Extinction?, 55 Fordham L. Rev. 1 (1986); and Zagrans, "Under Color of" *What* Law: A Reconstructed Model of Section 1983 Liability, 71 Va. L. Rev. 499 (1985).

Chapter 12

Defamation

Defamation is one of the most complex torts. The sources of the complexity lie in the historical origins of the law,[1] and in the difficulties of reconciling the important but often conflicting interests in the protection of reputation and freedom of speech. In 1964, the United States Supreme Court began the process of restriking the balance between these two interests that had been achieved by the common law. In New York Times Co. v. Sullivan, discussed in Section B, below, the Court held that defamation of public officials is speech entitled to the protection of the First Amendment to the United States Constitution. Later cases have expanded the reach of the first amendment into the law of defamation, and how much remains of the traditional law is somewhat in doubt.

Section A of this chapter contains a general description of the traditional law of defamation as it has developed apart from the constitutional cases. In Section B, we set out the principal lines of constitutional development. Section C sets out a proposal for a uniform act which seeks to bring about a more rational balance between the interests in reputation and in speech.

A. *The Traditional Law*

The law of defamation protects the interest in reputation. The basic elements of an action for defamation are:

(1) A defamatory statement. Not all insults are actionable; the general rule is that to be defamatory, a statement must hold the plaintiff up to "hatred, ridicule, or contempt."

(2) Publication. The basis of the plaintiff's cause of action is the harm suffered from the reaction of others and not hurt feelings. The defamatory statement must, therefore, be published—that is, communicated to a third person.

(3) Harm. In some circumstances, the plaintiff must prove actual harm from the publication of the defamatory statement in order to recover. In other instances, there is no need for such proof. The requirements with

1. The history of the law of defamation defies brief restatement. In general, see Donnelly, History of Defamation, 1949 Wis. L. Rev. 99; Veeder, The History and Theory of the Law of Defamation, 3 Colum. L. Rev. 546 (1903), and 4 Colum. L. Rev. 33 (1904).

respect to proof of harm are reflected in the categories of damages that may be recovered. There are two categories of compensatory damages: special and general. In addition, punitive damages may be recovered.

If the plaintiff is successful in establishing a prima facie case, the defendant may be able to avoid liability by setting up either of two defenses:

(1) Privilege. The privilege to publish a defamatory statement may be either absolute or qualified. An absolute privilege is available in situations in which the interest in free expression totally outweighs interests in reputation. A qualified privilege rests on a more limited interest of permitting free expression between the publisher and the audience.

(2) Truth. Truth is a defense to a suit for defamation, and is not part of the plaintiff's prima facie case.

1. What Constitutes Defamation

a. The General Standard

Since the interest which the law of defamation seeks to protect is the integrity of the plaintiff's reputation, the defamatory communication must do more than hurt the plaintiff's feelings. It must be of a nature to cause others to react adversely to the plaintiff. Defamation is traditionally defined as a statement that holds one up to hatred, ridicule, or contempt. A somewhat broader definition is supplied by §559 of the Restatement (Second) of Torts:

> A communication is defamatory if it tends so to harm the reputation of another as to lower him in the estimation of the community or to deter third persons from associating or dealing with him.

Even this definition is too limited for some courts. For example, in Youssoupoff v. Metro-Goldwyn-Mayer Pictures, Ltd., 50 T.L.R. 581 (C.A. 1934), the plaintiff, a Russian princess, claimed that the defendant's motion picture defamed her by portraying her as a woman who had been raped by the notorious Russian monk, Rasputin. Although the film did not suggest that the plaintiff was guilty of any misbehavior, the appellate court affirmed a lower court decision for the plaintiff. The court approved the trial judge's definition, which included statements causing persons "to be shunned or avoided," and added its own gloss by characterizing as defamatory "a false statement about a man to his discredit. . . ." To the defendant's assertion that the motion picture was not defamatory, the court responded (50 T.L.R. at 584):

> [T]his is the argument as I understand it: "To say of a woman that she is raped does not impute unchastity." From that we get to this, which was solemnly put forward, that to say of a woman of good character that she has

> been ravished by a man of the worst possible character is not defamatory. That argument was solemnly presented to the jury, and I only wish the jury could have expressed, and that we could know, what they thought of it, because it seems to me to be one of the most legal arguments that were ever addressed to, I will not say a business body, but a sensible body.

The medium of the defamatory communication does not have to be the written or spoken word; actions, gestures, pictures, and other visual representations may be defamatory. In Schultz v. Frankfort Marine Accident & Plate Glass Ins. Co., 152 Wis. 537, 139 N.W. 386 (1913), the court held that detectives who were "rough shadowing"—a form of surveillance designed to publicly harass and humiliate its object—the plaintiff had defamed him. And in Burton v. Crowell Publishing Co., 82 F.2d 154 (2d Cir. 1936), a photograph in an advertisement was held to be defamatory. The plaintiff in this case, a "widely known gentleman steeple-chaser," had posed for a picture showing him holding a saddle from which hung a large girth. The girth appeared to be attached to the plaintiff rather than the saddle. Characterizing the picture as "grotesque, monstrous, and obscene," the court commented on the unique way in which a picture can defame:

> If the advertisement is a libel, it is such in spite of the fact that it asserts nothing whatever about the plaintiff, even by the remotest implications. . . . [I]t is patently an optical illusion, and carries its correction on its face as much as though it were a verbal utterance which expressly declared that it was false. It would be hard for words so guarded to carry any sting, but the same is not true of caricatures, and this is an example; for notwithstanding all we have just said, it exposed the plaintiff to overwhelming ridicule. [82 F.2d at 155.]

In Masson v. The New Yorker Magazine, Inc., 111 S. Ct. 2419, 2430, 115 L. Ed. 2d 447, 469 (1991), the Supreme Court ruled that a misquotation of the plaintiff in a publication is capable of being defamatory:

> A fabricated quotation may injure reputation in at least two senses, either giving rise to a conceivable claim of defamation. First, the quotation might injure because it attributes an untrue factual assertion to the speaker. An example would be a fabricated quotation of a public official admitting he had been convicted of a serious crime when in fact he had not.
>
> Second, regardless of the truth or falsity of the factual matters asserted within the quoted statement, the attribution may result in injury to reputation because the manner of expression or even the fact that the statement was made indicates a negative personal trait or an attitude the speaker does not hold.

In general, see Comment, Fabricated Quotations as Cause for Libel Recovery by a Public Figure, 57 U. Chi. L. Rev. 1353 (1990).

By and large, parodies and satires have been held not to be defamatory on the ground that reasonable people would not take such publications to be statements of actual facts. See, e.g., Hustler Magazine v. Falwell, 485 U.S. 46, 108 S. Ct. 876, 99 L. Ed. 2d 41 (1988), involving a parody of liquor advertisement in which the plaintiff, a well-known religious leader, was portrayed as having a sexual dalliance with his mother in an outhouse. The jury found that the parody was not defamatory because no reasonable person would believe the parody to be true.

Defamation litigation often results when the content of the publication focuses on sex. Clearly defamatory are accusations that the plaintiff is an adulterer. Other statements like those in *Youssoupoff* and *Burton* may raise eyebrows but do not accuse the plaintiff of sexual misbehavior. A random sampling includes Vigil v. Rice, 74 N.M. 693, 397 P.2d 719 (1964), in which a doctor's report to school authorities that a young student was pregnant was ruled defamatory; Sauerhoff v. Hearst Corp. 538 F.2d 588 (4th Cir. 1976), in which the court ruled that a married plaintiff was defamed when the defendant referred to a woman who was not the plaintiff's wife as his "girl friend"; Clark v. American Broadcasting Companies, 684 F.2d 1208 (6th Cir. 1982), *cert. denied,* 460 U.S. 1040 (1983), which held that a television documentary on street prostitution showing the plaintiff walking toward the camera was capable of creating the impression that the plaintiff was a prostitute; and Mazart v. State, 109 Misc. 2d 1092, 441 N.Y.S.2d 600 (Ct. Cl. 1981), which held that a statement that the plaintiffs were "members of the gay community" was defamatory.

The business world also furnishes its share of defamation cases. Statements that the plaintiff is a bad credit risk or that he cheats his customers are defamatory. Merchants who criticize a competitor's goods in a way that impugns the latter's integrity may also be liable for defamation. See, e.g., Rosenberg v. J. C. Penney Co., 30 Cal. App. 2d 609, 86 P.2d 696 (1939) (defendant's comment that plaintiff's gym shorts were "poorly made seconds or prison-made merchandise" was defamatory in light of plaintiff's known claim to sell only first-grade goods). A merchant may suffer harm to reputation in more unusual ways, such as in Braun v. Armour & Co., 254 N.Y. 514, 173 N.E. 845 (1930), which held that an advertisement listing a kosher meat market as a seller of Armour's Star Bacon was defamatory.

It is not unreasonable for the law to expect people to have a certain toughness of hide, and there are a variety of vulgarisms which generally are not considered defamatory. Common epithets such as "bastard" and "son of a bitch," because they are almost never taken in a literal sense, are only mildly offensive except to the most sensitive. Given the proper circumstances, however, even these epithets may be defamatory. See, e.g., Capps v. Watts, 271 S.C. 276, 246 S.E.2d 606 (1978), in which the words "paranoid sonofabitch" were actionable where they could be found to impute qualities to the plaintiff which were incompatible with the exercise of his office as an administrator of a state association for the blind. And in

Spence v. Flynt, 816 P.2d 771 (Wyo. 1991), *cert. denied,* 112 S. Ct. 1668 (1992), the court held that summary judgment was not appropriate in a case involving a vulgar diatribe against a lawyer for representing another person in a suit against Hustler Magazine.[2] But opprobrious terms describing one's personal outlook are not generally actionable. The court in Raible v. Newsweek, Inc., 341 F. Supp. 804 (W.D. Pa. 1972), found the characterization "bigot" not defamatory, stating that descriptions of a person's political, religious, economic, or sociological philosophies are not defamatory. A federal appeals court has called terms such as "fascist" and "fellow traveler" amorphous expressions of opinion that cannot defame. Buckley v. Littell, 539 F.2d 882 (2d Cir. 1976), *cert. denied,* 429 U.S. 1062 (1977). An accusation that the plaintiff was a Communist was held defamatory in Cahill v. Hawaiian Paradise Park Corp., 56 Haw. 522, 543 P.2d 1356 (1975), but not defamatory in Korry v. International Telephone & Telegraph Corp., 444 F. Supp. 193 (S.D.N.Y. 1978). Whether or not the charge that one is a Communist or a Communist sympathizer is defamatory has been an on-again, off-again proposition in American law. For cases from the 1920s through the early 1950s which show how courts' attitudes have changed with the changing political relationship between the United States and the Soviet Union, see Annotation, 33 A.L.R.2d 1196 (1954).

The statement does not have to be taken as defamatory by the general public to be actionable. It suffices if the statement is perceived to be defamatory by a smaller community such as the one in which the plaintiff works. See Sharratt v. Housing Innovations, Inc., 365 Mass. 141, 310 N.E.2d 343 (1974). Occasionally, courts have been asked to make moral judgments about the values which lead the audience to react adversely to the statement; and some have argued that a plaintiff's reputation must suffer in the eyes of "right-thinking" people for a statement to be defamatory. In general, American courts have rejected this formulation, preferring the view that a statement is defamatory if so perceived by a significant segment of the community. As Justice Holmes stated in Peck v. Tribune Co., 214 U.S. 185, 190, 29 S. Ct. 554, 556, 53 L. Ed. 960, 962-963 (1909): "No conduct is hated by all. That it will be known by a large number, and will lead an appreciable fraction of that number to regard the plaintiff with contempt, is enough to do her practical harm." And in Grant v. Reader's Digest Assn. Inc., 151 F.2d 733 (2d Cir. 1945), *cert. denied,* 326 U.S. 797 (1946), the court stated, with respect to an accusation that the plaintiff was a legislative representative of the Communist party (151 F.2d 734-735):

> A man may value his reputation even among those who do not embrace the prevailing moral standards; and it would seem that the jury should be allowed

2. The language used by the defendant to describe the plaintiff might be appropriate in an "adult" magazine sold from behind the counter and enclosed in a plastic wrapper, but not in a family publication like this. Those who are curious as to the statement will have to go the case.

> to appraise how far he should be indemnified for the disesteem of such persons. . . . We do not believe, therefore, that we need say whether "right-thinking" people would harbor similar feelings toward a lawyer, because he had been an agent for the Communist Party, or was a sympathizer with its aims and means. It is enough if there be some, as there certainly are, who would feel so, even though they would be "wrong-thinking" people if they did.

Not all courts, however, ignore the values of the audience. In Connelly v. McKay, 176 Misc. 685, 28 N.Y.S.2d 327 (1941), the defendant had falsely accused the plaintiff, who ran a gas station and guest house catering to truck drivers, of informing the Interstate Commerce Commission of truckers who violated Commission regulations. There is no question about how truck drivers would regard such a person, but the court held that the statement was not defamatory, relying in part on §559 of the Restatement of Torts,[3] which provided:

> The fact that a communication tends to prejudice another in the eyes of even a substantial group is not enough if the group is one whose standards are so anti-social that it is not proper for the courts to recognize them.

Following *Connelly* in this regard is Burrascano v. Levi, 452 F. Supp. 1066 (D. Md. 1978), *aff'd,* 612 F.2d 1306 (4th Cir. 1979).

Some persons, such as those with a history of criminal activity, have been held to be "libel-proof" with respect to certain sorts of statements. See, e.g., Jackson v. Longcope, 394 Mass. 577, 476 N.E.2d 617 (1985); Ray v. Time, Inc., 452 F. Supp. 618 (W.D. Tenn. 1976), *aff'd,* 582 F.2d 1280 (6th Cir. 1978). In the latter case, the plaintiff was the person convicted of killing Martin Luther King. In Guccione v. Hustler Magazine, Inc., 800 F.2d 298 (2d Cir. 1986), *cert. denied,* 479 U.S. 1091 (1987), the plaintiff, the publisher of Penthouse magazine, was held to be libel-proof with respect to an accusation that he had committed adultery. The libel-proof concept was rejected in Liberty Lobby, Inc. v. Anderson, 746 F.2d 1563 (D.C. Cir. 1984), *vacated on other grounds,* 477 U.S. 242, (1986), in which the court expressed doubt about its ability to determine whether the plaintiff's reputation had already been so badly damaged that it could not be further harmed by a new libel. In general, see Note, Libel Proof Plaintiffs—Rabble Without a Cause, 67 B.U. L. Rev. 993 (1987), and Note, Libel-Proof Plaintiffs and the Question of Injury, 71 Tex. L. Rev. 401 (1992).

b. Interpretation of the Statement

The general rule is that if the statement about the plaintiff is capable of several meanings, one of which is not defamatory, the plaintiff must establish

3. The quoted language also appears in Comment e of §559, Restatement (Second) of Torts.

that the audience would take the statement in its defamatory sense. For example, in Washington Post Co. v. Chaloner, 250 U.S. 290, 39 S. Ct. 448, 63 L. Ed. 987 (1919), the defendant published a story that the plaintiff "shot and killed John Gillard, while the latter was abusing his wife, who had taken refuge at Merry Mills, Chaloner's home." The trial judge had ruled as a matter of law that the story implied that the plaintiff had committed murder. In reversing, the Supreme Court stated (250 U.S. at 293-294, 39 S. Ct. 449, 63 L. Ed. at 989):

> Counsel for [plaintiff] admit (and properly so) that, upon the authorities, a published item saying "C shot and killed G," without more, would not be libelous per se—it does not set forth the commission of a crime in unambiguous words. And we are unable to conclude that, as matter of law, addition of the words "while the latter was abusing his wife, who had taken refuge at Merry Mills, Chaloner's home" would convert such a statement into a definite charge of murder. On the contrary they might at least suggest to reasonable minds that the homicide was without malice.

Illinois follows the *innocent construction rule*—the plaintiff cannot recover if the statement is capable of a nondefamatory meaning. See Chapski v. Copley Press, 92 Ill.2d 344, 442 N.E.2d 195 (1982).

The plaintiff is not limited to the words of the statement in attempting to establish its defamatory meaning (although, as will be seen, if resort to extrinsic facts is necessary, that statement may not be actionable without proof of special damages). Extrinsic facts necessary to make the statement defamatory are called the *inducement* and the defamatory meaning based on such facts is called the *innuendo.* In Cassidy v. Daily Mirror Newspapers, Ltd., [1929] 2 K.B. 331, the defendant had published a story that one Cassidy had announced his engagement to "Miss X." The plaintiff was Mrs. Cassidy, and she proved that she lived with Cassidy as his wife (the inducement). The story would then have the meaning that she was an immoral woman in that she lived with Cassidy as his wife but without marrying him (the innuendo).

A further problem of interpretation involves a defamatory statement that makes no direct reference to the plaintiff. Proof that such a statement was taken by the audience to refer to the plaintiff is called the *colloquium.* A difficult problem is presented when the defendant has made a defamatory statement about a group of which the plaintiff is a member. If the group is sufficiently small so that the plaintiff is identifiable as the one defamed, then the action will be sustained. A statement in a newspaper editorial that the state treasurer and "all of the other people indicted by the Federal Grand Jury . . . (were) guilty" was held actionable where only the treasurer, the plaintiff, and one other person were indicted. Grove v. Morgan, 576 P.2d 1155 (Okla. 1978). A larger group was involved in Fawcett Publications, Inc. v. Morris, 377 P.2d 42 (Okla. 1962), *cert. denied,* 376 U.S. 513 (1964).

In this case, the plaintiff was permitted to recover based upon the statement that the football team of which he was a member used amphetamines, although there were 60 to 70 others on the team at the time. In Neiman-Marcus v. Lait, 13 F.R.D. 311 (S.D.N.Y. 1952), the defendants, in a book entitled U.S.A. Confidential, asserted that the saleswomen in a large department store were call girls. There were 382 saleswomen in all, and the action was brought by 30 of them. In dismissing their complaint, the court said (13 F.R.D. at 316):

> [W]here the group or class disparaged is a large one, absent circumstances pointing to a particular plaintiff as the person defamed, no individual member of the group or class has a cause of action. . . .
>
> Giving the plaintiff saleswomen the benefit of all legitimate favorable inferences, the defendants' alleged libel cannot reasonably be said to concern more than the saleswomen as a class. There is no language referring to some ascertained or ascertainable person. Nor is the class so small that it follows that defamation of the class infects the individual of the class. This Court so holds as a matter of law since it is of the opinion that no reasonable man would take the writers seriously and conclude from the publication a reference to any individual saleswoman.

In Barger v. Playboy Enterprises, Inc., 564 F. Supp. 1151 (N.D. Cal. 1983), *aff'd,* 732 F.2d 163 (9th Cir.), *cert. denied,* 469 U.S. 853 (1984), the court stated that if the group is larger than 25, members of the group cannot recover based upon defamatory statements about the group. In this case, the article depicted the sexual activities of the "brides" and "mommas" of the members of the Hell's Angels motorcycle gang. In general, see Note, Group Defamation: Five Guiding Factors, 64 Tex. L. Rev. 591 (1985); Annotation, 52 A.L.R. 4th 618 (1987).

2. Remedies

a. Damages

The rules governing damages for defamation follow the classic division between compensatory and punitive damages. While the awarding of punitive damages proceeds along conventional lines, the awarding of compensatory damages does not. There are two categories of compensatory damages—special and general damages, both of which are defined in a way unique to the law of defamation. Furthermore, for some types of defamation, the plaintiff will not be able to recover any damages unless there is proof of special damages. Thus, the rules of damages for defamation have importance not only in determining how much the plaintiff may recover, but also in determining whether he or she can recover at all. Whether the plaintiff is entitled to damages at all, and if so how much is also affected by the law relating to retraction.

(1) Special Damages

It is generally held that special damages are limited to pecuniary losses directly caused by the reaction of others to the defamatory statement. See Terwilliger v. Wands, 17 N.Y. 54 (1958), which, in spite of its age, is still a leading case on the point. Loss of credit, or of a job, or of customers are the typical sources of special damages. Such damages, then, do not arise because the plaintiff has been harmed emotionally, or even physically, but because others, motivated by the defamatory statement, refuse to do business with the plaintiff. But see O'Hara v. Storer Communications, Inc., 213 Cal. App. 3d 1101, 282 Cal. Rptr. 712 (1991), in which the court held that the plaintiff, a freelance public relations person, could recover, as special damages, the expenses in connection with psychiatric treatment for emotional harm resulting from the defendant's calling her a prostitute.

(2) General Damages

If the plaintiff has shown special damages, or if the case is one in which there may be recovery without having to prove them, the plaintiff is entitled to recover general damages. General damages include the mental anguish and associated economic losses that are not included under special damages. In addition, general damages are presumed to flow from certain kinds of defamation, and little in the way of proof has to be presented to support an award. The extent of indefiniteness of proof permitted is illustrated by Judge Wyzanski's charge to the jury in Curley v. Curtis Publishing Co., 48 F. Supp. 29, 34, 35, 36 (D.C. Mass. 1942):

> In a libel suit, the appropriate measure of damages is the loss of reputation suffered by the plaintiff, the physical pain which he has suffered, and the mental anguish which he has suffered. . . .
>
> You are entitled to take into account the standing of the plaintiff in the community and group in which he moves. You are entitled to take into account the extent of the publication of which complaint is made. All those are proper elements. . . .
>
> As to damages—damages are an element about which a Judge has no better knowledge than a jury. You are practical men. You know what the consequences practically are of articles which are defamatory and not true or privileged, and articles which are defamatory and are malicious.
>
> . . . [Y]our experience is sufficient to decide the matter, and twelve of you are much better estimators than I alone would be.

Because by their nature general damages cannot be established with precision, a court can exert little control over a jury's verdict. Unless the award shocks the judicial conscience or is the obvious result of passion or prejudice, reviewing courts are reluctant to overturn verdicts for such damages, whether the plaintiff complains that the award was inadequate or the defendant that it was excessive. See, e.g., Eulo v. Deval Aerodynamics, Inc., 47 F.R.D. 35 (E.D. Pa. 1969), *aff'd in part and reversed in part,* 430 F.2d 325 (3d Cir. 1970); *cert. denied,* 401 U.S. 974 (1971) (jury is the "supreme arbiter" of damage awards in defamation cases, and the court would not overturn the jury's verdict of 6 cents on a $300,000 claim); Kansas Electric Supply Co. v. Dun & Bradstreet, Inc., 448 F.2d 647 (10th Cir. 1971), *cert. denied,* 405 U.S. 1026 (1972) (the court was "extremely reluctant" to set aside the verdict of $100,000 even though no special damages were proven); and Time, Inc. v. Firestone, 424 U.S. 448, 96 S. Ct. 958, 47 L. Ed. 2d 154 (1976) (the court had "no warrant" for reexamining a $100,000 award for plaintiff's "anxiety and concern" over an inaccurate report of the grounds for her divorce).

(3) Punitive Damages

If the plaintiff proves that the defendant published the defamatory statement with malice, the plaintiff may be entitled to punitive damages. The malice that must be proved has been called actual malice, express malice, or malice in fact, and it has been defined variously as bad faith, ill will, hatred, intent to injure, vindictiveness, and wanton or reckless indifference to the plaintiff's rights. Wrongful motive may be almost impossible to prove, and courts accept evidence of other matters as indicia of malice, such as the defendant's knowledge of the falsity of the statement or the failure to try to verify the truth of the statement, failure to publish a retraction, excessive publication of the statement, or the presence of an overall scheme of harassment. One explanation of punitive damages is contained in Reynolds v. Pegler, 123 F. Supp. 36 (S.D.N.Y. 1954). The plaintiff won a jury verdict of one dollar for compensatory damages and a total of $175,000 in punitive damages from three defendants. In denying the defendants' motion to set aside the verdict for punitive damages as excessive, the court stated (125 F. Supp. at 37-38):

> In effect, the defendants urge that the giving of punitive damages is dependent upon, and must bear relationship to, the allowance of actual damages. But the applicable law is to the contrary and is too firmly rooted to admit of argument. . . .
>
> To adopt the contrary view now urged by the defendants would mean that a defamer gains a measure of immunity no matter how venomous or malicious his attack simply because of the excellent reputation of the defamed; it would mean that the defamer, motivated by actual malice, becomes the beneficiary of that unassailable reputation and so escapes punishment. It would require punitive damages to be determined in inverse ratio to the reputation of the one defamed.

b. Retraction

Under the traditional common law rule, a demand by the plaintiff that the defendant retract the defamatory statement was not a prerequisite to recovery. But if the defendant published a retraction, this would be taken into account in calculating damages. Although some courts have held that a retraction may affect only punitive damages, most take it into account with respect to compensatory damages as well. In general, see Eldredge, The Law of Defamation 543-563 (1978).

Beginning toward the end of the last century, a number of states enacted retraction statutes applicable to news media. Some statutes, like that of California (Cal. Civ. Code §48a), limit the plaintiff to actual damages unless a demanded retraction has not been published. Others, like that of Wisconsin (Wis. Stat. Ann. §895.05), make a demand for retraction a prerequisite for bringing the action. The constitutionality of retraction statutes has been attacked, with mixed results. The California statue was upheld in Werner v. Southern California Associated Newspapers, 35 Cal. 2d 121, 216 P.2d 825 (1950). The Montana statute, which requires a demand for retraction as a condition of bringing suit, was held unconstitutional in Madison v. Yunker, 589 P.2d 126 (Mont. 1978), under a state constitutional provision requiring that "a speedy remedy [be] afforded for every injury." A provision of the Arizona constitution that the "right of action to recover damages for injuries shall never be abrogated, and the amount recovered shall not be subject to any statutory limitation," was held in Boswell v. Phoenix Newspapers, 152 Ariz. 9, 730 P.2d 186 (1986), *cert. denied,* 481 U.S. 1029 (1987), to override that state's retraction statute.

c. Injunctions

As a general rule, injunctions against the publication of defamatory statements are not available, in large part because of the First Amendment to the United States Constitution prohibiting the abridgment of the freedoms of speech and the press. See Kramer v. Thompson, 947 F.2d 666 (3rd Cir. 1991), *cert. denied,* 112 S. Ct. 935 (1992); Smolla, Law of Defamation §9.13[1] (1986). But one case, Lothschuetz v. Carpenter, 898 F.2d 1200 (6th Cir. 1990), enjoined the further publication of a statement that had already been judicially determined to be defamatory.

3. The Libel-Slander Distinction

As was stated at the beginning of the subsection on damages, for some types of defamation the plaintiff must prove special damage to recover at all. The principal distinction is between *slander* (oral defamation) and *libel* (written defamation). Subject to important exceptions, there can be no recovery for slander absent proof of special damage, whereas no such proof is necessary to recover for libel. Whatever the historical justifications for this distinction, it has come under strong fire. One critic is A. P. Herbert, who penned a series of fictional and humorous English cases and published them as The Uncommon Law (1935). In Chicken v. Ham, Mr. Herbert, writing as the Lord Chancellor, observed (at p. 73):

> A layman, with the narrow outlook of a layman on these affairs, might rashly suppose that it is equally injurious to say at a public meeting, 'Mr. Chicken is a toad,' and to write upon a postcard, 'Mr. Chicken is a toad.' But the unselfish labours of generations of British jurists have discovered between the two some profound and curious distinctions. For example, in order to succeed in an action for slander the injured party must prove that he has suffered some actual and special damage, whereas the victim of a written defamation need not; so that we have this curious result, that in practice it is safer to insult a man at a public meeting than to insult him on a postcard, and that which is written in the corner of a letter is in law more deadly than that which is shouted from the house-tops. My Lords, it is not for us to boggle at the wisdom of our ancestors, and this is only one of a great body of juridical refinements handed down to us by them, without which few of our profession would be able to keep body and soul together.

In routine cases, the distinction between libel and slander, whether sensible or not, is easy enough to apply. But modern electronic communication has added new dimensions. Motion pictures were absorbed into the law of libel without much difficulty. A film is printed, even if what the customers see is a projection of the film. Radio and television, however, do not lend themselves so easily to classification. Videotaped and filmed programs on television would seem closely analogous to motion pictures, and some courts have held accompanying defamation to be libel. Live broadcasts are more difficult. They are oral and transitory, but have wide circulation, similar to newspapers and magazines. Predictably, different courts have reacted differently, some holding them to be slander, others libel. Some courts have introduced an additional refinement: if the words are off-the-cuff, the defamation is slander; if read from a script the defamation is libel.

Section 568A of the Restatement (Second) of Torts characterizes all broadcast defamation as libel, whether read from a script or not. In general, see Annotation, 50 A.L.R. 3d 1311 (1973). Some states have dealt with the problem by statute. See Eldredge, The Law of Defamation 86-90 (1978).

a. Slander

There can be no recovery for slander absent proof of special damage, unless what the defendant has said falls into the category of slander per se, in which event there may be recovery without proof of special damage. The theory behind making some statements actionable per se is that some charges are so serious that harm to the plaintiff's reputation resulting in economic loss is almost certain to follow. The four categories of slander per se are:

(1) Statements that the plaintiff has committed a crime. In general, not any crime will do. American courts usually take the position that the crime must be serious, one involving moral turpitude. Section 571 of the Restatement (Second) of Torts provides that the crime must be punishable by imprisonment in a state or federal institution or be regarded by the public as involving moral turpitude. Comment *g* defines moral turpitude as "shameful wickedness, so extreme a departure from ordinary standards of honesty, good morals, justice or ethics as to be shocking to the moral sense of the community." The illustrative offenses it lists range from those commonly considered grievous, such as treason, murder, arson, rape, criminal assault, and kidnapping, to those which are less abhorrent, such as bootlegging or filing fraudulent tax returns.

(2) Statements that the plaintiff has a loathsome disease. There are not many diseases which would lead people to regard the plaintiff with sufficient revulsion to justify the presumption of economic loss. In 1863, the Supreme Judicial Court of Massachusetts, in "George, The Count Joannes" v. Burt, 88 Mass. (6 Allen) 236, 239 (1863), stated that there were only three: "An action for oral slander, in charging the plaintiff with disease, has been confined to the imputation of such loathsome and infectious maladies as would make him an object of disgust and aversion, and banish him from human society. We believe the only examples which adjudged cases furnish are the plague, leprosy, and venereal disorders."

Should AIDS be added to the modern list? In McCune v. Neitzel, 235 Neb. 754, 457 N.W.2d 803 (1990), the trial judge ruled that a statement that the plaintiff had AIDS was slander per se. The defendant did not appeal from the ruling.

(3) Statements damaging to one's business, trade, or profession. The presumption that the plaintiff has suffered economic loss as a direct result of the defamation has its greatest justification in this category. A person's reputation is important to business, and loss of business is likely to follow when that reputation is disparaged. Thus, accusations that the plaintiff is a bad credit risk, or is dishonest or mismanages business affairs are actionable without proof of special damages. For example, in Demers v. Meuret, 266 Or. 252, 512 P.2d 1348 (1973), a statement that the plaintiff, an airport manager, was "a demented old man" who "might come out and chop up our airplanes with an axe," was held to be slander per se. The defamatory statement must relate to the plaintiff's qualifications to conduct his business, or to the way he conducts it. Thus, in Liberman v. Gelstein, 80 N.Y.2d 429, 605 N.E.2d 344 (1992), statements by a tenant that his landlord "threw a punch at me," "called my daughter a slut," and "threatened to kill me"

was held not to be slander per se because the statements were unrelated to the plaintiff as a landlord.

(4) Statements that a woman is unchaste. This category of slander per se was late in developing, having been created by statute in England in 1891. Many states have followed the English lead, sometimes by statute, other times by judicial decision. Men are not protected by this rule. Comment *c* to §574 of the Restatement (Second) of Torts suggests that the distinction between males and females may be unconstitutional, but does not speculate whether, if it is unconstitutional, the rule will be extended to males, or the category abandoned altogether.

At least one case has extended the category to include accusations of homosexual behavior. See Nowark v. Maguire, 22 App. Div. 2d 901, 255 N.Y.S.2d 318 (1964). For contrary holdings, see Moricoli v. Schwartz, 361 N.E.2d 74 (Ill. App. 1977), and Hayes v. Smith, 832 P.2d 1022 (Colo. App. 1991). In the latter case, the court observed (832 P.2d at 1025):

> For a characterization of a person to warrant a per se classification, it should, without equivocation, expose the plaintiff to public hatred or contempt. However, there is no empirical evidence in this record demonstrating that homosexuals are held by society in such poor esteem. Indeed, it appears that the community view toward homosexuals is mixed.

The court in Ward v. Zelikovsky, 623 A.2d 285 (N.J. Super. 1993), held that the categories of slander per se are not limited to these four, and ruled that a statement that the plaintiffs were "Jew haters" made to a predominantly Jewish audience was slander per se. The court felt that the "intellectual virus" the defendant accused the plaintiffs of having was similar to the "loathsome disease" category.

b. Libel

The rule that proof of special damage is not needed to support recovery in libel is modified in some states by the libel per quod-libel per se distinction. In the states distinguishing between the two kinds of libel, only libel per se is actionable without proof of special damage. To constitute libel per se, the statement must be defamatory on its face. This should not be confused with the "per se" of slander per se, which refers to the substance of the statement. If there is need to look outside the statement for facts which will make it defamatory, it is libel per quod, and the plaintiff must show special damage to recover. An exception to the libel per quod rule is that if the statement would have been slander per se if spoken, proof of special damage is not required.

There is some disagreement among commentators as to whether the majority of American jurisdictions observe the libel per se-libel per quod distinction or follow the English rule that special damage does not have to be proved in libel actions. Commentators also disagree about which view is the better rule of law. The first Restatement makes no note of the diverging course set by some American courts and points to the justifications for the English rule. Restatement of Torts, §569, Comment *b.* The Restatement, Second, calls the libel per se-libel per quod distinction a minority view and states that the rule's principal justification has been preempted by recent constitutional decisions. Restatement (Second) of Torts §569 Comment *b.* For the view that most states allow recovery in a libel action without proof of special damage and that this is the preferable position, see Eldredge, The Spurious Rule of Libel per Quod, 79 Harv. L. Rev. 733 (1966). For the view that most states observe the libel per se-libel per quod distinction and that it is the better mode of analysis, see Prosser, More Libel per Quod, 79 Harv. L. Rev. 1629 (1966). The two positions are discussed in Murnaghan, From Figment to Fiction to Philosophy—The Requirement of Proof of Damages in Libel Actions, 22 Cath. U.L. Rev. 1 (1972), in which the author concludes that there should be no recovery for general, unproven damages in any case.

4. Publication

To satisfy the requirement of publication, the plaintiff must show that the defamatory statement has been communicated by the defendant to a third person. The person who publishes the statement is liable even if it is a mere report of something heard from someone else. This is so even if the source of the story is carefully identified. And the person who makes a defamatory statement that is republished by another may also be subject to liability. Generally, however, a person is not liable for another voluntary and unauthorized repetition of defamatory matter unless the republication was the natural and probable consequence of the original communication. For example, in Oberman v. Dun & Bradstreet, Inc., 586 F.2d 1173 (7th Cir. 1978), a credit reporting agency was held not liable for defamatory material in a confidential report issued to a bank when a realty company obtained the report through a bank director who was a salesman for the realty company. The court ruled that it was not foreseeable that a confidential report would fall into the hands of a third party in this way.

A number of cases have arisen in which the defendant has written a letter to the plaintiff containing defamatory material, and the plaintiff has shown the letter to another. In general, the courts have concluded that the publication is by the plaintiff rather than the defendant. But there are circumstances in which the defendant will be responsible for the publication. In Hedgpeth v. Coleman, 183 N.C. 309, 111 S.E. 517 (1922), the defendant sent a letter to the plaintiff, a 14-year-old boy, accusing him of theft. The plaintiff showed the letter to his brother, who in turn showed it to their father. The court held the defendant responsible for the communication of the letter to the plaintiff's brother and father.

One "self-publication" context arising with increasing frequency involves a discharged employee's disclosure to a prospective employer of the grounds for the discharge. Holding that the former employer may be a publisher of the employee's statement of the grounds for the discharge are Churchey v. Adolph Coors Co., 759 P.2d 1336 (Colo. 1988), and Lewis v. Equitable Life Assurance Society, 389 N.W.2d 876 (Minn. 1986). In so ruling, the court in *Churchey* stated (759 P.2d at 1345):

> When the originator of the statement reasonably can foresee that the defamed person will be compelled to repeat a defamatory statement to a third party, there is a strong causal link between the originator's actions and the harm caused to the defamed person; this causal connection makes the imposition of liability reasonable. If publication could be based on the defamed person's freely-made decision to repeat a defamatory remark, however, the defendant would be held liable for damages which the plaintiff reasonably could have avoided. . . . Imposing liability for self-publication which is "likely" but not compelled would unnecessarily deter such communication.

Other courts have held that the "tort of compelled self-defamation" in this context should not be recognized. See, e.g., Layne v. Builders Plumbing Supply Co., 569 N.E.2d 1046 (Ill. App. 1991); Yetter v. Ward Trucking Corp., 585 A.2d 1022 (Pa. Super.), *appeal denied,* 529 Pa. 623, 600 A.2d 539 (1991). In general, see Note, A Unified Theory for Consent and Compelled Self-Publication in Employee Defamation: Economic Duress in Tort Law, 67 Tex. L. Rev. 1295 (1989).

Courts have taken different positions with respect to intrabusiness communications. Some courts have held that there is no publication when the communication takes place between persons within a business unit who are legitimately concerned with the matter being communicated. See, e.g., Mims v. Metropolitan Life Insurance Co., 200 F.2d 800 (5th Cir. 1952), *cert. denied,* 345 U.S. 940 (1953); Rowe v. Isbell, 599 So. 2d 35 (Ala. 1992). Other courts have held that there is a publication under these circumstances, and handle the matter as one involving a qualified privilege. See, e.g., Bals v. Verduzco, 600 N.E.2d 1353 (Ind. 1992). What if the communication is by the defendant to the plaintiff's agent? The court in Reece v. Finch, 562 So. 2d 195 (Ala. 1990) held that there was no publication.

One of the most complex problems in the law of defamation involves multiple publication in newspapers and magazines. Each successive republication constitutes a separate tort. With the development of mass communications most states applied the same rule to multiple but simultaneous publications. But the modern trend is toward the "single publication" rule, under which each edition is considered as one publication giving rise to only one cause of action. When the publication occurs in more than one state, very difficult conflict of laws problems are presented. See Leflar, McDougall, and Felix, American Conflicts Law 371-373 (4th ed. 1986).

5. The Basis of Liability

The basis of liability in defamation can be put briefly: aside from the malice necessary to defeat a conditional privilege, liability, with two exceptions, is strict, and the state of the defendant's mind is irrelevant. The plight of the defendant in Cassidy v. Daily Mirror Newspapers, Ltd., p. 881, above, illustrates this. Cassidy, who was also known as Corrigan, was well known in racing circles as a bon vivant and womanizer. At one racing meet, he posed for a photographer with a woman whom he identified as his betrothed. He gave the photographer permission to announce the engagement. The photographer sent the photograph to the defendant's newspaper, which published it with the caption, "Mr. M. Corrigan, the race horse owner, and [Miss X] whose engagement has been announced. . . ." The court affirmed a judgment entered on a jury verdict for the plaintiff, Cassidy's wife, notwithstanding that defendant did not know the fact which made the publication libelous, stating (2 K.B. at 341-342):

> It is said that this decision would seriously interfere with the reasonable conduct of newspapers. I do not agree. If publishers of newspapers, who have no more rights than private persons, publish statements which may be defamatory of other people, without inquiry as to their truth, in order to make their paper attractive, they must take the consequences, if on subsequent inquiry, their statements are found to be untrue or capable of defamatory and unjustifiable inferences. . . . To publish statements and inquire into their truth afterwards, may seem attractive and up to date. Only to publish after inquiry may be slow, but at any rate it would lead to accuracy and reliability.

In reaching its decision, the court relied on the classic strict liability case, E. Hulton & Co. v. Jones, [1910] A.C. 20. There the defendant printed a story in its newspaper written by a Paris correspondent, which in part ran: " 'Whist! there is Artemus Jones with a woman who is not his wife, who must be, you know—the other thing!' whispers a fair neighbor of mine excitedly to her bosom friend's ear. Really, is it not surprising how certain of our fellow-countrymen behave when they come abroad? Who would suppose by his goings on, that he is a churchwarden at Peckham?" The plaintiff was Thomas Artemus Jones, not of Peckham but from North Wales; nor was he a church warden. But he did produce witnesses who testified that they read the article and thought it referred to the plaintiff. Both the trial court and the House of Lords on appeal accepted the defendant's assertion that he had never heard of the plaintiff and had used "Artemus Jones" as a fictitious name. Nonetheless, judgment for the plaintiff on the jury verdict was affirmed. Lord Loreburn's opinion is, in part (at 23-24):

> Libel is a tortious act. What does the tort consist in? It consists in using language which others knowing the circumstances would reasonably think to be defamatory of the person complaining of and injured by it. A person charged with libel cannot defend himself by shewing that he intended in his own breast not to defame, or that he intended not to defame the plaintiff, if in fact he did both. He has none the less imputed something disgraceful and has none the less injured the plaintiff. A man in good faith may publish a libel believing it to be true, and it may be found by the jury that he acted in good faith believing it to be true, and reasonably believing it to be true, but that in fact the statement was false. Under those circumstances he has no defence to the action, however excellent his intention. If the intention of the writer be immaterial in considering whether the matter written is defamatory, I do not see why it need be relevant in considering whether it is defamatory of the plaintiff.

The law in this area has been stated as follows: "The question . . . is not who was aimed at, but who was hit." Laudati v. Stea, 44 R.I. 303, 306, 117 Atl. 422, 424 (1922). The problem of fiction generally is analyzed in a symposium, Defamation in Fiction, 51 Brooklyn L. Rev. 223-478 (1985).

One exception to strict liability relates to publication. The defendant is not liable absent intent to publish or negligence in publishing. For example, if the defendant accuses the plaintiff of something that is defamatory with the intent that no one other than the plaintiff hear it, the defendant is not liable if it is overheard without negligence on the defendant's part. Thus, in Harbridge v. Greyhound Lines, Inc., 294 F. Supp. 1059 (E.D. Pa 1969), it was held that the defendant was not liable for an allegedly defamatory statement to the plaintiff's wife in a telephone conversation with the plaintiff, when the wife, unknown to the defendant, was listening in on the plaintiff's telephone.

The other exception to strict liability involves dissemination. Section 581(1) of the Restatement (Second) provides that one who "delivers or transmits defamatory matter published by a third person is subject to liability if, but only if, he knows or has reason to know of its defamatory character." Under this rule, a variety of disseminators, such as newspaper distributors, libraries, and telegraph companies, have been relieved of the strict liability which otherwise would have attached. The second clause of §581, however, states that where the communication of defamatory matter occurs by way of TV or radio broadcast, the publisher is subject to the same liability as the original publisher.

6. Defenses

The law of defamation has developed a highly technical and labyrinthine set of defenses with which the defendant can meet the plaintiff's equally technical and labyrinthine prima facie case. These defenses are that the publication of the defamatory statement was privileged, and that the statement is true.

a. Privilege

The privilege to publish a defamatory statement may be either absolute or qualified. Both are complete defenses, but the latter may be lost under some circumstances, while the former cannot be lost at all. The defendant with an absolute privilege can, without liability, publish a statement known to be false and do it with the most evil of intentions. As might be expected, this complete immunity from liability will not be lightly granted and is generally limited to situations in which the communication is with the consent of the plaintiff, or is by a government official in the performance of governmental duties, or is between husband and wife, or is a political broadcast required under the federal "equal time" statute.

The defendant is free to publish a defamatory statement about the plaintiff if the latter has consented to it. In Cassidy v. Daily Mirror Newspapers, Ltd., p. 881, for instance, Cassidy himself could not recover since he was the source of the story and solicited its publication. One recurring problem is the letter of recommendation. The plaintiff who asks the defendant for such a letter does not necessarily consent to the inclusion of defamatory material. But if the plaintiff knows or has reason to believe that the defendant will include such material, it is arguable that there is consent. Such a situation might arise when the defendant, a former employer perhaps, has derogatory information which the plaintiff should expect the defendant to include in any reference letter. Richardson v. Gunby, 88 Kan. 47, 127 P. 533 (1912), illustrates how fine the line can get. The plaintiff requested one Neal to ask the defendant for information concerning a cement company, of which plaintiff was the secretary, and its officers. Defendant responded with a letter stating that "no one locally has any faith in the integrity or ability of its officers. Its secretary is regarded as one of the most tricky men in this community and a good man to leave strictly alone, and all of his projects." In a suit for libel based on this letter, the defendant argued that the plaintiff could not recover because he solicited the letter for the purpose of creating a cause of action, and thus consented to its publication. The court stated that this was correct as far as it went, but added the following qualification (88 Kan. at 54, 127 P. at 536):

> If, however, the plaintiff instigated or set on foot the inquiry for the purpose of ascertaining whether the defendant . . . was disseminating evil reports concerning the cement company or its officers, in order that such influences might be counteracted, or for any other proper purpose, and not for the

purpose of predicating an action for damages in his own behalf, he was not estopped from maintaining an action.

Consent to defamatory statements may also be based on contract, as in Joftes v. Kaufman, 324 F. Supp. 660 (D.C. 1971). In this case, the court ruled that the plaintiff has consented to the publications of allegedly defamatory letters explaining reasons for the plaintiff's discharge from his employment, the letters having been sent pursuant to a contractual grievance procedure initiated by the plaintiff.

The most important absolute privilege is extended to parties involved in the conduct of government affairs, whether they exercise a judicial, legislative, or executive function. This privilege rests on the notion that free expression and full disclosure of information is so essential to the proper functioning of the governmental process that it outweighs any private interest in reputation. Thus, it is usually held that the official participants in a judicial proceeding—judge, jury, attorneys, litigating parties, and witnesses—may make defamatory statements with impunity before and during a judicial proceeding as long as the statements relate to some part of the proceeding. See, e.g., Garfield v. Palmieri, 297 F.2d 526 (2d Cir.), *cert. denied,* 369 U.S. 871 (1962) (federal judge is not liable for defamatory matter contained in a court opinion); Lowenschuss v. West Publishing Co., 402 F. Supp. 1212 (E.D. Pa. 1975), *aff'd,* 542 F.2d 180 (3d Cir. 1976) (reporter of court opinions has an absolute privilege to reprint opinions containing defamatory matter); Binder v. Oregon Bank, 284 Or. 89, 585 P.2d 655 (1978) (testator is absolutely privileged to make defamatory statements in a private will since they are made preliminary to a judicial proceeding of probate); Bergman v. Hupy, 64 Wis. 2d 747, 221 N.W.2d 898 (1974) (attorney is absolutely privileged while initiating an investigation into possible criminal violations). The privilege attending communications made in the course of judicial proceedings is generally extended to those made in administrative proceedings of a judicial or quasi-judicial nature. In Mazzucco v. N.C. Board of Medical Examiners, 31 N.C. App. 47, 228 S.E.2d 529, *cert. denied,* 291 N.C. 323, 230 S.E.2d 676 (1976), the court held that the plaintiffs could not sue the individual members of a state medical board for statements uttered in connection with their investigations of charges made against a doctor. See also, Kelley v. Bonney, 221 Conn. 549, 606 A.2d 693 (1992) (teacher decertification proceeding is quasi-judicial).

The privilege is also available to members of state and national legislatures while they are functioning as such. It has been embodied in Article I, Section 6 of the Constitution of the United States: ". . . and for any Speech or Debate in either House, [the Senators and Representatives of Congress] shall not be questioned in any other Place."

The executive and administrative officers of the state and federal governments also have the absolute privilege. The federal rule is set forth in Barr v. Matteo, 360 U.S. 564, 79 S. Ct. 1335, 3 L. Ed. 1434 (1959), which held that the privilege attaches so long as the statement is made within the scope of the official's duty. The absolute privilege may not apply, however, if the communication impairs a constitutional right of the plaintiff. See Butz v. Economou, 438 U.S. 478, 98 S. Ct. 2894, 57 L. Ed. 2d 895 (1978). Moreover, although Barr v. Matteo stated that the privilege attaches no matter how minor the functionary, many states limit it to top officials.

Most of the cases which have dealt with communications between husband and wife have concluded that there is no publication. These cases have rested on the ancient fiction that the husband and wife are one, and that one cannot publish to himself. A more satisfying explanation, however, is that the nature of the marital relationship requires that the publication be absolutely privileged. For a discussion of the history of the husband and wife privilege in defamation law, see Eldredge, The Law of Defamation 416-417 (1978).

Under the Federal Communications Act of 1934 (47 U.S.C.A. 315), a radio or television broadcaster who permits a candidate for public office to use its station for campaign purposes must afford equal broadcasting opportunity to other candidates for the same office. This statute also prohibits the broadcaster from censoring the material so broadcast. The Supreme Court ruled in Farmers' Educational & Coop. Union v. WDAY, Inc., 360 U.S. 525, 79 S. Ct. 1302, 3 L. Ed. 2d 1407 (1959), that the broadcaster is absolutely immune from liability for defamatory statements made during equal time broadcasts.

Beyond those occasions calling for an absolute immunity from liability, there are many situations in which it is appropriate to afford a more limited protection to the publication of defamatory matter. The nature of the privilege depends on whether the communication is private or relates to a public matter. As to communications relating to private matters, Baron Parke suggested in Toogood v. Spyring, 1 C.M. & R. 181 (1834), that the existence of a qualified privilege depends on the interest of the publisher, the interest of the audience, or an interest common to both. This analysis has been generally followed by the courts and commentators.

The qualified privilege of the defendant to publish defamatory statements for self-protection is somewhat analogous to the privileges of self-defense and defense of property. It is proper for the defendant to protect against the plaintiff's statement by calling the plaintiff a liar, but only if that statement serves to explain the plaintiff's motives. For example, if the plaintiff accused the defendant of embezzlement, it would be proper for the defendant to state the plaintiff is the embezzler and is trying to cover up his own crime. It would be improper for the defendant to add that the plaintiff is a horse thief who for that reason cannot be believed. As to the nature of the privilege of reply, see generally Annotation, 41 A.L.R.3d 1083 (1972).

Marking out the limits of the qualified privilege based on the interests of the audience has been particularly troublesome. Generally, the privilege is not available to the idle gossip or the self-appointed watchdog of the community's morals. Thus, In Watt v. Longsdon, [1930] 1 K.B. 103 (Ct. App.), a letter from a friend of the plaintiff and his wife to the wife detailing the plaintiff's extramarital activities was not privileged. Beyond this, factors that are likely to be important are whether the defendant is a relative or personal adviser to the person to whom he communicates the information, and whether the defendant has been asked for the information. But the cases do not fall into any clear pattern. The Restatement (Second) of Torts is a satisfactory statement of the privilege:

> §595. PROTECTION OF INTEREST OF RECIPIENT OR A THIRD PERSON
>
> (1) An occasion makes a publication conditionally privileged if the circumstances induce a correct or reasonable belief that
>
> (a) there is information that affects a sufficiently important interest of the recipient or a third person, and
>
> (b) the recipient is one to whom the publisher is under a legal duty to publish the defamatory matter or is a person to whom its publication is otherwise within the generally accepted standards of decent conduct.
>
> (2) In determining whether a publication is within generally accepted standards of decent conduct it is an important factor that
>
> (a) the publication is made in response to a request rather than volunteered by the publisher or
>
> (b) a family or other relationship exists between the parties.

Cases in which the privilege has been found to exist are Lester v. Powers, 596 A.2d 65 (Me. 1991) (communication from alumna of college to college in connection with tenure review process of alumna's former teacher), and Erickson v. Marsh & McLennan Co., 117 N.J. 539, 569 A.2d 793 (1990) (communication from former employer of plaintiff to prospective employer in response to inquiry from the prospective employer).

One troublesome situation involving the interest of the audience is the furnishing of reports by credit agencies. The general rule in the United States is that such agencies are protected by a qualified privilege if the information is given out in response to a specific request and results from a careful investigation. See Annotation, 40 A.L.R.3d 1049 (1971). In some states, however, credit reporting agencies have no such privilege. See Hood v. Dun & Bradstreet, Inc., 486 F.2d 25 (5th Cir. 1973) *cert. denied,* 415 U.S. 985 (1974), and Bryant v. TRW, Inc., 689 F.2d 72 (6th Cir. 1982). The court in Retail Credit Co. v. Russell, 234 Ga. 765, 218 S.E.2d 54 (1975), in rejecting the majority rule, explained that consumers would be virtually unable to protect their reputations were the privilege to be recognized. The court added (234 Ga. at 770, 218 S.E.2d at 58):

> We cannot agree to this weighting of the scales against the individual who stands alone facing a commercial Goliath with the power to destroy—not

> necessarily through malice but perhaps merely from carelessness—his credit rating, commercial advantages, insurance protection and employment, all through the publication of erroneous reports concerning his affairs. . . . An individual living in a world more and more dominated by large commercial entities is less able to bear the burden of the consequences of a false credit or character report than the agency in the business of selling these reports.

See also Note, Protecting the Subjects of Credit Reports, 80 Yale L.J. 1035 (1971).

There are numerous examples of situations in which the publisher and the audience share a common interest. They include communications between members of a family, employees of a business, and members of various associations. The communication must relate, of course, to the shared interest. Thus, in Harbridge v. Greyhound Lines, Inc., p. 892, above, it was held that defendant's employees were privileged to discuss among themselves a shortage of money, for which the plaintiff was thought to be responsible, when all of the employees were by virtue of their offices concerned with the matter.

A somewhat narrower privilege applies to public statements about matters of public concern. The general rule is that fair comment on such matters as current political issues and endeavors in the arts, sciences, and sports are privileged insofar as the comment is one of opinion. However, the privilege does not extend to misstatements of fact. It has not always been easy to distinguish between opinion and fact for the purpose of this rule. For example, in Kellems v. California CIO, 68 F. Supp. 277 (N.D. Cal. 1946), a statement that the plaintiff's opposition to payment of income taxes was "treasonable" was held to be an expression of opinion; and in Myers v. Boston Magazine Co., 380 Mass. 336, 403 N.E.2d 376 (1980), a statement that the plaintiff is "the only sportscaster in town enrolled in a course in remedial speaking" was at most an opinion that his reading style needed improvement. On the other hand, in Eikhoff v. Gilbert, 124 Mich. 353, 83 N.W. 110 (1900), a statement that a candidate for the state legislature had "championed measures opposed to the moral interests of the community" was held to be an assertion of fact. A minority of states have extended the fair comment privilege to include statements of fact, at least under some circumstances. See Coleman v. MacLennan, 78 Kan. 711, 98 Pac. 281 (1908); Dairy Stores, Inc. v. Sentinel Publishing Co., 104 N.J. 125, 516 A.2d 220 (1986). The protection that is, and should be, extended to letters published by the media is discussed in Franklin, Libel and Letters to the Editor: Toward an Open Forum, 57 U. Colo. L. Rev. 651 (1986).

The qualified privilege to publish defamatory matter may be lost if the defendant abuses it. Courts generally assert that the privilege will be defeated only if the defendant is guilty of actual malice—ill will toward the plaintiff or reckless indifference to the plaintiff's rights. But it is clear that the courts have used this term much more loosely. According to §§599-605 of the Restatement of Torts,[4] the privilege is abused if the defendant does not believe in the truth of the defamatory matter, or even if believing it, does not have reasonable grounds for the belief. The privilege may also be forfeited if in publishing the defamatory matter, the defendant does not act for a proper purpose, that is, to protect the interest for which the privilege is granted in the first place. An abuse of privilege by publication with an improper purpose was involved in MacLean v. Scripps, 52 Mich. 214, 17 N.W. 815 (1883), in which a jury found that a newspaper published defamatory matter in order to create a sensation and for the sole purpose of increasing circulation. It is in the context of improper purpose that §603, Comment *a,* of the first Restatement places "ill will and spite":

> Thus, a publication of defamatory matter upon a privileged occasion if made solely from spite or ill will is an abuse and not a use of the occasion. However, if the publication is made for the purpose of protecting the interest in question, the fact that the publication is inspired in part by resentment or indignation at the supposed misconduct of the person defamed does not constitute an abuse of the occasion. On the other hand, if the publisher does not act to protect the particular interest in question, the occasion is abuse although he is not acting from spite or ill will.

The privilege may also be lost through excessive publication. Ordinarily, the purposes for which the privilege exists can be satisfied by limited publication. The employee who suspects a fellow employee of tapping the till need not call a press conference to alert the employer, nor announce it in front of other employees. Cf. Brown v. First National Bank of Mason City, 193 N.W.2d 547 (Iowa 1972).

b. Truth

"The greater the truth, the greater the libel," was the early response to truth as a defense to a prosecution for criminal libel. But on the civil side, truth has historically been a complete defense. It is not clear why this should be so. The gist of the plaintiff's claim is that the defendant has assaulted reputation, not character. Perhaps the law results from a moralistic judgment that the plaintiff is not entitled to a reputation that is not in fact deserved. The effect of making truth a defense is that the plaintiff comes into court with a spotless reputation. Given the difficulties the defendant may encounter in proving truth, this can be a tremendous advantage for the plaintiff.

4. The reference is to the first Restatement—the Restatement (Second) of Torts has been redrafted to take into account the constitutional cases in Section B.

One problem facing the defendant is the particularity with which the truth of the statement must be shown. The truth may differ in some respects from the statement, and the question is one of how great a difference will be tolerated. The defendant cannot prove the truth of a statement that the plaintiff stole a horse on January 15 by showing that it was a cow stolen on September 28, even if it does prove that the plaintiff is a thief. On the other hand, proof that the plaintiff stole the horse on January 16 ought to be close enough. At one time the courts tended to be sticklers for detail, and in one case, Sharpe v. Stephenson, 34 N.C. 348 (1851), the court stated that the defendant could not show the truth of a statement that the plaintiff had criminal intercourse with a certain person at a particular time and place with proof of criminal intercourse with that person but at a different time and place. However, hostility to truth as a defense has moderated over the years. In Fort Worth Press Co. v. Davis, 96 S.W.2d 416 (Tex. Civ. App. 1936), the court stated that substantial, not literal, truth is enough, and held that a statement that the plaintiff mayor had squandered $80,000 of public funds was true enough, although the actual amount was $17,500. And in Guccione v. Hustler Magazine, Inc., 800 F.2d 298 (2d Cir. 1986), *cert. denied,* 107 S. Ct. 1303 (1987), the court ruled that a statement that the plaintiff was an adulterer was true, although the plaintiff's actual adultery had ended with his divorce three years before the story was printed. The court stated that the "test is whether the statement, as it was published, had a different effect on the mind of the reader than the actual literal truth." 800 F.2d at 301-302.

7. Judge, Jury, and Burden of Proof

The Restatement (Second) of Torts in §613 sets out the commonly accepted rules for allocating the burden of proof between the plaintiff and the defendant. The plaintiff has the burden of proof as to most issues of fact that may arise in a defamation case. Thus, for example, the plaintiff must prove, as a part of his prima facie case, that the statement is defamatory and that the audience understood its defamatory meaning, and, if required, that he suffered special damages. The defendant has the burden of proving that the publication was privileged. However, the plaintiff has the burden of proving that a qualified privilege was abused by the defendant.

The rules relating to the allocation of functions between judge and jury are contained in §§614-619 of the Restatement (Second). Under these rules, the judge determines whether the statement could be taken as defamatory by the audience and whether the publication was privileged. The jury determines whether the statement was understood by the audience as defamatory, whether it is true, and whether a qualified privilege was abused.

Problem 38

You have just finished an interview with Gary Carlson, a professor in the chemistry department of Colchester College, a small, private liberal arts college. He wants to know if he can sue the National Journal for defamation. The National Journal is a weekly "supermarket" publication that carries a variety of sensational stories. Like other publications of the type, it has the reputation for playing loosely with the truth. The article is entitled "Drugs on Campus." The portion relating to Carlson is:

> In our investigation into drug use at American colleges and universities, we visited Colchester College. Given its bucolic location, you might think that drugs would not be a problem. That's what we thought, but we were wrong. The use of cocaine and marijuana is pervasive, not only by students but by the faculty and administration as well. For example, we heard of a party at which marijuana was freely available, and you can imagine the orgy when everyone got good and high. We asked Professor Gary Carlson, a self-styled expert on marijuana, about it, but he would not talk to our reporters. We did find out that Professor Carlson is a member of NORML (National Organization for the Repeal of Marijuana Laws), so his reluctance to speak on the record is understandable.

On the page on which this paragraph appeared was a photograph of Carlson and some students taken at his home. The photograph depicted an informal scene, in which most of the people, including Carlson, were smoking. The caption under the photograph said: "Drugs at College—Prof. Entertains Students at Home."

The story related to you by Carlson is that he has conducted several carefully controlled experiments designed to determine the effects of marijuana in general, and on AIDS victims in particular. He has used both students and non-students in the experiments, with the advance approval of the college administration and of the appropriate federal and state agencies. Carlson admits that he smoked marijuana a few times out of curiosity as a graduate student fifteen years ago, but not since then. Carlson does not know how the National Journal came into possession of the photograph. He occasionally conducted experiments in his home, and he thinks that the photograph was taken by someone present at one of them, who then gave the photograph to a National Journal reporter. The cigarette Carlson was smoking was not marijuana but an ordinary cigarette. He does not belong to NORML, although he has communicated with officials in the organization from time to time as a source of information.

Carlson is not particularly concerned with the effect the article might have on his own career. The university and the scientific communities are aware that his involvement with marijuana is limited to scientific studies and are unlikely to take the article seriously. The wags among his acquaintances have had a field day at his expense, however. Carlson's primary concern is with the impact on the college. Already some alumni and parents have sent letters expressing concern about the moral climate at Colchester. Since Carlson has tenure, he is not afraid that his position is in any danger, but a decline in the funds raised could have an adverse effect on the chemistry department as well as the college as a whole.

Based on your knowledge of the law of defamation gained from the text preceding this problem, prepare a memorandum for the file indicating:

1. A preliminary analysis of the law that you expect would control the claim;

2. What additional facts you will need to make an evaluation of Carlson's potential claim, where you are likely to be able to get the facts, and any problems you may encounter in the investigation; and

3. Your opinion as to whether in any event Carlson should carry the matter to suit. The following observations from Morris and Morris, Morris on Torts 376-378 (2d ed. 1980) may help you in this regard:

> A dishonored client who wants a lawyer to file a libel suit may be actuated by several different motives. The client may want compensation for financial losses caused by the slur. Usually the victim is outraged and would like to make the harasser squirm. Sometimes the complainant wants to grab a chance to receive a great deal of money. Perhaps the most decent goal of a person dishonored is an urgent need for exculpation and vindication. These motives seldom occur singly, and a defamed client often hopes to reach more than one objective.
>
> Counsel representing a smeared client whose major motive is the rehabilitation of reputation must proceed with circumspection. When vindication is the client's principal need, the wisest course may involve sacrificing other objectives in order to get a prompt, prominent, and full retraction. An out-and-out apology will often neutralize dishonor more effectively than successful litigation ending in a substantial judgment. An early and large money settlement without complete retraction is often unthinkable to one who urgently needs to clear his or her name; even though the dishonored person widely publicizes the settlement, the rancorous vilifier may, in replay, circulate the imputation that the victim seemed willing to sell honor for a price. Sometimes, especially when the defamation results in heavy financial losses, the astute counsel for a claimant may be able to persuade the libeler both to retract and to pay for all or part of the harm done. . . . The risk of incurring both liability and legal expenses in such a case may bring the libeler around not only to publishing a retraction but also to paying for all or some of the claimant's financial loss. Retraction, however, does not always protect one defamed from suffering extraordinarily large damages, recoverable only through litigation.
>
> When a disparaged person brings and loses a defamation suit, further resort to litigation will probably reestablish or reenforce the plaintiff's disrepute. The technical reasons for losing a libel suit are many and are rarely understood by the public. An honorable person who has been

defamed can lose a case on a number of grounds that have nothing to do with the plaintiff's deserved reputation. The victim can be defeated by the libeler's constitutional privileges of freedom of expression, the libeler's common law privilege, the plaintiff's inability to prove the right kind of fault or to establish the right kind of damages, and so on. The besmirched plaintiff's acquaintances, once the libel suit is lost, are likely to believe that the defamation was true; a plaintiff's ironclad proof of falsity is overshadowed when the court awesomely dismisses the case. Most claimants who genuinely desire a rehabilitated reputation should be advised not to sue when risk of failure is substantial.

A claimant who desires to litigate must be prepared, once started, to fight all the way to the end. The plaintiff must stand ready to appeal if the case is lost at the trial, since subsidence may imply an admission that the disparagement was true.

Counsel should view with special caution a proposal to bring suit on a subtle or somewhat trivial defamation. Like any witness, a disparaged plaintiff who takes the stand is subject to impeachment by cross-examination intended to show acts of misconduct evincing bad moral character; conviction of a crime involving moral turpitude, if such has been the case; or bad reputation for truth and veracity. Even one who can prove all elements of a postrevolution libel case may not be well served when his or her past has been less than perfect. The litigant's opponent may offer proof calculated to show that the claimant's "actual damages" could have resulted from widespread knowledge of misdeeds having no relation to the defendant's disparagement. Only plaintiffs with good records are likely to come out of a libel suit with better reputations than they had going in. Oscar Wilde unwisely sued on a libel that was proven true. The civil suit's sequel was an indictment, and Wilde was convicted. His two years' experience in prison is reflected in his woeful Ballad of Reading Gaol.

Defamation plaintiffs who collect substantial judgments have not necessarily acted in their best interests. Slurs are often less damaging than the derided person fancies. Defamations, like most communications, seldom are fully apprehended; many people who hear or read aspersions neither clearly identify the person affronted nor remember the scorn for long. Those well acquainted with the victim will generally not believe false accusations. Litigation, at its various stages and over a substantial period of time, republicizes the defamation. Fragments of trials and appeals are reported as they happen. Many who know that legal proceedings are in progress never follow their entire course; others who read about a final judgment often forget who won. When a defendant vigorously contests a suit for publishing a defamation, some people will sententiously say that so much smoke without some fire is unlikely.

The well-known victim of prominent and persistent vilification may have little to lose, other than legal costs, by bringing a libel suit. Some litigation victories are newsworthy and easily understood; they are especially exculpatory and reparative when judgment awards the plaintiff substantial damages. There are, then, only a modicum of cases in which counsel should recommend filing a defamation suit and prosecuting it vigorously to its conclusion.

B. The Constitutional Issues

In 1964, the Supreme Court of the United States ruled that defamation relating to public officials is entitled to the protection of the First Amendment to the Constitution of the United States. New York Times Co. v. Sullivan, 376 U.S. 254, 84 S. Ct. 710, 11 L. Ed. 2d 686 (1964). In this case, the plaintiff, an elected Commissioner of Public Affairs of Montgomery, Alabama, sued the New York Times and four individual defendants for an allegedly libelous statement made in a newspaper advertisement published in the Times. The statement accused city police of violating the civil rights of black students and of harassing Dr. Martin Luther King for his civil rights activities. Although the plaintiff was not named in the advertisement, he claimed that it referred to him because he supervised the Montgomery police department. He was successful in the Alabama courts, receiving a $500,000 judgment. The Supreme Court reversed, holding that a public official may not recover damages for defamation relating to his official conduct unless he proves that the defendant published the statement with actual malice. The Court defined actual malice as either knowledge of the falsity of the statement or "reckless disregard" of whether or not the statement is false. The Court also ruled that the plaintiff must establish malice with "convincing clarity," and that the Court will independently review the evidence to determine for itself that the plaintiff has discharged his heavy burden in this respect.[5] The Court based its decision on the commitment a democratic nation must have to uninhibited debate about important public issues and expressed its belief that a constitutional dimension to the law is necessary to prevent citizens from censoring their criticism of the government. According to the Court, the common law defense of truth is an inadequate safeguard (376 U.S. at 279, 84 S. Ct. at 725-726, 11 L. Ed. 2d at 706):

> Under such a rule, would-be critics of official conduct may be deterred from voicing their criticism, even though it is believed to be true and even though it is in fact true, because of doubt whether it can be proved in court or fear of the expense of having to do so. . . . The rule thus dampens the vigor and limits the variety of public debate. It is inconsistent with the First and Fourteenth Amendments.

In addition, the Court felt that critics of government officials should have the "fair equivalent" of the immunity enjoyed by public officials under Barr v. Matteo, discussed at p. 894, above.

5. In Bose v. Consumers Union of United States, Inc., 466 U.S. 485, 104 S. Ct. 1949, 80 L. Ed. 2d 502 (1984), the court reaffirmed its statement in *New York Times* that appellate courts must determine, after an independent review of the record, that the plaintiff has established malice with clear and convincing proof. In so doing, it rejected the "clearly erroneous" standard of appellate review of facts set out in Federal Rule 52(a).

Under *New York Times,* the two most important issues that would have to be dealt with in later cases concern the facts the plaintiff must prove to establish actual malice and the determination of who is a public official. As stated above, actual malice for constitutional purposes does not refer to the defendant's attitude toward the plaintiff, but rather toward the falsity of the statement; the plaintiff can recover only by establishing that the defendant knew the statement was false, or published it with reckless disregard of its falsity. As to the latter requirement, the Court in St. Amant v. Thompson, 390 U.S. 727, 730-731, 88 S. Ct. 1323, 1325, 20 L. Ed. 2d 262, 267 (1968) observed:

> "Reckless disregard," it is true, cannot be fully encompassed in one infallible definition. Inevitably its outer limits will be marked out through case-by-case adjudication, as is true with so many legal standards for judging concrete cases, whether the standard is provided by the Constitution, statutes, or case law. . . . [R]eckless conduct is not measured by whether a reasonably prudent man would have published, or would have investigated before publishing. There must be sufficient evidence to permit the conclusion that the defendant in fact entertained serious doubts as to the truth of his publication. Publishing with such doubts shows reckless disregard for truth or falsity and demonstrates actual malice.

Generally, the determination of whether actual malice has been proven with convincing clarity does not rest on any one factor, but results from a cumulation of evidence which is held to amount to reckless disregard of the truth. Cases in which plaintiffs have succeeded in establishing malice include Carson v. Allied News Co., 482 F. Supp. 406 (N.D. Ill. 1979), in which the defendant had distorted and altered facts contained in his source material and had fabricated entire conversations; and Goldwater v. Ginzburg, 414 F.2d 324 (2d Cir. 1969) *cert. denied,* 396 U.S. 1049 (1970), involving purported psychiatric evaluations of a presidential candidate. But the burden of proving actual malice clearly and convincingly is so heavy that few plaintiffs are able to meet it. For example, in Dickey v. CBS Inc., 583 F.2d 1221 (3d Cir. 1978), the trial court held that although the defendant was unconcerned whether the defamatory material it broadcast was true or not, it was nonetheless not liable because it had not in fact entertained serious doubts about the truth of the charges. The appellate court affirmed the decision, because it believed that CBS's reliance on the author of the statement, a veteran Congressman who knew the plaintiff and who refused to retract the charges, was justified. But, while the failure to investigate by itself will not necessarily constitute malice, the purposeful avoidance of the truth may well be enough. See Harte-Hanks Communications, Inc. v. Connaughton, 491 U.S. 657, 109 S. Ct. 2678, 105 L. Ed. 562 (1989).

Because the malice standard is difficult to meet, courts have decided many libel cases on motions for summary judgment, even though summary judgment is not ordinarily granted a defendant whose state of mind is at issue. For criticisms of this trend, see Nader v. de Toledano, 408 A.2d. 31 (D.C. App. 1979), *cert. denied,* 444 U.S. 1078 (1980), and Louis, Summary Judgment and the Actual Malice Controversy in Constitutional Defamation Cases, 57 S. Cal. L. Rev. 707 (1984). In Anderson v. Liberty Lobby, 477 U.S. 242, 106 S. Ct. 2505, 91 L. Ed. 2d 202 (1986), the Court ruled that the "clear and convincing" burden of proof applicable to the malice issue applies to the trial judge in deciding motions for summary judgment as well as to the jury. In general, see Oakes, Proof of Actual Malice in Defamation Cases: An Unsolved Dilemma, 7 Hofstra L. Rev. 655 (1979).

The question of who is a public official for the purposes of the *New York Times* rule has also been the subject of considerable litigation. In Rosenblatt v. Baer, 383 U.S. 75, 85-86, 86 S. Ct. 669, 676, 15 L. Ed. 2d 597, 605-606 (1966), the Court stated that the public official designation applies to government employees "who have, or appear to the public to have, substantial responsibility for or control over the conduct of governmental affairs," and to governmental positions important enough that "the public has an independent interest in the qualifications and performance of the person who holds it beyond the general public interest in the qualifications and performance of all government employees. . . ."

A wide assortment of public employees, no matter where in the hierarchy of officialdom, have been held to be public officials: clerk of county court (Theckston v. Triangle Publications, Inc., 242 A.2d 629 (N.J. Super.), *cert. denied,* 52 N.J. 173, 244 A.2d 302 (1968)); city police officer (Reed v. Northwestern Publishing Co., 124 Ill. 2d 495, 530 N.E.2d 474 (1988)); fire department captain (Miller v. Minority Brotherhood of Fire Protection, 463 N.W.2d 690 (Wis. App. 1990)); public school teacher (Kelley v. Bonney, 221 Conn. 549, 606 A.2d 693 (1992)); but not a high school principal (Ellerbee v. Mills, 262 Ga. 516, 422 S.E.2d 539 (1992)). The category of public officials has also been interpreted to include many persons not normally thought of as public employees. See Monitor Patriot Co. v. Roy, 401 U.S. 265, 91 S. Ct. 621, 28 L. Ed. 2d 35 (1971) (candidate for public office); Klahr v. Winterble, 4 Ariz. App. 158, 418 P.2d 404 (1966) (member of student senate at state university); Turley v. W.T.A.X., Inc., 94 Ill. App. 2d 377, 236 N.E.2d 778 (1968) (architect involved in construction of a public building and in a position to influence the expenditure of public funds); Doctors Convalescent Center, Inc. v. East Shore Newspapers, Inc., 104 Ill. App. 2d 271, 244 N.E.2d 373 (1968) (nursing home licensed by state and in which were patients who were wards of the state: ". . . one is a public official if he . . . is carrying out a function of government or is participating in acts relating to matters in which the government has substantial interest."). In Jenoff v. Hearst Corp., 453 F. Supp. 541 (D. Md. 1978), *aff'd,* 644 F.2d 1004 (1981), the court refused to rule that the plaintiff, a volunteer undercover police informant, was a public official, pointing out that the nature of his activities precluded such a designation. According to the court in

Bufalino v. Associated Press, 692 F.2d 266 (2d Cir. 1982), *cert. denied,* 462 U.S. 1111 (1983), the status of the plaintiff may have as much to do with how the story refers to him as with his actual status. The plaintiff was the town attorney, but the court refused to characterize him as a public official because the story about him only referred to him as an attorney; the story did not identify him as a public official, nor did the defendant establish that the plaintiff's name was recognized in the town as a public official.

In Curtis Publishing Co. v. Butts and Associated Press v. Walker, 388 U.S. 130, 87 S. Ct. 1975, 18 L. Ed. 2d 1094 (1967), the Supreme Court held that the *New York Times* rule should be extended to "public figures." Butts was a college athletic director and former football coach accused in a magazine article of furnishing his team's plays to the coach of a rival team. Walker was a retired Army general who took part in the events surrounding the use of federal troops to integrate a southern university. In his plurality of opinion, Justice Harlan explained that both Butts and Walker were public figures, Butts by virtue of his position, and Walker because he had voluntarily injected himself into a public controversy. Furthermore, both plaintiffs had access to the media so that they could refute false accusations, and both were of continuing interest to the public. However, Justice Harlan asserted in his opinion that a recovery by either plaintiff could not be viewed as a vindication of government policy, as was the case in *New York Times,* and he advanced a standard of liability that was less rigorous than the actual malice standard imposed on *New York Times* plaintiffs but more demanding than the common law. He suggested a rule by which a public figure could recover for defamation if it could be proved that the defendant's conduct has been "highly unreasonable" so that it constituted "an extreme departure from the standards of investigation and reporting ordinarily adhered to by responsible publishers." 388 U.S. at 155, 87 S. Ct. at 1991, 18 L. Ed. 2d at 1111. The majority, however, did not support this intermediate standard, preferring instead Chief Justice Warren's opinion adopting the *New York Times* standard for cases with public figure plaintiffs. Warren reasoned that the increasing concentration of power in private sectors of society means that many who are not public officials "are nevertheless, intimately involved in the resolution of important public questions or, by reason of their fame, shape events in areas of concern to society at large." 388 U.S. at 164, 97 S. Ct. at 1996, 18 L. Ed. 2d at 1116. For that reason, and because they have access to the media, Warren concluded that the *New York Times* standard should also be applied to public figure plaintiffs.

After the *Butts* and *Walker* cases were decided, a new category of matters of public interest or concern emerged in lower court cases. If the statements were determined to be related to a matter of legitimate public concern, the plaintiff had to meet the *New York Times* standard. This concept gained acceptance by a plurality of the Supreme Court in Rosenbloom v. Metromedia, Inc., 403 U.S. 29, 91 S. Ct. 1811, 29 L. Ed. 2d 296 (1971), in which the Court held that the plaintiff, a magazine distributor, could not recover for statements asserting that he sold obscene literature. Justice Brennan concluded in his plurality opinion that the *New York Times* privilege should apply to defamatory statements relating to private persons if the statements relate to matters of general or public interest. He emphasized society's interest in being informed about certain issues, and reasoned that its interest does not diminish merely because a private individual, however involuntarily, is involved.

The *New York Times* standard has been applied to nonmedia defendants where the plaintiff was a public figure or official. See, e.g., St. Amant v. Thompson, above; Garrison v. Louisiana, 379 U.S. 64, 85 S. Ct. 209, 13 L. Ed. 2d 125 (1964).

There was uncertainty following the decision in *New York Times* as to whether it would be constitutionally permissible to retain the traditional rule that the burden of proof as to truth is on the defendant. The matter was put to rest in Philadelphia Newspapers, Inc. v. Hepps, 475 U.S. 767, 106 S. Ct. 1558, 89 L. Ed. 2d 783 (1986), which held that the burden is on the plaintiff to prove the falsity of the statement.

Obviously, the Supreme Court in *New York Times* and later cases hoped that the more stringent malice standard would discourage the bringing of defamation suits. Whether it has or not is impossible to determine, because we cannot know what would have happened had strict liability continued as the permissible basis of liability. But it is apparent that defamation continues as a lively source of litigation. One commentator's explanation appears in Smolla, Let the Author Beware: The Rejuvenation of the American Law of Libel, 132 U. Pa. L. Rev. 1, 11 (1983):

> I contend that there are four contributing causes to the recent rejuvenation of American libel law. . . . The first factor is a new legal and cultural seriousness about the inner self. Tort law has undergone a relaxation of rules that formerly prohibited recovery for purely emotional or psychic injury, a doctrinal evolution that parallels the growth of the "me-generation." A second factor is the infiltration into the law of defamation of many of the attitudes that have produced a trend in tort law over the past twenty years favoring compensation and risk-spreading goals over fault principles in the selection of liability rules. A third cause of the new era in libel is the increasing difficulty in distinguishing between the informing and entertaining functions of the media. The blurring of this line between entertainment and information has affected the method and substance of communications in important ways and highlights the inadequacies of the current legal standards governing defamation actions. The final factor is doctrinal confusion, caused in large part by a pervasive failure to accommodate constitutional and common law values in a coherent set of standards that is responsive to the realities of modern communications. That doctrinal confusion is particularly telling in an environment where cultural trends, such as a heightened concern for the inner self, and legal trends, such as the trend in tort law in favor of strict liability, both work against the ideals of free expression.

In any event, it does not appear that money is a central motivation for pursuing defamation claims. According to one study, only 20 percent of defamation plaintiffs had compensation as the primary goal. Rather, plaintiffs are more concerned with revenge and correcting the record. See Bezanson, Libel Law and the Realities of Libel Litigation: Setting the Record Straight, 71 Iowa L. Rev. 226 (1985). It is just as well that money does not figure large in the decision to sue, for another study determined that defamation plaintiffs were successful in only 20 percent of the reported cases. Excluding two very large awards, recoveries averaged only $20,000, out of which the plaintiffs had to pay their costs and legal fees. Settlements averaged only $7,000 before costs and fees. Bezanson, The Libel Suit in Retrospect: What Plaintiffs Want and What Plaintiffs Get, 74 Calif. L. Rev. 789 (1986). The latter article appears in Symposium: New Perspectives in the Law of Defamation, 74 Calif. L. Rev. 677-926 (1986), which covers a wide range of topics.

Gertz v. Robert Welch, Inc.

418 U.S. 323, 94 S. Ct. 2997, 41 L. Ed. 2d 789 (1974)

MR. JUSTICE POWELL delivered the opinion of the Court.

This Court has struggled for nearly a decade to define the proper accommodation between the law of defamation and the freedoms of speech and press protected by the First Amendment. With this decision we return to that effort. We granted certiorari to reconsider the extent of a publisher's constitutional privilege against liability for defamation of a private citizen.

I

In 1968 a Chicago policeman named Nuccio shot and killed a youth named Nelson. The state authorities prosecuted Nuccio for the homicide and ultimately obtained a conviction for murder in the second degree. The Nelson family retained petitioner Elmer Gertz, a reputable attorney, to represent them in civil litigation against Nuccio.

[Respondent published an article in his magazine accusing the petitioner of being part of a Communist conspiracy against the police. The article also stated that petitioner belonged to two Marxist organizations. Petitioner brought this action for libel against the respondent in federal district court, and after the evidence was completed, the trial judge directed a verdict for petitioner on the liability issues, since it was undisputed that the article contained false statements which constituted libel per se. After a verdict for the petitioner of $50,000, the trial judge granted the respondent's motion for judgment notwithstanding the verdict on the ground that the article was about a matter of public interest and thus entitled to the protection of the *New York Times* rule, and that actual malice had not been convincingly demonstrated. The court of appeals affirmed.] . . .

III

We begin with the common ground. Under the First Amendment there is no such thing as a false idea. However pernicious an opinion may seem, we depend for its correction not on the conscience of judges and juries but on the competition of other ideas. But there is no constitutional value in false statements of fact. Neither the intentional lie nor the careless error materially advances society's interest in "uninhibited, robust, and wide-open" debate on public issues. New York Times Co. v. Sullivan, 376 U.S., at 270. They belong to that category of utterances which "are no essential part of any exposition of ideas, and are of such slight social value as a step to truth that any benefit that may be derived from them is clearly outweighed by the social interest in order and morality." Chaplinsky v. New Hampshire, 315 U.S. 568, 572 (1942).

Although the erroneous statement of fact is not worthy of constitutional protection, it is nevertheless inevitable in free debate. . . . Our decisions recognize that a rule of strict liability that compels a publisher or broadcaster to guarantee the accuracy of his factual assertions may lead to intolerable self-censorship. Allowing the media to avoid liability only by proving the truth of all injurious statements does not accord adequate protection to First Amendment liberties. . . . The First Amendment requires that we protect some falsehood in order to protect speech that matters.

The need to avoid self-censorship by the news media is, however, not the only societal value at issue. If it were, this Court would have embraced long ago the view that publishers and broadcasters enjoy an unconditional and indefeasible immunity from liability for defamation. Such a rule would indeed obviate the fear that the prospect of civil liability for injurious falsehood might dissuade a timorous press from the effective exercise of First Amendment freedoms. Yet absolute protection for the communications media requires a total sacrifice of the competing value served by the law of defamation.

The legitimate state interest underlying the law of libel is the compensation of individuals for the harm inflicted on them by defamatory falsehoods. We would not lightly require the State to abandon this purpose, for, as Mr. Justice Stewart has reminded us, the individual's right to the protection of his own good name "reflects no more than our basic concept of the essential dignity and worth of every human being—a concept at the root of any decent system of ordered liberty. The protection of private personality, like the protection of life itself, is left primarily to the individual states under the Ninth and Tenth Amendments. But this does not mean that the right is entitled to any less recognition by this Court as a basic of our constitutional system." Rosenblatt v. Baer, 383 U.S. 75, 92-93 (1963) (opinion of Stewart, J.). . . .

[W]e have no difficulty in distinguishing among defamation plaintiffs. The first remedy of any victim of defamation is self-help—using available opportunities to contradict the lie or correct the error and thereby to minimize its adverse impact on reputation. Public officials and public figures usually enjoy significantly greater access to the channels of effective communication and hence have a more realistic opportunity to counteract false statements than private individuals normally enjoy. Private individuals are therefore more vulnerable to injury, and the state interest in protecting them is correspondingly greater.

More important than the likelihood that private individuals will lack effective opportunities for rebuttal, there is a compelling normative consideration underlying the distinction between public and private defamation plaintiffs. An individual who decides to seek governmental office must accept certain necessary consequences of that involvement in public affairs. He runs the risk of closer public scrutiny than might otherwise be the case. And society's interest in the officers of government is not strictly limited to the formal discharge of official duties. As the Court pointed out in Garrison v. Louisiana, 379 U.S. 64, 77 (1964), the public's interest extends to "anything that might touch on an official's fitness for office. . . . Few personal attributes are more germane to fitness for office than dishonesty, malfeasance, or improper motivation, even though these characteristics may also affect the official's private character."

Those classed as public figures stand in a similar position. Hypothetically, it may be possible for someone to become a public figure through no purposeful action of his own, but the instances of truly involuntary public figures must be exceedingly rare. For the most part those who attain this status have assumed roles of especial prominence in the affairs of society. Some occupy positions of such persuasive power and influence that they are deemed public figures for all purposes. More commonly, those classed as public figures have thrust themselves to the forefront of particular public controversies in order to influence the resolution of the issues involved. In either event, they invite attention and comment.

Even if the foregoing generalities do not obtain in every instance, the communications media are entitled to act on the assumption that public officials and public figures have voluntarily exposed themselves to increased risk of injury from defamatory falsehoods concerning them. No such assumption is justified with respect to a private individual. He has not accepted public office nor assumed an "influential role in ordering society." Curtis Publishing Co. v. Butts, supra, 388 U.S., at 164 (opinion of Warren, C.J.). He has relinquished no part of his interest in the protection of his own good name, and consequently he has a more compelling call on the courts for redress of injury inflicted by defamatory falsehood. Thus, private individuals are not only more vulnerable to injury than public officials and public figures; they are also more deserving of recovery.

For these reasons we conclude that the States should retain substantial latitude in their efforts to enforce a legal remedy for defamatory falsehood injurious to the reputation of a private individual. . . .

We hold that, so long as they do not impose liability without fault, the States may define for themselves the appropriate standard of liability for a publisher or broadcaster of defamatory falsehood injurious to a private individual. This approach provides a more equitable boundary between the competing concerns involved here. It recognizes the strength of the legitimate state interest in compensating private individuals for wrongful injury to reputation, yet shields the press and broadcast media from the rigors of strict liability for defamation. At least this conclusion obtains where, as here, the substance of the defamatory statement "makes substantial danger to reputation apparent." This phrase places in perspective the conclusion we announce today. Our inquiry would involve considerations somewhat different from those discussed above if a State purported to condition civil liability on a factual misstatement whose content did not warn a reasonably prudent editor or broadcaster of its defamatory potential. Such a case is not now before us, and we intimate no view as to its proper resolution.

IV

Our accommodation of the competing values at stake in defamation suits by private individuals allows the States to impose liability on the publisher or broadcaster of defamatory falsehoods on a less demanding showing than that required by *New York Times.* This conclusion is not based on a belief that the considerations which prompted the adoption of the *New York Times* privilege for defamation of public officials and its extension to public figures are wholly inapplicable to the context of private individuals. Rather, we endorse this approach in recognition of the strong and legitimate state interest in compensating private individuals for injury to reputation. But this countervailing state interest extends no further than compensation for actual injury. For the reasons stated below, we hold that the States may not permit recovery of presumed or punitive damages, at least when liability is not based on a showing of knowledge of falsity or reckless disregard for the truth.

The common law of defamation is an oddity of tort law, for it allows recovery of purportedly compensatory damages without evidence of actual loss. Under the traditional rules pertaining to actions for libel, the existence of injury is presumed from the fact of publication. Juries may award substantial sums as compensation for supposed damage to reputation without any proof that such harm actually occurred. The largely uncontrolled discretion of juries to award damages where there is no loss unnecessarily compounds the potential of any system of liability for defamatory falsehood to inhibit the vigorous exercise of First Amendment freedoms. Additionally, the doctrine of presumed damages invites juries to punish unpopular opinion rather than to compensate individuals for injury sustained by the publication of a false fact. More to the point, the States have no substantial interest in securing for plaintiffs such as this petitioner gratuitous awards of money damages far in excess of any actual injury.

We would not, of course, invalidate state law simply because we doubt its wisdom, but here we are attempting to reconcile state law with a competing interest grounded in the constitutional command of the First Amendment. It is therefore appropriate to require that state remedies for defamatory falsehood reach no farther than is necessary to protect the legitimate interest involved. It is necessary to restrict defamation plaintiffs who do not prove knowledge of falsity or reckless disregard for the truth to compensation for actual injury. We need not define "actual injury," as trial courts have wide experience in framing appropriate jury instructions in tort action. Suffice it to say that actual injury is not limited to out-of-pocket loss. Indeed, the more customary types of actual harm inflicted by defamatory falsehood include impairment of reputation and standing in the community, personal humiliation, and mental anguish and suffering. Of course, juries must be limited by appropriate instructions, and all awards must be supported by competent evidence concerning the injury, although there need be no evidence which assigns an actual dollar value to the injury.

We also find no justification for allowing awards of punitive damages against publishers and broadcasters held liable under state-defined standards of liability for defamation. In most jurisdictions jury discretion over the amounts awarded is limited only by the gentle rule that they not be excessive. Consequently, juries assess punitive damages in wholly unpredictable amounts bearing no necessary relation to the actual harm caused. And they remain free to use their discretion selectively to punish expressions of unpopular views. Like the doctrine of presumed damages, jury discretion to award punitive damages unnecessarily exacerbates the danger of media self-censorship, but, unlike the former rule, punitive damages are wholly irrelevant to the state interest that justifies a negligence standard for private defamation actions. They are not compensation for injury. Instead, they are private fines levied by civil juries to punish reprehensible conduct and to deter its future occurrence. In short, the private defamation plaintiff who establishes liability under a less demanding standard than that stated by *New York Times* may recover only such damages as are sufficient to compensate him for actual injury.

V

Notwithstanding our refusal to extend the *New York Times* privilege to defamation of private individuals, respondent contends that we should affirm the judgment below on the ground that petitioner is either a public official or a public figure. There is little basis for the former assertion. . . .

Respondent's characterization of petitioner as a public figure raises a different question. That designation may rest on either of two alternative bases. In some instances an individual may achieve such pervasive fame or notoriety that he becomes a public figure for all purposes and in all contexts. More commonly, an individual voluntarily injects himself or is drawn into a particular public controversy and thereby becomes a public figure for a limited range of issues. In either case such persons assume special prominence in the resolution of public questions.

Petitioner has long been active in community and professional affairs. He has served as an officer of local civil groups and of various professional organizations, and he has published several books and articles on legal subjects. Although petitioner was consequently well-known in some circles, he had achieved no general fame or notoriety in the community. None of the prospective jurors called at the trial had ever heard of petitioner prior to this litigation, and respondent offered no proof that this response was atypical of the local population. We would not lightly assume that a citizen's participation in community and professional affairs rendered him a public figure for all purposes. Absent clear evidence of general fame or notoriety in the community, and pervasive involvement in the affairs of society, an individual should not be deemed a public personality for all aspects of his life. It is preferable to reduce the public figure question to a more meaningful context by looking to the nature and extent of an individual's participation in the particular controversy giving rise to the defamation.

In this context it is plain that petitioner was not a public figure. He played a minimal role at the coroner's inquest, and his participation related solely to his representation of a private client. He took no part in the criminal prosecution of officer Nuccio. Moreover, he never discussed either the criminal or civil litigation with the press and was never quoted as having done so. He plainly did not thrust himself into the vortex of this public issue, nor did he engage the public's attention in an attempt to influence its outcome. We are persuaded that the trial court did not err in refusing to characterize petitioner as a public figure for the purpose of this litigation.

We therefore conclude that the *New York Times* standard is inapplicable to this case and that the trial court erred in entering judgment for respondent. Because the jury was allowed to impose liability without fault and was permitted to presume damages without proof of injury, a new trial is necessary. We reverse and remand for further proceedings in accord with this opinion.

It is so ordered.

[The concurring opinion of JUSTICE BLACKMUN, and the dissenting opinions of CHIEF JUSTICE BURGER and JUSTICES DOUGLAS, BRENNAN and WHITE are omitted.]

At the retrial, the jury determined that the defendant was guilty of actual malice, and the trial judge entered judgment for the plaintiff on the verdict for $100,000 in compensatory damages, and for $300,000 in punitive damages. The judgment was affirmed on appeal in Gertz v. Robert Welch, Inc., 680 F.2d 527 (7th Cir. 1982), *cert. denied,* 459 U.S. 1226 (1983).

The first post-*Gertz* case to reach the Supreme Court was Time, Inc. v. Firestone, 424 U.S. 448, 96 S. Ct. 958, 47 L. Ed. 2d 154 (1976). The case arose out of a report of the plaintiff's divorce published in the defendant's magazine. The plaintiff and her husband had sued each other for divorce in Florida, the husband claiming extreme cruelty and adultery. The husband's petition was granted, but there was no specification of the grounds in the decree, beyond a statement that neither party "has shown the least susceptibility to domestication." The defendant reported that the plaintiff's husband was granted a divorce on grounds of extreme cruelty and adultery. After the defendant refused to print a retraction, the plaintiff brought this action. The Florida Supreme Court affirmed a judgment of $100,000 for the plaintiff, from which the defendant appealed. Writing for the majority, Justice Rehnquist rejected Time's contention that Mrs. Firestone was a public figure. In the Court's view the plaintiff had not assumed a role of special prominence in the affairs of society, since her prominence was limited to the Palm Beach social circle; she had not thrust herself into any public controversy in an attempt to influence its resolution; her involvement in the litigation was involuntary, since the legal system compelled parties seeking a divorce to dissolve their marriage judicially. The Court also emphasized that a public controversy was not to be equated with all controversies of interest to the public, warning that to do so would be to reinstate *Rosenbloom.* Justice Marshall in dissent argued that the majority had reinstated *Rosenbloom,* despite its protestations to the contrary, with its discussion of whether the plaintiff's divorce action was a matter of "public controversy." In Justice Marshall's view, the plaintiff was a public figure for the purposes of the divorce litigation. She had greater access to the media than do private persons generally, as evidenced by the fact that press coverage of her activities was frequent enough to warrant her subscribing to a press-clipping service; she had voluntarily assumed a position of social prominence and thus could be fairly held to have assumed the risk of defamatory statements; finally, she had held several press conferences during the course of her long divorce trial, which had attracted national media coverage.

In two cases, the Supreme Court held that the media cannot convert the plaintiff from a private figure to a public figure by simply making the plaintiff the subject of a story. In Hutchinson v. Proxmire, 443 U.S. 111,

99 S. Ct. 2675, 61 L. Ed. 2d 411 (1979), the Court ruled that a researcher applying for public financing was not a public figure. That the plaintiff's response to a statement criticizing his research project was carried by some newspapers did not mean that he had the kind of access to the media discussed in *Gertz*. The Court stated that the plaintiff's access to the media must predate the alleged defamatory statement, and must be of a "regular and continuing" nature. To the same effect is Wolston v. Reader's Digest Association, 443 U.S. 157, 99 S. Ct. 2701, 61 L. Ed. 2d 450 (1979).

As one court has stated, trying to draw the line between public figures and private individuals is "much like trying to nail a jellyfish to the wall." Rosanova v. Playboy Enterprises, Inc., 411 F. Supp. 440, 443 (S.D. Ga. 1976). A five-factor test for determining whether the plaintiff was a limited-purpose public figure was suggested by Fitzgerald v. Penthouse International, Ltd., 691 F.2d 666, 668 (4th Cir. 1982), *cert. denied,* 460 U.S. 1024 (1983):

> (1) the plaintiff had access to channels of effective communication; (2) the plaintiff voluntarily assumed a role of special prominence in a public controversy; (3) the plaintiff sought to influence the resolution or outcome of the controversy; (4) the controversy existed prior to the publication of the defamatory statements; and (5) the plaintiff retained public figure status at the time of the alleged defamation.

The cases tend to be context-specific, so generalizations are difficult to make. Holding plaintiffs to be public figures, either all-purpose or limited, are: Reuber v. Food Chemical News, Inc., 925 F.2d 703 (4th Cir.), *cert. denied,* 111 S. Ct. 2814 (1991) (whistleblowing scientist for National Cancer Institute); Rebozo v. Washington Post Co., 637 F.2d 375 (5th Cir.), *cert. denied,* 454 U.S. 964 (1981) (well-known friend of a former president); Carson v. Allied News Co., 529 F.2d 206 (7th Cir. 1976) (wife of late night talk show host); James v. Gannett Co., 40 N.Y.2d 415, 353 N.E.2d 834 (1976) (professional belly dancer). Holding the plaintiffs not to be public figures are Long v. Cooper, 848 F.2d 1202 (11th Cir. 1988) (discount wholesaler of satellite television equipment); Warford v. Lexington Herald-Leader Co., 789 S.W.2d 758 (Ky. 1990), *cert. denied,* 498 U.S. 1047 (1991) (assistant college basketball coach); Dodrill v. Arkansas Democrat Co., 265 Ark. 628, 590 S.W.2d 840 (1979), *cert. denied,* 444 U.S. 1076 (1980) (attorney suspended from practice).

In Dun & Bradstreet, Inc. v. Greenmoss Builders, Inc., 472 U.S. 749, 105 S. Ct. 2939, 86 L. Ed. 2d 593 (1985), the Supreme Court held that proof of *New York Times* malice is not required to support an award of presumed or punitive damages if the story does not involve a matter of public concern. The Court went on to hold that a credit report is not a matter of public concern.

The Supreme Court in *Gertz* specifically left it to the states to determine whether a malice or negligence standard should be applied in cases of private individuals as plaintiffs. Most courts considering the issue have opted for negligence. See, e.g., Rouch v. Enquirer & News of Battle Creek,

440 Mich. 238, 487 N.W.2d 205 (1992); Capuano v. Outlet Co., 579 A.2d 469 (R.I. 1990). Adopting the malice standard is Gugliuzza v. K.C.M.C., Inc., 606 So. 2d 790 (La. 1992). Liability for punitive damages is discussed in Note, Punitive Damages and Libel Law, 98 Harv. L. Rev. 847 (1985).

Gertz did not involve purely private defamation—a private individual suing a non-media defendant. Some courts have altered the common law basis of liability in favor of negligence in these cases. See, e.g., Jacron Sales Corp. v. Sindorf, 276 Md. 580, 350 A.2d 688 (1976). Other courts have continued to apply strict liability. See, e.g., Harley-Davidson Motorsports, Inc. v. Markley, 279 Ore. 361, 568 P.2d 1359 (1977); Denny v. Mertz, 106 Wis. 2d 636, 318 N.W.2d 141, *cert. denied,* 459 U.S. 883 (1982). Some light may have been shed on this issue by the various opinions in Dun & Bradstreet, Inc. v. Greenmoss Builders, Inc., 472 U.S. 749, 105 S. Ct. 2939, 86 L. Ed. 2d 593 (1985). Five justices, one who concurred in and four who dissented from, the result in that case specifically addressed whether *Gertz* should be limited to media defendants and agreed at least on that point that it should not. This issue is discussed in Smolla, *Dun & Bradstreet, Hepps,* and *Liberty Lobby:* A New Analytic Primer on The Future Course of Defamation, 75 Geo. L.J. 1519 (1987).

Another issue discussed by Professor Smolla in this article is whether public officials and figures have any "private" lives to which the malice standard would not apply. Professor Smolla suggests that courts might be receptive to distinguishing between public officials for that purpose, according those well up in the "policymaking hierarchy" little in the way of private lives, with increasing privacy as cases move down the ladder of the hierarchy.

Milkovich v. Lorain Journal Co.

497 U.S. 1, 110 S. Ct. 2695, 111 L. Ed. 2d 1 (1990)

CHIEF JUSTICE REHNQUIST delivered the opinion of the Court. Respondent J. Theodore Diadiun authored an article in an Ohio newspaper implying that petitioner Michael Milkovich, a local high school wrestling coach, lied under oath in a judicial proceeding about an incident involving petitioner and his team which occurred at a wrestling match. Petitioner sued Diadiun and the newspaper for libel, and the Ohio Court of Appeals affirmed a lower court entry of summary judgment against petitioner. This judgment was based in part on the grounds that the article constituted an "opinion" protected from the reach of state defamation law by the First Amendment to the United States Constitution. We hold that the First Amendment does not prohibit the application of Ohio's libel laws to the alleged defamations contained in the article.

[The article that was the basis of the suit appeared in a newspaper owned by respondent Lorain Journal, and] bore the heading "Maple beat the law with the 'big lie,' " beneath which appeared Diadiun's photograph and the words "TD Says." The carryover page headline announced ". . . Diadiun says Maple told a lie." The column contained the following passages:

> . . . A lesson was learned (or relearned) yesterday by the student body of Maple Heights High School, and by anyone who attended the Maple-Mentor wrestling meet of last Feb. 8.
>
> A lesson which, sadly, in view of the events of the past year, is well they learned early.
>
> It is simply this: If you get in a jam, lie your way out.
>
> If you're successful enough, and powerful enough, and can sound sincere enough, you stand an excellent chance of making the lie stand up, regardless of what really happened.
>
> The teachers responsible were mainly Maple wrestling coach, Mike Milkovich, and former superintendent of schools, H. Donald Scott.
>
> Anyone who attended the meet, whether he be from Maple Heights, Mentor, or impartial observer, knows in his heart that Milkovich and Scott lied at the hearing after each having given his solemn oath to tell the truth.
>
> But they got away with it.
>
> Is that the kind of lesson we want our young people learning from their high school administrators and coaches?
>
> I think not.

Petitioner commenced a defamation action against respondents . . . alleging that the headline of Diadiun's article and the 9 passages quoted above "accused plaintiff of committing the crime of perjury, an indictable offense in the State of Ohio, and damaged plaintiff directly in his lifetime occupation of coach and teacher, and constituted libel per se."

[The Court's detailing of the proceedings below is omitted. The result of those proceedings is that summary judgment in favor of the respondents was affirmed on the ground that "the article in question was constitutionally protected opinion." Certiorari was granted "to consider the important questions raised by the Ohio courts' recognition of a constitutionally-required 'opinion' exception to the application of its defamation laws."] We now reverse.

Since the latter half of the 16th century, the common law has afforded a cause of action for damage to a person's reputation by the publication of false and defamatory statements.

In Shakespeare's Othello, Iago says to Othello:

> Good name in man and woman, dear my lord.
> Is the immediate jewel of their souls.
> Who steals my purse steals trash;
> 'Tis something, nothing; 'Twas mine, 'tis his, and has been slave to thousands;
> But he that filches from me my good name
> Robs me of that which not enriches him,
> And makes me poor indeed.

Act III, scene 3.

Defamation law developed not only as a means of allowing an individual to vindicate his good name, but also for the purpose of obtaining redress for harm caused by such statements. As the common law developed in this country, apart from the issue of damages, one usually needed only allege an unprivileged publication of false and defamatory matter to state a cause of action for defamation. The common law generally did not place any additional restrictions on the type of statement that could be actionable. Indeed, defamatory communications were deemed actionable regardless of whether they were deemed to be statements of fact or opinion. See, e.g., Restatement of Torts, §§565-567. As noted in the 1977 Restatement (Second) of Torts §566, Comment *a:*

> Under the law of defamation, an expression of opinion could be defamatory if the expression was sufficiently derogatory of another as to cause harm to his reputation, so as to lower him in the estimation of the community or to deter third persons from associating or dealing with him. . . . The expression of opinion was also actionable in a suit for defamation, despite the normal requirement that the communication be false as well as defamatory. . . . This position was maintained even though the truth or falsity of an opinion—as distinguished from a statement of fact—is not a matter that can be objectively determined and truth is a complete defense to a suit for defamation.

However, due to concerns that unduly burdensome defamation laws could stifle valuable public debate, the privilege of "fair comment" was incorporated into the common law as an affirmative defense to an action for defamation. "The principle of 'fair comment' afford[ed] legal immunity for the honest expression of opinion on matters of legitimate public interest when based upon a true or privileged statement of fact." 1 F. Harper & F. James, Law of Torts §5.28, p. 456 (1956) (footnote omitted). As this statement implies, comment was generally privileged when it concerned a matter of public concern, was upon true or privileged facts, represented the actual opinion of the speaker, and was not made solely for the purpose of causing harm. See Restatement of Torts, supra, §606. "According to the majority rule, the privilege of fair comment applied only to an expression of opinion and not to a false statement of fact, whether it was expressly stated or implied from an expression of opinion." Restatement (Second) of Torts, supra, §566, Comment *a.* Thus under the common law, the privilege of "fair comment" was the device employed to strike the appropriate balance between the need for vigorous public discourse and the need to redress injury to citizens wrought by invidious or irresponsible speech.

[The Court's discussion of the earlier Supreme Court cases imposing constitutional restraints on the common law of defamation is omitted.]

Respondents would have us recognize, in addition to the established safeguards discussed above, still another First Amendment-based protection for defamatory statements which are categorized as "opinion" as opposed to "fact." For this proposition they rely principally on the following dictum from our opinion in *Gertz* [v. Robert Welch, Inc., 418 U.S. 323, 94 S. Ct. 2997, 41 L. Ed. 2d 789 (1974)]:

> Under the First Amendment there is no such thing as a false idea. However pernicious an opinion may seem, we depend for its correction not on the conscience of judges and juries but on the competition of other ideas. But there is no constitutional value in false statements of fact.

418 U.S., at 339-340, 94 S. Ct., at 3007 (footnote omitted).

Read in context, . . . the fair meaning of the passage is to equate the word "opinion" in the second sentence with the word "idea" in the first sentence. Under this view, the language was merely a reiteration of Justice Holmes' classic "marketplace of ideas" concept. See Abrams v. United States, 250 U.S. 616, 630, 40 S. Ct. 17, 22, 63 L. Ed. 1173 (1919) (Holmes, J., dissenting) ("[T]he ultimate good desired is better reached by free trade in ideas . . . the best test of truth is the power of the thought to get itself accepted in the competition of the market").

Thus we do not think this passage from *Gertz* was intended to create a wholesale defamation exemption for anything that might be labeled "opinion." . . . Not only would such an interpretation be contrary to the tenor and context of the passage, but it would also ignore the fact that expressions of "opinion" may often imply an assertion of objective fact.

If a speaker says, "In my opinion John Jones is a liar," he implies a knowledge of facts which lead to the conclusion that Jones told an untruth. Even if the speaker states the facts upon which he bases his opinion, if those facts are either incorrect or incomplete, or if his assessment of them is erroneous, the statement may still imply a false assertion of fact. Simply couching such statements in terms of opinion does not dispel these implications; and the statement, "In my opinion Jones is a liar," can cause as much damage to reputation as the statement, "Jones is a liar." . . .

Apart from their reliance on the *Gertz* dictum, respondents do not really contend that a statement such as, "In my opinion John Jones is a liar," should be protected by a separate privilege for "opinion" under the First Amendment. But they do contend that in every defamation case the First Amendment mandates an inquiry into whether a statement is "opinion" or "fact," and that only the latter statements may be actionable. They propose that a number of factors developed by the lower courts (in what we hold was a mistaken reliance on the *Gertz* dictum) be considered in deciding which is which. But we think the " 'breathing space' " which " 'freedoms of expression require in order to survive,' " is adequately secured by existing constitutional doctrine without the creation of an artificial dichotomy between "opinion" and fact.

Foremost . . . a statement on matters of public concern must be provable as false before there can be liability under state defamation law, at least in situations, like the present, where a media defendant is involved. Thus, unlike the statement, "In my opinion Mayor Jones is a liar," the statement, "In my opinion Mayor Jones shows his abysmal ignorance by accepting the teachings of Marx and Lenin," would not be actionable. . . . [A] statement of opinion relating to matters of public concern which does not contain a provably false factual connotation will receive full constitutional protection.

Next, [protection is provided] for statements that cannot "reasonably [be] interpreted as stating actual facts" about an individual. . . . This provides assurance that public debate will not suffer for lack of "imaginative expression" or the "rhetorical hyperbole" which has traditionally added much to the discourse of our Nation.

The *New York Times-Butts* and *Gertz* culpability requirements further ensure that debate on public issues remains "uninhibited, robust, and wide-open," New York Times [Co. v. Sullivan], 376 U.S., at 270, 84 S. Ct., at 720 [(1964)]. Thus, where a statement of "opinion" on a matter of public concern reasonably implies false and defamatory facts regarding public figures or officials, those individuals must show that such statements were made with knowledge of their false implications or with reckless disregard of their truth. Similarly, where such a statement involves a private figure on a matter of public concern, a plaintiff must show that the false connotations were made with some level of fault as required by *Gertz*.

We are not persuaded that, in addition to these protections, an additional separate constitutional privilege for "opinion" is required to ensure the freedom of expression guaranteed by the First Amendment. The dispositive question in the present case then becomes whether or not a reasonable factfinder could conclude that the statements in the Diadiun column imply an assertion that petitioner Milkovich perjured himself in a judicial proceeding. We think this question must be answered in the affirmative. . . . This is not the sort of loose, figurative or hyperbolic language which would negate the impression that the writer was seriously maintaining petitioner committed the crime of perjury. Nor does the general tenor of the article negate this impression.

We also think the connotation that petitioner committed perjury is sufficiently factual to be susceptible of being proved true or false. A determination of whether petitioner lied in this instance can be made on a core of objective evidence by comparing, *inter alia,* petitioner's testimony [in two proceedings below.]

The numerous decisions discussed above establishing First Amendment protection for defendants in defamation actions surely demonstrate the Court's recognition of the Amendment's vital guarantee of free and uninhibited discussion of public issues. But there is also another side to the equation; we have regularly acknowledged the "important social values which underlie the law of defamation," and recognize that "[s]ociety has a pervasive and strong interest in preventing and redressing attacks upon reputation." Rosenblatt v. Baer, 383 U.S. 75, 86, 86 S. Ct. 669, 676, 15 L. Ed. 2d 597 (1966). Justice Stewart in that case put it with his customary clarity:

> The right of a man to the protection of his own reputation from unjustified invasion and wrongful hurt reflects no more than our basic concept of the essential dignity and worth of every human being—a concept at the root of any decent system of ordered liberty.
>
> The destruction that defamatory falsehood can bring is, to be sure, often beyond the capacity of the law to redeem. Yet, imperfect though it is, an action for damages is the only hope for vindication or redress the law gives to a man whose reputation has been falsely dishonored.

Id., at 92-93, 86 S. Ct., at 679-680 (Stewart, J., concurring).

We believe our decision in the present case holds the balance true. The judgment [below] is reversed and the case remanded for further proceedings not inconsistent with this opinion.

Reversed.

[The dissenting opinion of JUSTICE BRENNAN is omitted.]

Milkovich has been seen as changing the law that made "opinion" immune to defamation litigation; that is, if the statement were defined as opinion, there could be no recovery in defamation based on it. See Anderson, Is Libel Law Worth Reforming?, 140 U. Pa. L. Rev. 487, 507 (1991). An example of the impact *Milkovich* has had on the courts is Unelko Corp. v. Rooney, 912 F.2d 1049 (9th Cir. 1990). In a nationally televised program, the defendant stated that he had tried a product made by the plaintiff called "Rain-X," advertised to be a "one-step, wipe-on automotive glass coating that repels rain, sleet and snow on contact and takes up where windshield wipers leave off!" The defendant stated over the air that he had tried the product and that "[i]t didn't work." In a decision rendered before *Milkovich,* the trial judge entered summary judgment in favor of the defendant on the ground that the statement was one of opinion, not of fact. The court of appeals disagreed with this assessment of the case, stating that "a factfinder could conclude that Rooney's statement that Rain-X 'didn't work' implied an assertion of objective fact." 912 F.2d at 1055. Perhaps the plaintiff should have left well enough alone, however, for the court of appeals affirmed the trial court, ruling that the plaintiff had failed to prove that the statement was false. In Yetman v. English, 168 Ariz. 71, 811 P.2d 323 (1991), the defendant said of the plaintiff at a political meeting, "What kind of a communist do we have up here that thinks it's improper to protect your interests?" The court held that in the context, whether the statement was an assertion of fact, or was "political invective or hyperbole" and thus protected opinion, was an issue of fact for the jury.

Other courts, however, have given defendants more leeway in using very derogatory expressions to describe plaintiffs. For example, in Phantom Touring, Inc. v. Affiliated Publications, 953 F.2d 724 (1st Cir.), *cert. denied,* 112 S. Ct. 2942 (1992), the defendant newspaper carried a story suggesting that the plaintiff was misleading the public in the marketing of a production of "Phantom of the Opera" by failing to call clear attention to the fact that the plaintiff's production was not the more popular Andrew Lloyd Webber version. In affirming the dismissal of the complaint, the court ruled that expressions such as "rip-off," "fraud," and "a snake-oil job" could not reasonably be found to be anything other than expressions of opinion. In Hickey v. Capital Cities/ABC, Inc., 792 F. Supp. 1195 (D. Or. 1992), the plaintiff supplied animals for medical research. The defendant's broadcast characterized the plaintiff's operations as "a black market in stolen pets," "a low, repulsive crime," and "a rotten trade." The court granted the defendant's motion for summary judgment.

Milkovich does not, of course, preclude a state from according more protection to speech under state law than does the U.S. Supreme Court under the Constitution. In Immuno AG. v. J. Moor-Jankowski, 77 N.Y.2d 235, 567 N.E.2d 1270 (1991), the Court of Appeals of New York did extend broader protection to speech than did the court in *Milkovich.* The plaintiff sued the defendant, the editor of a scientific journal, for publishing a letter critical of the plaintiff's plans for hepatitis research on chimpanzees in West Africa. The court read *Milkovich* as establishing a rule that "except for special situations of loose, figurative, hyperbolic language, statements that contain or imply assertions of provably false fact will likely be actionable." 77 N.Y.2d at 245, 567 N.E.2d at 1275. On this test, the court believed it could be found that the letter did contain statements of fact. The court ruled, however, that under New York law, the "full context" of the statement should be taken into account, and that the letter as a whole

> would not have been viewed by the average reader of the Journal as conveying actual facts about plaintiff [and] it would be plain to the reasonable reader of this scientific publication that [the letter writer] was voicing no more than a highly partisan point of view.

77 N.Y.2d at 255, 567 N.E.2d at 1281.

One important factor to the court was that the defamation appeared in a letter to the editor.

> The public forum function of letters to the editor is closely related in spirit to the "marketplace of ideas" and oversight and informational values that compelled recognition of the privileges of fair comment, fair report and the

> immunity accorded expression of opinion. These values are best effectuated by according defendant some latitude to publish a letter to the editor on a matter of legitimate public concern—the letter's author, affiliation, bias and premises fully disclosed, rebuttal openly invited—free of defamation litigation. A publication that provides a forum for such statements on controversial matters is not acting in a fashion "at odds with the premises of democratic government and with the orderly manner in which economic, social, or political change is to be effected" (Garrison v. Louisiana, 379 U.S. 64, 75, [85 S. Ct. 209, 216, 13 L. Ed. 2d 125 (1964)]), but to the contrary is fostering those very values.

Id., 567 N.E.2d at 1281-1282.

Problem 39

In what way would your analysis of Problem 38, set out at the end of Section A, p. 900, be altered as a result of the constitutional developments discussed in this section?

C. *Legislative Reform of the Law of Defamation*

Recent years have seen growing dissatisfaction with the way in which the law of defamation, including the constitutional rules, strikes the balance between the interest in reputation and the interest in free speech. As one critic of the defamation scene observed:

> The present law of libel is a failure. It denies most defamation victims any remedy, and at the same time chills speech by encouraging high litigation costs and occasional large judgments.

Anderson, Is Libel Law Worth Reforming?, 140 U. Pa. L. Rev. 487, 550 (1991).

Another critic of the current law of defamation is Professor Bezanson, who argued for change in The Libel Tort Today, 45 Wash. & Lee L. Rev. 535, 556 (1988):

> At least in the mass communication, or media, setting, the libel tort today represents a very different set of interests from those reflected in the common law tort. The interests are essentially regulatory and punitive. The libel tort today represents a civil penalty for general publication in an irresponsible manner of an injurious falsehood about a person or entity. A finding of falsity is based on the content of the challenged statement and the subjective intent of the publisher, not on its meaning as understood in the real dynamics of

> actual communication. Injury is premised upon the logical consequences of the false fact and attendant emotional stress, not on community-based perceptions of reputation and harm. Irresponsibility is based on judicially-created standards of journalistic process and editorial judgment, not on concepts of privilege that reflect social value and abjure judgments of fault.
>
> Whatever may be said against or in favor of such a tort, it is a far cry from the common law concepts of reputation, compensation, publication, and privilege. For those whose interest is in protecting reputation, today's libel tort fails in almost all respects to do so. It underprotects the community-based interest in reputation, and overprotects the reputationally-unrelated interests in truth, responsible journalism, and freedom from emotional harm. For those whose interest is in protecting the press from unnecessary inhibition and government control of the standards of journalism, today's libel tort is anathema, for the chief consequence of libel today is inhibition of the press from violating judicially-crafted standards of journalism. Finally, for those who placed faith in the privileges created by New York Times Co. v. Sullivan and its progeny, today's libel tort must be discouraging, if not utterly devastating, for it falls substantially short of safeguarding press freedom and fails to safeguard individual reputation as well.
>
> Whether in our instinct for reform we should return to the imperfectly realized common law interests or formulate new approaches that depart from both our present and our past, we need to build change on an understanding of where we are today and how we got there. For my part, today's libel tort is profoundly and fundamentally disquieting in a society that attempts to strike a balance between reputation and freedom of expression. Change in the libel system is therefore an imperative. But this should be neither a shocking nor an unsettling conclusion, for change is the one common thread that extends throughout the libel tort's long and arduous history.

Objections of this sort are not new. But as yet, legislatures have not attempted broad intervention into defamation law, as they have with respect to personal injury law—no doubt because constitutional law substantially circumscribes the permitted scope of legislative action.

Nonetheless, a movement has emerged for legislative reformation of the law of defamation—a reformation that is much more sweeping than the recent legislative reforms of tort law. The movement began with the Libel Reform Project of the Annenberg Washington Program. Under the direction of Professor Rodney A. Smolla, the project developed its comprehensive "Proposal for the Reform of Libel Law" in 1988. The basic thrust of the proposal is to provide an alternative to damage actions in which the truth or falsity of the statement would be determinative. See Smolla and Gaertner, The Annenberg Libel Reform Proposal: The Case for Enactment, 31 Wm. & Mary L. Rev. 25 (1989). That facet of the proposal has emerged in a series of drafts of a Uniform Defamation Act prepared by the National Conference of Commissioners on Uniform State Laws, the latest of which is dated March 23, 1993, although there are significant differences between the two proposals. The Act would permit a defendant to submit an "offer of termination" to the plaintiff. To be effective, the offer would have to stipulate that the defendant does not assert the truth of the statement, and offer to publish a correction. If accepted by the plaintiff, the action would be dismissed; if rejected, the plaintiff's recovery, if any, would be limited to economic damages. The Act would also permit the plaintiff to bring an action for "vindication," rather than for damages. The central issue would be the falsity of the statement; the fault of the defendant would not be relevant, nor would the defendant be able to rely on a conditional privilege.

The proposed Act met with substantial opposition from a variety of quarters, and the Reporter has recommended that it be withdrawn from further consideration by the Commissioners. Part of the Uniform Defamation Act has survived for further consideration by the Commissioners, however, and was approved by them in the form of the Uniform Correction or Clarification of Defamation Act. The current draft of this proposed Act provides in part:

UNIFORM CORRECTION OR CLARIFICATION OF DEFAMATION ACT

SECTION 2. REQUEST FOR CORRECTION OR CLARIFICATION

(a) A person may not maintain an action for defamation unless the person has made a timely and adequate request for correction or clarification from the defendant or unless the defendant has made a correction or clarification.

(b) A request for correction or clarification is timely if it is made within the period of limitation for defamation actions, but a person who, within 90 days after knowledge of the publication, fails to make a good faith attempt to request a correction or clarification may recover only provable economic loss.

(c) A request for correction or clarification is adequate if it:

(1) is made in writing and reasonably identifies the person making the request;

(2) specifies with particularity the statement alleged to be false and defamatory and, to the extent known, the time and place of publication;

(3) states the alleged defamatory meaning;

(4) specifies the circumstances that give rise to the defamatory meaning if that meaning arises from other than the express language of the publication; and

(5) states that the alleged defamatory meaning is false.

(d) If an adequate request has not previously been made, service of a [summons and complaint] stating a [claim for relief] for defamation and containing the information required in subsection (c) constitutes an adequate request for correction or clarification.

(e) The period of limitation for a defamation action is tolled during the period provided in Section 5(a) for responding to a request for correction or clarification.

SECTION 3. DISCLOSURE OF EVIDENCE OF FALSITY

(a) A publisher may ask that a person requesting a correction or clarification disclose reasonably available information material to the falsity of the allegedly defamatory statement. If a correction or clarification is not made, a person who unreasonably fails to disclose the information after a request to do so may recover only provable economic loss.

(b) When a person supplies the information pursuant to subsection (a) of this section, a correction or clarification is timely if published within 25 days after receipt of such information or 45 days after receipt of a request pursuant to Section 2, whichever is later.

SECTION 4. EFFECT OF CORRECTION OR CLARIFICATION

If a timely and sufficient correction or clarification is made, a person may recover only provable economic loss caused by the defamatory publication, as mitigated by the correction or clarification.

SECTION 5. TIMELY AND SUFFICIENT CORRECTION OR CLARIFICATION

(a) A correction or clarification is timely if it is published before, or no later than 45 days after, receipt of a request pursuant to Section 2.

(b) A correction or clarification is sufficient if it:

(1) is published with a prominence and in a manner and medium reasonably likely to reach substantially the same audience as the publication complained of;

(2) refers to the statement being corrected or clarified and:

(i) corrects the statement;

(ii) in the case of defamatory meaning arising from other than the express language of the publication, disclaims an intent to communicate that meaning or to assert its truth; or

(iii) in the case of a statement attributed to another person, identifies that person and disclaims an intent to assert the truth of the statement; and

(3) is communicated to the requester if a request has been made.

(c) A correction or clarification is published in a medium reasonably likely to reach substantially the same audience as the publication complained of if it is published in a subsequent issue or edition or broadcast of the original publication.

(d) If a subsequent issue or edition or broadcast of the original publication will not be published within the time limits established for a timely correction or clarification, a correction or clarification is published in a manner and medium reasonably likely to reach substantially the same audience as the publication complained of if:

(1) it is timely published in a reasonably prominent manner in:

(i) another medium likely to reach an audience reasonably equivalent to the original publication: or

(ii) if the parties cannot agree on another medium, the newspaper with the largest general circulation in the region in which the original publication was distributed;

(2) reasonable steps are taken to correct undistributed copies of the original publication, if any; and

(3) it is published in the next practicable issue or edition, if any, of the original publication.

(e) A correction or clarification is timely and sufficient if the parties agree in writing that it is timely and sufficient. . . .

SECTION 7. OFFER TO CORRECT OR CLARIFY

(a) If a timely correction or clarification is no longer possible, a publisher at any time before trial may offer to make a correction or clarification. The offer must be made in writing to the person harmed by the publication and contain:

(1) the publisher's offer to:

(i) publish, at the person's request, a sufficient correction or clarification; and

(ii) pay the person's reasonable expenses of litigation, including attorney's fees, incurred before publication of the correction or clarification; and

(2) a copy of the proposed correction or clarification and the plan for its publication.

(b) If the person accepts in writing an offer to correct or clarify pursuant to subsection (a):

(1) the person is barred from commencing an action against the publisher based on the statement; or

(2) if an action has been commenced, the court shall dismiss the action against the defendant after the defendant complies with the terms of the offer.

(c) A person who does not accept an offer made in conformance with subsection (a) may recover in an action based on the statement only:

(1) damages for provable economic loss caused by the statement; and

(2) unless the person failed to make a good faith effort to request a correction or clarification pursuant to Section 2(b) or failed to disclose information pursuant to Section 3, reasonable expenses of litigation, including attorney's fees, incurred before the offer.

(d) On request of either party, a court shall promptly determine the sufficiency of the offered correction or clarification. The amount of reasonable expenses of litigation, including attorney's fees, specified in subsections (a)(1)(ii) and (c)(2) of this section, shall be determined by the court.

Chapter 13

Invasion of Privacy

The right to recover for invasion of privacy had its genesis in a law review article—The Right to Privacy, 4 Harv. L. Rev. 193 (1890)—written by Samuel D. Warren and Louis D. Brandeis. The article was prompted by what Warren viewed as outrageous reporting by the Boston newspapers of his and his wife's social activities. In an impassioned indictment of the "yellow journalism" of the day, Warren and Brandeis wrote (4 Harv. L. Rev. at 196);

> The press is overstepping in every direction the obvious bounds of propriety and of decency. Gossip is no longer the resource of the idle and of the vicious, but has become a trade, which is pursued with industry as well as effrontery. To satisfy a prurient taste the details of sexual relations are spread broadcast in the columns of the daily papers. To occupy the indolent, column upon column is filled with idle gossip, which can only be procured by intrusion upon the domestic circle. The intensity and complexity of life, attendant upon advancing civilization, have rendered necessary some retreat from the world, and man, under the refining influence of culture, has become more sensitive to publicity, so that solitude and privacy have become more essential to the individual; but modern enterprise and invention have, through invasions upon his privacy, subjected him to mental pain and distress, far greater than could be inflicted by mere bodily injury.

Before 1890, privacy as such had no legal protection. But thereafter courts, and occasionally legislatures, built on the ideas of Warren and Brandeis and almost all states now recognize, in some form, the right to recover for invasion of privacy. Most courts have followed the analysis advanced by Prosser in an article from which the following excerpts are taken:

Prosser, Privacy

48 Calif. L. Rev. 383, 390-403, 405-406 (1960)

[In this article, Prosser undertakes a comprehensive survey of right to privacy cases, and concludes that not one tort but rather a set of four torts, each protecting a different interest, has emerged.]

I. Intrusion

[Prosser first discusses the early cases falling into this category, which involved physical intrusions into such places as the plaintiff's home or hotel room.]

The principle was, however, soon carried beyond such physical intrusion. It was extended to eavesdropping upon private conversations by means of wire tapping and microphones; and there are three decisions, . . . which have applied the same principle to peering into the windows of a home. . . . The tort has been found in the case of unauthorized prying into the plaintiff's bank account. . . .

It is clear, however, that there must be something in the nature of prying or intrusion, and mere noises which disturb a church congregation, or bad manners, harsh names and insulting gestures in public, have been held not to be enough. It is also clear that the intrusion must be something which would be offensive or objectionable to a reasonable man, and that there is no tort when the landlord stops by on Sunday morning to ask for the rent.

It is clear also that the thing into which there is prying or intrusion must be, and be entitled to be, private. . . . On the public street, or in any other public place, the plaintiff has no right to be alone, and it is no invasion of his privacy to do no more than follow him about. Neither is it such an invasion to take his photograph in such a place, since this amounts to nothing more than making a record, not differing essentially from a full written description, of a public sight which any one present would be free to see. . . .

It appears obvious that the interest protected by this branch of the tort is primarily a mental one. It has been useful chiefly to fill in the gaps left by trespass, nuisance, the intentional infliction of mental distress, and whatever remedies there may be for the invasion of constitutional rights.

II. Public Disclosure of Private Facts

. . . First, the disclosure of the private facts must be a public disclosure, and not a private one. There must be, in other words, publicity. It is an invasion of the right to publish in a newspaper that the plaintiff does not pay his debts, or to post a notice to that effect in a window on the public street or cry it aloud in the highway; but, . . . it has been agreed that it is no invasion to communicate that fact to the plaintiff's employer, or to any other individual, or even to a small group, unless there is some breach of contract, trust or confidential relation which will afford an independent basis for relief. . . .

Second, the facts disclosed to the public must be private facts, and not public ones. Certainly no one can complain when publicity is given to information about him which he himself leaves open to the public eye, such as the appearance of the house in which he lives, or the business in which he is engaged. . . .

. . . The decisions indicate that anything visible in a public place may be recorded and given circulation by means of a photograph, to the same extent as by a written description, since this amounts to nothing more than giving publicity to what is already public and what any one present would be free to see. . . .

Third, the matter made public must be one which would be offensive and objectionable to a reasonable man of ordinary sensibilities. All of us, to some extent, lead lives exposed to the public gaze or to public inquiry, and complete privacy does not exist in this world except for the eremite in the desert. Any one who is not a hermit must expect the more or less casual observation of his neighbors and the passing public as to what he is and does, and some reporting of his daily activities. The ordinary reasonable man does not take offense at mention in a newspaper of the fact that he has returned from a visit, or gone camping in the woods, or that he has given a party as his house for his friends; and very probably Mr. Warren would never have had any action for the reports of his daughter's wedding. The law of privacy is not intended for the protection of any shrinking soul who is abnormally sensitive about such publicity. It is quite a different matter when the details of sexual relations are spread before the public gaze, or there is highly personal portrayal of his intimate private characteristics or conduct. . . .

III. False Light in the Public Eye

. . . One form in which [this tort] occasionally appears . . . is that of publicity falsely attributing to the plaintiff some opinion or utterance. A good illustration of this might be the fictitious testimonial used in advertising. . . . More typical are spurious books and articles, or ideas expressed in them, which purport to emanate from the plaintiff. In the same category are the unauthorized use of his name as a candidate for office, or to advertise for witnesses of an accident, or the entry of an actor, without his consent, in a popularity contest of an embarrassing kind.

Another form in which this branch of the tort frequently has made its appearance is the use of the plaintiff's picture to illustrate a book or an article with which he has no reasonable connection. . . .

Still another form in which the tort occurs is the inclusion of the plaintiff's name, photograph and fingerprints in a public "rogues' gallery" of convicted criminals, when he has not in fact been convicted of any crime. . . .

The false light need not necessarily be a defamatory one, although it very often is, and a defamation action will also lie. It seems clear, however, that it must be something that would be objectionable to the ordinary reasonable man under the circumstances, and that, as in the case of disclosure, the hypersensitive individual will not be protected. . . .

The false light cases obviously differ from those of intrusion, or disclosure of private facts. The interest protected is clearly that of reputation, with the same overtones of mental distress as in defamation. There is a resemblance to disclosure; but the two differ in that one involves truth and the other lies, one private or secret facts and the other invention. Both require publicity. There has been a good deal of overlapping of defamation in the false light cases, and apparently either action, or both, will very often lie. The privacy cases do go considerably beyond the narrow limits of defamation, and no doubt have succeeded in affording a needed remedy in a good many instances not covered by the other tort.

It is here, however, that one disposed to alarm might express the greatest concern over where privacy may be going. The question may well be raised, and apparently still is unanswered, whether this branch of the tort is not capable of swallowing up and engulfing the whole law of public defamation; and whether there is any false libel printed, for example, in a newspaper, which cannot be redressed upon the alternative ground. If that turns out to be the case, it may well be asked, what of the numerous restrictions and limitations which have hedged defamation about for many years, in the interest of freedom of the press and the discouragement of trivial and extortionate claims? Are they of so little consequence that they may be circumvented in so casual and cavalier a fashion?

IV. Appropriation

. . . [T]here are a great many decisions in which the plaintiff has recovered when his name or picture, or other likeness, has been used without his consent to advertise the defendant's product, or to accompany an article sold, to add luster to the name of a corporation, or for other business purposes. . . .

It is the plaintiff's name as a symbol of his identity that is involved here, and not his name as a mere name. There is, as a good many thousand John Smiths can bear witness, no such thing as an exclusive right to the use of any name. . . . It is when he makes use of the name to pirate the plaintiff's identity for some advantage of his own, as by impersonation to obtain credit or secret information, or by posing as the plaintiff's wife, or providing a father for a child on a birth certificate, that he becomes liable. It is in this sense that "appropriation" must be understood.

On this basis, the question before the courts has been first of all whether there has been appropriation of an aspect of the plaintiff's identity. It is not enough that a name which is the same as his is used in a novel, a comic strip, or the title of a corporation, unless the context or the circumstances, or the addition of some other element, indicate that the name is that of the plaintiff. . . .

Once the plaintiff is identified, there is the further question whether the defendant has appropriated the name or likeness for his own advantage. . . . [I]t has been held that the mere incidental mention of the plaintiff's name in a book or a motion picture or even in a commentary upon news which is part of an advertisement, is not an invasion of his privacy; nor is the publication of a photograph or a newsreel in which he incidentally appears.

It seems sufficiently evident that appropriation is quite a different matter from intrusion, disclosure of private facts, or a false light in the public eye. The interest protected is not so much a mental as a proprietary one, in the exclusive use of the plaintiff's name and likeness as an aspect of his identity. It seems quite pointless to dispute over whether such a right is to be classified as "property." If it is not, it is at least, once it is protected by the law, a right of value upon which the plaintiff can capitalize by selling licenses. . . .

Courts have overwhelmingly adopted Prosser's "four tort" approach to privacy law, and, not surprisingly, the Restatement of Torts (Second) has incorporated this approach into §§652A-652E dealing with invasions of privacy. (Prosser was the Reporter for the Restatement of Torts (Second) when these sections were drafted and approved.) Given the judicial approval of Prosser's approach, the following also incorporates that organization. But judicial acceptance of Prosser does not mean that there is agreement as to the values that underlie the tort. A number of commentators have disagreed with Prosser on that score. For example, Professor Blaustein, in his article, Privacy as an Aspect of Human Dignity: An Answer to Dean Prosser, 39 N.Y.U. L. Rev. 962 (1964), argues in favor of a single tort, having as its purpose the protection of personal dignity. A different view is advanced in Post, The Social Foundations of Privacy: Community and Self in the Common Law Tort, 77 Calif. L. Rev. 957 (1989); the author argues that the purpose of privacy law should be to protect "rules of civility." Professor Benzanson, in *The Right to Privacy* Revisited: Privacy, News, and Social Change, 1890–1990, 80 Calif. L. Rev. 1133 (1992), asserts that privacy law should protect persons' control of information. The following overview of Prosser's four torts should enable you to draw at least some tentative conclusions on that score.

A. *Intrusion*

Hamberger v. Eastman

106 N.H. 107, 206 A.2d 239 (1964)

The plaintiffs, husband and wife, brought companion suits for invasion of their privacy against the defendant who owned and rented a dwelling house to the plaintiffs. . . .

The declaration in the suit by the husband reads as follows:

"In a plea of the case, for that the defendant is the owner of a certain dwelling house . . . which was, and still is, occupied by the plaintiff and his family as a dwelling house on a weekly rental basis; that said dwelling house is located adjacent to and abutting other land of the defendant whereon the defendant maintains his place of residence, together with his place of business.

"That, sometime during the period from October, 1961, to October 15, 1962, the defendant, wholly without the knowledge and consent of the plaintiff, did willfully and maliciously invade the privacy and sanctity of the plaintiff's bedroom, which he shared with his wife in their dwelling house, by installing and concealing a listening and recording device in said bedroom; that this listening and recording device, which was concealed in an area adjacent to the bed occupied by the plaintiff and his wife was attached and connected to the defendant's place of residence by means of wires capable of transmitting and recording any sounds and voices originating in said bedroom.

"That, on or about October 15, 1962, plaintiff discovered the listening and recording device which defendant had willfully and maliciously concealed in his bedroom, and the plaintiff, ever since that time and as a direct result of the actions of the defendant, has been greatly distressed, humiliated, and embarrassed and has sustained and is now sustaining, intense and severe mental suffering and distress, and has been rendered extremely nervous and upset, seriously impairing both his mental and physical condition, and that the plaintiff has sought, and still is under, the care of a physician; that large sums have been, and will be in the future, expended for medical care and attention; that because of his impaired mental and physical condition, the plaintiff has been and still is unable to properly perform his normal and ordinary duties as a father and as a husband, and has been unable to properly perform his duties at his place of employment, and has been otherwise greatly injured."

The declaration in the suit by the wife is identical, with appropriate substitutes of the personal pronoun, and omission of the allegation of inability to perform duties at her place of employment.

In both actions the defendant moved to dismiss on the ground that on the facts alleged, no cause of action is stated. The Court . . . reversed and transferred the cases to the Supreme Court without ruling.

KENISON, C.J. The question presented is whether the right of privacy is recognized in this state. There is no controlling statute and no previous decision in this jurisdiction which decides the question. Inasmuch as invasion of the right of privacy is not a single tort but consists of four distinct torts, it is probably more concrete and accurate to state the issue in the present case to be whether this state recognizes that intrusion upon one's physical and mental solitude or seclusion is a tort. . . .

We have not searched for cases where the bedroom of husband and wife has been "bugged" but it should not be necessary—by way of understatement—to observe that this is the type of intrusion that would be offensive to any person of ordinary sensibilities. What married "people do in the privacy of their bedrooms is their own business so long as they are not hurting anyone else." Ernst and Loth, For Better or Worse 79 (1952). The Restatement, Torts, §867 provides that "a person who unreasonably and seriously interferes with another's interest in not having his affairs known to others . . . is liable to the other." As is pointed out in Comment *d* "liability exists only if the defendant's conduct was such that he should have realized that it would be offensive to persons of ordinary sensibilities. It is only where the intrusion has gone beyond the limits of decency that liability accrues. These limits are exceeded where intimate details of the life of one who has never manifested a desire to have publicity are exposed to the public. . . ."

The defendant contends that the right of privacy should not be recognized on the facts of the present case as they appear in the pleadings because there are no allegations that anyone listened or overheard any sounds or voices originating from the plaintiffs' bedroom. The tort of intrusion on the plaintiffs' solitude or seclusion does not require publicity and communication to third persons although this would affect the amount of damages. . . . The defendant also contends that the right of privacy is not violated unless something has been published, written or printed and that oral publicity is not sufficient. Recent cases make it clear that this is not a requirement.

If the peeping Tom, the big ear and electronic eavesdropper (whether ingenious or ingenuous) have a place in the hierarchy of social values, it ought not to be at the expense of a married couple minding their own business in the seclusion of their bedroom who have never asked for or by their conduct deserved a potential projection of their private conversations and actions to their landlord or to others. Whether actual or potential such "publicity with respect to private matters of purely personal concern is an injury to personality. It impairs the mental peace and comfort of the individual and may produce suffering more acute than that produced by a mere bodily injury." III Pound, Jurisprudence 58 (1959). The use of parabolic microphones and sonic wave devices designed to pick up conversations in a room without entering it and at a considerable distance away makes the problem far from fanciful.

It is unnecessary to determine the extent to which the right of privacy is protected as a constitutional matter without the benefit of statute. For the purposes of the present case it is sufficient to hold that the invasion of the plaintiffs' solitude or seclusion, as alleged in the pleadings, was a violation of their right of privacy and constituted a tort for which the plaintiffs may recover damages to the extent that they can prove them. "Certainly, no right deserves greater protection, for, as Emerson has well said, 'solitude, the safeguard of mediocrity, is to genius the stern friend.' " Ezer, Intrusion on Solitude: Herein of Civil Rights and Civil Wrongs, 21 Law in Transition 63, 75 (1961).

The motion to dismiss should be denied.

Remanded.

All concurred.

Many intrusion cases are like *Hamberger* in that they involve physical invasions of the plaintiff's property. See, e.g., Engman v. Southwestern Bell Telephone Co., 591 S.W.2d 78 (Mo. App. 1979), and Gonzales v. Southwestern Bell Telephone Co., 555 S.W.2d 219 (Tex. Civ. App. 1977). In both of these cases telephone company employees entered the homes of the plaintiffs to remove telephones after service had been terminated. In *Gonzales,* the fact that the plaintiffs were not at home at the time of the entry did not defeat their claim. And in *Engman,* the court ruled that the telephone company tariff, pursuant to which the defendant retained title to telephones and was authorized to enter customers' premises to remove them, did not insulate the defendant from liability. In connection with the latter case, consider Florida Publishing Co. v. Fletcher, 340 So. 2d 914 (Fla. 1976), *cert. denied,* 431 U.S. 930 (1977) in which the court ruled that a newspaper reporter covering a story about a fire at the plaintiff's home had consent by "custom and usage" to enter the home with a fire marshal and a police officer investigating the fire.

Nader v. General Motors Corp.

25 N.Y.2d 560, 255 N.E.2d 765 (1970)

FULD, C.J. On this appeal, taken by permission of the Appellate Division on a certified question, we are called upon to determine the reach of the tort of invasion of privacy as it exists under the law of the District of Columbia.

The complaint, in this action by Ralph Nader, pleads four causes of action against the appellant, General Motors Corporation, and three other defendants allegedly acting as its agents. The first two causes of action charge an invasion of privacy, the third is predicated on the intentional infliction of severe emotional distress and the fourth on interference with the plaintiff's economic advantage. This appeal concerns only the legal sufficiency of the first two causes of action, which were upheld in the courts below as against the appellant's motion to dismiss.

The plaintiff, an author and lecturer on automotive safety, has, for some years, been an articulate and severe critic of General Motors' products from the standpoint of safety and design. According to the complaint—which, for present purposes, we must assume to be true—the appellant, having learned of the imminent publication of the plaintiff's book "Unsafe at Any Speed," decided to conduct a campaign of intimidation against him in order to "suppress plaintiff's criticism of and prevent his disclosure of information" about its products. To that end, the appellant authorized and directed the other defendants to engage in a series of activities which, the plaintiff claims in his first two causes of action, violated his right to privacy.

Specifically, the plaintiff alleges that the appellant's agents (1) conducted a series of interviews with acquaintances of the plaintiff, "questioning them about, and casting aspersions upon [his] political, social . . . racial and religious views . . . ; his integrity; his sexual proclivities and inclinations; and his personal habits" . . . ; (2) kept him under surveillance in public places for an unreasonable length of time . . . ; (3) caused him to be accosted by girls for the purpose of entrapping him into illicit relationships . . . ; (4) made threatening, harassing and obnoxious telephone calls to him . . . ; (5) tapped his telephone and eavesdropped, by means of mechanical and electronic equipment, on his private conversations with others . . . ; and (6) conducted a "continuing" and harassing investigation of him. . . .

[The court first determines that the law of the District of Columbia controls the disposition of this case, and that the District of Columbia would recognize a cause of action for invasion of privacy based on the right to be free from intrusions into private matters.]

It should be emphasized that the mere gathering of information about a particular individual does not give rise to a cause of action under this theory. Privacy is invaded only if the information sought is of a confidential nature and the defendant's conduct was unreasonably intrusive. Just as a common-law copyright is lost when material is published, so, too, there can be no invasion of privacy where the information sought is open to public view or has been voluntarily revealed to others. In order to sustain a cause of action for invasion of privacy, therefore, the plaintiff must show that the appellant's conduct was truly "intrusive" and that it was designed to elicit information which would not be available through normal inquiry or observation.

The majority of the Appellate Division in the present case stated that *all of "[t]he activities complained of"* in the first two counts constituted actionable invasions of privacy under the law of the District of Columbia. We do not agree with that sweeping determination. At most, only two of the activities charged to the appellant are, in our view, actionable as invasions of privacy under the law of the District of Columbia. . . .

Turning, then, to the particular acts charged in the complaint, we cannot find any basis for a claim of invasion of privacy, under District of Columbia law, in the allegations that the appellant, through its agents or employees, interviewed many persons who knew the plaintiff, asking questions about him and casting aspersions on his character. Although those inquiries may have uncovered information of a personal nature, it is difficult to see how they may be said to have invaded the plaintiff's privacy. Information about the plaintiff which was already known to others could hardly be regarded as private to the plaintiff. Presumably, the plaintiff had previously revealed the information to such other persons, and he would necessarily assume the risk that a friend or acquaintance in whom he had confided might breach the confidence. If, as alleged, the questions tended to disparage the plaintiff's character, his remedy would seem to be by way of an action for defamation, not for breach of his right to privacy.

Nor can we find any actionable invasion of privacy in the allegations that the appellant caused the plaintiff to be accosted by girls with illicit proposals, or that it was responsible for the making of a large number of threatening and harassing telephone calls to the plaintiff's home at odd hours. Neither of these activities, howsoever offensive and disturbing, involved intrusion for the purpose of gathering information of a private and confidential nature.

As already indicated, it is manifestly neither practical nor desirable for the law to provide a remedy against any and all activity which an individual might find annoying. On the other hand, where severe mental pain or anguish is inflicted through a deliberate and malicious campaign of harassment or intimidation, a remedy is available in the form of an action for the intentional infliction of emotional distress—the theory underlying the plaintiff's third cause of action. But the elements of such an action are decidedly different from those governing the tort of invasion of privacy, and just as we have carefully guarded against the use of prima facie tort doctrine to circumvent the limitations relating to other established tort remedies, we should be wary of any attempt to rely on the tort of invasion of privacy as a means of avoiding the more stringent pleading and proof requirements for an action for infliction of emotional distress.

Apart, however, from the foregoing allegations which we find inadequate to spell out a cause of action for invasion of privacy under District of Columbia law, the complaint contains allegations concerning other activities by the appellant or its agents which do satisfy the requirements for such a cause of action. The one which most clearly meets those requirements is the charge that the appellant and its codefendants engaged in unauthorized wiretapping and eavesdropping by mechanical and electronic means. . . . In point of fact, the appellant does not dispute this, acknowledging that, to the extent the two challenged counts charge it with wiretapping and eavesdropping, an actionable invasion of privacy has been stated.

There are additional allegations that the appellant hired people to shadow the plaintiff and keep him under surveillance. In particular, he claims that, on one occasion, one of its agents followed him into a bank, getting sufficiently close to him to see the denomination of the bills he was withdrawing from his account. From what we have already said, it is manifest that the mere observation of the plaintiff in a public place does not amount to an invasion of his privacy. But, under certain circumstances, surveillance may be so "overzealous" as to render it actionable. Whether or not the surveillance in the present case falls into this latter category will depend on the nature of the proof. A person does not automatically make public everything he does merely by being in a public place, and the mere fact that Nader was in a bank did not give anyone the right to try to discover the amount of money he was withdrawing. On the other hand, if the plaintiff acted in such a way as to reveal that fact to any casual observer, then, it may not be said that the appellant intruded into his private sphere. In any event, though, it is enough for present purposes to say that the surveillance allegation is not insufficient as a matter of law. . . .

We would but add that the allegations concerning the interviewing of third persons, the accosting by girls and the annoying and threatening telephone calls, though insufficient to support a cause of action for invasion of privacy, are pertinent to the plaintiff's third cause of action—in which those allegations are reiterated—charging the intentional infliction of emotional distress. However, as already noted, it will be necessary for the plaintiff to meet the additional requirements prescribed by the law of the District of Columbia for the maintenance of a cause of action under that theory.

The order appealed from should be affirmed, with costs, and the question certified answered in the affirmative.

[The concurring opinion of BREITEL, J., is omitted.]

For an interesting account of this case by the plaintiff's attorney, see Speiser, Lawsuit 1-118 (1980). The complaint had asked for $2 million in compensatory and $5 million in punitive damages; the case was settled before trial for $425,000.

As *Nader* illustrates, invasion of privacy by "intrusion" is not limited to physical invasions of the plaintiff's premises. Whether the plaintiff has unlawfully intruded into the plaintiff's "space" has arisen in a variety of contexts:

Eavesdropping. See, e.g., Billings v. Atkinson, 489 S.W.2d 858 (Tex. 1973) (telephone wiretapping); Dietemann v. Time, Inc., 449 F.2d 245 (9th Cir. 1971) (use of hidden camera and microphone by which conversation with plaintiff in his den relayed to tape recorder in automobile parked nearby). In both cases, the defendants were held to have invaded the plaintiffs' privacy.

Unwanted Telephone Calls. See, e.g., Beneficial Finance Co. v. Lamos, 179 N.W.2d 573 (Iowa 1970) (repeated telephone calls by a creditor to plaintiff, relating to debt, at latter's place of business not an invasion of privacy). See generally, Haiman, Speech v. Privacy: Is There a Right Not to Be Spoken To?, 67 Nw. L. Rev. 153 (1972).

Excessive Surveillance. See, e.g., Galella v. Onassis, 353 F. Supp. 196 (S.D. N.Y. 1972), *decree modified,* 487 F.2d 986 (2d Cir. 1973) (photographer's conduct in recording daily lives of wife and children of assassinated ex-president an invasion of privacy); Johnson v. Corporate Special Services, 602 So. 2d 385 (Ala. 1992) (observation of worker's compensation claimant outside his home to determine legitimacy of claim not an invasion of privacy).

Sexual Harassment. See, e.g., Busby v. Trustwal Systems Corp., 551 So. 2d 322 (Ala. 1989) (repeated offensive questions, comments and physical contacts an invasion of privacy).

B. Public Disclosure of Private Facts

Diaz v. Oakland Tribune, Inc.

139 Cal. App. 3d 118, 188 Cal. Rptr. 762 (1983)

BARRY-DEAL, A.J. Plaintiff Toni Ann Diaz (Diaz) sued the Oakland Tribune, Inc., owners and publishers of the Oakland Tribune (The Tribune), and Sidney Jones (Jones), one of its columnists, for invasion of privacy. Diaz claimed that the publication of highly embarrassing private facts in Jones' March 26, 1978, newspaper column was unwarranted and malicious and caused her to suffer severe emotional distress. The jury awarded Diaz $250,000 in compensatory damages and $525,000 in punitive damages ($25,000 against Jones and $500,000 against the Tribune). Judgment was entered on February 14, 1980. Defendants' motion for a new trial based on insufficiency of the evidence, errors of law, and excessive damages was denied. This timely appeal followed. As discussed below, we reverse the judgment because of instructional errors.

The facts are for the most part undisputed. Diaz is a transsexual. She was born in Puerto Rico in 1942 as Antonio Diaz, a male. She moved to California from New York in 1964. Suffice it to say that for most of her life Diaz suffered from a gender identification problem and the anxiety and depression that accompanied it. She testified that since she was young she had had the feeling of being a woman. . . . In 1975 gender corrective surgery was performed by the Stanford staff.

According to Diaz the surgery was a success. By all outward appearances she looked and behaved as a woman and was accepted by the public as a woman. According to her therapist, Dr. Sable, her physical and psychological identities were now in harmony.

Diaz scrupulously kept the surgery a secret from all but her immediate family and closest friends. She never sought to publicize the surgery. She changed her name to Toni Ann Diaz and made the necessary changes in her high school records, her social security records, and on her driver's license. She tried unsuccessfully to change her Puerto Rican birth certificate. She did not change the gender designation on her draft card, however, asserting that it would be a useless gesture, since she had previously been turned down for induction.

Following the surgery she no longer suffered from the psychological difficulties that had plagued her previously. In 1975 she enrolled in the College of Alameda (the College), a two-year college. . . .

In spring 1977, she was elected student body president for the 1977-1978 academic year, the first woman to hold that office. Her election and an unsuccessful attempt to unseat her were reported in the College newspaper, the Reporter, in the May 17, June 1, and June 14, 1977, editions. At no time during the election did Diaz reveal any information about her sex-change operation.

In 1977 Diaz was also selected to be the student body representative to the Peralta Community College Board of Trustees (the Board). Diaz's selection as student body representative, together with her photograph, appeared in the June 1977 issue of the Peralta Colleges Bulletin.

Near the middle of her term as student body president, Diaz became embroiled in a controversy in which she charged the College administrators with misuse of student funds. The March 15, 1978, issue of the Tribune quoted Diaz's charge that her signature had improperly been "rubber stamped" on checks drawn from the associated students' accounts.

On March 24, 1978, an article in the Alameda Times-Star, a daily newspaper, mentioned Diaz in connection with the charge of misuse of student body funds.

Shortly after the controversy arose, Jones was informed by several confidential sources that Diaz was a man. Jones considered the matter newsworthy if he could verify the information. Jones testified that he inspected the Tribune's own files and spoke with an unidentified number of persons at the College to confirm this information. It was not until Richard Paoli, the city editor of the Tribune, checked Oakland city police records that the information that Diaz was born a man was verified. The evidence reveals that in 1970 or 1971, prior to the surgery, Diaz was arrested in Oakland for soliciting an undercover police officer, a misdemeanor.

On March 26, 1978, the following item appeared in Jones' newspaper column: "More Education Stuff: The students at the College of Alameda will be surprised to learn their student body president, Toni Diaz, is no lady, but is in fact a man whose real name is Antonio.

"Now I realize, that in these times, such a matter is no big deal, but I suspect his female classmates in P.E. 97 may wish to make other showering arrangements."

Upon reading the article, Diaz became very depressed and was forced to reveal her status, which she had worked hard to conceal. Diaz testified that as a result of the article she suffered from insomnia, nightmares, and memory lapses. She also delayed her enrollment in Mills College, scheduled for that fall.

In her complaint Diaz did not charge that any of the information was untrue, only that defendants invaded her privacy by the unwarranted publicity of intimate facts. Defendants defended on the ground that the matter was newsworthy and hence was constitutionally protected.

At trial the jury returned a special verdict and found that (1) defendants did publicly disclose a fact concerning Diaz; (2) the fact was private and not public; (3) the fact was *not* newsworthy; (4) the fact was highly offensive to a reasonable person of ordinary sensibilities; (5) defendants disclosed the fact with knowledge that it was highly offensive or with reckless disregard of whether it was highly offensive; and (6) the disclosure proximately caused injury or damage to Diaz.

In this appeal defendants challenge the jury's finding on issues Nos. (2) and (3) above. Defendants also urge instructional error and attack the awards of compensatory and punitive damages. Before we address these issues, it is useful briefly to discuss the competing rights involved herein: the right to privacy and the right to free speech and press.

Background

The concept of a common-law right to privacy was first developed in a landmark article by Warren and Brandeis, The Right to Privacy (1890) 4 Harv. L. Rev. 193, and has been adopted in virtually every state. The specific privacy right with which we are concerned is the right to be free from public disclosure of private embarrassing facts, in short, "the right to be let alone." (Melvin v. Reid (1931) 112 Cal. App. 285, 289, 297 P. 91.) . . .

The public disclosure cause of action is distinct from a suit for libel or "false light," since the plaintiff herein does not challenge the accuracy of the information published, but asserts that the publicity is so intimate and unwarranted as to outrage the community's notion of decency. . . .

Of course, the right to privacy is not absolute and must be balanced against the often competing constitutional right of the press to publish newsworthy matters. . . . The First Amendment protection from tort liability is necessary if the press is to carry out its constitutional obligation to keep the public informed so that they may make intelligent decisions on matters important to a self-governing people. (See Cox Broadcasting Corp. v. Cohn, supra, 420 U.S. at pp. 491-493, 95 S. Ct. at pp. 1044-1045.)

However, the newsworthy privilege is not without limitation. Where the publicity is so offensive as to constitute a "morbid and sensational prying into private lives for its own sake, . . .' " it serves no legitimate public interest and is not deserving of protection. (See Virgil v. Time, Inc., supra, 527 F.2d at p. 1129; Rest. 2d Torts, §652D, Com. *h.*)

As discerned from the decisions of our courts, the public disclosure tort contains the following elements: (1) public disclosure (2) of a private fact

(3) which would be offensive and objectionable to the reasonable person and (4) which is not of legitimate public concern. . . .

Instructional Error

At the outset defendants urge that the trial court misinstructed the jury (1) on the right to privacy and (2) that defendants had the burden of proving newsworthiness. We agree and find that either of these errors was prejudicial and requires reversal.

1. The Right to Privacy

Plaintiff Diaz proffered a jury instruction properly defining the right to privacy.[12] However, the trial court, sua sponte, added the following language: "It prevents business or government interests from misusing information gathered for one purpose in order to serve other purposes, or to embarrass us. *This right should be abridged only when there is a compelling public need.*" (Emphasis added.)

The language contained in the last sentence was taken from White v. Davis (1975) 13 Cal. 3d 757, 120 Cal. Rptr. 94, 533 P.2d 222. The trial court misplaced its reliance on that case. In *White,* supra, plaintiff challenged covert police surveillance of University of California at Los Angeles students in their classrooms. There, the court required the *government* to demonstrate a " 'compelling public need' " for the intrusion. (Id., at p. 775, 120 Cal. Rptr. 94, 533 P.2d 222.) That case did not attempt to balance the competing rights of free speech and press against the right to privacy. Rather, it recognized the heavy burden on the government to justify interference with First Amendment freedoms. (Id., at pp. 767-773, 120 Cal. Rptr. 94, 553 P.2d 222.)

Unlike the government's activity in *White,* defendants' publication of the article is a preferred right which is not encumbered by the presumption of illegality. Defendants enjoy the right to publish information in which the public has a *legitimate interest.* (See Briscoe v. Reader's Digest Association, Inc., supra, 4 Cal. 3d at p. 541, 93 Cal. Rptr. 866, 483 P.2d 34; Virgil v. Time, Inc., supra, 527 F.2d at pp. 1128-1129; Rest. 2d Torts, supra, §652D, Com. *d.*) To require that the article meet the higher " 'compelling public need' " standard would severely abridge this constitutionally recognized right of free speech and press.

After examining the entire record, we cannot say that this error was harmless. The instruction misstated the law concerning defendants' right

12. The complete instruction reads as follows: "The California Constitution provides that all persons have an inalienable right of privacy. It is the right to live one's life in seclusion, without being subjected to unwarranted or undesirable publicity. In short, it's the right to be left alone."

to publish newsworthy matters and necessarily lessened plaintiff's burden of proof. Since plaintiff's verdict may have rested on this erroneous theory, the judgment must be reversed. . . .

2. The Burden of Proving Newsworthiness

[The court ruled that the burden to prove that the story lacked newsworthiness is on the plaintiff; its discussion of this point is omitted.]

The Public Disclosure Tort

1. Private Facts

Defendants next argue that the evidence establishes as a matter of law that the fact of Diaz's original gender was a matter of public record, and therefore its publicity was not actionable.[16] In support of their contention defendants rely on Cox Broadcasting Corp. v. Cohn, supra, 420 U.S. 469, 95 S. Ct. 1029, 43 L. Ed. 2d 328. That reliance is misplaced.

Generally speaking, matter which is already in the public domain is not private, and its publication is protected. . . .

In *Cox Broadcasting Corp.*, the Supreme Court ruled that Cohn, the father of a deceased rape victim, could not maintain a disclosure action against media defendants who identified Cohn's daughter as the victim during the television coverage of the murder trial. (Cox Broadcasting Corp. v. Cohn, supra, 420 U.S. at pp. 496-497, 95 S. Ct. at 1046-1047.) Central to the court's conclusion was the fact that the reporter obtained the victim's name from the indictment, which had been shown to him in open court. (Id., at p. 496, 95 S. Ct. at 1046.)

In a very narrow holding, the court ruled that a state may not impose sanctions on the accurate publication of the name of a rape victim obtained from judicial records which are maintained in connection with a public prosecution and which themselves are open to public inspection. (Id., at p. 491, 95 S. Ct. at 1044.) Importantly, the court expressly refused to address the broader question of whether the truthful publication of facts obtained from public records can ever be subjected to civil or criminal liability. (Ibid.)

Because of its narrow holding, *Cox Broadcasting Corp.* gives us little guidance.

Here there is no evidence to suggest that the fact of Diaz's gender-

16. Defendants do not challenge the jury's findings that (1) the matter was publicized and (2) the fact was highly offensive to a reasonable person. There is ample evidence in the record to support these findings.

corrective surgery was part of the public record. To the contrary, the evidence reveals that Diaz took affirmative steps to conceal this fact by changing her driver's license, social security, and high school records, and by lawfully changing her name. The police records, upon which Jones relied, contained information concerning one Antonio Diaz. No mention was made of Diaz's new name or gender. In order to draw the connection, Jones relied upon unidentified confidential sources. Under these circumstances, we conclude that Diaz's sexual identity was a private matter.

We also do not consider Diaz's *Puerto Rican* birth certificate to be a public record in this instance. In any event, defendants did not rely on that document and cannot be heard to argue that the information contained therein is public.

Moreover, matter which was once of public record may be protected as private facts where disclosure of that information would not be newsworthy. (See Briscoe v. Reader's Digest Association, Inc., supra, 4 Cal. 3d at pp. 537-538, 93 Cal. Rptr. 866, 483 P.2d 34 [publication of identity of ex-offender for past crime was held to be improper]; Melvin v. Reid, supra, 112 Cal. App. at pp. 290-291, 297 P. 91 [disclosure of plaintiff's past life as a prostitute, seven years after she reformed, was actionable].)

2. Newsworthiness

As discussed above, whether the fact of Diaz's sexual identity was newsworthy is measured along a sliding scale of competing interests; the individual's right to keep private facts from the public's gaze versus the public's right to know. . . . In an effort to reconcile these competing interests, our courts have settled on a three-part test for determining whether matter published is newsworthy: " '[1] the social value of the facts published, [2] the depth of the article's intrusion into ostensibly private affairs, and [3] the extent to which the party voluntarily acceded to a position of public notoriety.' " (Briscoe v. Reader's Digest Association, Inc., supra, 4 Cal. 3d at p. 541, 93 Cal. Rptr. 866, 483 P.2d 34.)

Defendants argue that in light of Diaz's position as the first female student body president of the College, her "questionable gender" was a newsworthy item. As a subsidiary contention, they assert that the issue of newsworthiness should not have been submitted to the jury. We address the latter contention first.

a. *Newsworthiness as a Jury Question*

Whether a publication is or is not newsworthy depends upon contemporary community mores and standards of decency. . . . This is largely a question of fact, which a jury is uniquely well-suited to decide. . . .

Defendants argue that the right to publish would suffer at the hands of a jury which, unlike the trial judge, would be more likely to use a general verdict in order to punish unpopular speech and persons. In Virgil v. Time, Inc., supra, 527 F.2d 1122, the Court of Appeals for the Ninth Circuit in a California case recognized this danger. However, that court concluded that any risk of prejudice may be checked by close judicial scrutiny at the stages of litigation such as summary judgment, directed verdict, and judgment notwithstanding the verdict. (Id., at p. 1130.) Our trial court judges are entirely capable of correcting such jury overreaching. . . .

b. Newsworthiness as a Matter of Law

Next, defendants urge that, as the first female student body president of the College, Diaz was a public figure, and the fact of her sexual identity was a newsworthy item as a matter of law. We disagree.

It is well settled that persons who voluntarily seek public office or willingly become involved in public affairs waive their right to privacy on matters connected with their public conduct. . . . The reason behind this rule is that the public should be afforded every opportunity of learning about any facet which may affect that person's fitness for office. . . .

However, the extent to which Diaz voluntarily acceded to a position of public notoriety and the degree to which she opened her private life are questions of fact. . . . As student body president, Diaz was a public figure for some purposes. However, applying the three-part test enunciated in *Briscoe,* we cannot state that the fact of her gender was newsworthy per se.

Nor does the fact that she was the first woman student body president, in itself, warrant that her entire private life be open to public inspection. The public arena entered by Diaz is concededly small. Public figures more celebrated than she are entitled to keep some information of their domestic activities and sexual relations private. . . .

Nor is there merit to defendant's claim that the changing roles of women in society make this story newsworthy. This assertion rings hollow. The tenor of the article was by no means an attempt to enlighten the public on a contemporary social issue. Rather, as Jones himself admitted, the article was directed to the students at the College about their newly elected president. Moreover, Jones' attempt at humor at Diaz's expense removes all pretense that the article was meant to educate the reading public. The social utility of the information must be viewed in context, and not based upon some arguably meritorious and unintended purpose.

Therefore, we conclude that the jury was the proper body to answer the question whether the article was newsworthy or whether it extended beyond the bounds of decency.

Insufficient Evidence of Malice

Defendants next urge that the award of punitive damages was improper, since there was insufficient evidence to support a finding of malice on the part of either defendant. The evidence demonstrated that Jones published the article without first contacting Diaz, although he knew that the information contained therein would have a "devastating" impact on her. He testified that he attempted to obtain Diaz's telephone number from his unidentified sources but was unsuccessful. He admitted that he never telephoned the College in order to contact Diaz. Jones also stated that his comment about Diaz's classmates in "P.E. 97" making other shower arrangements was a joke, an attempt to be "flip."

In order to justify the imposition of punitive damages, "the defendant ' ". . . must act with the intent to vex, injure, or annoy, or with a conscious disregard of the plaintiff's rights." ' " (Taylor v. Superior Court (1979) 24 Cal. 3d 890, 895, 157 Cal. Rptr. 693, 598 P.2d 854, emphasis omitted) . . . Viewing the article as a whole, as well as Jones' conduct in preparing the article, we cannot say as a matter of law that there was insufficient evidence to support a finding of malice.

Here Jones knew that Diaz would certainly suffer severe emotional distress from the publicity alone. Nevertheless, he added to the indignity by making Diaz the brunt of a joke. The defendants' knowledge of the extent and severity of plaintiff's injuries is relevant to a finding of malice. . . . The jury could reasonably have inferred from these facts that Jones acted with the intent to outrage or humiliate Diaz or that he published the article with a conscious disregard of her rights.

The fact that Jones verified the story with unidentified sources does not negate the finding of malice. The jury could well have concluded that Jones' effort to discuss the article with Diaz was de minimis when compared to the magnitude of the expected harm. This is especially true since Jones was under no deadline to publish this article. Under these circumstances, the jury could have reasonably concluded that Jones' conduct evidenced a callous and conscious disregard for Diaz's privacy interests. . . . Accordingly, the jury acted well within its discretion in awarding punitive damages.

The Oakland Tribune, Inc., was also liable for punitive damages since the newspaper publishing company reviewed and approved Jones' article for publication. . . .

We are mindful of the dangerous, inhibiting effect on speech and press a large punitive damage award can have. . . . If upon retrial the plaintiff recovers a judgment, we caution the trial court to scrutinize strictly any award of punitive damages to ensure that it is not used to silence unpopular persons or speech and that it does not exceed the proper level necessary to punish and deter similar behavior. . . .

Excessive Compensatory Damage Award

Finally, defendants urge that the compensatory damage award was excessive. The jury awarded Diaz $250,000, largely for emotional and psychological injury caused by the article. Diaz's special damages for psychotherapy approximated $800.

The evidence adduced at trial established that following the publication of the article Diaz became very depressed and withdrawn. She suffered from insomnia and experienced nightmares. She had frequent memory lapses and experienced difficulty in her social relationships. As a result, in September 1978 she began psychotherapy treatments with Allen Sable, Ph.D.

The actual injury involved herein is not limited to out-of-pocket loss. It generally includes "impairment of reputation and standing in the community, personal humiliation, and mental anguish and suffering." (See Gertz v. Robert Welch, Inc., supra, 418 U.S. at p. 350, 94 S. Ct. at p. 3012.) The harm Diaz alleged to have suffered is not easily quantifiable, and the amount of damages must necessarily be left to the sound discretion of the jury. . . .

As a rule all presumptions are in favor of the judgment. . . . A reviewing court must not interfere with the verdict unless it can be said that it was the result of "passion or prejudice" on the part of the jury. . . .

Here the jury fixed the damages after hearing the evidence and being properly instructed. The evidence of Diaz's emotional distress and suffering was uncontradicted. That Diaz was able to earn high marks in her classes after the incident does not necessarily minimize or negate the emotional trauma she suffered and will continue to suffer.

Also, the trial judge denied a motion for a new trial based on this same issue. While that determination is not binding upon this court, it is entitled to great weight. . . .

The jury and the trial judge were in the best position to evaluate the scope and severity of Diaz's injuries. They heard the testimony and observed the witnesses. Although the amount of the award is high, it cannot be said that it is so grossly disproportionate, considering the past and future pain and humiliation, as to be excessive as a matter of law.

The judgment is reversed.

SCOTT, ACTING, P.J., concurs. [The concurring opinion of FEINBERG, J., is omitted.]

The court in *Diaz* did not indicate a clear distinction between public figures and private persons, as does the post-*New York Times* law of defamation, for the purposes of the public disclosure tort. Nor does §652D of the Restatement (Second) of Torts. This section bases liability on whether the matter "would be highly offensive to a reasonable person" and "is not of a legitimate concern to the public." The comments refer to "the customs of the time and place," and to "the customs and conventions of the community." It is, Comment *h* states, a "matter of the community mores." Even a motion picture actress, this comment asserts, is entitled to keep some aspects of her life to herself.

But in California, public disclosure of the plaintiff's sex life is not always actionable. In Sipple v. The Chronicle Publishing Co., 154 Cal. App. 3d 1040, 201 Cal. Rptr. 665 (1984), the court upheld summary judgment in a case in which the defendants published the fact that the plaintiff was a homosexual. The plaintiff had grabbed the arm of a person about to shoot the then President Ford. In reporting the story, the defendants disclosed the fact that the plaintiff was a "prominent member of the San Francisco gay community." The court ruled that the fact of the plaintiff's homosexuality was a public, rather than a private, fact because he was well known in various homosexual communities. The court also ruled that in any event, the plaintiff's homosexuality was newsworthy. As to this, in California the newsworthiness of a story may be as much influenced by the style in which the information is presented as by its substance:

> Moreover, and perhaps even more to the point, the record shows that the publications were not motivated by a morbid and sensational prying into appellant's private life but rather were prompted by legitimate political considerations, i.e., to dispel the false public opinion that gays were timid, weak and unheroic figures and to raise the equally important political question whether the President of the United States entertained a discriminatory attitude or bias against a minority group such as homosexuals.

4 Cal. 3d at 1049, 201 Cal. Rptr. at 670.

Some courts do, however, give considerable weight to whether the plaintiff is a public figure. One of the leading cases is Sidis v. F-R Pub. Corp., 113 F.2d 806 (2d Cir.) *cert. denied,* 311 U.S. 711 (1940). The plaintiff as a child was a mathematical genius; he had lectured to distinguished mathematicians at the age of 11, and graduated from Harvard when he was 16. He dropped from public view for several years, until an article published by the defendant in The New Yorker, entitled "Where Are They Now," detailed the idiosyncratic habits and characteristics of the plaintiff and brought him back to the public gaze. In affirming the trial judge's dismissal of the action, the court said (113 F.2d at 809):

> William James Sidis was once a public figure. As a child prodigy, he excited both admiration and curiosity. Of him great deeds were expected. In 1910, he was a person about whom the newspapers might display a legitimate

intellectual interest in the sense meant by Warren and Brandeis, as distinguished from a trivial and unseemly curiosity. But the precise motives of the press we regard as unimportant. And even if Sidis had loathed public attention at that time, we think his uncommon achievements and personality would have made the attention permissible. Since then Sidis has cloaked himself in obscurity, but his subsequent history, containing as it did the answer to the question of whether or not he had fulfilled his early promise, was still a matter of public concern. The article in The New Yorker sketched the life of an unusual personality, and it possessed considerable popular news interest.

We express no comment on whether or not the news worthiness of the matter printed will always constitute a complete defense. Revelations may be so intimate and so unwarranted in view of the victim's position as to outrage the community's notions of decency. But when focused upon public characters, truthful comments upon dress, speech, habits, and the ordinary aspects of personality will usually not transgress this line. Regrettably or not, the misfortunes and frailties of neighbors and "public figures" are subjects of considerable interest and discussion to the rest of the population. And when such are the mores of the community, it would be unwise for a court to bar their expression in the newspapers, books, and magazines of the day.

The court in *Sidis* took the position that "once a public figure, always a public figure," a position with which some other courts have agreed. See, e.g., Montesano v. Donrey Medial Group, 99 Nev. 644, 668 P.2d 1081 (1983), *cert. denied,* 466 U.S. 959 (1984). Other courts, including California's, have rejected this notion. In Briscoe v. Reader's Digest Association, Inc., 4 Cal. 3d 529, 483 P.2d 34, 93 Cal. Rptr. 866 (1971), for example, the complaint alleged that the defendant named the plaintiff in a magazine article on truck hijacking in connection with an 11-year-old incident in which the plaintiff hijacked a truck and had a gun battle with the police. The complaint also alleged that, following the incident, the plaintiff became rehabilitated and led a respectable life, and that the article caused his daughter and his friends to scorn and abandon him. In ruling that the complaint stated a cause of action, the court stated (4 Cal. 3d at 543, 483 P.2d at 44, 93 Cal. Rptr. at 876):

> We do not hold today that plaintiff must prevail in his action. It is for the trier of fact to determine (1) whether plaintiff has become a rehabilitated member of society, (2) whether identifying him as a former criminal would be highly offensive and injurious to the reasonable man, (3) whether defendant published this information with a reckless disregard for its offensiveness, and (4) whether any independent justification for printing plaintiff's identity existed. We hold today only that, as pleaded, plaintiff has stated a valid cause of action, sustaining the demurrer to plaintiff's complaint was improper, and that the ensuing judgment must therefore be reversed.

Not all courts have accepted the tort of public disclosure of private facts. In Hall v. Post, 323 N.C. 259, 372 S.E.2d 711 (1988), the court asserted that with respect to facts that are "newsworthy," the free speech clause of the First Amendment to the Constitution of the United States generates constitutional problems. If the disclosed facts are private, the tort would overlap intentional infliction of emotional harm. The court concluded (323 N.C. at 269-270, 372 S.E.2d at 717):

> [A]ny possible benefits which might accrue to plaintiffs are entirely insufficient to justify adoption of the constitutionally suspect private facts invasion of privacy tort which punishes defendants for the typically American act of broadly proclaiming the truth by speech or writing.

The Florida Star v. B.J.F.

491 U.S. 524, 109 S. Ct. 2603, 105 L. Ed. 2d 443 (1989)

JUSTICE MARSHALL delivered the opinion of the Court.

Florida Stat. §794.03 (1987) makes it unlawful to "print, publish, or broadcast . . . in any instrument of mass communication" the name of the victim of a sexual offense.[3] Pursuant to this statute, appellant The Florida Star was found civilly liable for publishing the name of a rape victim which it had obtained from a publicly released police report. The issue presented here is whether this result comports with the First Amendment. We hold that it does not.

[The plaintiff reported to the county sheriff's department that she had been raped and robbed by an unknown person. The report of the department contained the name of the plaintiff, and was put in the press room, where it was seen by a reporter for the defendant's newspaper. The reporter prepared a story for the "Police Reports" section of the newspaper, which included the name of the plaintiff. The story was published as written, although the naming of a rape victim was contrary to the policy of the paper. The plaintiff sued the sheriff's department and the defendant, alleging a violation of §794.03. The plaintiff settled with the department before trial for $2,500.

At the trial, the plaintiff testified as to the emotional harm she suffered as a result of the article, stemming in part from phone calls to her mother from a man who said that he would rape her again. The trial judge denied the defendant's motion for a directed verdict, and the jury returned a verdict against the defendant for $75,000 in compensatory and $25,000 in punitive

3. The statute provides in its entirety:

> Unlawful to publish or broadcast information identifying sexual offense victim.— No person shall print, publish, or broadcast, or cause or allow to be printed, published, or broadcast, in any instrument of mass communication the name, address, or other identifying fact or information of the victim of any sexual offense within this chapter. An offense under this section shall constitute a misdemeanor of the second degree, punishable as provided in §775.082, §775.083, or §775.084.

Fla. Stat. §794.03 (1987).

damages. The trial judge offset the amount paid by the sheriff's department against the compensatory award. The judgment for the plaintiff on the jury verdict was affirmed by the Florida District Court of Appeal, and the Florida Supreme Court denied review.]

II

The tension between the right which the First Amendment accords to a free press, on the one hand, and the protections which various statutes and common-law doctrines accord to personal privacy against the publication of truthful information, on the other, is a subject we have addressed several times in recent years. Our decisions in cases involving government attempts to sanction the accurate dissemination of information as invasive of privacy, have not, however, exhaustively considered this conflict. On the contrary, although our decisions have without exception upheld the press' right to publish, we have emphasized each time that we were resolving this conflict only as it arose in a discrete factual context.

The parties to this case frame their contentions in light of a trilogy of cases which have presented, in different contexts, the conflict between truthful reporting and state-protected privacy interests. In Cox Broadcasting Corp. v. Cohn, 420 U.S. 469, 95 S. Ct. 1029, 43 L. Ed. 2d 328 (1975), we found unconstitutional a civil damages award entered against a television station for broadcasting the name of a rape-murder victim which the station had obtained from courthouse records. In Oklahoma Publishing Co. v. Oklahoma County District Court, 430 U.S. 308, 97 S. Ct. 1045, 51 L. Ed. 2d 355 (1977), we found unconstitutional a state court's pretrial order enjoining the media from publishing the name or photograph of an 11-year-old boy in connection with a juvenile proceeding involving that child which reporters had attended. Finally, in Smith v. Daily Mail Publishing Co., 443 U.S. 97, 99 S. Ct. 2667, 61 L. Ed. 2d 399 (1979), we found unconstitutional the indictment of two newspapers for violating a state statute forbidding newspapers to publish, without written approval of the juvenile court, the name of any youth charged as a juvenile offender. The papers had learned about a shooting by monitoring a police band radio frequency and had obtained the name of the alleged juvenile assailant from witnesses, the police, and a local prosecutor.

Appellant takes the position that this case is indistinguishable from *Cox Broadcasting*. Alternatively, it urges that our decisions in the above trilogy, and in other cases in which we have held that the right of the press to publish truth overcame asserted interests other than personal privacy, can be distilled to yield a broader First Amendment principle that the press may never be punished, civilly or criminally, for publishing the truth. Appellee counters that the privacy trilogy is inapposite, because in each case the private information already appeared on a "public record," and because the privacy interests at stake were far less profound than in the present case. In the alternative, appellee urges that *Cox Broadcasting* be overruled and replaced with a categorical rule that publication of the name of a rape victim never enjoys constitutional protection.

We conclude that imposing damages on appellant for publishing B.J.F.'s name violates the First Amendment, although not for either of the reasons appellant urges. Despite the strong resemblance this case bears to *Cox Broadcasting,* that case cannot fairly be read as controlling here. The name of the rape victim in that case was obtained from courthouse records that were open to public inspection, a fact which Justice White's opinion for the Court repeatedly noted. . . . Significantly, one of the reasons we gave in *Cox Broadcasting* for invalidating the challenged damages award was the important role the press plays in subjecting trials to public scrutiny and thereby helping guarantee their fairness. That role is not directly compromised where, as here, the information in question comes from a police report prepared and disseminated at a time at which not only had no adversarial criminal proceedings begun, but no suspect had been identified.

Nor need we accept appellant's invitation to hold broadly that truthful publication may never be punished consistent with the First Amendment. Our cases have carefully eschewed reaching this ultimate question, mindful that the future may bring scenarios which prudence counsels our not resolving anticipatorily. See, e.g., Near v. Minnesota ex rel. Olson, 283 U.S. 697, 716, 51 S. Ct. 625, 75 L. Ed. 1357 (1931) (hypothesizing "publication of the sailing dates of transports or the number and location of troops"); see also Garrison v. Louisiana, 379 U.S. 64, 72, n.8, 74, 85 S. Ct. 209, 215, n.8, 216, 13 L. Ed. 2d 125 (1964) (endorsing absolute defense of truth "where discussion of public affairs is concerned," but leaving unsettled the constitutional implications of truthfulness "in the discrete area of purely private libels"). . . . We continue to believe that the sensitivity and significance of the interests presented in clashes between First Amendment and privacy rights counsel relying on limited principles that sweep no more broadly than the appropriate context of the instant case.

In our view, this case is appropriately analyzed with reference to such a limited First Amendment principle. It is the one, in fact, which we articulated in *Daily Mail* in our synthesis of prior cases involving attempts to punish truthful publication: "[I]f a newspaper lawfully obtains truthful information about a matter of public significance then state officials may not constitutionally punish publication of the information, absent a need to further a state interest of the highest order." 443 U.S., at 103, 99 S. Ct., at 2671. . . .

. . . Appellee argues that a rule punishing publication furthers three closely related interests: the privacy of victims of sexual offenses; the physical safety of such victims, who may be targeted for retaliation if their names become known to their assailants; and the goal of encouraging victims of such crimes to report these offenses without fear of exposure.

At a time in which we are daily reminded of the tragic reality of rape, it is undeniable that these are highly significant interests, a fact underscored by the Florida Legislature's explicit attempt to protect these interests by enacting a criminal statute prohibiting much dissemination of victim identities. We accordingly do not rule out the possibility that, in a proper case, imposing civil sanctions for publication of the name of a rape victim might be so overwhelmingly necessary to advance these interests as to satisfy the *Daily Mail* standard. For three independent reasons, however, imposing liability for publication under the circumstances of this case is too precipitous a means of advancing these interests to convince us that there is a "need" within the meaning of the *Daily Mail* formulation for Florida to take this extreme step. . . .

First is the manner in which appellant obtained the identifying information in question. As we have noted, where the government itself provides information to the media, it is most appropriate to assume that the government had, but failed to utilize, far more limited means of guarding against dissemination than the extreme step of punishing truthful speech. That assumption is richly borne out in this case. B.J.F.'s identity would never have come to light were it not for the erroneous, if inadvertent, inclusion by the Department of her full name in an incident report made available in a pressroom open to the public. . . .

That appellant gained access to the information in question through a government news release makes it especially likely that, if liability were to be imposed, self-censorship would result. Reliance on a news release is a paradigmatically "routine newspaper reporting techniqu[e]." *Daily Mail,* 443 U.S., at 103, 99 S. Ct., at 2671. The government's issuance of such a release, without qualification, can only convey to recipients that the government considered dissemination lawful, and indeed expected the recipients to disseminate the information further. Had appellant merely reproduced the news release prepared and released by the Department, imposing civil damages would surely violate the First Amendment. The fact that appellant converted the police report into a news story by adding the linguistic connecting tissue necessary to transform the report's facts into full sentences cannot change this result.

A second problem with Florida's imposition of liability for publication is the broad sweep of the negligence per se standard applied under the civil cause of action implied from §794.03. Unlike claims based on the common law tort of invasion of privacy, see Restatement (Second) of Torts §652D (1977), civil actions based on §794.03 require no case-by-case findings that the disclosure of a fact about a person's private life was one that a reasonable person would find highly offensive. On the contrary, under the per se theory of negligence adopted by the courts below, liability follows automatically from publication. This is so regardless of whether the identity of the victim is already known throughout the community; whether the victim has voluntarily called public attention to the offense; or whether the identity of the victim has otherwise become a reasonable subject of public concern—

because, perhaps, questions have arisen whether the victim fabricated an assault by a particular person. Nor is there a scienter requirement of any kind under §794.03, engendering the perverse result that truthful publications challenged pursuant to this cause of action are less protected by the First Amendment than even the least protected defamatory falsehoods: those involving purely private figures, where liability is evaluated under a standard, usually applied by a jury, of ordinary negligence. . . .

Third, and finally, the facial underinclusiveness of §794.03 raises serious doubts about whether Florida is, in fact, serving, with this statute, the significant interests which appellee invokes in support of affirmance. Section 794.03 prohibits the publication of identifying information only if this information appears in an "instrument of mass communication," a term the statute does not define. Section 794.03 does not prohibit the spread by other means of the identities of victims of sexual offenses. An individual who maliciously spreads word of the identity of a rape victim is thus not covered, despite the fact that the communication of such information to persons who live near, or work with, the victim may have consequences as devastating as the exposure of her name to large numbers of strangers. . . .

When a State attempts the extraordinary measure of punishing truthful publication in the name of privacy, it must demonstrate its commitment to advancing this interest by applying its prohibition evenhandedly, to the small-time disseminator as well as the media giant. Where important First Amendment interests are at stake, the mass scope of disclosure is not an acceptable surrogate for injury. A ban on disclosures effected by "instrument[s] of mass communication" simply cannot be defended on the ground that partial prohibitions may effect partial relief. . . .

III

Our holding today is limited. We do not hold that truthful publication is automatically constitutionally protected, or that there is no zone of personal privacy within which the State may protect the individual from intrusion by the press, or even that a State may never punish publication of the name of a victim of a sexual offense. We hold only that where a newspaper publishes truthful information which it has lawfully obtained, punishment may lawfully be imposed, if at all, only when narrowly tailored to a state interest of the highest order, and that no such interest is satisfactorily served by imposing liability under §794.03 to appellant under the facts of this case. The decision below is therefore

Reversed.

[The concurring opinion of JUSTICE SCALIA is omitted.]

JUSTICE WHITE, with whom THE CHIEF JUSTICE and JUSTICE O'CONNOR join, dissenting.

"Short of homicide, [rape] is the 'ultimate violation of self.' " Coker v.

Georgia, 433 U.S. 584, 597, 97 S. Ct. 2861, 2869, 53 L. Ed. 2d 982 (1977) (opinion of White, J.). For B.J.F., however, the violation she suffered at a rapist's knife-point marked only the beginning of her ordeal. A week later, while her assailant was still at large, an account of this assault—identifying by name B.J.F. as the victim—was published by The Florida Star. As a result, B.J.F. received harassing phone calls, required mental health counseling, was forced to move from her home, and was even threatened with being raped again.

Yet today, the Court holds that a jury award of $75,000 to compensate B.J.F. for the harm she suffered due to the Star's negligence is at odds with the First Amendment. I do not accept this result.

The Court reaches its conclusion based on an analysis of three of our precedents and a concern with three particular aspects of the judgment against appellant. I consider each of these points in turn, and then consider some of the larger issues implicated by today's decision.

I

The Court finds its result compelled, or at least supported in varying degrees, by three of our prior cases: Cox Broadcasting Corp. v. Cohn, 420 U.S. 469, 95 S. Ct. 1029, 43 L. Ed. 2d 328 (1975); Oklahoma Publishing Co. v. Oklahoma County District Court, 430 U.S. 308, 97 S. Ct. 1045, 51 L. Ed. 2d 355 (1977); and Smith v. Daily Mail Publishing Co., 443 U.S. 97, 99 S. Ct. 2667, 61 L. Ed. 2d 399 (1979). I disagree. None of these cases requires the harsh outcome reached today.

Cox Broadcasting reversed a damages award entered against a television station, which had obtained a rape victim's name from public records maintained in connection with the judicial proceedings brought against her assailants. While there are similarities, critical aspects of that case make it wholly distinguishable from this one. First, in *Cox Broadcasting,* the victim's name had been disclosed in the hearing where her assailants pleaded guilty; and, as we recognized, judicial records have always been considered public information in this country. . . . In fact, even the earliest notion of privacy rights exempted the information contained in judicial records from its protections. See Warren & Brandeis, The Right to Privacy, 4 Harv. L. Rev. 193, 216-217 (1890). Second, unlike the incident report at issue here, which was meant by state law to be withheld from public release, the judicial proceedings at issue in *Cox Broadcasting* were open as a matter of state law. Thus, in *Cox Broadcasting,* the state-law scheme made public disclosure of the victim's name almost inevitable; here, Florida law forbids such disclosure. See Fla. Stat. §794.03 (1987).

These facts—that the disclosure came in judicial proceedings, which were open to the public—were critical to our analysis in *Cox Broadcasting.* The distinction between that case and this one is made obvious by the penultimate paragraph of *Cox Broadcasting*:

> We are reluctant to embark on a course that would make *public records generally available to the media* but would forbid their publication if offensive. . . . [T]he First and Fourteenth Amendments will not allow exposing the press to liability for truthfully publishing information *released to the public in official court records. If there are privacy interests to be protected in judicial proceedings, the States must respond by means which avoid public documentation or other exposure of private information.* . . . Once true information is disclosed in *public court documents open to public inspection,* the press cannot be sanctioned for publishing it.

Cox Broadcasting, supra, at 496, 95 S. Ct., at 1047 (emphasis added).

Cox Broadcasting stands for the proposition that the State cannot make the press its first line of defense in withholding private information from the public—it cannot ask the press to secrete private facts that the State makes no effort to safeguard in the first place. In this case, however, the State has undertaken "means which avoid [but obviously, not altogether prevent] public documentation or other exposure of private information." No doubt this is why the Court frankly admits that "*Cox Broadcasting* . . . cannot fairly be read as controlling here.". . .

II

We are left, then, to wonder whether the three "independent reasons" the Court cites for reversing the judgment for B.J.F. support its result.

The first of these reasons relied on by the Court is the fact "appellant gained access to [B.J.F.'s name] through a government news release." "The government's issuance of such a release, without qualification, can only convey to recipients that the government considered dissemination lawful," the Court suggests. So described, this case begins to look like the situation in *Oklahoma Publishing,* where a judge invited reporters into his courtroom, but then tried to forbid them from reporting on the proceedings they observed. But this case is profoundly different. Here, the "release" of information provided by the government was not, as the Court says, "without qualification." As the Star's own reporter conceded at trial, the crime incident report that inadvertently included B.J.F.'s name was posted in a room that contained signs making it clear that the names of rape victims were not matters of public record, and were not to be published. The Star's reporter indicated that she understood that she "[was not] allowed to take down that information" (i.e., B.J.F.'s name) and that she "[was] not supposed to take the information from the police department." Thus, by her own admission the posting of the incident report did not convey to the Star's reporter the idea that "the government considered dissemination lawful"; the Court's suggestion to the contrary is inapt.

Instead, Florida has done precisely what we suggested, in *Cox Broadcasting,* that States wishing to protect the privacy rights of rape victims might do: "respond [to the challenge] by means which *avoid* public documentation or other exposure of private information." 420 U.S., at 496, 95 S. Ct., at 1047 (emphasis added). By amending its public records statute to exempt rape victims' names from disclosure, Fla. Stat. §119.07(3)(h) (1983), and forbidding its officials from releasing such information, Fla. Stat. §794.03 (1983), the State has taken virtually every step imaginable to prevent what happened here. This case presents a far cry, then, from *Cox Broadcasting* or *Oklahoma Publishing,* where the State asked the news media not to publish information it had made generally available to the public: here, the State is not asking the media to do the State's job in the first instance.

Unfortunately, as this case illustrates, mistakes happen: Even when States take measures to "avoid" disclosure, sometimes rape victims' names are found out. As I see it, it is not too much to ask the press, in instances such as this, to respect simple standards of decency and refrain from publishing a victims' name, address, and/or phone number.[6]

Second, the Court complains that appellant was judged here under too strict a liability standard. The Court contends that a newspaper might be found liable under the Florida court's negligence per se theory without regard to a newspaper's scienter or degree of fault. Ante, at 2612. The short answer to this complaint is that whatever merit the Court's argument might have, it is wholly inapposite here, where the jury found that appellant acted with "reckless indifference towards the rights of others," 2 Record 170, a standard far higher than the *Gertz* standard [Gertz v. Robert Welch, Inc., 418 U.S. 323, 94 S. Ct. 2997, 41 L. Ed. 2d 789 (1974)] the Court urges as a constitutional minimum today. Ante, at 2612. B.J.F. proved the Star's negligence at trial—and, actually, far more than simple negligence; the

6. The Court's concern for a free press is appropriate, but such concerns should be balanced against rival interests in a civilized and humane society. An absolutist view of the former leads to insensitivity as to the latter.

This was evidenced at trial, when the Florida Star's lawyer explained why the paper was not to blame for any anguish caused B.J.F. by a phone call she received, the day after the Star's story was published, from a man threatening to rape B.J.F. again. Noting that the phone call was received at B.J.F.'s home by her mother (who was babysitting B.J.F.'s children while B.J.F. was in the hospital), who relayed the threat to B.J.F., the Star's counsel suggested:

> [I]n reference to the [threatening] phone call, it is sort of blunted by the fact that [B.J.F.] didn't receive the phone call. Her mother did. And if there is any pain and suffering in connection with the phone call, it has to lay in her mother's hands. I mean, my God, she called [B.J.F.] up at the hospital to tell her [of the threat]—you know, I think that is tragic, but I don't think that is something you can blame the Florida Star for.

2 Record 154-155.

While I would not want to live in a society where freedom of the press was unduly limited, I also find regrettable an interpretation of the First Amendment that fosters such a degree of irresponsibility on the part of the news media.

Court's concerns about damages resting on a strict liability or mere causation basis are irrelevant to the validity of the judgment for appellee.

But even taking the Court's concerns in the abstract, they miss the mark. Permitting liability under a negligence per se theory does not mean that defendants will be held liable without a showing of negligence, but rather, that the standard of care has been set by the legislature, instead of the courts. The Court says that negligence per se permits a plaintiff to hold a defendant liable without a showing that the disclosure was "of a fact about a person's private life . . . that a reasonable person would find highly offensive." Ibid. But the point here is that the legislature—reflecting popular sentiment—has determined that disclosure of the fact that a person was raped is categorically a revelation that reasonable people find offensive. And as for the Court's suggestion that the Florida courts' theory permits liability without regard for whether the victim's identity is already known, or whether she herself has made it known—these are facts that would surely enter into the calculation of damages in such a case. In any event, none of these mitigating factors was present here; whatever the force of these arguments generally, they do not justify the Court's ruling against B.J.F. in this case.

Third, the Court faults the Florida criminal statute for being underinclusive: §794.03 covers disclosure of rape victims' names in " 'instrument[s] of mass communication,' " but not other means of distribution, the Court observes. Ante, at 2612-2613. But our cases which have struck down laws that limit or burden the press due to their underinclusiveness have involved situations where a legislature has singled out one segment of the news media or press for adverse treatment, see, e.g., *Daily Mail* (restricting newspapers and not radio or television), or singled out the press for adverse treatment when compared to other similarly situated enterprises, see, e.g., Minneapolis Star & Tribune Co. v. Minnesota Commr. of Revenue, 460 U.S. 575, 578, 103 S. Ct. 1365, 1368, 75 L. Ed. 2d 295 (1983). Here, the Florida law evenhandedly covers all "instrument[s] of mass communication" no matter their form, media, content, nature, or purpose. It excludes neighborhood gossips because presumably the Florida Legislature has determined that neighborhood gossips do not pose the danger and intrusion to rape victims that "instrument[s] of mass communication" do. Simply put: Florida wanted to prevent the widespread distribution of rape victims' names, and therefore enacted a statute tailored almost as precisely as possible to achieving that end. . . .

Consequently, neither the State's "dissemination" of B.J.F.'s name, nor the standard of liability imposed here, nor the underinclusiveness of Florida tort law requires setting aside the verdict for B.J.F. . . .

III . . .

Of course, the right to privacy is not absolute. Even the article widely relied upon in cases vindicating privacy rights, Warren & Brandeis, The Right to

Privacy, 4 Harv. L. Rev. 193 (1890), recognized that this right inevitably conflicts with the public's right to know about matters of general concern—and that sometimes, the latter must trump the former. Resolving this conflict is a difficult matter, and I fault the Court not for attempting to strike an appropriate balance between the two, but rather, fault it for according too little weight to B.J.F.'s side of [the] equation, and too much on the other.

I would strike the balance rather differently. Writing for the Ninth Circuit, Judge Merrill put this view eloquently:

> Does the spirit of the Bill of Rights require that individuals be free to pry into the unnewsworthy private affairs of their fellowmen? In our view it does not. In our view, fairly defined areas of privacy must have the protection of law if the quality of life is to continue to be reasonably acceptable. The public's right to know is, then, subject to reasonable limitations so far as concerns the private facts of its individual members.

Virgil v. Time, Inc., 527 F.2d 1122, 1128 (1975), *cert. denied,* 425 U.S. 998, 96 S. Ct. 2215, 48 L. Ed. 2d 823 (1976). . . .

I do not suggest that the Court's decision today is a radical departure from a previously charted course. The Court's ruling has been foreshadowed.

In Time, Inc. v. Hill, 385 U.S. 374, 383-384, n.7, 87 S. Ct. 534, 539-540, n.7, 17 L. Ed. 2d 456 (1967), we observed that—after a brief period early in this century where Brandeis' view was ascendant—the trend in "modern" jurisprudence has been to eclipse an individual's right to maintain private any truthful information that the press wished to publish. More recently, in *Cox Broadcasting,* 420 U.S. at 491, 95 S. Ct., at 1044, we acknowledged the possibility that the First Amendment may prevent a State from ever subjecting the publication of truthful but private information to civil liability. Today, we hit the bottom of the slippery slope.

I would find a place to draw the line higher on the hillside: a spot high enough to protect B.J.F.'s desire for privacy and peace-of-mind in the wake of a horrible personal tragedy. There is no public interest in publishing the names, addresses, and phone numbers of persons who are the victims of crime—and no public interest in immunizing the press from liability in the rare cases where a State's efforts to protect a victim's privacy have failed.

Consequently, I respectfully dissent.

In Cape Publications, Inc. v. Hitchner, 549 So. 2d 1374 (Fla. 1989), *appeal denied,* 493 U.S. 929 (1989), the court held that the publication of a story involving child abuse, which included the names of the persons involved, was newsworthy and could not be made the basis of an invasion of privacy action, notwithstanding a Florida statute that prohibited the disclosure of child abuse proceedings. The prosecutor in the case had shown the file to the reporter.

C. *False Light*

Godbehere v. Phoenix Newspapers, Inc.

162 Ariz. 335, 783 P.2d 781 (1989)

FELDMAN, VICE CHIEF JUSTICE.

Richard G. Godbehere, a former Maricopa County Sheriff, and several deputies and civilian employees of the sheriff's office (plaintiffs) brought this action against Phoenix Newspapers, Inc., the publisher of The Arizona Republic and Phoenix Gazette, and fourteen editors and reporters of the two newspapers (publishers), for libel and false light invasion of privacy. The trial court granted publishers' motion to dismiss for failure to state a claim as to the invasion of privacy claims, but refused to dismiss the other counts of the complaint. Plaintiffs appealed and the court of appeals affirmed. We granted review to determine whether Arizona should recognize a cause of action for false light invasion of privacy, and if so, what the proper standard should be. . . .

Facts

In the spring and summer of 1985, publishers printed over fifty articles, editorials, and columns (the publications) about plaintiffs' various law enforcement activities. The publications stated that the plaintiffs engaged in illegal activities, staged narcotics arrests to generate publicity, illegally arrested citizens, misused public funds and resources, committed police brutality, and generally were incompetent at law enforcement. Plaintiffs alleged in their eighteen-count complaint that the publications were false, damaged their reputations, harmed them in their profession, and caused them emotional distress. Publishers moved to dismiss all eighteen counts of the complaint for failure to state a claim, and the court dismissed the false light invasion of privacy claims. . . .

On appeal, plaintiffs argued that Arizona should follow the Restatement (Second) of Torts §652E (1977) (hereafter Restatement), which provides in part:

> One who gives publicity to a matter concerning another that places the other before the public in a false light is subject to liability to the other for invasion of his privacy, if
>
> (a) the false light in which the other was placed would be highly offensive to a reasonable person, and
>
> (b) the actor had knowledge of or acted in reckless disregard as to the falsity of the publicized matter and the false light in which the other would be placed.

Discussion . . .

B. Privacy in Arizona

Arizona first recognized an action for invasion of privacy in Reed v. Real Detective Publishing Co., 63 Ariz. 294, 162 P.2d 133 (1945). Reed involved the unauthorized publication of the plaintiff's photograph. Subsequently, our court of appeals recognized the Restatement's four-part classification of the tort.

Although most jurisdictions that recognize a cause of action for invasion of privacy have adopted the Restatement standard of "highly offensive to a reasonable person" or a similar standard, Arizona courts of appeals' decisions have imposed a stricter standard. Rather than following the Restatement, these decisions have held that where the damage alleged is emotional, the plaintiff must prove the elements of the tort of intentional infliction of emotional distress in addition to proving invasion of privacy. To recover for invasion of privacy, a plaintiff must show that the defendant's conduct was "extreme and outrageous." No other state requires a plaintiff to prove that the defendant committed "outrage" in a false light action.

Publishers urge this court to adopt the court of appeals' view. They argue that there is no need for an independent tort of false light invasion of privacy because the action overlaps two other recognized torts: defamation and intentional infliction of emotional distress. These, publishers contend, cover the field and permit recovery in meritorious cases, thus making the false light action an unnecessary burden on the media's first amendment rights. To consider this argument, we must examine the distinctions between the false light action and the torts of intentional infliction of emotional distress and defamation.

C. False Light Invasion of Privacy and Intentional Infliction of Emotional Distress

Arizona has turned to Restatement §46 to define intentional infliction of emotional distress, also known as the tort of outrage. This section provides:

> (1) one who by extreme and outrageous conduct intentionally or recklessly causes severe emotional distress to another is subject to liability for such emotional distress, and if bodily harm to the other results from it, for such bodily harm.

The element of "extreme and outrageous conduct" requires that plaintiff prove defendant's conduct exceeded "all bounds usually tolerated by decent society . . . and [caused] mental distress of a very serious kind." . . .

Publishers emphasize that actions for both intentional infliction of emotional distress and invasion of privacy provide compensation for emotional distress or damage to sensibility. Thus, the injury from both torts is similar. Although this may be true, the fact that two different actions address the same injury is no reason to refuse to recognize torts that protect against different wrongful conduct. For example, three victims may suffer broken legs in the following ways: (1) a defendant negligently drives a car into the first victim's car; (2) a defendant's defective product injures the second victim; and (3) a defendant, without justification, attacks the third. Each victim would have a different tort claim: negligence, strict liability, and battery. The fact that each victim suffers the same type of injury does not preclude recognizing separate tort actions. Each tort theory developed separately to deter and provide redress against a different type of wrongful conduct.

Thus, the fact that outrage and invasion of privacy both provide redress for emotional injury does not persuade us that the actions are "merged" or that plaintiffs should be required to prove the former in an action for the latter. The outrage tort protects against conduct so extreme that it would induce "an average member of the community . . . to exclaim, 'outrageous!' " Restatement §46 Comment *d.* False light invasion of privacy, however, protects against the conduct of knowingly or recklessly publishing false information or innuendo that a "reasonable person" would find "highly offensive." Although false publication may constitute outrageous conduct and vice versa, it is also true that the same wrongful conduct will not always satisfy the elements of both tort actions. Because each action protects against a different type of tortious conduct, each has its place, and the common injury should not abrogate the action.

Nor do we believe that recognizing the false light action without requiring plaintiffs to prove outrage will circumvent the "stringent standards" of the emotional distress tort. The standards for proving false light invasion of privacy are quite "stringent" by themselves. For example, the plaintiff in a false light case must prove that the defendant published with knowledge of the falsity or reckless disregard for the truth. This standard is as stringent as the intentional infliction of emotional distress requirement that the plaintiff prove the defendant "intentionally or recklessly caused" the emotional distress. . . .

We conclude, therefore, that the two torts exist to redress different types of wrongful conduct. Situations exist where a jury could find the defendant's publication of false information or innuendo was not outrageous but did satisfy the false light elements. Thus, we believe the tort action for false light invasion of privacy provides protection against a narrow class of wrongful conduct that falls short of "outrage," but nevertheless should be deterred.

D. Invasion of Privacy and Defamation

A second argument advanced by publishers is that little distinction exists between a tort action for false light invasion of privacy and one for defamation. Thus, because defamation actions are available, they argue, Arizona need not recognize false light invasion of privacy. Again, we disagree.

Although both defamation and false light invasion of privacy involve publication, the nature of the interests protected by each action differs substantially. A defamation action compensates damage to reputation or good name caused by the publication of false information. To be defamatory, a publication must be false and must bring the defamed person into disrepute, contempt, or ridicule, or must impeach plaintiff's honesty, integrity, virtue, or reputation.

Privacy, on the other hand, does not protect reputation but protects mental and emotional interests. Under this theory, a plaintiff may recover even in the absence of reputational damage, as long as the publicity is unreasonably offensive and attributes false characteristics. However, to qualify as a false light invasion of privacy, the publication must involve "a major misrepresentation of [the plaintiff's] character, history, activities or beliefs," not merely minor or unimportant inaccuracies. Restatement §652E Comment *c*.

Another distinction between defamation and false light invasion of privacy is the role played by truth. To be defamatory, a publication must be false, and truth is a defense. A false light cause of action may arise when something untrue has been published about an individual, or when the publication of true information creates a false implication about the individual. In the latter type of case, the false innuendo created by the highly offensive presentation of a true fact constitutes the injury.[2]

2. A good example of a false light cause of action based on implication is Douglass v. Hustler Magazine, Inc., 769 F.2d 1128 (7th Cir. 1985), *cert. denied,* 475 U.S. 1094, 106 S. Ct. 1489, 89 L. Ed. 2d 892 (1986). In Douglass, the plaintiff posed nude, consenting to the publication of her photographs in Playboy magazine. Her photographer subsequently left the employ of Playboy for Hustler magazine, a publication of much lower standing in the journalistic community. He sold her photographs to Hustler, which published them. The plaintiff sued for the nonconsensual use of the photographs. Plaintiff had no cause of action for defamation, because essentially, there was nothing untrue about the photographs. She posed for them and, as published, they did not misrepresent her. She also had no claim for outrage. She voluntarily posed for the photographs and consented to their publication in Playboy. Publication was not "outrageous," as it may have been if she were photographed without her knowledge and the photos published without her initial consent. However, the court upheld her recovery for false light invasion of privacy. The jury may have focused on the differences between Playboy and Hustler and concluded that to be published in Hustler, as if she had posed for that publication, falsely placed her in a different light than the Playboy publication. 769 F.2d at 1138.

Thus, although defamation and false light often overlap, they serve very different objectives. The two tort actions deter different conduct and redress different wrongs. A plaintiff may bring a false light invasion of privacy action even though the publication is not defamatory, and even though the actual facts stated are true. . . .

F. Free Speech Considerations

As in defamation, a public official in a false light action must always show that the defendant published with knowledge of the false innuendo or with reckless disregard of the truth. Any doubt about the application of the actual malice element of the false light tort to public figures has been eliminated. In Hustler Magazine, Inc. v. Falwell, 485 U.S. 46, 108 S. Ct. 876, 99 L. Ed. 2d 41 (1988), the Supreme Court held that a public figure plaintiff must prove Times v. Sullivan actual malice in order to recover for intentional infliction of emotional distress. Although Hustler was an intentional infliction case, the language used by the Court is so broad that it applies to any tort action relating to free speech, particularly "in the area of public debate about public figures." See *Hustler,* 485 U.S. at 53, 108 S. Ct. at 881.[6] Additional protection for free speech comes from the principle that protection for privacy interests generally applies only to private matters. . . .

G. Is False Light Available in This Case?

Finally, publishers contended that even if we recognize false light actions, the action does not lie in this case. They argue that not only do the publications discuss matters of public interest, but plaintiffs have no right of privacy with respect to the manner in which they perform their official duties. We agree. . . .

A number of jurisdictions take the position that because false light is a form of invasion of privacy, it must relate only to the private affairs of the plaintiff and cannot involve matters of public interest. It is difficult to conceive of an area of greater public interest than law enforcement. Certainly the public has a legitimate interest in the manner in which law enforcement officers perform their duties. Therefore, we hold that there can be no false

6. To this point, we have spoken of false light as requiring that the plaintiff show actual malice. Restatement §652E seems to state that requirement, but the Caveat to that section states that the Institute "takes no position" on whether, under some circumstances, a nonpublic figure may recover for false light invasion of privacy where he does not show actual malice but does show negligent publication. *See also* Restatement §652E comment on clause (b). Because this case does not present the issue, we also take no position on the validity of a false light action for negligent publication. Suffice it to say that in this case, where we deal with publications concerning public officers performing public duties, the First Amendment controls.

light invasion of privacy action for matters involving official acts or duties of public officers.

Consequently, we adopt the following legal standard: A plaintiff cannot sue for false light invasion of privacy if he or she is a public official and the publication relates to performance of his or her public life or duties. We do not go so far as to say, however, that a public official has no privacy rights at all and may never bring an action for invasion of privacy. Certainly, if the publication presents the public official's private life in a false light, he or she can sue under the false light tort, although actual malice must be shown.

The Supreme Court has held that "the public official designation applies at the very least to those among the hierarchy of government employees who have, or appear to the public to have, substantial responsibility for or control over the conduct of governmental affairs." Rosenblatt v. Baer, 383 U.S. 75, 85, 86 S. Ct. 669, 676, 15 L. Ed. 2d 597 (1966). Police and other law enforcement personnel are almost always classified as public officials. The publications at issue concern the discharge of their public duties and do not relate to private affairs. Therefore, plaintiffs have no claim for false light invasion of privacy.

We affirm the trial court's dismissal of the false light claim. Because we disagree with the court of appeals' reasoning, we vacate that opinion and remand to the trial court for further proceedings consistent with this opinion.

Notwithstanding opinions like that in *Godbehere,* some commentators have argued the false light tort completely overlaps other torts, and for that reason should not be recognized as a distinct category of invasion of privacy. This point was first made in Kalven, Privacy in Tort Law—Were Warren and Brandeis Wrong?, 31 Law & Contemp. Prob. 327 (1966). More recently, the anti-false light cudgel was taken up by Professor Kelso in his article, False light Privacy: A Requiem, 32 Santa Clara L. Rev. 783 (1993). Professor Kelso characterized the tort as "Prosser's Folly" and asserted that

> [n]one of the cases Prosser cited in support of false light privacy came close to recognizing such a tort. False light existed only in Prosser's mind.

Id. at 788.

Professor Kelso surveyed over 600 cases, and concluded that in none of them was false light essential to the outcome. The "core" of the false light case, he stated, "lies elsewhere, in defamation, in misappropriation, or in intentional infliction of emotional distress." Id. at 785.

D. *Appropriation*

Carson v. Here's Johnny Portable Toilets, Inc.,
698 F.2d 831 (6th Cir. 1983)

BAILEY BROWN, SENIOR CIRCUIT JUDGE.

This case involves claims of unfair competition and invasion of the right of privacy and the right of publicity arising from appellee's adoption of a phrase generally associated with a popular entertainer.

[The defendant rented and sold "Here's Johnny" portable toilets. The expression, "Here's Johnny" was used to introduce the plaintiff, Johnny Carson, a well-known late night talk host. The plaintiff sued to enjoin the defendant for unfair competition and violation of his trademark rights, and for invasion of privacy and publicity rights.]

After a bench trial, the district court issued a memorandum opinion and order, Carson v. Here's Johnny Portable Toilets, Inc., 498 F. Supp. 71 (E.D. Mich. 1980), which served as its findings of fact and conclusions of law. The court ordered the dismissal of the appellants' complaint. On the unfair competition claim, the court concluded that the appellants had failed to satisfy the "likelihood of confusion" test. On the right of privacy and right of publicity theories, the court held that these rights extend only to a "name or likeness," and "Here's Johnny" did not qualify.

I

[The court affirmed the decision of the trial judge with respect to the unfair competition and trademark violation claims.]

II

The appellants also claim that the appellee's use of the phrase "Here's Johnny" violates the common law right of privacy and right of publicity. The confusion in this area of the law requires a brief analysis of the relationship between these two rights.

In an influential article, Dean Prosser delineated four distinct types of the right of privacy: (1) intrusion upon one's seclusion or solitude, (2) public disclosure of embarrassing private facts, (3) publicity which places one in a false light, and (4) appropriation of one's name or likeness for the defendant's advantage. Prosser, Privacy, 48 Calif. L. Rev. 383, 389 (1960). This fourth type has become known as the "right of publicity." . . .

Dean Prosser's analysis has been a source of some confusion in the law. His first three types of the right of privacy generally protect the right "to be let alone," while the right of publicity protects the celebrity's pecuniary interest in the commercial exploitation of his identity. Thus, the right of privacy and the right of publicity protect fundamentally different interests and must be analyzed separately.

We do not believe that Carson's claim that his right of privacy has been invaded is supported by the law or the facts. Apparently, the gist of this claim is that Carson is embarrassed by and considers it odious to be associated with the appellee's product. Clearly, the association does not appeal to Carson's sense of humor. But the facts here presented do not, it appears to us, amount to an invasion of any of the interests protected by the right of privacy. In any event, our disposition of the claim of an invasion of the right of publicity makes it unnecessary for us to accept or reject the claim of an invasion of the right of privacy.

The right of publicity has developed to protect the commercial interest of celebrities in their identities. The theory of the right is that a celebrity's identity can be valuable in the promotion of products, and the celebrity has an interest that may be protected from the unauthorized commercial exploitation of that identity. In Memphis Development Foundation v. Factors Etc., Inc., 616 F.2d 956 (6th Cir.), *cert. denied,* 449 U.S. 953, 101 S. Ct. 358, 66 L. Ed. 2d 217 (1980), we stated: "The famous have an exclusive legal right during life to control and profit from the commercial use of their name and personality." Id. at 957.

The district court dismissed appellants' claim based on the right of publicity because appellee does not use Carson's name or likeness. It held that it "would not be prudent to allow recovery for a right of publicity claim which does not more specifically identify Johnny Carson." 498 F. Supp. at 78. We believe that, on the contrary, the district court's conception of the right of publicity is too narrow. The right of publicity, as we have stated, is that a celebrity has a protected pecuniary interest in the commercial exploitation of his identity. If the celebrity's identity is commercially exploited, there has been an invasion of his right whether or not his "name or likeness" is used. Carson's identity may be exploited even if his name, John W. Carson, or his picture is not used. . . .

In this case, Earl Braxton, president and owner of Here's Johnny Portable Toilets, Inc., admitted that he knew that the phrase "Here's Johnny" had been used for years to introduce Carson. Moreover, in the opening statement in the district court, appellee's counsel stated:

> Now, we've stipulated in this case that the public tends to associate the words "Johnny Carson," the words "Here's Johnny" with plaintiff, John Carson and, Mr. Braxton, in his deposition, admitted that he knew that and probably absent that identification, he would not have chosen it.

That the "Here's Johnny" name was selected by Braxton because of its identification with Carson was the clear inference from Braxton's testimony irrespective of such admission in the opening statement.

We therefore conclude that, applying the correct legal standards, appellants are entitled to judgment. The proof showed without question that appellee had appropriated Carson's identity in connection with its corporate name and its product.

Although this opinion holds only that Carson's right of publicity was invaded because appellee intentionally appropriated his identity for commercial exploitation, the dissent, relying on its interpretation of the authorities and relying on policy and constitutional arguments, would hold that there was no invasion here. We do not believe that the dissent can withstand fair analysis.

The dissent contends that the authorities hold that the right of publicity is invaded only if there has been an appropriation of the celebrity's "name, likeness, achievements, identifying characteristics or actual performances." . . .

It should be obvious from the majority opinion and the dissent that a celebrity's identity may be appropriated in various ways. It is our view that, under the existing authorities, a celebrity's legal right of publicity is invaded whenever his identity is intentionally appropriated for commercial purposes. We simply disagree that the authorities limit the right of publicity as contended by the dissent. It is not fatal to appellant's claim that appellee did not use his "name." Indeed, there would have been no violation of his right of publicity even if appellee had used his name, such as "J. William Carson Portable Toilet" or the "John William Carson Portable Toilet" or the "J.W. Carson Portable Toilet." The reason is that, though literally using appellant's "name," the appellee would not have appropriated Carson's identity as a celebrity. Here there was an appropriation of Carson's identity without using his "name."

With respect to the dissent's general policy arguments, it seems to us that the policies there set out would more likely be vindicated by the majority view than by the dissent's view. Certainly appellant Carson's achievement has made him a celebrity which means that his identity has a pecuniary value which the right of publicity should vindicate. Vindication of the right will tend to encourage achievement in Carson's chosen field. Vindication of the right will also tend to prevent unjust enrichment by persons such as appellee who seek commercially to exploit the identity of celebrities without their consent.[4]

The dissent also suggests that recognition of the right of publicity here would somehow run afoul of federal monopoly policies and first amendment proscriptions. If, as the dissent seems to concede, such policies and proscriptions are not violated by the vindication of the right of publicity where the celebrity's "name, likeness, achievements, identifying characteristics or

4. Appellee did not brief and make the policy and constitutional arguments relied upon in the dissent. Instead, the appellee confined its argument to the straightforward proposition that the right of publicity is limited to appropriation of the celebrity's "name or likeness."

actual performances" have been appropriated for commercial purposes, we cannot see why the policies and proscriptions would be violated where, as here, the celebrity's identity has admittedly been appropriated for commercial exploitation by the use of the phrase "Here's Johnny Portable Toilets."

The judgment of the district court is vacated and the case remanded for further proceedings consistent with this opinion.

CORNELIA G. KENNEDY, CIRCUIT JUDGE, dissenting.

I respectfully dissent from that part of the majority's opinion which holds that appellee's use of the phrase "Here's Johnny" violates appellant Johnny Carson's common law right of publicity. While I agree that an individual's identity may be impermissibly exploited, I do not believe that the common law right of publicity may be extended beyond an individual's name, likeness, achievements, identifying characteristics, or actual performances, to include phrases or other things which are merely associated with the individual, as is the phrase "Here's Johnny." The majority's extension of the right of publicity to include phrases or other things which are merely associated with the individual permits a popular entertainer or public figure, by associating himself or herself with a common phrase, to remove those words from the public domain.

The phrase "Here's Johnny" is merely associated with Johnny Carson, the host and star of "The Tonight Show" broadcast by the National Broadcasting Company. Since 1962, the opening format of "The Tonight Show," after the theme music is played, is to introduce Johnny Carson with the phrase "Here's Johnny." The words are spoken by an announcer, generally Ed McMahon, in a drawn out and distinctive manner. Immediately after the phrase "Here's Johnny" is spoken, Johnny Carson appears to begin the program.[1] This method of introduction was first used by Johnny Carson in 1957 when he hosted a daily television show for the American Broadcasting Company. This case is not transformed into a "name" case simply because the diminutive form of John W. Carson's given name and the first name of his full stage name, Johnny Carson, appears in it. The first name is so common, in light of the millions of persons named John, Johnny, or Jonathan that no doubt inhabit this world, that, alone, it is meaningless or ambiguous at best in identifying Johnny Carson, the celebrity. In addition, the phrase containing Johnny Carson's first stage name was certainly selected for its value as a double entendre. Appellee manufactures portable toilets. The value of the phrase to appellee's product is in the risque meaning of "john" as a toilet or bathroom. For this reason, too, this is not a "name" case.

I. Policies Behind Right of Publicity

The three primary policy considerations behind the right of publicity are succinctly stated in Hoffman, Limitations on the Right of Publicity, 28 Bull.

1. It cannot be claimed that Johnny Carson's appearances on "The Tonight Show" are the only times at which a performer is introduced with the phrase "Here's ________." Numerous

Copr. Socy. 111, 116-122 (1980). First, "the right of publicity vindicates the economic interests of celebrities, enabling those whose achievements have imbued their identities with pecuniary value to profit from their fame." Id. at 116. Second, the right of publicity fosters "the production of intellectual and creative works by providing the financial incentive for individuals to expend the time and resources necessary to produce them." Limitations on the Right of Publicity, supra, 118. Third, "[t]he right of publicity serves both individual and societal interests by preventing what our legal tradition regards as wrongful conduct: unjust enrichment and deceptive trade practices." Limitations on the Right of Publicity, supra, 118.

None of the above-mentioned policy arguments supports the extension of the right of publicity to phrases or other things which are merely associated with an individual. First, the majority is awarding Johnny Carson a windfall, rather than vindicating his economic interests, by protecting the phrase "Here's Johnny" which is merely associated with him. . . . There is nothing in the record to suggest that "Here's Johnny" has any nexus to Johnny Carson other than being the introduction to his personal appearances. The phrase is not part of an identity that he created. In its content "Here's Johnny" is a very simple and common introduction. The content of the phrase neither originated with Johnny Carson nor is it confined to the world of entertainment. The phrase is not said by Johnny Carson, but said of him. Its association with him is derived, in large part, by the context in which it is said—generally by Ed McMahon in a drawn out and distinctive voice[5] after the theme music to "The Tonight Show" is played, and immediately prior to Johnny Carson's own entrance. Appellee's use of the content "Here's Johnny," in light of its value as a double entendre, written on its product and corporate name, and therefore outside of the context in which it is associated with Johnny Carson, does little to rob Johnny Carson of something which is unique to him or a product of his own efforts.

The second policy goal of fostering the production of creative and intellectual works is not met by the majority's rule because in awarding publicity rights in a phrase neither created by him nor performed by him, economic reward and protection is divorced from personal incentive to produce on the part of the protected and benefited individual. Johnny Carson is simply reaping the rewards of the time, effort, and work product of others.

Third, the majority's extension of the right of publicity to include the phrase "Here's Johnny" which is merely associated with Johnny Carson is not needed to provide alternatives to existing legal avenues for redressing wrongful conduct. The existence of a cause of action under section 43(a) of the Lanham Act, 15 U.S.C.A. §1125(a) (1976) and Michigan common law does much to undercut the need for policing against unfair competition

---

other performers are introduced with the phrase "Here's ________," using their first name, last name or full name.

5. Ed McMahon arguably has a competing publicity interest in this same phrase because it is said by him in a distinctive and drawn out manner as his introduction to entertainers who appear on "The Tonight Show," including Johnny Carson.

through an additional legal remedy such as the right of publicity. The majority has concluded, and I concur, that the District Court was warranted in finding that there was not a reasonable likelihood that members of the public would be confused by appellee's use of the "Here's Johnny" trademark on a product as dissimilar to those licensed by Johnny Carson as portable toilets. In this case, this eliminates the argument of wrongdoing. Moreover, the majority's extension of the right of publicity to phrases and other things merely associated with an individual is not conditioned upon wrongdoing and would apply with equal force in the case of an unknowing user. With respect to unjust enrichment, because a celebrity such as Johnny Carson is himself enriched by phrases and other things associated with him in which he has made no personal investment of time, money, or effort, another user of such a phrase or thing may be enriched somewhat by such use, but this enrichment is not at Johnny Carson's expense. The policies behind the right of publicity are not furthered by the majority's holding in this case. . . .

. . . I would affirm the judgment of the District Court on this basis as well.

Understandably, the commercial exploitation involved in the appropriation cases almost always involves famous people—those who are familiar enough to the public to be exploited. But one of the first privacy cases in this country involved a private person whose picture was used in connection with an advertisement by an insurance company. The court in Pavesich v. New England Life Ins. Co., 122 Ga. 190, 50 S.E. 68 (1905) upheld the plaintiff's cause of action for invasion of privacy.

The plaintiff's identity can be appropriated in ways other than the use of the plaintiff's name or likeness, as the court in *Carson* makes clear. The court in Midler v. Ford Motor Co., 849 F.2d 460 (9th Cir. 1988), for example, held that the plaintiff's right of publicity was appropriated by the defendant in an advertisement using a voice very much like the plaintiff's, singing one of the plaintiff's hit songs.

While the law may protect the plaintiff against appropriation of small segments of the plaintiff's identity, there may be less protection if what is appropriated is the plaintiff's whole life. In Spahn v. Julien Messner, Inc., 18 N.Y.2d 324, 221 N.E.2d 543 (1966), the plaintiff, a very successful major league pitcher, sued the defendant for the latter's unauthorized biography of the plaintiff. The court held that truth is a complete defense in cases involving reports about newsworthy events and people. But, the court ruled, if the biography is "fictionalized," the plaintiff may be able to recover. This latter aspect of appropriation law of *Spahn* was found constitutionally wanting in Time, Inc. v. Hill, 385 U.S. 374, 87 S. Ct. 534, 17 L. Ed. 2d 456 (1967).

The plaintiffs were a family that had been held prisoner in their homes for several hours by three escaped prisoners. An article in "Life," a magazine published by the defendant, was based on that incident, and on a later novel and play called "The Desperate Hours" depicting a similar incident, although there were many factual differences between the actual events and later novel and play. The plaintiffs' claim alleged that the magazine article intended to, and did, create the impression that the novel and play accurately portrayed what happened to the plaintiffs. A judgment for the plaintiffs was affirmed by the Court of Appeals of New York, but was reversed by the Supreme Court, which ruled that to recover based on the falsity of the article, the plaintiffs had to establish *New York Times* malice—that is, that the defendant either knew that the article was false, or acted in reckless disregard of its truth or falsity.[1]

What if the appropriation is not for the clearly commercial purposes involved in *Carson*? In Zacchini v. Scripps-Howard Broadcasting Co., 433 U.S. 562, 97 S. Ct. 2849, 53 L. Ed. 2d 965 (1977), the plaintiff was a "human cannonball" who performed at various fairs. The defendant, over the objection of the plaintiff, filmed the plaintiff's act, and broadcast it in full (the film lasted 15 seconds) as a segment on the evening news over one of its television stations. The Ohio Supreme Court upheld summary judgment in favor of the defendant, in part on First Amendment grounds (47 Ohio St. 2d 224, 235, 351 N.E.2d 454, 461):

> The press, if it is to be able to freely report matters of public interest, must be accorded broad latitude in its choice of how much it presents of each story or incident, and of the emphasis to be given to such presentation. No fixed standard which would bar the press from reporting or depicting either an entire occurrence or an entire discrete part of a public performance can be formulated which would not unduly restrict the "breathing room" in reporting which freedom of the press requires. The proper standard must necessarily be whether the matters reported were of public interest, and if so, the press will be liable for appropriation of a performer's right of publicity only if its actual intent was not to report the performance, but, rather, to appropriate the performance for some other private use, or if the actual intent was to injure the performer.

The Supreme Court reversed, ruling that the First Amendment did not protect the broadcasting of the plaintiff's act in full.

1. The attorney for the plaintiffs in the Supreme Court was Richard M. Nixon.

There is some confusion as to whether *Hill* is an appropriation or false light case. The plaintiff's cause of action was based on a New York statute providing for a recovery by "Any person whose name, portrait or picture is used within this state for advertising purposes or for the purposes of trade without the written consent" of that person. But the Supreme Court in *Zacchini,* discussed below, characterized the action as one involving false light. If *Hill* really is a false light case, however, it adds nothing to the law, at least as that law is set out in the Restatement (Second); proof that the defendant knew or acted in reckless disregard of the falsity is a part of the plaintiff's case under §652E.

Chapter 14

Commercial Torts: Misrepresentation and Interference with Business Relations

A. Misrepresentation

In this section, we shall consider the tort liability of one who misleads and thereby harms another by means of false representations in the course of business dealings. We are all familiar with the classic example of the con artist defrauding an unsuspecting victim, and it is hardly surprising that the law should provide a remedy in those relatively rare instances in which the con artist is brought into court. The vast majority of misrepresentation cases, however, are not so clear. Considerable leeway exists within which persons in a bargaining relationship may deal sharply with one another and may take advantage of each other's ignorance or lack of experience. One of the tasks in the cases that follow will be to trace the fine line that separates hard, effective bargaining from actionable misrepresentation. This task is made more difficult by the unreliability of morality as a guide. As we shall see, there are situations in which courts impose liability even when the misrepresentation was totally innocent; there are other situations in which recovery will be denied even when it can be shown that the plaintiff was willfully misled.

The following formulation appears in Pace v. Parrish, 122 Utah 141, 144-145, 247 P.2d 273, 274-275 (1952), and will suffice as a starting point for analysis of this subject:

> This being an action in deceit based on fraudulent misrepresentations, the burden was upon plaintiffs to prove all of the essential elements thereof. These are: (1) That a representation was made; (2) concerning a presently existing material fact; (3) which was false; (4) which the representor either (a) knew to be false, or (b) made recklessly, knowing that he had insufficient knowledge upon which to base such representation; (5) for the purpose of inducing the other party to act upon it; (6) that the other party, acting reasonably and in ignorance of its falsity; (7) did in fact rely upon it; (8) and was thereby induced to act; (9) to his injury and damage.

The rules that govern liability for fraudulent misrepresentation are set forth in §§525-549 of the Restatement (Second) of Torts and generally reflect the elements set forth above. (The Restatement divides its coverage of misrepresentation into two chapters: Chapter 22, which includes the above-mentioned sections and which covers business transactions; and Chapter 23, which covers nonbusiness transactions.) The Restatement also contains rules establishing liability for concealment and nondisclosure (§§550 and 551), negligent misrepresentation (§§552, 552A and 552B), and innocent misrepresentation (§552C).

Before addressing the substantive elements of the tort, it is useful to consider briefly the subject of damages as it relates to recovery for misrepresentation. The first and most basic principle is that the plaintiff must have suffered actual harm in order to recover on a theory of misrepresentation. See, e.g., Casey v. Welch, 50 So. 2d 124 (Fla. 1951); Dilworth v. Lauritzen, 18 Utah 2d 386, 424 P.2d 136 (1967). See generally McCleary, Damage as Requisite to Rescission for Misrepresentation, 36 Mich. L. Rev. 1, 227 (1937). As for the measure of the plaintiff's recovery in a misrepresentation case, there are two basic rules: the "out-of-pocket" rule, and the "benefit-of-the-bargain" rule. The former sounds classically in tort, and measures the recovery by the difference in value between what the plaintiff gave up in the business transaction and what was received. The latter, which rings of contract, measures the recovery by the difference in value between what the plaintiff actually received and what would have been received had the defendant's representations been true. The out-of-pocket rule looks backward, and seeks to restore the plaintiff to the position held before the transaction; the benefit-of-the-bargain rule looks forward, and seeks to place the plaintiff in the same position that would have been held after the transaction had the defendant's representations not been false. The Restatement does not provide for recovery for emotional harm damages in misrepresentation actions, even when the misrepresentation is intentional. Most courts follow the Restatement in this regard, and disallow such damages. See, e.g., Crowley v. Global Realty, Inc., 124 N.H. 814, 474 A.2d 1056 (1984). The court did state, however, that evidence of emotional distress is relevant to "enhanced compensatory damages," which are recoverable in New Hampshire in cases of aggravated wrongdoing. Some courts have allowed damages for emotional harm in fraud cases. See, e.g., Kilduff v. Adams, Inc., 219 Conn. 314, 593 A.2d 478 (1991). In general, see Merritt, Damages for Emotional Distress in Fraud Litigation: Dignitary Torts in a Commercial Society, 42 Vand. L. Rev. 1 (1989); Annotation, 11 A.L.R.5th 88 (1993).

The basic difference between these two measures of recovery may best be seen by means of a concrete example. Suppose that *A* sells a house to *B* and fraudulently misrepresents the condition of the property. Assume that the actual value of the house is $20,000; that the sale price is $30,000; and that the value of the house if the representations had been true would be

$35,000. Under the out-of-pocket rule, if successful in a misrepresentation action, *B* would receive $10,000—the difference between what was paid and what was actually received. Under the benefit-of-the-bargain approach, *B* would recover $15,000—the difference between what was actually received and what would have been received had *A*'s representations been truthful. The former measure of recovery is similar to rescission in equity, a remedy traditionally available as an adjunct to a contract action. However, rescission involves the returning by the plaintiff of the property to the defendant and the refunding by the defendant of the total purchase price. The out-of-pocket rule in misrepresentation cases does not involve giving up the property (which the plaintiff may wish to retain), but instead involves the payment by the defendant of an amount of money which, together with the plaintiff's retention of the property, will make the plaintiff whole.

To some extent, the damages rule will depend upon the type of case presented. Given the decidedly contract flavor of the benefit-of-the-bargain rule, it is not surprising that in most instances plaintiffs in misrepresentation actions will be limited to damages measured by the out-of-pocket rule. (There are cases, of course, in which the out-of-pocket rule will actually give the plaintiff a higher recovery—do you see how?) However, the provisions of the Restatement (Second) of Torts provide a fairly flexible approach. Section 549 of the Restatement (Second) of Torts extends the benefit-of-the-bargain rule to all cases of fraudulent misrepresentation, providing the plaintiff can prove damages "with reasonable certainty." Sections 552 and 552B, imposing liability upon a defendant who negligently supplies false information in the course of defendant's business, profession, or employment, or in a transaction in which the defendant has a pecuniary interest, speak in terms of compensating the plaintiff for both out-of-pocket and consequential pecuniary losses. And §552C, permitting recovery in some cases involving innocent misrepresentation, limits the measure of damages to out-of-pocket losses. As you work through the cases in this section, you should be alert to the importance of the damages issue, and in every instance you should consider whether the plaintiff might have sought alternative remedies to those apparently considered by the courts.

1. The Nature of the Defendant's Representation

Adams v. Gillig

199 N.Y. 314, 92 N.E. 670 (1910)

On and prior to June 2, 1908, the plaintiff was the owner in fee simple of a lot of land one hundred feet front and about one hundred and sixty feet in depth, situated on the east side of Elmwood avenue in the city of Buffalo, and also of two other lots of land fronting on Highland avenue in said city, and which run back to and adjoin the first-mentioned lot. The lots fronting on Highland avenue had houses on them, and the lot fronting on Elmwood avenue was vacant. The immediate neighborhood of said lots, so far as the same have been built upon, is devoted exclusively to residences.

The defendant sought to purchase a portion of the plaintiff's lot fronting on Elmwood avenue and stated that he desired to purchase the same for residence purposes. The negotiations were carried on with the plaintiff's agents, and the defendant stated to the representative of the plaintiff's agents and also to the agents themselves that he intended to build dwellings upon the lot if purchased. The plaintiff's agents communicated to her the statement of the defendant and his offers, and she asked her agents if they were sure the sale would not affect the value of the remaining vacant lot, and she was told by her agents that the defendant would build either single or double houses upon the lot so to be purchased.

The representations of the defendant that he intended to build dwellings on the lot to be purchased by him were false and fraudulent and made with the intent to deceive the plaintiff. The plaintiff relied upon the representations of the defendant that he intended to build dwellings upon the lot when purchased, and believing such statements to be true, executed and delivered to him a deed of sixty-five feet front and one hundred and sixty feet in depth in consideration of $5,525.

During all the time that the defendant was negotiating for the purchase of the lot in question he intended to build a public automobile garage thereon, which fact was unknown to the plaintiff and which the defendant fraudulently concealed from her.

On the day following the purchase of said lot the defendant instructed his architect to prepare plans for a garage to be built thereon to cover substantially the entire lot, and in less than two weeks thereafter he entered into a contract for the erection of such garage.

The plaintiff without delay communicated with the defendant and offered to procure another site for his garage, pay all the expenses he had incurred up to that time and restore the consideration he had paid for the property if he would reconvey the property to her. This the defendant refused to do. The plaintiff was deceived by said misrepresentations of the defendant and the construction of the proposed garage will greatly damage the remaining property belonging to the plaintiff. It will decrease the value of the remaining vacant lot on Elmwood avenue about one-half, and the value of her lots, with houses fronting on Highland avenue, about one-fourth. The referee found in favor of the plaintiff and directed a reconveyance of the property. From the judgment entered upon the report of the referee an appeal was taken to the Appellate Division of the Supreme Court where it was affirmed by a divided court.

CHASE, J. Any contract induced by fraud as to a matter material to the party defrauded is voidable. There are many rules as to what constitutes an inducement by fraud, and also affecting the general statement that any contract will be set aside for fraud, that have been established as necessary to protect the rights of all the parties to a contract, which need not be stated in this discussion, except so far as they affect the particular transaction under consideration.

It may be assumed that promises of future action that are a part of the contract between the parties, to be binding upon them, must be stated in the contract. An oral restrictive covenant, or any oral promise to do or refrain from doing something affecting the property about which a written contract is made and executed between the parties, will not be enforced, not because the parties should not fulfill their promises and their legal and moral obligations, but because the covenants and agreements being promissory and contractual in their nature and a part of, or collateral to a principal contract, the entire agreement between the parties must be deemed to have been merged in the writing. The value of a writing would be very seriously impaired if the rule mentioned in regard to including the entire agreement in such writing is not enforced.

A strict enforcement of such rule tends to greater security and safety in business transactions and leaves less opportunity for dishonesty and false swearing, induced, perhaps, by a change of purpose or a failure to obtain the result that was anticipated when the transaction was originally consummated and reduced to writing. Such rule makes it necessary for the parties to a written contract to include everything therein pertaining to the subject-matter of the principal contract, and if by mistake or otherwise an oral agreement, a part of the transaction, is omitted from the writing, it can only be made effective and enforceable by a reformation of the writing, so that the same shall include therein the entire agreement between the parties. The rule is quite universal that statements promissory in their nature and relating to future actions must be enforced if at all by an action upon the contract. It is unnecessary to decide or discuss the question whether under some possible circumstances the courts will not in equity lay hold of false statements that are contractual in their nature to prevent the consummation of a fraud.

It is not claimed on this appeal that the defendant made promises which became a part of the contract, or that the deed could be reformed by including therein restrictive covenants. The rule in regard to including the entire agreement between the parties in the writing does not take away or detract from the general rule by which a contract can always be set aside for fraud affecting the transaction as to a material fact that is not promissory in its nature. Any statement of an existing fact material to the person to whom it is made that is false and known by the person making it to be false and which is made to induce the execution of a contract, and which does induce the contract, constitutes a fraud that will sustain an action to avoid the contract if the person making it is injured thereby.

We have in this case findings by the trial court sustained by the record, which show that the defendant purposely, intentionally and falsely stated to the plaintiff that he desired to purchase a portion of her vacant lot for the purpose of building a dwelling or dwellings thereon. He must have known that if he thereby induced her to convey to him such portion of the lot and his intention to build a garage thereon was carried out it would injure her to an extent in excess of the full consideration to be paid by him to her for such lot.

The plaintiff relied upon the defendant's honesty and good faith in the purchase, and was apparently willing to take her chances of a subsequent change in his intention, or of his selling the lot to another whose intentions and purposes might be entirely different.

The simple question in this case is, therefore, whether the alleged intention of the defendant to build a dwelling or dwellings upon the lot which he sought to purchase is such a statement of an existing material fact as authorizes the court to cancel the deed because of the fraud.

The distinction between a collateral agreement as a part of a contract to do or not to do a particular thing, and a statement and representation of a material existing fact made to induce the contract may be further profitably considered.

A promise as such to be enforceable must be based upon a consideration, and it must be put in such form as to be available under the rules relating to contracts and the admission of evidence relating thereto. It may include a present intention, but as it also relates to the future it can only be enforced as a promise under the general rules relating to contracts.

A mere statement of intention is a different thing. It is not the basis of an action on contract. It may in good faith be changed without affecting the obligations of the parties. . . .

This case stands exactly as it would have stood if the plaintiff and defendant before the execution and delivery of the deed had entered into a writing by which the defendant had stated therein his intention as found by the court on the trial and the plaintiff had stated her acceptance of his offer based upon her belief and faith in his statement of intention, and it further appeared that the statement was so made by the defendant for the purpose of inducing the plaintiff to sell to him the lot, and that such statement was so made by him falsely, fraudulently and purposely for the purpose of bringing about such sale.

Intent is of vital importance in very many transactions. In the criminal courts it is necessary in many cases for jurors to determine as a question of fact the intent of the person charged with the crime. Frequently the life or liberty of the prisoner at the bar depends upon the determination of such question of fact. In civil actions relating to wrongs, the intent of the party charged with the wrong is frequently of controlling effect upon the conclusion to be reached in the action. The intent of a person is sometimes difficult to prove, but it is nevertheless a fact and a material and existing fact that must be ascertained in many cases, and when ascertained determines the rights of the parties to controversies. The intent of Gillig was a material existing fact in this case, and the plaintiff's reliance upon such fact induced her to enter into a contract that she would not otherwise have entered into. The effect of such false statement by the defendant of his intention cannot be cast aside as immaterial simply because it was possible for him in good faith to have changed his mind or to have sold the property to another who might have a different purpose relating thereto. As the defendant's intention was subject to change in good faith at any time it was of uncertain value. It was, however, of some value. It was of sufficient value so that the plaintiff was willing to stand upon it and make the conveyance in reliance upon it.

The use of property in a particular manner changes from time to time and restrictive covenants of great value at one time may become a source of serious embarrassment at a later date. The fact that restrictive covenants cannot ordinarily be drawn to bend to changed conditions has made many purchasers disinclined to accept conveyances with such covenants. A restrictive covenant in a deed may be of sufficient importance to justify a refusal by a contractee to accept a conveyance subject to such conditions. A person in selling property may be quite willing to execute and deliver a deed thereof without putting restrictive covenants therein and in reliance upon the good faith of express, unqualified assurances of the present intention of the prospective purchaser. In such case the intention is material and the statement of such intention is the statement of an existing fact.

Unless the court affirms this judgment, it must acknowledge that although a defendant deliberately and intentionally, by false statements, obtained from a plaintiff his property to his great damage it is wholly incapable of righting the wrong, notwithstanding the fact that by so doing it does in no way interfere with the rules that have grown up after years of experience to protect written contracts from collateral promises and conditions not inserted in the contract.

We are of the opinion that the false statements made by the defendant of his intention should, under the circumstances of this case, be deemed to be a statement of a material, existing fact of which the court will lay hold for the purpose of defeating the wrong that would otherwise be consummated thereby. . . .

We do not concede the accuracy of the statement made before us on behalf of the defendant to the effect that false statements similar to the one made by the defendant to induce the execution of the deed by the plaintiff are common in business transactions, but if true, and controversies arise over the retention of the fruits of such frauds, and the fraudulent inducement is conceded or proven beyond reasonable controversy, the transactions will not have the approval and sanction of the courts.

The judgment should be affirmed, with costs.

CULLEN, C.J., GRAY, VANN, WERNER, WILLARD, BARTLETT and HISCOCK, JJ., concur.

Judgment affirmed.

Vulcan Metals Co. v. Simmons Manufacturing Co.

248 F. 853 (C.C.A.N.Y. 1918)

[This is an appeal from two cases which were tried together in the district court. The first case was a deceit action brought by Vulcan Metals Company (Vulcan) against Simmons Manufacturing Company (Simmons) based upon misrepresentations allegedly made by Simmons to Vulcan in the course of the sale by Simmons to Vulcan of tools, dies and equipment, including patents, for the manufacture of vacuum cleaners. The second case was an action by Simmons against Vulcan on three notes given by Vulcan as part of the purchase price. In the second case, Vulcan raised the misrepresentations by way of defense and counterclaim. The evidence introduced during the trial in the district court is described as follows in the syllabus to the court's opinion:

"[The misrepresentations upon which Vulcan relies] were of two classes—those touching the efficiency of the vacuum cleaner; and, second, that no attempt had been made to market the machines by the Simmons Manufacturing Company.

"The first of these classes is substantially the same as those contained in a booklet issued by the Simmons Manufacturing Company for the general sale of the vacuum cleaners. They include commendations of the cleanliness, economy, and efficiency of the machine; that it was absolutely perfect in even the smallest detail; that water power, by which it worked, marked the most economical means of operating a vacuum cleaner with the greatest efficiency; that the cleaning was more thoroughly done than by beating or brushing; that, having been perfected, it was a necessity which every one could afford; that it was so simple that a child of six could use it; that it worked completely and thoroughly; that it was simple, long-lived, easily operated, and effective; that it was the only sanitary portable cleaner on the market; that perfect satisfaction would result from its use; that it would last a lifetime; that it was the only practical jet machine on the market; and that perfect satisfaction would result from its use, if properly adjusted. The booklet is in general the ordinary compilation, puffing the excellence and powers of the vacuum cleaner, and asserting its superiority over all others of a similar sort. Flynn [a broker acting on behalf of Simmons] made a demonstration of the cleaner to Freeman [one of Vulcan's promoters and an indorser of the notes] with borax sprinkled upon the carpet, and allowed him to take one for experiment, which he retained for some time.

"The second class of misrepresentations was that the Simmons Manufacturing Company had not sold the machine, or made any attempt to sell it; that they had not shown it to any one; that it had never been on the market, and that no one outside of the company officials and the men in the factory knew anything about it; that they had manufactured 15,000 of them, but before making any attempt to market it they had been told by their agent that it would be a mistake for them to attempt to sell these along with their ordinary line, which was furniture; that on that account they had withdrawn them from the market and had never made any attempt to put them out. Sweetland, one of the promoters of the Vulcan Metals Company, Incorporated, swore that Flynn had stated that the machines had been marketed, but marketed successfully. There was therefore a discrepancy between the testimony of these two representations, but for the purposes of the action it is not here material, since the complaint was based upon the representation that the machines had not been sold.

"There was evidence that the machines, when exploited by the Vulcan Metals Company, Incorporated, proved to be ineffective and of little or no value, and that their manufacture was discontinued by that company not very long after they had undertaken it. There was also evidence that several of the Western agents of the Simmons Manufacturing Company had had the machines in stock and had attempted to market some of them; that they had been unsuccessful in these efforts, owing for the most part to the fact that the water pressures, where they had been sold, had not been sufficient to establish the necessary vacuum. . . ."

The district court directed a verdict in favor of Simmons in both actions, and from judgments entered thereon Vulcan appealed.]

L. HAND, J. (after stating the facts as above). The first question is of the misrepresentations touching the quality and powers of the patented machine. These were general commendations, or, in so far as they included any specific facts, were not disproved; e.g., that the cleaner would produce 18 inches of vacuum with 25 pounds water pressure. They raise, therefore, the question of law how far general "puffing" or "dealers' talk" can be the basis of an action for deceit.

The conceded exception in such cases has generally rested upon the distinction between "opinion" and "fact"; but that distinction has not escaped the criticism it deserves. An opinion is a fact, and it may be a very relevant fact; the expression of an opinion is the assertion of a belief, and any rule which condones the expression of a consciously false opinion condones a consciously false statement of fact. When the parties are so situated that the buyer may reasonably rely upon the expression of the seller's opinion, it is no excuse to give a false one. And so it makes much difference whether the parties stand "on an equality." For example, we should treat very differently the expressed opinion of a chemist to a layman about the properties of a composition from the same opinion between chemist and chemist, when the buyer had full opportunity to examine. The reason of the rule lies, we think, in this: There are some kinds of talk which no sensible man takes seriously, and if he does he suffers from his credulity. If we were all scrupulously honest, it would not be so; but, as it is, neither party usually believes what the seller says about his own opinions, and each knows it. Such statements, like the claims of campaign managers before election, are rather designed to allay the suspicion which would attend their absence than to be understood as having any relation to objective truth. It is quite true that they induce a compliant temper in the buyer, but it is by a much more subtle process than through the acceptance of his claims for his wares.

In the case at bar, since the buyer was allowed full opportunity to examine the cleaner and to test it out, we put the parties upon an equality. It seems to us that general statements as to what the cleaner would do, even though consciously false, were not of a kind to be taken literally by the buyer. As between manufacturer and customer, it may not be so; but this was the case of taking over a business, after ample chance to investigate. Such a buyer, who the seller rightly expects will undertake an independent and adequate inquiry into the actual merits of what he gets, has no right to treat as material in his determination statements like these. The standard of honesty permitted by the rule may not be the best; but, as Holmes, J., says in Deming v. Darling, 148 Mass. 504, 20 N.E. 107, 2 L.R.A. 743, the chance that the higgling preparatory to a bargain may be afterwards translated into assurances of quality may perhaps be a set-off to the actual wrong allowed by the rule as it stands. We therefore think that the District Court was right in disregarding all these misrepresentations.

As respects the representation that the cleaners had never been put upon the market or offered for sale, the rule does not apply; nor can we agree that such representations could not have been material to Freeman's decision to accept the contract. The actual test of experience in their sale might well be of critical consequence in his decision to buy the business, and the jury would certainly have the right to accept his statement that his reliance upon these representations was determinative of his final decision. We believe that the facts as disclosed by the depositions of the Western witnesses were sufficient to carry to the jury the question whether those statements were false. It is quite true, as the District Judge said, that the number of sales was small, perhaps not 60 in all; but they were scattered in various parts of the Mountain and Pacific States, and the jury might conclude that they were enough to contradict the detailed statements of Simmons that the machines had been kept off the market altogether. . . .

The next question is as to whether any such misrepresentations were conclusively cured by the recital in the contract of purchase as follows: "The party of the first part [the Simmons Company] has been engaged in the manufacture of a certain type of vacuum cleaning machines, and the parties of the first and second part [the National Suction Cleaner Company] have been engaged in the sale thereof."

We all agree that an adequate retraction of the false statement before Freeman executed the contract would be a defense. Whether this be regarded as terminating the consequences of the original wrong, or as a correction of it, is of little importance. Further, we agree that, even if Freeman had in fact never learned of the retraction, it would serve, if given under such circumstances as justified the utterer in supposing that he would. For example, a letter actually delivered into his hands containing nothing but a retraction would be a defense, though it abundantly appeared that he had never read it. His loss might still be the consequence, and the reasonable consequence, but for the letter, of the original fraud; but the writer would have gone as far as necessary to correct that fraud, and we should not be disposed to hold it as an insurer that its correction should be effective. . . . I . . . do not think that [the recital in this contract] was certain to catch the eye of the reader, and that therefore neither was the defendant's duty of retraction inevitably discharged, nor, what is nearly the same thing, did the defendant show beyond question that Freeman actually saw it. As a retraction the recital was a defense, and the defendant had the burden of proof. As notice to Freeman actually conveyed, it may have been only evidence upon the causal sequence between the wrong and the injury; but we attach no great significance to that distinction. The fact that he signed the contract appears to us to be some evidence upon which the jury might say that he could not have seen the recital. That depends upon how much importance they think he attached to the original representation, and that depends in turn upon what they thought of his story. If they did believe that the representation was of critical consequence in his decision, they might infer that he did not see it, or he would not have gone on without some explanation. The very silence of the testimony upon the question might be taken to infer that he had not noticed it, even at the trial, just as it might also be taken to indicate that he had fabricated the whole story, and hoped the recital would escape the notice of the defendant. In any event, the interpretation of the whole transaction appears to us not to be so clear that reasonable people might not come to opposite conclusions upon it, and that involves a submission to the jury. It is perhaps of some importance that no allusion to the recital appears in the record.

It results from the foregoing that the judgment in the action for deceit must be reversed. In the action upon the notes the judgment upon the notes will be affirmed, because the Vulcan Metals Company, Incorporated, did not make any offer to return the machines, tools, and patents, which were not shown to be without any value, and consequently it was in no position to rescind. The judgment in that action dismissing the counterclaim must, however, be reversed, since the counterclaim involved the same facts as the complaint in the action for deceit. . . .

Judgment in the action of deceit reversed, and new trial ordered. Judgment in the action on the notes affirmed so far as it gives judgment on the notes, and reversed so far as it dismisses the counterclaim, and new trial upon the counterclaim ordered.

[Upon rehearing, the court dismissed Vulcan's counterclaim on the notes.]

Swinton v. Whitinsville Savings Bank

311 Mass. 677, 42 N.E.2d 808 (1942)

[A demurrer to the declaration was sustained by the trial court. The plaintiff appealed.]

QUA, J. The declaration alleges that on or about September 12, 1938, the defendant sold the plaintiff a house in Newton to be occupied by the plaintiff and his family as a dwelling; that at the time of the sale the house "was infested with termites, an insect that is most dangerous and destructive to buildings"; that the defendant knew the house was so infested; that the plaintiff could not readily observe this condition upon inspection; that, "knowing the internal destruction that these insects were creating in said house," the defendant falsely and fraudulently concealed from the plaintiff its true condition; that the plaintiff at the time of his purchase had no knowledge of the termites, exercised due care thereafter, and learned of them about August 30, 1940; and that, because of the destruction that was being done and the dangerous condition that was being created by the termites, the plaintiff was put to great expense for repairs and for the installation of termite control in order to prevent the loss and destruction of said house.

There is no allegation of any false statement or representation, or of the uttering of a half truth which may be tantamount to a falsehood. There is no intimation that the defendant by any means prevented the plaintiff from acquiring information as to the condition of the house. There is nothing to show any fiduciary relation between the parties, or that the plaintiff stood in a position of confidence toward or dependence upon the defendant. So far as appears the parties made a business deal at arm's length. The charge is concealment and nothing more; and it is concealment in the simple sense of mere failure to reveal, with nothing to show any peculiar duty to speak. The characterization of the concealment as false and fraudulent of course adds nothing in the absence of further allegations of fact.

If this defendant is liable on this declaration every seller is liable who fails to disclose any nonapparent defect known to him in the subject of the sale which materially reduces its value and which the buyer fails to discover. Similarly it would seem that every buyer would be liable who fails to disclose any nonapparent virtue known to him in the subject of the purchase which materially enhances its value and of which the seller is ignorant. The law has not yet, we believe, reached the point of imposing upon the frailties of human nature a standard so idealistic as this. That the particular case here stated by the plaintiff possesses a certain appeal to the moral sense is scarcely to be denied. Probably the reason is to be found in the facts that the infestation of buildings by termites has not been common in Massachusetts and constitutes a concealed risk against which buyers are off their guard. But the law cannot provide special rules for termites and can hardly attempt to determine liability according to the varying probabilities of the existence and discovery of different possible defects in the subjects of trade. The rule of nonliability for bare nondisclosure has been stated and followed by this court. . . . It is adopted in the American Law Institute's Restatement of Torts, §551. See Williston on Contracts (Rev. ed.) §§1497, 1498, 1499.

The order sustaining the demurrer is affirmed, and judgment is to be entered for the defendant.

So ordered.

The court in Obde v. Schlemeyer, 56 Wash. 2d 449, 353 P.2d 672 (1960), held that a selling home owner does have an affirmative duty to disclose the presence of termites to the buyer. Such a duty of disclosure, the court said, exists whenever "justice, equity, and fair dealing" require it.

Ingaharro v. Blanchette

122 N.H. 54, 440 A.2d 445 (1982)

KING, C.J. The plaintiff, Walter J. Ingaharro, after buying a house and lot from the defendants, Jacques E. Blanchette and Theresa Blanchette, brought an action against the defendants for negligent misrepresentation concerning the adequacy of the water supply serving his new home.

In June of 1978, the parties entered into a purchase-and-sale agreement for real property which was located in Candia, New Hampshire. The agreement contained a merger clause stating that all representations were expressed in the writing. The writing made no reference to the water supply. . . .

The defendants, with their three children, had lived on the property for about ten years before selling the real estate to the plaintiff in July of 1978. During the ten-year period, the defendants had experienced some problems with the water supply, and they had hired professionals to redrill two of their three wells. Even with the redrilled wells, the defendants had to conserve water, especially in the summer. All of the neighbors in the surrounding area in which the property was located experienced the same problems with their water supply.

Before they sold the property to the plaintiffs, the defendants made no statements regarding the adequacy of the water supply. When the plaintiff viewed the property, before entering into the purchase-and-sale agreement, he noticed the defendants' swimming pool. He did not ask about the source of water for the pool and was not informed that the pool was filled by bringing in water from elsewhere. The plaintiff also observed that the toilets in the house had not been flushed. Again he asked no questions, even though this measure is commonly used to conserve water.

After the plaintiff had taken possession of the property, the water supply failed. He called the defendants, and although they tried to assist him, the defendants were not able to correct the problem. The defendants then informed him that there was a water problem in the summer, but that the supply of water was increased in the fall. During the next year, the plaintiff experienced more water problems and as a result brought this action against the defendants.

The Master . . . concluded that the defendants' failure to inform the plaintiff of seasonal inadequacy in the water supply constituted negligent misrepresentation. The master concluded that the defendants were aware or should have been aware of the defect and he determined that the plaintiff could not have discovered the defect upon a reasonable inspection. The defendant, therefore, had an obligation to disclose such information. Concluding that the plaintiff reasonably relied on the defendants' omission, and that the inadequate water supply was material to the parties' contract, the master found for the plaintiff and awarded damages by multiplying the well-drilling cost per foot by the average depth of wells in the area where the property is located. The Superior Court . . . approved the master's recommendation, and the defendants appealed to this court. We reverse.

The essential elements of negligent misrepresentation are a negligent misrepresentation by the defendant of a material fact and justifiable reliance by the plaintiff. . . . The defendants argue that there can be no finding of negligent misrepresentation by mere omission in this case. We agree. The master erroneously relied on Colby v. Granite State Realty, Inc., 116 N.H. 690, 366 A.2d 482 (1976) for the proposition that the seller has a duty to disclose latent defects. In *Colby,* this court concluded that the buyer has no duty to inspect, but can rely on the seller's representations. Id. at 691, 366 A.2d at 484. Buyers cannot successfully claim misrepresentation in the absence of some form of representation.

We find no evidence in the record to support the conclusion that the defendant had a duty to disclose the inadequacy of the water supply. Without such a duty, mere silence is not sufficient for misrepresentation. . . . Some courts have concluded that, in some instances, the seller of property can have a duty to disclose defects. The defect must be a concealed defect known to the seller, unknown to the buyer and incapable of detection by the buyer's reasonable inspection. Obde v. Schlemeyer, 56 Wash. 2d 449, 452, 353 P.2d 672, 674-675 (1960). Additionally, the defect must be dangerous to property or life. Id. at 452, 353 P.2d at 674. The facts of this case do not give rise to a duty to disclose.

Even if a seller has no duty originally, partial disclosure by a seller creates a duty for full disclosure. . . . Additionally, this court has concluded that if a seller makes a representation and later learns that the statement is false, he must reveal the learned information to the buyer. . . . Here, no representations were made that would give rise to a duty of further disclosure.

In the instant case, the defendants had no duty to disclose the inadequacy of the water supply because the master found that "[t]he defendants may have honestly believed the [water] system met the standards of adequacy." Although the master found that the plaintiff relied on the omission and that the water supply was material to the parties' contract, these factors alone cannot make the defendants liable for negligent misrepresentation. . . .

The record indicates that a real estate broker, acting on the defendants' behalf, may have informed the plaintiff that the water supply was adequate. Because the trial court made no findings, we remand this issue to the trial court for further consideration of whether the salesman's statement constituted a misrepresentation and whether the salesman was acting as the defendants' agent. . . .

Reversed and remanded.

All concurred.

The cases in this subsection presume an intent on the defendant's part to deceive the plaintiff and present the question of what sort of conduct by the defendant will amount to a misrepresentation of fact sufficient to form the basis for tort liability. Although these cases do not raise the point, it should be fairly obvious that the defendant need not actually use words or employ language in order to misrepresent material facts. Thus, in Salzman v. Maldaver, 315 Mich. 403, 24 N.W.2d 161 (1946), the court refused to dismiss a complaint that alleged that the defendant, who sold a number of stacks of damaged aluminum metal sheets to the plaintiff, had deliberately misled the plaintiff by placing an undamaged sheet on the top of each stack of damaged sheets, under circumstances where it was impractical for the plaintiff to move the stacks in order to check their condition for himself. Similarly, in Jones v. West Side Buick Auto Co., 231 Mo. App. 187, 93 S.W.2d 1083 (1936), the turning back of the odometer of a used car by the defendant-seller was held sufficient to constitute a misrepresentation of the number of miles the car had previously been driven. (In 1972, Congress enacted the Motor Vehicle Information and Cost Savings Act, 15 U.S.C. §1901 et seq., rendering it illegal to change the odometer with the intent to alter the number of miles shown. Violations are punishable by substantial fines. The court of appeals in Edgar v. Fred Jones Lincoln-Mercury of Oklahoma City, Inc., 524 F.2d 162 (10th Cir. 1975) held that the federal act did not preempt the common law of the states imposing liability for fraudulent misrepresentation.)

The classic formulation of the rule that a misstatement of present intention may be sufficient to constitute an actionable misrepresentation of fact is that of Lord Bowen in Edgington v. Fitzmaurice, L.R. 29 Ch. Div. 459, 483 (1882): "[T]he state of a man's mind is as much a fact as the state of his digestion."

One of the most interesting issues relating to the nature of the defendant's representation involves the distinction between fact and opinion. Generally speaking, misrepresentations of fact are actionable, while misrepresentations of opinion are not. So many exceptions have been grafted onto the basic rule, however, that one may well doubt its continued utility. The difficulty is that almost any statement of opinion which occurs in the course of bargaining can be viewed, at least by implication, as involving an assertion of fact. Consequently, the distinction between fact and opinion is difficult to make, and results often appear to be in conflict. Purely conclusory words are unlikely to be viewed as statements of fact. Thus, in Cooper & Co. v. Bryant, 440 So. 2d 1016 (Ala. 1983), the description of a house with a cracked foundation as being in "excellent" condition was not a misrepresentation of fact. On the other hand, the court in Ragsdale v. Kennedy, 286 N.C. 130, 209 S.E.2d 494 (1974), held that a jury could find that descriptions of a corporation as a "gold mine" and a "going concern" were misrepresentations of fact. And in Pietrazak v. McDermott, 341 Mass. 107, 167 N.E.2d 166 (1960), the builder-seller of a house was held liable for having told the purchaser that there would be no water in the cellar, the court concluding that such a statement carried with it the implication that the construction of the house was such as to preclude the entry of water. In contrast, the builder-sellers of a house were held not liable as a matter of law in Yerid v. Mason, 341 Mass. 527, 170 N.E.2d 718 (1960), after having told the purchasers that a drain would be installed to cope with wetness in the cellar and that the purchasers would have no further trouble with water. The drain was installed, but the cellar flooded anyway.

The Restatement (Second) of Torts defines a misrepresentation of opinion as one that expresses only the uncertain belief of the maker regarding the existence of a fact, or the maker's judgment regarding "quality, value, authenticity, or other matters of judgment." (§538A.) In stating the opinion, however, liability may attach if the defendant implies that there are facts justifying the opinion that the defendant knows do not exist, or if the defendant implies, falsely, that there are no facts inconsistent with the opinion. (§539). On the subject of liability for misstatements of opinion see Casey, Misrepresentation of Opinion: Statement of Fact Distinguished from Statement of Opinion, 28 B.U. L. Rev. 352 (1948); Keeton, Fraud: Misrepresentations of Opinion, 21 Minn. L. Rev. 643 (1937).

Related to the distinction between fact and opinion is the distinction, sometimes encountered in the cases, between misrepresentations of fact and misrepresentations of law. Although some courts have expressed reluctance to allow recovery when someone misstates a legal conclusion (see §545, Restatement of Torts, Second), it is misleading to assume that misrepresentations of law are never actionable. In Dawe v. American Universal Insurance Co., 120 N.H. 447, 417 A.2d 2 (1980), the Supreme Court of New Hampshire affirmed a decision for the plaintiff where the defendant's claims adjuster had misrepresented to an insured her rights and had induced the insured to sign a release on the false understanding that the release would not preclude the bringing of further claims for future medical expenses against the defendant insurance company.

A recurring fact pattern involves deliberate misstatements made in the course of sales negotiations as a means of gaining an advantage on the question of price. Such statements may be made by either purchasers or sellers. In Kabatchnick v. Hanover-Elm Building Corp., 328 Mass. 341, 103 N.E.2d 692 (1952), the plaintiff, a lessee of property, alleged that the lessor had asserted during negotiations that he had received another, higher offer and that the lessee would have to meet it or lose the property. In fact, no such offer had been received by the lessor. The Massachusetts court overruled the defendant-lessor's demurrer and sent the case to trial. In contrast, the Supreme Court of South Carolina found the complaint insufficient in Warr v. Carolina Power & Light Co., 237 S.C. 121, 115 S.E.2d 799 (1960), where the plaintiff alleged that she had been fraudulently induced to sell a parcel of land to a purchasing agent for the defendant utility company who had misrepresented to her the company's plans for using the property and had misrepresented the price he had been authorized to pay for the land. See generally Goldfarb, Fraud and Nondisclosure in the Vendor-Purchaser Relation, 8 W. Res. L. Rev. 5 (1956).

As the *Swinton, Obde,* and *Ingaharro* cases, above, suggest, the subject of fraudulent nondisclosure has received a considerable amount of judicial attention. Other cases that have held that nondisclosures are not actionable are Nei v. Boston Survey Consultants, Inc., 388 Mass. 320, 446 N.E.2d 681 (1983) (surveyor hired by seller of house did not disclose to buyer knowledge of an unusually high water table that increased the cost of septic tank installation), and Cooper & Co., Inc. v. Bryant, 440 So. 2d 1016 (Ala. 1983) (real estate broker hired by seller did not disclose to buyer crack in foundation of house). Section 551 of the first Restatement of Torts, to which the court in *Swinton* makes reference, has been revised. The original §551 had placed a duty upon actors to disclose in three basic situations: where a fiduciary or other similar relation of trust and confidence exists between the parties; where subsequently acquired information is recognized by the actor to make untrue or misleading a previous representation; and where the actor subsequently ascertains that a misrepresentation not originally made for the purpose of being acted upon is about to be acted upon by the other party to the business transaction. The second of these situations is illustrated in a decision by the Supreme Court of Ohio that suggests the relative liberality with which courts today are likely to impose duties to disclose. In Miles v. McSwegin, 58 Ohio St. 2d 97, 388 N.E.2d 1367 (1979), a judgment for the plaintiffs was affirmed when the defendant real estate broker, who had described the property purchased by the plaintiffs as "a good sound house," subsequently learned that the house was infested with termites. See also Bursey v. Clement, 118 N.H. 412, 387 A.2d 346 (1978).

Section 551 of the Restatement (Second) describes two additional circumstances under which a duty to disclose will arise: where, with respect to "facts basic to the transaction," the actor knows or believes that disclosure of additional matters is necessary to prevent a partial statement of the facts from being misleading; and where the actor knows that the other party is about to enter into the transaction under a mistake as to such facts and that the other party, "because of the relationship between them, the customs of the trade or other objective circumstances, would reasonably expect a disclosure of those facts." These additional provisions greatly enlarge the circumstances under which a duty to disclose will be imposed. It remains to be seen whether it makes sense any longer to speak, as the court in *Swinton* spoke, of "the rule of nonliability for bare nondisclosure." A number of cases indicate a judicial willingness to expand nondisclosure liability, particularly in the context of real estate transactions. In Reed v. King, 145 Cal. App. 3d 261, 193 Cal. Rptr. 130 (1983), the court ruled that a claim by a buyer against the seller of a house and his real estate broker was improperly dismissed; the complaint alleged that the defendants had not disclosed that the house was the site of a multiple murder, which substantially lowered the market value of the house. In Easton v. Strassburger, 152 Cal. App. 3d 90, 199 Cal. Rptr. 383 (1984), the court ruled that the seller's real estate broker was liable not only for failing to disclose to the buyer defects in the land of which he actually knew, but also for failing to act reasonably to discover such defects, here the susceptibility to earth slides of the land on which the house was built.

A rule even more protective of buyers was adopted in Johnson v. Davis, 480 So. 2d 625 (Fla. 1985), where the court stated "that where the seller of a home knows of facts materially affecting the value of the property which are not readily observable and are not known to the buyer, the seller is under a duty to disclose them to the buyer. This duty is equally applicable to all forms of real property, new and used." 480 So. 2d at 629.

2. Scienter, Negligence, and Strict Liability

Derry v. Peek

14 App. Cas. 337 (House of Lords, 1889)

[This action was brought by Sir Henry William Peek against the chairman of the Plymouth, Devonport and District Tramways Company, William Derry, and four company directors for having fraudulently misrepresented to him that the company was authorized in moving its carriages to use steam power instead of horses, thereby inducing him to purchase shares in the company. By a special act of Parliament (45 & 46 Vict. c. clix), the company had been authorized to build certain tramways.]

By sect. 35 the carriages used on the tramways might be moved by animal power and, with the consent of the Board of Trade, by steam or any mechanical power for fixed periods and subject to the regulations of the Board.

By sect. 34 of the Tramways Act 1870 (33 & 34 Vict. c. 78), which section was incorporated in the special Act, "all carriages used on any tramway shall be moved by the power prescribed by the special Act, and where no such power is prescribed, by animal power only."

In February 1883 the appellants as directors of the company issued a prospectus containing the following paragraph:—

"One great feature of this undertaking, to which considerable importance should be attached, is, that by the special Act of Parliament obtained, the company has the right to use steam or mechanical motive power, instead of horses, and it is fully expected that by means of this a considerable saving will result in the working expenses of the line as compared with other tramways worked by horses."

Soon after the issue of the prospectus the respondent, relying, as he alleged, upon the representations in this paragraph and believing that the company had an absolute right to use steam and other mechanical power, applied for and obtained shares in the company.

The company proceeded to make tramways, but the Board of Trade refused to consent to the use of steam or mechanical power except on certain portions of the tramways.

[As a result of the decision of the Board of Trade,] the company was wound up, and the [plaintiff] in 1885 brought an action of deceit against the [defendants] claiming damages for the fraudulent misrepresentations of the defendants whereby the plaintiff was induced to take shares in the company.

[At the trial, the plaintiff and defendants testified that they were aware that the consent of the Board of Trade was necessary for the company to use steam power, but that they either assumed that consent had been given or would be given in due course.

[The trial judge dismissed the plaintiff's action, concluding that the defendants believed that the company had the authority described in the prospectus, that their belief in this regard was not unreasonable, and that their conduct was not so reckless or careless that they should be held liable in deceit. The decision of the trial judge was reversed by the Court of Appeal (COTTON L.J., SIR J. HANNEN, and LOPES L.J.), who held that although the defendants honestly believed their statement to the plaintiff was true they made it without any reasonable ground for believing it to be true, and therefore should be liable to make good to the plaintiff the loss suffered by him in purchasing the shares. The defendants appealed from the decision of the Court of Appeal to the House of Lords, where the decision of the intermediate court was unanimously set aside and the decision of the trial judge restored.]

LORD HERSCHELL:—

My Lords, in the statement of claim in this action the respondent, who is the plaintiff, alleges that the appellants made in a prospectus issued by them certain statements which were untrue, that they well knew that the facts were not as stated in the prospectus, and made the representations fraudulently, and with the view to induce the plaintiff to take shares in the company.

"This action is one which is commonly called an action of deceit, a mere common law action." This is the description of it given by Cotton L.J. in delivering judgment. I think it important that it should be borne in mind that such an action differs essentially from one brought to obtain rescission of a contract on the ground of misrepresentation of a material fact. The principles which govern the two actions differ widely. Where rescission is claimed it is only necessary to prove that there was misrepresentation; then, however honestly it may have been made, however free from blame the person who made it, the contract, having been obtained by misrepresentation, cannot stand. In an action of deceit, on the contrary, it is not enough to establish misrepresentation alone; it is conceded on all hands that something more must be proved to cast liability upon the defendant, though it has been a matter of controversy what additional elements are requisite. I lay stress upon this because observations made by learned judges in actions for rescission have been cited and much relied upon at the bar by counsel for the respondent. Care must obviously be observed in applying the language used in relation to such actions to an action of deceit. Even if the scope of the language used extends beyond the particular action which was being dealt with, it must be remembered that the learned judges were not engaged in determining what is necessary to support an action of deceit, or in discriminating with nicety the elements which enter into it.

[An extended treatment of the authorities is omitted.]

Having now drawn attention, I believe, to all the cases having a material bearing upon the question under consideration, I proceed to state briefly the conclusions to which I have been led. I think the authorities establish the following propositions: First, in order to sustain an action of deceit, there must be proof of fraud, and nothing short of that will suffice. Secondly, fraud is proved when it is shewn that a false representation has been made (1) knowingly, or (2) without belief in its truth, or (3) recklessly, careless whether it be true or false. Although I have treated the second and third as distinct cases, I think the third is but an instance of the second, for one who makes a statement under such circumstances can have no real belief in the truth of what he states. To prevent a false statement being fraudulent, there must, I think, always be an honest belief in its truth. And this probably covers the whole ground, for one who knowingly alleges that which is false, has obviously no such honest belief. Thirdly, if fraud be proved, the motive of the person guilty of it is immaterial. It matters not that there was no intention to cheat or injure the person to whom the statement was made. . . .

In my opinion making a false statement through want of care falls far short of, and is a very different thing from, fraud, and the same may be said of a false representation honestly believed though on insufficient grounds. . . . [T]he whole current of authorities, with which I have so long detained your Lordships, shews to my mind conclusively that fraud is essential to found an action of deceit, and that it cannot be maintained where the acts proved cannot properly be so termed. . . . But for the reasons I have given I am unable to hold that anything less than fraud will render directors or any other persons liable to an action of deceit.

At the same time I desire to say distinctly that when a false statement has been made the questions whether there were reasonable grounds for believing it, and what were the means of knowledge in the possession of the person making it, are most weighty matters for consideration. The ground upon which an alleged belief was founded is a most important test of its reality. I can conceive many cases where the fact that an alleged belief was destitute of all reasonable foundation would suffice of itself to convince the Court that it was not really entertained, and that the representation was a fraudulent one. So, too, although means of knowledge are . . . a very different thing from knowledge, if I thought that a person making a false statement had shut his eyes to the facts or purposely abstained from inquiring into them, I should hold that honest belief was absent, and that he was just as fraudulent as if he had knowingly stated that which was false. . . .

I quite admit that the statements of witnesses as to their belief are by no means to be accepted blindfold. The probabilities must be considered. Whenever it is necessary to arrive at a conclusion as to the state of mind of another person, and to determine whether his belief under given circumstances was such as he alleges, we can only do so by applying the standard of conduct which our own experience of the ways of men has enabled us to form; by asking ourselves whether a reasonable man would be likely under the circumstances so to believe. I have applied this test, with the result that I have a strong conviction that a reasonable man situated as the defendants were, with their knowledge and means of knowledge, might well believe what they state they did believe, and consider that the representation made was substantially true. . . .

I think the judgment of the Court of Appeal should be reversed. [LORD HALSBURY, L.C., LORD WATSON, LORD BRAMWELL and LORD FITZGERALD delivered concurring opinions.]

Order of the Court of Appeal reversed; order of [the trial judge] restored.

International Products Co. v. Erie R.R.

244 N.Y. 331, 155 N.E. 662 (1927)

ANDREWS, J. Early in August, 1921, the plaintiff was expecting a valuable shipment consigned to it to arrive in New York on the steamer Plutarch. It was an importer selling the goods received to other customers. Consequently it was necessary that such goods should be stored until resold, either in ordinary warehouses or in one maintained by some carrier, who might in turn send them over its lines to the ultimate consumer.

The plaintiff . . . arranged, while no definite contract was executed, that the goods when they arrived should be stored at the railroad company's warehouse docks.

The Plutarch was to dock in Brooklyn. There the Erie would receive the goods on its own lighters, transfer them to New Jersey and then ship them on upon the order of the plaintiff. . . .

The Plutarch reached Brooklyn between August 10th and August 15th and was unloaded in three or four days. The goods in question were covered by insurance until they reached the warehouse. Naturally the plaintiff was desirous of protecting itself from that time forward and to protect itself it was essential that the particular warehouse in which they were stored should be made known to the insurer. Therefore on August 17th, giving this reason for its question, it inquired of the defendant where the goods would be stored. The latter, taking time to obtain the required information, replied they were docked at dock F, Weekawken. From this reply the plaintiff had the right to infer that the goods were already received and stored. It immediately thereafter obtained its insurance, giving the same information to the insurer.

The answer was erroneous. In fact the goods were not received from the steamer by the defendant until August 27th and August 31st. The plaintiff's officer, however, having charge of the transaction did not know but what the representation was true, nor did the plaintiff itself know that it was not, unless it is a fact that under no circumstances might the defendant have obtained possession of the goods from the Plutarch without a so-called "delivery order" signed by the plaintiff. The latter did know that such an order was not given until August 26th, but in the hurry of business, dealing with a responsible party, we have no reason to suppose that the Plutarch might not have delivered the goods trusting to receive the "delivery order" if necessary later. Certainly nothing in the testimony negatives this conclusion. We have then the false assurance as to an existing fact, given by one who had arranged to become and who in fact subsequently did become bailee of these goods, to the owner, to enable it to obtain valid insurance thereon and in reliance upon which the owner acted.

One-half of the goods were in fact stored when they arrived not on dock F but on dock D, both docks belonging to the defendant. When the formal bill of lading prepared by the defendant some time later was returned to it early in September a close examination of certain stamps impressed upon it would have revealed the truth. It was not discovered, however. In November dock D with the goods stored thereon was destroyed by fire. The plaintiff could obtain no insurance because of the misdescription in the policy. It, therefore, seeks to recover the insurance it would have been entitled to had it not given the misdescription in reliance on the statement of the defendant. The defendant denies liability on any theory, either of tort or of contract. . . .

Confining ourselves to the issues before us we eliminate any theory of fraud or deceit. Had they been present other questions would arise. We come to the vexed question of liability for negligent language. In England the rule is fixed. "Generally speaking there is no such thing as liability for negligence in word as distinguished from act." (Pollock on Torts [12th ed.], p. 565; Fish v. Kelby, 17 C.B. [N.S.] 194.) Dicta to the contrary may be found in earlier cases. But since Peek v. Derry (L.R. 14 A.C. 337), although what was said was not necessary to the decision, the law is clearly to the effect "that no cause of action is maintainable for a mere statement, although untrue, and although acted upon to the damage of the person to whom the statement is made unless the statement be false to the knowledge of the person making it" (Dickson v. Reuters Telegram Co., Ltd., L.R. 1877, 3 C.P. Div. 1), or as said elsewhere "we have to take it as settled that there is no general duty to use any care whatever in making statements in the way of business or otherwise, on which other persons are likely to act." (9 Law Quarterly Review, 292.) And the same principle has been applied in equity although it had been supposed that here, at least, there was often a remedy for negligent misrepresentation.

These cases have not been without criticism. The denial, under all circumstances, of relief because of the negligently spoken or written word, is, it is said, a refusal to enforce what conscience, fair dealing and the usages of business require. The tendency of the American courts has been towards a more liberal conclusion. The searcher of a title employed by one, who delivers his abstract to another to induce action on the faith of it, must exercise care. So must a physician who assures a wife that she may safely treat the infected wound of her husband or hired by another, examines a patient and states the result of his diagnosis. So of a telegraph company, stating that a telegram was delivered when in fact it was not. And the liability of such a company to the receiver for the erroneous transcription of a telegram has also sometimes been placed on this ground.

In New York we are already committed to the American as distinguished from the English rule. In some cases a negligent statement may be the basis for a recovery of damages. . . .

Obviously, however, the rule we have adopted has its limits. Not every casual response, not every idle word, however damaging the result, gives rise to a cause of action. Chancellor Kent might not be held responsible for an error in one of his "Battery opinions." As he himself said, they cost nothing and bind no one. Liability in such cases arises only where there is a duty, if one speaks at all, to give the correct information. And that involves many considerations. There must be knowledge or its equivalent that the information is desired for a serious purpose; that he to whom it is given intends to rely and act upon it; that if false or erroneous he will because of it be injured in person or property. Finally the relationship of the parties, arising out of contract or otherwise, must be such that in morals and good conscience the one has the right to rely upon the other for information, and the other giving the information owes a duty to give it with care. An inquiry made of a stranger is one thing; of a person with whom the inquirer has entered or is about to enter into a contract concerning the goods which are or are to be its subject is another. Even here the inquiry must be made as the basis of independent action. We do not touch the doctrine of caveat emptor. But in a proper case we hold that words negligently spoken may justify the recovery of the proximate damages caused by faith in their accuracy.

When such a relationship as we have referred to exists may not be precisely defined. All that may be stated is the general rule. In view of the complexity of modern business each case must be decided on the peculiar facts presented. The same thing is true, however, in the usual action for personal injuries. There whether negligence exists depends upon the relations of the parties, the thing done or neglected, its natural consequences, and many other considerations. No hard and fast line may be drawn.

Here, as we view the facts, the duty to speak with care if it spoke at all, rested on the defendant. We have it about to become the bailee of the plaintiff's goods; the inquiry made by him with whom it was dealing for the purpose as it knew of obtaining insurance; the realization that the information it gave was to be relied upon and that if false the insurance obtained would be worthless. We have an inquiry such as might be expected in the usual course of business made of one who alone knew the truth. We have a negligent answer, untrue in fact, actual reliance upon it, and resulting proximate loss. True the answer was not given to serve the purposes of the defendant itself. This we regard as immaterial.

If there was negligence justifying a recovery we cannot hold the plaintiff guilty of contributory negligence as a matter of law. Whether or not it should have discovered the error by an inspection of the bill of lading when it received it was a question of fact.

We have confined our decision to the precise issues before us. We do not consider what might be the result under other conditions or whether a recovery might not be had upon other grounds. If the testimony is to be interpreted as the defendant claims it should be; if the statement as to the dock was a mere expression of present intention, still it might be claimed that under the circumstances due care required notice if such intention was subsequently changed. Or under either interpretation it might be said some principle of estoppel might be applied. Or if we are to take the wider view of contracts sometimes proposed, then that a recovery on this theory is permissible. All this we pass by. Such questions we will consider when they are required by the decision we must reach. Until then we express no opinion.

The judgment appealed from should be affirmed, with costs.

CARDOZO, C.J., POUND, CRANE and LEHMAN, J.J., concur; KELLOGG, J., absent.

Judgment affirmed.

The holding of the New York court in the *International Products Co.* case is recognized in most American jurisdictions and is reflected in §552 of the Restatement (Second) of Torts. Liability will be imposed on those who, in the course of their businesses or professions, or in other transactions in which they have pecuniary interests, negligently supply false information for the guidance of others in their business transactions. As mentioned earlier at the beginning of this section, §552B limits the damages for negligent misrepresentation to those necessary to compensate the plaintiff for the pecuniary harm thereby caused, including the traditional out-of-pocket measure and other consequential pecuniary losses. The plaintiff may not, however, recover the benefit of the bargain. As subsequent materials will reveal, these rules governing negligent misrepresentation are most frequently applied to persons, such as accountants, who are in the business or profession of supplying information to be used in making business decisions. But the rule has been held inapplicable in a case in which the plaintiff alleged that he relied on information in the Wall Street Journal about bonds in which he invested. The information turned out to be false, and the plaintiff's action for negligent misrepresentation was dismissed. See Gutter v. Dow Jones, Inc., 22 Ohio St. 3d 286, 490 N.E.2d 898 (1986).

Johnson v. Healy

176 Conn. 97, 405 A.2d 54 (1978)

PETERS, J. This case arises out of the sale of a new one-family house by its builder, the defendant John J. Healy, to the plaintiff, Ronald K. Johnson. The plaintiff bought the house, located in Naugatuck, in 1965, for $17,000. Between 1968 and 1971, the house settled in such a way as to cause major displacements in various foundation walls, and substantial damage to the sewer lines. In 1971, the plaintiff instituted this law suit alleging misrepresentation and negligence on the part of the defendant builder-vendor. The court below found for the plaintiff on the claims of misrepresentation, for the defendant on the claims of negligence, and assessed damages. Both parties have appealed from these conclusions of law, and from the assessment of damages.

I

The claims of misrepresentation are based on the following facts, which are amply supported by the evidence below. As part of the negotiations leading to the contract of sale of the house, the plaintiff inquired about the quality of its construction. The defendant replied that the house was made of the best material, that he had built it, and that there was nothing wrong with it. These representations were relied upon by the plaintiff and induced him to purchase the house. The damage which the house sustained because of its uneven settlement was due to improper fill which had been placed on the lot beneath the building at some time before the defendant bought the lot, as a building lot, in 1963. On the basis of these findings, the trial court concluded that the defendant had made an express warranty coextensive with the doctrine of implied warranty of workmanship and habitability in cases involving the sale of new homes by a builder. . . .

The defendant . . . assigns as error the trial court's conclusion that the defendant bore responsibility for a condition of which he had no knowledge, actual or constructive. The trial court found that the defendant's representations, although innocent, amounted to an express warranty of workmanlike construction and fitness for habitation. Since those representations reasonably induced reliance in the purchase of the house, the defendant was held liable despite the absence of written warranties concerning the fitness or condition of the home in the contract of sale or the deed of conveyance.

The scope of liability for innocent misrepresentation has varied with time and with context, in American law generally and in this court. Traditionally, no cause of action lay in contract for damages for innocent misrepresentation; if the plaintiff could establish reliance on a material innocent misstatement, he could sue for rescission, and avoid the contract, but he could not get affirmative relief. See Restatement (Second), Contracts §§304, 306, and Introductory Note to Chapter 13 (Tentative Draft No. 11, 1976). In tort, the basis of responsibility, although at first undifferentiated, was narrowed, at the end of the 19th century, to intentional misconduct, and only gradually expanded, in this century, to permit recovery in damages for negligent misstatements. At the same time, liability in warranty, that curious hybrid of tort and contract law, became firmly established, no later than the promulgation of the Uniform Sales Act in 1906. In contracts for the sale of tangible chattels, express warranty encompasses material representations which are false, without regard to the state of mind or the due care of the person making the representation. For breach of express warranty, the injured plaintiff has always been entitled to choose between rescission and damages. Although the description of warranty liability has undergone clarification in the Uniform Commercial Code, which supersedes the Uniform Sales Act, these basic remedial principles remain unaffected. At the same time, liability in tort, even for misrepresentations which are innocent, has come to be the emergent rule for transactions that involve a commercial exchange. See Restatement (Second), Torts [§552C.]

In Connecticut law, strict liability for innocent misrepresentation in the sale of goods is well established. As long ago as Bartholomew v. Bushnell, 20 Conn. 271 (1850), this court held (p. 275) that "[i]f a man sell a horse to another, and expressly warrant him to be sound, the contract is broken, if the horse prove otherwise. The purchaser, in such case, relies *upon the contract;* and it is immaterial to him, whether the vendor did, or did not, know of the unsoundness of the horse. In either case, he is entitled to recover all the damages, which he has sustained." For similar reasons, strict liability for innocent misrepresentation was imposed in a construction contract in E. & F. Construction Co. v. Stamford, 114 Conn. 250, 158 A. 551 (1932). In *Stamford,* the defendant's erroneous description of subsurface conditions materially affected the plaintiff's excavation costs. This court held the misrepresentation to be actionable, even though there was no allegation of fraud or bad faith, because it was false and misleading, "in analogy to the right of a vendee to elect to retain goods which are not as warranted, and to recover damages for the breach of warranty." Id., 258, 158 A. 553. *Stamford* quotes, with approval, from 3 Williston, Contracts §1512, p. 2689 (1920): " 'If a man makes a statement in regard to a matter upon which his hearer may reasonably suppose he has the means of information, . . . and the statement is made as part of a business transaction, or to induce action from which the speaker expects to gain an advantage, he should be held liable for the consequences of reliance upon his misstatement.' " Id., 259, 158 A. 554. *Bartholomew* and *Stamford* together make it clear that liability for innocent misrepresentation is not a novelty in this state, that such liability is based on principles of warranty, and that such warranty law is not confined to contracts for the sale of goods. . . .

On the facts of the case before us, as the trial court concluded, liability for innocent misrepresentation is entirely appropriate. Although the defendant vendor had built no houses other than this one, this information was not disclosed to the buyer until the sale had been concluded; the defendant had been otherwise engaged in the real estate business for about thirty years. Although indefinite, the defendant's statement that there was "nothing wrong" with the house could reasonably have been heard by the plaintiff as an assertion that the defendant had sufficient factual information to justify his general opinion about the quality of the house. In context, this statement of opinion could reasonably have induced reliance.

II

[The court affirms the trial court's ruling that negligence was not proven.]

III

The assessment of damages in the trial court was an award in the amount of $5,000 for breach of warranties and not for negligence. The plaintiff attacks this award as inadequate, since it does not measure damages by the cost of repairs. The defendant attacks the award as excessive because it does not measure the difference between the value of the property as warranted and as sold.

The plaintiff's claim for damages was twofold: $882.50 for sewer repairs occasioned by the settling of the foundation which damaged the sewer line, and $27,150 as an estimate, procured in 1971, for the cost of constructing a new foundation. The court specifically found that the cost of replacing the foundation would in all likelihood exceed the value of the house, originally purchased for $17,000.

Apart from the sewer repair costs, the plaintiff incurred, from 1965 to 1970, additional expenditures of $5,112 in connection with the house. These expenses were largely, but not exclusively, incurred in making repairs. The trial court concluded that, since a substantial part of the $5,112 was for repairs attributable to the faulty settlement of the house, he would allocate to damages an amount which, when added to the $882.50 sewer costs, would produce a total recovery of $5,000. The court noted that, in late 1971, when the plaintiff first complained to the defendant about problems with the house, the defendant offered to repurchase the property for the purchase price of $17,000 and the expense of repairs then represented by the plaintiff to approximate $5,000.

[The court held that the trial judge correctly ruled that the plaintiff could not recover the $27,150 cost of replacing the foundation. The court observed that while recovery of the cost of repairs normally satisfies the rule that warranty damages should put the plaintiff in the position he would have been in had the property been in the warranted condition, if the cost of repairs significantly exceeds the loss in value, "policy dictates limitation to diminution of value to avoid unreasonable economic waste."]

The proper test for damages was the difference in value between the property had it been as represented and the property as it actually was. This standard is notoriously more difficult to apply than to state. Reasonable costs of repair may therefore sometimes furnish a reasonable approximation of diminished value. Reliance expenses often serve as a surrogate for damages otherwise inaccessible to proof. See the classic articles, Fuller & Perdue, "The Reliance Interest in Contract Damages: 1," 46 Yale L.J. 52 (1936-1937), and Fuller & Perdue, "The Reliance Interest in Contract Damages: 2," 46 Yale L.J. 373 (1936-1937). The trial court's reference to the $5,112 expended by the plaintiff with regard to the house would have been an acceptable resource for the inquiry into diminution of value, if only the $5,112 list had accurately distinguished between expenses for repairs and expenses for improvements. To the extent that reliance expenses are probative of losses incurred because of breach, they must be expenses demonstrably incident to breach. The tender of a particular sum by the defendant in negotiation of an aborted settlement is no more dispositive than is the plaintiff's unwillingness to agree to a rescission and to insist, as he had a right to do, on affirmative relief in damages.

Under these circumstances, the court's award of damages was in error, the judgment is set aside, and the case is remanded with direction to render judgment for the plaintiff to recover such damages as he may prove on a new trial limited to the issue of damages.

In this opinion the other judges concurred.

Tort liability for innocent misrepresentation is recognized in the Restatement (Second) of Torts:

§552C. MISREPRESENTATION IN SALE, RENTAL OR EXCHANGE TRANSACTION

(1) One who, in a sale, rental or exchange transaction with another, makes a misrepresentation of a material fact for the purpose of inducing the other to act or to refrain from acting in reliance upon it, is subject to liability to the other for pecuniary loss caused to him by his justifiable reliance upon the misrepresentation, even though it is not made fraudulently or negligently.

(2) Damages recoverable under the rule stated in this section are limited to the difference between the value of what the other has parted with and the value of what he has received in the transaction.

CAVEAT

The Institute expresses no opinion as to whether there may be other types of business transactions, in addition to those of sale, rental and exchange, in which strict liability may be imposed for innocent misrepresentation under the conditions stated in this Section.

Although the court in the *Johnson* case mingles principles of tort and warranty law, there may be some utility in keeping them separate in determining liability for innocent misrepresentation. Indeed, it may be important to keep both tort and warranty principles separate from equitable principles of restitution. The following comment to §552C of the Restatement attempts to explain why these distinctions may be necessary.

b. Relationship to action for restitution or breach of warranty. The remedy provided in this Section is very similar to that afforded under the law of restitution. It differs, however, in a material respect. The plaintiff is permitted to retain what he has received and recover damages, rather than rescind and seek restitution, in which case he must return what he received. The tort action for damages may have a definite advantage to the plaintiff in cases in which he is unable to restore what he received in its original condition; when he has made improvements or for other reasons finds it desirable to keep what he has received rather than return it; when he is barred from rescission by delay or has so far committed himself that he has lost the remedy by an election; or when for some other reason, such as the defendant's change of position, restitution is not available to him. It may even in many cases be a better solution from the point of view of the defendant himself, since it permits the transaction to stand, rather than be upset at a later date.

In view of the many similarities of the rule set forth in this Section to the restitutionary remedy, it is difficult to say with certainty whether this rule should be regarded as one of strict liability in the law of torts, eliminating the requirement of intent or negligence in making the representation, or one of the law of restitution, eliminating the requirement of rescinding and restoring the status quo. Under either classification the rule of this Section retains its usefulness.

It should be added that in cases involving the sale of goods, and probably in other transactions, a somewhat similar remedy has been available in the action for breach of warranty. The latter action, despite its historic relationship to tort, has been subject to important contract defenses, notably among them the parol evidence rule. This is made explicit by the Uniform Commercial Code. (See U.C.C. §2-202.) Further, in cases involving the sale of goods, most of the innocent misrepresentations made actionable by this Section would also be actionable under the Code on the theory of breach of warranty. But it does not necessarily follow that actions for damages founded upon innocent misrepresentation are preempted by the Code. The measure of damages provided by this Section differs from the traditional measure of damages for breach of warranty (now embodied in the Code). Under this Section, damages are solely restitutionary in character. In contrast, the measure of damages for breach of warranty includes compensation for benefit of the bargain and for consequential losses. This difference argues for viewing the tort action under this Section as unburdened by contract (or Code) defenses. However, this issue has gone virtually unnoticed in the jurisdictions that give damages in tort for innocent misrepresentation. In a case in which, as a practical matter, the amount recoverable under this Section is substantially the same as the amount recoverable for breach of warranty, the argument against recognition of defenses traditional to the warranty action loses much of its force.

3. Reliance and Contributory Negligence

Pelkey v. Norton

149 Me. 247, 99 A.2d 918 (1953)

TIRREL, J. This is an action "on the case" for deceit.

The plaintiff, who is a dealer in automobiles and trucks in the town of Topsham, alleged that he and the defendant entered into an agreement for the purchase and sale of a 1951 Packard automobile, by the terms of which the plaintiff sold the defendant a 1951 Packard automobile for a total sales price of $3,007.84, and in payment thereof, the defendant paid to the plaintiff the sum of $1,807.84 in cash and sold or, as the term is commonly used, "traded in" a truck towards the purchase price of the Packard automobile, for which the plaintiff "allowed" the defendant a credit on the purchase of $1,200, making payment in full.

The truck which the defendant sold or traded in was a 1947 Chevrolet truck. The plaintiff contends that at the time of their negotiation for the sale of the Packard automobile, the truck owned by the defendant was represented to be a 1949 Chevrolet truck by the defendant; whereas in truth and fact the truck was a 1947 model, and was known by the defendant to be a 1947 model, but was falsely represented by the defendant to induce the plaintiff to allow a greater amount as its trade-in value.

The undisputed testimony of witnesses for the plaintiff indicates the facts to be,—the plaintiff is an automobile dealer and had been for several years. On the date alleged in the declaration the defendant went to the place of business of the plaintiff and conversation was had between the parties concerning the sale by the plaintiff to the defendant of a 1951 Packard sedan. The selling price of the Packard, including extras, handling charges, and taxes, including the State sales tax, was $3,007.84. The defendant was the owner of a Chevrolet dump truck which he wished to "trade in" as part payment for the Packard sedan. It was, of course, essential for the plaintiff to know the year of manufacture of the truck in order to make the proper allowance as its "trade-in" value. The defendant informed the plaintiff it was a 1949 truck, saying: "I ought to know, I bought it new." The year of manufacture may be determined by securing serial and motor numbers imprinted on the frame and motor and by then referring to a certain book showing the year of manufacture. Included in the serial number is a key letter. The plaintiff by himself or his agents obtained certain numbers and a serial letter from the impression on the car. A mistake was apparently made in reading the letter Q as O. No serial letter O was revealed in the Dealers Book. The letter Q, if read correctly, would have informed the plaintiff that the Chevrolet truck was a 1947 model. The 1947 and 1949 models were of the same general appearance. The plaintiff then asked the defendant to show him the original bill of sale but was informed by defendant that it was at his son's house in North Yarmouth. The difference in the trade-in price between a 1949 model and a 1947 model was approximately $700. The plaintiff allowed the trade-in price of a 1949 model. Applications for registration of this same truck signed by the defendant and introduced by plaintiff as exhibits show the year model as a 1947. The plaintiff sold this truck to a third person as a 1949 model who later informed the plaintiff of the error in the date of the model and brought suit for damages against this plaintiff.

Upon completion of the plaintiff's evidence the defendant rested, and moved for a directed verdict for the defendant, which was granted, to which the plaintiff seasonably filed his exceptions. After the motion for a directed verdict was granted for the defendant, and before judgment was rendered, the plaintiff filed a motion for a directed verdict for the plaintiff, which motion was denied, and to which denial the plaintiff also took exceptions.

The plaintiff now prosecutes in this court on his exceptions to the granting of the motion for a directed verdict for the defendant and the denial of the motion for a directed verdict for the plaintiff.

The presiding Justice, in a short summation to the jury, before directing the verdict for the defendant, gave his reasons based on the case of Benjamin H. Coffin v. Winfred S. Dodge, 146 Me. 3, explaining to the jury that among the elements of deceit is one that a plaintiff in such a case must prove "that the plaintiff did not know the representation to be false, and by the exercise of reasonable care could not have ascertained its falsity."

In Coffin v. Dodge, supra, we said on pages 5 and 6: "In the case of Crossman v. Bacon & Robinson, 119 Me. 105, 109, the elements in deceit are stated to be '(1) a material representation which is (2) false and (3) known to be false, or made recklessly as an assertion of fact without knowledge of its truth or falsity and (4) made with the intention that it shall be acted upon and (5) acted upon with damage. In addition to these elements it must also be proved that the plaintiff (6) relied upon the representations (7) was induced to act upon them and (8) did not know them to be false, and by the exercise of reasonable care could not have ascertained their falsity. Every one of these elements must be proved affirmatively to sustain an action of deceit.' "

There is a well recognized exception to or limitation upon so much of the foregoing clause numbered (8) as requires proof that the plaintiff by the exercise of reasonable care could not have ascertained the falsity of the representation. . . .

The limitation on the foregoing clause numbered (8) is that one cannot escape liability for *intentional misrepresentation* on the ground that the plaintiff negligently relied thereon. In Bixler v. Wright, 116 Me. 133, 139 we said: "The law dislikes negligence. It seeks properly to make the enforcement of men's rights depend in very considerable degree upon whether they have been negligent in conserving and protecting their rights. But the law abhors fraud. And when it comes to an issue whether fraud shall prevail or negligence, it would seem that a court of justice is quite as much bound to stamp out fraud as it is to foster reasonable care.". . .

Many decisions hold that one guilty of actual fraud may not excuse his own wrongful acts by claiming that the person defrauded was guilty of contributory negligence.

In Eastern Trust & Banking Company v. Andrew W. Cunningham, 103 Me. 455, 465, 466, the court said:

> But the defendant contends further that if the plaintiff did not know, it ought to have known, and would have known but for its own negligence. We think this defense cannot avail. There are cases which hold that where one carelessly relies upon a pretence of inherent absurdity and incredibility, upon mere idle talk, or upon a device so shadowy as not to be capable of imposing upon anyone, he must bear his misfortune, if injured. He must not shut his eyes to what is palpably before him. But that doctrine, if sound, is not applicable here. We think the well settled rule to be applied here is that if one intentionally misrepresents to another facts particularly within his own knowledge, with an intent that the other shall act upon them, and he does so act, he cannot afterwards excuse himself by saying "You were foolish to believe me." It does not lie in his mouth to say that the one trusting him was negligent. In this case the fact whether or not there were funds in the Gardiner bank to meet the checks was peculiarly within the knowledge of the defendant. The rule is stated in Pollock on Torts, §252, as follows:—"It is now settled law that one who chooses to make positive assertions without warrant shall not excuse himself by saying that the other party need not have relied upon them. He must show that his representation was not in fact relied upon. In short, nothing will excuse a culpable misrepresentation short of

> proof that it was not relied upon, either because the other party knew the truth, or because he *relied wholly* on his own investigations, or because the alleged fact did not influence his actions at all." (Emphasis ours) . . .

This case has been twice quoted with approval by this court, to wit, in the cases of Bixler v. Wright and Eastern Trust & Banking Company v. Cunningham, both supra. The same doctrine was recognized in Elmer E. Harlow et al. v. Fred E. Perry, 113 Me. 239, when we said:

> We think the well settled rule to be applied here is that if one intentionally misrepresents to another facts particularly within his own knowledge, with an intent that the other shall act upon them, and he does so, he cannot afterwards excuse himself by saying, 'you were foolish to believe me.' It does not lie in his mouth to say that the one trusting him was negligent.

The present case is clearly distinguishable from Coffin v. Dodge, supra. The facts bring it within the limitation on the general rules laid down therein. In this record there is testimony which, if believed by the jury, would justify a finding that the defendant was guilty of an actual, intentional, false and fraudulent misrepresentation to the plaintiff. If so, negligence on the part of the plaintiff in reliance thereon was no defense to his action of deceit. There was sufficient evidence in this record to justify a finding by the jury of the existence of every essential element of actionable fraud.

On this record it was error to direct a verdict for the defendant and the plaintiff's exception thereto must be sustained. . . .

Exception to direction of verdict for the defendant sustained.

Pelkey follows the generally accepted rule that the plaintiff must rely upon the defendant's misrepresentation and the reliance must be justifiable under the circumstances. Thus, the plaintiff's actual knowledge of the facts will bar recovery. See, e.g., Williams v. Bisson, 142 Me. 83, 46 A.2d 708 (1946), wherein the plaintiff knew the true facts regarding erroneous recitals in a deed. And in Ex parte Leo, 480 So. 2d 572 (Ala. 1985) the plaintiff indicated by his conduct that he did not rely on representations as to the square footage of the house he bought from the defendant; the plaintiff had access to the house and had made some measurements himself. The difficult cases are those in which the plaintiff actually relies, but under circumstances where the defendant may argue that the plaintiff's reliance was unreasonable. Where the defendant has been guilty of actual fraud, a majority of courts have sided with Pelkey v. Norton in turning a deaf ear to the argument that the plaintiff should have discovered the truth. See Restatement (Second) of Torts §545A; Roda v. Berko, 401 Ill. 335, 81 N.E.2d 912 (1948). A classic statement of this position appears in Chamberlin v. Fuller, 59 Vt. 247, 256, 9 A. 832, 836 (1887): "No rogue should enjoy his ill-gotten plunder for the simple reason that his victim is by chance a fool." Section 540 of the Restatement (Second) makes clear that the recipient of a fraudulent misrepresentation of fact is justified in relying on its truth even if its falsity would have been revealed by an investigation. Of course, even in a case involving fraud, the plaintiff must justifiably rely on the misrepresentation. Unlike contributory negligence, however, justifiable reliance is determined by a subjective evaluation of the characteristics of a particular plaintiff in the circumstances of a particular case, rather than on the basis of an objective evaluation of what a reasonable person would have believed. Under §541 of the Restatement (Second), for example, reliance on fraudulent misrepresentation is not justified if the plaintiff knows it is false or if its falsity is obvious to the plaintiff.

On the other hand, when the misrepresentation is merely negligent and not fraudulent, contributory negligence will in most jurisdictions bar the plaintiff's recovery (see §552B, Restatement of Torts (Second)) or reduce it if comparative fault rules apply (see Halla Nursery, Inc. v. Baumann-Furrie & Co., 454 N.W.2d 905 (Minn. 1990)). In Estate of Braswell v. People's Credit Union, 602 A.2d 510 (R.I. 1992), the court ruled that contributory negligence will not bar recovery for pecuniary loss stemming from negligent misrepresentations in consumer transactions. In some states, contributory negligence will not bar a restitution claim based on negligent misrepresentation. See Wilson v. Came, 116 N.H. 628, 366 A.2d 474 (1976). And when the defendant is held strictly liable under §552C, above, the plaintiff is only required to show justifiable reliance on the innocent misrepresentation. Does it seem strange to you that innocent misrepresenters are treated more harshly than negligent misrepresenters with regard to the effects of the plaintiff's contributory negligence?

In any event, can you imagine a case in which a contributorily negligent plaintiff can plausibly argue justifiable reliance on the defendant's misrepresentation? Consider the following, arguably unusual case.

Corva v. United Services Automobile Association

108 A.D. 2d 631, 485 N.Y.S.2d 264 (1985)

Before SANDLER, J.P., and CARRO, BLOOM and KASSAL, JJ.

MEMORANDUM DECISION. . . .

Plaintiff was a passenger in an automobile on March 29, 1979 when it was involved in an accident with a motor vehicle owned by Donald Sabia. Plaintiff retained the firm of Mangiatordi & Corpina (M & C) to represent her. Sabia was insured by United Services Automobile Association (USAA). Upon notification of the accident USAA employed Dahle Lassonde & Co., Inc., (Dahle) and Jack L. Hall to protect its interests. Negotiations ensued between M & C and Dahle and Hall as a result of which the matter was settled for $15,000, allegedly because Dahle and Hall represented to M &

C that that was the limit of Sabia's coverage. The complaint alleges that Sabia carried insurance with USAA in excess of $15,000 and seeks compensatory and punitive damages. Dahle and Hall and USAA interposed separate defenses. Each set forth a cross-complaint against M & C asserting that M & C violated its duty of care to Corva by not independently verifying the policy limits in the policy of insurance issued by USAA and that therefore, in the event of a recovery by Corva against the cross-claimants, or any of them, those found liable to Corva will be entitled to indemnity or contribution from M & C.

M & C moved to dismiss the third and fourth party complaints. Special Term granted the motion. We reverse and reinstate these complaints. . . . Paragraph 15 of the complaint alleges:

> . . . That the aforesaid representations were made with the knowledge that they were false, or there should have been knowledge that they were false; or were made with wanton, gross and reckless disregard as to whether they were true or false, with a pretense of knowledge when in fact there was no knowledge, without taking the necessary and proper steps to ascertain the truth of the said representations which were ascertainable and available all with knowledge that the plaintiff was relying and would act upon said representations.

To the extent to which the cross-complaints seek contribution from M & C on the theory that M & C's violation of its duty of care to Corva contributed to the loss sustained, the cross-complaints would appear to be legally sufficient. It is of course well established that New York law permits an apportionment of damages among culpable parties "regardless of the degree or nature of the concurring fault" and that contribution is permitted even in favor of an intentional wrongdoer if the parties are subject to liability to plaintiff for damages for the same injury.

In dismissing the cross-complaints, Special Term . . . concluded that plaintiff could succeed in its main action only on showing that M & C had justifiably relied upon the misrepresentation alleged and that such a finding would be inconsistent with a determination that M & C had violated its duty of care to its client by not independently verifying the policy limits. The flaw in this analysis lies in the erroneous assumption that the standard for determining justifiable reliance in an action for fraud and misrepresentation is identical with the standard of reasonable care in a negligence or malpractice action. The standards are in fact quite different.

In discussing the requirement of justifiable reliance in a misrepresentation case, a leading authority observed:

> The plaintiff's conduct must not be so utterly unreasonable, in light of the information open to him, that the law may properly say that his loss is his own responsibility. . . . If he is a person of normal intelligence, experience and education, he may not put faith in representations which any such normal

> person would recognize at once as preposterous, as, for example, that glasses, once fitted, will alter shape and adapt themselves to the eye, or which are shown by facts within his observation to be so patently and obviously false that he must have closed his eyes to avoid discovery of the truth. . . . Prosser, Law of Torts (4th ed.) pp. 715, 716.

The standard of reasonable care in negligence or malpractice actions in obviously quite different, and it is clearly theoretically possible that M & C could have justifiably relied on the alleged misrepresentations for purposes of the plaintiff's action and still have been at fault in failing independently to inquire into the policy limits.

In the foregoing observations we of course intimate no opinion as to the merits of the cross-complaints. There is obviously something unappealing in the notion that someone who has deceived another should be entitled to contribution for the damage caused by the deception because the deceived person had imprudently relied on the truthfulness of the representation. All we decide here is that the cross-complaints may not be dismissed as a matter of law.

All concur.

4. Liability to Third Persons

Ultramares Corp. v. Touche

255 N.Y. 170, 174 N.E. 441 (1931)

CARDOZO, C.J. The action is in tort for damages suffered through the misrepresentations of accountants, the first cause of action being for misrepresentations that were merely negligent and the second for misrepresentations charged to have been fraudulent.

In January, 1924, the defendants, a firm of public accountants, were employed by Fred Stern and Co., Inc., to prepare and certify a balance sheet exhibiting the condition of its business as of December 31, 1923. They had been employed at the end of each of three years preceding to render a like service. Fred Stern & Co., Inc., which was in substance Stern himself, was engaged in the importation and sale of rubber. To finance its operations, it required extensive credit and borrowed large sums of money from banks and other lenders. All this was known to the defendants. The defendants knew also that in the usual course of business the balance sheet when certified would be exhibited by the Stern company to banks, creditors, stockholders, purchasers or sellers, according to the needs of the occasion, as the basis of financial dealings. Accordingly, when the balance sheet was made up, the defendants supplied the Stern company with thirty-two copies certified with serial numbers as counterpart originals. Nothing was said as to the persons to whom these counterparts would be shown or the extent or number of the transactions in which they would be used. In particular there was no mention of the plaintiff, a corporation doing business chiefly as a factor, which till then had never made advances to the Stern company, though it had sold merchandise in small amounts. The range of the transactions in which a certificate of audit might be expected to play a part was as indefinite and wide as the possibilities of the business that was mirrored in the summary.

By February 26, 1924, the audit was finished and the balance sheet made up. It stated assets in the sum of $2,550,671.88 and liabilities other than capital and surplus in the sum of $1,479,956.62, thus showing a net worth of $1,070,715.26. Attached to the balance sheet was a certificate as follows:

TOUCHE, NIVEN & CO.
Public Accountants
Eighty Maiden Lane
New York

February 26, 1924.

Certificate of Auditors

We have examined the accounts of Fred Stern & Co., Inc., for the year ending December 31, 1923, and hereby certify that the annexed balance sheet is in accordance therewith and with the information and explanations given us. We further certify that, subject to provision for federal taxes on income, the said statement, in our opinion, presents a true and correct view of the financial condition of Fred Stern & Co., Inc., as at December 31, 1923.

TOUCHE, NIVEN & CO.
Public Accountants

Capital and surplus were intact if the balance sheet was accurate. In reality both had been wiped out, and the corporation was insolvent. The books had been falsified by those in charge of the business so as to set forth accounts receivable and other assets which turned out to be fictitious. The plaintiff maintains that the certificate of audit was erroneous in both its branches. The first branch, the asserted correspondence between the accounts and the balance sheet, is one purporting to be made as of the knowledge of the auditors. The second branch, which certifies to a belief that the condition reflected in the balance sheet presents a true and correct picture of the resources of the business, is stated as a matter of opinion. In the view of the plaintiff, both branches of the certificate are either fraudulent or negligent. As to one class of assets, the item of accounts receivable, if not also as to others, there was no real correspondence, we are told, between balance sheet and books, or so the triers of the facts might find. If correspondence, however, be assumed, a closer examination of supporting invoices and records, or a fuller inquiry directed to the persons appearing on the books as creditors or debtors, would have exhibited the truth.

[The plaintiff corporation loaned money to Stern & Co. in reliance upon the audit certified by the defendant, and suffered losses when Stern & Co. went into bankruptcy.]

This action, brought against the accountants in November, 1926, to recover the loss suffered by the plaintiff in reliance upon the audit, was in its inception one for negligence. On the trial there was added a second cause of action asserting fraud also. The trial judge dismissed the second cause of action without submitting it to the jury. As to the first cause of action, he reserved his decision on the defendants' motion to dismiss, and took the jury's verdict. They were told that the defendants might be held liable if with knowledge that the results of the audit would be communicated to creditors they did the work negligently, and that negligence was the omission to use reasonable and ordinary care. The verdict was in favor of the plaintiff for $187,576.32. On the coming in of the verdict, the judge granted the reserved motion. The Appellate Division affirmed the dismissal of the cause of action for fraud, but reversed the dismissal of the cause of action for negligence, and reinstated the verdict. The case is here on cross-appeals.

The two causes of action will be considered in succession, first the one for negligence and second that for fraud.

(1) We think the evidence supports a finding that the audit was negligently made, though in so saying we put aside for the moment the question whether negligence, even if it existed, was a wrong to the plaintiff. [The court's description of the defendant's negligence is omitted.]

If the defendants owed a duty to the plaintiff to act with the same care that would have been due under a contract of employment, a jury was at liberty to find a verdict of negligence upon a showing of a scrutiny so imperfect and perfunctory. . . .

We are brought to the question of duty, its origin and measure.

The defendants owed to their employer a duty imposed by law to make their certificate without fraud, and a duty growing out of contract to make it with the care and caution proper to their calling. Fraud includes the pretense of knowledge when knowledge there is none. To creditors and investors to whom the employer exhibited the certificate, the defendants owed a like duty to make it without fraud, since there was notice in the circumstances of its making that the employer did not intend to keep it to himself. A different question develops when we ask whether they owed a duty to these to make it without negligence. If liability for negligence exists, a thoughtless slip or blunder, the failure to detect a theft or forgery beneath the cover of deceptive entries, may expose accountants to a liability in an indeterminate amount for an indeterminate time to an indeterminate class. The hazards of a business conducted on these terms are so extreme as to enkindle doubt whether a flaw may not exist in the implication of a duty that exposes to these consequences. We put aside for the moment any statement in the certificate which involves the representation of a fact as true to the knowledge of the auditors. If such a statement was made, whether believed to be true or not, the defendants are liable for deceit in the event that it was false. The plaintiff does not need the invention of novel doctrine to help it out in such conditions. The case was submitted to the jury and the verdict was returned upon the theory that even in the absence of a misstatement of a fact there is a liability also for erroneous opinion. The expression of an opinion is to be subject to a warranty implied by law. What, then, is the warranty, as yet unformulated, to be? Is it merely that the opinion is honestly conceived and that the preliminary inquiry has been honestly pursued, that a halt has not been made without a genuine belief that the search has been reasonably adequate to bring disclosure of the truth? Or does it go farther and involve the assumption of a liability for any blunder or inattention that could fairly be spoken of as negligence if the controversy were one between accountant and employer for breach of a contract to render services for pay?

The assault upon the citadel of privity is proceeding in these days apace. How far the inroads shall extend is now a favorite subject of juridical discussion. . . . In the field of the law of torts a manufacturer who is negligent in the manufacture of a chattel in circumstances pointing to an unreasonable risk of serious bodily harm to those using it thereafter may be liable for negligence though privity is lacking between manufacturer and user (MacPherson v. Buick Motor Co., 217 N.Y. 382). A force or instrument of harm having been launched with potentialities of danger manifest to the eye of prudence, the one who launches it is under a duty to keep it within bounds. Even so, the question is still open whether the potentialities of danger that will charge with liability are confined to harm to the person, or include injury to property. In either view, however, what is released or set in motion is a physical force. We are now asked to say that a like liability attaches to the circulation of a thought or a release of the explosive power resident in words. . . .

In Glanzer v. Shepard [233 N.Y. 236, 135 N.E. 275 (1922)] the seller of beans requested the defendants, public weighers, to make return of the weight and furnish the buyer with a copy. This the defendants did. Their return, which was made out in duplicate, one copy to the seller and the other to the buyer, recites that it was made by order of the former for the use of the latter. The buyer paid the seller on the faith of the certificate which turned out to be erroneous. We held that the weighers were liable at the suit of the buyer for the moneys overpaid. Here was something more than the rendition of a service in the expectation that the one who ordered the certificate would use it thereafter in the operations of his business as occasion might require. Here was a case where the transmission of the certificate to another was not merely one possibility among many, but the "end and aim of the transaction," as certain and immediate and deliberately willed as if a husband were to order a gown to be delivered to his wife, or a telegraph company, contracting with the sender of a message, were to telegraph it wrongly to the damage of the person expected to receive it. The bond was so close as to approach that of privity, if not completely one with it. Not so in the case at hand. No one would be likely to urge that there was a contractual relation, or even one approaching it, at the root of any duty that was owing from the defendants now before us to the indeterminate class of persons who, presently or in the future, might deal with the Stern company in reliance on the audit. In a word, the service rendered by the defendant in Glanzer v. Shepard was primarily for the information of a third person, in effect, if not in name, a party to the contract, and only incidentally for that of the formal promisee. In the case at hand, the service was primarily for the benefit of the Stern company, a convenient instrumentality for use in the development of the business, and only incidentally or collaterally for the use of those to whom Stern and his associates might exhibit it thereafter. Foresight of these possibilities may charge with liability for fraud. The conclusion does not follow that it will charge with liability for negligence.

[The opinion next discusses International Products Co. v. Erie R.R., above, and distinguishes it on the ground that there existed in that case a "determinate relation, that of bailor and bailee, with peculiar opportunity for knowledge on the part of the bailee as to the subject-matter of the statement and with a continuing duty to correct it if erroneous."]

From the foregoing analysis the conclusion is, we think, inevitable that nothing in our previous decisions commits us to a holding of liability for negligence in the circumstances of the case at hand, and that such liability, if recognized, will be an extension of the principle of those decisions to different conditions, even if more or less analogous. The question then is whether such an extension shall be made.

The extension, if made, will so expand the field of liability for negligent speech as to make it nearly, if not quite, coterminous with that of liability for fraud. Again and again, in decisions of this court, the bounds of this latter liability have been set up, with futility the fate of every endeavor to dislodge them. Scienter has been declared to be an indispensable element except where the representation has been put forward as true of one's own knowledge, or in circumstances where the expression of opinion was a dishonorable pretense. Even an opinion, especially an opinion by an expert, may be found to be fraudulent if the grounds supporting it are so flimsy as to lead to the conclusion that there was no genuine belief back of it. Further than that this court has never gone. Directors of corporations have been acquitted of liability for deceit though they have been lax in investigation and negligent in speech. This has not meant, to be sure, that negligence may not be evidence from which a trier of the facts may draw an inference of fraud (Derry v. Peek, [L. R.] 14 A.C. 337, 369, 375, 376), but merely that if that inference is rejected, or, in the light of all the circumstances, is found to be unreasonable, negligence alone is not a substitute for fraud.

Many also are the cases that have distinguished between the willful or reckless representation essential to the maintenance at law of an action for deceit, and the misrepresentation, negligent or innocent, that will lay a sufficient basis for rescission in equity. If this action is well conceived, all these principles and distinctions, so nicely wrought and formulated, have been a waste of time and effort. They have even been a snare, entrapping litigants and lawyers into an abandonment of the true remedy lying ready to the call. The suitors thrown out of court because they proved negligence, and nothing else, in an action for deceit, might have ridden to triumphant victory if they had proved the self-same facts, but had given the wrong another label, and all this in a State where forms of action have been abolished. So to hold is near to saying that we have been paltering with justice. A word of caution or suggestion would have set the erring suitor right. Many pages of opinion were written by judges the most eminent, yet the word was never spoken. We may not speak it now. A change so revolutionary, if expedient, must be wrought by legislation. . . .

Our holding does not emancipate accountants from the consequences of fraud. It does not relieve them if their audit has been so negligent as to justify a finding that they had no genuine belief in its adequacy, for this again is fraud. It does no more than say that if less than this is proved, if there has been neither reckless misstatement nor insincere profession of an opinion, but only honest blunder, the ensuing liability for negligence is one that is bounded by the contract, and is to be enforced between the parties by whom the contract has been made. We doubt whether the average business man receiving a certificate without paying for it and receiving it merely as one among a multitude of possible investors, would look for anything more.

(2) The second cause of action is yet to be considered.

The defendants certified as a fact, true to their own knowledge, that the balance sheet was in accordance with the books of account. If their statement was false, they are not to be exonerated because they believed it to be true. We think the triers of the facts might hold it to be false. . . .

In this connection we are to bear in mind the principle already stated in the course of this opinion that negligence or blindness, even when not equivalent to fraud, is none the less evidence to sustain an inference of fraud. At least this is so if the negligence is gross. . . .

We conclude, to sum up the situation, that in certifying to the correspondence between balance sheet and accounts the defendants made a statement as true to their own knowledge, when they had, as a jury might find, no knowledge on the subject. If that is so, they may also be found to have acted without information leading to a sincere or genuine belief when they certified to an opinion that the balance sheet faithfully reflected the condition of the business. . . .

Upon the defendants' appeal as to the first cause of action, the judgment of the Appellate Division should be reversed, and that of the Trial Term affirmed, with costs in the Appellate Division and in this court.

Upon the plaintiff's appeal as to the second cause of action, the judgment of the Appellate Division and that of the Trial Term should be reversed, and a new trial granted, with costs to abide the event.

POUND, CRANE, LEHMAN, KELLOGG, O'BRIEN and HUBBS, JJ., concur.

Judgment accordingly.

In Credit Alliance Corp. v. Arthur Andersen & Co., 65 N.Y.2d 536, 483 N.E.2d 110 (1985), the Court of Appeals of New York held that to be liable to third persons in negligence, "(1) the accountants must have been aware that the financial reports were to be used for a particular purpose or purposes; (2) in the furtherance of which a known party or parties was intended to rely; and (3) there must have been some conduct on the part of the accountants linking them to that party or parties, which evinces the accountants' understanding of that party or parties' reliance." 65 N.Y.2d at 551, 483 N.E.2d at 118. The Court of Appeals has made it clear that the accountant's knowledge that the third person will rely on the accountant's work is not enough to impose liability. See Iselin v. Landau, 71 N.Y.2d 420, 522 N.E.2d 21 (1988).

A broader rule of third person liability for negligent misrepresentation is contained in §552 of the Restatement (Second) of Torts, which in part provides:

> (1) One who, in the course of his business, profession or employment, or in any other transaction in which he has a pecuniary interest, supplies false information for the guidance of others in their business transactions, is subject to liability for pecuniary loss caused to them by their justifiable reliance upon the information, if he fails to exercise reasonable care or competence in obtaining or communicating the information.
>
> (2) [T]he liability stated in Subsection 1 is limited to loss suffered
>
> (a) by the person or one of a limited group of persons for whose benefit and guidance he intends to supply the information or knows that the recipient intends to supply it. . . .

Most courts that have considered the matter have opted for the Restatement rule. See, e.g., Bily v. Arthur Young & Co., 3 Cal. 4th 370, 834 P.2d 745, 11 Cal. Rptr. 2d 51 (1992); Bethlehem Steel Corp. v. Ernst & Whinney, 822 S.W.2d 592 (Tenn. 1991); First National Bank of Bluefield v. Crawford, 182 W. Va. 107, 386 S.E.2d 310 (1989).

A somewhat more restrictive rule than that expressed in *Ultramares* and *Credit Alliance* was adopted by the court in Selden v. Burnett, 754 P.2d 256 (Alaska 1988). The court held that in giving tax advice, an accountant is liable for negligent misrepresentation only to those the accountant specifically intends to rely on the advice, and then only if the accountant makes that intent known.

Other courts have gone beyond the scope of liability set out in the Restatement, and impose liability in favor of those who foreseeably rely upon the misrepresentation. See, e.g., H. Rosenblum, Inc. v. Adler, 93 N.J. 324, 461 A.2d 138 (1983); Citizens State Bank v. Timm, Schmidt, & Co., 113 Wis. 2d 376, 335 N.W.2d 361 (1983).

Critical of the expansion of accountants' liability to include those who foreseeably rely are Siliciano, Negligent Accounting and the Limits of Instrumental Tort Reform, 86 Mich L. Rev. 1929 (1988), and Goldberg, Accountable Accountants: Is Third-Party Liability Necessary?, 17 J. Legal Stud. 295 (1988).

To some extent, the subject of the liability of accountants and others for negligent misrepresentations has been supplemented by federal statutes and regulations governing the sale of securities in this country. Actions may be brought under several sections of the Securities Act of 1933 (15 U.S.C. §77) and the Securities Exchange Act of 1934 (15 U.S.C. §78) by investors financially harmed by misleading or fraudulent representations or nondisclosures accompanying the sale of securities. See generally Loss, Fundamentals of Securities Regulation 1016-1024 (2d Ed. 1988).

Although most of the cases have involved accountants and auditors, courts have extended third party liability to other occupations. See, e.g., First State Savings Bank v. Albright & Associates of Ocala, Inc., 561 So. 2d 1326 (Fla. App.), *rev. denied,* 576 So. 2d 284 (Fla. 1990) (land appraiser); Ossining Union Free School Dist. v. Anderson LaRocca Anderson, 73 N.Y.2d 417, 539 N.E.2d 91 (1989) (engineers and architects); John Martin Co., Inc. v. Morse/Diesel, Inc., 819 S.W.2d 428 (Tenn. 1991) (subcontractor).

Of considerable interest to the legal profession is the extent to which lawyers may be liable for misrepresentation to persons other than their clients. Two federal district court cases took opposite positions as to whether New York law under *Credit Alliance* would impose third person liability on lawyers. The court in Crossland Savings FSB v. Rockwood Insurance Co., 692 F. Supp. 1510 (S.D. N.Y. 1988), held that *Credit Alliance* only applies to accountants, and so refused to impose liability for negligent misrepresentation against an attorney in favor of one with whom the attorney was not in a contractual relationship. A different judge in the same federal district held in Vereins-Und Westbank, AG v. Carter, 691 F. Supp. 704 (S.D. N.Y. 1988), that *Credit Alliance* does apply to attorneys. Which of the two federal district judges is correct as to the liability of lawyers in New York may be unresolved, but it is clear that the Court of Appeals of New York will apply *Credit Alliance* to others besides accountants. See *Ossining Union Free School District,* cited above.

The failure of large numbers of federally insured savings and loan associations has resulted in a search for sources of compensation for the consequent losses that has focused on lawyers. One law firm agreed to a fine of $41 million for its misconduct in connection with the failure of one S & L. In general, see Langevoort, Where Were the Lawyers? A Behavioral Inquiry

Into Lawyers' Responsibility for Clients' Fraud, 46 Vand. L. Rev. 75 (1993); Symposium, 66 So. Cal. L. Rev. 985 (1993). The liability of lawyers to third persons for negligent misrepresentations in securities matters is discussed in Cohn, Securities Counseling for New and Developing Companies, ch. 20.11 (1993).

As a general rule, liability of a defendant found to have been guilty of intentional misrepresentation extends to those the defendant intends to, or has reason to foresee will, act in reliance on the representation. See Restatement of Torts (Second), §531; Bily v. Arthur Young & Co., cited above. Liability for innocent misrepresentation is limited under §552 C to sale, rental, and exchange transactions, and applies only when the defendant made a representation "of material fact for the purpose of inducing the other to act or to refrain from acting in reliance on it," and the other justifiably relied on the representation.

B. Interference with Business Relations

1. Intentional Interference with Contractual Relations

Wilkinson v. Powe

300 Mich. 275, 1 N.W. 2d 539 (1942)

BUSHNELL, J. Plaintiff Jay D. Wilkinson brought this action against defendants Powe and Stinson, individually and doing business as Shamrock Creamery, charging them with wrongfully procuring a breach of plaintiff's contract with certain farmers to haul their milk.

In 1932 plaintiff and his father, David Wilkinson, began to haul milk for farmers to the Oakland Creamery and built up their first milk route. Later, they ceased to deliver milk to the Oakland Creamery and began to deliver to the Shamrock Creamery. The Wilkinsons developed a second milk route in 1934 or 1935. A written agreement covering the year 1937 was entered into between the Wilkinsons and the farmers on their milk routes in December of 1936. The Wilkinsons agreed to haul milk to Pontiac creameries and the farmers agreed to pay them 25 cents per hundred. Prior to 1937, the arrangement between the Wilkinsons and the farmers was not evidenced by a written contract. The principal and heavier route was 97 miles and the other 94 miles. In April of 1937, David H. Wilkinson assigned all of his interest in the milk routes to plaintiff Jay D. Wilkinson.

Shortly after the execution of the written agreement, defendant Powe told the Wilkinsons that he wanted to take over the larger route and offered in exchange for the route the trade-in value of plaintiff's old truck, and told plaintiff he would give him a job in the creamery. Plaintiff then informed Powe of the existence of the written contract and refused to give up the route. About three months later Powe informed plaintiff that he would be required to replace the open stake racks on his trucks with insulated bodies because of a municipal ordinance. After plaintiff made this change in his trucks, he was unable to get his trucks into the creamery and the milk had to be handled by hand. This led to friction between the parties.

On May 29, 1937, defendant Powe sent a letter to the farmers doing business with plaintiff, worded as follows:

> For reasons which are vital to our business, we the Shamrock Creamery, have decided that on and after June 1st, we will purchase no milk except that which is picked up by our own trucks at the farm.
>
> Nothing on your part has occasioned or made necessary this change, and we are hopeful that you will continue to sell us your milk. Pursuant to the change made, our trucks will call at your place Tuesday afternoon, June 1st, to pick up your milk, if you desire to continue business with us.
>
> Trusting that our business relationship may continue and be of mutual benefit, I am,
>
> Yours very truly
> (Signed) *T. M. Powe,*
> SHAMROCK CREAMERY

The particular season of the year in which the letter was written was described by a witness as being the "lush" season for milk when the available supply is about double that of other months of the year. This letter resulted in a meeting of some of the farmers to consider the situation. As a result of the request made by some of these farmers at the meeting, defendants sent out a notice dated June 1, 1937, reading:

> We have agreed to let Jay D. Wilkinson's trucks continue to haul the milk they have been hauling to our milk plant for the first 10 days of June, 1937. Disregard the notices you received today May 31st until June 11th.

On June 10th, Powe wrote a letter to Wilkinson in which he said:

> We have caused to be served on all farmers affected by the same a duplicate of the attached letter. Due to a verbal agreement made in consideration of the wish of some of those affected the date stated was extended to June 11, 1937.
>
> Since we understand that you have a contract of some nature with many of the farmers in question we are inclosing a copy of said letter, so that you may govern yourself accordingly.

Wilkinson was unable to find another suitable market for milk after June 10th and was soon forced to abandon his routes. Defendants have since hauled the milk of practically all the farmers formerly under contract with plaintiff.

Plaintiff alleged in his declaration that defendants' object was to prevent him from protecting the farmers on his routes from false, fraudulent, and dishonest practices in the testing, weighing and price paid for milk. This was denied by defendants. They claimed their reason for deciding to haul the milk was that plaintiff failed to deliver the milk on time or in a proper condition, and that the action was taken to protect themselves and their customers by insuring a steady supply of good cream and wholesome milk. The testimony is in conflict on this point; but since the jury found for plaintiff, it must be assumed that they resolved this question against the defendants.

Plaintiff claimed damages in the sum of $5,000, and testified that each of his routes had a value of $2,000. The jury returned a verdict in the sum of $4,000. On a former trial by jury, a verdict of $5,000 was rendered and judgment entered thereon. Subsequently a new trial was granted. On this, the second trial, decision on a motion for directed verdict having been reserved, the trial judge entered a judgment for no cause of action. . . .

The crux of the [trial] court's opinion is expressed as follows:

> A factual situation justifying the submission of the issue to a jury for the assessment of the damages is not present. The jury verdict must be predicated upon a circumstance which does not take into consideration the defendants' right to discontinue its source of supply at any time. To find for the plaintiff is a sympathetic attempt to give legal security to one, who, in a precarious position, acted unwisely. . . . Without their acceptance (defendants) of the product the routes had no value. Lawful action, not unlawful action, then eliminated any value the routes may have had.

If the trial court is to be sustained, the judgment must stand on one of two grounds; first, that, in procuring the breach of contract, defendants were exercising what is often designated as a "superior" or "absolute" right, i.e., to refuse to accept further delivery of milk from plaintiff and, therefore, no justification was necessary; or second, that the injury, if any, was the result of defendants' refusal to accept deliveries of milk from plaintiff, and the breach of contract by the farmers was not the proximate cause of plaintiff's injury. [The court approves the principle laid down in Lumley v. Gye, above.] . . .

If the defendants in the instant case had merely refused to accept further delivery of milk by plaintiff, they would have been clearly within their legal rights, although this would have resulted in a breach of contract between plaintiff and the farmers. But defendants did more. Their letters of May 29th and June 1st show active solicitation of a breach of the contract and their refusal to accept delivery of milk was merely another step in bringing about the breach.

Almost analogous facts, so far as the principle is concerned, are found in Knickerbocker Ice Co. v. Gardiner Dairy Co., 107 Md. 556 (69 Atl. 405, 16 L.R.A. [N. S.] 746). In the *Gardiner* case, plaintiff Gardiner Company was engaged in the dairy business and required a large quantity of ice during the spring and summer months. In order to meet its requirements, it entered into a contract with the Sumwalt Company to deliver not exceeding 20 tons of ice a day until the completion of plaintiff's plant, then in the course of construction, at a price of $5 per ton, delivered. Sumwalt at the time was purchasing ice in large quantities from the defendant, Knickerbocker Ice Company, and when defendant learned of the contract between Gardiner and Sumwalt, it notified Sumwalt that it would refuse to deliver any ice whatever to it unless it refrained from delivering ice to Gardiner. Being compelled by the exigencies of its business to secure ice from Knickerbocker, and alarmed by the threat, Sumwalt breached its contract with Gardiner and advised it that this was done because of the action of Knickerbocker. Gardiner was thereby compelled to purchase ice directly from Knickerbocker at a price considerably greater and on less advantageous terms. The court discussed Lumley v. Gye, supra, and other authorities, and held that (p. 567):

> If the Knickerbocker company had simply refused to furnish the Sumwalt company with ice, the Gardiner company would not, for that reason alone, have a remedy against the Knickerbocker company. Such action would not necessarily be unlawful or wrongful, but, if the Knickerbocker company refused to furnish the Sumwalt company if it furnished the Gardiner company, although it knew it was under contract to do so, in order to get the business of the Gardiner company for itself on its own terms, then it was unlawful thus to interfere with the contract between the Sumwalt company and the Gardiner company. So, without further pursuing that branch of the case, we are of the opinion that the demurrer was properly overruled, as the declaration stated an actionable wrong, even if there had been no express allegation of malice.

The editor states in the annotations of 16 L.R.A. (N.S.) at page 747, that: "Although the doctrine is denied by some courts, the weight of authority at the present time sustains Knickerbocker Ice Co. v. Gardiner Dairy Co."

Substituting defendant for Knickerbocker, the farmers for Sumwalt, and plaintiff for Gardiner, there is a parallel in principle. Instead of refusing to sell, as in the *Gardiner* case, defendants in the instant case refused to purchase from the farmers unless they broke their contract with plaintiff and thereby brought about the breach.

Defendants' refusal to accept further deliveries of milk by plaintiff was wrongful in the light of the evidence in the instant case because it was done to accomplish an unlawful purpose, i.e., to bring about a breach of contract. It therefore follows that the problem of proximate cause disappears from consideration in the case. Defendants cannot be heard to say that they should not be held liable for the injury caused plaintiff by their unlawful acts merely because they could have caused the same injury by a lawful act.

The right to perform a contract and to reap the profits resulting therefrom, and the right to compel performance by the other party, is generally regarded as a property right. The direct consequence of defendants' acts was to destroy plaintiff's routes, and plaintiff is entitled to recover their value.

That a few of the farmers on the routes had not signed the contracts is beside the point. Plaintiff certainly had an understanding with them, and there is no testimony to show that they would not have continued to employ plaintiff to haul their milk if defendants had not interfered.

The damages allowed by the jury are supported by the testimony. The order for entry of judgment notwithstanding the verdict is vacated and the cause remanded for entry of judgment upon the verdict. Costs to appellant.

CHANDLER, C.J., and BOYLES, NORTH, STARR, WIEST, BUTZEL, and SHARPE, JJ., concurred.

The most famous decision imposing tort liability upon one who intentionally induces another to breach a contract with a third party is Lumley v. Gye, 2 El. & Bl. 216, 118 Eng. Rep. 749 (Q.B. 1853). The plaintiff had a contract with the singer Johanna Wagner (Richard Wagner's niece) whereby the latter was to perform exclusively for the former during the term of the contract. The defendant, knowing of the contract, "enticed and procured Wagner to refuse to perform" for the plaintiff. The court held that the plaintiff could recover damages for defendant's wrongful interference with the contract.[1] Although at first the doctrine established in Lumley v. Gye was approached somewhat hesitantly by both English and American courts (see Schofield, The Principle of Lumley v. Gye and Its Application, 2 Harv. L. Rev. 19 (1888)), it is now fully accepted both in England (see, e.g., Thompson v. Deakin, [1952] ch. 646) and in this country (see, e.g., Wilkinson v. Powe, above, and Restatement (Second) of Torts §§766-774A). A broad range of contractual relations are protected, including agreements which are unenforceable (see, e.g., Hill & Co. v. Wallerich, 67 Wash. 2d 409, 407 P.2d 956 (1965)), or terminable (see, e.g., Hammonds v. Aetna Casualty & Surety Co., 237 F. Supp. 96 (N.D. Ohio 1965)). These elements of unenforceability and terminability may affect the measure of damages to which the plaintiff is entitled, but they do not bar recovery against one who has intentionally interfered with the relationship.

In order to recover in these cases, the plaintiff must show that the defendant's interference with contractual relations was intentional—it is not enough that the defendant acted negligently. See §766(C), Restatement (Second) of Torts. However, even intentional interference will not always,

1. In the equally famous companion case, Lumley v. Wagner, 1 De G.M. & G. 604, 42 Eng. Rep. 687 (1852), the court enjoined Wagner from breaking her agreement not to perform for anyone other than the plaintiff.

or perhaps even usually, result in liability. Section 766 of the Restatement (Second) provides that the interference must be improper as well as intentional. According to the comments, both the purpose and the means used are relevant to the issue of whether the actor acted improperly. In addition, §767 lists seven factors to be taken into account in evaluating the defendant's conduct:

(a) the nature of the actor's conduct,
(b) the actor's motive,
(c) the interests of the other with which the actor's conduct interferes,
(d) the interests sought to be advanced by the actor,
(e) the social interests in protecting the freedom of action of the actor and the contractual interests of the other,
(f) the proximity or remoteness of the actor's conduct to the interference and
(g) the relations between the parties.

Where the contract interfered with is found to be against public policy, however, the plaintiff will not be allowed to recover. See Restatement (Second) of Torts, §774. Even legitimate contracts may be interfered with without liability, so long as such interference furthers some public interest. Thus in Brimelow v. Casson, [1924] 1 ch. 302, the defendants, representatives of an actors' union, were accused of having interfered with the contractual relationship between the plaintiff, who managed a burlesque troupe known as Wu Tut Tut Revue, and the operators of the various theaters in which the troup appeared. Evidence showed that the girls in the plaintiff's chorus line were grossly underpaid and as a result had been forced to take up prostitution. The defendants had persuaded the theater owners to refuse to honor their contracts with the plaintiff unless he paid the chorus girls higher wages, and as a consequence the troupe's tour through southern England was interrupted. Referring to what the judge on appeal called "the good sense of this tribunal," the plaintiff's complaint was dismissed.

The fact patterns in which these rules have been applied are varied. In Guard-Life Corp. v. S. Parker Hardware Manufacturing Corp., 50 N.Y.2d 183, 406 N.E.2d 445 (1980), the New York Court of Appeals held that an issue of fact was presented whether the defendant, in entering into an exclusive dealership contract with a Japanese manufacturer with knowledge that the plaintiff already had a similar (and inconsistent) contract with the manufacturer, induced the manufacturer not to deliver an order already placed with it by the plaintiff. And in Adler, Barish, Daniels, Levin & Creskoff v. Epstein, 482 Pa. 416, 393 A.2d 1175 (1978), *cert. denied,* 442 U.S. 907 (1979), the Supreme Court of Pennsylvania upheld an injunction in favor of a law firm against former salaried associates prohibiting them from contacting the law firm's clients in order to induce them to transfer their legal work to the new firm formed by the former associates. The court in Koeppel v. Schroder, 122 A.D.2d 780, 505 N.Y.S.2d 666 (1986) reached a different result, asserting that a client has an absolute right to terminate an existing relationship with an attorney without cause. To support recovery in such cases, the court stated that there must be a wrongful interference, such as that involving fraud. In general, see Johnson, Solicitation of Law Firm Clients by Departing Partners and Associates: Tort, Fiduciary, and Disciplinary Liability, 50 U. Pitt. L. Rev. 1 (1988).

Also of interest to the legal profession is Cross v. American Country Insurance Co., 875 F.2d 625 (7th Cir. 1989), which held that a liability insurer wrongfully interfered with an attorney's contingent fee contract by settling directly with the attorney's injured client. The insurer was aware that the attorney represented and had a contract with the injured person.

In a widely publicized case, a Texas jury returned a verdict in favor of Pennzoil based on the Texaco's conduct in enticing Getty Oil Company to back out of a merger agreement with Pennzoil. The verdict for the plaintiff of $7.53 billion in compensatory and $3 billion in punitive damages was affirmed in Texaco, Inc. v. Pennzoil Co., 729 S.W.2d 768 (Tex. App. 1987), *cert. dismissed,* 485 U.S. 994 (1988). Texas law required Texaco to post a bond in the amount of the verdict to appeal the decision. Texaco's unsuccessful challenge to that law is reported at Pennzoil Co. v. Texaco, Inc., 481 U.S. 1, 107 S. Ct. 1519, 95 L. Ed. 2d 1 (1987). For a discussion of the *Pennzoil* case from a variety of perspectives, see Symposium, 9 Rev. of Litigation 1 (1990).

As is typical of many areas in which concepts of tort and contract intersect, the damages issue has produced some confusion and controversy in these cases. By and large, a tort, rather than a contract, measure of damages has been accepted. See Restatement (Second) of Torts, §774A. Thus, instead of just basing damages on the position the plaintiff would have occupied had the defendant not interfered, courts have allowed successful plaintiffs to recover for all harm proximately resulting from the defendant's conduct. In an appropriate case the plaintiff will be allowed to recover for mental upset and suffering. Section 774A calls for recovery if the harm is "reasonably to be expected to result from the interference." The Oregon Supreme Court in Mooney v. Johnson Cattle Co., Inc., 291 Or. 709, 634 P.2d 1333 (1981), surveyed the law and adopted a modification of the Restatement rule. (In rejecting the Restatement formulation, the court observed in a footnote that even the Reporters conceded that existing case law did not support recovery.) Instead, the court ruled that to recover, the emotional distress "must be a common and predictable result of disrupting the *type* of relationship or transaction rather than a result 'reasonably to be expected' in the particular situation. . . ." 291 Or. at 718, 634 P.2d at 1338. This rule seems close to the Restatement (Second) of Contracts provision with respect to recovery for emotional harm. Section 353 calls for such recovery in breach of contract cases if the harm is a "particularly likely result" of the breach. Two judges dissented in *Mooney,* arguing that recovery for emotional harm for intentional interference with contract should be treated like any other intentional infliction of such harm, and should be controlled by Section 46, Restatement (Second) of Torts discussed in Section D of Chapter 11, above. Punitive damages also may be awarded in appropriate cases. See Duff v. Engelberg, 237 Cal. App. 2d 505, 47 Cal. Rptr. 114 (1965); Leigh Furniture and Carpet Co. v. Isom, 657 P.2d 293 (Utah 1982).

In general, see Cohen-Grabelsky, Interference with Contractual Relations and Equitable Doctrines, 45 Mod. L. Rev. 241 (1982), and Comment, An Analysis of the Formation of Property Rights Underlying Tortious Interference with Contracts and Other Economic Relations, 50 U. Chi. L. Rev. 1116 (1983).

2. Intentional Interference with Prospective Contracts

Tuttle v. Buck

107 Minn. 145, 119 N.W. 946 (1909)

This appeal was from an order overruling a general demurrer to a complaint in which the plaintiff alleged:

That for more than ten years last past he has been and still is a barber by trade, and engaged in business as such in the village of Howard Lake, Minnesota, where he resides, owning and operating a shop for the purpose of his said trade. That until the injury hereinafter complained of his said business was prosperous, and plaintiff was enabled thereby to comfortably maintain himself and family out of the income and profits thereof, and also to save a considerable sum per annum, to wit, about $800. That the defendant, during the period of about twelve months last past, has wrongfully, unlawfully, and maliciously endeavored to destroy plaintiff's said business, and compel plaintiff to abandon the same. That to that end he has persistently and systematically sought, by false and malicious reports and accusations of and concerning the plaintiff, by personally soliciting and urging plaintiff's patrons no longer to employ plaintiff, by threats of his personal displeasure, and by various other unlawful means and devices, to induce, and has thereby induced, many of said patrons to withhold from plaintiff the employment by them formerly given. That defendant is possessed of large means, and is engaged in the business of a banker in said village of Howard Lake, at Dassel, Minnesota, and at divers other places, and is nowise interested in the occupation of a barber; yet in the pursuance of the wicked, malicious, and unlawful purpose aforesaid, and for the sole and only purpose of injuring the trade of the plaintiff, and of accomplishing his purpose and threats of ruining the plaintiff's said business and driving him out of said village, the defendant fitted up and furnished a barber shop in said village for conducting the trade of barbering. That failing to induce any barber to occupy said shop on his own account, though offered at nominal rental, said defendant, with the wrongful and malicious purpose aforesaid, and not otherwise, has during the time herein stated hired two barbers in succession for a stated salary, paid by him, to occupy said shop, and to serve so many of plaintiff's patrons as said defendant has been or may be able by the means aforesaid to direct from plaintiff's shop. That at the present time a barber so employed and paid by the defendant is occupying and nominally conducting the shop thus fitted and furnished by the defendant, without paying any rent therfor, and under an agreement with defendant whereby the income of said shop is required to be paid to defendant, and is so paid in partial return for his wages. That all of said things were and are done by defendant with the sole design of injuring the plaintiff, and of destroying his said business, and not for the purpose of serving any legitimate interest of his own. That by reason of the great wealth and prominence of the defendant, and the personal and financial influence consequent thereon, he has by the means aforesaid, and through other unlawful means and devices by him employed, materially injured the business of the plaintiff, has largely reduced the income and profits thereof, and intends and threatens to destroy the same altogether, to plaintiff's damage in the sum of $10,000.

ELLIOTT, J. (after stating the facts as above).

It has been said that the law deals only with externals, and that a lawful act cannot be made the foundation of an action because it was done with an evil motive. In Allen v. Flood, [1898] A.C. 1, 151, Lord Watson said that, except with regard to crimes, the law does not take into account motives as constituting an element of civil wrong. . . . In Jenkins v. Fowler, 24 Pa. 308, Mr. Justice Black said that "malicious motives make a bad act worse, but they cannot make that wrong which, in its own essence, is lawful.". . .

Such generalizations are of little value in determining concrete cases. They may state the truth, but not the whole truth. Each word and phrase used therein may require definition and limitation. Thus, before we can apply Judge Black's language to a particular case, we must determine what act is "in its own essence lawful" . . . It is not at all correct to say that the motive with which an act is done is always immaterial, providing the act itself is not unlawful. Numerous illustrations of the contrary will be found in the civil as well as the criminal law.

We do not intend to enter upon an elaborate discussion of the subject, or become entangled in the subtleties connected with the words "malice" and "malicious." We are not able to accept without limitations the doctrine above referred to, but at this time content ourselves with a brief reference to some general principles.

It must be remembered that the common law is the result of growth, and that its development has been determined by the social needs of the community which it governs. It is the resultant of conflicting social forces, and those forces which are for the time dominant leave their impress upon the law. It is of judicial origin, and seeks to establish doctrines and rules for the determination, protection, and enforcement of legal rights. Manifestly it must change as society changes and new rights are recognized. To be an efficient instrument, and not a mere abstraction, it must gradually adapt itself to changed conditions. Necessarily its form and substance have been greatly affected by prevalent economic theories.

For generations there has been a practical agreement upon the proposition that competition in trade and business is desirable, and this idea has found expression in the decisions of the courts as well as in statutes. But it has led to grievous and manifold wrongs to individuals, and many courts have manifested an earnest desire to protect the individual from the evils which result from unrestrained business competition. The problem has been to so adjust matters as to preserve the principle of competition and yet guard against its abuse to the unnecessary injury to the individual. So the principle that a man may use his own property according to his own needs and desires, while true in the abstract, is subject to many limitations in the concrete. Men cannot always, in civilized society, be allowed to use their own property as their interests or desires may dictate without reference to the fact that they have neighbors whose rights are as sacred as their own. The existence and well-being of society require that each and every person shall conduct himself consistently with the fact that he is a social and reasonable person. The purpose for which a man is using his own property may thus sometimes determine his rights. . . .

Many of the restrictions which should be recognized and enforced result from a tacit recognition of principles which are not often stated in the decisions in express terms. Sir Frederick Pollock notes that not many years ago it was difficult to find any definite authority for stating as a general proposition of English law that it is wrong to do a wilful wrong to one's neighbor without lawful justification or excuse. But neither is there any express authority for the general proposition that men must perform their contracts. Both principles in this generality of form and conception, are modern and there was a time when neither was true. After developing the idea that law begins, not with authentic general principles, but with the enumeration of particular remedies, the learned writer continues: "If there exists, then, a positive duty to avoid harm, much more must there exist the negative duty of not doing wilful harm, subject, as all general duties must be subject, to the necessary exceptions. The three main heads of duty with which the law of torts is concerned, namely, to abstain from wilful injury, to respect the property of others, and to use due diligence to avoid causing harm to others, are all alike of a comprehensive nature." Pollock, Torts (8th ed.), p. 21. He then quotes with approval the statement of Lord Bowen that "at common law there was a cause of action whenever one person did damage to another, wilfully and intentionally, without just cause or excuse.". . .

It is freely conceded that there are many decisions contrary to this view; but, when carried to the extent contended for by the appellant, we think they are unsafe, unsound, and illy adapted to modern conditions. To divert to one's self the customers of a business rival by the offer of goods at lower prices is in general a legitimate mode of serving one's own interest, and justifiable as fair competition. But when a man starts an opposition place of business, not for the sake of profit to himself, but regardless of loss to himself, and for the sole purpose of driving his competitor out of business, and with the intention of himself retiring upon the accomplishment of his malevolent purpose, he is guilty of a wanton wrong and an actionable tort. In such a case he would not be exercising his legal right, or doing an act which can be judged separately from the motive which actuated him. To call such conduct competition is a perversion of terms. It is simply the application of force without legal justification, which in its moral quality may be no better than highway robbery.

Nevertheless, in the opinion of the writer this complaint is insufficient. It is not claimed that it states a cause of action for slander. No question of conspiracy or combination is involved. Stripped of the adjectives and the statement that what was done was for the sole purpose of injuring the plaintiff, and not for the purpose of serving a legitimate purpose of the defendant, the complaint states facts which in themselves amount only to an ordinary everyday business transaction. There is no allegation that the defendant was intentionally running the business at a financial loss to himself, or that after driving the plaintiff out of business the defendant closed up or intended to close up his shop. From all that appears from the complaint he may have opened the barber shop, energetically sought business from his acquaintances and the customers of the plaintiff, and as a result of his enterprise and command of capital obtained it, with the result that the plaintiff, from want of capital, acquaintance, or enterprise, was unable to stand the competition and was thus driven out of business. The facts thus alleged do not, in my opinion, in themselves, without reference to the way in which they are characterized by the pleader, tend to show a malicious and wanton wrong to the plaintiff.

A majority of the justices, however, are of the opinion that, on the principle declared in the foregoing opinion, the complaint states a cause of action, and the order is therefore affirmed.

Affirmed.

JAGGARD, J., dissents.

The court in Katz v. Kapper, 7 Cal. App. 2d 1, 44 P.2d 1060 (1935) was considerably less sympathetic to the plaintiff than was the court in *Tuttle.* In *Katz,* the plaintiff and the defendants were rivals in the wholesale fish business in Los Angeles. The complaint alleged that the defendants, with the "sole intention" of putting the plaintiff out of business, threatened customers of the plaintiff that if they continued to buy fish from the plaintiff, the defendants would open a retail store and sell fish at prices so low that the customers would be driven out of business. The complaint further alleged that the defendants did open a retail store and sold at lower than wholesale prices, resulting in many customers shifting their purchases from the plaintiff to the defendants. In affirming the order sustaining the defendants' demurrer to the complaint, the court stated (44 P.2d at 1062):

> It very clearly appears from the allegations of the complaint that the primary purpose of the defendants was to acquire for themselves the business of plaintiff's customers, and that the detriment which would result to plaintiff's business from the accomplishment of defendants' purpose was incidental thereto. This view must be taken of the complaint, notwithstanding the allegation that the sole purpose was to drive the plaintiff out of business. The defendants are not charged with making any effort to deprive plaintiff of his trade except by transferring the same to themselves. This is essentially business competition. The defendants did or threatened to do nothing other than to gain a business advantage proportionate to the losses sustained by plaintiff, and by the accomplishment of that end their purposes would have been satisfied. It cannot be said that the methods used by the defendants were unlawful. They threatened plaintiff's customers with the ruination of their businesses if they continued to trade with plaintiff, but a threat is not unlawful if it is to do a lawful thing. . . .
>
> The threats alleged in general terms are identified and particularized by the allegations that the defendants threatened to and did undersell the plaintiff and his customers at retail prices less than the wholesale prices at which the commodities could be purchased. These must be taken as the only acts of coercion either threatened or done, since no others are alleged. They were not unlawful nor were they committed in an unlawful manner. They related solely to the aims of the defendants to engage in business competition with plaintiff for the resulting business advantage to themselves. The fact that the methods used were ruthless, or unfair, in a moral sense, does not stamp them as illegal. It has never been regarded as the duty or province of the courts to regulate practices in the business world beyond the point of applying legal or equitable remedies in cases involving acts of oppression or deceit which are unlawful. Any extension of this jurisdiction must come through legislative action. In this case no questions of statutory law are involved. The alleged acts of defendants do not fall within the category of business methods recognized as unlawful, and hence they are not actionable. The demurrer to the complaint was properly sustained.

Baker v. Dennis Brown Realty, Inc.

121 N.H. 640, 433 A.2d 1271 (1981)

BROCK, J. This case is an action in tort for the intentional interference with a prospective contractual relationship brought by a prospective purchaser of certain real estate against the seller's real estate agent. The Concord District Court . . . found for the plaintiff and entered a judgment of $3,525.29. On the defendant's appeal, we affirm in part.

In June 1978, the plaintiff, Sharon Baker, was seeking to purchase a home in Concord and enlisted the services of Keeler Family Realty. An agent of that firm, Jody Keeler, examined the listings in the Multiple Listing Service and found a home that he thought could be of interest to the plaintiff. Because the defendant, Dennis Brown Realty, Inc., held an exclusive listing authorization from the home's owner, Sarah Landry, the plaintiff's real estate agent contacted the defendant firm to arrange for the plaintiff to be shown the home.

On June 22, 1978, the home was shown to the plaintiff by her own agent and an agent of the defendant firm, Faye Olson. In the event that the plaintiff was to purchase the home, the two real estate agencies involved would share equally in the sales commission under a co-brokerage agreement.

Upon seeing the property, the plaintiff immediately decided that she wished to buy it and offered $26,900, the *full* asking price. The two agents immediately drafted an unconditional purchase and sale agreement, which the plaintiff signed.

At about the same time another agent from the defendant firm, Douglas Bush, arrived on the premises. He informed the plaintiff and her agent that only the full asking price would be acceptable to the seller and asked to see the purchase and sale agreement. After reviewing the document, Mr. Bush insisted that two conditions be added to the agreement; bank financing and the sale of the plaintiff's home. Due to the plaintiff's particular situation, both she and her own agent advised Mr. Bush that these conditions were not necessary because she already had obtained bank financing for up to $33,000. Mr. Bush insisted, however, and she finally acquiesced to his demands.

By this time Faye Olson, the other agent of the defendant firm, had already cancelled other appointments that she had made to show the home. Twenty minutes later, however, Mr. Bush showed the home to his own clients, the Piars. He informed the Piars that there was an outstanding offer for the full asking price, and the Piars then offered $300 more. Mr. Bush then prepared a purchase and sale agreement for the Piars (buyers) to sign. Although he inserted a condition in the offer relating to bank financing, he did not insert a condition for the sale of the Piars home; a term he had insisted be placed in the plaintiff's offer. The Piars' offer and the plaintiff's offer were then communicated to the seller without anyone from the defendant firm notifying the plaintiff that a higher offer had been made for the home. Mr. Bush did not tell the seller about the possibility of obtaining a higher offer from the plaintiff and the seller accepted the Piars' offer. Because the Piars had dealt exclusively with the defendant firm the entire sales commission went to the defendant, and Mr. Bush received 35 per cent of that commission. Even if the plaintiff had made a higher offer and eventually purchased the home, the defendant firm and Mr. Bush would have received a substantially smaller commission due to the co-brokerage agreement.

The plaintiff was ultimately able to purchase a similar property in the same neighborhood, but at a price $3,100 greater than the amount that she had offered to purchase the Landry home. . . .

The defendant first argues that an offer to purchase real estate creates no legally protected interest or right if the offer is in fact not accepted. . . . However, the present action is not on the contract but rather is one in tort for the *intentional* interference with a prospective contractual relationship, . . . an action that has been recognized in this State for some time. . . . See also Hanger One, Inc. v. Davis Associates, Inc., 121 N.H. [586],—, 431 A.2d 792, 794 (1981). "One who, without a privilege to do so, induces or otherwise purposely causes a third person not to . . . enter into or continue a business relation with another is liable to the other for the harm caused thereby.". . .

The trial court, in ruling upon the parties' requests for findings of fact, found facts which clearly support its determination that the defendant's agent "purposely caused" the seller "not to enter into a business relation" with the plaintiff.

Once it has been established that the defendant induced or otherwise caused the seller not to enter into a contract with the plaintiff, a determination must be made as to whether the defendant's action was privileged. "An action for interference with contractual relations cannot succeed . . . where the defendant's actions were justified [or privileged] under the circumstances." Bricker v. Crane, 118 N.H. at 252, 387 A.2d at 323. As the seller's real estate agent, the defendant might have some degree of privilege in situations such as are involved here but certainly not an absolute one that would blanket him in complete immunity. Moreover, the burden is on the defendant to show that his actions were privileged. . . . Here, the trial court, after considering the evidence presented, ruled that the defendants' actions were not privileged. Because there is no transcript of the testimony below, we are in no position to say either that the trial court abused its discretion or that there was insufficient evidence to support its ruling.

Only one issue remains in this case and that is the question whether the damages awarded were speculative.

[The court then ruled that the correct measure of damages is the difference between the price of the home that the plaintiff actually purchased and plaintiff's offer on the home involved in this case.]

. . . It is the defendant's position that this award too is speculative because, had the defendant informed the plaintiff of the second offer on the home, a bidding contest or "auction" would have resulted, and it is impossible to determine where it would have stopped. No doubt there is some truth to this argument, and we cannot say with certainty what the result would have been had the defendant not isolated the plaintiff out of contention for the home. Nevertheless, " 'the difficulty of determining the sum which will recompense a person' wronged by another is no reason for not allowing the injured party damages.". . .

Judgment for the plaintiff in the sum of $3,100.

BATCHELDER, J., did not sit; the others concurred.

In general, courts have been less willing to protect interests in prospective business relations than they have been to protect interests in existing contracts. See Guard-Life Corp. v. S. Parker Hardware Manufacturing Corp., 50 N.Y.2d 183, 406 N.E.2d 445 (1980). However, the structure of the Restatement (Second) of Torts with respect to the former is similar to that with respect to the latter. Section 766B establishes the basic tort, and provides that one who "intentionally and improperly interferes with another's prospective contractual relation is subject to liability" for the pecuniary loss sustained. Section 767, listing the factors relevant to whether the actor acted improperly, applies to §766B as well as to §766 which deals with existing contracts. In addition, there is a separate §768 applicable only to §766B which permits interference in a competition context. According to this section, the interference is not improper if "wrongful means" are not used, the interference does not result in an unlawful restraint of trade, and its purpose is in part to advance the actor's interest in competition. The Supreme Court of Utah in Leigh Furniture and Carpet Co. v. Isom, 657 P.2d 293 (Utah 1982), concluded that the Restatement approach is too complex, and established the following as elements of the plaintiff's claim (657 P.2d at 304):

(1) that the defendant intentionally interfered with plaintiff's existing or potential economic relations,
(2) for an improper purpose or by improper means,
(3) causing injury to the plaintiff.

It is not clear how this differs from the Restatement. The court also stated that it would recognize privilege as a defense, although it did not indicate what sort of privilege it had in mind, other than by referring to an earlier case involving a first amendment claim of privilege to engage in a boycott. See Searle v. Johnson, 646 P.2d 682 (Utah 1982). In Caruso v. Local Union Number 690 of International Brotherhood of Teamsters, 100 Wash. 2d 343, 670 P.2d 240 (1983), the court held that an article in the defendant's magazine calling on Teamster members and "laboring people" not to do business with the plaintiff (the owner of a carpet store who had called police to remove trucks that blocked the driveway to his parking lot) was constitutionally privileged.

Examples can be cited in which courts have ruled that the defendant has crossed the line from proper competition to improper conduct (see, e.g., Monette v. AM-7-7 Baking Co., Ltd., 929 F.2d 276 (6th Cir. 1991)), and in which courts have ruled that the defendant has not crossed that line (see, e.g., Las Vegas-Tonopah-Reno Stage Line, Inc. v. Gray Line Tours of Southern Nevada, 106 Nev. 283, 792 P.2d 386 (1990)). But because different courts articulate the elements of the plaintiff's cause of action somewhat differently, and because of the difficulty of marking out the line between healthy competition and improper tactics, the cases do not fall into any consistent pattern.

Cases in which liability has been imposed for interference with prospective relationships have largely been limited to those involving contracts. Other types of expectancies have not received the same degree of legal protection from interference. Thus, in Trautwein v. Harbourt, 40 N.J. Super. 247, 123 A.2d 30, *cert. denied,* 22 N.J. 220, 125 A.2d 233 (1956), a plaintiff who complained that he had been willfully and maliciously excluded from a fraternal organization was denied relief as a matter of law. But cf. Deon v. Kirby Lumber Co., 162 La. 671, 111 So. 55 (1926), in which the court held that the plaintiff's allegation that the defendant had acted maliciously to deprive the plaintiff and his family of the society of their friends and neighbors stated a cause of action under Louisiana law. The only expectancies other than those related to prospective contracts to which the Restatement (Second) of Torts extends legal protection are the interests of a prospective donee in an inheritance or gift. See §774B of the Restatement (Second) of Torts.

Liability for interference with both existing and prospective contracts is discussed in Perlman, Interference with Contract and Other Economic Expectancies: A Clash of Tort and Contract Doctrine, 49 U. Chi. L. Rev. 61 (1982), and Note, Tortious Interference with Contract: A Reassertion of Society's Interest in Commercial Stability and Contractual Integrity, 81 Colum. L. Rev. 1491 (1981).

Note: Wrongful Discharge of Employees at Will

In Leigh Furniture and Carpet Co. v. Isom, p. 1025, above, the court stated the generally accepted view that there can be no recovery in tort based upon the defendant's interference with his own prospective contracts with the plaintiff. An exception to this rule has developed in a number of states with respect to "at will" employees—those whose employment arrangements enable the employer to discharge the employee at any time and for any reason. In some states, and under some circumstances, such employees have been able to recover damages in tort for "wrongful discharge." The argument for imposing liability was put forcefully, and somewhat dramatically, by the court in Sides v. Duke University, 328 S.E.2d 818 (N.C. App.), *rev. denied,* 314 N.C. 331, 333 S.E.2d 490 (1985). In upholding the complaint for wrongful discharge based on the plaintiff's refusal to give false testimony in a medical malpractice case against the defendants, the court stated (328 S.E.2d at 826):

> But none of the foregoing discussions of the at will doctrine, or any others that we have seen, focuses on what we believe is the fundamental fact upon which the at will doctrine rests, a fact that is crucial to this case, in our judgment. We refer to the obvious and indisputable fact that in a civilized state where reciprocal legal rights and duties abound the words "at will" can never mean "without limit or qualification," as so much of the discussion and the briefs of the defendants imply; for in such a state the rights of each person are necessarily and inherently limited by the rights of others and the interests of the public. An at will prerogative without limits could be suffered only in an anarchy, and there not for long—it certainly cannot be suffered in a society such as ours without weakening the bond of counter balancing rights and obligations that holds such societies together. Thus, while there may be a right to terminate a contract at will for no reason, or for an arbitrary or irrational reason, there can be no right to terminate such a contract for an unlawful reason or purpose that contravenes public policy. A different interpretation would encourage and sanction lawlessness, which law by its very nature is designed to discourage and prevent. We hold, therefore, that no employer in this State, notwithstanding that an employment is at will, has the right to discharge an employee and deprive him of his livelihood without civil liability because he refuses to testify untruthfully or incompletely in a court case, as plaintiff alleges happened here. One of the merited glories of this country is the multitude of rights that its people have, rights that are enforced as a matter of course by our courts, and nothing could be more inimical to their enjoyment than the unbridled law defying actions of some and the false or incomplete testimony of others. If we are to have law, those who so act against the public interest must be held accountable for the harm inflicted thereby; to accord them civil immunity would incongruously reward their lawlessness at the unjust expense of their innocent victims.

The following is a sampling of cases which have upheld tort liability, based on public policy considerations, for employees alleging wrongful discharge: Amos v. Oakdale Knitting Co., 331 N.C. 348, 416 S.E.2d 166 (1992) (employee who refused to work for less than statutory minimum wage); Tate v. Browning-Ferris, Inc., 833 P.2d 1218 (Okla. 1992) (employee who brought racial discrimination complaint); Gantt v. Sentry Insurance, 1 Cal. 4th 1083, 824 P.2d 680, 4 Cal. Rptr. 2d 874 (1992) (manager who supported employee's sexual harassment claim); Winkelman v. Beloit Memorial Hospital, 168 Wis. 2d 12, 483 N.W.2d 211 (1992) (employee who refused to perform nursing services for which she was not qualified); Peterson v. Browning, 832 P.2d 1280 (Utah 1992) (customs officer who refused to falsify tax and customs documents).

Some courts also permit wrongful discharge recovery in breach of contract actions. These courts have found an express or implied agreement to terminate only for cause, or have recognized an implied covenant of good faith and fair dealing in at will contracts. See, e.g., Luedtke v. Nabors Alaska Drilling, Inc., 834 P.2d 1220 (Alaska 1992); Merrill v. Crothall-American, Inc., 606 A.2d 96 (Del. 1992); Wieder v. Skala, 80 N.Y. 628, 609 N.E.2d 105 (1992). In the last case, the employee was an associate discharged by his law firm because he insisted that the firm report ethical violations of another associate.

An at will employee may also be protected by statute against arbitrary discharge. The Whistleblower Protection Act of 1989 protects federal employees from retaliation or threatened retaliation for reporting violations of law or "gross mismanagement, a gross waste of funds, an abuse of authority, or a substantial and specific danger to public health or safety. . . ." 5 U.S.C. §2302(b)(8) (Supp. III 1991). Some states have also enacted protective legislation. See, e.g., Montana's Wrongful Discharge From Employment Act, Mont. Code Ann. Ti. 39-2-901-914.

A number of courts have retained the traditional rule and refused to create a common law tort exception to the employment at will doctrine. See, e.g., Murphy v. American Home Products Corp., 58 N.Y.2d 393, 448 N.E.2d 86 (1983); Jarvinen v. HCA Allied Clinical Laboratories, Inc., 552 So. 2d 241 (Fla. 4th DCA 1989); Tulloh v. Goodyear Atomic Corp., 62 Ohio St. 3d 541, 584 N.E.2d 729 (1992).

A considerable amount of law review commentary favors recovery for wrongful discharge. See, e.g., Peck, Unjust Discharges from Employment: A Necessary Change in the Law, 40 Ohio St. L.J. 1 (1979); Minda, The Common Law of Employment at Will in New York: The Paralysis of Nineteenth Century Doctrine, 36 Syracuse L. Rev. 939 (1985); Linzer, The Decline of Assent: Employment At-Will as a Case Study of the Breakdown of Private Law Theory, 20 Ga. L. Rev. 323 (1986); Note, Protecting Employees at Will Against Wrongful Discharge: The Public Policy Exception, 96 Harv. L. Rev. 1931 (1983). Some commentators, however, defend the traditional rule. See, e.g., Harrison, The "New" Terminable-at-Will Employment Contract: An Interest and Cost Incidence Analysis, 69 Iowa L. Rev. 327 (1984); Epstein, In Defense of the Contract at Will, 51 U. Chi. L. Rev. 947 (1984). For a history of the at will doctrine, see Feinman, The Development of the Employment at Will Rule, 20 Am. J. Legal Hist. 118 (1976).

Wrongful discharge is the subject of the Model Employment Termination Act, 7A U.L.A. 66 (1993 Cum. Supp.), adopted by the National Conference of Commissioners on Uniform State Laws in August 1991. Except as otherwise permitted by the Act, an employer could not discharge an employee without "good cause." Good cause is defined as:

> (i) a reasonable basis related to an individual employee for termination of the employee's employment in view of relevant factors and circumstances, which may include the employee's duties, responsibilities, conduct (on the

job or otherwise), job performance, and employment record, or (ii) the exercise of business judgment in good faith by the employer, including setting its economic or institutional goals and determining methods to achieve those goals, organizing or reorganizing operations, discontinuing, consolidating, or divesting operations or positions or parts of operations or positions, determining the size of its work force and the nature of the positions filled by its work force, and determining and changing standards of performance for positions.

The Model Act leaves room for alterations by contract between the employer and the employee of the rights otherwise given the employee by the Act. If there is an express agreement, the good cause requirement can be waived if the employer agrees to pay the employee on termination one month's pay for each year of employment. Further, the discharge for good cause requirement does not apply to the termination of employment at the end of an expressly agreed-on specified period of employment "related to the completion of a specified task, project, undertaking, or assignment."

In general, see Perry, Deterring Egregious Violations of Public Policy: A Proposed Amendment to the Model Employment Termination Act, 67 Wash. L. Rev. 915 (1992).

Appendix

Introduction to Economic Analysis of Tort Law

Posner, Economic Analysis of Law

3-6, 10-14, 16-17 (4th ed. 1992)

§1.1 Fundamental Concepts

Many lawyers think that economics is the study of inflation, unemployment, business cycles, and other mysterious macroeconomic phenomena remote from the day-to-day concerns of the legal system. Actually the domain of economics is much broader. As conceived in this book, economics is the science of rational choice in a world—our world—in which resources are limited in relation to human wants. The task of economics, so defined, is to explore the implications of assuming that man is a rational maximizer of his ends in life, his satisfactions—what we shall call his "self-interest." Rational maximization should not be confused with conscious calculation. Economics is not a theory about consciousness. Behavior is rational when it conforms to the model of rational choice, whatever the state of mind of the chooser. And self-interest should not be confused with selfishness; the happiness (or for that matter the misery) of other people may be a part of one's satisfactions.

The concept of man as a rational maximizer of his self-interest implies that people respond to incentives—that if a person's surroundings change in such a way that he could increase his satisfactions by altering his behavior, he will do so. From this proposition derive the three fundamental principles of economics:

1. The first is the inverse relation between price charged and quantity demanded (the Law of Demand). If the price of steak rises by 10¢ a pound, and if other prices remain unchanged, a steak will now cost the consumer more, relatively, than it did before. Being rational and self-interested he will react by investigating the possibility of substituting goods that he preferred less when steak was at its old price but that are more attractive now because they are cheaper relative to steak. Many consumers will continue to buy as much steak as before; for them, other goods are poor substitutes even at somewhat lower relative prices. But some purchasers will reduce their purchases of steak and substitute other meats (or other foods, or different products altogether), with the result that the total quantity demanded by purchasers, and hence the amount produced, will decline. . . .

The Law of Demand doesn't operate just on goods with explicit prices. Unpopular teachers sometimes try to increase class enrollment by raising the average grade of the students in their classes; for, other things being equal, hard graders have smaller class enrollments than easy graders. The convicted criminal who has served his sentence is said to have "paid his debt to society," and an economist would find the metaphor apt. Punishment is, at least from the criminal's standpoint (why not from society's, unless the punishment is in the form of a fine?), the price that society charges for a criminal offense. The economist is led to predict that an increase in either the severity of the punishment or the likelihood of its imposition will raise the price of crime and therefore reduce its incidence. The criminal will be encouraged to substitute other activity. Economists call nonpecuniary prices "shadow prices."

2. The consumers in our steak example—and the criminal—were assumed to be trying to maximize their utility (happiness, pleasure, satisfactions). The same is presumably true of the producers of beef, though in the case of sellers one usually speaks of profit maximization rather than utility maximization. Sellers seek to maximize the difference between their costs and their sales revenues, but for the moment we are interested only in the lowest price that a rational self-interested seller would charge. That minimum is the price that the resources consumed in making (and selling) the seller's product would command in their next best use—the alternative price. It is what the economist means by the cost of a good, and suggests why (subject to some exceptions that need not trouble us here) a rational seller would not sell below cost. For example, the cost of making a lawn mower is the price the manufacturer must pay for the capital, labor, materials, and other resources consumed in making it. That price must exceed the price at which the resources could have been sold to the next highest bidder for them, for if the manufacturer had not been willing to beat that price he would not have been the high bidder and would not have obtained the resources. We postpone the complication that is introduced when the sellers of a resource price it higher than its alternative price.

A corollary of the notion of cost as alternative price is that a cost is incurred only when someone is denied the use of a resource. . . . Cost to the economist is "opportunity cost"—the benefit forgone by employing a resource in a way that denies its use to someone else. . . .

3. The third basic principle of economics is that resources tend to gravitate toward their most valuable uses if voluntary exchange—a market—is permitted. Why did the manufacturer of lawn mowers in an earlier example pay more for labor and materials than competing users of these resources? The answer is that he thought he could use them to obtain a higher price for his finished good than could competing demanders; they were worth more to him. Why does farmer *A* offer to buy farmer *B*'s farm at a price higher than *B*'s minimum price for the property? It is because the property is worth more to *A* than to *B,* meaning that *A* can use it to produce a more valuable

output as measured by the prices consumers are willing to pay. By a process of voluntary exchange, resources are shifted to those uses in which the value to consumers, as measured by their willingness to pay, is highest. When resources are being used where their value is highest, we may say that they are being employed efficiently.

§1.2 Value, Utility, Efficiency . . .

The use of the words "value" and "utility" to distinguish between (1) an *expected* cost or benefit (i.e., the cost or benefit, in dollars, multiplied by the probability that it will actually materialize) and (2) what that expected cost or benefit is worth to someone who is *not* risk neutral obscures a more dramatic distinction. This is the distinction between (1) value in a broad economic sense, which includes the idea that a risk-averse person "values" $1 more than a 10 percent chance of getting $10, and (2) utility in the sense used by philosophers of utilitarianism, meaning (roughly) happiness.

Suppose that pituitary extract is in very scarce supply relative to the demand and is therefore very expensive. A poor family has a child who will be a dwarf if he does not get some of the extract, but the family cannot afford the price and could not even if they could borrow against the child's future earnings as a person of normal height; for the present value of those earnings net of consumption is less than the price of the extract. A rich family has a child who will grow to normal height, but the extract will add a few inches more, and his parents decide to buy it for him. In the sense of value used in this book, the pituitary extract is more valuable to the rich than to the poor family, because value is measured by willingness to pay; but the extract would confer greater happiness in the hands of the poor family than in the hands of the rich one.

As this example shows, the term efficiency, when used as in this book to denote that allocation of resources in which value is maximized, has limitations as an ethical criterion of social decisionmaking. Utility in the utilitarian sense also has grave limitations, and not only because it is difficult to measure when willingness to pay is jettisoned as a metric. The fact that one person has a greater capacity for pleasure than another is not a very good reason for a forced transfer of wealth from the second to the first. Other familiar ethical criteria have their own serious problems. Although no effort will be made in this book to defend efficiency as the only worthwhile criterion of social choice, the book does assume, and most people probably would agree, that it is an important criterion. In many areas of interest to the economic analyst of law, such as antitrust, it is, as we shall see, the main thing that students of public policy worry about.

Many economists prefer a less controversial definition of efficiency that confines the term to purely voluntary transactions. Suppose *A* sells a wood carving to *B* for $10, both parties have full information, and the transaction has no effect on anyone else. Then the allocation of resources that is brought about by the transaction is said to be Pareto superior to the allocation of resources before the transaction. A Pareto-superior transaction is one that makes at least one person better off and no one worse off. (In our example, it presumably made both *A* and *B* better off, and by assumption it made no one worse off.) In other words, the criterion of Pareto superiority is unanimity of all affected persons. Now this is a very austere conception of efficiency, with rather few applications to the real world, because most transactions (and if not a single transaction, then a series of like transactions) have effects on third parties, if no more than by changing the prices of other goods (how?). In the less austere concept of efficiency used in this book—called the Kaldor-Hicks concept or wealth maximization—if *A* values the wood carving at $5 and *B* at $12, so that at a sale price of $10 (indeed at any price between $5 and $12) the transaction creates a total benefit of $7 (at a price of $10, for example, *A* considers himself $5 better off and *B* considers himself $2 better off), then it is an efficient transaction, provided that the harm (if any) done to third parties (minus any benefit to them) does not exceed $7. The transaction would not be Pareto superior unless *A* and *B* actually compensated the third parties for any harm suffered by them. The Kaldor-Hicks concept is also and suggestively called potential Pareto superiority: The winners could compensate the losers, whether or not they actually do.

Because the conditions for Pareto superiority are almost never satisfied in the real world, yet economists talk quite a bit about efficiency, it is pretty clear that the operating definition of efficiency in economics is not Pareto superiority. When an economist says that free trade or competition or the control of pollution or some other policy or state of the world is efficient, nine times out of ten he means Kaldor-Hicks efficient, as shall this book.

The dependence of even the Pareto-superiority concept of efficiency on the distribution of wealth—willingness to pay, and hence value, being a function of that distribution—further limits efficiency as an ultimate criterion of the social good. If income and wealth were distributed differently, the pattern of demands might also be different and efficiency would require a different deployment of our economic resources. Since economics does not answer the question whether the existing distribution of income and wealth is good or bad, just or unjust (although it can tell us a great deal about the costs of altering the existing distribution, as well as about the distributive consequences of various policies), neither does it answer the ultimate question whether an efficient allocation of resources would be socially or ethically desirable. Nor can the economist tell us, assuming the existing distribution of income and wealth is just, whether consumer satisfaction should be the dominant value of society. Thus, the economist's competence in a discussion of the legal system is limited. He can predict the effect of legal rules and arrangements on value and efficiency, in their strict technical senses, and on the existing distribution of income and wealth, but he cannot issue mandatory prescriptions for social change. . . .

§1.3 The Realism of the Economist's Assumptions

The reader who lacks previous acquaintance with economics may be troubled by what appear to be the severely unrealistic assumptions that underlie economic theory. The basic assumption, that human behavior is rational, seems contradicted by the experiences and observations of everyday life, though the contradiction is less acute once one understands that the concept of rationality used by the economist is objective rather than subjective, so that it would not be a solecism to speak of a rational frog. Even so, the assumptions of economic theory are one-dimensional and pallid when viewed as descriptions of human behavior—especially the behavior of such unconventional economic "actors" as the judge, the litigant, the parent, the rapist, and others whom we shall encounter in the economic analysis of law. However, abstraction is of the essence of scientific inquiry, and economics aspires to be scientific. Newton's law of falling bodies, for example, is unrealistic in its basic assumption that bodies fall in a vacuum, but it is still a useful theory because it predicts with reasonable accuracy the behavior of a wide variety of falling bodies in the real world. Similarly, an economic theory of law will not capture the full complexity, richness, and confusion of the phenomena—criminal or judicial or marital or whatever—that it seeks to illuminate. But its lack of realism in the sense of descriptive completeness, far from invalidating the theory, is a precondition of theory. A theory that sought faithfully to reproduce the complexity of the empirical world in its assumptions would not be a theory—an explanation—but a description.

The real danger for positive economics in general, and the positive economic theory of law expounded in many places in this book (especially in Part II) in particular, is the opposite of reductionism: Call it complicationism. When the economic analyst seeks to make a very simple economic model more complex, for example by bringing in (as we shall do many times in this book) risk aversion and information costs, he runs the risk of finding himself with too many degrees of freedom: that is, with a model so rich that no empirical observation can refute it—which means that no observation can support it, either.

All this is not to suggest that the analyst has a free choice of assumptions. An important test of a theory is its ability to explain reality. If it does a lousy job, the reason may be that its assumptions are insufficiently realistic; but we need not try to evaluate the assumptions directly in order to evaluate it. Judged by the test of explanatory power, economic theory is a significant (although only partial) success; so perhaps the assumption that people are rational maximizers of their satisfactions is not so unrealistic as the non-economist might at first think. Economic theory explains a vast number of market and nonmarket phenomena, such as the inverse correlation, mentioned in the first section of this chapter, between price ceilings and queues; the inverse correlation between rent control and the stock of housing; the positive correlation in financial markets between risk and expected return; the relation between futures prices and spot-market prices; the dependence of college enrollment on the financial returns to a college education; the fact that the best goods tend to be shipped the farthest distances and the worst consumed at home; and many others. Much of this book is concerned with proposing economic explanations for legal phenomena modeled in economic terms.

Calabresi, The Costs of Accidents

26-28, 69-72, 95-96 (1970)

Apart from the requirements of justice, I take it as axiomatic that the principal function of accident law is to reduce the sum of the costs of accidents and the costs of avoiding accidents. (Such incidental benefits as providing a respectable livelihood for a large number of judges, lawyers, and insurance agents are at best beneficent side effects.) This cost, or loss, reduction goal can be divided into three subgoals.

The first is reduction of the number and severity of accidents. This "primary" reduction of accident costs can be attempted in two basic ways. We can seek to forbid specific acts or activities thought to cause accidents, or we can make activities more expensive and thereby less attractive to the extent of the accident costs they cause. These two methods of primary reduction of accident costs are not clearly separable; a number of difficulties of definition will become apparent as we consider them in detail. But the distinction between them is useful because from it flow two very different approaches toward primary reduction of accident costs, the "general deterrence" or market method and the "specific deterrence" or collective method.

The second cost reduction subgoal is concerned with reducing neither the number of accidents nor their degree of severity. It concentrates instead on reducing the societal costs resulting from accidents. I shall attempt to show that the notion that one of the principal functions of accident law is the compensation of victims is really a rather misleading, though occasionally useful, way of stating this "secondary" accident cost reduction goal. The fact that I have termed this compensation notion secondary should in no way be taken as belittling its importance. There is no doubt that the way we provide for accident victims *after* the accident is crucially important and that the real societal costs of accidents can be reduced as significantly here as by taking measures to avoid accidents in the first place. This cost reduction subgoal is secondary only in the sense that it does not come into play until after earlier primary measures to reduce accident costs have failed. . . .

The third subgoal of accident cost reduction is rather Pickwickian but very important nonetheless. It involves reducing the costs of administering our treatment of accidents. It may be termed "tertiary" because its aim is to reduce the costs of achieving primary and secondary cost reduction. But in a very real sense this "efficiency" goal comes first. It tells us to question constantly whether an attempt to reduce accident costs, either by reducing accidents themselves or by reducing their secondary effects, costs more than it saves. By forcing us to ask this, it serves as a kind of general balance wheel to the cost reduction goal. . . .

The crucial thing about the general deterrence approach to accidents is that it does not involve an a priori collective decision as the correct number of accidents. General deterrence implies that accident costs would be treated as one of the many costs we face whenever we do anything. Since we cannot have everything we want, individually or as a society, whenever we choose one thing we give up others. General deterrence attempts to force individuals to consider accident costs in choosing among activities. The problem is getting the best combination of choices available. The general deterrence approach would let the free market or price system tally the choices.

The theoretical basis of general deterrence is not hard to find. The problem posed is simply the old one of allocation of resources which for years has been studied in the branch of economics called welfare economics; the free market solution is the one traditionally given by welfare economics. This solution presupposes certain postulates. The most important of these, and the only one we need consider now, is the notion that no one knows what is best for individuals better than they themselves do. If people want television sets, society should produce television sets; if they want licorice drops, then licorice drops should be made. The proportion of television sets to licorice drops, as well as the way in which each is made, should also be left up to individual choices because, according to the postulate, as long as individuals are adequately informed about the alternatives and as long as the cost to society of giving them what they want is reflected in the cost to the individual, the individual can decide better than anyone else what he wants. Thus, the function of the prices of various goods must be to reflect the relative costs to society of producing them, and if prices perform this function properly, the buyer will cast an informed vote in making his purchases; thus the best combination of choices available will be achieved.

The general deterrence approach treats accident costs as it does any other costs of goods and activities—such as the metal, or the time it takes, to make cars. If all activities reflect the accident costs they "cause," each individual will be able to choose for himself whether an activity is worth the accident costs it "causes." The sum of these choices is, ex hypothesis, the best combination available and will determine the degree to which accident-prone activities are engaged in (if at all), how they are engaged in, and who will engage in them. Failure to include accident costs in the prices of activities will, according to the theory, cause people to choose more accident-prone activities than they would if the prices of these activities made them pay for these accident costs, resulting in more accident costs than we want. Forbidding accident-prone activities *despite* the fact that they can "pay" their costs would, in theory, bring about an equally bad result from the resource allocation point of view. Either way, the postulate that individuals know best for themselves would be violated. . . .

For the theory to make some sense there is no need to postulate a world made up of economic men who consciously consider the relative costs of each different good and the relative pleasure derived from each. If the cost of all automobile accidents were suddenly to be paid out of a general social insurance fund, the expense of owning a car would be a good deal lower than it is now since people would no longer need to worry about buying insurance. The result would be that some people would buy more cars. Perhaps they would be teen-agers who can afford $100 for an old jalopy but who cannot afford—or whose fathers cannot afford—the insurance. Or they might be people who could only afford a second car so long as no added insurance was involved. In any event, the demand for cars would increase, and so would the number of cars produced. Indeed, the effect on car purchases would be much the same as if the government suddenly chose to pay the cost of the steel used by automobile manufacturers and to raise the money out of general taxes. In each case the objection would be the same. In each, an economist would say, resources are misallocated in that goods are produced that the consumer would not want if he had to pay the full extent of their cost to society, whether in terms of the physical components of the product or in terms of the expense of accidents associated with its production and use. . . .

I call the second approach to primary accident cost reduction specific or collective deterrence. At its extreme specific deterrence suggests that all decisions as to accident costs should be made collectively, through a political process. All the benefits and all the costs, including accident costs, of every activity would be evaluated together and a collective decision would be made regarding both how much of each activity should be allowed and the way in which each should be performed. (No one actually considers such a collective view of society either desirable or feasible, just as no one could accept a world of total general deterrence.)

General deterrence, although it cannot avoid collective valuation of accident costs, seeks to value accident costs on as individual a basis as possible. Specific deterrence would occasionally be forced to use the market, but ideally it would rely on the market only as a basis for broader collective judgments. Similarly, it might need to use the market to enforce its decisions, but it would do this only in as limited a way as possible.

In practice, specific deterrence takes a number of forms. It can be seen in a relatively pure form in decisions to bar certain acts or activities altogether. But the approach can be seen to operate even in many situations where no out-and-out bans on activities are imposed. Indeed, whenever accident costs are valued in relation to which activity causes them, a collective decision is implied, not only as to the value of the accident costs to the victim but also as to the value of the "cost-causing" activity or the way in which it was performed. In other words, activities are being collectively judged to be desirable or undesirable and are being subsidized or penalized accordingly. As we shall see, such penalties or subsidies would never be necessary in perfect specific deterrence and imply some use of the market, and hence of general deterrence notions. But they are a long way from the minimal degree of collective decisions that general deterrence, taken as a sole approach, would allow.

There are five major bases for specific deterrence as a goal of accident law. Not all of them would be accepted by everyone, but virtually everyone would accept at least one. The first is simply the antithesis of the basic postulate of general deterrence: individuals do *not* know best for themselves. The second, similar but more limited, is the notion that in deciding how many accident-causing activities we want, comparisons of nonmonetizable "costs" and "benefits" which the market cannot handle must be made. The third is that in making a decision for or against accidents we are not concerned solely with costs, however broadly defined, but must consider moral concepts. The fourth is that the inherent limitations in resource allocation theory, whether described in terms of income distribution, monopoly, or theory of the second best, require some collective decisions. The last is that general deterrence cannot efficiently reach some categories of activities and can almost never reach those very small subcategories of activities that we call acts, and that to reach these in an economically efficient way, collective action is needed.

Calabresi and Hirschoff, Toward a Test for Strict Liability in Tort

81 Yale L.J. 1055, 1060-1061, 1067-1069 (1972)

[The authors describe the "Learned Hand test" for negligence, see United States v. Carroll Towing Co., p. 203, above, concluding that, in theory at least, it accomplishes the objective of minimizing the sum of accident costs and avoidance costs. The authors proceed to suggest a strict liability test that will, as a practical matter, achieve greater efficiency:]

When a case comes to judgment under . . . the . . . Learned Hand [test,] a cost-benefit analysis is made by an outside governmental institution (a judge or jury) as to the relative costs of the accident and of accident avoidance. Liability would be placed on the party initially free of responsibility only if the *decider* found the benefits of avoidance (i.e., not incurring the cost of the accident) to be greater than the costs of such avoidance to that party. The strict liability test we suggest does not require that a governmental institution make such cost-benefit analysis. It requires of such an institution only a decision as to which of the parties to the accident *is in the best position to make the cost-benefit analysis between accident costs and accident avoidance costs and to act on that decision once it is made.* The question for the court reduces to a search for the cheapest cost avoider.

So stated, the strict liability test sounds deceptively simple to apply. Instead of requiring a judgment as to whether an injurer *should* have avoided the accident costs because the costs of avoidance were less than the foreseeable accident costs as the Learned Hand test does, the strict liability test would simply require a decision as to whether the injurer or the victim was in the better position both to judge whether avoidance costs would exceed foreseeable accident costs and to act on that judgment. The issue becomes not *whether* avoidance is worth it, but which of the parties is relatively more likely to find out whether avoidance is worth it. This judgment is by no means an easy one, but we would suggest that in practice it is usually easier to make correctly than is the judgment required under either the Learned Hand test or its reverse. It also implies a lesser degree of governmental intervention than does either of the Hand type tests.

[The authors demonstrate how their strict liability test would be applied in various tort areas, including products liability and ultrahazardous activities.]

The greatest differences among areas of strict liability go . . . to the question of the level of generality at which a decision is made with respect to the category or party best suited to make the appropriate cost-benefit analysis. In . . . ultrahazardous activities generally, the court-made decision that the blaster is best suited to make the cost-benefit analysis is at a high level of generality. In many jurisdictions the decision contemplates virtually no exceptions so long as the injury arises out of the risk which makes the activity ultrahazardous. The likelihood of foolish behavior by the victim or the unusual sensitivity of some victims are deemed to be best considered by the blaster. Some courts, it is true, have raised the question of whether there would be liability if a blaster blasted in what seemed to be a totally deserted place. The victim, these courts have in effect said, is better suited to gauge the costs of making his presence in such an unusual place known as against the costs of taking whatever risks may be attendant on being in a place unexpectedly. But some judges have in effect reasoned that such an exception, precisely because it would require more individualized judgments, might not be worth making. Perhaps an occasional victim would be better suited to make the cost-benefit analysis, but the administrative cost of dealing with such instances would not be worthwhile, given their presumed rarity.

In strict products liability, instead, the judgment, again court-made, that by and large producers are better suited than users to make the cost-benefit analysis is deemed much less generally applicable, and the manufacturer is allowed to try to show in each specific case that the user was in the best position to make the analysis. The questions asked as to the adequacy of warning and the appropriateness of use, and, in some jurisdictions, the availability of the defense of contributory negligence, suggest how far from certain courts are that the generalized premise that the producer is the cheapest cost avoider will apply to the individual case. As a result, a combination of judge and jury is allowed to find that given the availability of substitutes, the adequacy of warning and the capacity of an individual user to identify himself as being especially risky or especially safe, the general assumption as to who is better suited to compare the risks and benefits will not apply. That such determinations must be made in ways which are much more realistic than were analogous decisions in old assumption of risk cases, is the lesson of cases like *Henningsen* [see Chapter 7, p. 568]. But this in no way detracts from the judgment that in determining who is better suited to make a cost-benefit analysis in products liability cases, a fair degree of case by case analysis is worthwhile.

Workmen's compensation differs from both ultrahazardous activities and products liability in that the original decision was legislatively made. It also differs in that it tends to divide the decision of who is better suited to evaluate costs and benefits according to the *type of damage* rather than *type of accident.* We are not here concerned with the fact that workmen's compensation schedules are hopelessly out of date, but instead with the very fact that they deal with damages on a scheduled basis. The result of this is that the measure of damages for dignitary losses and even wage losses is that of the ordinary worker doing that job. If a great violinist mangles his hand in a steel mill, causing him extreme suffering and economic loss, that is his burden. One may contrast this with cases involving ultrahazardous activities where, except in very unusual situations, one takes one's victim as one finds him. On the other hand, the fact that a worker is warned that a machine is especially dangerous, or must be used in a given way, will not negate the employer's liability, short of extremes like wanton and wilful behavior by the victim.

Without going into further detail, one can discern a certain rationality in these cases as to the appropriate level of generality of the original liability decision and the exceptions made to it. This does not mean we agree with all of the cases, by any means. But it is not unreasonable to suppose that a violinist is the best evaluator of the relative advantages and costs of working a steel mill, with regard to the suffering he will feel if he loses his hand, while he is not as likely to be in that position with respect to blasting injuries. Similarly, a user of a product may be well suited to evaluate whether he wishes to use a given product in a given way despite a warning of danger, whereas an employee using that same product on the job would not be so suited. If we add to the foregoing considerations the administrative costs inherent in allowing an attempt to show an exception to the general rule, it is easy to understand the levels of generality which have in fact emerged.

Table of Cases

Principal cases are in italics.

Index